Children Moving

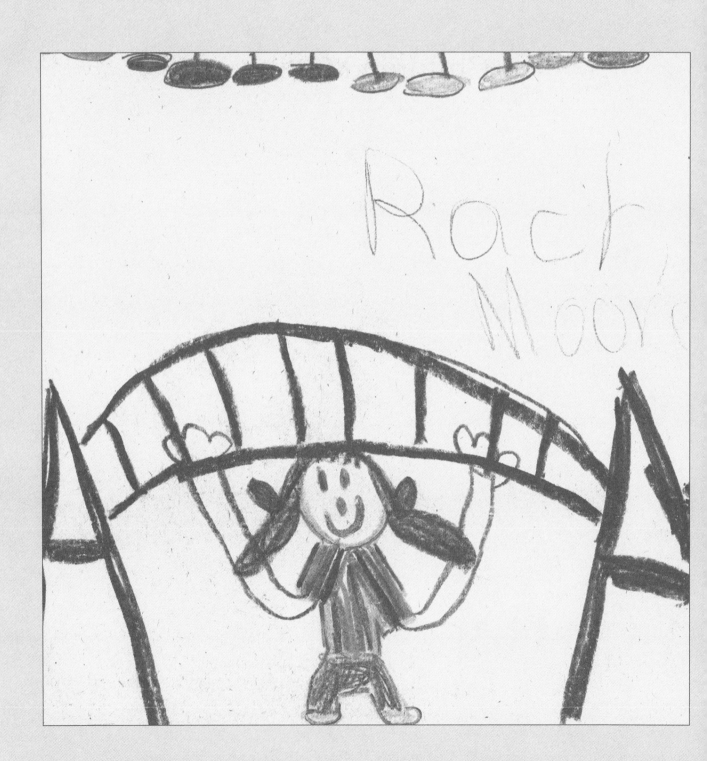

FOURTH EDITION

Children Moving

A Reflective Approach to Teaching Physical Education

George Graham
Virginia Polytechnic Institute and State University

Shirley Ann Holt/Hale
Linden Elementary School, Oak Ridge, Tennessee

Melissa Parker
University of North Dakota

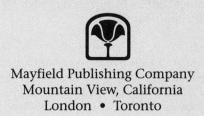

Mayfield Publishing Company
Mountain View, California
London • Toronto

Library of Congress Cataloging-in-Publication Data
Graham, George
    Children moving: a reflective approach to teaching physical education / George
Graham, Shirley Ann Holt/Hale, Melissa Parker. — 4th ed.
        p.   cm.
    Includes bibliographical references and index.
    ISBN 1-55934-921-2
    1. Physical education for children—Study and teaching—United States.
2. Physical education for children—United States—Curricula.   3. Movement
education—United States.   I. Holt/Hale, Shirley Ann.   II. Parker, Melissa.
III. Title.
GV443.G73   1998
372.86′044—dc21   97-51688
                                                                                          CIP

Manufactured in the United States of America
10   9   8   7   6   5   4

Mayfield Publishing Company
1280 Villa Street
Mountain View, California 94041

Sponsoring editor, Serina Beauparlant; production editor, Carla L. White; manuscript
editor, Beverley DeWitt; text designer, Anne Flanagan; design manager, Jean Mailander;
art manager, Robin Mouat; manufacturing manager, Randy Hurst. The text was set in
9.5/12 Stone Serif by AC & G and printed on 50# Quebecor Opaque by Quebecor Print-
ing Book Group, Kingsport.

Text credits. Page 368, By permission. From *Merriam-Websters Collegiate® Dictionary,
Tenth Edition.* © 1996 by Merriam-Webster, Incorporated; NASPE Content Standards
and Assessment Examples reprinted from *Moving Into The Future: National Standards for
Physical Education* (1995) with permission from the National Association for Sport and
Physical Education (NASPE), 1900 Association Drive, Reston, VA 20191-1599.

To a shared love of teaching children and a friendship that spans twenty years of professional writing.

Preface

When the first edition of *Children Moving* was published eighteen years ago, we could barely find solid evidence documenting why physical education should be included as an important part of school curriculums. In 1998 this has changed drastically! Today, for the first time ever, we have national research and consensus reports that solidly document the important contributions physical activity can make to one's health and well-being and also straightforward recommendations about what should be included in quality programs of physical education for children—and how that content should be taught. More than ever before, this fourth edition of *Children Moving* clearly defines and explains how teachers can start to "guide youngsters in the process of becoming physically active for a lifetime"—and heavily relies on these recent national documents to do so.

This edition frequently references three landmark national documents that were published after the third edition—the *Surgeon General's Report on Physical Activity,* published in 1996; the consensus report on physical activity sponsored by the National Center for Chronic Disease Prevention and Health Promotion, which was also published in 1996; and the *National Standards for Physical Education,* published by the National Association for Sport and Physical Education (NASPE) in 1995. These three documents, in addition to NASPE's *Developmentally Appropriate Guidelines for Children's Physical Education,* provide direction and guidance as to how a quality physical education program needs to be structured, along with suggested content for such programs.

George Graham was one of the co-authors of the *Developmentally Appropriate* document and also the NASPE Outcomes Project, the forerunner to the *National Standards.* Shirley Ann Holt/Hale was a co-author of the *National Standards for Physical Education.* Involvement in these national projects is one of the key reasons for the match between *Children Moving* and the recent national advances that have been made in substantiating the importance of physical activity and the translation of the research and con-

sensus reports into meaningful and worthwhile experiences for children. The fourth edition relies on these documents to be consistent with the national, state, and local directions to define the standards for what students should be learning in schools—and includes literally hundreds of practical learning experiences and assessments for reaching the goals and objectives outlined in the *National Standards.*

While recent information from the national documents is new, much remains from previous editions, especially our goal to keep the text both informal and practical. What we wrote in the preface to the first edition remains true in this fourth edition: "We are teachers of children first. And writers second. Individual insights, gained during years of teaching experience and ideas to enhance teacher success are sprinkled throughout the text. We hope that by sharing these experiences we can help others to enrich the lives of children."

So we begin the fourth edition of *Children Moving* by describing the "Value and Purpose of Physical Education for Children," which highlights many of the recommendations made in the recent national documents. This chapter is the first one in Part One, entitled "Introduction and Overview," which gives an overview of the skill theme approach. Chapters 2 and 3 define the skill theme approach, which is what the program suggested in *Children Moving* has come to be termed since we originally wrote about it in 1980. These two chapters also illustrate the connections between the skill theme approach and the *National Standards.* Chapter 4 has been expanded to include wellness as it relates to elementary physical education along with physical fitness as a product of a quality physical education program. Chapter 5 makes the case that schools are different from one another and that quality programs reflect those differences. The final chapter in Part One provides an overview of disabilities, the philosophy of inclusion in physical education, and our role in providing quality physical education for children with special needs.

Part Two, "Teaching Skills," contains nine chapters (7–15) that focus on the teaching process (also referred to as pedagogy), while Parts Three and Four focus on the actual content of the skill theme approach. Part Two begins with a chapter describing our "system" for determining the content children are ready to learn based on their developmental levels and interests (generic levels of skill proficiency) rather than on age or grade level. A revised chapter on planning (8) follows. The chapter has been revised and simplified from previous editions, and the analogy of planning for a trip is described in four steps. The next two chapters focus on practical ideas for developing a positive learning environment in which children can learn in a safe and enjoyable atmosphere (Chapter 9) while also providing practical techniques for children who may need extra help in learning how to function appropriately in a physical activity setting (Chapter 10). Because *Children Moving* describes a "child-centered," as opposed to "subject-centered," approach to teaching, it is important that teachers constantly observe children to determine the progress they are making so that lessons can be adjusted for individual differences. Chapter 11 describes some of the observation techniques used by reflective teachers, while Chapter 12 describes how teachers organize content into meaningful learning experiences by developing a logical progression of tasks (learning experiences), cues (critical elements), and challenges designed to truly make physical education classes a learning experience. In this edition of *Children Moving*, based on student and reviewer comments, we have replaced the term *extension* with *task*, *refinement* with *cue* (critical elements), and *application* with *challenge*. We think this will make it easier for the reader to understand the process of content development. Chapter 13 describes a variety of instructional approaches used by teachers to heighten the children's understanding and enjoyment of the lessons. Chapter 14, on assessment, has been substantially revised and includes a number of alternative assessment examples based on the authors' teaching and also the *National Standards*. Assessment icons 🖼 are used throughout the text to indicate performance assessments. In addition, the tool check for cognitive understanding is indicated with the icon ♟. The third icon you will find in the text ⚠ is an alert for strong emphasis on safety in a given situation. The final chapter (15) in Part Two includes a variety of practical ways teachers can assess their own teaching to determine if, and how, they are using the techniques employed by effective teachers of children's physical education.

The next two parts of *Children Moving* focus on the content of the skill theme approach. Chapters 16–18 describe how the concepts of space awareness, effort, and relationships are taught in the skill theme

approach. These revised chapters include references to the *National Standards* for both content and assessment ideas. They are followed by the skill theme chapters (19–31), which contain hundreds of learning experiences designed to help children learn the motor skills that are necessary for successful participation and enjoyment of a variety of physical activities and sports. Each skill theme chapter begins with an overview of the content followed by a description of a series of tasks 🅣, the critical element(s) or cues that are necessary to succeed at these tasks, and challenges 🅒 designed to maintain the children's interest in learning the tasks. The tasks are organized according to the Generic Levels of Skill Proficiency in a spiral progression from beginner to advanced.

Another change in the fourth edition has been to move the chapters on Skill Themes in Dance (20), Skill Themes in Gymnastics (25), and Skill Themes in Games (31) into Part Four. In past editions these three chapters had followed the skill theme chapters in a separate section. We made this decision based on our reviewers' recommendation, and they are now placed more clearly near the content that precedes the development of the skill themes. Chapter 20, "Skill Themes in Dance," follows the chapters on the movement concepts and "Traveling" (19). Chapter 25, "Skill Themes in Gymnastics," follows the chapters on "Jumping and Landing" (22) "Balancing" (23), and "Transferring Weight and Rolling" (24). Skill theme chapters on "Kicking and Punting" (26), "Throwing and Catching" (27), "Volleying and Dribbling" (28), "Striking with Rackets and Paddles" (29), and "Striking with Long Handled Implements" (30) immediately precede Chapter 31, "Skill Themes in Games." Although technically Chapters 20, 25, and 31 are not skill theme chapters, we have referred to them as such to make it easier for the reader. This placement provides a much stronger link between skill themes and the three content areas of elementary physical education.

Two chapters make up the final part, "The Future," in this fourth edition of *Children Moving*. The first describes some of the techniques teachers have successfully used to build support for their programs (Chapter 32). Chapter 33, the final chapter, once again includes our dreams for children's physical education as we enter the 21st century.

As with the past two editions, Shirley Ann Holt/Hale has revised the lesson plans designed to accompany *Children Moving* in her book, *On the Move* (4th Edition) based on her twenty-four years of teaching children at Linden Elementary School in Oak Ridge, Tennessee. And based on the recommendation of our reviewers and a number of other teacher educators, there is now an *Instructor's Manual to Accompany Children Moving.* Each chapter in the manual begins with an overview of the chapter content and includes key points for classroom lectures and discussions with overhead transparency masters, active learning experiences for both the classroom and the gym, computer lab assignments and other assignments to be completed outside of class, along with worksheets and test questions for each chapter. The *Instructor's Manual* was developed by Eloise Elliott, Ph.D., who has used previous editions of *Children Moving* in her classes for future physical education and classroom teachers at Concord College in Athens, West Virginia. In preparation for the development of the *Instructor's Manual to Accompany Children Moving,* Dr. Elliott also "sat in" on a semester-long course taught by George Graham that used *Children Moving* as the required text.

Acknowledgments

Needless to say, we are grateful to a number of people for assisting us in the process of revising *Children Moving.* Although we can't name everyone, we are especially grateful for the assistance of the following individuals:

- Dolly Lambdin, University of Texas, for her excellent and helpful reviews of this and previous editions of *Children Moving.*
- Casey Jones, formerly of Margaret Beeks Elementary School and now of Kipps Elementary School in Blacksburg, Virginia, for his excellent work with children, for his collaborative efforts with Virginia Tech, for allowing George Graham to do his spring teaching each year at his school, and most important for keeping quiet about George's theories that wobbled when he tried to put them into practice.
- The children at Linden Elementary School in Oak Ridge, Tennessee, who create as well as follow our dreams of physical education for children.
- The children, teachers, and principals of St. Mary's Elementary School in Grand Forks, North Dakota, for allowing Melissa Parker three years of teaching opportunities.
- Mexican Hat, Montezuma Creek, and Bluff Elementary Schools (San Juan County Schools, Utah) for accepting a stranger, Dr. Parker, with open arms and providing the teaching experience of a lifetime.
- To Rosa Edwards, Alanton Elementary School in Virginia Beach, Virginia; John Pomeroy, Roland E. Cook, and Fort Lewis Elementary Schools in Roanoke County, Virginia; and Larry Satchwell, Shiloh Elementary School in Lawrenceville, Georgia, for being such inspirations and wonderful role models for both beginning and veteran teachers.
- Clay Thurston, for his ability to capture children's movement through photography.
- The professionals at Mayfield Publishing for their patience and gentle prodding: Michelle Sordi and Serina Beauparlant, Sponsoring Editors; Carla White, Production Editor; Marty Granahan, Permissions Editor; Robin Mouat, Art Manager; and Beverley DeWitt for her attention to the many details of the editing process.
- Finally we want to thank the countless teachers and students who have made so many positive and helpful comments since the first edition of *Children Moving* was published. Your support and encouragement continues to be most appreciated.

Brief Contents

PART ONE: Introduction and Overview   1

Chapter 1   The Value and Purpose of Physical Education for Children   3
Chapter 2   The Skill Theme Approach   11
Chapter 3   Skill Themes, Movement Concepts, and the *National Standards*   21
Chapter 4   Physical Fitness and Wellness for Children   33
Chapter 5   Reflective Teaching   59
Chapter 6   Teaching Children with Special Needs   67

PART TWO: Teaching Skills   85

Chapter 7   Determining Generic Levels of Skill Proficiency   87
Chapter 8   Planning   97
Chapter 9   Establishing an Environment for Learning   111
Chapter 10   Maintaining Appropriate Behavior   127
Chapter 11   Observation Techniques   143
Chapter 12   Developing the Content   151
Chapter 13   Instructional Approaches   161
Chapter 14   Assessing Student Learning   175
Chapter 15   Understanding Your Teaching   199

PART THREE: Movement Concepts Defined   215

Chapter 16   Space Awareness   217
Chapter 17   Effort   235
Chapter 18   Relationships   251

PART FOUR: Skill Theme Development   275

Chapter 19   Traveling   277
Chapter 20   Skill Themes in Dance   307
Chapter 21   Chasing, Fleeing, and Dodging   327
Chapter 22   Jumping and Landing   343
Chapter 23   Balancing   367
Chapter 24   Transferring Weight and Rolling   395
Chapter 25   Skill Themes in Gymnastics   437
Chapter 26   Kicking and Punting   451
Chapter 27   Throwing and Catching   485
Chapter 28   Volleying and Dribbling   517
Chapter 29   Striking with Rackets and Paddles   555
Chapter 30   Striking with Long-Handled Implements   581
Chapter 31   Skill Themes in Games   617

PART FIVE: The Future   633

Chapter 32   Building Support for Your Program   635
Chapter 33   Physical Education for Tomorrow's Children   645

Contents

Preface   vii

PART ONE

Introduction and Content Overview   1

1

The Value and Purpose of Physical Education for Children   3

The Benefits of Physical Activity   4
The Purpose of Physical Education   7
The Characteristics of a Quality Physical Education Program   8
Summary   10
Reading Comprehension Questions   10
References   10

2

The Skill Theme Approach   11

Why Don't You Describe Such Activities as Duck, Duck, Goose and Kickball?   12
What Are Skill Themes?   12
What Is the Curriculum Diamond?   12
   Building a Foundation (Grades Pre-K–5)   13
   Exploring Possibilities (Grades 6–8)   13
   Developing Expertise (Grades 9–12)   13
What Are the Characteristics of the Skill Theme Approach?   13
   Characteristic 1   13
   Characteristic 2   15
   Characteristic 3   16
Isn't It Difficult to Maintain Youngsters' Interest in a Program That Emphasizes the Fundamentals?   16
What Does "Adjusting the Activities" Mean?   16
Where Is Physical Fitness in the Skill Theme Approach?   17
Where Do the Cognitive and Affective Domains Fit into the Skill Theme Approach?   17
What about Dance and Gymnastics?   17
Isn't This a Harder Way to Teach? How Do Experienced Teachers React to Developing the Content This Way?   17
How Do Classroom Teachers Feel about the Skill Theme Approach?   18
How Do Middle (Junior) and High School Physical Education Teachers Feel about the Skill Theme Approach?   18
Summary   19
Reading Comprehension Questions   19
References   20

3

Skill Themes, Movement Concepts, and the *National Standards*   21

Characteristics of Themes   22
Skill Themes and Movement Concepts   23
   The Wheel   25
   Context Variation   25
The *National Standards* and the Skill Theme Approach   27
   Background of *National Standards* Development   27
   Skill Themes and the Content Standards   29
Summary   31
Reading Comprehension Questions   32
References/Suggested Readings   32

4

Physical Fitness and Wellness for Children   33

Physical Fitness: A Definition   34
   Muscular Strength and Endurance   35
   Flexibility   35
   Cardiovascular Efficiency   35

Body Composition   35

Physical Fitness and the *National Standards for Physical Education*   36

Principles of Fitness Training   36

Children's Lifetime Physical Activity Model   36

Fitness in the Curriculum   37

Health-Related Fitness Components   37

Muscular Strength and Endurance   37

Upper Body Strength and Endurance   38

Activities/Exercises for Abdominal Strength and Endurance   38

Wall Push   38

Untimed Sit-Ups   38

Activities/Exercises for Upper Body Strength and Endurance   38

Flexed-Arm Hang   38

Reverse Pull-Ups   39

Walking Handy   39

Just a Piece of Paper   39

Flexibility   40

Activities/Exercises for Flexibility   40

Trunk and Shoulder Extensions   40

Trunk and Shoulder Rotation   40

Inner Thigh Stretch   40

Lying Knee Pull   40

Cardiovascular Efficiency   41

Activities/Exercises for Cardiovascular Efficiency   41

Cardiovascular Activities for Outside the Gym   44

Body Composition   45

Physical Fitness Testing   45

Incorporating Physical Fitness   49

A Final Thought on Fitness   50

Wellness   51

Nutrition   51

Personal Safety: Bicycle, Auto, Water, Fire   52

Drug, Alcohol, and Tobacco Abuse   53

Personal and Social Responsibility   53

Mental/Emotional Health   54

Final Thoughts on Wellness   55

Summary   55

Reading Comprehension Questions   56

References/Suggested Readings   56

5

Reflective Teaching   59

The Need for Reflective Teaching   60

Values of the Teacher   60

Class Size   61

Number of Class Sessions   63

Facilities and Equipment   63

Discipline   64

Context of the School   65

Summary   65

Reading Comprehension Questions   65

References   65

6

Teaching Children with Special Needs   67

The Philosophy of Inclusion   68

The Multidisciplinary Team   69

Individualized Education Program   69

Least Restrictive Environment   70

Implementing the IEP   70

Visual Impairments   71

Hearing Impairments   73

Physical Disabilities   75

Cerebral Palsy   76

Spina Bifida   78

Muscular Dystrophy   78

Health-Related Impairments   79

Asthma   79

Diabetes   79

Mental Retardation   80

Remedial Physical Education and Mental Retardation   80

Emotional Disturbance/Behavior Disorders   81

Learning Disabilities   82

A Final Thought   82

Summary   83

Reading Comprehension Questions   83

References/Suggested Readings   83

PART TWO

Teaching Skills   85

7

Determining Generic Levels of Skill Proficiency   87

Identifying Levels of Skill Proficiency   88
    Precontrol Level   88
    Control Level   88
    Utilization Level   88
    Proficiency Level   90

What Do We Mean by *Generic?*   90

Using the Generic Levels of Skill Proficiency in Teaching   91
    Which Task?   92
    How to Know If a Task Works   92

Final Insights about the Generic Levels of Skill Proficiency   93
    Multiple Skill Levels in a Class   93
    Control Level in Two Days a Week   93
    Proficiency Level Is Rare   94

Summary   94

Reading Comprehension Questions   95

References   95

8

Planning   97

Reflective Planning   98

A Four-Step Planning Process   99
    Step 1: Developing the Scope and Sequence   99
    Step 2: Devising a Yearly Overview   100
    Step 3: Determining Benchmarks   103
    Step 4: Detailing Daily Lesson Plans   104
        1. *Class Name*   105
        2. *Skill Level*   105
        3. *Length of Lesson (Time)*   105
        4. *Number of Meetings per Week*   105
        5. *Major Focus and Subfocus*   105
        6. *Objectives*   105
        7. *Materials/Equipment*   105
        8. *Organization/Management*   105
        9. *Introduction*   105
        10. *Task Development*   106
        11. *Closure*   107
        12. *Reflection*   108

Making Planning Enjoyable   108

Recording Progress   108

Lesson Design   108
    Interesting Lessons   109
    Appropriate Lessons   109
    Maximum Participation   109

Summary   109

Reading Comprehension Questions   110

References   110

9

Establishing an Environment for Learning   111

The Managerial Task System   113
    Getting Off to a Good Start   113
    Developing Protocols   115
    Establishing Rules and Expectations   115
    Establishing Gymnasium Routines   118
        Establishing a Positive Atmosphere   118
        Choosing Routines That Reflect a Positive Atmosphere   119
        Teaching Stopping and Listening Routines   121

The Instructional Task System   121

Teaching Skills for Establishing a Learning Environment   122
    Setting Performance Standards   122
    Maintaining Consistency   123
    Monitoring and Reacting   123

Teaching Safety Procedures   123

A Time for Reflection   125

Summary   125

Reading Comprehension Questions   125

References   126

10

Maintaining Appropriate Behavior   127

Increasing Appropriate Behavior   128
    Proactive Strategies   128
        Positive Interaction   129
        Eliminating Differential Treatment   130
        Prompting   130
    Reactive Approaches   130
        Ignoring Inappropriate Behavior   130

Nonverbal Teacher Interactions   131

Person-to-Person Dialogue   131

Decreasing Inappropriate Behavior   132

Desists   132

Time-outs   133

Planning Time   133

Behavior Contracts   134

Letters to Parents   134

Involving the Principal   134

Maintaining Appropriate Behavior in Entire Classes   135

Developing Personal and Social Responsibility   135

Class Rewards   138

Token Systems   138

Behavior Games   139

Corporal Punishment   139

Summary   139

Reading Comprehension Questions   140

References/Suggested Readings   140

11

Observation Techniques   143

Major Observation Techniques   144

Back-to-the-Wall   144

Scanning   145

Observation Foci   146

Safety   146

On-Task Behavior   147

Class Movement Patterns   147

Individual Movement Patterns   148

Combining Observation Aspects   148

Summary   149

Reading Comprehension Questions   149

References/Suggested Readings   150

12

Developing the Content   151

Overview of Content Development   152

Informing   152

The KISS Principle   152

Demonstrations   153

Pinpointing   153

Tasks (Extensions)   153

Cues (Refinements)   154

One Cue at a Time   154

Congruent Feedback   155

Challenges (Applications)   156

Assessing Your Content Development   157

Planning Format   157

Accommodating Individual Differences   157

Teaching by Invitation   158

Intratask Variation   158

Summary   159

Reading Comprehension Questions   159

References/Suggested Readings   159

13

Instructional Approaches   161

Direct Instruction   163

Task Teaching   165

Guided Discovery   167

Convergent Inquiry   167

Divergent Inquiry   168

Peer Teaching   169

Cooperative Learning   169

Child-Designed Instruction   170

Child-Designed Tasks   170

Contracts   171

Summary   173

Reading Comprehension Questions   173

References/Suggested Readings   173

14

Assessing Student Learning   175

Understanding the Purpose of Assessment   176

Assessing What Was Learned   176

Student Journals   177

Exit (or Entrance) Slips   178

Homework   179

Peer Observation   182

Event Tasks   182

Videotaping   184

Student Drawings   184

Student Displays   186

Teacher Observation   186

Portfolios   186

Assessing How Well It Was Learned   187

Assessing All Three Domains   190

Summarizing and Reporting Progress   191
Three Practical Systems   192
Hartinger System   192
Lambdin System   192
Metz System   193
Similarities   194
Finding the Time for Assessment   195
Summary   196
Reading Comprehension Questions   196
References/Suggested Readings   197

15

Understanding Your Teaching   199

Self-Reflection   200
Systematic Observation   200
Unassisted Techniques   201
Tape-Recording for Self-Analysis   201
Feedback Analysis   202
Lesson Content   203
Written Instruments   205
Student-Assisted Techniques   205
Teacher Pathway   205
Interaction Patterns   206
Practice Opportunities   206
Peer-Assisted Techniques   207
Practice Opportunities and Feedback Checklist   207
Duration Recording System   208
Combining Techniques   209
Being Observed   210
Finding Out More   211
Support Groups   212
Summary   212
Reading Comprehension Questions   213
References/Suggested Readings   213

PART THREE

Movement Concepts Defined   215

16

Space Awareness   217

Developing the Concept of Self-Space   220
Teaching the Concept of Self-Space   220

Learning Experiences Leading to Movement Concept Understanding   220
Exploring Self-Space   220
Curling, Stretching, and Twisting in Self-Space   221
Moving the Whole Body in Self-Space   222
Developing the Concept of General Space   222
Teaching the Concept of General Space   222
Learning Experiences Leading to Movement Concept Understanding   223
Exploring General Space   223
Scamper   223
Reducing the Size of the General Space   223
City Streets, Crowded Spaces   223
Dodging in General Space   224
Traveling Over, Under, and Around Obstacles in General Space   224
Obstacle Course   224
Developing the Concept of Directions   224
Teaching the Concept of Directions   225
Learning Experiences Leading to Movement Concept Understanding   225
Traveling in Different Directions   225
Moving Clockwise and Counterclockwise   225
Exploring Directions   225
Changing Directions on Signal   226
Turning While Moving in Different Directions   226
Developing the Concept of Levels   226
Teaching the Concept of Levels   226
Learning Experiences Leading to Movement Concept Understanding   226
Traveling and Freezing at Different Levels   226
Traveling with Body Parts at Different Levels   227
Rising and Sinking to Create Different Levels   227
Traveling While Rising and Sinking   227
Developing the Concept of Pathways   227
Teaching the Concept of Pathways   227
Learning Experiences Leading to Movement Concept Understanding   228
Exploring Pathways   228
Using Pathway Maps   228
Designing Pathways   229
Creating Follow-the-Leader Pathways   229
Traveling Pathways and Obstacles   229

Following-the-Dots Pathways   230

Combining Pathways, Levels, and Directions   230

Developing the Concept of Extensions in Space   230

Teaching the Concept of Extensions in Space   231

Learning Experiences Leading to Movement Concept Understanding   231

Exploring Extensions   231

Traveling and Extensions   232

Changing from One Extension to Another   232

Using Extensions and Imagery   232

Applying the Concepts of Space Awareness   232

Reading Comprehension Questions   233

References   233

17

Effort   235

Developing the Concept of Time   237

Teaching the Concept of Time   239

Learning Experiences Leading to Movement Concept Understanding   239

Exploring Time   239

Using Different Speeds in Self-Space   239

Moving at Different Speeds   240

Traveling and Freezing by Using Changes in Time   240

Combining Imagery and Time   240

Differentiating among Time Words   241

Combining Sport Skills and Time   241

Continually Changing in Time While Traveling   243

Developing the Concept of Force   243

Teaching the Concept of Force   243

Learning Experiences Leading to Movement Concept Understanding   243

Exploring Force   243

Traveling and Changing Force Qualities   244

Using Imagery and Force   244

Showing Contrasts of Force   244

Developing the Concept of Flow   246

Teaching the Concept of Flow   246

Learning Experiences Leading to Movement Concept Understanding   246

Traveling and Flow   246

Eliciting Flow Qualities   247

Following Flow Sentences   247

Practicing Flow Sequences   247

Using Flow Conversations   248

Combining Time, Force, and Flow   249

Applying the Effort Concepts   249

Reading Comprehension Questions   249

References   250

18

Relationships   251

Developing the Concept of the Relationships of Body Parts   252

Teaching the Concept of the Relationships of Body Parts   252

Activities Leading to Movement Concept Understanding   254

Identifying Body Parts   254

Balancing While Using Different Body Parts   254

Freezing on Different Body Parts   255

Traveling on Different Body Parts   255

Balancing on Matching and Nonmatching Parts   256

Round, Narrow, Wide, and Twisted Body Shapes   256

Changing from One Body Shape to Another   257

Traveling and Freezing in Different Body Shapes   257

Making Symmetrical and Nonsymmetrical Shapes   257

Creating Postcard Sculptures   259

Creating Body Shapes in the Air   259

Developing the Concept of Relationships with Objects   260

Teaching the Concept of Relationships with Objects   260

Activities Leading to Movement Concept Understanding   260

Traveling Over, Close To, Far Away, Inside   260

Traveling Over, Under, Close To, and Far Away from Equipment   262

Learning Onto/Off Concepts   263

Studying Over, Under, Around, In Front Of, and Behind Concepts   263

Traveling along Equipment   263

Traveling through Obstacles   264

Going Over and Under the Obstacle Course   265

Using Partners As Obstacles   265

Developing the Concept of Relationships with People   266

Alone in a Mass   267

Solo   267

Partners   267

Groups   268

Between Groups   268

Teaching the Concept of Relationships with People   268

Activities Leading to Movement Concept Understanding   268

Matching   268

Traveling and Matching   270

Mirroring   270

Matching and Mirroring   270

Traveling Alongside/Following   270

Following with a Group   271

Meeting/Parting   271

Forming Cooperative and Collaborative Relationships   271

Meeting and Parting in a Cooperative Group   272

Performing Solo   272

Applying the Concept of Relationships   272

Reading Comprehension Questions   273

References   274

PART FOUR

Skill Theme Development   275

19

Traveling   277

Fundamental Locomotor Skills   278

Walking   278

Running   278

Hopping   279

Leaping   279

Sliding   282

Galloping   282

Skipping   282

Levels of Skill Proficiency   282

Precontrol Level: Activities for Exploration   285

Traveling in General Space   285

Traveling with Different Locomotor Movements   285

Traveling in Different Ways   285

Traveling with Imagery   286

Traveling Through Rope Pathways   286

Traveling among the Large and Tall   286

Control Level: Learning Experiences Leading to Skill Development   287

Traveling with Different Locomotor Patterns   287

Sliding   287

Galloping   287

Hopping   287

Skipping   287

Leaping   288

Running   288

Traveling to Open Spaces   289

Performing Locomotor Sequences   289

Moving to Rhythms   290

Traveling in Confined Spaces   290

Traveling with Music   290

Traveling an Obstacle Course   291

Traveling in Different Directions   291

Slidestepping   292

Traveling in Different Pathways   292

The Locomotors Dance   292

The Follow-Me Dance   293

Traveling at Different Speeds   293

Traveling Using Different Directions, Levels, Pathways, and Locations   293

Changing Speeds to Music   294

A Dance of Water, Steam, and Ice   294

Slow-Motion Replay: The Sports Dance   294

Combination Locomotors   294

Utilization Level: Learning Experiences Leading to Skill Development   295

Traveling with a Partner: Matching Pathways   295

The Copy Cat Dance   297

Traveling with a Partner: Changing Speed and Direction   297

Shadowing   297

Meeting and Parting While Traveling with a Partner   299

Performing Rhythmical Patterns   299

Traveling to Express Age: The Fountain of Youth Dance   299

Traveling in Bound and Free Flow   300

Traveling to Tom Foolery Rhymes   300

Proficiency Level: Learning Experiences
Leading to Skill Development   300

Depicting Primitive Tribes Through Travel   301

Traveling to Show Tradition Versus
Change   301

Performing Rhythmical Patterns:
Tinikling   301

Traveling in Games and Sports   303

Traveling in Gymnastics   304

Reading Comprehension Questions   304

References   305

20

Skill Themes in Dance   307

The Purpose of Dance in Elementary
School   309

Dance Experiences   310

Rhythmic Experiences   310

Folk Dances   313

Creative Experiences   313

Design of Dance   314

Evaluation of Dance Making   316

The Content of Expressive Dance   316

The Process of Teaching Dance   317

Don't Call It Dance!   320

Begin Gradually   322

Start with a Cooperative Class   322

Use Props   322

Imagery   322

Start with Exciting Movement
Experiences   323

Dance to the Music   323

A Final Thought   323

Summary   323

Reading Comprehension Questions   324

References/Suggested Readings   324

21

Chasing, Fleeing, and Dodging   327

Chasing   328

Fleeing   328

Dodging   328

Levels of Skill Proficiency   328

Precontrol Level: Activities for
Exploration   330

Moving Obstacles   330

Traveling to Flee   332

Traveling to Dodge   332

Make-Believe Chase   332

Control Level: Learning Experiences Leading
to Skill Development   332

Dodging in Response to a Signal   332

Fleeing from a Partner   332

Dodging the Obstacles   333

Dodging with Quick Changes of
Direction   333

Overtaking a Fleeing Person (Catch-up
Chase)   333

Fleeing a Chaser (Frogs and Flies)   334

Utilization Level: Learning Experiences
Leading to Skill Development   334

People Dodge (Dodging Stationary
Obstacles)   334

Dodging and Faking Moves to Avoid a Chaser
(Freeze-and-Count Tag)   335

Dodging and Chasing As Part of a Team
(Octopus)   335

Dodging and Chasing One Person in a Mass
(Partner Dodge)   336

Dodging in a Dynamic Situation (Body-Part
Tag)   336

Dodging While Manipulating an Object   337

Proficiency Level: Learning Experiences
Leading to Skill Development   337

Continual Fleeing and Chasing with a Large
Group   338

Dodging While Maintaining Possession of an
Object   338

Chasing and Fleeing in a Game Situation   338

Chasing and Dodging Simultaneously (Snatch
the Flag)   339

Dodging in a Game Situation (Safety
Bases)   339

Dodging in a Game Situation (Pirate's
Treasure)   340

Using Team Strategy for Chasing, Fleeing, and
Dodging (Rip Flag)   340

Dodging While Manipulating an Object in a
Game Situation   341

Reading Comprehension Questions   341

References   342

22

Jumping and Landing   343

Fundamental Jumping Patterns   344

Levels of Skill Proficiency   344

Precontrol Level: Activities for
Exploration   345

Jumping and Landing: Different Patterns   345

Jumping for Distance   351

Jumping for Height   351

Jumping over a Swinging Rope   351

Control Level: Learning Experiences Leading
to Skill Development   351

Jumping and Landing: Basic Patterns   351

Standing Long Jump   352

Jumping for Height   352

Jumping over Low Obstacles: Hoops   353

Jumping over Low Obstacles: Hurdles   353

Jumping Rhythmically   354

Jumping in Rhythmical Sequences   354

Jumping a Turned Rope   355

Jumping a Self-Turned Rope   355

Jumping Using Buoyant and Yielding
Landings   356

Jumping to Form a Body Shape During
Flight   356

Traveling, Jumping, and Body Shapes   357

Performing Jumping Sequences and Making
Body Shapes   358

Jumping over Equipment Using Buoyant
Landings   358

Jumping on and off Equipment Using Buoyant
and Yielding Landings   358

Jump, Squash, TaDa   359

Jumping and Landing Task Sheets   359

Utilization Level: Learning Experiences
Leading to Skill Development   360

Jumping to Catch   361

Jumping to Throw   361

Jumping on a Bench   362

Throwing and Catching While Jumping   362

Jumping to an Accented Beat   363

Proficiency Level: Learning Experiences
Leading to Skill Development   363

Jumping with a Partner to Mirror Actions   363

Jumping with a Partner to Match Actions   364

Jumping with a Springboard   364

Jumping As Part of a Dance Creation   364

Jumping, Dancing, and Imagery   365

Hurdling Jumps   365

Reading Comprehension Questions   365

References   366

23

Balancing   367

Levels of Skill Proficiency   368

Precontrol Level: Activities for
Exploration   369

Balancing on Different Bases of Support   369

Balancing on a Wide Base of Support   371

Balancing in Different Body Shapes   371

Traveling and Stopping in Balanced
Positions   371

Traveling on Low Gymnastics Equipment   371

Balancing on Boards   372

Control Level: Learning Experiences Leading
to Skill Development   372

Balancing on Different Bases of Support   373

Tightening the Gymnastics Muscles   373

Counterbalance   373

Balancing Symmetrically and
Nonsymmetrically   374

Balancing in Different Body Shapes   375

The Gymnastics Dance   376

Performing Inverted Balances   377

Alignment of Body Parts   377

Doing Kickups   377

Traveling and Stopping in Balanced
Positions   378

Stationary Balances on Equipment   379

Traveling on Large Apparatus   382

Traveling While Balanced   382

Balancing Sequence   382

Balancing on Stilts   383

Balance Boards   383

Utilization Level: Learning Experiences
Leading to Skill Development   384

Balancing on Crates   384

Moving out of and into Balances by Stretching,
Curling, and Twisting   386

Traveling into and out of Balances by
Rolling   387

Performing Inverted Balances on
Equipment   387

Performing Sequences That Combine Stationary
Balances and Traveling on Mats   388

Proficiency Level: Learning Experiences Leading to Skill Development   390

Balancing While Supporting the Weight of a Partner   390

Balancing on Hanging Ropes   390

Transferring off Equipment with Weight on Hands   390

Performing Apparatus Sequences That Combine Stationary Balances and Traveling with Movement Concepts   392

Reading Comprehension Questions   392

References   393

24

Transferring Weight and Rolling   395

Levels of Skill Proficiency in Transferring Weight   396

Precontrol Level: Activities for Exploration of Weight Transfer   396

Locomotor Actions   396

Transferring Weight from Feet to Back   397

Transferring Weight from Feet to Hands   397

Transferring Weight onto and off Equipment   397

Control Level: Learning Experiences Leading to Skill Development in Weight Transfer   397

Transferring Weight to Hands across Mats   399

Transferring Weight from Feet to Back   399

Transferring Weight from Feet to Combinations of Body Parts   399

Stretching, Curling, and Twisting into Transfers   400

Performing Spring/Step Takeoffs   401

Performing Spring/Step Takeoffs onto Crates and/or Benches   401

Transferring off Low Apparatus (Bench, Crate, or Low Table)   402

Making Spring/Step Takeoffs with Sequences   402

Traveling over Low Apparatus   403

Transferring onto Low Apparatus   403

Transferring Weight from Feet to Hands   404

Transferring Weight to Hands by Stepping: Cartwheels   404

Utilization Level: Learning Experiences Leading to Skill Development in Weight Transfer   404

Transferring Weight to Hands: Walking   405

Transferring Weight to Hands and Twisting   405

Transferring Weight to Hands and Forming a Bridge   405

Transferring Weight onto Large Apparatus   406

Transferring Weight to Head and Hands on Apparatus   406

Transferring Weight onto Bars   408

Transferring Weight over Apparatus (Vaulting Box)   408

Transferring Weight along Apparatus   409

Transferring Weight by Rolling (Bench, Box, or Table)   409

Transferring Weight from Feet to Hands   410

Transferring Weight on Bars   411

Combining Skills on Mats   411

Combining Weight Transfer and Balances into Sequences on Mats and Apparatus   411

Proficiency Level: Learning Experiences Leading to Skill Development in Weight Transfer   413

Levels of Skill Proficiency in Rolling   413

Precontrol Level: Activities for Exploration of Rolling   417

Rounds   417

The Rocking Horse   417

Rolling Sideways   418

The Ball   418

Control Level: Learning Experiences Leading to Skill Development in Rolling   418

Twin Rockers   418

Log Roll   418

Egg Roll   418

Shoulders Sideways   419

Back Rocker   419

Through the Legs   420

Rolling Forward   420

Back Touch   420

Rolling from Different Positions   421

Rolling at Different Speeds   422

Back Shoulder   422

Handclasp Backward   422

Rolling Backward   423

Rolling in Different Directions   424

Rolling from Different Directions and Positions   424

Linking Rolls   425

Rolling Using Different Directions and Speeds   425

Jumping off Equipment, Landing, and Rolling   426

Jumping for Height, Landing, and Rolling   426

Jumping from Different Heights and Rolling   427

Jumping over Equipment, Landing, and Rolling   427

Rolling, Levels, Directions, and Jumping   428

Traveling, Jumping, Landing, and Rolling   429

Utilization Level: Learning Experiences Leading to Skill Development in Rolling   429

Busy Mat   429

Touch-and-Go Rolls   430

Rolling over Low Hurdles   430

Rolling on Low Equipment   430

Rolling off Low Equipment   431

Traveling and Rolling Between Pieces of Equipment   431

Rolling, Balancing, and Rolling   431

Rolling to Express an Idea   432

Throwing, Catching, and Rolling   432

Rolling onto Low Equipment   433

Balancing and Rolling on Equipment   433

Rolling to Meet and Part   433

Striking and Rolling   434

Catching, Throwing, and Rolling   434

Proficiency Level: Learning Experiences Leading to Skill Proficiency in Rolling   434

Reading Comprehension Questions   435

References   435

25

Skill Themes in Gymnastics   437

The Nature of Gymnastics   438

The Purpose of Gymnastics   439

The Content of Educational Gymnastics   440

Floor Experiences   441

Sequences   441

Apparatus Experiences   442

Outdoor Play Equipment As Gymnastics Apparatus   444

The Process of Teaching Educational Gymnastics   444

The Learning Environment   445

Gymnastics Equipment   445

Stations   446

Varying the Task   446

Demonstrating   447

Spotting   447

Club Gymnasts   448

A Final Thought   448

Summary   448

Reading Comprehension Questions   449

References   449

26

Kicking and Punting   451

Levels of Skill Proficiency in Kicking   452

Precontrol Level: Activities for Exploration of Kicking   452

Kicking a Stationary Ball from a Stationary Position   452

Kicking at Large Targets   453

Approaching a Stationary Ball and Kicking   453

Tapping the Ball (As in Soccer)   458

Control Level: Learning Experiences Leading to Skill Development in Kicking   458

Kicking on the Ground   458

Kicking in the Air   459

Kicking for Distance   459

Kicking to a Distance Zone   460

Kicking to Targets   460

Kicking to a Rolling Ball from a Stationary Position   461

Kicking to a Partner   462

Tapping the Ball along the Ground (Soccer Dribble)   463

Starting and Stopping   463

Traveling in Pathways   463

Dribbling around Stationary Obstacles   464

Keeping It Perfect: Zero, Zero   464

Utilization Level: Learning Experiences Leading to Skill Development in Kicking   465

Changing Directions: Tap/Dribble   465

Performing a Continuous Tap/Dribble and Change of Direction   465

Traveling and Kicking for a Goal   466

Playing One-on-One Soccer   466

Playing Soccer Golf   467

Kicking to a Partner from Various Angles   467

Kicking to a Traveling Partner   468

Passing to a Partner in General Space   469

Playing Two-on-One Soccer   469

Proficiency Level: Learning Experiences Leading to Skill Development in Kicking   469

Kicking at Small Stationary Targets   469

Kicking at a Moving Target   470

Playing Minisoccer   470

Playing Soccer Keep-Away   470

Playing Alley Soccer   471

Playing Cone Soccer   471

Levels of Skill Proficiency in Punting   472

Precontrol Level: Activities for Exploration of Punting   473

Dropping, Bouncing, and Kicking Lightweight Balls   473

Dropping and Punting   473

Control Level: Learning Experiences Leading to Skill Development in Punting   473

Punting for Consistency   473

Punting over Low Ropes   475

Punting with an Approach   475

Punting Different Types of Balls   478

Punting for Distance   478

Using Punting Zones   478

Punting for Accuracy   479

Punting for Height   479

Utilization Level: Learning Experiences Leading to Skill Development in Punting   480

Punting at Angles   480

Punting to a Partner   481

Receiving a Pass, Then Punting   481

Punting within a Limited Time   481

Playing Rush the Circle   481

Proficiency Level: Learning Experiences Leading to Skill Development in Punting   482

Receiving and Punting against Opponents   482

Punting While Traveling   482

Playing Punt-Over   482

Reading Comprehension Questions   483

References   483

27

Throwing and Catching   485

Levels of Skill Proficiency in Throwing   486

Levels of Skill Proficiency in Catching   491

Precontrol Level: Activities for Exploration   494

Throwing a Yarn Ball against the Wall   494

Throwing at a Large Target   494

Catching a Rolling Ball   494

Catching from a Skilled Thrower   495

Drop—Catch   495

Tossing to Self and Catching   495

Control Level: Learning Experiences Leading to Skill Development   496

Throwing Overhand   496

Throwing Underhand   496

Throwing Sidearm   497

Overs, Unders, and Sides   497

Bouncing a Ball to Self and Catching It   497

Throwing an Object to Different Levels and Catching It   498

Catching in Different Places around the Body   498

Throwing Overhand at a Stationary Target   499

Hit the Can   499

Bowling for Targets   499

Throwing Underhand to Hoops   500

Throwing to High Targets   500

Throwing Backhand to a Target   500

Throwing a Frisbee   501

Catching with a Scoop   501

Throwing a Ball against a Wall and Catching the Rebound   502

Throwing for Distance   503

Throwing and Catching with a Partner   503

Throwing and Catching over a Net with a Partner   504

Bench Bounce Catch   505

Utilization Level: Learning Experiences Leading to Skill Development   505

Moving to Catch   505

Throwing and Catching While Traveling   506

Throwing on the Move   506

Throwing to Make a Partner Move to Catch   506

Throwing to a Moving Target   507

Throwing for Distance and Accuracy   507

Target Backaway   508

Playing Frisbee Golf   508

Catching to Throw Quickly to a Partner   509

Catching to Throw Quickly to a Target   509

Throwing While in the Air   509

Proficiency Level: Learning Experiences
Leading to Skill Development   510

Playing Frisbee Stretch   510

Running the Bases   510

Throwing to Avoid a Defender   511

Playing Keep Away   511

Playing Hit the Pin   512

Playing Half-Court Basketball (modified)   512

Playing Frisbee Football   513

Playing Four-Person Football   514

Playing Team Handball (modified)   514

Playing Passball   515

Reading Comprehension Questions   515

References   516

28

Volleying and Dribbling   517

Volleying   518

Levels of Skill Proficiency in Volleying   518

Precontrol Level: Activities for
Exploration   518

Striking Balloons in the Air   518

Striking a Balloon Forward   519

Striking with Different Body Parts   519

Striking Lightweight Objects   519

Control Level: Learning Experiences Leading to
Skill Development   521

*Striking a Ball Noncontinuously with Different
Body Parts   521*

*Striking a Ball Upward (Underhand
Pattern)   522*

*Striking a Ball Upward with the Forearms (the
Bump)   522*

*Striking a Ball to the Wall (Underhand
Pattern)   523*

*Striking a Ball over a Line (Underhand
Pattern)   524*

Playing Hoop Volley (Underhand Pattern)   524

*Playing Four Square, Two Square (Underhand
Pattern)   525*

*Striking over a Low Net (Underhand
Pattern)   525*

Volleying to the Wall (Overhead Pattern)   526

*Volleying a Ball Upward (Overhead
Pattern)   526*

Volleying to a Partner (Overhead Pattern)   526

Playing Keep It Up   527

Playing One-Bounce Volleyball   527

Obstacle-Course Volley   527

Utilization Level: Learning Experiences Leading
to Skill Development   527

Volleying Game: Child Designed   527

*Striking a Ball Continuously with Different Body
Parts   529*

Volleying with the Foot   529

Playing Aerial Soccer   530

Volleying with a Volleybird   531

*Striking to the Wall, Varying Levels, Force, and
Body Position   532*

Volleying over a Net   532

Volleying Continuously to a Partner   533

Volleying Three on Three   533

Serving Underhand over the Net   534

Proficiency Level: Learning Experiences
Leading to Skill Development   534

*Striking with Different Body Parts While
Traveling   534*

Serving Overhand over the Net   535

Striking Downward with Force   536

Spiking   536

Volleying in a Line Formation   537

Playing Modified Volleyball   537

Dribbling   537

Levels of Skill Proficiency in Dribbling   538

Precontrol Level: Activities for
Exploration   540

Bouncing a Ball Down and Catching It   540

*Bouncing a Ball Down (Dribbling)
Continuously   540*

Dribbling and Walking   540

Control Level: Learning Experiences Leading to
Skill Development   540

All the Time Dribble   540

Dribble Like a Basketball Player   541

Dribbling at Different Heights   542

Dribbling and Looking   542

Switches   542

*Dribbling with the Body in Different
Positions   543*

*Dribbling in Different Places around the Body
While Stationary   543*

Dribbling and Traveling   544

Moving Switches   544

Utilization Level: Learning Experiences Leading to Skill Development   544

Dribbling and Changing Speed of Travel   544

Dribbling While Changing Directions   545

Starting and Stopping While Changing Directions   546

Dribbling in Different Pathways   546

Dribbling around Stationary Obstacles   547

Mirroring and Matching While Dribbling   548

Dribbling and Passing with a Partner   548

Dribbling against an Opponent: One on One   548

Proficiency Level: Learning Experiences Leading to Skill Development   549

Dribbling against Opponents: Group Situations   549

Now You've Got It, Now You Don't   550

Dribble Tag   550

Dribbling While Dodging   551

Dribbling and Passing in Game Situations   551

Making Up Fancy Dribbling/Passing Routines   551

Dribbling and Throwing at a Target   551

Dribble/Pass Keep Away   552

Small-Group Basketball   552

Reading Comprehension Questions   553

References   553

29

Striking with Rackets and Paddles   555

Levels of Skill Proficiency   556

Precontrol Level: Activities for Exploration   556

Paddle Balance   557

Balloon Strike (Lightweight Paddle)   561

Striking a Suspended Ball   561

Hit the Wall   562

Upward Bound   562

Control Level: Learning Experiences Leading to Skill Development   563

Downs   563

Ups   563

Ups and Downs   564

Up Against the Wall (Striking Forward)   565

Ups, Downs, and Forwards   565

Both Sides (of the Paddle) Now   566

Striking to Wall Targets   566

Striking for Distance (Varying the Force)   567

Striking for Hoops (Varying the Distance)   567

To the Wall—Sideways (Sidearm Forehand Pattern)   567

To the Wall Again—Sideways (Sidearm Backhand Pattern)   568

Striking at High and Low Targets   569

Hitting to Different Places   570

Striking through a Target   570

Striking an Object to Send It over a Net   571

Striking a Ball Rebounding from a Wall   571

Striking Continuously over and through a Target   572

Utilization Level: Learning Experiences Leading to Skill Development   572

From Both Sides Now   572

Hitting Cooperatively and Continuously with a Partner   573

Striking to Different Places around a Partner   573

Striking Overhead   574

Demonstrate the Skill of Striking Overhead   574

Striking Overhead over a Net   574

Striking Continuously Upward with a Group   574

Striking in Various Aerial Pathways in Gamelike Situations   575

Racket Call Ball   575

Proficiency Level: Learning Experiences Leading to Skill Development   576

Wall Ball   576

Racket Corner Ball   577

Racket Four Square   577

Minitennis   578

Aerial Net Games   578

Minitennis Doubles   579

Badminton Volleyball   579

Self-Designed Racket Games   579

Reading Comprehension Questions   580

References   580

30

Striking with Long-Handled Implements   581

Levels of Skill Proficiency   582

Precontrol Level: Activities for Exploration   589

Striking a Stationary Ball—Golf or Hockey   589

Striking to Large Targets—Hockey/Golf   590

Striking off a Batting Tee—Bats   590

Striking (Dribbling) a Ball in Self-Space—Hockey   591

Traveling Slowly While Striking a Ball—Hockey   591

Control Level: Learning Experiences Leading to Skill Development   591

Striking a Stationary Ball on the Ground—Hockey or Golf   592

Striking in the Air—Golf   592

Striking for Distance—Golf or Hockey   592

Striking to Targets—Hockey   594

Striking to a Target (Around the World)—Hockey   594

Striking a Stationary Ball—Bats   594

Level Swings—Bats   595

Striking a Stationary Ball for Distance—Bats   596

Striking Suspended Objects—Bats   597

Hit and Run—Bats   597

Striking to a Stationary Partner—Hockey   598

Traveling Slowly While Striking a Ball—Hockey   598

Traveling, Stopping, and Controlling the Ball—Hockey   599

Traveling and Changing Speeds—Hockey   599

Traveling and Striking While Changing Pathways—Hockey   600

Striking to Different Places—Hockey   600

Hitting a Stationary Ball from Different Places—Bats   601

Striking to Varying Distances—Golf   601

Throwing a Ball in the Air and Striking It—Bats   601

Striking a Self-Tossed Ball to Different Distances—Bats   602

Striking a Pitched Ball—Bats   602

Striking While Dodging Stationary Obstacles—Hockey   604

Utilization Level: Learning Experiences Leading to Skill Development   604

Grounders and Flies—Bats   604

Directing the Placement of an Object—Bats   605

Hitting to Open Spaces—Bats   605

Striking a Pitched Object Varying the Distance—Bats   606

Batting, Combining Distance and Placement   606

Striking to Targets at Various Distances—Golf   606

Playing Hoop Golf   606

Playing Hockey Bowl (Small Targets)   607

Directing the Air Pathway of the Struck Object—Golf   607

Dribbling and Changing Directions Backward—Hockey   607

Performing a Continuous Dribble and Change of Direction—Hockey   608

Pathways, Speeds, and Directions—Hockey   608

Traveling and Striking for a Goal—Hockey   608

One-on-One Hockey   610

Striking from a Stationary Position to a Moving Target—Hockey   610

Passing and Receiving on the Move—Hockey   611

Keeping It Moving—Hockey   611

Two-on-One Hockey   611

Proficiency Level: Learning Experiences Leading to Skill Development   612

Striking to Dodge an Opponent—Hockey   612

Keep Away—Hockey   612

Directing the Pathway, Distance, and Speed of an Object—Golf   613

Directing the Pathway, Distance, and Speed of an Object (Call Your Hit)—Bats   613

Whiffle Ball Golf   614

Minihockey   614

Six-Player Teeball   615

One-Base Baseball   615

Half Ball—Bats   616

Reading Comprehension Questions   616

References   616

31

Skill Themes in Games   617

The Purpose of Games in the Elementary School   618

Games Experiences   618

Invariant Game Skill Experiences   621

Dynamic Gamelike Skill Experiences   622

Games-Playing Experiences   623

The Process of Teaching Games   624

Selecting a Game   624

Predesigned Games   624

Modified Predesigned Games   624

Teacher-Designed Games   625

Teacher/Child-Designed Games   625

Child-Designed Games   626

Games Equipment   627

The Name of the Game   627

Group Size   628

   To Ref or Not to Ref?   628

   The Learning Environment   628

After-School Sport Programs   628

Child Development and Games   628

A Final Thought   629

Summary   629

Reading Comprehension Questions   630

References/Suggested Readings   630

PART FIVE

The Future   633

32

Building Support for Your Program 635

The Principal   636

Teachers in the School   637

Parents   638

The School Board   642

The Community at Large   642

Children As Advocates   643

Summary   643

Reading Comprehension Questions   643

References/Suggested Readings   643

33

Physical Education for Tomorrow's Children   645

Appendix   A1

Index   I1

PART ONE

Introduction and Content Overview

A quality program of physical education for children is much more than simply a bunch of activities that children enjoy for thirty minutes or so several times a week. A quality program of physical education has a definite purpose, has long-term goals, and is developmentally appropriate; in short, it makes a difference for children that lasts well beyond elementary school.

Chapter 1, "The Value and Purpose of Physical Education for Children," relies on several recently published documents developed by the Surgeon General of the United States, The National Center for Chronic Disease Prevention and Health Promotion, and the landmark document *Standards for Physical Education* developed by the National Association for Sport and Physical Education (NASPE). Together these documents define a clear and unified direction (outcomes) for programs of physical education while also suggesting a process (developmentally appropriate) that is in the best interests of children.

Chapter 2, "The Skill Theme Approach," answers many of the questions that teachers often ask when they are first exposed to the skill theme approach. Because the content is organized by skills and concepts rather than by games, gymnastics, and dance, for example, some teachers initially find the approach confusing. In Chapter 2, we use a question-and-answer format to respond to these questions; then, in Chapter 3, we define the skill themes and movement concepts. Chapter 3 also includes many of the reasons that support the use of a skill theme approach in children's physical education.

Chapter 4 complements Chapter 3 in describing how physical fitness concepts are interwoven throughout our lessons. It also provides numerous examples of ways children can learn to include activities that enhance their fitness outside of organized physical education classes. It's important that children learn to do this because most programs simply don't allow enough time to help children improve both their physical abilities and their fitness.

If every school were exactly alike, we could now proceed to provide examples of activities that would "work" in every situation. As you know, however, no two schools or programs of physical education are exactly alike. "Reflective Teaching" (Chapter 5) describes how teachers adapt and adjust their programs according to the particular characteristics of their school (e.g., the number of days per week they teach physical education, the available facilities and equipment) and their children (e.g., background, experience, type of community).

The final chapter in Part 1 focuses specifically on "Children with Special Needs." Chapter 6 provides an overview of some of the ways teachers can adapt their lessons to provide these children experiences in physical education that are both beneficial and encouraging.

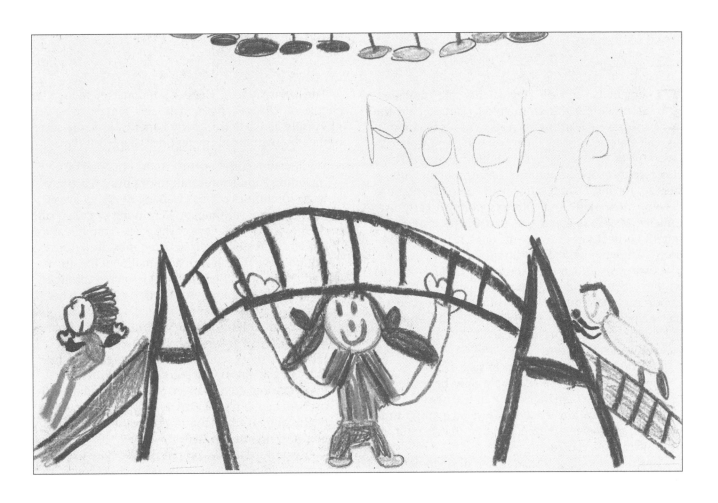

The Value and Purpose of Physical Education for Children

As the old man walked the beach at dawn, he noticed a young man ahead of him picking up starfish and flinging them into the sea. Finally catching up with the youth, he asked him why he was doing this. The answer was that the stranded starfish would die if left until the morning sun.

"But the beach goes on for miles and there are millions of starfish," countered the old man. "How can your effort make any difference?"

The young man looked at the starfish in his hand and then threw it to the safety of the waves. "It makes a difference to this one," he said.

——Donald Quimby

Elementary school curriculums are designed, among other things, to guide youngsters in the process of learning to read, write, use computers, calculate accurately, solve problems, and work collaboratively with others. In addition many schools also recognize the importance of introducing youngsters to art, music, and movement to enable them to develop their skills and interests from an early age. *Children Moving* is about one part of the elementary school curriculum—movement, or as it is more commonly known, physical education.

As we write this fourth edition of *Children Moving* we have better evidence than ever before about the important role a quality physical education program has the potential to play in the life of a child. We want to be very clear from the outset about how the authors view physical education.

Physical education *should not* be recess!

Physical education *should not* simply be a time to provide planning time for classroom teachers!

Physical education *should not* just be a "fun" time for children to expend excess energy that is built up from sitting in a classroom!

Physical education *should* be a developmentally appropriate educational experience designed to provide immediate and lifelong benefits—important benefits that are typically only taught in physical education classes.

Physical education curricula and instruction *should* emphasize enjoyable participation in physical activity and "help students develop the knowledge, attitudes, motor skills, behavioral skills, and confidence needed to adopt and maintain physically active lifestyles" (National Center for Chronic Disease Prevention and Health Promotion, 1997, p. 205).

Physical education *should* be an experience that *guides youngsters in the process of becoming physically active for a lifetime!*

Why?

The Benefits of Physical Activity

Schools that purport to educate the whole child, as many do in their mission statements, must recognize that physical education is a crucial part of that education. We all have bodies, and failure to educate them properly has serious consequences. These consequences outlined in Box 1.1 have never been scientifically documented more clearly than in the landmark document *Physical Activity and Health: A Report of the Surgeon General* (U.S. Department of Health and Human Services, 1996).

The 1996 Surgeon General's report concludes that people of all ages, both male and female, who are physically active derive many benefits. Here are some of the observations in the report (USDHHS, 1996):

- Significant health benefits can be obtained by including a moderate amount of physical activity (e.g., 30 minutes of brisk walking or raking leaves, 15 minutes of running, or 45 minutes of volleyball) on most, if not all, days of the week. Through a modest increase in daily activity, most Americans can improve their health and quality of life. (p. 4)
- Additional health benefits can be gained through greater amounts of physical activity. People who can maintain a regular regimen of activity that is of longer duration or of more vigorous intensity are likely to derive greater benefit. (p. 4)
- Physical activity reduces the risk of premature mortality in general, and of coronary heart disease, hypertension, colon cancer, and diabetes mellitus in particular. Physical activity also improves mental health and is important for the health of muscles, bones, and joints. (p. 4)
- Consistent influences on physical activity patterns among adults and young people include confidence in one's ability to engage in regular physical activity (e.g., self-efficacy), enjoyment of physical activity, support from others, positive beliefs concerning the benefits of physical activity, and lack of perceived barriers to physical activity. (p. 249)
- Physical activity appears to improve health-related quality of life by enhancing psychological well-being and by improving physical functioning in persons compromised by poor health. (p. 8)

Clearly, the accumulated evidence suggests that youngsters who are physically active stand to gain enormous health benefits. It's important to reemphasize, however, that this doesn't happen automatically. Programs must be carefully designed and implemented if they are to guide youngsters in the process of becoming physically active for a lifetime. (As Table 1-1 suggests, many programs still emphasize team sports more than lifetime activities.)

As anyone who knows children will quickly acknowledge, however, fears of heart disease, stress, or back pain in later years are not very real concerns for most eight- or ten-year-olds. To them, forty seems old! Fortunately children enter school loving to move and be active. As we know, one of the early tasks of primary-grade classroom teachers is to teach children to listen and stay in their seats. Most would prefer to be up and moving. The challenge of physical educators is not so much to instill a love of movement as it is to keep alive and channel this inborn urge to move so

Table 1.1   Activities Taught in Physical Education

Activity	Percentage of all courses*
Basketball	86.8
Volleyball	82.3
Baseball/softball	81.5
Flag/touch football	68.5
Soccer	65.2
Jogging†	46.5
Weight lifting or training†	37.3
Tennis†	30.3
Aerobic dance†	29.6
Walking quickly†	14.7
Swimming†	13.6
Handball†	13.2
Racquetball†	4.9
Hiking/backpacking†	3.0
Bicycling†	1.3

SOURCE: School Health Practices and Programs Study (1994), U.S. Department of Health and Human Services, p. 237.

* Percentage of all physical education courses in which more than one class period was devoted to each activity, by activity.
† Lifetime physical activities

that as individuals enter their adult years they will continue to enjoy being physically active and derive all of the benefits—physical, emotional, social—that come to those who have been physically active throughout their lifetime. How does that happen?

As with art and music, and many of the other subjects taught in elementary schools, the time devoted to physical education varies widely from school to school and from teacher to teacher. Children in some elementary schools, for example, "go to PE" twice a week with a "specialist" who has majored in physical education in college and has been certified by the state to teach physical education. In other schools children have daily physical education (also known as "gym" class for some strange reason) taught by the classroom teacher, who typically has a limited background in this subject area. The ideal situation, from the standpoint of the child, of course, is to have physical education every day, taught by a professional with an extensive background in children's physical education. Why, you ask? There are many reasons. One of the more obvious is changing lifestyles.

In times past many youngsters derived some of their physical education from playing with friends after school and on weekends. As one drove through neighborhoods, it was common to see children playing outside. Today, instead of playing outside after school, many children watch television and play computer games; consequently, many children are less physically

BOX 1.1   THE PHYSICALLY UNEDUCATED ADULT

Adults who are physically uneducated often find themselves in awkward and unpleasant situations. For example, they may:

■ Be overweight as a result of physical inactivity
■ Have chronic lower back pain
■ Have painful memories of being picked last when teams were chosen
■ Remember being laughed at because they couldn't catch a softball or were afraid of a volleyball
■ Recall being last whenever they ran laps
■ Dread the memory of never being able to do even one pull-up on the physical fitness test
■ Be uncomfortable starting, and maintaining, an exercise program
■ Feel like a "klutz" and make excuses to avoid physical activity
■ Believe that athletes were born that way
■ Not understand that there are virtually hundreds of ways to exercise and that they would enjoy some of them

BOX 1.2   ARE YOUNGSTERS PHYSICALLY ACTIVE TODAY?

The 1996 Surgeon General's report, *Physical Activity and Health,* cites a number of alarming statistics about physical activity patterns in adolescents and also about physical education programs. For example:

- Only about one-half of U.S. young people (ages 12–21 years) regularly participate in vigorous physical activity. One-fourth report no vigorous physical activity.
- Approximately one-fourth of young people walk or bicycle (i.e., engage in light to moderate activity) nearly every day.
- About 14 percent of young people report no recent vigorous or light-to-moderate physical activity. This indicator of inactivity is higher among females than males and among black females than white females.
- Males are more likely than females to participate in vigorous physical activity, strengthening activities, and walking or bicycling.
- Participation in all types of physical activity declines strikingly as age or grade in school increases.
- Among high school students, enrollment in physical education remained unchanged during the first half of the 1900s. However, daily attendance in physical education declined from approximately 42 percent to 25 percent.
- The percentage of high school students who were enrolled in physical education and who reported being physically active for at least 20 minutes in physical education classes declined from approximately 81 percent to 70 percent during the first half of this decade.
- Only 19 percent of all high school students report being physically active for 20 minutes or more in daily physical education classes.

SOURCE: From *Physical Activity and Health: A Report of the Surgeon General* (p. 8), by U.S. Department of Health and Human Services, 1996, Atlanta, GA: USDHHS, Centers for Disease Control and Prevention, National Center for Chronic Disease Prevention and Health Promotion.

fit than their counterparts in past years (Box 1.2). No doubt their motor skills are also inferior. These are the children who stand to benefit most from physical education. A child—or an adult, for that matter—who is not physically educated will fail to derive the benefits of regular participation in physical activity.

This book is designed to introduce you to a children's physical education program or approach that's designed for every child, from the least skilled child in a class to the most athletic youngster. The book explains the ways you can guide all children in positive directions, enabling them to develop the competence that leads to confidence in their physical abilities. This competence and this confidence eventually culminate in a desire to participate regularly in physical activity, because it has become an enjoyable and important part of their lives as children, as teens, and later as adults. In this chapter, we provide an overarching view of quality physical education by briefly responding to three fundamental questions:

1. What is the purpose of a quality physical education program?
2. What are the known benefits of a quality physical education program?
3. What are the characteristics of a quality physical education program for children?

No doubt you have noticed that each of these questions contains the term *quality.* We want to be honest with you from the beginning—not every physical education program is a quality program. Some are little more than organized recesses. Others year after year emphasize only a few team sports. Still others feature low organized games that are enjoyable but do little to enhance either the motor skills or the physical fitness of children.

BOX 1.3   CONTENT STANDARDS IN PHYSICAL EDUCATION

A physically educated person:

1. Demonstrates competency in many movement forms and proficiency in a few movement forms.
2. Applies movement concepts and principles to the learning and development of motor skills.
3. Exhibits a physically active lifestyle.
4. Achieves and maintains a health-enhancing level of physical fitness.
5. Demonstrates responsible personal and social behavior in physical activity settings.
6. Demonstrates understanding and respect for differences among people in physical activity settings.
7. Understands that physical activity provides opportunities for enjoyment, challenge, self-expression, and social interaction.

SOURCE: From *Moving into the Future: National Standards for Physical Education* (p. 1), by National Association for Sport and Physical Education, 1995, St. Louis: Mosby. With permission from the National Association for Sport and Physical Education (NASPE), 1900 Association Drive, Reston, VA 20191-1599.

The Purpose of Physical Education

What is the purpose of a quality physical education program? Several years ago, we would have offered you our own answer, because at that time there was no national consensus about the purpose of physical education. Today, for the first time ever in the physical education profession, a response to this question has been developed at the national level to provide physical education teachers with a general direction about the purposes of physical education. The National Association for Sport and Physical Education (NASPE), as part of an effort titled the Outcomes Project, spent several years developing content standards for physical education. To make the document straightforward and easy to understand, NASPE (1995) wrote it as a response to the question, "What is a physically educated person?" (Box 1.3).

The NASPE statement represents the ultimate goal of many physical education programs in school districts: to ensure that by the time youngsters graduate from high school they are physically educated. Needless to say, this definition implies that youngsters participate daily, or almost daily, in a quality program from an early age (ideally in preschool) through the twelfth grade (National Center for Chronic Disease Prevention and Health Promotion, 1997).

PE CENTRAL
http://pe.central.vt.edu/

▶ Throughout the fourth edition of *Children Moving* we will be referring to the 1996 report of the Surgeon General entitled *Physical Activity and Health* (U.S. Department of Health and Human Services, 1996) and also to NASPE's (1995) *National Standards for Physical Education.* Both of these documents appear in the reference list at the end of this chapter. If you use the Internet, however, you can learn more about them—and how to order them—by going to a Web site called PE Central, which is sponsored by Virginia Tech University. PE Central was created by Mark Manross and Todd Pennington. In addition to links to the Surgeon General's report and the *National Standards,* it also contains developmentally appropriate lesson ideas, ready-to-use assessments, conference and job announcements, kids' quotes, and links to other Web sites of interest to physical educators. The address, or URL, for PE Central is http://pe.central.vt.edu/. When you visit PE Central you will also find easy-to-use forms for sharing your lesson and assessment ideas with other physical educators. We encourage you to share some of your best ideas.

BOX 1.4 APPROPRIATE AND INAPPROPRIATE PHYSICAL EDUCATION PRACTICES

Component: Curriculum

Appropriate Practice: The physical education curriculum has an obvious scope and sequence based on goals and objectives that are appropriate for all children. It includes a balance of skills, concepts, games, educational gymnastics, rhythms, and dance experiences designed to enhance the cognitive, motor, affective, and physical fitness development of every child.

Inappropriate Practice: The physical education curriculum lacks developed goals and objectives and is based primarily upon the teacher's interests, preferences, and background rather than those of the children. For example, the curriculum consists primarily of large-group games.

Component: Development of Movement Concepts and Motor Skills

Appropriate Practice: Children are provided with frequent and meaningful age-appropriate practice opportunities which enable individuals to develop a functional understanding of movement concepts (body awareness, space awareness, effort, and relationships) and build competence and confidence in their ability to perform a variety of motor skills (locomotor, nonlocomotor, and manipulative).

Inappropriate Practice: Children participate in a limited number of games and activities where the opportunity for individual children to develop basic concepts and motor skills is restricted.

Component: Concepts of Fitness

Appropriate Practice: Children participate in activities that are designed to help them understand and value the important concepts of physical fitness and the contribution they make to a healthy lifestyle.

Inappropriate Practice: Children are required to participate in fitness activities, but are not helped to understand the reasons why.

Component: Cognitive Development

Appropriate Practice: Physical education activities are designed with both the physical and the cognitive development of children in mind.

Experiences which encourage children to question, integrate, analyze, communicate, and apply cognitive concepts, as well as gain a multicultural view of the world, are provided, thus making physical education a part of the total educational experience.

Inappropriate Practice: The unique role of physical education, which allows children to learn to move while also moving to learn, is not explored and recognized by instructors.

Children do not receive opportunities to integrate their physical education experience with art, music, and other classroom experiences.

Component: Affective Development

Appropriate Practice: Teachers intentionally design and teach activities throughout the year which allow children the opportunity to work together for the purpose of improving their emerging social and cooperation skills. These activities also help children develop a positive self-concept.

Teachers help all children experience and feel the satisfaction and joy which results from regular participation in physical activity.

Inappropriate Practice: Teachers fail to intentionally enhance the affective development of children when activities are excluded which foster the development of cooperation and social skills.

Teachers ignore opportunities to help children understand the emotions they feel as a result of participation in physical activity.

The Characteristics of a Quality Physical Education Program

Up to this point, we have written of the potential benefits and value of participating regularly in physical activity. As we have said several times, these benefits don't accrue automatically—they are specific to programs described as "quality" programs of physical education. But what do we mean by a "quality" program? What are its characteristics? See Box 1.4.

This question has been addressed succinctly in a document developed by the Council on Physical Education for Children (COPEC), the nation's largest professional association of children's physical education teachers. According to the COPEC (1992) position statement:

Component: Success Rate

Appropriate Practice: Children are given the opportunity to practice skills at high rates of success adjusted for their individual skill levels.

Inappropriate Practice: Children are asked to perform activities that are too easy or too hard, causing frustration, boredom, and/or misbehavior.

All children are expected to perform to the same standards without allowing for individual abilities and interests.

Component: Regular Involvement for Every Child

Appropriate Practice: Children participate in their regularly scheduled physical education class because it is recognized as an important part of their overall education.

Inappropriate Practice: Children are removed from physical education classes to participate in classroom activities and/or as a punishment for not completing assignments or for misbehavior in the classroom.

Component: PE and Recess

Appropriate Practice: Physical education classes are planned and organized to provide children with opportunities to acquire the physical, emotional, cognitive, and social benefits of physical education.

Inappropriate Practice: "Free-play," or recess, is used as a *substitute* for daily, organized physical education lessons. Free-play, in this case, is characterized by a lack of goals, organization, planning, and instruction.

Component: Active Participation for Every Child

Appropriate Practice: All children are involved in activities which allow them to remain continuously active.

Classes are designed to meet a child's needs for active participation in all learning experiences.

Inappropriate Practice: Activity time is limited because children are waiting in lines for a turn in relay races, to be chosen for a team, or due to limited equipment or playing games such as Duck, Duck, Goose.

Children are organized into large groups where getting a turn is based on individual competitiveness or aggressive behavior.

Children are eliminated with no chance to reenter the activity, or they must sit for long periods of time. For example, activities such as musical chairs, dodgeball, and elimination tag provide limited opportunities for many children, especially the slower, less agile ones, who actually need activity the most.

Component: Gender-Directed Activities

Appropriate Practice: Girls and boys are provided equal access to participation in individual, partner, small-group, and team activities. Both girls and boys are equally encouraged, supported, and socialized toward successful achievement in all realms of physical activity.

Statements by physical education teachers support leadership opportunities and provide positive reinforcement in a variety of activities which may be considered gender-neutral.

Inappropriate Practice: Girls are encouraged to participate in activities which stress traditionally feminine roles, whereas boys are encouraged to participate in more aggressive activities.

Boys are more often provided with leadership roles in physical education class. Statements by teachers reinforce traditional socialization patterns which provide for greater and more aggressive participation by boys and lesser and more passive participation by girls.

SOURCE: From *Developmentally Appropriate Physical Education Practices for Children: A Position Statement of the Council on Physical Education Practices for Children (COPEC)*, 1992, Reston, VA: National Association for Sport and Physical Education. Reprinted with permission.

Quality physical education is both developmentally and instructionally suitable for the specific children being served. *Developmentally appropriate* practices in physical education are those which recognize children's changing capacities to move and those which promote such change. A developmentally appropriate physical education program accommodates a variety of individual characteristics such as developmental status, previous movement experiences, fitness and skill levels, body size, and age. *Instructionally appropriate* physical education incorporates the best known practices, derived from both research and experiences teaching children, into a program that maximizes opportunities for learning and success for all children.

Knowledge of the educationally appropriate and inappropriate characteristics of programs enables teachers to understand, and reflect upon, the characteristics of their own programs—and the impact they may be having on children. When implemented, these characteristics are indices of a *quality* program of physical education. We have selected a number of these components to share with you at the outset of the book to help you understand our approach to children's physical education. These components help clarify what the concept of quality physical education for children means. In later chapters we will share additional components as they apply directly to the contents discussed in those chapters.

SUMMARY

Quality physical education programs for children have never been more important than they are today. The three overarching questions provide an introduction to the program and teaching process described in the text. The responses to the questions taken from the recent literature (1) define a physically educated person, (2) summarize the known benefits of physical education programs, and (3) define a quality physical education program for children as one that is developmentally appropriate.

READING COMPREHENSION QUESTIONS

1. Why are physical education programs for children today more important than ever? Cite several examples from your personal background to support your answer.
2. Chapter 1 suggests that the purpose of physical education programs in the schools is to "guide youngsters in the process of becoming physically active for a lifetime." Why is it important for teachers to have a straightforward statement like this? In one sentence provide your own statement describing the purpose of physical education in the schools.
3. This chapter lists a number of benefits of participating in physical education programs that have been documented in the research literature. Why do you think the list isn't longer? Describe several benefits that you think accrue from physical education that have yet to be supported in the literature.
4. Quality programs have been described as developmentally appropriate. Reflect on your past experiences in physical education, and provide examples of both appropriate and inappropriate practice. What, if any, long-term impact did these examples have on you? On others?
5. Both the Surgeon General's report on physical activity and health (USDHHS, 1996) and the *National Standards for Physical Education* (NASPE, 1995) are extremely important documents for the profession of physical education. Explain why these two documents are important, and list at least three ways you might use them to build support for your program of physical education with parents and administrators.

REFERENCES

Council on Physical Education for Children (COPEC). (1992). *Developmentally appropriate physical education practices for children: A position statement of the Council on Physical Education for Children.* Reston, VA: National Association for Sport and Physical Education.

National Association for Sport and Physical Education. (1995). *Moving into the future: National standards for physical education.* St. Louis, MO: Mosby.

Quimby, D. (1988). The starfish. *TEAM, 2(6).*

The National Center for Chronic Disease Prevention and Health Promotion, Centers for Disease Control and Prevention. (1997). Guidelines for school and community programs to promote lifelong physical activity among young people. *Journal of School Health*, **76**(6), 202–219.

U.S. Department of Health and Human Services (USDHHS). (1996). *Physical activity and health: A report of the Surgeon General.* Atlanta, GA: USDHHS, Centers for Disease Control and Prevention, National Center for Chronic Disease Prevention and Health Promotion.

CHAPTER 2

The Skill Theme Approach

Physical fitness, movement skills, concept and affective development should be emphasized throughout the curriculum. The greatest emphasis during the preschool and early elementary grades should be upon movement skill acquisition.

——NASPE, 1992

By now we hope you are asking questions like these:

- So what does developmentally appropriate physical education look like?

- What can a teacher do to help youngsters develop the skills and desire to become physically active for a lifetime?

Our answers to these questions are contained in what has come to be known as the "skill theme approach," which describes both the *content* of children's physical education (what is actually taught; detailed in Parts Three and Four of *Children Moving*) and also the teaching process, or *pedagogy* (described in Part Two of this book). This chapter answers the two questions above and also provides an overview of the skill theme approach and explains how it differs from elementary school physical education as taught in years past.

The program content described in Parts Three and Four may be different from what you experienced in elementary school. For example, in the upcoming chapters you might be expecting to find explanations of how to teach such games as Duck, Duck, Goose; Brownies and Fairies; Red Rover; Crows and Cranes; or even kickball and dodgeball. You might also expect to find the rules for softball or soccer. These games, and others like them, aren't in *Children Moving* for very good reasons.

Why Don't You Describe Such Activities as Duck, Duck, Goose and Kickball?

There are two major reasons why we don't include many of the so-called traditional activities. First, activities such as these, in which children are singled out to perform solo with everyone watching them, can be both embarrassing and discouraging when the less skilled children are "on center stage." Needless to say, children (or adults, for that matter) who are embarrassed or made to feel inadequate are hardly motivated to participate. One of our primary goals is to encourage children to develop positive attitudes about themselves and about physical activity so that they choose to be physically active throughout their lives. Games such as the ones named above are developmentally inappropriate in that they do not take into account the varying skill abilities of children within a class (COPEC, 1992) and thereby force some children into situations that make them unhappy and may lead them to dislike physical activity.

Second, these games emphasize "winning" more than learning. Another of our primary goals is to help children develop the movement competence that enables them to participate in physical activity successfully and with enjoyment. For this reason, we have organized our content, or suggested curriculum, around skill themes rather than the more complex movement forms of games, gymnastics, and dance.

What Are Skill Themes?

Skill themes are fundamental movements that are later modified into the more specialized patterns on which activities of increasing complexity are built. Once the basic skills are learned to a certain degree of proficiency, they can be combined with other skills and used in more complex settings, such as those found in dance, games, and gymnastics. The intent is to help children learn a variety of locomotor, nonmanipulative, and manipulative skills that they can use to enjoyably and confidently play a sport, for example, or perform a dance consisting of an intricate set of movements. The Curriculum Diamond (Figure 2.1), originally created by physical educators Dawn McCrumb and Wendy Mustain in 1995, illustrates this concept. The model was expanded and elaborated upon by George Graham, Ken Bell, and Catherine Himberg in 1996. The intention of this model is to help physical educators think about and design curriculums that will "guide youngsters in the process of becoming physically active for a lifetime." Grade levels are suggested in the model for illustration purposes only. Clearly decisions about when to introduce different content will need to be based on the progress made by the students in a given program.

What Is the Curriculum Diamond?

The Curriculum Diamond suggests a curricular focus corresponding to the grade level structure of most school districts across the United States—elementary, middle, and high school. It follows the recommendations of the National Center for Chronic Disease Prevention and Health Promotion (1977) and the *National Standards for Physical Education* (NASPE, 1995) by developing a broad foundation at the elementary and middle-school levels and then focusing on proficiency in a few movement forms at the high school level.

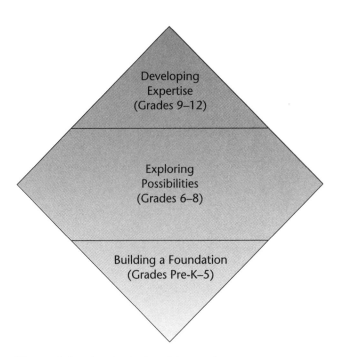

Figure 2.1 The Curriculum Diamond.

Building a Foundation (Grades Pre-K–5)

The bottom part of the diamond represents the earliest ages at which children are introduced to a wide range of skill themes and movement concepts. The focus is on developing a functional understanding of the concepts of space awareness, effort, and relationships. As children develop, they are introduced to a wide range of skill themes designed to encourage and assist them in beginning to acquire the fundamental competencies that will become the foundation skills for many of the sports and physical activities they will pursue as adolescents and adults. You will notice that the diamond widens as each layer is laid upon the foundational layer that precedes it—movement concepts and skill themes are constantly revisited based on the developmental and skill levels of the students being taught.

Exploring Possibilities (Grades 6–8)

In the middle-school years, you will notice that the diamond is at its widest but that it also rests upon the foundation that ideally was built in grades pre-K–5. At this point the focus shifts from building a foundation to utilizing it in a variety of movement forms. Skills continue to be developed and learned, but the focus is on exposing students to a broad array of content areas

designed to stimulate interest in lifetime and health-enhancing activities. It is this broad exposure to and exploration of movement and activity that will stimulate interest in the next part of the diamond.

Developing Expertise (Grades 9–12)

We hope that the exposure to many options in middle school stimulated student interest in a handful of lifetime and health-enhancing activities. When students enter high school, the diamond begins to narrow, suggesting that students will begin to make decisions about the activities they enjoy and desire to become proficient in. It is at this point that students choose electives based on the possibilities they explored in middle school. As students approach the peak, the focus narrows. This is the time when students develop the expertise that enables them to participate in several activities enjoyably and with confidence, thereby enabling them to accrue the benefits that come to those who remain physically active for a lifetime. This is the time when students refine the skill themes and movement concepts they learned in the early years for use in specific sports and physical activities.

What Are the Characteristics of the Skill Theme Approach?

There are three characteristics of the skill theme approach (content and pedagogy combined) that clearly distinguish it from the "primary use of dance, games, and gymnastic activities . . . considered the traditional 'activity' approach" (Gabbard, LeBlanc, & Lowy, 1987, p. 3).

Characteristic 1

Competence in performing a variety of locomotor, nonmanipulative, and manipulative motor skills is a major purpose of the skill theme approach.

The skill theme approach reflects the growing concern that children who participate in programs emphasizing games playing rather than motor skills learning don't necessarily improve their motor ability (Graham, 1987; Manross, 1992). The logical implication, of course, is that adults with inefficient motor skills tend to avoid physical activities that require them to use these poorly learned skills and as a consequence develop tendencies toward "couch potato-

BOX 2.1   CRITICAL ELEMENTS IN THE SKILL THEME APPROACH

One of the sample benchmarks for second-graders in the *National Standards* suggests that children be able to "identify four characteristics of a mature throw" (NASPE, 1995, p. 20). In the skill theme approach, as you will see in later chapters, we focus on children learning the critical elements. Manross (1992) interviewed twenty-five children who had been taught using a skill theme approach and twenty-five children whose curriculum consisted primarily of low organized games. As part of his study he asked the children to identify the critical elements (cues) of the overhand throw. It was clear that the children in the skill theme approach (Pendleton Elementary School) could describe many of the critical elements of a mature overhand throw, whereas the children at the other school (Eckland) really had not learned the critical elements. The table contains their responses.

Answer	No. of Times Stated
Pendleton (Skill Theme Approach)	
Turn your side to the target	17
Step with the opposite foot	15
Arm way back	10
Aim at target	9
Follow through	3
Step through with other foot	2
Let elbow lead	1
Twist body at waist	1
Bring arm straight over, not sidearm	1
Eckland (Low Organized Games)	
Get straight in front of target	4
Hold ball with tight grip	3
Bring hand back behind shoulder	3
Follow through	2
Try your best	2
Don't know	2
Practice	2
Don't be scared of the ball	2
Take a forward step	2
Throw hard	2
Aim at target	2
Don't strain arm	2
Try to throw sidearm	1
Hold your hand straight	1
Work on stance	1
Don't throw hard	1
Pretend it is hot object	1
Don't get nervous	1
Keep mind on throwing	1
Make sure they see good	1
Have a strong arm	1
Keep eye on ball	1

ism." See Box 2.1 for one example of the difference in outcomes of the two approaches.

A basic assumption is that a curriculum that is "scoped and sequenced" by skill themes provides students with the requisite skills for participating in adult versions of sports, dance, and the myriad other physical activities that are available today—and those that will be invented tomorrow. As physical educators we're able to help children learn these skills more quickly and with less frustration than they would if they attempted to learn the skills on their own.

The skill themes are generic, in the sense that they are not tied to any single sport or activity. Rather, they transcend, or cut across, structured activities. For example, jumping and landing (Chapter 22) is studied initially as a fundamental skill (one-foot takeoff to a two-foot landing) and later as a skill in the context of a game (jumping to catch), a dance (leaping in synchrony with a partner), and gymnastics (jumping and turning as part of a sequence).

Some skill theme chapters include rules for games (e.g., Chapters 21, 26, and 27), but these rules are suggested as part of the skill theme progression for children at more advanced levels (e.g., utilization and proficiency levels, as described in Chapter 7). To reach the more advanced levels, the children will spend

BOX 2.2 TEST YOUR MOTOR DEVELOPMENT IQ

Motor development, defined as "the process of change in an individual's movement behaviors . . . is both the underlying basis for and the end product of sound instruction in physical education" (Barnett & Merriman, 1992, p. 5). There are a number of misconceptions related to motor development, however. To test your "motor development IQ," indicate which of the statements below are true and which are false. The correct answers can be found in the Summary at the end of this chapter.

T F 1. Motor development is a finite process that ends at a predetermined age.

T F 2. All children at a given age can be expected to exhibit the same level of development in their motor skills.

T F 3. As children get older, their motor skills always get better.

T F 4. Reflexes have no influence on motor development past infancy.

T F 5. Most children perform the fundamental motor skills correctly.

T F 6. All children receive sufficient play opportunities involving physical activity to develop efficient and effective motor skills.

T F 7. Children have different levels of general motor ability, which influence their performance on all motor skills.

T F 8. There is only one correct form for each fundamental motor skill.

T F 9. Genetics alone determines the optimal level of motor development that an individual child will attain.

T F 10. Males always outperform females in motor skills.

SOURCE: From "Misconceptions in Motor Development," by B. E. Barnett and W. J. Merriman, 1992, *Strategies*, 5(3) 5–7.

---

considerable amounts of time on tasks devoted to learning these skills—initially in rather static environments—prior to using them successfully within the dynamic setting of an organized game, for example. In this book games are carefully selected (or designed) to enhance skill acquisition as part of a long-term progression rather than simply as a way to keep children "busy, happy, and good" for thirty minutes or so.

In addition to including a progression of tasks for developing each skill theme from the beginning level through the advanced (Part Four), each chapter includes information (written descriptions, diagrams, and/or photos) to assist the teacher in the process of observing children (this process is first described in Chapter 11) to help them develop efficient and biomechanically correct motor patterns (see Chapter 12).

Characteristic 2

The skill theme approach is designed to provide experiences appropriate to a child's developmental level, as opposed to age or grade level.

One of the many challenges of teaching is to match the content of the lesson to the abilities of the students (Chapter 12). As we all know, both grade level and age are unreliable indices of ability. A second characteristic of the skill theme approach is that it uses the students' developmental level as a guide for selecting the content to be taught. See Box 2.2 to assess your own knowledge of motor development.

The generic levels of skill proficiency (Chapter 7) serve as guides for assessing the abilities of the children and then selecting tasks that are matched to their abilities. If the majority of children in a class, for example, were unable to hit a ball against a wall continually so that it returned on a single bounce, we wouldn't require them to participate in a game requiring an even greater ability to strike the ball—for example, a game that required them to hit a ball to a partner (Chapter 29).

In the skill theme approach, the tasks are selected according to the children's abilities, not a predetermined calendar that implies that all children of the same grade develop at the same rate. This is especially important, for example, when the skill development of children may be limited because they have physical education classes only one or two days a week (Graham, Metzler, & Webster, 1991). In practice, this means that if three consecutive fourth-grade classes were taught by an experienced teacher using a skill theme approach, one class might be challenged with a more difficult series of tasks than another (Graham, Hopple, Manross, & Sitzman, 1993). And within each of the three fourth-grade classes, students might be challenged individually or in groups to undertake different tasks (Chapter 11).

We can use the skill of throwing (Chapter 27) to illustrate how a skill theme is developmentally sequenced. At the most basic level (precontrol), children are encouraged to throw a ball hard or to throw it far. These tasks lead to the development of greater trunk rotation and foot-arm opposition, for example, which combine with other critical components to form a mature (biomechanically efficient) throwing pattern. Throwing for distance, however, is only one type of throwing. As the children learn the components of an overhand throw for distance, they are challenged by tasks that involve throwing at targets, throwing to a partner, and throwing while moving. At more advanced levels (utilization and proficiency), they might be invited to participate in a game of Keep Away involving throwing, such as two against two or three against one (three throwers, one defender). The teacher bases these decisions, however, on the children's readiness rather than age or grade level. Throwing efficiently and effectively then becomes a focus that is interwoven and revisited as variations of this skill theme are revisited throughout the program.

Characteristic 3

The scope and sequence of the skill themes are designed to reflect the varying needs and interests of students over a period of years.

The third characteristic of the skill theme approach can be found within the scope and sequence recommendations (see Chapter 8 and Appendix A). Rather than focusing on the same skill theme for several weeks (in a three- or six-week unit, for example), we focus on a skill theme for brief periods and then revisit it at various times during the year. At the beginning levels (precontrol and control), we might spend only two or three days in a row on a skill theme. In fact, we might not even spend an entire class period on one skill theme. As children gain proficiency, expanding their motor repertoire, they become more interested in spending larger amounts of time (three or four days) on the same skill theme because the tasks are

more complex and involved, and their success rate is higher.

Revisiting the same skill theme several times during a year also allows the teacher to teach virtually the same lesson that was taught two or three months before. This is often necessary when the skill of the children doesn't improve noticeably. A teacher who remains on the same skill theme for many days in a row, however, is tempted to make the tasks harder (in an effort to alleviate the boredom of both the children and the teacher) than the children may be ready for.

Isn't It Difficult to Maintain Youngsters' Interest in a Program That Emphasizes the Fundamentals?

Ideally, children begin this program in preschool. When they do, this is really the only program they know, so their interest is high. When we introduce this program to children in the fourth and fifth grades for the first time, some initially have a difficult time adjusting, particularly the highly skilled children who enjoy playing games they dominate. In time, however, children learn to enjoy this program because they're improving. We also attempt to adjust the activities to the youngsters' skill level, and this makes the lessons more interesting.

What Does "Adjusting the Activities" Mean?

In essence, this is the concept of reflective teaching (Chapter 5). If a boy can't catch a ball, for example, then he isn't going to enjoy playing a game of softball in which the score is kept and winning is important. For this child we provide noncompetitive activities that he can succeed at. In the same class, however, a girl may have played softball on a team for several years and be very good. We try to provide her with gamelike activities related to softball in which she and a group of classmates may choose to keep score. In reading and math classes, for more effective learning the children are grouped by ability. Although it's harder to do this in physical education, we do provide different tasks based on the youngsters' ability. We group children by four skill levels: *precontrol, control, utilization,* and *proficiency.* Children at the precontrol level are unable consciously to control or replicate a particular movement. Control-level children are able to replicate particular movements that now respond more accurately to the child's intentions. Children at the utilization level are able to move automatically and reflexively and are therefore ready to study combinations of skill themes. Children at the proficiency level are challenged by repeating movements exactly or using movements in dynamic, unpredictable situations because they've gained control of the movement. (Skill levels are explained more fully in Chapter 7.) In addition, the tasks in each skill theme chapter are arranged from simple to complex, based on these four skill levels.

Where Is Physical Fitness in the Skill Theme Approach?

Physical fitness is an important part of the skill theme approach. As we explain in Chapter 4, it is interwoven throughout the program rather than confined to one separate unit. Our emphasis is not on *training* children so that they score well on a physical fitness test battery. Rather, we try to provide experiences that help them to understand and value the importance of physical fitness. We also try to help children enjoy physical activity so that they choose to make it a part of their daily lives (NASPE, 1995; U.S. Department of Health and Human Services, 1996). The success of the physical fitness component within the skill theme approach is measured, not by the children's scores on a physical fitness test battery, but by an assessment of their understanding of, attitudes toward, and enjoyment of physical activity.

Some of our lessons are devoted primarily to helping children understand and apply the important fitness concepts. In virtually every lesson we teach, however, we try to ensure that children are active the vast majority of the time, with a minimum of waiting, listening, and managing (Chapters 9 and 14), thereby enhancing their cardiovascular benefits. We also find that running laps or doing jumping jacks, for example, seem to be a waste of time when children can obtain the same benefits while also learning and enjoying physical activity—in playing tag games, learning new jump rope tricks, or perfecting a sequence of jumping and landing and rolling.

Where Do the Cognitive and Affective Domains Fit into the Skill Theme Approach?

As we do with the physical fitness aspect of the skill theme approach, we try to weave the important concepts of cognitive and affective dimensions into our lessons rather than deal with them as separate entities. Throughout the chapters, you will find examples and suggestions that might be labeled *cognitive* or *affective*—encouraging children to cooperate with one another in designing a game, for example, or to discover the most stable type of balance they might make. In this way we blend these important dimensions into the lessons instead of isolating them as separate units of learning.

What about Dance and Gymnastics?

Initially our focus is on helping children develop and learn the basic skills. As children learn these skills, the skills are placed into the contexts of dance and gymnastics (and also games). It's important to understand that the purpose of dance, gymnastics, and games extends beyond simply skill improvement. *Dance* is a form of expression by moving to rhythm alone or with others. *Gymnastics* is a series of acrobatic skills combined into smooth, repeatable sequences performed on the floor and/or apparatus to demonstrate strength, balance, and body control. *Games* are organized activities that use manipulative skills and are played for the enjoyment and satisfaction of cooperating and competing with others.

Dance, gymnastics, and games require skills that are best learned initially *outside* these contexts. It's ineffective to always practice the skills outside these contexts, however, so the contexts of dance, gymnastics, and games are interwoven throughout the movement concept and skill theme chapters (Parts Three and Four). The chapters on dance, gymnastics, and games (Chapters 20, 25, and 31, respectively) illustrate this technique.

An analogy with reading also illustrates this point. We teach children to read; as adults they choose what they'll read. Our goal is to provide a solid foundation for the variety of games, gymnastics, and dance situations the children will experience later as adolescents and adults. Right now the children might tell us they aren't interested in some skills. But twenty years from now, who knows?

Isn't This a Harder Way to Teach? How Do Experienced Teachers React to Developing the Content This Way?

Initially this approach is harder. Anything new is harder. Some teachers try it for a few weeks and give up. Others stick with it and find that, in the long run, it's better for the children. At times teachers find it's tempting to take the easy way. It's far less trouble, for example, to teach a game like kickball and then let the

BOX 2.3   WHO TAUGHT YOU TO THROW?

Box 2.1 (earlier in this chapter) contrasted the ability of children in a skill themes approach (Pendleton Elementary School) to recall the critical elements of a mature overhand throwing pattern with children whose curriculum consisted primarily of playing low organized games (Eckland Elementary School). As another part of his study Manross (1992) also asked the twenty-five children from each school to answer the question "Who taught you to throw?" The children's responses appear in this box. As you will see, children are keenly aware of who is teaching them!

Pendleton (Skill Theme Approach)

Physical education teacher	19
Dad	10
Coaches	7
Brother	1
Previous PE teacher	1
Other people	1
Neighbor	1
Cousin	1

Eckland (Low Organized Games)

Dad	11
Coaches	7
Friends	4
Watching others	2
Brother	2
Don't know	2
Watching ball games	1
No one	1
Sister	1
Family	1
Cousin	1
Myself	1
Physical education teacher	1

children play it for weeks on end. The outspoken, athletic children like it, and once the teams have been chosen, the teacher can sit back and simply watch the children play and settle the occasional argument. The problem, once again, as our experience and an increasing body of research suggests, is that the children don't learn much of anything in programs where they simply play games all the time. See Box 2.3 for a look at children's awareness of who is really teaching them.

How Do Classroom Teachers Feel about the Skill Theme Approach?

Some classroom teachers are very positive about the skill theme approach because they can relate it directly to their work in the classroom—in teaching children vocabulary, for example. These teachers also appreciate the fact that the program accommodates the variation in abilities that is typical of any class of children. Many teachers also consider the program's deemphasis on competition a welcome alternative to those programs that constantly pit one team against another in games in which the score is kept. They feel

not only that this is more consistent with the approaches they use in the classroom but also that it makes their jobs easier; the children don't come angrily into their rooms after physical education class, arguing about the scores or who cheated, for example.

How Do Middle (Junior) and High School Physical Education Teachers Feel about the Skill Theme Approach?

Clearly there are many views. Some teachers are enthusiastically supportive, realizing the importance of ensuring that children maintain positive attitudes about physical activity. Their job is much harder if their students have been "turned off" to physical education. Interestingly, a number of middle-school teachers, because of their students' poor motor skill development, have actually started emphasizing skill themes in their programs. These teachers realize that it's extremely difficult to excite students about sports and lifetime physical activity if they have yet to acquire the basic motor skills. The skill theme approach has no age or grade limits. It can be valuable for people of any age.

SUMMARY

There are many ways to organize the content (what is taught) in a physical education program for children. Probably the most common way is to group activities by games (e.g., soccer, basketball, volleyball), gymnastics, and dance. Our experience suggests, however, that when teachers do this they focus more on the rules of the game than on helping the children learn the prerequisite skills. Organizing the content this way is also somewhat narrow, because it limits children to activities that are in existence today, rather than encouraging them to think about novel ways of moving and creating movement opportunities. We believe that before children learn the rules of a game, for example, they first need to learn the skills that will allow them to play the game enjoyably; thus, we focus on skill learning.

The skill theme approach allows us to organize experiences that match the range of abilities possessed by the children in a given class—rather than trying to force them to play a game that may be boring for the highly skilled children and too hard for (thereby frustrating and even embarrassing) the poorly skilled children. This approach also provides opportunities to teach fitness concepts as part of our daily lessons. We know today that children can improve their skills and fitness simultaneously—and enjoy doing so. Teachers who use a skill theme approach are not faced with the dilemma of emphasizing either fitness or motor skills! Finally, throughout the program we attempt to create opportunities for children to think about and understand how and why they move (cognitive) as well as opportunities to feel good about themselves and their involvement with other children in the classes (affective). These are not presented as distinct lessons, however. We try to blend them into every lesson so that they are an integral part of the entire program—not just an isolated lesson or two throughout the year.

Note: All of the statements in Box 2.2 (Motor Development IQ Test) are false. They are all misconceptions about motor development.

READING COMPREHENSION QUESTIONS

1. Why aren't games such as basketball and Duck, Duck, Goose included in this book?
2. In your own words describe the skill theme approach. Use the Curriculum Diamond (Figure 2.1) as part of your explanation.
3. Three characteristics of the skill theme approach are listed in this chapter. Which provides the most compelling reason, in your opinion, for using a skill theme approach? Why?
4. The skill theme approach can be described as developmentally appropriate. How does this concept relate to the generic levels of skill proficiency?
5. When are children ready for "organized" games? Why wouldn't it be correct to respond to this question by suggesting an age or grade level?
6. Physical fitness is an important part of the skill theme approach, yet only one chapter addresses it. How can this be explained?
7. Physical activity can be used to teach important lessons about cooperating with others. How might these lessons be taught within a skill theme approach?
8. Do you think the skill theme approach should be used in middle schools? Why, or why not?

REFERENCES

Barnett, B. E., & Merriman, W. J. (1992). Misconceptions in motor development. *Strategies, 5*(3), 5–7.

Council on Physical Education for Children (COPEC). (1992). *Developmentally appropriate physical education practices for children: A position statement of the Council on Physical Education for Children.* Reston, VA: National Association for Sport and Physical Education.

Gabbard, C., LeBlanc, E., & Lowy, S. (1987). *Physical education for children.* Englewood Cliffs, NJ: Prentice-Hall.

Graham, G. (1987). Motor skill acquisition—an essential goal of physical education programs. *Journal of Physical Education, Recreation and Dance, 58*(8), 44–48.

Graham, G., Hopple, C., Manross, M., & Sitzman, T. (1993). Novice and expert children's physical education teachers: Insights into their situational decision-making. *Journal of Teaching in Physical Education, 12,* 197–214.

Graham, G., Metzler, M., & Webster, G. (1991). Specialist and classroom teacher effectiveness in children's physical education. *Journal of Teaching in Physical Education, 10*(4), 321–426.

Manross, M. (1992). *What children think, feel and know about the overhand throw.* Unpublished Master's thesis, Virginia Tech.

National Association for Sport and Physical Education (NASPE). (1992). *What is a physically educated person? Definition, outcomes and benchmarks.* Reston, VA: NASPE.

National Association for Sport and Physical Education (NASPE). (1995). *Moving into the future: National standards for physical education.* St. Louis, MO: Mosby.

The National Center for Chronic Disease Prevention and Health Promotion, Centers for Disease Control and Prevention. (1997). Guidelines for school and community programs to promote lifelong physical activity among young people. *Journal of School Health, 76*(6), 202–219.

U.S. Department of Health and Human Services. (1996). *Physical activity and health: A report of the Surgeon General.* Atlanta, GA: U.S. Department of Health and Human Services, Centers for Disease Control and Prevention, National Center for Chronic Disease Prevention and Health Promotion.

CHAPTER 3

Skill Themes, Movement Concepts, and the National Standards

A physical education program for children which begins with an organized sport is analogous to a language arts program beginning with a Shakespearean sonnet.

——Iris Welsh [student]

Typically, children who are learning to read are taught to recognize letters, then parts of words, then complete words, and finally sentences. Children who are studying mathematics learn to solve problems after they've grasped the basic functions of numbers and signs. Children learning to play a musical instrument study the scale before attempting a song. In physical education, however, children frequently are taught games, dances, or complex gymnastic stunts before they're able to perform the necessary skills. Too often, children know the rules for a game or the formation of a dance but don't have the skills needed for successful and enjoyable participation. Our way of teaching children how to participate effectively in various activities is to focus on the development of the necessary skills. We call this approach *teaching by skill themes.*

One of the easiest ways to understand skill themes is to think of a popular sport. Let's pick softball. What skills do people use when they play softball? The major ones include throwing, catching, batting, and running. Let's pick another popular sport—basketball. Throwing, catching, running, dribbling with hands, jumping and landing, and chasing and fleeing skills are used frequently in basketball. Obviously we could list a number of other sports. The point is that some of the same skills—for example, throwing, catching, and running—are used in both sports, and in many more sports that you know of. Thus if children learn to throw and catch, for example, their chances of playing and enjoying a sport such as softball or basketball increase, because they have a reasonable chance to succeed at that sport. We have termed these skills *themes* because they apply to many different sports, although the way they are used (the context) differs from one sport to another. Table 3.1 lists various skill themes and indicates which sports emphasize them.

Essentially, the notion is that these elements are learned in early life through the various activities performed (such as jumping, throwing, striking, and the like), and then when a new act is to be learned in later life, the student can piece together these elements in a more efficient way to achieve the new motor goal. The assumption is that by jumping over objects of various sizes, shapes, heights, et cetera, the student will have more effective "elements" for the performance of the next jumping tasks (e.g., the running long jump in high school).

Richard Schmidt, "Schema Theory: Implications for Movement Education"

Characteristics of Themes

In music, a theme recurs in different parts of a song, sometimes in exactly the same way, at other times in a slightly different form. The *Random House Dictionary of the English Language* defines *theme* as "a short melodic subject from which variations are developed." In physical education, various movements can be thought of as a theme.

By revisiting a moment—sometimes in the same context as before, and sometimes in a radically different context—we provide children with variations of a skill theme. These variations lead to proficiency as well as diversity. Jumping can be presented as jumping from an object—a box or a table—and landing softly. This movement can be revisited with a slight variation: jumping from an object and landing facing in a different direction from the takeoff position. Jumping for distance or leaping in synchronization with the leap of a partner would be radically different, yet the theme would still be jumping (Gallagher, 1984).

Some movements, such as jumping, traveling, and balancing, can be focused on in games, gymnastics, and dance contexts. Other movements, such as throwing and dribbling, are primarily used in only one of those three areas. Whenever possible, we point out to students the similarities in movements used in different contexts, to enhance students' cognitive understanding of the principles that underlie successful performance of a movement. We're not certain that this influences skill performance (transfer of learning), but it doesn't seem to have any adverse effects.

The instructor who teaches by themes can focus on helping children become skillful movers. Youngsters will have plenty of opportunities as they grow older to learn games, dances, and gymnastics activities, but first they must learn the basic skills needed for successful participation.

Many adults choose not to play tennis or swim or dance. They don't enjoy these activities because they

Fundamental activities such as running, jumping, skipping, sliding, catching, kicking and striking are the basic components of the games, sports and dances of our society. Children who possess inadequate motor skills are often relegated to a life of exclusion from the organized and free play experiences of their peers, and subsequently, to a lifetime of inactivity because of their frustrations in early movement behavior.

Vern Seefeldt, John Haubenstricker, Sam Reuschlein

Table 3.1 Skill Themes Used in Sports*

Skill Themes	Aerobics	Basketball	Football	Dance	Golf	Hockey	Martial Arts	Rock Climbing	Soccer	Softball	Tennis	Track and Field	Tumbling	Ultimate Frisbee	Volleyball
Traveling	X	X	X	X		X	X	X	X	X	X	X	X	X	X
Chasing, Fleeing, Dodging		X	X			X	X		X	X				X	
Jumping, Landing	X	X	X	X		X	X	X	X	X	X	X	X	X	X
Balancing	X	X	X	X	X	X	X	X	X	X	X	X	X	X	X
Transferring weight	X	X	X	X	X	X	X	X	X	X	X	X	X	X	X
Rolling		X	X			X	X						X		X
Kicking	X	X	X				X		X						
Punting		X							X						
Throwing		X	X						X	X	X	X		X	X
Catching		X	X						X	X				X	
Volleying									X						X
Dribbling		X				X			X						
Striking with rackets											X				
Striking with golf clubs					X										
Striking with bats										X					
Striking with hockey sticks						X									

*This table is only intended to suggest how various skill themes are applied in sports contexts.

don't possess the skills needed to participate successfully. An unskilled adult attempting to learn a complex set of dance steps may be embarrassed and frustrated. So too will the adult who is trying to learn to play tennis but cannot even hit the ball into the opponent's court.

As children become ready, they begin to combine skill themes and movement concepts into the movement forms that we typically identify as games, gymnastics, and dance. The key word, however, is *ready*. We try to lead children to these experiences gradually rather than forcing them into settings prematurely; for example, we have devised a variety of ways children can practice the skill of batting (Chapter 30) without placing them in a softball-like game. The way to turn a child on to a sport like softball is not to require the child to participate when the child knows (and all of the other children in the class know) that he or she will probably strike out every single time.

Our primary goal, then, is to provide children with a degree of competence leading to the confidence that encourages them to try—and enjoy—a variety of activities and sports. Our intent is to help children gain enough skill and confidence for them to participate enjoyably in many activities, not just a few traditional team sports, and avoid the abysmal failure and embarrassment that often result from a total lack of skill. By focusing on learning and practicing skills rather than on the rules or structure of a sport, we can dramatically increase the amount of practice the children actually receive, thereby heightening their opportunities to learn skills and their application to various sports and activities.

Skill Themes and Movement Concepts

The movement content of our program consists of more than just skill themes. We also focus on movement concepts. In fact, it's very difficult to focus on a skill theme for very long without introducing one or more movement concepts. The terms *skill themes* and *movement concepts* differentiate the movements (skill themes) from the ideas (movement concepts) used to modify or enrich the range and effectiveness of skill employment.

Table 3.2   Movement Concepts

Space Awareness (where the body moves)		Effort (how the body moves)		Relationships
Location:	Self-space and general space	Time:	Fast/slow Sudden/sustained	Of body parts: Round (curved), narrow, wide, twisted, symmetrical/nonsymmetrical
Directions:	Up/down Forward/backward Right/left Clockwise/ counterclockwise	Force: Flow:	Strong/light Bound/free	With objects and/or people: Over/ under, on/off, near/far, in front/behind, along/through, meeting/parting, surrounding, around, alongside
Levels:	Low/middle/high			With people: Leading/following, mirroring/matching, unison/contrast, alone in a mass, solo, partners, groups, between groups
Pathways:	Straight/curved Zigzag			
Extensions:	Large/small Far/near			

The distinction between movement concepts (Table 3.2) and skill themes (Table 3.3)* can be clarified by a comparison to grammar. Skill themes are always verbs—they're movements that can be performed. Movement concepts are always modifiers—they describe how a skill is to be performed. This distinction also clarifies how movement concepts are employed to embellish, enhance, or expand the quality of a movement. A verb by itself—*strike, travel, roll*—is typically less interesting than one that is modified by an adverb—*strike hard, travel jerkily, roll smoothly*. Skills can stand by themselves. You can roll or gallop or jump, but you can't slow or high or under. Concepts modify skills.

Our initial focus with the primary grade children is on learning and understanding the movement concept vocabulary (see Table 3.2); for this reason, the movement concepts are listed before the skill themes (see Table 3.3). We focus on movement concepts before skill themes because children in preschool and the primary grades spend a great deal of time studying vocabulary (learning new words), and many of the movement concepts are part of this vocabulary. This is also the time when children truly enjoy the challenge of learning, and moving, as they demonstrate their understanding of such words as *symmetrical, zigzag,* and *twisted*.

It's important to remember, however, that although the children are focusing on learning the movement concepts, they are also practicing the skill themes. As soon as the children begin to move, they are practicing one or more skill themes, even though they may

not be thinking about it at the time. For example, if we ask children to skip in a curved pathway, they may be thinking about the concept of *curve*, but they are also practicing skipping. If we ask them to land in a *low level* (from a jump), they are also getting jumping and landing practice. In later grades, the emphasis will shift from the low level (movement concept) to the quality of the landing—from the concept to the skill. In fact, however, this is an artificial separation, because the skill themes and movement concepts are constantly interacting.

ING-LY

▶ A game developed by Glenn Reif at the University of Maine helps clarify how the skill themes and movement concepts work together. Reif named the game Ing-ly. You will need five- by eight-inch index cards. On one side of each card, write one of the skill themes, ending in *-ing*. *Galloping* is a good example. On the other side of the card, write your responses (or the children's) to the question "Galloping *how*?" Although it may not be proper grammar, end all of your responses in *-ly* (e.g., *quickly, straightly, freely, widely*). The purpose of this game is obviously not to improve your grammar. It will, however, help you understand how the movement concepts and the skill themes work together. The first time you try this game, you may need to refer to Table 3.2 or 3.3. In time, however, you will be able to play Ing-ly without having to refer to either table.

---

* The major source for this explanation of skill themes and movement concepts is *Physical Education: A Movement Orientation,* 2nd ed., by Sheila Stanley, 1977, New York: McGraw-Hill.

Table 3.3   Skill Themes

Locomotor Skills

Walking
Running
Hopping
Skipping
Galloping
Sliding
Chasing, fleeing, and dodging

Nonmanipulative Skills

Turning
Twisting
Rolling
Balancing
Transferring weight
Jumping and landing
Stretching
Curling

Manipulative Skills

Throwing
Catching and collecting
Kicking
Punting
Dribbling
Volleying
Striking with rackets
Striking with long-handled implements

The Wheel

The interaction between the skill themes and movement concepts listed in Tables 3.2 and 3.3 can be represented schematically by five concentric circles (Figure 3.1). (For easy reference, we call this figure "the wheel," a term our students coined.) The two inner circles represent the skill themes; the three outer circles represent the movement concepts.

The first inner circle contains the general categories of the skill themes from Table 3.3: manipulative, non-manipulative, and locomotor skills. The next inner circle contains the breakdown of the skills in each category, such as walking and running for locomotor skills, balancing and rolling for nonmanipulative skills, and throwing and kicking for manipulative skills.

The outer circle contains the three categories of the movement concepts from Table 3.2: space awareness (where the body moves), effort* (how the body

moves), and relationships. The second circle from the outside subdivides each of the three movement concept categories. For example, space awareness is subdivided to include location and directions; the subdivisions of effort include time and force; and among the relationships subdivisions are body parts and people. Finally, in the third circle, the movement concepts are subdivided even further.

In the wheel, the two inner circles representing the skill themes are stationary. The three outer circles are connected to each other but are able to rotate around the two inner circles. This rotation illustrates the idea that the same movement concept can be used to enhance the development of different skills. The concept of *levels* in space, for example, is useful for refining such skills as catching, striking, volleying, and balancing. The concept of *fast* and *slow* can be applied to the study of such skills as traveling, rolling, dribbling, transferring weight, and dodging. At times, some concepts blend with other concepts. For example, *fast* or *slow* may modify *pathways,* and *forward* and *backward* may modify *over* and *under.*

Context Variation

Just learning the terminology for the movement concepts (see Table 3.2) and the skill themes (see Table 3.3) is of course not enough to begin actually teaching them. For this reason, we have developed thorough explanations for each of the movement concepts and skill themes, along with a plethora of activities, in subsequent chapters. Part Three of the book (Chapters 16, 17, and 18) contains the definitions and suggested activities for teaching the movement concepts. Part Four (Chapters 19 to 31) does the same for the skill themes.

In each chapter we organize the activities from the easiest to the hardest, from less to more complex. The content in each of the skill theme chapters is outlined in a figure that we call a progression spiral (Figure 3.2). The spiral is a graphic reminder that the same context (task) may be revisited and that, when appropriate, the context can be varied to give the learner a more difficult challenge.

The concepts of *fast* and *slow,* for example, can be used to increase the challenge of a task. But the use of the concept depends on the skill theme being studied. The context variation for the skill theme of rolling or of transferring weight can be made more difficult by challenging the children to move more slowly. But with a skill such as dribbling, which is easier to perform at a slower rate, the challenge "dribble faster" increases the complexity of the task. In short, there's no standard formula that can be used as a guide for

---

* Some movement analysis frameworks include the concept of space (direct and flexible) as a quality of movement. In our teaching, however, we use this concept so infrequently that we don't include it in our discussion of the qualities of movement.

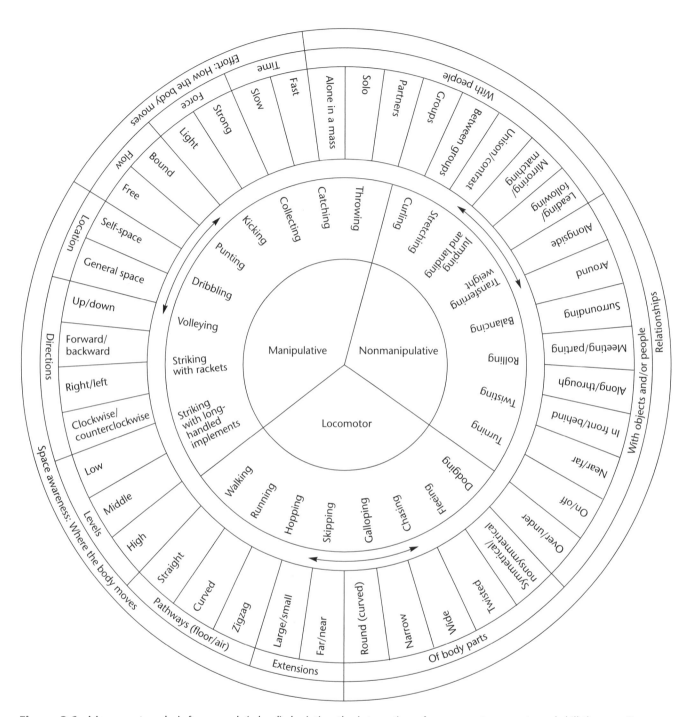

Figure 3.1 Movement analysis framework (wheel) depicting the interaction of movement concepts and skill themes. To enhance your understanding, mount the wheel on pieces of cardboard (a manila folder works well) or on poster board. Cut the wheel between the inner two and the outer three circles, and glue the outer three circles to one piece of cardboard. Attach the two inner circles to a second piece of cardboard and connect the two with a clasp that lets the inner circles rotate.

varying the contexts in which all skill themes are studied. Each skill theme is different.

The spirals aren't intended to suggest the length of time to be spent studying a particular theme. In reflective teaching, the context is varied when appropriate for a particular class or child.

Finally, the spiral represents a progression from the precontrol level up to the proficiency level (see Chapter 7). When the context of a movement is varied, many children regress to a previous level. This doesn't mean that children will drop from the utilization or proficiency level to a precontrol level each time the

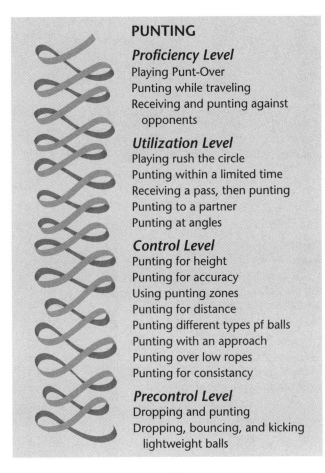

PUNTING

Proficiency Level
Playing Punt-Over
Punting while traveling
Receiving and punting against
    opponents

Utilization Level
Playing rush the circle
Punting within a limited time
Receiving a pass, then punting
Punting to a partner
Punting at angles

Control Level
Punting for height
Punting for accuracy
Using punting zones
Punting for distance
Punting different types pf balls
Punting with an approach
Punting over low ropes
Punting for consistancy

Precontrol Level
Dropping and punting
Dropping, bouncing, and kicking
    lightweight balls

Figure 3.2 Progression spiral illustrating the contextual variations in which skill themes can be studied.

context of a task is varied. But the teacher can expect to observe a variation in skill performance each time the context of a task is varied.

The progressions in Parts Three and Four are based on our knowledge of the pertinent literature and on years of teaching experience. But you may find that a different ordering of the context variations is more appropriate for a particular teaching situation. Each child, each class, each teaching environment differs from all others, and the reflective teacher adapts to these differences. See Box 3.1 for an example of one school's use of skill themes in its physical education curriculum.

The *National Standards* and the Skill Theme Approach

Since the third edition of *Children Moving* was published, *Moving into the Future: National Standards for Physical Education* (NASPE, 1995) has been completed. George Graham and Shirley Holt/Hale, two of the co-

authors of *Children Moving,* served on the task forces that developed these standards. As we have revised this edition of *Children Moving* we have attempted to show how the fourth edition and the *National Standards* fit together. We think this will be especially useful for those teachers who are interested in revising their programs to reflect the content suggested in the *National Standards.* Before describing how *Children Moving* might be used as a guide to developing a program designed on the *National Standards,* it seems important to provide a brief background of the process that led to the development of those standards.

Background of *National Standards* Development

In the late 1980s, the National Association for Sport and Physical Education (NASPE) formed a Blue Ribbon Task Force and asked its members to:

■ Define a person who is "physically educated"
■ Define "outcomes" and "benchmarks" that could serve as guidelines for constructing physical education program curriculums

The Outcomes Task Force worked on the project for more than five years, and each year, at NASPE's national conference, physical educators from throughout the United States were invited to review and critique the work. The Task Force then revised its work based on these recommendations and presented it again the following year. Over the several years' period, the work of the Task Force was reviewed by hundreds of physical educators and as a result reflects the collective wisdom of much of the profession. The result of this work, published in 1992, was a document entitled *The Physically Educated Person* (NASPE, 1992), which defined a physically educated person as an individual who:

■ HAS learned skills necessary to perform a variety of physical activities
■ IS physically fit
■ DOES participate regularly in physical activity
■ KNOWS the implications of and the benefits from involvement in physical activity
■ VALUES physical activity and its contributions to a healthful lifestyle

Outcome statements were also developed for each of the five parts of the definition, along with benchmarks for kindergarten, second, fourth, sixth, eighth, tenth, and twelfth grades.

Using the same process, NASPE built upon the foundation of the "Outcomes Project" to develop national content standards for physical education, including examples for assessment. The standards

BOX 3.1   ADAPTING THE SKILL THEME APPROACH

Since the first edition of *Children Moving* was published in 1980, a number of school districts throughout the United States have based their curricula on skill themes. In Gwinnett County (near Atlanta, Georgia) an overview of each area of the curriculum is described on a poster that many elementary schools in the county display on their walls. The poster is prominently displayed alongside math, reading, and science posters, an arrangement conveying the message that the teachers of Gwinnett County are dedicated to educating the total child.

Physical Education
K–5 Curriculum

The fundamental objective of the physical education program is to provide opportunities for the development of motor skills and physical fitness.

Skill Themes and Fitness Concepts
Students in grades K–5 will experience a developmentally designed program of skill and fitness development, including educational games, educational dance, and educational gymnastics. The following motor skills and fitness concepts are included:

- body awareness
- balancing
- chasing, fleeing, dodging
- kicking and punting
- striking with implements (short and long handled)
- rolling
- throwing and catching
- traveling
- volleying and dribbling
- transferring weight
- jumping and landing
- cardiorespiratory endurance
- flexibility
- muscular strength and endurance
- fitness testing

Becoming physically educated is a developmental process that begins in early childhood and continues throughout life. The physical education program involves the total child and includes physical, mental, social, and emotional growth experiences. The physical education program provides instruction that will enable the pursuit of physical fitness and a lifetime of physical activity.

Gwinnett County Public Schools

SOURCE: Reprinted with permission of Gwinnett County Public Schools, Gwinnett County, Georgia.

BOX 3.2 SAMPLE BENCHMARKS FOR NATIONAL STANDARD 1: MOVEMENT FORMS

A more detailed description of each benchmark, along with activities to teach it, is included in the *Children Moving* chapter(s) listed below at the end of each benchmark.

Kindergarten

1. Travels in forward and sideways directions using a variety of locomotor (nonlocomotor) patterns and changes directions quickly in response to a signal. (Chapters 16, 19)
2. Demonstrates clear contrasts between slow and fast movements while traveling. (Chapters 17, 19)
3. Walks and runs using mature form. (Chapter 19)
4. Rolls sideways without hesitating or stopping. (Chapter 24)
5. Tosses a ball and catches it before it bounces twice. (Chapter 27)
6. Kicks a stationary ball using a smooth, continuous running step. (Chapter 26)
7. Maintains momentary stillness, bearing weight on a variety of body parts. (Chapter 23)

Second Grade

1. Demonstrates skills of chasing, fleeing, and dodging to avoid others. (Chapter 21)
2. Combines locomotor patterns in time to music. (Chapter 19)
3. Balances, demonstrating momentary stillness, in symmetrical and nonsymmetrical shapes on a variety of body parts. (Chapter 23)
4. Receives and sends an object in a continuous motion. (Chapter 27)
5. Strikes a ball repeatedly with a paddle. (Chapter 29)

Fourth Grade

1. Throws, catches, and kicks using mature form. (Chapters 26, 27)
2. Dribbles and passes a basketball to a moving receiver. (Chapter 28)
3. Balances with control on a variety of objects (balance board, large apparatus, skates). (Chapter 23)
4. Develops and refines a gymnastics sequence demonstrating smooth transitions. (Chapter 25)
5. Develops and refines a creative dance sequence into a repeatable pattern. (Chapter 20)
6. Jumps and lands for height/distance using mature form. (Chapter 22)

Sixth Grade

1. Throws a variety of objects, demonstrating both accuracy and force (e.g., basketball, football, Frisbee). (Chapter 27)
2. Hand dribbles and foot dribbles while preventing an opponent from stealing the ball. (Chapters 26, 28)
3. Designs and performs gymnastics and dance sequences that combine traveling (Chapter 19), rolling (Chapter 24), balancing (Chapter 23), and weight transfer (Chapter 24) into smooth, flowing sequences with intentional changes in direction (Chapter 16), speed (Chapter 17), and flow (Chapter 17).
4. Keeps an object going continuously with a partner using a striking pattern. (Chapter 28)
5. Places the ball away from an opponent in a racket sport activity. (Chapter 29)

were published in 1995 (NASPE, 1995). They were especially important because they paralleled work that was also being done in other disciplines, such as math, science, and geography.

The skill theme approach, as defined in *Children Moving*, clearly addresses the *National Standards for Physical Education*, no doubt because two of the co-authors of this book served on the task forces that led to the development of these content standards. (George Graham served on the Outcomes Task Force

and Shirley Holt/Hale on the subsequent Standards and Assessment Task Force.)

Skill Themes and the Content Standards

Box 1.2 (in Chapter 1) lists the seven content standards for physical education from the *National Standards*. *Children Moving* addresses all of the standards throughout the text, but many readers will find Parts Three and Four of the book especially helpful for

BOX 3.3   SAMPLE BENCHMARKS FOR NATIONAL STANDARD 2: MOVEMENT CONCEPTS

A more detailed description of each benchmark, along with activities to teach it, is included in the *Children Moving* chapter(s) listed below at the end of each benchmark.

Kindergarten

1. Walks, runs, hops, and skips in forward and sideways directions and changes directions quickly in response to a signal. (Chapter 19)
2. Identifies and uses a variety of relationships with objects (e.g., over/under, behind, alongside, and through). (Chapter 18)
3. Identifies and begins to utilize the technique employed (leg flexion) to soften the landing in jumping. (Chapter 22)

Second Grade

1. Identifies four characteristics of a mature throw. (Chapter 27)
2. Uses concepts of space awareness and movement control to run, hop, and skip in different ways in a large group without bumping or falling. (Chapter 16)
3. Identifies and demonstrates the major characteristics of mature walking, running, hopping, and skipping. (Chapter 19)

Fourth Grade

1. Transfers weight from feet to hands at fast and slow speeds using large extensions (e.g., mule kick, handstand, cartwheel). (Chapter 24)
2. Accurately recognizes the critical elements of a throw made by a fellow student and provides feedback to that student. (Chapter 27)
3. Consistently strikes a softly thrown ball with a bat or paddle, demonstrating an appropriate grip. (Chapters 29, 30)

designing, delivering, and assessing the first two content standards. The first two content standards, and part of the general description for each one, follow:

1. *A physically educated person demonstrates competency in many movement forms and proficiency in a few movement forms.* The intent of this standard is the development of movement competence and proficiency. Movement competence implies the development of sufficient ability to enjoy participation in physical activities and establishes a foundation to facilitate continued motor skill acquisition and increased ability to engage in appropriate motor patterns in daily physical activities. In the primary years students develop maturity and versatility in the use of fundamental skills (e.g., running, skipping, throwing, striking) that are further refined, combined and varied during the middle school years. (NASPE, 1995, p. 2)
2. *A physically educated person applies movement concepts and principles to the learning and development of motor skills.* This standard concerns the ability of the learner to use cognitive information to understand and enhance motor skill acquisition and performance. During the lower elementary years emphasis is placed on establishing a movement vocabulary and initial application of introductory concepts (e.g., force absorption, principles governing equilibrium, application of force). Through the upper elementary and middle school years an emphasis is placed on learning more and increasingly complex concepts. (NASPE, 1995, p. 2)

Don't be frustrated if you do not understand a lot of this terminology. Phrases like "movement forms," "appropriate motor skill patterns," and "absorption of force" will become clearer as you read subsequent chapters in *Children Moving.* In fact, not only will the terminology become clearer but you will find many examples of how you can teach the skills and concepts suggested in the *National Standards* to children. It will also help to refer to Boxes 3.2 and 3.3, which contain sample benchmarks from the *National Standards.* After each sample benchmark you will see one or more chapter references that indicate where you can learn more about that specific benchmark and the activities that teachers use to help children achieve the suggested goal.

In many chapters we have also quoted sample benchmarks from the *National Standards* to assist you in understanding how the content of the *Children Moving* chapters can be developed to meet these benchmarks. When appropriate we have also included assessment examples in those *Children Moving* chap-

GUIDELINES FOR PROMOTING LIFELONG PHYSICAL ACTIVITY

The National Center for Chronic Disease Prevention and Health Promotion (NCCDPHP) makes the following recommendations for "developing students' mastery of and confidence in motor and behavioral skills for participating in physical activity:

■ Students should become competent in many motor skills and proficient in a few to use in lifelong physical activities.

■ Elementary school students should develop basic motor skills that allow participation in a variety of physical activities.

■ Older students should become competent in a select number of physical activities they enjoy and succeed in.

■ Students' mastery of and confidence in motor skills occurs when these skills are broken down into components and the tasks are ordered from easy to hard.

■ Students need opportunities to observe others performing the skills and receive encouragement, feedback, and repeated opportunities for practice during physical education class.

■ Active student involvement. . . . that focuses on building confidence may increase the likelihood that children and adolescents will enjoy and succeed in physical education and physical activity."

Source: (NCCDPHP, 1977, p. 209)

ters to assist you in determining how well your students are progressing in regard to the benchmarks.

In concluding this section on skill themes and movement concepts and how they are described in the *National Standards,* it is important to remember that the standards are not intended as a prescribed set of goals or outcomes to be achieved by all physical education programs. The *National Standards* document is not a national curriculum! As detailed in Chapter 5,

"Reflective Teaching," teachers must determine the goals of their program based on the specific characteristics of the schedule, the children, and the community. The suggested grade levels, for example, are only that—suggestions. The *National Standards* can be immensely helpful, however, as a well-thought-out document suggesting what many think ought to be included in a quality physical education curriculum that leads to physical activity for a lifetime.

SUMMARY

Teaching by skill themes focuses on developing children's competence in a variety of motor skills and movement concepts that will eventually enable the children to acquire confidence and enjoy physical activity throughout their lifetimes. Games, gymnastics, and dance typically require children to use combinations of motor skills and movement concepts that are developed only after a substantial amount of practice. Therefore, the teacher places emphasis on helping children acquire the skills and confidence necessary to participate eventually in games, gymnastics, and dance with enjoyment and confidence.

Teaching by themes also involves revisiting the same skills or concepts continually throughout the program at different times and in different contexts. In preschool and the primary grades, the focus is on learning the vocabulary associated with the movement concepts. Once this has been learned, the emphasis shifts to the skill themes. In fact, however, the skill themes and movement concepts constantly interact, as depicted in the movement analysis framework (wheel). The progression and activities for each of the skill themes are illustrated by a spiral. The spiral is a visual reminder that the child revisits each task to enhance skill acquisition and retention and that skills are best learned when they are presented in a progression from basic to advanced.

Support for the skill theme approach can be found in two recent national statements, the *National Standards for Physical Education* (NASPE, 1995) and *Develop-*

mentally Appropriate Physical Education Practices for Children (COPEC, 1992). Essentially, these sources recommend that physical education programs at the preschool and elementary school levels focus on helping children improve their fundamental motor skills in relatively simple environments. Physical fitness, rather than being a separate unit, is interwoven throughout the program as we help children understand and value its importance while they also learn to develop their own programs of physical fitness.

READING COMPREHENSION QUESTIONS

1. What do children need to learn in physical education before they're ready to play a game? Why?
2. What are movement concepts? How do they modify skill themes?
3. How can you distinguish skill themes from movement concepts?
4. What does revisiting themes mean?
5. What does the spiral indicate about skill development? (Use Figure 3.1, the wheel, to explain your answer.)
6. What skill themes relate generally to game contexts? To dance contexts? To gymnastic contexts?
7. Indicate how one skill theme can be used to modify another.
8. Give an example of how the space awareness concepts are important in varsity team sports.
9. Explain what the authors mean when they write that the skill themes may be used to develop a program that reflects the content suggestions in the *National Standards*.

REFERENCES/ RECOMMENDED READING

Council on Physical Education for Children (COPEC). (1992). *Developmentally appropriate physical education practices for children: A position statement of the Council on Physical Education for Children.* Reston, VA: National Association for Sport and Physical Education.

Gallagher, J. (1984). Making sense of motor development: Interfacing research with lesson planning. In J. Thomas (Ed.), *Motor skill development during childhood and adolescence* (pp. 123–138). Minneapolis, MN: Burgess.

Holyoak, C., & Weinberg, H. (1988). *Meeting needs and pleasing kids: A middle school physical education curriculum.* Dubuque, IA: Kendall Hunt.

National Association for Sport and Physical Education (NASPE). (1992). *The physically educated person.* Reston, VA: Author.

National Association for Sport and Physical Education (NASPE). (1995). *Moving into the future: National standards for physical education.* St. Louis, MO: Mosby.

Schmidt, R. A. (1977). Schema theory: Implications for movement education. *Motor Skills: Theory Into Practice, 2,* 36–48.

Stanley, S. (1977). *Physical education: A movement orientation* (2nd ed.). New York: McGraw-Hill.

The National Center for Chronic Disease Prevention and Health Promotion, Centers for Disease Control and Prevention. (1977). Guidelines for school and community programs to promote lifelong physical activity among young people. *Journal of School Health, 76*(6), 202–219.

Physical Fitness & Wellness for Children

Intelligence and skill can only function at the peak of their capacity when the body is healthy and strong.

—John F. Kennedy

The term *physical fitness* brings to children an image of Arnold Schwarzenegger, Jackie Joyner-Kersee, and Olympic athletes. Physical fitness testing all too often brings moans and negative memories of unattainable goals, a self-concept that suffered on each test day, group calisthenics, and running without pleasure. Many people view physical fitness as synonymous with physical education, attainable only through a strenuous exercise program. We believe physical fitness is an integral part of physical education, a product of a quality physical education program.

The first alarm on children's physical fitness was sounded in the mid-1950s in response to a comparison of fitness levels of American and European children. The Kraus-Weber test battery had a significant impact on physical education programs in schools, resulting in increased emphasis on exercises to improve physical fitness in children and youth. More recently physical fitness in childhood was linked to the prevention of cardiorespiratory and coronary disease in adults, as well as the degenerative diseases of hypertension and diabetes. Again, the alarm was sounded that children were not as physically fit as their counterparts of a generation ago. The result was a curricular shift to health-related fitness and a renewed emphasis on activities to boost fitness components.

Current research on fitness for children paints a much less negative picture than previously thought. Although not all children are as physically fit as we would like them to be, neither are they on a rapidly descending spiral. Children are among the most active, the most fit segment of our society (Simons-Morton, Parcel, & O'Hara, 1987). Young children are active by nature; movement is their learning. Physical fitness is a product of movement that provides children with confidence, skills, and enjoyment. Through quality physical education, fitness becomes a process, attained and maintained through health-related physical activity.

The Surgeon General's report (U.S. Department of Health & Human Services, 1996) shifted the focus from strenuous exercise as a prerequisite for health and fitness to physical activity and the development of an active lifestyle, with physical inactivity portrayed as "hazardous to health." With the new guidelines for physical activity, the long-standing frequency-intensity-duration formula for physical fitness now emphasizes physical activity for a lifetime. The formula recommended in the Surgeon General's report is:

- Frequency: most, preferably all, days of the week
- Intensity: moderate
- Duration: thirty minutes cumulative

The new frequency-intensity-duration formula places the focus on physical activity rather than calisthenics—and on making physical activity in childhood a habit that will lead to a physically active lifestyle in adulthood.

The importance of establishing physical activity habits in childhood is supported in the research. Children who are physically active are more likely as adults to participate in physical activities on a regular basis. Recognizing this critical link between childhood activity and adult lifestyle, the Centers for Disease Control's (CDC's) Guidelines for School and Community Programs to Promote Lifelong Physical Activity among Young People (U.S. Department of Health & Human Services, 1997) reminds us that physical activity programs for children are most likely to be effective when they:

- Emphasize enjoyable participation in physical activities that are easily done throughout life
- Offer a diverse range of noncompetitive and competitive activities appropriate for age and ability
- Give children the skills and confidence needed to be physically active

What follows in the section of this chapter devoted to fitness is an overview of physical fitness for elementary-age children. We discuss the components of physical fitness and, specifically, fitness for children. We delineate the place of physical fitness in the elementary education curriculum, testing for children, and fitness beyond the school.

The Surgeon General's report on physical activity and health recommends the following formula for exercise and health benefits: "All people over the age of 2 years should accumulate at least 30 minutes of endurance-type physical activity, of at least moderate intensity, on most—preferably all—days of the week"

(U.S. Department of Health & Human Services, 1996, p. 28).

Physical Fitness: A Definition

Physical fitness is the capacity of the heart, blood vessels, lungs, and muscles to function at optimum efficiency. In previous years, fitness was defined as the capacity to carry out the day's activities without undue fatigue. Automation, increased leisure time, and changes in lifestyles following the Industrial Revolution meant this criterion was no longer sufficient. Optimum efficiency is the key.

Physical fitness in the past focused on skill-related components—muscular strength, power, speed, agility, and endurance—components associated with performance in games and sports. In more recent years fitness has centered around those factors pertaining to a healthy lifestyle. Although the linkage between health-related fitness components and good health as adults may not be as strong as previously assumed (Corbin & Pangrazi, 1992), the attainment of a positive level of health-related fitness is a goal for all children. The components of health-related fitness are muscular strength and endurance, flexibility, cardiovascular efficiency, and body composition.

Muscular Strength and Endurance

Muscular strength is the amount of force a muscle can produce; *muscular endurance* is the muscle's ability to produce that force for a period of time. Children who are normally active and healthy possess sufficient leg strength for participation in activities. However, today there's growing concern over the upper body strength of children and adolescents. Fewer physical chores, coupled with an increase in sedentary activities, such as television and computers, have produced a generation of youngsters often described as excellent in the fine motor skills—using a mouse and a keyboard—but very weak in arm and shoulder strength. Lack of strength in the back and abdominal muscles is associated with poor posture and with lower back problems in later life. The vigorous physical activities that develop cardiovascular endurance also develop muscular strength and endurance in the legs. Upper arm and shoulder strength and abdominal strength are enhanced through activities that focus on supporting weight on hands, transferring weight involving hands, gymnastics balances requiring muscular tension, stretching actions of the trunk, and challenging activities on gymnastics and playground equipment (see Chapters 23 and 24, and later in this discussion).

Flexibility

Flexibility is the ability to use joints fully; it's the capacity of a joint to move through its potential range of motion. Very young children are extremely flexible, seemingly capable of moving their bodies in innumerable positions, literally tying themselves in knots. With few exceptions, children remain flexible throughout their elementary school years.

Flexibility can be increased through stretching the muscles, tendons, and ligaments. Activities that emphasize extending the range of motion, such as dance and gymnastics, help children attain and maintain flexibility. Activities that promote stretching actions and extending the range of motion are incorporated into the skill themes of transferring weight, rolling, and balancing within stretching, curling, and twisting actions. See Chapters 23 and 24 for appropriate tasks.

Flexibility is specific to each joint; therefore, we carefully select activities that increase flexibility in various muscle groups, that is, the legs, lower and upper back, and shoulders. Children benefit from being taught the concept of specificity and exercises to enhance each muscle group, so they develop a cognitive understanding of the relationship between individual exercises and the specific muscle group they enhance.

Children involved in competitive athletics may experience a lack of flexibility in certain muscles as other muscles are emphasized for the particular sport. All stretching actions should emphasize a static stretch, in which the child slowly moves the joint or muscle to its stretching point and holds the position, rather than bouncing to force the body into position. As we point out in Chapter 17, slowness of movement is a difficult concept for children to grasp, yet it is a most important one.

Cardiovascular Efficiency

Cardiovascular efficiency is the body's ability to undergo vigorous exercise for a long time. Children who are physically fit have sufficient endurance to participate in vigorous activities without undue fatigue. These children can participate longer and play harder than those less fit. Cardiovascular efficiency is developed through moderate to vigorous physical activity that increases the heart rate for extended periods of time. Jumping rope, jogging, swimming, and fitness walking are examples of aerobic activities that promote cardiovascular efficiency. Within our physical education classes, we plan activities to promote cardiovascular efficiency; see Chapters 19, 21, 22, 27, and 28, and later in this chapter for ideas.

Body Composition

Body composition is the amount of fat cells compared to lean cells in the body mass. Lean body mass is the nonfat tissue of muscles, bones, ligaments, and tendons. Body composition is measured by skinfold thickness. Skinfold thickness remains relatively constant until age seven, after which it gradually increases until puberty. For girls, the gradual increase continues throughout adolescence; for boys, the percentage of body fat levels off or decreases.

A certain amount of body fat is essential for good health, but an extremely high or low amount of body fat is unhealthy. With the nation's emphasis on leanness, children often have misconceptions about fatness versus leanness in body composition. Children also confuse body weight and body composition. Lean muscle mass actually weighs more than the same amount of fat tissue; therefore, body weight can't be used to determine body composition.

A person's percentage of body fat is determined by heredity, nutrition, and level of activity. Increased activity can decrease body fat; however, best results are obtained through a combination of activity and diet. Body composition is a fitness component that can't be changed in a short period of time; adjustments in nutritional habits and lifestyle must be carefully planned and continued for a long time. These changes require the involvement of not just the child but the child's family. It isn't enough to guide the child into healthy nutritional habits for school lunch and active participation during physical education and recess. To be successful, the nutrition/lifestyle package must be carried out at home as well as at school. We try to be extremely sensitive to parents' perceptions, emphasizing nutrition and activity for healthy living and trying to avoid negative assessment of the family's lifestyle and eating habits. (Nutrition and activity for good health are discussed later, in the Wellness section of this chapter.)

Physical Fitness and the *National Standards for Physical Education*

Standard 3: Exhibits a physically active lifestyle
Standard 4: Achieves and maintains a health-enhancing level of physical fitness

The *National Standards for Physical Education* (NASPE, 1995) recognize the importance of physical fitness for children, with an emphasis at the elementary level on the learning of skills, knowledge, and behaviors that will enable children to be physically active now and in their adult years. The focus for children in early elementary is the enjoyment of activity: positive participation in physical education, on the playgrounds of school and community and in active play. As children grow and mature, the focus is on an awareness of fitness concepts and their importance coupled with the development of skills and knowledge for regular participation in meaningful activity. In the *National Standards* fitness is viewed as a product of a physically active lifestyle; a physically active lifestyle is the product of movement competency and knowledge gained through the *process* of positive participation in physical activity.

Principles of Fitness Training

The components of fitness, both the health- and the skill-related ones, are developed through the principle of overload: exercising more today than yesterday and more tomorrow than today. Levels of fitness are increased by changes in the intensity, duration, and frequency of exercise. Running faster, farther, longer, and more often subjects the cardiovascular system, for example, to an increasing "load" and enables that system to adapt to higher performance levels.

The principles of fitness training—frequency, intensity, and time—when applied to children can best be stated as *fun, intrinsic motivation,* and *two C's: competence and confidence* (Corbin, 1986). All activities in physical education, including physical fitness, should be fun. Pain is not the name of the game in fitness for children. If fitness activities are fun and if children experience success, they will be intrinsically motivated to be physically active outside the school environment. They will be motivated to improve themselves. Children who participate in programs that are designed for maximum participation and provide challenges appropriate to skill levels develop confidence in themselves as they develop competence in the skills of physical education. This combination of competence and confidence motivates children to adopt lifestyles that include moderate to vigorous activity on a regular basis.

Children's Lifetime Physical Activity Model

Just as exercise, training, and fitness guidelines for children in the past were based on research for adults, adult physical activity guidelines for good health have also been imposed on children. With the shift to moderate activity and cumulative time throughout the day, the Children's Lifetime Physical Activity Model (C-LPAM) (Corbin & Pangrazi, 1994) has emerged as the "new" strategy for health risk reduction through physical activity. C-LPAM recognizes both a minimum activity standard for good health and an optimal functioning standard as "a goal for all children." This standard includes frequent (three or more) activity sessions per day, alternating bouts of moderate to vigorous activity with rest as needed, and sixty minutes per day of cumulative active play. Emphasis throughout the C-LPAM is on the development of skills with substantial practice time and energy expenditure, the learning of lifetime physical activities, and fitness through activity.

> ▶ The Surgeon General's report on physical activity and health (U.S. Department of Health & Human Services, 1996) recommends 30 minutes of cumulative activity of moderate intensity, preferably on a daily basis. Cumulative physical activity . . . periods of moderate (to vigorous) activity throughout the day: Is this not the natural pattern for children? A casual observation of children at play reinforces both the research findings that children are the most active segment of our population and that health fitness grows through cumulative intermittent periods of physical activity throughout each day. Physical educators need to plan all activities to capitalize on children's natural love of activity.

Fitness in the Curriculum

Research has shown that children can be trained in the components of fitness if (1) exercises are maintained at a rate of intensity high enough to produce the desired results, that is, Olympic-style training schedule, and (2) diversified programs of physical education are replaced with programs of just physical fitness a minimum of three times per week. Both these concepts, however, are in direct opposition to our beliefs about activity programs for children.

Caution must be used in involving children in intensive training programs or distance running because short-term gains may be outweighed by long-term detriments, for example, bone growth damage and lack of interest and motivation in later years.

Programs of strenuous calisthenics for children can result in "winning the battle but losing the war." We may develop fitness in children for the period of time they're under our control, but the negative feelings associated with the forced activity often lead to negative feelings toward activity and exercise that continue into adulthood.

> Fitness gives me joy feels all over.
>
> Ben Stewart

We try to present moderate to vigorous activity as an enjoyable experience so that children develop a positive attitude toward an active lifestyle. We also try to provide children and their parents with a sufficient knowledge of fitness and training concepts to be wise consumers of commercial fitness items, packaged programs, and health spas. As teachers, we can help children and their parents choose sports and activities to attain and maintain fitness and have fun doing so. We can also help students set realistic physical fitness goals for themselves. Fitness is a personal matter; its goal is self-improvement toward healthy living. Within our elementary physical education curriculum we can teach basic concepts of fitness, design our lessons to promote the fitness components, and help children build a repertoire of exercises for their personal use.

Health-Related Fitness Components

As noted earlier, health-related fitness includes five components: abdominal muscular strength and endurance, upper body muscular strength and endurance, lower back flexibility, cardiovascular efficiency, and body composition. Here we highlight concepts associated with each component as the concepts relate to elementary school children, and suggest some activities/exercises that help youngsters develop fitness in each area.

Muscular Strength and Endurance

It's important that teachers help children understand these critical concepts about muscular strength and endurance:

■ Muscular strength and endurance are important so that you can perform everyday activities without getting tired quickly
■ Muscular strength is specific: Different muscles require different exercises
■ Poor posture is often the result of poor muscle tone

Upper Body Strength and Endurance

The following muscular strength and endurance concepts are specific to the upper body:

- Upper body strength can be improved through chin-ups and the flexed-arm hang.
- The flexed-arm hang as an exercise should never be held for extended periods of time because of the possibility of elbow injury and/or extreme muscular fatigue.
- Girls may experience a decrease in upper body muscular strength and endurance with the onset of puberty.
- Muscular strength training with weights is not recommended for elementary age children.
- Lack of muscular strength in the upper trunk can be very discouraging for children; therefore, focus on the positive, e.g., on the flexed-arm hang or chin-ups rather than on pull-ups.

Activities/Exercises for Abdominal Strength and Endurance

Wall Push   Stand with your back against a wall, your feet only a few inches from the wall (Figure 4.1). Your knees should be slightly bent, with your arms at the sides of your body. Pull in your abdomen, and press your shoulders, small of back, and buttocks against the wall. Hold the position for five seconds.

Untimed Sit-ups   Lie flat on your back with your knees bent and your arms crossed on your chest. Gradually perform sit-ups.
Sit-up variations:

- Extend your arms forward. Shake your hands and arms as you curl up.
- Extend your arms forward. Clap your hands on the floor as you curl back to the mat.

Finger Walk   Lie flat on your back with your knees bent in the sit-up position. Extend your arms at your sides. Walk your fingers forward on the mat in the direction of your feet as you tighten your stomach muscles and raise your shoulders slightly off the mat. Gently lower your shoulders to the mat and repeat.

Activities/Exercises for Upper Body Strength and Endurance

Flexed-Arm Hang   In a pull-up position, palms facing forward, chin above the bar (Figure 4.2), hold the position for five to eight seconds without letting your chin touch the bar or drop below the bar. When holding for eight seconds feels comfortable, increase the duration to fifteen seconds.

 The flexed-arm hang should not be held for extended periods because of the possibility of elbow injury and/or extreme muscular fatigue.

Figure 4.1   Correct position for a wall push.

Figure 4.2   Correct position for flexed-arm hang.

Reverse Pull-ups   Hold the bar as in the flexed-arm position, chin above the bar, palms either forward or reversed. *Slowly* lower your weight to a hanging position by straightening your arms.

Walking Hands   Assume a push-up position with your body fully extended and your hands on the floor behind a line or tape mark (Figure 4.3). Walk your hands forward and backward over the line as you count 1-2-3-4; aim for sixty counts. Variation: Time for sixty seconds.

Just a Piece of Paper   Hold a piece of paper in one hand. On cue do the following:

- Wave hello to muscular strength; wave hello to your friends; wave here, there, everywhere.
- Pat the paper between your hands; pat the paper as you move to a low level and as you return.
- Pat the paper as you turn around and as you jump up and down.
- Crumple the paper in one hand; unfold it with the same hand.
- Tighten your hand into a fist around the paper; make a *big* muscle.
- Repeat with the other hand. Add variations.

Figure 4.3   Weight on hands improves upper body strength.

Cumulative minutes of activity/exercise at home can supplement time in physical education for fitness and good health. The activities/exercises in Box 4.1 can be performed at various times: on waking up, while getting ready for school, on the way to school, while studying, or while watching television.

BOX 4.1   STRENGTH AND ENDURANCE ACTIVITIES; EXERCISES FOR OUTSIDE THE GYM

Wake-up Time

- Before getting out of bed, tighten all the muscles in your body, rest your muscles, then tighten them again—hard! Can you tighten one part of your body at a time?

Getting Ready

- While you're wringing out the washcloth, squeeze and twist it as hard as you can. What does this movement strengthen?
- After putting on your shoes, lift both your feet and legs up and down from a sitting position. How many times can you do this without stopping? Can you hold both legs in the air for thirty seconds?

Going to School

- Hold a heavy book in one hand and see how many times you can lift it up and down by bending your elbow. Try lifting the book while keeping your arm straight.
- On the bus, put your feet underneath the seat in front of you and tighten your leg muscles to make them straight and stiff.

Studying

- Hold the sides of your chair, and pull as hard as you can, but don't bend your back.
- How hard can you push down on the desk with your hand and arm? Push and hold for thirty seconds.

Television Time

- Lie on your side, and lift one leg up and down in the air. Can you do each leg for a whole commercial?
- On your back, try to raise your legs, arms, and shoulders off the floor at the same time. Hold that position. This is called the *crunch*.
- Lie on your back. Place a pillow between your knees and try to curl up in a ball so that your nose touches the knees. How many times can you do this during one commercial?

Flexibility

These are the critical concepts children should understand about flexibility:

- Flexibility is joint specific. You may be very flexible in one joint and not in another
- You must continue to exercise to maintain flexibility
- Stretching exercises increase flexibility
- Stretching should be done slowly, without bouncing
- Stretching reduces the chance of injury in sports

Activities/Exercises for Flexibility

Trunk and Shoulder Extensions   Slowly extend both your arms overhead as high as possible and hold them for ten seconds.

Trunk and Shoulder Rotation   With your right arm at shoulder level, look and slowly turn to your left; hold ten seconds (Figure 4.4). Repeat the movement in the opposite direction.

Figure 4.4   Student holding the trunk and shoulder rotation position.

Inner Thigh Stretch   Sit on the floor with your legs spread apart and extended. Slowly lean forward with one arm on each side of one leg and hold the position (Figure 4.5). Repeat the exercise on the other leg.

Figure 4.5   Student performing the inner thigh stretch on the right leg.

Lying Knee Pull   Lie flat on your back with your legs extended and arms straight at your sides. Bring your left knee to your chest, grabbing under the knee with both your hands (Figure 4.6). Pull and hold your knee for five seconds. Repeat the exercise with your right leg. Remember to keep your extended leg straight and on the floor.

Figure 4.6   The lying knee pull exercise.

Box 4.2 contains suggestions for activities/exercises that can be done outside the gym to build flexibility.

BOX 4.2   FLEXIBILITY ACTIVITIES/ EXERCISES FOR OUTSIDE THE GYM

Wake-up Time

- Stretch all your body in all different directions; then wiggle like Jell-O on a plate.
- Lie on your stomach, and then reach back and grab your feet with your hands. Try to make a bowl shape with your body by raising up your chest and legs and rocking on your stomach.

Going to School

- Keep one arm straight, and swing it in a big circle from the front of your body to the back. Hold on tight to your books.
- Shake your leg each time you take a step. If you're wearing long socks, try to shake them down to your ankles. The vibration of the skin and muscles will help loosen you up.

Studying

- Hold your hands together behind your chair, keeping your arms straight. Can you feel which muscles are being stretched?
- Let your head fall to one shoulder, and then roll it around to the other shoulder. Be limp, but don't fall asleep.

In the Kitchen or Den

- Stand about three feet from the kitchen counter or a table. Lean toward it, holding onto the edge of the counter or table. Can you keep your legs straight and your feet flat on the floor?

Television Time

- Sit on the floor, and pull your feet up to your body with the bottoms of your feet together. Hold on to your feet; then use your elbows to push your knees to the floor. Next, try to touch your chest to your feet. What do you feel stretching this time?

Family Time

- Sit facing a partner with your legs spread apart and your feet touching your partner's feet. (If you're doing this exercise with your father or mother, your feet may touch only their ankles because their legs are much longer.) Hold hands; one partner leans back and slowly pulls the other partner so that he or she is stretching. Take turns stretching your partner.

Cardiovascular Efficiency

- The heart is a muscle that benefits from exercise, as do other muscles.
- Exercising makes your heart beat harder and faster and will help keep your heart strong and healthy.
- Being on an athletic team doesn't automatically increase your cardiovascular efficiency; active participation is necessary.

The Surgeon General's focus on the need for physical activity and the benefits of cumulative activity throughout the day highlights the importance of physical activity beyond instructional physical education. With many school programs not affording children daily physical education, activities beyond the gymnasium are critical for the accumulation of thirty minutes of activity daily as well as for establishing the pattern for a lifetime of daily participation. Jogging and jump-rope programs, physical activity and fitness clubs, and family activity participation are examples of physical activity beyond the instructional physical education program.

Activities/Exercises for Cardiovascular Efficiency.   In-school activities such as jumping rope and jogging can provide daily and enjoyable vigorous exercises for children. *Jump-rope clubs* can be organized

Figure 4.7 Both beginners and students with advanced skills find jumping rope fun.

Figure 4.8 Membership in a jogging club provides opportunities for children to improve their cardiovascular fitness. *Source:* PEANUTS © United Feature Syndicate, Inc.

at different skill and interest levels (Figure 4.7). Names—for example, Tigger the Tiger (basic jumps forward and backward), Dolphin Club (jumping for speed), Jimmie Cricket (tricks), Kanga and Roo (group jumping), and the Masters Club—provide motivation for children as they progress through different skills. Jump Rope for Heart, sponsored by the American Heart Association and the American Alliance for Health, Physical Education, Recreation, and Dance (AAHPERD), has contributed significantly to improved cardiovascular efficiency for children. Instructional booklets and information on organizing jump-rope teams are available from local chapters of the American Heart Association. Jump-rope clubs can be organized to meet before school, after school, or during recess. Many schools award certificates for participation in the activity.

Jogging clubs can also meet before school, after school, or during recess, depending on the teacher's and students' schedules (Figure 4.8). The following guidelines are helpful for organizing a jogging club:

■ Obtain written parental permission for each child's participation, including a health statement.

■ Teach children the correct foot placement for jogging: feet pointing straight ahead, absorbing force when landing.
■ Remind children in the beginning that jogging is not running at top speed or racing with others.
■ Joggers should build up distance gradually; as the teacher you will need to set the upper limits.

Children enjoy selecting names for their jogging clubs, such as Roadrunners, Jogging Jaguars, Snoopy and Woodstocks, and Linden Lions Jog Across America. Bulletin boards and displays portraying the theme add interest for children. For example, a Snoopy-Woodstock theme depicts Snoopy in sweatpants for his morning jog, followed by individual Woodstocks. Each child in the club has a personalized Woodstock. Stick-on numbers on the cafeteria, hallway, or gymnasium wall indicate the number of miles completed. The children post their Woodstocks near the number that corresponds to the miles completed. Classroom teachers, parent volunteers, the physical education teacher, or the child can do the record keeping. Each child's monthly chart (Figure 4.9) shows the number of laps completed per day; cumulative laps/miles are recorded across the chart.

Figure 4.9   Daily jogging chart.

Month _November_

Previous total _____ laps _5_____ miles _____

Name _Benning, Tom_____ Homeroom _4b_____

Number of Laps	1	2	3	4	(5)	6	7	(8)	9	10	11	(12)	13	14	(15)	16	17	18	(19)	20	21	(22)	23	24	25	(26)	27	28	29	30	31
30					✓			✓														✓				✓					
29																															
28																															
27																															
26																															
25																															
24																															
23																															
22																															
21																															
20												✓			✓				✓												
19																															
18																															
17																															
16																															
15																						✓				✓					
14																															
13																															
12																															
11																															
10																															
9																															
8																															
7																															
6																															
5																															
4																															
3																															
2																															
1																															

Additional in-school activities include *fitness clubs* to provide additional physical activity time within the school week, to increase play activities on the playground, and to foster cardiovascular fitness. Fitness clubs can provide additional skill practice for lifetime activities, choice activities to promote responsible decision making by children, and family activities outside the school setting. Such clubs become a cooperative effort among parents, the children, classroom teachers, and the physical education specialist as they all work together to promote increased physical activity and fitness. In the Super Active Kids Fitness Club (East Grand Forks, Minnesota), the physical education specialist devotes one class period per week to additional skill instruction in lifetime physical activity, classroom teachers assist children with record keeping, parents promote and assist children with at-home activity, and children gain physical skills and confidence as they assume responsibility for this portion of their health/fitness.

Students enjoy recording physical activity for a day (or longer) and coding the activity according to inten-

Figure 4.10 Adapted from: Physical Activity and Health: A Report of the Surgeon General, U.S. Department of Health and Human Services, Centers for Disease Control, 1996.

sity (less virorous, moderate, more vigorous) in relation to physical fitness. Figure 4.10 provides a sample scale for coding.

Cardiovascular Activities for Outside the Gym. Family fitness programs, such as a physical activity club (PAC), can provide additional activity for children outside the school setting. The research continues to show family support for physical activity and parental modeling as *the* important predictors for the adoption of regular physical activity by children (Stucky-Ropp & DiLorenzo, 1993). When designing a PAC, choose activities that are readily available in the community, the majority of which require no additional expense for the family. Promote physical activities that the family can enjoy together as well as those of special interest to children (Figure 4.11). Introduce the physical activity club to the parents with a letter of invitation and explanation; include in the letter a brief discussion of the health/fitness benefits of physical activity, the purposes of the club, and your goals for the students. Keep in touch throughout the year

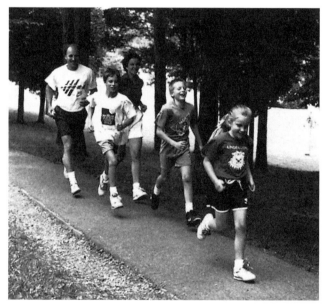

Figure 4.11 These parents promote good physical fitness habits by participating with their children in a cardiovascular activity.

Figure 4.12 Physical activity club recording sheet.

with updates on all PACs via the school newsletter, an annual PTA program, and notes to parents. A combination physical activity evening and health fair, with participation by parents is an excellent way to promote physical education and wellness.

Children can record their PAC participation on a chart like the one in Figure 4.12. Note that double credit is given for family participation with an older sibling or a parent. More cardiovascular activities that can be done outside the gym are suggested in Box 4.6.

Body Composition

The concept of body composition is difficult for children to understand. Activities that contribute to a decrease in body fat are the same as those that promote cardiovascular efficiency. The following con-

cepts are important for children at the elementary level:

- Body composition is affected by heredity, nutrition, and lifestyle
- A certain amount of body fat is essential
- Body fat is not the same as body weight

Further discussion of the role of nutrition and moderate exercise in relation to body composition and wellness can be found in the Wellness section of this chapter.

Physical Fitness Testing

Physical fitness assessments can be used to culminate a unit, to motivate students, as diagnostic screening

BOX 4.3   CARDIOVASCULAR ACTIVITIES FOR OUTSIDE THE GYM

Wake-up Time

- Before getting out of bed, lie on your back and kick your legs up in the air. Keep kicking them as fast and as long as possible, or move them in a circular motion, as if you were riding a bicycle.

Getting Ready

- Stand in front of the mirror and pretend you're boxing with yourself. How quickly can you swing and punch? How long?

Going to School

- Walk, skip, ride a bicycle, or even jog to school or the bus stop.
- If you ride in a car pool, run to the car before mom or dad gets there, and then count the number of times you can jump up and down before she or he arrives.

Family Time

- Put on some upbeat music and dance. See who can move around the most, longest, and best.

instruments, and/or as an ongoing process throughout the year. We strongly advocate using physical fitness assessments for screening purposes and as an ongoing process. If the physical fitness assessment is to be used as a diagnostic tool, administer the test in early fall. You can then use the test results to help develop yearly plans, assist youngsters in establishing personal fitness goals, and plan remedial programs for individual students. We recommend that children who have extremely low scores be given remedial fitness programs, individualized educational plans for their area(s) of weakness. The physical education teacher can counsel these students individually on ways to improve fitness through physical activity. Programs of activity and exercise can be designed for use at home, and parents can become active participants with their child.

Whether the physical fitness assessment is used as a screening tool in the fall, as a culminating experience for children, or as an ongoing process, it should be an educational endeavor. Each test item should be carefully explained, emphasizing the particular component being tested. All too often, children do poorly on an assessment because they do not understand the directions. Sufficient time should be allowed for practice so that children understand the proper techniques

and stretch their muscles. The purpose of the test is to motivate the children to do their personal best, not to trick them. We recommend not recording test scores of children below the fourth grade. Younger children can take the test as an educational experience, but the characteristics of young children don't promote maximum effort and extended concentration on a subject that is of more interest to the teacher than to them.

A key to successful testing is management of the time involved. Physical fitness assessment should not take an exorbitant amount of time. Carefully planning the testing and organizing the class can minimize the time necessary. Self- and peer assessments can greatly reduce the amount of teacher instructional time devoted to testing. For those times when direct teacher involvement in the testing is necessary, we've found it best to structure the study of the theme in games, gymnastics, or dance so the children can work independently while the teacher is involved in the fitness assessment. Thus the children can continue their study of the theme, their completion of the project, and their practice and refinement of skills.

Several commercial tests are available for fitness assessment. Further information on the specifics of each test, awards systems, and so forth, can be obtained by writing to the addresses in Box 4.4. When

BOX 4.4   PHYSICAL FITNESS TEST PACKAGES

Additional information concerning specific physical fitness packages, national norms, awards programs, and so on, may be obtained from the following sources:

Fitnessgram

Institute for Aerobics Research
12330 Preston Road
Dallas, Texas 75230

Physical Best

American Alliance for Health, Physical Education, Recreation and Dance (AAHPERD)
1900 Association Drive
Reston, Virginia 22091

President's Challenge

President's Council on Physical Fitness and Sports
450 5th Street, N.W., Suite 7103
Washington, D.C. 20001

using a fitness assessment that employs different standards for achievement, we recommend that the interpretation of the test scores be divided into health standards and fitness standards—that is, that the assessor determine what score represents a basic level of health fitness and what score is a measure of athletic fitness/skill performance. For tests with a criterion reference for health fitness, that score is the level needed for basic health. Scores at a much higher level are indicative of athletic performance fitness.

Assessment of children's physical fitness should not end with the completion of the test. The recording of scores should be done in a way that provides ownership to children, is personal and private for each individual, and assists children in setting fitness goals. Children can be active participants in the recording of their fitness scores following test completion. A

simple graph can be designed listing test items (Figure 4.13). Each child is provided his/her scores from the assessment. Using a highlighter the child colors in the portion of the bar corresponding to the score for each test item. Completion of the graph provides a visual representation for the child of the areas of fitness in the health fitness range, those above, and those needing remediation. When the children have recorded their scores and reflected on the assessment results, they can write in their journals their feelings about their test results and record their personal fitness goals for the year.

The focus of elementary physical education is the child; the focus of physical fitness should also be the child. No child should be asked to give more than his or her personal best. Scores from the assessment test are personal; they are not to be compared and not to be used for grading purposes. We recommend the following guidelines for the assessment of children's physical fitness:

▶ Fitness comes from being physically active. Being physically active comes from enjoyment of activity, competence in skills, and confidence in self. Enjoyment, competence, and confidence come from quality physical education.

■ Involve students in the assessment process, not just as participants in the test, but also in the recording of scores and interpretation of results. Personal involvement in the total process will facilitate acceptance of responsibility for fitness.

Figure 4.13 Personal fitness profile.

PERSONAL FITNESS PROFILE

Name _____ Homeroom _____

Test Item: Curl-ups   Score:

[   ]

　　　　　　　　　　　　Be Healthy Club   Super Healthy Club

Test Item: Shoulder Flexibiity   Score:

[   ]

　　　　　　　　　　　　Be Healthy Club   Super Healthy Club

　　　　　　　　　　　　　　　　　　　　　　Score: Left—
Test Item: Sit and Reach   Right—

[-]

　　　　　　　　　　　　Be Healthy Club   Super Healthy Club

Test Item: Push-ups   Score:

[   ]

　　　　　　　　　　　　Be Healthy Club   Super Healthy Club

Test Item: Pull-ups   Score:

[   ]

　　　　　　　　　　　　Be Healthy Club   Super Healthy Club

Test Item: One-mile Run   Score:

[   ]

　　　　　　　　　　　　Be Healthy Club   Super Healthy Club

■ Consider allowing children to select items from a test battery for each component to be assessed. For example, upper arm strength may be tested with pull-ups, chin-ups, modified pull-ups, or push-ups. Children may make individual choices from the battery.

■ Develop an assessment tool that meets your needs: times per week you see the children for physical education, entry level fitness for children, class size, your goals for fitness.

■ Assist the children in setting their personal fitness goals. Following the fall screening and graphing of scores, have the children record in their journals their personal goals for the year. Young children often need teacher assistance in setting realistic goals. All too often the school athlete is the measure of success for children. Instead, goals should be based on a reflection of assessments and increments of success.

■ Praise children's accomplishments at the lower end of the spectrum as well as those at the high-performance level. (In the fall the class cheered Molly's efforts on the mile run [21:00]; in the spring they cheered her accomplishments [16:34].)

Appropriate and inappropriate practices in regard to physical fitness tests are summarized in Box 4.5.

BOX 4.5   APPROPRIATE AND INAPPROPRIATE PHYSICAL EDUCATION PRACTICES

Component: *Physical Fitness Tests*

Appropriate Practice: Ongoing fitness assessment is used as part of the ongoing process of helping children understand, enjoy, improve, and/or maintain their physical health and well-being.

Inappropriate Practice: Physical fitness tests are given once or twice a year solely for the purpose of qualifying children for awards or because they are required by a school district or state department.

Appropriate Practice: Test results are shared privately with children and their parents as a tool for developing their physical fitness knowledge, understanding, and competence.

Inappropriate Practice: Children are required to complete a physical fitness test battery without understanding why they are performing the tests or the implications of their individual results as they apply to their future health and well-being.

Appropriate Practice: As part of an ongoing program of physical education, children are physically prepared so they can safely complete each component of a physical test battery.

Inappropriate Practice: Children are required to take physical fitness tests without adequate conditioning (e.g., students are made to run a mile after "practicing" it only one day the week before).

SOURCE: From *Developmentally Appropriate Physical Education Practices for Children: A Position Statement of the Council on Physical Education for Children (COPEC)*, 1992, Reston, VA: National Association for Sport and Physical Education. Reprinted with permission.

Incorporating Physical Fitness

Teaching the important physical fitness concepts is an important part of the physical education curriculum, but it doesn't happen by chance; it must be carefully planned. During the process of planning the daily lesson, keep in mind the components of fitness and the muscle groups involved in the activities outlined for the children. Not all lessons will lend themselves to incorporating fitness into the theme of study. Other types of activities that can be used to teach physical fitness concepts are dance aerobics, fitness circuits, and activities to enhance the specific fitness components.

Dance aerobics is similar to continuous calisthenics, except that various dance steps are added. A typical routine combines exercises for flexibility, muscular strength, and endurance with dance steps, jogging, or other locomotor movements. A number of aerobics videotapes, as well as exercises designed specifically for the classroom, are now available. Your school librarian may want to purchase several of these tapes for use throughout the school.

A fitness circuit can be set up around the perimeter of the gymnasium or playing field. Exercises and activities at each station focus on different muscle groups and fitness components; cardiovascular activities may be incorporated into the stations or performed as a total group. The number of stations must be sufficient to permit all students to be actively involved. The teacher can call for rotation between stations after a given number of repetitions or after a predetermined amount of time. Children enjoy doing the exercises to recorded music, rotating each time the music stops.

Fitness parcourses are permanent outdoor fitness circuits. Parcourses are commercially available, or parents and teachers can build them as a PTA project. A typical parcourse includes stations for exercising various muscle groups. At each station is a large sign or laminated poster with a graphic representation of the exercise and the number of suggested repetitions for both a beginner and an experienced participant.

Parcourse stations are often set up around a jogging track to promote cardiovascular activity, such as walking and jogging, as well as muscular strength and endurance and flexibility workouts. Parcourses are excellent opportunities for community and family involvement in physical fitness at the school environment after the normal school day ends as well as fitness for students during recess on non–physical education days.

Many traditional games and activities can be adapted for large-group fitness. Examine the game carefully to be sure all students can participate. Teacher-designed activities may also be used to focus on specific fitness components. The following are examples of teacher-designed or -adapted large-group fitness activities.

- *Here, There, Everywhere (cardiovascular efficiency):* When the teacher calls "Here," students run toward the teacher. When the teacher calls "There," students run where the teacher is pointing. When the teacher calls "Everywhere," students run freely in general space.
- *I See (cardiovascular efficiency, flexibility, muscular strength):* Children are in scattered formation facing the teacher. The teacher says in loud voice, "I see." The children answer in chorus, "What do you see?" The teacher responds, "I see all students moving in any direction without touching anyone." Children respond to this signal until the teacher again says, "I see." The children stop and answer, "What do you see?" The teacher responds with a new challenge—locomotor skills, push-ups, bend and stretch, or twisting actions, for example—making each challenge focus on a different muscle group and fitness component.
- *Heart Hustle (cardiovascular efficiency):* The teacher constructs a series of color-coded exercise/activity cards and places them blank side up on a table. Students select a card and perform the activity pictured on the card. At the end of the timed interval, the students return the cards to the table and select a different color. Possible activities include jumping rope, stationary running, speed walking, free-form dancing.
- *Magic Cars (cardiovascular efficiency, leg strength):* The teacher scatters carpet squares around the room. Students place their hands on the carpet square that is to be their magic car. On the signal, they begin traveling around the room by pushing the carpet square. When the teacher calls "Red light" or stops the music, all cars must stop and the children sit down. Children rest for a few seconds and begin to travel again. This is an excellent cardiovascular activity.

- *Sticky Popcorn (cardiovascular efficiency, leg strength):* Children are in scattered formation. The teacher gives the signal for the children to begin gently jumping in their own spaces . . . pop, pop, pop. With the second signal, individual children move toward a partner, touch shoulders, and continue jumping; now the two children jump up and down together . . . pop, pop, pop. With the next signal, the two partners join two other children; now the four jump together . . . pop, pop, pop. Each additional signal unites the groups: Four becomes eight and so forth until all are connected. Final signal: Cool down with a slow melt! Throughout the activity, the children are to jump together. Each segment of jumping is short in duration, no more than twenty to thirty seconds.

Physical fitness for all elementary school children can be enhanced through the cooperative efforts of the physical education specialist, the classroom teacher, and the child's parents. Physical activity and fitness clubs encourage children to participate in regular programs of physical activity. The child is recognized, not for attaining scores on a fitness test or for setting the school record in certain exercises, but for participating in activities that promote cardiovascular fitness, increase muscular strength and endurance, and improve flexibility. Children earn points for participating in selected activities or exercises during a portion of their recess time, for engaging in club or community physical activities after school hours, and for involving their families in activity. They receive rewards and recognition for achieving a preestablished level of regular activity. Parents are involved through verifying their child's activities outside school and participating actively with their children. Classroom teachers are encouraged to designate a corner of the room as a fitness learning/activity center and to engage the total class in a fifteen- to twenty-minute fitness break on non–physical education days. Thus, the child is encouraged to participate in physical activities on a regular basis, develops habits of including the family in these activities, and is rewarded at school for doing so.

A Final Thought on Fitness

The goal of physical education for children is to enable them to develop health and activity habits that will become a lifestyle throughout adolescence and adulthood. The two most important factors in attaining this goal at the elementary school level are that the children (1) enjoy the fitness activities and (2) master the basic skills of physical education that will enable them to participate successfully in the

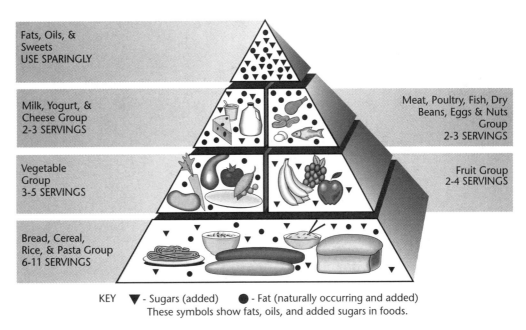

Figure 4.14 USDA Food Guide Pyramid. *Source:* From *Dietary Guidelines and Your Health* by U.S. Department of Agriculture, 1992, Rockville, MD.

activities that promote fitness. Only if fitness is fun will the children pursue it outside the two or three times they are with us in physical education class each week and on through middle school, high school, and beyond. Children must enjoy exercise and physical activity as well as understand and appreciate the importance of physical fitness if they are to develop lifelong health fitness habits.

Fitness for health is not the same as conditioning for competitive sports participation. We are teachers of children in physical education, not coaches striving for the "gold" in a sports program. Therefore, we focus on the teaching and learning of skills, knowledge, and behaviors that will enable children to be physically active today, tomorrow, and throughout their adult lives.

Wellness

In a broader sense, fitness is wellness . . . optimal health and well-being. In addition to physical fitness, wellness encompasses the dimensions of emotional, mental, spiritual, interpersonal/social, and environmental well-being (Fahey, Insel, & Roth, 1994). These dimensions translate for children into learning experiences in nutrition; personal safety (bicycle, auto, water, and fire); drug, alcohol, and tobacco abuse; personal and social responsibility; and mental/emotional health. Fitness in all of these areas results in optimal health and well-being—in other words, in wellness.

Nutrition

Busier schedules and more fast food meals have resulted in a decrease in good nutrition for America's families. A positive increase in physical activity—that is, organized sports, dance, and gymnastics clubs for children—has been coupled with a decrease in family meals at home. All too often the quickest meal is one from a drive-through, one that is high in fat and low in the balance of nutrients needed for good health.

Although elementary-age children may not be interested in nutrition for good health (after all, they are immortal), we have found they are very interested in nutrition as it relates to running, jumping, throwing, and being a better athlete. Thus, the appeal of athletics opens the door to educating children about the importance of eating fruits and vegetables, decreasing fats, attaining healthy body weight, and maintaining a balance of physical activity and nutrition as a daily pattern, a childhood pattern that becomes a lifestyle for wellness.

Children at the elementary level need an understanding of the Food Guide Pyramid (Figure 4.14), the

- Eating the right foods will help you be stronger and stay healthy.
- Food is the fuel that makes activity possible.
- Start each day with a good breakfast.
- Eat fruits and vegetables every day.

Figure 4.15
Young children learn traffic signals and safety through community-sponsored programs.

contribution of the major essential nutrients to building and maintaining healthy bodies, and the necessity of balancing exercise and nutrition in maintaining good health. As children approach puberty this balance between exercise and nutrition in maintaining proper body weight becomes very important for both boys and girls; however, for young children the emphasis on the balance is for good health.

Children enjoy learning about the following nutrition facts and their relationship to good health and movement performance:

■ Food is the fuel that makes activity possible; too little fuel, too little energy.
■ Foods are not "good" or "bad", balance is the key.
■ Carbohydrates supply energy to muscles for maximum performance. They are the main fuel source for the muscles.
■ Some fat is essential to supply energy, and to insulate and cushion vital organs.
■ Proteins are needed to form strong bones and muscles. They are the building blocks of body tissues.
■ Water makes up 50–70 percent of total body weight and is critical for survival. The more active you are, the more water you need.

▶ An excellent resource for educational information about nutrition and the important balance between nutrition and physical activity:
The American Dietetic Association
National Center for Nutrition and Dietetics
216 West Jackson Boulevard
Chicago, IL 60606-6995

Personal Safety: Bicycle, Auto, Water, Fire

Seat Belts . . . Always
Helmets . . . Always
Life Jackets . . . Always

The subjects of bicycle and automobile safety, fire safety, and water safety provide excellent opportunities for school and community cooperative endeavors as communities come together to provide demonstrations and hands-on activities in these areas of wellness. One such example is a summer playground project called "Safety City," which involves youngsters maneuvering "big wheels" and tricycles through miniature streets, learning traffic signals, and meeting police officers (Figure 4.15). From big wheels and tricycles the children advance to bicycle safety, with participation in activities stressing safe riding and consideration for others. Our experience with these cooperative endeavors has shown a positive, enthusiastic response from the adults as well as the children, an increased awareness of safety, and tremendous public relations for the schools.

FIRE SAFETY

Stop, drop, and roll.
Have a plan.
Stay low.

Drug, Alcohol, and Tobacco Abuse

With children experimenting with drugs, alcohol, and tobacco at increasingly younger ages, it is never too early to educate children on the risks of use and dangers of substance abuse. Classroom teachers and entire school systems have adopted a variety of programs to educate children on substance abuse, all with the overriding message, "Just say no." Our role as physical educators is that of supporting the classroom teachers in this endeavor, reinforcing the message, and as with all areas of wellness, serving as a model for children to emulate. Physical educators serve a key role for children in the area of substance abuse. With daily reports of professional athletes involved in substance abuse children receive a confusing message regarding the dangers of drugs and the consequences of use. We can provide positive role models and clear, consistent messages regarding abstinence.

> Drugs, alcohol, and tobacco can kill you.
> Say *YES* to physical activity, *NO* to drugs.

Much research and thought has been given to the reasons individuals use drugs. Two of those reasons are boredom and low self-esteem. A youngster actively involved in physical activity and sports is an active youngster. A youngster involved in a quality physical education program develops the skills for successful participation in a variety of sports/physical activities. A solid movement-skills base provides a positive self-image in this important area for children. Thus, physical education has the potential to contribute directly to a healthy, drug-free world for children.

Personal and Social Responsibility

> Respect for self.
> Respect for others.

The gymnasiums and playgrounds of our schools provide a rich environment for the development of personal and social responsibility. The physical activity setting provides a miniworld of emotional, interactive situations. Within this world of competition and cooperation, success and failure, and fast-moving action, children make a multitude of decisions on a daily basis. The development of personal and social responsibility—and its importance to the future of our society—is a reminder that we are teachers of children, not just skills, sequences, games, and dances.

The importance of personal and social responsibility is highlighted in the *National Standards for Physical Education*, being referred to in three of the seven standards:

- Demonstrates responsible personal and social behavior in physical activity settings
- Demonstrates understanding and respect for differences among people in physical activity settings
- Understands that physical activity provides opportunities for enjoyment, challenge, self-expression, and social interaction (NASPE, 1995)

Don Hellison's work on the development of personal and social responsibility through physical activity (Hellison, 1995) has served as the model for many physical education programs concerned with this critical area of wellness. Many have adopted Hellison's philosophy and adapted his model for acceptance of responsibility in physical education. Figure 4.16 (p. 54) shows Linda Masser's (1990) application of the Hellison model in and beyond the physical education setting.

While we as physical educators teach in an environment rich in opportunity for the development of personal and social responsibility, it is not enough simply to let children experience decision-making situations. We guide them in the development of

> Our coaches said drugs weren't cool
> If you take them you're a fool.
>
> If you smoke, you'll probably croak,
> And if you're in a gang,
> You'll lose the game.
>
> Choose your friends,
> Choose them well
> 'Cause if you don't, you might fail.
>
> We learned to deal with stress
> So we don't get in a mess.
> Violence isn't cool
> Obey the Golden Rule.
>
> When you do drugs and alcohol,
> You'll never do anything at all.
> Remember this, remember it right
> Drugs do nothing for your life.
>
> Coaches and parents say drugs aren't cool,
> We agree; we're not fools!
>
> P. Petrie (Grade 5)

Figure 4.16 Levels of responsibility. *Source:* From "Teaching for Affective Learning in Elementary Physical Education" by L. Masser, 1990, *JOPERD, 61,* pp. 18–19.

acceptance of responsibility through awareness talks, group meetings, counseling, reflection time, individual decision making, and our modeling of responsible personal and social actions (Hellison, 1995). Further discussion of Hellison's model for the development of personal and social responsibility can be found in Chapter 10, "Maintaining Appropriate Behavior."

Responsible adults develop from responsible children who have had opportunities to make decisions, to experience success and failure, to be accepted and to accept others. Acceptance of self and others leads to respect for self and others and to personal and social responsibility.

Mental/Emotional Health

Accept me as I am.
Love *me.*

The foundation of the young child's emotional health is self-esteem—how worthy and valuable the individual considers himself or herself (Anspaugh & Ezell, 1995). Everyone needs to be accepted and loved; children are no exception. We as teachers play a critical role in how children view themselves. Our reactions to their skill or lack of skill, our reaction to their mistakes and sometimes loss of control greatly affect their view of themselves. Children's opinions of themselves are established early and are very fragile. A quick, negative response can have a lasting effect on a child. Children with a strong sense of worth and importance are free to develop their potential, better able to resolve personal and interpersonal conflicts, and free to establish their independence and self-expression. R. M. Page and T. S. Page (1993) offer the following suggestions for fostering a positive classroom/gymnasium climate for emotional wellness:

- Quickly learn the names of students, call them by name, and show respect for each child.
- Be sensitive to diverse cultures, ethnicities, and races; strive to view children from their perspectives rather than your own.
- Expect no problems. Expect students to be competent, capable, and eager to learn.
- When problems arise, handle them immediately and consistently.

What's Your Level?

Level 4: Caring

Home: Helping take care of a pet or younger child

Playground: Asking others (not just friends) to join them in play

Classroom: Helping another student with a math problem

Physical education: Willingly working with anyone in the class

Level 3: Self-responsibility

Home: Cleaning room without being asked

Playground: Returning equipment used during recess

Classroom: Doing a science project not a part of any assignment

Physical education: Undertaking to learn a new skill through resources outside the physical education class

Level 2: Involvement

Home: Helping to clean up supper dishes

Playground: Playing with others

Classroom: Listening and doing classwork

Physical education: Trying new things without complaining and saying I can't

Level 1: Self-control

Home: Keeping self from hitting brother even though really mad at him

Playground: Standing and watching others play

Classroom: Waiting until appropriate time to talk with friends

Physical education: Practicing but not all the time

Level 0: Irresponsibility

Home: Blaming brothers or sisters for problems

Playground: Calling other students names

Classroom: Talking to friends when teacher is giving instructions

Physical education: Pushing and shoving others when selecting equipment

- Avoid sarcasm, ridicule, and belittling remarks; help students to do the same.
- Avoid all suggestions of criticism, anger, or frustration. Make personal corrections in private.
- Create an atmosphere in which children feel at ease.
- Arrange for a high ratio of successes to failures.
- Avoid encouraging competitiveness between students in learning activities.
- Demonstrate the characteristics of effective teachers: warmth, friendliness, fairness, a good sense of humor, enthusiasm, empathy, openness, spontaneity, adaptability, and a democratic governing style.

The American Academy of Pediatrics approaches wellness from a positive viewpoint with a focus on "solutions before problems." All adults—parents, teachers, caregivers—involved in children's lives have the responsibility to ensure that all children have:

Security—the feeling that they are safe and can trust themselves and others.
Order and organization, to help them make sense of the world around them.
Love—unconditional.
Understanding and patience that they in turn will model for others.
Truth and honesty from adults.
Identity, independence, and influence—a sense that they count.
Opportunities to explore and to expand their world freely and happily.
Nurturing guidance and discipline to help them learn self-control and self-respect.
Successful life experiences that give them a sense of personal competence and pride and enhance their self-esteem.

Self-esteem—the way people think and feel about themselves and how well they do things that are important to them—is formed at an early age as young children attempt daily tasks and perceive the reaction of nearby adults. Children's feelings about self continue to grow and change with reactions from parents, teachers, and peers as they progress through the elementary and middle-school years. Experiences in the gymnasium and on the playground, reactions from classroom teachers (and specifically teachers of physical education) have a large impact on children's self-esteem. We are teachers of children; our interactions with them, our actions, and our language affect not just the moment, but their lives.

Final Thoughts on Wellness

We are teachers of physical education. Many of us see the children on less than a daily schedule. We are faced with the teaching of skills while dealing with fire drills, assemblies, and photo-day interruptions. Now the teaching of wellness has entered our gymnasium! The introduction of wellness into the physical education curriculum does not mean a reduction of time for the teaching of physical education. The ideas presented in this chapter are concepts for coordination with the classroom teacher, for integration with community services. We can assist in this endeavor with quotes of the week, bulletin boards, items in the newsletter to parents, teachable moments, and the conscious integration of wellness into our curriculum. We have found the inclusion of wellness to be an asset, not a disruption, to our teaching of physical education.

SUMMARY

Physical fitness is the capacity of the heart, blood vessels, lungs, and muscles to function at optimum efficiency. In previous years, fitness was defined as the capacity to carry out the day's activities without undue fatigue; we are now recognizing that this condition may not be sufficient for healthy hearts and lungs. Optimum efficiency is the key.

Physical fitness in the past focused on skill-related components—muscular strength, power, speed, agility, and endurance—components associated with performance in games and sports. In more recent years fitness has centered around those factors pertaining to a healthy lifestyle, with an emphasis at the elementary level on the learning of skills, knowledge, and behaviors that will enable children to be physically active now and in their adult years. Fitness is a process/product of a physically active lifestyle; a physically active lifestyle is the product of movement competency and knowledge gained through the process of positive participation in physical activity.

Physical fitness for children includes a health-related screening each fall, setting of individual goals, a cognitive understanding of the components of fitness, and moderate to vigorous activity on a regular basis. It involves the physical education specialist, the classroom teacher, the child, and the parent(s). Physical fitness can be incorporated into the theme of study, added to the lesson as a group activity, and increased through after-school jogging/jump-rope clubs and fitness trails/parcourses. The focus of physical fitness for the elementary school child is the development of a positive attitude toward an active lifestyle, a knowledge of the concepts of fitness, and an understanding of how to attain and maintain personal fitness.

Wellness is optimal health and well-being. In addition to physical fitness, wellness encompasses the dimensions of emotional, mental, spiritual, interpersonal/social, and environmental well-being. For elementary school children these dimensions translate into learning experiences relative to nutrition, substance abuse, personal safety, personal/social responsibility, and mental/emotional health. Physical education and wellness are intricately woven together in the quest for optimal health and well-being for all children.

READING COMPREHENSION QUESTIONS

1. Define physical fitness. Why can we no longer define the level of fitness as the capacity to carry out the day's activities without undue fatigue?
2. What is the difference between health-related and athletic fitness?
3. Why do we emphasize health-related fitness in our programs?
4. Define cardiovascular efficiency. How is it developed? Name several activities that contribute to cardiovascular efficiency.
5. Within our physical education curriculum, what activities contribute to the development of muscular strength?
6. What does the phrase "specificity of flexibility" mean? What are the implications for physical education?
7. Explain the fitness component of body composition. What factors determine an individual's body fat?
8. How did the Surgeon General's 1996 report *Physical Activity and Health* change the focus on fitness for children?
9. How do the CDC guidelines for the promotion of physical activity among young people affect the physical education curriculum?
10. Define wellness. What are the components of wellness for children at the elementary school level?
11. Choose one wellness component. Design a strategy for working with the classroom teacher to teach that component. Include in your action plan the integrating of the component into physical education.
12. Design a plan for community involvement in the teaching of wellness.

REFERENCES/ SUGGESTED READINGS

American Academy of Pediatrics. (1996). *Solutions before problems*. Elk Grove Village, IL: Author.

Anspaugh, D. J., & Ezell, G. (1995). *Teaching today's health*. Boston: Allyn & Bacon.

Cooper, K. H. (1991). *Kid fitness*. New York: Bantam Books.

Corbin, C. B. (1986). Fitness is for children: Developing lifetime fitness. *Journal of Physical Education, Recreation and Dance, 57*(5), 82–84.

Corbin, C. B., & Pangrazi, R. P. (1992). Are American children and youth fit? *Research Quarterly for Exercise and Sport, 63*(2), 96–106.

Corbin, C. B., & Pangrazi, R. P. (1994). Toward an understanding of appropriate physical activity levels for youth. *Physical Activity and Fitness Research Digest, 1*(8), 1–7.

Fahey, T. D., Insel, P. M., & Roth, W. T. (1994). *Fit and well.* Mountain View, CA: Mayfield.

Hellison, D. (1995). *Teaching responsibility through physical activity.* Champaign, IL: Human Kinetics.

Kennedy, J. F. (1960). The soft American. *Sports Illustrated,* 13–15.

Masser, L. (1990). Teaching for affective learning in elementary physical education. *JOPERD, 61,* 18–19.

National Association for Sport and Physical Education (NASPE). (1995). *Moving into the future: National standards for physical education.* St. Louis, MO: Mosby.

Page, R. M., & Page, T. S. (1993). *Fostering emotional well-being in the classroom.* Boston: Jones & Bartlett.

Safrit, M. J. (1995). *Complete guide to youth fitness testing.* Champaign, IL: Human Kinetics.

Sallis, J. F., & McKenzie, T. L. (1991). Physical education's role in public health. *Research Quarterly, 62*(2), 124–137.

Simons-Morton, B. G., Parcel, G. S., & O'Hara, N. M. (1987). Children and fitness: A public health perspective. *Research Quarterly, 58*(4), 295–302.

Stucky-Ropp, R. C., & DiLorenzo, T. M. (1993). Determinants of exercise in children. *Preventive Medicine, 22,* 880–889.

U.S. Department of Health & Human Services. (1996). *Physical activity and health: A report of the Surgeon General.* Atlanta, GA: USDHHS, Centers for Disease Control and Prevention, National Center for Chronic Disease Prevention and Health Promotion.

U.S. Department of Health & Human Services (1997). *Guidelines for school and community programs to promote lifelong physical activity among young people.* Atlanta, GA: USDHHS, Centers for Disease Control and Prevention.

Weathers, W. (1983). *Physical fitness activity program for health-related physical fitness test.* Special Projects Report. Murfreesboro: Middle Tennessee State University, Department of Physical Education.

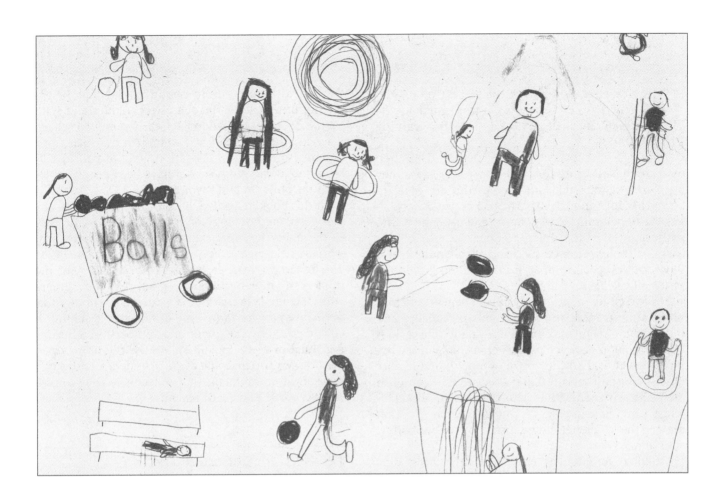

Reflective Teaching

5

The good teacher must relate his teaching to the world of his students as it is, not as he would like it to be.

——Herbert Foster

A search for rigid prescriptions of the right way to teach has largely been replaced with the search for propositional rules and principles to guide practice.

——Judith E. Rink

Physical education is more than recess, more than simply a time to play. As documented in the *National Standards,* it is a time for learning (NASPE, 1995).

In any physical education class you'll find children who are there because they must be, not because they want to be. And you'll find some who are eager to become skillful enough to participate in varsity athletics. We're determined to foster the development and enthusiasm of all the children in our classes. We want them all to experience success and pleasure and a sense of competence that leads to their becoming physically active for a lifetime.

No two children are exactly alike. There are obvious physical differences and more subtle personality and individual differences. What is exciting to one child is boring to another. Some youngsters are able to accomplish a great deal on their own; other children require almost constant monitoring if they are to accomplish anything. For each child who delights in the challenge and camaraderie of a team game, another prefers the challenge and satisfaction of individual activities.

Children are different, and so are the schools they attend. Some school buildings have open designs, but others are divided into permanent classrooms. Administrators can be strict, stultifying, or supportive. Fellow teachers can be cooperative or competitive, helpful or obstructive. Gymnasiums, plentiful physical education equipment, adequate field space, and small class sizes are basic necessities in some elementary schools; other schools view such facilities as frills. Parents are concerned, meddlesome, apathetic, helpful, or unavailable.

How is a teacher to succeed amid this diversity? We have no magical answers. But we are convinced that a linear approach* to teaching is not effective, and so we coined the term *reflective teaching.* The reflective teacher achieves success and professional satisfaction by employing a variety of teaching skills that interact effectively with the particular teaching environment.

The concept behind what we call reflective teaching is not new. Indeed, reflective teaching has probably been practiced since the beginning of formal education. Nor are we attempting to add another term to an already cumbersome educational jargon. We're trying to convey the concept that effective† teaching is situational rather than generic. For example, a teacher who succeeds in suburbia may fail in the ghetto, unless he or she adapts techniques and skills to the specific educational environment. For many teachers, the results of attempting to transplant pre-designed programs of education without considering the ecology of a given school have been disastrous for both the children and themselves.

In this book, reflective teaching doesn't refer to any particular methodology or style of teaching; it refers to the many teaching skills employed by individuals who are respected as master teachers (Graham, 1992). The reflective teacher is one who can design and implement an educational program that is congruent with the idiosyncrasies of a particular school situation. *Invariant teaching,* unlike reflective teaching, is characterized by the use of one approach in all teaching situations (see Table 5.1). We use the terms *reflective teaching* and *invariant teaching* to define and clarify *some* of the components that collectively seem to constitute "good" and "bad" teaching.

The Need for Reflective Teaching

The casual observer who visits a number of classes or schools may not be conscious of the differences in teaching environments. However, an experienced teacher is often aware of those differences and can describe how they influence students, teachers, and teaching (Borko & Livingston, 1989; Graham, Hopple, Manross, & Sitzman, 1993; Housner & Griffey, 1985). Each teaching environment is composed of a variety of factors, as Figure 5.1 illustrates.

Our conversations with teachers as well as our own experiences have revealed that the same characteristics substantially influence what are generally called good or bad teaching situations. The following six variables illustrate the need for reflective teaching: the values of the teacher, class size, the number of class sessions per week, facilities and equipment, discipline, and the context of the school. We'll now discuss these variables in detail.

Values of the Teacher

Clearly one of the most important variables is the personal attitudes and beliefs we, as teachers, bring to our teaching situation. Some physical education teachers, for example, are more interested in coaching than teaching—and their programs reflect a lack of planning and interest in high-quality physical education. Other physical education teachers are totally dedicated to their programs and spend countless hours

---

*Dwight Allen defined *linear thinking* as searching for the answer to a problem by investigating a single solution without considering feasible alternatives (Allen, 1975).

†We use the terms *successful teaching* and *effective teaching* to indicate a teaching process that results in the sought-after physical, affective, and cognitive gains.

Table 5.1   Comparison of Reflective Teaching and Invariant Teaching

Variable	The Reflective Teachers	The Invariant Teachers
Planning	Adjust lesson plans to differences between classes and children	Use the same plan for each primary grade and the same plan for each intermediate grade
Progression within and between lessons	Base progression on such factors as youngsters' (1) rate and extent of improvement; (2) physical skill needs; (3) interest in a particular topic or activity	Base progression on such factors as (1) six-week units; (2) amount of material to be covered in a semester or year; (3) a predetermined formula for progression
Methodology	Vary the methodology according to such factors as (1) kinds of children in the class; (2) purpose of the lesson; (3) ability of the children to accept responsibility	Employ the same methodology with all classes and hope that the children will eventually fulfill the teacher's expectations
Curriculum	Design curriculum for each unique class of children after examining the children to determine their abilities and needs	Use predetermined curricular content without considering such factors as children's ability, community influences, or children's interests
Equipment and facilities	Modify activities and lessons to available equipment and facilities	Teach activities and lessons that use available equipment and facilities
Discipline	Attempt to understand management problems and then seek the causes, modifying teaching procedure accordingly	Assume that the children are misbehaving and resort to punitive measures to modify individual and class behavior
Assessment	Regularly assess the children and also seek constructive criticism about their teaching from children and colleagues	Assess sporadically and often base assessment on whether children liked the lesson, how long they remained interested, and how well they behaved

planning new and interesting activities, as well as volunteering time with children before and after school. Still other physical education teachers view physical education as merely a break for the children from the routine of the classroom, so their programs consist primarily of fun activities for the children, with virtually no emphasis on learning.

In many schools, physical education is also the responsibility of the classroom teacher. Like physical education teachers, classroom teachers also vary in their views of the purpose and importance of physical activity in the lives of children. Some classroom teachers, for example, find time in their hectic schedules to develop programs for children that truly enhance the development of positive attitudes and learning as suggested in Chapter 1. In contrast, other classroom teachers view physical education as a break for the children and themselves—and rely on such old standbys as kickball, dodgeball, and Duck, Duck, Goose to keep the children entertained during physical education class.

Ideally, every teacher, whether classroom teacher or physical education teacher, would appreciate the importance of physical education for children and develop programs that are developmentally appropriate—and effective—for children. Realistically, however, there will always be some teachers who "fall back" on the ways things were done in the past rather than working to develop innovative programs for children. In addition to the values of the teacher, a number of other variables contribute to the ease, or difficulty, of developing quality programs of physical education for children.

Class Size

A variable that has particular impact on what a teacher is able to accomplish in physical education classes is the size of the classes. Physical education classes are historically the largest classes in a school. A person doesn't need much teaching experience to realize that the number of students within a given class, other variables excluded, significantly dictates what a teacher can accomplish. Lessons that are possible with twenty-five children are difficult, if not impossible, with one hundred children.

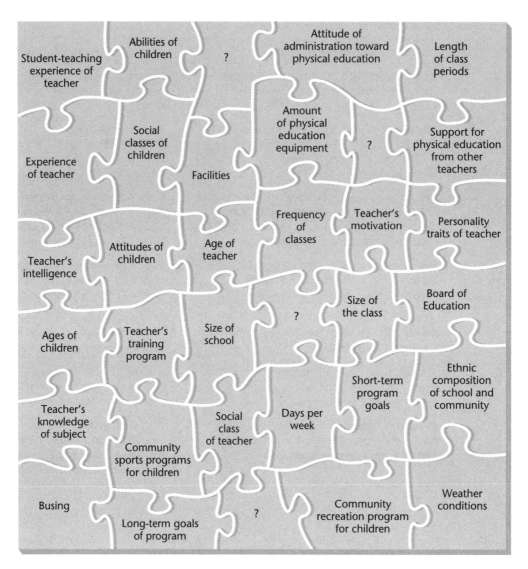

Figure 5.1   Interacting factors that contribute to the unique ecology of each school.

At the heart of complexity in the gym is *numbers.* That the teacher is one and the learners are many is a fact of life which shapes every aspect of the teacher's experience. What many outsiders fail to appreciate is that an average class contains a lot of kids for one person to handle *even if there were no intent to teach anything.* This failure particularly is true of parents who often feel qualified as experts on child management because they deal more or less successfully with their own children in groups rarely exceeding three or four.

Larry Locke, "The Ecology of the Gymnasium:
What the Tourist Never Sees"

HOW IMPORTANT IS QUALITY PHYSICAL EDUCATION TO YOU?

▶ Every teacher values some subjects and topics more than others. How important is physical activity for children in your philosophy of education? Will you be a teacher who "rolls out the ball" and finds excuses for not organizing and teaching lessons that are of true value to the children? Or will you be a teacher who develops a program that is truly beneficial for your children? What past and current experiences do you think are contributing to your view of the relative importance of physical education for children?

For teachers to do more than provide directions to a mass of children, they must have opportunities to observe and analyze and to give children feedback. The logistical problems of providing individual instruction for each child in a class of fifty children who meet for half an hour are overwhelming. The educational literature supports this viewpoint: "The more successful teachers did more tutorial teaching. They spoke to the class as a whole in order to provide structure and give general direction, but most of their actual instruction was given in small groups or to individuals" (Good, Biddle, & Brophy, 1975, p. 70). Class size can determine the teaching approach that a given teacher can use to foster a successful educational experience.

Number of Class Sessions

In addition to the values of the teacher and the size of classes, another influential variable that must be considered is the number of class sessions per week. Children in some schools, for example, have "organized" physical education only one day a week. Children in other schools have daily physical education. Obviously, the children who have instructional physical education for 180 days a year can learn significantly more than those who have physical education only 36 days a year. The challenge for the teacher is to make the difficult decisions about what can be learned in one or two days a week so that the children truly benefit from the program, rather than simply being exposed to a variety of activities (Graham, Metzler, & Webster, 1991).

In schools where children don't have daily physical education, the classroom teacher can play a vital role in reinforcing what the specialist has taught—and vice versa. When the classroom teachers and the physical education specialist work together closely, the children reap the benefits. Unfortunately, in many schools the classroom and physical education teachers, for a number of reasons, don't work closely together; consequently, there is little or no carryover between the classroom and the physical education lessons.

Facilities and Equipment

A fourth variable is the adequacy of the facilities and equipment within a particular school. Established programs of physical education often include adequate equipment supplies and a reasonable solution to the use of indoor space during inclement weather. In con-

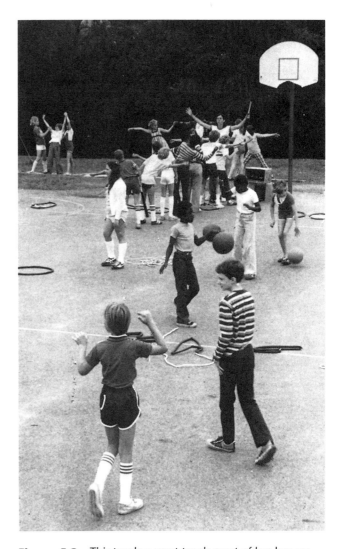

Figure 5.2 This teacher must teach most of her lessons outside because she doesn't have an appropriate indoor facility for physical education; her equipment may also be limited.

trast, fledgling programs of physical education frequently severely lack physical education equipment (Figure 5.2). In some schools, physical education classes are forced to use classrooms, cafeterias, or even hallways on rainy days.

Some teachers are masters of improvisation, but others can't function without adequate facilities and equipment. The teaching skills acquired during student teaching, when equipment and facilities were ideal, often must be adapted to less desirable conditions. You may find that there is only one ball per class instead of one ball per pupil. You may find yourself on a rainy afternoon teaching in a classroom instead of on a playground. Different environments call for different teaching skills.

Figure 5.3 Some teachers have a gymnasium or multipurpose room in which to teach physical education; they may have plenty of equipment.

Discipline

Another variable that contributes to the need for reflective teaching is generally referred to as *discipline*—the process of dealing with children who behave in ways the teacher considers unacceptable. The ability to discipline children effectively is a major concern in education today, among parents as well as teachers.

The ability to manage a class of children effectively is also one of the few teaching skills that educators agree is a prerequisite to successful teaching. A teacher must be able to create and maintain an appropriate environment if children are to learn. Some teachers are able to maintain desirable student behavior simply by glancing occasionally at certain children within a class. (Figure 5.3) Other teachers spend most of their time trying to maintain order. We believe that specific teaching skills can be effectively employed to create and sustain an appropriate environment (see Chapters 9 and 10).

Unfortunately, many textbooks—and many teachers—underplay the role of discipline. These texts and teachers assume that a "good" teacher doesn't have

discipline problems (Siedentop, 1991). Our experience suggests otherwise. During a teaching career, a teacher encounters many kinds of classes. Some will test the teacher's ability to maintain appropriate behavior; others are cooperative. Successful teachers are able to work effectively with both types of classes.

> Some inner-city youngsters often test their teachers according to rules governing their street corner behavior rather than by their teachers' middle-class rules and expectations. This testing by street corner rules happens to teachers and administrators in inner-city schools every day. And most of the teachers and administrators neither realize nor understand what is happening. Indeed, until you actually experience this testing—when all your middle-class niceties do not count a damn and you wonder why this kid is doing that to you because you are not as prejudiced as the others and you really want to help . . . —it will be hard, if not impossible, for you to understand what I am talking about.
>
> Herbert Foster, *Ribbin', Jivin' and Playin' the Dozens*

Context of the School

A sixth variable, certainly not the least important, that supports the need for reflective teaching is the context of the school. Some schools today are populated predominantly by children in transient situations, many of whom will move before the end of the school year. An increasing number of children are from homes in which both parents work outside the home and consequently are generally unavailable during the day or when the children return home after school. Rural schools continue to have children with needs different from those of children in suburban or inner-city schools. Moreover, it is typical today to have one or more children in a class who do not speak English, and it seems that more classes have mainstreamed children than ever before. Each of these situations, as well as the many variations that have not been described, presents interesting challenges to teachers—challenges that have no standard answers. The one constant in all of these situations is that children need caring, dedicated teachers, perhaps more than ever.

SUMMARY

The reflective teacher assesses the ecology of the teaching environment to define the variables that will determine the most effective physical education program for a particular situation. The teacher then plans the teaching process that will be most effective.

The teacher considers the characteristics of each class and the abilities of the individual students. A reflective teacher doesn't expect all children to respond in the same way or to achieve the same level of skill. Reflective teachers continually observe and analyze, a process that enables them to revise their expectations and adapt all the components of the program, thereby constantly improving the effectiveness of the program. The reflective approach to teaching requires that teachers constantly and accurately monitor as they attempt to design and implement a physical education program for a given school.

READING COMPREHENSION QUESTIONS

1. What is reflective teaching? What are its basic characteristics?
2. What does a linear approach to learning mean?
3. Why and how does class size affect teaching?
4. What factors, typically beyond the teacher's control, contribute to the dissimilarity of teaching situations?
5. Teachers have different belief and value systems that are formed before they ever enter a university. What are your beliefs about physical education? How do a person's beliefs influence the way he or she teaches physical education?
6. Can a teacher learn to discipline classes, or is maintaining appropriate behavior an inborn ability? Explain your answer.
7. In your own words, explain the major implication of reflective teaching.

REFERENCES

Allen, D. (1975). The future of education—Where do we go from here? *Journal of Teacher Education, 26,* 41–45.

Borko, H., & Livingston, C. (1989). Cognition and improvisation: Differences in mathematics instruction by expert and novice teachers. *American Educational Research Journal, 26*(4), 473–498.

Foster, H. L. (1974). *Ribbin', jivin' and playin' the dozens: The unrecognized dilemma of inner-city schools.* Cambridge, MA: Ballinger.

Good, T. L., Biddle, B. J., & Brophy, J. E. (1975). *Teachers make a difference.* New York: Holt, Rinehart and Winston.

Graham, G. (1992). *Teaching children physical education: Becoming a master teacher.* Champaign, IL: Human Kinetics.

Graham, G., Hopple, C., Manross, M., & Sitzman, T. (1993). Novice and experienced children's physical education teachers: Insights into their situational decision-making. *Journal of Teaching in Physical Education, 12,* 197–217.

Graham, G., Metzler, M., & Webster, G. (1991). Specialist and classroom teacher effectiveness in children's physical education: A 3-year study [Research monograph]. *Journal of Teaching in Physical Education, 4,* 321–426.

Housner, L. D., & Griffey, D. C. (1985). Teacher cognition: Differences in planning and interactive decision making between experienced and inexperienced teachers. *Research Quarterly for Exercise and Sport, 56,* 56–63.

Locke, L. F. (1975, Spring). The ecology of the gymnasium: What the tourist never sees. *Southern Association of Physical Education for College Women Proceedings.*

National Association for Sport and Physical Education (NASPE). (1995). *Moving into the future: National standards for physical education.* St. Louis, MO: Mosby.

Rink, J. (1996). Effective instruction in physical education. In S. J. Silverman and C. D. Ennis (Eds.). *Student learning in physical education* (pp. 171–198). Champaign, IL: Human Kinetics.

Siedentop, D. (1991). *Developing teaching skills in physical education* (3rd ed.). Mountain View, CA: Mayfield.

CHAPTER
6

Teaching Children with Special Needs

Movement is learning; movement is life. No matter how disabled a child, movement can make a difference in his/her life. Movement can help a child become oneself. If a child can move, he/she can become more a master of the environment rather than being controlled by it.

——Jane R. Evans

Public Law 94-142 (Education for All Handicapped Children–1975) and the Individuals with Disabilities Education Act (IDEA) of 1990 guarantee all children with disabilities from ages three to twenty-two a free and appropriate education in the least restrictive environment. That education includes physical education. The Educational Disabilities Act defines physical education as the development of physical and motor fitness, fundamental motor skills and patterns, and skills in aquatics, dance, games, and sports. IDEA further states that to the maximum extent appropriate, children with disabilities are to be educated with children without disabilities—that is, in their home school, in the classroom, and in the gymnasium that would be theirs if they had no disabilities.

Early interpretations of "least restrictive environment" led to the mainstreaming of children with disabilities for art, music, and physical education and to a somewhat limited exposure to the classroom environment of their peers, with the remainder of the day spent in a "special" education classroom. Parents of children with disabilities voiced concern at this separate but equal approach to education at the same time research was questioning the benefits of the approach. There was strong concern with the negative (and once affixed, everlasting) label of special education. Thus began the gradual move from mainstreaming to a philosophy of inclusion.

Figure 6.1 In individualized physical education classes, all children can be successful.

The Philosophy of Inclusion

Inclusion is a philosophy that says all children can learn, all children want to learn. The question is not whether children with disabilities are smart but *how* they are smart. The question is not whether they can develop skills in physical education, but *how* they can develop their skills. Discovering children's abilities and helping them learn what they are good at is critical to their success. Inclusion identifies and nurtures each student's unique abilities, recognizing that all children do better when the emphasis is on strengths (Oberti, 1993). Children with disabilities are children with conditions that affect the ways in which they learn and perform physical and motor skills and activities. Physical education programs that include children with disabilities have the same basic goals and objectives as physical education programs for all students. Programs that include students with disabilities are not corrective or rehabilitative; they are developmentally sound, sequential programs with special and/or specific accommodations for individuals (Stein, 1992).

Inclusion does not mean placement of all children with disabilities in the regular physical education program with no assistance and support for the teacher. It does mean that regular physical education is the right of all children, not something they have to earn. It means assistance for the child as needed and support for the teacher ranging from in-service, to training, to team teaching with an adapted physical educator. Inclusion, in brief, means education in the setting that would be offered if there were no handicapping conditions, with technical assistance and support personnel brought to the child. Inclusion begins with a teacher willing to accept all children, a teacher open and responsive to individuals and the unique needs of each (Figure 6.1).

This is not to say inclusion of students with disabilities in regular physical education classes is easy, especially during the early stages. The following guidelines will help teachers adopt positive attitudes in implementing the inclusion philosophy:

- Study the literature. When you learn that a child with a particular disability will be included in your program, go to the public library or a nearby university library and read in depth about the disability. The better informed you are about a child's disability, the better you will be able to teach the child. Many universities with medical libraries will research the disability at no cost and will be happy to assist in your understanding.
- Read the cumulative folder. Study the child's cumulative folder, records from previous multidisciplinary team (M-Team) meetings, and other available information. Personal notes from teachers, successes, and challenges are often included.
- Note special medical conditions. Be aware of any medical and/or physical problems that might contraindicate certain activities. Such conditions include osteogenesis imperfecta (brittle bones) and atlantoaxial subluxation (maladjustment of the cervical vertebrae in the neck).
- Introduce yourself to the child's parents. Take the initiative to become acquainted with the parents of a child with disabilities. Let them know you favor inclusion of all children and look forward to working with their child. Establishing an atmosphere of friendship and trust will serve you well as you work together for the success of the child in physical education.
- Become an active participant in the multidisciplinary team. Ask to be informed of all M-Team meetings that include children you teach; attend the meetings if the plan being developed or the discussion includes physical education.
- Don't be afraid to ask for assistance. Remember support services are to be provided for the child and for you, as needed, under the provisions of the Individuals with Disabilities Education Act.
- Become a member of a support group. The Internet is an excellent place to establish contacts with other physical educators working with children with disabilities. Ask questions; find out what others are doing; share your frustrations and your joys with others.

The Multidisciplinary Team

The appropriate education—both placement and curriculum—for each student with disabilities is determined by a multidisciplinary team called the M-Team. The M-Team is composed of all those involved in providing an appropriate education for the child: the classroom teacher, special educators, parents, and professionals from related services. Following an educational assessment by the school psychologist and

---

ESSENTIAL ELEMENTS OF INCLUSION PROGRAMS

- A full continuum of placement options and services. Placement and services must be determined for each student by a team that includes all stakeholders and must be specified in the Individualized Education Program (discussed later).
- Appropriate professional development, as part of normal work activity, for all educators and support staff associated with such programs.
- Adequate time, as part of the normal school day, to engage in coordinated and collaborative planning on behalf of all students.
- Class sizes that are responsive to student needs.
- Staff and technical assistance that is specifically appropriate to student and teacher needs.

SOURCE: From *NEA Today* (July 1996), Washington, DC: National Education Association.

---

other professionals as needed, the M-Team designs the educational program for the child, identifies services to be secured from outside agencies, and establishes the educational goals to be attained within the given school year.

For children whose disabilities reflect strong needs in the motor skills area, the physical education specialist may be asked to serve on the M-Team or to act as a consultant to the team. As a member of the M-Team, the physical education specialist provides input regarding the most enabling physical education environment for the child with disabilities. Physical education options may include full inclusion, inclusion with a teacher assistant, or remedial physical education in addition to the regular program. The goal of the last is assistance in specified areas for better functioning/performance in the regular physical education program.

Individualized Education Program

Education for a child diagnosed with disabilities is formulated through the individualized education program (IEP). Generally, the IEP is limited to curricular areas of special education and related services—instruction designed to meet the unique needs of the child and the related services necessary to help the child achieve maximum success. The IEP includes:

- A statement of the present level of the child's functioning
- Annual goals

- Short-term instructional objectives with time lines
- The extent to which the child will participate in the regular educational program
- Special services to be provided, including their duration and extent
- Plan for evaluation of annual goals

For some students with disabilities, the IEP addresses only a very limited part of their education, for example, speech; for others, the IEP may cover their total education. The IEP is a projection of what professionals and the parents think the child can accomplish. If the annual goals are inappropriate, the M-Team reassesses the child's curriculum and formulates new goals better suited to the child's needs. In many states, the M-Team also sets goals for the parents in working at home with the child. The IEP may specify time for motor skills development in addition to physical education or remedial assistance in perceptual, sensory-motor, balance, or body image areas. If special services are to be provided under the direction of the physical education teacher, the M-Team will inform the teacher of the decision, or the teacher will be asked to help develop the yearly plan.

Least Restrictive Environment

The least restrictive environment is the educational setting that is most appropriate and most enabling for the child with disabilities. To the maximum extent appropriate, children with disabilities are to be educated with nondisabled students; thus, the philosophy of inclusion.

Legal reasons aside, there are sound educational reasons for educating children with disabilities in the least restrictive environment. Research has shown that placing these youngsters with nondisabled children yields positive benefits in behavior and life skills. Educators have long agreed on the effectiveness of peer modeling in academics and skill acquisition among

children. Furthermore, the mainstreamed classroom and gymnasium more closely mirror the real world than do the classroom or physical education setting that consists entirely of children with disabilities. Most of the students with disabilities we see in our public schools will reside and work within our communities and participate in community activities. The least restrictive, more enabling educational environment should give students with disabilities the same opportunities to learn, to develop personal potential, to interact and mature socially that all other students receive.

Implementing the IEP

After the IEP has been written, it's the responsibility of all teachers working with the child with disabilities to implement it. For those children with an unrestricted classification, no adaptation of the environment or curriculum is necessary (Figure 6.2). For children with a modified classification, adaptation of the existing curriculum is warranted. Other children require an individualized remedial program. The inclusion of some children with disabilities in physical education classes requires considerable modification of existing environmental and curricular tasks.

Whether the IEP specifies an unrestricted, modified/adapted, or remedial program, we can no longer be content with letting the child be the scorekeeper. The program must be designed to develop the child's skills in gymnastics, games, and dance. Adaptations in tasks, as is true for all children, will permit the child with disabilities to participate, to achieve, and to develop skills commensurate with personal ability. With an understanding of basic concepts, an awareness of the children's needs, and knowledge of how to adapt the environment and/or the curriculum, the teacher can create the enabling environment for children with special needs. Children with disabilities can function in an elementary physical education envi-

Figure 6.2 Children with disabilities can successfully participate in physical education.

ronment that allows individual response, fosters performance at the individual's skill level, and is taught by teachers who observe, reflect, and make changes in light of children's needs.

Visual and hearing impairments, physical disabilities, and health-related impairments often necessitate a modification of the physical education program. Other disabling conditions include mental retardation, severe emotional disturbance, and learning disabilities. Any special adaptations for these conditions will be noted in the child's IEP. A brief description of each condition, its implications for physical education, and suggestions for program modifications follow in this chapter.

Visual Impairments

The two categories of visual impairment are blindness and partial sight. Approximately 1 percent of school-age children are seriously visually impaired, with impairments ranging from blindness to blurred/distorted vision, tunnel vision, and the ability to see out of the corners of the eyes only. Children with serious visual impairments may exhibit the following characteristics:

- Self-stimulating mannerisms, for example, stamping feet, rocking, clicking fingers, and turning the head from side to side. These mannerisms often result from boredom and lack of external stimulus.
- Awkward, clumsy total-body movements and poor motor skills from lack of experience and limited sensory information.
- Poor posture due to lack of visual modeling.
- Developmental lag of at least one year, often due to lack of stimulus and/or overprotective parents.
- Lack of fitness and tendency toward being overweight because of sedentary lifestyle.
- Difficulty dealing with abstractions and a limited conception of the "whole."
- Difficulty in conceptualizing boundaries.

The child with severe visual impairments needs auditory and tactile stimulation. As teachers, we need to encourage this child to venture beyond the known environment, to explore the gymnasium and the playground. We need to promote social interaction with peers as well as adults and to maximize learning through all the senses. IEPs for children with serious visual impairments focus on attention to sensory abilities, spatial awareness, and mobility. Visually impaired children need the maximum use of their proprioceptive, auditory, haptic, and spatial perceptions.

For visually impaired children, proprioceptive perception is important for maintaining balance. Body awareness and proprioceptive perception can be increased through activities that focus on the identification of body parts, awareness of the relationship of

▶ Ron, a child blind since birth, was mainstreamed into a physical education class. The class was studying balance—balance on different bases of support and balance in inverted positions (Chapter 23). Ron was working independently in the space defined by the boundaries of his gymnastics mat. Suddenly Ron cried aloud; the entire class stopped and turned in his direction. Nothing was wrong; Ron was experiencing for the first time the change in body position and perception that accompanies being balanced in an inverted position on the hands only. Ron apologized for disturbing the class, and activity continued. During sharing time at the end of the class, Ron shared his feelings of the experience and his excitement for more gymnastics.

body parts to each other, and the body part's position in space. Children can be asked to move individual body parts when the body part is named and to perform certain movements with the isolated body part, for example, swing or tap. Teachers can increase proprioceptive awareness by adding small weights to body parts and then instructing children to move the parts. The gymnastics skills of balancing on different body parts and in different positions also help this development.

The senses are also used to establish spatial awareness. Children who are blind have difficulty perceiving the relationship of objects in space and the spatial relationship of themselves to objects. Lateral and directional activities, such as identification of left and right sides; movement away from self—left, right, up, down, front, back; and positioning of self in relation to equipment (for example, a table or a chair) help develop this perception in children without the visual sense. Auditory cues help these children determine distance in space. Sound-emitting devices can be placed on stationary equipment and the equipment used with a partner to help measure distance, location in space, and pathways of travel. Young children can face sounds made at different locations and thus determine near and far. Older children can follow a bike rider by the sound of cardboard on the spokes or copy the pathway of a partner by changes in intensity of the sound.

One of the greatest disabilities of visually impaired children is lack of mobility. A mobility training program in the gymnasium as well as the outdoor play area increases the child's independence and thus the ability and desire to participate fully. Three-dimensional models of both the indoor and outdoor physical education environments, including permanent equipment, give visually impaired children the concrete, hands-on experience to develop a conception of the whole and the ability to move within the physical education space. The mobility training should also include a peer-guided tour of the environment and time for personal exploration of the environment, including full use of tactile and auditory senses. The blind child should be free to walk, crawl, and touch the gymnasium without the embarrassment of a class of onlookers; the teacher, parent, or a trusted adult should be present to answer questions and ensure safety.

There are no unique motor characteristics that result directly from visual impairments. However, most children with serious visual impairments lack the motor skills and patterns essential for successful participation in physical education activities due to lack of experience. Many aren't able to perform the basic skills of running, skipping, jumping, throwing,

and so on. The IEP for such children may include one-to-one instruction in these basic skills and movement patterns. Traditional teaching of locomotor skills and movement patterns relies heavily on the visual mode. The teacher of children with serious visual impairments will have to sharpen personal skills of movement analysis, clearly present the instruction, and provide effective feedback.

The inclusion of visually impaired children in physical education classes has implications for the teacher, the environment, and physical education equipment. Specific implications for the teacher include:

- Teaching with manual guidance accompanied by verbal directions.
- Remembering that the visually impaired child relies heavily on tactile perception. Manually guiding the visually impaired child can serve as the demonstration of the skill for other children, thus benefiting the group as well as the individual.
- Providing specific and immediate feedback. For profitable feedback, the teacher must thoroughly analyze movement skills and provide the verbal cues for correcting deviations.
- Using peer teaching to assist with the manual guidance and verbal feedback.
- Involving visually impaired children in small-group and partner activities rather than large-group situations.
- Avoiding activities that involve throwing and catching with fast speed and travel.
- Progressing from simple tasks in gymnastics and games to sequentially more difficult tasks to develop motor skill and cognitive complexity.
- Involving all children in the world of creative movement experiences and dance. Creative dance comes from the inner self; it is born of the senses. Vision is necessary only for the observer.

Adaptations in the environment include:

- Ensuring that the gymnasium is well lighted to help the child with residual vision.
- Varying the texture of the boundaries for game areas—dirt/grass for the play area, sand for the surrounding area.
- Making pathways between targets or bases three to four feet wide and of a different texture.
- Keeping the outdoor teaching area and the gymnasium well organized and consistent. Introduce new equipment to visually impaired children by means of three-dimensional models.
- Providing tactile markings on the floor as a reference for teaching stations, the center for teacher directions, water fountains, and so on.
- Placing guide ropes across the gymnasium or playground to permit the practice of locomotor skills

and freedom of travel. Tie a series of knots in the ropes to signal the approach of the boundary.

The inclusion of visually impaired children into physical education may necessitate such special equipment as:

- Brightly colored balls and objects for children with limited vision
- Sponge and foam balls for projectile activities
- Protection for the eyes; eyeglasses
- Audible beep balls for tracking and location
- Battery-powered electronic sound devices within large marker cones to serve as bases
- A large gymnastics mat to serve as "personal space" for balancing and transferring of weight activities.

Write to the American Foundation for the Blind, New York, NY 10011, for catalogs of special equipment.

We expect children with visual disabilities to participate to their fullest potential in physical education, trying not to let the child use the disability as an excuse to withdraw from activity and social interaction. Games situations that involve constant contact with the participants (for example, wheelbarrow travel and parachute activity) require the least adaptation. When new activities are introduced, having children with visual disabilities play in slow motion will help their orientation to the play environment and the rules. The use of the buddy system also helps these children participate in traveling activities. Note, however, that although young children naturally hold hands with partners, they do need to know the correct way to assist a visually impaired person. That is, the visually impaired person should grasp the guide's upper arm above the elbow, thus permitting the non-sighted person to maintain a sense of control rather than being led as if helpless.

Falls, scratches, and bruises are a part of physical education for children with serious visual impairments. Visually impaired children need to be permitted to recover on their own, maintain dignity, and attain maximum independence. The teacher must discuss with all members of the class the danger of being overprotective. With the exception of ball-handling/striking activities, the visually impaired child can function quite independently in physical education classes. Following orientation and mobility training, the teacher's task is simply to help the child develop skills and a belief in self.

Hearing Impairments

The term *hearing impairment* refers to hearing loss that can range from mild to profound. The disability includes those who have trouble hearing normal

> We strongly recommend a course in sign language for teachers with hearing-impaired children in their classroom or gymnasium. Think of how much better the hearing-impaired child will feel if she or he is greeted the first day of physical education by a teacher she or he can communicate with!

speech and those who can't understand even amplified speech. Approximately 5 percent of school-age children have a hearing loss that can affect learning, but only one in one thousand is profoundly deaf. The term *deaf* is rarely used to classify a hearing impairment; most individuals labeled deaf have some level of hearing, being able to understand speech with the help of amplification or by hearing combined with watching the speaker's lips, facial expressions, and gestures. The danger of labeling a child deaf is that it may cause peers to stop interacting with the child and may actually make the child functionally deaf as an adult.

The social domain is the greatest problem for children with serious hearing loss. The hearing-impaired young child doesn't engage in play experiences with other children; speech, if present, is garbled, and communication quite limited. Hearing-impaired children don't understand their role in the play experience and often withdraw, thus denying themselves the social interaction and development of motor skills that accompany play for young children. As children's games become more complex, the hearing-impaired child is likely to be left out of the activities. Rules are developed as the game is played; instructions are shouted in the midst of play. Without special assistance, the hearing-impaired child is unable to comprehend all the intricacies of the game. Thus, the child fails to develop the social skills learned through group interaction in play. Withdrawal from activity causes a developmental lag in motor skills.

The frustration of being unable to communicate, be understood by others, and express emotions in socially accepted ways often leads children with serious hearing impairments to express their emotions through physical means. Aggressive behavior is often the means of expressing negative emotions. Additional characteristics of a child with a serious hearing impairment may include:

- Slow development of inner and expressive language, often leading others to mistake the child as mentally retarded
- Poor pronunciation; garbled speech
- Absence of laughter
- Difficulty in dealing with abstractions due to slowness in developing inner language

Figure 6.3 Signing for physical education. *Source:* From "Signing for Physical Education," by C. B. Eichstaedt, 1978, with permission from the *Journal of Physical Education and Recreation, 49*(5), pp. 20–21. The journal is a publication of the American Alliance for Health, Physical Education, Recreation and Dance, 1900 Association Drive, Reston, VA 22091.

- Hyperactive appearance because of constant movement to maintain visual contact
- Lack of good balance in some hearing-impaired children caused by inner-ear damage
- Shuffling gait resulting from not hearing the sound of movement

Most children with hearing impairments function quite well in the regular physical education program. As a rule, adaptations in equipment or environment won't be necessary. However, the physical education teacher needs to modify certain aspects of teaching:

- Position yourself so the child with a serious hearing impairment can read your lips; be conscious of not turning your back when speaking; and be close enough for lip reading.
- Face the sun when outdoors so that the hearing-impaired child doesn't have to face the sun.

- Let the hearing-impaired child move freely in the teaching environment so that he or she can always be in the best position for hearing.
- Visually and manually demonstrate skills; don't rely on verbal directions alone.
- Remember, the hearing-impaired child can't read lips or hear a whistle across the playing field or gymnasium; accompany the auditory sound with large hand signals.
- Learn the basic sign language needed for communication. Figure 6.3 provides specific signs for physical education and basic communication.

Hearing-impaired children with a developmental lag in motor skills need additional physical education to develop the motor skills and movement patterns needed for successful participation in the regular program. Those with balance problems and vertigo due to damage to the inner ear need additional work in the

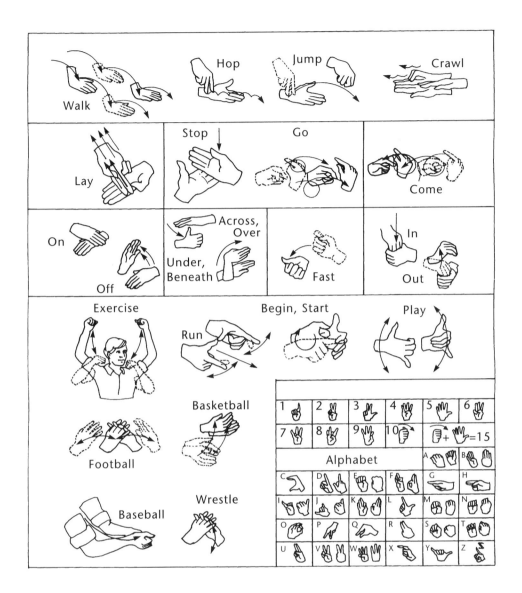

area of balance to develop maximum use of the visual and kinesthetic cues for balancing activities. Tumbling activities with rotation and climbing to heights on large apparatus should be done only with close adult supervision. Children who have poor motor skills and/or difficulty with balance are very conscious of how their abilities compare with those of their peers; a private place to practice can help overcome self-consciousness in attempting skills.

Like many children with disabilities, the child with a serious hearing impairment may be less skilled because of a lack of experiences. As teachers, we try to maximize strengths rather than focusing on the weakness, the inability to hear. The child will have to experience success in activities to build the self-esteem needed for eager participation and social interaction. The directions and simple activities that the class can grasp easily may have to be carefully explained to the child with a serious hearing impairment. Encourage the children to initiate conversation with the hearing-impaired child to help the child understand class activities, yet not patronize the youngster. We need to educate all children in our classes to interact with the hearing impaired, to accept their less-than-perfect speech, and to involve them in both physical education and play activities.

Physical Disabilities

Physical disabilities include conditions resulting in orthopedic handicaps, such as cerebral palsy and spina bifida, the crippling diseases of arthritis and muscular dystrophy, permanent loss of limbs, and the temporary disabilities caused by fractures. Other related health factors that can mean limited or restricted physical education for children include hemophilia, severe burns, congenital heart defects, and respiratory disorders.

Each child with a physical disability has different physical and motor capabilities, so the IEP must be designed to meet individual needs (Figure 6.4). The child's physical education program will include two aspects: (1) the IEP of exercises and activities to meet specific needs and develop motor skills and (2) any adaptations in the regular program of physical education. The following procedure is recommended when planning the program for children with physical disabilities:

1. Identify the child's clinical condition.
2. Determine what activities would be contraindicated based on medical recommendation.
3. Determine functional motor skills needed.
4. Select activities that will develop desired motor skills.
5. Adapt the physical education environment and equipment as needed to provide the program.

It's important to remember that the program will be designed in consultation with a physician and a physical therapist. As teachers, we aren't expected to make a clinical diagnosis or to prescribe a program of individualized remedial exercises without the assistance of trained medical professionals. The professionals familiar with the child's medical history will be valuable consultants to the M-Team developing the child's program (Box 6.1).

Figure 6.4 With minimal teacher assistance, this child participates successfully in the physical education program.

One of the keys to successful inclusion of children with disabilities is to promote the acceptance of those children by their peers. Many children have never been around children with disabilities and are hesitant about beginning conversations with them or engaging in activity. The physical education teacher should coordinate efforts with the classroom teacher to orient children to the nature of the disability, its correct name, any limitations it imposes, and the potential for activity. Sensitivity training for all children can include such physical activities as

■ Forming a circle, standing with legs shoulder-width apart, and rolling a playground ball across the circle while the *eyes are closed*
■ Playing a simple game with no verbal sound—no verbal clues for directions, rules, and stopping the action
■ Executing simple ball-handling and racket skills with the nondominant hand

Cerebral Palsy

Perhaps the most misunderstood of all children with disabilities are those with cerebral palsy. Because of the language and auditory disabilities and the lack of muscular control that often accompany cerebral palsy, the child is often labeled mentally retarded. Social acceptance and recognition of strengths are major obstacles for children with cerebral palsy. Cerebral palsy is a neurological impairment, an impairment caused by incomplete development of, or injury to, the central nervous system. Cerebral palsy may occur as a result of prenatal factors, injuries during birth, or postnatal conditions such as a serious childhood disease with a high fever or a head injury. Characteristics associated with cerebral palsy include:

■ Disabilities in visual, auditory, and perceptual development and in speech

BOX 6.1   WHAT DO I SAY? WHAT DO I DO? TIPS FOR TIMES WITH CHILDREN WHO HAVE DISABILITIES

■ Act naturally. Be you. There often is a tendency to either ignore a disabled child or over-attend. Like Goldilocks, pick the amount of attention that is "just right."

■ Assume the child is bright. Talk as you would to any child, until you are told to do otherwise. It is better to "talk up" to someone than to talk down.

■ Talk to the *child*, not to the attendant, parent, or teacher.

■ Establish eye contact. This may mean sitting down, comfortably half kneeling, or moving to one side (if the child cannot look straight ahead). Avoid standing behind the wheelchair and talking. Many children rely on facial cues, gestures, and clear hearing to understand all that you are saying.

■ Avoid simple yes/no questions. They make for dull, one-sided conversation—for anyone! Instead, ask about family, friends, activities. Don't ask, "Did you enjoy the circus?" but rather, "What did you see at the circus?" "Who did you go with?" and "Tell me about the elephants."

■ Wait for replies . . . patiently. Repeating a question too soon may interrupt a child who is attempting to formulate an answer.

■ Keep conversation about a child's wheelchair to a minimum, not because it is insulting (it isn't), but because often it is all people find to talk about (e.g., "I bet you can zoom around in that thing! I wish I had one. How fast does it go? Can I ride? How long do the batteries last?"). A little wheelchair talk is okay, but move to other topics that are more interesting to the child.

■ It is fine to use phrases like "I have to run now" to a child in a wheelchair, or "I see" to a child who is blind.

■ Many children cannot help drooling. Saliva won't kill you. Don't be hesitant to wipe someone's mouth (with their permission) or hold a hand that is wet.

■ Yes, touching is okay. Holding hands, hugging, or a pat on the back are appropriate if they are something you would do with any child. A pat on the head is not okay. Typically it is a condescending gesture. Appropriateness is the key. Keep in mind that some children are too affectionate and need to learn proper social interaction.

■ Roughhousing is great—provided you get clearance (ask the parents). Being "thrown around" is part of growing up!

■ Ask permission before you help a child. Ask the parents, too, if they are present—but ask the child first.

■ When lifting children, first show them and then tell them where they will be set down.

■ A child with a disability can misbehave just like any other child. Not to mince words: They can be snotty. Or they can be nice. Don't let yourself become so tolerant that you allow clearly unacceptable behavior.

■ Don't feel as if everything you have to say needs to be funny or light. Serious topics are welcomed. Some children appreciate a break from laughing because they cannot control that response very well.

Source: From Dave Taylor, *Project Active Newsletter, 12*(1), 1991, Joe Karp, (Ed.), Northshore School District, Bothell, WA. Used with permission.

■ Lack of concentration, distractability, overexcitability, and hyperactivity causing underachievement and poor behavior

■ Poor coordination and lack of balance, resulting in awkward movements and frequent falls

■ Difficulty in coordinating eye movements

■ Tendency toward seizures

The lack of coordination associated with cerebral palsy results in a delay in motor control. The child with cerebral palsy will benefit from the breakdown of skills to basic components and sequential presentation of those components. Due to either restricted or extraneous movements, the child with cerebral palsy expends a great deal of energy when performing physical activity; a decrease in endurance may result. The physical education program for a child with cerebral palsy should concentrate on perceptual motor activities—locomotor patterns, balance, response to rhythm, development of ocular control, and form perception—as well as the development of skills for successful participation. Additional exercises may be recommended by the physical therapist to focus on the following factors:

■ Muscle stretching to relieve contractures, prevent bone deformities, and permit fuller range of motion

■ Muscle awareness exercises to elicit conscious control

■ Relaxation techniques to help control contractures, rigidity, and spasms

■ Posture alignments

■ Gait training for walking patterns

■ Exercises/activities to increase muscular strength

For some children with cerebral palsy the only effect is a slight speech impairment; for others there is a total inability to control body movements. The physical education teacher will benefit from extensive reading concerning the type of cerebral palsy and from discussion with the physical therapist concerning special needs and the adaptation of equipment and activities for maximum participation.

Spina Bifida

Spina bifida is a congenital condition in which the bony elements of the spine don't close properly during development in the womb. The condition may result in a cystlike formation on the spinal column that contains part of the spinal cord, a protruding sac containing covering tissue, or a malformation with no protrusion of spinal cord. In mild cases of spina bifida, the only effects may be weak muscles and deviations in posture. Because spina bifida causes paralysis in the legs and a loss of sensation in the lower limbs, children with mild spina bifida benefit from weight-bearing activities to stimulate bone growth and circulation in the lower limbs as well as exercises/activities to develop muscular strength in the upper body.

Children with spina bifida have normal intelligence; they have the same play and social needs as all children. Adaptations in physical education will be those needed to accommodate their mode of transportation, that is, crutches or wheelchair. In addition to the areas of need noted above, it is necessary for children with spina bifida to develop skills for participation with their peers in physical education and skills for lifetime sports and activities in which they can be successful.

Like many children with disabilities, children with spina bifida benefit from the socialization inherent in physical education, in addition to learning and developing skills. Guiding this growth is perhaps the greatest contribution we as physical educators can make in educating children with disabilities.

Muscular Dystrophy

Childhood muscular dystrophy begins between the ages of two and six. It's an inherited disease; the exact nature of the inheritance isn't yet known. Muscular dystrophy is a progressive disease that affects the voluntary muscles, for example, legs and arms; involuntary muscles, such as the diaphragm, aren't affected. First affected are the muscles involved in walking and standing; the child with muscular dystrophy will

TEACHER

I will know you.
I will touch you and hold you
And smell and taste and listen
To the noises that you make—and the words, if
    any.

I will know you.
Each atom of your small, lonely
Aching, raging, hurting being
Will be known to me
Before I try to teach you.
Before I try to teach
I must first reach you.

And then, when I have come to know you,
    intimately,
I will insist, gently, gradually, but insist
That you know me.
And later, that you trust me
And then yourself.

Now, knowing each other, we will begin to know
    the world—
The seasons, the trees, animals, food, the other
    children,
The printed word, books,
The knowledge of what has gone before and been
    recorded.

Then as surely as I moved toward you
I will move away.
As I once insisted on being close to you,
Demanding entrance into your half wild world
Of fear and fantasy, refusing you aloneness.

So now, I move away.
As your words come and your walk quickens,
As you laugh out loud
Or read clearly and with understanding,
I stand behind you—no longer close—
Available, but no longer vital to you.

And you—you grow!
You are! You will become!

And I, the teacher,
I turn, with pride in you,
Toward my next child.

                                        Mary MacCracken

Source: In Touch, 1, 6, July 1978. Used with permission from National Mental Health Association.

begin to have difficulty maintaining posture, getting up from a chair, or walking up stairs. The degenerative nature of the disease causes the general deterioration of the muscle tissue and a replacement of muscle with fat. Thus the young child with muscular dystrophy initially appears quite healthy as the legs and arms maintain or increase in size.

The child with muscular dystrophy has a tendency to tire easily. Fine manual dexterity is gradually lost, and the progressive weakening of the muscles causes adverse postural changes. The IEP for the child with muscular dystrophy should concentrate on exercises to strengthen the muscles involved in the basic tasks of daily living, walking patterns, posture control, and stretching of contractures. However, these exercises must be selected in consultation with the child's physician. The child with muscular dystrophy should be kept actively involved in physical education to the extent the condition permits; inactivity only increases the atrophy of the muscles. Adaptations will be necessary as the child becomes dependent on crutches, braces, or a wheelchair.

Health-Related Impairments

Although not normally thought of as physical disabilities, several other health-related impairments can affect a child's full participation in physical education. The following disorders may require temporary adaptations in the child's environment or limitations in physical activity: juvenile arthritis, asthma, diabetes, heart defects, sickle cell anemia, severe burns, and respiratory disorders. The physical educator should review health records early in the school year, making note of any conditions that require monitoring and/or temporary adaptations. Open communication with the child's parents, rapport with the child, and an understanding of the particular disorder and its effects will result in maximum participation for the child as well as trust between you, the parents, and—most important—the child.

> ▶ The *National Standards for Adapted Physical Education* (U.S. Department of Education, 1994), is an excellent reference for further understanding of the unique attributes of learners with various disabilities and the considerations for successful inclusion of these children in our physical education programs.

Asthma

In increasing numbers children are affected by asthma, an allergic reaction that results in wheezing, coughing, tightening of the airways, and accumulation of mucus in the bronchial tubes. An asthmatic attack can be triggered by allergens, upper respiratory infections, or even robust laughing. The most common conditions we see in physical education are reactions to changes in the weather (especially cold weather) and to strenuous exercise (e.g., the mile run).

All too often in the past, physical educators treated lightly the asthmatic child with a note, an excuse from running, or a request for adaptation in activity. Asthma is a serious health problem for millions of children. Failure to attend to the condition can result in serious and sometimes life-threatening consequences for the child.

The following suggestions will be helpful in assuring maximum, healthy participation for children with asthma:

- Scan health records in the fall, noting children with asthma and/or serious allergies.
- Code your daily record system for individual reminders.
- Notify children with asthma and/or allergies and/or their parents prior to a day of extra-vigorous activity.
- Ask the child prior to the activity if he/she brought the inhaler to physical education.
- Consult with the parents of children with serious asthmatic conditions for any special safeguards or procedures.
- On days when adaptation is necessary, make needed modifications to provide maximum participation.

Diabetes

Another health impairment that necessitates our attention is Type 1, insulin-dependent diabetes. Although we may experience only one or two children with diabetes in our years of teaching, the child with diabetes requires our having a thorough understanding of the disorder, an awareness of the warning signs of low blood sugar, and the knowledge to instigate immediate emergency procedures.

The goal for a child with diabetes is to have the diabetes fit into daily life as opposed to daily life fitting into the diabetes treatment plan. Children with diabetes can be expected to participate fully in physical education. If their physical education is scheduled prior to lunch or in the late afternoon, a snack may be advised in anticipation of the physical activity. On days of extra-strenuous activity (e.g., the mile run), an extra snack may be provided by the parents. Children with diabetes react emotionally as well as physically to daily insulin, ketone checks, and a routine that is different from that of their friends. Confidence in self and acceptance by peers is very important for these children. Success in movement skills extends beyond the gymnasium to aid feelings of self-worth and social acceptance.

Mental Retardation

The term *mental retardation* refers to intellectual functioning that is significantly below average, accompanied by deficits in adaptive behavior. Children with mental retardation function two or more standard deviations below average on a standardized intelligence test. They have problems of maturation, learning, and/or social adjustment, which, to different degrees, result in a degree of independence or social responsibility lower than that expected for their age. These characteristics manifest themselves during the early developmental periods of life.

The physical skills of many children with mild or moderate retardation are average and above; the difficulties center around comprehending the instructions and following through to complete the assignment. The mentally retarded youngster can more easily understand and follow directions if we remember the following:

- Keep verbal directions to a minimum; when possible use both visual and verbal instructions.
- Communicate in a direct, simple, and meaningful manner.
- Present tasks within the child's current level of physical skills.
- Structure the environment for focus on tasks and a minimum of distractions.
- Maintain a routine so that the child knows what to expect.
- Provide repetition of experiences for overlearning.
- Minimize the number of variables to which the child must attend; simplify the task.
- Present the lesson in short segments; restate the task at regular intervals.
- Reinforce strengths with frequent praise; minimize weaknesses.

Mentally retarded children can perform simple gymnastics sequences and rhythmical routines and participate in skill development activities. The teacher's attentiveness to task presentation and lesson design will result in better learning, not just for children with cognitive deficits, but for all students.

> ▶ A number of children with Down syndrome have a condition called atlantoaxial subluxation, a maladjustment of the cervical vertebrae in the neck. Because of the possibility of serious injury, persons with atlantoaxial subluxation should not participate in any activities that place stress on the head and neck muscles. Down syndrome children with atlantoaxial subluxation should not be actively involved in inverted balances, rolling activities, or other gymnastics actions that could place stress on the head and neck.

Many mentally retarded children are lacking in areas of verbal expression and social interaction. Physical education classes can provide excellent opportunities for growth in both these areas. The following suggestions will help foster personal and social growth for the mentally retarded child:

- Engage the child in conversation. Ask questions; encourage a response.
- Be an attentive listener; listen when the child speaks.
- Create opportunities for cooperative activity that *actively* involve the child.
- Recognize achievements; share them with the whole class so that they can appreciate and share in the child's accomplishment.
- Encourage verbal expression of feelings.

Just as we as teachers must take an active role in interacting socially and verbally with mentally retarded children, we must also teach other students to do the same. The retarded child's initial response to another child's attempts at conversation or group participation may be silence; mentally disabled children may be unsure of themselves or not understand. Remind the other children to repeat the question or to reach out with a touch to include the disabled child in the group.

For all major disabilities and health-related impairments, excellent resources for furthering our understanding and the child's maximum development are available through the national foundations/organizations for each disability. These foundations may also be readily accessed via the Internet.

Remedial Physical Education and Mental Retardation

Although many children with mild or moderate mental retardation have average or above-average physical skills, others have physical skills that are far below average because of a lack of experience or as a sec-

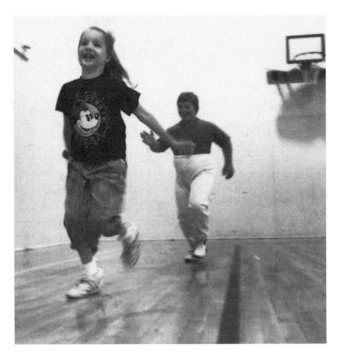

Figure 6.5 Locomotor activities are just as exciting to children with disabilities as they are to those without disabilities.

ondary characteristic of the disabling condition. For some mentally retarded children, the small-group physical education class can provide the "extra" practice they need to succeed in the regular physical education class. For these children, the remedial physical education class provides the environment for learning the basic skills of physical education that will enable them to participate successfully in the gymnasium and on the playground.

The content of the remedial physical education class centers around three areas of physical/motor skill development. The first area of concentration is mobility, balance, and muscular strength—hopping, jumping, and running; stepping onto a low platform or climbing the first rung of a ladder; walking a low balance beam or bench; and grasping a bar and lifting the body off the floor, taking weight on hands and feet. These areas contribute not only to success in physical education but also to greater independence throughout life (Figure 6.5).

The second area of concentration is physical fitness. Although the child's flexibility is often very good, muscular strength—both abdominal and upper body—and cardiovascular endurance are extremely poor. Most physical fitness testing and educational programs include activities for special populations (see Chapter 4).

The third content area is the basic manipulative skills of physical education—throwing, catching, drib-

bling, kicking, and so forth. Children who succeed in these three content areas will participate meaningfully in physical education, attain greater personal independence, and improve their recreational/leisure skills on the school playground and beyond.

Early testing of the motor skills of the children in the remedial physical education class will help the teacher develop the educational plan for each child. This plan should be based on the child's present level of functioning and include goals for the year. Although evaluation is ongoing, motor skills tests should be conducted at least by midyear and again in the spring. Records of activities and achievements can be kept in simple chart form. Remember, progress for these children is often very slow and is measured in small increments; charting their progress will help you recognize and praise achievements.

Emotional Disturbance/Behavior Disorders

In increasing numbers, children come to us with behavior disabilities: emotionally disturbed, behavior disordered, hyperactive, attention deficit disorder (ADD), attention deficit hyperactivity disorder (ADHD), distractive, aggressive, impulsive, and socially unacceptable. Children classified as emotionally disturbed/behavior disordered have deficiencies in at least one of the following: characteristics that facilitate learning, characteristics that promote interpersonal relationships, and characteristics that foster appropriate behavior under normal conditions. What classifies children with these characteristics as emotionally disturbed/behavior disordered is the persistence of the behavior, its severity, and its adverse effects on educational performance.

The role of the teacher is to control the learning environment while helping the child gain control. The following guidelines have implications for teachers of physical education:

- Provide a sense of order, structure, and dependability in the learning environment.
- Teach the child that verbal responses to frustration and conflict are acceptable but that physical aggression is not.
- Reinforce to the child that he or she is accepted even when the behavior is unacceptable.
- Establish short-range, achievable goals geared to the child's current level of functioning.
- Convey your expectations through your conduct and consistent messages.
- Avoid overreacting to extreme behavior; an emotional response from the teacher is counterproductive.

- Remember that what works for one child with emotional disturbance/behavior disorders may not work for another.

Physical activity has been shown to have a positive influence on children with behavior disorders/disruptive behaviors. These children benefit from physical education programs that emphasize fitness, balance, and basic movement; many have great difficulty with competitive games and sports. These children's past experiences in physical education have included a larger amount of time in nonactivity and a lesser degree of skill development due to behavior. The development of basic skills may require attention. Programs such as Hellison's Responsibility Model (Chapter 10) and programs with a cooperative rather than a highly competitive focus have been found to have a positive influence on the development of personal and social responsibility for these at-risk students.

Learning Disabilities

A specific learning disability is a disorder in one or more of the basic processes involving understanding or using language. According to the U.S. Department of Health and Human Services, the disability may manifest itself as an imperfect ability to listen, think, speak, write, spell, or do mathematical calculations. Children with learning disabilities have normal intelligence but, unlike other children, are unable to perform academically within the normal IQ range. Children with learning disabilities are typically characterized by hyperactive behavior, short attention spans, impulsiveness, poor self-concepts, and often a delay in play development.

The motor skills of children with learning disabilities are difficult to categorize. Some children with learning disabilities experience no motor delays; others demonstrate a number of delays. The most common difficulties include visual-motor coordination, fine motor coordination, bilateral coordination, and balance. Early IEPs for children with learning disabilities focused on perceptual-motor development; more recently the focus has been on sensory integration. Selection of the activities for the IEP must be based on assessment of the child's deficiencies. Not all learning-disabled children have motor/perceptual delays; not all have the same deficiencies.

Children with learning disabilities can be expected to participate fully in all physical education activities. Slight teaching modifications may be needed for individual students:

- To reduce hyperactive tendencies, prepare the lesson with several short activities in mind rather than one lengthy concentration.

- Give clear, brief instructions; ask the child to repeat the directions before beginning the activity.
- Use small learning steps, and praise the child's efforts and accomplishments. Remember, the attitude of the learning-disabled child is, "I can't."
- Use a positive behavior modification program if needed (Chapters 9 and 10).
- End the lesson with a brief relaxation period.

Teaching children with learning disabilities can be a most rewarding experience (Box 6.1). Teachers can help the youngsters develop socialization skills, motor skills many didn't know existed, and self-confidence. We believe that children with disabilities can benefit from physical education and from integration with others.

A Final Thought

All of us who work with special needs children in our classes know the joy as well as the challenge they bring to us:

Andy, a Down syndrome child who ran his endurance test for physical fitness with only one verbal expression, "Go."

Nate, who has multiple disabilities—blindness, mental retardation, and no language—who taught the children the power of touch and who rejected each playground ball until he felt the one in twenty-nine that he was using that day.

Paul, a mentally retarded child without sufficient arm strength to hang from a horizontal bar but with an 80 percent success rate at a ten-foot distance in basketball.

Each child is unique; each is special. Our task as teachers is to provide *all* students maximum opportunities to learn and to develop their personal potential.

> ▶ Children who have mild or moderate mental retardation, learning disabilities, or emotional disturbances but whose physical appearance does not manifest the disability are sometimes the least accepted by their peers. The class has the same expectations of them as of the nondisabled and becomes frustrated when they do not behave or respond as expected. The class response is usually due to the students' lack of awareness of the disability or knowledge of its characteristics. We as teachers must educate our students regarding specific disabilities. We must answer their questions, increase their awareness of the disability, and thus increase their understanding and acceptance of all children.

SUMMARY

Integrating children with special needs into regular educational settings is no longer a choice for teachers and administrators. The Individuals with Disabilities Education Act of 1990 guarantees each child with a disability a free and appropriate education in the least restrictive environment. The multidisciplinary team, commonly called the M-Team, determines the placement that constitutes the least restrictive environment.

The child's educational program, including annual goals and any special services, is written into the individualized education program (IEP). The IEP includes any individualized program in physical education—motor skills, perceptual-motor, and sensory development. Individualized programs are designed in consultation with medical specialists and other professionals with the expertise to help fashion the program that will best meet the child's needs.

With very few exceptions, children with disabilities can be included in physical education. Inclusion doesn't mean sitting on the sidelines keeping score or turning on the record player; inclusion means participating fully to the extent possible.

Most children with disabilities have had a limited number of childhood play experiences, so they're often deficient in social interaction and basic motor skills. Individualized programs of physical education can help close the developmental lags in motor skills; purposeful inclusion can assist in the development of social skills.

Each disability is different. Each child with a disability has needs specific to him or her. When a child with a disability enters our program, we need to increase our knowledge of the condition through extensive reading about the disability and its implications for physical education. We should consult with the child's medical doctor and physical therapist to determine appropriate activities for the individualized program and adaptations to facilitate full participation. We need to educate all children concerning the disability and orient them to the world of children with disabilities. By promoting the acceptance of all individuals and presenting a curriculum that focuses on the development of skills commensurate with ability, we can promote the acceptance of children with disabilities as contributing members of physical education classes.

READING COMPREHENSION QUESTIONS

1. What is the Individuals with Disabilities Education Act? What is its impact on physical education?
2. What is a multidisciplinary team? What is its function? Who serves on the M-Team?
3. What is an individualized education program? What does it include?
4. Name three characteristics of children with visual impairments. Discuss the implications of each characteristic in relation to physical education.
5. Physical education can serve as a laboratory for socialization of the hearing-impaired child. What adaptations, if any, are necessary for this objective to be accomplished?
6. Why are children with learning disabilities, behavior disorders, and mild retardation so often misunderstood?
7. Choose one physically disabling condition, and explain its implications for physical education. Discuss the adaptations involved in physical education for this child—adaptations for the child, adaptations for the total class, and adaptations for the teacher.

REFERENCES/ SUGGESTED READINGS

Auxier, D., & Pyfer, J. (1985). *Principles and methods of adapted physical education and recreation.* St. Louis, MO: Times Mirror/Mosby.

Craft, D. H. (Ed.). (1994). Inclusion: Physical education for all. *JOPERD 65*(1), 22–56.

Block, M. E., & Garcia, C. (Eds). (1995). *Including students with disabilities in physical education: A position statement.* Reston, VA: American Alliance for Health, Physical Education, Recreation and Dance.

Evans, J. R. (1980). *They have to be carefully taught: A handbook for parents and teachers of young children with handicapping conditions.* Reston, VA: American Alliance for Health, Physical Education, Recreation and Dance.

Liemohn, W., Winter, T., Bright, R., Shepherd, S., Battle, M., & Robertson, C. (1985). *Rigors and rhythms.* Knoxville: University of Tennessee.

MacCracken, M. (1978, July). Teacher. *In Touch, 1* (6).

Milne, D. C., Haubenstricker, J. L., & Seefeldt, V. D. (1991). Remedial motor education. *Strategies, 4*(4), 15–18.

National Education Association. (1996, July). *NEA Today.* Washington, D.C.: Author.

Oberti, C. (1993). Inclusion: A parent's perspective. *Exceptional Parent, 23*(7), 18–21.

Sherrill, C. (1993). *Adapted physical activity, recreation, and sport* (4th ed). Madison, WI: Wm. C. Brown & Benchmark.

Stein, J. (1992). Inclusive physical education. *TEPE 3*(5), 6–7.

U.S. Department of Education. (1994). *National standards for adapted physical education.* Washington, DC: U.S. Department of Education, Office of Special Education and Rehabilitation Services.

Winnick, J. (Ed). (1995). *Adapted physical education and sport* (2nd ed). Champaign, IL: Human Kinetics.

PART TWO

Teaching Skills

Part Two describes many of the teaching skills that teachers use to help children learn and enjoy physical activity. The initial chapter, Chapter 7, "Determining Generic Levels of Skill Proficiency," describes a system for matching class activities or tasks with the abilities of the children so that success rates can be high—and enjoyment frequent. As we know, neither age nor grade level are accurate indicators of a child's physical abilities. Chapter 7 provides a system for observing children that can enable the teacher to match the content of the lessons (which are organized according to the generic levels) with the children's abilities.

Chapter 8, "Planning," discusses lesson planning skills. A poorly planned or inappropriately organized lesson often will fail, regardless of a teacher's ability to interact with children. Chapter 8 describes step-by-step effective planning for the year and the day and covers such important points as how to record progress, design lessons, and actually enjoy planning.

Chapters 9 to 11—"Establishing an Environment for Learning," "Maintaining Appropriate Behavior," and "Observation Techniques," respectively—discuss skills used in the instruction process. Most of these skills involve direct interaction with children. Chapter 9 includes ideas for differentiating (a) physical education class as a learning experience from (b) recess. The chapter elaborates on various ways to establish the proper attitudes, how to foster a good atmosphere in the classroom, and how to set up safety procedures.

Chapter 10 provides practical ideas on discipline, including approaches for working with both individual children and entire classes. Specific examples from actual teaching situations illustrate how to increase appropriate and decrease inappropriate behavior and how to maintain proper behavior. The teacher is shown how to interact positively with the children; work with them one on one; apply "punishment," such as time-outs and desists; and follow worthwhile reward systems, such as class rewards, tokens, and behavior games.

Chapter 11 focuses on the process of teaching physical education and includes a format for observing classes that includes safety, on-task behavior, and the movements of the entire class and individual children. Teachers are also told how to use the two observation techniques of back to the wall and scanning and how to plan for observation.

One of the important reasons for developing the ability to observe children effectively is to make decisions about how to develop the content (Chapter 12). Reflective teachers constantly find themselves asking such questions as these: "Which tasks are appropriate for this class of children? Will the children benefit from a cue (refinement), or should the task be changed to a harder or easier one? This tasks is appropriate for the children, but they seem to be getting bored—how can their interest be maintained?" These are the questions that we respond to in Chapter 12 as we explain a process for developing the content and provide practical examples. This is an especially important chapter because all of the chapters in Parts Three and Four are based on this approach to content development.

Chapter 13, Instructional Approaches, provides an overview of a few of the techniques used by physical education teachers to create active learning experiences for children. This chapter describes a number of other approaches, beyond direct instruction, for example, task sheets, learning centers, peer teaching, cooperative learning, and guided discovery. Each of these alternatives provides a more engaging way for children to learn while at the same time more fully addresses the cognitive and affective goals of our physical education classes.

The final two chapters in Part Two, "Assessing Student Learning" (Chapter 14) and "Analyzing Your Teaching" (Chapter 15) both focus on attempting to determine how well lessons are going—for the children and for you as a teacher. In recent years educators have started to use alternative methods of assessing children. These techniques are ongoing (rather than a culminating experience at the end of a series of lessons) and are designed by teachers to assess specifically what they have been teaching. Some of the techniques are included in this chapter and include journals, exit slips, student drawings, and displays.

Successful teachers not only assess children, they also assess their teaching. Chapter 15 describes some of the techniques teachers use to do so—by themselves or with the assistance of students and/or colleagues. This chapter concludes by discussing the importance of support groups for teachers as one way to provide encouragement and comfort in a challenging profession. As in Part One, the ends of the chapters here in Part Two contain useful reading comprehension questions and references.

Determining Generic Levels of Skill Proficiency

Where parents have a voice in physical education programs, they usually insist that the curriculum includes the dances, games and sports skills of their culture. At the elementary level these activities are often preceded by the fundamental skills that are combined into more complex tasks as age and skill levels increase. . . . Teachers are to concentrate on the process of learning by selecting the appropriate content for whatever level of development the child demonstrates.

——Vern Seefeldt

One of the challenges of reflective teaching (Chapter 5) is matching a task (activity) to the ability of a child. If a task is appropriate, not too hard and not too easy, the child will typically remain interested, continue trying, and learn. If a task is too easy, however, the child will become bored and lose interest; too hard, and the child will want to do something else. Unfortunately, this rather oversimplified description is complicated drastically by the fact that we don't teach one child at a time—we typically teach twenty-five or more in a class. And the range of abilities within that class is typically a wide one.

One of the more obvious and accepted truths about teaching is that there is a range of ability within a given class. Some of the children may have never tried an activity, whereas others may have been playing it at home after school, or on a team, for several years.

From the outset we knew that describing and organizing activities according to the children's grade level would simply be inadequate. We discussed the possibility of organizing the curriculum according to the categories of beginner, intermediate, and advanced. We learned quickly, however, that even among the three of us who had been working together closely, there were different concepts of what constituted a beginning, an intermediate, and an advanced level of ability. We needed a classification system that would help us communicate with one another—and with you.

As we reviewed the literature, we came across a classification system developed by Stanley (1977), which we found to be descriptive and helpful in communicating the range of abilities related to a skill. She proposed four levels, which we have termed the *generic levels of skill proficiency* (GLSP): precontrol, control, utilization, and proficiency. As we discussed her system, we found that it was helpful to us and allowed us to describe and understand the range of motor abilities more accurately. We have organized and sequenced the content in the skill theme chapters by the GLSP. As you become familiar with these terms, we think you too will find them more descriptive and helpful than the beginner to advanced classifications. Before describing how we have used the GLSP throughout the text, we first need to define and describe each of the four skill levels.

Figure 7.1 Movements at the precontrol level are characterized by inconsistency, and successful skill performances are often accidental rather than intentional.

Identifying Levels of Skill Proficiency

Observable characteristics of each generic level of skill proficiency are listed in Box 7.1. The levels are also discussed below.

Precontrol Level

The *precontrol* (beginner) level is characterized by lack of ability to either consciously control or intentionally replicate a movement (Figure 7.1). For example, a child at the precontrol level who is bouncing a ball spends more time chasing after the ball than bouncing it—the ball seems to control the child. A child who tries to do a forward roll may complete a revolution on a mat or may get stuck, not rolling at all or rolling half forward and half to the side and finishing flat on the back. A child's efforts to strike a ball with a racket are characterized by frequent misses, mishits, and an inefficient and inconsistent striking pattern. Successful skill performances are a surprise! Most preschool and kindergarten children are at the precontrol level. By the time children are in the first grade, however, you'll observe some of them entering the control level.

BOX 7.1   OBSERVABLE CHARACTERISTICS OF THE GENERIC LEVELS OF SKILL PROFICIENCY

Precontrol Level

- Child is unable to repeat movements in succession; one attempt doesn't look like another attempt to perform the same movement.
- Child uses extraneous movements that are unnecessary for efficiently performing the skill.
- Child seems awkward and frequently doesn't even come close to performing the skill correctly.
- Correct performances are characterized more by surprise than by expectancy.
- When the child practices with a ball, the ball seems to control the child.

Control Level

- The child's movements appear less haphazard and seem to conform more to the child's intentions.
- Movements appear more consistent, and repetitions are somewhat alike.
- The child begins to perform the skill correctly more frequently.
- The child's attempt to combine one movement with another or perform the skill in relation to an unpredictable object or person is usually unsuccessful.
- Because the movement isn't automatic, the child needs to concentrate intensely on what he or she is doing.

Utilization Level

- The movement becomes more automatic and can be performed successfully, with concentration.
- Even when the context of the task is varied (slightly at first), the child can still perform the movement successfully.
- The child has developed control of the skill in predictable situations and is beginning to be able to move skillfully in unpredictable situations. The child can execute the skill the same way consistently.
- The child can use the skill in combination with other skills and still perform it appropriately.

Proficiency Level

- The skill has become almost automatic, and performances in a similar context appear almost identical.
- The child is able to focus on extraneous variables—an opponent, an unpredictable object, the flow of travel—and still perform the skill as intended.
- The movement often seems effortless as the child performs the skill with ease and seeming lack of attention.
- The movement can be performed successfully in a variety of planned and unplanned situations as the child appears to modify performance to meet the demands of the situation.

Control Level

The *control* (advanced beginner) level is characterized by less haphazard movements—the body appears to respond more accurately to the child's intentions. The child's movements often involve intense concentration because the movements are far from automatic (Figure 7.2). A movement that is repeated becomes increasingly uniform and efficient. At this level, a cartwheel the child performs is identifiable as a cartwheel; the child is able to travel in a previously identified direction while briefly taking full weight on the hands. When the child tries to throw a ball at a target, the ball usually travels in the direction of the target.

Some primary grade children are at the control level. You'll begin to observe that a few children involved in certain youth sports programs are at the next level, the utilization level. This is true only for their sport, however. For example, children involved in after-school gymnastics programs may be approaching the utilization level in the skill themes of rolling or transferring weight, but they may be at the precontrol level for throwing and catching or kicking a ball.

Utilization Level

The *utilization* (intermediate) level is characterized by increasingly automatic movements. A child at this level is able to use a movement in different contexts because he or she doesn't need to think as much about how to execute the movement (Figure 7.3). Dribbling a ball in a game situation is appropriate for a child at the utilization level. When children at the previous

Figure 7.2   Control-level movements often involve intense concentration.

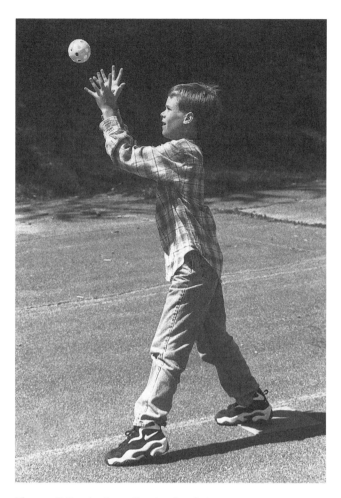

Figure 7.3   At the utilization level, movements are more reflexive and require less concentration.

level (control) try to dribble a ball, they spend more time chasing the ball than dribbling because they're unable to focus on dribbling a ball while trying to travel away from an opponent. A cartwheel, as one in a sequence of three movements, is also an appropriate task for a child at the utilization level.

As children get older, the gap between the skill levels widens. Children in the fourth and fifth grades who are involved in youth sports programs are often at the utilization level in the skill themes used in their sport, but not necessarily in other skills. In the same class, however, it's not uncommon to have children who have remained at the precontrol level, primarily because of their lack of activity beyond formally organized physical education classes.

Proficiency Level

The fourth level, *proficiency* (advanced), is characterized by somewhat automatic movements that begin to seem effortless. At this level the child gains control of

a specific movement and is challenged by the opportunities to employ that skill in changing environments that may require sudden and unpredictable movements (open skill) (Figure 7.4). The challenge of repeating movements exactly and with ever-increasing degrees of quality (closed skill) is also appropriate for children at this level. Rarely are elementary school children at the proficiency level in a skill. We do observe them, but they're certainly in a minority. In almost every instance, their proficiency is a result of their extensive involvement in after-school youth sports programs.

What Do We Mean by *Generic?*

Now that you have an understanding of the four levels of skill proficiency, it is important to explain what we mean by *generic*. Once again, our jobs as teachers would be much easier if every child had the same abil-

Figure 7.4 Children at the proficiency level are challenged by dynamic, unpredictable situations.

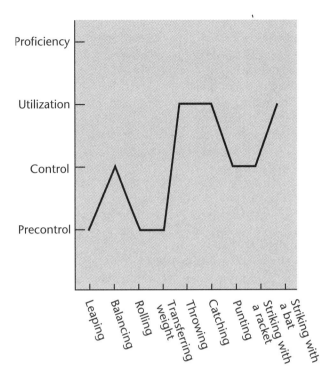

Figure 7.5 Hypothetical example representing a child's varying levels of proficiency in different skills.

ity—not only within a grade, but also for every skill. If this were so, we could, for example, merely observe a child kicking a ball at the utilization level and thereby determine that the child was also at the utilization level in throwing, balancing, and jumping and landing. As you know, however, this is not the case. A child may be at the utilization level in one skill and at the precontrol level in another. It's not uncommon for children in our classes to be skillful (utilization-level) throwers and catchers and at the precontrol level in the nonmanipulative skills of rolling, balancing, and transferring weight. By *generic*, then, we mean that the terms *precontrol, control, utilization,* and *proficiency* are used to describe a child's ability in every skill we teach—we don't use a different set of terms to describe the skill level for balancing, for example, and still another set of terms to describe the skill level for volleying. The hypothetical example in Figure 7.5 illustrates two points: (1) the GLSP apply to all of the skills we teach, and (2) children are typically at different skill levels for different skills.

Figure 7.5 also illustrates that age is not an accurate indicator of ability. If it were, all adults would be skillful at striking with a racket, for example, and we know this isn't true. We often observe fourth- and fifth-graders at the precontrol level when a new skill is introduced, one they have never practiced. Generally, however, because of their physical maturation and previous experiences, they move from the precontrol level more rapidly than the primary-grade children (although there are always exceptions).

Using the Generic Levels of Skill Proficiency in Teaching

The generic levels of skill proficiency provide a broad guideline for answering these questions: "What is the ability level of this class? What types of tasks and activities will be of value to them?" Although there will be a range of skill levels within any class, we as teachers make a judgment about the overall ability of the class. Then we modify the tasks for individuals using teaching by invitation and intratask variation as discussed in Chapter 12.

Essentially, each class we teach has certain characteristics (Chapter 5). Some fourth-grade classes are more skilled than others. Some are more enjoyable to work with. Some are more challenging than others. When we take these factors into consideration, we realize that the tasks that just worked so well for one class may need to be changed (made easier or harder) to meet the needs of the next class. The GLSP provide us with broad guidelines for doing so. For example, it is generally safe to assume that most of the children in school through first grade will be at the precontrol level.

In the upper grades, however, we typically find a few children who are at precontrol level, a number at control level, some at utilization level, and a few, especially in middle school, who might be at proficiency level. The higher the grade level, the greater the range of skill levels within a class.

Note that we use the levels of skill proficiency to describe a youngster's proficiency for each skill theme, e.g., kicking, jumping and landing, hitting a ball with a bat. The skill levels do *not* pertain to the movement concepts (Chapters 16 to 18) because the concepts aren't skills; they represent cognitive understanding expressed through versatile and efficient use of the skill themes. As you read further, this point will become clearer. For now, however, just remember that the four levels of skill proficiency apply to the skill themes only.

As reflective teachers we use the GLSP in two ways. First, we observe the students to determine their overall skill level. Second, we attempt to match the tasks to the skill level of the children in the class. For example, if we determine that the majority of the children in a class are at the precontrol level for the skill of kicking, we would not require them to play a proficiency-level game such as Alley Soccer or Cone Soccer (Chapter 26). Instead, we would ask them to practice precontrol tasks, such as kicking a stationary ball, from a standing position and then running to kick the ball.

Which Task?

As teachers gain experience and learn to use the GLSP, they become able to assess the overall skill level of a class rather quickly and determine which tasks will be helpful to that group (Graham, Hopple, Manross, & Sitzman, 1993; Housner & Griffey, 1985). For those who are new to the skill theme approach, or perhaps new to a school, it will take time and experience to learn the tasks that "work" with different grade and ability levels. Veteran teachers who have been teaching by skill themes know which tasks will work—and which will not. Beginning teachers, in contrast, will learn with practice the tasks that are most effective—and how to make them interesting and appealing to children of various grade levels. As you plan, espe-

cially when you start working with the skill theme approach, we recommend being prepared to deliver a series of tasks (ten to fifteen) in a lesson—not just one or two! Extensive planning will also help you learn the progression of tasks for each skill theme and movement concept. The chapters on Planning and Observation Techniques (Chapters 8 and 11) that follow will also help you better understand how to plan for lessons—and when to use a task and when to change to a new one.

Finally, it is important to remember that there is no single, correct way to deliver the tasks in a lesson. Some teachers, for example, prefer to start at the precontrol level (for a class at the control level) and quickly progress up the spiral with a series of tasks that serve as a warm-up and review for the children. Others prefer to start with a task or activity that most closely matches that class's GLSP. If a task is too hard, and children have high rates of failure and frustration, then a teacher who has planned well can move down the spiral to an easier task. That's why it is so important to plan a series of tasks rather than only one or two for a lesson.

How to Know If a Task Works

Chapter 11 on Observation Techniques explains in more detail how to know if a task works, but a quick overview of the process will be helpful here. A task works when youngsters are encouraged to be highly successful—they want to keep doing the task. Tasks that are too hard or too easy lead to frustration or boredom. The GLSP will help you match tasks to the ability level of the majority of the class so that children are not frustrated or bored. Again this is why we did not organize the book by grade levels: There is such a wide range of variance among classes at the same grade level. As you increase your understanding of the skill theme approach, you will find that it is relatively easy to change tasks and activities with classes.

When a class is required to play a sport or participate in a low organized activity, however, the teacher implicitly assumes that all of the youngsters have the same abilities and interests. The response of a sixth-grade boy to an opinion poll about a "flag football" unit (Figure 7.6) provides one potent example of how some children feel when they are all required to play a sport that requires proficiency-level skills. It also suggests why teaching the prerequisite skills for successful game playing, as opposed to playing games, is so important at the elementary school level—especially for those youngsters who have not reached the utilization or proficiency levels.

Figure 7.6 Sixth-grader's evaluation of a flag football unit.

Personal Opinion

Age: 12½   Sex: M

Answer the following questions:

1) What is the most important thing you have learned in flag football?

In flag football I learned, hold on I can sum it up with a couple of words! Absolutely nothing!

2) Did you enjoy the unit? Why? Why not?

No! I hated this unit! I'm sorry, but it stank! I pretty much hate any outdoor activity. Except Rollerblading, riding bicycles and basketball!

3) Is flag football appropriate to your age? Why?/Why not?

I don't know, and don't care! I Hate Football.

Final Insights about the Generic Levels of Skill Proficiency

Now that you're familiar with the four levels that constitute the GLSP, you need to be aware of three insights that will enhance your understanding of the levels and also help you apply them in your teaching situation.

Multiple Skill Levels in a Class

The first insight is that in the upper elementary and middle-school grades you can expect to have children in the same class at three different levels: precontrol, control, and utilization. Your challenge as a teacher is to determine the predominant skill level and then make adjustments for individuals through teaching by invitation or intratask variation (Chapter 12) and task sheets (Chapter 13), for example. In the preschool and primary grades, in contrast, many children will be at the precontrol and control levels—although there will always be an exception or two.

Control Level in Two Days a Week

The second insight we can offer is that in typical programs of elementary school physical education, in which children have physical education classes only twice a week, the children will reach the utilization level of most of the skill themes *only if they do something outside of class* (Graham, Metzler, & Webster, 1991). Unfortunately, an increasing number of children today are not physically active after school and on weekends. It is our observation that along with the decline in physical fitness (Chapter 1), children are also experiencing a decline in their skill levels from past years. The implication, of course, is that it is not uncommon for a teacher to use control-level tasks for children in the fourth and fifth grades—because the majority haven't developed their skills beyond that level. If we develop lessons using utilization- and proficiency-level tasks, we end up frustrating these children and convincing them that physical activity is not enjoyable because they are so inept.

Proficiency Level is Rare

Our third insight is that children who are at the proficiency level in a skill are the exception. Remember that the GLSP applies to skills, not ages. Thus anyone, regardless of age, can be at the precontrol level. The standards or criteria for each of the GLSP apply across the board to all skills and all ages. Consequently, we do not see many children at the proficiency level. In fact, it seems unlikely that many children can reach proficiency level simply by participating in a physical education program—unless that program is a quality, daily program. Typically children reach the proficiency level in a skill because they've been involved in an after-school sports program in which they practice the skill frequently or because a parent or older sister or brother is involved in a sport and the child consequently spends a lot of time practicing and receiving instruction in the backyard.

Overall, however, we do not observe children at proficiency level very often. For this reason, you will probably use the proficiency-level tasks we have listed in each of the chapters more as part of teaching by invitation and intratask variation (Chapter 12) than with entire classes of children. This does not mean, of course, that some of the children don't want to perform the proficiency-level tasks, especially the games. Children who are new to the skill theme approach, particularly those in the upper elementary and middle-school grades, constantly ask the question, "When do we get to play the game?" Our standard answer is, "At recess. At home. On the weekends." In time, as the children become accustomed to the skill theme approach and we're able to individualize the program to a greater extent, they no longer ask the question—at least, not as often.

Unfortunately, some teachers succumb to the pressure from the children to "play the game." In the long run, the children end up shortchanged—just as they do when their diet consists primarily of unhealthy snacks and fast food. Although it may not be as much fun as playing games such as kickball and dodgeball, a focus on learning and improving has the potential to help children eventually derive the benefits of regular involvement in physical activity. Failure to help children develop the prerequisite skills may mean that the children, as they age, come to feel inadequate and incompetent in physical activity. Just as it's easier for parents to let their children sit in front of the television for five or six hours a day, it's easier for teachers to let the children play kickball and dodgeball every day. But it's not better for the children!

SUMMARY

Organizing curriculum by grade level or age is convenient. Yet, because of the range of skills found at any grade level or age, age and grade level are inadequate indicators of children's skill levels. We adapted the concept of Generic Levels of Skill Proficiency (GLSP). Assessing children's skills in terms of these levels is a basis for planning appropriate activities. The four generic levels of motor skill proficiency are (1) precontrol, (2) control, (3) utilization, and (4) proficiency.

Children at the precontrol level are unable to consciously control or replicate a particular movement. At the control level, the child's body appears to respond more accurately to the child's intentions, and movements become increasingly similar. Movements are even more automatic and reflexive at the utilization level; children can use a movement in a variety of contexts. At the proficiency level, the child has gained control of a movement and is challenged by the goal of repeating movements exactly or using movements effectively in dynamic, unpredictable situations.

The generic levels of skill proficiency are task related—that is, a person at the utilization level in one skill may be at the control level in another skill. Age and skill level are not necessarily related.

READING COMPREHENSION QUESTIONS

1. What is the purpose of the GLSP? How are they used?
2. In your *own* words, explain the differences among the four levels of skill proficiency.
3. What do we mean by *generic?*
4. Why isn't age an indicator of motor skill proficiency?
5. Describe how the GLSP serve as a guide for selecting and matching tasks to the abilities of children within a class. Pick a skill theme, and describe how you would use the GLSP to help you make your decisions about which tasks to present.
6. Figure 7.5 shows a hypothetical example of a child's proficiency level at several skills. Use the form below to create your own graph. Select ten of the skill themes. Try to select ones that represent your range of abilities. Graph your skill levels. Which skill themes do you need to work on most? Why are you less advanced at these skills than at the others? Did you rate yourself at the proficiency level for any of these skills? If so, why do you think you attained the proficiency level for that skill? Answer the same questions if you're at the precontrol level for any of the ten skills you selected.

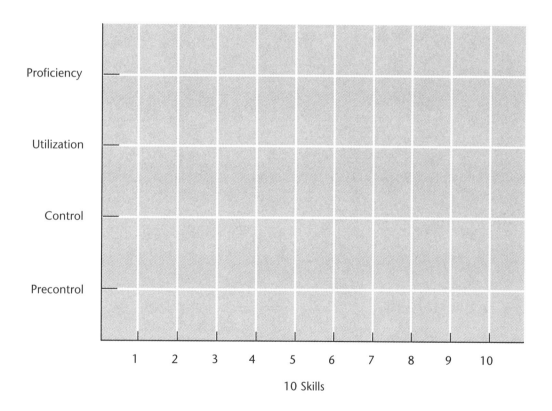

REFERENCES

Graham, G., Hopple, C., Manross, M., & Sitzman, T. (1993). Novice and experienced children's physical education teachers: Insights into their situational decision-making. *Journal of Teaching in Physical Education, 12,* 197–214.

Graham, G., Metzler, M., & Webster, G. (1991). Specialist and classroom teacher effectiveness in children's physical education: A 3-year study [Research monograph]. *Journal of Teaching in Physical Education, 4,* 321–426.

Housner, L. D., & Griffey, D. C. (1985). Teacher cognition: Differences in planning and interactive decision making between experienced and inexperienced teachers. *Research Quarterly for Exercise and Sport, 56,* 56–63.

Seefeldt, V. (1979). Developmental motor patterns: Implications for elementary school physical education. In C. Nadeau, W. Halliwell, K. Newell, & C. Roberts (Eds.), *Psychology of motor behavior and sport.* Champaign, IL: Human Kinetics.

Stanley, S. (1977). *Physical education: A movement orientation* (2nd ed.). New York: McGraw-Hill.

CHAPTER
8

Planning

"Will you please tell me which way I ought to go from here?"
"That depends a good deal on where you want to get to," said the Cat.
"I don't care much where," said Alice.
"Then it doesn't matter which way you go," said the Cat.

——Lewis Carroll

If you don't know where you are going, you will be lost when you get there.

——Yogi Berra

The next seven chapters focus on many of the techniques or skills that successful teachers use when they teach children. The first teaching skill we want to discuss is planning. We need to tell you right up front, however, that some of the material in this chapter will be new to you—and it won't be explained until later in the book. For this reason, you will probably want to review this chapter again after you have read the content chapters (Parts Three and Four), when the examples will probably make more sense to you.

Nevertheless, we think it is important to start at the beginning. Any good program begins with a good plan. For many teachers, however, planning is one of the least enjoyable aspects of teaching. And yet it's essential, because failure to plan appropriately can lead to lessons that are disastrous. Disorganization and spending an excessive amount of time on management characterize the lessons of the teacher who hasn't planned effectively.

Inappropriate planning can also have long-term implications. One of the important tasks of physical education is to provide a variety of learning experiences that give children a broad foundation of movement abilities. Children who are skillful in only a few activities, typically games, may be the products of programs characterized by inefficient planning. Instructors who don't plan are likely to teach only what they know well and the children enjoy, which often results in an unbalanced program over the years.

Because planning is typically done during the teacher's own time rather than during school time, there are strong temptations to avoid it. It can be much more pleasant to watch television, go to a ball game, or just go to bed early. But planning, even though you may consider it as onerous as homework, *is* necessary.

Reflective Planning

If all schools, all children, all facilities, all teachers, all communities, and all equipment were the same, we could simply provide you with a book of lesson plans that would be successful with every class you teach, no matter the situation. As you know, however, that isn't the case. Experienced teachers are able to plan lessons—and entire programs—that take into account the various unique characteristics of their teaching situation (Graham, Hopple, Manross, & Sitzman, 1993; Housner & Griffey, 1985).

The reflective planner considers many factors when trying to devise the best lessons possible under the circumstances. Planning can't be reduced to an exact for-

mula, but certain factors will always influence the effectiveness of a lesson. Each factor is important, and all interact to determine the teaching environment for which the reflective teacher must plan. When planning, we consider class size, frequency of class meetings, available equipment and facilities, personal characteristics of the children, and children's skill levels and interests.

Class size often determines the amount and types of information that can be presented. It's fairly safe to assume, for example, that a class of fifteen children will accomplish significantly more in a year's time than a class of sixty (Glass, Cahen, Smith, & Filby, 1979).

Frequency of class meetings is the second factor. Classes that meet once or twice a week accomplish far less than classes that meet daily because you can't present as much material in one or two days as you can in five (Kelly, 1989). And children, particularly the younger ones, tend to forget what they learned a week earlier.

To learn and understand a concept or skill, a child needs a multitude of experiences with a particular task or challenge. When the amount of *available equipment and facilities* is limited, each child has fewer opportunities to use the equipment. One result is that children learn more slowly than they would with adequate equipment that would increase learning opportunities.

Equipment also dictates which experiences can be presented. In gymnastics, for example, children who have progressed beyond the initial stages of skill development need apparatus—tables, beams—that allows them to work off the floor, because only with such equipment will they continue to be challenged. Similarly, nylon hose rackets are appropriate for children who are just beginning to learn to strike with implements. But paddles or rackets are essential if the children are to remain interested in and challenged by the skill theme of striking with implements.

Facilities also influence planning. Kicking can be studied briefly in a limited indoor space. But children can learn much more about kicking when they can practice it outdoors in a larger area. Thus, lack of adequate outdoor facilities may prevent you from devoting as much time as you'd like to a particular skill theme.

Similarly, the kind of available indoor space influences planning. Most teachers, for example, prefer to teach dance indoors. Hallways, classrooms with furniture pushed aside, school foyers—all these indoor areas can be used for teaching. But these aren't ideal settings for teaching many skill themes. It's extremely difficult, for example, to teach locomotor activities in a crowded classroom. However, you can effectively teach the movement concepts of symmetrical and nonsymmetrical shapes in a crowded, indoor area.

How responsible are the students? Children's ability to function in a variety of environments also influences planning (see Chapters 9 and 10). During the first few meetings of a class, you can gather observations about the *children's characteristics;* this information is useful when you plan lessons for a particular class. Some classes and some individual children can cooperate with others and work well in less than optimal circumstances.

The four factors just mentioned are easier to assess than *children's skill levels and interests.* You must have this information, though, to decide what tasks are appropriate and how to present those tasks. You want to challenge the students but not overwhelm them, so that they will continue to be interested and will want to learn.

If you decide that your class needs to be introduced to the concept of levels (Chapter 16), many factors, including the children's ages and abilities, will determine your plan for this lesson. Young, unskilled children often enjoy the challenge of taking different body parts into different levels—for example, "Can you move your elbow into low level?" "Can you move an ankle into high level?" Children in the intermediate grades might be bored by that task and so would probably learn more effectively if challenged to catch or strike a ball at different levels.

When teaching children in the upper grades, it's important to consider the types of movement experiences to which they've already been exposed. You'll want to take advantage of skills learned in earlier experiences, and you'll also want to avoid repetition of material with which students are already familiar. For example, if the children are proficient in the skills used in softball, you may decide to minimize the amount of time spent on the skill theme of striking with bats.

A Four-Step Planning Process

Although there are several ways teachers plan either alone or as a group when they develop a curriculum, we suggest a four-step planning process that provides children with a progression of learning experiences over several years. At this point in the book, much of the terminology will be new to you. Our recommendation is that you continue to read with the understanding that you'll return to this chapter after reading more of the book, when the examples we provide to illustrate the four parts of the planning process

will make a great deal more sense to you. Don't be frustrated, however, if you don't understand the meaning of every term we use—the definitions are in subsequent chapters. At this point, it's important that you understand the process itself—the four steps that describe one way to develop an overall plan for a physical education program.

The first step in planning is developing a curriculum scope and sequence for the entire five or six years of the program. Step 2 is developing a yearly plan from the program scope and sequence, deciding approximately how many days you will devote to the various movement concepts and skill themes for each grade taught that year. Step 3 involves deciding which aspects of each of the skill themes and movement and fitness concepts you'll focus on, with special attention to the cues or refinements (see Chapter 12) that you will be emphasizing. These are referred to as benchmarks or checkpoints. The final step, step 4, is the development of your daily lesson plans.

An analogy may help explain the process. Imagine that you and a friend are going on a trip. You are planning to drive several thousand miles. You would probably ask and answer four questions:

1. Where do we plan to end up? What do we plan to visit along the way?
2. How many days do we plan to stay in each location?
3. What will we use as our checkpoints (or benchmarks) along the way to determine how well our plan is working?
4. How will we organize each day?

Effective teachers ask, and answer, essentially the same four questions as they plan their programs. The planning process used by teachers employing a skill theme approach—one of asking and answering these four questions—is described (with examples) in the next section. We caution you that the process may appear complex but, just as with a long journey, taking it step by step makes it much easier.

Step 1: Developing the Scope and Sequence

The first step is deciding what you will include in your curriculum—and what you will not include. This is the *scope* of the curriculum. Teachers in Florida, for example, would probably not focus on ice skating or snow skiing, whereas teachers in Alaska and Minnesota would. Reviewing the curriculum scope tells us what is included—and what is not.

Just as in your imaginary trip with a friend, you will need to decide the sequence of your journey—where you will go first, second, and so on. The curriculum

Table 8.1 Movement Concept Scope and Sequence for Grades K–5

Movement Concept	K	1	2	3	4	5
Space Awareness						
Self-space	X	X				
General space	X	X	X			
Levels	X	X	X			
Directions	X	X	X			
Pathways	X	X	X			
Extensions			X	X		
Effort						
Time/speed	X	X	X	X	X	
Force			X	X	X	X
Flow			X	X	X	X
Relationships						
Body part identification	X					
Shapes	X	X	X			
Relationships with objects	X	X	X	X		
Relationships with people			X	X	X	X

Notes: This chart is intended only as an example. Reflective teachers will want to adapt this chart for their school.

X denotes that a movement concept is the major focus of lessons at a grade level. Concepts are studied at other grade levels but not as the primary focus of the lesson.

Table 8.2 Skill Theme Scope and Sequence for Grades K–5

Skill Theme	K	1	2	3	4	5
Traveling						
Walking	X	X				
Running	X	X				
Hopping	X	X	X			
Skipping	X	X	X			
Galloping	X	X	X			
Leaping	X	X	X	X		
Sliding	X	X	X	X		
Chasing, Fleeing, Dodging		X	X	X	X	X
Jumping and Landing	X	X	X	X	X	X
Balancing	X	X	X	X	X	
Transferring Weight			X	X	X	X
Rolling	X	X	X	X	X	X
Kicking			X	X	X	X
Punting					X	X
Throwing			X	X	X	X
Catching			X	X	X	X
Volleying				X	X	X
Hand Dribbling			X	X	X	X
Foot Dribbling			X	X	X	X
Striking with Rackets			X	X	X	X
Striking with Long-Handled Implements						
Bats				X	X	X
Golf clubs				X	X	X
Hockey sticks				X	X	X

Notes: This chart is intended only as an example. Reflective teachers will want to adapt this chart for their school.

X denotes that a skill theme is the major focus of lessons at a grade level. Concepts are studied at other grade levels but not as the primary focus of the lesson.

sequence provides an overview of the order in which the content will be taught—and at what grade levels. In the skill theme approach the movement concepts (Table 8.1) are emphasized in grades K–2 (visited first) and the skill themes (Table 8.2) in grades 3–5. This does not mean that first-graders never throw or kick in a skill theme approach but rather that the lesson focus is not on learning to throw or kick but on using movement concepts to enhance the effectiveness of those skills. In contrast, a concept like pathways is important as fourth- and fifth-graders participate in minigames in which they try to escape (flee) or catch (chase) others on the team. At the upper grades, however, the children have already learned the concept of pathways so we do not teach them the difference between straight, curved, and zigzag the way we do with the younger children.

As we have discussed in the previous chapters, *Children Moving* focuses on youngsters learning the various skills used in a variety of sports and physical activities, but not the official, adult versions of the sports, which are more developmentally appropriate for middle- and high school youngsters (Chapters 7 and 11). Consequently our organizing themes are not sports but skill themes and concepts (movement, fitness, and wellness). Tables 8.1 and 8.2 exemplify how we organize the content we teach—by grade levels to be consistent with the *National Standards* (NASPE, 1995). Note, though, that the grade levels merely serve as a general

indicator; the decisions about what to teach and when are based on observing the actual classes of children we teach (Chapters 7 and 11). So the first two question you will need to answer as a reflective teacher are

1. What do I want to include in my curriculum (scope)?
2. At what grade levels will I emphasize the various concepts and skills (sequence)?

Step 2: Devising a Yearly Overview

Continuing the analogy of a trip with a friend, the next step would be to decide how long you plan to spend at each destination. You will visit some places only briefly; at others you will spend several days. In curriculum development, once you have decided your scope and sequence the next step is to develop a yearly overview. How many days do you plan to spend teaching the movement concept "levels" to kindergarten children? How many days will you spend

Table 8.3   Yearly Overview for a Two-Day-a-Week Program: Kindergarten, Second, and Fourth Grades

Concept/Theme/Activity	K	2	4
Establishing a Learning Environment	6	4	3
Space Awareness	10	4	2
Effort	4	4	3
Relationships	6	4	3
Traveling	10	3	1
Chasing, Fleeing, Dodging	3	5	3
Jumping and Landing	4	4	3
Rolling	2	4	4
Balancing	4	4	4
Transferring Weight	2	3	4
Kicking and Punting	4	4	4
Throwing and Catching	4	6	6
Volleying	0	2	4
Dribbling	1	2	3
Striking with Rackets	2	4	4
Striking with Hockey Sticks	0	1	2
Striking with Golf Clubs	0	1	2
Striking with Bats	0	1	2
Fitness/Wellness Concepts	5	7	10
Field Day and Other Events	5	5	5
Total Days per Year	72	72	72

Note: Numbers represent days per year that a concept theme will be the *major* focus of a lesson. Numbers are intended for discussion only; the overview will be different from teacher to teacher.

teaching your fourth- and fifth-graders to strike with paddles?

Table 8.3 exemplifies the overview of a teacher who sees children twice a week (72 days a year) for physical education. It uses the kindergarten, second, and fourth grade levels to be consistent with the *National Standards* and provides one example of how many days a teacher might spend on the various concepts and skills in a given year. As you review Table 8.3 two facts should strike you:

- There aren't enough days for youngsters to learn everything recommended in the curriculum guides.
- The primary-grade emphasis is on the concepts; the upper-grade emphasis is on the skill themes.

Like Tables 8.1 and 8.2, Table 8.3 is for illustrative purposes only. As a reflective teacher you will want to ask and answer this question based on your specific teaching situation: "How many days a year will I be able to allocate to teaching each concept and skill theme?"

Once you have developed a yearly overview for your program, you'll need to translate it into a yearly calendar. Essentially, this involves deciding which skill themes or concepts you'll emphasize during which days of the school year. Most school districts provide planning calendars, and preparation of the yearly calendar can rather easily be done at the beginning of

the school year during planning days. Figure 8.1 shows one type of planning calendar.

Based on what we know about how children learn, it seems wise to distribute the throwing lessons over the year rather than to mass them together (Rink, 1996). If, for example, a teacher planned to teach throwing for three days of the year, two of the throwing lessons might be scheduled in September, the third in March. A teacher with a three-day-a-week program might have a total of nine throwing lessons. In such a case, the teacher might decide to devote three lessons in a row to throwing, but it's still better to spread the total number of lessons throughout the year. Continuing to revisit lessons helps the children better remember the key points; spending several days on a skill or concept and then not reviewing it for another year is much less effective. Again, it's important to emphasize that the children will actually practice throwing in more classes than just the ones that focus primarily on throwing. For example, the sessions dedicated to catching will typically offer many opportunities to throw. In these sessions, however, the teacher will focus on the way the children catch, not on the way they throw. Obviously, children don't become effective throwers in three lessons a year—it takes much more time and practice. It is possible for them to learn parts of the overhand throw, however, in three lessons a year. It is reasonable to expect, for example, that they can learn to step with the foot opposite the throwing hand or turn their nondominant side toward the target (see Chapter 12).

The beginning teacher will have to experiment with devising the lesson sequences. This process of sequencing lessons to enhance learning movement concepts or skill themes is a valuable one. With practice, you'll learn to predict, with increasing accuracy, the appropriate emphasis that you should place on a theme or concept in a given class. And experience helps you adjust the sequence of the lessons to account for individual differences within a class and among classes. Once you have outlined a sequence, you can rearrange that sequence without losing sight of the intended direction or progression of the skill theme or movement concept.

Here are helpful guidelines for developing your yearly overviews:

1. The first time you introduce a concept or theme, the children will need several lessons in a row to grasp the major ideas. Later in the year, they'll need less time. Mass the practice in the beginning of the year; distribute it later. During weeks 4 and 6, for example, you may devote four lessons to jumping and landing. For the remainder of the

Week 1 M T W T F	Week 2 M T W T F	Week 3 M T W T F	Week 4 M T W T F	Week 5 M T W T F	Week 6 M T W T F
Week 7 M T W T F	Week 8 M T W T F	Week 9 M T W T F	Week 10 M T W T F	Week 11 M T W T F	Week 12 M T W T F
Week 13 M T W T F	Week 14 M T W T F	Week 15 M T W T F	Week 16 M T W T F	Week 17 M T W T F	Week 18 M T W T F
Week 19 M T W T F	Week 20 M T W T F	Week 21 M T W T F	Week 22 M T W T F	Week 23 M T W T F	Week 24 M T W T F
Week 25 M T W T F	Week 26 M T W T F	Week 27 M T W T F	Week 28 M T W T F	Week 29 M T W T F	Week 30 M T W T F
Week 31 M T W T F	Week 32 M T W T F	Week 33 M T W T F	Week 34 M T W T F	Week 35 M T W T F	Week 36 M T W T F

Figure 8.1 Yearly planning calendar.

year, jumping and landing are the major focus of the lesson for only two days in a row. This same principle applies to any skill theme or movement concept: massed practice during initial learning, distributed practice later.

2. The older the children, the longer they're able to remain on the same skill theme. For example, children designing games or dances typically need several days in a row for this task. As the children become more skilled, you'll notice that it becomes easier to remain on a skill theme than it was initially.

3. It isn't very effective to focus on a skill once a year and then never revisit it. Three weeks of practice on the skill theme of rolling in February, for example, probably won't lead to the long-term learning that three weeks of practice, one week each in October, February, and April, will.

4. To get you started, a major task is generally appropriate for the focus of a day's lesson. If you think the children will find a single task too strenuous or

uninteresting, you may want to combine a major task from two different chapters. For example, you may want to combine the ideas under the heading Jumping a Turned Rope (Chapter 22) with the major task Traveling in Different Pathways (Chapter 19). This will give the children variety. Although most of our lessons focus on one major movement concept or skill theme, there's certainly no valid reason not to focus on two themes or concepts in a single lesson.

Our experience has been that it's often difficult for beginning teachers to develop a daily calendar. In an attempt to make this process easier (and better), we have provided four sample daily calendars in Appendix A. Two calendars are for classes that have physical education five times a week (180 days a year); two are for classes that meet twice a week (72 days a year). Two of the calendars are for kindergarten through grade two, and two are for grades three through six.

You'll find that you'll want to change these calendars as you plan your year, but they're a helpful start. To the right of each activity is a page number, which indicates where in *Children Moving* you can find a thorough explanation of each task and how it can be presented to children.

Once you've written your outline, use it only as a guide and change it as often and as much as the particular situation requires. You will want to write your outlines in pencil, leaving plenty of space for changes.

Learning is not totally predictable. If the study of a particular topic is going especially well, we don't change simply because the daily outline tells us to change. If several lessons on a particular topic have proven ineffective, it's possible to change to a different focus even though the daily outline calls for teaching three more lessons on that topic.

The children's needs and interests are the guide for the lessons to be presented. No outline, however theoretically sound it may be, can unfailingly reflect the progress and the interests of all the children being taught.

Step 3: Determining Benchmarks

Now that you and your friend have decided where you want to go on your imaginary trip and how long you plan to spend at various sites along the way, your next step is to determine checkpoints (or benchmarks) that you constantly check to be certain you are on the right road headed in the desired direction—in other words, to ensure that you don't get lost. In most cases, especially if you are not on an interstate highway, you would constantly check your map, highway signs, and anything else that would assure you that you are headed in the proper direction.

Good teachers do the same thing. They develop checkpoints to be sure the children are learning what they want them to be learning—and then constantly assess their progress along the way. These teachers don't wait until the fifth grade, for example, to assess what the children have learned (or not learned). They continually check to be sure the children are "getting it" before moving on—and revisit areas that have not been clear to the children.

The *National Standards for Physical Education* (NASPE, 1995) include sample *benchmarks* designed to serve as guides to what students are expected to be learning in our physical education programs. They are intended to serve as checkpoints along the way, assuring us that we are on the right course in guiding youngsters in the process of becoming physically active for a lifetime. They represent the "learnable pieces" that, when combined together, result in skill-

Table 8.4   Benchmarks for Assessing Catching Progress

Grade	Critical Element
2	Eye contact
3	Ready position
4	Hand and arm position
5	Absorption of force

Table 8.5   Benchmarks for Assessing Understanding of the Movement Concepts Symmetrical/Asymmetrical

Grade	Benchmark
K	Recognizes the difference between symmetrical and asymmetrical balances
1	"Completed four balances, two symmetrical and two asymmetrical" (NASPE, 1995, p. 19)
2	"Maintains stillness in balance for three seconds" (NASPE, 1995, p. 19)

ful performance and the development of a positive self-efficacy. Often the benchmarks are the critical elements or cues for various skills. Thus once a teacher makes the decision to spend a certain number of days on the skill of catching, for example, she will need to decide what the students are going to learn about catching—that is, the critical elements of catching. Remember that the students will not be able to become proficiency-level catchers in one year, but they can learn one or more catching cues that year. Table 8.4 provides one example of how a teacher might define the various critical elements of catching that will be emphasized from year to year. Assume that a teacher decides to teach the four catching cues in Table 8.4 to illustrate Content Standard 2 of the *National Standards*, which states, "Applies movement concepts and principles to the learning and development of motor skills" (NASPE, 1995, p. 21). The teacher could then decide which cues to emphasize each year to serve as benchmarks of student progress. These four phrases would provide a checkpoint to be sure that the children were actually remembering these cues, which would assist them on their journey to becoming competent and confident catchers.

For younger children the teacher might teach the difference between symmetrical and asymmetrical movements as described in the chapter on Space Awareness (Chapter 16). If the teacher wanted to adapt the assessment example from Content Standard 1 of the *National Standards*—"Demonstrates competency in many movement forms and proficiency in a few movement forms"—into a series of yearly benchmarks, they might look like the items in Table 8.5.

Table 8.6   Benchmarks for Assessing a Traveling, Rolling, and Balancing Sequence

Grade	Critical Element
4	Demonstrates a clear beginning and ending to the sequence
5	Demonstrates smooth transitions between the various skills (of traveling, rolling, and balancing)

Again for Content Standard 1, but with older children, the teacher might want to use the criteria for assessment suggested in a gymnastics example (traveling, balancing, and rolling) from the *National Standards for Physical Education* (NASPE, 1995, p. 33) and in Chapters 19, 23, and 24 of *Children Moving*. She might develop the checkpoints or benchmarks shown in Table 8.6.

The first three steps of the planning process involve long-range planning and some difficult decisions. Fortunately, however, you can make these decisions over a summer, for example, or over a year as you "pilot," or try out, a curriculum. Ideally, you make these decisions along with your fellow teachers as you talk about, reflect, and design a curriculum that will be successful for you in your district. The last step in the planning process, however, is one you do on your own: translating the scope and sequence completed in step 1, the yearly outline completed in step 2, and the benchmarks identified as part of step 3 into a daily lesson plan.

Just as on your imaginary trip with your friend, as a reflective teacher you will need to decide on the benchmarks that fit your program. You will see that in Parts Three and Four of *Children Moving*, along with the tasks and activities, we have also included the cues or critical elements that we emphasize in our teaching. You will see that they are consistent with the *National Standards for Physical Education* and will allow you to develop your own set of benchmarks to measure the progress of your children on their journey to becoming physically active for a lifetime. Thus the question we suggest you ask and answer for step 3 of the planning process is this: "What are the benchmarks or checkpoints that I will use to assess the progress my students are making?"

Step 4: Detailing Daily Lesson Plans

The final question a teacher asks as part of the planning process is "What tasks and cues will I teach each day in my lessons?" On your imaginary trip with your friend, you will also need to plan each day by answering questions like these: How far do we plan to drive? Where will we stop along the way? What will we see and do there? Where will we stop for the night? And, of course, each day's plan will often not work out exactly as imagined—for many reasons.

The same is true for teachers. Although daily learning plans rarely work out exactly as designed, you will want to develop them based on the decisions you made in the first three steps of the planning process. To assist you, we have included in Box 8.1 an example of a lesson plan for use with a skill theme approach. The plan is quite detailed because we think the detail is especially helpful to teachers planning to use a skill theme approach. In time, as you gain in experience and knowledge of children's abilities and interests, you will find that you can be less detailed. In the beginning, however, detailed planning of the sort we suggest here is an excellent way to understand how to teach the skill theme content.

Short-term planning is typically done after school and in the evenings. This is the step in which you take into account the specific variations among individuals and classes. Long-term planning is typically done before the school year begins, before you know the individual children you'll be teaching. Thus, it is in daily lesson planning that you can accommodate individual variations.

You can generate lesson ideas from a number of sources, including notes from classes, your own and others' observations, books, workshops, conferences, articles, and discussions. Planning for lessons involves sifting through sources and then designing lessons to match the needs and characteristics of a particular class to help them learn the benchmarks developed in the previous step of the planning process. We've found few, if any, predesigned lessons that worked for us as they supposedly worked for their authors. So instead of including specific lesson plans in *Children Moving* (with the exception of Box 8.1), we provide tasks for development to encourage you to develop your own plans.

To plan effectively, you need to consider the vital information in Box 8.1, which is useful for planning lessons and for improving teaching. It is presented here only as a guide; you may want to change it or adapt it to your particular style of lesson planning. This is the format that is also used in *On the Move* (Holt/Hale, 1998). We have intentionally included more detail than a typical plan contains so that we can provide a better understanding of how we develop the content in a lesson.

The sample lesson plan in Box 8.1 has twelve different parts. Each part, along with suggested modifications, is discussed in the order in which a plan is typically completed.

1. Class Name   This part isn't necessary for a classroom teacher. Physical education specialists may want to make a plan for each of their classes or, when their teaching load is particularly heavy, list the grade level (e.g., second/third grade) as a general guide. Another alternative is to just list the skill level of the class. Teachers with heavy loads, for example, thirty different classes in a week, use the same basic plan for each grade level and then make individual notes about different classes as suggested at the end of this form (part 12).

2. Skill Level   This gives the teacher a general idea of the skill level of the class. The information is based on observations and assessments.

3. Length of Lesson (Time)   This refers to the length of a class, for example, 10:00 to 10:30, or twenty-five minutes.

4. Number of Meetings per Week   This information is especially helpful for specialists who meet certain classes a different number of times per week from others.

5. Major Focus and Subfocus   The major focus of the lesson will be based on what you did in step 2 of the planning process when you decided which concepts and skill themes would be taught on which days of the school year. This provides you with the focus and purpose for that lesson or lessons. The subfocus also indicates which additional concepts and skill themes will be reinforced within that lesson. In the sample lesson plan in Box 8.1, the children will spend most of their time throwing and catching, but the teacher will emphasize their catching skill. In addition, they'll need to be aware of self-space and levels (Chapter 16), although these concepts will not be the major focus of the lesson because they have already been covered. In this lesson, throwing (Chapter 27) will also be a subfocus.

6. Objectives   The objectives for the lesson describe what the children are to *learn* during the lesson, not what they are to *do*. For example, stating that the children will throw and catch a ball in self-space is not an objective—it is a task. "The children will learn to catch a ball" is an objective. Unfortunately, this objective cannot be accomplished in a thirty-minute lesson; it will take many lessons, perhaps thousands of practice catches, before a child can be said to be truly able to catch a ball.

The objectives, then, are "learnable pieces" based on the benchmarks—something a child has a reasonable chance to learn in a single lesson. In the sample lesson in Box 8.1, the teacher will focus on two aspects (critical elements) of successful catching: teaching the children to (1) move their hands into a ready position before catching the ball and (2) extend their arms to avoid trapping the ball against their body. The teacher decided on these two cues after reading the chapter on catching (Chapter 27) and also from the example in the *National Standards for Physical Education* (NASPE, 1995, p. 20). The teacher will not simply provide chances to practice catching but will focus on teaching the children to use the hands and arms appropriately to catch a ball or an object. During the lesson she will continually pause and *remind* the children of the cue they need to work on. Sometimes she will *demonstrate* the cue. Sometimes she will *pinpoint* other youngsters as they use the critical elements in their catching (Chapter 12). As the children practice, the teacher will also move among them and provide feedback about how well they are using the cues. You will hear her constantly remind individual children to "get their hands into the 'ready' position" or to "reach for the ball." When the teacher observes individual children and then provides an analysis of how they are using a cue, the technique is called *specific, congruent feedback* (Chapter 12). Cues are extremely important; they are what the children can actually learn during a lesson (Graham, 1992).

7. Materials/Equipment   This section of the lesson plan is simply a list of equipment and materials that will be needed for the lesson. It serves as a handy checklist to make certain that everything is available prior to beginning the lesson. Given the hectic schedules of elementary schools, it's easy to forget a piece of equipment; the checklist is designed to prevent this from occurring.

8. Organization/Management   This section of the plan provides the teacher with a place to write down the different organizations and formats that'll be used during a lesson. Although this may not be necessary for experienced teachers, it's very helpful for beginning teachers; it leads them to think through the organizational formats that they might use during the lesson, thereby avoiding some of the problems that might occur, for example, when a teacher hasn't thought about how the children will move from one task to another.

9. Introduction   This extremely important part of the lesson "sets the tone" by providing the children with a cognitive scaffolding for what they'll learn—and why! Some teachers introduce the lesson as soon as the children arrive; others prefer to provide children with a chance to move for a few minutes first.

BOX 8.1   SAMPLE LESSON PLAN FOR SKILL THEME APPROACH

Catching

Class Name _____ Skill Level _____
Lesson Length _____
Number of Meetings per Week _____

Focus:	Catching
Subfocus:	Spatial awareness, underhand throwing
Objectives:	At the end of this lesson the children will have learned to 1. Move their arms in front of the body (elbows flexed) in preparation for catching the ball or beanbag 2. Extend their arms to catch the ball or beanbag CUES: Hands ready Extend
Materials/ Equipment	Various types of large, lightweight balls (plastic, beach balls, Nerf) Tennis balls, whiffle, yarn, small Nerf balls for stations Net, 6' x 8' (found in decorative section of drugstore) Small incline surface with sides (slide from backyard jungle gym; long box with sides, ends removed)
Organization/ Management	Children in self-space Children throw against a wall Stations: See diagram.

Introduction:

The skill we are working on today is actually one half of a two-part skill—throwing and catching. We are going to focus on catching—catching the ball with hands only. The skill of catching is important in many games we play as well as in junior high and high school sports like basketball, football, and softball.

Scattered around the room are different types and sizes of balls. Some are large, some are small, but all are lightweight so they will not hurt if they hit you when you are trying to catch. Spread out in general space and begin to toss the ball to yourself and catch it.

Task Development

1.0   As I observed you warming up, I noticed several of you were having trouble tossing the ball upward. Some balls were going far from your space; others were going back over your heads. Let's review the toss for a moment.

Cue   Hold the ball slightly in front of you with both hands. Toss the ball by lifting your arms upward, stopping the lifting when your arms are at shoulder height.

🅣 Practice again, tossing the ball only slightly above your head.

🅣 The toss looks much better. Now we are ready to concentrate on the catch. See if you can catch the ball

---

The "why" part of the introduction is especially important for the older grades and children in middle school (Graham, 1992).

10. Task Development   The section of the lesson plan that includes the tasks and activities for the lesson is referred to as the task development section. However, it includes much more than simply tasks or

activities. In the sample lesson plan in Box 8-1, we've provided a typical task development section that includes not only tasks (denoted by a 🅣), but also challenges (denoted by a 🅒). After you read Chapter 12, the meaning of each of these will become clearer to you as a way you can develop the tasks throughout a lesson. To provide a better "feel" for how teachers develop tasks, we have written the sample lesson in with your hands only. Sometimes it helps to let it bounce one time before you catch it. (*Model.*) Toss, bounce, catch. Ready? Begin.

Cue   Remember, bend your arms as you are getting ready for the catch. Think, "hands ready."

🅣 Toss the ball higher this time so the bounce will go as high as your head.

Cue   Reach for the ball. Don't wait and catch it against your body.

2.0   Stand approximately six to eight feet from the wall. Remember the bubble of your self-space and your neighbors'—don't stand too close. Toss the ball to the wall and catch it after it bounces one time.

🅣 Throw the ball just hard enough for it to rebound to you. Too much force will send it over your head.

🅣 Practice a couple of times more as I observe your readiness.

🅣 You appear to be ready to catch the ball as it rebounds from the wall without the bounce. When you feel comfortable, try this skill.

🅣 Return to your self-space scattered about the room. Toss the ball upward and catch it before it bounces.

🅒 See if you can catch the ball five times with no mistakes.

🅒 I will time you for thirty seconds. Try to toss and catch in your self-space without dropping the ball. (Older students: If we are 100% successful, I will never hear a ball touch the floor.)

Children at the precontrol level of skill development need mass practice and revisitation to the theme often. Station practice as revisitation will be enjoyable and beneficial.

Stations for Practice: Four stations are set up for practice of the skill we have been learning—catching. The stations are for fun but will give us additional practice

of our catching. Even professional athletes spend lots of time practicing the skill of catching.

Station 1: (Suspend a net approximately six feet above the floor, with the back corner higher than the front edge so the ball will roll off. (8-1/2" plastic balls) Toss the ball above the net. It will slowly roll down the net and drop off. Catch it before it bounces.

Station 2: (Use tennis balls, whiffle balls, yarn balls, Nerf balls.) Select a ball. Toss and catch it five times; you may let it bounce if you wish. After five catches, try another type of ball. Continue until you have used all the different types.

Station 3: (Use slide with raised edges, back against wall, slight incline; playground or plastic ball). Toss the ball up the slide. It will come back toward you quickly. Catch it first after one bounce, then before.

Station 4: Partner toss. Face your partner. First catch after a bounce and then without the bounce. When you are successful, you may take one step back if you wish.

Use this station to note individual visual tracking of the ball, hands/arms in ready position, and reaching for the ball.

Closure:

Our lesson today focused on throwing and catching. Which part were we concentrating on?

Do we catch with hands only or against the chest?

Show me the correct arm position for catching: correct, arms extended with elbows slightly bent.

Reflection:

Do the children get their arms/hands in ready position in preparation for the catch?

Do they extend their arms when they catch or do they still trap the ball against the chest?

Box 8-1 as a teacher might actually speak it to the children. In your plan you'll abbreviate the format presented here. Chapter 12 provides a more concise format for planning the task development section of the lesson.

11. Closure The closure, or conclusion, typically lasts no more than two or three minutes. The teacher

calls the children together and quickly reviews the key points of the lesson that were stated in the lesson objectives and emphasized throughout the class. As the sample lesson in Box 8-1 indicates, the teacher can phrase the closure in the form of questions. This is an especially important time to remind children of what has been emphasized throughout the class. It can also provide the teacher with important insights about whether the children have attained the lesson objectives (Graham, 1992).

12. Reflection   In a perfect world, there would be time at the end of every lesson for a teacher to reflect on the lesson just completed. Did I accomplish my objectives? Which tasks worked well? Which needed to be changed? What do I need to emphasize the next time I teach catching to this class?

In the real world, however, the teacher rarely has time to reflect on the lesson that was just taught—one class follows another, often with no break at all. However, the teacher usually has a few minutes in the day to jot down a few notes about what the children did or didn't accomplish. We suggest guiding the reflection by asking questions related to the objectives for the lesson. Realistically, the teacher often reflects about several classes that have been taught in a row and thus makes the best guess about what the children in those classes have learned and what might be changed in future lessons.

As you know, a well-developed plan can be somewhat lengthy, especially for beginning teachers. For this reason, many teachers find it helpful to write a brief outline on a five- by eight-inch card that they carry with them during the lesson as a handy reminder.

As you review these twelve steps for the lesson plan, you may find that certain steps are unnecessary for your situation. This is to be expected. We suggest that you adapt this format to meet your needs and then make plenty of copies for the year.

Making Planning Enjoyable

Planning is hard work. It takes time and energy to plan effective lessons that are exciting and interesting to children. Teachers who fail to plan well tend to return to old standbys—kickball, dodgeball, and four square—that contribute minimally to children's physical education.

You'll always be able to find something to do that is more interesting than planning lessons. So it's a good idea to devise ways to make planning easier and more fun. We've found the following ideas helpful:

- Set aside some time each day specifically for planning. Then you won't be constantly trying to find time to plan. Some people find that planning at school before they leave for home is effective; others prefer to arrive at school early to plan the day.
- Try to become excited about your plans. When you're excited about trying to present an idea in a new and interesting way, planning is fun, and you communicate your enthusiasm to your students.

- Don't hesitate to experiment. The worst that can happen is that a lesson won't work as planned. When this happens, we tell the children we were trying a new idea and it didn't work. Children understand and sometimes make worthwhile suggestions about how the idea might be improved.

When you set aside appropriate amounts of time, try new ideas, and attempt to make lessons exciting, planning becomes more enjoyable. And your attitude toward teaching will be affected. Most of us experience uncertainty when beginning a lesson (or anything else) for which we're unprepared. When you've planned a lesson thoroughly, the assurance and enthusiasm you feel can be contagious.

Recording Progress

A reflective teacher will want to record the progress that a particular class, group, or individual makes during a lesson. An elementary school physical education specialist may teach eight to twelve classes a day. Each group and each student will progress to a different degree and in a different way. A reflective teacher, whose approach takes these differences into consideration, will need notes on which to base the next day's (or week's) lessons.

You can write brief comments in a standard planning book or on index cards. Notes summarizing what was accomplished during a lesson help you plan the next day's lessons. Whenever possible, the day's schedule should include five or ten minutes between classes; you can use this time for recording observations and, if necessary, arranging equipment for the next class. When you don't have time to write, particularly when teaching a class as individuals, a cassette tape recorder is helpful. Just a few words on tape can help you remember the details of an important observation you made during the first lesson of the day. What seemed so clear at 9:00 A.M. is often opaque by 4:00 P.M.

Lesson Design

If children are to develop into skillful movers, they must do more than play games. Children need opportunities to practice skills in meaningful contexts. A successful teacher is able to create practice situations that are enjoyable, are appropriately designed, and allow for maximum participation. The teacher who can design interesting and exciting practice situations will rarely hear the question—asked so often by highly skilled unchallenged children—"When do we get to play a game?"

Interesting Lessons

Many children, particularly younger ones, don't understand the need to practice in order to become more skillful. Nor do they care. Children typically are interested only in the present and have little concern about the future, which seems remote. Young children more easily accept and enjoy lessons with immediate meaning. For example, we wouldn't teach second-graders how to turn on one foot (pivot) by having them perform a mass drill, because such an exercise would make little sense to them. We might have them jog around the gym and instruct them to "Spin around on one foot when you hear the drum and then continue jogging." On the next drumbeat we might ask them to "Pivot on the other foot" or to "Spin in the opposite direction." Later, when the children are able to travel dribbling a ball, we might ask them to "Spin on the drumbeat while continuing to dribble a ball." We don't teach skills as if all children really want to learn the skill because they intend to play on a varsity team in high school—they don't.

Variety in a lesson also makes the lesson more enjoyable. We try to give children a number of related practice opportunities in a single lesson, rather than having them practice the same skill the same way the entire lesson.

Appropriate Lessons

Children want to be challenged and successful at the same time. The ideal task is difficult enough so that the child can't do it as intended every time, yet easy enough so that the child is successful much of the time. If small children try to shoot a basketball through a ten-foot-high basket, their success rate may be so low that they'll quickly lose interest. If the same children are given options—for example, shooting at a basket seven feet high or shooting through a hoop suspended from a pole—their interest will remain higher for longer periods, and their skills will therefore improve.

Maximum Participation

One of the clearest differences between more effective and less effective teachers is that the students of more effective teachers actually spend more time practicing than do the children of less effective teachers (Rink, 1996; Siedentop, 1991). The value of practice may seem obvious, yet practice is frequently neglected, particularly in teaching games. When a class of thirty children practices a skill such as throwing or catching and uses only three or four balls, the children's skills will improve less than the skills of children whose teacher designs the same lesson so that there is a ball for every two children in the class.

Remember, though, that not all children have learned to practice on their own. Making more equipment available doesn't guarantee increased practice time. In fact, we've observed instances where the children in a class actually practiced more when there were only three or four balls available because most of the students in the class hadn't yet learned to work on their own.

SUMMARY

Planning is a crucial, although not necessarily the most enjoyable, part of the teaching process. Successful teachers plan effectively—not only their daily lessons, but also the entire program, as well as each year of the program. Plans are guides, not cast in stone. As you learn more about the school, the children, and the context of the teaching situation, plans change!

This chapter described four steps in the planning process. Step 1 is the development of a five- or six-year scope and sequence. Essentially the first step answers the questions "What will I teach?" and "In what grades?" Step 2 involves making the difficult decisions about how many days you will be able to focus on various skills and concepts—and which one should receive more or less emphasis. Benchmarks are formulated in step 3 as you determine when and how you will check to see what your children are learning. The final step is the creation of daily lesson plans. Twelve different parts of a lesson plan are described, along with examples to illustrate the process of planning daily lessons. The chapter concludes with ideas for creating lessons that are interesting, appropriate, and provide for maximum participation and success for the children.

READING COMPREHENSION QUESTIONS

1. What is meant by the term *reflective planning*? Think about your elementary school: Which contextual factors influenced the program and the way the teacher planned?
2. What might happen when a teacher does not bother to do steps 1 and 2 in the planning process and only plans day to day?
3. Tables 8.1 and 8.2 present sample scope and sequences for the movement concepts and skill themes. In your own words explain why some concepts and skills are not taught at various grade levels. Use specific concepts and skills in your explanation.
4. Using Table 8.3 as a guide select first, third, or fifth grade and do a yearly overview for that grade. Then write a brief analysis explaining what you changed from the grade before and after. So, for example, if you choose third grade, explain how your guide is different from ones for second and fourth grades.
5. Use the guide for planning daily lessons (Box 8-1) to plan one of your own lessons. Use one of the movement concept or skill theme chapters as a guide, but do not use the skills of throwing and catching.
6. Veteran teachers typically spend less time planning than beginning teachers. Why do you think this is often true?

REFERENCES

Glass, G. V., Cahen, L., Smith, M., & Filby, N. (1979, April–May). Class size and learning. *Today's Education*, pp. 42–44.

Graham, G. (1992). *Teaching children physical education.* Champaign, IL: Human Kinetics.

Graham, G., Hopple, C., Manross, M., & Sitzman, T. (1993). Novice and experienced children's physical education teachers: Insights into their situational decision-making. *Journal of Teaching in Physical Education, 12,* 197–217.

Holt/Hale, S. (1998). *On the move: Lesson plans to accompany children moving.* Mountain View, CA: Mayfield.

Housner, L., & Griffey, D. (1985). Teacher cognition: Differences in planning and interactive decision making between experienced and inexperienced teachers. *Research Quarterly for Exercise and Sport, 56,* 56–63.

Kelly, L. E. (1989). Instructional time: The overlooked factor in PE curriculum development. *Journal of Physical Education, Recreation and Dance, 60,* 29–32.

National Association for Sport and Physical Education (NASPE). (1995). *Moving into the future: National standards for physical education.* St. Louis, MO: Mosby.

Rink, J. E. (1996). Effective instruction in physical education. In S. Silverman and K. Ennis (Eds.), *Student learning in physical education* (pp. 171–198). Champaign, IL: Human Kinetics.

Siedentop, D. (1991). *Developing teaching skills in physical education* (3rd ed.). Mountain View, CA: Mayfield.

Establishing an Environment for Learning

A well run lesson that teaches nothing is just as useless as a chaotic lesson in which no academic work is possible.

——Walter Doyle

To teach effectively, it's necessary to establish an environment in which learning is supported and allowed to take place. Such an environment is a necessary, although not sufficient, condition for learning. Establishing the learning environment has been called a first-base skill—you can't get to home without getting on first, but getting there is only the first step to scoring a run (Rink, 1987). Without such an environment there is little chance that learning will occur, yet with it, learning is not guaranteed unless instructional activities are carried out. Establishing a learning environment involves using both managerial and instructional techniques to place students in contact with—and to keep them in contact with—the subject matter at a high success rate for as long as possible.

One of the easiest ways to think of the learning environment in physical education is as the working of two systems (Rink, 1993; Tousignant & Siedentop, 1983). Those systems—the instructional task system and the managerial task system—are important to the establishment of a climate conducive to effective learning. A *task system* can be defined as a regular pattern of practices used to accomplish the functions of a class. The *managerial task system* refers to the non-subject matter functions necessary for a class to run smoothly and efficiently over a period of time. The *instructional task system* refers to the subject-matter functions designed to see that children learn what we want them to by participating in physical education. Both types of systems need to be developed when establishing a learning environment. All too often physical education teachers establish a managerial system (Marks, 1988) but neglect to focus on an instructional system as well.

For each of these task systems certain teacher practices exist that ensure the system operates well. A well-functioning system establishes and maintains student responsibility for appropriate conduct, task involvement, and learning outcomes. These practices have come to be known as accountability measures (Doyle, 1980; Siedentop, 1991). These accountability measures are so important that without them both the instructional and managerial task systems become lax and may not even operate (Doyle, 1980). Traditional accountability measures in physical education are tests, grades, attendance, teacher reprimands, and punishment. This chapter will introduce you to a variety of other teacher practices that serve as accountability measures in establishing the managerial and instructional task systems necessary for a smoothly running class where learning occurs.

Although the development of the system sounds quite rigid, sterile, and certain, the type of system

> Classroom Management helps run an effective classroom, but doesn't solve the social problems.
>
> Don Hellison

developed reflects what we believe not only about physical education, but about education, children, and society. It reflects what we feel is important about our school, our gymnasium, our students, and ourselves. All systems must accomplish certain things—the smooth and consistent operation of the gym, for example—yet it is how the system is put into action that says who we are. For example, a managerial system that is solely teacher developed and directed indicates a belief that student input or helping students learn to make decisions isn't important. On the other hand, the complete lack of a managerial system could indicate an abdication by the teacher of all responsibility and a belief that it doesn't make any difference what we do (Ennis, 1995). However, systems that help students learn to make decisions about managerial (noninstructional) situations and instructional (learning) situations may indicate a belief that we have a responsibility to teach not only content but other goals as well. The National Standards indicate that one of the goals of physical education is to develop students who demonstrate responsible personal and social behavior in physical activity settings (NASPE, 1995). Although the accountability and managerial literature have largely developed from behavior management and business, where efficiency is paramount, there are models in which the development of responsibility and self-direction are important (Hellison, 1995). In these models, although initial efficiency may be slightly compromised and the teacher must be willing to relinquish some control, students gradually move toward more independent learning and responsibility.

It is our belief that physical education is child centered and students should develop increasing responsibility for their own behavior, attitudes, and learning. Therefore, the prevailing philosophy of this chapter is one of task systems that are designed to accomplish those goals. In other words, just like fitness and motor skill development, responsibility is part of the content with which students must stay in contact.

Of all the teacher practices involved in establishing a learning environment, one of the most important is also one of the least tangible and most easily compromised: teacher attitude or the translation of beliefs into practice. The teacher's self-image and feelings about teaching, about physical education, and about children all influence attitude. The teacher who is enthusiastic conveys this attitude to the children and as a result heightens their enthusiasm for physical education. The teacher who views physical education as a time for learning and work communicates this feeling to the children in the way he or she demands that all the children adhere to certain criteria for behavior.

The impact of teacher attitude on the learning environment is becoming clearer and clearer. A recent study illustrates the strength of teacher attitude on the atmosphere of a learning environment. Herbel and Parker (1995) studied middle-school boys in a basketball program who were constantly in trouble at school and at risk of dropping out. In the sports setting, however, the same students were well behaved and participated with no problems while actually helping each other (something that was not their normal pattern of behavior). When asked why they were different in the sports setting from school, the students' answer was plain and simple, "You listened to us." They expanded their answer to include having input into what occurred, being given responsibility for certain things, and not always being told what to do (especially about things that they interpreted as demeaning, e.g., dress, warm-up activities, etc.). Yet, these same boys were the ones who were off-task, rude, and disruptive in other classes. The power of the learning environment cannot be underestimated.

Some educators use the terms *developing a learning environment* and *discipline* as if they were synonymous, but we don't. Creating a learning environment is proactive; discipline is reactive. Discipline is required when a child's behavior is disruptive and the teacher needs to prevent the disruption from occurring again (see Chapter 10). When establishing a learning environment, the teacher focuses on fostering acceptable behavior and creating an atmosphere appropriate for a physical education class. Some discipline may be required in a physical education class, as in any class. An established, consistent, positive environment in the gymnasium, where the students know exactly what is expected of them, will reduce the need for discipline and stimulate enthusiasm for learning. The remainder of this chapter deals with ways teachers have been successful in developing both managerial and instructional task systems to establish a productive learning environment.

The Managerial Task System

The managerial task system establishes structures through which the physical education class becomes predictable and operates smoothly (Rink, 1993; Sieden-

top, 1991). When they begin school, most children have few preconceptions about how a physical education learning environment will be structured. Within a short time they learn to function according to the teacher's expectations. The managerial task system establishes the limits for behavior and the teacher's expectations for the students. Due to our beliefs in children developing responsibility for themselves and our dislike for constantly feeling as if it is our job to "control" students, the managerial task systems we develop focus not only on establishing an appropriate learning environment, but on having students take more and more responsibility for that environment. If youngsters are allowed to develop unacceptable behavior in physical education class, the teacher will find it increasingly difficult to alter their behavior. For this reason it's crucial that teachers establish an appropriate learning environment during their very first lessons with the students. How well they do this sets the tone for the remainder of the year. We've found the following techniques helpful in developing and holding students accountable for managerial task systems.

Getting Off to a Good Start

Typically, the first day a class meets, the teacher goes over the logistical and organizational rules and procedures she or he feels are essential for effective class functioning. Many times we've seen this done only in the first lesson via a lecture; the rules and procedures are never taught and never reviewed again, unless something goes wrong. In recent years, it has become increasingly obvious how really important the first few days of school are (Brooks, 1985; Brophy & Good, 1986; Krouscas, 1996): They establish the environment for the entire year. The students learn what behavior and attitude are appropriate in the gymnasium and what will be expected of them in physical education. It is then that they learn the class rules, both stated and unstated. When a situation arises and is consistently treated the same way, the students know the teacher means what has been said. This establishes the behavior and attitude that will typify a class for the remainder of the year. We've found the following suggestions helpful for getting off to a good start, and Figure 9.1 provides a checklist of items to ensure that you're ready for the beginning of the school year.

1. *Readying the gym.* Be certain that your gymnasium and materials are ready for the beginning of the year.

2. *Planning rules and routines.* Even if it is your plan to have students provide input into the rules and

Figure 9.1 Checklist for the beginning of school. *Source: Classroom Management for Elementary Teachers* by C. Evertson, E. Emmer, B. Clements, J. Sanford, & M. Worsham, 1984, Englewood Cliffs, NJ: Prentice-Hall.

CHECKLIST FOR THE BEGINNING OF SCHOOL

Item	Check When Done	Notes
1. Are your teaching areas and equipment ready?		
2. Have you decided your class rules, procedures, and consequences?		
3. Are you familiar with the parts of the school that you may use (halls, cafeteria, playgrounds, multipurpose room) and any procedures associated with their use?		
4. Do you have complete class rosters for each class you teach?		
5. Do you have file information on your students, including any comments from previous teachers and information on health problems?		
6. Do you know if any of your students have handicapping conditions?		
7. Do you have an adequate amount of equipment for all students?		
8. Have you established the procedure for the arrival and departure of the students from the physical education area?		
9. Are the children's name tags ready? Do you have some blank ones for unexpected students?		
10. Do you have your first day's plan of activities ready?		
11. Do you have rainy-day activities planned?		
12. Do you have a letter ready to send home to the parents with information about the school year and what materials or clothing the child will need to bring to school?		
13. Do you know how to obtain assistance from school staff members (e.g., school nurse, office personnel, resource teachers, and the custodians)?		

routines of the gymnasium, decide before you meet your students what general rules and routines are important and necessary for you. What is the general atmosphere you wish to create? In what way can you guide students? Even teachers who have students decide on rules and procedures often come prepared with generic guidelines (e.g., participation; treatment of others—students and teachers; safety; equipment) for operation of the gym. Students can then form specific rules within those guidelines. If you decide to develop the rules of the gym yourself, determine what procedures students need to follow for your gymna-

sium to run smoothly; decide what behaviors are acceptable and unacceptable; and develop a list of rules before the students' arrival. Regardless of how the rules are established, post them.

3. *Consequences.* As with rules, consequences need to be established for *appropriate* and *inappropriate* behavior. These, too, can be developed jointly or independently. They need to be communicated to students and followed through on consistently (see the next section for more about rules and consequences).

4. *Beginning-of-school activities.* Develop activities for the first few days of physical education that will involve students at a high success rate and have a whole-group focus (see Chapter 13). This gives you an opportunity to see who follows directions and to reinforce appropriate behavior and attitudes. Don't begin independent work until you are certain that individuals know what is expected of them. Teach the rules of behavior and expected attitudes as well as classroom procedures (e.g., what to do when arriving in class; how to take out, set up, and take down equipment; what to do in a fire drill). You can most easily do this by planning what the procedures will be, designing situations that allow students to practice the procedures, and teaching those procedures "in the gym." Spending time teaching behavior and attitudes at the beginning of the school year allows you to spend more time during the rest of the year teaching skills and much less time repeating what should have already become habit.

5. *Developing strategies for potential problems.* Anticipate problems in the content or gymnasium routine, and develop ways to prevent or reduce those problems.

6. *Monitoring.* In the early days, routinely check with students individually to determine how they're settling in and to gain other information that may be relevant to the physical education and school setting.

7. *Accountability.* Develop procedures that keep the students responsible for their work.

Developing Protocols

Research indicates that effective teachers develop gymnasium protocols that help their gyms run smoothly and minimize disruptions, thus maximizing students' learning time (Jones & Jones, 1990). These protocols consist of both rules and routines. *Rules* identify general expectations for behavior that cover a variety of situations. Though rules are intended to address both acceptable and unacceptable behavior, they quite often focus on inappropriate behavior. A concept that some teachers have found useful in changing the focus to the positive is explaining rules as guidelines to help children examine their behavior and attitudes as they affect themselves and others (Jones & Jones, 1990). *Routines* are procedures for accomplishing specific duties within a class. They are different from rules in that they usually refer to specific activities and are usually aimed at accomplishing tasks rather than forbidding behavior. Evidence has shown that effective teachers spend the first few days of the year teaching

protocols to their classes (Brophy & Good, 1986; Fink & Siedentop, 1989).

Protocols generally stay in effect for the school year (unless you find one that really isn't working or discover that something has been neglected). It is frustrating and time-consuming to repeat the protocols for new students or for students who were absent when they were taught. We have found it valuable to videotape the lessons at the beginning of the year when protocols are presented and taught. Then, when a new student joins the class the videotape can be used, either at school or at home, to orient that student to the protocols of your gymnasium. The tape is also a useful resource with parents at parent-teacher meetings to share classroom procedures or if needed to document the teaching of rules and routines to a class. This is also an especially good way to orient new students and remind others of safety procedures in class.

Establishing Rules and Expectations

The establishment of rules does more than provide the "laws" of the gymnasium, it sets the tone for the general atmosphere of the gym and conveys the teacher's beliefs about control and responsibility. If, for example, all the rules are developed by the teacher, are written as a series of "don'ts", and are narrow and punitive, this sends the message that the teacher is the ultimate control figure and children are merely persons to be controlled. If, however, children are allowed input and the rules are guiding and broader, allowing children some part in the decision making, then the message is that children are persons learning to be responsible; they are capable of making decisions and have self-worth. These messages may appear subtle, but they are very powerful to students. Therefore, our choice in the development of rules and routines is to be broad and guiding rather than narrow and restricting.

Children who understand the expectations within which they are to function are less likely to test the teacher's flexibility and more likely to cooperate. A few rules stated clearly and adhered to consistently by the teacher can be helpful to everyone. One set of guidelines that we have found effective—that help children examine their behaviors and attitudes—is an adaptation of Don Hellison's four levels of responsibility (Hellison, 1995) (Box 9.1). These guidelines are broad enough to encompass the aspects necessary for safe group survival in the gym while at the same time guiding students well beyond simple compliance.

Figure 9.2 shows how these guidelines can be translated into class rules. A discussion of the guidelines

BOX 9.1   RESPONSIBILITY LEVELS

Level I: Respecting the rights and feelings of others

Self-control
The right to be included
The right to peaceful conflict resolution

Level II: Participation and effort

Exploring effort
Trying new things
A personal definition of success

Level III: Self-direction

On-task independence
Personal plan
Balancing current and future needs
"Striving against external forces"

Level IV: Caring about and helping others

Prerequisite interpersonal skills
Compassion
Contributing member of the community and beyond
Without rewards

SOURCE: From *Teaching Responsibility Through Physical Activity* by D. Hellison, 1995, Champaign, IL: Human Kinetics. Used with permission.

can cover many things that are normally included in narrower rules. For example, respect for the rights and feelings of others can include all aspects of pushing, stopping and looking when the teacher talks, sportspersonship, interrupting, use of equipment, and the like. Participation and effort is broad enough to include the whole idea of trying hard (even when you might not want to), giving 100 percent, and the like. Interestingly enough these two guidelines alone encompass most of the rules we are accustomed to seeing in the gymnasium. The two other guidelines provide an extension that we consider important in our teaching. The third indicates that students should be able to work on their own, without the teacher's constant attention—a concept most of us relish. The fourth is one of our ultimate goals—that students be able to care for and help each other. This can include actions as small as handing stray balls back to their owners or as broad as helping another student learn a skill. We have found that when we establish this type of governing system and constantly adhere to it students learn to manage themselves and develop the concepts of personal and social responsibility that we desire as outcomes of our programs. With such a managerial system developed and in place we find that we are "managing" less, have more time for teaching, and have more fun teaching because we do not need to behave like police officers.

Rules are necessary for group survival and development. Figure 9.3 shows another set of gymnasium rules that teachers have found successful in eliciting the learning environment they desire. You may wish to establish different rules; if so, the following general guidelines may help you:

■ Explain why the rules are necessary. Children are far more cooperative with rules that make sense to them than with seemingly arbitrary regulations. In some cases children can help make the necessary rules.

Gymnasium Rules

Be nice to classmates, the teacher,
and the equipment.

Try everything—and try hard.

Do what you are supposed to do,
even when the teacher isn't looking.

Help others.

Figure 9.2   Translation of Hellison's (1995) responsibility levels into rules.

Physical Education Rules

1. Stop, look, & listen when you hear the signal. (Signal = whistle, freeze, lights out, & stop)

2. Participation = 100% every day—all day long.

3. Show good sportspersonship by playing fairly, following the rules, being honest, & cooperating.

4. Keep the noise level appropriate for the activity.
   Good Noise = Encouraging others.
   Bad Noise = Screeching and Screaming.

5. Treat others as you want to be treated. Work in your own space. Be helpful. Don't interrupt. Be courteous. Keep your hands to yourself.

6. Always remember SAFETY.
   Safety = wearing tennis shoes, moving under control, watching for others.

7. Handle equipment with care.

Figure 9.3   Gymnasium rules. *Source:* Denise Horpedahl, C. B. Eielson Elementary School, Grand Forks, ND.

- State rules positively. Whenever possible, avoid using the words "don't," "not," and "no."
- Keep the number of rules to a minimum. A good guide is to state no more than seven rules.
- Post rules in an attractive fashion so they can be seen and read easily.
- Make sure the children understand the rules. To teach rules most efficiently, first describe and demonstrate the desired behavior, then have the children rehearse the correct behavior (this usually takes more than one rehearsal), and finally provide feedback, especially the first time you ask the children to use a routine.
- Design, teach, post, and practice the consequences of breaking the rules.
- Especially in the beginning, prompt students toward appropriate behavior, and reinforce appropriate behavior. Let students know when they've done something correctly.

One of the obvious questions, although students don't always ask it, is "What happens when one of the rules is broken?" No matter how well we teach, some of the children will break some of the rules, so we find it helps at the outset of the year to describe the conse-quences for breaking a rule. These consequences are for relatively minor offenses; major offenses are discussed in Chapter 10.

The teacher needs to develop consequences appropriate to the particular teaching situation. Many teachers use a series of consequences similar to the following:

1. The first time a child violates a rule—for example, the child fails to stop and listen—give the child a *verbal* warning.
2. The second time a child violates a rule in the same class period, ask if the child "needs to sit out for a while." The child's response to this question is usually amazingly honest, and the question places the responsibility on the child for his or her actions.

Figure 9.4 Possible signals for attention.

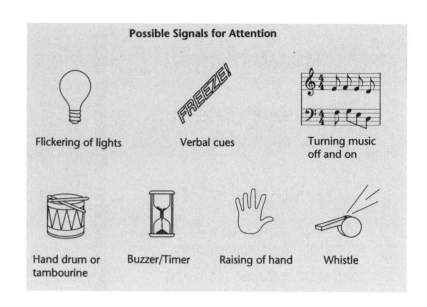

The child can reenter class when ready without consulting the teacher.

3. The third time a child violates a rule, have the child sit out until a personal plan can be developed regarding his or her actions (see Chapter 10). This usually means the remainder of the class. Although sitting out the remainder of the class may seem a bit harsh, as teachers we need to be able to teach. A continually disruptive child takes our attention away from other children who deserve it just as much.

As much as possible, the consequences for violating a rule should be noninterruptive. We try to deliver a consequence with a word or two and avoid interfering with the learning experiences of the rest of the class. One final comment about time-out: It is effective when the children find the lesson interesting. If the lesson is uninteresting, dull, or inappropriate for a child, then time-out becomes a reward rather than a consequence for off-task behavior.

Establishing Gymnasium Routines

Routines are procedures designed to help the gymnasium run smoothly and efficiently. Remember, routines are specific ways to accomplish certain tasks within a lesson; they should remain consistent as much as possible. Routines also reflect what we feel is important. Here are key areas in which physical education teachers find routines to be effective: entry to/exit from the gymnasium/playground; ways to handle, as well as obtain or return, equipment; signals for attention and starting and stopping activity

(Figure 9.4); the use of space; boundaries for work spaces; and "housekeeping" items like going to the restrooms, drinks, and leaving the room.

Routines can be taught to children just as you would teach content. To teach a routine, choose activities in which students can practice the routine. Describe the expectations for the routine (e.g., walk with the equipment to your space), have the children practice the routine, prompt the action often, and reinforce appropriate behavior. Follow this procedure for several days, and students will soon have the routines etched in their minds; you won't find yourself continually reminding children to walk when they pick up equipment.

Establishing a Positive Atmosphere   Though it may sound simple and inconsequential, one of the best things teachers can do to establish a productive classroom environment is to make the gymnasium a place students like to be (Herbel, 1996). The gym should be a warm, positive place where learning is enthusiastically pursued and teachers are excited about being there. One way to develop a positive gymnasium climate is to be sure there are many positive interactions. Positive reinforcement and praise need to dominate interactions with students. Students need to know when they have done something right. Unfortunately, many of the verbalizations in the gym are dominated instead by negative interactions: "I'm waiting for you to be quiet," "Any time now!!" and the like. Such comments are really nagging behaviors that are construed most often by students as negative. Positive statements such as "I like the way Denise is quiet" and "It's really helpful that Kevin is ready"

Figure 9.5 To become accustomed to them, these students practice routines for getting equipment.

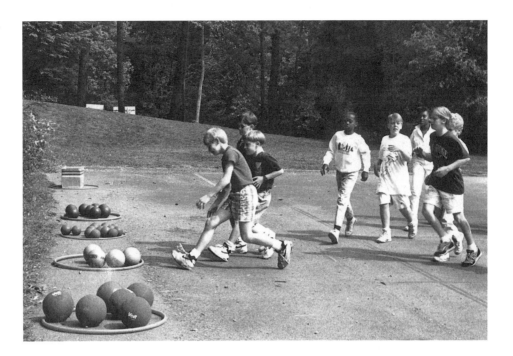

make strong contributions to a positive climate. (See Chapter 10 for ways to assess whether your interactions are positive or negative.) Other positive tone-setters might be brightening up the gym with posters and new paint or student artwork related to sports, or even music during warm-ups or extended activity periods.

Choosing Routines That Reflect a Positive Atmosphere   Routines do much to reflect what we think of students and what we believe about them and thus send very clear messages to students. By the nature of how they are implemented routines can tell students that they are competent and capable or dependent and not to be trusted. Martinek (1988) found that teachers developed learned helplessness in students by creating low expectations for them. Conversely, Herbel (1996) found that students, when given and taught seemingly high expectations for things such as responsibility and their own learning, lived up to them. Although some of the actions may be subtle, the difference in the two scenarios appears to center around how much perceived control the students have over some basic decisions. Routines that rob students of basic decisions or allow no alternative seem to cause resentment and let the students transfer responsibility for their actions to the teacher. Alternatively, routines that allow students some flexibility and decision making seem to empower them (Figure 9.5).

For example, routines are usually developed around restroom use. In some classes, students must either ask the teacher before they leave or use the restroom before they enter the gym. Both routines assume that students aren't responsible enough to make a "good" decision on their own. On the other hand, a restroom routine that involves a tag on the wall (similar to the key at a gas station) and allows the student to use the restroom whenever the "key" is there assumes that the student is capable of making the decision. Through the use of the "key" the teacher has helped structure and manage the decision, while at the same time allowing the student to make the main decision independently. Many of us will never forget the child who wet his or her pants because we said he or she "could wait."

Table 9.1 compares gymnasium routines that enable and don't enable students. The basic idea is that any decisions we can help students learn to make on their own serve to make them more independent and competent and to build feelings of self-worth and confidence, reducing behavior problems. Taking decisions students are capable of making away from them fosters dependence and usually creates behavior problems. The key factor is first teaching students to make decisions competently. The net result of this instruction is that we as teachers are freed from trivial decisions that detract from our ability to teach—and we have a classroom that manages itself.

BOX 9.2   LISTENING GAMES

In a successful learning environment, noise rarely exceeds a reasonable level that can be thought of as "busy noise." Hollering, shrieking, and yelling are appropriate at recess. In physical education class, the children shouldn't be expected to be silent, but they should be able to hear a teacher speaking in a reasonable tone, considerably below a shout. You can use the games described below to establish an appropriate noise level; the objective of these games is to teach the children to listen for the teacher as they move.

These listening games are designed to help the children learn to stop as quickly as possible when responding appropriately to the teacher's verbal challenge. Try not to single out children who are slow, and don't use penalties as a form of discipline. Embarrassment and punishment are both counterproductive; you want children to enjoy exercise, not to think of it as unpleasant.

Stop and Go

Children travel in general space in a scattered formation. Once the children are able to (1) walk without touching others and (2) stay far away from others as they walk, you can begin to play Stop and Go. When you say "Stop," the children should stop and freeze instantly. When you say "Go," they should begin to travel again.

Don't shout the signals—speak them, so that the children become accustomed to listening for your voice at a reasonable level.

Body Parts

This game focuses on the different body parts. Once the children have adjusted to Stop and Go, they enjoy the challenge of touching the floor with different body parts—elbow, seat, knee, wrist, waist, left hand, or right foot—as quickly as they can when you say "Stop."

Traveling

Once the children have learned to travel using different locomotor patterns, variations in these patterns are appropriate. Call out different ways of traveling—skipping, hopping, crab-walking, galloping—and challenge the children to change from one to another as rapidly as possible. You can increase the challenge of this game by combining traveling and the concept of direction—for example, gallop backward or hop to the right.

Circles

This game can be played on a painted playground surface or in a gymnasium. Before class, draw circles, trian-

Table 9.1   Routines That Promote (and Don't Promote) Decision Making

Task	Promotes	Doesn't Promote
Getting equipment	Spread equipment and have students walk to pick it up.	Hand out equipment.
Entering the gymnasium	Post initial activity; students begin to practice as soon as they enter.	Students line up, waiting for the teacher.
Choosing partners	Students choose partners with whom they can practice productively.	Teacher assigns partners.
Dress	Students choose appropriate clothing that allows them to participate freely.	Students wear uniforms.
Getting water	Students get a drink when they need it, if no one else is at the drinking fountain.	Drinking is permitted only before or after class.

gles, squares, and so on, on the ground. The object is for the children to move as quickly as possible to the shape you name; for example, if you call out "circle," the children stand on a circle as quickly as possible. You can use colors instead of or in combination with shapes if the surface you're using is painted various colors. The terms you use will be determined by your pupils' knowledge of colors and shapes.

Numbers

In one version of this game, the children stop with the appropriate number of body parts touching the ground. For example, if you call out "three," the children should stop with three body parts touching the ground.

In a second version, the children stop in groups. The number the teacher calls determines the size of the group. This game is helpful when you want the children to form into groups of three, four, or five in a hurry.

Combinations

As children learn each variation, they find it challenging and fun to play several games at once. For example, you might call out a body part or a color or a locomotor pattern or a number. Children thrive on increasingly difficult games.

Switch and Rotate

The purpose of this game is primarily to teach listening, but it's more appropriate for older children. The object of the game is to stay so close to a partner that when the teacher says "Stop" and the players freeze, the follower can still touch the leader. When the teacher says "Switch," the partners change roles, and the follower becomes the leader.

You can make this game more difficult by increasing the size of the group to three, then four, then five. The object of the game remains the same: Each child should be able to touch the person in front as soon as you say "Stop." When you add the challenge "Rotate," the leader goes to the end of the line and becomes a follower. Children find the challenge of listening and responding instantly while trying to remain close to the children in front of them fascinating. You can make this game more challenging by varying the locomotor patterns, for example, from walking to skipping to hopping to galloping to running.

Teaching Stopping and Listening Routines   One of the seemingly hardest routines to teach children in physical education is to stop activity quickly and listen to the teacher. When a teacher must spend time quieting the children so that the entire class can hear an explanation or comment, the amount of time left for activities is decreased. Physical activity, by its nature, is noisier than classroom activity, and children tend to be even louder on a playground than in a gymnasium. Thus it's imperative that children learn to respond quickly and appropriately to the teacher's signal for quiet. Listening games (Box 9.2) can be used to teach children to listen as they move and to respond quickly to the teacher's signals.

You might initially assign a criterion of five seconds as a reasonable amount of time for the children to stop and listen after they hear the stop signal. If the entire class stops and listens in five seconds or less, praise them. If they don't, explain that taking more than five seconds is too slow and have them practice again because it's a waste of time to take that long.

Gradually raise the standard as the children become more proficient. The children often view these races against the clock as fun games and delight in praise from the teacher when they perform well. They also enjoy trying to beat their own records. This approach provides far more time for activity and instruction. As the children learn the value of spending less time on management tasks, you can eliminate these races against the clock.

Teachers must be clear, concise, and to the point. As a general rule, once a class has begun, we try to keep our verbal explanations to less than one minute. Although this isn't always possible (or even appropriate), it does help to increase the children's willingness to stop and listen to us.

The Instructional Task System

It is not enough to create a reasonable place in which students are able to learn; we must also teach so students can learn. For us, the learning of motor skills and fitness concepts is the unique goal of physical education. It provides the focus that guides our actions as teachers and directs student attention as well as participation and attitudes. Student learning is therefore an important consideration in how we organize and maintain order in the gymnasium. Students are more likely to learn when expectations about organization, management, and learning are communicated. Although many of us are accustomed to these expectations as part of the managerial task system, they also are a component of the instructional task system. Simply, more learning occurs when students understand and value learning goals; when a task has a definite aim or focus; and when content is made personal, concrete, and familiar.

If students are to be held accountable for learning expectations that we have set, it is essential they accomplish the task as intended. Accountability in a managerial system is clear: If a student is asked to walk and instead runs, he or she is asked to start over again and walk. Accountability also exists with motor performance, but the strategies differ. Typically we have used testing as the major accountability system for learning in physical education. Unfortunately, testing occurs infrequently and only at the end of a unit. Authentic assessment practices have helped alleviate that problem (see Chapter 14). Yet, to truly learn and understand, students need ongoing accountability systems. Effective teachers utilize a variety of accountability practices to create effective instructional task systems that keep students on task, focused, and motivated to improve their performance. These are thoroughly developed in Chapter 12, but they are summarized here to reinforce the interrelatedness of the learning environment.

Varying the type of task builds accountability into the instructional task. The use of challenge tasks on a regular basis gives students the opportunity to focus their work as well as assess their learning on an informal, regular basis. Though there is no magic number or mix, we have found it a reasonable goal to always include one or two challenge tasks for every task we give. It has been our finding that appropriate, challenging content eliminates about 90 percent of the potential behavior problems in class.

Learning cues also provide students with an instructional accountability mechanism. Cues are simply short phrases or words that focus the learner on the salient aspects of the skill to be practiced. Usually one or two cues are all that students can remember at one time. If for every task presented the last thing the teacher did was to repeat the cues for the task, many students would be highly focused. Major cues are pro-

vided at the beginning of each control-through-proficiency-level task in the skill theme chapters.

Providing specific congruent feedback about students' performance increases the accountability for learning. Specific congruent feedback means feedback that is directly related to the cues given with the task and nothing else. If a teacher provides such feedback student performance is then more directed and focused.

Public challenges and recognition can also be used as instructional accountability systems. These systems need not be elaborate or time-consuming and can all be done in nonthreatening ways. Asking "How many did you catch? Five? Ten? Fifteen?" lets students assess themselves against a teacher-set standard, but at the same time does not embarrass the child. *Public recognition* at the end of class of several students or groups who did really well also has been used effectively by many teachers.

Whatever the strategy, to learn, students must have a focus for the activity and be held accountable for realizing the focus. Without focus and accountability students will lack motivation, not learn the intended content, and begin to behave in inappropriate ways.

Teaching Skills for Establishing a Learning Environment

The preceding sections emphasized the importance of managerial and instructional task systems as well as the tasks necessary to create them. A variety of generic skills is also used by effective teachers to help create and maintain these systems. Such skills include setting performance standards, maintaining consistency, and monitoring and reacting to students.

Setting Performance Standards

Effective teachers set high but reasonable expectations for students and communicate them to the children. These expectations apply to both managerial and instructional aspects of the class. We've found that an easy way to do this is to teach with a *critical demandingness* (Brophy & Evertson, 1976), which means that we set standards and consistently adhere to them so that the children know exactly what is expected. For example, we've established performance standards for

Students don't need to be fearful of a teacher to listen to them.

Mark Murdock, practicum student, after his first time teaching sixth grade many of the daily management tasks, such as putting away equipment or lining up to go back to the classroom.

Performance standards are really a way for teachers to communicate exactly what they expect. When these expectations are clear, the children understand what the teacher desires. For example, children know that they're to put away the ball if the teacher has clearly stated this expectation. When the expectation isn't clear, however, several children may throw their ball from halfway across the gym, hoping that somehow the ball will land in the appropriate container or location. But the expectation is that children will *place*, not throw, the ball into the appropriate box (or hoop). Unfortunately, some classes need several practice episodes before the children learn that the teacher means business. The children need to learn that putting the ball away rather than throwing it isn't something the teacher hopes they do—it's something the teacher *insists* they do. This avoids the chaos and disruption that can occur when standards for performance aren't set and adhered to.

Maintaining Consistency

When establishing a classroom atmosphere, it's very important that teachers be consistent in what they expect from one day to the next, to avoid *slippage* (letting the children become lax as the year progresses). The management techniques suggested by Kounin (1970) outline effective ways to maintain consistency.

Students learn best when the gymnasium is a predictable place to be. Rules and routines must be followed in a habitual fashion. For example, if children are allowed one day to take out equipment mats by dragging them across the floor but the next day four people are required to carry each mat, what Doyle (1979) calls ambiguity exists: The students really don't know what is expected of them. These misleading practices must be eliminated, and the function of the gymnasium must follow a set routine so that procedural aspects of the class occur the same way each time.

Monitoring and Reacting

The following techniques are effective for monitoring and subsequently handling student behavior during class:

- Keep movement patterns unpredictable. Vary the way you move through the class during activity, and stand in various places to instruct the class.
- Scan the class frequently to "catch students being good." To scan, quickly look across the class in a predetermined direction, usually left to right, at regular intervals.
- Provide clear and precise directions, and repeat them at least once for clarity; then ask questions to check for understanding.
- Maintain *withitness*, the quality of appearing to have eyes in the back of your head (Kounin, 1970).
- *Overlap* (attend to two issues simultaneously) (Kounin, 1970).
- Avoid *dangles* (issues left in midair) (Kounin, 1970).
- Avoid *flipflopping* (terminating one activity, starting another, and returning to the first activity) (Kounin, 1970).
- Use *targeting* (direct your interactions toward the appropriate student) (Siedentop, 1991).
- Display the skill of *timing*. As a general rule, the shorter the lag time between student action and teacher behavior, the better (Siedentop, 1991).

Using these skills enables a teacher to avoid what Kounin (1970) calls the *ripple effect*, which occurs when one class member involves several others in a rapidly spreading circle of off-task behavior. The classic example of the ripple effect resulting from ineffective targeting and timing is attempting to identify who started a fight:

Teacher: All right, who started the fight?
   Ted: Ray pushed me first.
  Ray: Well, Ted threw a rock at me.
  Ted: But I was aiming for Bobby because he called me a dumbbell.

If a teacher practices these techniques consistently and regularly, the functioning of the gymnasium is more likely to progress in a manner that enhances learning. Furthermore, discipline problems, although they won't vanish, will be curtailed.

Teaching Safety Procedures

Although teaching safety procedures could logically be included within the managerial task system, it is so important that we have chosen to address it separately. We discuss it in generic terms here, but we also include specific safety aspects in each skill theme development chapter: these are coded with the safety icon ⚠.

A major responsibility of every physical education teacher is to provide students with a safe learning environment, both physically and psychologically (Siedentop, 1991). You as a teacher are entrusted with the safety of students in your class. That responsibility cannot be given to anyone else. As with other aspects of the learning environment, safety needs to be

Figure 9.6 Checklist for a productive learning environment.

CHECKLIST FOR A PRODUCTIVE LEARNING ENVIRONMENT

Item	Check When Done	Notes
1. Were rules reviewed?		
2. Were rules followed?		
3. Was positive feedback given when students practiced a procedure correctly?		
4. Were directions and demonstrations given so all children could see and hear?		
5. Was inappropriate behavior stopped immediately?		
6. Were rules and procedures posted so all could see and read them?		
7. Was equipment gotten safely and efficiently?		
8. Did all children know the stop signal?		
9. Were any new students spoken to individually at least once?		
10. Did class begin immediately when students entered the area?		
11. Was students' appropriate behavior rewarded in some way?		
12. Were the designed consequences administered to all students who displayed inappropriate behavior?		

taught. We can't expect children to learn and practice safety simply by listening once or twice to explanations of safety procedures. Although you should certainly plan for safety, it is ultimately the conduct of the task where safety is most important.

General safety procedures can easily be taught at the beginning of the school year by incorporating them with and encompassing them by other gymnasium rules and routines. These safety procedures must be explained and then taught as well as practiced.

We've found that special safety procedures, ones that deal with specialized equipment or unique situations, are most effectively taught at the time that situation arises. Again, the procedures shouldn't be

glossed over; students should thoroughly understand them before you proceed. When specific safety rules are presented and taught, it is again a good time to videotape the teaching—for students who may be absent, for those who tend to forget, or in case of legal action.

It's beneficial to explain why selected behaviors are inappropriate and safety procedures necessary. Explaining the possible harmful consequences of actions helps children understand the need for stated practices. As with all ongoing gymnasium rules, the consequences of breaking safety rules must be stated; they might easily be included in the general rules for behavior. The children need to understand that safety is *their* responsibility as well as the teacher's when activity begins. Student safety should be the first thing the teacher observes for when the children begin a task (see Chapter 11). Proper task progressions are also critically important to the safety of students. A student must possess all the prerequisite skills before beginning a new task. A teacher who skips from the precontrol level to the proficiency level when students are still at the precontrol level has not followed a proper progression. The teacher, in this case, is simply asking for safety and legal problems. Accurate records of lesson and unit plans allow teachers not only to establish proper progressions but also to document them.

Students need to behave safely in a safe environment. They also need to feel safe about what they are doing in class. Students who feel comfortable about what they are doing and are willing to participate fully by experiencing appropriate task progressions tend to behave safely, because they are challenged by the task at hand yet feel able to accomplish it.

As physical educators, we have always been conscious of safety, but in today's world of increasing legal action against teachers, we simply have to become more cautious and thorough in all that we do. To do anything less risks student injury as well as legal action.

A Time for Reflection

Quite often it's very easy to forget what actually happened in a class—how much you accomplished, what you didn't accomplish, what was understood and misunderstood. Figure 9.6 is a checklist of the critical aspects presented in this chapter; you may want to refer to it often at the beginning of the year. As the year progresses, you may want to use the checklist once a day or even once a week. If you consistently find items that aren't checked, you may want to begin to modify some of your teaching behaviors.

SUMMARY

A teacher must distinguish physical education class from recess. Once children truly understand the difference between purposeful practice (physical education class) and "doing your own thing" (recess), they're far more willing to participate in the development of a learning environment.

A new teacher needs to begin to develop both the managerial and instructional task systems of a learning environment immediately, as does the teacher working with a new class. Designing lessons that involve the children in activity most of the time is one positive approach to establishing a learning environment. Excessive management time and waiting time, often the result of poor organization, tend to hinder the creation of an appropriate atmosphere.

When children have acquired suitable listening skills and safety practices, when they accept the responsibility for their own actions and cooperate with others, the alternatives for class organization are increased significantly. The teacher who clearly states and consistently adheres to rules of behavior and standards for performance will have productive lessons and enthusiastic students.

READING COMPREHENSION QUESTIONS

1. What is the difference between physical education class and recess?
2. What is discipline? How does discipline differ from establishing a learning environment?
3. What are three activities you can use to teach children to listen in a physical education environment?
4. List five guidelines for establishing rules of behavior in the gymnasium.
5. In your words, what does *critical demandingness* mean?
6. Why are the first lessons of the year so important? List five suggestions for those lessons.
7. Why are effective monitoring skills important? Name three monitoring skills a teacher should employ.

8. What are task systems? What are the task systems in physical education?
9. Define *accountability measures*. List three accountability measures for each of the task systems in physical education.

REFERENCES

Brooks, D. M. (1985). The first day of school. *Educational Leadership, 42*(8), 76–78.

Brophy, J., & Evertson, C. (1976). *Learning from teaching: A developmental perspective.* Boston: Allyn & Bacon.

Brophy, J., & Good, T. (1986). Teacher behavior and student achievement. In M. Wittrock (Ed.), *Handbook of research on teaching,* (328–375), New York: Holt, Rinehart & Winston.

Doyle, W. (1979). Making managerial decisions in classrooms. In D. L. Duke (Ed.), *Classroom management: Seventy-eighth yearbook of the National Society for the Study of Education, Part 2.* Chicago: University of Chicago Press.

Doyle, W. (1980). *Student mediating responses in teaching effectiveness.* Denton, TX: North Texas State University (ERIC No. ED 187 698).

Doyle, W. (1986). Classroom management and organization. In M. Wittrock (Ed.), *Handbook of research on teaching,* (392–431), New York: Holt, Rinehart & Winston.

Ennis, C. (1995). Teacher's responses to noncompliant students: The realities and consequences of a negotiated curriculum. *Teaching and Teacher Education, 11*(5), 445–460.

Fink, J., & Siedentop, D. (1989). The development of routines, rules, and expectations at the start of the school year. *Journal of Teaching in Physical Education, 8*(3), 198–221.

Hellison, D. (1995). *Teaching personal and social responsibility through physical activity.* Champaign, IL: Human Kinetics.

Herbel, K. (1996). *Youth, basketball and responsibility: A fairy tale ending.* Unpublished master's thesis, University of North Dakota, Grand Forks.

Herbel, K., & Parker, M. (1995). *Same story, different setting: A case study of a program for at-risk youth.* Paper presented at the Northern Rocky Mountain Educational Research Convention, October, Jackson Hole, WY.

Jones, V., & Jones, L. (1990). *Comprehensive classroom management.* Boston: Allyn & Bacon.

Kounin, J. (1970). *Discipline and group management in the classroom.* New York: Holt, Rinehart & Winston.

Krouscas, J. (1996). No substitute for the first day of school. *Strategies, 10*(1), 5–8.

Marks, M. (1988). *Development of a system for the observation of task structures in physical education.* Unpublished doctoral dissertation, Ohio State University, Columbus.

Martinek, T. (1988). Conformation of the teacher expectancy model: Student perceptions and causal attributions of teacher behavior. *Research Quarterly for Exercise and Sport, 59,* 118–126.

National Association for Sport and Physical Education (NASPE). (1995). *Moving into the future: National standards for physical education.* St. Louis, MO: Mosby.

Rink, J. (1987). *The learning game: A baseball theory of teacher effectiveness.* Unpublished manuscript.

Rink, J. (1993). *Teaching physical education for learning* (2nd ed.). St. Louis, MO: Mosby.

Siedentop, D. (1991). *Developing teaching skills in physical education* (3rd ed.). Mountain View, CA: Mayfield.

Tousignant, M., & Siedentop, D. (1983). The analysis of task structures in physical education. *Journal of Teaching in Physical Education, 3*(1), 45–57.

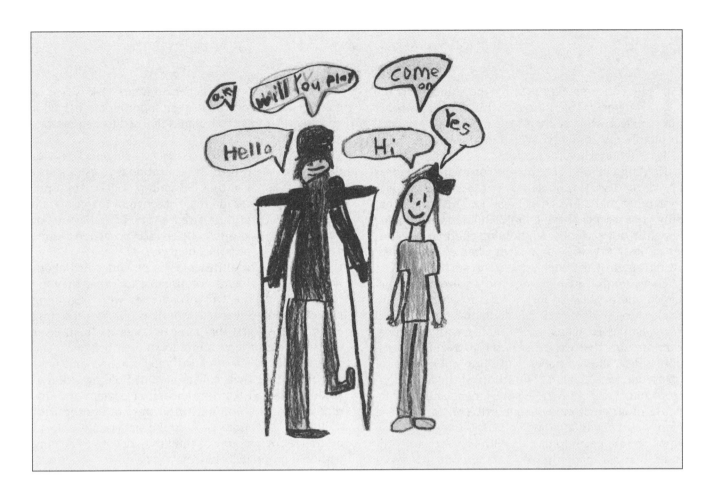

CHAPTER 10

Maintaining Appropriate Behavior

The thing that worries me is my lesson may not be good enough and students will get bored and be disruptive.

The only thing I am anxious about is if they [the students] decide to go berserk.

I am most worried that the students won't want to work as a team, that they will want to just mess around.

I am most worried that the students won't give full participation—won't listen—and I will revert back to the typical militaristic-like style.

I am anxious about discipline.

—University students before teaching sixth grade for the first time

The concerns expressed by the students in the statements that introduce this chapter probably reflect what many teachers feel: Will I be able to handle my students? Will they do what is right? What will I do when they don't?

Holding children accountable for their behavior is one of the least enjoyable tasks of teaching, but it is something that all teachers must do. The notion that only poor teachers have to hold children accountable is simply not accurate. Yet, holding children accountable is less likely to be a problem when effective managerial and instructional task systems are in place.

Consistently maintaining the environment designed and established for the class is second only to establishing it. Some call this discipline, but the word *discipline* has so many varied, and mostly negative, connotations that we have chosen to avoid it. Discipline most often implies punishing some type of inappropriate behavior. That, for us, is the last resort. From our viewpoint, the establishment and maintenance of an environment supportive of learning is a more positive and appropriate perspective. We follow a positive approach to dealing with behavior and attitudes that are inappropriate, an approach that lets a teacher both create a positive atmosphere and teach students appropriate behavior for the gymnasium. In

such a situation, the teacher's primary task is first to employ techniques that create appropriate behavior and second, to use techniques that reduce inappropriate behavior.

We define *appropriate behavior* as student behavior that is consistent with the educational goals of a specific educational setting (Siedentop, 1991). Appropriate behavior is *not* the mere absence of inappropriate behavior; rather, it is itself a set of behaviors or actions. These positive behaviors or actions must replace the inappropriate behavior.

It's normal for all teachers to be concerned about how to hold students accountable for what they are "supposed" to do. Our experiences with beginning and experienced teachers as well as our own teaching experiences suggest that most teachers ask themselves questions about responding to student behavior. The difference between so-called good teachers and poor teachers is not their concern about holding children accountable—all teachers encounter deviant and disruptive behavior and must find ways of dealing with it. Rather, the more successful teachers are able to minimize the amount of time they devote to dealing with inappropriate behavior.

Even the teacher who develops managerial and instructional task systems, establishes and explains rules of behavior, teaches with a critical demandingness, and sets and adheres to performance standards can't be sure that a class will perform as expected. In many classes there will be some children who find it difficult to function in a school environment, not only in physical education but in other classes as well. Occasionally an entire class has difficulty adhering to the behavioral boundaries the teacher has established.

Whether it is one, several, or most of the children who are unable to abide by the rules, your first response might well be to examine your performance as a teacher. When children react in unexpected ways, you may, upon reflection, find that their reactions are justified. Children are incredibly honest. A teacher may not want to know or believe that a lesson is a dud, but the children will let the teacher know. Occasionally it's the teacher's behavior, rather than the children's, that needs to be changed.

If you determine that the lesson is appropriate and your performance as a teacher is satisfactory, you can then look for other causes for disruptive behavior. Try not to view disruptive behavior as a personal affront. Instead, deal with it in two phases: reacting appropriately in the short term and seeking to understand the cause in the long term.

Comparing a referee or an umpire's job with the teacher's need to hold children accountable places a teacher's job in perspective. Those referees respected

> The class proceeded through its parody of education, following a formula validated in a thousand classrooms I have visited and countless thousands I have not. The first step in the formula is an assumption, an untested hypothesis which becomes valid merely because (and as soon as) it is assumed. Children who do not easily take the imprint of their teacher's own education and values, who are not ductile enough to be drawn wire-thin so that they may slip through traditional holes in the fabric of society—these are not "promising children" and the best that can be hoped for from them is good behavior (silence) and early withdrawal (dropout). Since silence is their most positive attribute, they should be left unmolested during the class hour so long as they practice that virtue.
>
> Perhaps worst of all the many dreadful aspects of this assumption is that *the children know it.* They know—and will tell you, as they told me, if they are asked—that a few of them are regarded as "good material" and the rest are nothing: "ever' time I go to her class, she make me feel like I was nothin'." Snapper, Rubbergut's half brother, said it. He said it for all the children who drown in the well of silence.
>
> Daniel Fader, *The Naked Children*

by players and coaches share the following characteristics: They're fair, consistent, accurate, and unemotionally involved. As teachers, we should keep these good characteristics in mind as we reflect on how to help children work within our guidelines.

Although a referee's job is less enjoyable than a player's or coach's, at least to us, it's an important aspect of organized sport. Similarly, maintaining the learning environment is an important role for a teacher. In physical education, as in sports, there will be violations and infractions.

Our goal is to help children become intrinsically motivated so that they can benefit from and enjoy physical activity. In some situations, this motivation will occur naturally, so few of the techniques described will be necessary. In other teaching situations, however, many of the techniques will be needed. In either situation, the goal is to use fewer and fewer of these techniques so that the children participate in physical education because they like it and feel it is valuable rather than because of an external reward or motivator. Our explanation of effective techniques for helping children work within our guidelines is divided into three steps: increasing appropriate behavior, decreasing inappropriate behavior, and maintaining whole-class appropriate behavior.

Increasing Appropriate Behavior

When behavior doesn't conform to the expectations established for the specific setting, the teacher must first attempt to increase appropriate behavior. Six techniques teachers have found useful for increasing appropriate behavior are positive interaction, eliminating differential treatment, prompting, nonverbal teacher interactions, ignoring inappropriate behavior, and person-to-person dialogue. Three of these techniques are proactive—that is, they are to be used in the absence of inappropriate behavior; the other three are reactive, to be used in response to inappropriate behavior.

Proactive Strategies

Teachers can do many things to increase the likelihood of students' behaving appropriately. And, many of these things can be done proactively to increase the likelihood that appropriate behavior will prevail.

Positive Interaction   As discussed in Chapter 9, one of the most powerful things a teacher can do to create an environment where students want to be is to make the gymnasium a positive place. One of the

most convincing means of creating a positive environment is to interact with students in a positive way when they behave in an appropriate manner. In essence, this approach emphasizes the positive rather than the negative. Many children who are known throughout the school as "discipline problems" have become accustomed to hearing nothing but negative comments about their behavior. Catching them in the act of doing something right and praising them for it can dramatically change their behavior (Siedentop, 1991).

But note that praise shouldn't be contrived and meaningless, offered with no genuine feeling, as is often the case. Give praise frequently but not so profusely that it seems trivial. And give it only when a child actually displays appropriate behavior. All children are capable of receiving some type of praise— catch them being good!

This sounds like common sense, but research (Siedentop & Taggart, 1984) and our experiences have shown that this isn't the prevalent mode of operation in the gym. Siedentop and Taggart (1984) found that "punitive and corrective interaction" were the most frequent forms of communication (p. 105). You can stand at many gymnasium doors and hear statements like these: "I'm waiting for you!" "Ssshh!" "Ben, whenever you sit down, we'll start," and "Kari, carry the ball." Although these statements aren't openly negative, they in fact reinforce the inappropriate behavior of certain children and ignore the appropriate behavior of a large majority of students. They are what might be called nagging behaviors. Instead, the following list includes examples of positive verbal (left-hand column) and nonverbal interactions. For an idea of how you're doing, have a student make a simple tally or videotape a class and critique your own behavior:

Verbal positive statements	Nonverbal positive interactions
Good	High five
Terrific	Smiling
Right	Clapping
Nice job	Thumbs up
Way to go	Winking
That's it	Pat on the back
Thank you	Shaking hands
Great	Giving an OK sign
You did it this time	
Beautiful	
Excellent	
Nicely done	
OK	
All right	

Every person needs recognition. It is expressed cogently by the lad who says, "Mother, let's play darts. I'll throw the darts and you say 'Wonderful.'"

Dale Baughman

	Name called	Reprimand	Positive Interaction
Mike	|||			||
Sue			
Rich	||				
Bill			
Don	~~||||~~ ||||	||||	~~||||~~
Billie					

Figure 10.1 Chart for identifying differential treatment of students.

Eliminating Differential Treatment Often a stranger can walk into a classroom and after a few minutes pick out the "discipline problems" in a group of children he or she has never seen before. Frequently these are the children whose names the teacher is constantly calling out: "Rico, are you listening?" "Sarah, sit down, please." (By the way, saying "please" doesn't automatically make something a positive interaction!) It is not uncommon to see the same children singled out repeatedly. Typically these children are masters of their craft—they know exactly how far they can go without actually being held accountable. Because they covet adult attention, these children persist in their behavior (and as long as we reinforce their behavior by acknowledging it, they become even more skilled at it). So, avoid singling out these children whenever possible.

One way to spot differential treatment of students in your classes is to tape-record a few lessons. Place a tape recorder in the gymnasium or attach it to a belt around your waist. (This observation and assessment technique is discussed further in Chapter 15.) After you've taped several lessons, listen to the tapes and record the number of times you call each child's name and the number of reprimands or desists as well as positive comments you issue to individual children.

A simple way to record your tally is to use a copy of the class roster that has three columns to the right of the names (Figure 10.1). The first column is a tally for each time you call a child's name; the second column is a tally for each time you reprimand or interact negatively with a specific child, and the third column is for tallying positive comments or interactions. After you complete your tallies, single out the same few children and/or interact negatively with those children, you know you need to take steps to change your teaching behavior (see Chapter 15).

Prompting Prompting is a teacher behavior that reminds students what is expected of them. Some teachers find themselves prompting appropriate behavior only after inappropriate behavior has occurred. This is not the most effective way to use prompts. Prompts should be used as a positive tool as often as possible, rather than as a negative interaction.

For example, it is more beneficial to say, "Remember to walk as you go to pick up equipment," than "I told you to WALK!" or even "Can't you remember by now that you are supposed to walk?" Used as in the first example, prompting is a proactive response rather than a reactive response. Initially you should prompt students quite frequently about what behavior is appropriate; later, you will probably need to prompt only when a new or different situation arises.

Reactive Approaches

Interacting positively, eliminating differential treatment, and prompting are all proactive strategies for increasing appropriate behavior. They can be used as a means of preventing inappropriate behavior. The three strategies that follow are reactive strategies designed to increase appropriate behavior. They are intended for use after the inappropriate behavior has occurred—as ways of reacting to it. Ignoring inappropriate behavior, nonverbal interactions, and person-to-person dialogue are all strategies teachers can use as responses to inappropriate behavior that are designed to increase appropriate behavior.

Ignoring Inappropriate Behavior The opposite of emphasizing appropriate behavior with positive interactions is ignoring inappropriate behavior. Many of us find that praising appropriate behavior is hard, but ignoring inappropriate behavior is even more difficult. Inappropriate behavior can be ignored when it meets the following three criteria:

1. It is of short duration and is not likely to spread or persist.
2. It is a minor deviation.

3. Reacting to it would interrupt a lesson or call attention to the behavior.

Student behaviors that could be ignored in a physical education setting include occasional calling out during discussions, brief whispering, short periods of inattentiveness or nonpractice, and occasional continuation of activity after the stop signal. Thus, unless a behavior is harmful to other students, causes a safety problem, or seriously disrupts other students, reacting to it would consume too much of your energy, interrupt your lessons constantly, and detract from your classroom climate.

To be completely effective, teachers must ignore minor inappropriate behavior while simultaneously praising appropriate behavior. Yet, when we've become accustomed to saying, "Sh-h," "Hurry up!" "I'm waiting for you to get quiet," or "Tommy!!!" it's not easy to change to phrases such as, "Jody was quiet when she heard the stop signal," "Terrific, you were ready to go in ten seconds today," and "Jimmy, you showed thoughtfulness when you helped Jay up after he fell down." Such interactions, which can create appropriate behaviors in children, imply, for many of us, that the teacher is letting Tommy or the students who aren't yet quiet get away with inappropriate behavior. For many of us this is a risky action because the perceived implication is that our control is in jeopardy. In reality, the teacher who ignores simple inappropriate behavior while praising appropriate behavior is teaching children what desired behavior is while simultaneously creating an atmosphere that is warm and conducive to learning.

There's a subtle innuendo with the praising appropriate behavior/ignoring inappropriate behavior scenario. For example, if a teacher used *both* sets of examples described in the previous paragraph, what message would the students receive? The answer is confusion. Students would assume they could receive reinforcement and adult attention for either appropriate or inappropriate behavior.

Ignoring inappropriate behavior is for many of us a very uncomfortable and awkward act. A good way to assess your skill in praising the good and ignoring the inappropriate is to tape-record your lessons and count how often you say something positive and the number of times you say something negative. Remember that even little things such as "Hurry up!" and "Sh-h" count as negative interactions. Don't be surprised at what you first discover about your behavior; look at it as a challenge to improve.

Nonverbal Teacher Interactions   A number of simple nonverbal techniques are often sufficient to prompt appropriate student behavior. Sometimes just the physical proximity of the teacher will solicit the desirable behavior from some students. For example, when giving directions or speaking to the class as a whole, the teacher merely stands near the student displaying inappropriate behavior. Another technique for increasing appropriate behavior is to borrow the equipment the student is using for purposes of demonstration. Finally, even less obvious actions often work. For example, simple eye contact or a signal, such as nodding the head, will redirect the student.

Person-to-Person Dialogue   Another successful technique for increasing appropriate behavior is the person-to-person dialogue. Arrange a time to meet with a child away from the class (though not immediately before or after). You might say to the child, "Willie, you don't seem to be enjoying our physical education class. I'd like you to come to my office after school today so that we can talk about it." The purpose of this meeting is to try to determine the reasons for the child's behavior in your class. This is *not* a time for a lecture; instead, teacher and pupil should have a dialogue. We've found that a statement such as the following enables many children to begin a discussion of their concerns: "Willie, I'd like to talk to you about physical education class. Is there something I do that bothers you?"

This statement takes the focus from the child and places it on the teacher. Many children are quite candid about what's bothering them. Remember, this is a dialogue, not a lecture. Explaining to the child something about how and why you teach is constructive and often productive. Lecturing the child about behavior or threatening the child with future punishments is counterproductive. This dialogue is not teacher-to-child but person-to-person. Often the temptation to lecture, accuse, or blame a child is strong, but succumbing to this temptation is the quickest way to destroy any rapport between student and teacher. If a child trusts you enough to talk candidly about personal concerns and you threaten or lecture, communication ceases. Many children—especially those who need individual attention the most—have been betrayed before, so they're likely to be sensitive and wary (Figure 10.2). Use of teacher power in this situation reinforces a child's belief that teachers are untrustworthy and that being honest only gets him or her into more trouble.

Some children never want to participate in physical education class. A person-to-person dialogue is often helpful here, as is a conference with the child's other teachers. Some children are simply being obstinate or are genuinely lazy. Others may be afraid of participating in physical activity because they've already had

Figure 10.2   This teacher uses person-to-person dialogue to reach an alienated student.

unsatisfactory experiences at home or on the playground. If a child has a legitimate reason, we respect the child and attempt to create a satisfactory alternative. Transferring the child to another physical education class or arranging a one-to-one teaching situation often leads, in time, to participation with the regular class. Forcing a child to participate in physical education classes without first understanding the reason for the reluctance may not be in the child's best interests. Once you understand why a child is reluctant to participate, you can make an informed decision about the most appropriate course of action.

Decreasing Inappropriate Behavior

Although our first approach in dealing with inappropriate behavior is to attempt to increase appropriate behavior, we all know this doesn't always work. At times a teacher must decrease inappropriate behavior. When this is necessary, the teacher should have a repertoire of strategies available. Teachers in physical education have found the following techniques useful: desists, time-outs, planning time, behavior contracts, letters to parents, and involving the principal. Note that many of the techniques fit the psychological definition of the term *punishment*—they decrease the likelihood of an inappropriate behavior recurring by applying undesirable consequences to the behavior. These techniques should *not* be emotionally laden, associated with acts of anger, or said in a raised voice.

Also, any action the teacher takes to decrease inappropriate behavior should be accompanied by actions to build appropriate behavior.

Nowhere in our discussion will you find strategies that advocate physical exercise as a technique to reduce inappropriate behavior. In a word, physical exercise (sit-ups, push-ups, running laps, etc.) should never be used as a technique to hold children accountable for their behavior. Our goal is that children acquire the skills and desire to be physically active for a lifetime; using physical activity as punishment is counterproductive to that goal. Instead of learning to love activity, children will hate activity because of its association with punishment. The following are all techniques that can be used to react to inappropriate behavior in an attempt to reduce and eliminate it.

Desists

Sometimes it is impossible to ignore inappropriate behavior. When that is the case, one of the most common and useful ways to react to the behavior is with a desist. A desist is a verbal statement that tells a child to stop doing something. Using desists effectively can result in behavior change. Kounin (1970) established several conditions that must be present for a desist to be effective:

1. *A desist must be clear.* "Ellen, stop doing that" isn't enough. The desist must contain exact information about what the student is doing wrong. For example, "Ellen, stop hitting the basketball with the tennis racket; it'll ruin the tennis racket" is clear and specific. The student knows exactly what she is doing wrong.
2. *A desist must be firm.* Firmness is the degree to which the teacher follows through on the desist, making sure the student knows that the teacher means what was said. Brooks (1985) found that teachers who giggled or laughed after they delivered desists weren't taken seriously. Moving a bit closer to the student, looking the student momentarily in the eyes, and keeping a straight face when delivering the desist all communicate the teacher's firmness.
3. *A desist must be well timed.* The behavior must desist immediately, before it's allowed to spread to other students.
4. *A desist must be appropriately targeted.* It must be directed at the original offender, not a second or third party.
5. *A desist mustn't be harsh.* Kounin found that rough desists simply upset children and weren't effective.

Figure 10.3 A time-out temporarily removes a child who is off-task from activity.

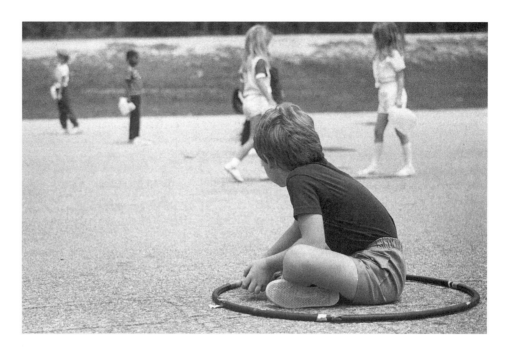

Firmness doesn't mean harshness or punitiveness; it is simply meaning what you say.

Time-Outs

A time-out is like a penalty box in hockey. During a time-out, a child, either through choice or at the request of the teacher, withdraws from class for a specified amount of time or until ready to return and function according to the class rules (Figure 10.3). When ready to return to class, the child simply rejoins the activity or reports to the teacher for instructions. Teach the time-out procedure with all other procedures at the beginning of the year so you can subsequently give a time-out as a standard penalty without disrupting the rest of the class. Here are some other considerations for effective use of time-outs:

1. The student must find physical education enjoyable; if not, the time-out may be a reward instead of a punishment.
2. The time-out area should be a clearly designated place where social contact with classmates isn't possible.
3. The length of a time-out can be at the discretion of the child or the teacher. If the child determines the length, then the child must take responsibility for determining when he or she is capable of returning. Some teachers prefer to specify the length of the time-out, for example, three minutes. If the time-out is to be timed, an egg timer or a clock

helps children determine when the specified amount of time has passed.

Planning Time

Planning time (DeLine, 1991) is a peer-directed alternative to time-outs. It is designed for inappropriate behavior involving two students interacting with one another. When students sit alone, as in a time-out, they do not have the opportunity to discuss or resolve their problems. Planning time, by contrast, provides students who do not demonstrate appropriate behavior a chance to resolve their conflict. During planning time, students who have conflicts go to a small area of the gymnasium designated as the "planning area," where they are required to sit together and develop a resolution. To be allowed to rejoin class, they must present to the teacher a verbal plan on how to work together or how to change their behavior. In other words, No Plan, No Play!

Be aware that, as with any educational strategy, students need to be taught how to use planning time effectively. Cues and questions (Box 10.1) can be posted on the wall to prompt students toward appropriate behavior. Students can then read and review the prompts to assess the nature of their behavior as well as develop an alternative. Essentially, planning time allows students who are "in trouble" to get "out of trouble." As with any new technique, learning to do it takes time, but the result is a class that cooperates more and students who learn to resolve their differences.

BOX 10.1   POSSIBLE CUES AND QUESTIONS FOR PLANNING TIME

What class rule weren't you following?
What behavior will you need to change in order to follow the rules?
What plan will you develop to make sure the behavior doesn't occur again?
Is your plan workable?
How will you know if your plan works?
What things can you do to make class a better place for you and everyone else?

Don Hellison (1995) has developed a version of planning time for individual students. In his version, the student whose behavior does not meet standards must develop a personal plan. The personal plan is actually a less formal variation of a behavior contract (see the following section) in which the student presents the teacher with a personal plan about how his or her behavior will change.

Behavior Contracts

A behavior contract is a formal agreement between a student and the teacher regarding behavior in the physical education setting. The contract includes a statement of the desired behavior, the contingencies (how much, for how long), and the rewards that will be earned if the behavior and the contingencies are met (Siedentop, 1991). When using a behavior contract, remember that students must have a role in defining all three aspects of the contract: behavior, contingencies, and rewards. After all three have been agreed upon, it is very important that both parties (sometimes a third party as a witness) sign the agreement. The student should be made aware of the importance of the agreement and, just as the teacher does, view it as a formal agreement, not to be taken lightly. Figure 10.4 is an example of a behavior contract with one student.

Letters to Parents

Desists, time-out, planning time, and behavior contracts work with some children but not with others. When a child continues to misbehave and present problems, a written report to the parents can be effective in obtaining that child's cooperation. But this technique should be used only after other approaches have proved unsuccessful.

The written report lists specific violations (Figure 10.5). The child is to have the report signed by a par-ent and then return it to you. Such a report is usually followed by improvements in behavior. When that occurs, you should send home another report, as soon as possible, that enumerates the improvements as clearly as the earlier report cataloged the violations. This second report congratulates the child on improved behavior and, like the first one, requires a parent's signature.

This is not to suggest that the written report to parents need be used only as a measure to decrease inappropriate behavior. The teachers of St. Andrew's Episcopal School in Austin, Texas, found that a "good letter" (Figure 10.6) was one of the most effective strategies in their program for increasing support for the program and generating good will with parents (D. Lambdin, personal communication, July 1991). In the St. Andrew's program, a "good letter" was sent home with every deserving student during one marking period each year. The response from parents was gratifying. Many commented on how wonderful it was that teachers took time to let parents know about good behavior.

Involving the Principal

Sending a disruptive child to the principal may or may not be successful. When you send a child to the principal, you're acknowledging—to yourself and to the child—your inability to cope with the situation. You're also placing the child in a situation you can't control.

Some principals are positive and helpful in working with disruptive children. Others use threats or corporal punishment, techniques likely to temporarily improve the child's behavior but permanently damage the child's enthusiasm and trust.

Only when you've tried every other possible technique to deal with behavior detrimental to the child and classmates should you send a child to the principal. If you must do this, we hope yours is a principal

Figure 10.4 Typical behavior contract. *Source:* Adapted from *Developing Teaching Skills in Physical Education,* 3rd ed., by D. Siedentop, 1991, Mountain View, CA: Mayfield.

BEHAVIOR CONTRACT

Kim Thomas and Mr. Diller agree that the following plan will be in effect for the next two weeks.

Starting date _____ Ending date _____

Kim will

1. Not interrupt other students' work by trying to knock their equipment away

2. Not disturb class by talking while the teacher is talking

3. Participate in all activities and try hard to improve her skills in throwing

Mr. Diller will

1. Give Kim individual help on throwing

2. Count one point for each day that Kim meets the three points stated above

3. Let Kim help with the physical education equipment for one week if she earns five points during the two weeks of the contract

Signed _____

_____

_____

who can help you and the child to better understand each other's needs and situations, so that you can work together more successfully.

Maintaining Appropriate Behavior in Entire Classes

Some classes have a more difficult time than others learning to abide by the class rules. When the traditional means of establishing a learning environment don't result in the desired outcome, it's necessary to use more sophisticated techniques. Four approaches that have proven successful are incorporating a system for developing student responsibility, class rewards, token systems, and behavior games.

Developing Personal and Social Responsibility

Because physical education largely focuses on the development of motor skills and fitness, teachers quite often ignore social and personal development—the very thing that is usually needed when an entire class seems unable to respond appropriately. Hellison (1995) states that it is usually assumed that students

Figure 10.5 Behavior report for parents.

ELEMENTARY SCHOOL
PHYSICAL EDUCATION BEHAVIOR REPORT

NAME _____ DATE _____

Educational research has consistently shown that when a teacher spends class time managing discipline problems, less teaching and student learning occur. Disruptive behavior, therefore, is a primary reason for poor student achievement.

We regret to inform you that your child exhibited the following misbehavior during physical education class today:

_____ Fought with others		_____ Refused to participate	
_____ Argued with others		_____ Lazy; no hustle or energy	
_____ Mistreated equipment		_____ Late to class	
_____ Disrupted the work of others		_____ Disruptive in hallway	
_____ Discourteous to others		_____ Continually off-task; not following teacher's directions	
_____ Frequently clowned, acting foolish and silly		_____ Spoke using foul language	
_____ Talked while teacher was talking		_____ Did not listen to teacher	

Teacher's Comments: _____

_____

_____

Please discuss today's incident with your youngster. We are concerned about the harm your child's behavior is causing himself/herself and his/her classmates. We will keep you informed of your child's behavioral progress during the coming weeks.

Thank you for your cooperation.

TEACHER _____

PARENT'S SIGNATURE _____

will be under control and that cooperation will automatically result in stability. As we know, such bliss does not occur automatically. The social responsibility model of physical education specifically focuses on empowering students to take responsibility for their own bodies and lives in the face of a variety of barriers and limitations and on teaching students that they have a social responsibility to be sensitive to the rights, feelings, and needs of others.

Hellison (1995) has developed a system for leading youngsters initially to become responsible for their own behavior and then, in time, to work successfully with other students. His ideas were mentioned in

Chapter 9 as an underlying philosophy for establishing a learning environment. Here we develop them specifically for use with those classes that have a hard time accepting responsibility for their actions. It's important to point out that this approach is not a quick fix for class problems, but a shift in thinking and action that permeates all activities in class. It is a philosophic approach to teaching that places the focus on creating personal and social responsibility using physical activity as the medium.

Hellison's approach uses a four-level series of guidelines to define what responsibility means and what students are to take responsibility for. The guidelines serve

Figure 10.6 "Good" letter for parents.

ELEMENTARY SCHOOL
PHYSICAL EDUCATION BEHAVIOR REPORT

Name _____ Date _____

Educational research has shown that when a teacher spends class time managing discipline problems, less teaching and less learning occur. Therefore, when disruptive behavior is nonexistent in a class situation, greater student achievement is likely to result.

We are glad to inform you that ____*(child's name)*____ behavior in physical education class consistently exhibits the following exemplary behaviors:

_____ Listens to the teacher   _____ Is courteous to others

_____ Is on-task, following   _____ Treats equipment with
              directions   care

_____ Is eager to participate   _____ Plays safely

Your child is doing a wonderful-terrific-dynamite job in physical education and we are proud of him/her. You are to be commended for preparing your youngster to function so well in school. We are more effective teachers because of your efforts.

Thank you for your cooperation.

TEACHER: _____

as a loose progression of goals for the class. Hellison's four levels of awareness are self-control, effort and participation, self-direction, and caring and helping (see Figure 9.2 and Box 9.1). For each of the levels, various instructional strategies exist to help students experience and interact with the ideas. It is through this interaction (teaching) that students begin to develop more responsibility for themselves and for the well-being of their classmates. The description given here is not sufficient to implement the social responsibility model. If you are interested in implementing this approach, a complete description is given in Hellison's 1995 text, *Teaching Responsibility Through Physical Activity.*

I have tried to respond to what children say rather than to what I expect or want them to say. Responding to children in this way is not a natural act; I have often been chagrined or embarrassed to discover myself listening to myself (rather than to the child) and answering a question both unasked and unintended. Or, worst of all, I have an answer that was not only unwanted but unmanageable by the child. In this, as in so much else, adult responses are inferior to children's, for children are usually too wise to burden adults with information they cannot handle.

Daniel Fader, *The Naked Children*

BOX 10.2   FORMAT FOR A BEHAVIOR GAME

1. The class is divided into four groups. Groups are allowed to choose a name for their team.
2. It is emphasized that each team can win and that teams are competing against a behavior criterion rather than against each other.
3. Four to six behavior rules are explained thoroughly.
4. Rewards are discussed and decided on by the group.
5. The game is explained. Points will be awarded each time a signal goes off (the students won't know when the signal will occur). The teacher will check each group when the signal occurs. If all team members are behaving according to the rules, the team gets one point. If any team member is breaking any of the rules, the team gets no point.
6. A cassette audiotape is preprogrammed with a loud noise to occur periodically (a bell or buzzer works well). Eight signals are programmed. The intervals between the signals vary. Several tapes are preprogrammed. When class begins, the teacher simply turns on the tape recorder with the volume up (often he or she doesn't know when the signals will occur).

7. When the signal occurs, the teacher quickly glances at each team and makes a judgment on their behavior. Teams that win a point are praised and told about their point. Teams that do not win a point are told why. (After doing this for a few days, the teacher can usually manage this kind of behavior game easily, not taking more than fifteen or thirty seconds at each signal to record and announce points.)
8. At the end of the period, the teacher totals the points and posts the scores for the day.
9. At the end of a specified period (ranging from one day to as long as eight weeks), the rewards are earned by each team that has met the criterion.
10. If one player on a team loses more than two points for his or her team two days in a row, the team meets and decides whether this player should sit out from gym class for a day (this "doomsday" contingency very seldom needs to be used).
11. With each consecutive game played, it is possible to reduce the number of signals per class and increase the length of the game. As good behavior becomes the norm for the class, the game can gradually be phased out.

SOURCE: From *Developing Teaching Skills in Physical Education* (3rd ed.), (pp. 113–115), by D. Siedentop, 1991, Mountain View, CA: Mayfield.

Class Rewards

With class rewards the class as a whole has the opportunity to earn rewards for abiding by the class rules. The first step is to establish a reward that will have meaning to students of a particular age—posters, banners, and free time have been used successfully. When an entire class does well for a day (week, month), it receives the reward. For example, if a class consistently does better than the performance standards established for management tasks over a given period of time, it receives a poster or banner to display in its room. Some teachers provide a reward for a class-of-the-week. We prefer, however, that rewards not be exclusionary. Every class should be able to earn a reward every week. Competition should be limited to the class against a standard, not the class against other classes.

Token Systems

Time-out penalizes disruptive behavior; a token system rewards desirable behavior. A token system is a program with academic, organizational, or managerial outcomes accompanied by a system in which students can earn "tokens" that can be exchanged for various rewards (Siedentop, 1991). The intent is to reward appropriate behavior and so encourage all children to behave appropriately.

The teacher initially explains to the class that a particular rule or procedure is being violated or not being accomplished as efficiently as possible. In doing this, the teacher must define very clearly the behaviors that are to be improved. After the behaviors have been defined, rewards must be developed. This is best done with the students' input, by having them rank the awards the teacher has offered, according to their desirability. The higher the ranking, the more the students will be motivated by the reward; the lower the ranking, the greater the probability it won't do much to encourage children to change their behavior. After the behaviors and rewards have been established, the rate of exchange must be agreed upon: how many tokens it will take to acquire the different rewards.

Successful rewards to be earned in physical education have included public recognition (name boards, photo boards, names in school newsletter), extra physical education time, free-choice time (at the end of class or the end of the week), special privileges (helping the teacher with other classes or before school), field trips, equipment use (borrowing equipment to use at home and on weekends), and T-shirts. Regardless of what reward is established, its effectiveness is based on the children's having had a part in the decision.

Once the behavior has been specified and the rewards agreed upon, then it must be decided how many "tokens" it will take to earn a certain reward. For example, five minutes' free time at the end of class might cost three tokens, whereas a T-shirt might cost fifty tokens. Just as in a store, different merchandise costs different amounts, and if you don't have the money (tokens), you can't buy it. It is also important to specify ahead of time when the tokens can be redeemed, for example, only on Fridays.

After all aspects of the token system are in place, the project begins. For example, the teacher explains to the class that some students aren't stopping and listening as soon as they hear the signal. Beginning today, the teacher explains, he'll check off on a class list the names of the students who don't stop and listen within five seconds after the signal is given. Students who have less than five checks during class will earn one token.

As the project progresses, in an effort to get classes off the token system, gradually increase the number of tokens it takes to receive an award and/or increase the length of time between token redemptions. Once children have learned to abide by the rules that are vital for the successful functioning of a large group, the token system becomes unnecessary.

Behavior Games

A more sophisticated and persuasive approach to class discipline is the use of a behavior game in which appropriate behavior is learned via the game (Siedentop, 1991). Certain standards for performance are established, and all the students in a class have the opportunity to earn the reward. The teacher can modify this format by raising the standards gradually, decreasing the number of signals, and extending the time period over which the game is played from one week to two weeks to a month. The purpose of this game is to elicit the desired behavior, so that the behavior game eventually can be eliminated. Behavior games aren't intended to be a permanent feature of a program; they can be effectively employed when the behavior of a class as a group is exceptionally deviant. As with class rewards, the key to success is a reward that the class as a whole finds desirable. Remember, what appeals to one class may not appeal to another. See Box 10.2 for one suggested format for a behavior game.

Corporal Punishment

We're unalterably opposed to corporal punishment. For some teachers a spanking or a paddling seems to be—inappropriately—a cathartic that may help the teacher but is more likely to harm the child. There are times when the temptation to paddle or strike a continually misbehaving child is almost overwhelming. And yet, according to our observations, it is the same few children who receive the vast majority of the paddlings. Obviously, this shows that for many children paddling doesn't achieve the desired result. And simultaneously it proves to these children that physically striking another person is a legitimate alternative when no other course of action appears effective. Interestingly, many of the children who repeatedly receive corporal punishment are being punished for fighting or hitting others. Occasionally a first paddling achieves the desired result. But the result is only temporary and has little effect on long-term behavior; in fact, corporal punishment could become a negative reinforcer. One cannot help but wonder about the long-term impact of such an experience on a child. Use of corporal punishment is inhumane, ineffective, and an admission of failure.

SUMMARY   Maintaining a learning environment is the presence of appropriate behavior that supports the educational goals of the specific situation. During the time needed to establish a learning environment, behavior inappropriate for the setting may occur. When it does, the teacher should first make certain that the lesson plans are pedagogically sound. If they are, then it is appropriate to focus on the students' behavior. It's important to understand that problems with inappropriate behavior are normal; *all* teachers will encounter some children who are off-task.

There are two phases to managing inappropriate behavior: the immediate (short-term) response to the situation and the long-term strategy. The long-term strategy involves recognizing the need to prevent the recurrence of the behavior by finding out what triggered it and developing ways of helping students learn more constructive means for dealing with inappropriate behavior. Short-term techniques give a teacher practical skills to use instantly when undesirable behavior occurs. Only after the teacher has acquired and consistently used these techniques with positive results is she or he comfortable with addressing the long-term aspects of inappropriate behavior. The techniques are simply a way of dealing with the immediate inappropriate behavior; as a learning environment is developed and students accept the responsibility for their own behavior, such techniques should no longer be needed and can gradually be faded out.

When inappropriate behavior first occurs, the teacher should use the techniques for increasing appropriate behavior: positive interaction, eliminating differential treatment, prompting, ignoring inappropriate behavior, nonverbal teacher interactions, and person-to-person dialogue. For those times when teachers find it necessary to decrease inappropriate behavior, successful techniques include desists, time-outs, planning time, behavior contracts, letters to parents, and involving the principal. Remember that strategies to reduce inappropriate behavior should *always* be accompanied by techniques to increase appropriate behavior. Techniques for refocusing an entire class that is off-task include incorporating a system for developing student responsibility, class rewards, token systems, and behavior games.

READING COMPREHENSION QUESTIONS

1. What should your first step be when you find most of the students in your class misbehaving? Why?
2. Why have we chosen not to use the word *discipline?*
3. What are the two phases in dealing with inappropriate behavior in the gymnasium?
4. What is the first strategy for maintaining an effective learning environment in the gymnasium? What techniques can be used to accomplish this goal?
5. Why are positive interactions with students so important, especially in the beginning of the year?
6. When should you ignore inappropriate behavior?
7. What does differential treatment of children mean? How can you determine whether you are doing this?
8. What is the major point to remember in a person-to-person dialogue with a student?
9. What is the second strategy for handling inappropriate behavior in the gymnasium? What techniques can you use to accomplish this goal?
10. What are the characteristics of an effective desist?
11. What is a time-out? What points should you remember when using a time-out? When is a time-out not effective? How does planning time differ?
12. When is a letter to parents useful? What should you include in the letter?
13. What is a token system? Describe how one works.
14. What is a behavior game? How is it played?
15. Why should many of the techniques discussed in this chapter *not* be as the school year progresses?

REFERENCES/ SUGGESTED READINGS

Brooks, D. (1985). The first day of school. *Educational Leadership, 42*(8), 76–78.
DeLine, J. (1991). Why can't they get along? Developing cooperative skills through physical education. *Journal of Physical Education, Recreation and Dance, 62*(1), 21–26.
Fader, D. (1971). *The naked children.* New York: Macmillan.

Hellison, D. (1995). *Teaching responsibility through physical activity.* Champaign, IL: Human Kinetics.

Hellison, D., & Templin, T. (1991). *A reflective approach to teaching physical education.* Champaign, IL: Human Kinetics.

Kounin, J. (1970). *Discipline and group management in classrooms.* New York: Holt, Rinehart & Winston.

Siedentop, D. (1972, June). Tilting at windmills while Rome burns. *Quest,* Vol. XIII pp. 94–97.

Siedentop, D. (1991). *Developing teaching skills in physical education* (3rd ed.). Mountain View, CA: Mayfield.

Siedentop, D., & Taggart, A. (1984). Behavior analysis in physical education and sport. In Heward, W., Heron, T., Hill, B., & Trap-Porter, J. (Eds.) *Focus on behavior analysis in education.* Columbus, OH: Charles Merrill.

Observation Techniques

It is vital for a teacher to observe children, whatever the subject or situation. It is through observation that the successful teacher assesses the moods, attributes, needs, and potential of individuals and groups.

——E. Mauldon and J. Layson

Locke (1975) provided the following description of a two-minute segment of a class of thirty-four fourth-grade students:

Teacher is working one-on-one with a student who has an obvious neurological deficit. She wants him to sit on a beam and lift his feet from the floor. Her verbal behaviors fall into categories of reinforcement, instruction, feedback, and encouragement. She gives hands-on manual assistance. Nearby two boys are perched on the uneven bars and are keeping a group of girls off. Teacher visually monitors the situation but continues to work on the beam. At the far end of the gym a large mat propped up so that students can roll down it from a table top, is slowly slipping nearer to the edge. Teacher visually monitors this but continues work on the beam. Teacher answers three individual inquiries addressed by passing students but continues as before. She glances at a group now playing follow-the-leader over the horse (this is off-task behavior) but as she does a student enters and indicates he left his milk money the previous period. Teacher nods him to the nearby office to retrieve the money and leaves the beam to stand near the uneven bars. The boys climb down at once. Teacher calls to a student to secure the slipping mat. Notes that the intruder, milk money now in hand, has paused to interact with two girls in the class and, monitoring him, moves quickly to the horse to begin a series of provocative questions designed to reestablish task focus.

After painting this picture of the complexity of teaching, Locke aptly reminds us:

That was only 120 seconds out of the 17,000 the teacher spent that day in active instruction. A great deal of detail was unobserved or unrecorded over those two minutes, and nothing in the record reflected the invisible train of thought in the teacher's mind.

It is obvious from the above description that observation is not only complex, but also critical. The ability to *observe*—to see with understanding—is crucial for a reflective teacher. The instructor who designs and implements a successful physical education program must be able to observe perceptively, accurately, and continuously and then translate the information gained from the observation into usable material.

Coaches will easily and readily talk of observing very detailed movements of their players in both practice and game situations. When untrained coaches and players have been compared with physical education teachers on their ability to observe and analyze movement, the coaches and players scored significantly higher than the teachers, who had degrees in physical education (Hoffman, 1977).

> ▶ Be gentle with yourself. Don't be disappointed initially if, in the relative tranquility after you've finished teaching, you find that you made some apparently obvious errors. Observation appears easy to the spectator, but the complexity of teaching and observing movement can be fully appreciated only when one assumes the role of the teacher. In time and with practice, you'll become increasingly satisfied with your ability to observe and analyze movement.

Yet, there is evidence that observation skills can be learned (Hoffman, 1977; Kniffen, 1985; Wilkinson, 1986). Data from these studies indicate that the ability to detect errors in a fundamental skill can be learned in a relatively short time period. It should be noted that none of these studies were conducted in a field setting.

Accurate observational analysis is difficult in a non-teaching or poorly managed environment. The complexity increases considerably, however, when the teacher attempts to observe the movement and behavioral characteristics of individual children while simultaneously monitoring the work of an entire class during a physical education lesson (Barrett, 1977, 1979, 1983). Beginning teachers should not be dismayed by the complexity of the observation tasks; not only can the skills be learned, but they also become easier as the teacher becomes more comfortable with the content and the teaching environment. (See Figure 11.1 for one suggestion that can help.)

The process of observation involves two aspects: how to observe and what to observe. Observation techniques, or how to observe, are generic, regardless of what is observed. What to observe, or the observation focus, can be broken into four categories: safety, on-task behavior, class movement patterns, and individual movement patterns. The remainder of this chapter introduces you to two successful observation techniques and then explains the different foci of observation.

Major Observation Techniques

There are many observation techniques that can help a teacher, but the two that we've found most valuable are the *back-to-the-wall* and *scanning* techniques. Although they seem quite simple, it has been our experience that many teachers are unaware of these two techniques.

Back-to-the-Wall

To determine whether the class is functioning appropriately, a teacher must be in a position to observe the

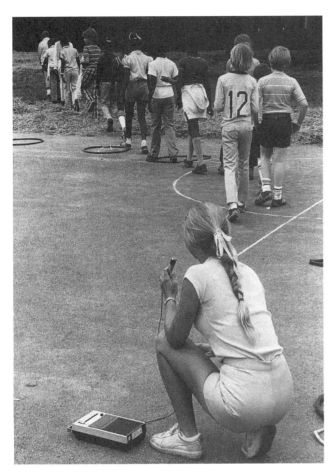

Figure 11.1 Using a tape recorder is a quick, convenient way for a teacher to record observations.

entire class. This position is called *back-to-the-wall* (Figure 11.2). The teacher stands outside the area in which the children are working, so that she or he can see the entire class. When the teacher enters the middle of an instructional area, he or she is unable to see part of the class (Figure 11.3).

The ability to observe all that is going on, particularly with classes that are difficult to manage, is important for both effective classroom management and comprehensive observation. Once the teacher is sure that a class is capable of working without constant monitoring, he or she can ignore the back-to-the-wall technique, except when using it to observe the whole class.

Remember, though, that the teacher who is in a position to observe an entire class isn't necessarily observing effectively. It's not unusual for a teacher to become so focused on the movement or behavior of a particular individual or group that she or he becomes oblivious to other children within the class.

Scanning

The teacher who wants to observe the class as a whole can maintain an appropriate focus by scanning (Siedentop, 1991). Using a left-to-right sweep, the teacher can glance at an entire class in just a few seconds and accurately assess how all the children are working. For example, if you want to determine the number of children who are actively practicing a given movement, you could quickly observe the class

Figure 11.2 Using the back-to-the-wall technique, this teacher can view all the children simultaneously.

Figure 11.3 Ineffective teacher position for observation.

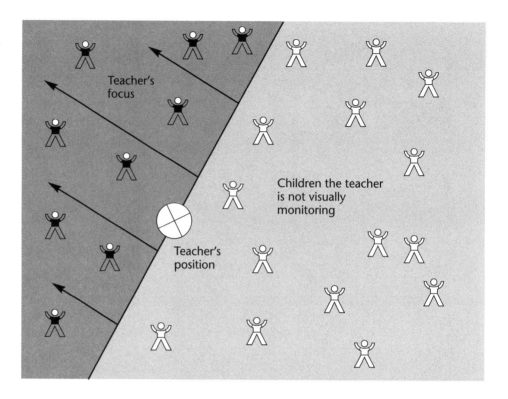

Teacher's focus

Children the teacher is not visually monitoring

Teacher's position

from left to right, counting as you scan. By comparing the number practicing a particular movement with the total number of children in the class, you can rapidly (in no more than fifteen seconds) assess the way the class is working. This observation technique can be used for obtaining information about the appropriateness of the movement, the behavior of an entire class, or the behavior of individuals within the class.

Both the back-to-the-wall technique and scanning should be used with all of the observation foci described in the next section. They are helpful in determining the safety of the activity as well as the behavioral, instructional, and managerial aspects of the class.

Observation Foci

When teaching physical education, a person is constantly bombarded by seemingly hundreds of ideas in just a few seconds, so here we've provided a procedure that we've found valuable for observing and understanding all that goes on in our classes. Because teaching is so complex, it's important that a teacher know what to look for in a particular lesson prior to conducting the lesson itself. This requires some advance planning (Chapter 8). When we don't plan beforehand, we often find it difficult to decide what to

observe during a lesson, so our lessons lack focus or direction. It's almost as if we were just "doing things" with children rather than actually teaching. For this reason, when we plan, it is helpful to divide our observation into four categories: safety, on-task behavior, class movement patterns, and individual movement patterns.

Safety

The teacher's initial and constant attention must always be directed toward the children's safety. Whenever you observe an unsafe situation, remember that safety must take priority over everything else going on in the lesson. If you have stated a task in such a way that the children are responding unsafely, stop the class, and restate the task. If equipment is unsafe or being used unwisely, stop the class to make the use of the equipment safe. Safety is the initial focus of any lesson and must be the uppermost consideration as you work with children.

We teach the children about safety as well so that they're able to understand some of the hazards they may encounter if they aren't careful. Initially, we explain the reasons for our safety procedures, to enable children to better understand and make intelligent decisions about their own safety. That's not enough, however. We need to constantly be aware of unsafe conditions. The following are several of the safety precautions we constantly keep in mind as we observe the classes. Certain of these precautions are also described in Chapter 9.

1. The children are required to work independently without pushing, shoving, tripping, or otherwise interfering with other children.
2. The children are required to work in a space reasonably distant from others (the concept of self-space). When the youngsters get too close, for example, when striking with rackets, we stop the lesson and make them adjust their space.
3. Depending on the surface, our children work in tennis shoes or barefoot. We don't allow stockinged feet, especially on hardwood or linoleum floors because they're so slippery. The children enjoy sliding, but this is a definite hazard.
4. In lessons on skill themes, such as rolling, transferring weight, and balance (gymnastics context), we don't allow I Dare You and Follow the Leader games or touching and pushing.
5. Unless otherwise indicated, in lessons in which gymnastics apparatus is being used, we allow only one child on the equipment at a time. This condition changes once the learning environment has been effectively established.

Legal liability is an increasing concern of teachers, particularly those of physical education. We strongly encourage you to be certain to teach safety rules similar to those just described and to include the rules in the written lesson plan so that they're part of a permanent record in the unfortunate event you have to document safety precautions. Most of these safety rules should be taught in the first few weeks of school (Chapter 9) and then reinforced throughout the year. Again, as you observe, make sure safety is constantly the forefront of your focus.

On-Task Behavior

Once you've observed that the environment is safe, your next focus is to determine whether children are on-task. Are they actually doing what you asked them to do? For example, if you asked your class to throw and catch with a partner, are they indeed doing so? Or are they kicking the ball; running around chasing one another; not working with a partner but in groups of four or five? If so, these are off-task behaviors, and you need to attend to them immediately. Stop the lesson!

There are three reasons why children may be off-task:

1. The children are trying, but the task was stated unclearly. You must restate the task.
2. The task is too hard or too easy (success rate information will help you here). Many of the children are either bored or frustrated. In either event, restate or change the task.
3. The children haven't yet learned to be on-task. If so, you'll have to once again practice the appropriate behavior in physical education class (Chapter 9). Although this isn't particularly enjoyable for either the children or you, it's necessary because constant off-task behavior simply can't be tolerated; it's not fair to either you or the children, especially those children who are working so hard to be on-task and do what you ask.

The reality of teaching, unfortunately, is that every class always has one or two children who tend to be off-task more than others. What do you do with them? After all, it's not fair to punish the entire class because of the behavior of one or two children. Refer to Chapters 9 and 10 for ideas about appropriate behavior.

Class Movement Patterns

When you've determined that the class is working safely and on-task, begin observing the entire class to see how they're accomplishing the task. Constantly be on the alert, however, for unsafe and off-task situations.

As you scan the entire class to see how they're moving, you'll make one of three decisions, based on what you observe the majority of the children doing. Your choices are to: (1) change the task, (2) provide a cue, or (3) present a challenge to the children without changing the task. Chapter 12 will discuss these three content development decisions in detail. We mention them here to emphasize that these content-development decisions need to be based on what you observe, not on an arbitrary time allotment that doesn't take into account, for example, the abilities and interests of the children. As part of making the decision you will also want to ask if the task is really helping the students learn what they need to know (Rink, 1996). If, for example, your goal for a lesson is

> ▶ One study (Graham, Hopple, Manross, & Sitzman, 1993) that compared student and experienced teachers found that veteran teachers provided children with far fewer tasks than the novice teachers. The novices believed that they had to "get through all of the tasks in their plan." In contrast, the veteran teachers were focused on the children. If a task was "right," they stayed with it for long periods of time.

to guide children to reach a content standard such as "applies critical elements to improve personal performance in fundamental and selected specialized motor skills" (NASPE, 1995, p. 33) and the skill you have chosen is the use of "large extensions in weight transfer," then you will want to be sure that the way the children have understood and are practicing the tasks is really leading to the use of large extensions. This is easy to decide, but much harder to implement with thirty children in a physical education class.

Let's take another example. Say that for this lesson you've decided that your second-graders need practice throwing overhand and your goal is to begin to teach "four characteristics of a mature throw" (NASPE, 1995, p. 20). You select a series of tasks from Chapter 27. You also decide that your major focus for this lesson will be the use of opposition—that is, that the children step with the foot opposite their throwing arm. Once you've defined the task and explained the cue ("Throw the ball as hard as you can against the wall. Remember to step with the foot on the other side of your body from your throwing arm."), observe to see which children are using opposition and which ones aren't. If you observe that most of the children aren't using opposition, stop the class and remind them to use opposition (or remind children individually). You may also demonstrate the correct performance yourself, or pinpoint as models several children who are using opposition. Then the children can return to their practice.

Be sure to observe the responses of the children to determine whether they are performing as the cue indicates. Remember that the cue (opposition) is what you actually expect the children to *learn* in this lesson.

Individual Movement Patterns

Teaching children individually is something we try to do as teachers. Obviously, however, it's not an easy job. Chapter 12 describes two approaches to working with individuals: teaching by invitation and intratask variation. Use of these approaches involves the ability to observe individuals and yet maintain the focus on the entire class. This may sound easy; it isn't.

We encourage teachers to focus initially on the entire class using the scanning technique described earlier. By working with individuals (intratask variation) too early, the teacher may lose focus on the entire class. We've seen this happen frequently with beginning teachers. The teacher becomes so involved helping an individual child that he or she loses focus on the entire class and may suddenly look up to find that a number of children are off-task or that an

unsafe condition has developed. This is *not* to suggest that teachers shouldn't work with children individually—we certainly should and do. But teachers must make sure that they don't become so involved with one child that they forget to concentrate on the whole class. As Locke's vignette suggests, doing so is a real challenge.

When we work with individuals, we essentially use the same process we use for the entire class. We vary the task for different children or we provide challenges (intratask variation). If you ever have an opportunity to watch a master teacher, you'll see that this teacher is constantly using intratask variation as he or she travels from child to child while simultaneously remaining conscious of the entire class, their safety, and their on-task behavior. Now you can better understand why it's so important to spend time establishing a learning environment at the beginning of the year.

Combining Observation Aspects

Our description of the four observation foci of the lesson—safety, on-task behavior, class movement patterns, and individual movement patterns—was rather easy to follow. When teaching, however, a teacher is rarely able to focus on any one aspect at a time. As

> Recently I observed a teacher attempting to teach a child how to run and kick a stationary ball. The child was unable to adjust her run to enable her to arrive at the ball in a proper kicking position. After each unsuccessful attempt (the ball barely moved; the child appeared almost to step on the ball rather than kick it), the teacher would say to the child, "No, that's not it!" The child knew she had failed as she watched the ball erratically dribble away from her foot, and yet the teacher offered no prescription for improvement. Rather than stating results the student can readily observe, the successful instructor offers a prescription for practice, that is, a cue.

> The first time I taught the whole class [twenty-six children] I had a great deal of trouble seeing individuals in the class. All I saw, no matter how hard I tried, was a mass of individuals. I couldn't see individual performances.
>
> Fran McGillan (as a junior in college, the first time he taught an entire class of twenty-six children)

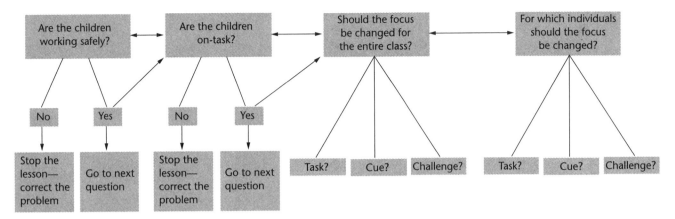

Figure 11.4 Questions reflective teachers use to guide observation.

Locke's vignette suggests, the teacher must concentrate simultaneously on the four aspects. Figure 11.4 is a schematic overview of the four major questions that we ask ourselves when we teach. Note that the arrows between the questions go both ways, indicating that the observation focus isn't linear but that there's a constant interplay between the questions.

SUMMARY

Observing—the ability to see with understanding—is a crucial skill for the reflective teacher. Successful observers use two techniques: remaining on the periphery of the class (back-to-the-wall) and periodically checking to see what the entire class is doing (scanning). A second critical aspect of accurate and successful observation is planning ahead of time. By planning ahead, a teacher knows what he or she will be looking for in regard to the lesson's objectives. The key focal points for observation are safety, on-task behavior, class movement patterns, and individual movement patterns; these four are interrelated.

Changing tasks to make them easier or harder, determining which cue the children will benefit from the most, and recognizing when to challenge the children all rely on the observation process. Another part of the process of observing effectively is to analyze the children's success rate.

READING COMPREHENSION QUESTIONS

1. In reflective teaching, what is the purpose of observation?
2. Why is observation in physical education so difficult?
3. Describe how you would use the scanning and back-to-the-wall techniques in your teaching.
4. In your own words, explain the key focal points regarding safety that a reflective teacher watches for.
5. What does off-task behavior look like? Give three examples.
6. Imagine you are teaching children to kick a ball to a partner. Briefly describe what you might observe that would cause you to change the task to make it easier or harder.
7. In the same imaginary situation, describe what you might observe that would cause you to provide a kicking cue rather than to change the task.
8. Again, assuming the same teaching situation, describe what you might observe that would cause you to provide a kicking challenge rather than changing the task or the cue.

REFERENCES

Barrett, K. R. (1997). We see so much but perceive so little: Why? *Proceedings: 1977 National Conference of the National College for Physical Education for Men and the National Association for Physical Education of College Women.* Chicago: Office of Publications Services, University of Illinois.

Barrett, K. R. (1979). Observation for teaching and coaching. *Journal of Physical Education and Recreation, 50*(1), 23–25.

Barrett, K. R. (1983). A hypothetical model of observing as a teaching skill. *Journal of Teaching in Physical Education, 3*(1), 22–31.

Graham, G., Hopple, C., Manross, M., & Sitzman, T. (1993). Novice and experienced children's physical education teachers: Insights into their situational decision making. *Journal of Teaching in Physical Education, 12,* 197–214.

Hoffman, S. J. (1977). Toward a pedagogical kinesiology [Monograph 28]. *Quest,* 38–48.

Kniffen, M. (1985). *The effects of individualized video tape instruction on the ability of undergraduate physical education majors to analyze selected sport skills.* Unpublished doctoral dissertation, The Ohio State University, Columbus.

Locke, L. F. (1975, Spring). The ecology of the gymnasium: What the tourist never sees. *Southern Association of Physical Education for College Women Proceedings.*

Mauldon, E., & Layson, J. (1965). *Teaching gymnastics.* London: MacDonald & Evans.

National Association for Sport and Physical Education (NASPE). (1995). *Moving into the future: National standards for physical education.* St. Louis, MO: Mosby.

Rink, J. E. (1996). Effective instruction in physical education. In S. Silverman and K. Ennis (Eds.), *Student learning in physical education* (pp. 171–198). Champaign, IL: Human Kinetics.

Siedentop, D. (1991). *Developing teaching skills in physical education* (3rd ed.). Mountain View, CA: Mayfield.

Wilkinson, S. (1986). *Effects of a visual discrimination training program on the acquisition and maintenance of physical education students' volleyball skill analytic ability.* Unpublished doctoral dissertation, The Ohio State University, Columbus.

CHAPTER
12

Developing the Content

*Elementary school students should develop basic motor skills that allow partici-
pation in a variety of physical activities. Students' mastery of and confidence in
motor skills occurs when these skills are broken down into components and the
tasks are ordered from easy to hard. In addition, students need opportunities to
observe others performing the skills and to receive encouragement, feedback,
and repeated opportunities for practice during physical education class.*

——National Center for Chronic Disease Prevention and Health Promotion, 1997

*In order to maximize the development of self-esteem, it is important to create
learning opportunities that match the task difficulty with the learner's developmental capabilities. Children love to be challenged. Succeeding at a task that is
too easy gives little pleasure. In contrast, causing children to work just a bit
beyond their current skill can produce optimal growth. In order to do that,
teachers should sequence tasks in a developmental order before presenting them
to children as challenges.*

——Linda Bunker

One of the major responsibilities of a teacher is to select and sequence the content of a lesson (Chapter 8). During the actual lesson the reflective teacher determines how effectively the tasks or activities are helping the students accomplish the goals of that lesson—and makes changes accordingly. Tasks or activities that are too difficult for the children often lead to frustration, resulting in off-task behavior. Tasks that are too easy often lead to boredom, again resulting in off-task behavior (Csikszentmihalyi & Csikszentmihalyi, 1988). One of the challenges for the physical education teacher, then, is to carefully select and sequence tasks that allow children to feel successful—and that result in learning and improvement.

Teaching would be much easier if lesson plans worked perfectly, exactly as designed. In fact, however, reflective teaching is a dynamic process—the teacher is constantly involved in making decisions: Is this task too hard? Should I provide the children with a cue? Are they getting bored? How can I change this task to make it more interesting? Are the children benefiting from this task?

We have attempted to assist you with developing the content by organizing the movement concept chapters (Chapters 16 to 18) and the skill theme chapters (Chapters 19 to 31) in developmentally appropriate progressions based on the generic levels of skill proficiency (Chapter 7). These chapters are helpful guidelines, but as you plan you will no doubt want to add additional tasks and also modify some of the tasks to better match your particular teaching situation (Chapter 5). We don't intend that you use the progressions we have suggested in these chapters exactly as written, especially if you are an experienced teacher. We know, however, they will be extremely valuable for novice teachers and those who are new to the skill theme approach. Because you will be changing some of these tasks as you teach, as well as providing children with cues and challenges during a lesson, it is important that you understand the "system" we have used to develop the content in each of these chapters. In the final part of this chapter we describe two techniques, teaching by invitation and intratask variation, that teachers use to adjust for differences in ability within the same class of children.

Overview of Content Development

In the process of content development developed by Rink (1993), a teacher performs four functions during a lesson to help children learn the various concepts and skills that constitute the content of the program: (1) *informing* the children, that is, providing information about the concepts or skills and describing how

the tasks are to be done; (2) extending *tasks*, that is, making them easier or harder, according to the ability of the children; (3) refining tasks, that is, providing children with *cues* or "critical elements" that will help them become more efficient in performing a skill or task; and (4) applying the task by inventing *challenges* that are designed to motivate the children to continue practicing or to show them how the task can be applied.

We have adapted Rink's system of content development and refer to extensions as *tasks*, refinements as *cues*, and applications as *challenges* throughout this book. In the following sections we define and give examples of each of the four aspects of content development beginning with the process of informing students.

Informing

Effective teachers are good communicators (Graham, Hussey, Taylor, & Werner, 1993; Rink, 1996). They provide clear and interesting explanations and descriptions so that the children can easily understand the information. When we provide information to children, we try to follow several guidelines: the KISS principle and the use of demonstrations and pinpointing.

The KISS Principle   The KISS principle (Keep It Short and Simple) is a good guideline to follow when talking to children. The problem we face as teachers is that we have much to tell the children about a concept or skill, but the children aren't really interested in listening for very long; they want to move. Although there are exceptions, we try to limit our instruction to just what the children need to know.

One of the traps teachers easily fall into is spending five or more minutes telling (and demonstrating) all they know about a skill or activity. There is a lot to tell the children—the problem is that the children can't possibly remember all that information when it is provided in a single "minilecture." Think of a skill or exercise you know well. It would be easy for you to talk for five minutes on how to hit a ball with a bat or the correct way to do a "crunch," for example. The children won't remember all of this, however. If you don't believe it, try an experiment with one of your classes. Give them a minilecture. During the next class, use the technique described in Chapter 14, Helping Murgatroid, to see what they actually are able to recall from your minilecture. We believe you'll find that information provided in small bits throughout a lesson seems to be more effective than long-winded explanations that children don't remember.

Figure 12.1 This teacher uses pinpointing (demonstration by two or more children) to help the class more clearly understand the concept she is emphasizing.

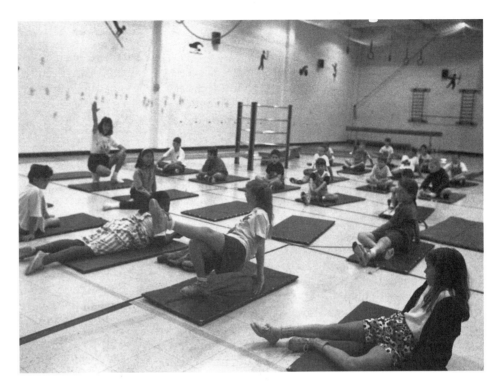

Demonstrations   In addition to keeping our explanations brief and to the point, we also try to demonstrate whenever possible (Rink, 1996; Sharpe, Hawkins, & Wiegand, 1989; Southard & Higgins, 1989). This is helpful to the children who are visual, as opposed to auditory, learners and necessary for the increasing number of children in our classes who do not speak English. Demonstrations of motor skills need to be done correctly, and they must emphasize the part or parts that the children need to pay attention to—the instep, the elbow, the shoulder, the hands—so that children can clearly see how that part is to be used and how it fits into the total movement. This seems obvious, yet it is amazing to see how often teachers don't provide the children with a demonstration or fail to demonstrate slowly enough or emphasize a part, so that the demonstration is just not helpful to children. If you videotape some of your lessons, as we suggest in Chapter 15, you will be able to ascertain quickly the effectiveness of your demonstrations.

Pinpointing   There are times when we choose not to demonstrate or are unable to demonstrate a skill for the children. In these instances, *pinpointing*—inviting several children to do the demonstration—can be an effective technique (Figure 12.1). The children are encouraged when they see that their peers can demonstrate the skill or technique. When possible we try to select two or more children to do the pinpoint-

ing; in this way we avoid placing children who are uncomfortable performing in front of other children in a solo situation.

As you will see in the movement concept and skill theme chapters (Chapters 16 to 31), each section (activity) begins by providing the children with some information about how a particular task is to be done, for example, the equipment needed, the space in which the activity will take place, the rules, and whether the children will be working alone or with others. These are considered informing tasks and for that reason are not designated as tasks, cues, and challenges. Ideally, the informing part of the lesson is both brief and clear so that the children can quickly begin practicing the starting task with few questions.

Tasks (Extensions)

Once the children have been provided with a starting task, the next step in the development of the content is to observe the children to determine whether the task is too easy (the children are able to do it easily with no apparent challenge), too hard (the children are occasionally successful, but many are unable to do the task with success), or simply unproductive (the children just aren't benefiting from the task). In any of these cases, the teacher will want to change (extend) the task so that more of the children can be successful. Each of the movement concept and skill theme chapters (Chapters 16 to 31) provides a suggested progression of tasks (extensions) for children. The tasks are marked with the symbol ⓣ.

Tasks that are "just right" allow children to succeed at the task about 80 percent of the time (Berliner, 1984; Brophy, 1983; Rosenshine, 1983; Siedentop, 1991). This is a very rough estimate, but it provides a measure for determining whether to change a task. Tasks that children can accomplish at high rates of success are ones that they will continue working at—tasks that are too easy or too hard prompt off-task behavior or the question, "When can we do something else?"

Cues (Refinements)

Once a task is judged to be appropriate, the teacher can provide cues to help the children perform the skill more efficiently. Cues are also referred to as critical elements (NASPE, 1995). Providing cues is one of the most valuable roles a teacher can perform (Landin, 1994; Masser, 1987, 1993; Rink, 1996). Cues help children understand how to perform a skill. In the overhand throw for distance, for example, it is important that children learn to step with the foot opposite the throwing hand. When landing from a jump, it is important that the children learn to bend, not only at the knees, but also at the hips and ankles. These tips or cues (refinements) help children learn skills more efficiently than they would by trial and error. The cues (critical elements) are listed at the beginning of each series of tasks for skill themes and movement concepts. (Figure 12.2, taken from Chapter 29, shows how the tasks, cues, and challenges are presented in the movement concept and skill theme development chapters.) This will help you observe the children to determine which cue or refinement will best help the children improve their skill performance. In addition to helping the children learn the correct ways of performing a skill, emphasizing cues can also provide the children with a checklist of the important critical elements that they will need when they decide to play a sport on their own outside of school. Children who attend physical education class for an hour or less a week obviously don't have enough time to reach the utilization or proficiency levels. We do know, however, that they can learn the critical elements so at least they will recall how to perform a skill appropriately (Manross, 1992).

When you begin to read and use the information in the skill theme chapters, you will notice that no cues are provided with the tasks at the precontrol level of the generic levels of skill proficiency (GLSP) (Chapter 7). This is because youngsters at that level have had minimal experience with even attempting a given

STRIKING WITH BOTH SIDES OF THE PADDLE

Setting   Each child has a paddle (foam or wood) and a ball (foam, dead tennis ball), and a carpet square or some other way to define self-space.

Cues

Flat Paddle   (Place your paddle flat on the floor. Now pick it up and see if you can keep it as flat as it was on the floor—the same angle.)

Stiff Wrist   (Pretend you have a cast.)

Tasks/Challenges

ⓣ In tennis or racketball or badminton players use both sides of the paddle. Let's try this. Keep hitting the ball up. Try to hit the ball with one side of the paddle, then the other.

ⓣ If this is easy, see if you can use both sides of the paddle and both sides of the body. Try not to always strike the ball when it is right in front of you.

ⓣ Can you make a rainbow with the ball—hit it on one side of your body and then the other so that the ball travels in a rainbow shape? Remember, if you miss the ball and have to chase it, go back to your self-space before you start striking again.

ⓒ How many rainbows can you make? Each time the ball goes over your head it counts as one. Five rainbows without a miss would be excellent.

Figure 12.2   Sample presentation of tasks, cues, and challenges for one skill theme.

movement. We want them to first explore the skill until they have at least a general idea of how it feels and what is required to do it successfully. You can understand that if, for example, you have never attempted a movement, it will not be very helpful to be told four or five cues that will have little meaning—and that you will no doubt not remember. Obviously we must emphasize safety, but explanation and demonstration of the critical elements can begin once youngsters have a basic understanding of the movement and are moving to the control level. At this point in the learning curve they are often more receptive to learning the cues because they have discovered that they are not very adept at the skill and would like to know how to do it more efficiently and effectively.

You will also notice that the cues change from the control to the utilization and then the proficiency levels. This is because the movements are used differently

BOX 12.1   FOURTH-GRADE ASSESSMENT EXAMPLE FROM THE
NATIONAL STANDARDS FOR PHYSICAL EDUCATION

Standard 1: Movement Forms

Peer Observation
Have partners observe the preparatory phase of a designated skill in an attempt to ascertain the correct use of critical elements. For example, student A will throw a ball toward a target five times using the overhand pattern while student B observes the performance, focusing on a single critical element during the preparatory phase (e.g., opposite foot forward, side to target, arm pulled way back). The observing student gives a "thumbs-up" if the critical element is correct; if it is incorrect, the observing student tells what is needed to improve the movement.

Criteria for Assessment
a. Thrower displays the critical element that is the focus of the observation.
b. Observer makes an accurate judgment on the performance.

SOURCE: From NASPE, 1995, p. 33.

at each of the GLSP. For example, youngsters at the proficiency level in landing from a jump do not need to be told to "bend their knees"—they learned that when they were at the control level. So just as the tasks change for each of the GLSP, so do the cues.

Each of the movement concept and skill theme development chapters provides numerous cues that the children will find helpful for enhancing the quality of their movements. The challenge for you as a teacher is to select the cue that will be most helpful for the class you are teaching. Beware of the temptation to tell the children too much at once. As suggested in the *National Standards,* we want the children not only to hear the cues but to remember them. Box 12.1 provides one example of how you might assess your children to determine how well they are learning the critical elements.

One Cue at a Time   Generally we try to focus on one cue at a time in our instructions. For example, to a class of second-graders we might provide instruction and demonstrate the cue of stepping with the lead foot when batting (Chapter 30). We would then ask the children to continue the task—batting off a tee against a wall or fence—while we circulate and provide feedback to the children.

If you can imagine this setting, you realize that the children may need several other cues. Some, for example, will not be swinging in a horizontal plane; some may not be swinging the bat appropriately on the

backswing or following through appropriately. The problem, however, is that children at this age (and many adults for that matter) can concentrate (effectively) on only one cue at a time. By focusing on one cue at a time, we heighten the chances that the children will learn this cue (Rink, 1996; Rink & Werner, 1989). Once the children have learned this cue—that is, they are *actually* stepping with the lead foot as they swing (this may not happen in a single lesson)—we move on to another cue. We may change the task, as suggested in the batting progression in Chapter 30, but the cue remains the same.

Congruent Feedback   As the children practice a task, the teacher circulates among them, providing feedback (Figure 12.3). Again, there are many cues the teacher might provide in the form of feedback. We try, however, to provide congruent feedback, that is, feedback that is consistent with what we told the children to think about when practicing the skill (Belka, Conner, & Bowyer, 1991; Rink, 1996; Rink & Werner, 1989). For example, during instruction (informing) we might ask the children to think about stepping with the lead foot as they are batting; the feedback we provide, therefore, would be about how they are (or are not) stepping with the opposite foot. We might say:

"Rachel, good step."
"Nick, don't forget to step when you swing."
"Jennifer, remember to step."
"Tommy, way to step."

Figure 12.3 Congruent teacher feedback can help children understand and improve their movement.

Interestingly, both the children and the teacher seem to benefit from this type of feedback. The children hear a consistent message—and are able to remember the cue. The teacher is able to focus quickly on a specific part of a movement while moving among the children, rather than attempting to analyze every child's batting swing. The feedback analysis checklist (Figure 15.1) is a tool to help you analyze the type of feedback you provide to the children—and also to whom you provide it.

Challenges (Applications)

In addition to informing (providing information to the children), presenting a logical progression of tasks and activities, and providing cues to the children, a teacher may also present challenges (applications) to the children to maintain their interest in a task. Even when children are doing a task and succeeding at high rates, there comes a time when they are ready to move on to another task. The problem, of course, is that as teachers we are not always able to provide another task that is just a little bit harder; in some instances, a task is much harder, and if we ask the children to do this task before they are ready, many of the children will fail.

Let's take the example of batting. A logical progression from striking a ball from a batting tee is to strike a suspended object (Chapter 30). If the equipment and facilities to suspend objects are available, the children can logically proceed to this task when they are ready.

If the teacher does not have the necessary facilities and equipment, however, the children's next task might be to hit a ball pitched by a partner. This is much more difficult for the children. But there is an alternative to changing the task, one that can maintain their interest in continuing to strike a ball from a batting tee.

The teacher can provide a challenge, or application, to the children that will interest them in continuing that task for a longer period of time, thereby allowing the teacher time to continue providing feedback about the way they are (or aren't) stepping with the lead foot when they bat. The following are examples of challenges:

> "If this is easy for you, you may want to try batting a smaller ball; if it is hard for you, you may want to try batting a larger ball."
> "Every time you hit the ball, say a letter of your last name."
> "See how many times in a row you can hit the ball without hitting the tee or missing the ball."
> "Try to hit the fence (wall) with the ball on a fly three times in a row."

The challenges are marked in the movement concept and skill theme chapters (Chapters 16 to 31) with the symbol Ⓒ to provide you with examples that may be helpful to you in your teaching. It is important to realize that these challenges do not substantively change the task; rather, they are designated to maintain the children's interest in that task. In gamelike

Table 12.1   Sample Part of a Lesson Plan Using a Content Development Format   *Children's objectives: Children will learn to swing their arms on the takeoff and bend their knees when they land from a jump.**

Tasks 🅣	Cues	Challenges 🅒
Jump over your rope, taking off and landing on two feet. See how high you can get.	Swing both arms—hard!	Make a different shape with your rope. Continue two-foot takeoff and landing jumps.
Jump using a one-foot takeoff and two-foot landing.	Bend your knees when you land.	See if you can land perfectly still-frozen on three landings in a row.
Make your rope into a circle. Let's try a hop—one foot to the same foot—into and out of the circle.	Bend your knee when you land.	How many times can you hop into and out of your rope circle without touching the other foot to the ground? (*Then try the other foot.*)
Lay your rope in a straight line. Stand next to your rope. How far away can you jump from it? (*Two-foot takeoff and landing.*)	Swing both arms—hard!	Now get a piece of masking tape from the wall. Lie on the floor. Touch your feet to the rope. Put the masking tape near your head. Can you jump your own height?
Now run and jump. Take-off (*one- or two-foot*), and land on two feet. Try to take off very close to your rope.	Swing your arms as you get ready to take off. Bend your knees when you land.	Move the masking tape to where your feet first hit the floor on your landing. See if you can jump even farther next time.

*This progression is taken from Chapter 22, "Jumping and Landing."

settings, a challenge of keeping score, either cooperatively or competitively, would be a logical application for that task.

Some teachers find it easier to use challenges in their teaching than others. As we increase our understanding of how children at different ages think—and their sense of humor—it becomes easier to create challenges for them. Preschool children, for example, can be challenged simply by being asked to perform a task with a ball, hoop, or carpet square of a different color. Some middle-school children enjoy the challenge of competing against a friend to see who can be more successful. We have provided a few examples of challenges in the subsequent chapters, but the best ones are those you create as you come to know the children you are teaching.

Assessing Your Content Development

The final chapter in Part Two, "Understanding Your Teaching" (Chapter 15), provides you with a way to determine how you are developing the content (see Figure 15.2). Ideally, you will find that your lessons include a number of cues that relate to the tasks the children are doing in that lesson. Lessons that consist entirely of tasks followed by challenges are considered undesirable sequences (Belka & Short, 1991). Desirable task sequences consist of a more varied pattern that includes a mix of tasks, relevant cues, and challenges as needed (Belka & Short, 1991).

Planning Format

Chapter 8 discussed planning and the various aspects of a lesson that teachers typically include in their plans. Now that you understand the process of content development, we want to share an alternative way to plan that some teachers have found effective (Rink, 1993; Siedentop, Herkowitz, & Rink, 1984). This alternative relates specifically to how a teacher writes the activities for the day. Essentially, a three-column format is used—tasks are listed in the first column; cues, in the middle column; and challenges, in the last column. For each task, the teacher writes at least one cue and one challenge in the same row; the cue(s) and challenge(s) are designed to correspond to the task the children will be practicing.

Table 12.1 provides an example of part of a lesson that was planned using this format. This format for planning is especially useful for beginning teachers and those who are new to this process of content development. Rather than carrying the entire plan with them as they teach, some teachers briefly summarize the lesson by writing a key word or two for each of the tasks, cues, and challenges on a five- by eight-inch card, which can be easily carried in a pocket for quick reference during a lesson.

Accommodating Individual Differences

We have described a process for developing the content that enables children to truly learn and benefit from physical education lessons (Rink, 1993). As you know, however, the process is made even more complicated by the fact that children in our classes have different skill levels and interests. Although we have no magical solutions, we do want to suggest two techniques that can help you to accommodate individual differences within a class—that is, to match the challenge of a task with the ability of the child (Csikszentmihalyi & Csikszentmihalyi, 1988). We have termed these two techniques *teaching by invitation* and *intratask variation*.

Teaching by Invitation

One of the ways a teacher can adjust for individual differences is to extend an invitation to the children to decide some of the parameters of a given task (Graham, 1992). The teacher makes the statement to the entire class, and each child then decides which task he or she wants to participate in. The following are examples of teaching by invitation:

> "You may want to continue dribbling in self-space, or you may want to begin dribbling and walking in general space."
>
> "Working alone or with a partner, design a sequence . . . "
>
> "You may want to continue batting from the tee, or you may want to work with a partner, taking turns pitching a ball to each other."
>
> "You may want to continue striking a ball with your paddle, or you may want to try striking a shuttlecock."
>
> "You decide how far away you want to be from the goal when you kick."
>
> "In groups of two or three, make up a game . . . "

If you choose to use this technique, you will find that most of the children make truly intelligent decisions about the tasks in which they choose to participate. As in every instance, there will be a few children who, in your judgment, make questionable decisions. Overall, however, we think you will find that your children will choose tasks that allow them to be successful—and yet are not too easy (Csikszentmihalyi & Csikszentmihalyi, 1988).

Intratask Variation

Teaching by invitation allows the children to make decisions about the task they prefer to work on. Intratask variation, by contrast, is a technique in which the teacher makes the decision to extend a task for individuals or small groups within the class (Graham, 1992). The teacher bases this decision on his or her knowledge of the children's abilities and interests. Typically, intratask variation is a rather private interaction between one or more children and the teacher, who makes a task easier or harder to better match the skill level of the children. The following are examples of intratask variation:

> "Todd, why don't you try striking a balloon instead of a ball?"
>
> "Jim, you may want to practice dribbling behind your back and between your legs." (Other children are practicing dribbling and staying in self-space.)
>
> "Eloise and Starla, why don't you two make up a partner sequence that has rolling and transferring weight in it." (Other children are practicing rolling in backward directions.)
>
> "I would like the four of you to move over to the next field and make up a game that has kicking and dribbling with your feet in it." (Other children are practicing dribbling with their feet; these four have been playing soccer for several years and are adroit at kicking and foot-dribbling. They move to the other field and quickly begin a 2 v 2 soccer game.)

Unfortunately, intratask variation is not a 100 percent guaranteed panacea that will allow you to adjust tasks satisfactorily to meet the needs of every child in a class. As with most teaching techniques, intratask variation is effective with some children in some classes some of the time.

One of the ways a teacher can heighten the potential success of intratask variation is to explain to the children, prior to using the technique, that at various times in a lesson they will be asked to do different things. Understanding why this is being done—they already know that there is a wide range of skill levels within the class—will enable the children to realize that the teacher is not "playing favorites," but rather helping children benefit more from physical education class.

When using intratask variation, the teacher can also make the point that children at the higher skill levels, utilization and proficiency (Chapter 7), have most likely acquired these skills because of the activities they pursue after school and on weekends; the teacher can add that unfortunately most schools do not provide enough physical education time for children to progress to the higher levels of skill proficiency.

SUMMARY

One of the truly important tasks for a physical education teacher is to develop the content in ways so that children can learn and benefit from the activities. This chapter defines and illustrates four functions that teachers might use in developing the content. The first function is informing, or presenting information to children—ideally in brief instructional episodes accompanied by demonstration and/or pinpointing. Once an initial task has been presented, the teacher needs to decide whether to make the task easier or harder. The rate of success is one measure to use in determining whether to make a task easier or harder. The third function in content development is providing cues to children that heighten their understanding and efficiency at performing a given skill or activity. Teachers should provide only one cue at a time and ensure that the feedback they provide is congruent (that is, that it is about that cue). The last teacher function is providing challenges to the children to maintain their interest in a task, rather than moving on to a harder task. Teachers can use two techniques to adjust lessons for individual differences. In teaching by invitation, the teacher allows the children to make decisions, whereas in intratask variation, the teacher decides which tasks are most appropriate for children of different skill levels.

READING COMPREHENSION QUESTIONS

1. Can children simply play games and, as a result, learn the basic motor skills? What about children of differing abilities and interests?
2. Define developing the content, and explain why it is an important part of teaching physical education.
3. Pick a skill or movement concept with which you are familiar. Provide several examples of tasks designed to help children learn that skill or concept. Be sure to provide both easier and harder tasks.
4. Why is providing cues an important teaching skill for physical education teachers? What might be the result when a teacher provides no cues or does so ineffectively?
5. Refer to Table 12.1. Using the skill or concept you chose in question 3, write at least five tasks in one column. In a second column, write alongside each task a cue that you might use when teaching that task. In a third column, write a challenge for each of the tasks in the first column. Remember that the task, the cue, and the challenge need to work together—that is, they need to complement one another.
6. As a teacher, do you think you are more likely to use teaching by invitation or intratask variation? Explain your answer.

REFERENCES/ SUGGESTED READINGS

Belka, D. E., Conner, K. C., & Bowyer, G. R. (1991, April). *Quality and congruency of task presentations and teacher verbal feedback in preservice peer teaching episodes.* Revision of a paper presented at the International Association for Physical Education in Higher Education World Congress, Atlanta, GA.

Belka, D. E., & Short, C. J. (1991, January). *Implementing a content sequencing model in physical education instruction.* Paper presented at the International Association for Physical Education in Higher Education World Congress, Atlanta, GA.

Berliner, D. (1984). The half-full glass: A review of research on teaching. In P. Hosford (Ed.), *Using what we know about teaching.* Alexandria, VA: Association for Supervision and Curriculum Development.

Brophy, J. (1983). Classroom organization and management. *The Elementary School Journal, 83,* 265–286.

Bunker, L. K. (1991). The role of play and motor skill development in building children's self-confidence and self-esteem. *The Elementary School Journal, 91*(5), 467–471.

Csikszentmihalyi, M., & Csikszentmihalyi, I. S. (Eds.) (1988). *Optimal experience: Psychological studies of flow in consciousness.* New York: Cambridge University Press.

Graham, G. (1992). Teaching children physical education. Champaign, IL: *Human Kinetics.*

Graham, K. C., Hussey, K., Taylor, K., & Werner, P. (1993). A study of verbal presentations of three effective teachers [Abstract]. *Research Quarterly for Exercise and Sport, 64,* 87A.

Landin, D. (1994). The role of verbal cues in skill learning. *Quest, 46,* 299–313.

Masser, L. (1987). The effects of refinement on student achievement in a fundamental motor skill in grades K through 6. *Journal of Teaching in Physical Education, 6*(2), 174–182.

Masser, L. (1993). Critical cues help first grade students' achievement in handstands and forward rolls. *Journal of Teaching in Physical Education, 12,* 301–312.

National Center for Chronic Disease Prevention and Health Promotion. (1997). Guidelines for school and community programs to promote lifelong physical activity among young people. *Journal of School Health, 67*(6), 202–219.

Rink, J. E. (1993). *Teaching physical education for learning.* St. Louis, MO: Mosby–Year Book.

Rink, J. E. (1996). Effective instruction in physical education. In S. Silverman and K. Ennis (Eds.), *Student learning in physical education* (pp. 171–198). Champaign, IL: Human Kinetics.

Rink, J. E., & Werner, P. H. (1989). Qualitative measures of teaching performance scale (QMTPS). In P. W. Darst, D. B. Zakrasjeck, & V. H. Mancini (Eds.), *Analyzing physical education and sport instruction* (2nd ed.). Champaign, IL: Human Kinetics.

Rosenshine, B. (1983). Teaching functions in instructional programs. *The Elementary School Journal, 83,* 335–351.

Rosenshine, B., & Stevens, R. (1988). Teaching functions. In M. E. Wittrock (Ed.), *Handbook of research on teaching.* New York: Macmillan.

Sharpe, T. L., Hawkins, A., & Wiegand, R. (1989). Model/practice versus verbal/rehearsal introductions of systems skills within an individually prescribed instructional system. *Journal of Teaching in Physical Education, 9*(1), 25–38.

Siedentop, D. (1991). *Developing teaching skills in physical education* (3rd ed.). Mountain View, CA: Mayfield.

Siedentop, D., Herkowitz, J., & Rink, J. (1984). *Elementary physical education methods.* Englewood Cliffs, NJ: Prentice-Hall.

Southard, D., & Higgins, T. (1989). Changing movement patterns: Effects of demonstration and practice. *Research Quarterly for Exercise and Sport, 58*(1), 77–80.

Werner, P., & Rink, J. E. (1989). Case studies of teacher effectiveness in second grade physical education. *Journal of Teaching in Physical Education, 8*(4), 280–297.

Instructional Approaches

Here is Edward Bear, coming downstairs now, bump, bump, bump, on the back of his head, behind Christopher Robin. It is, as far as he knows, the only way of coming downstairs, but sometimes he feels that there really is another way, if only he could stop bumping for a moment and think of it.

——A. A. Milne

Instructional approaches? Organizational strategies? Teaching style? Teaching strategies? Instructional formats? What is what? When should which one be used? What are they? The choices often seem confusing—even the definitions seem confusing. Though referred to by a variety of names, instructional approaches, organizational strategies, teaching strategies, and instructional formats all refer to *how* content is delivered to the students—the different ways that a teacher organizes for the delivery of instruction—rather than to *what* is delivered (Rink, 1993; Siedentop, 1991). Teaching style, on the other hand, refers to the instructional and managerial atmosphere of the gymnasium (Siedentop, 1991). Whether the gym is warm, positive, businesslike, demanding, easygoing—are all part of the teacher's style. This chapter focuses on what we have chosen to call instructional approaches: various ways that the teacher can organize and deliver the content to children. We have found six instructional approaches—direct instruction, task teaching, guided discovery, peer teaching, cooperative learning, and child-designed instruction—to be most useful in our teaching (Table 13.1).

"Which strategy should I use when?" "Which is the best?" are both common questions. Yet, the answer to the questions is, "It all depends." The appropriate instructional approach depends on a number of things. The teacher's beliefs about the ultimate purpose of education and the goal of a lesson should play a vital part in the instructional approach used in a class, yet both must be tempered by other aspects. The skill and preference of the teacher, the characteristics of the students, the nature of the content, and the context in which the teaching is taking place (Siedentop, 1991) all affect which instructional approach might be best for a certain class at a certain time.

Your teaching skills as well as your personal preferences should factor into the instructional approach you choose to use. Your "comfort zone" is a legitimate ingredient in how you choose to deliver content to the children. This is not to say you shouldn't ever stretch your limits, but that teachers generally are more effective when they are using strategies that "fit" them. As teachers grow and develop they acquire new strategies and see a need for new approaches to accomplish the goals they have set for their classes.

The characteristics of the children in your classes have a significant impact on the instructional approach that you choose. How much responsibility is the class ready for? How many decisions are the students capable of sharing? Will the lesson fail if the students are allowed to choose between several activities? These are some of the other considerations a teacher must take into account. For example, if the teacher believes students should be responsible for their own decisions and should direct their own learning, then direct instruction might seem to be contradictory to the teacher's goals. But for children who have never been given the responsibility to make decisions about their own learning or been taught any self-direction, a

Table 13.1 Characteristics of Six Instructional Approaches

Instructional Approach	Goal	Teacher Skills	Characteristics Children Need	Content	Context
Direct instruction	Efficient skill learning	Clarity	Beginning learners New students	Specific skills	Whole class
Task teaching	Skill learning + independence	Ability to monitor multifaceted environment	Independent working skills	Already learned skills; self-assessment; product-oriented tasks	Large spaces
Inquiry	Skill learning + problem solving	Questioning	Beginning learners	Exploration	Whole class
Cooperative learning	Skill learning + group inter-dependence; individual responsibility	Ability to design meaningful tasks	Independent working skills	Complex sequences; basic skills	Groups
Child-designed	Skill learning + self-responsibility	Ability to guide and monitor	Ability to use time wisely; independent working skills	Use of learned skills	Groups
Peer teaching	Skill learning + cooperation	Active monitoring	Independent working skills	Simple, clear cues; limited performance	Large spaces

Figure 13.1 Using the direct instruction approach, this teacher can effectively communicate specific content to the class as a whole. Teaching the class as a whole is an effective method of organizing instruction.

It takes experience, including defeat, failure, and frustration, to develop skills as a teacher. It takes years to become established in a new community and then more time to develop an organization strong enough to fight oppressive schools effectively. With the best will in the world, it also takes years to learn to build the right tone in a class and equip the room sensibly, to develop an eye for children in trouble, to know how to support students and how to make demands on them without oppressing them, to know when to add something new or step back and leave the children alone. Teaching is no simple matter. It is hard work, part craft, part art, part technique, part politics, and it takes time to develop ease within such a complex role. However, for many of us the effort makes sense, for one gets the opportunity to see young people grow while one has a positive and caring role in their lives.

Herbert Kohl, *On Teaching*

design complex routines and sequences, a child-designed or guided discovery strategy may be more effective.

The environment or context in which the learning is taking place is an additional factor that influences the instructional approach that is used. This is especially true of facilities and equipment. If a task or lesson requires that students be spread out over a large space (such as a field), making it difficult to provide continuous feedback to and verbal communication with the children, a task-teaching strategy may be appropriate. In a situation in which safety is a paramount issue, as in a first experience with large apparatus in gymnastics, direct instruction may be more appropriate.

Whatever instructional approach is chosen, it should be based on careful consideration of the goals of the lesson, the skills and preferences of the teacher, the characteristics of the children, the content, and the context. One approach is better than the other only for a particular situation.

child-designed program would most likely lead to chaos. Instead, the teacher might choose to use direct instruction while at the same time giving children limited or structured choices, thus teaching them how to make responsible decisions.

Different content may lend itself to different instructional approaches. If you are trying to teach a basic skill a direct instructional strategy may be the most effective. Alternately, if the children are asked to

Direct Instruction

Direct instruction is by far the most common approach used in physical education classes (Figure 13.1). It has been called by a variety of names, active instruction (Siedentop, 1991) and interactive teaching (Rink, 1993) being two of the most common. In direct instruction the teacher directs the responses of the students: by telling them what to do, showing them how to practice, and then directing their practice. Students usually work as a whole class or in small groups. As children practice, the teacher evaluates what they are doing and provides more instruction. Each teacher decision (instruction) is based on the responses the students gave to the previous task. The content is communicated by the teacher, and the pacing of the lesson is controlled by the teacher. Usually the entire class practices the same task or a variation of that task.

Direct instruction is effective when the teacher's goal is to have students learn a specific skill and perform that skill correctly in a specified manner. For example, if your goal is to teach the underhand throw, you want children to step with the foot opposite the throwing hand, extend the arm, and follow through. At this point, direct instruction would be an appropriate instructional choice—some children might learn the correct way of throwing without your assistance, but many would not. Direct instruction is not an appropriate approach for children who are beginners, however, and not developmentally ready to produce a mature skill pattern.

Direct instruction utilizes all the components of effective teaching, but five are particularly important:

1. Initially the teacher gives the student a clear idea of what is to be learned. The teacher or a student *correctly* demonstrates the skill, along with the important cues. For example, the teacher who is focusing on landing from a jump emphasizes in the demonstration that for a soft, quiet landing, the ankles and knees must be flexed prior to landing.
2. The second aspect is to give explanations and instructions clearly and repeat the cues often. At the end of a lesson, we often ask the children to repeat the cues so that we know whether we've been effective. The answers to the question "What are the important things to remember when you're trying to land softly and quietly from a jump?" will tell you whether the children have really remembered your teaching cues related to soft, quiet landings.
3. Next, the teacher gives specific feedback. In our example, the children now practice flexing their knees and ankles prior to landing; the teacher specifically tells them how well they're flexing their knees and ankles. The teacher tells the children *exactly* what they are (or are not) doing correctly so that they can improve. Once the children have the "big" idea—soft, quiet landings—the teacher helps them land softly and quietly by structuring appropriate tasks and giving them information about how well they perform. The teacher proceeds in small steps, but at a brisk pace.

4. One of the most important and obvious factors in the direct approach is often overlooked. Children need *considerable* opportunities for practice if they're actually going to *learn* to land softly and quietly. For this reason we always try to structure the learning situation so that the children have plenty of practice. Most of the time we're able to arrange the environment so that children rarely, if ever, have to wait. We try to ensure that all the children are active a minimum of 60 percent of the lesson, more when possible.
5. High success rates are also important for learning, especially the basic skills. We try to provide tasks that allow children to be successful about 80 percent of the time. This motivates the children and also allows them to grasp one skill before moving on to the next level. If children can't land softly and quietly when they jump from the floor, for example, then obviously they won't be able to land effectively when they jump from a bench or a wooden box.

Each of these components is developed and explained in more detail in Chapter 12.

Direct instruction calls for a specific response, one the teacher is looking for and helps the children to produce. Just any response is not acceptable. For example, if you want to teach the children to use opposition when they throw overhand, you'll need to give them plenty of practice opportunities and feedback to be certain that they step with the opposite foot before moving on to another aspect of the overhand throw. If you don't require the children to practice stepping with the opposite foot until the movement is overlearned, they will quickly forget the concept of opposition once the task changes. Then, you'll find yourself continually reminding children to "Step with the opposite foot when you throw." The proof of this statement can be found in any high school softball class: Watch the students play a game and see how many are inefficient throwers who've never learned the concept of opposition when they throw. They were *taught* the concept, but never to the point of *learning* it.

Direct instruction works well for beginning teachers or teachers who haven't worked with a group of students for a long while. Once the teacher has established a productive learning environment, teaching by invitation or intratask variation (Chapter 12) is helpful for changing the tasks to meet the needs of individual students within the direct instruction approach. This strategy also requires less time for organization than the other approaches, an important consideration for teachers who meet their students only once or twice a week.

Figure 13.2 Arrangement of stations (learning centers) in the teaching space.

Direct instruction should not be confused with a militaristic style of teaching in which everyone does the same thing, the same way, at the same time, and on cue. Remember, style is reflected in the atmosphere of the gym, and direct instruction is one way in which content can be delivered to the students. Direct instruction can be combined with a militaristic style, but that doesn't foster the positive atmosphere we support. We would much rather see direct instruction combined with a warm, caring, and positive style.

Task Teaching

A task-teaching instructional approach allows different students to practice different tasks at the same time. This approach is often called station teaching or learning centers. In our approach, task teaching includes stations and task sheets. With either option, different students practice different, specified tasks, often at their own pace, throughout the lesson.

Stations provide several activity areas (or learning centers) in the teaching space, each with a different task, through which students rotate during the class. See Figure 13.2 for an example of stations that could be used to practice a variety of skills during one lesson.

Task sheets provide another task-teaching option that allows children to practice at their own pace. Each child is given a task sheet (Figure 13.3), which contains a progression of activities. After successfully completing each task, the student records it on the task sheet, with that day's date, and then asks the teacher, a parent, another student, or an older child to observe the accomplishment and sign the sheet. Initially, we have entire classes work on the same task sheet at the same time. As children learn to use task sheets, we let them pick from task sheets on several different skill themes.

Task teaching provides students with a structured opportunity to work on their own or with partners, but

it can create management problems. To manage stations and task sheets more easily, first explain all the stations or the task sheet to the class. Tell them what they are supposed to do, and, if they are to have activities verified, who is to do the verification (teacher or another student). Second, make sure the managerial aspects are quite explicit. Designate the areas in which activities are to occur or where specific stations are located. Design, explain, and teach a rotation system between areas or stations. With stations, we initially have students change stations on a signal. Once children are able to function using this strategy, they can be allowed to choose the stations at which they'd like to work (though we usually limit the number of stu-

> ▶ I recently walked into a large multipurpose room full of thirty second-graders. As I sat to watch, I noticed that six very diverse activities were taking place: striking with hockey sticks in a game situation, doing pull-ups, jumping rope, shooting at targets, wall-climbing, and jumping and landing using a vaulting horse. The teacher was walking around from group to group talking to the children, offering feedback and encouragement but no instructions or managerial directions. At this point, I started to look more closely. *All* the children were active and on task. The noise level was productive; there was no screaming or yelling. Children were moving from activity to activity as they saw fit. Some were recording scores on wall charts. The teacher was never asked to make the decisions of a referee in the game. Children calmly retrieved stray equipment without interfering with other activities or sending the mob to chase a stray ball. These were seven-year-olds. I then asked the teacher how this situation came to be. His response: "I taught them at the beginning of the year the rules for Fridays (the designated day for choice activities), and we practiced."

Figure 13.3 Task sheet.

Name _____   Teacher _____

BALANCE TASK SHEET

Date Accomplished	Verification	Challenge
		I am able to walk forward the entire length without falling off.
		I am able to walk leading with my right side the entire length without falling off.
		I am able to walk leading with my left side the entire length without falling off.
		I am able to walk backward the entire length without falling off.
		I am able to walk forward (with my hands folded on my head) the entire length without falling off.
		I am able to walk forward the entire length with an eraser balanced on my head.
		I am able to walk backward the entire length with an eraser balanced on my head.
		I am able to walk along the beam, pick up a beanbag, and walk to the other end without falling off.
		I am able to walk along the beam, balance on one knee, and walk to the other end without falling off.
		I am able to walk the entire length of the balance beam without falling off, keeping my eyes closed all the way.
		I am able to bounce a ball across the beam without a miss.
		I am able to roll a ball along a beam without either the ball or myself touching the ground.
		I am able to walk along the beam, do a complete turn on one foot only, and walk to the end without falling off.
		I am able to walk along the beam twirling a hoop on one arm, without falling off.
		I am able to walk along the beam balancing a wand in one hand without falling off.
		I am able to hop along the beam on one foot without falling off.
		I am able to throw a ball back and forth to a partner ___ times without a miss, while standing on the end of the beam.
		I am able to jump rope on a balance beam ___ times without a miss.
		I am able to do a forward roll on the beam.
		I am able to jump onto the beam from a spring board without losing my balance.
		I am able to . . . .
		I am able to . . . .
		I am able to . . . .

dents at any one station or area). Eventually students can rotate from one station to another at their own discretion. Post necessary cues and directions at each station or practice area (Figure 13.4). This technique substantially reduces the time spent in providing additional instruction and management. Third, check with the students frequently to see how they're doing; move around the room. Fourth, start slowly, with only a few (maybe three) stations or a small task sheet (maybe five items) at the end of a lesson. It has been our experience that children enjoy working on task sheets and at stations, especially as a culminating activity, but they need guidance if this approach is to succeed for them and you.

With task teaching children won't all be involved in the same activity simultaneously; they and the teacher need to be ready to have more than one activity happening at the same time. Making task teaching work efficiently demands complex organizational and managerial skills on the part of the teacher. To benefit from the task-teaching approach, students need to have good independent working skills and to be able to function without close teacher supervision. Stopping when asked, rotating systematically, and not interfering with others are skills that students need to practice before they can use stations effectively.

A task instructional approach works well when students are practicing skills that have already been

Figure 13.4 Writing directions on poster boards and posting them at task-teaching stations can increase time spent in activity.

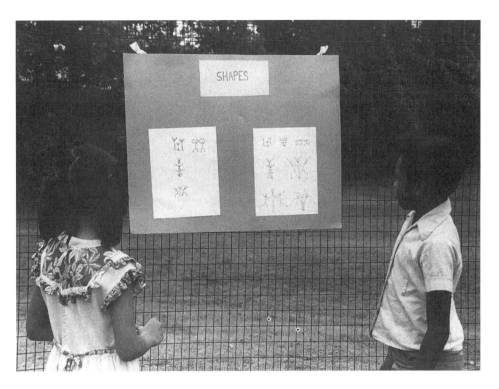

taught, with self-assessment, and with product-oriented tasks. The approach is not very effective for introducing new or complex skills. Task teaching works best with simple tasks that can be clearly and completely described and that have a clear goal—for example, make ten throws that hit the target and then take a step back.

One advantage of the task-teaching approach is that it allows you to set up areas that don't require students to wait in line for turns, thus making up for limitations in space and equipment. If, for example, in a balance unit you have a limited number of balance boards and balance beams, you can design tasks for each piece of equipment and have students rotate among the stations. Task-teaching instructional approaches also work well when children have to be spread out over a large space and verbal communication is difficult.

Guided Discovery

Guided discovery, an approach some call teaching through questions (Siedentop, 1991), a cognitive strategy (Rink, 1993), inquiry learning (Harrison, Blakemore, Buck, & Pellett, 1996), or problem solving, is designed to have children think and solve problems rather than copy the teacher's or another student's correct performance. In this approach, the teacher typically gives the task by asking questions. The teacher most often describes how the task will be practiced and some measure of success, but exactly how to perform the task is left to the child to explore and interpret. For example, the teacher may say, "From your spot on the floor, try to kick the ball to the wall both in the air and on the ground." The child knows how to practice (from the spot on the floor, kick) and a little about success (to the wall, in the air, and on the ground), but the rest is left up to the child.

We use two versions of guided discovery, convergent and divergent. One asks children to find multiple answers to a task, whereas the other encourages children to find a single answer.

Convergent Inquiry

Convergent inquiry encourages children to discover the same answer(s) to a series of questions the teacher asks. The teacher guides the children toward one or more correct answers. Several educators (Doolittle & Girard, 1991; Thorpe & Bunker, 1989; Werner & Almond, 1990) have successfully adapted this approach to teaching game skills and strategies. Mosston (1981) suggested that children can discover ideas, similarities, dissimilarities, principles (governing rules), order or system, a particular physical activity or movement, how, why, limits (the dimension of "how much," "how fast," etc.), and other elements. When we want children to learn one of these elements, we often use the discovery approach to increase their involvement.

It's important that the teacher formulate in advance the questions to be asked so that he or she can determine the correct sequence of questions that will lead the children to the solution. The teacher must ask questions in relevant small steps, rather than spanning too wide a gap. Equally important, the teacher needs to wait for the answer rather than becoming impatient and telling the answer.

The following sequence illustrating Mosston's (1981) classic slanty rope technique is a very good example of convergent inquiry encouraging children to find ways to avoid eliminating others from activity. This excerpt is from page 166 of his work.

Step 1: Ask two children to hold a rope for high jumping. Invariably they will hold the rope horizontally at a given height (for example, at hip level).

Step 2: Ask the group to jump over. Before they do so, you might want to ask the rope holders to decrease the height so that everybody can be successful.

Step 3: After everyone has cleared the height, you ask, "What shall we do now?" "Raise it!" "Raise it!" is the answer—always! (The success of the first jump motivates all to continue.)

Step 4: Ask the rope holders to raise the rope just a bit. The jumping is resumed.

Step 5: "Now what?" "Raise it!" the children will respond.

Step 6: Raising the rope two or three more times will create a new situation, a new reality. Some children will *not* be able to clear the height. In traditional situations these children will be *eliminated* from the jumping, and only some will continue; there will be a constantly diminishing number of active participants. The realization of individual differences becomes real; the *design* for opportunity for all has not yet come about.

Step 7: Stop the jumping and ask the group, "What can we do with the rope so that nobody will be eliminated?" Usually one or two of the following solutions are proposed by the children: (*a*) Hold the rope higher at the two ends and let the rope dip in the center. (*b*) Slant the rope! Hold the rope high at one end and low at the other.

Divergent Inquiry

In divergent inquiry, the teacher outlines a problem and then challenges the children to find many answers. This technique encourages children to find movement alternatives. A typical divergent question is, "Find at least three different ways to travel under the hoop (supported on cones) and at least three different ways to travel over the hoop."

In the divergent inquiry approach, the teacher must be careful not to impose personal values on the children's responses. The emphasis is on obtaining a *variety* of responses, not a single answer. For this reason, Mosston (1981) warned of two verbal behavior patterns that we try to avoid when using divergent inquiry. "You can do better than that" in response to a child's movement indicates that the teacher doesn't really value the response or that the teacher has a particular response in mind. Another counterproductive verbal behavior is a statement such as "Stop. Everyone watch Penny." After Penny finishes her movement, the teacher says, "Terrific, Penny." This behavior by the teacher, although perhaps innocent in nature, suggests to students that there's a right answer and therefore encourages the children to attempt to find a correct answer (convergent) rather than searching for a variety of alternatives, the goal of divergent inquiry.

In contrast, two productive verbal behaviors might include such statements as these:

"Now that you have found two ways, try to make the third one quite different."
"Stop. Everyone watch this half of the class. Good! Now, let's watch the other half. Great."

These two statements allow the teacher to provide feedback while at the same time encouraging creativity and diversity of responses.

Teachers who use guided discovery effectively can provide feedback that encourages exploration and problem solving rather than a single right answer. These teachers can also structure questions (tasks) that challenge children in small, sequential steps. These questions are based on a detailed knowledge of the content and knowing what should come next. Teachers using the guided-discovery approach are also masters at providing prompts to children—encouraging them to keep practicing by trying different ways or looking for different solutions.

We've found guided discovery especially helpful for encouraging children to think on their own to discover new and different approaches to performing skills and to solve questions related to teamwork and strategy. Guided discovery is also important for those children who aren't developmentally ready to learn a mature version of a skill, but simply need opportuni-

Teachers have to learn how to provide transitions for their pupils. It is not possible for most young people to make choices after five or six years of being told what to do every minute they are in school. It is equally hard for them to share resources, help other students, or decide what they want to learn after years of being expected to hoard, compete, and conform. Transitional situations often have to be provided. Some students need workbooks for a while; others want to memorize times tables or have weekly spelling tests. Young people are no different from adults. When faced with new possibilities they want something old and predictable to hold onto while risking new freedom. Inexperienced teachers often make the mistake of tearing down the traditional attitudes their students have been conditioned to depend upon before the students have time to develop alternative ways of learning and dealing with school. In their impatience they become cruel to students who do not change fast enough or who resist change altogether. One just cannot legislate compassion or freedom. Teaching as a craft involves understanding how people learn; as an art it involves a sensitive balance between presenting and advocating things you believe and stepping away and encouraging your students to make their own sense of your passion and commitment.

Herbert Kohl, *On Teaching*

Teaching was easy. All you did was tell them and they did it.

Fourth-grader after teaching a self-designed game to another group

ties to explore the movement. It is often the strategy we use at the precontrol level when students are exploring a new skill. It provides children a chance "to try things out" without a specific focus or direction.

Peer Teaching

Peer teaching is an instructional approach that uses peers in pairs or small groups to actively teach one another. In peer teaching the teacher plans the tasks and communicates them to the children; the children assume the roles of providing feedback and assessing. Demonstration of the task is shared between the children and the teacher. Often the teacher will demonstrate initially and the children, as peer teachers, will repeat the demonstration as necessary. A simple example of peer teaching would be using peers to help teach the overhand throw. After initial instructions and practice, children divide into pairs. Their task is to "coach" their partner to see if the partner brings the arm way back, steps forward on the opposite foot, and

follows through. If the partner does, then he or she gets a "thumbs up"; if the partner doesn't, the peer teacher tells the partner what to correct next time.

For peer teaching to be an effective instructional approach, the skill to be taught should be simple, the cues for observation very clear, and the performance easily measured. It is helpful to post the cues on the wall so that the peer "teachers" can remember them. Many teachers start out by using one peer teaching task in a lesson and then expand as the children become more competent teachers.

Children must be able to work cooperatively and independently for peer teaching to be a success. They must be responsible enough to take seriously the task of teaching another student. Children are asked to provide feedback as well as analyze performance; therefore, they must know the cues and what the skill looks like. The teacher, besides having to design the task, must be able to provide feedback to the peer teachers to assist them in their teaching.

Peer teaching can work with any content, but it works best when the skills are simple, there are clear criteria for observation, and the performance is limited and easily measured. For example, peer teaching works well with basic skills but is much more difficult with dynamic and strategic skills.

Children thoroughly enjoy being the teacher, but for the strategy to be successful they must be able to both analyze skill and provide feedback—something the teacher can help them learn through her or his presentation of the task.

Cooperative Learning

Cooperative learning is a relatively new instructional approach to physical education. In cooperative learning, group work is carefully designed to promote group interdependence and individual responsibility. Three common cooperative learning formats are "pairs-check," "jigsaw," and "co-op, co-op" (Kagan, 1990).

In pairs-check, children are in groups of four with two partner-pairs in each group. Each pair practices a task, teaching each other as in peer teaching. The two pairs then get together to assess each other to see if they are achieving the same outcomes, to provide

Figure 13.5 Child-designed activities allow teachers to work with children as individuals.

further feedback, and to practice. For example, the pairs-check strategy could be used to teach dribbling with the hands. After the initial task is given, pairs would work with each other, focusing on using the fingerpads, having the knees bent, and keeping the hand on top of the ball. Then, when each pair thought they had mastered the task, they would come together to check each other. In this sense, pairs-check is much like peer teaching.

In the jigsaw format, children are usually in groups of three or four. Each child becomes an "expert" on one aspect of a skill or task by working with the children who are "experts" from other groups. Children then return to their "home" group and teach their group their piece of the skill. The jigsaw format can be used quite effectively to teach activities with multiple parts while simultaneously developing interdependence.

Co-op, co-op is a cooperative learning format in which small groups are used to create a project with many components (Grineski, 1996). Each small group is responsible for one component of the larger project. The co-op, co-op format can be used to have children create a dance sequence in which several elements are to be portrayed. For example, in the dance depicting African American heritage described in Chapter 20, one group might develop the concept of slavery, another the concept of freedom, another the concept of strength as a people, another dispersal, another gathering, and another respect. Each group would then bring their piece to the full dance.

Cooperative learning works equally well with children who have highly developed responsibility skills or with children who need to learn to work together. Research suggests that cooperative learning has affective as well as cognitive benefits (Slavin, 1990). Teachers must be skilled in designing tasks that are meaningful to children.

A variety of content, from basic skills to complex sequences, can be adapted for use with cooperative-learning strategies. To find out more about cooperative learning in physical education, we suggest you read Steve Grineski's (1996) book, *Cooperative Learning in Physical Education.*

Child-Designed Instruction

Child-designed instructional approaches allow the child to be the center of the learning activities (Figure 13.5). In these strategies the teacher serves as a guide or mentor. There are several child-designed strategies; child-designed tasks and contracts are the two we use most often.

Child-Designed Tasks

Child-designed tasks urge children to design their own activities. This approach encourages creativity in children and also lets them invent and develop activities that match their skill levels or the skill level of the

Figure 13.6 Individual contract.

Time	Activity	Goal	Partner

Name _____

Contract for _____ 19 _____
                        (date)

COMMENTS:

1) Did you accomplish your goal?

2) What do you need to work on during the next class?

3) Do you want to tell me about the class?

group in which they're working. Within the context of various lessons we ask children to design their own games, dances, and gymnastic routines. See Chapters 20, 25, and 31 for examples of child-designed activities.

Contracts

As children become accustomed to working on their own, the teacher can use independent contracting to make instruction more personal. A teacher who uses independent contracting is saying to the students, "I trust you to make intelligent and responsible decisions about what you need to practice."

We've used the written contract illustrated in Figure 13.6. Each child writes down the skill or activity she or he will be practicing or playing, the goal to be achieved, the time to be spent practicing each activity, and (when appropriate) the name of a practice partner. Recognizing the dynamic nature of a physical education class, we let the children change their contracts during class, provided that they write down all changes. We encourage the children to save time by coming to physical education class with their contracts already completed for that day. In the final few minutes of a class, we ask the children to evaluate their accomplishments for that day.

Contracts can be used in physical education classes in a variety of ways. When you first use independent contracting, it is wise to restrict each child to a single skill theme or even a certain aspect of the skill theme or unit. For example, some teachers have used contracts as a culminating activity to let students decide how they want to complete their learning on a specific topic.

For teachers who want to try to incorporate child-designed strategies into their teaching but aren't sure where to begin, we have found the following suggestions helpful. Moderation is the key to success. If you simply say to children, "Make up your own game; it has to include throwing and catching" or "Write a contract about what you want to do in physical education," the results can be disastrous. We know from experience. Try to give children more specific instructions for designing activities:

> "Design beginning and ending movements for the balance, roll, balance sequence you've been practicing."
>
> "You've been practicing five movements: leaping, spinning, sinking, exploding, and freezing. Use them in a sequence that flows together smoothly."
>
> "We have been practicing dribbling for the past few lessons and will continue to do so for another week. Design a contract that tells what you will do each day for the first five minutes of class to practice your dribbling skills."

Several activities also serve to hold students accountable for working productively while working on their own. Reflection time allows children to spend time thinking about what they accomplished for the day and what they want to accomplish during the next class. It also lets children think about how much effort they put into accomplishing their independent tasks. You can set aside a few minutes at the beginning or end of class to have students reflect. Reflection is enhanced if children put their thoughts in writing. (See Chapter 14 for use of student journals.) Student sharing at the end of a lesson lets children offer their opinions about what they did or share their accomplishments with others. Teaching others what they have developed or learned also provides a strong accountability mechanism. As with any instructional format, teacher feedback and reinforcement are vital to the success of the approach: child-designed instruction teacher responses encourage children to stay on task, while at the same time providing reinforcement for the decisions the students are making.

INSTRUCTIONAL APPROACHES CITED IN THE *NATIONAL STANDARDS FOR PHYSICAL EDUCATION*

▶ The instructional strategy of peer teaching is referred to in the *National Standards for Physical Education* (NASPE, 1995) as a sample second-grade benchmark under Standard 5: Demonstrates responsible personal and social behavior in physical activity settings. The sample benchmark states: "Assists partner by sharing observations about skill performance during practice" (p. 25). The approach is also cited as a sample fourth-grade benchmark under Standard 2: Applies movement concepts and principles to the learning and development of motor skills. That sample benchmark states: "Accurately recognizes the critical elements of a throw made by a fellow student and provides feedback to that student" (p. 34).

The use of child-designed instructional strategies is identified as a sample sixth-grade benchmark under Standard 1: Demonstrates competency in many movement forms and proficiency in a few movement forms. The sample benchmark states: "Designs and performs gymnastics and dance sequences that combine traveling, rolling, balancing, and weight transfer into smooth, flowing sequences with intentional changes of direction, speed, and flow" (p. 46). These strategies are also referred to as a sample sixth-grade benchmark under Standard 3: Exhibits a physically active lifestyle. This benchmark states: "Participates in games, sports, dance, and outdoor pursuits both in and out of school based on individual interests and capabilities" (p. 50).

To function productively with a child-designed approach, children need to be highly motivated, be self-directed, and have the skills to work independently. They need to be knowledgeable about making use of the time and materials available to them. The teacher must be skilled in designing the initial task—and then must let the students work on their own, making their own decisions and their own mistakes. This is very hard for many of us to do. Child-designed strategies work well after the basic skill has been learned. They are especially useful with dynamic situations, when children are at different skill levels, and as culminating activities.

SUMMARY

An instructional approach can be defined as the way in which a teacher presents lesson content to a class. One of the myriad of questions that a teacher must answer is "Which instructional approach should I use?" The answer depends on a number of factors, the primary one being the teacher's goal for a particular lesson or series of lessons. Six instructional approaches (summarized in Table 13.1) can be used to deliver the lesson content to students.

The direct instructional approach is effective when students are to learn a specific skill technique. A task-teaching approach is helpful when having students practice a skill they have already learned. The inquiry approaches stimulate thinking and students' involvement on a cognitive level. Peer teaching fosters cooperation and provides repeated practice and feedback for children. Cooperative learning develops group-relation skills as well as stimulating cognitive involvement. Child-designed approaches encourage creativity and inventiveness; they involve children in creating their own learning experiences.

Each approach has its strengths, and each requires different student and teacher skills. Which strategy to select depends on the teacher's goals. One of the challenges reflective teachers face is analyzing both their students' and their own needs and skills and matching them with the goals of the lesson. Ideally, over a period of weeks, both the teacher and the children learn to work effectively no matter which instructional strategy is selected.

READING COMPREHENSION QUESTIONS

1. What is an instructional approach? Explain the differences among the six instructional approaches presented in this chapter.
2. What criteria might the teacher use in selecting a particular instructional approach for use with a class?
3. Give examples of convergent and divergent inquiry, written in the actual form in which they would be stated.
4. Select a skill theme from one of the skill theme chapters (Chapters 19, 21 through 24, 26 through 30) and develop a task sheet similar to the one in Figure 13.3. Include at least six different tasks, ranging from precontrol through utilization levels.
5. Why do we say that a direct instructional approach may not be the best for children who are not developmentally ready?
6. Using the skills of throwing and catching against a defense, design a task sequence using the jigsaw cooperative learning strategy.
7. What strategies can a teacher employ to begin to use child-designed approaches for instruction? Give an example of how one strategy might be developed for a group of eleven- or twelve-year-olds.
8. How can different instructional approaches be used to help students meet various National Standards for physical education?

REFERENCES/ SUGGESTED READINGS

Doolittle, S., & Girard, K. (1991). A dynamic approach to teaching games in elementary PE. *Journal of Physical Education, Recreation and Dance, 62*(4), 57–62.

Grineski, S. (1996). *Cooperative learning in physical education.* Champaign, IL: Human Kinetics.

Harrison, J., Blakemore, C., Buck, M., & Pellett, T. (1996). *Instructional strategies for secondary school physical education* (4th ed.). Dubuque, IA: Brown & Benchmark.

Kagan, S. (1990). The structural approach to cooperative learning. *Educational Leadership, 47*(4), 12–16.

Kohl, H. (1976). *On teaching.* New York: Schocken.

Milne, A. A. (1926). *Winnie the Pooh.* New York: Dutton.

Mosston, M. (1981). *Teaching physical education* (2nd ed.). Columbus, OH: Merrill.

National Association for Sport and Physical Education (NASPE). (1995). *Moving into the future: National Standards for physical education.* St. Louis, MO: Mosby.

Rink, J. (1993). *Teaching physical education for learning* (2nd ed.). St. Louis, MO: Mosby.

Slavin, R. (1990). Research on cooperative learning: Consensus and controversy. *Educational Leadership, 47*(4), 52–55.

Siedentop, D. (1991). *Developing teaching skills in physical education* (3rd ed.). Mountain View, CA: Mayfield.

Thorpe, R., & Bunker, D. (1989). A changing focus in games teaching. In L. Almond (Ed.), *The place of physical education in the schools.* London: Kogan Page.

Werner, P., & Almond, L. (1990). Models of games education. *Journal of Physical Education, Recreation and Dance, 61*(4), 23–27.

Assessing Student Learning

The primary goal of assessment should be seen as the enhancement of learning, rather than simply the documentation of learning.

——NASPE, 1995

Do you ever wonder what children really learn in physical education? Do you sometimes feel that even after "testing" you still don't know what the children actually can do? Do you occasionally feel that testing really doesn't help the students? Do you ever feel that testing is a waste of time and simply takes time away from teaching? If so, you are not alone. Educators in all fields, including physical education, are calling for more meaningful, practical, and worthwhile assessment methods (Wiggins, 1992). Although not a panacea, performance assessment methods—many of which are labeled authentic or alternative assessment—are a possible solution to these issues.

Performance assessments are measures in which students actually demonstrate the skills, knowledge, or attitudes that the teacher wants to assess (Hopple, 1995). These measures are considered authentic when they are conducted in real-to-life contexts. They require students to apply what they have learned to situations that relate directly to present or future everyday life. The context is thus relevant and meaningful. Authentic assessment is part of the whole learning process, not tacked on to the end of the unit, but incorporated into the unit on a daily basis. Feedback is given to students during the assessment process so that learning can take place during assessment. Assessment and instruction are no longer separated—one informs the other.

Understanding the Purpose of Assessment

Assessment essentially asks two questions: What was learned? and How well was it learned? The first question deals with content; the second, with the nature of the performance and the level to which it was done. Assessment also serves the dual purpose of providing feedback to the learner as to the two assessment questions as well as providing the teacher with information about the program and student learning.

Assessing What Was Learned

Assessment of "what" was learned answers this question: What should children know and be able to do? Designing performance assessments to answer this question is not always easy, largely because we are not used to thinking clearly about our outcomes. We tend to think about what we are going to have students do and activities to engage children rather than what the result will be ("Questioning our motives," 1996). Yet, several things can help us focus on what we want students to be able to do and know. The *National Standards for Physical Education* (NASPE, 1995) outline essential learning for all students in physical education. When those standards are translated into specific benchmarks or goals, they provide us with a clear direction about what it is we want students to learn. The skill theme chapters in *Children Moving* provide activities for meeting those standards. Thus, the first step in assessment is to establish outcomes for your physical education program.

After deciding upon the outcomes, the next step is to determine how the learning will be assessed. Traditionally, in physical education we have measured learning, usually at the end of a unit, using standardized tests based on normative criteria. The current assessment movement calls for assessment to be more meaningful and worthwhile. Assessment should be tied to instruction and provide students with information that will fuel their interests ("Questioning . . . ", 1996). A good assessment model supports students' desire to learn. Such an assessment model calls for us as teachers to relinquish some of the control we have held over assessment and give it to the students.

To meet these new demands, a variety of performance-based assessment alternatives have been developed that focus on high-priority objectives and significant outcomes for students. These alternatives are authentic and designed to take place in the real-life setting of day-to-day activities in or outside the gym and physical education class, not on artificially contrived "test" days. All the assessment alternatives are formative in nature, providing students with ongoing and continual feedback about their performance, rather than summative, providing feedback only as a culminating event. In addition, because our goals for physical education include cognitive and affective, as well as psychomotor, outcomes, assessment occurs in all three domains. There are many performance assessments available to physical education teachers. We have chosen ones that best fit the content we are teaching and ones that we know work.

In *Children Moving* we call performance assessments that are designed primarily to provide feedback to the learner *challenges*. You will find these challenges in all the skill theme chapters. These tasks are designed to let students, on a regular basis, self-assess how they are doing with the skill being taught. They also serve to focus the children and keep them practicing the task.

> Because the student is the primary client of all assessment, assessment should be designed to improve performance, not just monitor it.
>
> Grant Wiggins

BOX 14.1   JOURNALS IN THE *NATIONAL STANDARDS FOR PHYSICAL EDUCATION*

Journals are referenced three times in the *National Standards for Physical Education* (NASPE, 1995):

As a Sample Sixth-Grade Assessment Option under Standard 2: Applies movement concepts and principles to the learning and development of motor skills

The sample assessment states: "Students are asked to perform a self-assessment of their progress in throwing different types of objects (e.g., Frisbee, football, softball, deck tennis rings) and record this information in their journal. Moreover, they should describe the differences and similarities in throwing these objects and discuss which objects were easy/difficult to throw. Criteria for assessment: (a) correctly identifies personal status on the use of critical elements of throwing, (b) identifies differences and similarities that occur when applying principles of throwing to different objects, and (c) describes which objects they found easy/difficult to throw" (p. 49).

As a Sample Second-Grade Assessment Option under Standard 4: Achieves and maintains a health-enhancing level of physical fitness

The sample assessment states: "Following a discussion of muscular strength and endurance appropriate for second graders and participation in different activities that focus on climbing, hanging, and taking weight momentarily on their hands, have the children write in their journals about their strength in climbing, hanging, and taking weight on hands. Assist each child in setting a goal for themselves. Have the children illustrate their journal entries with a drawing of themselves. Ask them to circle the body parts (muscles) used for hanging, climbing, and supporting weight on hands. Criteria for assessment: (a) established appropriate goal relative to muscular strength and endurance and (b) correctly identifies the body parts involved in hanging, climbing, and taking weight on hands" (p. 24).

As a Sample Second-Grade Assessment Option under Standard 7: Understands that physical activity provides opportunities for enjoyment, challenge, self-expression, and social interaction

The sample assessment states: "At different times throughout the year, students are requested to write and/or draw in their journals:

■ How they felt when they scored a goal, made a basket, or kicked a ball really far.

■ How they felt when they missed the ball for the kick or hit.

■ How they felt when the class tried an activity for the first time.

■ Their favorite activities in physical education class.

Criteria for assessment: (a) identifies feelings associated with successes and failures and (b) expresses these feelings in their journal" (p. 29).

Sometimes these challenges occur at the end of a series of tasks and sometimes in the middle, but they are built right into the tasks that we give students.

In this section we have chosen to focus on ten performance assessments that are designed to provide feedback to the teacher as well as the student. These are broader than the challenges, often assessing the cognitive and affective, as well as the psychomotor, domains. And, with the exception of the student journal, these assessment options provide a product that can be scored. In the skill theme chapters we include suggestions (identified with the assessment icon 🖼) as to where these assessments might be used. The examples show how we make assessment part of our daily teaching, not a separate entity at the end of a unit. Although we focus on a limited number of assessment options here, many more are available. We hope that these suggestions will allow you to develop other options that are specific to your situation. When you find an assessment option that really works, we invite you to share it with us.

Student Journals   Student journals (Box 14.1) are like diaries. They are written records of participation, results, responses, feelings, perceptions, or reflections about actual happenings or outcomes (NASPE, 1995). Student journals provide a wonderful opportunity to assess the affective (Cutforth & Parker, 1996) domain of our teaching. Students can simply be asked to write down their feelings, or they can be asked to respond to structured questions to assess more specific goals (Figure 14.1). These journals often yield fascinating

BOX 14.2   EXIT SLIPS IN THE *NATIONAL STANDARDS FOR PHYSICAL EDUCATION*

Exit slips are referenced in the *National Standards for Physical Education* (NASPE, 1995):

As a Sample Second-Grade Assessment Option under Standard 2: Applies movement concepts and principles to the learning and development of motor skills

The sample assessment (listed as an event task) states: "Have students pretend that Rapunzel recently enrolled in your school. She knows nothing about catching a ball. Students are asked to explain what Rapunzel needs to know to catch a ball thrown to her from the front at about chest high. Instruct the students to imagine themselves practicing with Rapunzel and providing feedback after each attempted catch. Have them imagine looking for the critical elements (ready position, hand and arm position, eye contact, and absorption of force). Criteria for assessment: (a) identifies critical elements of catching and (b) uses appropriate feedback to improve performance" (p. 21).

Teacher Question: How do you feel about today's tournament compared to the others, when you were playing with smaller teams?

Brenda: I liked the two-on-two game better than the tournament.

Justin: Bad, it's harder to win.

Dustin: It was the best tournament I played in.

Casey: It was funner than others because you [could] play the whole thing.

Beau: It sucked. Because too many people and the teams sucked and I got in a fight.

Figure 14.1 Sample journal question with student responses. *Source:* From Steve Sorenson and Brad Rempel, as quoted in "Promoting Affective Development in Physical Education: The Value of Journal Writing" by N. Cutforth and M. Parker, 1996, *JOPERD, 67*(7), pp. 22. Used with permission from American Association of Health, Physical Education, Recreation, and Dance.

insights into how children perceive physical education class.

Remember, the purpose of journals is for students to reflect on their feelings, growth, frustrations, joys, and successes regarding physical activity and physical education. Students have to feel safe in doing that. One sure way to stifle the honesty and reflectivity of the students is to grade journals and/or correct writing skills. The purpose of journals is to give students a venue for writing honestly and freely.

Exit (or Entrance) Slips   Exit slips (Box 14.2) are written pieces that allow the teacher to assess specific learning goals for the lesson. The slips quite often contain two or three questions or ask the student to write in some form about specific learning cues or affective goals for the lesson (Figure 14.2).

Helping Murgatroid provides another format for exit slips. This is how we use Helping Murgatroid; modify the instructions to fit your situation:

The lesson is being taught in a multipurpose room that becomes a cafeteria from 11:30 A.M. to 1:00 P.M. On one side of the room, lunch tables are permanently set up. Before beginning the lesson, the teacher places pencils and pieces of paper on the lunch tables, enough for each child in the upcom-

BOX 14.3   HOMEWORK IN THE *NATIONAL STANDARDS FOR PHYSICAL EDUCATION*

Homework is referenced as a parental report in the *National Standards for Physical Education* (NASPE, 1995):

As a Sample Second-Grade Assessment Option under Standard 5: Demonstrates responsible personal and social behavior in physical activity settings

The sample assessment states: "Students are given the assignment to select and practice at home several movement skills (e.g., balancing on one foot, catching a tossed ball) on which they need additional work. They must record what they did and for how long, and have their parents sign the record at the end of the week. Criteria for assessment: (a) identifies correctly the skills needing additional work, (b) practices identified skill at least three times a week for 15 minutes, and (c) records performance accurately and neatly" (p. 26).

ing class. The lesson begins as normal. At some point, the teacher stops the lesson and says to the children, "Remember several weeks ago we were practicing throwing? What I want you to do now is sit at one of the lunch tables so that you each have a piece of paper and a pencil. Then I want you to write a note to your friend Murgatroid. Murgatroid is not a very good thrower. List five cues that might help Murgatroid become a better thrower. As soon as you are finished, you can return to the other side of the 'gym' and continue working on your jumping-and-landing sequence."

The entire Helping Murgatroid process takes less than five minutes, but it can be enormously helpful in assessing what the children remember from past lessons. Figure 14.3 provides three examples of Helping Murgatroid cues written by children. Which set of responses would you be satisfied with?

Homework   Homework (Box 14.3) is work a student completes outside of the physical education class. It can be a record of student regularity, progress, process, or product participation or some other written work. Quite often we ask parents to verify the work. Physical education homework is similar to reports of reading done at home, and we have found homework quite useful, especially in terms of fitness

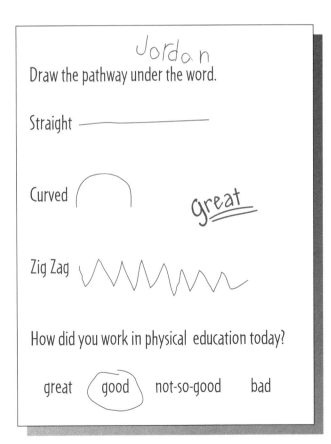

Figure 14.2   Exit slips.

1. use both hands

2. try throwing over your head

3. move your feet apart a little

4.

5.

---

1. hold the ball in one hand and when you throw step with the oposite foot.

2. follow through

3. keep your ey on the target

4. put your side to the target

5. throw hard enough to get it to the target but dont throw to hard

---

1. watch my friends first.

2. then you try.

3. then well help you throw strat.

4. then you would try.

5. then you would get it right

Figure 14.3 Sample responses to the question, "What cues would you suggest to help Murgatroid become a better overhand thrower?"

From the teacher's perspective, the management of journals and exit slips is the key to their success (or lack of it). Four guidelines may help:

■ *Determine the major purpose of the journal or exit slip.* Limit the scope initially. Focus on learning cues, on behavior, or on students' thoughts about the lesson—choose one. Expand the scope when you feel comfortable.

■ *Decide on a format for writing.* Because students are not accustomed to writing in physical education, their writing may initially be shallow and unfocused. Therefore, we have found it useful to provide students with a question to answer. As students become accustomed to writing, the level of the question may be increased to ask for more open-ended responses.

■ *Organize writing procedures.* To effectively respond to journals, many teachers use journals with only two or three classes at a time and then switch to another group of classes at the end of a marking period. We have found it most effective to keep the journals in the gym (and sometimes with classroom teachers) in containers by class. This way you can

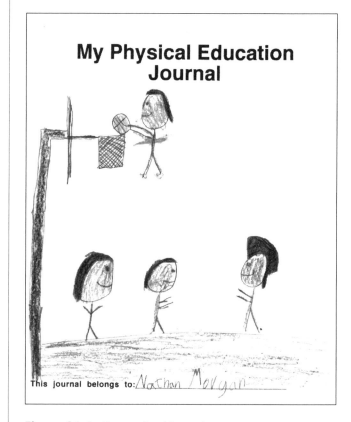

Figure 14.4 Personalized journal cover

Figure 14.5   Child's class journal.

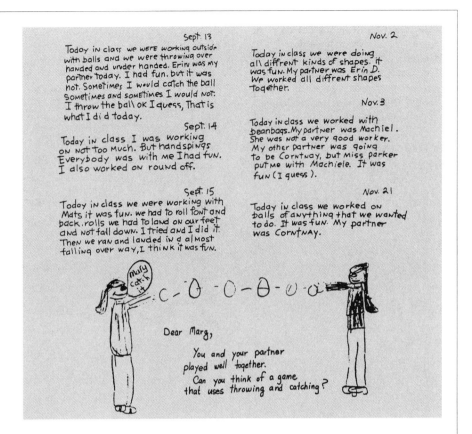

Sept. 13
Today in class we were working outside with balls and we were throwing over handed and under handed. Erin was my partner today. I had fun. but it was not. Sometimes I would catch the ball Sometimes and sometimes I would not. I throw the ball ok I guess, That is what I did today.

Sept. 14
Today in class I was working on not too much. But handsprings Everybody was with me I had fun. I also worked on round off.

Sept. 15
Today in class we were working with Mats it was fun. we had to roll font and back. rolls we had To land on our feet and not fall down. I tried and I did it. Then we ran and landed in a almost falling over way, I think it was fun.

Nov. 2
Today in class we were doing all diffrent kinds of shapes. it was fun. My partner was Erin D. We worked all diffrent shapes together.

Nov. 3
Today in class we worked with beanbags. My partner was Machiel. She was not a very good worker. My other partner was going to be Corntnay, but miss parker put me with Machiele. It was fun (I guess).

Nov. 21
Today in class we worked on balls of anything that we wanted to do. It was fun. My partner was Corntnay.

Dear Marg,
You and your partner played well together.
Can you think of a game that uses throwing and catching?

read them when you get the chance and don't have to hunt them down. One of the best ways to encourage children to keep a journal is to let them personalize it (Figure 14.4). We have used everything from college blue books to manila folders to laminated construction paper. Usually we have students write for about three minutes at the end of class. Some teachers prefer the beginning of class if they want students to reflect on their previous journal entry before class (Figure 14.5).

■ *Read and respond.* One key aspect of journals and exit slips is providing feedback to students (Figure 14.6). Teachers need to respond to student writing. Responses can be short, snappy phrases (e.g., "Good job!") or longer, probing questions. Generally, it takes less than a minute to respond to each student's entry, but the minutes add up. To manage the time, some teachers have students do journals or exit slips only once a week; others have the children do them for every lesson but review them only once a week; still others use them with selected classes only.

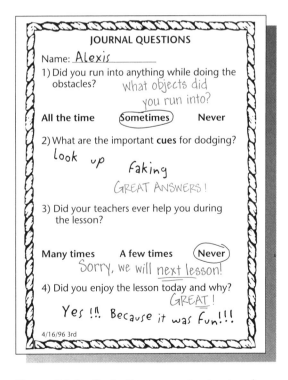

JOURNAL QUESTIONS

Name: Alexis

1) Did you run into anything while doing the obstacles?   *What objects did you run into?*

All the time   (Sometimes)   Never

2) What are the important **cues** for dodging?

look up   Faking   *GREAT ANSWERS!*

3) Did your teachers ever help you during the lesson?

Many times   A few times   (Never)   *Sorry, we will next lesson!*

4) Did you enjoy the lesson today and why?   *GREAT!*

Yes !!!. Because it was Fun!!!

4/16/96 3rd

Figure 14.6   Student's response to structured journal questions, with teacher feedback.

Figure 14.7 Homework assignment: fitness. *Source:* From Super Active Kids Program Instructor's Manual (unpublished manuscript) by B. Entzion et al., 1991, Grand Forks: University of North Dakota, Department of Health, Physical Education and Recreation.

After School/Weekend Exercise Records

After School/Weekends	Activity	After School/Weekends
	Jump Rope	
	Jogging/Walking	
	Soccer	
	Basketball	
	Football	
	Swimming	
	Dancing	
	Hiking	
	Gymnastics	
	Biking	
	Tennis	
	Other (_____)	
	Did Nothing	

Parent Signature
Date: ___/___/___

Parent Signature
Date: ___/___/___

Instructions:

1. When your child does an activity for at least 20 minutes, draw around the box to highlight it (more than 20 minutes still only counts as one activity credit).

2. Write which day the activity was done in the box. Use the letters M, T, W, R, F, or S.

3. Sign and date the record, and cut it out for your child to bring to school.

or activity participation. Figure 14.7 illustrates a form for recording and verifying out-of-class assignments.

Peer Observation   Peer observation (Box 14.4) of students by other students can be used to assess competence in performance of skills and demonstration of selected critical elements. Peer observation is easily built into tasks by asking students to work as partners and to provide each other with selected feedback regarding performance. For example, while working on dribbling with the hands, one student can be asked to watch the other and see if the partner uses the fingerpads, bends the knees, and has a staggered stance.

To more fully tie assessment to instruction and learning, the partner can provide feedback to the performer to help him or her improve. On a more formal basis, students can record their observations for later use by the teacher (Figure 14.8). The key aspect is for the teacher to define the cues clearly enough so that the partner can observe and comment. Children are incredibly honest when evaluating their own skills. Some educators have called for involving students in the evaluation of all their work (Willis, 1996).

Event Tasks   Event tasks (Box 14.5) are performance tasks that can be completed within a class period or

BOX 14.4 PEER OBSERVATION IN THE NATIONAL STANDARDS FOR PHYSICAL EDUCATION

Peer observation is referenced five times in the *National Standards for Physical Education* (NASPE, 1995):

As Sample Second- and Fourth-Grade Assessment Options under Standard 1: Demonstrates competency in many movement forms and proficiency in a few movement forms

The sample second-grade assessment states: "Students are asked to work on balancing on different bases of support (e.g., two hands and one foot, hands and knees, headstand). Students should balance in four different positions, two using symmetrical shapes and two using asymmetrical shapes. Students are asked to draw their favorite symmetrical and asymmetrical balances on papers, labeling 'S' and 'A,' respectively. Students now select a partner who will observe their balances and then indicate on the paper: (1) if the drawn figures were labeled correctly and (2) if the balances were held for 3 seconds. Criteria for assessment: (a) completes four balances, two—symmetrical and two—asymmetrical, (b) correctly labels balances 'S' and 'A', (c) maintains stillness in balance for three seconds, and (d) observer correctly assesses the appropriateness of the labels and the extent to which the performer was still" (p. 19).

The sample fourth-grade assessment states: "Have partners observe the preparatory phase of a designated skill in an attempt to ascertain the correct use of critical elements. For example, student A will throw a ball toward a target five times using the overhand pattern while student B observes the performance, focusing on a single critical element during the preparatory phase (e.g., opposite foot forward, side to target, arm pulled way back). The observing student gives a 'thumbs up' if the critical element is correct; if incorrect, the observing student tells what is needed to improve. Criteria for assessment: (a) thrower displays the critical element that is the focus of the observation and (b) observer makes an accurate judgment on the performance" (p. 33).

As Sample Second- and Fourth-Grade Assessment Options under Standard 2: Applies movement concepts and principles to the learning and development of motor skills

The sample second-grade assessment states: "Using an appropriate size ball, students practice throwing at a target on the wall alternating with a partner in five throw turns. The students should be instructed to concentrate on the critical elements of throwing as taught by the instructor (i.e., ready position, arm preparation opposite side to the target, step with leg opposite the throwing arm, follow-through, accuracy of throw). After each bout of five throws the partner gives feedback on one of the critical elements by drawing a smiley face on a score sheet each time the element is employed as instructed. Note changes in performance with subsequent five throw bouts. Criteria for assessment: (a) recognizes critical elements of basic movement pattern and (b) adjusts conditions for success following feedback" (p. 20).

The sample fourth-grade assessment states: "Students observe a classmate in a performance showing combinations of various basic skills used in a changing environment. The observer analyzes the skills performed for maturity of movement by determining the critical elements used or missing. For each skill combination, students must first identify if the performance represents a mature pattern. If the performance has critical elements missing, students must identify those missing elements. Finally, they should suggest ideas for either practice or use of available cues to improve performance. Criteria for assessment: (a) accurately identifies the critical elements required of the various movement skills, (b) recognizes the presence or absence of critical elements during performance, and (c) suggests appropriate practice activities" (p. 35).

As a Sample Second-Grade Benchmark under Standard 5: Demonstrates responsible personal and social behavior in physical activity settings

The sample assessment states: "Students are given a task of practicing the underhand throw at a target with a partner. Students may choose the type and size of ball, distance from the target (enough distance to produce a throw, not a toss), and the height of the target. Partners assist each other by marking a score sheet for accuracy for each of the five throws. Partners change roles after five throws. Take as many turns as time allows. Criteria for assessment: (a) chooses appropriate ball and placement of target for personal competence, (b) records partner's performance accurately and honestly, (c) assists partner by speaking politely and taking turns, and (d) assumes personal responsibility for the results of the activity" (p. 27).

Screen and Roll				
Name	Score	Feet Planted	Roll to Basket	Screen to Side
Mr. Ell	9	yes	yes	yes
Adam	14	yes	yes	yes
Matthew	7	no	yes	yes
Riley	15	yes	yes	yes
Roel	8	yes	yes	yes
Melissa	2	yes	no	no
Chris	13	yes	yes	yes
Mark	5	no	no	no
Rafael	5	yes	yes	no
Ashley	7	yes	yes	yes
Wade	4	sorta	Yes	yes

Figure 14.8 Example of recorded performance observation. *Source:* From Dwayne Ell, student teacher, Central Middle School, East Grand Forks, Minnesota. Used with permission.

Things Needed: 2 people, A small ball, open space

The two people toss the ball back and forth, one throwing high the other low (above knees). Then when one player says switch the other player thows high and the other low. The when someone says freeze both players freeze for five seconds. *great game* How to score

When the other player doesn't catch it, does low when they should of threw high or when they threw it out of bounds.

Figure 14.9 An event task: child's self-designed game

portion of it. A task may be entirely psychomotor, such as the development of a self-designed game, or it may include other aspects, such as writing about the game. See Figure 14.9 for a self-designed game used as an event task.

Videotaping Videotape (Box 14.6) can provide a final, permanent product for gymnastics sequences, dances, or self-designed games. It can also let students display their knowledge and skill with respect to critical aspects of a skill. One possible task is to have students videotape themselves performing a certain skill and then analyze the critical cues for that skill. Likewise, students can videotape each other and provide "color commentary" regarding the performance.

Student Drawings Children love to draw, and we have found drawing one of the most rewarding assessment tools (Box 14.7). The options for student drawing are endless. Children can be asked to draw about themselves, what a sequence looks like, what a skill looks like, what they liked best. Figure 14.10 shows a student drawing used as an assessment piece.

Figure 14.10 Second-grader's drawing of the cue of using the shoelaces to kick.

BOX 14.5   EVENT TASKS IN THE *NATIONAL STANDARDS FOR PHYSICAL EDUCATION*

Event tasks are referenced six times in the *National Standards for Physical Education* (NASPE, 1995):

As Sample Kindergarten, Second-, and Fourth-Grade Assessment Options under Standard 1: Demonstrates competency in many movement forms and proficiency in a few movement forms

The sample kindergarten assessment states: "Students will perform the 'Dance of the Locomotors' in which they travel in different ways through general space. Upon hearing the signal from the teacher, the students will change to the locomotor pattern named by the teacher. Repeat the dance, but this time upon the signal to change locomotor patterns, the students will respond by selecting any locomotor pattern they desire. The teacher should encourage creative modes of travel. Criteria for assessment: (a) demonstrates a variety of locomotor skills, (b) identifies and models locomotor movements shown by the teacher, and (c) exhibits correct locomotor skill when the skill is named by the teacher" (p. 7).

The sample second-grade assessment states: "Students are asked to design and practice a movement sequence of three different locomotor skills. Following the practice period, students demonstrate their movement sequence for the class. Criteria for assessment: (a) demonstrates three different locomotor movements, (b) demonstrates mature pattern for each locomotor skill, and (c) demonstrates smooth transitions between locomotor patterns" (p. 19).

The sample fourth-grade assessment states: "Students are asked to combine a balance, a roll, and a traveling action into a gymnastics sequence. The sequence must include all the components and a clear beginning and ending. Criteria for assessment: (a) exhibits a balance, a roll, and a traveling action during the performance, (b) demonstrates a clear beginning and ending to the sequence, and (c) demonstrates smooth transitions between the various skills" (p. 33).

As a Sample Fourth-Grade Assessment Option under Standard 2: Applies movement concepts and principles to the learning and development of motor skills

The sample assessment states: "Students are requested to design a game of throwing and catching for one or two persons to play. The game must include the underhand throwing skill that has been taught in class. Students write a description of the game so students in another class could, after reading the information, play the game. They are also asked to describe how the critical elements of the skill might change when used in different situations. Criteria for assessment: (a) game incorporates use of underhand throwing and catching skills, (b) description of game adequately identifies needed skills and critical elements of each, and (c) description accurately describes how critical elements might change under varying conditions" (pp. 34–35).

As a Sample Sixth-Grade Assessment Option under Standard 5: Demonstrates responsible personal and social behavior in physical activity settings

The sample assessment states: "Students, working in pairs, are given the opportunity to design and practice a gymnastics sequence using a combination of skills that they have learned during class. The students are instructed to choose skills at their own ability level and those that they 'can really polish.' Students are told they will be evaluated on their choice of skills and their form, rather than on the level of difficulty of the skills they choose. Criteria for assessment: (a) chooses skill of an appropriate difficulty, (b) follows rules specific to the selected skill, (c) uses practice time appropriately, and (d) shares practice space with others in the class" (p. 55).

As a Sample Second-Grade Assessment Option under Standard 7: Understands that physical activity provides opportunities for enjoyment, challenge, self-expression, and social interaction

The sample assessment states: "Students are asked to express a variety of feelings (e.g., happiness, sadness, anger, frustration, joy) during a creative movement or dance lesson through the use of a variety of shapes, postures, and movements. Students are asked to discuss with the class situations in physical activity that bring about these feelings. Criteria for assessment: (a) uses movement to communicate feelings and (b) verbally expresses feelings that result from participation in physical activities" (p. 29).

BOX 14.6   VIDEOTAPING IN THE *NATIONAL STANDARDS FOR PHYSICAL EDUCATION*

Videotaping is referenced three times in the *National Standards for Physical Education* (NASPE, 1995):

As a Sample Second-Grade Assessment Option under Standard 1: Demonstrates competency in many movement forms and proficiency in a few movement forms

The sample assessment states: "Students are asked to skip, gallop, and jump off a low box. A camera is set up in one corner of the gym to record their performance. Each student is asked to go in front of the camera and perform the specified movement patterns. The teacher uses a checklist to assess the extent to which mature and skilled patterns have been obtained. Criteria for assessment: (a) exhibits mature form for each of the movement patterns and (b) demonstrates consistent and smooth performance" (p. 19).

As a Sixth-Grade Assessment Option under Standard 2: Applies movement concepts and principles to the learning and development of motor skills

The sample assessment states: "Partners videotape each other while striking a ball resting on a batting tee (five times) and while striking a ball thrown by a pitcher (five times). They review the tape with their partner and self-assess according to the criteria presented to them in class. Based on this information they write a description of one or more of the following: the critical elements of batting; the consistency of their movement patterns; the differences in cues available when striking from a tee (closed skill) versus striking a pitched ball (open skill); and practice suggestions for improvement in each skill. Criteria for assessment: (a) accurately describes the criteria for good batting, (b) accurately assesses their own consistency of performance, (c) accurately identifies cues available in open or closed skills, and (d) selects appropriate practice options based on the differences between the two skills" (p. 49).

As a Second-Grade Assessment Option under Standard 5: Demonstrates responsible personal and social behavior in physical activity settings

The sample assessment states: "Students are videotaped while working on gymnastics equipment. Students' performance is judged according to whether they have worked productively, safely, and cooperatively with others. The teacher records the extent to which each of the criteria are met by the class as well as by each student. (Recording instances of noncompliance in most cases will be the most efficient way to record this information.) The teacher shares the assessment results with the students to develop an awareness of undesirable behavior and assist in making improvements. Criteria for assessment: (a) works on assigned task in a productive manner, (b) works safely (no crashes and with an awareness of each other), and (c) exhibits cooperative behaviors (taking turns, supportive comments, assisting each other with moving equipment)" (p. 26).

Student Displays   Student displays (Box 14.8) are public displays of student work that communicate what the children have learned. These can take a variety of forms, from posters on which students have drawn a person displaying a skill and labeling the cues, to photographs, to bulletin boards.

Teacher Observation   Teacher observation (Box 14.9) is the most common form of assessment utilized in physical education classes. It is generally employed to assess psychomotor performance but can be used to assess the affective domain as well. There are many tools that a teacher may use to record observational information, including anecdotal records, checklists, rating scales. See Chapter 11 on Teacher Observation for specific examples.

Portfolios   Portfolios (Box 14.10) are collections of student work gathered over a period of time, usually a school year, but for elementary physical education a portfolio could follow a student for his or her entire elementary career. A portfolio is much like a scrapbook; it can include entries that are made up of some of the many other types of assessment tasks. Some teachers prefer to do portfolios for one unit only.

The first consideration with a portfolio is its purpose. It is quite difficult to select items without a sense of purpose. Common purposes include keeping track of

BOX 14.7   STUDENT DRAWING IN THE *NATIONAL STANDARDS FOR PHYSICAL EDUCATION*

Student drawing is referenced twice in the *National Standards for Physical Education* (NASPE, 1995):

As a Sample Second-Grade Assessment Option under Standard 2: Applies movement concepts and principles to the learning and development of motor skills

The sample assessment states: "Students are provided with a drawing of a hand print and are asked to color the portion of the hand that is used in mature dribbling. Students may also be asked to draw an entire person dribbling to show the overall critical elements of this movement task. Criteria for assessment: (a) correctly identifies portion of hand used in mature dribbling and (b) identifies the critical elements of dribbling" (p. 20).

As a Sample Kindergarten Assessment Option under Standard 7: Understands that physical activity provides opportunities for enjoyment, challenge, self-expression, and social interaction

The sample assessment states: "Students are asked to work together in a group to create a 'Physical Education Book' for their classroom. Each child is to draw activities that represent physical education class. With assistance from the classroom teacher, sentences can be added to describe the activity. Criteria for assessment: (a) willingly participates in the project, (b) identifies several activities that are enjoyable, and (c) expresses positive feelings when describing the activity" (p. 14).

progress, providing students a way to assess their own accomplishments, and determining the extent to which learning objectives have been achieved. For example, if one of the purposes of your physical education class is helping students practice a healthy lifestyle, their portfolios might include various pieces that attest to their knowledge of fitness, activities they do to stay fit, and indications of how they value fitness. Many of the products of the assessment options discussed in this chapter could be included in a portfolio. For example, a fitness portfolio might include some of the following artifacts: results of a health-related fitness test given at the beginning of the school year, goals set as a result of that test, activities in which the student participated to achieve the goals set, weekly homework sheets that document physical activity, a fitness written report, results of a fitness test later in the year, an indication of how well established personal goals were met, and finally, goals for the summer. The teacher may specify some items in the portfolio, but because the portfolio is a personal record, the student should be allowed and encouraged to decide which items will most strongly "make the case."

Assessing How Well It Was Learned

Scoring rubrics allow the teacher to determine how well the performance was achieved. Rubrics are the scoring criteria by which student performance is judged. They are designed to measure both process and product—the journey as well as the destination.

Scoring rubrics are designed to let *both* teacher and student know how well or to what level the learning occurred. They set forth the guidelines by which learning is evaluated. Unlike traditional grading scales, rubrics are written before instruction begins and shared with the students at the beginning of instruction. In other words, students have a standard by which to judge their performance and thus can receive feedback during instruction. In this sense rubrics serve as a formative evaluation process and link assessment to instruction. They are yet another

BOX 14.8   STUDENT DISPLAYS IN THE NATIONAL STANDARDS FOR PHYSICAL EDUCATION

Student displays are referenced three times in the *National Standards for Physical Education* (NASPE, 1995):

As a Sample Sixth-Grade Assessment Option under Standard 3: Exhibits a physically active lifestyle

The sample assessment states: "Students are instructed to develop a chart that can be used to identify opportunities in the school and community for regular participation in physical activity. Various information can be included on the chart including the type of activity, the providing body, the address and phone number of the providing body, cost to participate, special equipment requirements, registration dates, and time of involvement. Students should be encouraged to gather the information and to organize the chart for ease of locating information about the various activities. Information can be summarized by creating a general class chart created from the information on the individual charts. Criteria for assessment: (a) completes the chart relative to the number of community opportunities, (b) provides accurate information in the chart in terms of the amount and type of information provided for each activity, and (c) organizes and presents ideas well" (pp. 51–52).

As a Fourth-Grade Assessment Option under Standard 5: Demonstrates responsible personal and social behavior in physical activity settings

The sample assessment states: "Students create an activity wall chart comparing differences in safety practices, rules, procedures, and etiquette for each physical activity presented in class during the course of the year. Criteria for assessment: (a) identifies appropriate safety practices, rules, etc., for the chosen activities and (b) recognizes similarities and differences among activities" (p. 40).

As a Sample Fourth-Grade Assessment Option under Standard 7: Understands that physical activity provides opportunities for enjoyment, challenge, self-expression, and social interaction

The sample assessment states: "Students are asked to create a mural entitled, 'Favorite Activities in Physical Education,' using butcher paper that is then placed around the gym walls. (Invite classroom teachers, administrators, and parents to see the children's work.) Criteria for assessment: (a) willingly participates in the class project and (b) art work shows enjoyment of activity" (p. 43).

---

way that assessment becomes an open part of instruction, not something that is hidden from students.

When writing rubrics, all important criteria should be addressed. The criteria are written in levels. The top level is most often written as the optimal level of performance for the task that is to be achieved by the students, at that point in their development at that time. Our view is that the top level should be challenging, yet achievable.

Most rubrics are written with four to six levels. Each successive level is somewhat easier to achieve than the previous one because the standards are lower. You must decide what an acceptable level of performance is. The levels between the highest and lowest should be graduated. See Figure 14.11 for an example of a scoring rubric for movement sequence and Figure 14.12 for one for writing self-designed games.

> Whenever a value is set forth which can only be attained by a few, the conditions are ripe for widespread feelings of personal inadequacy. An outstanding example in American society is the fierce competitiveness of the school system. No educational system in the world has so many examinations, or so emphasizes grades, as the American school system. Children are constantly being ranked and evaluated. The superior achievement of one child tends to debase the achievement of another.
>
> Morris Rosenberg, *Society and the Adolescent Self-Image*

BOX 14.9   TEACHER OBSERVATION IN THE NATIONAL STANDARDS FOR PHYSICAL EDUCATION

Teacher observation is referenced seven times in the *National Standards for Physical Education* (NASPE, 1995):

As Sample Kindergarten, Second-Grade, and Fourth-Grade Assessment Options under Standard 1: Demonstrates competency in many movement forms and proficiency in a few movement forms

The sample kindergarten assessment states: "The student will be asked to travel through general space with a steady run, and upon a designated signal, perform the next locomotor action announced by the teacher (e.g., walk, hop, gallop). Upon observing the student's performance, the teacher marks on a checklist mastery of the various critical elements (e.g., arm swing, balance, foot placement). Criteria for assessment: (a) demonstrates selected critical elements of locomotor skills and (b) responds with correct locomotor skill as named by the teacher" (p. 6).

The sample second-grade assessment states: "Students are requested to demonstrate the skills introduced in class as the teacher observes their performance and records the satisfactory use of the critical elements of the skills on a checklist. Criteria for assessment: (a) demonstrates critical elements of the selected skills over several trials" (pp. 18–19).

The sample fourth-grade assessment states: "Students are asked to receive and send a basketball pass to a partner on the move. The teacher observes the passing and uses a checklist to annotate the performance. Criteria for assessment: (a) receives the pass and sends it in one motion, (b) passes ahead of the moving player (receiver does not have to stop), and (c) receiving student cuts into a space to receive the pass" (p. 32).

As a Sample Fourth-Grade Assessment Option under Standard 2: Applies movement concepts and principles to the learning and development of motor skills

The sample assessment states: "After initial practice of a skill the teacher gives the students a cue to improve per-

formance. The teacher records the names of those students who are having difficulty practicing with an intent to use the information given to them. Criteria for assessment: (a) practice shows definite intent to use the information given them to improve performance and (b) stays with the focus given by the teacher until that aspect of performance is not a problem" (p. 34).

As a Sample Second-Grade Assessment Option under Standard 3: Exhibits a physically active lifestyle

The sample assessment states: "The teacher identifies and records the names of those students who do not engage in activities (playground or in class) that require sustained moderate physical activity. Criteria for assessment: (a) initiates participation in vigorous activity and (b) sustains vigorous activity for more than ten minutes" (p. 22).

As Sample Fourth- and Sixth-Grade Assessment Options under Standard 5: Demonstrates responsible personal and social behavior in physical activity settings

The fourth-grade sample assessment states: "The teacher monitors on-task and off-task activity for each student several times during a unit and records the extent of on-task activity. Each student is observed at least once in four intervals of one minute set aside for this purpose. Criteria for assessment: (a) demonstrates on-task activity 90% of the time" (p. 39).

The sixth-grade sample assessment states: "The teacher is beginning a new unit on an activity in which students have had instruction in previous years. The teacher holds a class discussion to present the safety rules and procedures for the class and to assess the degree to which students are able to anticipate, identify, and develop appropriate procedures to make the environment safe and maintain proper care of the equipment used. Criteria for assessment: (a) identifies the critical dimensions of safety for the activity and (b) establishes rules and procedures that adequately address the potential safety problems of the activity" (p. 55).

BOX 14.10   PORTFOLIOS IN THE *NATIONAL STANDARDS FOR PHYSICAL EDUCATION*

Portfolios are referenced three times in the *National Standards for Physical Education* (NASPE, 1995):

As a Sample Sixth-Grade Assessment Option under Standard 3: Exhibits a physically active lifestyle

The sample assessment states: "Students are asked to select a favorite physical activity. With teacher assistance, the student should set a goal for improvement and plan a 10 to 15 minute daily practice period. Furthermore, the student should keep a log of the actual practice that took place in accordance with the plan. In-class or out-of-class time may be used to accomplish the task. Evidence of improvement is gathered and maintained in a portfolio that includes the log, established goals, rationale for selecting the activity and the goals, and any other evidence of participation in the activity. Criteria for assessment: (a) selects appropriate goal, (b) develops appropriate plan, (c) meets goal, and (d) presents project well" (p. 51).

As a Sample Fourth-Grade Assessment Option under Standard 6: Demonstrates understanding and respect for differences among people in physical activity settings

The sample assessment states: "Working in a group of three or four members, students will choose a country of interest and a dance native to that country. Students will learn the dance and teach it to other members of the class. Each group will examine all the dances presented for similarities and differences and attempt to determine reasons for similarities and differences. A portfolio consisting of a description of the country and why it was chosen, the selected dance and why it was chosen, and interpretative descriptions of the similarities and differences of the various dances presented in class will be submitted by each group. Criteria for assessment: (a) willingly participates in learning games, dances, and activities from other parts of the world, (b) accepts lesson in a positive manner, (c) recognizes similarities and differences between dances from different countries, and (d) identifies reasons for similarities and differences among dances of various countries" (p. 42).

As a Sample Fourth-Grade Assessment Option under Standard 7: Understands that physical activity provides opportunities for enjoyment, challenge, self-expression, and social interaction

The sample assessment states: "Students are requested to develop a portfolio illustrating games, gymnastics, or dances in which they frequently participate. Students shall then select their favorite activity in the portfolio and write a paragraph telling why this is their favorite. Ask them to share their portfolio with the class and describe their favorite activity. Criteria for assessment: (a) selects activities that are personally interesting and rewarding, (b) explains why they have selected a particular activity as their favorite, and (c) willingly shares their portfolio and favorite activity with the class" (p. 43).

Assessing All Three Domains

We do not teach only motor skills and fitness. For us, there are clear affective and cognitive goals in our programs. Therefore, we must also assess those goals. The examples provided in the previous section include assessment ideas in all three domains. Assessments for motor skills and fitness include homework and peer observation. Assessment of the affective domain can occur in the form of student journals. The cognitive domain can be assessed through exit slips (e.g., Helping Murgatroid) or simply by checking for under-

standing with questions during class identified in skill themes chapters by the check for cognitive understanding icon ▲. What the move to more authentic assessment has provided teachers are noninvasive, instructional ways to assess all three domains.

Also, in recent years it has become increasingly obvious to us that physical education programs that are limited to one or two days a week have less impact on children than daily programs of physical education (Graham, Metzler, & Webster, 1991). Although it may not be possible for children to reach utilization or proficiency level in a skill such as throwing in the limited

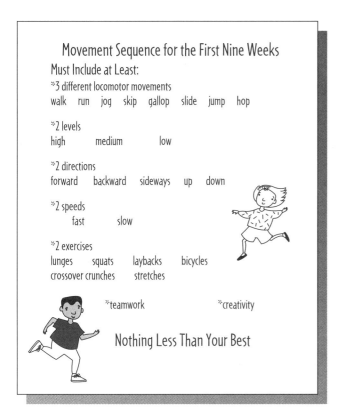

Movement Sequence for the First Nine Weeks

Must Include at Least:

*3 different locomotor movements
walk   run   jog   skip   gallop   slide   jump   hop

*2 levels
high   medium   low

*2 directions
forward   backward   sideways   up   down

*2 speeds
        fast   slow

*2 exercises
lunges   squats   laybacks   bicycles
crossover crunches   stretches

        *teamwork   *creativity

Nothing Less Than Your Best

(a)   Movement Sequence Event Task

Figure 14.11   Event task with scoring rubric.
Courtesy of: Megin DeMoss, Rose Hill, Kansas.

Rubric for Movement Sequence

4 – Shows Creativity

3 – Shows Teamwork

2 – Included All Criteria

1 – Included Some Criteria

NA – No Attempt Was Made

(b)   Scoring Rubric for Movement Sequences

Note: This rubric assumes all previous (lower level) criteria as components of the next higher level.

time allotted to physical education, it is realistic to expect that children can at least learn the key cues for the points that we emphasize in our programs. Although that is not totally satisfactory, it does represent progress. It is encouraging to realize that even though all of the children in our program are not throwing at the utilization level, they do know how to throw correctly if, and when, they choose to throw on their own.

Summarizing and Reporting Progress

At some point most all teachers are required to summarize and report children's progress to parents and others. This summative evaluation provides parents and children with an indication of what the child has learned and where he or she is with respect to the essential learning in physical education. It also provides teachers with information about their program—what has been accomplished and what needs to be worked on. For physical education teachers, reporting has always been nothing short of a nightmare due to the sheer numbers of children we teach.

Scoring Rubric for Writing Self-Designed Games

3. Includes all equipment needed, number of players, space needed, and a clear description of how to play and how to score.

2. Includes equipment, players, space, and an OK description of how to play and score.

1. Includes only some of the criteria.

Figure 14.12   Scoring rubric for writing self-designed games.

Physical Education Skill Sheet
1 - 5th Grades

Name _____   Dates _____

The skills listed below should be accomplished by the time your child has completed the fifth grade. (A check (✔)
in front of the skill shows the student is proficient in that task.) This sheet will be following your child through grades 1-5.

MOVEMENT CONCEPTS
___ Quick starts/stops on signal
___ Understands general space
___ Understands self-space
___ Moving in different
      directions
___ Knows right/left
___ Change direction quickly
___ Moving at 3 different levels
___ Travel different pathways
___ Repeat specific pathways
___ Moving at different rates

TRAVELING
___ Crawling
___ Walking
___ Running
___ Skipping
___ Sliding
___ Galloping

JUMPING
___ Two feet to two feet
___ Hop
___ Leap
___ One foot to two feet
___ Run and jump
___ Distance
___ Height
___ Rhythmic jumping
___   long rope
___   short rope
___ Over obstacles
___ Jump and turn
___ Control/soft landing

ROLLING
___ Log roll
___ Forward roll

___ Backward roll
___ Shoulder roll
___ Variation roll
___ Jump off, land, & roll
___ Jump over, land, & roll
___ Dive roll

BALANCING
___ One leg
___ Different body shapes
___ Tripod
___ Bridge
___ Walk on low beam
___ Walk on high beam
___ Variety of stunts on beam
___ Small base of support
___ Pushing
___ Pulling
___ Lifting
___ Climbing rope (1/3 up)
___ Climbing rope (2/3 up)
___ (Option) (top)
___ Cartwheel
___ Roundoff

KICKING
___ Stationary ball on the run
___ Ball rolled by someone
___ Distance
___ Dribbling the ball
___ Dribbling around obstacles
___ Kicking at a target
___ Passing to a partner
___ Use various parts of the foot
___ Accuracy
___ Moving target
___ Accuracy while traveling
___ One-to-one situation
___ Volleying to self

___ Kick to a target against a
      defense
___ Gamelike situation

THROWING
___ Body mechanics
___ To self
___ To wall
___ Stepping w/opposite foot
___ Using more body parts to
      increase the force
___ Follow through
___ To stationary target
___ To partner
___ Accuracy while traveling
___ Accuracy to a traveling
      partner
___ Hit a moving target
___ Dynamic situation
___ Against an opponent
___ Without being intercepted
___ Accuracy w/consistency
___ Gamelike situation

CATCHING
___ Body mechanics
___ To self at various heights
___ Thrown by a skilled thrower
___ Bounce to self & catch
___ Catch at different levels
___ Catch in different directions
___ Catch with an implement
___ Catch wall rebound
___ Stationary partner
___ Moving with partner
___ In the air
___ Outmaneuvering defender
___ Intercept

___ Off-balance catching
___ Gamelike situation

VOLLEYING
___ Striking balloon with hand
___ Striking balloon w/other
      parts
___ Striking ball with hands
___ Striking ball w/other parts
___ Striking balloon w/partner
___ Striking ball w/partner
___ Striking ball to target (over)

DRIBBLING
___ Bounce ball - stationary
___ Bounce ball - moving
___ Bounce ball (eyes up)
___ Using either hand
___ Changing directions
___ Around stationary obstacles
___ Traveling - changing hands
___ Change speed of dribbling
___ Keep ball away from
      opponent
___ Gamelike situation

**STRIKING WITH RACKETS AND
PADDLES**
___ Striking a balloon
      (repeatedly)
___ Self-tossed ball
___ Striking a ball up/down
      (repeat)
___ Against the wall (repeat)
___ Over the net (repeat)
___ With a partner
___ Performing
      offensive/defensive moves
___ Gamelike situation

LONG HANDLED IMPLEMENTS
___ Striking stationary
      object/floor
___ Striking off a batting tee
___ Traveling - object on floor
___ Striking suspended object
___ Striking to stationary partner
___ Striking to stationary target
___ Striking a pitch ball
___ Strike self-toss ball
___ Traveling - dodging
      stationary objects
___ Traveling - dodging moving
      objects
___ Pass to moving partner
___ Pass & receive while moving
___ Striking for distance
___ Direct speed, distance, &
      pathway of object
___ Gamelike situation (hockey)
___ Gamelike situation (bat)

PUNTING
___ Drop ball, then punt
      (alternate)
___ Distance
___ Accuracy
___ Catch pass, then punt
___ Gamelike situation

MUSIC
___ Claps to a beat
___ Moves to a beat
___ Follows a specific
      pattern/dance (moderate
      difficulty)
___ Creative movement

Figure 14.13   Carbon-backed form for tracking students' progress. *Source:* Developed by
Karyn Hartinger, Portland, Oregon. Used with permission.

The three systems discussed here have made reporting practical, formative, and ongoing—providing a record over time.

Three Practical Systems

Hartinger System   Karyn Hartinger developed her system as a practical and realistic way of following or tracking the progress of several hundred children over a period of several years. She used the movement concept and skill theme chapters to outline the important skills and concepts she wanted her children to learn throughout elementary school (Figure 14.13). She then arranged with her school district to print the form on carbon-backed paper so that there are six copies of each individual form.

The first year, Hartinger writes the name of each child on an individual form. That year she assesses the progress of each child, checks the appropriate lines, then tears off the top page for the parents. She keeps the five copies (carbons), which give her an automatic record. The second year, when she gets ready to assess

the child's progress, she simply writes in the date for that year on the first carbon copy, checks the new lines on which the child has made satisfactory progress, and sends the top carbon to the parents. For years three through five, the parents continue to receive the top carbon. A child who attends the school where Karyn teaches thus receives a report during each of his or her five years at the school.

Another advantage of the Hartinger system is that it gives the teacher a practical approach to evaluating the curriculum. Each year the teacher will have to focus on the skills and concepts included in the progress report if the child is expected to make progress. This has a subtle advantage of keeping the teacher on-task regarding a curriculum's scope and sequence.

Lambdin System   Dolly Lambdin's system (Figure 14.14), a form sent home at the time of each report period, lists the objectives or benchmarks for the report period under the broader standard that is a goal of her physical education program. Students then

Figure 14.14 Lambdin reporting system. Used with permission.

SAMPLE REPORT CARDS

Essential for Good Health-A Physically Active Lifestyle

Childs Name _____   Class_____

I CAN   Physical Education Report
4th 6 week period 1993-94
Grade 4

Your child has rated his/her ability level in the space next to each skill. If my rating is different from your child's rating you will see my rating in GREEN. Please ask your child "What do these letters you wrote mean?" Hopefully you will get a thoughtful answer like, "I put L for learning because I can do that some of the time, but not all the time." If my rating is different you may also want to ask why s/he thinks they are different. There may be a very good reason. Encourage your child to think about what s/he needs to work on and celebrate new skills.   Thanks, Dolly Lambdin

B = Beginning—I can do it once in a while
L = Learning—I can do it most of the time—but I have to really think about it
M = Mastered—I can always do it—It is easy for me
P = Problems—I have problems with this

In physical education we learn to move our bodies and objects with skill and confidence.

Short Rope Jumping Skills
____ Forward single bounce   ____ Forward double bounce
____ Backward single bounce   ____ Backward double bounce
____ Cross arms   ____ Front to back
____ Skier   ____ Jump, side swing, jump

Long Rope Jumping Skills   **Dance**
____ Jump   ____ Belle Kawe
____ Run in and jump

Body Management (Gymnastics)
____ Backward shoulder roll
____ Forward shoulder roll
____ Weight on hands and land lightly
____ Jump off bench and land lightly, bending knees
____ Perform a movement sequence

We encourage and support each other and make class a good place to learn.
____ I listen during instructions   ____ I move safely
____ I follow the directions   ____ I am kind to others
____ I do quality work   ____ I like to move

- -

Thanks for reading this 4th report card. Have your child return this slip for a "playdough" treat.
    Child's Name_____   Parent's Signature_____
Walk, jog, bike, EXERCISE with your children!!! Enjoy a healthy lifestyle.

evaluate themselves on a "beginning," "learning," "mastered," "I have problems" scale (actually precontrol, control, utilization, and proficiency, put into kids' language). If the child's rating differs from hers, Lambdin marks hers in a different color ink. At the end of the year the report-period sheets are summarized on one sheet for the permanent record.

Metz System   Rick Metz and colleagues at Chipeta Elementary School in Colorado Springs also use student self-evaluation. At the beginning of the school year, the teachers at Chipeta Elementary send home a copy of the physical education standards and outcomes used at Chipeta. These standards are grouped in six areas: object manipulation, coordination, sportspersonship/self-control, respect for others/teamwork, listens/follows directions, participation, and other. The Chipeta outcomes are keyed to both the Colorado and the *National Standards for Physical Education* (which are also provided to parents in the first-of-the-year packet). Quarterly, with the report card, the specific goals or benchmarks addressed during that report period are sent home (Figure 14.15). The

Figure 14.15 Sample quarterly benchmarks (Metz system). Used with permission from Susan Stevens, Chipeta Elementary School, Colorado Springs, Colorado.

GRADE ONE

Quarter 1

1. Object Manipulation: The child will
   a. alternate tosses (right and left hands) with 2 juggling scarves.
   b. toss an 8-1/2" playground ball above head, clap hands 1 time, and catch ball before it bounces.
   c. balance a peacock feather for 15 seconds on palm of hand, 10 seconds on 1 finger, 10 seconds on back of hand with both right and left hands.
   d. strike a playground ball against a wall (handball action) for more than 1 time.
   e. Quarters 1–4 kindergarten benchmarks continued as a review.

2. Coordination: The child will
   a. walk a 2" line without losing balance.
   b. Quarters 1–4 kindergarten benchmarks continued as a review.

3. Sportsmanship/Self-Control: The child will
   a. demonstrate different sportsmanship "contacts" with opponents at the end of a contest (high 5, low 5, handshake, etc.).
   b. Quarters 1–4 kindergarten benchmarks continued as a review.

4. Respect for Others/Teamwork: The child will
   a. work together as part of a group during the 1/2-hour class without needing time-out for self-control.
   b. Quarters 1–4 kindergarten benchmarks continued as a review.

5. Listens/Follows Directions: The child will
   a. wait for a specific "go" signal before continuing an activity (verbal or music).
   b. Quarters 1–4 kindergarten benchmarks continued as a review.

6. Participation:
   a. Quarters 1–4 kindergarten benchmarks continued as a review.

7. Additional Comments/Areas: The child will
   a. explain the reason for using a seatbelt while in an automobile.
   b. Quarters 1–4 kindergarten benchmarks continued as a review.

benchmarks are lettered A through H (though rarely are all letters used) to correspond with the boxes on the report form (Figure 14.16). At the end of each report period, achievement of specific objectives is sent home. To assist in the reporting, students assess themselves at the end of each term. All students have a notebook containing the form, and the form is also on the computer. Grades 5 and 6 students help the first- through third-graders complete their forms. The form is carbon backed, so that one copy can be kept as part of the permanent record.

Similarities   Both the Lambdin and the Metz systems involve student self-assessment. These teachers found that student self-assessment is not only accu-

rate and honest but increases student learning while integrating instruction and assessment. The assumptions of both systems are that when children think about their own learning, they attend more carefully to that learning. Both teachers have found that students are very good and honest at assessing their own

> To begin with, I've found that there is no one else like me, anywhere, like snow flakes. No one else feels completely the way I do. No one else sees things in the same scope as I do. So my first discovery about myself is that I'm me.
>
> From a High School Composition

CHIPETA ELEMENTARY SCHOOL   DATE _____ - _____
SCHOOL DISTRICT #11 COLORADO SPRINGS
STUDENT SELF-EVALUATION IN PHYSICAL AND WELLNESS EDUCATION
EDUCATORS: MR. RICK METZ, MRS. SUSAN STEVENS and MR. MIKE GARCIA

Marking System: Student's Name _____
   X = Bench Mark Learned
        (N = National Standard achieved)   Homeroom Teacher _____
        (C = Colorado Standard achieved)   Grade Level _____

Benchmark General Area: Quarter 1   Quarter 2   Quarter 3   Quarter 4
   (see explanation below)

1. Object Manipulation   N2/C1

2. Coordination   N1/C1

3. Sportsmanship/Self-Control   N5

4. Respect for Others/Teamwork   N6

5. Listens/Follows Directions   N5/C5

6. Participation   N4/C3

7. Additional Comments/Areas   N3,7/C2,4

- -

Benchmark General Areas

1. Object Manipulation = Hand-eye, foot-eye coordination in throwing, catching, striking, kicking, handling balls (basketballs, soccer balls, footballs, nerf balls, yarn balls) and objects (beanbags, hoops, wands, bats, frisbees, etc.).

2. Coordination = Walking, running, skipping, galloping, sliding, crawling, jumping, hopping, leaping, jump rope activities, tumbling activities, stomp board, and carpet square activities.

3. Sportsmanship/Self-Control = Self-reactions to situations, accepting decisions, accepting winning and losing.

4. Respect for Others/Teamwork = Sharing and caring, stations, mass activities.

5. Listens/Follows Directions = Leadership, followership.

6. Participates = "Open mind" to new activities.

7. Additional Comments/Areas = Examples: strength, fitness tests, concept learning.

Figure 14.16   Metz reporting form. *Source:* Used with permission from Susan Stevens, Chipeta Elementary School, Colorado Springs, Colorado.

abilities. Additionally, the approach helped these teachers—even though they kept lots of records—find the time, energy, and ability to assess each child more accurately. You will note that none of these systems uses "grades": All the teachers found that grades did not communicate much to the parents or the students. Lambdin's system, in fact, led to the study and possible redesign of the school report card.

Finding the Time for Assessment

Time has always been an issue in physical education. Some would argue that even authentic assessment takes time away from activity. In some senses that may be true, but the information gathered from and provided by the assessment options is critical to children's learning, to instructional decisions that meet the needs of the child, and to the design of the program. What this assessment movement has done is mesh evaluation with instruction. The two are no longer separate entities, but pieces of the same puzzle. Assessment is an ongoing process that occurs in every lesson, simply by the nature of the tasks students do. Assessment is instruction. Assessment is simply teaching well.

No instructor who teaches several hundred children each week—as many physical education instructors do—has the time needed to use all the assessment techniques described in this chapter. But a reflective teacher is aware of these techniques and uses them with different classes for different purposes. Perhaps you'll have one class at a time keeping logs. And you may be able to send only one written report a year to parents.

Select from the various assessment techniques those that are most appropriate; each technique provides a different type of information. For example, journals provide fascinating insights into how children are progressing in designing their own games or dances, but a checklist would be far less appropriate for that purpose. In contrast, a checklist is useful for assessing children's individual abilities in a new situation—for example, for a class of kindergarten children or during a teacher's first year in a new school.

Even when you narrow down the assessment options to be used with your classes, time can still be an issue. For example, it's counterproductive to assess one child while the others stand in line waiting their turn. There are at least four ways to minimize the waiting time for children during assessment:

1. Set up stations or learning centers (Chapter 13). Stay at one of the stations, and use that station as the assessment station. If you plan to do this, be certain the children are familiar with the other stations so that you can devote most of your time to

helping with the assessments rather than explaining procedures at the other stations.

2. Ask the classroom teacher (or another teacher, paraprofessional, parent, or high school student) to assist with the class. The assistant can either help some children while you work with the other children or supervise most of the class while you work with a few children at a time.

3. Videotape the children so that you can make your judgments about skill levels and progress during your planning time or after school.

4. Use a tape recorder as you teach, and use the class list as a guide for observing each child; then make comments about the child's ability level and improvement.

SUMMARY

Assessment answers two questions: What was learned? and How well was it learned? The first question deals with content; the second, with the nature of the performance and the level of achievement.

Assessment also provides a direct measure of teaching effectiveness. No longer is assessment an "end-of-the-unit thing"; now it is an ongoing process that happens on a daily basis in physical education classes. This type of assessment is known as authentic assessment. Authentic assessment is directly linked with instruction, not separated from it. In this way, instruction and assessment inform the whole learning process.

Many authentic assessment options exist. The ones we have chosen to focus on include journals, exit slips, homework, peer observation, event tasks, videotaping, student drawings, student displays, teacher observation, and portfolios. These assessment options can be used to assess student learning, report progress to parents, and discover individual children's needs and interests. Progress reports to children's parents are the preferred mode of reporting student progress whenever feasible.

READING COMPREHENSION QUESTIONS

1. What is authentic assessment? How does it differ from traditional assessment modes?
2. What are the purposes of assessment in physical education?
3. What does it mean to tie assessment to instruction and the whole learning process?
4. What are five options available for authentic assessment?
5. What is the purpose of having children keep a journal? How does the journal differ from the other assessment options?
6. What are scoring rubrics? How do they work?
7. Select one of the three reporting systems (Hartinger, Lambdin, or Metz) and provide an argument for using that system as opposed to the other two. Imagine you are actually teaching as your write your answer.
8. Explain why assessment is necessary in children's physical education.

**REFERENCES/
SUGGESTED READING**

Cutforth, N., & Parker, M. (1996). Promoting affective development in physical education: The value of journal writing. *JOPERD, 67*(7), 19–23.

Entzion, B., Fairchild, M., Parker, M., Pemberton, C., Steen, T., Taylor, D., & Whitehead, J. (1991). Super active kids program instructor's manual. Unpublished manuscript, University of North Dakota, Department of Health, Physical Education and Recreation, Grand Forks.

Graham, G., Metzler, M., & Webster, G. (1991). Specialist and classroom teacher effectiveness in children's physical education. *Journal of Teaching in Physical Education, 10*(4), 321–426.

Hopple, C. (1995). *Teaching for outcomes in elementary physical education.* Champaign, IL: Human Kinetics.

Melograno, V. J. (1994). Portfolio assessment: Documenting authentic student learning. *JOPERD, 65*(8), 50–61.

NASPE (1995). *Moving into the future: National standards for physical education.* St. Louis, MO: Mosby.

Questioning our motives. (1996). *Education Update, Association for Supervision and Curriculum Development, 38*(4), 5.

Wiggins, G. (1992). Creating tests worth taking. *Educational Leadership, 50*(8), 26–33.

Wiggins, G. (1993). *Assessing student performance.* San Francisco: Jossey-Bass.

Willis, S. (1996). On the cutting edge of assessment. *Education Update, Association for Supervision and Curriculum Development, 38*(4), 1, 4–7.

Understanding Your Teaching

Of all the things teachers undertake, the most important, it seems to me, is doing the thinking of teaching *or the reflecting about the complexities of their work. . . . Learning is continuous as reflective teachers engage in the work of thinking and doing. . . . In this way,* learning is central to teaching.

——Anna Richert

Teaching is an incredibly complex activity. Teachers plan lessons and teach them. To do this we choose content, determine how to deliver it, deliver it, and assess the results. We also talk with students, parents, school administrators, school counselors, custodians, and other teachers. We observe student performances, read student journals and portfolios, and evaluate student work. We comfort fearful children and weary parents. We cultivate hope, coax commitment, and celebrate joy. This list could go on and on, and it represents only a portion of what is necessary to the work of good teaching. And equally as important as doing all these things is the thinking that is associated with doing them (Richert, 1995).

One of the characteristics of successful teachers is that they continue to wonder, worry, and reflect on what is happening in their classrooms and gymnasiums. These teachers learn by inquiring into their practice. They think about their experiences in order to make sense of them. When faced with a situation for which there is no easy or certain answer, they engage in the process of reflective inquiry. They gather as much information as possible about the situation that puzzles them, then scrutinize the information to determine how they will act in the future. Most often this process is informal—we all engage in it to some extent to answer the millions of questions we encounter in our work on a daily basis. Occasionally the process is more formal. Either way, it is this constant and ongoing process of reflection that provides the basis for learning in teaching. It is this process of learning in teaching that makes good teaching responsive to the uncertainties of the rapidly changing world of which it is a part (Richert, 1995).

Reflective teachers work to improve their teaching and the learning of their students throughout their teaching careers. Unfortunately, reflection and inquiry into teaching are left largely to the individual teacher. Historically, a number of informal (and in many cases inaccurate) approaches to obtaining information about teaching have been used. For example, an assessment based on how much the students like a teacher doesn't provide much useful information about that teacher's performance, nor does a principal's evaluation based on a five-minute, once-a-year visit to the gymnasium. Some student teachers receive feedback from their supervisors that is both helpful and accurate. Few teachers, however, continue to receive throughout their teaching careers the amount and type of feedback vital to improving teaching performance.

The notion that, upon certification, a teacher knows all there is to know about how and what to

Elementary school physical education teachers have been observed who clocked as little as three and a half minutes of significant face-to-face contact with other adults between the hours of 7:30 A.M. and 4:30 P.M. The teacher can be psychologically alone in a densely populated world. The physical (architectural) isolation of the gym located away from the political heartland of the school and the social isolation of the physical educator role which may make the teacher peripheral to the real business of the school, both seem to sustain and intensify the feelings of isolation. Teaching physical education in some schools is a lonely job, awash in an endless sea of children.

Larry Locke, "The Ecology of the Gymnasium:
What the Tourist Never Sees"

teach and requires little, if any, assistance is quickly being discredited. In its place there is growing acceptance of the belief that teachers, if they are to progress in their teaching, can benefit from reflection, guidance, and assistance. Although some school districts provide mentors for beginning teachers, few arrange for ongoing assistance and development opportunities throughout the teaching years. For this reason, this chapter focuses on helping teachers reflect on their own teaching.

Self-Reflection

Housner (1996) suggests that ongoing reflection regarding one's knowledge, beliefs, instructional practices, and teaching effectiveness is essential to ongoing professional growth. Self-reflection allows a teacher to reflect and act upon the struggles and successes encountered in teaching (Stroot, 1996). Self-reflection can be accomplished through a journal or an audiotaped log—or some other method of maintaining a record of thoughts and reflections. These reflections often lead teachers to identify concerns and begin to think about how to reduce problems and enhance the learning environment. When specific concerns are identified or interests arise, systematic observation can be employed to obtain more formal and reliable information.

Systematic Observation

Systematic observation allows you to obtain clear, detailed information regarding various aspects of your

BOX 15.1   ACTIONS OF EFFECTIVE TEACHERS

Research has shown that effective teachers—whether classroom or physical education teachers—share similar behaviors. Effective teachers:

■ Give students time to learn by devoting a high percentage of time to the academic subject.
■ Communicate high, yet realistic, expectations for students.
■ Establish routines and organizational structures which lead to a positive classroom management climate.
■ Present meaningful and challenging tasks where students are highly successful.
■ Move the class forward with determined direction.
■ Communicate the content clearly and hold students accountable for completing tasks.
■ Assess students' skill progress closely and change practice to fit students' needs.
■ Communicate warmth through clear, enthusiastic presentations.

Source: From "Improving Your Teaching through Self-Evaluation" by B. Cusimano, P. Darst, & H. van der Mars, 1993, October, *Strategies,* p. 28. Used with permission.

teaching. Again, in view of the usual lack of assistance teachers receive, you can carry out many of the techniques we include in this chapter on your own or with the assistance of another teacher, a videotape, or an "untrained" observer.

Regardless of who is collecting the information on your teaching, the first step is deciding what you as a teacher want to look at. These "targets" may stem directly from your self-reflection or from the variables that have been shown to be related to effective teaching (Silverman & Ennis, 1996). Box 15.1 enumerates some of the actions, gleaned from research on teaching, of effective teachers. We have stated that establishing a learning environment is a necessary but not sufficient condition for student learning. Therefore, if nothing else seems to fit, determining whether you have indeed set up a learning environment may be a good place to start. The checklists in Box 15.2 can help you decide what to look for, based on your questions about teaching.

Unassisted Techniques

You can learn much about your teaching without relying on others for observation, interpretation, or analysis. You can learn, for example, the amount of time you spend actually talking to the entire class or to individuals within a class. You can discover which children receive most of your attention and whether you spend more time discussing their movement or

their behavior. How do children react to your teaching performance? How, and how often, do you use positive or negative comments? How much time do the children spend getting out or putting away equipment? You can answer these and other key questions with self-assessment techniques.

Tape-Recording for Self-Analysis   One of the simplest techniques for analyzing your teaching performance is to tape-record your verbal interactions and instruction. If you strap a portable cassette tape recorder around your waist, you'll be able to record both interactions with individual children and instructions to the entire class. The children quickly become accustomed to seeing the tape recorder, and before long they forget about it. By taping different classes, you can obtain answers to such important questions as these:

■ What percentage of a lesson did I spend talking to the entire class? To groups? To individuals?
■ Are my verbal comments clear? Do I repeat myself frequently?
■ What percentage of my comments to the children are positive? Negative? Neutral? Do I nag children?
■ Do I interact with many children in a class? Or do I focus on just a few, constantly calling their names?
■ How do I develop the lesson content?

These and many other questions can be answered by making tape recordings. Finding the answers

BOX 15.2 DETERMINING WHAT TO OBSERVE

If you're having problems with inappropriate behavior, select one or more of the following:

1. Look at your plans for potential breakdowns.
2. Transcribe all your instructions to the class, and check for clarity. Did you know what was supposed to happen?
3. Videotape a lesson to analyze your time. Was there an extreme amount of management time? Waiting time?
4. Record your feedback. Did you handle inappropriate behavior promptly and consistently, or did you nag often?

Ways to analyze your answers to these questions and obtain some helpful insights are discussed in the remainder of the chapter.

To check the atmosphere of your class, do one or more of the following:

1. Tally your feedback.
2. Check for differential treatment of students.
3. Check student interaction patterns.

To assess the instructional environment, select from the following:

1. Check your task development.
2. Assess each student's practice opportunities.
3. Check the general use of class time.
4. Tally feedback with specific attention to skill feedback.

---

involves defining what you want to assess, listening to the tape, tallying the number of times each behavior occurs or recording the length of time something occurs, and then determining percentages.

Feedback Analysis   Feedback, the information the teacher provides to individual or small groups of children about the quality of their movement or behavior based on observation, is one aspect of teaching that can be analyzed from an audiotape. (An analysis can be made from a videotape only if you have a cordless microphone that permits you to hear your individual interactions with children. The microphone on most videocameras is unable to pick up teacher-child interactions in the relatively noisy environment of a playground or gym.)

The teacher feedback form (Figure 15.1) allows you to analyze your feedback by tallying each comment you make to children. Depending on the lesson, and your interest, you may simply want to total the amount and type of feedback you give to children. You may also want to determine which children receive your feedback—and what type of feedback they receive. If you want to analyze total feedback, simply tally each feedback statement, placing it in one of the categories defined below. (If you want to analyze feedback to individual children, see the discussion of Figure 15.7 later.)

There are several categories on the teacher feedback form (Figure 15.1). You may want to use all of them or

just one or two. Your first choice is specific versus general feedback.

Specific feedback has to do either with the child's skill or with the child's behavior. If, however, there is no way for the child to tell (based just on the statement) whether the feedback is about skill or behavior, the feedback is *general.* "Good" is probably the most common general feedback statement heard in physical education lessons, followed closely by "OK." If the feedback is specific, the next step is to determine whether it is about *skill* (movement) or *behavior.* For each specific feedback statement, simply answer the question, "Was that about skill or behavior?" Then, ask yourself whether the child to whom it was provided would perceive the statement as *positive, corrective,* or *negative.* In addition, you may want to determine whether the feedback was *congruent* or *incongruent* with the cues of the lesson and, specifically, with what you asked the children to think about when you last gave instruction. Congruent feedback relates directly to what you said immediately before the children began their activity. Incongruent feedback, in contrast, might be about something the children were never told or hadn't been reminded of for several weeks. This sounds complicated, but as the process is broken down it will become easier. A number of examples are provided to show you how the checklist works.

Assume that the children are practicing striking with paddles (Chapter 29) and the teacher is focusing

Teacher Feedback

Teacher: _____   Date: _____
Grade/Activity: _____   # of Pupils: _____
Start time: _____ End time: _____ Elapsed time: _____

FEEDBACK	BEHAVIOR FEEDBACK		SKILL FEEDBACK				
	Praise	Scold	Positive	Corrective	Negative	Congruent	Incongruent
Specific							
General							
Total							
Rate/Minute							

Rate/Minute _____ _____ _____ _____ _____ _____ _____
COMMENTS:

Figure 15.1 Teacher feedback form.

on teaching them to turn their sides to the target so that they can swing more efficiently. The following are examples of feedback and the way each statement would be coded on the teacher feedback form:

- "Marilyn, that swing was great! You really turned your side to the target." (Specific, Skill, Positive, Congruent)
- "Terrific." (General, Positive)
- "Mark, remember to keep your eye on the ball." (Specific, Skill, Corrective, Incongruent)
- "Christine, stay in your own space." (Specific, Behavior, Scold)
- "Kakki, way to keep your side to the target." (Specific, Skill, Positive, Congruent)
- "Good side, Rosie." (Specific, Skill, Positive, Congruent)
- "Side, Steve." (Specific, Skill, Corrective, Congruent)

When you tally your various feedback statements, you will have a profile that lets you know what type of

feedback you tend to give. Additionally, you can determine a feedback rate per minute to find out how much feedback you give. Don't worry if your feedback pattern doesn't initially appear as you would like it to be—after all, anything we do takes practice. The good news is that adjusting feedback is relatively easy (van der Mars, 1987).

Lesson Content Another useful type of information you can get from audio- or videotape is how you develop the content of the lesson when you teach. As described in Chapter 12, there are three categories of information you may wish to collect regarding your lessons: the tasks you give the children, the cues you provide, and the challenges you offer. The tasks are the activities you actually ask the students to do. Examples are asking the children to bounce a ball in self-space and to bounce a ball while traveling in general space. Cues are the hints you provide the children to help them perform the task more effectively or correctly. Examples would be "fingerpads" and "bend

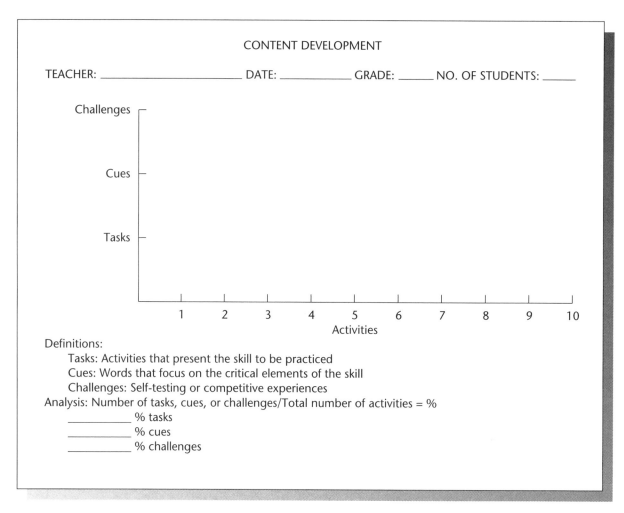

Figure 15.2   Content development graph.

your knees." Cues always seek to improve the quality of the student performance and are listed at the beginning of each task segment in the skill theme chapters. Challenges shift the focus to using the skill in a more demanding or testing situation. These are most often self-testing or competitive situations.

Figure 15.2 is a graph for determining how content is developed in a lesson. Before using it, listen to your tape and write down, in order, every task, cue, and challenge presented during the class session. Then categorize each as a task, cue, or challenge. (For this project, record only tasks, cues, or challenges that are given to the entire class, not feedback or suggestions that are given to individual students.)

After you have labeled the tasks, cues, and challenges, plot them on the graph in the order in which they occurred. Once you have finished, you will have a picture of how your lesson progressed. In most cases you will find that tasks are followed by cues, although this pattern will vary, depending on the purpose of

the lesson, student ability, and so on. Challenges are usually offered after several tasks and cues or toward the end of the lesson, although this will vary as well.

Data on feedback and content are only two examples of information you can collect from a tape recording of your teaching. For most of the questions you want to ask about your teaching, you can develop similar, uncomplicated systems that will give you the specific information you want to know. The secret to developing such systems is to define the behavior (what you want to observe or listen to) very precisely so that you can tell when it does and doesn't happen. It doesn't help very much to say, "I want to find out if I was clear or not when I talked to students"; you need to define what "clear" means to you. It could mean that students didn't have to ask you questions about how to do a task after you gave the task; it could mean that you didn't mumble and slur your words when you gave a task; or it could mean that you didn't have to turn the tape recorder up to 9 to be able to hear

DIRECTIONS: Circle the face that best describes your teacher for each statement.

My teacher gives me good directions.

My teacher will repeat his or her directions if someone misunderstands them.

My teacher gives me a second chance to learn what I need to learn if I didn't the first time.

My teacher talks to me politely and wants me to do the same to him or her and my classmates.

My teacher makes me behave.

My teacher calls on me or my classmates by name.

My teacher keeps me working during the entire class.

Figure 15.3 Form for assessing student reaction to teaching performance.

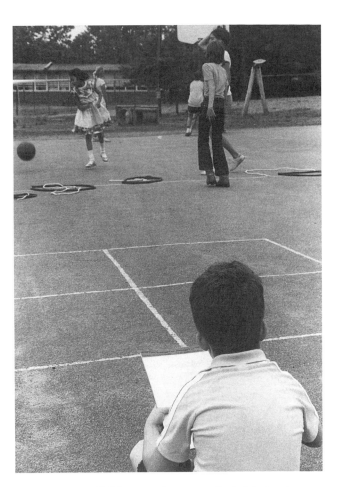

Figure 15.4 Children can learn to collect data teachers can use to understand their teaching performance.

yourself. Whatever it is, define it, and then try to assess it by listening to your tape.

Once you've obtained baseline data about your teaching performance, you can measure improvement over a period of weeks or months. You may find it challenging to set teaching goals for yourself: "During this class I want to interact at least once with every child in the class," or "During this class I want to make at least 80 percent of my comments positive." When you listen to a tape after a class, you'll learn whether you've achieved your goal.

Written Instruments A written instrument, completed by the children, can provide information about your teaching. The children can circle appropriate faces (Figure 15.3) to indicate their responses. You can hand out the answer sheets and then read the questions to the whole class. When you read the questions to the entire class, you minimize reliance on children's ability to read.

Be careful in interpreting the results of such an instrument, and remember that it is only one of many techniques that can be used to obtain information about your teaching performance. Judiciously

employed, however, such an instrument can provide valuable insights about the children's reaction to your teaching.

Student-Assisted Techniques

Mature, responsible students can occasionally help you assess your teaching performance by using techniques that they can learn in just a few minutes (Figure 15.4). These methods can provide information that cannot be obtained by the unassisted techniques.

Teacher Pathway Give the student a sketch of the teaching area—the gym or playground. Have the student trace the pathway that you make during the lesson. This is especially helpful when you're learning to increase your effectiveness as an observer (Chapter 11). You can also teach the student to make a mark on the pathway each time you interact individually with a child.

Figure 15.5 Interaction checklist.

INTERACTION CHECKLIST

Teacher Observed: _____ Date: _____
Start Time: _____ End Time: _____

Student's Name	Types of Interaction			
	Talked To	Smiled At	Touched	Total
Nick	||		|	3
Tom	|||	|		4
Carlos	||			2
Melinda		|		1
Abbey	|||||		||	7
Total Interactions	12	2	3	17

COMMENTS:

Interaction Patterns It's important to interact, verbally or nonverbally, with each child during each lesson. You can use an interaction checklist (Figure 15.5) to obtain information about your patterns of interaction with an entire class.

Select a student who knows the names of all the children in the class. Give that student a checklist form on which you've listed the names of the entire class. Ask the student to make a tally, in the appropriate column, across from the name of each child you talk to, touch, or smile at during one class period. At the conclusion of the lesson, you can use the completed checklist to analyze your teaching pattern.

You may also find interesting information in an analysis of the gender and race of the children you interact with. If you're unintentionally favoring one group over another, you should be aware of that.

Another type of analysis enables you to determine whether there's a disparity in your interactions with different children. Are you interacting more with the most skilled children than with the least skilled ones? Or do the interaction patterns indicate some other distribution of attention? Again, you can use the information on an interaction checklist that a student has filled in. For example, identify a most skilled and a least skilled group—each group should include about 25 percent of the class. From an analysis of the interactions with each group and a comparison of these two interaction patterns, you determine the group to which you are devoting more time.

Practice Opportunities Effective teachers give children plenty of practice opportunities. One way to indirectly assess the number of practice opportunities

Figure 15.6 Practice opportunities checklist.

Date _____

Teacher _____ Observer_____

Theme of Lesson _____

OBSERVATIONAL DATA

Practice Opportunities

Name of Children	ROLL	CATCH	KICK	THROW

students are getting in a class is to teach a student helper to observe and record the number of practices for selected students (Figure 15.6). You may want to select the children to be observed, or the student helper can select two or more children to observe. This technique works best when the lesson focuses on easily observed movements, such as rolls, catches, or kicks, that can be written on the form before the lesson.

Peer-Assisted Techniques

Some children could learn to use the data-gathering systems described below, but it's more realistic to seek the assistance of a colleague who's willing to help you assess your teaching performance. Such an arrangement can be mutually beneficial, because the systems described in this section can be easily adapted for use

in a classroom setting. Thus, if there's only one physical education specialist in the school, a classroom teacher could work as peer assistant with the specialist.

Practice Opportunities and Feedback Checklist
This system goes a bit further than the practice opportunities checklist (Figure 15.6) and the teacher feedback form (Figure 15.1) described in the previous sections. Using the form shown in Figure 15.7, a colleague selects several children, without your knowledge, and records their practice opportunities. She also codes feedback statements you make to the students being observed. Each statement is coded as related to the child's movement or behavior, and each statement is coded as positive or negative when possible—that is, if the statement is clearly positive or negative. Neutral statements are not recorded under the behavior heading.

Figure 15.7 Practice opportunities and teacher feedback checklist.

Teacher _WANDA_   Observer _JUDY_   Date _FEBRUARY 12_

Theme of Lesson _KICKING AND CATCHING_

OBSERVATIONAL DATA

| Name of Children | Practice Opportunities | | | Teacher Feedback | | | |
| | | | | MOVEMENT | | BEHAVIOR | |
	KICKS		CATCHES	POSITIVE	NEGATIVE	POSITIVE	NEGATIVE
MARK	⊪ ⊪ ⊪		⊪ ⊪⊪	⊪	⊪	⊪	
CARMELITA	⊪ ⊪		⊪⊪	⊪⊪		⊪	
TODD	⊪ ⊪ ⊪ ⊪		⊪ ⊪ ⊪ ⊪	⊪⊪		⊪	⊪
JEFF	⊪ ⊪ ⊪		⊪ ⊪		⊪	⊪	⊪⊪
SUSIE	⊪ ⊪ ⊪ ⊪		⊪ ⊪ ⊪	⊪⊪	⊪	⊪	⊪

The statement "Nice catch, Carmelita" would be coded on the checklist as Movement, Positive. The statement "Jeff, you never listen!" would be coded as Behavior, Negative. This observation system is relatively simple to learn and can be used reliably after just a few minutes of practice.

Duration Recording System Duration recording looks at teacher performance through what the students are doing. This system, which is a bit more difficult to use than the teacher feedback form, includes four categories of student behavior: (1) instruction time, (2) management time, (3) activity time, and (4) waiting time. The total amount of time, in minutes and seconds, is determined for each of the four categories, allowing the teacher to see how the class spent its time. Minutes and seconds can be converted into

percentages, so that you can compare one lesson with another.

The duration recording form (Figure 15.8) contains five time bars, each representing seven minutes, tick-marked in fifteen-second increments. The form defines the codes the peer assistant should use to report what is happening: A for activity, I for instruction, M for management, and W for waiting. The peer assistant records the exact time the lesson begins—the time at which the teacher gives a starting signal or the children begin to practice one or more activities. (Alternatively, you can analyze a videotaped lesson.) From that moment until the end of the lesson, the peer assistant, using a watch with a second hand, marks the time bars to reflect what is happening in the class. When there is a change in student behavior, the assistant indicates the change by writing the

Figure 15.8   Duration recording form.

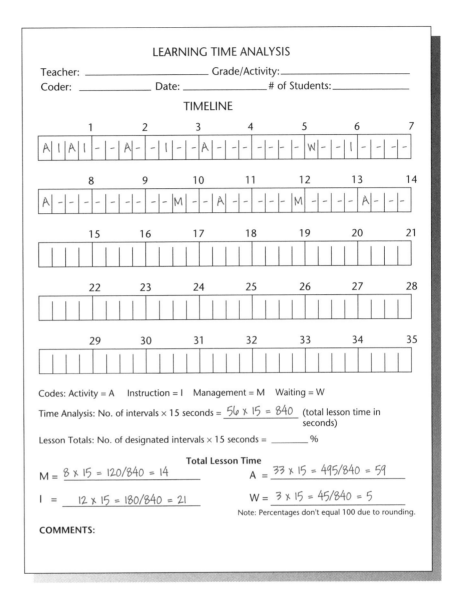

appropriate letter in the next space on the bar. At the end of the lesson, the time is recorded. The peer assistant uses the definitions and examples in Table 15.1 as guides to accurate coding. It is important to remember to code what 51 percent (or more than half) of the students are doing and to code what is happening for the majority of the segment. So, if only ten of twenty-five students are active or if fifteen students are active but only for five seconds of the fifteen-second segment, a W would be recorded (if the students are waiting for a turn).

After the lesson, the teacher uses the information on the duration recording form to figure out what percentage of class time was spent in each category. The following procedure should be used: Add up the seconds for each of the four categories. Divide each category total by the total lesson time in seconds, and then multiply each by 100. The calculations at the bottom of Figure 15.8 illustrate how the percentages for that sample lesson were determined.

In the beginning, the peer assistant may be uncertain about how to code a particular event. This is not uncommon when one is learning to use any type of analysis system. The assistant should make a decision and then code other such events the same way. That will enable you to compare a succession of lessons to determine what progress you're making.

Combining Techniques

Many observation systems have been developed to analyze the teaching performance of physical education teachers (Anderson, 1980; Darst, Zakrajsek, & Mancini, 1989; Rink, 1985; Siedentop, 1991). As you

Table 15.1   Duration Recording System Coding Guide

Category	Definition	Examples
Activity	Time when most students (51 percent or more) are involved in physical movement consistent with the specific goals of the particular lesson (Figure 15.9).	Performing exercises; designing a game, dance, or gymnastic sequence; participating in a group or individual game; providing assistance for a partner
Instruction	Time when students have an opportunity to learn. They may be receiving verbal or nonverbal information. Most students (51 percent or more) are *not* engaged in physical activity (Figure 15.10).	Listening to a lecture, watching the teacher or another student demonstrate a skill, participating in a class discussion, answering teacher's questions
Management	Time when the opportunity to learn is *not* present. Most students (51 percent or more) are involved in activities only indirectly related to class learning activity. There is no instruction, demonstration, or practice.	Changing activities, numbering off for an activity, listening for roll call, getting out or putting away equipment, getting into line
Waiting	Time not defined by the other three categories (Figure 15.11).	Waiting for class to begin, or waiting for instruction to resume when it has been interrupted by another teacher, student messenger, parent, principal, or public address system; waiting in line for a turn

Source: Adapted from an instrument developed by the Physical Education Department, Ohio State University, Columbus, Ohio. Used with permission.

Figure 15.9   During activity time, the children are involved in movement that is consistent with the teacher's goals.

become accustomed to using different systems, you can begin to code additional teacher or student behavior simultaneously—for example, how many students are off-task at a particular moment or how many positive and negative feedback statements you make. Remember that what is measured or how it is measured is less important than the continuing effort to systematically assess and improve your teaching performance. Relying on your subjective judgment ("I think I'm getting better") or that of a colleague ("That lesson looked good") is not nearly as effective as collecting and analyzing relatively objective data that you can refer back to in a few days, months, or even years.

Being Observed

Because many of us are reluctant to be observed while we teach, it may be less threatening to begin your assessment process with the unassisted or student-assisted techniques. When you've progressed to the point where you want more complex data and can no longer use students to help obtain data, be thoughtful about whom you ask to observe you. We've found it easier and more comfortable to use a colleague who is a friend and nonjudgmental, someone you're willing to expose both your good points and weaknesses to. For most of us, it takes a while to build up to this point—take it slowly.

Always remember that you're obtaining this information to help improve your teaching. The informa-

Figure 15.10 During instructional time, the opportunity to learn is present but the students aren't active.

tion is yours to do with as you wish; no one else needs to see it unless you want them to. When viewed this way, assessing your teaching performance can be interesting and challenging, not threatening (Hellison & Templin, 1991).

Finding Out More

The observation and reflection techniques just discussed are based to a large degree on information from research on teaching—the things that have been found to affect student learning of skills. Many teachers may want to find out more—they may desire to know if their teaching is successfully accomplishing the student learning they desire. To find this out, you will want to use the authentic assessment options discussed in Chapter 14 and found throughout the skill theme chapters. If you consistently find that students do not learn what you intend them to, then you may want to use some of the techniques outlined in this chapter to try to discover if some of the basic constructs of effective teaching are not aligned in your teaching the way you want them to be.

Additionally, many of the techniques discussed in this chapter deal largely with student learning of psychomotor and cognitive goals (e.g., activity time relates directly to the learning of psychomotor goals). If you have affective and cognitive goals in your lesson, you may want to revise these instruments or devise others that allow you to discover how much time you are spending with these goals. Again, a num-

Figure 15.11 Waiting time can include the minutes when students are waiting for class to begin.

ber of teachers have found that keeping a teacher jour-nal, much like a diary, allows them to look back on their own teaching over time and provides revealing insights into the nature of their work. The important point to remember is to reflect on your own teaching in an effort to continually find ways to enhance student learning. Employing systematic observation without the purpose of improving teaching to improve learning is a fruitless, time-consuming under-taking that often produces only defensive behavior.

Support Groups

The techniques described for analyzing one's teaching are effective approaches to improving performance. But successful teaching is more than using specific teaching behaviors in predetermined ways. Teaching can never be totally reduced to specific formulas of behavior that guarantee success for all teachers with all classes (Hellison & Templin, 1991; Schon, 1987). However, systematic observation can help answer some questions and provide information that can influence a teacher's success. There are other questions that require careful thought and analysis, questions that cannot be answered solely by systematic observa-tion. Sometimes we need to sit down with colleagues who'll listen carefully and help us understand (ana-lyze) a particular situation. This is what a support

group does. Teachers form support groups to build helping relationships between two or more individu-als who've learned to trust one another. These individ-uals share their concerns, questions, dreams, and hopes about themselves as teachers.

If you're not careful, teaching can be a lonely and difficult profession. As a poster depicting an exhausted teacher at the end of an obviously difficult day reminds us: "No one ever said teaching was going to be easy." When your teaching isn't going well, or when you've had a spectacular day, a support group can provide comfort and encouragement or share your excitement. It's reassuring to have a stable group of colleagues who'll listen carefully, verbally applaud your successes, and help you analyze your concerns.

Most teachers occasionally complain about teach-ing conditions, parents, administrators, or fellow teachers. We all have our down days. Within a support group, however, complaining is inappropriate because it's often toxic and tends to contaminate the thinking of others. A support group is designed to make people feel better about their teaching, not worse.

Teaching will never be an exact, predictable science. There will always be some art to teaching effectively. Self-reflection, systematic observation techniques, and support groups are three approaches to improving both teaching performance and one's personal satisfac-tion and enthusiasm for teaching.

SUMMARY

Teaching is a developmental process. Because effective teaching involves learn-ing, it is a continuous, lifelong process. Teachers who want to become more effec-tive can use various techniques to reflect on their teaching. These techniques, which include self-reflection and systematic observation, are classified into three categories: (1) unassisted, (2) student-assisted, and (3) peer-assisted.

When no one is available to help, teachers can use written instruments and videotape or audiotape to obtain information about teaching performance. A teacher's pathways, interaction patterns, and the number of practice opportuni-ties given to children can be documented with student assistance. A peer can pro-vide even more technical information by using a feedback and practice opportunities checklist or a duration recording system.

A very different but equally valuable aid is the support group. Such a group, made up of fellow teachers, can provide comfort and encouragement for all par-ticipants. When a group of peers actively listens to each other's questions and helps clarify each other's thoughts, the teaching attitude of all the members is improved.

READING COMPREHENSION QUESTIONS

1. Identify two reflective techniques you can use by yourself. What information can you obtain from each technique?
2. When would you want to use written instruments?
3. What is the use of knowing the pathway you traveled during class?
4. What kind of analysis can you make from student-teacher interactions?
5. How does the combined feedback and practice opportunities checklist (Figure 15.7) work?
6. What is duration recording? What categories does it contain? How is each category defined?
7. How does a duration recording system work?
8. What are support groups? What is their value?
9. What is the value of self-reflection?

REFERENCES/ SUGGESTED READINGS

Anderson, W. G. (1980). *Analysis of teaching physical education.* St. Louis, MO: Mosby.

Cusimano, B., Darst, P., & van der Mars, H. (1993, October). Improving your teaching through self-evaluation. *Strategies,* 26–29.

Darst, P. W., Zakrajsek, D. B., & Mancini, V. H. (Eds.). (1989). *Analyzing physical education and sport instruction.* Champaign, IL: Human Kinetics.

Hellison, D., & Templin, T. (1991). *A reflective approach to teaching physical education.* Champaign, IL: Human Kinetics.

Housner, L. (1996). Innovation and change in physical education. In S. Silverman & C. Ennis (Eds.), *Student learning in physical education: Applying research to enhance instruction.* Champaign, IL: Human Kinetics.

Locke, L. F. (1975, Spring). The ecology of the gymnasium: What the tourist never sees. *Southern Association of Physical Education for College Women Proceedings* pp 38–50.

Richert, A. (1995). Introduction. In T. Russell & F. Korthagen (Eds.) *Teachers who teach teachers: Reflections on teacher education* (1–7). London: Falmer Press.

Rink, J. (1985). *Teaching physical education for learning.* St. Louis, MO: Mosby.

Schon, D. A. (1987). *Educating the reflective practitioner.* San Francisco: Jossey-Bass.

Siedentop, D. (1991). *Developing teaching skills in physical education.* Mountain View, CA: Mayfield.

Silverman, S., & Ennis, C. (1996). *Student learning in physical education: Applying research to enhance instruction.* Champaign, IL: Human Kinetics.

Stroot, S. (1996). Organizational socialization: Factors impacting beginning teachers. In S. Silverman & C. Ennis (Eds.), *Student learning in physical education: Applying research to enhance instruction.* Champaign, IL: Human Kinetics.

van der Mars, H. (1987). Effects of audiocueing of teacher verbal praise on students' managerial and transitional task performance. *Journal of Teaching in Physical Education, 63,* 48–59.

Movement Concepts Defined

The three chapters in Part Three explain the concepts of space awareness (Chapter 16), effort (Chapter 17), and relationships (Chapter 18) and present ideas for teaching them to children. Because these are concepts rather than actual skills, levels of skill proficiency are not discussed. As children study space awareness, effort, and relationships, they learn to demonstrate, through movement, their understanding of the meaning of each concept. Once children have acquired this functional understanding, the concept is used primarily as a subfocus to enhance the range and quality of skill development that result from the study of the various skill themes (Part Four).

CHAPTER
16   Space Awareness

All movement takes place in space. Because children who develop a keen space sense will be better able to move safely as they travel through physical education environments, it's beneficial to focus on the concept of space awareness at the beginning of the physical education program.

Children can be made aware of the different aspects of space and then challenged to think about spatial considerations as they engage in game, gymnastics, and dance experiences. As children move their bodies in different ways through varying spatial conditions, they begin to feel and understand space in new ways. As relationships between the body and space become clear, adeptness at controlling movements in functional or expressive physical education activities is enhanced. For example, children learn to maneuver across a large span of climbing equipment, traveling around, over, and under other youngsters without bumping any of them or losing control of their own movements. See Box 16.1 for information on space awareness from the *National Standards for Physical Education*.

Recall from earlier chapters that the movement analysis framework consists of both movement concepts and skill themes. Space awareness—where the body moves—is one of the three categories of movement concepts. The space awareness categories are shaded in the movement analysis framework wheel (Figure 16.1). The position of space awareness on the wheel indicates that it is a movement modifier or concept. In other words, it describes *how* a skill is to be performed as opposed to stating *what* skill is to be performed.

The space awareness section is subdivided into five categories that delineate various aspects of space: location, directions, levels, pathways, and extensions. In turn, each of these categories is further subdivided into specific components that are the working or teachable aspects of space awareness. For example, the location category is subdivided into general space and self-space. Study Figure 16.1 to determine all the subdivisions for each of the separate aspects of space. It helps to think of the three outermost portions of the wheel as three levels of the same idea. The first level, or outside ring, describes the idea, the second ring gives the categories that make up the idea, and the third ring defines what is found in each category.

Activities in this section are planned as beginning tasks not only to introduce but also to teach children the five categories of space indicated in the second ring of the wheel (Figure 16.2). Children *must* understand these concepts before they attempt to apply them in conjunction with skill themes.

BOX 16.1 SPACE AWARENESS IN THE *NATIONAL STANDARDS FOR PHYSICAL EDUCATION*

The movement concept of space awareness is referenced in the *National Standards for Physical Education* (NASPE, 1995) under Standard 2: Applies movement concepts and principles to the learning and development of motor skills. The standard speaks of the child learning to apply concepts like pathways, levels, range, and directions to locomotor patterns to extend movement versatility, varying the direction and level of a locomotor pattern, identifying and performing the movement concepts, and transferring appropriate concepts from one movement skill to another.

Sample benchmarks for space awareness include:

- Walks, runs, hops, and skips, in forward and sideways directions, and changes directions quickly in response to a signal. (K)
- Uses concepts of space awareness and movement control to run, hop, and skip in different ways in a large group without bumping into others or falling. (2)
- Transfers weight from feet to hands at fast and slow speeds using large extensions. (4)
- Designs and performs gymnastics and dance sequences that combine traveling, rolling, balancing, and weight transfer into smooth, flowing sequences with intentional changes in direction, speed, and flow (6).

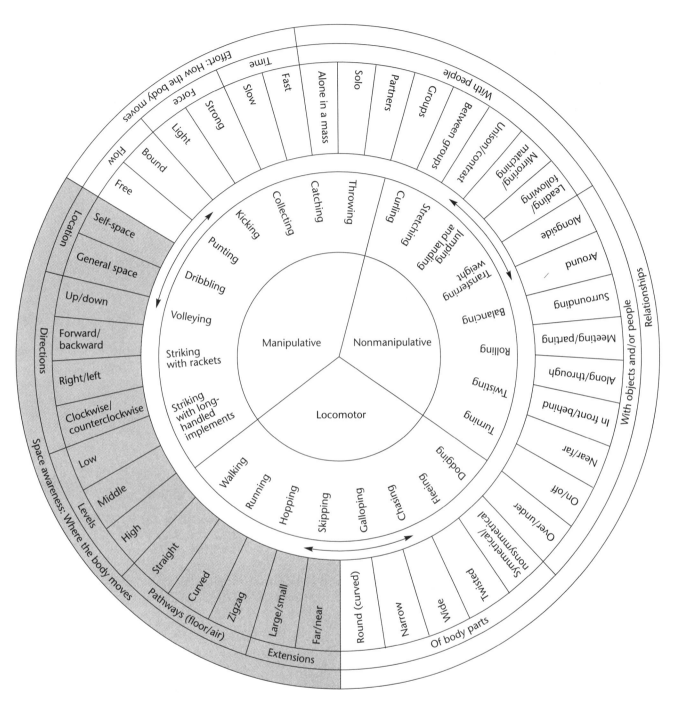

Figure 16.1 Movement analysis framework: space awareness concepts.

We usually begin by acquainting children with the two basic orientations of *location:* self-space and general space. These two ideas are crucial to all future learning; they're the foundation upon which everything else is built. *Self-space* is all the space that the body or its parts can reach without traveling away from a starting location. *General space* is all the space within a room, an outdoor teaching space, or a boundary that the body can penetrate by means of locomotion. At the precontrol level space awareness denotes the ability to move throughout the work/play area without bumping others. At the utilization and proficiency levels the ability to see open spaces, to move to open spaces, and to throw/kick to open spaces is a key element in successful games play.

Figure 16.2 This young girl, appropriately challenged, is enthralled with the process of exploring space.

The remaining four categories of space describe the relationships of the body to the space aspects of directions, levels, pathways, and extensions. *Directions* in space are the dimensional possibilities into which the body or its parts move or aim to move—up and down, forward and backward, right and left, clockwise and counterclockwise. *Levels* in space are divided into low, middle, and high. Low level is the space below the knees. Medium level is the space between the knees and the shoulders when the child is in a standing position. High level is the space above the shoulders. *Pathways* in space are the floor patterns (straight, curved, and zigzag) the body can create by traveling through space. The term *pathways* also denotes the possible floor or air patterns of a thrown or struck object—for example, the arched flight of a basketball set shot or the curved path of a pitcher's curveball.

The category *extensions* includes the size of movements of the body or its parts in space (for example, small arm circles or large arm circles) and the distances from the center of the body that the parts reach to carry out a movement. The tennis serve a skilled player performs is a far extension, whereas the tennis serve a beginner executes is often close to the body.

The ideas for developing each space concept are stated in direct terms. Remember, though, that the method used to study each concept can be varied according to your purposes and the characteristics of the children in your class (see Chapter 13).

Developing the Concept of Self-Space

We've found that the best way to teach the concept of *location* is to focus on its two components—self-space and general space—separately. We first teach self-space and then proceed to general space. You should repeat all the activities involved in teaching self-space and general space until it's clear that the students understand the distinction between the two concepts as well as the need to use space effectively.

 An understanding of self-space and general space plus starting and stopping on signal are crucial for students' safety.

If children understand the concept of self-space, their awareness of movement possibilities in the space immediately surrounding their bodies increases. Without a keen sense of the relationship of self-space to surrounding space, children's range of potential movements is restricted. When young children are introduced to a wide repertoire of movement skills in self-space, they begin to build a foundation of nonlocomotor skills (such as twisting and turning) that can be used to enhance the development of concepts and of other skills (Figure 16.3).

Teaching the Concept of Self-Space

To teach the self-space concept, we give the children learning experiences they can accomplish in one location, without traveling. The absence of locomotion enhances kinesthetic awareness of stretching, curling, twisting, and swinging (nonlocomotor) movements, as well as builds the children's movement vocabularies.

Learning Experiences Leading to Movement Concept Understanding

EXPLORING SELF-SPACE

Setting: Children scattered throughout general space

Tasks/Challenges:

🅣 While standing in a place all by yourself, not traveling anywhere else, move your arms in as many places as possible around your body. Pretend that you're on an island in the middle of shark-infested waters, and all your friends are on islands of their own. You can't reach your friends on their islands, and they can't reach you. You're stranded.

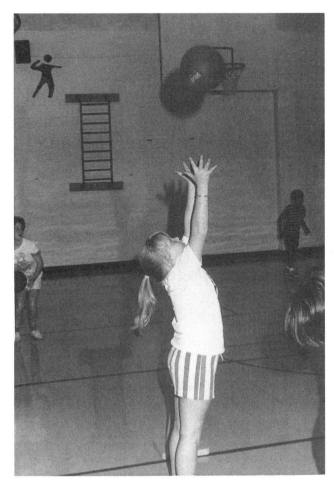

Figure 16.3 Sufficient space to work safely is crucial to skill development.

🅣 This time, while in a place by yourself, move your legs all around you. Try places that you think are hard to get to, like behind you or way out to the side; come very close to falling off your island.

🅣 Once you think that you're very good with moving your arms and legs without leaving the space you're in, choose other parts you can move without leaving your space. Use parts you think would be really hard to move around in your space without moving your whole body from your island. Explore your whole island.

The area that you've just explored is called *self-space;* it's like your own island or armor that travels with you wherever you go. Your self-space belongs to you, and no one else is allowed in it unless you let them. Remember too that you're not allowed in anyone else's self-space unless they invite you.

Even with the best analogies in the world, it's sometimes difficult for children, both young and old, to understand the concept of self-space. When this happens, we've used hoops, carpet squares, ropes shaped into circles, and X's marked on the floor to help children differentiate and remember what their self-space really looks like. As soon as children properly understand what self-space is and are able to consistently remain in self-space, you can remove these prompts.

Each individual is surrounded by a self-space as he or she travels—the possible movements into space immediately surrounding the body will be the same regardless of location. But children will understand this concept most easily if they learn it while remaining stationary. Staying in one location will clarify for the children the difference between the movements possible in the space immediately surrounding the body and the movements possible when the body travels through a general space.

CURLING, STRETCHING, AND TWISTING IN SELF-SPACE

Setting: Children scattered throughout general space

Tasks/Challenges:

🅣 While staying in self-space, where you can't touch anyone else, curl your body up very tightly so that you look like a little ball. Now that you're curled up, begin to stretch, ever so slowly, until you're stretched as tall and wide as possible. As you stretch, remember that you can't leave your own space. You're in your own birdcage. Slowly stretch just one arm, then the other arm. Slowly stretch only one leg, then the other leg. Don't forget to stretch your fingers and toes while you are in self-space.

🅣 Pretend that you're trying to reach the cookie jar that is on a shelf at the very top of your cage. Stretch as tall as you can to get it. Now, just as you have two cookies in your hand, your mother walks in. Sink very quickly back to the floor and make yourself very small to hide.

🅣 This time, a big spider is on the floor of the cage, near your feet. Stretch tall; you're trying to reach the top rungs of your cage to pull yourself up out of the spider's way. Now the spider climbs to the top; shrink slowly to get away from the spider.

🅣 Now that you've practiced your stretching and curling actions, you're going to add twisting actions to them. You want to twist your *whole* body, not just one part. To start, make believe the cookie jar is on the very back of the shelf, behind two boxes; as you

Figure 16.4 These children are learning to travel safely through general space—one of the first objectives of movement concept teaching.

stretch, twist your body so you can get to the cookie jar.

T Stretch toward the top of the birdcage (as you did to get away from the spider). Now pretend that suddenly you have an itch in the middle of your back. Hold on to the top of the cage with one hand and try to scratch your back with your other hand.

T Pretend that you have an itch in the middle of your back that is impossible to reach. Twist your body in different directions as you attempt to reach the itch. Stretch, curl, and twist body parts in self-space to scratch the itch.

C See how many body parts you can stretch in self-space. How many different ways can you curl without moving from your self-space? Isolate different body parts for twisting in self-space.

MOVING THE WHOLE BODY IN SELF-SPACE

Setting: Children scattered throughout general space

Tasks/Challenges:

T So far, all you've done in self-space is to curl, stretch, and twist; you haven't really moved your whole body using any kind of specific movement. This time, let's practice walking in place in self-space. Remember that you can't go anywhere off your island or out of your birdcage—that's all the area you have.

Other actions to practice in self-space: skipping, hopping, jumping, and turning slowly like a music box dancer.

Developing the Concept of General Space

General space is all the space within a room or boundary into which an individual can move by traveling away from the original starting location (self-space).

We help the children learn different ways of traveling safely through general space by providing appropriate movement tasks (Figure 16.4). Once the children are able to travel safely (without bumping or losing control) in general space, they're ready to experience more complex tasks that include several concepts in combination, such as speed, pathways, and directions. Manipulating balls as one travels through general space is an even more difficult challenge.

Teaching the Concept of General Space

The learning experiences in this section are designed to help children learn to travel safely and efficiently through general space. You can increase the complexity of the activities by focusing on the concepts of speed, pathways, and directions and on the manipulation of objects through general space. Traveling in general space is an excellent warm-up or limbering activity that you can use each day; it also provides additional opportunities for practice of the various locomotor skills.

Learning Experiences Leading to Movement Concept Understanding

EXPLORING GENERAL SPACE

Setting: Children scattered throughout general space

Tasks/Challenges:

🅣 Find a space by yourself within the boundaries of our work area. I'll know you're ready when I see you standing very still in a space where you can't touch anyone else. When I say "Go," begin to walk around the room, trying not to come near anyone else and at the same time not leaving any empty spaces in the room. On signal (*verbal signal or drumbeat*), stop very quickly right where you are. When you stop, you shouldn't be able to touch anyone else.

This area that you just moved in is called *general space;* it's all the space available for you to move in. As you move in general space, your self-space goes with you, like a bubble that surrounds you, so that you're protected.

🅣 Let's try the same activity again, but this time move a little faster through general space. Remember that as you move and when you stop, you shouldn't be able to touch anyone else.

 Increase the speed only when you observe that the children are able to travel without bumping into one another; for some classes this will take several days. Always start slowly.

🅣 This time, instead of walking through general space, you're going to jog (*or skip, leap, hop, gallop, etc.*) through general space. Remember to always stay as far away from other people as you can. Think about visiting different places in the area, such as the corners and the middle of the area.

After you give the stop signal, you can further concept development by giving the children feedback, for example:

1. *Praise youngsters who stop in isolated areas.*
2. *Praise youngsters who stop quickly and safely.*
3. *Point out congested or vacant spaces.*
4. *Praise youngsters who've avoided collisions by traveling defensively.*

SCAMPER

Setting: Children scattered throughout general space

Tasks/Challenges:

🅣 Travel throughout general space, constantly moving to an open space. When you arrive at that open space, quickly move to another one when someone invades your open space or you see a second or a third open space.

🅣 Travel throughout general space looking for an open space. When you see an open space, pretend you are throwing a ball to that space, then quickly travel to that space to "catch" the ball. Look for another open space, "throw," and travel again.

🅣 Travel throughout general space looking for an open space. Each time you travel to an open space, claim that space as your own by calling "yes." Then quickly move to a new open space.

REDUCING THE SIZE OF THE GENERAL SPACE

Setting: Children scattered throughout general space facing the teacher, who is positioned at the edge of the general space. (*All the children will be moving within the boundaries. When you want the space to become smaller, take a step or two toward the center of the general space—the idea is a whole wall moving forward at one time.*)

Tasks/Challenges:

🅣 Spread out and find a space by yourself. On the signal, begin to travel on your feet in general space, not touching anyone else. The hard part this time will be that I'm going to keep making your space smaller as you move. For me to do that, you must always stay in front of me; I'll keep moving forward until your general space is very small.

CITY STREETS, CROWDED SPACES

Setting: Children divided into two groups in a reduced amount of general space as in the previous activity

Tasks/Challenges:

🅣 Let's move within this reduced amount of space as if we were in a crowded city. We will begin walking at a moderate speed to avoid bumping others on the crowded streets. On signal, increase the speed of your walking as if you were in rush-hour traffic. Remember, no collisions.

🅣 Now move very slowly, because the area is congested. Increase your speed again.

T Group 1, stand very still in your self-space. You are the tall buildings in the city; you may be tall and wide or just tall. Group 2, walk throughout the general space without bumping other walkers or the buildings. Listen for the signal to increase or decease your speed. (*Switch the groups after thirty seconds.*)

DODGING IN GENERAL SPACE

Setting: Children divided into two groups: half the children on one side of the work area, half on the other side

Tasks/Challenges:

T Let's practice our moving in general space in a game. The object of the game is for both groups to get to the other side of the area without touching anyone else. The hard part is that both groups will be moving at the same time. Remember, all of you in both groups are trying to switch sides without touching anyone else. I'll watch very carefully to see if I can find anyone touching.

T Now, instead of walking, you're going to gallop (*or skip, hop, jump, etc.*) to the other side.

⚠ *Permit children to travel at fast speeds, such as running, only after they have mastered stopping on signal and moving with no collisions.*

TRAVELING OVER, UNDER, AND AROUND OBSTACLES IN GENERAL SPACE

Setting: Small obstacles (hoops and ropes on the floor, milk crates, and low benches) spread out in various places around the area

Tasks/Challenges:

T Travel around the space without touching any piece of equipment or any other person. You may go over, under, or around any of the obstacles, but don't touch anyone or anything. Remember, if someone else is at a piece of equipment, go on to another one; don't wait in line.

ASSESSMENT EXAMPLE
from the National Standards for Physical Education

Teacher Observation/Observational Record

The teacher uses a checklist to assess the degree to which a class or individual students can identify a "good personal space," work in "personal space,"

and move in "general space" during a manipulative lesson.

Criteria for Assessment

a. Finds a personal space within general space that provides maximum room to work
b. Stays in or returns to personal space during lesson
c. Moves with an awareness of others as well as space available within general space

NASPE (1995, p. 7)

OBSTACLE COURSE

Setting: Jump ropes, wands, hoops, yardsticks, crates, and similar small equipment placed around the edge of the work area

Tasks/Challenges

T Today you are going to design an obstacle course for our traveling in general space. What is an obstacle course? Right, an area to travel through without bumping into things or going outside the boundaries. Select two or three pieces of the small equipment, and place them on the floor; you may wish to place them so they are touching or so that they connect with the equipment of the person working next to you. (*Allow two to three minutes for the children to construct the obstacle course.*)

Walk throughout general space, avoiding the obstacles placed on the floor; travel without touching the equipment or any other person.

T Travel in a way other than walking.

Developing the Concept of Directions

Directions in space are the dimensional possibilities into which the body or its parts move or aim to move—up and down, right and left, forward and backward, clockwise and counterclockwise. There is no universally correct direction; direction is a function of the body's orientation in space. Forward and backward, for example, depend on the way a person is facing rather than a location in a room. Left and right refer to the respective sides of the body, not a certain wall or location in a gymnasium. Because the concepts of right and left (sideways) and clockwise and counterclockwise require cognitive as well as physical maturation for correct execution, it's not uncommon to find that children learn the directions forward and backward and up and down before they learn the directions right and left and clockwise and counterclockwise.

Teaching the Concept of Directions

The learning experiences in this section provide ideas for helping children understand the concepts of forward and backward, up and down, sideways, clockwise and counterclockwise, and right and left. As the children become more capable, the complexity of the tasks is increased—the children are challenged to combine two or more direction concepts and to move in different directions in relation to objects or people.

Learning Experiences Leading to Movement Concept Understanding

TRAVELING IN DIFFERENT DIRECTIONS

Setting: Children scattered throughout general space

Tasks/Challenges:

🅣 On the signal, walk as you usually walk, with the front of your body going first. This direction is called *forward.*

🅣 This time, walk with your back going first. This direction is called *backward.* Sometimes going backward is hard because you have to look over your shoulder to see where you're going.

🅣 Now walk with one side of your body going first. This direction is called *sideways.* You can move to either your right or left side. Let's practice both ways. First move with your right side going first. When you hear the beat of the drum (*if you don't have a drum, use a tin can, a baby rattle, or a New Year's noisemaker*), change so that your left side goes first.

🅣 Skip forward, walk slowly backward, slide from side to side like an ice skater, and jump up and down as though you were on a pogo stick.

MOVING CLOCKWISE AND COUNTERCLOCKWISE

Setting: Children scattered throughout general space

Tasks/Challenges:

Rotation *describes movement in a clockwise or a counterclockwise direction. When we want children to turn, spin, or pivot, using the terms* right *and* left *is inaccurate. Instead, the terms* clockwise *and* counterclockwise *indicate the appropriate direction in which to move.*

🅣 Look down at the floor. Imagine that there's a clock on the floor in front of you. Slowly turn around, turning in the direction the hands on the clock move. This direction is called *clockwise.* Now turn in the other direction. This direction is called *counterclockwise.*

🅣 Now practice the different directions some more. See if you can spin clockwise on one foot. Now change and spin counterclockwise on the same foot.

🅣 Swing your arms in the direction you want to spin and see if you can spin all the way around before you stop. Swinging your arms will help you spin farther. Remember to swing in the direction you want to go.

 Is it easier to spin in a clockwise or a counterclockwise direction? Why do you think so? Find a partner. One of you spin or jump and turn while the other watches. See if your partner can tell you whether you were spinning (turning) in a clockwise or a counterclockwise direction. Take turns.

🅣 This time try jumping. Stay in your self-space, and jump and turn all the way around so that you land facing the same direction you were facing when you started. Bend your knees to land in a balanced position.

🅣 Practice turning clockwise and counterclockwise when you jump. Can you turn farther in one direction than the other?

🅣 Now you're going to try something different. Travel in general space. When you hear one drumbeat, spin in a clockwise direction and keep traveling. When you hear two drumbeats, spin in a counterclockwise direction and keep traveling. If you hear three drumbeats, change the way you're traveling, for example, from a skip to a slide. Do you think you can remember all this? Let's see!

You can also teach and reinforce the concepts of clockwise and counterclockwise when working with several of the skill themes, by having the children dribble in a clockwise or counterclockwise direction, for example, or push a puck with a field hockey stick in both directions.

EXPLORING DIRECTIONS

Setting: Children scattered throughout general space

Tasks/Challenges:

🅣 In your self-space, point with the body part named in the direction that I call out. (*You can continue the list with any body part.*)

With your foot, point forward.
With your elbow, point backward.
With your hip, point to the left.
With your left foot, point forward.

As you point, make sure the direction you're pointing to is very clear—so I could easily tell which way to go if you were pointing out a direction to me.

CHANGING DIRECTIONS ON SIGNAL

Setting:　Children scattered throughout general space

Tasks/Challenges:

🅣 Now that you know the directions, move a little faster when you practice them, and mix them all up. On the signal, begin to travel in general space in a forward direction. After that, each time you hear the signal, change the direction you're moving in. For example, if you start out moving in a forward direction, the first time you hear the signal change to a sideways direction; the next time you hear the signal change to a backward direction; and the next time change back to a sideways direction. Remember to make your directions very clear.

While the children are waiting for the signal, have them think about how they're going to change direction.

🅣 This time, change not only the direction of your travel, but also the locomotor movement you use, for example, gallop forward, walk backward, or slide to the right.

🅣 This time the changes of direction are going to be a bit harder. They'll be in code. One beat of the drum means forward. Two beats of the drum mean sideways. Three beats of the drum mean backward. Spread out in general space in a space by yourself. When you hear the beat of the drum, begin to travel in the direction indicated by the code. When you hear the next beat of the drum, change and travel in the direction that it indicates. Listen very carefully to the drumbeats because I might try to trick you.

TURNING WHILE MOVING IN DIFFERENT DIRECTIONS

Setting:　Children positioned around the perimeters of the gymnasium, facing the walls

Tasks/Challenges:

🅣 Spread out around the outside of the room and face the wall. When you hear the drumbeat, begin to travel around the space by using a sliding pattern. As the drum beats again, turn, without stopping, to face the inside of the room—keep sliding. Each time the drum beats, change the way you're facing, and continue moving sideways. When you do this, I'm looking for turns that are smooth and slides that don't stop as you turn.

Developing the Concept of Levels

Levels are the horizontal layers in space where the body or its parts are positioned or can move. *Low level* is the space below the knees, close to the floor. A stamp or twist of the foot is an action at a low level. Crawling, creeping, or rolling are locomotor actions performed at a low level.

Medium level is the space between low level and high level—the area between the knees and shoulders. Catching a thrown ball, for example, typically occurs in middle level.

High level is the space above the shoulders, toward the ceiling. Although one can't move the whole body into high level, actions such as stretching the arms up high or standing on the balls of the feet bring body parts into a high level. A jump can take much of the upper body into a high level, while part of the body remains at a medium or low level because of the pull of gravity.

Teaching the Concept of Levels

The learning experiences in this section give children movement challenges that help them learn to move the body, body parts, and objects into different levels in space.

Learning Experiences Leading to Movement Concept Understanding

TRAVELING AND FREEZING AT DIFFERENT LEVELS

Setting:　Children scattered throughout general space

Tasks/Challenges:

🅣 Spread out and find a space by yourself. On signal, begin to travel in general space. When you hear the drumbeat, stop where you are, with your whole body at a low level.

T This time, travel, and on the signal stop with your body at a low level and a body part at a high level. Make it very clear which part is at a high level.

T This time, when you stop, stop with your body at a medium level. Remember that a low level means below your knees, a medium level is from about your knees to your shoulders, and a high level is above your shoulders.

TRAVELING WITH BODY PARTS AT DIFFERENT LEVELS

Setting: Children scattered throughout general space

Tasks/Challenges:

T Travel around general space with as many of your body parts as possible at a low level. Remember that your body parts should always be at a low level when you're traveling, not just when you freeze.

T As you travel this time, try to have as many body parts as possible at a medium level. Remember that it isn't possible to have all body parts at a medium level as you travel because your feet always have to be on the floor, but have as many parts as possible at a medium level and none at a high level.

T This time as you travel, have as many parts as possible at a high level. This activity is harder than the other two, so be very careful that all possible body parts are at a high level.

RISING AND SINKING TO CREATE DIFFERENT LEVELS

Setting: Children scattered throughout general space

Tasks/Challenges:

T Find a space by yourself, and get into a low position that you like. I'm going to beat the drum very slowly eight times. As I beat the drum, rise very slowly to the eight beats until you attain a position of stillness with as many body parts as possible at a high level. Remember to rise slowly. But also remember that you have only eight beats in which to get to a high level, so judge your movement so you get there in time. After you've reached your high position, on the next eight beats slowly sink

back to your low position. The sequence then goes like this: a low position, eight beats to get to a high still position, eight beats to return to your low position. Let's try it.

TRAVELING WHILE RISING AND SINKING

Setting: Children scattered throughout general space

Tasks/Challenges:

T As you travel around the space this time, I'll give you drumbeats to guide your actions. The drumbeats will be in counts of four, with the accent on the first beat. Start by traveling at a low level. On the accented first beat, quickly jump and stretch into a high level and then immediately return to a low level of travel until the next accented beat. Your movement should look like this: travel low, jump high, travel low, jump high, travel low, and so on. Make your jump very clear and as high as possible and your travel at a low level very clear. I should be able to easily tell the difference between the two levels.

Developing the Concept of Pathways

A pathway is an imaginary design that the body or its parts when moving through space create along the floor or through the air. A pathway is also the trail of an object (a ball or hockey puck) as it travels from one player to another or toward a goal.

At first, young children may have difficulty understanding the concept of pathways in space. However, a class of young children can become enthralled with the process of discovering and experimenting with the many pathways the body can travel. A teacher can plan experiences that enable youngsters to recognize pathways and to effectively use knowledge of pathways to improve control of travel. For instance, even very young children can come to understand that a curved or angular pathway is effective for avoiding collisions when traveling through a crowd.

Teaching the Concept of Pathways

Children learn to travel in straight, angular, and curved pathways, and in combinations of these pathways, by experiencing the activities in this section. More difficult learning experiences involve manipulating various objects in pathways and traveling in relation to others along various pathways. (Figure 16.5)

Figure 16.5 Spacial awareness becomes very important when manipulating objects in general space.

Learning Experiences Leading to Movement Concept Understanding

EXPLORING PATHWAYS

Setting: Tape markings on the floor similar to those shown in Figure 16.6; children scattered throughout general space

Tasks/Challenges

🅣 Today you're going to learn about pathways. A line that doesn't turn or twist and is always straight is called a *straight pathway*. A line that circles around is called a *curved pathway*. A semicircle is a curved pathway. A line that looks like a lot of Z's put together is a *zigzag pathway*. Now find a space on one of the pathways marked on the floor. Travel along that pathway on your feet; be able to tell me what kind of pathway it is when I ask you.

🅣 This time as you travel, change your direction, sometimes going forward along your pathway, sometimes sideways, and sometimes backward. Try out all directions on your pathway.

🅣 Now change the way that you travel along your pathway. Sometimes you may want to hop, sometimes leap, sometimes run. Find at least four different ways that you can travel along your pathway.

During the activity, have the children regularly change places so that they're on a different pathway.

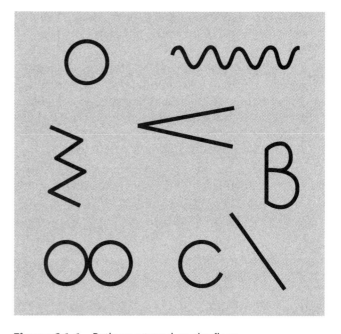

Figure 16.6 Pathways taped on the floor.

USING PATHWAY MAPS

Setting: A card, similar to the ones shown in Figure 16.7, for each child

Tasks/Challenges

🅣 Take a card and find a space by yourself. Travel on your feet and follow the pathway indicated on your card. Pretend that your card is a map showing

Figure 16.7 Pathway cards.

Card 1   Card 2   Card 3

the route to take to get to a new place. Keep practicing your pathway until you're very sure it's just like the one on the card and you can do it the best you can. Be able to tell me the name of the pathway you're following whenever I ask you.

C Now trade cards with someone else and practice that pathway until you think it's perfect.

DESIGNING PATHWAYS

Setting: Children scattered throughout general space

Tasks/Challenges:

T Pick a spot on the wall across the room from you. Remember where your spot is, and in your mind plan a pathway that will take you from where you are now to that spot. Think about it a long time so you can remember it when you start to move. When I give the signal, travel along your made-up pathway until you get to the spot you've picked out. Stop when you get there. On the next signal, travel back to the place you started from, following the same pathway you took coming over. This is similar to following a path through the woods: You can't go off the path or you'll get lost.

C Now I am *not* going to give you the signal any more. Practice your pathway on your own until you have memorized and can repeat it exactly every time.

CREATING FOLLOW-THE-LEADER PATHWAYS

Setting: Sets of partners scattered throughout general space

Tasks/Challenges:

T Find a partner and stand in a space together. I'll know that you're ready when I see each of you

standing quietly in your space. Decide which of you is going to be the leader. On the signal, the leader travels a pathway to somewhere else in the room. On the second signal, the leader stops, and the follower moves along the same pathway the leader took until the follower catches up with the leader. After doing this three times, the leader and follower switch places. The secret is for the follower to watch the leader very closely. In the beginning, the leader should not make up hard pathways. Followers, remember to copy the leaders' pathways exactly.

TRAVELING PATHWAYS AND OBSTACLES

Setting: Half the class positioned throughout general space; the other half, around the perimeter of the space

Tasks/Challenges:

T Now you're going to travel in pathways that go around, over, and under obstacles in your way. Always remember that your classmates are the obstacles, so you have to be very careful of them. You can't touch anyone else. People who are obstacles must remember to stay very still so as to not interfere with anyone who's moving. Obstacles, go find a position in a space by yourself that you can hold still. It can be any position that you like—a bridge, a statue, or a balance. Those of you on the side of the space, pick a point on the other side of the room and plan a pathway to get there. Remember that your pathway can go over, under, or around any of the obstacles. Think about it and really make it different from anything you've done before.

Give the children a few seconds to plan their pathway and the obstacles time to select their position.

On the signal, follow your pathway to the point you picked on the other side of the room. Freeze when you get to the point you picked. On the next signal, try to retrace your pathway until you get back to your starting position.

Ⓖ Now, on your own, practice your pathway four times. Remember to avoid running into other trav-

elers as you cross the space. Always have a clear beginning and end to your pathway.

When all have completed their pathways, have the students switch places and perform the activity. You can enhance activities such as these by asking children who're doing the activities correctly to demonstrate for the rest of the class.

MR. JENNING'S KINDERGARTEN CLASS DISCOVERS PATHWAYS

Teacher: Hey gang! How did we get to the physical education space today?

Children: We walked!

Teacher: Yes! And what parts of our bodies did we use?

Children: Our feet . . . our legs.

Teacher: You got it! Tell me, did we leave a trail behind us? Any footprints on the floor?

Children: No! (*Loud and laughing*)

Teacher: I don't see any either. But what if your shoes were muddy. Would we have left a trail?

Children: Yeah! But Mrs. Farmer (*the principal*) sure would be mad!

Teacher: I think she would be, too! But if we did leave muddy footprints from your classroom all the way to the physical education space, what would our path look like?

Children: Long . . . Messy . . . We go by the library.

Teacher: I think you're all right. I have an idea . . . Let's look at the chalkboard. Here's your room way over here and this is where the physical education space is. Look at our pathway. Although we didn't leave any real footprints, we did follow a path. We follow this same pathway each time we come to the physical education space. Tell me, is our path just one straight line or did we make any turns?

Children: We turned when we came out of the room. At the library.

Teacher: You people are sharp today. Hey! Can you think of any other pathways you follow each day?

Children: We go to lunch . . . Walk to school . . . Down to the playground.

Teacher: We follow a lot of pathways each day. Let's see if we can have some fun with pathways today. Pick a spot somewhere on the outside edge of the room (for example, a brick, a picture) and when I say "Go," you stand up and walk in a straight line to your spot and freeze. Here we go!

Setting: A pencil plus a card with dots randomly plotted on it for each child; carpet squares on the floor in a pattern similar to that of the dots on the card

Tasks/Challenges:

Ⓣ Connect the dots on your card to form any design you like. After you've finished connecting the dots, follow the path that you drew from one carpet square to the other. Make sure you know the type of pathway you've designed because I might ask you.

Ⓖ Now trade maps with someone else. Follow that person's map. Figure out if that pathway is different from yours.

COMBINING PATHWAYS, LEVELS, AND DIRECTIONS

Setting: A task sheet, similar to that in Figure 16.8, for each child

Tasks/Challenges:

Ⓣ This activity lets you combine pathways, levels, and directions. It's also a good way to test yourself. Once you think you're able to perform a challenge, have a friend watch you and sign the line on the task sheet beside the challenge. When you're finished, I'll come and check you out. You may use a friend to help you if you want extra help.

Younger children can use a smile face instead of having someone else initial the sheet.

Developing the Concept of Extensions in Space

Extensions in space are best understood as two separate possibilities. First, extensions are spatial relationships of body parts to the entire body. Body extremities can be held in close to the body, as in a curl, or they can

Figure 16.8 Task sheet for pathways, levels, and directions.

Name _____ Teacher _____

Pathways, Levels, and Directions Task Sheet

Date	Who Watched	Challenge
		I can walk forward in a straight pathway.
		I can walk backward in a straight pathway.
		I can walk sideways in a straight pathway.
		I can walk forward in a curved pathway.
		I can walk backward in a curved pathway.
		I can walk forward, low, and curved.
		I can walk backward, high, and zigzag.
		I can run sideways, medium, and curved.
		I can slide backward, medium, and zigzag.
		I can
		I can
		I can
		(Make up three things you can do on your own using pathways, levels, and directions.)

be opened up, as in a stretch. Extensions are also the size of movements in space. Movements with extremities held close to the body are *small movements,* such as putting a golf ball; those with the extremities extended or opened up are *large movements,* such as driving a golf ball.

Teaching the Concept of Extensions in Space

The concept of extensions is taught through learning experiences that give children an operational understanding of the differences between large and small, as well as near and far extensions (movements).

Learning Experiences Leading to Movement Concept Understanding

EXPLORING EXTENSIONS

Setting: Children scattered throughout general space

Tasks/Challenges:

Ⓣ Find a space by yourself. With your hands, explore all the space close to your body. Remember to not reach very far from your body; this is an extension near your body. We call it a *near* extension.

T Now, without leaving your self-space, explore all the space that is far away from your body. Try to reach as far as you can without leaving your space. Remember to explore above and behind as well as in front of you. This is called an extension that is far away from your body. We call it a *far* extension.

TRAVELING AND EXTENSIONS

Setting: Children scattered throughout general space

Tasks/Challenges:

T Travel around the room. When you hear the beat of the drum, stop in a position where your body reaches as far into space as possible. Be very sure that all possible body parts are as far away from the center of your body as you can get them.

T This time as you travel, when you hear the drum-beat, stop with all body parts as close to your body as possible. Remember to keep all your body parts as close to yourself as you can.

T Now try traveling with change. When you hear the sound of the drum, jump high into the air, extend-ing your arms and legs as far away from your body as possible. When you land, hold a position very still, with all body parts very close to the center of your body. Really try to make a clear difference between the far and near extensions.

CHANGING FROM ONE EXTENSION TO ANOTHER

Setting: Children scattered throughout general space

Tasks/Challenges:

T Find a space by yourself, and get into a tight posi-tion you like. I'll beat the drum six times, in slow beats. On the first six beats, gradually extend all body parts far away from body. On the next six beats, slowly move to your tight curled posi-tion. The movement then goes like this: first a tight, curled position; on six beats, slowly move to a spread-out position; on the next six counts, slowly move back to a near extension. Try to make the extensions you use very clear. We'll practice this activity a number of times so you can work on doing your best possible.

USING EXTENSIONS AND IMAGERY

Setting: Children scattered throughout general space

Tasks/Challenges

T As you travel around general space, pretend you're carrying an object you don't want anyone to see or that you're trying to hide or protect something, such as a baby bird, a million-dollar jewel, or a lot of money. As you walk, think very carefully about how you'd actually carry the object you've chosen.

T Now, instead of having an object you want to hide, you have one you're proud of and want to show off—maybe a trophy that you just won. How would you carry it? Go!

 In which activity did you use a near or small extension? In which activity did you use a large or far extension?

Applying the Concept of Space Awareness

Self-space and general space are often appropriate beginning concepts for children who have had little experience in formal physical education classes. One of the important skills that children need to develop early is the ability to occupy an area or to travel in an area while maintaining awareness of others. Self-space and general space are helpful concepts to use when teaching these skills.

The concepts of directions, levels, and pathways are usually introduced after children have developed the ability to differentiate self-space from general space. Until the children actually acquire a functional under-standing of directions, levels, and pathways (high, medium, low levels; forward, sideways, backward direc-tions; straight, zigzag, and curved pathways), the obser-vational focus is primarily on the concept rather than on correct performance of a particular skill. For exam-ple, if you ask the children to throw so that the ball starts off at a high level, you're less interested in the actual mechanics of throwing than in the child's ability to release the ball at a high level. Once you're confident that the children are able to apply the concepts, you can focus more on appropriate skill technique.

Most children take a longer time to grasp the con-cepts of right and left, air pathways, and extensions. Thus it's wise to introduce the other concepts to chil-dren before focusing on these three ideas.

The ability to understand the concept of right and left is related to cognitive maturation. Some children will need more time and more practice opportunities than others to master left and right. Many children easily acquire cognitive understanding of the concepts of extensions and air pathways for objects, but most require a certain degree of skill before they can express these ideas in movements (Figure 16.9). Children with immature throwing and kicking patterns, for example, have difficulty propelling objects so that they travel in different (but intended) air pathways. Children with immature striking or catching patterns are unable to consistently catch or strike an object far from or near to the body.

If you wait until children have developed the skills that are related to these concepts, you'll find that the pupils grasp the concepts more easily than if you try to teach the concepts and then the skills. There's no universally successful sequence for the introduction of these concepts. The reflective teacher uses all available information and makes judgments about the most appropriate time, sequence, and duration for introducing and studying the concepts of space awareness and the application of the concepts to specific skill-practice situations.

Figure 16.9 To respond to the challenge of catching while traveling, this child must have a functional understanding of the concept of space.

READING COMPREHENSION QUESTIONS

1. What is the primary reason for focusing on the concept of space at the beginning of a physical education program?
2. What does the term *space awareness* mean? What are the characteristics of someone who is "aware of space"?
3. What directions in space are studied in this program? Why do children find some directions harder than others to understand?
4. Distinguish the three levels of space from one another.
5. List the three types of pathways an individual might travel. Explain the difference between a floor pathway and an air pathway.
6. Give two examples each of a far extension and of a near extension.
7. Why do we have children study self-space while stationary rather than traveling?
8. What does it look like when children are able to travel safely in general space?

REFERENCES

National Association for Sport and Physical Education (NASPE). (1995). *Moving into the future: National standards for physical education.* St. Louis, MO: Mosby.

CHAPTER 17   Effort

Too often teachers make no conscious, planned attempt to help children understand the effort concepts of time, force, and flow and the application of these concepts to specific skills.* Many teachers don't feel comfortable teaching these concepts, which are vague and abstract. It is not like teaching a child to strike a ball with a paddle, where the objective of striking is obvious and the result easily perceived. Despite the hesitancy of many teachers to undertake the teaching of effort concepts, there is agreement that an applied understanding of these concepts is essential in skill development, from beginning through advanced levels. See Box 17.1 for information on effort from the *National Standards for Physical Education.*

The concept of effort defines how the body moves. The concept is divided into three components: time, force, and flow, which are defined by observable characteristics that can be taught to children. Figure 17.1 conceptualizes this idea and puts it into perspective with the other movement concepts and skill themes. The effort category is in the shaded portion of the framework. The outside ring defines the concept, the second ring states the components of the concept, and the third ring defines the three components.

---

*Some movement analysis frameworks include the concept of space (direct and flexible) as a quality of movement. In our teaching, however, we use this concept so infrequently that we've chosen not to include it in the discussion of the qualities of movement.

Highly skilled (proficiency level) movers have developed an internalized, almost reflexive knowledge of the proper amount and degree of time, force, and flow. They're able to adjust the quality of movements in relation to the demands of a situation—harder or softer, faster or slower, bound or free.

We begin to teach effort concepts to children by providing experiences to help them understand the contrasts of fast-slow, strong-light, and bound-free. Once the children have grasped the differences between the extremes, we focus on the concepts as they apply to specific skills (such as throwing, striking, and transferring weight) and in different situations (for example, to assist in the expression of an idea or to accomplish a particular strategy). As children become more skillful, we focus on the gradations among the extremes. To illustrate, initially we might ask children to travel rapidly and to travel slowly. As children develop the ability to differentiate between the extremes, we focus more on the movement possibilities that occur between the extremes—faster, slower, accelerating, decelerating, sudden changes of speed.

Many of the activities in this chapter use imagery to help children distinguish among different effort concepts. It's important to keep in mind that the focus is on the movement qualities of the various images rather than on the images. For example, when we say "Move like a hippo," we're not asking the children to pretend to be hippos; we're using this task to help the children envision a slow, lumbering movement. Box 17.2 and Chapter 20 contain additional information

BOX 17.1 EFFORT IN THE *NATIONAL STANDARDS FOR PHYSICAL EDUCATION*

The movement concept of effort is referenced in the *National Standards for Physical Education* (NASPE, 1995) under Standard 2, Applies movement concepts and principles to the learning and development of motor skills. The standard speaks of an emphasis on the child's establishing a beginning movement vocabulary (fast/slow speeds, light/heavy weights) and applying appropriate concepts to performance. The standard also emphasizes the ability of the child to identify and perform movement concepts in order to enhance the quality of the movement.

Sample benchmarks for effort include:

- Demonstrates clear contrasts between slow and fast movements while traveling. (K)
- Designs and performs gymnastics and dance sequences that combine traveling, rolling, balancing, and weight transfer into smooth, flowing sequences with intentional changes in direction, speed, and flow. (6)

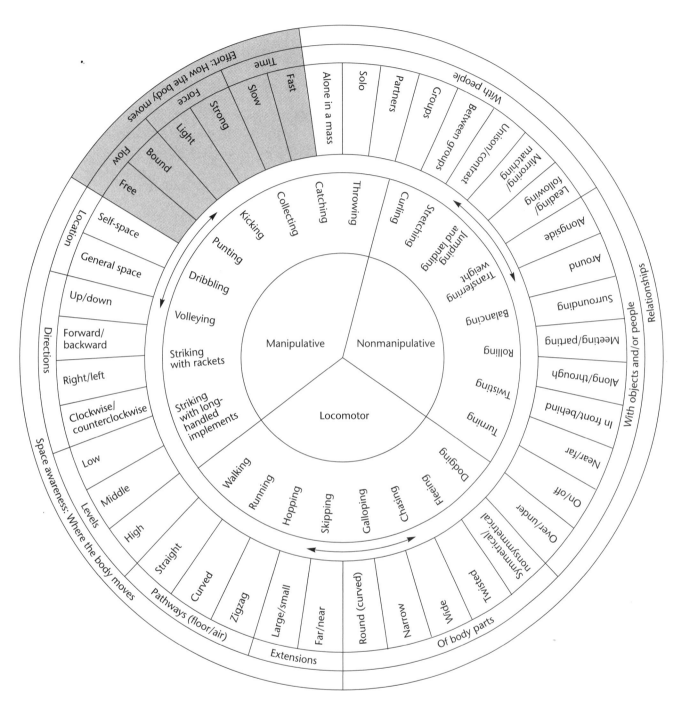

Figure 17.1 Movement analysis framework: Effort concepts.

about the appropriate use of imagery in teaching movement.

Developing the Concept of Time

Time to a young child is the ticktock of a watch, the cuckoo on a clock, or the numbers racing by on a digital timepiece. When spoken of in relation to move-ment, time is fast—being able to run like the wind; being the fastest in the class; zip, dash, zoom (Figure 17.2).

In an activity in which speed is often the measure of success, children often have difficulty comprehend-ing slowness and seeing the importance of this rate of movement. Yet the performer executing a walkover on the balance beam grasps the concept of slowness, as does the leaping dancer who seems to remain

BOX 17.2   IMAGERY AND MOVEMENT

Much has been said about imagery and movement, specifically related to dance. We've all had the experience of asking children to "show a flower growing," only to discover that instead of exploring the movement possibilities available, the children were pretending to be flowers. Herein lies the pitfall of imagery: Concept development isn't pretending; it's understanding.

To be beneficial, the teaching of movement concepts and ultimately dance must first be involved with children learning a movement vocabulary and then relating it to other ideas (much like the development of movement skills before relating them to game play). This notion implies that we must talk about movement first and use images to lead to an understanding or enhancement of that movement. It precludes moving or dancing "about"

something (anger, fear, excitement, horses, etc.) or pretending to be something (a piece of fruit, a cowboy, a flower, an airplane, etc.).

Mary Joyce (1980) developed three useful phases regarding dance and imagery that can be easily applied to any creative movement:

1. Images that lead to movement: "Make your back curved like a banana."
2. Images that arise from movement: "You're in a curved shape. What else do you know that is curved?"
3. Images as a basis for movement: "What kind of movement might a banana do?"

Always remember to talk about the movement first and the image second.

Figure 17.2   These young children are enjoying the sensation of running—a fast movement.

suspended in the air while the hands and arms express a certain feeling or emotion.

Changes in the time of a movement usually occur without forethought as children adapt to different situations—speeding up or slowing down to maintain

possession, to avoid being tagged, to get in open space and receive a pass. Many movements and specific skills dictate the rate of movement (Figure 17.3). A handspring is done quickly, but a back walkover is performed slowly. In some activities, the child is free

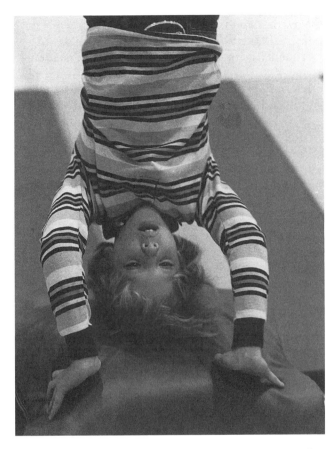

Figure 17.3   Slowness is necessary in executing a transfer like this.

to assess a situation and then perform a skill at the best rate. For example, a movement executed quickly in dance or gymnastics elicits feelings of power and speed; the same movement executed slowly expresses the ultimate in control.

We begin teaching the concept of time to young children by contrasting extremes. Gradually we advance to work that focuses on degrees of speed along a continuum—the ability to execute movements at varying speeds for the purpose of adapting, changing, or creating a situation.

Teaching the Concept of Time

The learning experiences that follow are designed to help children develop a functional understanding of time by contrasting fast and slow actions of the total body and body parts as well as by focusing on acceleration-deceleration. *When the children are traveling fast, try to keep the activity period short to avoid undue fatigue.*

Learning Experiences Leading to Movement Concept Understanding

EXPLORING TIME

Setting: Children scattered throughout general space

Tasks/Challenges:

🅣 Find a space by yourself. Without leaving your space, move with the beat of the drum. The beat will be very loud and quick to begin with, so you'll want your movements to be very sharp and quick. The trick to having very quick actions it to make them very short; something that's really quick can't go on for very long. This action is called a *sudden* movement.

🅣 This time the beat of the drum will be slower and longer. Try to move your whole body as slowly as the drumbeats, much like a balloon floating through the air or a feather being dropped from a high building. Think about moving every part of your body slowly, not just your arms but your head, shoulders, back, stomach, legs, everything. This action is called a *sustained* movement.

USING DIFFERENT SPEEDS IN SELF-SPACE

Setting: Children scattered throughout general space

Tasks/Challenges:

🅣 In a space by yourself, bring your hands together very slowly, as if to catch an insect that might try to fly away. At the very last moment before your hands are going to touch, quickly separate them as if you're surprised to find out that the insect is a bee. When you do your slow movements, remember to make them very slow but to always keep your hands moving; make your quick movements so quick that they're like flashes of lightning.

🅒 Let's try those movements five more times. You can bring your hands together any way you want as long as you do so slowly, and then quickly take them away any way you want. Remember to make your slow and quick movements as clear as they can be. Five times. Go.

🅣 Now, on your own, find other body parts that you can bring together slowly and then quickly pull apart. Try to find at least three combinations. Practice each movement so that the difference between fast and slow is very clear.

This activity is more difficult than it sounds because it asks for extremes of a movement. You can have children practice this activity over and over; always ask for faster and slower actions than the children previously exhibited.

MOVING AT DIFFERENT SPEEDS

Setting: Children scattered throughout general space

Tasks/Challenges:

Ⓣ On the signal, move as fast as you can, but remain in self-space; on the next signal, freeze in a balanced position that you can hold very still. Remember to try to go as fast as you can, but you must be able to stop on the signal without falling over.

Ⓣ Now, on the start signal, move as slowly as you can. Try to move very slowly, but always keep moving. On the stop signal, freeze in a balanced position. Remember to stay in your self-space.

Ⓣ Your first movement was at a fast speed; your second, at a slow speed. Could you tell the difference? Again, you're going to practice both fast and slow speeds. Try to make the movements very clear so I can really tell the difference between them. As you move, I'll call out "Fast" or "Slow," and you change your speed accordingly. So if I call out "slow," move very slowly, and if I call out "fast," move fast. Listen very carefully because I might try to trick you. Make your fast really fast and your slow really slow.

Once the children demonstrate an understanding of speed in self-space, you can transfer these same tasks to traveling in general space.

TRAVELING AND FREEZING BY USING CHANGES IN TIME

Setting: Children scattered throughout general space

Tasks/Challenges:

Ⓣ This time, begin your traveling with a quick explosion of speed, and keep going at a fast speed; then freeze very quickly in a balanced position. The movement should be like this: Begin really fast as if you've been shot out of a cannon, then move fast as if you're running from someone, then freeze quickly as if someone has surprised you and you can't move. Make each segment of your traveling very clear so that I can tell when you change from one part to the other. I'll give you the start signal, then you're on your own.

Ⓒ Now that you've practiced sudden starts, traveling fast, and then freezing, you're going to make up a sequence using those speeds. Choose one sudden-start, fast-travel, and freeze position that you really like, and practice it until you can do it smoothly and with control. Each of the three parts should be very clear and very different from one another. After you think the sequence is really good, practice it three more times. Remember to start and end in the same place each time. Your three movements should look the same every time, as if they'd been videotaped.

Ⓣ Now begin very slowly, as a car does on a cold morning. As you warm up, gradually increase your speed until you're moving fast. Then, freeze suddenly. The sequence should look like this: a slow start, a gradual increase to fast speed, then a freeze. This is different from your last traveling action, so make that difference very clear.

Ⓒ Now make up a sequence that includes a slow start that gradually increases to a fast speed and suddenly freezes. Practice the sequence until you're ready to show someone else, who, after seeing it, should be able to tell you what the three parts were.

Children often equate slowness with heavy, jerky, stiff actions rather than with graceful movement. Examples of slow-moving animals can be useful here. Box 17.3 also contains hints for helping children learn to design movement sequences.

COMBINING IMAGERY AND TIME

Setting: Children scattered throughout general space

Tasks/Challenges:

Ⓣ This time you're going to practice traveling the way different things that move fast or slow do. Remember that you aren't really trying to act like the things you're pretending to be; you're just trying to move at the speed they move. Let's practice one movement. On the signal, move as a turtle would move. Think carefully about it—a turtle moves very slowly. Now try moving as fast as a rabbit. Go really quickly.

Ⓣ How does a new race car move? Let's try to go as fast as a race car can. There's only one thing different about this race car: It goes so fast that it can't make any noise. So go as fast as a silent race car. Change your race car to an old jalopy trying to go uphill; the car is really tired and old, so remember that it goes very slowly.

BOX 17.3   DESIGNING SEQUENCES

Helping children learn how to design movement sequences if much like helping them learn how to design their own games (see Chapter 31). Following are several tips we've found helpful when beginning to have children design sequences.

1. It takes time.
2. Structure the sequence into a simple form that is easily remembered, for example, a starting shape, a middle moving phase based on a specific aspect of movement, an ending shape.
3. Practice the starting and ending shapes separately before adding the middle movement.
4. Initially, provide a beginning signal, some time to practice (twenty to twenty-five seconds), and then an ending signal.
5. During the first stages, prompt the children during the movement aspect about exactly what movements need to be included (change of level, speed, etc.).
6. Have children repeat their sequence several times. The middle movement aspect may vary slightly each time, but the beginning and end should remain constant.
7. In some way hold the children accountable for what they've created, for example, divide the class in half and have them present their sequence, present their sequence to another person, or write it down.

As the children's ability to design sequences increases, you can gradually relax some of these guidelines, but we've found these steps useful for both the students and the teacher when children first begin to create movement sequences.

SOURCE: Adapted from *First Steps in Teaching Creative Dance to Children*, 2nd ed., by Mary Joyce, 1980, Palo Alto, CA: Mayfield.

Some classes enjoy and can accept the responsibility for making the sounds of race cars and jalopies. You'll have to use your judgment about whether to encourage the sounds, which can be either productive or detrimental, depending on the circumstances.

🅣 Now pretend that the fair is in town and you're going to go with your friends tonight to ride all the rides and eat all kinds of food. How excited are you? Really let your excitement show as you go home from school. Try it. Now, instead of going to the fair, you're going home, and you know you'll be in trouble because your mom told you not to take any more cookies from the cookie jar and you got caught taking the last two.

🅣 You're the fastest sprinter in the Olympics and are in the starting blocks waiting for the gun to go off. Go. Now you're a distance runner just about to start a ten-mile race; you have a long way to go, and you don't want to wear yourself out.

🅣 You're a mouse running from a cat. Now you're a hippopotamus with a full stomach trying to run.

DIFFERENTIATING AMONG TIME WORDS

Setting: Children scattered throughout general space

Tasks/Challenges:

🅣 Show me the difference among the words "dash," "waddle," "dart," and "crawl." First, dash. Go. Now, waddle. Go. Now, dart. Go. Next, crawl. Remember to change speeds with each word so the speeds are very clear.

🅣 Let's try them again. Listen very carefully because I'm going to start calling them out faster and you'll have to change quickly from one to the other.

Other pairs of words can be used to elicit changes in time: creep/explode, pop/sneak, gallop/totter, slither/stride. See Box 17.4 for other action words that can be used in teaching the various effort concepts.

COMBINING SPORT SKILLS AND TIME

Setting: Children scattered throughout general space

Tasks/Challenges:

🅣 Before beginning, I want you to think of your favorite television or sports character. Be sure you can tell me who it is when I ask, because this is important. After you decide who your favorite character is, choose one action she or he performs that you really like. For example, if you choose a

BOX 17.4   ACTION WORDS

When you're teaching the effort concepts, action words help elicit many of the responses desired. For the exercise to be productive as well as exciting, students need to have more than a few common words repeated over and over. Here are some possibilities.

Single Action Words

Traveling Actions			Nontraveling Actions				Stopping Actions	
Run	Hop	Creep	Flick	Squeeze	Contract	Dangle	Pause	Collapse
Dash	Skate	Sneak	Jerk	Compress	Fold	Jab	Stop	Slide
Dart	Jump	Slither	Twitch	Explode	Splatter	Slash	Freeze	Flop
Skip	Bounce	Crawl	Writhe	Spread	Punch	Chop	Anchor	Crumble
Gallop	Slide	Step	Stab	Tense	Pull	Saw		
Stamp	Kick	Stride	Grip	Relax	Press	Drip		
Whirl	Spin	Shuffle	Release	Push	Lower	Drag		
Waddle	Totter							

Sinking Actions			Rising Actions			Vibratory Actions	
Melt	Spin	Screw	Evaporate	Spin	Swell	Shake	Wriggle
Flop	Turn	Hammer	Float	Pop	Inflate	Rattle	Squirm
Drop	Slink	Spread	Rise	Grow	Lift	Vibrate	Snake
Collapse	Squash	Deflate	Turn	Blossom		Gyrate	Whisk
Pounce	Shrink	Crumple				Tumble	

Sentences of Action Words

Run—freeze—skip	Slither—inflate—explode	Rise (turn)—twitch—skip
Dart—collapse—pop	Squeeze—jump—release	Gallop—stamp—screw
Grow—spin—deflate	Creep—pounce—explode	Jump—freeze—jab
Writhe—jerk—pop	Skip—pause—flop	Chop—whirl—slash

Descriptive Words (for use with action words)

Droopy	Excited	Light	Springy	Spikey	Square
Tired	Heavy	Tense	Carefree	Sharp	Angular
Happy	Strong	Floppy	Carefully	Rounded	Curvy
Greedy	Loving	Gentle	Fierce	Soft	Hard
Prickly	Spongy	Big	Small	Enormous	Tiny
Bubbling	Nervous	Unsure	Confident	Bold	Afraid

Nonsense Words

Snickersnack	Spelunk	Krinkle	Blump
Gallumph	Brip	Siczac	Crickcrock
Cavort	Bruttle-brattle	Swoosh	Snap-crackle
Flip-flop	Achoo	Kerumph	Wheezey
Grunch	Hic-up	Squizzog	

SOURCE: From *Education Through the Dance Experience* by David Docherty, 1975, Bellingham, WA: Educational Designs and Consultants. Used with permission from the author.

famous football quarterback as your favorite person, you might pick "throwing the bomb" as your favorite action. Think carefully to pick your person and action.

T Now, on the signal you'll perform the action you chose as if it were on video set at a fast speed—in a fast motion instead of slow motion. Repeat your fast-motion action four times, each time making the motion faster and faster.

T Now do the same action as if it were in slow motion, just like instant replays. Make sure there's a clear difference between your fast and slow motions. I should be able to tell just from watching which motions are fast and which ones are slow.

CONTINUALLY CHANGING IN TIME WHILE TRAVELING

Setting: Children scattered throughout general space

Tasks/Challenges:

T As you're standing in your self-space, pick a point across the room you want to focus on. All the traveling you do will be directed toward that point. On the signal, slowly begin to travel around the point you've chosen, much like a lion stalking its prey. Gradually increase your speed so you're traveling at your maximum speed. Just before you reach the spot you've chosen, slow down, slowly circle, then suddenly pounce. The differences in the speeds at which you travel should be very clear. Thus your sequence should go like this: Pick a point to focus on, start slowly circling toward that point, gradually pick up speed until you're going really fast, then gradually slow down and suddenly pounce toward your spot.

C Now that you have the idea, pick a new spot and practice your circling routine five times so that it's very good. Try to make it the best that you can because we're going to show some of them to the class. Slow should be really slow, fast really fast, and the pounce as quick as lightning.

To help clarify this activity, choose three or four children who are successfully completing it to demonstrate (they can all demonstrate at the same time). Reinforce the notions of gradually increasing speed and the sudden contrast of the pounce.

Developing the Concept of Force

Force is the contrast of muscular tensions. The extremes are *strong* and *light,* but there are obvious gradations between the extremes. Just as *speed* to a young child is "as fast as you can go," *force* often means trying to bat a ball as hard as possible, whether the situation calls for a bunt or an outfield placement. A preschooler is likely to use the same degree of force to throw a ball three feet as to throw it ten yards.

We usually introduce the concept of force by combining it with a skill that has been developed to the control level, preferably to the utilization level. For example, think of the child at a precontrol level who is learning to strike a moving ball. The youngster is so fully concentrating attention on making contact with the ball that the concept of force is an unnecessary and probably confusing thought. Hard and easy hits can come later, once the child is able to hit a ball consistently.

A dancer exemplifies the qualities of strong and light movement while expressing aggression, strength, and power; the gymnast exemplifies the qualities in a free-floor exercise routine (tumbling on a large mat) while combining firm and fine actions and balancing in a demonstration of muscular control and strength.

Teaching the Concept of Force

This section provides suggestions for helping children to understand the concept of force. The learning experiences presented help youngsters develop an operational understanding of the strong (firm) and light (fine) actions of body parts and of the entire body (Figure 17.4). *Actions of concentrated movement and muscular tensions are very tiring; keep the activity periods short.*

Learning Experiences Leading to Movement Concept Understanding

EXPLORING FORCE

Setting: Children scattered throughout general space

Tasks/Challenges:

T In your own space, with your whole body, make a statue that shows how strong you are. (A strong force is also called "heavy" or "firm.") Now practice the activity again, but think about making *every* muscle in your body strong, even your head, neck, stomach, back, hands, and feet.

T Now make a statue that is very light, such as a ghost would be. Your statue should be so light that it would blow away if a strong wind came along.

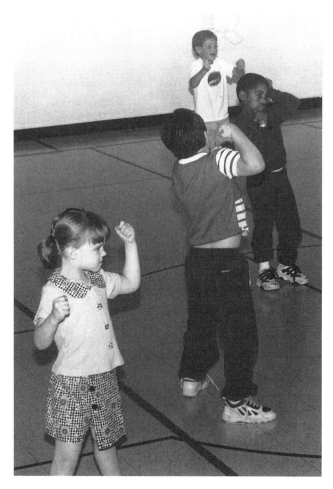

Figure 17.4 Young children's attempts at strong shapes show a beginning understanding of the concept.

This is what is called a light force. Try a light shape again, such as a leaf floating through the wind.

T When I beat the drum, change from a strong to a light statue and then back.

TRAVELING AND CHANGING FORCE QUALITIES

Setting: Children scattered throughout general space

Tasks/Challenges:

T This time you're going to travel around the whole space. But as you travel, try to be as strong as you can be. You're an indestructible and all-powerful force; make all your body parts strong.

T Now, as you travel, make yourself as light as can be, just as if you were floating away. All your muscles should be loose, not tight at all; make your entire body light.

USING IMAGERY AND FORCE

Setting: Children scattered throughout general space

Tasks/Challenges:

T This time you're going to use different images you know to help understand the force qualities. On the signal, think of yourself as a pat of butter left out on a hot day. All day long you sit in the hot sun, all weak and melted. Then suddenly someone puts you in the refrigerator, and in a little while you feel strong and solid again. Remember to make it clear with your whole body what it's like to be weak, and then make it clear with your whole body when you're strong again.

The imagery sequences you design provide experiences in extreme contrasts. Focus on the degrees along the continuum (the subtle changes) in conjunction with the actual skill, such as jumping and landing, or balancing. For tips on observing children during activity, see Box 17.5.

SHOWING CONTRASTS OF FORCE

Setting: Children scattered throughout general space

Tasks/Challenges:

T Now you're going to show the force differences between things. On the signal I'll call out an idea; you show me what the idea looks like by moving either strong or light. Make it very clear which you are: strong or light.

Young children often equate the concept of strong force with the concept of size. Be careful to not pair all imagery examples as such—for example, big-firm or small-fine.

Ideas:
1. *Bank robber.* You're a bank robber about to hold up the richest bank in the country; now you're the teller at the window that is getting held up; now you're the courageous person who comes in and stops the robbery and saves the teller.
2. *Frosty the Snowman.* You're going to show the life of Frosty the Snowman. First you're a single snowflake falling through the air; then you're several snowflakes that are beginning to stick together to make a shape; now you're the solid, sturdy snowman that can't be knocked over; and finally you're the snowman melting slowly as the sun comes out.
3. *Punch/flick.* Now we're going to use words to help us tell the difference between strong and light

---

BOX 17.5   OBSERVING DURING ACTIVITY

When concentrating on developing tasks, it's quite easy to forget to really look at the students and the responses they're making. Here's a practical way to observe them: After you give a task and before saying anything to the class, move to the outside of the area, and observe for ten to fifteen seconds. You should quickly assess these three questions:

1. Are the children working safely without interfering with others?
2. If any equipment or apparatus is involved, is it being used within the context of the lesson?
3. Is the assigned task appropriate for the developmental level of the class and of interest to the class?

When you can answer yes to all three questions, look at the aspects you've determined to be important for the specific skill being practiced, and extend or refine the task as appropriate.

---

movements. The first two words are "punch" and "flick." I'll give you a story and you make the movements that go with it. One movement should be strong, the other light. Make each movement very clear. Pretending that you're a boxer, punch your opponent as hard as you can. Now, just flick a fly off your mother's freshly baked chocolate cake.

4. *Creep/pounce.* The words "creep" and "pounce" can help us learn strong and light movements. Let's try it. You're playing Hide-and-Seek; creep very quietly from your hiding place so no one will see or hear you. Now, you're creeping up to catch your runaway kitten. You've found her and are ready to pounce and grab her before she runs away again. Ready, pounce. Oops, you missed. Which movement was strong and which was light? (*Check for cognitive understanding.*)

5. *Sneak/scare.* This time you're going to show light and strong actions when I use the words "sneak" and "scare." Let's pretend your brother has a letter from his girlfriend. You want to know what it says, so you sneak up behind him to find out. You can't read over his shoulder, so you figure if you scare him, he'll drop the letter and run. Go. You need to sneak, then scare.

6. *Float/collapse.* Have you ever seen a hang glider? It's like a big kite that floats through the air, but a person is floating with it, just as if he or she were attached to a kite. You're now a hang glider, sail-

ing over the mountains. Go. Oh, no—all the wind suddenly died; your hang glider is crashing to the ground. You just collapse as you hit the ground.

7. *Glide/stomp.* You're a very good skater, and today you go roller-skating. You're at the local roller-skating rink, gliding along, having a grand time. Now something sticks to your skate; you don't fall, but you have to stomp your skate really hard to try to get the object off. Clearly show the difference between your light and strong movements.

8. *Raindrop/thunderstorm.* You're a raindrop in a gentle spring rain, a rain that makes all the flowers bloom and the grass turn its greenest green. Now you're a raindrop in a bad summer thunderstorm—you know, a storm where the wind blows so hard you think the trees will fall down and the sky turns very dark. Remember to make it very clear which raindrop is strong and which one is light.

9. *Friends/foes.* Now you're going to show strong and light as you greet your friend and then as you meet an enemy. Pretend you're walking down the street and see an old friend. How would you greet her? Now play as if you've just seen the biggest bully in the school. How would you greet him? Which force was light and which one was strong? (*Check for cognitive understanding.*)

10. *Ant/rock.* Imagine what an ant trying to lift a rock feels like. Try hard; you're the only hope of the

Figure 17.5 To elicit bound flow, the teacher challenged these children to travel while balancing beanbags on their heads.

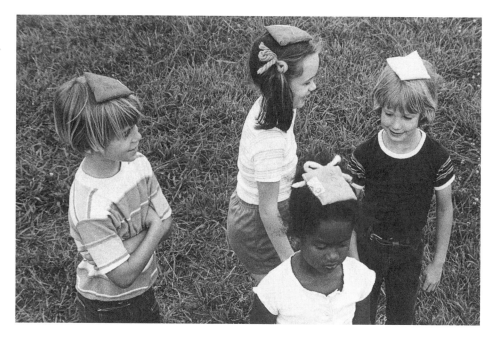

rock getting off the ground. Now you're a strong person trying to lift the same rock that the ant lifted. How are your actions different?

11. *Olympic weight lifter.* You're an Olympic weight lifter going for the gold medal; this is the heaviest weight you've ever lifted. As you pretend, remember to keep your entire body strong. Even show in your face that you're strong. Now you're lifting a five-pound bag of flour. How easy is it for you? Make your whole body light as you show this action. All your muscles should be loose, as if they're hardly being used at all.

Developing the Concept of Flow

Watch a very young child running down a hill. The actions are unstoppable, almost out of control, until the child reaches the bottom. A batter's swing at a baseball, the smash a tennis player executes, a gymnast's giant swing on the high bar—all these are examples of *free flow* in movement. It seems that the performer is lost in the movement; the movement, not the performer, seems to control the situation.

Bound actions are stoppable, cautious, and restrained. The performer is in control at all times. Pushing a heavy object, traveling an angular pathway while trying to stay within boundaries, executing a slow cartwheel with a pause for a handstand before traveling on are all examples of *bound flow*. See Figure 17.5 for one suggestion for helping children understand bound flow.

Teaching the Concept of Flow

This section provides learning experiences designed to help children understand and demonstrate the difference between the free flow and bound flow. The activities encompass a variety of movements that are important for both skill performance and safety. *Music can greatly enhance the feel of bound and free flow.*

Learning Experiences Leading to Movement Concept Understanding

TRAVELING AND FLOW

Setting: Children scattered throughout general space

Tasks/Challenges:

T On the signal, travel around the room and pause the instant you hear the stop signal. I'm really looking for stops that happen suddenly, without you taking any extra steps. Freeze dead in your tracks. This kind of movement—jerky and with lots of stops—is said to have *bound* flow. In other words, it doesn't flow very smoothly.

Children tend to anticipate the teacher's signals. Make stop signals close together and frequent so this activity will be successful.

T This time as you travel around the space, pretend you're completely free, like an eagle soaring high, a prisoner who just was let out of jail, or a really happy person who has no cares in the world. Make your traveling seem as if it has no end; it could just keep going and going. This type of movement is said to have *free* flow; it doesn't stop, much like a balloon or cloud floating in the air.

ELICITING FLOW QUALITIES

Setting: Children scattered throughout general space

Tasks/Challenges:

T This time I'm going to give you some actions to help you practice bound flow. Pretend to do each action that I tell you, always showing the bound flow of what you're doing. Remember, bound flow can be stopped and is generally slow and sometimes jerky.

1. Press the floor with your hands and feet as you move. Make sure you keep a bound flow throughout the whole motion.
2. Pretend you're pushing a heavy box.
3. Now carry a glass of milk that is too full without spilling any of it.
4. Play as if you're pulling from the bottom of a well a full bucket of water on a pulley.

T Now I'll give you some actions that require free flow. Free flow can be harder than bound flow, so really concentrate on making your movements seem as if they could go on forever. Make it very clear that these are free movements and unstoppable.

1. Pretend to flick away a fly.
2. This time you're really mad at your brother. Slash your arms through the air to show how really mad you are.
3. You're cooking bacon on the stove and the grease starts to spatter; jerk your head and arms away so you won't get burned.

T This next action will combine free and bound flow. Raise your arm high above your head with bound flow, stoppable at any moment. Let your arm fall freely downward in an unstoppable action.

FOLLOWING FLOW SENTENCES

Setting: Children scattered throughout general space

Tasks/Challenges:

T On the board are a number of sentences. The first one says "Walk, run, jump." On the signal, begin to

travel, using the sentence as your guide. The words are clear; the commas mean to pause or hesitate, and the periods mean to stop. Make it very clear where your pauses are and when you stop. Repeat the action of the sentence three times.

Other possible sentences: "Walk, sneak, pounce; leap, stamp, twist; creep, hop, flop."

T What you just did was an example of bound flow. Now you're going to turn the same thing into free flow. This time, on the signal, you're going to follow the same sentences but without the punctuation marks—in other words, no commas and no periods or no pauses or stops. So you'll start at the beginning of the sentence and keep going all the way through; no one should know when you're going to change to the next action. Your action should just flow smoothly, one action leading to the next. When you get to the end of a sentence, just start over again. On the signal, let's start with the first sentence.

Children enjoy using interpretations of different punctuation marks, such as the comma, exclamation point, and question mark, as different ending shapes.

C Now that you're so good at the sentences, you're going to make up one of your own. On the board is a list of words. (*Such words as "walk," "shrink," "gallop", "skip," "explode," "jump," "roll," and "hop" are good to use.*) Choose three of the words, and make your sentence. Put punctuation in, because punctuation is the key to when you stop or pause. Practice your sentence five times with the punctuation in it; then practice it five times without punctuation. Practice it very carefully, because we'll show some of the sentences to the class. It should be obvious when the punctuation is and isn't in the sentence.

PRACTICING FLOW SEQUENCES

Setting: Children scattered throughout general space

Tasks/Challenges:

T This time, there are two columns of words on the board, but no punctuation. You're going to join the words together to make a sequence. The first column of words reads "melt," "inflate," "slither," "shrink." On the signal, practice the words in the order you see them. It is your choice when to change from one word to the next. Go.

Now, do the second column of words: "jump," "spin," "stride," "pop."

Figure 17.6 Task sheet for time, force, and flow.

Name _____ Teacher _____

Time, Force, and Flow Task Sheet

Date	Who Watched	Challenge
		Find three body parts that you can move at a slow speed.
		Find three body parts (different from the ones in the first challenge) that you can move at a fast speed.
		Find four ways to move while showing free and light qualities.
		Find two movements that you can first make strong and slow and then make light and fast.
		Find any movement you want that combines two aspects of the effort concept (**time:** fast-slow, **force:** strong-light, **flow:** bound-free). After you finish, write down your movements and the concepts they included.

Movement   Concept

_____   _____

_____   _____

_____   _____

_____   _____

Which sequence gave you a bound feeling? Which one a free feeling? (*Check for cognitive understanding.*)

C Now go back and practice each sequence three times, making it very clear each time which one is bound and which one is free.

USING FLOW CONVERSATIONS

Setting: Children with partners, scattered throughout general space

Tasks/Challenges:

Children beginning sequence work often need guidance in restricting the length of the sequence; generally two or three actions are appropriate for the initial sequence.

T Now you're going to work with a partner and talk to your partner. The only catch is that neither of you can use your voice to talk. You're going to talk with your body. One of you needs to be bound and the other one free; go ahead and decide that now. Ready? This is how you'll talk: The partner who is bound will talk about being imprisoned and not being allowed to go out to see the world; the partner who is free will talk about how wonderful it is to roam and explore and run up and down the hills; in other words, what it's like to be free. Now, one of you start; with your body talk about your aspect. Keep your sentence very short. As you move, your partner listens or watches. After you make your statement, stop; your partner then answers with a statement, and you listen. When your partner finishes, you again provide an answer. The whole conversation should go back and forth until each of you has moved five times.

C After you've completed the conversation once, go back and practice it twice more so that it's very clear who's free and who's bound. I know this is a bit hard to understand, so let me go over it one more time. You and your partner are going to talk about bound and free flow with your body actions, not your voices. Just as in any conversation, it's a give and take. One of you will make a short body action sentence and then the other one will answer. Each of you gets to talk five times and then it ends. After you've finished once, go back and practice two more times. Remember that two people can't talk at once, so listen when your partner is talking. "Still" is the word.

It really helps to find at least one twosome (ideally more) doing the activity correctly and have them demonstrate. Be patient; the task will take time if the children are to really develop their conversations. Children should switch roles after sufficient time, to practice the other aspect of flow.

COMBINING TIME, FORCE, AND FLOW

Setting: Children scattered throughout general space

Tasks/Challenges:

T The task sheet (*Figure 17.6*) for today will allow you to practice combining the concepts of time, force, and flow. After you practice each challenge so that you feel it's as clear as you can make it, find a friend to watch you. If the friend feels you've done the challenge correctly, she or he signs her or his name in the blank; if not, you'll have to go back

and practice some more. I'll walk around the class, and at any time I can ask you to show me any challenge you've marked off. If you have any questions, ask me.

Applying the Effort Concepts

We focus on concepts until the children have learned the basic terminology related to the effort qualities of movement. When the children are able to accurately demonstrate the differences between the extremes of each concept, we no longer focus on the concept. Instead, we focus on how the concept relates to the performance of a particular skill: fast dribble, fluid roll, or light gallop. We want the children to learn the effort concepts so that they can apply the concepts to actual skill-learning situations.

The ability to use gradations of movement qualities distinguishes the inept performer from the skilled one, the sloppy movement from the polished one. An individual can learn to execute the basic requirements of a cartwheel, for example, so that it can be recognized as a cartwheel. But when that cartwheel is executed in a ragged, uneven, uncontrolled manner, it is clearly and easily distinguishable from a cartwheel performed by an experienced, trained gymnast. We teach children to apply the qualities of movement to their skill performances to help them become skillful movers.

Generally, the concept of time (fast-slow) is easier for children to grasp than either the concept of force (strong-light) or the concept of flow (bound-free). For this reason, you may need to focus more on force and flow than on time. Time can be studied as an applied concept—fast and slow skips, rolling fast and rolling slowly, accelerated and decelerated change of levels—before force or flow. The difference is that in teaching a concept, our observational focus is primarily on the children's ability to understand and apply the effort concept. In contrast, when we use a concept as a subtheme, we know that the children already understand the concept from previous lessons, and therefore our teaching focus is primarily on the skill and how it can be executed by using varying movements.

READING COMPREHENSION QUESTIONS

1. How is a movement performed fast different from the same movement performed slowly?
2. How is a movement executed with strong force different from the same movement performed with light force?

3. How is a movement performed with bound flow different from the same movement performed with free flow?
4. Initially, the extremes, rather than the gradations, of the effort concepts are emphasized. Why?
5. When is slowness an important concept? List several movements.
6. What does the term *acceleration-deceleration* mean? Answer by using examples from the text or from your own experiences.
7. What does focusing on the movement quality of an image rather than on the image itself mean? This statement will help you: "Imagine that the floor is covered with peanut butter six inches deep."
8. When do you change from focusing on the effort concept to focusing on how the concept relates to the performance of a particular skill?
9. What is the purpose of teaching children to apply the qualities of movement to their skill performances?

REFERENCES

Joyce, M. (1980). *First steps in teaching creative dance to children* (2nd ed.). Palo Alto, CA: Mayfield.

National Association for Sport and Physical Education. (1995). *Moving into the future: National standards for physical education.* St. Louis, MO: Mosby.

Relationships

Our lives are made up of relationships—to people and to objects—that occur not only in physical education classes but in everyday life. Driving to and from work in an automobile, maneuvering through a crowded aisle in a supermarket, or dodging around an icy spot on a sidewalk—all these activities involve complex, dynamic relationships. And each relationship involves several contextual variables (bodies, body parts, and objects) in simultaneous interaction.

The movement concept of relationship defines with whom or with what the body moves; it gives meaning to the interaction between individuals and their environment. The concept is divided into three major components: relationships of body parts, relationships with people, and relationships with objects and/or people. In turn, each of these constructs is defined by observable characteristics that can be taught to children. Figure 18.1 conceptualizes this idea, putting it in perspective with the other movement concepts and skill themes. The relationship category is in the right-hand side of the movement framework. The outermost ring defines the concept, the second ring presents the three components of the concept, and the third ring defines the aspects of the three components.

When teaching the relationship concepts, we typically begin with the simplest relationships for children to understand—the self relationships. Because so many young children are still at the "I" stage, the initial lesson focus is simply identifying body parts and their relationship to one another, followed by body part shapes. As the children develop a functional understanding of the relationships among body parts, we shift the emphasis to moving in relation to different objects and also one another. In preschool settings, many of the relationship concepts will be new to children. In the primary grades, however, some of these concepts will simply be a review for the children, and therefore the lessons can progress rather rapidly. The third category of concepts, relationships with others, is typically combined with the study of other concepts and skill themes. Initially the focus is on working with partners, and when the children develop the social and physical maturity needed to collaborate with three or four others, we're able to include tasks that require them to work in groups.

When teaching the relationship concepts it's easy to forget that the purpose is to have the children actually *know* what each relationship concept means. This analogy may help. Imagine that one of us is going to come and teach a class of your second-graders. Prior to teaching, we might ask whether your children know the relationship concepts. If you say yes, we'd assume that the children can make a sym-

metrical shape or a nonsymmetrical shape when asked to do so. Or we'd assume that the youngsters know the difference between mirroring and matching, over and under, and so forth. "Knowing" doesn't mean that the concepts were taught; knowing means that the children are able to show their understanding through their movement. In other words, the children have *functional understanding*.

Another illustration further makes this point. If one of us were going to teach a second-grade art class, we might ask the teacher whether the children know their colors. If the teacher says yes, we'd assume that the children know the difference among red, brown, black, orange, and so forth. We'd further expect that they can readily use these colors in the lesson we would teach. If the teacher says the children don't know their colors, however, we'd design our lesson to help them learn their colors.

Developing the Concept of the Relationships of Body Parts

Before children can focus on the relationships among body parts, they need to be able to identify specific body parts. Thus, it's essential that each child acquire a functional vocabulary of body part names. Examples of tasks that can be used in teaching this vocabulary include:

1. Pointing to the ceiling with the elbow (knee, nose) (Figure 18.2)
2. Touching the floor with the wrist (waist, stomach)
3. Traveling around the room and on the signal stopping and touching heels (shoulders, heads) with another person.

Once the children have learned the names of the body parts, lessons focus on making shapes (round, narrow, wide, twisted, symmetrical, and nonsymmetrical) and using body parts in relation to one another. For example, we might ask children to:

1. Travel and stop in a twisted shape
2. Change from a symmetrical to a nonsymmetrical shape
3. Make a wide shape during flight
4. Move their feet so that they're higher than their head

Teaching the Concept of the Relationships of Body Parts

This section of the chapter provides suggestions for teaching children to identify and use different body

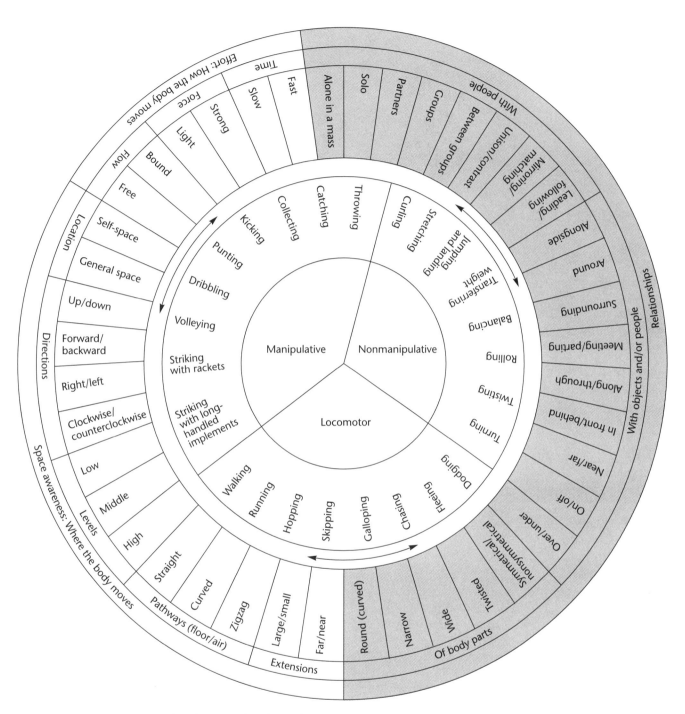

Figure 18.1 Movement analysis framework: relationship concepts.

parts and to develop an understanding of how different body parts can relate to one another. Suggestions for teaching the concepts of various body shapes and body part shapes also are presented. You can use any body parts for the activities given here, but with the tasks that require balancing, be careful to not use parts that will elicit balances that may be too complex for some students. For example, when using parts such as the head and hands, make it clear that other parts can be used in conjunction with them.

Figure 18.2   "Point to the door with your elbow." This young girl responds to the teacher's challenge.

Activities Leading to Movement Concept Understanding

IDENTIFYING BODY PARTS

Setting: Children in self-space (on a carpet square; on an X on the floor)

Tasks/Challenges:

🅣 I'm going to call out different body parts. Touch the body parts I call out as quickly as possible when you hear them. Remember to pay close attention to what I'm saying, because I may start to go faster or try to trick you. Ready? Remember, touch each body part as I call it out.

Body parts can include nose, arm, chin, ankle, ear, foot, elbow, temple, wrist, neck, shoulder, eyebrow, eye, teeth, cheek, leg, forehead, knee, thumb, mouth, side, hip, lip, earlobe.

🅣 This time, instead of just touching a body part as I name it, you'll have to touch whatever hand I call out to the different body parts I call out. This activity will be harder, because you'll have to remember which is your right and which is your left. For example, if I say "Right hand to left knee," touch your right hand to your left knee. Try to do this as quickly as possible, but be careful in deciding what

body parts to use. Just to help you out, let's review right and left. Raise your right hand. (*Check to see that they're correct.*) Ready? Let's try it.

Body parts used can include left hand to right knee, right hand to left elbow, left hand to left shoulder, right hand to left knee, left hand to left foot.

🅣 This time you're going to play a game with finding body parts, similar to Simon Says, except you don't have to sit out if you miss. Here's how to play. I'll call out "Simon says to touch your toes" and you'll touch your toes. But if I don't say "Simon says," then you aren't supposed to do it. So if I just say "Touch your toes," you aren't supposed to touch your toes, because Simon didn't say to do it. Pay attention, because the game will start to go very quickly. Remember I'm watching to see if you touch the right parts and how quickly you can do it.

🅣 This time, instead of touching your hands to different body parts, you're going to touch two different body parts together. For example, I'll call out "Knee to elbow" and you'll touch your knee to your elbow. You'll have to think hard on this one. Ready? I'm looking to see if you can get the correct different parts together.

Possible body part combinations include knee to elbow, hands to waist, head to knees, foot to shoulder, knee to foot, elbow to wrist, back of wrist to back of knee (Figure 18.3).

BALANCING WHILE USING DIFFERENT BODY PARTS

Setting: Each child on a carpet square

Tasks/Challenges:

🅣 Find a carpet square for yourself, and sit on the square. I'll know that you're all ready when I see everyone seated on a carpet square. This time when I call out a body part, you should put that body part on the carpet square and make a shape with the rest of your body, leaving the one part that I called out on the carpet. So if I call out "Elbow," put your elbow on the carpet, and then make a shape with the rest of your body. When you make your shape, be sure to hold it very still so I can see what part is on the carpet and what your shape looks like. Ready? Let's try it.

Shapes that you hold very still are called *balances*, almost like statues. Let's try this activity again; make your balances and shapes very clear and still.

🅣 Now you're going to balance on different numbers of body parts. I'll call out a number of parts; you

Figure 18.3 "Touch ears with hands." These young children, who are at the "I" stage, benefit from tasks designed to clarify the relationships among body parts.

balance by touching that number to the floor. Count your parts touching the floor very carefully because I'll be coming around and asking you how many parts are on the floor and which parts they are.

Four parts
Three parts
More than four parts
Two parts
One part

For each number, offer suggestions or hints, or have several students demonstrate the possible combination of parts. Also mix up the order in which the parts are called out.

FREEZING ON DIFFERENT BODY PARTS

Setting: Children scattered in general space

Tasks/Challenges:

🅣 You're going to travel around the space on your feet. When you hear the stop signal, touch the body part I call out to the floor. So if I call out "Elbow" as you stop, touch your elbow to the floor. As you move, be very careful to stay in a space by yourself, so you don't touch anyone when you're trying to touch different body parts to the floor. This activity will start to go very fast, so touch the parts to the floor as quickly as possible, and make it very clear which part is touching the floor.

Body parts can include arm, ankle, foot, leg, side, hip.

🅣 When you travel this time, instead of touching body parts to the floor, touch the body parts I call out to one other person. So if I call out "Heels," stop, touch your heels to the heels of one other person, and then freeze. As you do this, make the touching parts very clear; don't just stand beside the other person. To be safe, make sure as you touch that you stop first and then touch easily so no one gets hurt. The idea is to quickly and easily touch and then be ready to go again. Ready?

Body parts can include wrist, shoulder, forehead, knee, thumb, arm, ankle, foot, elbow, leg, side, hip.

TRAVELING ON DIFFERENT BODY PARTS

Setting: Children scattered in general space

Tasks/Challenges:

This time, instead of balancing on different body parts, you're going to travel on different body parts. What body parts do we usually travel on? Let's start with the feet, just to get warmed up. Make sure to travel in all the space and to stay on your feet.

🅣 Now try something a little different: the hands and feet. Remember to travel with your hands and feet both touching the floor at some time. Ready? Make sure you actually go someplace, and be careful of others.

T This time you're going to make up your own way of traveling using different body parts. As you do this, make sure that I can tell from just looking at you what body parts you're using for traveling; you should be using two different body parts to move around the room. Practice your new way of traveling until you can do it so it looks professional. Be very careful to watch where you're going and not touch anyone else.

BALANCING ON MATCHING AND NONMATCHING PARTS

Starting: Each child in a personal space

Tasks/Challenges:

T This time, instead of balancing on a certain number of parts, you're going to balance on parts that are alike and parts that are different. Parts that are alike are called *matching* parts. What parts do you have that are matching or alike? (*Children respond "Hands," "Feet," etc.*) Good; let's try to balance on some of those parts. First let's try an easy one: the feet. Now, how about the knees? Think up one of your own. Make sure that the parts you use are matching parts.

T Now pick one set of matching parts and make up a balance that you like and practice it until you can hold it very still. Be sure you know the name of the matching parts you're balancing on because I'll come around and ask some of you, just to make sure.

T This time you're going to balance on different parts. *Different* parts are parts that don't match each other; they aren't alike. What are some possible combinations of different parts? (*Children respond "Knee and elbow," "Back and hands," etc.*) Let's try some. First, try the seat and the feet. Now try the shoulders and the elbows. What about the knees and the elbows? Now, make up one combination on your own.

T Now pick one set of different parts and make up your own balance. Practice your balance until you can hold it very still. Be sure the different parts you're using are very clear, because I might ask you what they are.

ROUND, NARROW, WIDE, AND TWISTED BODY SHAPES

Setting: Each child in a personal space

Tasks/Challenges:

T Today you're going to learn about different shapes you can make with your bodies. Everyone find a self-space so that you can't touch anyone else. The first shape you're going to make is a pretzel. All of you try to make a pretzel out of your body; hold very still. This shape is called a *twisted* shape.

T Now, try a twisted shape on your own. As you do so, make sure your whole body is twisted, not just your arms and legs. Try to twist your stomach, too.

T The next shape is a circle. Try to make your whole body look like a circle. This is called a *round* shape.

T Now try to make up a different round shape by yourself. Make sure that your whole body is making the round shape and that it is very round. Remember, round things have no bumps in them.

T This time you're going to make a skinny shape. Try to make your body as skinny as possible, so skinny that if you turned sideways, no one would be able to see you. This is called a *narrow* shape.

T Find another narrow shape by yourself. Make it as skinny as possible, as if you were trying to hide.

T What do you think the opposite of narrow is? *Wide,* right. Make your body as wide as possible.

T Try another wide shape by yourself. Remember to get as wide as possible, as if you were trying to stop someone from getting around you.

C This time pick your favorite kind of shape, and make it, holding it very still. I'm going to come around and guess which type of shape it is, so make your shape as clear as possible. Your shape should be wide, narrow, round, or twisted.

T Things are going to be a little harder this time. Still staying in your own space, you're going to make a wide shape. Then, when I give the signal, change your wide shape to a narrow shape, and hold it very still. The difference between the wide and narrow shape should be very clear. Make a wide shape, and hold it. Now change that wide shape to a narrow shape.

T Try it again—another wide shape; change to a narrow.

T Now, a third.

T This time pick the shape you liked the most, and practice it until it changes very easily from wide to narrow. Work on it until it's your best and both shapes are very clear.

T You thought the last activity was hard? This one is even harder! Think you can do it? You're going to change from a twisted shape to a round shape. So find your twisted shape. Got it? On the signal, change that twisted shape to a round shape.

T Now, let's try another twisted to round shape. Go.

T And a third twisted to round shape. Make sure that your twisted shape is really twisted and your round shape is very round. I should be able to easily tell the difference between the two shapes.

C Now, pick the shape you liked the most. You need to practice your favorite one so that your move from twisted to round is very smooth, like a professional, and that your shapes are so clear the principal could easily tell the difference if he or she walked in.

CHANGING FROM ONE BODY SHAPE TO ANOTHER

Setting: Children in self-space moving to a drumbeat

Tasks/Challenges:

T You'll really need to be in your self-space for this activity, so make sure you're as far away from everyone else as you can be. Again you're going to change from one shape to another, but I'm going to give you drumbeats to help. You're going to move from a round shape to a wide shape, but instead of just doing it on your own, you'll have six beats of the drum to get from the round shape to the wide shape and then six beats to get back to your round shape. Listen now while I give you the beats of the drum. Does everyone understand? You'll start in a round shape and on the six beats of the drum open to a wide shape. You'll hold your wide shape very still, and then on the next six beats of the drum you'll return to your round shape. Let's try it. Find your round shape.

T Let's try it again; this time find different round and wide shapes.

T Now, let's do a third set of shapes.

C You're now going to practice one set of shapes four more times, so you can make it really good. Pick your favorite shapes. Remember as you move to make each shape very clear, and make sure that the movement goes with the beats of the drum.

Pinpoint two or three children who are succeeding with the activity, and ask them if they'd like to show it to the class.

T You're going to make the shapes a little different this time. Instead of opening up on six beats and closing on six, you're going to open up on one

quick beat and then close slowly on six. So the sequence will now go like this: Start in a round shape; on the beat, quickly open up to a wide shape, and hold it still; then on the next six beats of the drum, slowly return to your round shape. Try it—round shape. Remember that you must open from the round to the wide shape very, very quickly, as if you were a flash of lightning.

Pinpoint several children to show the activity to the rest of the class.

C Now practice your favorite shapes four times. Remember not only to make the quick shape sudden and the slow shape sustained but also to make your round and wide shapes very clear. To look really good, remember to hold the beginning and the end very still so that we all know when you started and when you finished.

For the distinction between the movement concepts of body shapes and the skills needed to achieve those shapes, see Box 18.1.

TRAVELING AND FREEZING IN DIFFERENT BODY SHAPES

Setting: Children traveling in general space

Tasks/Challenges:

T Instead of making shapes in your self-space, this time you're going to travel around the space and on the signal make the shape I call out. For example, if you're traveling and I call out "Twisted," on the signal, make a twisted shape. As you make your shapes, be sure they're very clear so that I can easily tell what they are. If I can't tell what they are, I'll have to ask you. As you travel, be careful of your classmates.

T Now, as you stop to make your shape, try to do it as quickly as possible, almost as if you just froze in that shape when you stopped. Remember frozen shapes; don't fall over *(Figure 18.4)*.

MAKING SYMMETRICAL AND NONSYMMETRICAL SHAPES

Setting: Children in self-space

Tasks/Challenges:

T You've already learned about wide, narrow, round, and twisted shapes. This time you're going to learn about two different kinds of shapes. The words

BOX 18.1   STRETCHING, CURLING, TWISTING, AND TURNING

There is a subtle, yet important, distinction between the *movement concepts* of round, narrow, wide, and twisted (body shapes) and the *skills* of stretching, curling, twisting, and turning. When the children are in the process of actually moving—the "ing" part—it is technically a skill; once they have arrived, it is technically a concept. For example, when a child has arrived at a twisted shape, it is considered a concept. When the child is in the process of twisting, however, it is technically a skill (i.e., an actual movement). For this reason, you will find the movements of stretching, curling, twisting, and turning listed under the nonmanipulative category of the skill themes (Chapter 2) and the tasks for helping children achieve quality stretches, twists, turns, and curls described primarily in Chapters 23, 24, and 25. The tasks for helping children learn the difference between the movement concepts of round, narrow, wide, and twisted are described in this chapter. In actuality, this distinction is important only from a theoretical standpoint—the children don't necessarily need to understand this distinction. They just need plenty of opportunities to understand the meaning of the concepts (which we describe in this section) and truly develop their abilities to stretch, curl, twist, and turn.

Figure 18.4   "Freeze in a low and wide shape." This task requires children like this young girl to consider relationships among body parts.

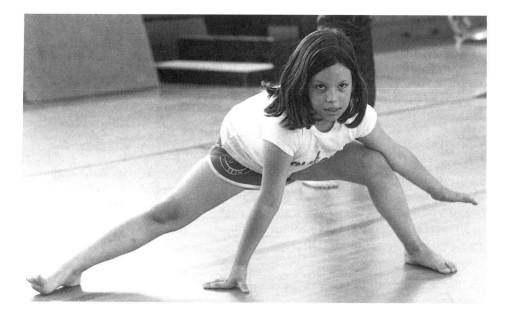

describing these shapes are hard, so listen carefully. First, find a body shape that looks exactly alike on both sides of your body; in other words, if you were cut in half, both sides of you would look alike. This is called a *symmetrical* shape.

🅣 Try making a symmetrical shape. Remember, both sides of your body must look exactly alike *(Figure 18.5)*.

🅣 Now find a shape in which the two sides of your body don't look alike. In other words, if you were cut in half, each side would have a different shape. This is called a *nonsymmetrical* shape.

🅣 Do another nonsymmetrical shape. Remember, both sides must be different.

🅣 Since you now know the difference between symmetrical and nonsymmetrical, let's find three more

Figure 18.5 Symmetrical and nonsymmetrical shapes.

balances of each shape. First do symmetrical; remember, both sides are alike. Try to make each of your balances very clear so I can tell without thinking what kind of shape it is.

🅣 Now do nonsymmetrical shapes. Find three more nonsymmetrical shapes. Try to make the sides of your body as different as possible so no one could possibly confuse your shape with a symmetrical one.

🅒 Once you've found three more nonsymmetrical shapes, practice your favorite one five extra times so you can show it to the whole class. (*Half the class demonstrates their favorite nonsymmetrical shape, and then the other half shows their favorite nonsymmetrical shape.*)

CREATING POSTCARD SCULPTURES

Setting: Museum postcards of statues, one postcard for every child. Children love to play the roles of statues and sculptors but tend to get silly during this activity. Warn them that no horseplay will be allowed. Also caution them to place others only in shapes they can hold without too much difficulty, so no one gets hurt.

Tasks/Challenges:

🅣 You're going to pretend that you're sculptors who are creating great statues. To do this you'll need a partner. When I say "Go," find a partner, and sit beside your partner. I'll know you're ready when I see everyone seated beside a partner. Each set of partners has two postcards of statues; you're going to form each other into these statues. Decide which partner will be the sculptor first; the sculptor then decides which statue to make the partner into. The trick is to try and make each statue both symmetri-

cal and nonsymmetrical, so it will be a little different from the postcard picture. First, make the statue just as it is on the card, as closely as possible to what you see. Then, if the statue is symmetrical, change it to nonsymmetrical; if it's nonsymmetrical, make it symmetrical. Mold each statue very carefully, and be sure you can tell me which statue is symmetrical and which is nonsymmetrical. After you make your statue, trade places with your partner.

🅣 This time you're going to design your own statues. You'll still need your partner. Go ahead and decide which of you is to be the sculptor first. Make your first statue symmetrical. The statue stays symmetrical until the signal. At the signal, move to someone's else's statue and redesign it to suit yourself. On the next signal, move to another new statue and redesign it. Keep doing this until you're told to change. When you hear the change signal, change places with whatever statue you're with.

Let's practice once. Form your partner into a symmetrical statue. (*Allow at least one minute.*) Now, move to another statue and remake it, still into a symmetrical shape. Do you have the hang of it? (*Select several children for demonstration.*) Go to the next statue.

🅣 Now trade places with the statue you've just made. The activity changes a little this time; you're going to create nonsymmetrical statues. Ready? Without moving to a new place, form a nonsymmetrical statue out of your partner.

🅣 Change to a new statue, and then change this statue to a nonsymmetrical shape. Remember: *Nonsymmetrical* means that both sides of the body are very different from each other.

🅣 Change one more time. Make this your best statue yet.

CREATING BODY SHAPES IN THE AIR

Setting: Boxes, benches, low beams, and milk crates set up around the space. Figure 18.6 shows a typical equipment setup.

Tasks/Challenges:

🅣 Now you're going to combine all the different kinds of body shapes that you've practiced so far. What you're going to do may be hard, but it'll be fun. Remember that as you work, all the rules for gymnastics apply. (*See Chapters 9 and 25 for establishing an environment for learning and for the rules of a gymnastics environment.*) Three or four of you will be at a piece of equipment at once. One at a time,

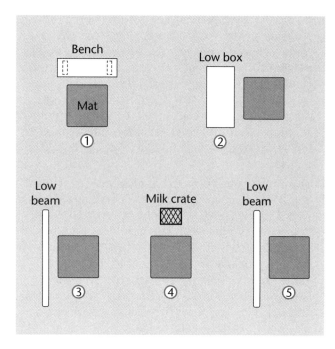

Figure 18.6   Equipment setup.

you'll each jump off the equipment and make a shape in the air. I'll call out a shape, and each time you jump, try to make that shape in the air. Let's start with a wide shape. Make sure that you land on your feet after the jump, and don't crash to the ground. See if you can hold your landing as still as a statue.

After a while, change to narrow, twisted, round, symmetrical, and nonsymmetrical shapes.

Ⓣ Now that you've been through all the shapes separately, you may practice them in any order you wish. Make the shapes so clear that I don't have to ask you what they are. Remember to land on your feet.

Developing the Concept of Relationships with Objects

Some concepts are studied in relation to objects; others have more meaning when they're practiced in relation to people. The concepts of *on* and *off, along, through, over, under, around,* and *surrounding* apply primarily to relationships with objects. The concepts of *near* and *far, in front, behind,* and *alongside* are generally studied as person-to-person relationships. Because objects are more predictable (less dynamic) than children, however, we first focus on the concept of rela-

tionships with objects and then relationships with people.

It's interesting to note that children frequently identify a lesson by the object they related to rather than by the concept they studied. For example, after a lesson in which hoops were used to study the concepts of traveling over, under, and through, children might say, "Hey, that was fun! Are we going to play with hoops again tomorrow?" In time, however, children begin to understand and use the terminology that we use. For instance, a child might say, "It's easier to go over and under the hoop than to go through the hoop."

Within the context of a game or a dance lesson, specific terms are classified as objects. In dance, for example, wands, streamers, newspapers, or scarves are considered objects. Goals, boundaries, nets, and targets are objects with which the child learns relationship concepts within a game context. See Box 18.2 for information from the *National Standards* on relationships.

Teaching the Concept of Relationships with Objects

The activities in this section will enhance the children's awareness and ability to function effectively in relation to the objects that exist in various physical activity contexts.

Activities Leading to Movement Concept Understanding

TRAVELING OVER, CLOSE TO, FAR AWAY, INSIDE

Setting: A hoop or a rope for each child (Figures 18.7 and 18.8)

Tasks/Challenges:

Ⓣ To warm up, travel *over* your piece of equipment in any way you want to. As you travel, make sure that you actually go over the equipment, not around it.

Ⓣ This time as you travel over your equipment, try to stay as *close to* the equipment as possible. Try to keep as much of your body as possible close to the equipment, not just one body part.

Ⓣ Now, instead of being close to the equipment, try to have as many body parts as possible as *far away* from the equipment as possible. Only the parts that are really used to support your body should be near the equipment. Make sure that your whole body is

BOX 18.2   RELATIONSHIPS IN THE *NATIONAL STANDARDS FOR PHYSICAL EDUCATION*

The movement concept of relationships is referenced in the *National Standards for Physical Education* (NASPE, 1995) as a sample kindergarten benchmark under Standard 2: Applies movement concepts and principles to the learning and development of motor skills. The sample benchmark states that a child "identifies and uses a variety of relationships with objects, e.g., over/under, behind, alongside, through" (p. 8).

Figure 18.7   Construction of a hoop. Cut hoops from half-inch plastic air conditioner or water pipe. Make the connection with a dowel rod held in place with staples or tacks. You can also use special pipe connectors or fuse with heat to close the gap. For a 30-inch diameter hoop, you'll need 95 inches of pipe; for a 36-inch hoop, you'll need 113 inches of pipe; and for a 42-inch hoop, you'll need 132 inches of pipe.

as far away as possible, not just the upper parts of your body.

❶ The activity is a little harder now. Start on the *outside* of your equipment, put your weight down on your hands *inside* the hoop (*or a circle made with a rope*), and then continue to travel over the equipment. Make sure that you shift your weight to your hands inside the hoop (*rope*) at some point.

❶ These are all relationships that your body can have to equipment or other people. We can go over things, we can be close to things, we can be far away from things, or we can go inside things. Practice all four of these relationships on your own: over, close to, far away, and inside. See if you can find three ways to do each relationship. Be sure you know which ones you're practicing, because I'll come around and ask you.

If you say you're going to come around and ask the children questions or see their work, Do It! *Otherwise, the children may soon stop believing you.*

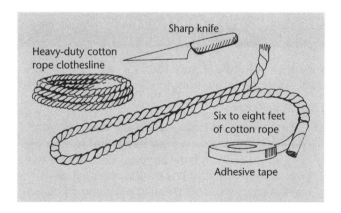

Figure 18.8   Construction of a rope. Use half-inch cotton rope. The cotton will eventually loosen up and give, so different shapes can be made with it. Single ropes should be from six to eight feet long. After you cut the ends of the rope, tape the ends to prevent fraying. You can use tape of different colors to quickly identify the length of the rope, e.g., green for a six-foot rope, red for a seven-foot rope, and yellow for an eight-foot rope.

Figure 18.9 Construction of hurdles. Hurdles can be made from plastic bleach or milk jugs and rolled newspaper held together with masking tape. A more permanent type of hurdle can be made from wood and dowel rods.

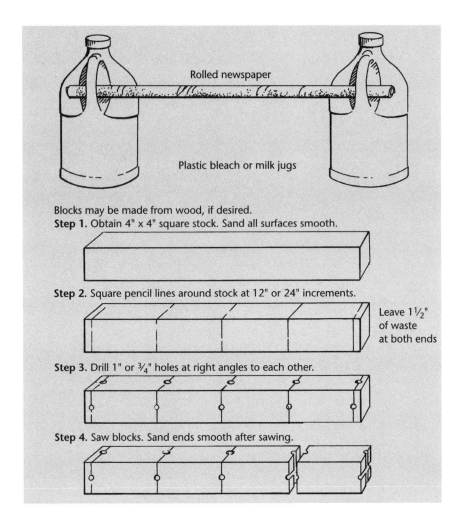

Rolled newspaper

Plastic bleach or milk jugs

Blocks may be made from wood, if desired.
Step 1. Obtain 4" x 4" square stock. Sand all surfaces smooth.

Step 2. Square pencil lines around stock at 12" or 24" increments.

Leave 1½" of waste at both ends

Step 3. Drill 1" or ¾" holes at right angles to each other.

Step 4. Saw blocks. Sand ends smooth after sawing.

TRAVELING OVER, UNDER, CLOSE TO, AND FAR AWAY FROM EQUIPMENT

Setting: A hurdle (Figure 18.9) for each child in the class, scattered throughout the space

Tasks/Challenges:

🅣 To begin, travel *over* the hurdle any way that you can; you can jump, use your hands and feet, or use only your hands. Whatever you do, make sure that you can land on your feet on the other side without falling down. This is called *going over* an object. Sometimes when we try to go over an object, we cheat and actually go around the side of it. Make very, very sure that you really do go over and not around.

🅣 Now, instead of going over the hurdle, you're going to go *under* it. This will be hard because the hurdle isn't very far off the ground. You'll really have to scrunch up. Try to do it without upsetting the hurdle.

🅣 Now, let's try going under in different ways. Sometimes go under feet first, sometimes head first, sometimes on your back, and sometimes on your stomach. Be careful; always know where your body is, even those parts that you can't see.

🅣 One more activity. This time you're going to put part of your weight on your hands and bring your feet down in different places around the hurdle. To begin, bring your feet down very *close to* the hurdle. You may take your feet across the hurdle or simply leave them on one side; whatever you do, be sure your feet come down close to the hurdle.

🅣 Now try bringing your feet down *far away from* the hurdle. Make sure that every time your feet touch the floor, they're far away from the hurdle.

🅣 Now, as you work, your feet can be close to the hurdle or far away, but sometimes have your feet land close to each other, sometimes spread far apart from each other. Be able to tell me if your feet are close together or far apart when I ask you. Remember, *close together* means almost so close that nothing could get between, and *far apart* means spread out so much that a person could crawl through.

LEARNING ONTO/OFF CONCEPTS

Setting: A low box or a milk crate for each student, scattered throughout the space.

Tasks/Challenges:

T You're now going to learn two more types of relationships: *onto* and *off*. I think you probably already know what these two ideas mean, but let's practice them just to make sure. Find at least three ways to get onto and off your piece of equipment. I'm really looking for very different ways to get onto and off the equipment.

C After you find three ways, practice the way you like best four extra times, so that you can show it to the class. Make it really special.

T I'm going to make the activity a little harder this time by combining different types of relationships. When I say "Go," each of you get a hoop and place it on the floor beside your box. Travel *into* the hoop before you travel *onto* and *off* the box. So, your sequence will involve three different relationships: into, on, and off. Find three different ways to do this. Make them very different from each other. Go.

Pinpoint several children who are doing the activity correctly and/or who've found very creative ways to accomplish the activity to demonstrate their actions for the rest of the class. Be sure to use a variety of students so that the rest of the class has a number of different creative ideas to base their work on.

T Now you're going to make up a sequence of the relationships you practiced with the box and hoop. You must include the concepts of *off, onto,* and *into* in your sequence. Once you find a sequence that you really like, practice it until you can do it from memory and it looks the same each time.

STUDYING OVER, UNDER, AROUND, IN FRONT OF, AND BEHIND CONCEPTS

Setting: A streamer, such as one used in rhythmic gymnastics, for each child; paper and pencils (You can make streamers from two-inch-wide crepe paper or from surveyors tape cut into four- to ten-foot lengths.)

Tasks/Challenges:

T Just to warm up, practice moving your streamer anywhere around your body. Remember to always try to keep the streamer in the air. To do this, you'll have to keep the streamer moving all the time; you can't let it stop, or it'll touch the floor.

T Now that you know how to keep the streamer in the air, try to make it go *over, under, around, in front of,* and *behind* different body parts, such as your head, legs, and trunk. As you do this, think about what relationship each position has to each body part. Remember, you must keep the streamer moving at all times.

T Now you're going to pretend you're Olympic gymnasts. Make up a sequence in which your streamer goes over, under, around, in front of, and behind two different body parts. After you make up a sequence that you like, practice it until it looks the same each time and you can do it from memory. It's very important that you remember exactly what you did, because we're going to do something really special with it.

T Do you remember your sequence? Now you're going to write it down on a piece of paper and exchange the paper with a friend. Your friend will try to do your sequence, and you will try to do your friend's sequence just by reading the directions on the paper, so make it very clear which parts you went over, under, around, in front of, and behind.

C Now practice your friend's sequence until you think you've learned it perfectly. When you think you're ready, ask your friend to watch you do the sequence. In a few minutes I'll ask for volunteers to show routines that clearly have all five of these concepts.

This series of activities is also very good for developing the concept of free flow.

TRAVELING ALONG EQUIPMENT

Setting: Low balance beams or benches set up around the room

Tasks/Challenges:

T So far we've learned the relationships of *on, off, over, in front of, under, around,* and *behind.* Now we're going to learn the relationship of *along.* At your piece of equipment, each of you, one at a time, should travel along the beam or bench by walking. Make sure that you travel from one end of

Figure 18.10 As children travel cautiously through a narrow space, each child constantly monitors her or his relationship to the obstacle.

the beam or bench to the other. This relationship of *along* means being on a piece of equipment and traveling from one part of it to another.

🅣 If it's easy for you to walk on the beam, try some other ways. Try a slide. If you need help keeping your balance, spread your arms out to either side.

As children progress with learning traveling on or along equipment, you can increase the complexity of the activities by changing the locomotor pattern required for traveling. Patterns can include hopping, skipping, running, waddling. Before you change the pattern, be sure the children are able to advance safely to the next pattern. In other words, don't have them run on the balance beam before they can keep their balance at a fast walk.

🅣 This time, we're going to be funny by combining two different relationships while you travel along the bench. Have some of your weight on the bench and some on the floor. For example, have one hand and foot on the bench and one hand and foot on the floor, or have both your feet on the bench and both your hands on the floor. The idea is to place part of your weight on the equipment and part on the floor. Make sure that I can tell where your weight really is.

🅒 Make up one way you like to travel with part of your weight on the floor and part on the bench,

and practice it so that you can show the class. Try to give your movement a name.

TRAVELING THROUGH OBSTACLES

Setting: Hoops on foam supports; a ladder spread throughout general space

Tasks/Challenges:

🅣 So far we have practiced traveling over, under, around, in front of, behind, and along. Now we are going to practice traveling *through* obstacles. Look around the area. You will see hoops standing up straight on foam supports. You will also see a ladder on its side. See if you can travel through the hoops and the ladder without touching the sides. Start going through at a slow speed *(Figure 18.10)*. If that is easy, gradually go through at a faster speed.

🅣 If you can travel through the obstacle without knocking it down or touching it at a fast speed, then try going through it in a backward direction—slowly at first and then faster and faster.

🅒 See if you can go through the obstacle three times without touching it in a forward direction at a fast speed. See if you can travel through three times in a backward direction without touching the obstacle.

Figure 18.11 Moving in relationship to a rolling hoop is a fascinating challenge for the skilled child.

T This game is called rolling hoops. You may work alone or with a partner. The object is to travel through a rolling hoop without touching it so that the hoop keeps rolling after you travel through it (*Figure 18.11*). If you work with a partner, ask your partner to roll the hoop slowly or to make it spin by throwing it so that the hoop spins back to the thrower. Try to go through the hoop when it changes direction and starts back to the thrower.

GOING OVER AND UNDER THE OBSTACLE COURSE

Setting: An obstacle course made by placing elastic or regular ropes at various heights around the room. Chairs, volleyball standards, and benches can be used to anchor the ropes.

Tasks/Challenges:

T You can see that the whole room is now a giant maze. Your task is to go through the maze by going over or under the ropes. Everyone can move at once, but be sure to not touch anyone else as you find your way through the maze.

T Now that you've gone through the maze at least once, I'm going to make the activity harder. This time, try to go over some of the high ropes that

you went under and to go under some of the low ropes that you went over. Be very careful to not touch anyone else, and try not to touch the ropes. This will take a lot of concentration—pretend the ropes are electric fences that will shock you if you touch them.

This is a good initial activity because you can set it up before class and then have the children help you take it down if you don't want to use it for the entire class. Children really enjoy this activity.

USING PARTNERS AS OBSTACLES

Setting: Partners in a self-space

Tasks/Challenges:

T Things are going to change a little this time. Instead of using equipment as obstacles, you're going to use partners (*Figure 18.12*). To warm up, partner 1 freezes in any shape he or she likes and can hold still. Partner 2 finds as many ways as possible to go over, under, around, and through the shape, without touching the obstacle. When partner 2 has found two ways to do each of the four movements, he or she changes places with the partner.

Figure 18.12   Using partners as obstacles.

T Now, partner 1 makes a shape and holds it while partner 2 finds three ways to go over that shape without touching it. Make sure you're actually going over the shape, not around it. After you've found three ways to go over the shape, trade places with your partner.

T To make things a bit harder, this time as you cross the low-level shape, try to match it. So if your partner is in a small round shape, you want to be in a small round shape in the air as you cross over your partner. Your partner on the floor makes three different shapes and then switches. I'll be watching to see how closely the two shapes match each other.

T This time, instead of matching, you're going to try to look the opposite as you cross. So if your partner is in a round, curled shape, you want to be in a wide, spread-out shape. After you do this three times, trade places.

T Let's make the activity even more difficult. Partner 1 forms a shape, and partner 2 crosses the shape. Partner 2 now makes a shape for partner 1. Partners keep taking turns making shapes and crossing them. Every time you cross a shape, you immediately stop and form a shape for your partner to cross. Let's try it. Each partner should make three shapes and then stop.

T Let's work on making the movement smoother so it flows together well. This time, cross the shape, and smoothly and immediately go into your shape, as if you just flowed into it. The person getting up should begin movement as soon as her or his shape has been crossed. Partners should perform as if they can read each other's mind and are continually changing places.

It may help to plan your shapes ahead of time. Talk about your shapes first, so you know exactly what you're going to do. Remember, you must go over your partner, not around.

T This will be the hardest activity yet. Each set of partners should mark off their own space. No one else can travel in this space, and the partners can't travel out of it. This is very important, so do it now. You must be able to show me the boundaries to your space when I ask.

Now that you have your space, here's what you'll be doing. Both of you will be traveling on your feet in your space. Suddenly, one of you will stop and make a low-level shape; when this happens, the other person quickly travels over the shape, and then both of you continue traveling. Do this again, with the other partner making the shape. The whole movement is split second and unpredictable. No one knows when a shape will be made, and it is barely made before it's crossed. The action goes like this: Both of you travel, one of you stops and makes a low-level shape, the other one crosses the shape, and you keep moving. The object is to perform this movement three times without breaking the flow of the movement or bumping into each other. Let's give it a try.

The secret to this task is to react as soon as you see your partner beginning to make a shape. You have to anticipate, somewhat like making an interception in football. Try again and see if you can move more smoothly, with fewer breaks and jerks.

Developing the Concept of Relationships with People

When children understand the concept of relationships with people, they have increased awareness of the interplay that occurs—in games, dance, and gymnastics—among the persons involved in the movement. Such interplay occurs, for example, when dancers converge and move around, between, and beside each other; paired acrobats balance and flip each other; trapeze artists catch and throw each other; and soccer players work as a unit to advance a ball downfield.

Children often think of relationships to others simply as children working with other children. The term *relationships,* as we use it in physical education, is generally unknown to children. When teaching youngsters about relationships with people, we focus on alone in a mass, solo, partners, groups, and between groups. These relationships can occur is a variety of ways: Each child dribbles a ball in general space (alone in a mass); one child demonstrates a sequence before an entire class (solo); a child mirrors or matches the

▶ Project Adventure has developed a number of initiative or group problem-solving activities that involve the use of relationships to objects, to other people, and to the environment. These activities are great fun, especially for older students, and develop the concepts of relationships in a myriad of enjoyable and beneficial ways. For more information about other activities, see *Cowtails and Cobras II: A Guide to Games, Initiatives, Rope Courses and Adventure Curriculum* by Karl Rohnke (Dubuque, IA: Kendall Hunt, 1989).

movement of a partner(s); children meet or part in a dance with a group to express an idea (groups); and individuals work with others as a team to accomplish a task against another team (between groups).

Alone in a Mass

This relationship occurs when all children move simultaneously, with no intent of observing one another. It's frequently seen in lessons that use a problem-solving or guided discovery approach. The children are indirectly relating to one another as they move throughout general space. In contrast to a solo relationship, the children say they feel they're truly on their own, even though they're surrounded by classmates. A child is alone in a mass when dribbling his or her own ball through general space. So too is each child when an entire class is running simultaneously to a predetermined location.

Solo

A solo relationship exists between an individual and the audience the person is performing before and who is observing the person. Examples are the pitcher on a baseball team, a featured performer in a ballet, and a gymnast. Because some children experience unpleasant pressure or tension when they're the center of attention, we make solo performances voluntary rather than mandatory. This is particularly important for the poorly skilled child, who often feels increased tension and pressure when asked to perform in front of an audience. For this reason, we always try to pinpoint two or more children. Some children, however, enjoy the challenge of solo performances and actually seem to do better when watched by a group. The feeling experienced when moving and being observed by others is an interesting phenomenon and one that we want children to explore, but in a safe, nonthreatening environment. In all classes we discourage the chil-

Figure 18.13 Working with a partner increases the fun of physical activity.

dren from laughing at or criticizing the performances of other children.

Partners

Partners are two individuals relating to each other through their movements (Figure 18.13). As children become increasingly skilled and socially mature, we introduce the partner relationship. Partner relationships include two dancers moving in synchronization to express harmony or peace, two people paddling a canoe, and two synchronized swimmers performing a routine together. Relationship concepts introduced as children work with partners (or groups) include

1. Meeting and parting—traveling toward or away from a partner.
2. Unison and contrast—both partners intentionally do the same thing (unison), or they intentionally do the same thing in different ways (contrast)
3. Leading and following—one partner leads, the other follows
4. Matching—partners are side by side and attempt to duplicate one another's movements instantaneously (to make the same movement at the same time)
5. Mirroring—partners face one another and form the reverse reproduction of the partner's movements, as if looking in a mirror

Figure 18.14a Youngsters match shapes in a study of balance.

Groups

Group cooperative relationships occur when more than two children work together for a common purpose. These relationships include children working together to express an emotion in dance, to build a shape supporting one another's weight, or as a team trying to keep a ball from touching the floor, but without catching it.

As the size of the group increases, so too does the complexity of the relationship. A partner relationship involves being aware of one other child; a successful group relationship necessitates an awareness of two or more children. The difficulty of decision making also increases proportionately with the size of the group. The concepts of meeting and parting, unison and contrast, and leading and following all become increasingly challenging as the size of a group increases.

We typically assign specific tasks to children in groups. This enables the children to develop the skills of moving in relationship to others before they try group tasks that require them to make decisions—such as those required when children make up a game or invent a sequence. Asking children who've had little opportunity to work in groups to make group decisions about their work has proved counterproductive. Once children become proficient at group relationships, however, they are challenged by the adventure and creative opportunities of group decision making.

Between Groups

A between-group relationship occurs when two or more children relate to two or more children. It's the most complex of relationships because it involves not only being aware of one's own group but a responsibility to relate to another group. This relationship is extremely challenging, as demonstrated by the wide appeal of sports that match one team against another. We initially keep intergroup relationships small (two to three on a side) and try to allow choices about whether to participate in an intergroup relationship.

Between-group relationships can be competitive (working with a group to outmaneuver another group) or collaborative (two groups striving for a common goal). We usually begin with collaborative relationships and provide children the opportunity to choose competitive activities. See Box 18.3 for additional information on competitive intergroup relationships.

Teaching the Concept of Relationships with People

The following activities are designed to improve children's ability to function successfully with other individuals and groups in a variety of situations.

Activities Leading to Movement Concept Understanding

MATCHING

Setting: Partners in a self-space

Tasks/Challenges:

🅣 Stand alongside a partner. Partner 1 should make a shape, and partner 2 should try to copy it exactly *(Figure 18.14a, b)*. Try to make the shapes so alike that you look like twins. After five shapes, partners should change places, with partner 2 now making the shapes while partner 1 copies them. Work hard to make the shapes exactly alike.

BOX 18.3   COMPETITION

Many intergroup relationships are competitive, with one group attempting to perform more skillfully than the other group. The emphasis on winning creates an intense emotional involvement that can produce disturbing feelings in some children. We talk with children about these feelings, which usually occur in competitive, predesigned team situations, and we explain to the youngsters how they can understand these feelings and deal with them effectively. Cooperative situations, in which children in a group work to accomplish a common goal, involve relationships that are easier for young children to handle.

Some might suggest that competitive relationships between groups are inappropriate for children. The affective and cognitive ramifications of competition include the feelings associated with winning and losing, false feelings of superiority or inferiority, and determination to beat an opponent. Our experience has been that competitive relationships, with many affective and cognitive ramifications, occur anyway, at recess or after-school situations, so we're convinced that it's the teacher's responsibility to help children develop a healthy attitude about competitive situations.

It's important for children to understand that it's acceptable to choose to not participate in a competitive situation if they feel threatened or insecure. Similarly, children should understand that everyone makes mistakes in games, and that when they make mistakes, the other children are not unhappy with them as individuals but rather with the situation. These affective concepts aren't typically included in a discussion of relationships between groups. But it's in these types of relationships that we so often observe children developing the distaste and disaffection for physical activity that can endure for a lifetime if not dealt with effectively. And so we believe that it's important to discuss them.

Figure 18.14b A child matches a partner's rocking movement.

⊤ These types of shapes are said to *match*; they look alike as much as possible. Now you're going to make matching balances a little harder by playing Follow the Leader. On the signal, partner 1 leads by traveling; partner 2 follows. On the stop signal, you both stop, and the follower—partner 2—matches the balance the leader—partner 1—makes. As you make your shapes, try to match exactly what your partner does. Your whole body should do this, not just your trunk. After four turns, switch places. Be sure that when you're the leader you make a shape that your partner can actually do—not one that's too hard.

TRAVELING AND MATCHING

Setting: Partners traveling in general space

Tasks/Challenges:

⊤ Now you'll perform matching actions while traveling instead of being still. With your partner, make up five ways that you can travel and then perform the movements side by side at the exact same time, as if you're both part of a marching band that does everything alike. Practice doing the movements together so you do them at exactly the same time. It may help to count to yourselves as you move.

MIRRORING

Setting: Partners in a self-space

Tasks/Challenges:

⊤ This time you're going to try something a little different. Face your partner; partner 1 will be the leader and partner 2 the follower. The leader will make a balance, and the follower will then make the same balance, only opposite. For example, if partner 1 uses his right arm to do something, partner 2 uses her left arm. Make five statues, and then trade places. Work very hard to make every part of the statue the exact opposite of what you see. These types of actions are called *mirroring* actions because the effect is that of looking in a mirror.

MATCHING AND MIRRORING

Setting: Partners in a self-space

Tasks/Challenges:

⊤ This activity tests how well you understand the difference between mirroring and matching. With your partner, make a matching balance. On the signal, change that balance so that you mirror each other.

It helps to have a group that is doing the activity correctly demonstrate it for the class.

⊤ With your partner, now try to find five more balances that you can change from matching to mirroring. I'm going to come around as you practice and ask to see at least one of your combinations, so be sure you know the difference. If you have questions, ask now.

⊤ This time, the activity will be harder. Instead of copying a still statue your partner makes, you're going to mirror your partner's movements. Remember that this is still in your own space and that there's no traveling. So if your partner moves his or her left arm down, you move your right arm up. Make four moves and change places. This is hard. Think about it.

⊤ This time, try to tell a story with your mirroring actions, such as a baby first seeing herself in the mirror, your mother putting on her makeup, or your father shaving. Practice your story until you can do it the same way three times in a row. Then we'll have the class try to guess what you're saying.

TRAVELING ALONGSIDE/FOLLOWING

Setting: Traveling in general space with a partner

Tasks/Challenges:

⊤ Though we haven't really discussed it, often you were practicing another type of relationship when you followed your partner around the space: *leading and following*. So far you've always followed from behind the other person; now let's try it differently this time, with you traveling alongside or next to your partner as you follow. One person is still the leader and the other the follower, but you

> When children begin to work with others in collaborative and competitive situations involving a manipulative skill, the skill level tends to deteriorate briefly if they're concentrating on the relationship. This should be expected and explained. The children, though, do need to have a certain level (control level) of manipulative ability before beginning these situations, or the activity will become very frustrating to them.

both move as if you were a team of horses: beside each other. Each of you should take five turns leading and then switch places. This activity is harder, so you have to watch very closely what your partner does. Start out with very easy moves.

T Now try to speed it up a little. Watch carefully. Try to follow exactly.

The leader must be aware of the follower's capabilities so that the leader challenges the partner but doesn't frustrate the partner with movements that are too difficult.

FOLLOWING WITH A GROUP

Setting: Traveling in general space with a group

Tasks/Challenges:

T This time, you're going to try another type of following: from behind, with four or five of you in a group. The first person in line is the first leader and leads the group all over the room. Then on the signal, the first person goes to the end of the line, and the second person becomes the leader; this change continues until everyone has had a chance to lead. The secret is to stay far enough apart so that you can see. The activity is just like Follow the Leader.

T This time you're going to make the activity a little more challenging. I'm *not* going to give you the signal to change anymore. Your group will have to make up its own change signal, such as a hand clap. You'll start as you did before, with the first person leading. Then at some time the second person in line will give the change signal and at the same time start traveling a new way. When this happens, the whole line starts to follow the new leader, and the old leader goes to the back of the line. The hard part is that you're going to do this without stopping the movement; the line must always keep moving. The same process continues until everyone has had a chance to be the leader. Remember, it's always the second person in line who gives the change signal.

MEETING/PARTING

Setting: Partners working in self- and general space

Tasks/Challenges:

T Now you're going to work with partners again. First you and your partner are going to work only with your hands while seated in your self-space. Very slowly, try to bring your hands as close to your partner's as you can without touching them. As soon as your hands are close, pull them as far away as you can without moving your body.

T This relationship is called *meeting and parting*. To make it a little easier, I'm going to give you a drumbeat to go by. On the six slow counts of the drum, bring your hands as close as possible without touching them, and freeze. Then, on a sudden loud beat, quickly pull your hands as far away as possible, as if you don't want them to touch poison.

T Now try meeting and parting with your whole body. In a small space, use the six slow drumbeats to bring your bodies as close together as possible without touching, and then freeze. On the sudden beat, quickly pull away. The secret is to pull away quickly, as if you were a flash of lightning, and then freeze very still.

T The activity will be harder this time. You'll still have the same partner, but you both will be separated. You're all going to travel around the room, and on the beat of the drum quickly come toward your partner and freeze very close to each other, just for a few seconds, and then begin your traveling again. Do this every time you hear the signal. The secret is to always know where your partner is. Maintain eye contact.

T This time, as you and your partner meet on the sound of the signal, come together as if you're greeting a friend you haven't seen in a long time; then, as you get right up to each other, you realize that you really don't know the person. It could be really funny.

FORMING COOPERATIVE AND COLLABORATIVE RELATIONSHIPS

Setting: Groups of four traveling, throwing, and catching in a large space

Tasks/Challenges:

T So far, all our relationships with people involved how we moved with those people. You're now going to work on a few different types of relationships that involve not only how you move with people but also how you think. In your group of four, you're going to travel in a line spread out across the field toward the goal. As you travel, throw the ball back and forth to each other, always trying to stay the same distance apart. Imagine a marching band moving across the field but throwing a ball as they move. The secret is that the receivers move slightly ahead of but not toward the passers and the passers throw the ball ahead of the receivers so that they don't have to come back to catch it. This type of relationship is called a *cooperative* relationship, because everybody has to work together to make it work.

This idea works well if a lined field (such as a football field) is available and the children can follow the lines as guides.

T Now you're going to change the cooperative relationship a little. You're still going to work with your group to move the ball across the field while staying the same distance apart, but two people who are going to try to steal the ball while it is in the air will be coming toward you. It will be really hard to resist the temptation to go close to your own players to try and help them, but remember you have two goals: to stay away from your teammates and to not let the other two people steal the ball. It really does help to stay away from the other people on your team.

This is called a *collaborative* relationship, because you have to work with the people on your team to keep the two other people from getting the ball. Let me give you a few more hints on how to make such a relationship work really well. First, when it's your turn to receive the ball, move slightly in front of the passer so the passer can easily throw the ball to you. Second, pass before the defender gets close to you; when you're free to pass, don't wait until the defender is so close that you're forced to pass.

As the children become more proficient with these activities, you may want to try manipulative skills other than throwing, such as kicking, passing, or striking.

MEETING AND PARTING IN A COOPERATIVE GROUP

Setting: Groups in a general space

Tasks/Challenges:

T This time, instead of meeting and parting with a partner, you're going to meet and part with a small group. Your group forms a group shape: Remember: close, but not touching. Then on the signal, suddenly leave, as if you're in a hurry, but take only a few steps and by yourself freeze into a shape you like. On the next signal, slowly come back to your group and form the same group shape with which you started. To repeat, start with a group shape, on the signal quickly leave and form a shape of your own, and on the next signal return to the first group shape—almost as if someone were playing a movie forwards, backwards, forwards, backwards.

C Let's work on this activity with one series that you really like. Practice it so it works out the same each time. This will involve hard thinking. It may help to count your steps so you know exactly how far to move. It also helps to not laugh too much. Who knows, you could be stars!

PERFORMING SOLO

Setting: Groups of six, each group with a foam ball and cones to define their area; pencil and paper for each child.

Tasks/Challenges:

T You're going to play a bunch of small dodgeball games—only six people in a group. Start with two people on the outside. When you get hit, do *not* sit out, but become a thrower on the outside, so in the end there will be many throwers and one person in the middle. But I have another activity for you to think about while you're doing this. I want you to be able to tell what it's like to be in the middle, what all you have to think about, who and what you have to watch out for. When you finish one game, just start another one. The last two players left in the middle are the first throwers in the next game. Remember to think about what it's like in the middle.

T Now you're going to write down your thoughts about what it was like in the middle. In case you're wondering, this is another type of relationship: a *solo* relationship, which means that there are many people around you, but it's each person for him- or herself. Write down what you thought.

After the youngsters have had some time to write, briefly discuss the feelings of being in a solo relationship when each child is the center of attention. Point out that some people (probably the highly skilled) like being solo, but others (probably the lower skilled) prefer to not be solo.

Applying the Concept of Relationships

The concept of relationships with objects and people (Figure 18.15) is a beginning theme in the gymnastics and dance areas as the children are taught the concepts of over, under, inside, outside, along, and onto. There the focus is on whether the child understands the concept rather than whether she or he can accomplish the skill involved. For example, you'd observe whether a child was actually jumping symmetrically over a hurdle rather than whether she was crossing

Figure 18.15 This group of children is working together for a common purpose.

without knocking it over. Once you're sure that the child understands the concept, begin to focus on the skill. Once a particular concept has been learned, it can also be used for expressive purposes in dance.

We don't introduce the concept of relationships with objects in the games area until children have reached at least the control level (Chapter 7). Children must learn to manipulate objects with some consistency before they can reasonably be expected to manipulate them in relation to objects or people. If children are given tasks involving manipulative skills and relationships too early, they become frustrated and bored.

The concept of relationships with others is the last concept we introduce. Socially, children enjoy working near other children at a very young age, but often physically and cognitively they aren't able to function effectively in relationship to others. For example, children at the precontrol level don't possess enough skill to be able to consistently work with a partner—when such children are asked to throw an object back and forth to partners, only one out of three throws is likely to reach the partner. Therefore, it's best not to deal with relationships with others as a *concept* until the children's skills are adequate and they've matured enough socially so that their abilities are enhanced when they work with other children. There are no magical ages or times for introducing the different relationship concepts. Each teacher must reflect on information about the environment, the children, the skill, and personal ability as a teacher to determine the best time for introducing the concept of relationships.

READING COMPREHENSION QUESTIONS

1. List three examples each of relationships of body parts, relationships with objects, and relationships with people (total of nine examples).
2. What does the term *functional understanding* mean?
3. Define symmetrical and nonsymmetrical by listing examples of each concept.

4. We recommend that you teach the concept of relationships with objects before teaching relationships with people. Why?
5. What does the term *alone in a mass* mean? What does *solo* mean?
6. We recommend that solo performances and intergroup experiences be voluntary, not required. Why?
7. Explain the difference between mirroring and matching.
8. What factors should you consider when making decisions about the most appropriate times to introduce the various relationships?

REFERENCES

National Association for Sport and Physical Education (NASPE). (1995). *Moving into the future: National standards for physical education.* St. Louis, MO : Mosby.

PART FOUR

Skill Theme Development

Chapters 19 to 31 discuss the content of the skill themes we focus on in our physical education programs. Each chapter begins with an introduction to the skill theme; the introduction includes a discussion of the skill theme's characteristics and how the theme can be applied to teaching children. It's tempting to skip the introduction and get to the actual lesson ideas, but we recommend that you carefully read the introduction so that you'll be able to adapt the skill theme to your particular needs. Obviously you'll change some of the ideas; an understanding of the skill as taught to children will help you make these adaptations.

Each skill theme chapter (except Chapters 20, 25, and 31) is arranged in a logical progression, from precontrol through proficiency levels as explained in Chapter 7. This progression is accompanied by what we call a progression spiral, which outlines the content of each skill theme. Each line in the spiral corresponds to a section in the chapter that explains how to develop that idea. The progressions are presented as a series of tasks (not lessons) that you will be able to develop based on the skill level and abilities of the classes you teach.

Each series of tasks begins by describing the space and equipment you will need. At the precontrol level children are exploring a movement and therefore cues are not provided. At the next three generic skill levels, however, cues are provided before the actual task(s). You are reminded that it is probably most effective to focus on only one of these cues at a time. The reason we provide several at the beginning of the series of tasks is to allow you to observe your children to determine which cue will be the most appropriate for them. Following the cues are one or more suggested tasks (which are designated with the symbol Ⓣ) and also challenges (which are designated with the symbol Ⓒ). As you recall, tasks, cues, and challenges were described in Chapter 12, Developing the Content. In addition you will also find suggested Assessments (Chapter 14) to help you determine how well the children are understanding the concepts and skills you are teaching.

Chapters 20, 25, and 31 are discussions of how dance, games, and gymnastics are incorporated into the skill theme approach. You will not find a series of rules for games, dance steps, or gymnastic stunts in these chapters. To do so would violate the very premise upon which *Children Moving* is based—children have different needs and interests! If we were to provide a series of games organized by grade level, for example, we would be assuming that all of the children had the ability to play those games successfully. And we know that is not true. Thus the three chapters on dance, games, and gymnastics are placed in Section Four closest to the skill themes that typically are used in those movement forms. Gymnastics (Chapter 25), for example, follows directly behind chapters on jumping and landing, balancing, and transferring weight and rolling. We hope this will enable you to see how skill themes are taught in gymnastics-like lessons. In fact, the children often refer to lessons on rolling and transferring weight as gymnastics. That's fine with us as long as they are learning the skills that eventually lead to success and participation not only in gymnastics but also in dance and games.

Finally, we encourage you to change the suggested progressions and implied methodology to suit your students' needs and your teaching goals. Our suggestions are certainly not prescriptions. The chapters in Part Four are ordered in the progression we'd use to organize our yearly plan (discussed in Chapter 7), but you should reflect on your situation and design the curriculum for *your* children.

CHAPTER
19

Traveling

Children are first capable of changing the location of their bodies at about three months of age, when they turn over from their backs onto their stomachs. Unless seriously handicapped, they'll soon begin to crawl, then creep. At about one year, they'll take their first step. And by the time they enter school, they'll exhibit relatively mature walking and running patterns. Unlike other skills—such as throwing, catching, and striking—the basic locomotor patterns develop naturally in most children.

Most school-age youngsters, therefore, are beyond the precontrol level in walking and running. Nevertheless, the teacher's first task is to evaluate traveling performance to ensure that any youngsters who exhibit severely immature or inefficient patterns will receive remedial assistance. Most children attain a mature walking pattern through experience. Verbal cues from the teacher, plus the modeling of the correct pattern, will help children with inefficiencies. Continued deviations (e.g., toes turned out or in) signal the need for a thorough physical examination by a pediatrician.

Similarly, it's important to ascertain how many students can perform the fundamental locomotor skills that emerge from the walk-run pattern: hopping, leaping, sliding, galloping, and skipping. Young children need much practice of each skill when the skills are introduced, and they also need distributed practice of the locomotor skills throughout the primary grades. Young children inexperienced in different locomotor skills may not be able to give the correct locomotor response to a verbal command because they often lack cognitive understanding rather than motor performance. We've found that modeling is the best way for young children to learn these skills; the children follow the example of the teacher and other children who've mastered the skill. It's also important to name the locomotor skill each time you or others demonstrate it to the children.

By approximately age eight, we expect children to be able to execute the locomotor skills of hopping, leaping, sliding, galloping, and skipping in response to a verbal command. This expectation implies that children recognize the word and the action it represents and that they've mastered the skill. Consequently, most of the activities in this chapter are geared to the precontrol and control levels. At the utilization and proficiency levels, traveling most often occurs as combinations of skill themes, such as traveling while dribbling, or in a game, dance, or gymnastics context, for example, traveling to run bases. See Box 19.1 for information on traveling from the *National Standards*.

Fundamental Locomotor Skills

Walking

Walking is a process of alternately losing balance and recovering it while moving forward in an upright position. While moving forward, the body should display little up and down or side to side movement. The arms and legs move in opposition. A mature walking pattern looks smooth and is accomplished in an easy manner.

When assessing the walking pattern of young children, look for the following inefficiencies:

1. Bouncy walk—too much vertical push
2. Excessive swing of the arms away from the sides
3. Failure to swing the arms at the shoulders
4. Feet held too close together so that the entire body looks jerky as the child walks
5. Feet held too far apart—duck walk
6. Toes turned out
7. Toes turned in—pigeon-toed
8. Head too far forward—body leaning forward before the lead foot touches the ground

Running

During the earliest stage of running (at about twenty-four months), a child's new speed produces precarious balance. The child makes exaggerated leg movements. In particular, the knee of the recovery leg swings outward and then around and forward in preparation for the support phase. This knee action is accompanied by the foot of the recovery leg toeing out. These exaggerated movements gradually disappear as the legs become longer and stronger.

Most school-age youngsters are able to run at a relatively fast speed and are fairly successful at changing direction while running. In a mature running pattern (observed when the children are attempting to run at maximum velocity), each leg goes through a support phase and a recovery phase, and the full sequence produces two periods of nonsupport. The essentials of the mature running pattern are the following (Wickstrom, 1977, pp. 37–57):

1. The trunk maintains a slight forward lean throughout the stride pattern.
2. Both arms swing through a large arc and in synchronized opposition to the leg action.
3. The support foot contacts the ground approximately flat and nearly under the center of gravity.
4. The knee of the support leg bends slightly after the foot has made contact with the ground.

BOX 19.1   THE SKILL OF TRAVELING IN THE *NATIONAL STANDARDS FOR PHYSICAL EDUCATION*

The movement skill of traveling is referenced in the *National Standards for Physical Education* (NASPE, 1995) under Standard 1: Demonstrates competency in many movement forms and proficiency in a few movement forms. The standard speaks of the child achieving mature forms of locomotor skills, using patterns in combinations, and combining locomotor and manipulative skills in increasingly dynamic and complex environments.

Sample benchmarks for traveling include:

- Travels in forward and sideways directions using a variety of locomotor (nonlocomotor) patterns and changes direction quickly in response to a signal. (K)
- Walks and runs using mature form. (K)
- Combines locomotor patterns in time to music. (2)
- Develops and refines a creative dance sequence into a repeatable pattern. (4)
- Designs and performs gymnastics and dance sequences that combine traveling, rolling, balancing, and weight transfer into smooth, flowing sequences with intentional changes in direction, speed, and flow. (6)

Figure 19.1 Hopping pattern.

5. Extension of the support leg at the hip, knee, and ankle propels the body forward and upward into the nonsupport phase.
6. The recovery knee swings forward quickly to a high knee raise, and simultaneously the lower leg flexes, bringing the heel close to the buttock.

Use the key observation points in Box 19.2 to assess running patterns. The illustrations of "correct" and "incorrect" patterns help you answer the questions you should ask yourself as you evaluate a youngster's performance.

Hopping

A hop is a springing action from one foot, in any direction, to a landing on the same foot (Figure 19.1). The knee seldom straightens fully; the work of the ankle joint is primarily what accomplishes the push into the air and the absorption of the landing shock.

Leaping

A leap is an extension of a run—greater force is used to produce a higher dimension than a run (Figure 19.2).

BOX 19.2   KEY OBSERVATION POINTS: RUNNING

Leg Action

Does the knee of the child's recovery leg swing forward and backward rather than outward, around, and then forward?

NO   YES

Arm Action

Do the child's arms move forward and backward in opposition to the legs without crossing the midline?

NO   YES

Do the child's arms stay close to the body throughout the action?

NO   YES   NO   YES

Trunk Position

Does the child's trunk lean slightly forward?

NO   YES

Foot Placement

Is the child's support foot approximately flat when it contacts the ground?

NO   YES

Mature Stage

When children are at the mature stage of running, do their runs look similar to the following sequence?

Figure 19.2 Leaping pattern.

Figure 19.3 Sliding pattern.

A one-foot takeoff propels the body upward to a landing on the opposite foot. Arm opposition is the same as for the run. There's an emphasis on body extension for height or for distance. Upon touching the floor, the landing leg bends to absorb the force of the body.

Sliding

A slide is a combination of a step and a run. The lead step is quickly followed by the free foot closing to replace the supporting foot (Figure 19.3). The lead foot quickly springs from the floor into a direction of intended travel. The weight is primarily on the balls of the feet. The sequence is repeated for the desired distance. The same foot always leads in a slide, producing an uneven rhythm: step-close, step-close, step-close.

Galloping

A gallop is an exaggerated slide in a forward direction. The lead leg lifts and bends and then thrusts forward to support the weight. The rear foot quickly closes to replace the supporting leg as the lead leg springs up into its lifted and bent position. The rhythm is uneven, the same as that of a slide.

Skipping

A skip is a combination of a step and a hop, first on one foot and then on the other foot (Figure 19.4). The pattern has the alternation and opposition of the walk plus the same-sided one-foot hop. The skip has an uneven rhythm.

Levels of Skill Proficiency

In many schools, usually in communities where parents provide their preschoolers with a wealth of movement experiences, most five- and six-year-old children will already have mastered the traveling skills, and their classmates will be quick to catch on. However, we have observed some situations in which a number of the students were unable to perform many locomotor skills beyond walking and running. Such children need basic precontrol-level travel experiences so they will learn to:

1. Crawl along the floor
2. Creep on hands and knees
3. Walk along a line on the floor
4. Crawl underneath a low bar without touching it

Figure 19.4 Skipping pattern.

5. Step over a low obstacle without touching it

Precontrol-level experiences provide a multitude of exploration experiences in travel: traveling in different ways, exploring various locomotor patterns, the world of imagery and travel, and traveling just for the sheer enjoyment of moving. Once youngsters can identify and perform the basic modes of travel relatively easily, they are ready for control-level challenges.

Control-level challenges include mastery of the different locomotor patterns. Following mastery of the basic skills, the children can attempt variations of those skills: walking at a low level, skipping backward, galloping, changing direction on signal, and running in a crowded room without touching anyone. Next, the youngsters can try traveling rhythmically or expressively: skipping to the uneven beat of the teacher's drum, running and leaping on the accented beat, walking as if on hot sand, and walking mechanically, like a robot.

Once children are easily able to perform a variety of locomotor skills and can use their travel abilities to carry out a primary objective, they're ready for utilization-level activities. At this point, an involvement in challenging situations can refine and expand the youngsters' repertoires of travel skills.

The children can combine two or more travel operations into a short sequence, such as run-jump-roll, or run-leap-turn in air-run. They can try to perform another skill while traveling: keeping a long ribbon from touching the ground by traveling swiftly, or striking a balloon and traveling to keep it up.

Children can improvise or plan in detail expressive travel for short dance phrases, focusing on:

1. The purpose, idea, or theme of the phrase—harmony, a battle, autumn
2. The most appropriate pathway of travel—straight, angular, curved, or symmetrical

3. The specific travel skills to be incorporated—running, leaping, collapsing
4. The travel qualities to be exhibited—smooth-flowing, jagged-jerky

The youngsters can use effective travel skills and strategic pathways in dynamic game situations:

1. React quickly to a batted ball by charging forward, to the left or right, to collect a ground ball and throw accurately to a teammate
2. Run a planned pass pattern, using fakes and quick changes of direction to lose an opponent and receive a ball a teammate throws

When students consistently use a variety of travel skills and pathways effectively in game, dance, and gymnastics settings, they're ready to put all the elements together through participation in proficiency-level experiences.

■ Games: Youngsters play teacher- and/or student-designed games that demand alert and accurate performance of travel skills and strategic use of travel pathways while performing another skill, for example, dribbling.
■ Dance: Students and teacher work together to design dance studies. Specific travel pathways and locomotor skills are decided upon, practiced, revised, and refined. This process ends in a completed dance that clearly reflects the theme or idea that stimulated the study.
■ Gymnastics: Students and teacher cooperatively design travel patterns and select specific locomotor skills (as well as positions of stillness, i.e., balances) for individual or group gymnastics routines.

Our progression spiral on page 284 shows the sequence for developing the skill theme of traveling at the precontrol, control, utilization, and proficiency levels.

Traveling

■ **PROFICIENCY LEVEL**

Traveling in gymnastics
Traveling in games and sports
Performing rhythmical patterns: Tinikling
Traveling to show tradition versus change
Depicting primitive tribes through travel

■ **UTILIZATION LEVEL**

Traveling to Tom Foolery rhymes
Traveling in bound and free flow
Traveling to express age: The Fountain of Youth Dance
Performing rhythmical patterns
Meeting and parting while traveling with a partner
Shadowing
Traveling with a partner: changing speed and direction
The Copy Cat Dance
Traveling with a partner: matching pathways

■ **CONTROL LEVEL**

Combination locomotors
Slow-Motion Replay: The Sports Dance
A Dance of Water, Steam, and Ice
Changing speeds to music
Traveling using different directions, levels, pathways, and locations
Traveling at different speeds
The Follow-Me Dance
The Locomotors Dance
Traveling in different pathways
Slidestepping
Traveling in different directions
Traveling an obstacle course
Traveling with music
Traveling in confined spaces
Moving to rhythms
Performing locomotor sequences
Traveling to open spaces
Traveling with different locomotor patterns
    Running
    Leaping
    Skipping
    Hopping
    Galloping
    Sliding

■ **PRECONTROL LEVEL**

Traveling among the large and tall
Traveling through rope pathways
Traveling with imagery
Traveling in different ways
Traveling with different locomotor movements
Traveling in general space

Figure 19.5 After challenging a class to travel about a general space, the teacher can observe individual children for possible inefficiencies.

Precontrol Level: Activities for Exploration

The activities that follow are designed to introduce children to the fundamental locomotor patterns and to help them explore the skill of traveling.

TRAVELING IN GENERAL SPACE

Setting: Children scattered throughout general space

Tasks/Challenges:

🔵 On the signal, travel any way you wish in general space. Avoid colliding with others, and stop without falling when you hear the drum.

🔵 Change to a different way to travel. . . . Some of you are hopping; some are galloping; most are running. Travel throughout general space any way except running. Watch out for others as you travel.

🔵 See how many different ways you can travel on your feet, sometimes traveling on one foot, sometimes on two feet, sometimes on one foot and then the other.

🔵 Show me three different ways you can travel on your feet.

TRAVELING WITH DIFFERENT LOCOMOTOR MOVEMENTS

Setting: Children scattered throughout general space

Tasks/Challenges:

🔵 When we explored different ways to travel, some of you were hopping, some were walking, some were galloping. Let's explore the different locomotor skills as we travel in general space (*Figure 19.5*). Travel throughout general space with your favorite locomotor movement; I will name the ones I see: walking, running, galloping . . . .

🔵 Travel throughout general space with a *hop*, staying on one foot. Switch to the other foot after several hops so you will not become tired and lose your balance.

🔵 Travel throughout general space with a *jump*, two feet to two feet. Make some of your jumps small and low, some of them long, some of them high in the air.

🔵 Travel throughout general space with a *gallop*, one foot always staying in front of the other. Can you gallop backward?

🔵 Travel throughout general space with a *run*, always looking for the open spaces. Remember to stop on the signal, without falling down.

🔵 Thus far, you have traveled by hopping, jumping, galloping, and running; you were already very good at walking. Of those five locomotor actions, choose your favorite three and practice them as if you were going to teach them to someone who does not know how to do them—perfection!

TRAVELING IN DIFFERENT WAYS

Setting: Children scattered throughout general space

Figure 19.6   These children are enjoying traveling at a low level.

Tasks/Challenges:

🅣 Travel throughout general space on two feet. On the signal, change the way you are traveling, yet remain on your feet.

🅒 How many different ways can you travel on your feet?

🅣 Travel throughout general space on two feet and two hands; travel forward, backward, sideways on your feet and hands.

🅣 Travel throughout general space on body parts other than your feet. How many different combinations of body parts can you use for travel?

TRAVELING WITH IMAGERY

Setting: Children scattered throughout general space

Tasks/Challenges:

🅣 Travel throughout general space like a rabbit, jumping from two feet to two feet; travel like a frog, jumping from pad to pad.

🅣 Travel throughout general space, walking as if in sticky mud or a sea of peanut butter.

🅣 Walk like a robot. March like a soldier.

🅣 Travel throughout general space like a large elephant. Will your steps be heavy or light?

🅣 Travel like a tall giraffe, with your head above the clouds.

🅣 Run quietly, like deer through the forest.

Figure 19.7   Rope pathways as an obstacle course.

🅣 Slither like a snake. Crawl like an inchworm, then like a snail *(Figure 19.6)*.

The imagery of animals for movement is almost endless. Always remind children of the movement with a simple lead question, such as "How does a giraffe move?"

TRAVELING THROUGH ROPE PATHWAYS

Setting: An obstacle course of marker cones and ropes on the floor to form varying pathways of different widths for travel (Figure 19.7).

Tasks/Challenges:

🅣 On the signal, travel around the cones and between the rope boundaries without touching them. I will time you for thirty seconds. Try to finish with a perfect score—no touches.

🅒 Challenge yourself to travel throughout the obstacle course three times with no collisions with others or the items in the course.

TRAVELING AMONG THE LARGE AND TALL

Setting: Children with partners, scattered throughout general space

Tasks/Challenges:

🅣 Stand in your self-space, stretching in all directions to be sure you have a clear self-space; it is not important that you be near your partner. Partners A, stand in your self-space, extending your arms to make a very large, wide shape. Partners B, travel throughout general space with any locomotor pattern you wish; avoid touching anyone traveling or a stationary wide shape. *Have partners switch travel and stationary activities after one or two minutes of travel.*

🅣 Partners A, stand in your self-space with a tall, narrow shape. Partners B, run throughout general space with no collisions; always look for open spaces as you travel. *Switch activities after one or two minutes.*

Control Level: Learning Experiences Leading to Skill Development

Control-level experiences are designed to help children master the basic locomotor skills and to expand their traveling abilities. The learning experiences challenge youngsters to use different traveling patterns with other concepts, such as speed and direction.

A note about cues: Although several cues are listed for many of the learning experiences, it's important to focus on only one cue at a time. That way, the children can really concentrate on that cue. Once you provide feedback to the children and observe that most have learned a cue, then it's time to focus on another one.

TRAVELING WITH DIFFERENT LOCOMOTOR PATTERNS

Setting: Children scattered throughout general space

Cues	
Heads Up	(Keep your head up for good balance and to avoid collisions with others.)
Balanced Stops	(Spread your feet apart and lower your hips slightly to maintain your balance when you stop.)

Tasks/Challenges:

🅣 On signal, travel any way you wish in general space. Avoid colliding with others, and stop without falling when you hear the drum.

SLIDING

Cue	
Buoyant Landings	(Make light, "springy" actions as you travel.)

🅣 Raise your right arm and point toward the far side of the blacktop (gymnasium). On the signal, use a slide step to travel across the area. When your left foot almost touches your right foot, step again quickly to the side with your right foot.

🅣 Slide across the area like a dancer, arms extended to the side and your body stretched upward as you "leap."

🅣 Slide like a basketball player with your knees bent, hips lowered, and arms extended in front.

GALLOPING

Cue	
Same Foot Forward	(Keep the same foot in front as you gallop.)

🅣 On the signal, gallop in general space, keeping the same foot in front throughout the action.

🅣 Now lead with the other foot as you gallop.

HOPPING

Cue	
Up, Up, Light, Light	(Make light, quick actions as you hop.)

🅣 Hop on one foot five times, and then hop on your other foot five times. Continue to alternate hopping on your right foot and then your left foot until you hear the signal to stop.

SKIPPING

Cue	
Lift Your Knees	(Lift your knees, swing your arms . . . step, hop.)

🅣 Now that you can hop and gallop, try skipping. Skip throughout general space until you hear the signal to stop.

Developmentally, children progress from a gallop to a skip only on the dominant side, then to a mature skipping pattern (Figure 19.8).

Figure 19.8   Children seem to skip for the sheer pleasure they experience in doing so!

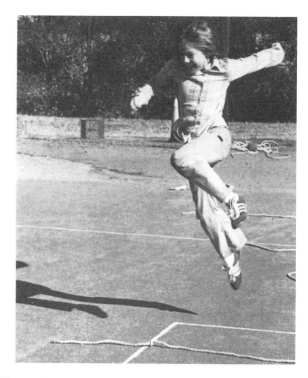

Figure 19.9   The airborne sensation that results from combining a run and a leap thrills this youngster.

LEAPING

Cue

Arms Up . . . Stretch   (Lift your arms; stretch your arms and legs as you leap.)

🅣 We did leaping when we worked on jumping and landing. Who can remember what a leap is? Right, it's taking off on one foot and landing on the other, with the body airborne between the takeoff and landing (*Figure 19.9*). Travel in general space by running. After running three steps, leap high in the air, and when you land, continue to run. Your travel will be this: Run, run, run, leap; run, run, run, leap. . . . **Remember to land softly by bending your knee.**

🅣 I'm going to number you off in 1s and 2s. The 1s will be spread around the room in a curled shape close to the floor. The 2s will run throughout the room, leaping over the curled 1s without touching them. On the signal, the 2s will collapse to the floor in curled shapes. The 1s will count with me, "One, two, three," and then pop up and begin running and leaping over the 2s.

Repeat the activity several times for endurance.

RUNNING

Cue

Light on Your Feet   (Make light, buoyant landings for quick steps.)

🅣 Now that you can move without bumping others and stop on signal, try running throughout general space. Cover as much area as you can. Be sure your entire foot contacts the floor, not just your toes.

ASSESSMENT EXAMPLE
from the National Standards for Physical Education

Teacher Observation/Observational Record

The student will be asked to travel through general space with a steady run, and upon a designated signal perform the next locomotor action announced by the teacher (e.g., walk, hop, gallop). Upon observing the student's performance, the teacher marks on a checklist mastery of the various critical elements (e.g., arm swing, balance, foot placement).

Criteria for Assessment

a. Demonstrates selected critical elements of locomotor skills

b. Responds with correct locomotor skill as named by teacher

NASPE (1995, p. 6)

ASSESSMENT EXAMPLE
from the National Standards of Physical Education

Event Task/Observational Record

Students will perform a "Dance of Locomotors" in which they travel in different ways through general space. Upon hearing a designated signal from the teacher, students will change to the locomotor pattern named by the teacher. Repeat the dance, but this time upon the signal to change locomotor pattern the students will respond by selecting any locomotor pattern they desire. The teacher should encourage creative modes of travel.

Criteria for Assessment

a. Demonstrates a variety of locomotor skills
b. Identifies and models locomotor movements shown by the teacher
c. Exhibits correct locomotor skill when the skill is named by the teacher

NASPE (1995, p. 7)

TRAVELING TO OPEN SPACES

Setting: Children scattered throughout general space

Cues	
Heads Up	(Keep your head up for good balance and to avoid collisions with others.)
Balanced Stops	(Spread your feet apart and lower your hips slightly to maintain your balance when you stop.)

Tasks/Challenges:

🅣 In your self-space, look around the work space. Do you see open spaces that no one has taken as their space? On the signal, run to that open space. When you arrive, stop and look for another open space; run to that space.

🅣 Travel throughout general space, always looking for the open spaces. This time you will only pause at an open space long enough to see your next open space.

🅒 I will time you for sixty seconds of travel. Your task is to travel throughout general space always looking for and moving to open spaces with no collisions.

PERFORMING LOCOMOTOR SEQUENCES

Setting: On index cards (or slips of paper placed inside film cylinders), write a sequence of locomotor movements—for example, "Walk, hop, gallop"—one sequence card per child.

Cues	
Heads Up	(Keep your head up for good balance and to avoid collisions with others.)
Pause and Go	(Pause momentarily; then continue your locomotor movement.)
Balanced Stops	(Spread your feet apart and lower your hips slightly to maintain your balance when you stop.)

Tasks/Challenges:

🅣 Think of your favorite locomotor movement that you've practiced. On signal, use that movement to travel in general space. I should be able to identify the locomotor movement by watching you travel.

🅣 There are cards spread around the wall. When I say "Go," get a card, and bring it back to your space. Read your card. Each card contains a movement sentence: three locomotor movements separated by commas. What does a comma mean in your reading? Right—pause. After each locomotor movement you'll pause. Your sequence will be travel, pause; travel, pause; travel, freeze. Practice your movement sentence until you can do it the same way three times.

Children whose reading level reflects ways to end a sentence enjoy freezing with an image of a period, an exclamation, or a question mark.

ASSESSMENT EXAMPLE
from the National Standards of Physical Education

Event task—observational record

Students are asked to design and practice a movement sequence of three different locomotor skills. Following the practice period, students demonstrate their movement sequence for the class.

Criteria for Assessment

a. Demonstrates three different locomotor movements

b. Demonstrates mature pattern of each locomotor skill

c. Demonstrates smooth transitions between locomotor patterns

NASPE (1995, p. 19)

MOVING TO RHYTHMS

Setting: Children scattered throughout general space

Cues	
Heads Up	(Keep your head up for good balance and to avoid collisions with others.)
Pause and Go	(Pause momentarily; then continue your locomotor movement.)

Tasks/Challenges:

🅣 Listen to the drumbeat. I'll beat a cadence of one, two, three, four, and then you'll clap the same. Listen. (*Beat drum four times in even rhythm.*) Now clap. Walking and running are both even rhythms. Let's try again. Listen, then clap.

🅣 Let's walk the rhythm of the beat. Listen to the speed. (*Beat four times in even rhythm, slowly.*) Ready? Walk as I beat the drum. Clap as you walk.

🅣 You'll need to walk more quickly or slowly now, depending on the beat of the drum. I'll pause between each segment so you can hear the change in rhythm.

🅣 Now run to the beat of the drum. It's an even rhythm but a faster speed. Be sure you listen for the beat. Ready, go.

TRAVELING IN CONFINED SPACES

Setting: Large marker cones designating general space for travel; children scattered throughout this space

Cues	
Heads Up	(Keep your head up for good balance and to avoid collisions with others.)
Open Spaces	(Look for open spaces as you travel.)
Speed Check	(Slow your speed slightly to avoid others.)

Tasks/Challenges:

🅣 For today's class, the area inside the cones is your city, and you cannot go out of the city until class is over. Travel throughout the city in any locomotor pattern you wish.

🅣 This time, the city has begun to shrink and will keep doing so—so watch the cones. *Begin to move the cones closer in as the children become more adept at moving without bumping into each other or falling down.*

TRAVELING WITH MUSIC

Setting: Children scattered throughout general space; music with appropriate even and uneven beats for different locomotor movements; hoops, one per child, at the edge of the space

Cues	
Heads Up	(Keep your head up for good balance and to avoid collisions with others.)
Balanced Stops	(Spread your feet apart and lower your hips slightly to maintain your balance when you stop.)

Tasks/Challenges:

🅣 Walk, skip, gallop, or hop throughout general space without touching anyone else. Remember, you may have to move to the right or left to avoid bumping into someone else. When I give the signal, stop quickly with both your feet on the floor.

🅣 I've selected music for each of our locomotor movements. The first is for skipping. Listen to the beat. Is it an even or uneven rhythm? Right, skipping is an uneven rhythm. Begin skipping when you hear the music. Stop when the music stops.

🅣 Now listen to the music for the gallop; it's also uneven (*Pause, play music.*) Ready? Gallop.

🅣 The music for hopping is short and quick. Clap the rhythm. Is it even or uneven? Hop on one foot to the music.

🅣 I've saved your favorite locomotor movement until last. What is it? Running. Run quietly so you'll hear the music stop.

Children tend to practice only their favorite locomotor skill when the task is open. We find it helps to specify each skill in addition to "your choice" or "your favorite."

🅣 This is a game like musical chairs, except that you are never out. When the music begins, travel

Figure 19.10 An obstacle course.

Bamboo pole placed on milk crates

Table

Hoop placed on floor

Low balance beam

Hoop placed on milk crates

throughout the whole space using the traveling action that I call out. When the music stops find a space inside a hoop as quickly as possible. Each time I will remove some of the hoops. The trick is that someone must be in every hoop, but any number of people can be inside the hoops when there are not enough left.

TRAVELING AN OBSTACLE COURSE

Setting: An obstacle course of hoops, bamboo poles, low beams, and other items (Figure 19.10).

Cues	
Heads Up	(Keep your head up for good balance and to avoid collisions with others.)
Pause, Look, Go	(Pause momentarily to avoid others who are also moving.)

Tasks/Challenges:

🅣 You've worked on various locomotor skills and on moving with control. Using a combination of a hop, skip, gallop, leap, walk, and slide, move through the obstacle course without touching other people, the hoops, or the bamboo poles.

TRAVELING IN DIFFERENT DIRECTIONS

Setting: Children scattered throughout general space

Cues	
Heads Up	(Keep your head up for good balance and to avoid collisions with others.)
Hips over Feet	(Keep your body centered over your feet for good balance and quick changes of direction.)

Tasks/Challenges:

🅣 You have learned six directions. Let's name them together: forward, backward, right, left, up, and down. This time as you walk, run, or hop, change directions as you travel.

🅣 Begin walking forward. On the signal, change directions and walk backward. Exaggerate your movements so you look like a toy soldier or robot.

🅣 On the signal, run in a forward direction. When you hear the drum, slow your speed, and run to the side or backward. Take only a few steps; then continue running forward.

🅣 Pretend you're going to draw a square with one foot. Hop forward, backward, to the right, and to the left to draw your square.

🅒 This time, we will really see how well you can travel in different directions. I will call out a traveling action and a number. If the number is even, travel forward; if it is odd, travel backward.

Remember to do this task only with students who know the difference between odd and even numbers. It can be quite embarrassing for students not to know how to travel because of their math skills.

SLIDESTEPPING

Setting: Children scattered throughout general space

Cues	
Heads Up	(Keep your head up for good balance and to avoid collisions with others.)
Hips over Feet	(Keep your body centered over your feet for good balance and quick changes of direction.)

Tasks/Challenges:

🅣 Use a sliding action (a slidestep) to travel toward the far end of the field. On the signal, change the direction of your slidestep.

🅣 Using the slidestep, travel eight steps to the right, then eight steps to the left. Stop and balance on one foot. Repeat eight steps to the left, eight steps to the right. Stop and balance in a wide shape. This combination of travel and balances is the ingredients of the folk dance "Seven Jumps." Many folk dances use this slidestep.

🅒 In a small group of four, six, or eight persons, use a combination of slidesteps and balances to create your own version of "Seven Jumps." Practice with your group until you are ready to show the dance to the class. We will then videotape the dances for your portfolios.

 With the establishment of criteria, videotape is an excellent means for assessing children's work. Refer to Chapter 14 for details on assessment.

TRAVELING IN DIFFERENT PATHWAYS

Setting: Children scattered in general space

Cues	
Heads Up	(Keep your head up for good balance and to avoid collisions with others.)
Hips over Feet	(Keep your body centered over your feet for good balance with changes in direction and/or pathways.)

Tasks/Challenges:

🅣 A while ago you learned three different pathways. Who remembers what they were? That's right:

straight, curved, and zigzag. This time, change your pathway as you travel. Begin by walking in a straight pathway. On the signal, change to a curved pathway. **Exaggerate your movements so that the pathway is really quite curved.**

🅣 This time, practice traveling in a zigzag pathway. **Remember, zigzag looks like the letter Z; make really sharp angles.**

🅣 On the signal, begin traveling in a straight path. You may use any form of traveling that you wish. When you hear the drum, change to another pathway. The next time you hear the drum, change your pathway again.

🅣 This will be a test of how well you can travel using the different pathways. The game is like Follow the Leader. When I say "Go," find a partner whose skill in traveling is about the same as yours. Go. Now, the shorter one of you will be the first leader. You are to travel using any traveling action you like and as many different pathways as possible. The follower will try to copy your every move. But don't make it so hard that your follower can't possibly keep up with you. Make it a fun game. When you hear the signal, you must be able to stop without falling over or touching each other. After three times as a leader, switch positions.

THE LOCOMOTORS DANCE

Setting: Class divided into groups of five to eight persons; paper and pencil for each group

Cues	
Heads Up	(Keep your head up for good balance and to avoid collisions with others.)
Hips over Feet	(Keep your body centered over your feet for good balance with changes in direction and/or pathways.)

Tasks/Challenges:

🅣 You have practiced hopping, skipping, galloping, sliding, leaping, and running. You have traveled in different directions and pathways. In your group, combine the locomotors with directions and pathways to create a dance of locomotors. You will need to decide:

■ the amount of space you'll need
■ a leader or changes in leaders
■ which locomotors and what directions and pathways

When you have created your dance, record it on paper, and practice it several times; then we will watch them. The criteria for observation will be correct execution of the locomotors, cooperative work with your group, and creative ideas in the dance.

THE FOLLOW-ME DANCE

Setting: Instrumental music with a strong beat (e.g., hoedown or country music); children scattered throughout general space, facing the teacher

Cues	
Heads Up	(Keep your head up for good balance and to avoid collisions with others.)
Hips over Feet	(Keep your body centered over your feet for good balance and quick changes of direction.)
Balanced Stops	(Spread your feet apart and lower your hips slightly to maintain your balance when you stop.)

Tasks/Challenges:

T We're going to practice our locomotor skills today; we'll combine the skills with rhythm and keeping the beat in self-space. This is called Follow Me, country western style. Spread throughout general space, facing me. I'll move to the right, the left, forward, and backward. You'll mirror my direction. So if I go left, you go right; if I go forward, you go backward. I'll hop, jump, gallop, slide, walk, and move in other ways. After each locomotor phrase, you'll stop in self-space and do such things as touch your hands to your heels, nod your head forward and backward, cross your knees as in a Charleston, and so on. You only need to watch and follow me.

Keep all activities in a count of eight—for example, eight slides to the left, eight slides to the right, stop, touch hands to heels in time with the music; one, two, three, four, five, six, seven, eight; gallop forward eight steps, gallop backward eight steps, stop, clap hands in time with the music: one, two, three, four, five, six, seven, eight.

TRAVELING AT DIFFERENT SPEEDS

Setting: Sheets of newspaper stacked at the edge of the gymnasium; children scattered throughout general space

Cues	
Heads Up	(Keep your head up for good balance and to avoid collisions with others.)
Pause and Go	(Check your speed slightly to avoid others.)

Tasks/Challenges:

T Each of you will need one sheet of newspaper. After you get your sheet, unfold it and place it against your chest, holding it at your shoulders. At the signal, begin running; you'll no longer have to hold your newspaper. What will happen to the newspaper when you stop running? Ready, go.

T Try running at different speeds, sometimes very fast, sometimes very slowly, to see if the paper will stay up.

TRAVELING USING DIFFERENT DIRECTIONS, LEVELS, PATHWAYS, AND LOCATIONS

Setting: Several sets of task cards: one set that names single locomotor actions (e.g., walk, run, or hop); a second set that names different directions; a third set that names different levels; a fourth set that names different locations (general and self-space); and a final set that names different pathways. *It is helpful to color-code the different sets.*

Cues	
Heads Up	(Keep your head up for good balance and to avoid collisions with others.)
Hips over Feet	(Keep your body centered over your feet for good balance with changes in direction and/or pathways.)

Tasks/Challenges:

T Choose a card from each color (stack), and return to your self-space. You are going to travel using the directions on the cards you have. For example, if your cards say "Walk," "Backward," "Low," and "General Space," you walk backward at a low level in general space.

T This time, change one card of the same color with the person next to you. Now move according to the new directions.

The combinations here are endless. You could trade as many cards as you like until the children have practiced a multitude of combinations.

C With the last set of cards that you have, practice the action until you think it is so clear that anyone could figure it out just by watching you. (*Give children time to practice.*) Now, when I say "Go," choose a partner whom you can work with well. Show your partner your sequence, and see whether he or she can guess what your cards said. Now, switch: Watch your partner's sequence, and you guess.

CHANGING SPEEDS TO MUSIC

Setting: Recordings of music at 78, 33, and 16 rpm or variable speed control; children scattered throughout general space

Cues

Heads Up	(Keep your head up for good balance and to avoid collisions with others.)
Speed Check	(Slow your speed slightly to avoid others.)
Balanced Stops	(Spread your feet apart and lower your hips slightly to maintain your balance when you stop.)

Tasks/Challenges:

T Listen to the music; it will start slowly and gradually increase in speed to a fast rhythm. Do you think you can run with a gradual increase and decrease in your speed? Match your running speed with the music. Begin slowly and gradually increase to your fastest speed; as the music begins to slow, decrease your speed to a jogging pace.

A DANCE OF WATER, STEAM, AND ICE

Setting: Children scattered throughout general space

Cues

Pause and Go	(Pause between actions to emphasize changes.)
Exaggerate	(Exaggerate movements and shapes for emphasis.)

Tasks/Challenges:

T Let's think about how water changes form as the temperature changes. At normal temperature, water is a liquid whose molecules are moving at a medium speed. As the temperature increases, the water molecules move faster and faster until the water is transformed into steam. As the temperature decreases, the molecules move more and more slowly until they finally freeze, forming ice. Let's put this story into a creative dance. As I tell the story, you'll travel with changes in speed as the molecules increase their speed, decrease their speed, and freeze.

SLOW-MOTION REPLAY: THE SPORTS DANCE

Setting: Children scattered throughout general space

Cues

Pause and Go	(Pause between actions to emphasize changes.)
Exaggerate	(Exaggerate movements and shapes for emphasis.)

Tasks/Challenges:

T Think about how the players move when a film is shown in slow motion or when the sports announcer replays a special segment from a game. I want each of you to think of your favorite moment in a sport. Is it when the quarterback breaks away to run for a touchdown, or was it when you scored the winning soccer goal? Perhaps it was the throw of the javelin at the Olympics or the relay team running at the track meet. Decide what kind of locomotor movement would portray your favorite moment. Combine your movements as in a slow motion replay. How would you begin—in what position? How will the replay end? Practice the segment until you can do it three times the same way, just like a replay. Remember, it's slow motion. We'll look at the movements when you're ready.

Other ideas for creative dance and travel include walking through a thick jungle, walking through a completely dark and haunted house, walking on the ledge of an eighty-story building, traveling across a high wire on a windy day, traveling during an earthquake.

COMBINATION LOCOMOTORS

Line dances, as well as traditional folk and square dances, are combinations of locomotor skills and nonlocomotor body actions. While there are excellent resources available for the teaching of such dances (see Chapter 20, Box 20.3),

BOX 19.3   THE GRAPEVINE STEP

The grapevine step is used in many line dances as well as in intermediate folk dances; it may be done to the right or to the left. Children enjoy combining it with forward and backward steps and turns to create new dances.

Cue: Front, Side, Back, Side

Count 1: Cross right foot over in front of left foot.
Count 2: Step to left on left foot.
Count 3: Cross right foot behind left foot.
Count 4: Step to left on left foot.

The Grapevine Step

we encourage our students—and you as teachers—to create new line, square, and folk dances. See Boxes 19.3 and 19.4.

▶ Folk dances are combinations of locomotors—combinations into specific steps, changes in directions, and partner/group formations. Here are some examples of beginning and intermediate folk dances appropriate for elementary-age children with no previous dance experience:

Beginning Dances	Intermediate Dances
Seven Jumps (Denmark)	Virginia Reel (United States)
Greensleeves (England)	Gustav's Skol (Sweden)
Cshebogar (Hungary)	Kavelis (Lithuania)
Jump Jim Joe (United States)	LaRaspa (Mexico)
Teton Mountain Stomp (United States)	Troika (Russia)
Kinderpolka (Germany)	Mayim! Mayim! (Israel)

Utilization Level: Learning Experiences Leading to Skill Development

The learning experiences in this section challenge children to travel in increasingly complex ways. Tasks are designed to develop the travel skills used in many dance, game, and gymnastics sequences.

A note about cues: Although several cues are listed for many of the learning experiences, it's important to focus on only one cue at a time. That way, the children can really concentrate on that cue. Once you provide feedback to the children and observe that most have learned a cue, then it's time to focus on another one.

TRAVELING WITH A PARTNER: MATCHING PATHWAYS

Setting: Sets of partners scattered throughout general space

BOX 19.4   THE MARGIE DANCE

Description: This line dance was choreographed in honor of Margie Hanson and presented at a retirement tribute for her at the 1992 American Alliance for Health, Physical Education, Recreation and Dance (AAHPERD) National Convention.

Music: "I'd Like to Teach the World to Sing," Metromedia Records, KMD1051.

Formation: Lines

Counts and Steps:
1-2—Introduction, sway with body or hands.
3-4—Hands in air and sway to the right, left, right, and left.
5-8—Walk to right and give a high five greeting on step 8.
1-4—Walk to left and give a high five greeting on step 4.
5-8—Hands in air and sway to the right, left, right, and left.
1-4—Join and raise hands.
5-8—Lower hands.
1-4—"Thank you" in sign language (see illustration below), two times.
5-8—"I love you" in sign language (hold two middle fingers down and keep pinky, index finger, and thumb up) and raise hands.

Repeat dance three more times. At the end, hug your neighbors in this world and give them some N and G's, which means tell them some nice and good things.

"Thank you" in sign language

SOURCE: From *Rhythmic Activities and Dance* (pp. 87–88) by J. P. Bennett and P. C. Riemer, 1995, Champaign, IL: Human Kinetics.

Cue

Heads Up   (Keep your head up for good balance and to avoid collisions with others.)

Tasks/Challenges:

🅣 Stand back to back with a partner. When I say "Go," each partner travels in the direction he or she is facing. That is, each of you travels away from your partner. When you hear the drum, stop, turn around, and return to your partner with the exact pattern and locomotor movements you used before (*Figure 19.11*). Return at the same speed you used to travel away from your partner.

🅣 Earlier you learned that there are three pathways. (*See "Space Awareness," Chapter 16.*) What are they?

Figure 19.11 Traveling in pathways away from and toward a partner.

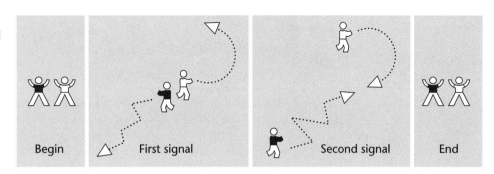

Begin   First signal   Second signal   End

(*Ask for answers.*) All patterns are made up of those pathways or combinations of those pathways. This time as you travel away from your partner, be aware of the pathways you use. On your return, copy the same pathways.

🅣 Stand beside your partner. This time as you travel, use a slidestep to move away from your partner. Remember to return using the same pathway.

🅣 Select a partner, and decide who's to be the first leader. When the follower says "Go," the leader travels across the field with a combination of straight, curved, and zigzag pathways. When the leader stops, the follower then travels the same pattern. The other partner then designs the pattern. (*For tips on helping children learn to design floor patterns for dance, see Box 19.5.*)

THE COPY CAT DANCE

Setting: Music, such as "Dueling Banjos," that features copy phrases; sets of partners scattered throughout general space.

Cue

Heads Up (Keep your head up for good balance and to avoid collisions with others.)

Tasks/Challenges:

🅣 Earlier this year you practiced traveling with a partner, copying pathways. This time you will copy not only pathways with your partner, but also locomotors and directions. For your beginning, you may choose to stand beside or behind your partner. Partner A will travel away from Partner B as the first phrase of music plays; Partner B will then travel with the exact pattern and locomotor. The dance continues as one partner leads and the other copies. Listen to the phrases of the music to time the length of your travel.

TRAVELING WITH A PARTNER: CHANGING SPEED AND DIRECTION

Setting: Sets of partners scattered throughout general space

Cues

Heads Up   (Keep your head up for good balance and to avoid collisions with others.)
On Your Toes (Keep your weight on the balls of your feet for quickness.)

Tasks/Challenges:

🅣 Stand facing a partner approximately three feet apart: One of you is the leader; the other, the follower. The leader slides to the right or left, changing directions quickly. The follower tries to stay directly across from the leader at all times. I'll give the signal every sixty seconds for you both to switch positions. Note that by adding dribbling a ball and defensive arm position to this pattern, we form an offensive-defensive drill in basketball.

SHADOWING

Setting: Sets of partners scattered throughout general space

Cues

Heads Up   (Keep your head up for good balance and to avoid collisions with others.)
On Your Toes (Keep your weight on the balls of your feet for quickness.)

Tasks/Challenges:

🅣 Choose a partner whose speed and ability to change directions are very similar to yours. Partner

BOX 19.5   DESIGNING FLOOR PATTERNS FOR DANCE

The floor patterns created in dance experiences and the locomotor movements used are important components of creative dance. The patterns created as the dancer moves can tell a story, set a mood, or portray an idea. The various ways of travel used in dance and the patterns created aren't accidental; they're planned and carefully designed. When designing the travel pattern of a dance, teacher and children can focus upon the following concerns:

1. What idea stimulated the dance? Was it a music selection? A bullfight? A wiggly snake?
2. What qualities are inherent in the theme of the dance or the music selection? Is the tempo slow, moderate, or fast? Is the rhythm even or uneven? Is the music harmonious? Vibrant? Mellow?
3. What pathway best expresses the feelings or emotions you sense? Advancing, attacking? Retreating? Collapsing? Gathering? Departing? Wavy? Angular? Jagged?

It's a good idea to have the children keep notes and diagram their pathways as they design them, for several reasons. First, they will clearly visualize what the floor pattern looks like and be better able to evaluate its suitability for the dance. Second, children usually use several classes to put together a completed dance and often fail to remember ideas they had in earlier classes. Third, when children finish a dance, they take with them a written record of their accomplishments.

It's often beneficial to post several examples of pathways around the room on the walls, to give children an idea of what's expected. Another effective teaching aid is to post drawings of locomotor skills and positions of stillness that the children have experienced. Rather than trying to diagram a sequence from memory, youngsters can look at these posters and select movements to incorporate along their floor patterns.

Even those of us with no artistic abilities can trace beautiful diagrams using an opaque projector!

Zigzag path   Straight path   Curved path

1 stands approximately two feet behind partner 2. When I say "Go," partner 2 travels quickly, changing directions with sharp turns to the right and to the left; partner 1 attempts to stay within an arm's distance at all times. When you hear the drum hit, stop without colliding or losing your balance. Partner 1 now stands in front, ready to be the new leader. Keep your eyes on your partner's waist when you're the follower.

MEETING AND PARTING WHILE TRAVELING WITH A PARTNER

Setting: Sets of partners scattered throughout general space

Cue	
Heads Up	(Keep your head up for good balance and to avoid collisions with others.)

Tasks/Challenges:

🅣 This task is called Leapin' Lizards. On the signal, you are to travel throughout the general space. On the cue "Leapin' Lizards," find a partner as quickly as possible, travel side by side for a few steps, then leap in unison and split up to continue traveling using the new pattern I call out. The next time you hear the signal, find a new partner, travel and do two leaps, then split to travel in a new way. We will continue until the number of leaps gets to five.

🅣 This time, instead of partners find a group of three whenever you hear the cue. Make sure all of you leap at the same time. With a larger group it is harder to coordinate your leaps. It might help if one person calls out "One, two, three, leap."

PERFORMING RHYTHMICAL PATTERNS

Setting: Hoops, one per child, scattered throughout general space

Cues	
Heads Up	(Keep your head up for good balance.)
Soft Landings	(Bend your knees for a soft landing.)

Tasks/Challenges:

🅣 Jump in and out of your hoop with a four-four rhythm: two jumps in, two jumps out, or three jumps in, one jump out. Maintain an even tempo by clapping the four counts as you jump.

I'll clap the rhythm I want you to use for your jumps: one, two, three, four. Let's all clap the rhythm together before we begin our jumps. (*Group practices with teacher as leader.*)

🅒 Practice until you can match the rhythm three times with no mistakes.

🅣 Try your jumping pattern in and out of the hoop with the music. Remember, you may choose a three-one or a two-two pattern in and out.

TRAVELING TO EXPRESS AGE: THE FOUNTAIN OF YOUTH DANCE

Setting: Children scattered throughout general space

Cue	
Exaggerate	(Exaggerate your actions and gestures for expression.)

Tasks/Challenges:

🅣 Using combinations of locomotor movements, body language, and gestures, tell the story of an old, old person who discovers the Fountain of Youth. Let me set the stage for you. An old, old person is walking down the street. The person feels weary, tired, without enough energy to hold his or her head high. While walking down the street, the oldster sees a bottle in a gutter. An examination of the bottle reveals the words Fountain of Youth Juice. Puzzled, hesitant, yet desperate, the oldster takes a drink and then a few more. The transformation begins. . . . The old person is changed into an ecstatic youth who dances merrily down the street. Think of the following as you prepare your dance:

What type of movements would the old person use? Jerky or smooth? Slow or fast?
What body posture and what hand gestures would the old person assume?
How would the oldster approach the bottle?
Will the transformation occur quickly or be rather slowly executed?

How would you contrast the oldster's movements with those of the ecstatic youth: type of travel, speed, level, gestures?

TRAVELING IN BOUND AND FREE FLOW

Setting: Children scattered throughout general space

Cues

Exaggerate	(Exaggerate your actions and gestures for expression.)
Free Flow	(Unstoppable from beginning to end)
Bound Flow	(Jerky; stoppable at any moment)

Tasks/Challenges:

🅣 Here are two additional ideas for short dance phrases based on imaginary situations. First, a rag doll comes to life for a brief period of time. One interpretation is that the rag doll slowly comes to life with jerky, uncoordinated (bound) movements, falls over, and has trouble gaining control and balance; the doll gradually improves and is then running and leaping, turning in the air (free), and enjoying life. Then the doll suddenly stops, slowly walks back to the starting location, sits and sighs, freezes, and is a doll once again.

🅣 Second, a balloon filled with helium escapes from the hands of its owner, floats across the sky, leaks, and falls back to earth.

These types of dance experiences are often short, culminating the practice of travel patterns. Discuss with the children the travel qualities and movement concepts (space awareness, effort) appropriate for each activity. Each dance should have a clear beginning, rise to a climax, and then wind down to a conclusion.

TRAVELING TO TOM FOOLERY RHYMES

Setting: Children divided into groups of four; Tom Foolery rhymes written on cards and placed around the room, enough cards for one per group. *Some children may be able to write their own rhymes.*

Cues

Exaggerate	(Exaggerate your actions and gestures for expression.)
Free Flow	(Unstoppable from beginning to end)
Bound Flow	(Jerky; stoppable at any moment)

Tasks/Challenges:

🅣 In your group, make up a humorous sequence to the rhythmic pattern of the Tom Foolery rhyme written on your card. You decide the rhythm of the chant and the locomotor patterns you'll use to accompany the rhyme. Travel around the room with your chosen locomotor patterns, chanting the rhyme as you go.

Here are the Tom Foolery rhymes:

Soft feet, gentle, quick run:
    Pit-a-pat, pit-a-pat, pit-a-pat, jump back!

Swaying, rocking steps:
    See-Saw Mar-ger-y Daw,
    Jack shall have a new mas-ter.
    He shall have but a pen-ny a day,
    Be-cause he won't work an-y fast-er.

Skipping:
    Here's a word to the wise:
    Don't get soap in your eyes!
    I hope the dope who thought up soap
    Has to eat it—I repeat it, Eat It!

Bouncy jumps:
    Boinggg, boinggg, boingg, boingg, boingg, bammmm!

Proficiency Level: Learning Experiences Leading to Skill Development

The following learning experiences encourage youngsters to use their travel skills and knowledge of travel patterns in combination with other skills to design and perform dances, gymnastics routines, and strategic game maneuvers.

A note about cues: Although several cues are listed for many of the learning experiences, it's important to focus on only one cue at a time. That way, the children can really concentrate on that cue. Once you provide feedback to the children and observe that most have learned a cue, then it's time to focus on another one.

DEPICTING PRIMITIVE TRIBES THROUGH TRAVEL

Setting: Class divided into two groups

Tasks/Challenges:

Ⓣ Dance can be a story without words. You're going to tell the story of primitive tribes through shapes and actions. (*Show children cave drawings of tribal dances.*) Use your imagination as you look at the drawings. How do you think these people lived? What was their work? What was home like for them—did they have a home? Now let's put your ideas into movement terms. At what level would the people move? Would their movements be flowing or sustained, jerky or smooth?

Your dance will tell the story of two primitive tribes. Part 1 of your dance will show how the people live as a group. Show through your movements and gestures the life of a person in a primitive tribe. Part 2 of your dance will portray the two tribes discovering each other, their fear of the unknown, and their battle to defend their territory. In Part 2, each group begins with the movements portraying preparation for battle. The battle will consist of approach, attack (*with no contact*), and a retreat.

The following questions will help you design your movements for this dance story:

1. Will your travel be fast or slow when preparing for battle, approaching the enemy, retreating from the battle?
2. How can your gestures best represent the punching, jabbing, kicking, slashing actions of battle?
3. Will your travel be low, with angular actions, or high and smooth?
4. As you retreat from battle, how will your travel show caution, fear, injury?

TRAVELING TO SHOW TRADITION VERSUS CHANGE

Setting: Class divided into two groups

Tasks/Challenges:

Ⓣ Dance doesn't always tell a story. Sometimes dance is a study in form—the shapes we can make with our bodies, the spatial patterns we create as a group. Group 1 will represent tradition. The characteristics of tradition your body shapes and group travel can show might be a firm, solid shape, such

as a square, the group forms; identical and simultaneous group movements; use of a small amount of space; and firm, sustained quality—control at all times.

Group 2 will represent the forces of change. The characteristics of change include individualized shapes, travel in different directions, use of a large amount of space, and a variety of movements. Working together as a group, design a dance that combines at least five shapes and three locomotor patterns to portray the characteristics of your group.

When we look at the tradition group, we should see oneness, sturdiness, caution; the shapes and actions of the change group should portray individuality, risk taking, and freedom.

Dance that tells a story can easily become only pantomime. Children will need guidance in avoiding exactly replicating gestures and using more total body movement and space.

PERFORMING RHYTHMICAL PATTERNS: TINIKLING

Setting: Sets of tinikling poles, approximately twelve feet in length, either made from bamboo poles or purchased commercially. Each set of poles will accommodate four children—two for tapping the poles and two for jumping (Figure 19.12).

Cues	
Weight Balanced over Poles	(Keep your shoulders and hips over the poles.)
Feet In, In, Out, Out	(Your feet go inside, inside the poles, then outside, outside the poles.)

Tasks/Challenges:

Ⓣ Tinikling is a rhythmical activity that involves coordinated stepping, hopping, jumping actions with the tapping of long bamboo poles. In the beginning position, the bamboo poles are approximately two feet apart; they're tapped down on the floor twice: tap, tap. The poles are then brought together for two counts: tap, tap. This pattern is

Figure 19.12   Basic tinikling setup.

repeated: apart, apart, together, together. This opening and closing position is maintained while dancers step or jump in and out without touching the poles. Let's do the action of the poles with our hands; clap the rhythm with me: out, out, in, in. (*Demonstrate with your hands apart, apart, together, together.*) This is the action of the bamboo poles for all our tinikling skills: out, out, in, in.

T Divide into groups of four. Two persons clap the four-four rhythm; the other two persons practice the tapping action with the poles.

We find it helps to tape the ends of the poles where the children grip them to prevent the bamboo poles from cracking and pinching the children's fingers.

T You now know how to clap the four-four rhythm and to tap the bamboo poles to that rhythm. Now you'll learn the basic single-step pattern.

Stand on your left foot; hop two times on your left foot. Step on your right foot between the lines; transfer your weight to your left foot between the lines. Hop on your right foot two times outside the

Figure 19.13 shows the single-step pattern. Have the children stand outside the parallel tape lines on the floor. Their right sides should be toward the tape lines.

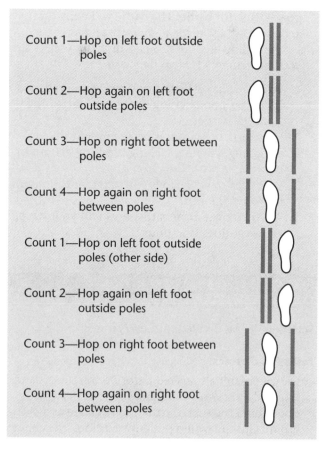

Count 1—Hop on left foot outside poles

Count 2—Hop again on left foot outside poles

Count 3—Hop on right foot between poles

Count 4—Hop again on right foot between poles

Count 1—Hop on left foot outside poles (other side)

Count 2—Hop again on left foot outside poles

Count 3—Hop on right foot between poles

Count 4—Hop again on right foot between poles

Figure 19.13   Tinikling: single-step pattern.

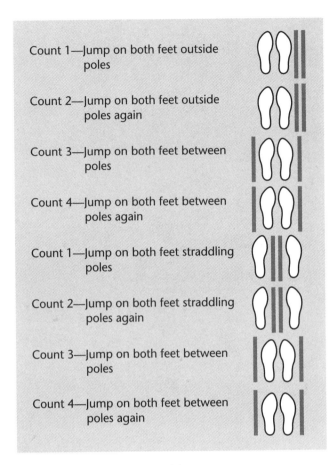

Figure 19.14   Tinikling: double-step pattern.

Count 1—Hop on left foot outside poles

Count 2—Hop again on left foot outside poles

Count 3—Step on right foot between poles

Count 4—Step on left foot between poles

Count 1—Hop on right foot outside poles

Count 2—Hop again on right foot outside poles

Count 3—Step on left foot between poles

Count 4—Step on right foot between poles

Figure 19.15   Tinikling: hopping.

lines. Repeat the action to the left. Clap the four-four beat as you hop.

C Practice until you can perform the pattern four times with no mistakes. You'll then be ready to practice the single-step pattern with two persons tapping the poles. Remember, your feet go in, in, out, out while the poles go out, out, in, in.

T After you feel comfortable with the single-step pattern, try the double-step or the hopping pattern (*Figures 19.14 and 19.15*). When you're really good, you can create a new pattern with a four-four or three-four beat.

Students with advanced tinikling skills enjoy the action with four poles—two poles crossed over two poles—and the combination of basic tinikling actions with gymnastics stunts, for example, cartwheels and walkovers between the poles as they move apart.

TRAVELING IN GAMES AND SPORTS

The ability to travel in games is often what separates the skilled player from the average player. Many children can throw and catch accurately and with control while they're stationary, but they regress to a precontrol level when travel is added. Thus, traveling is an important part of the utilization and proficiency sections of the games skills chapters. Games-related tasks that incorporate traveling are discussed in Chapter 21, "Chasing, Fleeing, and Dodging," and in Chapters 26 through 30: "Kicking and Punting," "Throwing and Catching," "Volleying and Dribbling," "Striking with Rackets and Paddles," and "Striking with Long-Handled Implements," respectively.

Figure 19.16 Children's travel patterns in gymnastics.

Leah, Missy, Heather, Sheri,

1. curved to start
   – come up and cartwheel one at a time
2. Turn and Roll.
3. Turn and ½ split
4. Get up and cartwheel
5. Neal down and roll
6. Jump up – Run and Leap.
7. Run – cartwheel – Run
8. Run a little and Leap
9. End two go out 10 steps and turn
   Cartwheel into pair – Curl-up and end.

TRAVELING IN GYMNASTICS

Traveling in gymnastics supplies the buildup of force necessary for many Olympic stunts, for example, handsprings and roundoffs (Figure 19.16). The floor patterns the travel creates form an important component of gymnastics routines. Travel in relation to gymnastics is discussed in Chapters 22, 23, and 24: "Jumping and Landing," "Balancing," and "Transferring Weight and Rolling," respectively.

READING COMPREHENSION QUESTIONS

1. What components of traveling are taught in a program of physical education for children?
2. What does "naturally developing skill" mean? List two examples.
3. List the fundamental locomotor skills that emerge from the walk-run pattern.
4. Describe a mature running pattern. Do all children have mature running patterns? Do all adults? Explain.

5. What are the differences among a hop, a leap, a slide, and a gallop?
6. Describe how travel is studied at the proficiency level in games, gymnastics, and dance.
7. How can you use a Tom Foolery rhyme to stimulate different ways of traveling?
8. What is tinikling?

REFERENCES

Bennett, J. P., & Riemer, P. C. (1995). *Rhythmic activities and dance.* Champaign, IL: Human Kinetics.

National Association for Sport and Physical Education (NASPE). (1995). *Moving into the future: National standards for physical education.* St. Louis, MO: Mosby.

Wickstrom, R. L. (1977). *Fundamental motor patterns,* 2nd ed. Philadelphia: Lea & Febiger.

CHAPTER 20   Skill Themes in Dance

One of the great values in the education of children comes from the experience of making their own forms to express, to communicate, to enjoy. Each child is unique in his individualism and in his environment. He needs a chance to say what he is, how he feels, what his world means to him.

——Ruth L. Murray

Movement skills and concepts form the curricular base for elementary physical education. Dance, educational gymnastics, and games/sports skills are the content areas through which these skills and concepts are explored, mastered, and applied. The development of the curricular content for the movement skills and concepts—that is, the skill themes—is found in Chapters 16–19, 21–24, and 26–30 of this text. Guidance on teaching these skill themes within the content areas of dance, gymnastics, and games/sports is found in Chapters 20, 25, and 31.

Movement skills and concepts would be of little value to the mover without the applications that challenge the learner. Skill themes would lose their richness without their infusion into games, gymnastics, and dance. We have chosen to place this chapter addressing skill themes in dance immediately after the skill theme of traveling due to the large number of tasks and challenges within "Traveling" (Chapter 19) as well as the concept chapters of "Space Awareness," "Effort," and "Relationships" (Chapters 16–18) that relate directly to dance. Other skill theme chapters with direct linkages to dance include "Chasing, Fleeing, and Dodging" and "Jumping and Landing" (Chapters 21–22), with less direct linkages in "Balancing" and "Transferring Weight and Rolling" (Chapters 23–24).

Dance is probably the most difficult teaching area, for the same reason that games teaching is the easiest. Most teachers have an extensive background in games playing, but few teachers have experience as dancers. And most of us do teach best what we know best. Many teachers, because of their limited background in dance, omit dance altogether or have only a few dance experiences in their programs. Others shy away from teaching dance, unsure of children's reactions and fearing a negative response from the class. Yet one needs only to teach Theresa Purcell's "Spaghetti Dance" (1994, pp. 83–86) to realize that the dance is as much fun for the teacher as for the children actively involved in spaghetti that "moves in a box, jumps in boiling water, and slithers down a wall."

None of the authors of this book is a dancer, yet each of us has learned to give children exciting, interesting, and educational dance experiences. In fact, dance has become one of the most enjoyable areas for

BOX 20.1 THE MOVEMENT MOVEMENT

When we are children most of us can run and tumble and roll in the grass. We can yell and laugh and cry. We can sing our inner songs and dance our personal dances. Our feelings are visible in our actions. When we're unhappy, we stomp and mope. When we're happy we turn cartwheels and splash in puddles. Our imaginations have a direct line to our arms and legs. We can take giant steps and be giants. We can flap our arms and they will fly us away over houses and mountains. We can do all of this and more, for a while.

And then, somewhere between five and twenty, we stop.

We stop running just for the fun of it. We stop letting out the shouts and belly laughs. We stop looking at the treetops and start walking the city sidewalks staring at the pavement. We begin, somewhere along the line, to "keep a stiff upper lip," to put "starch" in our spines, to speak softly and when spoken to. Our behavior becomes "acceptable" and, in the process, we are cut off bit by bit from ourselves and therefore from each other. If my impulses can't get through to me, how can I possibly share them with you? As we lose touch with our bodies, our heads take over and begin to monitor our actions, to restrict our responses until the simple interaction of chil-

dren becomes an elaborate and inaccurate communication system between Brain A and Brain B.

Jules Feiffer pictures one of these disconnected, clever heads floating around complaining about its headless, funny-looking, malfunctioning body. "It's lucky," Feiffer's head says, "that I need my body to carry my head around . . . otherwise . . . out it would go."

Too drastic.

We can fit our heads back onto our bodies. We can rediscover the links between the headbone and the toebones. We can regain the freedom to spread our arms out wide; to run and shout without feeling awkward or embarrassed. We can learn to fall down, jump up, and bend over without breaking. We can unlock the sounds of our sadness and our joy. We can tune in to the beat of our pulse and stamp our feet to our inborn sense of rhythm. We can explore the sounds and the gestures of our feelings and our dreams. We can reclaim our bodies and our voices; free them to rediscover our inherent sense of balance and design, and use them to show each other who we are and what we hope to be.

SOURCE: "The Movement Movement," by Ken Jenkins, in *California Living: The Magazine of the San Francisco Sunday Examiner and Chronicle,* Jan. 25, 1976, p. 19. Used with permission.

BOX 20.2 DANCE AND THE *NATIONAL STANDARDS FOR PHYSICAL EDUCATION*

The *National Standards for Physical Education* (NASPE, 1995) links to dance in the content statement " . . . opportunities for enjoyment, challenge, self-expression, and social interaction," as well as with " . . . competency in many movement forms and proficiency in a few" and the application of " . . . movement concepts and principles to the learning and development of motor skills."

The following are sample benchmarks for dance in elementary physical education:

- Demonstrates clear contrasts between slow and fast movement while traveling. (K)*
- Combines locomotor patterns in time to music. (2)
- Develops and refines a creative dance sequence into a repeatable pattern. (4)
- Designs . . . dance sequences that are personally interesting. (4)
- Designs and performs . . . dance sequences that combine traveling, rolling, balancing, and weight transfer into smooth flowing sequences with intentional changes in direction, speed, and flow. (6)
- Recognizes the role of . . . dance in getting to know and understand self and others. (6)

*Grade-level guidelines for expected student learning

most of us to teach because of the children's enthusiasm and excitement about dance. We're convinced that individuals who've had a minimum of formal training in dance can learn to teach it successfully.

The Purpose of Dance in Elementary School

One of the keys to providing children with successful dance experiences is to develop an understanding of dance and its purpose in an educational program. When we teach games, our purpose isn't to produce varsity athletes. Similarly, when we teach dance, our purpose isn't to train children to become professional dancers. Few, if any, physical education teachers have the expertise to train children to become professional dancers, and few children want to dance professionally. Dance experiences in physical education classes should give children

1. The ability to use their bodies to express feelings and attitudes about themselves and others
2. A sense of self-satisfaction that can be derived from effectively using one's body as an instrument of expression

3. Enjoyment and appreciation of dance as a worthwhile experience for all, not for just a few
4. An appreciation of dance as an art medium that can have value for both the participant and the spectator
5. The ability to interpret and move to different rhythms

When children begin school, many are still in tune with their bodies as instruments of expression (Box 20.1). The task of the teacher of young children is not so much to teach them how to use their bodies as instruments of expression as to enhance the expressive abilities that the bodies of young children already possess. Sue Stinson (1988) refers to it as rediscovering the magic deep inside and using the magic to transform movement into dance. By helping children at an early age to become aware of how they use their bodies for expressive purposes, we can help each child avoid a mind-body dichotomy. We're able to help children develop an increasing awareness of their bodies as instruments for the expression of feelings and ideas. See Box 20.2 for information on dance in the *National Standards for Physical Education*.

Figure 20.1 The teacher challenges a class to rhythmic movement at high level.

Dance Experiences

Dance experiences for children can be classified into three types: rhythmic experiences; folk, ethnic, or square dances; and creative dance. In rhythmic experiences, children learn about different rhythms; they develop an awareness of rhythm and the ability to move in relation to various beats. In folk/cultural dances, children are taught dances that are part of a society's heritage. These dances are often taught in coordination with classroom studies, for example, the culture of Greece or the pioneer period of American history. In creative/expressive dance, children express feelings and ideas through movement. Whereas folk dance and rhythmic experiences often call for a correct response, there are no right or wrong answers in creative dance. Children are asked to provide interpretations or responses to a particular problem or situation. Individual responses are encouraged; diversity is valued.

Prior to learning structured dance forms, children need experiences in locomotor movements and response to rhythm. They need to move about in free space before they are asked to move within the set formations of circles, squares, and such. They need to move freely in response to their own internal rhythm before moving to music. For these reasons, our focus in dance for young children is on rhythmic experiences and creative dance.

Rhythmic Experiences

Rhythmic experiences for children are designed to assist them in becoming competent and confident in recognizing and moving to rhythm. Children respond to the beat and the tempo of an external rhythm; they walk, skip, and gallop to their internal rhythm and to external rhythms. At the precontrol level, the rhythmic experiences are chosen to reinforce the movement concepts and themes the children are already studying. They may move body parts (head, feet, knees) to a simple beat played on a drum, tambourine, or wood block (Figure 20.1). After experiencing the locomotor movements freely at their own tempo, children may be asked to walk three beats in one direction and change directions on the fourth beat. In this combination of skill (walking) and movement concept (direction), children are now matching the tempo of their movements to that imposed by the external beat. Figure 20.2 illustrates several rhythmic instruments that can be used to provide the beat. Children may echo the beat by moving body parts or swinging the total body at fast or slow tempo to match a verbal rhythm. Moving body parts in self-space in accompaniment to a beat enhances children's body awareness (Figure 20.3).

Once the children are able to move (1) to their internal tempo and (2) to an external beat imposed by the teacher's voice or a simple instrument (e.g., a drum, shaker, clacker), music is introduced. The music should have a steady beat; although it provides the beat for the movements, it should accompany, not dominate, the children.

Once children have grasped the basic concepts of rhythm and are able to respond correctly to different beats, they enjoy the addition of a manipulative to the rhythmic experiences. Streamers, scarves, pizza circles, lummi sticks, and playground balls are examples of equipment that enhances rhythmic experiences for children. Initial activities focus on individual responses to rhythm. Following this exploration phase, teacher-designed routines are used to elicit a group response to a given rhythm. These control-level experiences are

Figure 20.2 Easy-to-make rhythm instruments.

DRUMS

Tin can drum

Remove the top and bottom on any size tin can. Cut two circles, about an inch larger in diameter than the tin can, from an inner tube. Punch about six small holes around the edge of each rubber circle. Place one circle over each end of the can. Tighten by lacing strong string or nylon cord through the holes. Bells or bottle caps may be added for additional sound.

Bleach (or milk) jug drum

Screw top of jug and secure with tape or glue. Hit with dowel rod. The children can decorate the jug with paint or colored tape.

CLACKER

Cut two pieces of board to the same size. Drill holes in one end of each board and join the boards with nylon cord or wire. The children can decorate the boards.

SHAKERS

Tube shaker

Cover one end of an empty paper towel tube with heavy paper or aluminum foil. Fill with small round stones or dried beans. Then cover the other end. The children can decorate the shaker.

Pie pan shaker

Place small round stones or dried beans in an aluminum pie pan. Staple another pie pan of the same diameter onto the top of the first pan.

Balloon shaker

Pour sand, rice, beans, or a combination of these ingredients into a balloon. Partially inflate the balloon and tie the end.

Cup shaker

Partially fill a paper or plastic cup with small stones, beans, or bottle caps. Tape another cup on top of the filled cup.

designed to involve the children in working together as a group, responding correctly to the rhythm, and remembering a sequence of movements and/or actions to be performed. Most of the ideas for our teacher-designed routines come from observing children during their exploration of the manipulative, listening to the music, and matching action to tempo and beat. Rhythmic group routines are excellent for promoting physical education at assemblies, PTA programs, and community functions (see Chapter 32).

The amount of time a teacher can spend on rhyth-mic group routines depends to a great extent on how often physical education is scheduled. When physical education classes meet only twice a week, for example, more time is spent on mastery of the basic skills involved in the rhythmic experiences, for example, rope jumping, ball handling, and such.

Children at the utilization and proficiency levels focus on creating new lummi stick routines, designing individual and partner jump rope routines (Figure 20.4), and using ball-handling skills in routines to music, e.g., Harlem Globetrotters (see Chapter 28).

Figure 20.3 This child travels to the rhythmic pattern played on a rhythm drum by a classmate.

Children at these levels of rhythmic experiences combine various movement qualities and patterns with their manipulative skills, for example, floor patterns, directions, levels, phrases, and variations in rhythm: double time, half time, and so on.

It isn't sufficient for the teacher to say, "Today we're going to design a jump rope routine. Find a partner and get started." As teachers, we provide guidelines for the routine. We tell the children the limitations we're imposing, such as the number of persons in a group, the length of the routine, the minimum number of skills to be included, and the music to be used (if this is a teacher decision). Children also need to know the necessary inclusions in the routine that are to be group decisions, for example, directions, pathways, floor patterns, and levels, as well as basic skills to be performed. If the teacher selects the music, there is maximum participation by the children during class, because all can practice to the same music. If each group of children selects the music, the variety of music is greater, but practice time is limited.

One of the most difficult parts of child-designed rhythmic or folk dance experiences is the time factor, that is, the matching of the length of the routine to the length of the music. Children often need guidance in choosing whether to add skills, repeat phrases, or repeat the entire routine.

Figure 20.4 For these partners jumping rope becomes a rhythmic dance experience.

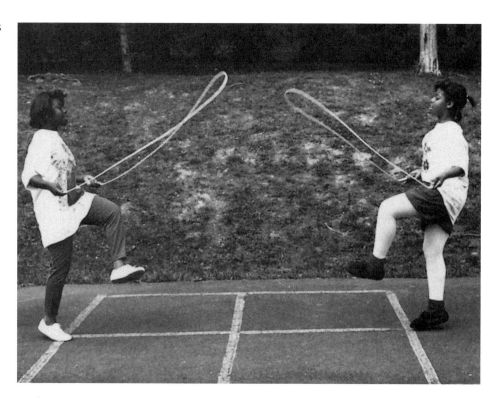

BOX 20.3   FOLK DANCE INFORMATION SOURCES

Additional information on folk/cultural dances can be obtained from the following sources:

J. P. Bennett and P. C. Riemer, *Rhythmic activities and dance,* 1995, Champaign, IL: Human Kinetics.

The Carper, Bailey, Steele Travelers, *Appalachian clogging and hoedown,* Bill Carper, 1537 4th Avenue, Charleston, WV 25312.

L. K. Czarnowski, *Folk dance teaching cues,* 1963, Palo Alto, CA: National Press.

J. A. Harris, A. M. Pittman, and M. S. Waller, *Dance awhile: Handbook of folk, square, contra and social dance,* 1988, New York: Macmillan.

E. Patrick Napier, *Kentucky mountain square dancing,* Christmas Dance School, Berea College, CPO 287, Berea, KY 40404.

S. Powell, *The clogger's book of Appalachian square dance figures,* 1983, Huron, OH: Burdick Enterprises.

R. H. Hipps and W. E. Chappell, *World of fun folk dances,* 1970, United Methodist Church, P.O. Box 871, Nashville, TN 37202.

Folk Dances

Folk and square dances (line and country) are the cultural dances of a society. Ranging from simple to very complex, they involve a series of actions with one or more of the following: a stated progression, verses and a chorus, locomotor and nonlocomotor actions, formations, changes in directions, right and left discrimination, and designated music.

When older children, who have acquired competence in rhythm and movement, study folk dances from different countries, they carry out a variety of locomotor and nonlocomotor actions to music. They learn formations for dances, moving to musical phrases, repetition of pattern, and so on. They're able to analyze the folk dances according to spatial awareness, effort qualities, and relationships. Based on the patterns of movement, formations, and specific steps they have learned, upper elementary and middle school students create new dances.

The following guidelines may be helpful when introducing students to structured dance forms (Weikart, 1989).

- Start with free-space movement; allow students to move about the room with no set formation. Then proceed to simple circle and line dances with no changes in direction.
- Provide multiple opportunities for students to practice locomotor and nonlocomotor sequences in different combinations to a variety of music.
- Begin with dances that require neither partners nor holding hands.

- Choose dances that do not specify the use of the right or left foot.
- Select music with a strong underlying beat; the musical phrases should be distinct and in groupings of eight or sixteen beats.
- Use no more than five minutes of the class time for teacher instructions.

See Box 20.3 for sources of additional information about folk dances.

Creative Experiences

Creative and rhythmic experiences in dance aren't separated in our programs; many of the creative experiences are performed to rhythm. In fact, it isn't uncommon for us to switch the focus several times during a lesson, sometimes focusing on the rhythm of the movement, other times focusing on the expressive qualities of the movement. When concentrating on rhythmic experiences, the primary focus is on the children's ability to move to the rhythm. In contrast, creative experiences are intended to provoke creativity and expression. Creative experiences for children are designed to evoke the expressiveness and lack of body inhibition so characteristic of the young child.

At the precontrol level, experiences are designed to help children develop sensitivity and awareness to movement by focusing on fundamental body actions and travel skills. Stretching, curling, bending and skipping, galloping, and leaping are movements frequently used with precontrol children. Initially it's a good idea to focus on giving children opportunities to

Figure 20.5 Many children are enthusiastic and excited about dance.

explore a wide range of movement possibilities (Figure 20.5). Once this has been accomplished, shift the emphasis to the spatial quality of the movements. For example, have the children do a complete, full stretch or a very tight curl, and use the movement concepts to enhance the children's sensitivity to the potential of movement. The primary emphasis, however, is still on the movement rather than the body's expressive or communicative possibilities.

At the control level, begin to clarify for children the expressive and communicative aspects of movement. The focus now centers more on the effort and relationship concepts (Chapter 3). Box 20.4 describes the effort and relationship concepts used for expressive dance. Through these concepts, movement is explored as a tool for expressing an idea, attitude, or feeling. Movement is no longer studied primarily as an entity in and of itself; it's viewed as a medium of expression. Challenge the children to structure their movements to an imposed beat or rhythmic pattern, or have them verbalize how their movements feel and describe their emotional reactions to classmates' expressive movements.

Children at the utilization level have learned to efficiently perform the movements studied at the precontrol level and to modify the movements intentionally by focusing on different movement concepts. At this level, children can begin to structure their communicative movements into organized forms. This structuring is often termed *sequencing* or *phrasing*.

It's usually a good idea to narrow the focus of a sequence or phrase to one, two, or at most three skills and concepts. When youngsters at this level are given too many possibilities, they're often unable to decide where to begin. The ability to move, however, combined with a working knowledge of movement concepts, enables pupils to elicit varying and qualitative responses to a single challenge. See Box 20.5 for sequencing suggestions.

Dance making—structuring several sequences or phrases into a whole—is the focus at the proficiency level. The idea behind a dance can be stimulated by an infinite variety of sources, such as machines, natural phenomena (flowers, snow flakes), sculpture, music, poetry, or painting. Dance making involves both design and evaluation.

Design of Dance

We've found it valuable to have upper grade children view the dance-making process as composed of the following procedures:

1. Selection of the purpose, idea, or theme of a dance
2. Identification of appropriate movements and movement concepts to express the intended idea, attitude, feeling, or theme
3. Design of a powerful opening statement for the dance
4. Design of a series of actions rising to a climax

BOX 20.4   EXPRESSIVE AND COMMUNICATIVE ACTIVITIES

Time

Travel or gesture in slow motion.
Travel to an externally imposed beat or rhythmic pattern, such as a handclap or drumbeat.
Rise and sink suddenly or slowly.

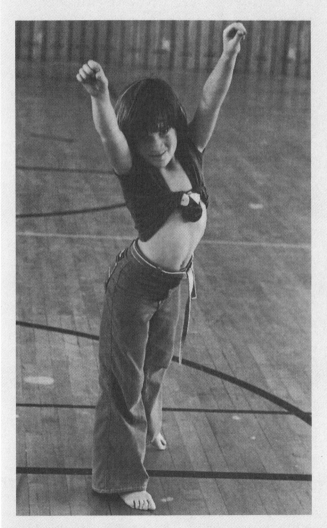

A child freezes in a strong pose.

Flow

Combine two travel skills, such as running and leaping, always moving smoothly.

Display hesitant, jerky, mechanical flow to create the illusion of being a robot.
Feel and observe the differences in combining a step with a turn, first with smooth, continuous flow, then with pauses (stillnesses) interspersed between each step and turn.

Force

Travel or perform nonlocomotor actions to a strong beat.
Travel or perform nonlocomotor actions to light, gentle, delicate music.
Freeze in a strong, dramatic pose.

Youngsters explore the expressive possibilities of partner formation.

Relationships

Experience the sensation of matching, mirroring, or shadowing the movements of a partner.
Explore the expressive possibilities of group formations—for example, sculpture for the city park, or a mountain range.
Experience the feeling of contrasting the movements of a partner—for example, as one partner rises the other sinks, or one partner travels in a geometric path (square) while the other travels in a random path.

BOX 20.5   SEQUENCE ACTIVITIES

- Design a sequence that combines light, gentle, delicate leaps with smooth, fluent step-turns interspersed with dramatic stillnesses.
- Combine appropriate travel skills and gestures with the rhythmic patterns of several Tom Foolery rhymes (see Chapter 19).
- Have groups of children organize into group formations and then continually transform themselves into different formations.
- Design a sixty-second phrase depicting the plight of a caravan of lost travelers crossing the Sahara.

5. Design of the portion of the dance that is to be the climax or peak of the action
6. Design of the resolution or concluding statement of the dance

The possibilities for dance making are infinite. Two examples illustrate how dances can be designed to portray different emotions or thoughts. The first is an abstract dance contrasting tradition with the forces of change. One group arranges itself as a solid square facing in one direction. Symmetrical movements prevail. Actions are firm, sustained. The other group is scattered widely, facing in random directions. Nonsymmetrical movements, free use of space, and variety are used.

The second dance is based on the theme of freedom. Joyous, vibrant movements prevail. Free use of space, meeting, and parting are appropriate. Displays of strength, courage, or pride are also suitable.

See Box 20.6 for insight into working with children as they create their own dance. The focus is on the creative process, not the making of the dance.

Evaluation of Dance Making

The evaluation of dance making is a continual process that results in constant refinement and revision. Children need to be satisfied with the final product. Evaluation examines all movement skills and concepts the teacher and children have incorporated into the dance. Considerations include the following:

- Beginning location and pathway of each youngster—how the children choose to locate themselves at the beginning of the dance and the pathway they choose to express various feelings
- Selection of travel skills (leaping, skipping) and the quality with which they're performed—whether

the children are using a variety of travel skills and executing them clearly and precisely as intended with the desired impact
- Relationship of the children to one another—whether the children are reacting to one another with sensitivity and whether the timing, strength, and speed of their responses are appropriate
- Flow of the dance—how the parts of the dance are connected to give a unity of expression

The Content of Expressive Dance

The movement framework, depicting the interaction of skill themes and movement concepts (Chapter 3), is used as the foundation for expressive dance experiences for children. The majority of skill themes categorized under locomotor skills (walking, running, hopping, skipping, and galloping) and nonmanipulative skills (turning, twisting, rolling, balancing, transferring weight, jumping and landing, and stretching and curling) are used in expressive dance. Virtually all the movement concepts (Chapter 3) are used to heighten and expand the child's ability to express feeling and emotion through movement (see Table 20.1).

The focus in expressive dance is not simply on executing a particular movement—a turn or a balance—but on performing the movement so that it communicates the message the child intends it to. Once children are able to perform turns efficiently, they can begin to experiment with different qualities of turning. Slow, hesitant turns or fast, sudden turns are two possibilities. Eventually these qualities of turning can be used to express inner feelings or attitudes. For example, slow, hesitant turns might be used to depict sadness or uncertainty; sudden, quick turns could be used to express anger, frustration, or perhaps

Table 20.1 Overview of the Content and Rationale of Teaching Expressive Dance to Children

We Want Children to Acquire:	By Learning a Movement Vocabulary of:	That Can Be Used to Express Emotions and Thoughts Such As:	Stimulated by Catalysts Such As:
An ability to use their bodies as a means of expression	Movement concepts	Friendship	Sounds
	Space awareness	Warmth	Music
The sense of self-satisfaction	Effort	Anger	Poetry
that can be derived through	Relationships	Unhappiness	Art
expressive movement	Skill themes	Peace	History
An enjoyment and appreciation	Locomotor	Hostility	Motion pictures
of dance	Nonmanipulative	Joy	Personal experiences
An ability to interpret and move		Satisfaction	
to different rhythms		Harmony	

SOURCE: Adapted from "Educational Dance," by K. R. Barrett, in *Physical Education for Children: A Focus on the Teaching Process,* by B. Logdson et al., 1977, Philadelphia: Lea & Febiger. Used with permission from the publisher.

Figure 20.6 The quality of a movement communicates the message.

joy. Turning, by itself, communicates little. It's the quality of the turn that communicates a message, just as it's the quality of any movement that is expressive (Figure 20.6). This is the reason why it's so important to give children a movement vocabulary if they're to become expressive movers.

The Process of Teaching Dance

Teaching creative dance is different from teaching functional movements. A functional movement is performed correctly or incorrectly, and the teacher's task is to guide the child toward an appropriate execution. Dance movements, performed to express an idea or emotion, are more difficult to define clearly, and so the teacher's task is different.

Because the child is trying to express a feeling or an idea, observation and feedback are also more complex. In games and gymnastics, the purpose of a movement is obvious; this isn't true in creative dance. When teaching dance, the teacher initially encourages, expands, and embellishes rather than correcting or refining. As the teacher comes to know the children and understand them as individuals, and as the children begin to trust the teacher, the children will seek sensitive and supportive feedback from the teacher. Remember, though, that human expression is very fragile and easily misinterpreted. Nothing stifles expression more quickly than insensitivity or lack of

BOX 20.6   CHILDREN DESIGNING THEIR OWN DANCE: A DESCRIPTION OF A PROCESS

One of the goals in teaching dance is to work with children so that they learn to design dances to express feelings or thoughts that are important to them. This description of the process of creating a dance tells how one teacher worked with a group of upper grade children, assisting them to create their own dance. The description is intended to reveal the process of creating dances; it isn't presented as a predesigned dance to be taught to other children.

Background

The population of the community in which the children in this class lived was predominantly black. The eight children in this group wished to create a dance that expressed pride and respect for their African American heritage.

We began by using several methods to develop an outline for the dance:

1. One student wrote a short paper describing what he considered the most important events in the movie *Roots*.
2. The school librarian provided several sources of information. Individual students read and outlined these sources for the remainder of the group.
3. Several students interviewed teachers and classmates about their family backgrounds. They also asked people to describe what emotions they had about their heritage.

Without question, the movie *Roots* had the biggest influence in determining the students' conception of black history. The pride and courage of Kunta Kinte and his descendants were the qualities the children wanted most to exhibit in their dance.

An Outline of the Dance

After gathering and reviewing this information, we discussed a sequential outline for the dance. It was agreed that:

1. We'd begin by depicting, in some way, the period of slavery.
2. The arrival of freedom would be expressed. Interestingly, the children didn't want this portion of the dance to be happy or exhilarating, for several reasons. They felt that blacks were always free, despite slavery, that many freedoms were long in coming, and that the struggle for equality continues today.
3. Upon arrival of freedom, it was important to display the pride and courage of African Americans in overcoming many injustices, both as individuals and as a people.
4. The conclusion of the dance would be spiritual, exhibiting respect and thankfulness to God for blessing a cherished people.

Creation of the Dance

Children focused on each section of the dance before putting it all together. For each portion the youngsters needed to decide upon and write on paper the

1. Beginning location of each dancer
2. Sequential travel pathway of each dancer or of the entire group

Travel Pattern for "Freedom"

Travel pathways
   Random: dancers weaving in, out, and around one another
Qualities
   Smooth, wavy, uncertain, looking to others for help
Actions
   Wavy gesturing of arms, held upward for protection or reaching out
   Slow stepping, with changes in direction and levels

3. Expressive qualities they intended to exhibit in their movements
4. Sequence of specific gestures and travel skills incorporated to express desired qualities

Once the group could perform one section to the teacher's and their own satisfaction, work was begun on the next phase of the dance.

Slavery

After discussing the accumulated information, the children agreed to begin the dance by exhibiting the qualities and actions of field slaves laboring under a hot sun.

Freedom

This phase of the dance was the most difficult for the children. After experimenting with several ideas, the youngsters asked if they could select music to serve as background for the dance. They thought that if they had appropriate music as a stimulus, they'd be able to solve their dilemmas. After listening to several cuts from the *Roots* soundtrack album, the children unanimously agreed that the words and slow pulse of the song "Many Rains Ago (Oluwa)" was perfect for their purposes. They decided to express freedom by simply putting down their tools and slowly and smoothly beginning to interweave with one another, making eye contact with others for the first time. This was intended to express changed circumstances, in which they were free and proud but still struggling. During this phase, the youngsters' facial features exhibited fear and uncertainty about the future. The travel pattern was random.

Gathering Together: Strength As a People

To express their solidarity and pride as a people, the children's random travel began to be directed toward the center of the room where they gathered one by one, grasped one another's hands tightly, and formed a strong, unified statue.

From this point the youngsters were able to complete their dance with little teacher suggestion or intervention.

Dispersing: Strength As Individuals

Youngsters dispersed from center stage with new vigor and traveled along definite travel patterns.

Gathering Again: Strength, Pride, Confidence

Children leaped to the center of the room, where suddenly and simultaneously they clasped hands with one another overhead and formed a statue.

Respect and Thankfulness to God

From the statue position, youngsters slowly bowed and traveled to semicircle formation. Slowly they dropped to their knees, and then slowly they raised their hands and heads upward.

Conclusion: We Are Strong and Proud

Youngsters slowly bent to curled position. . . . Suddenly and simultaneously they rose on knees to grasp one another's hands to form a statue as a final statement of strength and pride.

Travel Pattern for "Gathering Again: Strength, Pride, Confidence"

Travel pathways
  All dancers suddenly and simultaneously gather in the middle with a run, leap, and turn
  Qualities
  Strong, confident, proud, smooth, and fluent
Actions
  Smooth, fluent leap and landing, when dancers grasp each other's hands overhead and freeze into a stillness

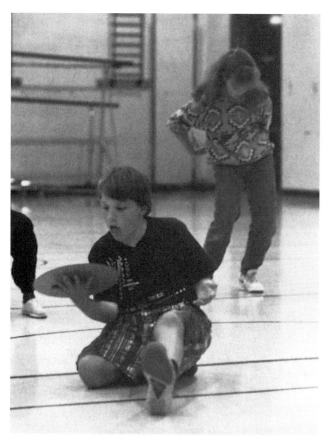

Figure 20.7   A pizza circle dance is fun for everyone.

understanding. The teacher of creative dance needs to be constantly aware of how easily creativity is threatened. The incident described in Box 20.7 illustrates how fragile a child's creativity is.

You don't have to be a dancer to be a successful teacher of children's dance. The following ideas may be helpful for those teachers unsure of their ability to teach dance, unsure of their students' reactions, yet searching for ways to develop effective programs of creative dance.

Don't Call It Dance!

Children who've had little exposure to creative dance experiences often react negatively to the prospect of studying dance. Children in the upper grades have been known to express their hostility to the idea with groans, frowns, sighs, and even emphatic refusals to participate. This resistance can be understood when you realize that too often, children in the upper elementary grades have had few opportunities to move creatively. Too often even those few opportunities have been poorly presented. Children have been forced, for example, to participate in uninteresting, unstructured forms of dance that had no purpose or reason for involvement that was apparent to the children.

When that happens, children turn away from the joy of dance instead of becoming excited about creative movement. For this reason, we recommend that you involve the children in enjoyable, challenging movement experiences without labeling the lesson as *dance* (Figure 20.7). People in Motion, an integrated project of art, music, and physical education (Figure 20.8) with a focus on sport and physical activity, is

Figure 20.8   Children combine shapes and actions from favorite sports for a group dance.

BOX 20.7   THE AWFUL BEGINNING: A TRUE STORY, UNFORTUNATELY

I looked across the desk at my big girl. She'd come for help in planning her semester schedule.

"Look," I said, "you have some electives. Why don't you take a course or two for fun? You've worked hard and really should take something outside your major that will be pleasurable."

"Like what?" she asked.

My eyes scanned the college schedule of courses. "Like Dr. Mann's Creative Writing or Dr. Camp's Painting for Beginners or something like that."

She threw back her head and laughed. "Who me? Paint or write? Good grief, Dad, you ought to know better than that!"

"And this," I thought, "is the awful ending."

It was not always like this. I remembered an early golden September day when I went to my garage studio and gathered together my easel, paintbrushes, and watercolors. I sensed someone was watching me and looked up from my activity to see her framed in silhouette in the doorway. The breeze and the sun tiptoed in the gold of her curls. Her wide blue eyes asked the question, "Whatcha doin'?"

"I'm going to the meadow to paint," I said. "Want to come along?"

"Oh, yes." She bounced on her toes in anticipation.

"Well, go tell Mommy and get your paints." She was off but returned in no time carrying the caddy I had made to hold her jars of paint and her assortment of brushes.

"Paper?" she asked.

"Yes, I have plenty of paper. Let's go."

She ran down the hill before me, pushing aside the long soft grasses of the meadow. I watched closely for fear of losing her golden top in the tops of the goldenrod. She found a deserted meadowlark's nest and we stopped to wonder at it. A rabbit scurried from under our feet. Around us yellow daisies and goldenrod nodded in friendly greeting. Above, the sky was in infinite blue. Beyond the meadow, the lake slapped itself to match the blue of the sky.

On the lake, a single white sailboat tipped joyously in the breeze. My daughter looked up and saw it. "Here!" she said.

Trusting her wisdom as I always did, I set up our easels. While I deliberated over choice of subject and color, she had no such problem. She painted with abandonment and concentration and I left her alone, asking no questions, making no suggestions, simply recognizing uncontaminated creative drive at work.

Before I had really begun, she pulled a painting off her easel.

"There!" she said. "Want to see?" I nodded.

I cannot describe the sense of wonder that flooded over me as I viewed her work. It was all there—that golden September day. She had captured the sunlight in her spilled yellows, the lake in her choppy, uneven strokes of blue, the trees in her long, fresh strokes of green. And through it all, there was a sense of scudding ships and the joyousness of wind that I experience when I sail, the tilting and swaying of the deck, the pitching of the mast. It was a beautiful and wondrous thing and I envied her ability to interpret so honestly, so uninhibitedly, so freshly.

"Are you going to give it a name?" I suggested.

"Yep! Sailboats!" she responded, as she taped another sheet of paper to the easel.

There wasn't a single sailboat in the picture.

She began school the following week. One dreary November day she came into my study with a sheet of paper in her hand.

"Daddy," she asked, "will you help me draw a sailboat?"

"Me? Help you draw a sailboat?"

My eyes turned to the wall where her golden September painting hung in a frame I had made for it.

"Me? Help you draw a picture of a sailboat? Why, sweetheart, I could never paint a picture like the one over there. Why don't you paint one of your own?"

Her blue eyes looked troubled.

"But, Daddy, Miss Ellis doesn't like my kind of painting."

She held up her sheet of paper in the middle of which was a dittoed triangle.

"Miss Ellis wants us to make a sailboat out of this."

And that was the awful beginning!

James A. Smith

SOURCE: James A. Smith, "The Awful Beginning", Today's Education, April 1972. Used with permission.

Figure 20.9 Class groups enjoy practicing meeting and parting relationships.

one example of this type of movement experience/dance. As the youngsters become comfortable with dance and their awareness of dance as exciting and stimulating grows, the stigma attached to the word *dance* will disappear.

Begin Gradually

The class's first experiences with creative dance need not last for an entire class session. A few minutes at the beginning or end of a class are often sufficient to introduce creative movement concepts—and simultaneously build your confidence as a teacher of creative dance. A short creative dance activity at the beginning of class can serve as a review of a concept related to the skill theme for the day, for example, twisting and turning actions in Shadow Boxing (dance) before their use in the skill theme of balance (gymnastics). A short creative dance activity at the conclusion of an active lesson can also be effective. While the children lie on the floor, eyes closed, ask them to move only their fingers (toes, arms, legs, elbows) to the music. Short segments of lively music are most effective. The children, whose eyes are closed, are less inhibited; the teacher, whose eyes are open, sees the creative dance potential that seems to be an inborn characteristic of the young child. At Linden Elementary each lesson designed for primary children includes "A Moment of Dance," a few minutes, usually at the beginning of the lesson, for self- and/or general space dance activity.

Start with a Cooperative Class

Some classes are more agreeable to work with than others. Select a class that is generally cooperative as

the first one to which you'll teach creative dance (Figure 20.9). You don't need to start dance programs with all your classes at the same time. Instead, pick one class that you feel comfortable with. As your confidence builds, start dance programs in other classes. Use the first class as a testing ground for your ideas.

Use Props

Creative dancers derive great pleasure and satisfaction from focusing on how they can move their bodies. In contrast, immature dancers often feel insecure when asked to focus on how they're moving. Props can serve as catalysts, redirecting the child's attention and so reducing self-consciousness. The use of such props as scarves, newspapers, balloons, dowel rods, stretch nylon, and even shadows can effectively divert the attention of uncertain children from their bodies. For example, when attempting to duplicate the light, airy movements made by a floating sheet of newspaper, the child focuses attention on moving as the newspaper does, rather than on trying to travel lightly. As confidence builds, the children gradually focus their attention on their own movements.

Imagery

Imagery is the use of a creative stimulus as a catalyst for movement. Many people believe, inaccurately, that imagery provides the content of dance. The content of expressive dance is movement; imagery is a helper. Asking children to use imagery as the content of expressive dance is similar to asking children to write a story when they have a vocabulary of only fifty words. One or two extraordinarily intelligent pupils might do well. Most, however, would fail miserably because they hadn't yet acquired the tools needed for successful story writing.

The same principle can be applied to expressive dance. Children must be provided with the tools of dance, the ability to use a variety of movements effectively. Only when children have developed these skills can they successfully combine the movements into dances that express what they want to communicate. Movement vocabularies, however, aren't acquired through imagery, as the following example illustrates.

A teacher focusing on the concept of slow, heavy movement may ask children to travel as if the floor were coated with six inches of peanut butter. But using the peanut butter image without first teaching the concept of slow and heavy travel is of little value. Children who are adept at such movements at the beginning of the class will remain adept. Those individuals who were unable to travel slowly and heavily might move in the desired manner when stimulated by the image of a peanut butter floor, but they won't have acquired a functional understanding of slow, heavy movement as a concept that can be transferred to other movement situations. In short, imagery can be useful as a reinforcer for certain movements, but imagery by itself doesn't enhance the quality of children's expressive movement.

Start with Exciting Movement Experiences

Fast, vigorous, large movements are attractive and appealing to young children. A lesson that focuses on running, leaping into the air, landing, and rolling evokes the exuberance associated with speed and flight. Gradually the teacher can begin to focus on the quality of the leaps, the effectiveness of the landings, and the use of gestures while in flight.

Dance to the Music

One of the most devastating experiences for poorly skilled or less confident children occurs when a teacher plays some music and simply says, "Today is a dance lesson. Go ahead and dance to the music." This can be a terrifying task for youngsters with no background or confidence in creative movement and no vocabulary of functional movements. The challenge "Move to the music" may be appropriate later, when children put together the movements they have acquired, but it is not appropriate in the early stages of teaching creative dance to children.

A Final Thought

One instructor's initial attempts at teaching creative dance are still vivid. She recalled teaching to a second-grade class an entire lesson that focused on running, jumping, and turning to different rhythms. Afterward she remarked to a friend that it was the best workout the children had experienced the entire year and added that she was going to teach another lesson because of the physical fitness benefits. After another lesson was received as enthusiastically as the first, she was struck with the realization that the reason the children had been so actively involved was that they were totally immersed in the exciting atmosphere that was generated by exploring fast and slow turns, acceleration and deceleration leading into jumps. The children loved creative dance.

The physical education instructor who doesn't offer creative movement experiences is being professionally irresponsible. You may be more qualified to teach gymnastics or games, but you'll always be teaching some children who might eventually choose creative dance as their primary form of participation in the motor domain. Depriving children of opportunities to experience creative movement is no more acceptable than eliminating all opportunities to practice throwing and catching. You may have to devote much time and work to developing a successful program. But any teacher, even one who has little background in creative dance, can provide children with effective creative movement experiences. Dance ideas within themes are found throughout the skill theme chapters with a concentration in the locomotors of Chapter 19, "Traveling."

SUMMARY   Teachers who lack experience and educational background in dance find it difficult to teach dance to children. But any teacher who's willing to try new and possibly unfamiliar ideas can learn to successfully teach children's dance. Children look forward to and enjoy dance experiences that are presented appropriately.

Because of the ages and abilities of children in elementary schools, we've found creative or expressive dance to be the most successful. Creative dance is also consistent with the nature and characteristics of young children, who are already adept at fantasizing and expressing their thoughts and feelings through movement.

The content of expressive dance is derived from the movement concepts and the majority of locomotor and nonmanipulative skill themes. The initial emphasis is on executing particular movements. As children learn to perform these skills efficiently, the emphasis shifts to varying the quality with which the movement is executed.

Children should have both rhythmic and expressive dance experiences. In rhythmic experiences, the focus is on moving in relation to different rhythmic beats. In contrast, creative dance experiences focus on expressive interpretation by children as they expand their movement vocabulary for communicating feelings and moods.

Through a process of trial and error, we've discovered numerous techniques that help make dance lessons for children both interesting and educational. For example, we suggest that teachers initially avoid the word *dance* because it has negative connotations for some children. Inexperienced dance teachers may find it helps to begin by teaching dance to one cooperative class. Using props and designing lessons that are vigorous and action-packed are also strategies that help excite children about dance.

READING COMPREHENSION QUESTIONS

1. What should dance in the elementary school provide for children?
2. Identify three dance forms. Where does each form fit into a curriculum, and why?
3. What skill themes and movement concepts generally appear in dance content?
4. What is the focus of expressive dance?
5. What is the role of imagery in dance? What must children possess before they can effectively use imagery?
6. Expressive dance can be classified into what two types of experiences? What is the primary focus of each experience, and how does the purpose differ at each proficiency level?
7. What is sequencing?
8. What is dance making? What procedures must be included in dance making?
9. How can you evaluate dance making?
10. What cues do the authors give for starting to teach creative dance?

REFERENCES/ SUGGESTED READINGS

Austin, G., & Lipscomb, B. (1989). *Movement and dance.* London: Cassell Publishers. (Teaching cards, booklet, and audiocassette.)

Barlin, A. L. (1979). *Teaching your wings to fly.* Santa Monica, CA: Goodyear.

Bennett, J. P., & Riemer, P. C. (1995). *Rhythmic activities and dance.* Champaign, IL: Human Kinetics.

Benzwie, T. (1988). *A moving experience.* Tucson, AZ: Zephyr Press.

Boorman, J. (1969). *Creative dance in the first three grades.* New York: McKay.

Buchoff, R., & Mitchell, D. (1996). Poetry workouts. *Strategies, 10*(1), 18–21.

Carroll, J., & Lofthouse, P. (1969). *Creative dance for boys.* London: MacDonald & Evans.

Davis, J. (1995). Laban movement analysis: A key to individualizing children's dance. *JOPERD, 66*(2), 31–33.

Docherty, D. (1977). *Education through the dance experience.* Bellingham, WA: Educational Designs and Consultants.

Fleming, G. A. (1976). *Creative rhythmic movement.* Englewood Cliffs, NJ: Prentice-Hall.

Fleming, G. A. (Ed.). (1981). *Children's dance.* Reston, VA: AAHPERD.

Joyce, M. (1980). *First steps in teaching creative dance* (2nd ed.). Palo Alto, CA: Mayfield.

Joyce, M. (1984). *Dance technique for children.* Palo Alto, CA: Mayfield.

Mehrhof, J. H., Ermler, K., & Kovar, S. (1993). Set the stage for dance. *Strategies, 6*(7), 5–7.

Murray, R. L. (1975). *Dance in elementary education* (3rd ed.). New York: Harper & Row.

National Association for Sport and Physical Education (NASPE). (1992). *Outcomes of quality physical education programs.* Reston, VA: Author.

National Association for Sport and Physical Education (NASPE). (1995). *Moving into the future: National standards for physical education.* St. Louis, MO: Mosby.

Purcell, T. M. (1994). *Teaching children dance: Becoming a master teacher.* Champaign, IL: Human Kinetics.

Russell, J. (1975). *Creative movement and dance for children.* Boston: Plays, Inc.

Slater, W. (1974). *Teaching modern educational dance.* London: MacDonald & Evans.

Smith, J. A. (1972, April). The awful beginning. *Today's Education.*

Stinson, S. (1988). *Dance for young children: Finding the magic in movement.* Reston, VA: AAHPERD.

Stinson, S. W. (1993). Voices from schools—The significance of relationship to public school dance students. *JOPERD, 64*(5), 52–56.

Weikart, P. S. (1989). *Teaching movement and dance,* 3rd ed. Ypsilanti, MI: High Scope Press.

Willis, C. M. (1995a). Creative dance education—Establishing a positive learning environment. *JOPERD, 66*(4), 16–20.

Willis, C. M. (1995b). Creative dance—How to increase parent and teacher awareness. *JOPERD, 66*(5), 48–53.

CHAPTER
21

Chasing, Fleeing, and Dodging

Since ancient times children have delighted in countless chasing, fleeing, and dodging games. These games all challenge children to evade a chasing player through dodging and fleeing. Such sports as basketball, hockey, soccer, and football are simply more elaborate forms of these games using the same elements. Physical education programs can build on the innate pleasure that children experience from playing these games. By providing a variety of challenging tasks and game situations, a teacher can help youngsters develop chasing, fleeing, and dodging skills (see our progression spiral, page 329).

Experience suggests that it's best to focus on chasing, fleeing, and dodging skills after children have developed a working understanding of space awareness concepts and have mastered fundamental traveling skills. Many consider chasing, fleeing, and dodging to be the utilization and proficiency levels of traveling. Although they do require traveling skills of a higher level, chasing, fleeing, and dodging also involve the use of some tactical skills in combination with other skill themes. Therefore, we have chosen to address these skills in a separate chapter.

Chasing, fleeing, and dodging tasks and games using these skills are best played outdoors in large, grassy areas. Box 21.1 notes what the *National Standards for Physical Education* say about chasing, fleeing, and dodging.

Chasing

Chasing is traveling quickly to overtake or tag a fleeing person. In many game situations, the fleeing player is given a head start and allowed time to run away before the chaser can begin traveling. The fleeing player tries to avoid being caught or tagged. Thus, the chaser needs to be able to run at full speed and to react quickly to changes in the direction of the fleeing player's travel.

Fleeing

Fleeing is traveling quickly away from a pursuing person or object. In most game situations, the fleeing person tries to keep as much distance as possible between himself or herself and the chaser. However, when the pursuer does close in, the fleeing player uses any maneuver possible to avoid being tagged—the fleeing person dodges, changes direction quickly, or runs full speed. This continual demand on the fleeing player, to react quickly to emerging, threatening situations, is what makes tag games such thrilling activities for children.

Dodging

Dodging is the skill of quickly moving the body in a direction other than the original line of movement. This includes any maneuver a person undertakes to avoid being touched by a chasing person. Dodging may occur while a person is fleeing or stationary. Effective dodging actions include quick fakes, twisting, and stretching.

Levels of Skill Proficiency

We've found that most school-age children are familiar with a variety of tag and dodging games. But some youngsters whose chasing, fleeing, and dodging skills are at the precontrol or control level of proficiency have limited success in playing these games; that is, although many children can chase, flee, and dodge, they can't perform these skills effectively in dynamic game situations. In a game of tag, for instance, the child doing the chasing is often unable to overtake or tag any of the fleeing players and quickly tires of playing the game. In their classic study of children's games, Iona Opie and Peter Opie (1969) noted that

BOX 21.1 CHASING, FLEEING, AND DODGING IN THE *NATIONAL STANDARDS FOR PHYSICAL EDUCATION*

The skill theme of chasing, fleeing, and dodging is referenced in the *National Standards for Physical Education* (NASPE, 1995) as a sample second-grade benchmark under Standard 3: Exhibits a physically active lifestyle.

The sample benchmark states that a child "sustains activity for longer periods of time while participating in chasing or fleeing, traveling activities in physical education, and/or on the playground" (p. 23).

Chasing, Fleeing, Dodging

■ **PROFICIENCY LEVEL**

Dodging while manipulating an object in a game situation
Using team strategy for chasing, fleeing, and dodging (Rip Flag)
Dodging in a game situation (Pirate's Treasure; Safety Bases)
Chasing and dodging simultaneously (Snatch the Flag)
Chasing and fleeing in a game situation
Dodging while maintaining possession of an object
Continual fleeing and chasing with a large group

■ **UTILIZATION LEVEL**

Dodging while manipulating an object
Dodging in a dynamic situation (Body-Part Tag)
Dodging and chasing one person in a mass (Partner Dodge)
Dodging and chasing as part of a team (Octopus)
Dodging and faking moves to avoid a chaser (Freeze-and-Count Tag)
People Dodge (dodging stationary obstacles)

■ **CONTROL LEVEL**

Fleeing a chaser (Frogs and Flies)
Overtaking a fleeing person (Catch-up Chase)
Dodging with quick changes of direction
Dodging the obstacles
Fleeing from a partner
Dodging in response to a signal

■ **PRECONTROL LEVEL**

Make-Believe Chase
Traveling to dodge
Traveling to flee
Moving obstacles

chasing games were often plagued with arguments and ended prematurely in heated disputes.

A teacher's initial task, therefore, is to help youngsters develop those skills prerequisite to becoming a capable chaser, fleer, or dodger in various game situations. In school situations where preschool youngsters' opportunities to play with other children are limited, a teacher may need to provide precontrol-level chasing, fleeing, and dodging activities—for example:

1. Running as fast as possible from one location to another
2. Traveling around a room and changing the direction of travel quickly when a signal is sounded
3. When a signal is given, quickly performing a designated dodging maneuver
4. Running as fast as possible away from a partner; on the signal, running quickly toward a partner

Children who can competently perform a variety of quick, dodging maneuvers while running fast are at the control level. A teacher can provide challenging tasks designed to have these children keep their eyes focused on a target child and react quickly to the movements of that child by chasing, fleeing from, or dodging the target child. Such tasks include

1. Staying as close as possible to a fleeing, dodging partner
2. Chasing after a person who has been given a slight head start and is fleeing
3. Trying to run across a field while dodging one or more chasers

When children can effectively dodge a chasing person and can react quickly and accurately to others' swift, darting movements, they're ready for utilization-level activities. Now the youngsters' chasing, fleeing, and dodging skills enable them to enjoy testing their abilities in ever-changing and complex game environments. Challenging activities include the following:

1. The players of one team flee and/or dodge the players of an opposing team while controlling an object (such as a football, Frisbee, or basketball).
2. One team chases down the members of an opposing team; that is, instead of fleeing their chasers, one team tries to run past them without being touched.

Many of the utilization- and proficiency-level learning experiences involve teams. See Box 21.2 for tips on partner and team formation.

At the proficiency level, children are able to use chasing, fleeing, and dodging skills effectively in a wide variety of game contexts. Both the chasers and

the fleeing, dodging players are skilled. At times the chaser gets the target; at other times the fleeing, dodging player escapes. Advanced chasing, fleeing, and dodging skills are evident in situations such as the following:

1. A runner in a football-type game darts quickly past the defense, dodging around the players who are chasing the runner.
2. A soccer player dribbles a ball past a defense player by faking one way and then traveling quickly in the opposite direction.
3. A defense player in a football-type game runs twenty to thirty yards to overtake an offensive runner heading for a score.
4. A basketball player races down court to score a layup even though a defense player is chasing right behind.

In elementary school settings, children at the proficiency level enjoy playing teacher- and student-designed games in which chasing, fleeing, and dodging are the primary movements.

Precontrol Level: Activities for Exploration

Activities at the precontrol level are designed to help children explore the skills of chasing, fleeing, and dodging in simple situations. Before beginning any practice with this theme, children should be at the control level of traveling and have had ample practice with space awareness.

 When working with chasing, fleeing, and dodging activities that involve a finish line, make sure that the line is far away from any obstructions. This precaution allows the children to run through the finish line at full speed safely.

MOVING OBSTACLES

Setting: Children scattered in general space

Tasks/Challenges:

Ⓣ At the signal, travel in general space. Make sure that you look up so that you can avoid collisions with others.

Ⓣ This time make your travel faster but still avoid others.

Have half the children move to one side of the room and half to the other.

Ⓣ On the signal, both lines will try to walk to the opposite side of the room without touching anyone else.

BOX 21.2   AVOIDING BEHAVIOR PROBLEMS WHEN FORMING PARTNERS OR TEAMS

Many activities for children involve working with a partner. In some classes, the act of finding a partner creates many behavior problems. Children argue over who is going to be whose partner, other children are left out, the time used in deciding partners takes longer than the task itself, and then children want to change partners. The same problems occur, even more so, when dividing children into groups and/or teams. For avoiding such problems as much as possible, we've found the following techniques helpful:

Getting Partners

1. Put a time limit on how long children can take to choose partners, e.g., "by the time I count to 5."
2. Put restrictions on who may be partners, e.g., "someone you've never worked with before," "the person sitting next to you," "the person who sits next to you in class," or "someone you know you can work with in a productive manner."
3. Decide ahead of class who'll be partners.
4. Hand out color codes (pieces of paper, stickers, or marking-pen marks on the hand) at the beginning of class; the children who match up are partners.

Dividing into Groups and/or Teams

1. Have children choose partners; then put one partner on one team and one on another. This works well for making teams equal.
2. Assign each student a color or number (the number of colors or numbers equals the number of groups you desire) at the beginning of the year or month. When groups are to be formed, simply say, "Reds here," "Blues here," "Purples here," and "Greens here." (This is also an efficient way to take roll in your class.)
3. Divide teams by certain generic characteristics, e.g., eye color, month of birth, number of siblings, or first letter of names.
4. Divide groups ahead of time.

Whatever you do, don't take more than sixty seconds, and most importantly, don't alienate anyone. Under no circumstances should selecting partners or dividing children into groups be a popularity contest.

T This time travel with three body parts touching the floor. Still no touching.

T Now you will cross the space using different levels. Everyone who has blue eyes will travel with his or her body parts high in the air; those with brown eyes should travel at a low level and those with green or gray eyes, at a medium level.

T This time you can choose any way you wish to travel, but go at a medium speed.

T Try jogging or running, if you feel ready.

C You have ten points to start; subtract one point for every collision. Try to end with all ten points.

Begin slowly. Have children walk. Gradually increase speed as you observe the children traveling competently and without collisions.

Because of the exciting nature of chasing, fleeing, and dodging activities, children's speed tends to increase, sometimes to unsafe levels. Monitor the speed of activities, always reminding children that they must be able to stop and change directions without falling. They should be able to tag someone without pushing.

TRAVELING TO FLEE

Setting: All children spread out in a space (an outside grassy space is best) about twenty yards by twenty yards

Tasks/Challenges:

T You've all played games in which you had to run away from someone who was chasing you. This time you are going to have an imaginary chaser. On the signal practice fleeing from your chaser by walking very quickly. On the next signal, stop. Remember, everyone is moving, so look up.

T This time, practice fleeing your chaser by running.

T How fast can you move to get away from your chaser?

TRAVELING TO DODGE

Setting: Carpet squares, hoops, milk jugs, or ropes spread out on the floor as obstacles

Tasks/Challenges:

T On the signal, travel around the general space without touching anyone else or any of the objects on the floor. Be sure to keep your head up so you can avoid collisions.

T How many different ways can you find to avoid the obstacles?

T This time try and go as fast as you can with no collisions and avoiding all the objects.

MAKE-BELIEVE CHASE

Setting: Children spread out in general space

Tasks/Challenges:

T On the signal, try to catch your make-believe partner. Your partner is very quick, so you will really have to work hard to catch him or her. Remember, everyone is chasing, so look up to avoid collisions.

T This time, you will chase your dog, who got off the leash. You want to catch your dog before she gets to the street.

You will notice that we have eliminated all dodgeball activities from the development of dodging skills. We feel that throwing an object at another person, with the intent of hitting the person, subtly supports violence and goes against what we know and believe about acceptable practice.

Control Level: Learning Experiences Leading to Skill Development

Learning experiences at the control level are designed to allow children to practice chasing, fleeing, and dodging in relatively static situations. Often chasing, fleeing, and dodging are combined with only a single other variable.

A note about cues: Although several cues are listed for many of the learning experiences, it's important to focus on only one cue at a time. That way, the children can really concentrate on that cue. Once you provide feedback to the children and observe that most have learned a cue, then it's time to focus on another one.

DODGING IN RESPONSE TO A SIGNAL

Setting: Children scattered in general space

Cues	
Fake	(Step/lean one way; go the other.)
Split Second	(Make your moves quicker than light.)

Tasks/Challenges:

T Now you're going to become really sneaky. As you travel throughout the general space, when you hear the signal, pretend that you are going in one direction and then quickly change and go in a different direction.

T This time, whenever you hear the signal, try not to let anyone know which direction you'll travel; try to fake them out.

T Now, instead of me giving you the signal, you'll fake on your own. Whenever you come to another person, pretend that you're going to go one way, but go another. Really try to confuse the other person so he or she doesn't know where you'll be going. **Make your move quickly once you decide which way you're going.**

C See if you can travel and dodge for twenty seconds without colliding with anyone.

FLEEING FROM A PARTNER

Setting: Partners about ten feet apart

Cue	
Split Second	(Make your moves quicker than light.)

Tasks/Challenges:

🅣 Face your partner. On the signal, walk slowly toward each other until you are as close as you can be without touching. Then, quickly jump back, as if you're scared, and walk backward to your starting position, keeping a close watch on your partner.

🅣 This time, you're going to do the activity a little differently because you seldom would move slowly to get away from someone. Try to move a little quicker and faster as you flee or go away from your partner. Just remember to not go so fast that you fall down.

🅣 Now, instead of walking away from your partner, try jogging.

DODGING THE OBSTACLES

Setting: Low- and medium-height objects placed around the room as obstacles

Cues	
Split Second	(Make your moves quicker than light.)
Change Speed	(Use changes of speed to avoid the obstacles.)
Change Direction	(Use changes of direction to avoid the obstacles.)

Tasks/Challenges:

🅣 On the signal, travel around the general space without touching anyone else or any of the obstacles on the floor. Everything is poison. Be sure to watch for other people as well as the objects.

🅣 This time try to move through the area a little faster.

🅒 I will time you for thirty seconds. See if you can travel for that long with no touches.

Children never seem to tire of this task, regardless of their skill level. As the children's skill levels increase, decrease the space between obstacles or use more obstacles to increase the complexity of the task.

DODGING WITH QUICK CHANGES OF DIRECTION

Setting: Children scattered in general space

Cues	
Fake	(Step/lean one way; go the other.)
Split Second	(Make your moves quicker than light.)

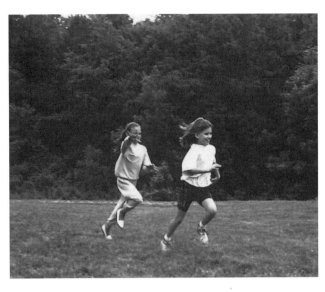

Figure 21.1   Chasing, fleeing, dodging situations are favorites of all youngsters.

Tasks/Challenges:

🅣 This is very similar to what you practiced before. Travel around in the general space. When you come close to someone, get as close as possible, and then quickly dodge away and look for another person to approach. There should be a clear burst of speed as you dodge away from the person—as if you're trying to escape. Remember, watch out for others.

🅣 Dodging with speed as you did is called *darting*. This time practice getting as close to the person you approach as you can before quickly darting away. Make the dart very clear.

🅒 Practice until you can make five darts in a row without having to stop.

OVERTAKING A FLEEING PERSON (CATCH-UP CHASE)

Setting: Partners scattered in general space

Cues		
Runner:	Split Second (Make your moves quicker than light.)	
	Fake (Step/lean one way; go the other.)	
	Change Direction (Use changes of direction to avoid the chaser.)	
Chaser:	Watch the Hips (Watch the hips of the runner to tell his or her next move.)	

Tasks/Challenges:

🅣 With a partner you're going to play Catch-up Chase (*Figure 21.1*). On the first signal, the front

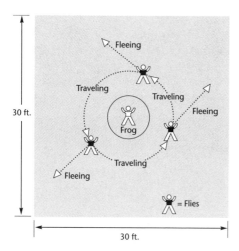

Figure 21.2   Setup for Frogs and Flies.

partner darts away from the back partner. After three seconds, another signal is sounded, and the second partner, who has remained still, chases after the first partner, trying to tag him or her before I blow the stop whistle in twenty seconds. For the next round, switch places. You must always stay inside the boundaries. So the activity goes like this: Start together. On the first signal, partner 1 takes off running. On the second signal, partner 2 takes off and tries to catch partner 1 before I blow the whistle in twenty seconds.

 Let's go again. Remember never to give up, even if the runner keeps getting away. See if you can use all the moves you know.

This task is appropriate when the children have learned to travel in general space without bumping into one another. Initially, children can perform this task more easily (and safely) in large areas, because they're able to focus more on their partners and less on avoiding other children.

FLEEING A CHASER (FROGS AND FLIES)

Setting: Six people in a group. See Figure 21.2 for setup.

Cues

Runner:	Split Second (Make all your moves quicker than light.)
	Fake (Step/lean one way, go the other.)
	Change Direction (Use changes of direction to avoid the chaser.)
Chaser:	Watch the Hips (Watch the hips of the runner to tell his or her next move.)

Tasks/Challenges:

 This task is designed to let you practice fleeing from a chaser. It's called Frogs and Flies. The chaser is the frog, and the runners are the flies. There will be six people in a group—one frog and five flies. The frog, who is in the middle circle, tells the flies how to travel. The flies then travel in a circle around the frog. When the frog gets to his or her feet, all the flies run toward the outside of the square, trying not to get tagged. A fly who is tagged helps the frog the next time. When all the flies are caught, the last fly caught becomes the new frog. Frogs, be sure and change the traveling action each time.

Multiple games can go on at once, but be sure there is ample space between games so that the fleeing children do not disrupt another game. Mark the boundaries clearly.

This is an appropriate place to use an exit slip (Chapter 14) to assess whether the children know the difference between chasing, fleeing, and dodging and the cues associated with each.

Utilization Level: Learning Experiences Leading to Skill Development

Children at the utilization level are ready to test their skills in increasingly complex and gamelike situations. In these experiences, children will have to fake and dodge quickly in reaction to the deceptive movements of others.

A note about cues: Although several cues are listed for many of the learning experiences, it's important to focus on only one cue at a time. That way, the children can really concentrate on that cue. Once you provide feedback to the children and observe that most have learned a cue, then it's time to focus on another one.

PEOPLE DODGE (DODGING STATIONARY OBSTACLES)

Setting: Carpet squares or Xs on the floor to indicate where taggers are to stand. Children divided into two groups.

Cues

Split Second	(Make your moves quicker than light.)
Fake	(Step/lean one way; go the other.)
Change Direction	(Use changes of direction to avoid the tagger.)

Tasks/Challenges:

 One group of you are taggers and the other dodgers. Taggers stand on the Xs (or carpet squares) marked on the floor. Both feet must always be on the X (or carpet square). The dodgers start on one side of the room and try to get to the other side of the room without being tagged. After five runs, switch places. If you get tagged, try to figure out how to avoid being tagged the next time.

 Now the activity gets a little harder. If you're tagged, you must freeze right where you're tagged and become a tagger. Dodgers, this will get really hard at the end, so be on your toes.

Videotaping students chasing, fleeing, and dodging in the People Dodge activity would be an appropriate way to assess their use of chasing, fleeing, and dodging in a more complex situation. The videotape also lets students view their own performance and analyze their skills.

DODGING AND FAKING MOVES TO AVOID A CHASER (FREEZE-AND-COUNT TAG)

Setting: Groups of six, each with a space about the size of a quarter of a basketball court

Cues	
Dodgers:	Split Second (Make your moves quicker than light.)
	Fake (Step/lean one way; go the other.)
	Change Direction/Change Speed (Use changes of direction and speed to avoid the chaser.)
Chasers:	Watch the Hips (Watch the hips of the runner to tell his or her next move.)
	Teamwork (Decide your plan for catching together.)

Tasks/Challenges:

 This chasing and fleeing game will really make you work hard. You can't be slow; if you are, you'll be caught. Make sure you know where your boundaries are. Two people will start out as chasers—you decide who they'll be. The other four players are runners. On the signal, the chasers have one minute to try to catch all the runners. If tagged, a runner has to freeze and then count to ten out loud before starting to run again. The object is for the taggers to catch all the runners at the same time. After the first minute, change taggers and play again. Remember, the taggers have to try to catch everyone, and no one can go outside the boundaries.

 When children tag one another, they can be quite rough, sometimes knocking others over. Here are two rules which have helped us: (1) A tag is only a touch, not a slap or hit, and (2) all tags must be on the shoulders or below.

DODGING AND CHASING AS PART OF A TEAM (OCTOPUS)

Setting: Class divided into two groups. Tape or chalk marks on the floor approximately an arm's length apart to designate where the members of one team must place their feet (Figure 21.3).

Cues	
Split Second	(Make your moves quicker than light.)
Fake	(Step/lean one way; go the other.)
Change Direction	(Use changes of direction to avoid the tagger.)

Tasks/Challenges:

 To play this game, half of you will be taggers, and you must stand on the marks on the floor. You can't move either of your feet from your mark. The other half of you are dodgers. You'll begin at this end of the room and try to travel through the taggers without being touched. After the dodgers make it to the other side of the room, return around the outside of the room, and keep trying to get through the taggers until you hear the stop signal. On the stop signal, switch places.

 This time things are going to be a little harder for the taggers. Instead of just tagging the dodgers, the taggers have to tag the left knees of the dodgers with their right hands.

> In some school yards we've observed classes of children playing a game popularly called Bombardment, Killer, or Murder Ball. As these names imply, the game can be dangerous. Typically, a class is divided into two teams, with a middle line separating each team. Each team throws a hard ball in an attempt to strike players on the opposing team; the teams often throw from close range and toward an unsuspecting child. We don't support this activity. There are many other dodge-type experiences you can plan that are safer, allow more children to participate, and are more apt to result in skill development.

Figure 21.3 Setup for Octopus.

You can change these directions to several combinations of body parts—for example, right hand–right knee, left hand–right knee, left hand–right elbow.

T This time, let's make it harder for the dodgers. Taggers can now move one foot to tag. The other foot has to be on the mark.

DODGING AND CHASING ONE PERSON IN A MASS (PARTNER DODGE)

Setting: Partners spread apart on a field

Cues

Dodgers: Split Second (Make your moves quicker than light.)
Fake (Step/lean one way; go the other.)
Change Direction/Change Speed (Use changes of direction and speed to avoid the chaser.)

Chasers: Watch the Hips (Watch the hips of the runner to tell his or her next move.)

Tasks/Challenges:

T For this game, you and your partner are on opposite teams. One of you is a tagger; the other one is a dodger. On the signal, the taggers will spread out inside the boundaries, and the dodgers will line up on this side of the field. On the next signal, the dodgers will try to get to the other side of the field

without being touched by their partners, the taggers. The trick is that each dodger can be tagged only by the partner. When the dodgers get to the other side, they return to the starting line by going around the outside of the field and continue to travel across the space until they hear the stop signal. On the stop signal, trade places with your partners.

T This time I'm going to decrease the space to half the size it was. Ready? Go again.

C Can you stay untagged until the signal sounds?

DODGING IN A DYNAMIC SITUATION (BODY-PART TAG)

Setting: Groups of ten: eight runners and two chasers

Cues

Dodgers: Split Second (Make your moves quicker than light.)
Fake (Step/lean one way: go the other.)
Change Direction/Change Speed (Use changes of direction and speed to avoid the chaser.)

Chasers: Watch the Hips (Watch the hips of the runner to tell his or her next move.)
Teamwork (Decide your plan for catching together.)

Tasks/Challenges:

Ⓣ This activity is called Body-Part Tag. The object, if you are a tagger, is to tag the runners on the named body part or, if you're a runner, to avoid being tagged on the named body part. Chasers, try to touch the runners on the body part I call out. Any runners you tag must freeze. The tagged runners can be unfrozen if they're tagged by a free runner on a body part other than the tagged part. The taggers will have one minute to try and catch all the runners. At the end of one minute, start again with two new taggers. You must stay inside your boundaries. "Shoulders." Go.

DODGING WHILE MANIPULATING AN OBJECT

Setting: Areas about the size of a basketball key circle, marked off on the floor or the pavement; two or three children occupying each circle

Children should be at the utilization level in dribbling before attempting this task (Figure 21.4).

Cues	
Dodgers:	Protect the Ball (Keep your body between the ball and the other players.) Fake (Step/lean one way; go the other.) Change Direction/Change Speed (Use changes of direction and speed to avoid the chaser.)
Taggers:	Watch the Hips (Watch the hips of the runner to tell his or her next move.)

Tasks/Challenges:

Ⓣ The object of this game is to dribble a ball and at the same time try to take a ball away from someone else. Here's how it works. Each of you in your circle will be dribbling a ball. As you dribble the ball, you'll be trying to knock the other players' balls out of the area while keeping your ball from being knocked away. If your ball gets knocked out, just go get it and start again.

Figure 21.4 At the utilization level, these children are enjoying the thrill and excitement of chasing, fleeing, and dodging while manipulating an object.

Proficiency Level: Learning Experiences Leading to Skill Development

Children at the proficiency level are ready to use their skillful chasing, fleeing, and dodging abilities in a variety of complex and ever-changing, gamelike situations. In the experiences provided here, two teams of players are required to chase, flee, and dodge one another. Although some activities are included here, when children are at the proficiency level of chasing, fleeing, and dodging they are in actuality using those skills in combination with manipulative skills. Thus, appropriate activities would be gamelike, proficiency-level manipulative activities in which chasing, fleeing, and dodging skills lend the strategic dynamics to the game. See proficiency-level tasks in the manipulative skill theme chapters, (Chapters 26 through 30).

A note about cues: Although several cues are listed for many of the learning experiences, it's important to focus on only one cue at a time. That way, the children can really concentrate on that cue. Once you provide feedback to the children and observe that most have learned a cue, then it's time to focus on another one.

CONTINUAL FLEEING AND CHASING WITH A LARGE GROUP

Setting: Children scattered throughout the space: three taggers (with blue armbands); the rest, dodgers

Cues

Dodgers:	Split Second (Make your moves quicker than light.)
	Fake (Step/lean one way; go the other.)
	Change Direction/Change Speed (Use changes of direction and speed to avoid the chaser.)
Taggers:	Watch the Hips (Watch the hips of the runner to tell his or her next move.)
	Teamwork (Decide your plan for catching together.)

Tasks/Challenges:

🅣 This task is very much like freeze tag, except that when you are tagged, you must freeze with your legs wide apart and your hands clasped to your head. You can then be "freed" by any free player crawling through your legs. There will be three taggers, each with a blue armband.

Note: It is virtually impossible for the taggers to catch all the dodgers, so set a time for play (e.g., three to five minutes) and switch taggers.

DODGING WHILE MAINTAINING POSSESSION OF AN OBJECT

Setting: A rumble rhumba (Figure 21.5) and a beanbag for each child

Cues

Dodgers:	Split Second (Make your moves quicker than light.)
	Fake (Step/lean one way; go the other.)
	Change Direction/Change Speed (Use changes of direction and speed to avoid the chaser.)
Chasers:	Watch the Hips (Watch the hips of the runner to tell his or her next move.)

Tasks/Challenges:

🅣 For this game, you will need a rumble rhumba tied around your waist with one beanbag in it (*Figure 21.6*). When I say "Go," you will try to snatch the beanbags from other people's rumbles without having yours snatched. If you snatch a beanbag, it goes

Figure 21.5   To make a rumble rhumba, you'll need a one-gallon plastic jug (e.g., an empty milk or water container) and one yard of clothesline cord. Cut the bottom inch from the jug, and make two holes on either side of the handle. Then, run a length of clothesline through the holes, and tie the jug (open end up) around the waist.

Figure 21.6   Rumble rhumba in position around the waist.

in your rumble. The other rules are (1) you can take a beanbag only from a rumble, not someone's hands; (2) you can't protect your rumble with your hands; and (3) you can't touch anyone.

🅒 How many points can you get? Score one point for each beanbag you snatch; subtract five points if yours is taken.

In many primitive tribal games, the tribes believed that the chaser was evil, magic, or diseased and that the chaser's touch was contagious. Although today's games are a far cry from fleeing possible death, one has a hard time believing otherwise when observing the intensity and all-out effort children fleeing a chaser display!

CHASING AND FLEEING IN A GAME SITUATION

Setting: Groups of six, each with a ball; enough flag belts (of two colors) for all the youngsters; a space about twenty yards by ten yards.

Cues

Offense: Toward Goal (Always move toward your goal.)

Fake (Step/lean one way; go the other.)

Change Direction/Change Speed (Use changes of direction and speed to avoid the chaser.)

Defense: Watch the Hips (Watch the hips of the runner to tell his or her next move.)

Teamwork (Decide your plan for catching together.)

Tasks/Challenges:

T Each group of six should divide into two teams, each with a different-colored flag belt. One team will start with the ball. On the signal, a player on the team with the ball (team 1) tries to pass or run the ball from its goal line to other team's goal line without the ball touching the ground or team 2's grabbing the flag of the player with the ball. If a flag is grabbed, the ball touches the ground, or the goal line is crossed, the other team gets the ball.

CHASING AND DODGING SIMULTANEOUSLY (SNATCH THE FLAG)

Setting: Start with groups of about six children; as the children become more proficient, you can increase the size of the groups.

Cues

Dodgers: Split Second (Make your moves quicker than light.)

Fake (Step/lean one way; go the other.)

Change Direction/Change Speed (Use changes of direction and speed to avoid the chaser.)

Chasers: Watch the Hips (Watch the hips of the runner to tell his or her next move.)

Tasks/Challenges:

T This game pits each player against every other player. The object is to snatch the flag from another player's belt without losing your own flag and while staying within the designated boundaries. If your flag is pulled off, another player can put it back on and you can keep on playing. You *can't* put your own flag back on. You've really got to watch all the other players and move to stay out of their way. Remember all the turning, twisting, and jumping dodges.

C How many points can you accumulate? Score one point for every flag you take; subtract three points for every time your flag is taken.

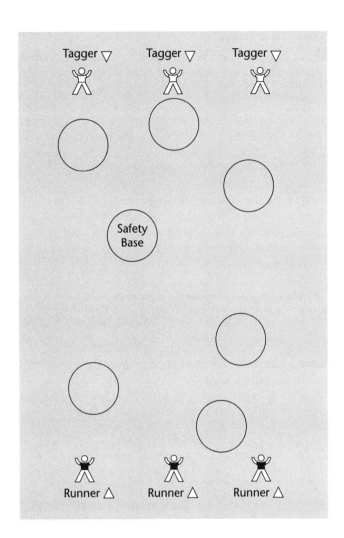

Figure 21.7 Setup for Safety Bases.

DODGING IN A GAME SITUATION (SAFETY BASES)

Setting: A large marked-off area, containing hoops as safety bases (Figure 21.7); teams of no more than five

Cues

Dodgers: Split Second (Make your moves quicker than light.)

Fake (Step/lean one way; go the other.)

Change Direction/Change Speed (Use changes of direction and speed to avoid the chaser.)

Chasers: Watch the Hips (Watch the hips of the runner to tell his or her next move.)

Teamwork (Decide your plan for catching together.)

Tasks/Challenges:

T This task is called Safety Bases. The object is for one team of runners, team 1, to cross the space without being touched by a team of taggers, team 2. Team 1 begins at one end of the field; the taggers on team 2 begin at the other end. On the signal, the runners try to cross the field without being tagged; the taggers try to stop any runners from getting across the field. The runners are safe—can't be tagged—when they're in any of the hoops. The runners have about one minute to cross the field. After two turns, you'll switch places. The safety bases will help, but use them wisely—only as a last resort when you're about to be tagged. Don't just stand in them the whole time.

DODGING IN A GAME SITUATION (PIRATE'S TREASURE)

Setting: A marked-off square playing area with a hoop in its center and a beanbag inside the hoop (Figure 21.8); groups of five

Cues

Offense (sailors):	Split Second (Make your moves quicker than light.)
	Fake (Step/lean one way; go the other.)
	Change Direction/Change Speed (Use changes of direction and speed to avoid the chaser.)
Defense (pirate):	Watch the Hips (Watch the hips of the runner to tell his or her next move.)

Tasks/Challenges:

T This chasing, fleeing, and dodging task is called Pirate's Treasure. The object is for the free players to try and steal the treasure, which is in the beanbag, from the middle of the space and return it to the outside of the space without being tagged by the pirate, who is protecting the treasure. There are five players in each group: one pirate and four sailors trying to get the treasure. The pirate's job is to protect the treasure from the sailors. On the signal, the sailors have two minutes in which to steal the treasure from inside the hoop and get it to the outside of the square without being touched by the pirate. If the sailors get the treasure to the outside or the two-minute limit is reached, play starts over again,

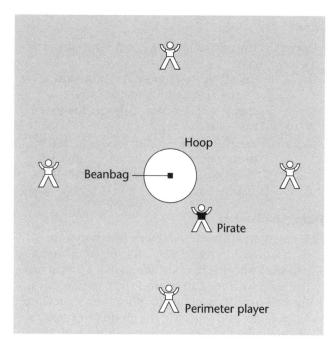

Figure 21.8   Setup for Pirate's Treasure.

and a new pirate tries to protect the treasure. The pirate cannot go inside the hoop.

USING TEAM STRATEGY FOR CHASING, FLEEING, AND DODGING (RIP FLAG)

Setting: A flag belt with two flags on it for each team member; each opposing team member has a different-colored flag. Groups of eight: four players on each team.

Cues

Dodgers:	Split Second (Make your moves quicker than light.)
	Fake (Step/lean one way; go the other.)
	Change Direction/Change Speed (Use changes of direction and speed to avoid the chaser.)
Chasers:	Watch the Hips (Watch the hips of the runner to tell his or her next move.)
	Teamwork (Decide your plan for catching together.)

Tasks/Challenges:

T The name of this task is Rip Flag. The object is to see how many of the other team's flags you can get without losing your own. One team begins at each end of the space. On the signal, both teams move into the playing area, and each team tries to snatch as many flags as possible from the other team's belts while preventing the other team from stealing their own flags. On the next signal, all play stops, and the teams return to their sidelines and count how many flags they were able to steal.

 For a journal entry at this point, you might ask children how they feel about their chasing, fleeing, and dodging ability.

DODGING WHILE MANIPULATING AN OBJECT IN A GAME SITUATION

Setting: This activity requires utilization-level skills in the manipulative activity you choose to use. It can be done with virtually any manipulative skill; the most common are dribbling and passing with the hands or feet, throwing and catching, or striking with a hockey stick. Whatever skill you choose, you will need one ball per group and appropriate other equipment. Groups of ten: five on a team.

Cues

Offense:	Split Second (Make your moves quicker than light.)
	Fake (Step/lean one way; go the other.)
	Change Direction/Change Speed (Use changes of direction and speed to avoid the chaser.)
Defense:	Watch the Hips (Watch the hips of the runner to tell his or her next move.)
	Teamwork (Decide your plan for catching together.)
	Play the Ball (Force the pass by playing the ball first.)

Tasks/Challenges:

🅣 This game is like Keep Away. There will be five on each team. You must clearly mark your boundaries, which can be no larger than half a basketball court. The object is for your team to keep the ball away from the other team. Here are the rules:

Figure 21.9 Goal line for manipulative activity Keep Away.

1. A ball can be stolen only on a pass; it cannot be taken when someone else has control of it.
2. No one can hold onto the ball longer than five seconds before passing it.
3. There can be no direct hand-offs; the ball must be passed.
4. If the ball goes out of bounds, it belongs to the other team.

🅣 We are going to change the game a little this time. You will keep your same teams, but each team will be trying to score by getting the ball across a goal line. All you have to do is get the ball across the line; the trick is that you cannot throw or hit it across until you are in the striking zone marked on the floor (*Figure 21.9*). The difference between this game and the last one is that now you should be moving in one direction, not all over.

READING COMPREHENSION QUESTIONS

1. List the differences among chasing, fleeing, and dodging.
2. Describe three effective dodging movements.
3. What are the characteristics of each of the four levels of skill proficiency for chasing, fleeing, and dodging?
4. Rank the following tasks by placing the number 1 in front of the easiest (most basic), the number 2 in front of the next more difficult, and so on.
   ( ) A defensive player in a football-type game pursues an offensive runner.

( ) You travel around the room. On a signal, you change directions as quickly as possible.

( ) You stay as close as you can to your partner, who'll try to get away from you.

( ) One team chases the members of an opposing team.

5. What is a fake? Give several examples of when a fake might be used.

6. Why do you use large areas when introducing the chasing, fleeing, and dodging skills?

7. Why have we eliminated dodgeball activities from the development of dodging skills?

8. What are some important cues to give when you're teaching fleeing? List at least three.

9. When a child is tagged during a tag game, what is one alternative to eliminating the child until a new game begins?

10. Killer (also called Bombardment) is a game that has been played for years in elementary schools. What is our reason for not recommending it?

11. What are two strategies for offense and two for defense that apply when chasing, fleeing, and dodging while manipulating an object?

REFERENCES

National Association for Sport and Physical Education (NASPE). (1995). *Moving into the future: National standards for physical education.* St. Louis, MO: Mosby.

Opie, I., & Opie, P. (1969). *Children's games in street and playground.* New York: Oxford University Press.

CHAPTER 22   Jumping and Landing

343

Jumping is a locomotor pattern in which the body propels itself off the floor or apparatus into a momentary period of flight. As an isolated maneuver or in combination with other basic patterns, jumping—particularly the flight phase when the body is unsupported in the air—is a fascinating body action.

A jump is performed for one of two reasons: (1) to raise the body vertically (straight up) for height or (2) to raise the body with a forward momentum to travel over a distance. Children who learn to jump effectively for height and distance are prepared for a multitude of game, dance, and gymnastics activities in which the performer needs to be a skilled jumper. See Box 22.1 for information on jumping and landing from the *National Standards for Physical Education*.

Fundamental Jumping Patterns

Wickstrom (1977, p. 63) suggested that infants are developmentally capable of performing a jumping action when they're approximately twenty-four months old. He described the types of jumps preschool children achieve in terms of progressive difficulty:

Jump down from one foot to the other.
Jump up from two feet to two feet.
Jump down from two feet to two feet.
Run and jump from one foot to the other.
Jump forward from two feet to two feet.
Jump down from one foot to two feet.
Run and jump forward from one foot to two feet.
Jump over object from two feet to two feet.
Jump from one foot to same foot rhythmically.

It's safe to assume that, within an average class of young children, some will be incapable of performing one or more of these jumping tasks. Initial observa-

tions will probably reveal a wide range of jumping abilities. Typically, kindergarten students are at the precontrol level. Their jumps usually achieve little height or distance, and they jump on two feet to ensure that they maintain their balance. Children at this level seem to be jumping merely to enjoy the sensation of momentarily losing contact with the ground and the challenge of maintaining balance upon landing (Figure 22.1). A teacher can build on this natural fascination by providing learning activities that progressively lead children toward the mature performance of jumping and landing in different dance, game, and gymnastics situations. (See our progression spiral on page 350.)

The fundamental jumping pattern consists of the following five basic variations:

1. Two-foot takeoff to a one-foot landing
2. Two-foot takeoff to a two-foot landing
3. One-foot takeoff to a landing on the same foot (hop)
4. One-foot takeoff to a landing on the other foot (leap)
5. One-foot takeoff to a two-foot landing

However, the specific actions of the body in performing a jump vary according to the purpose or intention—for example, jumping to catch or jumping to dismount from apparatus.

Levels of Skill Proficiency

When we begin to focus on jumping, we have children think of the skill as three successive phases:

1. Takeoff: Actions of the body as it's propelled off the ground
2. Flight: Actions of the body while it's off the ground and in the air

BOX 22.1   THE SKILL OF JUMPING AND LANDING IN THE *NATIONAL STANDARDS FOR PHYSICAL EDUCATION*

The movement skill of jumping and landing is referenced in the *National Standards for Physical Education* (NASPE, 1995) as a sample fourth-grade benchmark under Standard 1: Demonstrates competency in many movement forms and proficiency in a few movement forms. The standard speaks of the child's developing the ability to control use of the movement pattern and demonstrating sequential motor skills, for example, running into a jump. The sample benchmark states that a child "jumps and lands for height/distance using mature form" (p. 32).

Figure 22.1 This young child, jumping up and down like a bouncing ball, is enjoying the sensation of propelling his body off the ground for a momentary period of flight.

3. Landing: Actions of the body as it reestablishes contact with the ground

Our key observation points illustrate the correct and incorrect forms for the takeoff, flight, and landing phases as well as illustrating the mature stage. Box 22.2 contains key observation points for jumping for height and landing; Box 22.3 shows the key observation points for jumping for distance.

Following the initial exploration of jumping "just for fun," we explore jumping for height and distance, jumping a rope, and different patterns of jumping and landing. As they experiment with different takeoff and landing combinations, children begin to sense which takeoff procedures result in the highest jumps as opposed to which result in the longest jumps. They find that actions of the legs, arms, torso, and head during the flight phase influence the trajectory of the jump. They come to recognize the unique giving action of the ankles, knees, and hips in absorbing the shock of landing.

During the control level phase of our work on jumping and landing, children begin to accurately

perform the basic jumping variations using vigorous takeoffs and balanced, controlled landings. At this point, we also emphasize the flight phase of children's jumps. For example, we encourage them to begin to explore bodily actions in flight, such as the following:

Jumping and making body shapes in the air
Jumping and gesturing with an arm (for example, punching)
Jumping and twisting the trunk
Jumping and turning

Low apparatus is used to create new jumping situations, such as:

Jumping over hurdles and hoops
Jumping onto and off low equipment

Once children can repeatedly jump to fulfill a variety of objectives and their jumps continually exhibit a mature pattern, utilization-level tasks are appropriate:

Jumping on an accented beat
Performing a series of light, gentle leaps
Jumping to catch a ball
Jumping to mount or dismount apparatus

Performers at the proficiency level are able to jump high enough to carry out complex maneuvers in the air and to use a variety of jumping actions to express a feeling, idea, or attitude. Examples of proficiency-level performances include:

Jumping and throwing a ball to a target
Hurdling
Leaping reception of a football against an opponent
Standard patterns of jumping (for example, long jump, high jump)

Precontrol Level: Activities for Exploration

The following activities are designed for exploration of jumping. Through these activities children will begin to discover different types of jumps as well as jumps that take them high and jumps that take them far.

JUMPING AND LANDING: DIFFERENT PATTERNS

Setting: Ropes (one per child) placed around the edge of the teaching area

Tasks/Challenges:

🅣 At the edge of our working space are ropes. Select a rope and place it in a straight line in your self-space. Jump over the rope and land on the other side without falling down.

BOX 22.2   KEY OBSERVATION POINTS: JUMPING FOR HEIGHT AND LANDING

Takeoff

Do the child's hips, knees, and ankles flex in a crouch as the child prepares to jump?

Do the child's arms extend vigorously forward and then upward upon takeoff, reaching full extension above the head at liftoff?

Flight

Does the child's body extend fully in the air during the jump—especially the arms?

Landing

Do the child's ankles extend in preparation for landing?
Do the child's hips, knees, and ankles flex to absorb the shock of landing?

Mature Stage

When children are at the mature stage of jumping for height, do their jumps look similar to the following sequence? The hips, knees, and ankles flex in a preparatory crouch. The jump begins with a vigorous forward and upward lift by the arms. The thrust is continued by forceful extension at the hips, knees, and ankles. The body remains in extension until the feet are ready to retouch, and then the ankles, knees, and hips flex to absorb the shock of landing.

SOURCE: From *Fundamental Motor Patterns* (2nd ed.) by R. L. Wickstrom, 1977, Philadelphia: Lea & Febiger.

BOX 22.3   KEY OBSERVATION POINTS: JUMPING FOR DISTANCE

Takeoff

Do the child's arms extend vigorously forward and then upward upon takeoff, reaching full extension above the head at liftoff?

NO   YES

Are the child's hips, knees, and ankles fully extended at takeoff? Is the takeoff angle at 45° or less?

NO   YES

Flight

Does the child bring the legs forward and the arms downward in preparation for landing?

NO   YES

Landing

Do the child's heels contact the ground first?
Are the child's knees flexed and the arms thrust forward at the moment of contact?

NO YES

Mature Stage

When children are at the mature stage of jumping for distance, do their jumps look similar to the following sequence? The arms extend vigorously forward and then upward upon takeoff, reaching full extension above the head at liftoff. The hips and knees are extended fully, with the takeoff angle at 45° or less. In preparation for landing, the arms are brought downward and the legs thrust forward until the thighs are parallel to the surface. The center of gravity of the body is far behind the base of support (feet) upon contact, but at the moment of contact, the knees are flexed and the arms are thrust forward to maintain the momentum to carry the center of gravity beyond the feet.

SOURCE: From *Fundamental Motor Patterns* (2nd ed.) by R. L. Wickstrom, 1977, Philadelphia: Lea & Febiger.

Jumping and Landing

■ **PROFICIENCY LEVEL**

Hurdling jumps
Jumping, dancing, and imagery
Jumping as part of a dance creation
Jumping with a springboard
Jumping with a partner to match actions
Jumping with a partner to mirror actions

■ **UTILIZATION LEVEL**

Jumping to an accented beat
Throwing and catching while jumping
Jumping on a bench
Jumping to throw
Jumping to catch

■ **CONTROL LEVEL**

Jumping and landing task sheets
Jump, Squash, TaDa
Jumping on and off equipment using buoyant and yielding landings
Jumping over equipment using buoyant landings
Performing jumping sequences and making body shapes
Traveling, jumping, and body shapes
Jumping to form a body shape during flight
Jumping using buoyant and yielding landings
Jumping a self-turned rope
Jumping a turned rope
Jumping in rhythmical sequences
Jumping rhythmically
Jumping over low obstacles: hurdles
Jumping over low obstacles: hoops
Jumping for height
Standing long jump
Jumping and landing: basic patterns

■ **PRECONTROL LEVEL**

Jumping over a swinging rope
Jumping for height
Jumping for distance
Jumping and landing: different patterns

🔵 Explore different ways to jump over your rope, sometimes taking off on one foot and landing on two, sometimes taking off on two feet and landing on two.

🔵 Jump high in the air as you travel over your rope.

🔵 Stand at one end of your rope with a foot on either side of it. See if you can jump the distance of your rope.

⚠️ It is important to stress from the beginning that children land on their feet when jumping, not fall to the floor when they land.

🔵 Arrange your rope in a shape different from a straight line—for example, a circle or a rectangle. Jump into the shape and out the other side. Jump across your new rope shape.

JUMPING FOR DISTANCE

Setting: Ropes (one per child) placed around the edge of the teaching area; strips of masking tape (one per child) on the wall

Tasks/Challenges:

🔵 Place your rope on the floor away from others. Jump over your rope, landing as far from your rope as possible.

🔵 Place your piece of masking tape on the floor. Lie down with your feet touching the tape, and place the rope by the top of your head. If you have trouble, ask a friend to help. The distance from the rope to the tape is how tall you are. Standing behind your rope, try to jump your height.

🟢 Can you jump even farther than your height?

JUMPING FOR HEIGHT

Setting: Streamers hung at various heights from a rope stretched along the work area

Tasks/Challenges:

🔵 Jump to see if you can touch the streamers hanging from the rope.

🔵 Run and jump to touch the streamers.

JUMPING OVER A SWINGING ROPE

Setting: Class divided into groups of threes, each group with a "long" rope

Tasks/Challenges:

🔵 In your groups of three, you are going to take turns jumping over a swinging rope. Two of you will gently swing the rope while the third person jumps. After five jumps, trade places.

🟢 Practice for ten jumps without a mistake.

Control Level: Learning Experiences Leading to Skill Development

At the control level, we encourage children to practice both long and high jumps until their landings are balanced and controlled. We also provide opportunities for exploring variations in the flight phase of the jump and jumping in relation to different rhythms.

A note about cues: Although several cues are listed for many of the learning experiences, it's important to focus on only one cue at a time. That way, the children can really concentrate on that cue. Once you provide feedback to the children and observe that most have learned a cue, then it's time to focus on another one.

JUMPING AND LANDING: BASIC PATTERNS

Setting: Ropes (one per child) placed around the edge of the teaching area

Cue

Squash   (Bend your knees to absorb the force and maintain balance when you land.)

Tasks/Challenges:

🔵 When we first worked on jumping, you explored different ways to jump over your rope—just for fun. Place your rope in a straight line on the floor; choose three of your favorites from those different types of jumps and practice jumping over your rope, landing each time in a balanced position without falling down. Bend your knees when you land so that your landings are very quiet.

🔵 Jump over your rope, taking off on two feet and landing on two feet.

🔵 Position yourself approximately ten feet from your rope. Approach your rope with a series of running steps; jump over your rope, taking off on one foot and landing on two feet.

Using a series of running steps to approach your rope, take off on one foot and land on the opposite foot on the other side of your rope. Taking off on one foot and landing on the opposite foot is called a leap.

 Change the shape of your rope from a straight line to a circle, rectangle, or triangle. Standing just outside the rope shape, take off on one foot and jump inside your shape, landing on the same foot. What locomotor did you just do with this jump? A hop. Hop into and out of your rope.

Peer assessment of the different jumping patterns would be beneficial at this point. Review Chapter 14 for specific examples of assessments.

STANDING LONG JUMP

Setting: Ropes (one per child) placed around the edge of the work area; large color/panel gymnastics mats; strips of masking tape (one per child) on the wall

Cues	
Squash	(Bend your knees to absorb the force and maintain balance when you land.)
Swing Forward	(Swing your arms forcefully forward for maximum distance.)

Tasks/Challenges:

 Stand at one end of your rope with the rope between your feet. Bend your knees and swing your arms in preparation for the jump. Taking off on two feet and landing on two, jump forward as far as you can, trying to jump the full length of your rope.

 Remember when you practiced jumping your height by placing a piece of masking tape on the floor at the place of your feet and your rope on the floor the distance from your feet to your head. Try that jump again, taking off on two feet and landing on two feet. If you jump farther than your height, move the tape to where your heels first landed.

 Standing at one end of the mat, jump as far as you can toward the other end of the mat. Count your score by the number of panels you jumped over. **Remember to bend your knees and swing your arms in preparation for the jump, then swing your arms forward for a really far jump.** Keeping your arms stretched forward will also keep you from falling backward when you land!

The three tasks just described work well in station format for practice of the two-foot to two-foot standing jump.

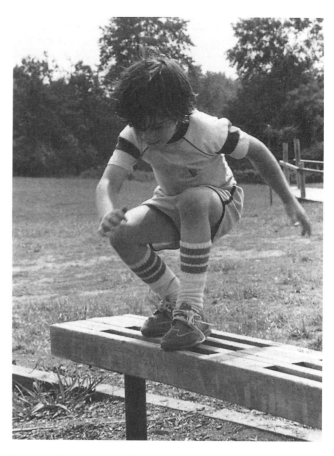

Figure 22.2   This child is learning to land safely by jumping off a low bench onto grass. Inside, children can jump from milk crates or boxes onto mats.

JUMPING FOR HEIGHT

Setting: Balloons suspended at various heights from a stretched rope; milk crates or low boxes (packed with newspaper) at large gymnastics mats

Cues	
Squash	(Bend your knees to absorb the force and maintain balance when you land.)
Swing Upward	(Swing your arms upward for good height.)

Tasks/Challenges:

 Scatter throughout general space and jump high in the air, returning to the floor in your same self-space. Take off on two feet and land on two feet.

 Jump high in the air, taking off on two feet and landing on two feet. Swing your arms upward; this will help you jump higher.

T Positioned around the work area are milk crates and boxes stuffed with newspaper on large gymnastics mats. Standing on the box or crate, jump high in the air and land on two feet on the mat in front of the box or crate (*Figure 22.2*). **Remember to swing your arms upward, reaching for the sky, to gain maximum height on your jump.**

T Travel throughout general space; on the signal, jump high in the air by taking off on one foot and landing on the opposite foot. This is the leap we practiced earlier; swing your arms upward as you jump to stay airborne as long as possible.

T Positioned around the work area are balloons suspended from stretched ropes. Using a two-foot takeoff and a two-foot landing, jump to touch the balloons like a basketball player trying to tap the ball on the jump.

T Approach the balloon with a series of running steps using a one-foot takeoff and a one-foot landing on the opposite foot to jump for the balloon. Which type jump gives your more height: A two-foot takeoff or a one-foot takeoff? A standing jump or a running approach to the jump?

ASSESSMENT EXAMPLE
from the National Standards for Physical Education

Teacher Observation/Observational Record

Students are requested to demonstrate the skills introduced in class as the teacher observes their performance and records the satisfactory use of the critical elements of the skills on a checklist.

Criteria for Assessment

a. Demonstrates critical elements of the selected skills (jumping and landing) over several trials

NASPE (1995, pp. 18–19).

JUMPING OVER LOW OBSTACLES: HOOPS

Setting: Hoops (one per child) scattered throughout the teaching area

Cues	
Squash	(Bend your knees to absorb the force and maintain balance when you land.)
Swing Upward	(Swing your arms upward for good height.)
Swing Forward	(Swing your arms forcefully forward for maximum distance.)

Tasks/Challenges:

T Jump over your hoop. As your feet touch the ground, freeze your body perfectly still; this means you must bend your ankles, knees, and hips as you land. **Think of your feet sinking into the floor as if the floor were a sponge.**

C Practice jumping over your hoop with two-foot takeoffs and landings until you can land without falling three times in a row. Can you then do the same three perfect landings with a one-foot takeoff and a two-foot landing?

T Travel throughout general space, leaping over hoops. **Remember to extend your arms up for good height as you leap.**

JUMPING OVER LOW OBSTACLES: HURDLES

Setting: One hurdle (cones and rolled newspaper or rope) per child

Cues	
Squash	(Bend your knees to absorb the force and maintain balance when you land.)
Swing Upward	(Swing your arms upward for good height.)

Tasks/Challenges:

T Standing just behind your hurdle, jump over it, using a two-foot takeoff and a two-foot landing. Try to be really high when you cross the top—**push with your toes; reach for the sky** (*Figure 22.3*).

T Now as you jump over the hurdle, try to use the different types of jumps you have learned. Try the easiest ones first and then the most difficult ones.

C Practice each jump until you can do it three times with a soft landing and without touching the crosspiece.

T Stand approximately six feet behind your hurdle. Approach the hurdle with quick, running steps. Jump over your hurdle using a one-foot takeoff and a two-foot landing.

T When you can clear the hurdle without touching the crossbar and land without falling down, approach the bar with quick, running steps. Jump over the bar using a one-foot takeoff and then land on the opposite foot; continue with a few quick, running steps before you stop. Wow! You look ready for the Olympics.

Figure 22.3 At the control level, youngsters enjoy running and jumping over low obstacles.

JUMPING RHYTHMICALLY

Setting: Carpet squares scattered throughout general space; a recording of the sounds of tools and machines; a recording of "Pop Goes the Weasel"

Cues

Spring, Spring	(Quick, springy landings for the fast beat.)
High Jumps, Full Squash	(Full squash following the high jumps.)
Heads Up	(Keep your head and shoulders up for good balance.)

Tasks/Challenges:

T Inside your carpet square, jump while keeping beat with the drum. You'll have to listen carefully, because the drumbeat will change at different times. **To do this without losing the beat, take little jumps so that your feet barely leave the floor.** In other words, you'll be almost bouncing on your toes.

For the next task, play the record or tape of the sounds of tools and machines. (Children enjoy electronic/synthesizer music.)

T This time, instead of a drumbeat you'll hear the sounds of different machines and tools that you're familiar with. Staying inside your carpet square, take little jumps, keeping time with the tool and machine sounds you hear. The sounds will change often, so be alert, and take little bouncy jumps on your toes.

T Again, the drumbeat will guide your jumps. As you hear the slow beat, take big, high jumps. When you hear the quick beat, take small jumps. This maneuver involves careful listening, so be prepared to change at any time. Make sure that your jumps are clearly big on the slow beats and really little on the fast beats; adjust the height of your jump for fast (low) and slow (high).

Place the carpet squares in a circle with approximately six to eight inches between each carpet.

C Let's combine our jumping and rhythmic response to "Pop Goes the Weasel." Select a carpet square, and stand on it without moving it from the circle. We will stay on our carpet squares, our self-space, during the verse of the song. Follow the leader (me) during that portion as we do self-space actions—stretching, twisting, clapping, tapping, jogging in place, and so forth. When we come to the "Pop" in the song, jump from your carpet square to the next one—clockwise around the circle. Be ready for new nonlocomotor actions in self-space when you land.

Choose a new leader for the self-space actions after each jump. Younger students enjoy singing "Pop Goes the Weasel" along with or instead of the recording.

The folk dance "Jump Jim Joe" is an excellent activity for the practice of rhythmical jumping. Young children enjoy the repetitive nature of the jumping in the dance.

JUMPING IN RHYTHMICAL SEQUENCES

Setting: Children scattered throughout general space

Cues

Spring, Squash	(Springy landings to continue travel; full squash to stop.)
Heads Up	(Keep your head and shoulders up for good balance.)
Swing Upward	(Swing your arms upward for good height.)

Tasks/Challenges:

T This time, you're going to travel and then jump and travel again, always keeping the same rhythm.

To begin, you'll all practice the same travel jump pattern, which will go like this: Run, run, leap/run, run, leap. As you move, all of you will say together "Run, run, leap" so you can stay together. Let's practice saying that and keeping the same tempo before beginning to move. (*Practice saying the phrase in tempo.*) As you jump and run this time, remember to stay with the voices; everyone should be jumping at the same time if you're all together.

T Now instead of saying the phrase, you're going to clap it as you go. You'll have to remember what to do on your own.

C Now that you can follow the phrase that I designed for you, you're going to make up your own and follow it. Your phrase should contain two traveling actions followed by one jumping pattern. You should repeat the sequence three times before coming to a stop. Practice the whole thing until you think that it's the best you can do. As you begin, it helps to say to yourself what you're supposed to be doing, just as you did in the previous activity. When you think you know it, go to clapping instead of saying it. When you're really good, practice doing it with no noise at all. Remember: two traveling actions followed by one jumping action, repeated three times. Keep the same rhythm throughout each part of the sequence. (*Pinpoint several children who've created an interesting sequence—they don't have to be the most skilled children in the class.*)

JUMPING A TURNED ROPE

Setting: Class divided into groups of two or three, each group with one long rope. *If the children are in groups of two, attach one end of the rope to a fence post, pole, or chair.* Mark a box on the floor at the center of the rope for the jumper and an X on the floor where the turner or turners stand.

Cues

Jumpers:	Heads Up (Keep your head and shoulders up for good balance.)
	Jump, Jump (Small, springy jumps with very little height.)
Turners:	One, Two, Three (Swing the rope back and forth before the first swing over the head, counting "One, two, three"; this will help the jumper be ready.)
	Smooth Turns (Turn the rope with large, smooth swings.)

Tasks/Challenges:

T At your ropes, two people will turn and one person will try to jump. Jumpers should try to stay in the box marked on the floor as you jump. After fifteen jumps, trade positions.

T When you can successfully jump the rope by starting in the middle, try to start from the outside: run in and jump. Turners: Turn the rope so it turns toward the jumper—the front-door approach. Jumpers: Start your run as soon as the rope touches the floor.

C Create a new rhyme as you jump the long rope. *Record the children's rhymes in a booklet of "Jump Rope Rhymes."*

JUMPING A SELF-TURNED ROPE

Setting: Ropes of different lengths so that each child has a personal rope of the proper length

Cues

Heads Up	(Keep your head and shoulders up for good balance.)
Jump, Jump	(Small, springy jumps with very little height.)

Tasks/Challenges:

T Practice jumping your rope by turning it over your head (*Figure 22.4*). Some of you will find that jumping forward is easier; others will find that jumping the rope as it turns backward is easier. Be sure you try jumping both ways.

T If you're having trouble, bring the rope over your head, and stop it on the floor in front of your feet, and then jump over the rope. As you become successful, go a little faster, and don't let the rope stop so much. As you practice, you will find yourself stopping the rope less.

T When you become successful at jumping in one direction (forward or backward) without missing, try jumping in the other direction.

C Set a goal for yourself of the number of jumps you want to make without a mistake.

T Try jumping with the different types of jumps we have learned—two feet to two feet, one foot to the other foot, two feet to one foot, and so forth.

Figure 22.4 Jumping rope is a favorite pastime of children.

JUMPING USING BUOYANT AND YIELDING LANDINGS

Setting: Children scattered throughout general space; paper and pencil available outside work area

Cues	
Yielding Landings	(Bend your knees to absorb the force when you land, as if sinking into the floor.)
Swing Upward	(Swing your arms upward for good height.)
Heads Up	(Keep your head and shoulders up for good balance.)

Tasks/Challenges:

T Jump three times in a row on two feet, pausing between each jump. This is called a yielding landing.

T This time, jump three times in a row using a two-foot takeoff and a two-foot landing without pausing between each jump. This is a buoyant landing. **Spring up quickly after each jump.**

T Now, jump twice in a row, the first time with a buoyant landing and the second time with a yielding landing. Make sure that your landings are clearly different so that I can tell which one you're doing simply by watching.

T This time on the signal, jump high, turn in the air, land balanced, and freeze. Again, use yielding landings.

T Now, jump high, turn in the air, and upon landing collapse to the floor, curl, and freeze. **Remember to use your arms to help you turn in the air.**

T Try this one: Jump high, turn in the air, and upon landing collapse to the floor, curl, and freeze for an instant—and then quickly resume traveling. Make your moves very smooth so that they really go together and you know exactly what you're doing and what comes next. Use your arms to help you get up in the air. Strive for a yielding landing.

C So far I've made up all your jumping and traveling patterns. On your piece of paper (*pass out paper to the youngsters*), write down a jumping/traveling pattern that you'd like to do yourself. After you've written it down, practice it until it goes smoothly and you know it by heart. Make sure that you always begin and end in the same place, which is one way you know you're doing the same thing each time. I should be able to tell what you're doing and the type of landing by watching you. If I can't, I'll ask you.

JUMPING TO FORM A BODY SHAPE DURING FLIGHT

Setting: Children scattered throughout general space, each with a hurdle or a rope in a shape on the floor

Cues	
Yielding Landings	(Bend your knees to absorb the force when you land, as if sinking into the floor.)
Swing Upward	(Swing your arms upward for good height.)
Heads Up	(Keep your head and shoulders up for good balance.)

Tasks/Challenges:

T Jump over your equipment, and form a narrow body shape while you're in the air. A narrow body shape is very skinny. **Remember to make all the**

Figure 22.5 Children learn to jump off apparatus and land safely.

parts of your body skinny, not just one part. Practice your shape until it's as skinny as it can be. (*Figure 22.5*)

Ⓒ Now think of five more skinny body shapes that you can make while you're in the air. Practice all the shapes until they're the best you can do. I'll come and ask each of you to show me your best shape, so be ready. **Remember not to fall over on your landings; your feet should stick as if you had glue on them.** What kind of landings will you need?

Ⓣ This time you're going to jump using wide body shapes in the air. A wide shape is very big and spread out, like a wall. **Remember as you jump to make your whole body wide in the air, by stretching your arms and legs outward from your body.** Practice your shape until it's as wide as it can be.

Ⓒ Now that you know what a wide shape is, think of five more wide shapes you can make when you jump. Let them be really different, even weird.

Practice all the shapes until they're the best you can do. I'm going to ask some of you to show your wide shapes, so work hard.

Pinpoint several children who are using wide shapes.

Ⓣ This time, you're going to learn some new names for body shapes. First, you're going to make symmetrical shapes in the air. A *symmetrical* shape looks exactly alike on both sides. For example, if I were to cut you in half from head to toe, you'd look the same on both sides. At your equipment, practice making a symmetrical shape in the air. Be sure that both sides of your body look exactly alike.

Ⓒ Create five more symmetrical shapes with your jumps.

Ⓣ This time you're going to do nonsymmetrical jumps. In a *nonsymmetrical* jump, both sides of your body look really different. So if I were to cut you in half, one arm might be up in the air and the other one out to the side, or one leg might be going forward and the other one backward. In other words, one side shouldn't look like the other one. In your space, create a nonsymmetrical jump. **Remember to absorb force when you land by bending your knees.**

Ⓒ Create five nonsymmetrical jumps you can do in the air.

Ⓣ Try to do wide, symmetrical jumps. Find three that you really like, and practice them.

Ⓣ Now try to find three narrow, symmetrical jumps. After you do that, find three wide, nonsymmetrical jumps and three narrow, nonsymmetrical jumps. I'm going to ask some of you to show your jumps to the class, so make them the best that they can be.

Ⓣ Approach your hurdle or rope shape with a series of running steps. Jump in the air, making a wide shape. **Land in a balanced position without falling down.**

Ⓣ Try your other shapes in the air combined with your short running approach.

 Students should attempt running, jumping, and making shapes while airborne only after they have demonstrated safe landings in self-space—absorbing the force by bending the knees and landing in a balanced position without falling forward.

TRAVELING, JUMPING, AND BODY SHAPES

Setting: Children scattered throughout general space

Cues

Buoyant Landings	(Bend your knees as you land, then spring up quickly.)
Swing Upward	(Swing your arms upward for good height.)
Heads Up	(Keep your head and shoulders up for good balance.)

Tasks/Challenges:

T As you travel around the room, make the kind of jump that I've called out each time you hear the drumbeat. The jump may simply be wide, or it may be narrow and nonsymmetrical. You'll have to be alert to what I'm saying as well as watching out for others. We'll use buoyant landings so that we can be ready to travel again. Remember to make your shapes as clear as you possibly can.

PERFORMING JUMPING SEQUENCES AND MAKING BODY SHAPES

Setting: Note cards with various body-shape sequences written on them, each sequence containing at least four different body shapes (e.g., wide; wide symmetrical; narrow nonsymmetrical; narrow); children scattered throughout general space, each with a sequence card

Cues

Buoyant Landings	(Bend your knees as you land, then spring up quickly.)
Yielding Landings	(Bend your knees to absorb the force when you land, as if sinking into the floor.)
Swing Upward	(Swing your arms upward for good height.)
Heads Up	(Keep your head and shoulders up for good balance.)

Tasks/Challenges:

T On your card are listed four body shapes. You're going to make up a sequence of jumps that shows those body shapes in the air. To do this, you'll first travel a bit and then jump, showing the first body shape; then you'll travel again and jump and show the second body shape listed; you'll travel again and jump using the third body shape; you'll travel one more time and jump showing the last body shape. So your sequence should be like this: Travel, jump; travel, jump; travel, jump; travel, jump, freeze. Repeat the sequence enough times so that you can do it the same way each time. Memorize it.

When it's memorized, show the sequence to a friend. **Remember, use buoyant landings between jumps and a yielding landing after your last jump.**

JUMPING OVER EQUIPMENT USING BUOYANT LANDINGS

Setting: Pairs of hurdles around the room, spaced so that children can jump the first and then the second hurdle

Cues

Buoyant Landings	(Bend your knees as you land, then spring up quickly.)
Yielding Landings	(Bend your knees to absorb the force when you land, as if sinking into the floor.)
Heads Up	(Keep your head and shoulders up for good balance.)

Tasks/Challenges:

T Earlier in our work, you practiced taking off on one foot and landing on the opposite foot, as in a leap. This is the action you use to clear a hurdle. Approach the first hurdle with quick, running steps; jump over the first hurdle with the one-foot to one-foot action; use a buoyant landing to continue your travel and jump over the second hurdle.

C Practice this activity until you seem to just pop over the first and then the second hurdle.

JUMPING ON AND OFF EQUIPMENT USING BUOYANT AND YIELDING LANDINGS

Setting: Boxes, low benches, milk crates, and other low equipment around the room

Cues

Buoyant Landings	(Bend your knees as you land, then spring up quickly.)
Yielding Landings	(Bend your knees to absorb the force when you land, as if sinking into the floor.)
Heads Up	(Keep your head and shoulders up for good balance.)

Tasks/Challenges:

T Jump onto a piece of equipment, and use a buoyant landing to quickly spring off with another jump to the floor. **You should barely touch the equipment before you are off again and back to**

the floor, almost as if you were on a spring-board—no stopping between jumps.

T This time, jump onto the piece of equipment using a yielding landing, hold still on top of the equipment a couple of seconds, then jump to the floor with another yielding landing. **Remember, on this jump, your knees should really bend and you should be able to hold still when you finish.**

T Try jumping onto the equipment with the different jumps we have learned—two feet to two feet, one foot to two feet, and so on. Sometimes use a buoyant landing on the equipment so that you can quickly jump off; sometimes use a yielding landing on the equipment, pausing before you jump off. Always use a yielding landing on two feet when you jump off the equipment to the floor.

 Which landing is used for a quick, springy action to continue movement? Which landing is used for landing and holding still?

ASSESSMENT EXAMPLE
from the National Standards for Physical Education

Teacher Observation (video)/Observational Record

Students are asked to skip, gallop, and jump off a low box. A camera is set up in one corner of the gym to record their performance. Each student is asked to go in front of the camera and perform the specified movement patterns. The teacher uses a checklist to assess the extent to which mature and skilled patterns have been attained.

Criteria for Assessment

a. Exhibits mature form for each of the movement patterns
b. Demonstrates consistent and smooth performance

NASPE (1995, p. 19)

JUMP, SQUASH, TaDa

Setting: Low benches, low balance beam, folded mats positioned throughout general space; children divided into groups for stations

Cues	
Squash	(Bend your knees to absorb the force and maintain balance when you land.)
Swing Upward	(Swing your arms upward for good height.)
Heads Up	(Keep your head and shoulders up for good balance.)

Tasks/Challenges:

T Have you ever watched gymnasts perform a stunt and then extend their arms high above their heads? Why do you think they do this movement? They do it to regain balance and proper body alignment after the gymnastics action. In the cartoon "Calvin and Hobbes," Calvin called this recovery the "TaDa" of gymnastics, the recovery to a balanced position no matter what has happened during the movement. Let's add that action to our jumping and landing work today. Jump from your mat (bench, beam) with a two-foot takeoff and a two-foot landing. Jump for maximum height, squash into a balanced position, then extend your arms to the sky as you say "TaDa."

T Jump off your mat (bench, beam) with a quarter turn in the air. Land in a balanced position; recover with a full extension. **Don't forget the TaDa!**

T When a friend gives you a thumbs-up for a good landing on your quarter turn, you may want to try a one-half turn. Practice turning your body clockwise and counterclockwise.

T Jump off the mat (bench, beam), make a shape in the air, land in a balanced position, and recover with a full gymnastics extension.

T Combine jumping off the low equipment, landing, and rolling in a gymnastics sequence; finish your sequence by returning to a standing TaDa.

 Use the previous task only if children have mastered rolling from Chapter 24 or in combination with work from that chapter.

(See Chapter 24 for additional combination tasks, as well as for transferring off low apparatus.)

JUMPING AND LANDING TASK SHEET

Setting: A jumping and landing task sheet (similar to the example in Figure 22.6) for each child

Cues	
Buoyant Landings	(Bend your knees as you land, then spring up quickly.)
Yielding Landings	(Bend your knees to absorb the force when you land, as if sinking into the floor.)
Heads Up	(Keep your head and shoulders up for good balance.)
Swing Upward	(Swing your arms upward for good height on the jump)
Swing Forward	(Swing your arms forcefully forward for maximum distance.)

Figure 22.6 Task sheet for jumping and landing.

Name ————————————— Teacher —————————————

Jumping Task Sheet

Verification	Challenge
	I can jump starting on two feet and landing on two feet.
	I can jump from two feet to one foot.
	I can jump from one foot to the other foot.
	I can hop from one foot to the same foot.
	I can jump from one foot to two feet.
	I can jump, turn in the air, and land without falling.
	I can jump off a box and land without falling.
	I can jump off a box, turn in the air, and land without falling.
	I can run and jump over a block and cane and land without falling.
	I can turn a jump rope myself and jump 15 times without missing.
	I can
	I can
	I can

Select cues appropriate to the tasks on the sheet (e.g., jumping forward, jumping upward, jumping and continuing action, jumping/landing with a stop of movement).

Tasks/Challenges:

C This task sheet lets you test the jumping skills you've practiced so far. Whenever you've practiced a challenge and think you can do it correctly, ask a friend to watch you. If your friend thinks you've done the challenge well, the friend signs her or his name on the sheet next to the challenge.

Utilization Level: Learning Experiences Leading to Skill Development

At the utilization level, we provide contexts that help children use jumping and landing in combination with other movements, with complicated rhythms, and as a means for expression. We make the manipulative learning experiences more difficult by selecting different objects for the children to throw. We start with beanbags; then, as the children improve, we switch to whiffle balls, foam footballs, and, for the highly skilled, tennis balls.

A note about cues: Although several cues are listed for many of the learning experiences, it's important to focus on only one cue at a time. That way, the children can really concentrate on that cue. Once you provide feedback to the children and observe that most have learned a cue, then it's time to focus on another one.

JUMPING TO CATCH

Setting: Low benches, chairs, or milk crates scattered throughout general space; sets of partners with beanbags, plastic balls, foam footballs, tennis balls

Cues	
Yielding Landings	(Bend your knees to absorb the force when you land, as if sinking into the floor.)
Swing Upward	(Swing your arms upward for a full extension and added height on the jump.)

Tasks/Challenges:

🅣 One partner stands on the low bench (chair, milk crate) and then jumps from the bench to catch the ball your partner tosses. Catch the ball while in the air. After three jumps, switch catcher-thrower positions with your partner. Hint for the thrower: Stand close and begin the toss as soon as your partner begins to jump.

For the next task, clear the general space of benches, crates, and other obstacles.

🅣 Pairs, scatter throughout general space. See how many times you can jump and catch without a mistake; count your score only if you catch the ball before you land. After three trials, switch thrower/catcher as you did earlier.

🅣 When the activity becomes easy for you and your partner, try throwing the ball so your partner has to reach to the left or to the right to make the catch.

🅣 Throw the ball so your partner is forced off the ground to catch it; this means that you have to throw the ball to a point above where the catch will actually be made. This is a high-level catch—feet off the floor, arms extended above the head

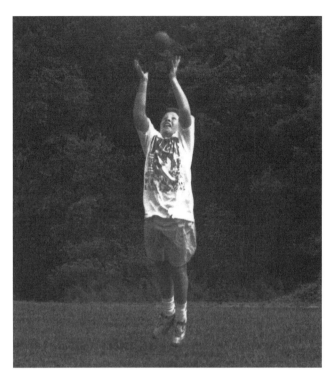

Figure 22.7 Catching at high level combines jumping and stretching.

(*Figure 22.7*). Throwers: It helps to pick a spot on the wall (tree, telephone pole) to aim at.

🅣 Try both one- and two-foot takeoffs.

🅣 Switch with your partner after five throws. You are now the catcher; your partner will throw the ball above your head, so you must jump for the catch.

🅣 When you are confident throwing and catching while jumping, you and your partner can add a new element—traveling. Practice running, jumping, and catching in the air. For the two of you to do this task well, your partner will need to make a good throw. At first, run and jump from right to left; then, run and jump from left to right.

🅣 When you are able to make at least three catches in a row, run away from the thrower—that is, start close to and run away from your partner, as you might in a football game.

JUMPING TO THROW

Setting: Low benches, chairs, or milk crates throughout general space; sets of partners with whiffle balls, tennis balls, footballs

Cues

Yielding Landings	(Bend your knees to absorb the force when you land, as if sinking into the ground.)
Vertical Jumps	(Jump upward, not outward, to throw.)

Tasks/Challenges:

T Stand ten to twelve feet from your partner. Jump from the bench (chair, crate) and throw the ball to your partner before you land. Try to throw the ball so your partner can catch it easily. Switch with your partner after four jumps/throws.

Clear the general space of benches, crates, and other obstacles.

T Pick a target, such as a target on the wall (or a basketball backstop, a hoop, or a stationary partner). Jump and throw the ball to the target.

C When you hit the target five times in a row, move farther away from the target. It counts as a successful throw only if you hit the target and make your throw while in the air.

T As this activity gets easier, trying running, jumping, and throwing to the target.

JUMPING ON A BENCH

Setting: Low benches scattered throughout the work area

Cues

Squash	(Bend your knees to absorb the force and maintain balance when you land.)
Arms Extended	(Extend your arms outward for good balance.)

Tasks/Challenges:

T You will work one at a time on the bench. Travel to the middle of the bench; jump upward, taking off and landing on two feet on the bench. **Focus your eyes on the end of the bench.**

T When you're able to do this activity several times without falling off, practice landing on only one foot. Hold your balance on the bench before your other foot comes down on the bench. Try to hold your balance for two or three seconds.

C Design a sequence along the bench that includes at least two different jumps. For example, hop on one foot along the bench, jump and turn so that you land facing the opposite direction, and travel back to the start using small leaps. At first, your jumps won't be very high, but as you get better, you'll want to make them higher. Practice your sequence until you can do it three times in a row without falling off.

When you observe that children are competent and comfortable with different types of jumps on the bench, they may progress to low and medium balance beams. This is an excellent opportunity for intratask variation.

THROWING AND CATCHING WHILE JUMPING

Setting: A court, its boundaries marked with a rope or a net (size of court is determined by space available; the larger the court, the more difficult the game)

Cues

Buoyant Landings	(Bend your knees as you land, then spring up quickly—to throw or travel.)
Yielding Landings	(Bend your knees to absorb the force, and sink into a balanced position.)

Tasks/Challenges:

T The game you're going to play will give you a chance to practice throwing and catching while jumping. The object is to have the ball touch the floor on the opposite side of the net. Here are the rules:

1. There are three players on a team.
2. There is one team on each side of the rope (or net).
3. A player must be off the floor when the ball is thrown or caught.
4. At least two players on your team must touch the ball before it is thrown back over the rope (net).
5. Points are scored when the ball lands out of bounds, the ball hits the floor in bounds, or a player throws or catches the ball while that player's feet are touching the ground.

This game can also be played cooperatively: Both teams work together to see how many times the ball can cross the rope or net without breaking any of the rules. A point is scored each time the ball crosses the net. A good score to aim for is ten throws in a row across the net without breaking a rule.

JUMPING TO AN ACCENTED BEAT

Setting: Children scattered throughout general space, each with a hoop

Cue	
Buoyant Landings	(Bend your knees, then spring up quickly to travel.)

Tasks/Challenges:

Ⓣ When I beat the drum, jump into and out of your hoop every time you hear the drumbeat.

Ⓣ Now take off on two feet, and land on two feet. As the drumbeat gets faster, be ready to jump by having your knees bent and your arms flexed. Try to land on only the balls of your feet, which means that your heels won't touch the ground.

Ⓣ Take off on one foot, and land on the same foot.

Ⓣ Try to keep up with the beat—it's going to get faster and faster. When one leg gets tired, change to the other leg.

Ⓣ Listen as I beat the drum. The first beat is louder than the others. This is called an *accented* beat. Use one-or two-foot takeoffs and landings, but jump on only the accented beat. The first beat will be accented; the next three beats will be unaccented.

Proficiency Level: Learning Experiences Leading to Skill Development

At the proficiency level, dynamic dance, game, and gymnastics experiences are designed to help youngsters use, refine, and enjoy their jumping abilities. Children almost always jump in relation to objects or other people (or both) and use jumping for both expressive and functional purposes (Figure 22.8).

A note about cues: Although several cues are listed for many of the learning experiences, it's important to focus on only one cue at a time. That way, the children can really concentrate on that cue. Once you provide feedback to the children and observe that most have learned a cue, then it's time to focus on another one.

JUMPING WITH A PARTNER TO MIRROR ACTIONS

Setting: Two pieces of equipment (benches, tables, or vaulting boxes) about fifteen feet apart, with a large mat on the floor between; children with partners

Figure 22.8 In games, children use the ability to jump while catching a rebounding ball.

Cues	
Yielding Landings	(Bend your knees to absorb the force, and sink into a balanced position.)
Buoyant Landings	(Bend your knees as you land, then spring up quickly.)
Heads Up	(Keep your head and shoulders up for good balance.)

Tasks/Challenges:

Ⓣ You and your partner are going to mirror each other's jumps. *Mirroring* means that you face each other and copy the other's movements, as if you were looking in a mirror. Therefore, if your partner uses the left arm, you'll use your right arm. To start, decide which of you will be the first leader. The leader makes up the first jump and shows it to the partner. Then you both face each other and do that jump at the same time, mirroring each other exactly. This activity will be hard at first, because you'll have to take off at the same time, jump the same height, and do everything exactly together. Start with some easy jumps and then go to harder ones. Each person takes three turns as leader and then switches. Again, make your jumps look like a reflection of your partner's. **Don't forget: Yielding and buoyant landings will be part of the mirror action.**

Pinpoint several pairs who are mirroring jumps accurately.

T As you get better at mirroring your partner, you may want to include such actions as gesturing in the air, turning in the air, or rolling after landing. **This will really take a lot of work; you may want to count out everything before you do it.**

JUMPING WITH A PARTNER TO MATCH ACTIONS

Setting: Two pieces of equipment (benches, tables, or vaulting boxes) about fifteen feet apart, with a large mat on the floor between; children with partners

Cues	
Travel, Jumps, & Landings	(Everything must match your partner—travel, jumps, and landings.)
Heads Up	(Keep your head and shoulders up for good balance.)

Tasks/Challenges:

T Now that you've become very good at mirroring a partner's actions and jumps, you're going to try matching jumps. *Matching* means that you do the same thing at the same time; thus, if you're facing your partner, your actions look the opposite of your partner's. If you use your right leg, then your partner must also use the right leg. Again, decide which of you will be the first leader. The leader makes a jump and faces the partner; the two of you then match jumps. Take three turns as leader, and then switch. Start with easy jumps. **Counting will help you match starting each jump.**

T Once you've become quite good at matching jumps with your partner while facing each other and standing still, try this: Travel a short distance together, and then, at a set point, do matching jumps in the air. This activity will be hard. You must pick a starting point, count exactly how

many steps you'll travel before you jump, and then jump and land. First, by yourself practice the traveling by itself and then the jump by itself; then, combine the traveling and jumping. Finally, try to do the task with your partner. The sequence is this: Travel, jump, land, freeze—all movements exactly matching those of your partner. You two should look like twins.

T To the sequence you just made up, add a second traveling action and a second jump.

JUMPING WITH A SPRINGBOARD

Setting: Springboards positioned throughout the work space with sufficient large mats for safe landings

Cues	
Push	(Push hard with your feet and legs as you contact the board.)
Swing Upward	(Swing your arms upward for good height.)
Squash	(Bend your knees and spread your feet for a stable, soft landing.)

Tasks/Challenges:

T Using the nearest springboard, run and jump, using a two-foot landing/takeoff on the board; spring up high and land on two feet on the mat.

T As you become good at going off the springboard and landing without falling over, add a turn in the air as you jump so that you end up facing the place where you started. **Remember to bend your knees and spread your feet apart when you land.**

T When you're able to do this activity, try a complete 360° turn in the air before you land. To get all the way around, you'll have to throw your arms up and around in the direction that you want to turn.

JUMPING AS PART OF A DANCE CREATION

Setting: Children divided into small groups, no more than four per group

Cues	
Individual cues as needed	

Tasks/Challenges:

C Now you're going to use jumps to make up a dance. The main actions of the dance will all use different jumps. First think of a theme for your dance, such as a fight. If you use that idea, your jumps will contain such gestures as punching, slashing, jabbing, protecting, and retreating.

As a group, think of what you want your dance to say. Once you've decided the theme, try to put together a series of jumps that express that idea. You'll be using your jumps and other movements to tell a story. It may be that you all move at the same time, or that two of you move and then the other two move. Your dance needs to have a definite beginning and a definite end, with at least six different jumps in the middle. Try to make the dance look really professional. This will take a while to do; I'll be available to help each group as they work. Toward the end of class, we'll show the dances to the rest of the class.

JUMPING, DANCING, AND IMAGERY

Setting: Children divided into small groups, no more than four per group.

Cues
Individual cues as needed

Tasks/Challenges:

C Jumps can be used to create a dance about the things around you (the flight of a bird, leaves in the wind, etc.). This time, you're going to make up a dance that uses one of these things as its main idea. Jumps will communicate that idea to your audience. You must decide in your group what natural thing you'd like to communicate in a dance using jumps.

After you've decided, begin to develop your dance, keeping the following ideas in mind:

1. The actions you're demonstrating should clearly portray your theme.
2. The starting location of each person should be clear.
3. The dance should rise to a climax and then wind down to a conclusion.
4. The jumps and gestures you're using to communicate your ideas should be the most effective ones you can create.

5. The pathways used in the dance should be clear.

At the end of class, we'll show all the dances you want to the class.

HURDLING JUMPS

Setting: A series of hurdles set up throughout the work area, with sufficient space between for children to run between jumping over each; stopwatches at starting line (optional)

Cues
Foot to Foot	(Opposite: one foot to the other foot.)
Extend	(Front leg upward and forward.)
Heads Up	(Keep your head and shoulders up for good balance.)

Tasks/Challenges:

T In this activity you'll be *hurdling*, which is sprinting over barriers, called hurdles, placed along the way. Begin behind the first hurdle, and run to the end of the line of hurdles. Each time you come to a hurdle, jump it and keep going. Run to the end of the line, come back to the first hurdle, and start again. Start your jump *before* you reach the hurdle by extending your front leg upward and forward. Try to get over the hurdles by barely clearing them rather than jumping really high over them. You need a horizontal rather than a high vertical jump for hurdles.

Use low barriers at first so that youngsters can focus on proper technique without worrying about clearing the obstacles. Once children begin to exhibit quality hurdling actions, you can gradually increase the height of the barriers. Milk crates spread apart with bamboo poles supported between them are satisfactory barriers.

C As you feel you're getting better at hurdling, time yourself and see if you can improve each time. You can use one of the stopwatches available at the starting line of each row of hurdles.

For transferring weight over apparatus (vaulting box), see Chapter 24.

READING COMPREHENSION QUESTIONS

1. Name the two basic reasons for performing jumps.
2. What are the three phases of a jump?
3. List in order of difficulty the different takeoff and landing patterns for jumping.

4. What does a precontrol jump look like?
5. What are the characteristics of jumping and landing at each of the four skill levels? For example, what does a utilization-level jump look like?
6. What is the focus of the jumping and landing activities for the control and proficiency levels? (The introductory text to each section will get you started.)
7. Describe a low obstacle that children can safely practice jumping over.
8. What is the difference between a buoyant landing and a yielding landing?
9. Describe a sequence for teaching young children to jump rope.

REFERENCES

National Association for Sport and Physical Education (NASPE). (1995). *Moving into the future: National standards for physical education.* St. Louis, MO: Mosby.

Wickstrom R. L. (1977). *Fundamental motor patterns,* 2nd ed. Philadelphia: Lea & Febiger.

CHAPTER
23

Balancing

erriam Webster's Collegiate Dictionary, Tenth Edition defines balance as "stability produced by even distribution of weight on each side of the vertical axis," and also as "an aesthetically pleasing integration of elements." There's no extraneous motion, no flagrant waving of arms to maintain position, no near topple or wobble from side to side. The center of gravity is clearly over the base of support.

The elementary school child attempting to do a headstand, walk a beam, or ride a skateboard encounters different types of static and dynamic balance challenges. Among the key teaching concepts in providing balance experiences are these:

1. It's easier to balance over a wide base of support than a narrow base.
2. The center of gravity should be aligned over the base of support for stationary balance (Figure 23.1).
3. Extensions to one side of the body beyond the base of support necessitate extensions in the opposite direction for counterbalance.

Static balance involves maintaining a desired shape in a stationary position; gymnastics balances, headstands, and handstands are examples. *Dynamic* balance involves maintaining an on-balance position while moving, starting, or stopping. Dynamic balance occurs in weight transference, jumping, throwing, catching, and all forms of travel. Balance as a concept is discussed in Chapters 19, 22, 24, and 27 as it applies to learning specific skills. See Box 23.1 for information on balancing from the *National Standards for Physical Education.*

Levels of Skill Proficiency

At the precontrol level, children sporadically achieve balance; it's often more coincidental than intentional. Activities at this level are designed to introduce weight bearing and stillness as prerequisites to balance. Appropriate tasks include:

1. Exploring the use of different body parts as bases of support
2. Using wide bases to balance
3. Stopping in balanced positions

The child at the control level is ready to focus on holding stationary supports for several seconds, balancing on smaller bases, and maintaining inverted balances. Appropriate tasks include:

1. Supporting weight on combinations of body parts (for example, head and hands)
2. Momentarily supporting weight on hands alone
3. Balancing on more narrow bases and in inverted positions
4. Holding stationary balances on various types of large apparatus

The child at the utilization level is ready to study balancing on equipment and in dynamic situations, combining balance with locomotion and weight transference. Appropriate tasks include:

1. Combining stationary balances with actions on benches, tables, and beams
2. Moving from an on-balance to an off-balance position

Figure 23.1 Center of gravity over base of support.

BOX 23.1   THE SKILL OF BALANCING IN THE *NATIONAL STANDARDS FOR PHYSICAL EDUCATION*

The movement skill of balancing is referenced in the National Standards for Physical Education (NASPE, 1995) under Standard 1: Demonstrates competency in many movement forms and proficiency in a few movement forms. The standard speaks of the child's taking weight momentarily on hands, showing clear shapes in balance activities, performing gymnastics sequences with partners, and acquiring the basic skills of gymnastic activities.

Sample benchmarks for balance include:

- Maintains momentary stillness, bearing weight on a variety of body parts. (K)
- Balances, demonstrating momentary stillness, in symmetrical and nonsymmetrical shapes on a variety of body parts. (2)
- Balances with control on a variety of objects (balance boards, large apparatus, skates). (4)
- Develops and refines a gymnastics sequence demonstrating smooth transitions. (4)
- Designs and performs gymnastics and dance sequences that combine traveling, rolling, balancing, and weight transfer into smooth, flowing sequences with intentional changes in direction, speed, and flow. (6)

---

3. Moving into and out of balances with stretching, curling, and twisting actions

Proficiency-level balance tasks focus on maintaining balance on inverted and narrow bases. Children practice moving into and out of stationary balances with changes in time, dynamic balances on narrow equipment, and combining/contrasting balance-time factors in sequences on the floor and on apparatus. Appropriate tasks include:

1. Extensions away from the body when balanced on a narrow base
2. Partner and group balances
3. Rapid turns and twists into balanced positions
4. Dismounts (from apparatus) that conclude with landings in balanced, stationary positions

The sequence for developing the skill theme of balancing at the precontrol, control, utilization, and proficiency levels is shown in our progression spiral on page 370.

Precontrol Level: Activities for Exploration

Activities at the precontrol level are designed to provide exploration of the concept of balance, supporting weight on different body parts as bases of support and in different shapes. As children explore the concept of balance, they begin to maintain simple stationary balances and to stop in balanced positions while traveling.

BALANCING ON DIFFERENT BASES OF SUPPORT

Setting: Carpet squares or small mats placed throughout general space, with sufficient room between for children to work without bumping others

Tasks/Challenges:

🅣 Balance on different bases of support on your mat. Your base of support is the body parts that are holding you in the balance. See how many body parts can be bases of support. Hold each balance as you count to yourself three seconds: "one thousand one, one thousand two. . . "

🅣 Try different combinations of body parts as you create your balances.

🅣 Let's list all the body parts you've used as bases of support for your balances. (*List on chalkboard or flipchart as students give responses.*) Do you see some body parts listed as bases of support that you didn't try? Take a few minutes to try all the combinations.

Balancing

■ **PROFICIENCY LEVEL**

Performing apparatus sequences that combine stationary balances and traveling
 with movement concepts
Transferring off equipment with weight on hands
Balancing on hanging ropes
Balancing while supporting the weight of a partner

■ **UTILIZATION LEVEL**

Performing sequences that combine stationary balances and traveling on mats
Performing inverted balances on equipment
Traveling into and out of balances by rolling
Moving out of and into balances by stretching, curling, and twisting
Balancing on crates

■ **CONTROL LEVEL**

Balance boards
Balancing on stilts
Balancing sequence
Traveling while balanced
Traveling on large apparatus
Stationary balances on equipment
Traveling and stopping in balanced positions
Doing kickups
Alignment of body parts
Performing inverted balances
The Gymnastics Dance
Balancing in different body shapes
Balancing symmetrically and nonsymmetrically
Counterbalance
Tightening the gymnastics muscles
Balancing on different bases of support

■ **PRECONTROL LEVEL**

Balancing on boards
Traveling on low gymnastics equipment
Traveling and stopping in balanced positions
Balancing in different body shapes
Balancing on a wide base of support
Balancing on different bases of support

Some children will watch others in class, often the more skilled students, and attempt to copy their balances. This can result in injury to the less skilled. A reminder to the group and/or to the less confident students of what the teacher is looking for eliminates this potential problem.

T Now I'll name the body parts that I want to be the bases of support. First, hand(s) and feet. Be creative in your balance. Although you're all using the same base of support, the gymnastics balances may be very different.

Additional exploration: feet and head, knees and elbows, stomach, base of spine, and shoulders in combination with other body parts.

 Sometimes children attempt to balance on body parts that aren't appropriate for supporting weight. Don't let youngsters balance in unsafe positions that could result in stress or injury.

C Balance on your favorite bases of support, holding the balance very still. Let's pretend I am going to take a photo of the balance—no wiggles, no wobbles.

 Young children enjoy labeling on a large stick figure the body parts that can serve as bases of support. Refer to Chapter 14, "Assessing Student Learning," for the use of cognitive assessment in physical education.

BALANCE ON A WIDE BASE OF SUPPORT

Setting: Carpet squares or small mats placed throughout general space with sufficient room between for children to work without bumping others

Tasks/Challenges:

T On the mat (ground), create a four-part balance on your hands and lower legs; have your hands under your shoulders and your legs approximately the same distance apart as the width of your hips. This wide base of support creates a very stable balance.

T Move your hands toward each other and your legs toward each other until they touch. Do you feel stable now? Could I push you over?

T Explore the concept of wide to narrow balances with different bases of support: hands and feet, knees and elbows.

BALANCING IN DIFFERENT BODY SHAPES

Setting: Carpet squares or small mats placed throughout general space, with sufficient room between for children to work without bumping others

Tasks/Challenges:

T Create a gymnastics balance on a wide base of support. Create a wide body shape by extending free body parts outward from your trunk (free body parts are those you're not using as bases of support).

T Create a narrow-shape gymnastics balance on the base of your spine—long and thin like a piece of spaghetti. Keep all free body parts close to your trunk.

T Create a curled-shape gymnastics balance on your chosen base of support. Free body parts can be tucked close to the body, or they may be added to the curled shape by bending them in the curve.

T Create a twisted-shape gymnastics balance. Use your two feet as your base of support and twist your body like a pretzel.

TRAVELING AND STOPPING IN BALANCED POSITIONS

Setting: Children scattered throughout general space

Tasks/Challenges:

T Travel through general space any way you choose. On the signal, stop and create a gymnastics balance with two feet and two hands touching the floor.

Additional exploration: two feet and one hand, base of spine, two knees and one hand. . .

T Travel again, but this time balance on three body parts when you hear the signal. Think which three parts you're going to use before traveling. Ready? Go.

Additional exploration: four body parts, five body parts, two body parts.

TRAVELING ON LOW GYMNASTICS EQUIPMENT

Setting: Jump ropes; low balance beams; two- by four-inch planks; low, narrow benches; and tape pathways arranged on the floor (Figure 23.2).

Tasks/Challenges:

T Travel on the different pieces of equipment without losing your balance and falling off.

Additional exploration: travel backward; travel with your arms above your head; walk with a beanbag on your head.

Figure 23.2 Equipment arrangement for traveling.

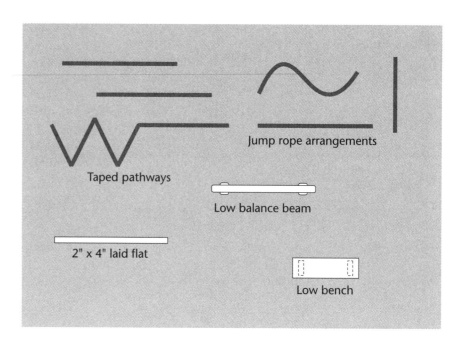

Taped pathways

Jump rope arrangements

Low balance beam

2" x 4" laid flat

Low bench

BALANCING ON BOARDS

Setting: Square, rectangle, and circular balance boards arranged as a station for the study of balance (Figure 23.3).

Tasks/Challenges:

T Balance on a balance board without falling off or letting the edges of the board touch the ground. You may want a partner to stand in front of the balance board to help when you first step up; place your hands on the partner's shoulders for support.

T Explore standing with your feet shoulder-width apart and with your feet close together. Which gives you better balance on the board?

Control Level: Learning Experiences Leading to Skill Development

Learning experiences at the control level focus on maintaining the stillness and control of a balance. Children balance on increasingly smaller bases of support, while holding the body in inverted positions, and in stationary balances on apparatus. These experiences begin to provide the ingredients for a movement repertoire of balances that may be included in sequences involving traveling and other balances. *Several of the tasks explored at the precontrol level will be repeated at the control level, with the focus on refinement cues.*

Rectangular

24"

10"

1½" metal pipe

Square top, square bottom

16"

16"

4" square base

Round top, round bottom

14"

2" round base

Figure 23.3 Construction of balance boards of various shapes.

A note about cues: Although several cues are listed for many of the learning experiences, it's important to focus on only one cue at a time. That way, the children can really concentrate on that cue. Once you provide feedback to the children and observe that most have learned a cue, then it's time to focus on another one.

BALANCING ON DIFFERENT BASES OF SUPPORT

Setting: Carpet squares or small mats scattered throughout general space with sufficient room between for children to work without bumping others

Cues

Stillness	(No wiggles, no wobbles—hold perfectly still for three seconds.)

Tasks/Challenges:

T Earlier in the year we explored balancing on different bases of support. Balance on different bases of support on your mat or carpet square. See if you can remember which body parts can serve as good bases for gymnastic balances.

T Listed on the board (flipchart) are the body parts that serve as bases of support. I will call the combination of body parts; you create the balance with that base—for example, feet and hands. What other body parts can you use with your feet to create a good base for gymnastic balances?

T Create balances using the following combination of bases: head and hands, head and knees, head and feet; elbows and knees; elbows, feet, and head; stomach only; base of spine only; shoulders, upper arms/elbows, and head.

T Create balances by adding your chosen base or bases to the following:

feet and _____
head and _____
elbows and _____

C From all the balances you have practiced, choose three of your favorites, each showing a different combination of body parts as bases of support. Practice until you can hold each balance three seconds without moving or losing your balance. When you are ready, show your balances to a partner, who will give you a "thumbs up" if you hold the balance stationary for three seconds.

TIGHTENING THE GYMNASTICS MUSCLES

Setting: Carpet squares and/or small mats scattered throughout general space, with sufficient room for children to work without collisions

Cues

Stillness	(No wiggles, no wobbles—hold perfectly still for three seconds.)
Tight Muscles	(Muscular tension is the key to holding the balance.)

Tasks/Challenges:

T Balance on your favorite base of support, holding the balance very still. Tighten the muscles of the body parts supporting your balance to maintain stillness.

T Balance on a different base of support. Tighten the muscles of the free body parts to hold a stretched or curled shape very still.

T Assume your favorite balance position. See if you can tighten the muscles without changing the appearance of your balance. You should look the same but feel the tightening inside.

C Continue to practice your balances with a focus on tightening the muscles without changing the appearance of the balance. As I walk by you, I should feel the tightness in the extended arm or leg if I touch you.

This tightening of the muscles is a key factor in holding the balance very still without extraneous movement and in maintaining the position.

COUNTERBALANCE

Setting: Carpet squares or small mats scattered throughout general space, with sufficient room between mats for children to work safely

Cues

Stillness	(No wiggles, no wobbles for three seconds.)
Tight Muscles	(Muscular tension is the key to holding the balance.)
Extensions	(Extend free body parts for stability in your balance.)

Tasks/Challenges:

T Balance on one foot. Extend your arms and leg, holding the balance very stationary. Repeat the balance, extending arms but not leg. Which balance is easier to maintain? Right, the one with arms and free leg extended in opposite directions. This is the concept of counterbalance. Extensions to one side of the body necessitate extensions in the opposite direction.

🅣 Balance on the base of your spine. Extend free body parts to one side only; repeat with the extension in the opposite direction.

🅣 Explore balances on different bases of support, extending your body parts in different directions from your body for counterbalance.

BALANCING SYMMETRICALLY AND NONSYMMETRICALLY

Setting: Carpet squares and/or small mats scattered throughout general space, with sufficient room for children to work safely

Cues	
Tight Muscles	(Muscular tension is the key to holding the balance.)
Extensions	(Extend free body parts for stability in your balance.)
Smooth Transitions	(Move slowly from one balance to the next for a smooth transition.)

Tasks/Challenges:

🅣 Balance on the base of your spine, with your arms and legs extended outward. Create exactly the same shape on both sides of your body. This is called a *symmetrical* shape; both sides of the body look the same.

🅣 Keeping the same base of support, change your free body parts, still creating a symmetrical shape.

🅣 Balance on your chosen base of support. Create a symmetrical shape (Figure 23.4). Now change to a *nonsymmetrical* shape—the sides look different— while balanced on that same base.

🅣 Balance on your shoulders, back of head, and arms. Create a symmetrical shape with your legs. Change to a nonsymmetrical shape and then back to a symmetrical one.

🅣 Repeat this three-part symmetrical, nonsymmetrical, symmetrical sequence; slowly change your legs into the different shapes. This smoothness in transition is an important component of gymnastics.

Figure 23.4   These youngsters maintain stillness in symmetrical and nonsymmetrical balances.

ASSESSMENT EXAMPLE
from the National Standards for Physical Education

Peer Observation

Students are asked to work on balancing on different bases of support (e.g., two hands and one foot, hands and knees, headstand). Students should balance in four different positions, two using symmetrical shapes and two using asymmetrical shapes. Students are asked to draw their favorite symmetrical and asymmetrical balances on paper, labeling "S" and "A," respectively. Students now select a partner who will observe their balances and then indicate on the paper: (1) if the drawn figures were labeled correctly and (2) if the balances were held still for 3 seconds.

Criteria for Assessment

a. Completes four balances—two symmetrical and two asymmetrical
b. Correctly labels balances "S" and "A"
c. Maintains stillness in balance for three seconds
d. Observer correctly assesses the appropriateness of the labels and the extent to which the performer was still

NASPE (1995, p. 19)

BALANCING IN DIFFERENT BODY SHAPES

Setting: Small mats and/or carpet squares scattered throughout general space, with sufficient room for children to work safely

Cues	
Tight Muscles	(Muscular tension is the key to holding the balance.)
Extensions	(Extend free body parts for stability in your balance.)
Smooth Transitions	(Move slowly from one balance to the next for a smooth transition.)

Tasks/Challenges:

🅣 Remember when we explored basic body shapes for physical education. Who can name the four shapes? Wide, curled, twisted, narrow, that's right. Let's create balances that show each of those shapes. Now that you have learned to balance on different bases of support, try to have a different base of support for each of your balances.

🅣 Let's focus on wide-shape balances. Create wide-shape balances with different bases of support. Remember, extensions of arms and legs away from the body create wide shapes.

🅒 I'm going to put on some background music for a few minutes. Create three balances that show wide shapes; each balance is to have a different base of support. Challenge yourself with a level of difficulty that tests your skills. When the music stops, we will look at the balances.

🅣 Now let's create gymnastics balances that show narrow shapes. Remember, we create narrow-shape balances by holding body parts close to each other. How many different narrow balances can you create?

🅣 Create a narrow balance on the base of your spine. **Stretch your legs and arms outward to counterbalance.**

🅣 Create two new narrow balances, one at a low level, the other at medium level.

🅣 You can create a curled (round) shape by curling your spine forward or arching your spine backward. Free body parts may be tucked close to the body, or they may be added to the curled image by bending in the curve. Create a curled gymnastics balance on your chosen base of support.

🅣 Create a curled-shape gymnastics balance in which the spine curls forward; slowly change into a curled-shape balance with your spine arched backward.

🅣 Stand in a balanced position, with both feet as bases of support for your weight. Create a twisted shape by turning your body to the right or the left without moving your feet. Now balance, using your left foot and the lower portion of your right leg as bases of support. Create a twisted shape from this base.

🅣 Create twisted shapes by rotating your trunk, arms, legs, neck, ankles, and wrists while balanced on different bases of support.

🅣 Balance on three body parts. Create a twisted shape by rotating free body parts, for example, arms, legs, trunk, neck. Create two more twisted-shape balances on various bases of support.

🅒 Think of all the balances you have created today. They represent four shapes: wide, narrow, curled, twisted. Review the balances you did; choose your favorite balance for each shape. On each signal, show me your favorite wide, narrow, curled, and twisted shape balance. **Concentrate on holding each perfectly still and moving smoothly from balance to balance.**

 Peer Observation. Using stick figures, draw each of your four balances, one representing each of the four shapes. Label the body shape of each figure. After you have drawn and labeled your balances, exchange papers with a neighbor, who will be the "gymnastics judge." Show each of your balances to your neighbor for evaluation (Figure 23.5). (Refer to Chapter 14, "Assessing Student Learning," for the use of peer observation as assessment.)

Figure 23.5 Student balance drawings and peer assessment results.

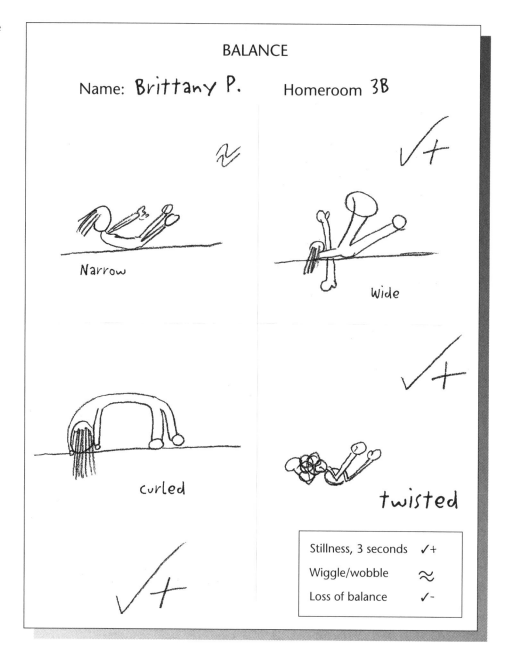

C Working in groups of four, create a balance statue in which each person partially supports another. Each person should represent one of the four basic shapes; wide, narrow, curled, and twisted. After you make the body-shape statue, convert it to a movable monster by moving as a unit in either self-space or general space.

Cues

Tight Muscles	(Muscular tension is the key to holding the balance.)
Extensions	(Extend free body parts for stability in your balance.)
Smooth Transitions	(Move slowly from one balance to the next for a smooth transition.)

THE GYMNASTICS DANCE

Setting: Children scattered throughout general space

Tasks/Challenges:

T Let's create a gymnastics dance that focuses on body shapes and balance. I will select one person to form a statue by holding a gymnastics balance with a wide base of support. Hold your wide balance as others come and go.

🅣 Each person in the group will slowly add to the statue by making a wide, narrow, curled, or twisted shape and touching the first statue with *one* body part.

🅣 That looks really good; the shapes are clear and the balances are stationary. After everyone in the group has added to the statue by making a balance and touching the first person, begin to move slowly from the original wide-shape balance that was the first one created without disturbing others in the group. I will touch you as a signal for you to move from the main statue. Use a locomotor movement or a turning action to move from the group.

🅣 On the signal, move slowly back into the large balance statue, with clear shapes and stillness. Move away again, forming an individual statue by yourself with a different base of support and different shape from the one you used before.

PERFORMING INVERTED BALANCES

Setting: Small mats and/or carpet squares scattered throughout general space, with sufficient room between mats for children to work without bumping others

Cues	
Tight Muscles	(Tighten your abdominal muscles to hold the inverted balance—stretch toward the sky!)
Equal Weight	(Take weight equally on all body parts that are bases of support.)

Tasks/Challenges:

🅣 Balance with your head and two feet as your base of support.

 When performing an inverted balance involving the head, it's important to distribute the body weight equally among all body parts serving as the base of support.

🅣 Balance on your head and hands, with your knees resting on your elbows (Figure 23.6).

🅣 When performing these inverted balances, concentrate on taking your weight equally on the following bases:

1. Head and knees
2. Head, hands, one foot
3. Back of head, shoulders, arm

Figure 23.6   Inverted balance on head and hands.

🅣 Explore other inverted balances that you can safely hold for three seconds (Figure 23.7).

ALIGNMENT OF BODY PARTS

Setting: Small mats and/or carpet squares scattered throughout general space, with sufficient room for children to work safely

Cues	
Tight Muscles	(Tighten your abdominal muscles to hold the inverted balance—stretch toward the sky!)
Alignment	(Toes over knees, over hips, over shoulders to form a straight line.)

Tasks/Challenges:

🅣 Repeat your balance on head and hands with knees resting on elbows. **Concentrate on tightening your abdominal muscles to align your hips over your shoulders.**

🅣 Balance on your head and hands, with your trunk and legs extended toward the ceiling. Form a triangular base with your weight equally distributed on your head and hands. **Stretch your body like a straight line, aligning hips over shoulders, feet over hips. Pretend your toes are attached by a string to the ceiling . . . stretch.**

DOING KICKUPS

Setting: Large gymnastics mats and/or small mats that will not slip scattered throughout general space, with sufficient room for children to work safely

Cues	
Tight Muscles	(Tighten your abdominal muscles to hold the inverted balance—stretch toward the sky!)
Alignment	(Toes over knees, over hips, over shoulders to form a straight line.)

Figure 23.7 Other inverted balances.

Tasks/Challenges:

T Place one foot in front of the other (front-back stance); lean forward, and place your hands on the floor shoulder-width apart, fingers pointing forward. Using your back leg as a lever, kick your leg upward so that your weight is supported on your hands only.

C Practice counting seconds as you balance on your hands.

With practice, the success rate for balancing on hands is very high, but practice must be massed and distributed.

 Teach the children to come safely out of an off-balance weight-on-hands position by twisting the trunk slightly to bring the feet down in a new place.

TRAVELING AND STOPPING IN BALANCED POSITIONS

Setting: Children scattered throughout general space

Cues	
Stillness	(Hold your balance perfectly still—no wiggles, no wobbles.)
Tight Muscles	(Muscular tension is the key to holding the balance.)
Extensions	(Extend free body parts for stability in your balance.)

Tasks/Challenges:

T We worked earlier on traveling through general space and creating a gymnastics balance when we stopped. Let's review those skills: Travel through general space any way you choose. On the signal, stop and create a gymnastics balance with two hands and one foot touching the floor.

T This time, change your way of traveling. If you ran before, skip or gallop through general space. On the signal, stop and create a balance with four body parts as bases of support. Think of the four parts you will choose before traveling.

T Repeat the travel, stop, balance sequence with different combinations of body parts as bases of support and different ways to travel.

C Remember the balance you created with four bases of support? Think of the balance you created with two bases. Now you are going to make a sequence of two travels and two stationary balances. Your sequence will be this: Travel, stop and balance on four bases; travel, stop and balance on two bases of support. I'll give the signal for travel each time. You will decide the ways you are going to travel; use the balances you just practiced. We will practice several times so you can repeat the travel, balance sequence exactly the same each time.

C After you have completed your two-part sequence and feel good about your travel and balances, create a larger sequence by adding other ways to travel and additional balances—for example, three bases,

Figure 23.8   Construction of a balance beam.

Figure 23.9   Construction of a wooden sawhorse.

five bases. How about going from five bases of support to one base, with travel between the balances? Remember, there are ways to travel other than on your feet.

STATIONARY BALANCES ON EQUIPMENT

Setting: Various pieces of gymnastics apparatus arranged throughout general space: low tables, boxes, benches, climbing frames, low balance beams, and sawhorses. (See Figures 23.8, 23.9 and 23.10 for plans for constructing balance beams, sawhorses, and balance benches, respectively.)

Cues

Stillness	(Hold your balance perfectly still—no wiggles, no wobbles.)
Tight Muscles	(Muscular tension is the key to holding the balance.)
Extensions	(Extend free body parts for stability in your balance.)

Tasks/Challenges:

🅣 Earlier in the year we explored traveling safely on gymnastics equipment. Select the piece of apparatus you want to begin working on; spend a few

Figure 23.10 Construction of a balance bench.

Figure 23.11 These children transfer floor skills to apparatus by practicing nonsymmetrical balances on equipment.

minutes exploring the apparatus until you are comfortable on this new surface and height. Travel forward and backward on the apparatus. Try some of the balances you did on the floor/mat surface on the apparatus (*Figure 23.11*).

🔵 Perform your balances at different places on the apparatus: on the top, near one end, in the middle, on a low rung, underneath. Try some balances with a combination of bases on the floor and on the apparatus.

🔵 Balance on your hands only on the low bench, low beam, or crate (*Figure 23.12*). The chart on the wall (*Figure 23.13*) will provide examples of balances that do not require you to be inverted when you balance on hands only on the equipment.

Create a balance on the apparatus, then move slowly to another part of the apparatus for your second balance. Can you create a combination of travel and three different balances?

 After you create three balances on the first piece of apparatus, move to another piece of gymnastics apparatus and create balances on that apparatus. You may be able to repeat balances from before or you may need to create balances on different bases of support to suit the different apparatus. Continue rotating to the various pieces of apparatus until you've created three balances on each piece of apparatus.

When children first begin this type of gymnastics, they may not be able to move independently from apparatus to apparatus. We have found it best in the beginning to assign the children to groups and rotate the stations.

 Create combinations of balances and travel on each of the pieces of apparatus.

 Choose your favorite piece of apparatus for a sequence. Create a sequence of four balances and four different ways to travel on that apparatus. Select different combinations of body parts as your bases of support, and be creative in your ways to travel on the apparatus. Don't forget different levels and directions as you create your sequence.

Portfolio: Record your sequence on paper using stick-figure drawings and writing; place the sequence in your portfolio. We will return to this work later in the year when we work on approaches and dismounts from apparatus.

Permit the children to attempt balances on apparatus only after they can safely hold the balances for three to five seconds on the floor/mats.

Figure 23.12 Maintaining stillness while balancing on different body parts becomes a challenge on various pieces of apparatus.

Figure 23.13 Noninverted, hands-only balances on apparatus.

TRAVELING ON LARGE APPARATUS

Setting: Large apparatus—benches, tables, beams, commercial gymnastics equipment—arranged in open space

Cues	
Eyes Forward	(Focus on a spot on the wall or the end of the beam, keeping your head up for good balance.)
Extensions	(Extend your arms for good balance as you travel.)

Tasks/Challenges:

🅣 Travel forward and backward on the large apparatus. **Focus your eyes on something stationary to help maintain your balance as you travel.**

🅣 Sometimes travel with your center of gravity close to the apparatus—that is, lower your hips. Sometimes travel with your center of gravity high—for example, walk on your tiptoes with your body stretched toward the ceiling.

🅣 Walk forward the length of the beam or bench; make a half turn and walk forward again. The secret to the turn is to take your weight on the balls of your feet and then pivot and quickly drop your heels so they make contact with the beam.

🅣 Practice turning both clockwise and counterclockwise while traveling forward and backward.

🅣 Walk to the center of the apparatus, and lower your hips into a squat position. Execute your turn in this low-level position.

TRAVELING WHILE BALANCED

Setting: Large apparatus—benches, tables, beams, commercial gymnastics equipment—arranged in open space

Cues	
Eyes Forward	(Remember to focus your eyes on something stationary when you travel.)
Extensions	(Extend your arms for good balance when doing your locomotors.)

Tasks/Challenges:

🅣 Travel on the apparatus using a series of gallops, hops, or skipping steps. You'll probably want very little height when you perform these skills on the apparatus.

🅣 Travel across the apparatus on four body parts.

🅣 If you are comfortable doing forward rolls on the mats, try rolling slowly forward across the apparatus. **Pretend you are executing the skill in slow motion; tighten your abdominal muscles for control.**

 Students should perform rolling on apparatus only after demonstrating mastery of the rolls on the floor or mats.

🅒 Perform the tasks on each piece of apparatus.

🅣 Add changes in directions and levels to your locomotors on the apparatus.

BALANCING SEQUENCE

Setting: Large apparatus—benches, tables, beams, commercial gymnastics equipment—arranged in open space

Cues	
Eyes Forward	(Remember to focus your eyes on something stationary when you travel.)
Smooth Transitions	(Move smoothly between balances and travels.)

Note: Individuals, sometimes classes, may need reminders of earlier cues, for example, Stillness, Extensions, Tight Muscles.

Tasks/Challenges:

🅣 Remember those balances you created on apparatus earlier in the year. You recorded them on paper and placed them in your portfolio. We are now going to revisit that lesson to create a sequence of traveling and balancing on your favorite piece of apparatus. Your task will be to design a sequence of traveling and balancing on one piece of equipment. You will choose either sequence A or sequence B.

Sequence A: Create a sequence of traveling combined with balancing on different bases of support. Your sequence must contain three balances with different bases and at least two travels.

Sequence B: Create a sequence of traveling combined with balancing in the basic body shapes. Your sequence must contain the four basic shapes—wide, narrow, curled, twisted—and at least three travels.

Practice your sequence on the floor and then on the apparatus. When you have the sequence memorized, let a friend watch it to see if

1. The bases of support are clear.
2. The balances are stationary.
3. The travels are smooth.

T You have refined your sequence nicely with a friend giving pointers. Now we need to add the beginning shape and the ending of the sequence. Begin your sequence on the apparatus positioned in what you wish to be your starting shape. The beginning shape you choose will be determined by your first action: travel or balance. Think of the level you need, and the direction, as well as the shape.

T Now that you have a beginning shape, let's focus on the ending of your sequence. Earlier in the year we studied jumping and landing—jumping for height and landing safely. We will review those skills and then you can select the type of jump/land action with which you want to end your sequence. *Review jumping off apparatus (Chapter 22) with the children, emphasizing safe landings and body shapes in the air.*

C On the assignment table you will find the forms for sequence A or B. The paper is divided into three parts: beginning shape, travel and balances, and dismount. Using stick figures to represent your balances, write/draw your sequence, remembering the number of balances needed for the sequence. When you can repeat the sequence without referring to your paper, ask a friend to watch it. After the friend watches your "dress rehearsal," come to me for your final assessment.

 This type of event task can easily become an assessment of children's work. Specifics for development of criteria and rubrics can be found in Chapter 14, "Assessing Student Learning."

BALANCING ON STILTS

Setting: Several stations in general space at which children can experience/practice dynamic balance; tin can stilts (see Figure 23.14 for instructions for making them) at some of the stations; wooden stilts (see Figure 23.15) at others; marker cones placed around the general space

Cue

Heads Up   (Eyes focused forward, shoulders erect.)

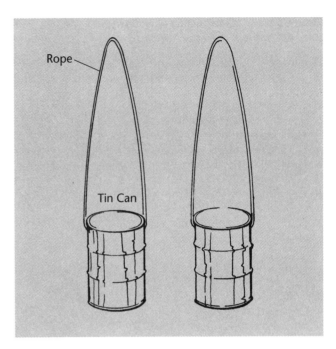

Figure 23.14 Construction of tin can stilts from discarded rope and large cans from the school cafeteria: (1) Cut two holes in the top sides of the cans; (2) string rope through the holes and tie it together inside each can. To use the stilts, children put each foot on a can and pull on the rope with their hands.

Children first experiencing this type of dynamic balance can develop confidence on tin can stilts before progressing to regular stilts.

T Walk forward on the tin can stilts. You'll have to take smaller steps than you would when walking normally.

T Walk backward.

T Walk around the marker cones.

T After you've mastered walking on the tin can stilts, you're ready for the higher wooden stilts. It's easier to mount the stilts from an elevated position, such as from a step or chair.

T Walk forward, backward, and sideways.

T Walk around the marker cones.

T Shift your weight to one stilt; lift your other leg, and swing it around.

T Jump forward with small steps.

BALANCE BOARDS

Setting: Balance boards set up as one of several stations at which children can experience static and dynamic balance

Figure 23.15 Construction of wooden stilts. (Each board makes one set of stilts.)

Directions:

1. Cut twelve inches from one end of the board.
2. Cut the twelve-inch board in half.
3. Cut the six-inch board diagonally in half for the steps.
4. Cut the remaining seven-foot board lengthwise to make two two-inch by seven-foot poles.
5. Nail or bolt the steps to the poles.

Materials:
One board, 2" x 4" x 8'
Nails or bolts

Cues

Heads Up	(Eyes focused forward, shoulders erect.)
Extensions	(Extend arms to the sides for good balance.)

Tasks/Challenges:

🅣 Remember when we did balances on boards earlier in the year. You practiced balancing on the different boards and learned that a wide base of support—feet shoulder-width apart—created a more stable balance on the boards, as in all balances. Practice your balance skills on the boards. Try to maintain your balance, without partner support, for several seconds.

🅣 When you can stand on the board for five seconds without the support of your partner and without losing your balance, you're ready to try the tasks written on the chart:

1. Slowly move your arms above your head. What happens to your center of gravity? (*Right—it moves upward.*)
2. Slowly move from a standing to a squat or low curl position. Which is more stable? Why is the low position more stable? (*When working on large apparatus, remember that we're better balanced when the center of gravity is low.*)
3. Catch a ball thrown by your partner; toss the ball to your partner.

Write additional tasks on flip charts or task cards near the balance board. Balance board activities can also be recorded on a task sheet (see Figure 23.16).

Utilization Level: Learning Experiences Leading to Skill Development

Learning experiences at the utilization level combine balancing and transferring weight for a contrast in stillness and action. Experiences include balancing in dynamic environments and transferring weight into stationary, still balances on various bases of support, as well as approaches to and dismounts from apparatus. Tasks that involve sequences of movement, on the floor and on apparatus, are particularly important and valuable. Children make decisions about the combination of movements and select and invent ways for one balance or action to move smoothly into another.

A note about cues: Although several cues are listed for many of the learning experiences, it's important to focus on only one cue at a time. That way, the children can really concentrate on that cue. Once you provide feedback to the children and observe that most have learned a cue, then it's time to focus on another one.

BALANCING ON CRATES

Setting: Milk crates and boxes (stuffed with newspaper or computer packing materials and taped closed so they will support a child's weight) positioned throughout general space, with sufficient room between for children to work safely

Cues

Tight Muscles	(Muscular tension is the key to holding the balance.)
Extensions	(Extend free body parts for balance/counterbalance.)
Alignment	(Position yourself over your base of support or extend free body parts for counterbalance.)

Tasks/Challenges:

🅣 In our previous work on balance, you explored balancing on different bases of support and in differ-

Figure 23.16 Task sheet for balance board activities. Younger children enjoy drawing the smile face for completed tasks; older children can record the date of successful completion.

Name _Melissa_

Homeroom _4b_

Balance Board Task Sheet

Draw a smile face beside those activities you can successfully complete.

I am able to:

_____ Balance on the board standing on two feet

_____ Sit in a balance position on the board

_____ Change from a standing to a sitting position on the board without losing balance

_____ Raise my hands high above my head while standing on the board

_____ Balance on the board standing on one foot

_____ Catch a ball tossed to me by a friend

_____ Toss a ball to a friend without losing my balance

New ideas by me:

_____ clap my hands 3 times

_____

_____

ent shapes. You practiced holding balances stationary while performing them on mats, on low equipment, and on large apparatus. Review your balances on different bases of support on the crate or box (Figure 23.17). Many of the balances that were easy for you to perform on the mat or the low equipment will be more difficult on the crate or box because of the added height and the size of the surface.

T Create a series of balances without ever leaving the surface of the crate or box. Transferring from one balance to the next will now be a major part of the sequence.

T Create a sequence of balances on your crate or box that includes an approach to the crate, a transfer

onto the crate, a series of balances on the crate, and a dismount from the crate. You may choose to focus on either bases of support or different shapes.

Select tasks from Chapter 24, "Transferring Weight and Rolling," for a review of approaches to and dismounts from low equipment.

T Select a partner to work with for a sequence on the crates. Explore matching symmetrical and nonsymmetrical balances on the crates or boxes. You may choose to work side by side matching shapes or face to face to mirror shapes.

C Design a partner sequence of symmetrical and nonsymmetrical balances on the crate or box. Your sequence must contain the following:

Figure 23.17 This child reviews balancing on different bases of support on a crate/box.

1. Three symmetrical and two nonsymmetrical balances
2. A minimum of three different bases of support
3. An approach to the crates or boxes and a dismount

Your sequence should represent a double image. Not only will your balances match those of your partner, but also the transitions between will be the same action and the same speed.

 Videotape: When you and your partner have completed your sequence, we will videotape it. You and your partner can then evaluate your sequence using the guidelines we discussed in class. Following your initial evaluation, you may wish to make some changes in your sequence. (*The children's sequences provide an excellent means of assessing their gymnastics skills. Refer to Chapter 14, "Assessing Student Learning," for examples of videotape analysis/assessment.*)

MOVING OUT OF AND INTO BALANCES BY STRETCHING, CURLING, AND TWISTING

Setting: Sufficient mats for children to work safely without bumping others as they practice

Cues

Line of Gravity	(Extending beyond your line of gravity will make you lose your balance unless you have an extension for counterbalance.)
Smooth Transitions	(Move smoothly through the transition from balance to balance.)

Tasks/Challenges:

Ⓣ Balance on a very narrow base of support. Stretch your free body parts in one direction away from the base. When you begin to lose your balance, you have moved just beyond the "line of gravity." At the moment of moving beyond the line of gravity—of moving off balance—transfer your weight to a new base of support.

Ⓣ Balance on one foot. Stretch forward until you are off balance; transfer your weight to your hands and feet in a new balance.

Ⓣ Balance on favorite bases of support. Extend free body parts with a stretching action to move into a new balance.

Ⓣ Balance on your head and hands with knees on elbows as in a three-point stand or tripod. Push with your hands, tuck your head, and curl your back to roll out of the balance. Make a new stationary balance after the rolling action.

Ⓣ Explore curling your spine to roll out of different balances until you find three balances that you can use the curling action to get out of and into a new balance.

Ⓣ Balance on the base of your spine only, as in a V-seat. After you have held the balance very still, twist your trunk until the action moves you off balance and into a new balance with a different base of support.

Ⓣ Balance on two hands and one foot, with the free leg extended. Twist your trunk and the free leg until you transfer to a new balance on hands and feet.

Ⓒ Practice balances with different bases of support and moving out of the balance by either stretching, curling, or twisting. When you are comfortable with one of each, put them together in a sequence as follows: balance, stretching action into new balance, curling action into new balance, twisting action into new balance. Your sequence will include four stationary balances and three transitions.

Figure 23.18 Children at an advanced level can balance in various shapes and on various body parts.

Additional balances with stretching, curling, and twisting actions can be found in Chapter 24, "Transferring Weight and Rolling."

TRAVELING INTO AND OUT OF BALANCES BY ROLLING

Setting: Sufficient mats for children to balance and roll without bumping into others as they practice

Cues	
Stillness and Action	(Remember to hold your balance perfectly still for three seconds, then move smoothly through the rolling action.)
Rounded Body	(Keep your back round and your chin tucked for a good roll.)

Tasks/Challenges:

🅣 Rock backward into a shoulder stand; hold the balance for three seconds, and then roll either forward or backward (*Figure 23.18*).

Children functioning at the utilization level in balancing should also have mastered rolling forward and backward.

🅣 Balance in a headstand for three seconds; then, press with your hands, and roll forward.

🅣 Balance with your weight on your hands, slowly lower yourself to the mat, and roll forward. **Remember to tuck your chin and curl your back.**

🅣 Transfer your weight from your feet to your hands; pause in the handstand; then, make a quarter turn, and transfer your weight back to your feet.

PERFORMING INVERTED BALANCES ON EQUIPMENT

Setting: Boxes or crates, benches, and/or low tables arranged for balancing, with sufficient mats around them for children to work safely

Cues	
Tight Muscles	(Remember to tighten the abdominal muscles plus free body parts for stillness in your balances.)
Alignment	(Position yourself over your base of support or extend free body parts for counterbalance.)

Tasks/Challenges:

🅣 Balancing in an inverted position on a piece of apparatus is quite different from balancing on the

Figure 23.19   Various equipment for balancing.

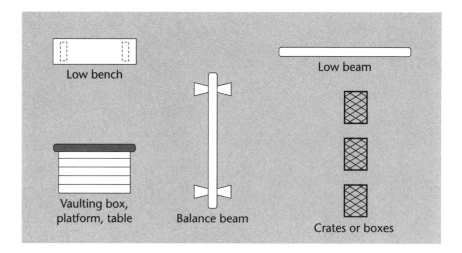

mats or the floor. The position of your hands is often quite different, and the surface is much smaller. Perform the balances until you are quite comfortable and skilled with them on the low equipment before you attempt them on the higher, more narrow apparatus (*Figure 23.19*).

🅣 Balance on your shoulders, back of your head, and arms. Stretch your legs upward.

🅣 Balance on your head and hands in a tripod position.

🅣 Balance on your head and hands with your legs extended toward the ceiling (*Figure 23.20*).

🅣 Balance on your hands only in an inverted balance.

🅣 While balanced on your hands only, turn slightly, bringing your feet down to the floor beside the beam, bench, or crate. This is the safety skill you will need when you become overbalanced.

🅣 Perform your inverted balance on the larger pieces of apparatus—vaulting box, balance beam, climbing frames.

 1. Inverted balances on apparatus should be attempted only after children show mastery of the balances on the floor/mats. Always have a mat area available for children to use to practice before performing their balances on apparatus.

2. Position yourself at the station where children are doing inverted balances; be sure you maintain a visual scan of the entire class.

PERFORMING SEQUENCES THAT COMBINE STATIONARY BALANCES AND TRAVELING ON MATS

Setting: A floor gymnastics area designed using available mats

Figure 23.20   A student at the utilization level balances on equipment in an inverted position.

Figure 23.21 Child's sequence to music, showing use of rolling; weight transfer; balance; and concepts of narrow, wide, curled, and directions.

Cues

Stillness in Balances	(Tighten the muscles to hold the balance very still.)
Smooth Transitions	(Make transitions between balances very smooth, whether they're fast or slow.)
Extensions	(Extend free body parts for aesthetic appeal as well as good balance.)
Alignment	(Position yourself over your base of support or extend free body parts for counter-balance.)

Tasks/Challenges:

🅣 Create a sequence that combines stationary balances and travel. As with an Olympic routine, design your sequence to cover the length of the mat as well as each corner. Your sequence must include the following:

1. A minimum of six balances, each with a different base of support
2. A minimum of three travels, with a change in direction and level
3. At least two inverted balances
4. A beginning and an ending shape

🅣 Add contrasts in time of actions—some fast, some slow—and changes in force—some powerful movements, some delicate—to add interest to your sequence.

🅒 Tomorrow we're going to practice the routines to music. If you like, bring a cassette tape of music from home, or you may select from those we have. You will then practice your routine with the music until you can repeat it three times exactly the same. (*See Figure 23.21 for an example of a routine.*)

Gymnastics routines are excellent projects for assessment of children's gymnastic skills and their understanding of the critical cues. Refer to Chapter 14, "Assessing Student Learning," for guidelines for developing criteria and rubrics.

Proficiency Level: Learning Experiences Leading to Skill Development

At the proficiency level, balance is studied on the floor and on various pieces of apparatus in combination with time and force factors to express contrast in power, stillness, and excitement in sequences. Children are encouraged to perfect the flow of their movements from one position to another and to develop their use of focus and full extension.

Although often not readily available, such activities as unicycling, skating, skiing, and surfing are challenging dynamic balancing experiences for children at the proficiency level. Sometimes these experiences can be provided during field trips or after-school programs.

A note about cues: Although several cues are listed for many of the learning experiences, it's important to focus on only one cue at a time. That way, the children can really concentrate on that cue. Once you provide feedback to the children and observe that most have learned a cue, then it's time to focus on another one.

BALANCING WHILE SUPPORTING THE WEIGHT OF A PARTNER

Setting: Sufficient mats for children to work safely without bumping others

Cues	
Wide Base	(A wide base of support provides greater stability.)
Extensions	(Extensions beyond the line of gravity require extensions in the opposite direction for counterbalance.)

Tasks/Challenges:

🅣 Working with your partner, create a balance that shows one wide and one narrow shape. You and your partner must be helping each other by partially supporting the other's weight.

🅣 Create different balances with your partner in which you are partially supporting each other's weight. If you are not the same weight, which of you will be the supporting partner?

🅣 Create a balance in which the base partner is supporting the weight of the top partner in an inverted position.

 Base partner: Your bases of support—for example, your arms and legs—should be no farther apart than the width of your hips and shoulders. *Top partner:* Make sure you put your weight over your partner's arms and hips, never in the middle of the back, which is unsupported.

🅒 Create two new balances supporting your partner's weight (*Figure 23.22*). You will need to make decisions based on the weight of both partners: Will you partially support each other, or will one of you totally support the other? Draw your two balances on a sheet of paper and post them at the partner balance center.

The combination of partner/group balancing, tumbling, and dance has evolved into an activity called Acrosport. Groups perform routines of supportive dynamic and static balances connected by tension balance positions.

BALANCING ON HANGING ROPES

Setting: Hanging ropes with sufficient mats below for children to work safely

Cue	
Tight Muscles	(Tighten your muscles to support body weight and maintain balance on ropes.)

Tasks/Challenges:

🅣 On a hanging rope, support your weight with both hands, then your hands and your legs, and finally one hand. Create each of the basic shapes—wide, narrow, curled, twisted—with your free body parts (*Figure 23.23*). Perform your balances on the hanging ropes with your head upward.

🅣 Create a series of symmetrical and nonsymmetrical shapes while supporting your weight on the rope (*Figure 23.24*).

 Permit inverted balances on the hanging ropes at low height and only for children with sufficient upper arm/shoulder strength.

TRANSFERRING OFF EQUIPMENT WITH WEIGHT ON HANDS

Setting: Gymnastics apparatus positioned throughout general space, with sufficient mats for children to work safely

Figure 23.22 Student-created balances supporting a partner.

Figure 23.23 Head-up balances on hanging ropes.

Cues

Alignment	(Feet over hips, over shoulders, over hands for a straight-line weight on hands.)
Tight Muscles	(Muscular tension is the key to holding the balance.)

Tasks/Challenges

T Balance momentarily on your hands on the apparatus, make a quarter turn, and transfer your weight from your hands to your feet on the mat. **Remember the cues for safety as you land.**

Figure 23.24 This student creates a symmetrical balance on a hanging rope.

 Practice this skill on the floor and on the low apparatus to be sure you can turn to the right or to the left.

⚠ Be sure students have mastered this skill on the floor/mats and on the low apparatus before they attempt it on higher, narrower apparatus.

PERFORMING APPARATUS SEQUENCES THAT COMBINE STATIONARY BALANCES AND TRAVELING WITH MOVEMENT CONCEPTS

Setting: Gymnastics apparatus positioned throughout general space, with sufficient mats and spacing for children to work safely

Cues

Individual cues as needed

Tasks/Challenges:

Ⓒ Select a piece of equipment that will be your choice for your final gymnastics project. Your assignment will be the design of a sequence combining station-ary balances and travel in relation to that piece of apparatus. The sequence must include the following:

1. An approach to the apparatus and a mount onto the apparatus
2. A series of stationary balances and travels on the apparatus
3. A dismount from the apparatus

You can add excitement and interest to your sequence with

1. Contrasts in fast and slow actions
2. Turning, twisting, curling actions
3. Changes in levels and directions
4. Combinations of slow, controlled movements and quick, sharp movements
5. Inverted balances and actions

Practice your sequence as if you were preparing for the Olympics. When you have completed and timed it with your music, show it to a friend and then to me. We will videotape the sequence for inclusion in your portfolio.

READING COMPREHENSION QUESTIONS

1. In your own words, define *balancing*. Be sure to include the meanings of *base of support* and *center of gravity*.
2. Draw or diagram (stick figures are best) the three key teaching concepts that are emphasized in providing balance experiences.
3. What is the difference between a static balance and a dynamic balance?

4. What are the characteristics of balancing for each of the skill levels? For example, what does a precontrol-level balance look like?
5. List three concepts or skills typically used as subthemes with balance.
6. List five different pieces of equipment that children can use to practice balancing. Include a task you might use with each piece of equipment.
7. What does *inverted balance* mean?
8. Why are jumping and landing studied in conjunction with balances on apparatus?
9. How is transfer of weight typically combined with balancing to present challenging tasks to children at the utilization and proficiency levels?

REFERENCES

National Association for Sport and Physical Education (NASPE). (1995). *Moving into the future: National standards for physical education.* St. Louis, MO: Mosby.

CHAPTER
24
Transferring Weight and Rolling

To travel—walking, running, leaping, rolling, stepping, springing, sliding—is to transfer weight on hands, on feet, on different body parts. The infant creeping on trunk and elbows is transferring weight, as is the toddler shifting weight from side to side during the beginning phase of walking unassisted, the gymnast performing a walkover, the Russian dancer executing a series of rapid mule kicks, the athlete poised to shift her weight to fake an opponent, and the dancer collapsing to the floor in an expression of grace and control. Locomotion is transfer of weight.

Probably the most common form of weight transfer is from foot to foot. In its simplest form, this is walking. At an advanced level—and when combined with the stretching, curling, and twisting actions of layouts and with full body twists—it demands extraordinary kinesthetic awareness, muscular strength, and control. See Box 24.1 for information on weight transfer from the *National Standards for Physical Education*.

Levels of Skill Proficiency in Transferring Weight

Children at the precontrol level are still trying to achieve control of their bodies when they transfer weight to different body parts. They enjoy traveling on body parts other than their feet, and they enjoy exploring apparatus. Activities at the precontrol level include:

1. Traveling on specific body parts (such as feet and seat or hands and feet)
2. Transferring weight by sliding, slithering, or creeping

Children at the control level are ready to transfer their weight onto specific body parts, such as the back for rolling actions and the hands for inverted balances and travel. Activities at the control level focus on:

1. Stretching, curling, and twisting into transfers
2. Transferring weight following step-and-spring takeoffs
3. Transferring weight onto and off equipment using different body parts
4. Transferring weight from feet to hands

Children at the utilization level are ready to transfer their weight onto their hands for travel and balances, for spring takeoffs, and for walkovers. At this level, weight is also transferred by rolling. At the utilization level, the child tries movements that combine the transfers onto specific body parts with stretching and twisting. Challenging activities include:

1. Vaulting over apparatus
2. Mounting apparatus by using inverted positions

3. Traveling on apparatus with curling actions

Children proficient in transferring weight enjoy the transfer from foot to foot with aerial actions between the contacts. They combine stretching, curling, and twisting with flight onto, off, and over apparatus. Proficiency-level weight transference includes many Olympic-style stunts and specific gymnastics apparatus. These tasks are best taught by trained coaches in club gymnastics.

The progression in gymnastics is from mats on the floor to low apparatus with a large surface to higher apparatus with a narrow surface. Our progression spiral (page 398) presents the full spectrum of weight transfer, from the precontrol level to the proficiency level. Alternative ways of further developing the ideas are discussed in Chapter 13.

Precontrol Level: Activities for Exploration of Weight Transfer

Tasks at the precontrol level are designed for the exploration of transferring weight to different body parts. Through this exploration children will begin to develop an awareness of the body parts best suited for weight transfer.

LOCOMOTOR ACTIONS

Setting: Children scattered throughout general space

Tasks/Challenges:

🅣 All locomotor movements are actions of transferring weight. When you walk, hop, skip, or gallop, you transfer your weight from foot to foot. Let's review some of the locomotor movements. Travel throughout general space with a skip or gallop.

🅣 Travel with a jump—two feet to two feet.

🅣 Hop on one foot. Do you transfer weight to different body parts when you hop? No, you move on one foot only.

Additional exploration:

🅣 Travel and jump high in the air like a basketball player.

🅣 Travel and jump over a brook; a large, flat rock; a puddle. This jump is sometimes called a leap—taking off on one foot and landing on the other.

🅣 Explore other ways to travel throughout general space, transferring weight from feet to feet: twirl, spin, slide. . . .

BOX 24.1   THE SKILL OF TRANSFERRING WEIGHT IN THE *NATIONAL STANDARDS FOR PHYSICAL EDUCATION*

The movement skill of transferring weight is referenced in the *National Standards for Physical Education* (NASPE, 1995) under Standard 1: Demonstrates competency in many movement forms and proficiency in a few movement forms.

Sample benchmarks for transferring weight include:

■ Develops and refines a gymnastics sequence demonstrating smooth transitions. (4)
■ Designs and performs gymnastics and dance sequences that combine traveling, rolling, balancing, and weight transfer into smooth, flowing sequences with intentional changes in direction, speed, and flow. (6)

Ⓣ Explore traveling on body parts other than your feet: slither, crawl, walk like a crab. . . .

✳ When you skip, you transfer weight from what body part to what body part? When you jump, you transfer from what to what? What is the difference between a jump and a hop?

TRANSFERRING WEIGHT FROM FEET TO BACK

Setting: Individual mats and/or carpet squares throughout general space, with sufficient room between for children to work safely

Tasks/Challenges:

Ⓣ Squat on your feet with your back rounded like an egg. Transfer your weight from your feet to your back with a rocking action.

Ⓣ Transfer your weight from your feet to your rounded back, and return to your feet with the rocking action.

Ⓣ Give the rocking action a little extra effort, transferring your weight from feet to rounded back, to feet, and then returning to a standing position.

TRANSFERRING WEIGHT FROM FEET TO HANDS

Setting: Large gymnastics mats and/or small mats that will not slide as children transfer weight, scattered throughout general space

Tasks/Challenges:

Ⓣ Transfer your weight from your feet to your hands to your feet, momentarily taking your weight on your hands only.

Wedge mats or folded/rolled mats may be easier for children just beginning to take weight on their hands and/or for those uncomfortable with transfer from standing position to mat on floor.

TRANSFERRING WEIGHT ONTO AND OFF EQUIPMENT

Setting: Low gymnastics equipment—benches, tables, balance beams, and so on—scattered throughout general space

Tasks/Challenges:

The focus for exploration of equipment at the precontrol level is safety—getting on and off equipment with personal safety and without creating an unsafe situation for others.

Control Level: Learning Experiences Leading to Skill Development in Weight Transfer

Tasks at the control level are designed to help children transfer their weight to specific body parts—feet to back, to hands, to head and hands—as they travel and/or balance. For children to maintain control of their bodies during weight transfer is the goal at this level.

A note about cues: Although several cues are listed for many of the learning experiences, it's important to focus on only one cue at a time. That way, the children can really concentrate on that cue. Once you provide feedback to the children and observe that most have learned a cue, then it's time to focus on another one.

■ PROFICIENCY LEVEL
Club gymnastics
Olympic-style transfers

■ UTILIZATION LEVEL
Combining weight transfer and balances into sequences on mats and apparatus
Combing skills on mats
Transferring weight on bars
Transferring weight from feet to hands
Transferring weight by rolling (bench, box, or table)
Transferring weight along apparatus
Transferring weight over apparatus (vaulting box)
Transferring weight onto bars (parallel bars, climbing frame)
Transferring weight to head and hands on apparatus (box, beam, table)
Transferring weight onto large apparatus
Transferring weight to hands and forming a bridge
Transferring weight to hands and twisting
Transferring weight to hands: walking

■ CONTROL LEVEL
Transferring weight to hands by stepping: cartwheels
Transferring weight from feet to hands
Transferring onto low apparatus
Traveling over low apparatus
Making spring/step takeoffs with sequences
Transferring off low apparatus (bench, crate, or low table)
Performing spring/step takeoffs onto crates and/or benches
Performing spring/step takeoffs
Stretching, curling, and twisting into transfers
Transferring weight from feet to combinations of body parts
Transferring weight from feet to back
Transferring weight to hands across mats

■ PRECONTROL LEVEL
Transferring weight onto and off equipment
Transferring weight from feet to hands
Transferring weight from feet to back
Locomotor actions

TRANSFERRING WEIGHT TO HANDS ACROSS MATS

Setting: Small mats (carpet squares or ropes stretched on the floor) scattered throughout general space with sufficient room between for children to work safely

Cues

Strong Muscles	(Strong arms and shoulders—no collapse.)
Stretch Your Legs	(Extend your legs upward—stretch to the sky.)

Tasks/Challenges:

⊤ When we were exploring transferring weight, you practiced taking your weight on your hands and bringing your feet to the floor at the same place. Practice taking your weight on your hands and bringing your feet down safely at a new place—to the right or the left of their original place.

⊤ Now you are going to transfer your weight from your feet to your hands to travel across your mat or rope. Begin at one end of your mat (carpet square or rope), transfer your weight to your hands, and bring your feet down on the other side. You will travel across your mat by transferring your weight to your hands and back to your feet.

You may want to begin in a squat position with your feet on the floor and your hands on the other side of the rope or carpet square, or relatively close to your feet on the mat. Transfer your weight to your hands and bring your feet down a short distance away—just over the rope or carpet square.

Ⓒ When you are comfortable taking your weight on your hands a longer time and you are landing safely, kick your legs higher in the air to remain on your hands even longer. **Stretch your legs as you kick them higher.**

⊤ Stand at the side of your mat (square, rope) in a front-back stance. Extend your arms upward. Step forward with your lead foot, and transfer your weight to your hands. Bring your feet to the floor on the opposite side of your mat (square, rope). If you stretch your trunk and legs as you transfer your weight to one hand and then the other, you will begin to do a cartwheel.

TRANSFERRING WEIGHT FROM FEET TO BACK

Setting: Small mats and/or carpet squares scattered throughout general space

Cues

Rounded Back	(Keep your back rounded, body curled for a good roll.)
Push with Your Hands	(Remember to push with your hands so your head does not get stuck when you roll.)

Tasks/Challenges:

⊤ Remember when you did the rocking action by transferring your weight from your feet to your rounded back. We are going to use that action now for a roll. Transfer your weight from your feet to your rounded back. As you rock back to your shoulders, push with your hands to roll backward across the mat. Remember to push hard with your hands so your neck doesn't get stuck.

If this is the children's first experience with rolling, follow the teaching progression for rolling in the second half of this chapter. If this is a revisitation, review the progression carefully with the children.

 Rolling backward is a weight-transfer skill. What body part do you transfer *to* in a backward roll? Feet to what?

⊤ Think of the forward roll. When you do a forward roll, you transfer your weight from your feet to what? What is *the* critical cue for rolling? Now travel across your mat, transferring your weight, as in a forward roll.

 When you can successfully complete your transfer of weight with a forward or a backward roll, maintaining a rounded back, ask a friend to observe the roll. That person will then record the date and initial the roll on your gymnastics checksheet in your portfolio. (*Refer to Chapter 14, "Assessing Student Learning," for the use of peer observation for assessment in physical education.*)

 Forward and backward rolls should always be optional for children; insisting that students perform specific rolls can result in serious neck injuries.

TRANSFERRING WEIGHT FROM FEET TO COMBINATIONS OF BODY PARTS

Setting: Small mats and/or carpet squares scattered throughout general space, with sufficient room between for children to safely transfer weight

Figure 24.1   Transfer of weight from feet to other body parts.

Cues

Strong Muscles	(Strong arms and shoulders for the transfer to hands—no collapse.)
Rounded Back	(Curl your back and body for all rolling skills.)
Stretch Your Legs	(Extend your legs upward, as if there is a string attached pulling you to the sky.)

Tasks/Challenges:

Ⓣ Transfer your weight from your feet to other combinations of body parts as you travel across your mat or carpet square. Always return to your feet (*Figure 24.1*).

STRETCHING, CURLING, AND TWISTING INTO TRANSFERS

Setting: Small mats and/or carpet squares scattered throughout general space

Cues

Smooth Transitions	(Move smoothly through the transition from balance, to off balance, to balance.)
Tight Muscles	(Tighten your abdominal muscles as you transfer weight, for control of the action.)

Tasks/Challenges:

 Balance on one foot. Bend at the waist, extending your arms forward and your free leg backward. Stretch your arms forward until you are off balance; then transfer your weight to your hands and next to your curled back to roll forward out of the balance.

⚠ Children should demonstrate a mastery of rolling forward with a rounded back before they attempt this task.

T Balance on your knees and one hand. Extend your free arm under your body, twisting your trunk until your weight transfers to your shoulder and new bases of support. Twist gently into the new balance.

T Balance in a shoulder stand with your weight on your shoulders, upper arms, and head, stretching your legs toward the ceiling. Twist your legs and trunk, bringing your feet to the mat behind you in a new balance.

T Balance on your chosen base of support. Twist until you are momentarily off balance; transfer your weight onto a new base of support.

T Balance on your chosen base again. Use different stretching, curling, and twisting actions to transfer onto new bases of support.

PERFORMING SPRING/STEP TAKEOFFS

Before practicing spring and step takeoffs in weight transfer, children should be at the control level of jumping and landing (Chapter 22).

Setting: Large gymnastics mats throughout general space

Cues	
Heads Up	(Keep your head and shoulders erect for a balanced landing.)
Soft Landings	(Bend your knees on landing to absorb the force.)

Tasks/Challenges:

T Approach your gymnastics mat from a distance of ten to twelve feet. Just before you reach the mat, use a two-foot takeoff to spring high in the air; land softly in the center of the mat. The *spring takeoff* in gymnastics is very similar to the approach on the diving board.

The spring takeoff is used for gymnastics skills requiring power—e.g., mounts onto beams and parallel bars, hand-

springs, and vaulting. It is a jump for height; that is why the arms are extended upward. It is also the takeoff used for a basketball jump ball or rebound.

T Approach the mat, spring off your two feet, make a quarter turn, and land in a balanced position. Now try the turn in the opposite direction.

T When you are comfortable with the quarter turn, try a half turn. Remember to practice both clockwise and counterclockwise turns.

T Approach the mat from the distance of ten to twelve feet. Using a *step takeoff,* land on your two feet in the center of the mat.

The step takeoff is the takeoff used for gymnastics skills requiring slow control. Who can give some examples of those? Right, walkover and cartwheels. It is also the takeoff needed for a lay-up in basketball.

PERFORMING SPRING/STEP TAKEOFFS ONTO CRATES AND/OR BENCHES

Setting: Milk crates positioned against large gymnastics mats

⚠ Place the crates against mats to prevent them from sliding.

Cues	
Heads Up	(Keep your head and shoulders erect for a balanced landing.)
Easy On	(Slowly absorb weight on crate—with control.)

Tasks/Challenges:

T Approach the crate or bench from a distance of ten to fifteen feet. Using either a spring or a step takeoff, land in a balanced position on the crate.

C Practice each takeoff until you can transfer your weight onto the crate or bench in a balanced position three times.

T Approach the crate or bench, use a spring takeoff, and transfer your weight to your feet and hands on the crate or bench. **Remember to take your weight momentarily on your hands and then softly lower your body to the crate or bench.**

T Approach the crate or bench, use a step takeoff, and transfer your weight momentarily to your hands only on the crate or bench. **Remember, strong arms for weight on hands.**

TRANSFERRING OFF LOW APPARATUS (BENCH, CRATE, OR LOW TABLE)

Setting: Benches, crates, and/or low tables surrounded by mats and positioned throughout general space

Cues

Rounded Back   (Keep your back rounded, body curled with chin tucked for a good roll.)

Soft Landings   (Bend your knees on landing to absorb the force.)

Tasks/Challenges:

 Transfer your weight off the bench or crate by assuming a kneeling position, placing your hands on the mat, slowly lowering your weight to the mat, and rolling forward.

⚠ Transferring off apparatus by rolling should be introduced only after children have mastered rolling on the floor/mats.

 Transfer your weight off the bench or low table with a jump. Make a wide body shape by extending your arms and legs while in the air. Land in a balanced position on two feet on the mat. **Remember to keep your head and shoulders erect as you jump.**

 Transfer off the bench or low table with a jump, making curled, narrow, and twisted shapes while in the air, and then each time land in your balanced position.

 Transfer off the bench or low table with a jump, turning in the air so that you land facing a different direction. Remember to twist your shoulders in the direction you wish to turn.

 When you are comfortable with a quarter turn, try to execute a half turn in the air so you land facing a different direction.

Revisit/review "Jumping to Form a Body Shape During Flight," in Chapter 22, for additional tasks. Although specific tasks for transferring weight with large apparatus aren't listed until the utilization level, children at the precontrol and control levels need exploration time on large apparatus to become familiar with the equipment and to gain confidence moving on it (Figure 24.2).

MAKING SPRING/STEP TAKEOFFS WITH SEQUENCES

Setting: Benches, crates, and/or low tables surrounded by mats

Figure 24.2 Traveling over, under, and through apparatus builds youngsters' skills transferring weight to a variety of body parts, as well as their comfort with the equipment.

Cues

Soft Landings   (Absorb the force; land softly *on* and *off* the equipment.)

Smooth Transitions   (Move with *control* from balance, to transfer, to balance. . . .)

Rounded Back   (Remember, a curled body with chin tucked for all rolls.)

Children should be able to tell you the critical cues for the skills and demonstrate the individual skills before combining skills in sequences.

Tasks/Challenges:

 Approach the bench (crate, table), and use either a step or a spring takeoff to transfer onto it. Decide what body parts are going to serve as your first bases of support before you begin; this will determine whether you use a step or a spring takeoff.

 Create a series of four balances by transferring your weight to different body parts on the bench (crate, table).

Review "Balancing on Different Bases of Support," "Balancing in Different Body Shapes," and "Balancing Symmetrically and Nonsymmetrically" in Chapter 23.

Figure 24.3 Equipment setups for transfer of weight when traveling over low apparatus.

T Transfer off the bench (crate, table) in one of the following ways: (1) jumping and turning, (2) jumping and making a shape while in the air, (3) rolling, or (4) using a transfer that you have created.

 Have the student tell you if the transfer off the low apparatus includes inversion or weight on hands; if so, be sure the student demonstrates mastery on the floor/mats before attempting a transfer off the low apparatus.

TRAVELING OVER LOW APPARATUS

Setting: Milk crates, benches, low tables, hurdles, and milk jug/rolled-newspaper or dowel-rod "hurdles" throughout general space (Figure 24.3)

Cues

Strong Muscles	(Strong arms and shoulders— no collapse.)
Stretch Your Legs	(Extend your legs upward— stretch to the sky.)

Tasks/Challenges:

T Travel over the various pieces of low equipment by transferring your weight from your feet to your hands to your feet. At the hurdles and the newspaper or dowel rods, place your hands on the mat on the other side of the hurdle or rod, and then transfer your weight over, landing on your feet. At the benches and milk crates, place your hands on the equipment, take your weight on your hands only, and land on your feet on the opposite side of the equipment.

C As you become comfortable taking your weight on your hands, kick higher toward the ceiling, stretching your legs and trunk.

TRANSFERRING ONTO LOW APPARATUS

Setting: Benches, crates, and/or low tables surrounded by mats in general space

Cues

Strong Muscles	(Strong arms and shoulders for transfer onto hands.)
Soft Landings	(Absorb the force on feet and/or hands and lower body gently onto apparatus.)

Tasks/Challenges:

T Use the benches (crates, low tables) to practice transferring your weight onto equipment. Transfer your weight from your feet to your hands on the equipment by springing off your two feet and landing on your hands and feet. Take your weight momentarily on your hands, then softly lower to your feet; don't jump onto the equipment.

T Using your spring takeoff, transfer your weight to your hands and knees on the apparatus. Yes, you still take your weight momentarily on your hands only.

T Use a front-back stance and step into the transfer, momentarily taking your weight on your hands only on the equipment, then lowering your total body onto additional body parts. Be sure your hands are firmly planted on the equipment so you won't slip when you transfer to hands only.

Setting: Large gymnastics mats scattered throughout general space, with sufficient room between for children to work safely

Cues

Strong Muscles	(Strong arms and shoulders to take weight on hands.)
Stretch to the Sky	(Stretch your trunk and legs upward.)
Alignment	(Feet over hips, over shoulders, over hands—in a straight line.)

Tasks/Challenges:

 Transfer your weight from your feet to your hands to your feet, momentarily taking your weight on your hands only. Reach downward, not forward, with your hands; **stretch your legs toward the ceiling and tighten your stomach muscles to maintain your balance.**

You may want to begin in a squat position with your hands and feet touching the floor. Transfer your weight to your hands by kicking your feet in the air.

Use a step action to transfer your weight to your hands; try to have your shoulders directly over your hands when you kick your legs up.

 When you are comfortable with your feet being just a few inches off the floor, begin to kick your feet higher in the air.

 Practice until you can balance for three seconds on your hands. Transfer your weight back to your feet in their original position each time.

 Teach children in the practice stages of taking weight on hands to twist the trunk, doing a quarter turn and bringing feet down to the floor safely, if they begin to overbalance. This prevents falling on the back in the event of an overbalance.

 Journal: Record in your journal the date on which you successfully take your weight on your hands for three seconds. Describe the feeling of "weight on hands." (*Refer to Chapter 14, "Assessing Student Learning", for the use of journals in physical education.*)

Setting: Large gymnastics mats throughout general space, with sufficient room for children to work safely

Cues

Strong Muscles	(Strong arms and shoulders to take weight on hands.)
Stretch	(Stretch your trunk and legs toward the sky—legs straight.)

Tasks/Challenges:

 Using a step action, alternate transferring your weight to your feet and to your hands, returning to your feet in a step action, as in a cartwheel. Your weight transfers momentarily from your foot, to your foot, to your hand, to your hand, to your foot, to your foot.

 Experiment beginning the cartwheel by facing the mat or by standing sideways with one shoulder toward the mat. You may choose either starting position.

 As you feel comfortable with the foot-foot-hand-hand-foot-foot transfer, try to make a straight pathway with your feet and hands along the mat.

 Practice leading first with your right and then with your left side so you can do a cartwheel in either direction.

 Practice until you can perform your cartwheel in a straight line three times.

 Portfolio: When you can perform your cartwheel in a straight line, with legs fully stretched in the air, ask a partner to assess the skill. Record the date on your gymnastics checklist in your portfolio. (*Refer to Chapter 14, "Assessing Student Learning," for guidelines on assessment.*)

 Transfer your weight to your hands, as in the cartwheel. While you are balanced in the inverted position, bring your feet together, twist a half turn, and bring your feet down quickly to face the opposite direction; this is a roundoff.

Children won't master gymnastics tasks in only one or two thirty-minute lessons. A station format plus revisitation (see Chapter 13) provides opportunities for distributed practice of skills.

Utilization Level: Learning Experiences Leading to Skill Development in Weight Transfer

Children at the utilization level of transferring weight learn to transfer their weight to their hands for longer

Figure 24.4 This child is discovering one of the ways to transfer weight across large apparatus.

periods of time and in combinations with stretching, curling, and twisting actions. Tasks are designed to teach children to transfer weight onto, over, and from large apparatus (Figure 24.4). The tasks also emphasize the development of more complex sequences involving weight transference.

A note about cues: Although several cues are listed for many of the learning experiences, it's important to focus on only one cue at a time. That way, the children can really concentrate on that cue. Once you provide feedback to the children and observe that most have learned a cue, then it's time to focus on another one.

TRANSFERRING WEIGHT TO HANDS: WALKING

Setting: Large gymnastics mats throughout general space, with sufficient room for children to work safely on transfers

Cues	
Strong Muscles	(Strong arms and shoulders for weight on hands.)
Stretch	(Stretch your trunk and legs toward the sky—legs straight.)
Alignment	(Feet over hips, over shoulders, over hands—in a straight line.)

Tasks/Challenges:

Ⓣ When you are confident and comfortable balancing on your hands for three seconds, try walking on your hands.

⚠️ Children should attempt walking on their hands only if they have sufficient upper body strength to support weight in the inverted position for several seconds and can move into and out of a balance on their hands only with control.

TRANSFERRING WEIGHT TO HANDS AND TWISTING

Setting: Large gymnastics mats throughout general space, with sufficient room for children to work safely on transfers

Cues	
Strong Muscles	(Strong arm and shoulder muscles for weight on hands.)
Stretch	(Stretch your trunk and legs toward the sky—legs straight.)
Alignment	(Feet over hips, over shoulders, over hands—in a straight line.)

Tasks/Challenges:

Ⓣ Transfer your weight to your hands, twist your body a half turn, and bring your feet to the floor so that you are facing the opposite direction.

Ⓣ While balanced on your hands, slowly walk on your hands a half turn to face the opposite direction.

TRANSFERRING WEIGHT TO HANDS AND FORMING A BRIDGE

Setting: Large gymnastics mats throughout general space

Cues

Strong Muscles	(Strong arms and shoulders for supporting weight on hands.)
Tight Muscles	(Tighten the abdominals for control.)
Extend	(Stretch from your fingertips to your toes as you transfer from feet to hands to feet.)

Tasks/Challenges:

T Using a step action, transfer your weight to your hands with sufficient force to continue the forward motion. Your feet should remain in the steplike stance as they move upward over your hands. Just before your feet contact the floor, bring them together, and bend your knees slightly. You will then balance in a "bridge" with your feet and hands supporting your weight. Keep your legs in the steplike stance throughout the transfer.

T As your feet contact the surface, push with your hands to continue your transfer to a standing position. This transfer without a pause is a walkover.

TRANSFERRING WEIGHT ONTO LARGE APPARATUS

Setting: Large apparatus—benches, tables, vaulting boxes, balance beams, parallel bars, large climbing frames—placed around the gym. *(Many transfers at the utilization and proficiency levels of transferring weight are specific to particular pieces of apparatus; the name of the apparatus appears in parentheses following the task title.)*

Cues

Heads Up	(Keep your head and shoulders erect as you approach the apparatus.)
Soft Landings	(Absorb the force on your feet and/or hands and lower your body slowly to the apparatus.)

Tasks/Challenges:

T Transferring weight onto large apparatus in gymnastics usually includes an approach to build momentum, a spring or step takeoff, and the transfer onto the apparatus. Approach the apparatus from about fifteen feet. Using a spring takeoff, transfer your weight from your feet on the floor to your feet and hands on the apparatus (box, beam, table). **Remember, you will need a spring takeoff for power and/or height; a step takeoff is a slower way to transfer weight.**

T Transfer your weight to your feet and hands with your body curled in a tuck position. (Model.)

T Transfer your weight to your feet and hands with legs extended in a straddle position. (Model.)

T Transfer your weight to your feet and hands in a "wolf" position: one knee bent, one leg straight (*Figure 24.5*). (Model.)

T Approach the apparatus from the sides as well as the front. Practice both spring and step takeoffs to transfer your weight to various body parts on the apparatus. Remember, you will need a spring takeoff for power and/or height; a step takeoff is a slower way to transfer weight.

Many of the control-level tasks for transferring weight onto and off low apparatus can be repeated for large apparatus (Figure 24.6). This is good practice because it enables children to adjust comfortably to the increased height and narrower surface of large apparatus.

TRANSFERRING WEIGHT TO HEAD AND HANDS ON APPARATUS (BOX, BEAM, TABLE)

Setting: Large apparatus placed throughout general space, with sufficient mats for children to work safely

Cues

Heads Up	(Keep your head and shoulders erect as you approach the apparatus.)
Strong Muscles	(Strong arm and shoulder muscles to support weight on apparatus.)
Soft Landings	(Absorb the force on your feet and/or hands and lower your body slowly to the apparatus.)

Tasks/Challenges:

T Approach the apparatus, and use a spring takeoff to transfer your weight to your hands and head on the apparatus. Push hard with your legs on the takeoff for sufficient height and time for the transfer, taking your weight first on your hands only and then gently, with control, on your head and hands.

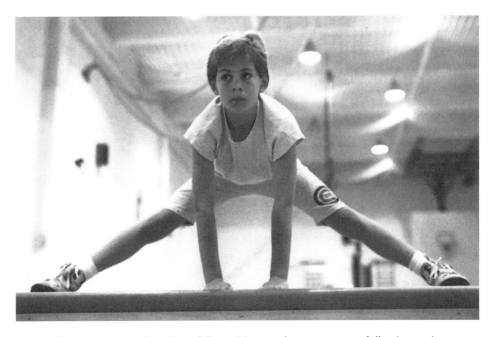

Figure 24.5 Tuck, wolf, and straddle positions on large apparatus following spring takeoffs.

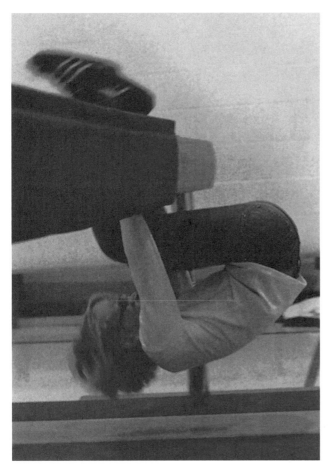

Figure 24.6 This youngster practices transferring weight onto and off equipment using different body parts.

 Have the children approach the box, beam, or table from the end rather than the side for this transfer to head and hands. This allows sufficient space for rolling across the apparatus if they overbalance.

 Teach the children to roll slowly across the apparatus if they overbalance on the head-and-hands transfer; teach them to transfer weight back to their feet on the floor if they do not have sufficient push to move into the inverted position on the apparatus.

Cues

Heads Up	(Keep your head and shoulders erect as you approach the apparatus.)
Strong Muscles	(Strong arm and shoulder muscles to support weight on apparatus.)
Soft Landings	(Absorb the force on your feet and/or hands and lower your body gently onto the apparatus.)

Tasks/Challenges:

🅣 Standing under the apparatus, use a spring takeoff to transfer your weight to your hands on a high bar. Hanging on the bar, pull up with your arms as you swing your legs over a lower bar and balance in a sitting position.

🅣 Approach the apparatus with a series of steps. Using a spring takeoff, grasp the bar with your hands and jump up. Push really hard with your arms to lift your body above the bar; balance with your hands and upper thighs on the bar. Swing a leg over the bar so you can straddle the bar.

🅣 Approach the apparatus with a series of steps. As you step under the bar, grasp the bar with your hands, and kick your rear leg forcefully upward to bring your hips to the bar. Keeping your arms bent and pulling your body close to the bar, assume a pike position by bending at the hips. The momentum of the leg kick will cause your body to circle the bar. Balance on your hands and upper thighs on the bar.

🅒 You have now practiced jumping into a hip mount and doing a hip circle with the body in a pike position. Practice these skills until you master them. Then add them to your gymnastics checklist in your portfolio.

🅒 Approach the apparatus from the back, front, and side; practice both spring and step takeoffs to transfer your weight to various body parts on the apparatus.

TRANSFERRING WEIGHT ONTO BARS (PARALLEL BARS, CLIMBING FRAME)

Setting: Large apparatus placed throughout general space, with sufficient mats surrounding for safety

TRANSFERRING WEIGHT OVER APPARATUS (VAULTING BOX)

Setting: Vaulting boxes, with sufficient mats for safety, in general space

Cues

Heads Up	(Keep your head and shoulders erect as you approach the apparatus.)
Strong Muscles	(Strong arm and shoulder muscles to support weight on apparatus.)
Soft Landings	(Bend your knees for a controlled landing.)

Tasks/Challenges:

 Approach the vaulting box with light running steps, keeping your weight on the balls of your feet. Using a spring takeoff, plant your hands firmly on the box, shoulder-width apart. Travel over the vaulting box, landing on your two feet on the mat.

⚠ Position yourself at the vaulting station when children are transferring weight over the apparatus. As a spotter, you should not help the children perform the skill, but you can help prevent serious injury from a fall. Because spotting techniques differ for each skill, you should consult a gymnastics text before attempting to spot students in specific gymnastics tasks.

 Now transfer over the box by placing your hands shoulder-width apart on the apparatus, bringing your legs up between your arms in a tuck or curled position. Pause momentarily on the box in this curled shape; then jump forward to the mat.

🅣 Push harder with your hands this time to bring your body into a curled position, and push yourself over the box without pausing in the tuck position on top of the box.

⚠ Children should attempt vaulting over the box with a curled, straddle, or wolf vault only after they have mastered transferring onto apparatus with these techniques.

🅣 Transfer over the vaulting box by bringing your feet and legs together, stretched to one side, as you cross over the box. Place your hands shoulder-width apart on the box, and shift your weight to one hand as you swing your legs over the box. Push off from the vaulting box with the supporting hand, landing on two feet with your back to the vaulting box. This is called a flank vault. That spring takeoff we practiced earlier becomes increasingly important as you work on mounts onto and transfers over large apparatus.

🅣 Transfer your weight onto the vaulting box in a wide shape by placing your hands shoulder-width apart and stretching your legs to either side of the box, supporting your weight momentarily on your feet and hands. From a standing position on the vaulting box, transfer your weight to your feet by jumping to the mat. You will need a really strong takeoff to gain the height for this transfer.

 Transfer your weight over the vaulting box by taking your weight on your hands, shoulder-width apart, and bringing your feet over the box in the stretched, wide shape. Keep your head and shoulders erect to prevent losing your balance. This is called a straddle vault. Do not attempt this vault without the spotter (teacher or qualified adult) at the station.

⚠ Always have the children tell you which vault they are attempting and whether they are stopping on top or transferring over before they begin their approach. This allows you to be ready for the proper spotting of that skill.

TRANSFERRING WEIGHT ALONG APPARATUS

Setting: Stationary bar, tables and benches of various heights, vaulting boxes, balance beam, and a stage

Many of the gymnastics skills learned on the floor and on low equipment (Figure 24.7) can also be performed on large apparatus. Before children try them on the large apparatus, they should review the skills on the floor/mats, then on the low equipment, concentrating on the skill and its critical cues.

TRANSFERRING WEIGHT BY ROLLING (BENCH, BOX, OR TABLE)

Setting: Benches, vaulting boxes, and/or tables of various heights, surrounded by sufficient mats for children to work safely

Cues

Rounded Back	(Keep your back curled, chin tucked for a good roll.)
Control	(Tight muscles, slow-motion action for control throughout the roll.)

Tasks/Challenges:

 Remind children to position themselves at one end of the bench, box, or table to start the roll so that they will have enough surface to complete the rolling action.

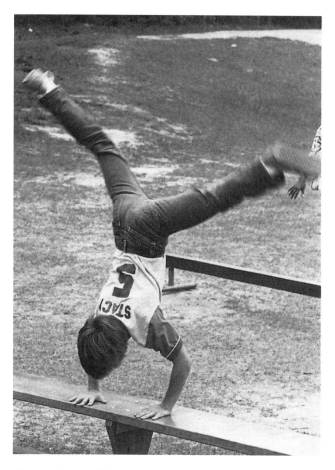

Figure 24.7 Ability to transfer weight to travel along low equipment is a prerequisite for transferring weight on large apparatus.

T Transfer your weight to your feet and hands on the bench, box, or table, with your back curled. Place your thumbs and the sides of your palms on top of the bench or box, with your hands and fingers on the sides of the apparatus. (Although this position is quite different from that used for rolling on mats, it provides a steady grip and constant awareness of the width of the surface.) Tuck your head, and slowly roll forward across the apparatus.

T Transfer your weight to your feet and hands with a curled back. Slowly transfer to your curled back and hands for rolling backward across the bench, box, or table. Extend your hands above your head to hold onto the sides of the box or bench; place your head to one side, and roll backward over one shoulder.

T Roll backward on the apparatus by transferring your weight from your curled back to one bent knee with one leg extended. This backward transfer is often easier when balancing on the small surface.

 Permit students to transfer weight by rolling across the apparatus only after they have demonstrated sustained control of the rolling action on the low apparatus. They should be able to stop the movement at any point in the rolling action.

TRANSFERRING WEIGHT FROM FEET TO HANDS

Setting: Tape lines on the gym floor, with sufficient space between for children to work safely; low benches surrounded by mats

Cues

Strong Muscles	(Strong arms and shoulders to take weight on hands.)
Stretch	(Stretch your trunk and legs toward the sky—legs straight.)
Muscular Tension	(Maintain tension through arms, trunk, and legs for full extension—stretched for cartwheels, arched for walkovers.)

Tasks/Challenges:

T Practice a cartwheel on a tape line on the floor until you can do it perfectly three times. Now transfer your weight from your feet to your hands in a cartwheel on the low bench.

Teaching by invitation or intratask variation is very effective when working with transferring weight on apparatus. Permit only those children who are clearly ready to do so to practice inverted weight transference along apparatus (Figure 24.8).

T Transfer your weight from your feet to your hands, as in a walkover, on the bench.

T Transfer your weight from your feet to your hands, slowly execute a half turn, and bring your feet down on the apparatus surface facing the opposite direction.

 Teach children to push with their hands to move the body away from the bench and to transfer weight to their feet on the floor if they feel off balance or unable to complete the transfer after inverting.

C Create three ways to transfer your weight while moving along the apparatus. Consider changes in levels and directions of travel. Diagram and/or describe your transfers on paper. Show your three

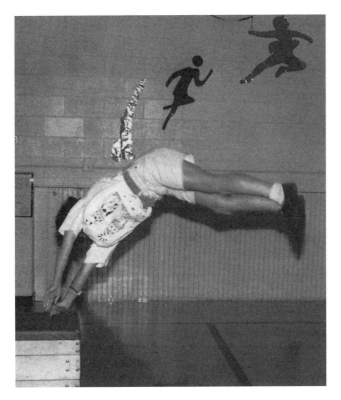

Figure 24.8 This student practices transferring off apparatus, taking weight on hands.

transfers to a friend; ask the friend to give you pointers to make your transfers even better.

 Children working together, as in the preceding task, can be an excellent type of assessment. Refer to Chapter 14, "Assessing Student Learning," for more information on peer assessment.

TRANSFERRING WEIGHT ON BARS

Setting: Parallel bars and/or large climbing frame, with sufficient mats surrounding

Cues	
Strong Grip	(Maintain a strong grip on the bars to work safely.)
Strong Muscles	(Strong arm and shoulder muscles to maintain control on the bars.)

Tasks/Challenges:

T Transfer your weight to different body parts as you move from bar to bar on the parallels or other climbing apparatus. Make some of your transfers very slowly; others, quickly.

T Circle the bar with your body curled, in a pike position.

T Use twisting actions to move your body off balance and into the transfer.

COMBINING SKILLS ON MATS

Setting: Large gymnastics mats in general space, with sufficient room between for children to work safely

Cues
Individual cues as needed

Tasks/Challenges:

C Travel the length of your mat, transferring your weight from your feet to other body parts, in various combinations to create a sequence. For example:

- Perform slow movements and then very quick movements for contrast.
- Do movements that show strength and then movements that demonstrate slowness and smooth control.
- Perform twisting, turning actions—for example, a roundoff, weight on your hands, a 360-degree turn on your hands.
- Travel the length of your mat, combining a balance, a jump, a roll, and a hands/feet action.
- Travel the length of your mat, transferring your weight from your feet to your hands, followed by a roll and an ending balance.

COMBINING WEIGHT TRANSFER AND BALANCES INTO SEQUENCES ON MATS AND APPARATUS

Setting: Large and small gymnastics apparatus, the large apparatus positioned in general space

Cues
Individual cues as needed

Tasks/Challenges:

Gymnastics routines on mats and apparatus are combinations of weight transfers and balance. Children at the utilization and proficiency levels of balance and weight transfer are ready for sequences involving combinations of

Figure 24.9 Sample assignment for utilization- or proficiency-level weight-transfer and balance sequence.

Name _____

Final Project: Gymnastics

Grade 6: (a) mat sequence, (b) equipment sequence

Alone; with a partner: mirror, side by side

1. Beginning
    A. Approach:
        distance, starting point, pathway
        <u>walk</u>, run, leap, roll, walkover, cartwheel
        other _____
    B. Takeoff:
        spring, <u>step</u>
2. Development of sequence: Mix <u>in any order</u> for interest.
    A. Balances:
        minimum of four body shapes/four different bases of support
    B. Actions:
        minimum of three
        stretch curl; twist turn
    C. Transfers:
        movement
        feet to hand, back, head/hands
        (headstands, cartwheels, rolls, etc.)
    D. Inversion:
        minimum of two
3. Ending shape or dismount
    A. Music selection: ninety seconds
    B. On back side of page, list the progression of section 2;
        illustrate it if you wish.

skills and travel. Figure 24.9 gives an example of an assignment, plus guidelines for completing it.

ASSESSMENT EXAMPLE
from the National Standards for Physical Education

Event Task/Observational Record

As the final project in gymnastics, students are to design a 90-second routine for either mats or apparatus. They may choose to work alone or with a partner; the partner relationship may be mirror or side-by-side. The routine must include an approach, development, and ending shape or dismount. The development portion of the routine must include the following: a minimum of four balances of different shapes and bases of support, a minimum of three locomotor and/or nonlocomotor actions, weight transfer, and at least two inversions. The selection of music for the routine is a student decision. The routine is to be diagrammed or written on paper and practiced until the sequence is memorized in its entirety. The routine will be videotaped for inclusion in student portfolios.

BOX 24.2   THE SKILL OF ROLLING IN THE *NATIONAL STANDARDS FOR PHYSICAL EDUCATION*

The skill theme of rolling is referenced in the *National Standards for Physical Education* (NASPE, 1995) as sample kindergarten and sixth-grade benchmarks under Standard 1: Demonstrates competency in many movement forms and proficiency in a few movement forms.

The sample kindergarten benchmark states that a child "rolls sideways without hesitating or stopping" (p. 6). The sample sixth-grade benchmark states that a child "designs and performs gymnastics and dance sequences that combine rolling, balancing, and weight transfer into smooth, flowing sequences with intentional changes in direction, speed, and flow" (p. 46).

Criteria for Assessment

a. Routine includes all necessary components: approach, balances, weight transfers, inversion, dismount (ending shape)
b. Routine matches music in length
c. Demonstrates changes in tempo in routine
d. Selects balances and weight transfers that can be correctly performed (i.e., skills matched to personal gymnastic ability)
e. Maintains stillness in balances
f. Displays creativity in routine design
g. Transitions between movement are smooth

NASPE (1995, pp. 47–48)

Proficiency Level: Learning Experiences Leading to Skill Development in Weight Transfer

Tasks at the proficiency level focus on increasing the horizontal and/or vertical distance of the weight transfer, as well as the intricate maneuvers (twisting and curling actions) that the body and its parts perform as weight is transferred from and received by different body parts. Examples include hands-only vaulting; performing stretching and twisting actions while airborne; and dismounting from apparatus by transferring weight from hands to feet combined with aerial twists, turns, and curls.

Activities at this level use specific gymnastics equipment and more closely resemble Olympic-style stunts. These skills are most often learned through club gymnastics. We do not teach them to the total class because very few children attain this level of performance. For those children who are ready to learn these skills or already proficient in these tasks, we provide individual teaching or coaching (see Chapter 25).

Levels of Skill Proficiency in Rolling

Children find the sensations of rolling—dizziness, loss of perception, and not knowing where they are or how they'll finish a roll—fascinating. The feeling of not knowing where you are or where you will end up, which is characteristic of a child's first attempts at rolling, is both intriguing and perplexing. And so children love to roll. As children become adept at rolling, the fascination of traveling upside down is augmented by the pleasure of being able to roll in different directions and at various speeds. See Box 24.2 for information on rolling from the *National Standards for Physical Education*.

Rolling is the act of transferring weight to adjacent body parts around a central axis. In physical education classes, rolling is generally dealt with in a gymnastics context, as a transference of weight. In gymnastics, safety through rolling is a skill introduced early to help children avoid crashing to the floor when they lose their balance. In dance and games, rolling is dealt with briefly to increase the children's range of movement and to enhance expressive abilities (see the progression spiral on page 414).

The precontrol level of rolling is characterized by exploration of various ways in which the body is able to be round. This exploration includes rocking actions from the head to feet on the back and stomach. At this level, children are challenged when asked to perform actions such as rocking back and forth like a rocking chair or rolling in a stretched position like a log. Rocking in a ball-like position, in preparation for rolling, is

Rolling

■ **PROFICIENCY LEVEL**

Club gymnastics

■ **UTILIZATION LEVEL**

Catching, throwing, and rolling
Striking and rolling
Rolling to meet and part
Balancing and rolling on equipment
Rolling onto low equipment
Throwing, catching, and rolling
Rolling to express an idea
Rolling, balancing, and rolling
Traveling and rolling between pieces of equipment
Rolling off low equipment
Rolling on low equipment
Rolling over low hurdles
Touch-and-go rolls
Busy Mat

■ **CONTROL LEVEL**

Traveling, jumping, landing, and rolling
Rolling, levels, directions, and jumping
Jumping over equipment, landing, and rolling
Jumping from different heights and rolling
Jumping for height, landing, and rolling
Jumping off equipment, landing, and rolling
Rolling using different directions and speeds
Linking rolls
Rolling from different directions and positions
Rolling in different directions
Rolling backward
Handclasp backward
Back shoulder
Rolling at different speeds
Rolling from different positions
Back touch
Rolling forward
Through the legs
Back rocker
Shoulders sideways
Egg roll
Log roll
Twin Rockers

■ **PRECONTROL LEVEL**

The Ball
Rolling sideways
The Rocking Horse
Rounds

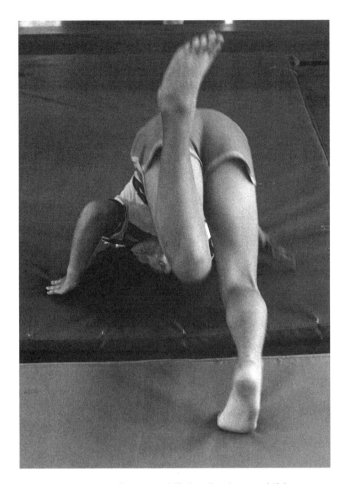

Figure 24.10   Rolling is a skill that fascinates children.

also explored at this level. When a child first begins to roll, the arms and hands are of little use (Figure 24.10). The child may "get over," but the whole body usually uncurls in the middle of the roll and the child lands sitting down.

At the control level, children become capable of controlling their bodies while rolling. They are able to roll in different directions, using their arms and hands to push while the body stays curled. The emphasis at this level is on control and the ability to roll in various situations. Rolls are performed as floor activities, and rolling is developed as a safety skill. Tasks such as the following can be presented to children:

1. Changing the direction of the rolls—backward, sideways, forward
2. Changing the speed of the rolls—fast or slow
3. Rolling from different positions—starting from low or standing positions and different balances (on one foot, two feet, or three body parts)
4. Combining jumping, landing, and rolling
5. Traveling and rolling

At the utilization level, children no longer have to "think about" staying round and are able to use the roll in combination with other skills and on equipment and large apparatus. Additionally, they can use rolling as an expressive form and in combination with manipulative skills. Activities such as the following challenge children at this level:

1. Rolling with something in their hands
2. Rolling after catching an object
3. Rolling on or over low equipment
4. Combining rolling with other locomotor forms as an expressive movement

Children proficient in rolling enjoy rolling over high equipment and aerial rolls. They also combine rolling as a means of weight transfer between various forms of balance and other forms of weight transference. At this level, children are capable of difficult and sophisticated rolls, but because of safety considerations, the teacher's skills, equipment requirements, and the student-teacher ratio of physical education classes, we do not teach them. Such rolls as dive rolls; rolls along high, narrow equipment; and rolls from aerial positions are better left to club gymnastics.

Children who master the skill of rolling are able to participate comfortably and safely in activities that involve the risk of being off balance and falling, because they possess sufficient recovery techniques. This skill also gives children a fluid way to connect different balancing actions and to change direction and/or speed in a dynamic, unpredictable situation.

When introducing the skill of rolling, we prefer to have one mat for each child. When we don't have a mat for each child, we use as many mats as possible. We've found that a good ground rule for any rolling situation is to have only one child at a time on the mat. This does *not* mean that the other children must stand in line and wait; they can stand around the mat and roll, in turn, as soon as the mat is empty. Sometimes we set up learning centers to prevent long waits in line. Grassy areas or carpeting can also serve as appropriate areas for practicing rolling. When children roll on or over equipment, we make sure that the surrounding area is covered with mats.

The key observation points in Box 24.3 show the correct and incorrect forms for rolling. Observe children carefully to help them overcome any problems with rolling.

Finally, as with any weight-bearing activity, it is critical to give careful consideration to the physical maturity and skill of each child. Before they're ready to attempt "traditional" forward and backward rolls, children *must be able to support their body weight with their arms.* We believe that children should not be

BOX 24.3   KEY OBSERVATION POINTS: ROLLING

1. Do the child's hands and arms receive the body weight evenly at the beginning of the roll without the body collapsing to one side?

2. Does the child's head slide through as the weight goes from the hands to the upper back and leave the mat as soon as the shoulders touch?

3. Do the child's arms come off the mat as soon as the shoulders touch?

4. Does the child's body stay curled and the roll end on the feet?

5. When children are at the mature stage of rolling, do their rolls look similar to the following sequence?

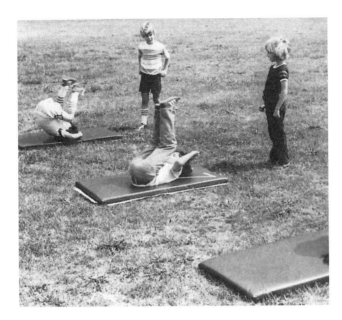

Figure 24.11 Smaller mats are adequate for introducing children to rolling; larger mats can be used for rolling in sequences and in relation to apparatus.

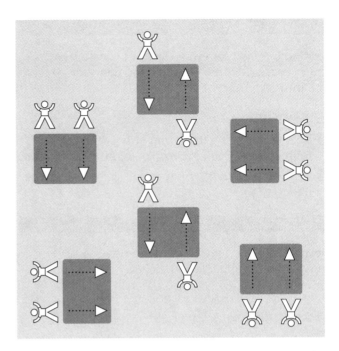

Figure 24.12 Mat positions that minimize the likelihood children will rock or roll into each other.

forced to do any specific forward or backward roll. We are especially concerned about asking children to do "traditional" backward and forward rolls when they haven't yet developed the strength they need to protect themselves from back and neck injuries. Thus, we have provided illustrations of the hand and body positions for a variety of rolls.

Precontrol Level: Activities for Exploration of Rolling

At the precontrol level children explore arching or rounding their bodies as a prerequisite to rolling. Once they are able to curve their bodies, they explore rocking and rolling actions that can be used for traveling and transferring weight.

ROUNDS

Setting: A mat (Figure 24.11), space on a mat, or a carpet square in a grassy area for each child; children positioned so that they will not rock into each other (Figure 24.12)

Tasks/Challenges:

🅣 On your mat try to find as many ways as possible to make your body so that it is round. Three different ways would be good.

THE ROCKING HORSE

Setting: A mat, space on a mat, or a carpet square in a grassy area for each child; children positioned so that they will not rock into each other

Tasks/Challenges:

🅣 In self-space, you're going to pretend what it is like to be a rocking horse. But this rocking horse can do special things. First, you want to find out what it is like to rock on your back. To rock on your back, you must make your back round, because flat things can't rock.

🅣 Now your special rocking horse is going to try and rock on its stomach. Remember to make your stomach round so you can rock smoothly.

🅣 Now your are going to try and do what no rocking horse has ever done: You are going to try and rock on your side. Can you make your side round? Try it.

🅣 Your rocking horse is just getting warmed up, so let's see if it can go faster. See if you can rock so fast on your back that it takes you up to your feet.

🅣 Now see if you can keep rocking on your back without stopping, almost as if you can't stop. If it helps, use your hands and arms.

ROLLING SIDEWAYS

Setting: A mat for every child or two or a large grassy space; children positioned so that they do not roll into each other

Tasks/Challenges:

🅣 Now we are going to try something different: rolling sideways, like a log. Try to roll slow and fast.

🅣 Can you find another way to roll sideways? Maybe like an egg?

THE BALL

Setting: A mat for every child or two or a large grassy space; children positioned so that they do not roll into each other

Tasks/Challenges:

🅣 Can you make your body like a ball? How many ways can your ball move around your space? Remember, only round balls roll.

Control Level: Learning Experiences Leading to Skill Development in Rolling

At the control level, children learn to roll in different directions and from different positions so they're able to perform other movements safely and to use rolling as a response to a fall. Children also practice rolling as a conclusion to jumping and landing.

A note about cues: Although several cues are listed for many of the learning experiences, it's important to focus on only one cue at a time. That way, the children can really concentrate on that cue. Once you provide feedback to the children and observe that most have learned a cue, then it's time to focus on another one.

TWIN ROCKERS

Setting: Partners side by side on a mat or in a grassy area, with enough space between them so that they do not hit each other

Cues

"C" Bodies   (Curve your body like the letter C to rock.)

Tasks/Challenges:

🅣 To warm up a bit, practice rocking back and forth on your mat. See if you can make your rocks very smooth.

🅣 This time you are going to play a game called Twin Rockers. You and your partner will be side by side. On the signal, you'll start to rock on your back. The challenge is to rock the same way and at the same time as your partner so that you look like twins.

🅣 This time, rock on your stomach.

🅒 Now see if you and your partner can develop two other Twin Rockers. Practice them until you can do them so that they match exactly.

LOG ROLL

Setting: A mat for every child or two or a large grassy space; children positioned so that they do not roll into each other

Cues

Stretch Arms   (Stretch your arms above your head.)
Straight Body   (Straighten your body.)
Feet Together   (Bring your feet tight together.)

Tasks/Challenges:

🅣 See if you can roll to the right and to the left with your log roll. Practice until you can go both ways just as smoothly.

🅣 This time try and make your log roll go in a straight line. Try to go from one end of your mat (a medium-sized, three-foot by five-foot or four-foot by six-foot mat) to the other without rolling off.

🅣 Try changing the speed of your log roll: Sometimes roll slowly as if you were rolling on flat land and sometimes move quickly as if rolling downhill.

🅣 If you feel comfortable doing the log roll with your hands over your head, try to do it with your arms at your sides.

🅒 Try to make a sequence of log rolls: for example, one slow to the right, two quickly to the left, one slow to the right, and then repeat the sequence. Be sure to stay in your space or on your mat.

 Portfolio: Children can write their sequences out, date them, and include them in their portfolios as an assessment task.

EGG ROLL

Setting: A mat for every child or two or a large grassy space; children positioned so that they do not roll into each other

Figure 24.13 Arm positions for keeping ankles and knees together during the Egg Roll.

Cues

"C" Bodies	(Curve your body like the letter C to roll.)
Hold Knees	(Hold your knees together, either from the outside or from the inside out; *see Figure 24.13*.)

Tasks/Challenges:

T This time try to roll sideways like an egg in a curled position. Practice rolling this egg in different directions—sometimes left, sometimes right.

T Try rolling on different body parts—shoulder, back, even upper legs.

T In your space or on your mat, practice using the egg roll to travel. Can you roll around the whole space?

T Roll at different speeds around your space or mat.

SHOULDERS SIDEWAYS

Setting: A mat for every child or two or a large grassy space; children positioned so that they do not roll into each other

Cues

Drop	(Drop one shoulder to the mat.)
Tuck	(Tuck the elbow and knee of the dropped shoulder under.)
Roll	(Roll over.)

Tasks/Challenges:

T This time we are going to roll over a shoulder. To do that you need to start on your hands and knees,

drop one shoulder to the mat, tuck your elbow and knee under your body, and roll over. Your roll should take you back up to your hands and knees. (*Demonstrate the roll.*) Let's all do it together this first time. Ready? Hands and knees, drop, tuck, roll. Good.

T Practice the roll on your own. **Say the cues out loud as you go, to help you remember the process.** Do one roll across your mat, get up, and try another one. You know you are really good when you can come up to your hands and knees each time.

T Once you feel comfortable rolling in one direction, try dropping the other shoulder and rolling that way.

C See if you can do three rolls in each direction that stay round throughout the whole roll.

T If you feel really good about rolling on your shoulder from your hands and knees, you may want to try it from a squatting position. The cues are the same; just the starting position changes.

BACK ROCKER

Setting: Each child with a space at a mat or in a large grassy area; children positioned so that they do not roll into one another; music conducive to rocking and a boom box

Cues

"C" Back	(Round your back like the letter C.)
Tuck	(Tuck your chin to your chest.)
Knees to Chest	(Pull your knees to your chest and hold.)

Tasks/Challenges:

T Remember when we explored rocking horses and did Twin Rockers? This time we are going to try a back rocker. Start by squatting down with your back to the mat, place your fingers on the floor, slowly transfer your weight backwards to the mat, and as your back reaches the mat, tuck your chin in, bring your knees to your chest and wrap your arms around them, and rock backward until your head touches the mat. Rock forward to your starting position. Watch me as I show you. (*Demonstrate.*) Squat, lower, tuck, knees, rock.

T Practice the back rocker on your own. Don't ever go over your head. See how smoothly you can make the rock.

As you rock, try to come back up to your feet at the end. What does it take to do this?

 See if you can keep your back rocker going for as long as I play the music. *(Play music in increasingly longer intervals, beginning with about five to ten seconds.)*

THROUGH THE LEGS

Setting: Each child with a space at a mat or in a large grassy area; children positioned so that they do not roll into one another

Cues	
Hands	(Your hands should be on the floor on the outside of your knees.)
Lean	(Lean forward.)
Hike	(Hike your bottom up high into the air.)
Look	(Look back through your legs.)
Tip	(Tip over; place the top of your shoulders on the mat.)

⚠ We do not force children to do a specific roll. Some may still prefer to roll over their shoulder at this point. If so, we place the emphasis on being round and staying in control. Gradually, we encourage children to move to positions higher than their hands and knees—for example, squatting—and to start the roll from there.

Tasks/Challenges:

 Now we are going to try rolling forward. This roll goes over your head. To do it, begin in a squat position, lean forward, hike your seat up in the air, look through your legs, and tip over. Everyone watch me do it once. *(Demonstrate.)* Now, let's do it together on the cues. Hands, lean, hike, look, tip.

 Now practice on your own. Practice once across your mat. **Say the cues as you roll so you don't forget them.** Get up and go again.

 See if you can do three rolls that stay round all the way.

 When you can stay round all the way through the roll, you may want to try and return to a standing position after the roll. The starting position is the same.

ROLLING FORWARD

Setting: Each child with a space at a mat or in a large grassy area; children positioned so that they do not roll into one another

Cues	
"C" Back	(Round your back like the letter C.)
Tuck	(Tuck your chin to your chest.)
Hike	(Hike your bottom up high into the air.)
Push	(Push off so much with your arms that your shoulders and the back of your neck—not your head—touch the mat first. Imagine that there is paint on the top of your head; try not to get any on the mat.)

⚠ Children should not be forced to roll over their heads if they cannot support their body weight with their hands or are uncomfortable with the roll.

Tasks/Challenges:

 Now we are going to try a forward roll. Squat down at your mat and place your hands on the mat just to the outside of your knees. Make your back really round like the letter C. Tuck your chin all the way down to your chest. Hike your bottom way up in the air. Push with your arms and roll. Watch me while I show you how it will look. *(Demonstrate.)* Practice once with me, altogether as we say the steps: hands *(Figure 24.14)*, C, tuck, hike, push, and roll.

⚠ Some children may be more comfortable doing a shoulder roll. Encourage them to concentrate on roundness and tucking, while gradually trying to get them to raise their starting position farther off the ground to kneeling or squatting.

 Now practice on your own. Do one roll, get up, and start again. Roll straight across the mat. Say the cues aloud as you practice so you won't forget them.

 See if you can do three forward rolls that stay round from beginning to end *(Figure 24.15)*.

 If you feel really good about your forward roll, try to come up to your feet at the end.

 See if you can do five forward rolls that the Olympic judges would give a "10."

BACK TOUCH

Setting: Each child with a space at a mat or in a large grassy area; children positioned so that they do not roll into one another

Figure 24.14   Hand positions on forward roll.

Figure 24.15   If children keep their chins close to their knees as they roll, they'll be able to stay in a round shape.

Cues

"C" Back	(Round your back like the letter C.)
Hands Behind Head	(Clasp your hands behind your head with your elbows sticking out to the sides; *see Figure 24.16*.)

Tasks/Challenges:

🅣 Start by squatting down with your back to the mat, clasp your hands behind your head with your elbows out as far as possible, slowly transfer your weight backwards to the mat, and as your back slowly reaches the mat, tuck your chin in, bring your knees to your chest, and rock backward as far

Figure 24.16   Hand-clasp position for Back Touch.

as possible until your weight is on your elbows. Rock forward to your starting position. Watch me as I show you. (*Demonstrate.*) Practice it once with me: squat, clasp, lower, tuck, knees, rock.

🅣 When you feel comfortable bringing your weight back on your elbows, challenge yourself a little more—try to make your feet touch the mat over your head. Then rock back to the starting position.

🅒 Try to do five rocks in which your feet touch the mat over your head.

ROLLING FROM DIFFERENT POSITIONS

Setting: Each child with a space to roll on a mat or grassy area

Cues

Round Body	(Round your back and tuck your chin for a good roll.)
Strong Muscles	(Use strong arms and shoulders to slowly transfer weight to the roll.)

Tasks/Challenges:

T So far you have been starting your rolls from a low position, close to the mat. Now we are going to try starting your rolls from different positions. The first position we will try may be easier than the low position you have been using. It is called a straddle position. Watch me as I show you.

Stand behind your mat with your feet wide apart; stretch your hands to the ceiling. Now put your hands on the mat almost between your feet (don't reach forward), tuck your chin to your chest, and roll forward. You will land sitting down. As with all rolls, keep your back rounded. Let's practice one together as we say the steps out loud: feet apart, stretch arms, hands on mat, tuck chin, slowly roll.

T Practice the straddle roll on your own until you can do it slowly and smoothly.

T Now that you can roll from the squatting position and the straddle position, see if you can find other positions from which to roll. You may want to try your knees, standing, one leg, and one arm. **Each time, remember to use strong muscles to lower slowly to the mat.** Try to find four different starting positions.

C Choose the starting position you like most. See if you can do four rolls from that position that stay rounded and lower slowly to the mat. When you think you can, ask a friend to watch you and give "thumbs up" for each roll that you do correctly.

ROLLING AT DIFFERENT SPEEDS

Setting: Each child with a space to roll on a mat or grassy area without rolling into each other.

Cues	
Round Body	(Round your back and tuck your chin and knees for a good roll.)
Arms	(Your arms are your brakes and accelerator for these rolls.)

Tasks/Challenges:

T Do you remember when you worked on traveling at different speeds? Now you are going to roll at different speeds: Sometimes you will roll fast, sometimes you will roll slowly, and sometimes you will roll at a medium speed. Practice now doing rolls at different speeds. Your speed should be so clear that I can tell which speed it is just by watching. I shouldn't have to ask you.

C Now I am really going to give you a challenge. I'll call out a speed, and you roll at that speed. I'll be watching to see if you really roll at the speed I call out.

BACK SHOULDER

Setting: Each child with a space at a mat or in a large grassy area; children positioned so that they do not roll into one another

Cues	
Round Body	(Round your back and tuck your chin and knees for a good roll.)
Arm to Side	(Keep the arm of the shoulder you are going to roll over out to the side of your body.)
Head to Side	(Tuck your head to one side as you go over.)

Tasks/Challenges:

T We are going to try rolling backward over a shoulder with our hands on the mat to push. Watch me as I show you what it looks like. (*Demonstrate.*) Squat with your back to the mat with your hands on the floor in front of you, push with your hands and rock backward to the mat, bring the arm of the shoulder you are going to roll over out to the side of your body and the other arm back over your head, tuck your head to one side, push with your arms, and roll over that shoulder. Let's practice one together as we say the steps: Squat, hands in front, push and rock back, arm to sides, tuck head, roll (*Figure 24.17*).

T Now practice the back shoulder roll on your own, each time saying the steps so that you don't forget them.

T When you feel good about going over one shoulder, try to tuck your head the other way and go over that shoulder.

C Try to do four backward rolls that stay round all the way through. When you think you can do it, raise your hand and ask me to come watch or have a friend watch.

HANDCLASP BACKWARD

Setting: Each child with a space at a mat or in a large grassy area; children positioned so that they do not roll into one another

Figure 24.17 Hand and head positions for back shoulder roll.

Cues

Round Body	(Round your back and tuck your chin and knees for a good roll.)
Hands Behind Head	(Clasp your hands behind the base of your head.)

Tasks/Challenges:

 Now we're going to practice rolling backward. It will be almost like when we did the rocking action with our hands behind our head, except this time we will try to roll over. Watch me as I show you what it looks like. (*Demonstrate.*) Squat with your back to the mat, clasp your hands behind the base of your head with your elbows sticking out to the sides, sit down quickly, tucking your knees and chin to your chest, and roll completely backward. Your weight should be on your elbows. Let's practice one together while I say the steps out loud: squat, clasp, sit, tuck, roll.

 Practice the backward roll this way on your own. Remember, one roll at a time. **Stay round.**

 If children cannot roll over backward, allow them to practice rocking back and forth with the elbows out. In no case should anyone apply force to a child's hips to attempt to help the child "get over."

ROLLING BACKWARD

 Children should not attempt to roll backward with the "traditional" backward roll until they can support their bodies with their arms. Until then, have them practice with their hands clasped at the base of their heads or have them do a shoulder roll. Force should never be applied to the hips to help a child "get over."

Setting: Each child with a space at a mat or in a large grassy area; children positioned so that they do not roll into one another

Cues

Mickey Mouse Ears	(Hands back by shoulders, fingers pointing toward shoulders, thumbs near ears.)
Tight Ball	(Keep a tight, round shape all the way through the roll.)
Push	(Push with your arms all the way through the roll.)

Tasks/Challenges:

 Now you are going to do a backward roll that goes over your head and uses your arms to push. This combines the two backward rolls you have done before. Watch me as I show you what this one looks like. (*Demonstrate.*) Start from a squatting position, place your hands on the floor in front of you, push and rock backward, tuck your knees and chin tight to your chest, bring your hands to your shoulders and make Mickey Mouse ears, *push* with both arms, and roll over your head. Let's do it together. Squat, hands in front, push, rock back, tuck, hands to shoulders, *push* and roll. Practice rolling backward (*Figure 24.18*).

 Practice on your own. Remember to say the hints as you roll.

When trying to roll backward, children often get stuck and roll no further, usually because they

1. *Make a flat rather than a round shape (knees move away from the chin), so they find it virtually impossible to roll.*
2. *Fail to place their hands in the proper position and thus are unable to push with the force needed to complete the roll.*

Figure 24.18   Hand positions for backward roll.

Practicing to overcome these two critical errors will enable children to roll backward.

C Do two backward rolls that stay tight and round. When you can do them, yell "yes!"

T A little more practice with the backward roll: This time, try to roll so that you can land on your feet instead of your knees at the end of the roll.

This is a good time to use teaching by invitation or intratask variation to let children practice the rolls they need to work on.

T This time, you are going to practice your backward rolls with a partner. Your partner will be your coach. He or she will watch and tell you if you have followed all the hints for the backward roll: tight ball, Mickey Mouse ears, push, and land on feet. After three tries, switch places.

 Peer Observation: This task works well as a peer observation opportunity, even with young children, provided the cues are simple and clear. It also gives children an opportunity to take responsibility for helping someone else learn.

ROLLING IN DIFFERENT DIRECTIONS

Setting: Each child with a space on a mat or grassy area to roll

Cues	
Round Body	(Round your back and tuck your chin and knees for a good roll.)
Three Directions	(Make sure you roll backward, sideways, and forward.)

Tasks/Challenges:

T You have practiced rolls that went sideways, forward, and backward. Now you are going to put all

three together. Practice rolls from all three directions—one roll at a time. Remember as you work that only one of you rolls on the mat at a time; however, as soon as the person ahead of you finishes, you can roll. I shouldn't see anyone standing in line, just rolling from all places around the mat.

T This time I am going to add one more thing to what I would like to see. Each time you roll, try to end up on your feet, not your knees or your seat.

T Decide which roll is the hardest for you to do. Practice that roll until you feel it is as good as your others.

ROLLING FROM DIFFERENT DIRECTIONS AND POSITIONS

Setting: Each child with a space on a mat or grassy area to roll

Cues	
Round Body	(Round your back and tuck your chin and knees for a good roll.)
Strong Muscles	(Use strong arms and shoulders to slowly transfer weight to the roll.)

Tasks/Challenges:

T We are going to combine two things you have done: rolling in different directions and rolling from different positions. There are many combinations. Why not start by rolling forward from a standing position? You can use any version of forward, backward, and sideways rolls you want.

T Next roll backward from a sitting position.

T Now roll sideways from a squatting position.

T On your own, practice as many ways to roll as you can think of. You should always be able to tell me the direction of your roll and the position you are starting from.

C Now that you've practiced on your own, find three different direction/position combinations that you like, and practice them until they are very smooth and flowing. Be able to tell me what position and direction you are using, and then we will show them to the class.

 This would be an appropriate place to use an exit slip (see Chapter 14) that asks the children to record the three combinations of rolls used and react to the difficulty they had in making the sequence flow together.

LINKING ROLLS

Setting: A large mat or a soft grassy space for each child to roll

Cues

Round Body	(Round your back and tuck your chin and knees for a good roll.)
Strong Muscles	(Use strong arms and shoulders to control your body from one roll to the next.)
Smooth Transfer	(Pause between rolls.)

Tasks/Challenges:

T Now you get a chance to do what you have wanted to do for a long time: more than one roll at a time. First, practice by doing two forward rolls in a row. When you can do two smoothly, balance and try two more. To make the links look good, the transfer between rolls should be smooth. To make it smooth, pause for a second and then go into your next roll. Use only a pause, not a stop.

T When you feel comfortable doing forward rolls, try two backward rolls.

T Try sideways rolls: one, then a pause, then two.

T This time we are going to put together a sequence of three different rolls. For starters try forward, backward, forward. There should be one pause or balance in your sequence.

C Now make up your own sequence. It should have three or four rolls, pauses, and two directions. When you can do your sequence really well, ask a friend to watch. See if your partner can name the sequence of rolls. Then watch your partner's sequence and name the rolls.

▶ Having children do multiple (more than two) rolls in a row is not helpful—and can be dangerous. When more than two rolls are asked for in a sequence, some other movement or a balance should come between them.

ROLLING USING DIFFERENT DIRECTIONS AND SPEEDS

Setting: Each child with a space on a mat or grassy area to roll. Two bags: one containing index cards with a speed category on each card and the other containing index cards with a direction on each card; the number of cards in each bag should equal or exceed the number of children in the class. Paper and pencil for each child.

Cues

Round Body	(Round your back and tuck your chin and knees for a good roll.)
Arms	(Your arms are your brakes and accelerator.)

Tasks/Challenges:

T Here's another combination—directions and speeds. This means, for example, that sometimes you will roll backward at a fast speed and sometimes at a slow speed. Practice on your own using all three speeds—fast, medium, and slow—combined with all three directions—forward, backward, sideways. That makes nine different ways you can roll; practice all of them.

T Now you are going to draw your speeds and directions out of a bag. On the signal, one at a time come and draw one card from each bag. One card will have a direction on it, and the other card will have a speed on it. The two cards together will give you the direction and speed you are to practice.

T Now for the hardest rolling task yet. Imagine you are in the Olympics and you are going to do a rolling sequence that combines directions and speeds. Let's start with this sequence: forward, fast; pause, backward, slow; forward, fast. The sequence is written on the board in case you forget.

C Now make up your own combination. Practice it until it flows together well. When you finish, write it down. You can use the example on the board as a guide to tell you how to write it. Practice your combination three more times.

The previous task can be used as an assessment task by having children record the sequence as an entry in their portfolios. This is also an opportune time to use a teacher or student observation (checklist, videotape) to assess the critical cues of rolling.

JUMPING OFF EQUIPMENT, LANDING, AND ROLLING

Setting: A low box or milk crate placed against every mat the children are using for rolling. (You can sometimes get milk crates from the local dairy. Low boxes can be made by filling soft-drink cases (24-can size) with flat newspapers and taping the outside of the boxes shut securely. Place crates or boxes against the mat so that they won't slide.)

Cues	
Jump, Land, Roll	(Jump; land on your feet; then roll.)
Strong Muscles	(Use strong muscles to lower slowly to the roll.)
Round Body	(Round your back and tuck your chin and knees for a good roll.

The cues for the following tasks focus largely on rolling, not on jumping and landing. This assumes that children have already mastered jumping and landing. If they crash when they land or do not use soft landings, you will want to revisit jumping and landing (Chapter 22) before progressing.

 The first observation you need to make after children begin this task is whether they are landing on their feet before they roll. Quite often, children begin dive-rolling here. If they do, stop the task immediately, and refocus or provide another demonstration that shows the correct way.

Tasks/Challenges:

🅣 You're now going to jump off a box (crate), land, and then roll. There's a box (crate) at the end of your mat. One at a time, jump off the box (crate), land on your feet, and then roll. Go slowly at first until you get the hang of it. Always be sure to land on your feet. The next person can go as soon as the person in front gets off the mat. Don't rush, but go quickly.

 Make sure children jump up, not out. When they jump out, they push against the box or crate, sending it sliding across the floor, which causes them to fall.

🅣 It's getting harder. This time, change the direction of your jump. Sometimes jump backward, sometimes sideways, and sometimes forward; then roll in any direction you want. If you aren't sure about jumping backward, just try stepping off until you get used to it.

🅣 We're going to change the activity again. This time, you'll still jump off in different directions, but you'll roll in the same direction as the jump. So if you jump sideways, you roll sideways; if you jump backward, you roll backward.

JUMPING FOR HEIGHT, LANDING, AND ROLLING

Setting: A low box or milk crate placed against every mat the children are using for rolling

Cues	
Jump, Land, Roll	(Jump; land on your feet; then roll.)
Strong Muscles	(Use strong muscles to lower slowly to the roll.)
Round Body	(Round your back and tuck your chin and knees for a good roll.)

Tasks/Challenges:

🅣 This time, instead of changing directions, you're going to practice jumping higher off the boxes (*crates*), still landing and rolling. Do you remember when we worked on jumping? What do you do to make your jump go higher? **Right—you bend your knees and throw your arms up as if you were reaching for the sky.** To warm up, just practice jumping high off the box (*crate*) and landing on your feet. If you fall on the landing, you know that you're jumping too high.

🅣 Now add a roll after your jump and landing. Everything should be in control. If you're falling on your landing or crashing into your roll, you'll know that you're jumping too high. Try it: high jump, land, and roll.

🅣 So far, most of what I've been seeing are jumps, lands, and rolls in forward directions. Go back and add different directions to your high jumps.

Jumping backward from the equipment is difficult for some children, as well as scary. Have the youngsters first step backward if they're hesitant or fearful.

Figure 24.19 Stations to facilitate jumping from different heights, landing, and rolling.

 Permit children to jump backward only to a height that they can control when they land. They should be able to land on their feet, on balance, absorbing their weight.

Remember, you're practicing jumping, landing, and rolling from the equipment that's at your station.

JUMPING FROM DIFFERENT HEIGHTS AND ROLLING

Setting: Boxes and benches of varying heights at stations around the room (Figure 24.19); arrows pointing from station to station on the floor; children in groups of four. Mats at each station

Cues

Jump, Land, Roll	(Jump, land on your feet, and then roll.)
Strong Muscles	(Use strong muscles to lower slowly to the roll.)
Round Body	(Round your back and tuck your chin and knees for a good roll.)

Tasks/Challenges:

 We're working at stations for this task, which will give you practice jumping from objects of different heights. This is how the activity works. There will be four of you at each station. On the signal, you'll begin to practice jumping, landing, and rolling from the equipment at your station. On the next signal, stop, rotate to the station the arrow on the floor points to, and then start all over again.

JUMPING OVER EQUIPMENT, LANDING, AND ROLLING

Setting: A hurdle set up at the end of each mat; see Chapter 18 (Figure 18.9) for hurdle construction details

Cues

Jump, Land, Roll	(Jump, land on your feet, and then roll.)
Strong Muscles	(Use strong muscles to lower slowly to the roll.)
Round Body	(Round your back and tuck your chin and knees for a good roll.)

 The hurdle should be only so high that children are able to jump it without difficulty and land in control (see Chapter 22). The hurdle should be an obstacle to cross, not a challenge to jump. Our hurdles are no higher than about eight to twelve inches and may be as low as three to four inches.

Tasks/Challenges:

 Your task now is to jump over the hurdle, land, and roll. Remember, just as in jumping off objects, you must land on your feet before you roll.

Figure 24.20 Task sheet for rolling.

Name _____ Teacher _____

Rolling Task Sheet

Verification	Challenge
	I can roll forward, coming up to my feet.
	I can roll sideways, coming up to my feet.
	I can roll backward, coming up to my feet.
	I can jump, land, and roll forward.
	I can jump, land, and roll sideways.
	I can jump, land, and roll backward.
	I can jump over a block and cane, land, and roll, coming back to my feet.
	I can roll over the block and cane without knocking it over.
	I can jump, land, change directions, and roll.
	I can jump, twist in the air, land, and roll without falling down.
	I can jump off a box, land, and roll without falling down.
	I can jump off a box in different directions, land, and roll.
	I can jump off a low box, make different body shapes in the air, land, and roll.
	I can jump off a box, twist in the air, land, and roll without falling down.
	I can

🅣 This time, change the direction of your jump. Sometimes try to jump sideways and backward as well as forward.

🅣 Now change the direction of your roll after the jump to match the direction of the jump. So if you jump backward, roll backward. **Controlled jumps and round rolls are our goal.**

🅣 You can also change the speed of the jump and of the roll. This time, practice mixing up the speeds of the jump and roll. In other words, you might mix a slow-motion jump with a fast roll or combine a fast jump and a fast roll. Make whatever speeds you use very clear.

ROLLING, LEVELS, DIRECTIONS, AND JUMPING

Setting: A jumping and rolling space for each child; a task sheet (Figure 24.20) for each child

Cues

Jump, Land, Roll	(Jump, land on your feet, and then roll.)
Strong Muscles	(Use strong muscles to lower slowly to the roll.)
Round Body	(Round your back and tuck your chin and knees for a good roll.)

Tasks/Challenges:

 Today I'll give you the chance to test yourself and see how well you can do the rolls you've been practicing. I'll also give you time to practice the rolls that have been hardest for you. Each of you has a task sheet. Your challenge is to do all the tasks on the sheet. When you think you can do something well, have a friend watch you; if the friend thinks you did the challenge correctly, the friend puts his or her initials on the sheet. The area has been set up so that there's space to practice each challenge.

This task can serve as a self- and/or peer assessment. When completed, it can be included in the child's portfolio.

TRAVELING, JUMPING, LANDING, AND ROLLING

Setting: Mats spread throughout general space with sufficient space between for travel

Cues	
Jump, Land, Roll	(Jump, land on your feet, and then roll.)
Strong Muscles	(Use strong muscles to lower slowly to the roll.)
Round Body	(Round your back and tuck your chin and knees for a good roll.)

Tasks/Challenges:

🔵 Now you're going to use only the mats, but you're going to jump, land, and roll at your mats all on your own. Practice jumping, landing, and rolling in different directions at your mat. Remember, you can start or end at any place around the mat, so there should be no lines.

🔵 This time, begin to travel around the outside of the mat. When the mat is empty, take a little jump, land, and roll. You'll almost be jumping from a moving position, but not quite. You'll travel, jump, pause, and roll, so you really come to a short stop before you roll. If you crash, you're going too fast. One person on the mat at a time.

🔵 Here's a new challenge. Instead of just jumping this time, try jumping over the corners of the mat; then land, and roll. Remember to practice all the different jumps you learned: one foot to the other, one to the same, two to one, one to two, and two to two.

🔵 Now I'll challenge you even further. As you jump the corners of the mat, add a twist or turn in the air

before you land. You still have to land on your feet before you roll.

Utilization Level: Learning Experiences Leading to Skill Development in Rolling

At the utilization level children no longer focus on rolling as an isolated skill but concentrate on using rolling for other purposes. Children develop the ability to combine rolling with other skills, such as catching and throwing. Much of their rolling at this level is directed toward its use as a form of weight transfer between balances. Additionally, rolling is used to transfer weight onto, from, and over large apparatus.

Because at this level rolling is most often used, not as an isolated skill, but as an act of weight transference, many tasks at the utilization level of rolling are included in the earlier weight transference section of this chapter. When that occurs, reference is provided.

A note about cues: Although several cues are listed for many of the learning experiences, it's important to focus on only one cue at a time. That way, the children can really concentrate on that cue. Once you provide feedback to the children and observe that most have learned a cue, then it's time to focus on another one.

BUSY MAT

Setting: Three or four children at a mat

Cues	
Jump, Land, Roll	(Jump, land on your feet, and then roll.)
Strong Muscles	(Use strong arms and shoulders to lower smoothly to the roll.)
Round Body	(Round your back and tuck your chin and knees for a good roll.)

Two tips:

1. *If students are not able to safely decide who is to roll when, specify the order in which they'll roll before they begin.*
2. *This is an exhausting task; if children are really doing it well, they usually can't maintain it for a long time.*

Tasks/Challenges:

🔵 This is a game called Busy Mat. It'll really give you a workout, so get ready. The object of the game is to always have someone rolling on the mat while the others are traveling around the outside of the mat. As soon as one person finishes rolling, another person should start. The timing should be split second. Everyone should always be moving either on the outside by jumping and landing or on the mat by rolling. Let's do a practice round.

TOUCH-AND-GO ROLLS

Setting: A place to roll for each child

Cues	
Off Balance	(Be slightly off balance toward the mat as you land.)
Strong Muscles	(Use strong arms and shoulders to smoothly lower to the roll.)
Round Body	(Round your back and tuck your chin and knees for a good roll.)

Tasks/Challenges:

 Now you're going to practice making your jumps, landings, and rolls more professional. You've been coming to a clear stop after landing and before rolling. Now you're going to roll with no hesitation. Your feet should barely touch the floor before you're into the roll. Your roll just flows, but your feet still have to hit the floor before you roll. **To do this, you'll really have to bend your knees on landing, let your arms absorb your weight, and make sure your shoulders are round.**

 Practice making your jumps so that you land **a little off balance right before you move into the roll.** You are trying to make it as smooth as possible, as if to save yourself from crashing. No stopping—touch and go.

 Make sure you sometimes change the direction of your land and roll, making it backward or sideways as well as forward and still keeping your touch-and-go actions.

ROLLING OVER LOW HURDLES

Setting: A low hurdle at each mat

⚠ The height of the hurdle should be low enough so that children can put their hands on the ground on the other side with no effort. Hurdles may be as low as three to four inches and no higher than ten to twelve inches. Hands must be on the floor before the feet leave the floor.

Cues	
Strong Muscles	(Use strong arms and shoulders to slowly lower into the roll.)
Round Body	(Round your back and tuck your chin and knees for a good roll.)
Hands on Floor	(Start with your hands on the floor on the other side of the hurdle.)

Tasks/Challenges:

⊙ Place your hands on the mat on the other side of the hurdle and try to roll over the hurdle without touching it. **You really have to raise your bottom in the air and push off with your legs. Remember to tuck your head to keep your body round. As you do this, make sure that your arms really give when your feet leave the floor. Bending your arms a little as you push off helps you let yourself down softly.**

ROLLING ON LOW EQUIPMENT

(See Transferring Weight by Rolling [Bench, Box, or Table] earlier)

⚠ Rolling on equipment should be introduced only after children have mastered rolling on the floor/mats.

Setting: Low, wide benches and tables around the room with mats under them

⚠ At this point, the equipment should be low and wide, not more than eighteen inches off the floor.

Cues	
Round Back	(Round your back and tuck your chin and knees for a good roll.)
Control	(Tight muscles, slow-motion action for control throughout the roll.)

Tasks/Challenges:

⊙ At your piece of equipment, get on it in any way you like, and practice rolling on the top of it, lengthwise; then get off in any way you like. To do this place your thumbs and the sides of your palms on the top of the bench, with your hands and fingers on the side of the bench. Although this position is very different from the one you use for rolling on mats, it provides a steady base on equipment. Tuck your head and slowly roll forward on

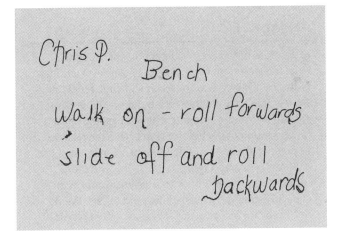

Figure 24.21 Child's rolling sequence.

the equipment. If you fall off a lot, you may want to go to a wider piece of equipment.

T As you practice now, try to make your rolls very smooth.

T Now try to roll backward by very slowly transferring your weight to a rounded back. Extend your hands above your head to hold onto the sides of the equipment, place your head to one side, and roll slowly over your shoulder.

C Now you're going to make up a sequence using all you've practiced. First figure out how you want to get on the equipment; you don't have to get on by rolling. When you're on the equipment, roll along the equipment, get off any way, and roll after your dismount. The sequence will go like this: Get on, roll along, get off, roll on the mat. Practice on your own until your sequence looks the same each time you do it.

Practice your sequence three more times, just to make sure that it's really in your memory. When you finish, write it down (*Figure 24.21*).

ROLLING OFF LOW EQUIPMENT

Setting: Low boxes, benches, and tables scattered throughout the space; mats around and under each piece of equipment. Children *must* be able to reach the mat from the equipment.

Cues	
Round Body	(Keep your back round and tuck your chin and knees for a good roll.)
Strong Muscles	(Use strong arms and shoulders to lower slowly into the roll.)

Tasks/Challenges:

T Assume a kneeling position at the end of your piece of equipment, place your hands on the mat, slowly lower your weight to the mat, and roll forward.

T Once you feel comfortable with one piece of equipment, try another one.

 This task should be preceded by the task of rolling over low hurdles. To do this activity safely, children must be able to absorb their body weight with their arms.

TRAVELING AND ROLLING BETWEEN PIECES OF EQUIPMENT

Setting: Two pieces of low, wide equipment placed about two to three feet apart at each station; mats under, around, and between all equipment

Cues	
Round Body	(Keep your body round and tuck your chin and knees for a good roll.)
Control	(Use tight, strong muscles to roll slowly.)

Tasks/Challenges:

T This next activity is similar to others you have done. As you can see, there are two pieces of equipment at each station. Your task now is to get on the first piece of equipment, roll one way on it, travel to the second piece of equipment without touching the floor, roll a different way on the equipment, jump to get off, and roll on the mat. The sequence goes like this: Get on, roll, travel across, roll another way, jump off, roll. Practice these ideas.

C Now pick one sequence that you really like, and practice it until it's smooth and fluid. There should be no breaks, and you shouldn't have to stop and think about what comes next. Make sure you land on your feet after you jump off before you roll.

ROLLING, BALANCING, AND ROLLING

(See also Traveling into and out of Balances by Rolling in Chapter 23, "Balancing")

Setting: Mats around the room large enough for children to roll and balance

Cues

Round Body	(Keep your back round and tuck your chin and knees for a good roll.)
Control	(Tight, strong muscles to roll slowly.)

Tasks/Challenges:

T You worked on balancing before; now you're going to combine balancing and rolling. At your mat, practice rolling forward into a symmetrical balance. Try to roll right into the balance so that there's no pause between the roll and the balance.

T This time try to focus on the connection between the roll and the balance. **Instead of stopping after the roll and before the balance, see if you can roll right into the balance.**

T Most of you are balancing on very stable body parts, such as knees and hands. This time, try some body parts that aren't quite so stable and see if you can still balance.

T Now try rolls from different directions—backward and sideways—and still roll straight into the balance. Hold the balance still. **Shifting some of your weight backward, just as you balance, might make your balances a little easier.**

ROLLING TO EXPRESS AN IDEA

Setting: A soft, grassy area; children in pairs

Cues

Round Body	(Keep your back round and tuck your chin and knees for a good roll.)

Tasks/Challenges:

T This time you're going to roll to express an idea. You're going to pretend and tell a story by rolling. The first thing you're going to tell is being scared. Here's how it works. Your partner will come close to you and pretend to scare you, without using words. You're so scared that you fall down and roll backward trying to get away. Make sure that your roll really shows that you're afraid; it should be a very stiff roll. After two turns, switch places with your partner.

C You're going to tell a desert story this time. Have any of you seen those old Westerns on television where tumbleweeds go blowing across the desert, with nothing stopping them? Well, you're going to

AERIAL ROLLS

▶ Because of safety considerations, the student-teacher ratio, the varied student skill level, and the high skill level required to teach and spot aerial rolls, we feel that they are best left to the private setting. To explain this to the students who are capable of such tasks, we simply say that we don't have the facilities to practice the rolls and don't want to encourage the children who aren't ready to try them. The more skilled students can instead use physical education class for refining their skill or helping others. We do not advocate teaching aerial or dive rolls in physical education classes.

be a tumbleweed, just blowing and rolling all over the desert. Remember, a tumbleweed is loose and bouncy as the wind just bumps it along.

C Instead of being a loose piece of tumbleweed, this time you're going to be a seed. The wind is blowing you all over; you're bouncing all around. Suddenly, the wind stops and you sprout roots and start to grow. When you start to grow, remember the ideas we talked about earlier about rising and spreading. Your sequence goes like this: the wind blows you around, the wind stops, you send out roots and grow into a big tree or flower.

THROWING, CATCHING, AND ROLLING

Setting: A soft grassy area (or if done inside, a very large mat [like a wrestling mat] or a space completely covered with smaller mats); children in pairs; a variety of objects (beanbags, Frisbees, balls) for each set of partners to throw and catch

Cues

Tuck Shoulder	(Tuck your shoulder so that it is round.)
Round Body	(Round your back and tuck your chin and knees for a good roll.)

Tasks/Challenges:

T With your partner, throw and catch the beanbag. Throw so that your partner has to really stretch to catch the beanbag. **Remember to make your partner stretch; you have to throw at a point away from your partner.**

T Now that you're stretching to catch, as soon as you catch the beanbag, roll in the direction you had to stretch to catch the beanbag. Keep the beanbag in your hand as you roll. Remember the whole sequence: Stretch to catch, catch, and then roll.

🅣 Now, for just a little while, practice throwing and catching the beanbag to yourself. Throw to yourself so that you have to jump to catch the beanbag in an off-balance position and then roll to break the fall from being off balance. The hardest part is throwing so that you force yourself to be in an off-balance position.

🅣 Now go back to working with your partner. Try the same task. Throw so that your partner has to first catch the beanbag in an off-balance position and then roll after catching it. Catchers, make sure you're really off balance and have to roll to recover your balance or so that you won't be hurt. Throwers, really force the catchers off balance when they catch.

🅣 Once you feel comfortable with a beanbag, try using another object, such as a Frisbee or football.

Successful throwing and catching with partners depends on throwers' ability to force the catchers to be off balance or to move to catch. Before exposing children to these ideas, make sure they're at the utilization level of throwing and catching.

ROLLING ONTO LOW EQUIPMENT

Setting: Benches or low boxes with mats surrounding them

Cues
Round Body   (Round your back and tuck your chin and knees for a good roll.)
Control   (Tight muscles, slow-motion action for control throughout the roll.)

Tasks/Challenges:

🅣 Use a roll to get onto your piece of equipment. Stand at the end of the equipment. Place your thumb and the sides of your palms on the top of the equipment and your hands and fingers on the sides of the equipment; then slowly lower into a forward roll to get on the equipment. Get off in any way you like.

🅣 Now I'm going to add to your task. Roll onto the equipment, travel any way that you want while on the equipment, jump to get off, land, and roll. Again, make sure that you're actually using a roll to get onto the equipment.

SPOTTING

▶ The question of spotting—physically assisting a child with a skill—often arises with gymnastics activities. Our experience in our programs and with other programs is that spotting often encourages children to attempt a skill before they're ready, and frequently the child won't even attempt the skill unless assisted. If skills are developed progressively, children will perform on equipment with no spotting.

If, because of the nature of a skill or the equipment on which it is performed, we feel a child might fall, we often find it sufficient to have someone stand beside the student as the student practices, to break any fall that might occur. We rarely physically help a child perform a skill.

BALANCING AND ROLLING ON EQUIPMENT

Setting: Tables, benches, and beams spread throughout the room, with mats surrounding all the equipment

Cues
Round Body   (Round your back and tuck your chin and knees for a good roll.)
Control   (Tight muscles, slow-motion action for control throughout the roll.)
Stillness   (Keep balances motionless.)

Tasks/Challenges:

🅣 At your equipment, practice mounting the equipment, balancing on the equipment, rolling out of the balance, and dismounting. Make sure your rolls out of the balances are going in the direction that seems natural for the balance, not necessarily the easiest way for you.

🅣 Now, keep the same balances, but for each balance find at least one more roll, going in a different direction than the first roll. Thus, you should have two rolls out of each balance, each roll going in a different direction.

🅒 See if you can develop five balances and rolls that you can do so they are smooth and round.

ROLLING TO MEET AND PART

Setting: Groups of five; a large grassy area or wrestling mats

Cues

| Smoothness | (Make your rolls flow smoothly into and out of each other.) |
| Planned Pauses | (Be sure any stops in your routine are on purpose.) |

Tasks/Challenges:

T You're going to work with the idea of meeting and parting. There will be five people in each group. Start by spreading apart from one another and coming together by traveling on your feet. When you get together, make any group shape that you want and hold it still for a few seconds. Next, each of you leaves your group by rolling away and freezing in a shape by yourself. You need to plan your rolls so that all of you come together at the same time to form the group shape and you know exactly when to roll away.

C Practice your routine until you can repeat it three times in a row, always doing it the same way. When you've done that, we will show the routines to the rest of the class.

 Videotaping routines provides an excellent assessment option for seeing if children can both use the rolling cues and incorporate them with smoothness to express an idea.

STRIKING AND ROLLING

Setting: A large grassy area; a plastic ball or training volleyball or the like for each person; children by themselves initially and then in pairs

Cues

| Tuck Shoulder | (Tuck your shoulder so that it is rounded.) |
| Round Body | (Round your back and tuck your chin and knees for a good roll.) |

Tasks/Challenges:

T In a space by yourself, strike a plastic ball with any body part so that you fall off balance when you strike and have to roll in the direction that you're falling. Make sure that you really strike the ball before you roll and roll in the direction that you're

falling, not some other direction.

T Try to strike the ball so that you have to roll in directions other than forward, such as backward and sideways.

T Now work with a partner. The partner throws the ball to you; you try to strike the ball back to your partner, roll, and be ready for the next throw. The thrower should always throw the ball so the striker really has to reach for it. After five strikes, change places.

CATCHING, THROWING, AND ROLLING

Setting: A large grassy area; partners; one ball or beanbag per pair

Cues

| Tuck Shoulder | (Tuck your shoulder so that it is round.) |
| Round Body | (Round your back and tuck your chin and knees for a good roll.) |

Tasks/Challenges:

T This is a really tough task. Your partner will throw you a ball so that you have to stretch and roll to catch it. Your job is to try to throw the ball back to your partner as you begin the roll. The secret is to keep your eyes open and try to catch with your throwing hand. Remember, you must throw as you begin the roll, not after you've rolled. After five times, switch places.

Proficiency Level: Learning Experiences Leading to Skill Development in Rolling

At the proficiency level children enjoy aerial rolls that defy gravity and intricate combinations of rolls with other movements. Due to time limitations, equipment requirements, safety aspects, and the normal student-teacher ratio we do not teach skills at this level. However, if you have students who have progressed to this level and enjoy the sensation these types of movements produce, encourage them to pursue out-of-school gymnastics clubs. These organizations allow children to increase their skill level beyond what we can do in a class setting.

READING COMPREHENSION QUESTIONS

1. List several examples of weight transfer.
2. What is the most common example of weight transfer?
3. Children at the precontrol, control, utilization, and proficiency levels are ready for what types of weight-transfer experiences?
4. Which relationship concepts are typically used as a subfocus in the study of weight transfer?
5. What does the question "Do the feet come down with control?" mean?
6. What are weight-transfer tasks at the utilization level designed to do?
7. What is a spring takeoff?
8. Define *rolling* and *rocking.*
9. How is rolling used in dance and in games?
10. In what way is rolling a safety skill?
11. What are the characteristics of rolling for each of the four skill levels? For example, what does a control-level roll look like?
12. What is our position on spotting?
13. What problems does a child usually encounter when rolling backward?
14. What are the safety issues of back rolls? When should children be alllowed to practice back rolls?
15. Why don't we advocate teaching aerial rolls in physical education class?

REFERENCES

National Association for Sport and Physical Education (NASPE). (1995). *Moving into the future: National standards for physical education.* St. Louis, MO: Mosby.

CHAPTER
25

Skill Themes in Gymnastics

If gymnastics is to be for everyone, including the handicapped child, then all children cannot be asked to do the same gymnastic movement at the same time, in exactly the same way, for clearly some children are going to be underchallenged and some are going to be overchallenged.

——Andrea Boucher

The skill themes of balancing and transferring weight, coupled with jumping and landing and traveling, form the foundation of educational gymnastics. As was stated earlier in the text, movement skills and concepts form the curricular base for elementary physical education, with dance, educational gymnastics, and games/sports skills as the content areas through which these skills and concepts are explored, mastered, and applied. The development and mastery of skills would be of little value if left in isolation, without infusion into games, gymnastics, and dance. Thus, we have chosen to place "Skill Themes in Dance" (Chapter 20), "Skill Themes in Gymnastics" (Chapter 25), and "Skill Themes in Games" (Chapter 31), not in a separate section of the text, but among the skill theme chapters themselves. This chapter integrates the skills of traveling, jumping and landing, balancing, and transferring weight, as well as the concepts of space awareness, effort, and relationships, into the content area of educational gymnastics.

The Nature of Gymnastics

The self-testing nature of gymnastics is challenging to children. They constantly ask themselves, "Can I balance in this position without falling? Can I walk this curb? Can I stand on my head? Can I climb this tree and hang by my arms?" These self-testing challenges meet the criteria of effective teaching/learning in several ways.

First, children receive immediate feedback regarding the skill: "Yes, I can do a headstand," or "No, I am still losing my balance." Second, the feedback is personal and not dependent on others; children do not have to rely on others to determine whether they are successful at the task (Figure 25.1). Third, the self-challenging tasks of gymnastics are a natural part of children's world; their environment, coupled with their curiosity and love of movement, creates multiple opportunities for climbing, hanging, supporting weight on different body parts, balancing, rolling, and so on. Finally, the self-testing nature of gymnastics permits younger children who are still in the egocentric stage of development to participate fully and successfully in a personal challenge without the necessity of team play or cooperative work with other children.

Children are exposed to advanced, competitive gymnastics through television coverage of the Olympics as well as by watching local club gymnasts on the playgrounds and in their neighborhoods. Children without a background of gymnastics experiences often enter our gymnasiums saying, "I can't do those things" or asking "Will we do back handsprings today?" Our task is to present gymnastics for children in a way that is both challenging and appropriate for

Figure 25.1 The joy of gymnastics can be instantaneous, as this student discovers by balancing successfully.

all students in our classes. The preceding two chapters, "Balancing" and "Transferring Weight and Rolling," coupled with jumping, landing, and locomotion provide the skills of educational gymnastics appropriate for elementary physical education.

To children, the self-testing, risk-taking nature of gymnastics brings excitement; to the teacher, it brings the challenge of creating a safe environment (Figure 25.2). We as teachers must always be sure the equipment arrangement, class organization, and selection of tasks maximize safety for our students. There must be a match between student and task, with intratask variation to allow for individual differences. The skills must progress from simple to complex, and the students must master each task before moving to the more complex. The teacher must never require that all students perform the same task. Performance of a certain skill must never be linked to a "grade" in physical education. The gymnastics tasks presented must be challenging to the less skilled, yet not boring to the highly skilled; tasks that are too easy or too difficult can lead to boredom and frustration. As a result, chil-

BOX 25.1   EDUCATIONAL GYMNASTICS AND THE *NATIONAL STANDARDS FOR PHYSICAL EDUCATION*

The *National Standards for Physical Education* (NASPE, 1995) cites the following sample benchmarks for educational gymnastics in elementary physical education:

- Rolls sideways without hesitating or stopping (K)*
- Maintains momentary stillness, bearing weight on a variety of body parts. (K)
- Balances, demonstrating momentary stillness, in symmetrical and nonsymmetrical shapes on a variety of body parts. (2)
- Balances with control on a variety of objects (balance board, large apparatus, skates). (4)
- Develops and refines a gymnastics sequence demonstrating smooth transitions. (4)
- Transfers weight from feet to hands at fast and slow speeds using large extensions (e.g., mulekick, handstand, cartwheel). (4)
- Designs and performs gymnastics . . . sequences that combine traveling, rolling, balancing, and weight transfer into smooth, flowing sequences with intentional changes in direction, speed, and flow. (6)

*Grade-level guidelines for expected student learning

Figure 25.2 Children challenge themselves on the floor/mats before attempting balances on apparatus.

dren may create their own agenda and an unsafe environment for learning in gymnastics. Finally, the mastery of gymnastics skills is a slow process and must not be rushed by us as teachers or by our students.

The Purpose of Gymnastics

Educational gymnastics as taught in physical education is not the same as Olympic gymnastics; the two have related but different purposes. In educational gymnastics, we don't train children to become competitive gymnasts; rather, we provide experiences to teach children to maneuver their bodies effectively against the force of gravity and challenge them to test themselves in appropriate environments on both the floor and apparatus. We attempt to provide our students with a foundation of gymnastics experiences that increases their skills and introduces them to the types of activities that are characteristic of gymnastics.

The *National Standards for Physical Education* (NASPE, 1995) supports the inclusion of educational gymnastics in elementary physical education. See Box 25.1 for the sample benchmarks specific to gymnastics in the elementary school curriculum contained in the National Standards.

The specialization of skills for competitive, Olympic-style gymnastics is reserved for club gymnastics and after-school programs with trained gymnastics specialists and coaches. These programs provide the training needed for specialization in specific stunts, required routines, and advanced aerial skills. Children interested in Olympic-style gymnastics or advanced work beyond the level of educational gymnastics can enroll in programs sponsored by youth agencies or private clubs. Some schools offer after-school programs for students who want additional practice in gymnastics.

BOX 25.2   APPROPRIATE AND INAPPROPRIATE PHYSICAL EDUCATION PRACTICES

Component: Gymnastics

Appropriate Practices: Children are encouraged to develop skills appropriate to their ability and confidence levels in noncompetitive situations centering around the broad skill areas of balancing, rolling, jumping and landing, and weight transfer.

Children are able to practice on apparatus designed for their confidence and skill level, and can design sequences which allow for success at their personal skill level.

Inappropriate Practices: All students are expected to perform the same predetermined stunts and routines on and off apparatus, regardless of their skill level, body composition, and level of confidence.

Routines are competitive, are the sole basis for a grade, and/or must be performed solo while the remainder of the class sits and watches.

Source: From *Developmentally Appropriate Physical Education Practices for Children: A Position Statement of the Council on Physical Education for Children* (COPEC), 1992, Reston, VA: National Association for Sport and Physical Education. Reprinted with permission.

Specializing in and teaching Olympic-style gymnastics in physical education class can educate a few students, but the majority will be left behind and the risk of injury for the less skilled students will increase. Educational gymnastics programs are designed to assist all children, regardless of ability, to improve their gymnastics skills—to become better able to control their bodies in the variety of planned and unplanned encounters they will have, as children and as adults, with the force of gravity (Box 25.2).

Do we exclude Olympic stunts from our curriculum? Not at all. Children at the utilization and proficiency levels who have a background in gymnastics experiences and the proper body control often use Olympic stunts as a response to a gymnastics task. When children use a handstand, walkover, or cartwheel, for example, the maneuver should be identified as such. With children who do have a background of gymnastics, we discuss the stunts they have chosen in response to the task given. We decide whether the response is appropriate for physical education class or best reserved for club gymnastics; for example, we consider whether the stunt requires a spotter and whether the other children will be tempted to imitate a stunt beyond their capabilities that could result in injury.

Other children in class may ask for help in learning a specific stunt or in perfecting one they've seen and are practicing on their own. The teacher's guidance is very important in these instances. As teachers, we can assess the child's skill level and the difficulty of the stunt. If these match, we can give the verbal cues and/or assistance to enable the child to learn the skill correctly and safely.

The Content of Educational Gymnastics

The content of educational gymnastics derives from the skill themes of balance, weight transference, and rolling in combination with jumping, landing, and traveling. The content also includes such concepts as directions, levels, and pathways as well as the actions of stretching, curling, and twisting. These concepts and actions are incorporated into the gymnastics themes only after children have experienced them in isolation and/or in games and dance. For example, children do not study twisting into and out of balances before they have an understanding of the action of twisting.

Before studying a skill theme in educational gymnastics, children need an understanding of the concept of balance in gymnastics—maintaining stillness in a position and holding that position for three to five seconds. Many children can take weight on their hands momentarily or balance in a headstand for one to two seconds but cannot hold the position stationary for five seconds. Children need early experiences in aligning body parts for balance and tightening the muscles to maintain balance as prerequisites to skill themes in educational gymnastics. Children fall out of inverted balances because the body parts are not properly aligned over the base of support and muscular tension is not sufficient to hold the proper alignment. Introductory and review lessons focusing on these fundamental skills will contribute to a safer environment in which students experience balance and weight transference activities.

Educational gymnastics is divided into floor experiences and apparatus experiences. Floor experiences are

Figure 25.3 Exploring basic shapes on apparatus follows balances on the floor/mats.

movements executed on grass, mats, or carpeting that don't require equipment to enhance the challenge. Apparatus experiences involve moving in relation to one or several pieces of equipment (tables, benches, beam, bars, vaulting boxes, and playground apparatus). Although apparatus adds excitement to gymnastics, children can experience very challenging, rewarding work in educational gymnastics with floor experiences only.

Even in a program rich in gymnastics apparatus, children should spend a large amount of time on floor/mat experiences before they begin work on apparatus. Balance, weight transference, and rolling activities should be mastered on mats and carpet squares before they are attempted on low or high gymnastics apparatus. Many of the movements performed on the floor will be replicated on apparatus, but the height and narrowness of the surfaces may increase the difficulty of the task. Students begin apparatus work on low, larger surfaces—that is, crates/boxes, low beams, and benches—before they work on higher, more narrow pieces of apparatus (Figure 25.3).

Floor Experiences

Children at the precontrol level in educational gymnastics explore balancing on different body parts as bases of support, balancing on wide bases, and balancing in different shapes. They learn to curve their bodies into rounded shapes and to maintain the rounded shape for rocking/rolling. They also learn to transfer weight safely on and off equipment and apparatus.

Control-level experiences include rolling from different positions and in different directions. Inverted

balances are introduced, with a strong emphasis on alignment of body parts and muscular tension to maintain balance. The concept of stillness is studied in combination with weight-transfer actions and as a contrast to rolling. Beginning at the control level, children are challenged with combinations of skills and the combination of skills and concepts, for example, moving from a two-part balance into a three-part balance on new bases of support or balancing in a wide body shape at different levels.

Control-level experiences also introduce children to sequences in gymnastics. Beginning-level sequences may be as simple as a beginning shape, followed by three balances on different bases of support and an ending shape. As children become more competent in gymnastics and more confident in the process, sequences become increasingly complex, with combinations of transfer actions and stillness. These sequences still include a beginning and an ending shape.

More advanced and increasingly complex sequences of movements are enjoyable and challenging to utilization-level children, who have developed control over movements executed singularly. Gymnastics sequences for these children include stretching, curling, twisting, and/or rolling actions as transitions between balances, as well as combinations of balances, weight-transfer actions, and traveling.

Maintaining weight on hands, exploring the state of being "almost off" balance, and taking part or all of a partner's weight are appropriate proficiency-level tasks for children in educational gymnastics. Students at this level enjoy focusing on the quality of movement execution in gymnastics. The concepts of acceleration and deceleration, strong and light, bound and free are added to sequences. Matching or mirroring the movements of a partner, repeating sequences of several gymnastics movements, and experiences that involve several students supporting one another's weight are all proficiency-level gymnastics floor experiences.

Sequences

A sequence in gymnastics can be compared to a recital piece in music. Once the children have learned the skills, they are to memorize and then repeat them in exactly the same order with exactly the same balances and actions. This is one of the most difficult parts of sequencing for children. They enjoy creating, but not memorizing for repetition. Recording the sequences with paper and pencil helps children retain them. They may record their gymnastics sequences with drawings and stick figures, and the class may devise a system of notation for balances and actions. You as a

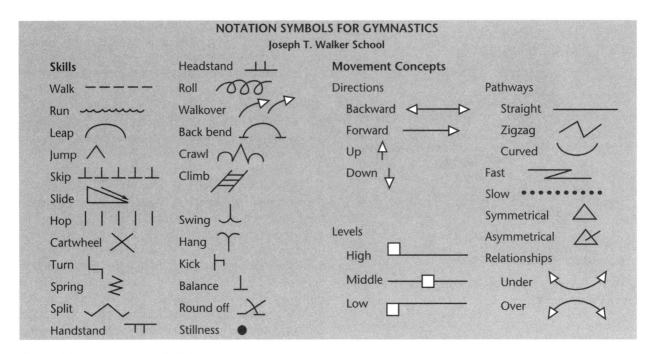

Figure 25.4 Notation symbols for gymnastics. *Source:* Steve Sanders, Joseph T. Walker School, Marietta, GA. Used with permission.

teacher may develop a method of recording sequences that will be used in all your gymnastics classes. Figure 25.4 shows a gymnastics notation system developed by Steve Sanders while working with students at the Walker School in Marietta, Georgia.

The notation system, which was inspired by Rudolf Laban's notation in dance, uses a symbol for each framework element most frequently used in gymnastics. For example, low level is represented by ⌑—, movement in a backward direction is represented by ⟵⟶, a roll is represented by ᴕᴕᴕ, and a movement performed at a slow speed is represented by ⋯⋯. In a written description of a gymnastics movement, the skill is listed first, and the movement concepts are written underneath the skill.

Sanders viewed the system as a way of enhancing the children's movement vocabulary so that they would better understand the meanings of the terms in the movement analysis framework. He also wanted to enhance the amount of thought and creativity that the students put into building their gymnastics sequences. You may choose to have children create their own notation systems, or you may create one with the children to use throughout your program.

Apparatus Experiences

Once children demonstrate control of their bodies in educational gymnastics floor experiences, have an understanding of safety in gymnastics, and understand the concept of sequences, we introduce them to experiences on apparatus. Balance beams, parallel bars, side horses, vaulting boxes, and still rings are Olympic gymnastics equipment. Some elementary schools have this official gymnastics apparatus, but many elementary school programs use benches, tables, chairs, hoops, the edge of a stage, climbing ropes, and climbing frames to provide gymnastics experiences on apparatus. Unofficial equipment is often more compatible with the children's abilities, and children have fewer preconceived notions about what is expected when they practice movements on an unfamiliar/nontraditional piece of equipment.

You can introduce the children to a piece of apparatus by encouraging them to explore the equipment and to discover safe ways to get on and off it. A child at the precontrol level can start by walking along a low beam or bench (Figure 25.5), jumping from a chair or low table, hanging from a climbing rope at a low height, or traveling along a climbing frame. Obstacle courses designed from available equipment—tables, benches, chairs, hoops, ropes—are also challenging to children at this level as they learn the concepts of under, over, along, and through. Some children will begin immediately to explore the apparatus; other children will be more cautious. Never force any child onto a piece of apparatus.

Children at the control level, while continuing to explore apparatus, can begin to focus on different

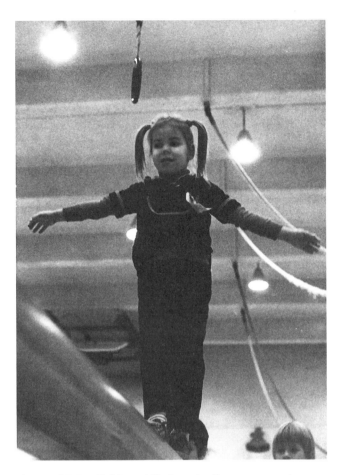

Figure 25.5 Children skilled on the floor move on to apparatus.

Figure 25.6 Creating new shapes on apparatus challenges children at higher skill proficiency levels.

Figure 25.7 Rolling on a bench is a challenge for this utilization-level student.

ways to move in relation to the equipment. They can try different ways of traveling along a beam, hanging from a bar or rope, jumping from a table or chair, or traveling from side to side on a climbing frame. They can balance on different bases of support (Figure 25.6) and combine traveling with stationary balances on apparatus. Sequence work at the control level might include transferring weight onto the apparatus, balancing and traveling on the apparatus, and traveling off the apparatus. Skills that were mastered during the floor experiences present a new challenge to children as they attempt them on various pieces of gymnastics apparatus.

Children at the utilization level can try different ways to get onto equipment, vaulting over equipment, and forming shapes in flight while moving from apparatus to the floor. Apparatus experiences that involve supporting weight on different body parts, transferring weight on equipment (Figure 25.7), nonsymmetrical balances, and inverted balances are also appropriate for children at this level.

When children reach the proficiency level, they should continue to focus on increasingly demanding balances, shapes, ways of traveling, and ways of supporting body weight. As with gymnastics experiences on the floor, the children should be encouraged to focus on the quality of their movements as they practice repeating movements exactly and combining movements into sequences that flow together smoothly and fluently.

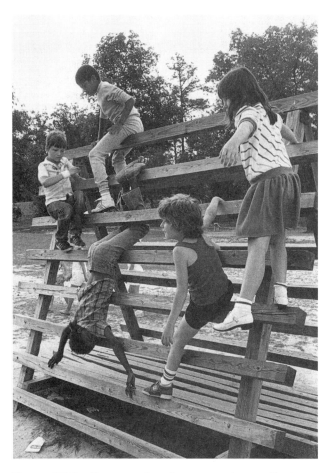

Figure 25.8 Playground equipment can be an effective tool for teaching different body shapes while balancing.

Outdoor Play Equipment As Gymnastics Apparatus

Outdoor playground equipment can serve as gymnastics apparatus in schools that have no indoor equipment and/or indoor physical education facility and as an additional avenue of exploration for children who've experienced indoor gymnastics (Figure 25.8). Children at the precontrol and control levels can focus on body control on various pieces of equipment. Children at the utilization and proficiency levels will be challenged by the complexity of structure, the number of bars, the distance between bars, and the variety of levels on playground equipment. Horizontal ladders, parallel bars, jungle gyms, monkey bars, and telephone pole balance beams can be used for rolling, balancing, and transferring weight on apparatus. (See Chapters 23 and 24 for these activities.)

Very often the key to successfully teaching gymnastics on the playground is the positioning of the playground equipment: grouping versus isolated pieces of equipment. If the playground equipment is grouped,

several pieces can easily accommodate a class of twenty-five to thirty children. But if the playground arrangement is such that instruction to the group on various apparatus as well as to individuals isn't possible, cable spools and milk crates can be added to supplement large apparatus.

Children's work on playground apparatus should begin with a study of the proper use of the equipment—the acceptable and unacceptable activities on the apparatus—and correct ways of getting on and off the apparatus. In early fall, let the children explore the various pieces of apparatus; this will lead to questions from the children and class discussions about what is permitted during both physical education class and recess. Any safety rules needed should be developed cooperatively by teacher and students; the rules may vary for younger and older children.

The use of playground equipment in physical education class will lead to increased use of that equipment during recess, which may make classroom teachers uncomfortable with children on the equipment. However, a booklet of the rules established for physical education class and for recess will help the classroom teacher be more at ease. The use of apparatus during physical education can be very different from the use of apparatus during recess; it's our responsibility to be sure children understand the difference.

The Process of Teaching Educational Gymnastics

Teaching gymnastics is different from teaching either dance or games because of the self-testing nature of gymnastics and because apparatus is used. Successful educational gymnastics teachers are able to match interesting and challenging tasks to the children's ability levels. This is a teaching skill learned only with time and practice.

Some teachers avoid gymnastics because they are concerned about the safety of the children and are afraid that children might be injured; some administrators are hesitant to include gymnastics in the curriculum for the same reasons. Injury is always a possibility in physical education classes. When the focus is on educational gymnastics (as opposed to Olympic-style stunts) and when the experiences are presented sequentially and in an appropriate environment, gymnastics is no more dangerous than other physical education activities. The following ideas relating to the learning environment and the teaching of educational gymnastics help create successful and safe experiences for children.

The Learning Environment

From the initial lessons, children learn spatial awareness of their movements and the movements of others. They are taught not to interfere with others attempting their gymnastics work, either by touching or talking to them. Concentration on the task is essential in gymnastics.

An appropriate learning environment in gymnastics emphasizes safety throughout. Encourage the children to be responsible for their own safety. Stress that if they don't think they can do something, they should either not do it or ask you for help. Games of I Dare You and Follow the Leader are inappropriate in gymnastics classes. Remember, following the progression outlined in the spirals for gymnastics skills and mastering a skill before attempting the next is critical for safety. Gymnastics classes are not the place for off-task behavior; being off-task in games and/or dance may result in behavior that is inappropriate, but off-task behavior in gymnastics can lead to injury. When we encourage children to be responsible for themselves (Figure 25.9), they will rely less on us and more on themselves to determine what is appropriate. Acceptance of responsibility and self-reliance are goals of physical education; they are major goals in teaching gymnastics.

Gymnastics Equipment

Gymnastics apparatus is heavy, cumbersome, and difficult for one person to move. In some situations, gymnastics would never be taught if the teacher had to move the gymnastics equipment alone. Children can be taught to move gymnastics equipment correctly during the first few lessons in which the apparatus is used (Figure 25.10). Once they learn to maneuver the apparatus safely and efficiently, the children can set up or take down a gymnastics environment in a short time. The following guidelines should be followed when children move gymnastics apparatus:

1. An adequate number of children (as determined by the teacher) must be present before equipment can be moved.
2. Children are to lift the equipment together and lower it together, being careful of toes and fingers.
3. Each piece of apparatus has its own storage space to which it is to be returned.

Moving gymnastics apparatus correctly is as important a part of the children's learning in educational gymnastics as working safely on the apparatus. Taking the time during the initial lessons to teach them the

Figure 25.9 Children are encouraged to be responsible for themselves and their own safety.

Figure 25.10 Teaching children early to transport apparatus safely and efficiently can reduce management time.

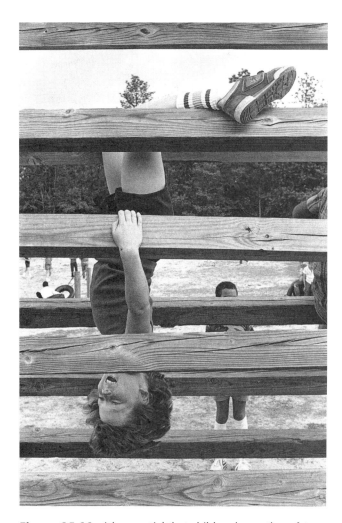

Figure 25.11 It's essential that children know the safety rules before performing any inverted balance.

proper procedure will help create a safe environment for gymnastics and increase valuable instructional time in subsequent lessons.

Stations

Initial gymnastics lessons for children at the precontrol level focus on floor experiences with large-group instruction. During this time, the children learn how to control their bodies when balancing, transferring weight, and rolling; they also learn about safety in gymnastics and working independently. After children demonstrate the ability to work safely and independently, allowing the class to work at stations (learning centers) can be a most efficient method of providing maximum participation on gymnastics apparatus. The stations are set up in different parts of the teaching area (see Chapter 13), with groups working on the same or different skills on the various

> **SAFETY RULES**
>
> ▶ Rules for working safely on mats and apparatus should be explained, demonstrated, and enforced very carefully (Figure 25.11). We suggest posting the rules where the children can see them as they work. (See Chapter 9, "Establishing an Environment for Learning," for additional suggestions.)

pieces of equipment. Sample tasks include jumping from a low table or chair onto a mat, landing, and rolling; traveling different ways along a bench or beam; climbing a rope; practicing taking weight on hands; and traveling onto and off a table.

This method of organization allows the use of various pieces of equipment and eliminates long lines. Tasks for the stations can be written on poster boards and taped to the wall near each station. This increases practice time: The children can read the directions and begin work immediately. The number of stations and complexity of the setup are guided by the following considerations:

1. How many stations will the total available space accommodate?
2. Are there enough mats to place under and around each piece of equipment?
3. Is the space surrounding the station adequate for the children to practice getting off the equipment—e.g., jumping, landing, and rolling—safely?
4. Is the space between the stations sufficient to allow the children to work without interfering with those at the adjoining station?
5. Does the setup provide the teacher the freedom to move throughout the learning environment, giving individual assistance as needed?

Varying the Task

When all the children in a class are expected to perform the same skill the same way, two things are likely to happen. Many of the children in the class will be bored because they can already perform the task successfully. Some of the children will be frightened because the task is too difficult for them, and they know it. When you offer children some choices about how they'll perform a task, each child can select an appropriate level of activity. For example, it's unlikely that all the children in a particular class will be able to do a handstand. Some children may not be strong enough to support all their body weight on their hands; some won't be able to land safely if they lose their balance. Instead of telling the entire class to do a

---

THE LITTLE GYMNAST

▶ *Come with us, now, to a very nice place where little children swing on rings.*
Where laughter is king—and happiness queen—and everyone likes who they are.

On a little green island called Mercer, in a big blue Washington lake surrounded by trees, is a wonderful building assembled by people who think it's important for children to play. And learn. And find out what they can do.

The building is called the Jewish Community Center, and children come from miles around to follow a Pied Piper of a man named Robin West.

Robin grew up in South Africa and then went to college at the University of Saskatchewan in Canada. Now he teaches movement, tumbling and gymnastics to hundreds of boys and girls in the United States. One of his favorite classes is "kiddie gymnastics," for little gymnasts, four to six.

Most four-year-olds already know how to run, jump and play when they come to their very first day of kiddie gymnastics. But in no time at all, Robin can open their eyes to hundreds of new ways to move, swing, roll, bend and balance their bodies with success.

"Success for everyone" is the motto in kiddie gymnastics. It's such a simple motto—so easy to follow—

that sometimes even Robin and the children's parents must stop to remind themselves of its magic.

A child is a butterfly in the wind. Some can fly higher than others; but each one flies the best way it can. Why compare one against the other? Each one is different. Each one is special. Each one is beautiful.

In kiddie gymnastics, everyone flies and nobody fails. There's plenty of praise for the attempt well-tried. To balance on a beam for the very first time is discovery. To be praised and applauded for the very same motion is joy.

In just a few short weeks the children in Robin's class have learned to move with a confidence, poise and imagination that surprises and pleases both themselves and their parents.

But they've also learned something else along the way. You can see it in their eyes when they tug so gently on Robin's bushy black beard. You can see it in the way they lie on their backsides and stare at the ceiling and giggle. It's as if they've learned something deep and exciting about themselves.

"I'm me . . . I'm special . . . I can try."

"If I make a mistake, it's all right. I'll start over . . . I'll learn . . . I'll get better."

"Look at my friend. I'm helping him stand on his head. He's special, too."

"We're good. We're children. We're okay."

Dan Zadra

Source: Dan Zadra, "The Little Gymnast," *Young Athlete Magazine,* June 1976, p. 8. Reprinted with permission.

---

handstand, you could tell the children to find a way to place some or all of their weight on their hands. An instruction that allows for individual differences in ability affords all children an opportunity for success.

Demonstrating

Some teacher feel that because they aren't skilled gymnasts themselves, they won't be able to teach gymnastics effectively. Certainly a thorough background in a teaching area is an asset in teaching. But even teachers who aren't skilled gymnasts can provide children with appropriate gymnastics experiences. In educational gymnastics, the instructor doesn't need to be able to demonstrate a skill correctly, because the children are never expected to perform the same skill the same way. If you want to give children additional ideas or to emphasize a particular movement quality or concept, you can invite some of the more proficient children to

demonstrate for the rest of the class. This technique has the added advantage of reinforcing those children who are working especially well.

Spotting

Spotting—the practice of physically assisting children as they perform a movement—isn't commonly used in educational gymnastics classes. Children who depend on such help are likely to be unsure and even afraid unless a teacher is nearby. And, conversely, spotting encourages children to attempt movements they may not be ready for. We've observed a number of programs, including our own, in which children have progressed to a relatively high level of skill proficiency without any spotting. To say we do not "spot" children when they are performing skills in educational gymnastics is not to say we do not strongly believe in safety for all children in the gymnastics set-

Some of the children who are working on gymnastics at an outside club or program may come to class with gymnastics skills that exceed your teaching knowledge and ability. Because you're responsible for the safety of all the children, the activities of these club gymnasts may cause you some uneasiness.

If you explain your concern to these children, you'll find that they appreciate your candor. Tell these young gymnasts that you're working to learn about the movements they're practicing. Assure them that once you're skilled enough to help them practice appropriately and safely, you'll be delighted to have them resume practice in class.

This approach makes it clear that you aren't criticizing but instead are respecting their proficiency. Students will, in turn, respect you for acknowledging your limitations and seeking their cooperation, and teacher-student rapport will be enhanced.

ting. Throughout the skill themes for gymnastics, you will have noted the safety icon (▲) emphasizing safety tips for the teacher.

Club Gymnasts

Some children in your classes may be studying gymnastics independently, perhaps in a club or recreation program. Most of these club gymnasts are more skilled than the other children—many are at the proficiency level in many skills—and so provide an interesting dimension to gymnastics lessons. The other children will look to the club gymnasts as models and sources for new ideas. The presence of club gymnasts in a gymnastics class results in an interesting blend of child-created gymnastics skills and Olympic gymnastics skills.

A Final Thought

Teaching educational gymnastics is, in some ways, more difficult than teaching Olympic gymnastics. In Olympic gymnastics, the desired outcomes are clear—the teacher wants the children to learn to execute predetermined skills in specific ways. The desired outcomes of educational gymnastics are less easily defined. The skills to be learned aren't predetermined, nor are they to be executed in one correct way. Instead, the teacher helps the children to improve their abilities to move in relation to the force of gravity, to learn self-confidence and self-reliance in interpreting tasks and determining the best ways to execute skills. Often it's more difficult for a teacher to share decisions with children than it is for the teacher to make the decisions. You'll find, however, that the process of sharing decisions in educational gymnastics can be exciting for you the teacher and rewarding for the children, regardless of their gymnastics abilities.

SUMMARY

Because of the self-testing nature of gymnastics, most children are fascinated by the challenge of attempting to defy the force of gravity. It's important to distinguish educational gymnastics from Olympic gymnastics. Educational gymnastics focuses on enhancing each child's ability to maneuver the body more effectively against the force of gravity. Olympic gymnastics emphasizes the learning of specific gymnastics stunts, usually for the purpose of entering individual or team competition.

Many gymnastics movements are learned on the floor (mats) first and then practiced on apparatus. Gymnastics apparatus can be purchased, or equipment available in schools—such as tables, chairs, and benches—can be adapted to serve the same purposes.

Because of the increased likelihood of injury in gymnastics, it's important to establish an appropriate learning environment so that children avoid games like Follow the Leader or I Dare You. Gymnastics tasks can be presented in ways that allow for individual differences, and this should be done so that children aren't tempted to try movements they aren't ready for.

READING COMPREHENSION QUESTIONS

1. Why do children find balancing, transferring weight, and supporting weight on different body parts fascinating skills?
2. What are the purposes of Olympic gymnastics and educational gymnastics?
3. What are the two types of experiences in educational gymnastics? Describe each type.
4. What activities are taught at the different levels of skill proficiency for both types of educational gymnastics experiences?
5. How are children introduced to equipment?
6. What are the considerations in teaching gymnastics?
7. Why is it important to vary the task in gymnastics?
8. Why is teaching Olympic gymnastics somewhat easier than teaching educational gymnastics?

REFERENCES

Boucher, A. (1978). Educational gymnastics is for everyone. *Journal of Physical Education and Recreation, 49*(7), 48–50.

Cameron, W. McD., & Pleasance, P. (1971). *Education in movement—gymnastics.* Oxford: Basil Blackwell.

Carroll, M. E., & Garner, D. R. (1984). *Gymnastics 7–11: A lesson-by-lesson approach.* London: Falmer Press.

Holbrook, J. (1974). *Movement activity in gymnastics.* Boston: Plays, Inc.

Kirchner, G., Cunningham, J., & Warrell, E. (1970). *Introduction to movement education.* Dubuque, IA: Brown.

Mauldon, E., & Layson, J. (1965). *Teaching gymnastics.* London: MacDonald & Evans.

Morison, R. (1969). *A movement approach to educational gymnastics.* London: Dent.

O'Quinn, G. (1978). *Developmental gymnastics.* Austin: University of Texas Press.

Parent, S. (Ed). (1978, September). Educational gymnastics. *Journal of Physical Education and Recreation,* 31–50.

Teaching children gymnastics (video). (1994). Champaign, IL. Human Kinetics.

Trevor, M. D. (1985). *The development of gymnastics skills.* Oxford: Basil Blackwell.

Werner, P. H. (1994). *Teaching children gymnastics: Becoming a master teacher.* Champaign, IL: Human Kinetics.

Williams, J. (1974). *Themes for educational gymnastics.* London: Lepus Books.

Zadra, D. (1976, June). The little gymnast. *Young Athlete Magazine,* 8.

Note: Although several of the references for educational gymnastics are older books, the reader is encouraged to pursue their location for reading and possible purchase; they are excellent resources in the teaching and content of educational gymnastics.

C H A P T E R
26

Kicking and Punting

A young boy kicking a stone along the sidewalk as he walks home from school, a neighborhood game of Kick the Can, kickball on the school playground at recess, an aspiring athlete practicing the soccer dribble, and the professional punter—all are executing a similar movement: the kick. This movement requires accuracy, body control, point of contact, force, and direction. Some children seem to perform the kick with intense concentration; others, effortlessly.

We try to give children a variety of opportunities to practice kicking so that they'll develop a foundation of kicking skills that they can use in different situations. We emphasize the development of mature kicking patterns by focusing on experiences designed to elicit such patterns. For example, kicking for distance leads to the development of a mature kicking pattern, but this isn't true of kicking for accuracy. See Box 26.1 for information from the *National Standards for Physical Education* on kicking and punting.

Levels of Skill Proficiency in Kicking

Children at the precontrol level of kicking are challenged by the task of simply making contact with a stationary ball. They explore kicking a variety of balls, kicking balls just for fun at large targets, and tapping a ball as in the beginning skills of soccer. Appropriate precontrol-level tasks include:

1. Kicking a ball from a stationary position
2. Running to kick a stationary ball
3. Tapping a ball along the ground while moving behind it

At the control level, children are introduced to contacting a ball with different parts of the foot—inside, outside, back, and front. They're also given challenges that involve dribbling with either foot, at various speeds, and in different directions. Appropriate control-level activities include:

1. Sending a ball along the ground or through the air to a partner
2. Kicking toward a target
3. Making quick kicks
4. Starting/stopping, changing directions with the soccer dribble

Children at the utilization level of kicking are able to kick for both distance and accuracy. They enjoy and learn from the challenge of one-on-one Keep Away situations (trying to prevent another child from getting the ball), which combine the skills of tapping a ball along the ground with the skills needed to dodge an opponent. Dynamic game situations children at the utilization level enjoy can involve:

1. Kicking a ball to a target while on the run
2. Kicking for accuracy while trying to maneuver around an opponent
3. Differentiating high from low kicks

Children who've reached the proficiency level in kicking enjoy group participation with more players, more complex relationships, and the excitement of strategy development. Sample tasks include:

1. Kicking for a target against defense
2. Gamelike situations
3. Kicking at moving targets

The entire spectrum of kicking experiences, from precontrol through proficiency, is represented in our progression spiral on page 454. The tasks are stated in terms that imply a direct approach (see Chapter 13), but teachers are encouraged to vary the approach according to the purpose of the lesson and the characteristics of the class.

The key observation points in Boxes 26.2 and 26.3 illustrate correct and incorrect ways of kicking along the ground and in the air, respectively. Ask yourself the questions in the boxes as you observe the youngsters in action.

Precontrol Level: Activities for Exploration of Kicking

At the precontrol level, we want children to make contact with a stationary ball for kicking. When they are able to do this, we add an approach to a stationary ball and tapping a ball gently along the ground.

KICKING A STATIONARY BALL FROM A STATIONARY POSITION

Setting: A variety of plastic, foam, and rubber balls for kicking, placed around the gymnasium approximately ten feet from the wall

Tasks/Challenges:

Ⓣ Stand behind a kicking ball. Kick the ball really hard so it travels to the wall.

Ⓒ Practice until you can kick the ball three times in a row to the wall.

Ⓣ Practice kicking with one foot and then with the other foot.

Ⓣ Practice kicking the ball, making it go sometimes along the ground, sometimes in the air.

 What determines whether the ball travels along the ground or in the air?

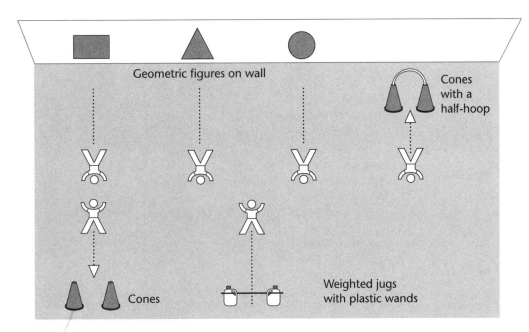

BOX 26.1   THE SKILLS OF KICKING AND PUNTING IN THE
NATIONAL STANDARDS FOR PHYSICAL EDUCATION

The movement skills of kicking and punting are referenced in the *National Standards for Physical Education* (NASPE, 1995) under Standard 1: Demonstrates competency in many movement forms and proficiency in a few movement forms. The standard speaks of the child's demonstrating progress toward mature status and acquiring some specialized skills basic to the movement form.

Sample benchmarks for kicking and punting include:

■ Kicks a stationary ball using a smooth, continuous running step. (K)
■ Throws, catches, and kicks using mature form. (4)

Figure 26.1   Target arrangement for kicking at large targets.

Ⓣ Move outdoors and practice your kicking in an open space for maximum distance.

KICKING AT LARGE TARGETS

Setting: Large targets on the wall at low level; free-standing targets placed four to five feet from the wall (Figure 26.1); a variety of plastic, foam, and rubber balls for kicking

Tasks/Challenges:

Ⓣ Stand behind your kicking ball. Kick the ball toward the target, trying to hit it.

Ⓣ Try kicking at the different types of targets. Which is your favorite? Which is your best for accuracy?

Ⓣ Choose your favorite target; stand eight feet away from the target and kick. When you can hit the target two times in a row, take a giant step backward and try from that distance.

APPROACHING A STATIONARY BALL AND KICKING

Setting: Balls for kicking, placed around the gymnasium approximately ten feet from the walls (Figure 26.2)

Tasks/Challenges:

Ⓣ Stand three to four feet behind the kicking ball. Approach the ball and kick it forward to the wall.

■ **PROFICIENCY LEVEL**

Playing Cone Soccer
Playing Alley Soccer
Playing Soccer Keep-Away
Playing Minisoccer
Kicking at a moving target
Kicking at small stationary targets

■ **UTILIZATION LEVEL**

Playing two-on-one soccer
Passing to a partner in general space
Kicking to a traveling partner
Kicking to a partner from various angles
Playing Soccer Golf
Playing one-on-one soccer
Traveling and kicking for a goal
Performing a continuous tap/dribble and change of direction
Changing directions: tap/dribble

■ **CONTROL LEVEL**

Keeping It Perfect: Zero, Zero
Dribbling around stationary obstacles
Traveling in pathways
Starting and stopping
Tapping the ball along the ground (soccer dribble)
Kicking to a partner
Kicking a rolling ball from a stationary position
Kicking to targets
Kicking to a distance zone
Kicking for distance
Kicking in the air
Kicking on the ground

■ **PRECONTROL LEVEL**

Tapping the ball (as in soccer)
Approaching a stationary ball and kicking
Kicking at large targets
Kicking a stationary ball from a stationary position

BOX 26.2   KEY OBSERVATION POINTS: KICKING ALONG THE GROUND

Soccer Dribble

Does the child contact the ball for the dribble behind the ball, rather than on top?

Dribble/Kick for Distance

1. Does the child make contact with the instep (shoelaces) of the foot, not with the toes?

2. Is the child's trunk inclined slightly backward for the kick?

BOX 26.3   KEY OBSERVATION POINTS: KICKING IN THE AIR

1. Does the child make contact below the center of the ball, not on top?

2. Is the child's kicking foot extended for contact on the shoelaces, not on the toes?

3. Does the child's kicking leg bend in preparation for the kick and follow through after contact?

4. Does the child's trunk incline slightly backward for the kick?

Mature Stage

When children are at the mature stage of kicking, do their kicks look similar to the following sequence? The approach to the ball involves one or more steps, with the distance just prior to the kick covered with a leap. The kicker is airborne in the approach. The knee of the kicking leg is slightly flexed because of the leap just prior to kicking. The trunk is inclined backward prior to and during contact. The kicker disperses the momentum of the kick by hopping on the support leg and stepping in the direction of the object that was struck.

SOURCES: "Developmental Sequence of Kicking," mimeographed materials, by V. Seefeldt and J. Haubenstricker, presented at the University of Georgia, Athens, June 1978; *Fundamental Motor Patterns,* 2nd ed., by R. L. Wickstrom, 1977, Philadelphia: Lea & Febiger.

Figure 26.2 Arrangement for the approach and kick of a stationary ball.

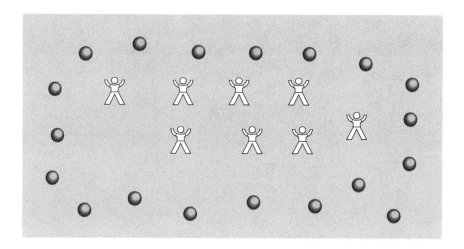

T Alternate kicking with your right foot and your left foot so you will be skilled at using either foot.

C Practice until you can successfully approach and kick to the wall three times. Success equals foot contacting the ball, and ball contacting the wall.

TAPPING THE BALL (AS IN SOCCER)

Setting: Children scattered throughout general space, with foam balls at their feet

Tasks/Challenges:

T Gently tap the ball from one foot to the other, using the inside of your foot.

T On the signal, begin tapping the ball from foot to foot; continue until you hear the signal to stop.

C I will time you for thirty seconds. Try to continue tapping between your feet for the full amount of time.

T Walk through general space, tapping the ball from foot to foot—left, right, left, right—as you go. Keep the ball between your feet throughout the travel.

T Walk through general space, tapping the ball from foot to foot, avoiding collisions with others. This means you must control for the tap and control for no collisions.

After a couple of years, the eight-and-a-half-inch inexpensive plastic balls become partially deflated; they can't be inflated. These half-life plastic balls are excellent for kicking. We mark them with a large K so children know which balls are for kicking, which ones for dribbling. Playground and kickballs can also be partially deflated for beginning practice and for use indoors.

Control Level: Learning Experiences Leading to Skill Development in Kicking

At the control level, we want children to make consistent contact with a ball. We provide a variety of kicking experiences that include kicking for accuracy, kicking in different directions, and partner relationships. We encourage use of different parts of each foot and greater control of speed and directions.

A note about cues: Although several cues are listed for many of the learning experiences, it's important to focus on only one cue at a time. That way, the children can really concentrate on that cue. Once you provide feedback to the children and observe that most have learned a cue, then it's time to focus on another one.

KICKING ON THE GROUND

Setting: A variety of balls for kicking—foam, plastic, rubber—placed around the gymnasium approximately ten feet from the wall (Figure 26.2)

Cues	
Shoelaces	(Contact the ball with your instep—your shoelaces or Velcro tabs—not your toes.)
Behind the Ball	(Contact the ball directly *behind* center for travel forward at a low level.)

Tasks/Challenges:

T When we were exploring kicking, you kicked balls that were positioned on the ground with you standing behind them. You also kicked balls placed on the ground with you running to the ball. Prac-

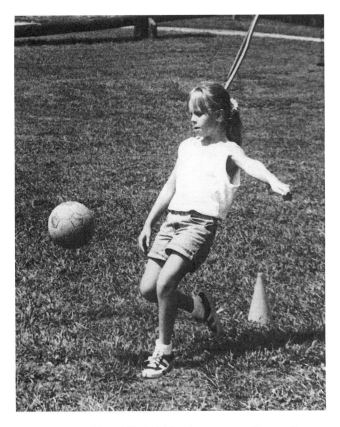

Figure 26.3 The skill of kicking improves with practice.

tice kicking the ball to the wall from both starting positions.

T Kick the ball hard so it hits the wall with enough force to rebound back to you.

Place a series of two-inch tape markers on the walls of the gym, approximately three feet above the floor.

T Kick the ball so it hits the wall below the tape line. **Remember, contact the ball directly behind center so it will travel at a low level.**

T Practice your kicking with both your right and your left foot (Figure 26.3). In game situations, you need to be skilled with both feet.

C Practice kicking with each foot until you can kick three times in a row with each foot, the ball contacting the wall below the tape line.

T The balls for kicking are scattered around the edge of the gymnasium. Begin traveling in general space, avoiding collisions with others or the balls on the floor. On the signal, approach the ball nearest you and kick it toward the wall. Quickly retrieve the ball you kicked and place it ten to twelve feet from the wall. You are now ready to move again. Ready? Travel in general space. Remember to listen for the signal to kick.

KICKING IN THE AIR

Setting: A variety of balls for kicking—foam, plastic, rubber—placed around the gymnasium approximately ten feet from the wall (Figure 26.2)

Cues

Shoelaces	(Contact the ball with your instep—your shoelaces or Velcro tabs—not your toes.)
Under the Ball	(Contact the ball *below* center for travel upward through the air.)
Step-Hop	(Step-hop on your nonkicking leg to complete a running approach.)

Tasks/Challenges:

T When we were exploring kicking, you kicked balls that were positioned on the ground with you standing behind them and you kicked balls placed on the ground with you running to the ball. Practice kicking the ball to the wall from both starting positions.

T Assume a starting position five to six feet behind the ball. Approach the ball for the kick; immediately after you kick the ball, take a small hop on your nonkicking leg, and then step forward in the direction of the kick. This step-hop checks your forward momentum.

T Practice your kicking with the step-hop, sending the ball through the air so it contacts the wall above the tape line.

C Practice kicking through the air until you can successfully complete the aerial kick five times.

KICKING FOR DISTANCE

Setting: Balls for kicking placed in a large circle on the playground (Figure 26.4); children positioned inside the circle, facing outward

Cues

Shoelaces	(Contact the ball with your instep—your shoelaces or Velcro tabs—not your toes.)
Behind the Ball	(Contact the ball directly *behind* center for travel at a low level, along the ground.)
Under the Ball	(Contact the ball *below* center for travel upward through the air.)
Step-Hop	(Step-hop on your nonkicking leg to complete the running approach.)

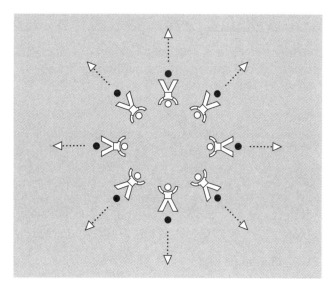

Figure 26.4   Circular pattern for distance kicking.

Tasks/Challenges:

T Stand inside the circle, just behind a ball, facing away from the center of the circle. You are going to practice kicking along the ground and in the air. There's enough room for you to kick as hard as you wish. Practice your first series of kicks standing just behind the ball—no running approach. Kick the ball so it travels along the ground, at low level. After you kick, retrieve the ball and quickly bring it back to your starting place for the next kick.

T Now kick the ball with your nonpreferred foot. Does the ball travel as far?

T Kick the ball with your preferred foot, sending it through the air. Remember to stand just behind the ball for the kick.

 What is the key for sending the ball along the ground? In the air? Where on the foot do you make contact for both kicks?

T Place the ball on the ground, and take three or four steps back from the ball. Approach the ball with three or four running steps, and then kick the ball along the ground (*in the air*). **Don't forget the step-hop on the nonkicking leg as you make contact.**

C Practice kicking both along the ground and through the air. Challenge yourself to kick farther each time. Can you attain that distance both along the ground and in the air?

Numbering the balls 1, 2, 3, 4, and so forth, eliminates confusion about which ball belongs to which child.

KICKING TO A DISTANCE ZONE

Setting: Marker cones or plastic milk cartons placed at ten-foot intervals across the playground, numbered consecutively so the children can see the numbers from the kicking line (Figure 26.5)

Cues	
Shoelaces	(Contact the ball with your instep—your shoelaces or Velcro tabs—not your toes.)
Under the Ball	(Contact the ball *below* center for travel upward through the air.)
Step-Hop	(Step-hop on your nonkicking leg to complete a running approach.)

Tasks/Challenges:

T Place the ball you are going to use at the kicking line. Approach the ball from about five to six feet. Kick the ball so it travels as far as possible through the air. Note the number of the zone in which the ball first contacts the ground. Kick five times, trying to improve your distance.

C Try to kick the ball so that it lands in the same zone three times in a row.

KICKING TO TARGETS

Setting: A series of targets of different heights arranged throughout the gymnasium (Figure 26.6); a variety of balls for kicking

Cues	
Shoelaces	(Contact the ball with your instep—your shoelaces or Velcro tabs—not your toes.)
Under the Ball	(Contact the ball *below* the center for travel upward through the air.)
Behind the Ball	(Contact the ball directly *behind* center for travel at a low level, along the ground.)
Watch the Ball	(Focus on the ball, not the target, until the ball leaves your foot.)

Tasks/Challenges:

T Spaced around the gym are targets for kicking—suspended hoops, marker cones to kick between and to hit, ropes hung between chairs for kicking over, tape squares on the wall.

I'll assign you to a station; at that station practice kicking at the target. Place the ball at the kick-

Figure 26.5 Numbered distance zones.

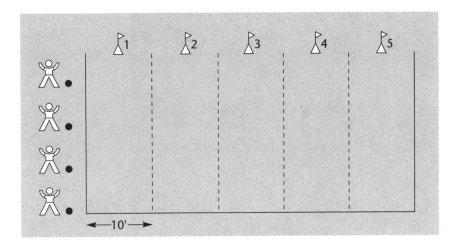

Figure 26.6 Targets for kicking.

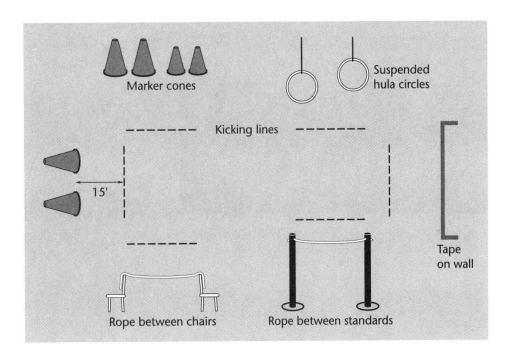

ing line. Approach the kicking line with two or three steps before you make contact. After your turn, retrieve the ball and return to your group to wait your next turn. Continue practicing at your station until the signal is given to change to another kicking station. You may need to adjust your force when you're kicking to hit a target (*Figure 26.7*).

Here's what you'll do at the different stations. At the hoops, kick the ball through the circle. At the large and small marker cones, kick the ball hard enough to make the cone fall over. At the rope between the chairs and the rope stretched between the standards, kick the ball so it travels over the rope. At the marker goals, kick the ball along the ground between the cones. At the tape square, kick the ball so it touches the wall inside the square.

Weighted jugs, cones, or tape marks on the wall can serve as goals. Vary the width of the goal according to individuals' abilities.

KICKING A ROLLING BALL FROM A STATIONARY POSITION

Setting: Partners positioned ten to twelve feet from each other, each pair with a ball for kicking

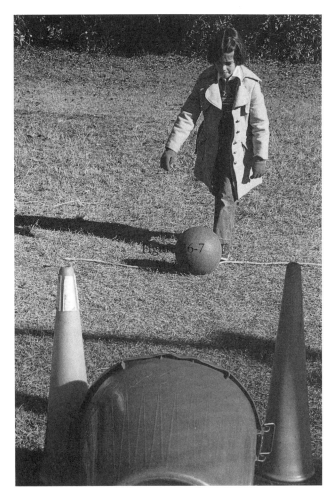

Figure 26.7 As they practice, children will discover that the force required to kick a ball for accuracy is initially different from that required to kick for distance.

Cues

Shoelaces	(Contact the ball with your instep—your shoelaces or Velcro tabs—not your toes.)
Behind the Ball	(Contact the ball directly *behind* center for travel at a low level.)
Under the Ball	(Contact the ball *below* center for travel through the air.)
Watch the Ball	(Focus on the ball, not your partner, until the ball leaves your foot.)

Tasks/Challenges:

🅣 Partner 1: Roll the ball along the ground to partner 2. Partner 2: Kick the ball so it travels back to partner 1. Kick only hard enough for the ball to travel to your partner.

🅣 Practice the kick along the ground with both your right foot and your left foot.

🅣 Practice the kick through the air to your partner. Sometimes in game situations you want to kick along the ground; sometimes you need to kick in the air.

🅒 Practice until you can kick the ball along the ground five times to your partner so your partner does not have to move from self-space to retrieve the ball—five times with the left foot, five times with the right.

🅒 Can you meet the challenge of kicking the ball through the air so your partner does not have to move to retrieve it? Give it a try!

KICKING TO A PARTNER

Setting: Partners facing each other, fifteen to twenty feet apart, each pair with a ball for kicking

Cues

Sender:	Shoelaces (Contact the ball with your instep—your shoelaces or Velcro tabs—not your toes.)
	Behind the Ball (Contact the ball directly *behind* center for travel at low level, along the ground.)
	Watch the Ball (Focus on the ball, not your partner, as you kick and as you receive.)
Receiver:	Trap (Stop the ball by placing your foot on top, slightly behind the ball.)

Tasks/Challenges:

🅣 Kick the ball along the ground to your partner so he or she can stop it with the foot without moving from self-space. This is called *trapping* the ball. To trap, place your foot slightly behind the ball, above the center back.

🅣 Practice sending and receiving—kicking and trapping—with your partner. Always stop (trap) the ball before kicking it back to your partner.

🅒 Practice until you can kick five times to your partner so he or she can trap without moving from self-space.

🅒 When you are comfortable with your skill and can kick accurately five times, take a large step backward and repeat the task. Practice at different distances to determine your maximum distance for accuracy with your partner.

TAPPING THE BALL ALONG THE GROUND (SOCCER DRIBBLE)

Setting: Children scattered throughout general space, with plastic (foam, rubber) balls for kicking; listening position is one foot resting on the ball

Cues

Tap, Tap	(Gently tap the ball so that it stays within three to four feet of you at all times.)
Inside of Foot	(Tap the ball with the inside of your foot—left and right.)
Open Spaces	(Look for open spaces as you travel.)

Tasks/Challenges:

🅣 When we were exploring kicking, you practiced tapping the ball between your feet, inside to inside. Practice that skill of gently tapping back and forth.

🅣 On the signal, begin traveling through general space, tapping the ball with the inside of your foot. When you hear the signal, quickly place one foot on top of the ball, slightly behind center, to stop the momentum—trap the ball.

🅣 Alternate tapping on your right foot and then your left foot; turn your feet out like a duck.

🅒 On the signal, begin traveling in general space, tapping the ball in the soccer dribble. Try to travel and tap with alternate feet and without letting the ball get away from you or colliding with another person. Ready? Tap, tap. . . .open spaces.

🅒 Now dribble in general space. See if you can keep it up for thirty seconds without colliding ball to ball or person to person.

As the children improve, you can increase the time to forty-five seconds and then to one minute.

🅣 Begin traveling in general space, dribbling the soccer ball as you go. Gradually increase your speed, keeping the ball within three to four feet of you at all times. Increase and decrease the speed of your travel, adjusting the force of your kick as you increase and decrease the speed.

🅒 I will time you again for a thirty-second dribble. Challenge yourself to dribble at your personal maximum speed—with soccer ball and body control.

STARTING AND STOPPING

Setting: Children scattered throughout general space, each with a ball for kicking

Cues

Tap, Tap	(Gently tap the ball so that it stays within three to four feet of you at all times.)
Inside of Foot	(Tap the ball with the inside of your foot—left and right.)
Trap	(Stop the ball by placing your foot on top, slightly behind the ball.)

Tasks/Challenges:

🅣 Begin dribbling in general space. When you hear the signal, quickly trap the ball. **Maintain a balanced, ready position** *(weight centered over support leg)* **so that you can move again quickly.** Ready? Begin.

This activity provides practice in stopping the ball quickly. Frequent signals will be needed: ten seconds of dribbling, stop; thirty seconds of dribbling, stop. . . .

🅣 Travel through general space, dribbling as you go. Each time you meet another person, trap the ball quickly with your foot, execute a quarter turn, and continue dribbling. The ability to stop and start quickly is an important offensive skill that helps you maintain control of the ball and avoid your opponents.

🅒 Test your dribbling and trapping skills with this two-minute activity: On the signal, begin dribbling in general space. Each time you hear the drum or meet another person, stop quickly, trapping the ball with one foot; execute a quarter turn; and continue dribbling. Your goal is to stop-start for two minutes without losing control of the ball or bumping another person or ball. The signal at the end of the two minutes will be a double drumbeat. **Look for the open spaces.**

TRAVELING IN PATHWAYS

Setting: Various pathways taped on the floor or spray-painted on the grass; children scattered throughout general space, each with a ball for kicking

Cues

Tap, Tap	(Gently tap the ball so that it stays within three to four feet of you at all times.)
Inside/Outside	(Use both the inside of your foot and the outside of your foot—left and right—to tap the soccer ball.)

Tasks/Challenges:

T On the ground are straight, curved, and zigzag pathways. Travel through the formations using the soccer dribble, traveling at a speed you can control—no collisions, no loss of the ball. Be sure to travel all the pathways.

T As you tap/dribble the different pathways, you begin to discover that the inside of the foot is perhaps not always the best surface to use for the tap/dribble. Practice the tap/dribble with the outside of your foot as well as the inside. **Keep the tap gentle—with control.**

DRIBBLING AROUND STATIONARY OBSTACLES

Setting: Marker cones and/or milk jugs positioned throughout general space; a kicking ball for each child

Cues	
Tap, Tap	(Gently tap the ball so that it stays within three to four feet of you at all times.)
Inside/Outside	(Use both the inside of your foot and the outside of your foot—left and right—to tap the soccer ball.)
Heads Up	(Keep your head up to avoid collisions—people, obstacles, soccer balls.)

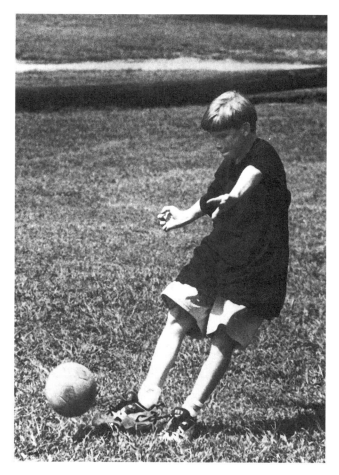

Figure 26.8   Dribbling, kicking, and punting require visual focus and concentration.

Tasks/Challenges:

T Tap/dribble the ball throughout general space, alternating contact with your right foot and your left foot. Avoid bumping into the cones (jugs) with either the ball or your body. Travel in zigzag and curved pathways to avoid the obstacles. Your visual range must now include the ball you're dribbling, other people, the balls they're using, and the obstacles (*Figure 26.8*).

T Tap/dribble in general space. Each time you approach an obstacle, trap the ball, execute a quarter turn to either the right or the left, and continue dribbling.

T Vary the speed of your travel—sometimes approach a cone (jug) very quickly, sometimes slowly.

T Tap/dribble in general space. As you near a cone (jug), tap the ball gently with the inside of your right foot, passing the ball to the left of the cone (jug). Quickly continue the dribble.

T Tap/dribble in general space. As you near a cone (jug), tap the ball gently with the inside of your left foot, passing the ball to the right of the cone (jug).

T Tap/dribble in general space. As you near the cone (jug), tap the ball gently with the outside of your right foot, passing the ball to the right of the cone (jug).

T Tap/dribble in general space. As you near a cone (jug), tap the ball gently with the outside of your left foot, passing the ball to the left of the cone (jug).

C This time as you practice dribbling, trapping, and turning, pretend you have 100 points. If the ball you are dribbling contacts a cone (jug), subtract 10 points from your score. If you have a collision with another person, subtract 25 points. Try to complete your practice with 100 points!

KEEPING IT PERFECT: ZERO, ZERO

Setting: Marker cones and/or milk jugs positioned throughout general space; a kicking ball for each child

Cues

Tap, Tap	(Gently tap the ball so that it stays within three to four feet of you at all times.)
Inside/Outside	(Use the inside of your foot and the outside of your foot—left and right—to tap the soccer ball.)
Heads Up	(Keep your head up to avoid collisions—people, obstacles, soccer balls.)

Tasks/Challenges:

C Thus far in our tap/dribble study, you've practiced dribbling with control, trapping with one foot, avoiding obstacles, changing the speed of your travel, and tapping the ball to the right or the left, as in passing. The game of Keeping It Perfect: Zero, Zero will give you a chance to test these skills.

Each of you has a perfect score of zero. The object of the game is to still have the perfect score at the end of the two minutes of activity. On the signal, begin to tap/dribble in general space. You may travel at any speed you choose, increasing and decreasing your speed as you wish. When you hear the drum, trap the ball immediately; I'll give a verbal "go" for you to continue.

You earn negative points if you

1. Don't trap the ball within two seconds of the drumbeat (–1)
2. Bump into another person or the ball they're dribbling (–1)
3. Bump into a marker cone (–1)

The key is control. Ready? Go.

You can use this activity to focus on specific skills. For example, in the first two minutes, children are to travel in general space (control); in the second two minutes, they are to travel in each area of the gymnasium (speed); in the third two minutes, they are to zigzag around as many cones as possible (passing, accuracy).

At the end of each two minutes, stop, rest, and calculate your scores. Remember, a perfect score is zero.

Utilization Level: Learning Experiences Leading to Skill Development in Kicking

At the utilization level, we focus on providing experiences for applying kicking skills in unpredictable situations of increasing complexity. Performing skills on the move and in relation to an opponent are important challenges. A great degree of accuracy and control is the goal at this level.

A note about cues: Although several cues are listed for many of the learning experiences, it's important to focus on only one cue at a time. That way, the children can really concentrate on that cue. Once you provide feedback to the children and observe that most have learned a cue, then it's time to focus on another one.

CHANGING DIRECTIONS: TAP/DRIBBLE

Setting: Children scattered throughout general space, each with a ball for kicking

Cues

Tap, Tap	(Gently tap the ball so that it is always within your control—no more than three to four feet from you—even with increased speed.)
Middle of Ball	(Contact directly behind the middle of the ball, using the insides, outsides, and heels of your feet for the dribble.)

Tasks/Challenges:

T Begin traveling in general space, tapping the ball three to four feet in front of you as you go. When you are comfortable with your control of the dribble, tap the ball ahead of you, run quickly beyond the ball, tap it gently with your heel, quickly turn, and continue the dribble. Be sure you run *beyond* the ball to tap the front of it; contact on top of the ball will cause you to fall.

PERFORMING A CONTINUOUS TAP/DRIBBLE AND CHANGE OF DIRECTION

Setting: Children scattered throughout general space in an outdoor grassy or blacktop area

Cues

Tap/Tap	(Tap the ball with control so that it stays within three to four feet of you at *all* times.)
Inside/Outside/ Heels of Feet	(Tap the ball with different parts of your feet as you dribble.)
Heads Up	(Keep your head up to avoid collisions—people, soccer balls.)

Figure 26.9 Setup for combination dribble and kick with varying degrees of force.

Tasks/Challenges:

🅣 You learned to change the direction of the ball by tapping it to the right or left with the inside or outside of your foot. And you just learned one method of changing direction front to back. Travel within the boundaries on the playground using changes of direction to avoid contact with others and to avoid crossing the outside boundaries. Your task is continuous dribbling. Ready? Begin.

🅣 Approach a boundary quickly; use the heel tap to change the direction of the dribble at the last moment, to prevent crossing the boundary.

🅣 Purposely approach some other students; use a pass to the right or left to avoid contact with them.

🅒 Challenge yourself by increasing your speed to the maximum rate you can travel with a controlled dribble and frequent changes of direction.

TRAVELING AND KICKING FOR A GOAL

Setting: Hoops or milk jugs scattered throughout general space; marker cones for goals (Figure 26.9)

Cues	
Behind the Ball	(Contact the ball directly *behind* center for travel along the ground.)
Gentle Taps/Hard Kicks	(Gently tap the ball for the dribble; kick hard for the goal.)

Tasks/Challenges:

🅣 Travel at your own speed and tap the ball while avoiding obstacles and other people. On the signal, travel quickly to an open space, and kick for the goal. Retrieve the ball; begin dribbling again, listening for the signal to kick for the goal.

🅣 Practice dribbling around obstacles and kicking for the goal on your own; I won't give the signal for the kick.

PLAYING ONE-ON-ONE SOCCER

Setting: Sets of partners in general space; kicking balls; marker cones (milk jugs) for goals

Cues	
Gentle Taps/Hard Kicks	(Gently tap the ball for the dribble; kick hard for the goal.)
Heads Up	(Keep your head up to avoid collisions—people, soccer balls.)
Inside/Outside/Heels of Feet	(Tap the ball with different parts of your feet as you travel.)
Offense:	Open Spaces. . . Look for Them, Move to Them
Defense:	Trap or Tap to Gain Possession

Tasks/Challenges:

🅣 Select a partner whose tap/dribble skills are very similar to your skills. Cooperatively decide the boundaries for your area; a small area provides more practice. Partner 1 begins to travel and dribble the soccer ball within that area; partner 2 attempts to gain possession of the ball by using the

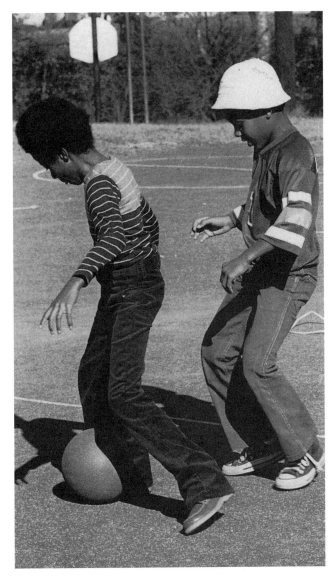

Figure 26.10 This youngster tries to keep the ball away from his partner using only his feet—no touching.

feet to trap the ball or tap it away (*Figure 26.10*). Follow these rules:

1. Contact the ball, not the person.
2. Gain possession of the ball; don't kick it away.
3. If you gain possession of the ball, begin your dribble as the offensive player; your partner will be the defense.

If partners are unmatched in skill, give a signal for the change from offense to defense. That is, each time partner 2 gains possession of the ball, that person will give it back to partner 1, who continues to tap/dribble until the signal to switch positions is given.

T Within your area, set up two marker cones (milk jugs) as a goal. Partner 1 will tap/dribble until within scoring range (*ten to twelve feet of the goal*)

and then kick for the goal. Partner 2 will attempt to gain possession of the ball, using the feet only. After each kick for the goal, switch positions.

C You may want to design a game using the skills of the soccer dribble and kicking for the goal. Work cooperatively with your partner to decide the rules of the game, scoring, boundaries. Can you think of a name for your game? (*See Chapter 31.*)

PLAYING SOCCER GOLF

Setting: Obstacle course arrangement (Figure 26.11); a kicking ball for each child

Cues	
Behind the Ball	(Contact the ball directly *behind* center for travel along the ground.)
Under the Ball	(Contact the ball slightly *below* center for travel upward through the air.)
Gentle Taps/Hard Kicks	(Gently tap the ball for the dribble; kick hard for the goal.)

Tasks/Challenges:

C The game of Soccer Golf involves the skills of dribbling in pathways, kicking for a goal, and kicking over a low height. The playground is arranged as a golf course. Your task is to complete the course with the fewest number of kicks. There are boxes to dribble around, zones to zigzag through, hoops to kick into, and poles to kick over. Count your kicks as you proceed through the course. When you finish the course, begin again, trying to lower your score.

To decrease waiting time, have the children begin at different holes on the course rather than having everyone start at the first hole.

KICKING TO A PARTNER FROM VARIOUS ANGLES

Setting: Partners positioned fifteen to twenty feet from each other, each pair with a kicking ball

Cues	
Behind the Ball	(Contact the ball directly *behind* center for travel along the ground.)
Foot, Not Toes	(Kick the ball with the inside or the outside of your foot, not with your toes.)
Kick Hard	(Kick the ball with enough force to send it to your partner.)

Figure 26.11   Soccer Golf course arrangement.

Figure 26.12   Kicking to a traveling partner.

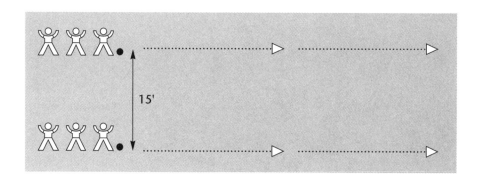

Tasks/Challenges:

⊤ Review the skill of kicking along the ground so that your partner can trap the ball without moving. When you are comfortable with the kick, take three to four steps to the right so you are at an angle to your partner. Kick the ball from this position so it travels directly to your partner. Kick with the inside of your right foot and the outside of your left foot until you can kick four out of five times directly to your partner with each foot.

⊤ Move to the left three to four steps from your original position. Kick the ball to your partner from this angle. Practice the kick with the inside of your left foot and the outside of your right foot. Then practice with the outside of your left foot and the inside of your right foot.

⊤ Position yourself at different angles in relation to your partner, and practice kicking to your partner from these positions. The ability to kick at different angles is important in passing the ball to teammates and in kicking for a goal in games.

KICKING TO A TRAVELING PARTNER

Setting: Sets of partners at one end of the playing field, approximately fifteen feet from each other; one partner with the ball for kicking (Figure 26.12)

Cues	
Behind the Ball	(Contact the ball directly *behind* center for travel along the ground.)
Inside of Foot	(Kick the ball with the inside of your foot, not with your toes.)
Kick Hard	(Kick the ball with enough force to send it to your partner.)
Sender:	Ahead of Partner (Kick beyond your partner.)
Receiver:	On the Move (Don't stop and wait for the ball.)

Tasks/Challenges:

⊤ Travel the length of the playing field, passing the ball to each other as you travel. Remember to pass to your partner while you are *on the move;* don't stop to execute the kick.

T Pass the ball *ahead* of your partner so he or she can continue jogging, rather than having to stop to receive the pass.

The second set of partners may begin their travel/pass when the partners in front of them are one-third the distance of the field, or you may signal when each set of partners is to begin traveling.

PASSING TO A PARTNER IN GENERAL SPACE

Setting: Sets of partners in general space, each set with a ball for kicking

Cues	
Heads Up	(Keep your head up to avoid collisions—people, soccer balls.)
Pass at an Angle	(Use the inside/outside of your feet [right/left] to send the ball to your partner.)
Pass to the Open Space	(Kick the ball to the open space ahead of your partner.)

Tasks/Challenges:

T Travel in general space, dribbling and passing to your partner. All other players will be traveling and passing at the same time, so it is important that you be aware of others and of passing to open spaces. Ready? Begin.

C Challenge yourself always to pass the ball ahead of your partner—to the open space. If you are successful, your partner will never have to stop to receive the pass. Try for five successful completions: open space, partner on the move.

PLAYING TWO-ON-ONE SOCCER

Setting: Groups of three in general space; marker cones for goals; balls for kicking

▶ Kicking (passing) at angles and kicking (passing) to the open space are two of the most critical skills for game play. They provide the "bridge" between skill mastery in a static situation and successful skill execution in a dynamic environment.

Cues	
Pass at an Angle	(Use the inside/outside of your feet [right/left] to send the ball to your partner.)
Pass to the Open Space	(Kick the ball to the open space ahead of your partner.)
Gentle Taps/Hard Kicks	(Gently tap the ball for the dribble; kick hard to pass and to make a goal.)

Tasks/Challenges:

C Form groups of three; two of you will be offensive players, and one of you will be a defensive player. The two offensive players will tap/dribble and pass to each other within the boundaries of your soccer area. The defensive player will attempt to gain possession of the ball by intercepting passes or tapping the ball away on the dribble.

Each team will have possession of the ball (*offense*) for two minutes. See how many goals you can score within that interval. The offensive team must execute at least two passes before attempting a kick for the goal.

Proficiency Level: Learning Experiences Leading to Skill Development in Kicking

At the proficiency level, we give children opportunities to use the skill of kicking in group games and for learning the strategy of offensive/defensive participation. Children play self-designed games, or the teacher chooses the games. These games involve relationships that are made increasingly complex by the number of players and types of strategies required.

A note about cues: Although several cues are listed for many of the learning experiences, it's important to focus on only one cue at a time. That way, the children can really concentrate on that cue. Once you provide feedback to the children and observe that most have learned a cue, then it's time to focus on another one.

KICKING AT SMALL STATIONARY TARGETS

Setting: Sets of marker cones six feet apart to serve as targets; a line for kicking fifteen to twenty feet from each target (Figure 26.13)

Cues	
Individual cues as needed	

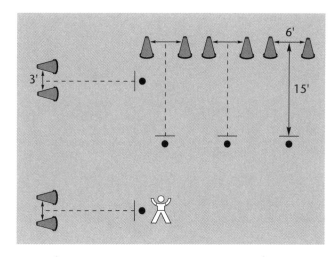

Figure 26.13 Kicking at small targets.

Tasks/Challenges:

T Each person will have ten kicks at the goal; mentally record your personal score. After each person has kicked ten times, move the cones closer together until they are three feet apart. Now kick ten times at this target. Compare this score with your score for the six-foot target.

T Position yourself at an angle facing the target. Repeat the tasks, kicking at an angle rather than in a direct line to the target. Compare your scores to your direct-line kicks.

C Set a personal goal for successful kicks. Practice to meet that goal for both direct and angle kicks.

KICKING AT A MOVING TARGET

Setting: Hoops suspended from a rope hanging from a frame, wall bars, or outdoor playground equipment (partners may also hold hoop for each other)

Cue	
Ahead of the Target	(Kick the ball to the open space just beyond the moving target.)

Tasks/Challenges:

T Partner 1 starts the suspended hoop swinging or moves back and forth, holding the hoop in the hand. Partner 2, approximately ten to twelve feet away, kicks the ball at the moving target, attempting to kick the ball through the hoop. After five trials, partners change places.

This learning experience reinforces "kicking to the open space" and "kicking at angles," which were introduced earlier. Remind children to kick the ball to the space where the hoop will swing, not to the space where the hoop is when they execute the kick, thus the concepts of angle and open space target!

PLAYING MINISOCCER

Setting: Milk jugs and marker cones as boundaries; children in groups of four, six, or eight

Cues	
Offensive:	Pass at an Angle to Teammates
	Pass to Open Space (Pass ahead of the receiver.)
	Body between Ball and Opponent (Keep your body between the ball and the defender at all times; quickly switch the tap/dribble to the outside foot.)
Defensive:	Tap or Trap

Tasks/Challenges:

C With your group, design a game of Minisoccer, using the skills we have been practicing. Cooperatively decide the rules, scoring, and the boundaries. I will place only one limitation on the game: Each member of the offensive team must dribble the ball before making a kick for the goal.

PLAYING SOCCER KEEP-AWAY

Setting: Children in teams of three to six; large open space

Cues	
Offensive:	Pass at an Angle to Teammates
	Pass to Open Space (Pass ahead of the receiver.)
	Body between Ball and Opponent
Defensive:	Close the open spaces (Move quickly to close the open spaces.)

Tasks/Challenges:

C The object of Soccer Keep-Away is to keep the ball away from your opponents using the tap/dribble and passing skills you have been practicing. There

Figure 26.14 Alley Soccer.

is no kicking for the goal, only passing and dribbling, in the game. To begin the game, one person throws the ball (two hands, overhead) in from the sideline. Play continues with the ball being dribbled and passed as the other team attempts to gain possession by trapping, intercepting, or gaining control of the dribble. At the end of each three minutes of play, I will signal for the other team to execute the throw-in to begin a new game.

Alley Soccer and Cone Soccer (below) are proficiency-level games that demand combinations of skills. Because it is rare that all the students in a class will be ready for this type game at the same time, some children will benefit from practicing different types of kicking while others are playing the game (see Chapter 31).

PLAYING ALLEY SOCCER

Setting: A playing field divided into five equal alleys (Figure 26.14); marker-cone goals six feet apart at each end of the field; six-member teams

Cues

Offensive: Kick at an Angle to Teammates
Pass to Open Space
Body between Ball and Opponent
Defensive: Close the Open Spaces (Move quickly to close the open spaces.)

Figure 26.15 Cone Soccer. Dimensions of the playing area may be adjusted to the size of the available area and the number of players.

Tasks/Challenges:

Ⓒ Alley Soccer is an activity that uses dribbling, passing, and kicking for a goal. Each team has six players—one player for each alley plus a goalie. Players may travel the length of their alley but can't cross into another alley. Your task is to dribble, avoid the opponent in your alley, pass to teammates, and kick for the goal. At regular intervals, I'll give the signal to rotate alleys; this rotation will allow each of you to play each position.

PLAYING CONE SOCCER

Setting: A marker cone placed at either end of the playing area with a circle (spray paint or marking dust) ten feet in diameter surrounding each cone (Figure 26.15); teams of two to six members

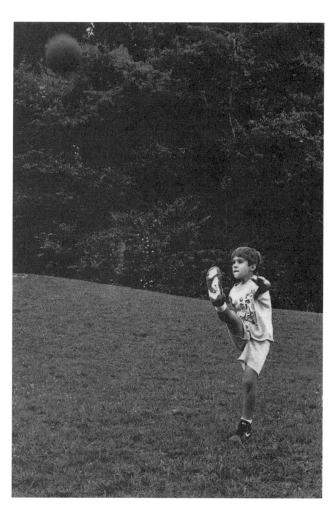

Figure 26.16   This child practices punting, a difficult skill for youngsters to master.

Cues

Offensive: Kick at an Angle to Teammates
Pass to Open Space
Gentle Taps to Dribble/Hard Kicks to
the Target
Body between Ball and Opponent
Defensive: Close the Open Spaces

Tasks/Challenges:

Ⓒ Cone Soccer emphasizes dribbling, passing, and
kicking for accuracy. The object of the game is to
kick the ball, knock over the other team's cone, and
protect your own cone. No one is allowed inside
the circle to kick or to defend. If one team makes
body contact, the other team gets a free kick on the
spot; everyone must be three feet away for the free
kick.

*A good way to form teams for equal skill is to ask children
to select a partner and then place the selected partners on
opposite teams.*

Levels of Skill Proficiency in Punting

Punting is a form of kicking: A ball is released from the
hands and kicked while it is in the air. This is a difficult skill for children to master (Figure 26.16). Because
the punt involves a complex coordination of body
movements—moving the body forward, dropping the
ball accurately, and kicking it before it reaches the
ground—we have found it best to introduce the punt
after children have practiced other types of kicking.

When children first try to punt, they toss the ball
up and then "kick" it with a knee or leg rather than
the foot. Often the novice punter will contact the ball

after it bounces. We give children at the precontrol level round, lightweight balls and balloons, challenging them to contact the "ball" with the foot before it touches the ground.

Children at the control level are challenged to consistently contact the ball for the punt, to drop rather than toss the ball, and to move forward to make contact rather than standing in one place. When children can consistently contact the ball with the foot before the ball hits the ground, we begin to expand the basic skill with experiences that include:

1. Punting for distance
2. Punting for height
3. Punting different types of balls
4. Punting for accuracy

At the utilization level, experiences are designed to combine punting with other factors. Appropriate activities include:

1. Punting to a partner
2. Catching and punting within a limited time

At the proficiency level, children are able to punt in relation to unpredictable, dynamic situations, such as might occur in a football or a rugby game.

Ideas for varying the contexts in which punting skills can be practiced are presented in our progression spiral on page 474. As in previous chapters, we encourage you to alter the method of organization, as suggested in Chapter 13. Box 26.4 contains key observation points illustrating correct and incorrect punting. Ask yourself the questions in the box as you observe children punting.

Precontrol Level: Activities for Exploration of Punting

At the precontrol level, children explore punting different types of lightweight balls, sometimes with a bounce before contact, sometimes contacting the ball before it touches the ground. At this level we are not concerned with mastery, but with children enjoying a variety of experiences as an introduction to the skill of punting.

DROPPING, BOUNCING, AND KICKING LIGHTWEIGHT BALLS

Setting: Lightweight balls (plastic, foam) positioned around the perimeter of the gym, approximately fifteen feet from the wall

Tasks/Challenges:

🅣 Drop the ball to the floor. After the first bounce, contact the ball with your shoelaces, sending it to the wall.

🅣 Try the kick with your right foot and with your left foot to determine which is your preferred foot for punting.

🅒 With your preferred foot, drop and kick the ball after the bounce five times. Repeat several times to determine your personal best.

DROPPING AND PUNTING

Setting: Kicking balls (plastic, foam) positioned around the perimeter of the gym, approximately fifteen feet from the wall

Tasks/Challenges:

🅣 Stand behind the kicking line, holding the ball in both hands. Drop the ball and kick it to the wall, making contact before the ball touches the floor. This drop-kick action is called a *punt*.

Children who are having difficulty with the drop-kick action can benefit from practicing punting with a balloon. This helps them understand the concept of dropping— rather than tossing—the object to be punted.

Control Level: Learning Experiences Leading to Skill Development in Punting

At the control level, children need experiences to develop consistency in contacting the ball for the punt. After they can consistently make contact, they are provided opportunities to punt different types of balls, to increase distance on the punt, and to improve accuracy.

A note about cues: Although several cues are listed for many of the learning experiences, it's important to focus on only one cue at a time. That way, the children can really concentrate on that cue. Once you provide feedback to the children and observe that most have learned a cue, then it's time to focus on another one.

PUNTING FOR CONSISTENCY

Setting: Lightweight balls for punting, placed around the perimeter of the gym, approximately twenty feet from the wall

Punting

■ **PROFICIENCY LEVEL**

Playing Punt-Over
Punting while traveling
Receiving and punting against opponents

■ **UTILIZATION LEVEL**

Playing Rush the Circle
Punting within a limited time
Receiving a pass, then punting
Punting to a partner
Punting at angles

■ **CONTROL LEVEL**

Punting for height
Punting for accuracy
Using punting zones
Punting for distance
Punting different types of balls
Punting with an approach
Punting over low ropes
Punting for consistency

■ **PRECONTROL LEVEL**

Dropping and punting
Dropping, bouncing, and kicking lightweight balls

Cues

Shoelaces	(Contact the ball with your instep—your shoelaces or Velcro tabs—not your toes.)
Eyes on the Ball	(Watch the ball until it contacts your foot.)
Drop	(Drop the ball for the punt; don't toss it upward.)

Tasks/Challenges:

T When we worked on punting earlier, you punted just for fun. Sometimes the ball went through the air, sometimes backward over your head, and sometimes nowhere! Today we will begin to practice punting so we can consistently kick the ball forward through the air. Stand behind the ball, holding it in both your hands at waist height. Take a small step on your nonkicking leg, then extend your kicking foot for contact on the shoelaces. Drop the ball as you swing your kicking leg forward; contact the ball just before it touches the floor (ground).

C Punt the ball five times. How many times did you contact the ball before it touched the floor (ground)? Continue your practice until you make three or more contacts.

T Good, you are now consistently contacting the ball before it touches the floor (ground). Now let's focus on the ball consistently traveling forward when you punt. Continue your practice with sets of five punts; mentally record how many times in each set you are successful at punting with your shoelaces and sending the ball forward to the wall.

PUNTING OVER LOW ROPES

Setting: Ropes suspended between standards or across chairs at a height of four to six feet; lightweight balls for punting

Cues

Extend	(Extend your foot to contact the ball with your shoelaces, not your toes.)
Eyes on the Ball	(Watch the ball until it contacts your foot.)
Drop	(Drop the ball for the punt; don't toss it upward.)

Tasks/Challenges:

T Stand approximately ten feet behind the rope. Punt the ball so it travels over the rope. Retrieve the ball and punt from the opposite side of the rope.

C Give yourself a point each time you are successful at punting the ball over the rope. How many points can you make out of ten trials?

PUNTING WITH AN APPROACH

Setting: Lightweight balls for punting, placed around the perimeter of the gym, approximately twenty feet from the wall (*If indoor space is not sufficient for this task, move the class outside and punt away from the circle, Figure 26.4.*)

Cues

Nonstop Approach	(Take a few running steps; then punt without stopping your forward momentum.)
Step-Hop	(Make your last step before contact a step-hop on your nonkicking leg, so that you'll be airborne for the punt.)

Tasks/Challenges:

T Take a series of quick steps forward. As your kicking leg moves back to front for the contact with the ball, hop slightly on your supporting leg so you are actually airborne for the contact. Quickly straighten your kicking leg at the moment of contact. (*Demonstrate or ask a child to demonstrate the step-hop action.*)

T Continue to practice the approach and punt. As you become more comfortable with the step-hop action, you will probably want to lean slightly backward as you kick, to counterbalance the forceful swing of your kicking leg.

C Practice until you can punt successfully three times in a row. When I watch your punting action, I should see the following:

1. A series of quick steps
2. Your body airborne for contact
3. The ball being dropped, not tossed
4. Your instep (your shoelaces) making contact with the ball

BOX 26.4   KEY OBSERVATION POINTS: PUNTING

1. Does the child drop the ball rather than toss it in the air for the punt?

NO   YES

2. Is the child's kicking foot extended for contact on the instep (shoelaces) rather than with the toes?

NO   YES

3. Does the child make contact at the right height for a 45-degree angle of flight rather than too soon or too late?

NO   YES

Mature Stage

When children are at the mature stage of punting, do their punts look similar to the following sequence? The child makes a rapid approach of one or more steps that culminates in a leap just before contact. If a leap does not precede contact, the child can enhance the forward momentum by taking a large step. The child makes contact with the ball at or below knee level as a result of having released the ball in a forward and downward direction. The momentum of the swinging leg carries the punter upward off the surface and forward after contact.

SOURCES: Adapted from "Developmental Sequence of Punting," mimeographed materials, by V. Seefeldt and J. Haubenstricker, presented at the University of Georgia, Athens, June 1978; *Fundamental Motor Patterns,* 2nd ed., by R. L. Wickstrom, 1977, Philadelphia: Lea & Febiger.

PUNTING DIFFERENT TYPES OF BALLS

Setting: A variety of balls for punting—plastic, foam, deflated rubber, nerf footballs—placed around an outdoor teaching area

Cues

Extend	(Extend your foot to contact the ball with your shoelaces, not your toes.)
Eyes on the Ball	(Watch the ball until it contacts your foot.)
Drop	(Drop the ball for the punt; don't toss it upward.)
Step-Hop	(Make your last step before contact a step-hop on your nonkicking leg, so that you'll be airborne for the punt.)

Tasks/Challenges:

🄣 Scattered around the practice area are punting balls of different types and sizes. Practice punting with each type of ball, using your running approach and airborne action for the kick.

🄒 Practice with each type of ball until you can punt successfully three out of five times.

🄣 Select a football for punting. What is very different about this ball? Yes, all the others are round. Hold the football with one end facing the direction in which the ball is to travel; all your other actions are the same as for punting other types of balls. Compare how well you're able to punt the football with your success with the other types of balls.

When footballs are added to the selection, some children may want to practice punting only with the footballs; encourage the children to practice punting with each type of ball.

PUNTING FOR DISTANCE

Setting: A variety of balls for punting; colored jugs for use as markers; children positioned at one end of an outdoor practice area

Cues

Extend	(Extend your foot and your kicking leg for a really good punt.)
Step-Hop	(Make your last step before contact a step-hop on your nonkicking leg, so that you'll be airborne for the punt.)
Kick Hard	(Kick hard to send the ball really far.)

Tasks/Challenges:

🄣 Take a series of running steps, and punt the ball as far as possible. Place a colored jug at the spot where the ball first touches the ground, and then try to punt beyond that spot. Remember, making the ball travel at a 45-degree angle when you punt it gives you the best distance. **To achieve that angle, extend your foot and contact the ball just before it touches the ground.**

Continue to practice your punting, trying to extend your distance with each punt. Each time you better your distance, move your marker to that spot. **Straightening your kicking leg when you contact the ball will increase your power for distance.**

When a new factor (distance) is added, children may modify their kicking patterns. Some may need verbal cues as they practice.

USING PUNTING ZONES

Setting: Colored tape, spray paint, marker cones, or colored streamers to mark a series of target zones, each approximately fifteen feet in length (Figure 26.17); a variety of balls for punting (*Target zones may be numbered, color-coded, or named for states, professional teams, etc.*)

Cues

Extend	(Extend your foot and your kicking leg for a really good punt.)
Step-Hop	(Make your last step before contact a step-hop on your nonkicking leg, so that you'll be airborne for the punt.)
Nonstop Approach	(Take a few running steps; then punt without stopping your forward momentum.)

Tasks/Challenges:

🄣 Approach the kicking line with a series of running steps; punt the ball for maximum distance. Mentally note the zone the ball first lands in. Retrieve the ball and be ready for another turn.

A key component in punting for distance is practice. Keeping the same distances and codes (colors, names) for zones permits children to check themselves against their best during previous lessons.

Figure 26.17 Punting zones.

PUNTING FOR ACCURACY

Setting: Colored tape, spray paint, marker cones, or colored streamers to mark a series of target zones, each approximately fifteen feet in length (Figure 26.17); a variety of balls for punting

Cues

Extend	(Extend your foot and your kicking leg for a really good punt.)
Step-Hop	(Make your last step before contact a step-hop, so that you'll be airborne for the punt.)
Hard Kick, Soft Kick	(Use a hard kick for maximum distance, a soft kick for shorter distances.)

Tasks/Challenges:

T We previously used the target zones in punting for distance. Now we will use them to focus on accuracy—making the ball land within a particular area. Practice punting with a running approach to review the skill and to determine the zone that is your best distance. Try to punt the ball consistently to that zone.

C Punt the ball five times, attempting to make it land within the same zone each time.

T Punt the ball so it lands within the first target zone. To do that you must adjust the amount of force behind the kick.

T Choose a zone midway between the first target zone and your best distance. Punt the ball so it lands within that target zone.

C Select three zones as your targets. Practice until you can successfully punt three out of five balls into each of those zones.

T Repeat the process for your three selected zones using each type of ball—foam, deflated rubber, soccer ball, football. Compare your accuracy with the different types of balls.

Being able to adjust force to kick a shorter distance is an important punting skill for games play and one that does not come easily for children. Encourage them to select zones of varying distances, not just their maximum.

PUNTING FOR HEIGHT

Setting: Colored tape, spray paint, marker cones, or colored streamers to mark a series of target zones, each approximately fifteen feet in length (Figure 26.17); a variety of balls for punting.

Cues

Under the Ball	(Contact the ball *below* center to send it upward and forward.)
Eyes on the Ball	(Watch the ball until it contacts your foot.)
Kick Hard	(Make a firm step-hop and swing of leg for good height.)

Tasks/Challenges:

T Sometimes in a game you want the ball to travel in a high aerial path rather than at a 45-degree angle

Figure 26.18 Punting at angles.

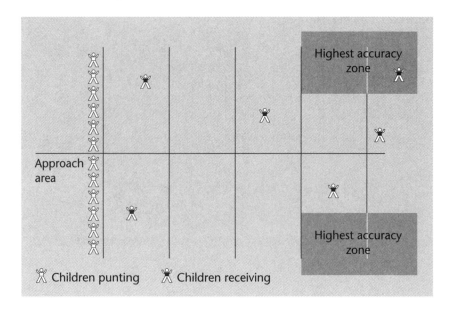

so that you can adjust the forward distance of the punt. What did we learn earlier about contacting a ball to send it upward rather than forward? Right, contact must be made directly underneath the ball for travel upward. You will also get more height on the punt if you contact the ball closer to waist height. Take a series of small steps, then punt the ball so it travels as high as possible.

Ⓣ Punt the ball high in the air; see if you can catch it before it touches the ground.

⚠ Because of the hazard of running to catch while looking up, this task must be done in a large outdoor field space. If such a space is not available, some children can practice punting for height while others practice punting for distance.

Ⓣ Select one of the first three target zones as your target area. Punt the ball so it travels in a high aerial path to that zone.

Children highly skilled in punting for accuracy will enjoy the challenge of smaller targets, such as hoops.

Utilization Level: Learning Experiences Leading to Skill Development in Punting

At the utilization level, we provide punting experiences in dynamic situations. This encourages children to use punting skills in combination with other factors, such as time and accuracy. To stress relationships with a partner, focus on punting so that a partner can catch the ball or punting shortly after receiving a throw from a partner.

A note about cues: Although several cues are listed for many of the learning experiences, it's important to focus on only one cue at a time. That way, the children can really concentrate on that cue. Once you provide feedback to the children and observe that most have learned a cue, then it's time to focus on another one.

PUNTING AT ANGLES

Setting: Spray paint, marker dust, or milk jugs to mark target zones divided by width and length (Figure 26.18); lightweight balls for punting

Cues

Extend to Target   (Extend your kicking foot and leg toward the target, to the right or left.)

Individuals and/or classes may need reminders of earlier cues (e.g., Eyes on the Ball, Drop, Step-Hop)

Tasks/Challenges:

Ⓣ Practice punting into the different target zones—to the right and to the left of where you're standing.

Ⓣ Select a target zone, and practice until you can consistently punt the ball into that zone. Then select a zone on the opposite side.

Ⓒ Practice until you can select a target zone, tell a partner which one you've chosen, and then punt three out of five balls into that zone. How about five out of five?

PUNTING TO A PARTNER

Setting: Colored tape, spray paint, marker cones, or streamers to mark target zones, each approximately fifteen feet long; partners, each pair with a light-weight ball for punting

Cues	
Eyes on the Ball	(Watch the ball—not your partner—until it contacts your foot.)
Step-Hop	(Make your last step before contact a step-hop, so that you'll be airborne for the punt.)
Adjust	(Adjust your power to match the distance your partner is from you.)

Tasks/Challenges:

🅣 Using the target zones as a measure of distance, tell your partner where to stand for the two of you to punt to each other; choose a distance at which both of you have been successful. Punt the ball so your partner can catch it without moving more than a couple of steps.

🅣 Punt so your partner can catch without moving from self-space.

🅣 From behind the kicking line, practice punting to your partner in each of the target zones: near/far, right/left angles.

🅣 Punt some balls high and lofty, others at a 45-degree angle.

RECEIVING A PASS, THEN PUNTING

Setting: Partners scattered throughout general space in an outdoor area; a variety of balls for punting—playground, soccer balls, footballs

Cues	
Eyes on the Ball	(Watch the ball, not your partner.)
Step-Hop-Punt	(Take a couple of steps only; then punt.)

Tasks/Challenges:

🅣 Select a partner with whom you can work well independently. Separate to a distance at which you can both throw and catch successfully. Partner 1 throws the ball to partner 2; partner 2 receives the ball and then quickly takes a couple of steps and punts the ball across the playing field. Your goal is to punt as quickly, yet correctly, as possible. Alternate positions as passer and punter.

 With children throwing, catching, and punting, space awareness can be a safety factor. Organize this activity with all passes and punts traveling in the same direction—across the playing area or end to end, not in multiple directions.

PUNTING WITHIN A LIMITED TIME

Setting: Partners scattered throughout general space in an outdoor area; a variety of balls for punting—playground, soccer balls, footballs

Cues	
Eyes on the Ball	(Watch the ball, not your partner.)
Step-Hop-Punt	(Take a couple of steps only; then punt.)

Tasks/Challenges:

🅒 Partner 2 throws the ball to partner 1. As soon as partner 1 receives the pass, partner 2 begins to count "one alligator, two alligators, three alligators." After receiving the pass, partner 1 punts it across the playing field as quickly as possible, trying to complete the punt before partner 2 counts "three alligators." Partner 1 retrieves the ball and switches positions with partner 2. Follow all the proper steps, even though you're punting quickly.

PLAYING RUSH THE CIRCLE

Setting: A spray-paint or marker-dust circle drawn on a field, with a diameter of ten feet or larger, and a passing line approximately fifteen feet from the edge of the circle (Figure 26.19); children with partners; a variety of balls for punting—playground, soccer balls, footballs

Cues	
Eyes on the Ball	(Watch the ball, not your partner.)
Step-Hop-Punt	(Take a couple of steps only; then punt.)

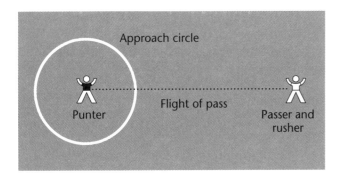

Figure 26.19   Partner pass-and-rush punting: Rush the Circle.

Tasks/Challenges:

Ⓒ Select a partner whose throwing/catching skills are similar to yours. The punter will be positioned inside the circle; the passer will be approximately twenty feet away, behind the passing line. The passer throws the ball from behind the passing line. When the punter receives the catch, the passer runs toward the circle, trying to reach the circle before the punter can kick the ball. The punter punts the ball as quickly as possible when he or she receives the pass. In other words, the punter tries to punt the ball before the passer reaches the circle.

At this level of punting and kicking combined with throwing and catching, some children will enjoy developing point systems and minigames for each task. Others will continue to enjoy practicing the skill in the dynamic environment.

Proficiency Level: Learning Experiences Leading to Skill Development in Punting

Punting experiences at the proficiency level lead to the ability to punt accurately and for distance in dynamic and unpredictable situations. The relationships are more complex. Emphasis is on punting while traveling and on working with others in game situations.

A note about cues: Although several cues are listed for many of the learning experiences, it's important to focus on only one cue at a time. That way, the children can really concentrate on that cue. Once you provide feedback to the children and observe that most have learned a cue, then it's time to focus on another one.

RECEIVING AND PUNTING AGAINST OPPONENTS

Setting: Groups of three, each group with a ball for punting

> **Cues**
>
> Focus on the ball, not your opponents.
> Drop—don't toss—the ball, even under pressure.
> Remember the approach, even with opponents.
> Individual cues as needed

Tasks/Challenges:

Ⓣ Working in groups of three, two partners will assume the offensive positions of passer and punter. The other player will be the defense, attempting to block the punt. Offense: Partner 1 (the passer) throws the ball to partner 2 (the punter) from a distance of about twenty feet. Partner 2 punts the ball down the playing field. Defense: Rush the punter, starting from the twenty-foot distance at which the passer is standing, to tag the punter before the punter releases the kick. You can't begin the rush until the punter receives the pass.

Alternate positions until each person has been the punter, the passer, the defense.

PUNTING WHILE TRAVELING

Setting: Spray paint, marker dust, or milk jugs to mark distance zones approximately fifteen feet in length; a variety of balls for punting

> **Cues**
>
> | | |
> |---|---|
> | Nonstop Approach | (Take a few running steps; then punt without stopping your forward momentum.) |
> | Step-Hop | (Make your last step before contact a step-hop on your nonkicking leg, so that you'll be airborne for the punt, even with a longer approach.) |

Tasks/Challenges:

Ⓣ Run with the ball the distance to two target zones, then quickly punt the ball. Focus on accuracy of contacting the ball for forward travel.

Ⓣ Focus on making the ball land accurately in a specific zone.

Ⓣ Focus on punting for maximum distance.

PLAYING PUNT-OVER

Setting: Spray paint or marker dust to mark target zones, approximately ten feet in length; teams of four

Figure 26.20   Punt-Over

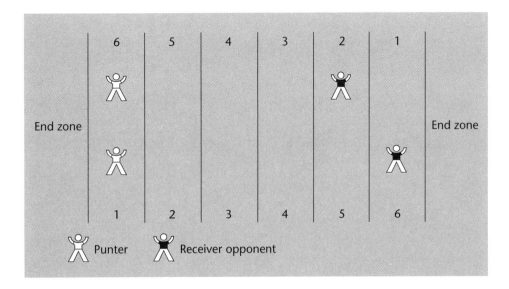

or six players; a choice of football or playground ball for each team

Cues

Individual cues as needed

Tasks/Challenges:

Ⓒ The object of the game Punt-Over is to punt the ball over your opponents so it lands in the end zone. You can play it in groups of four or six. Here are the basic rules:

1. Play begins with the punting team in their first zone; one person punts the ball toward the opposite end zone.

2. If the opponents catch the ball, they advance forward one zone before they punt.

3. If the opponents retrieve the ball short of the end zone, they punt from that spot.

4. The games consists of alternate punts; the number of points awarded for landing in the end zone corresponds to the zone from which the ball was punted (*Figure 26.20*).

The groups decide cooperatively:

1. If the defensive team catches the ball on the punt, can they run to the opposite end zone to score?

2. Can members of the opposite team rush the punter after the punter has received the pass?

READING COMPREHENSION QUESTIONS

1. What is the difference between a kick and a punt?
2. What is a mature kicking pattern? What is a mature punting pattern?
3. What kicking tasks lead to the development of a mature kicking pattern?
4. Describe appropriate kicking tasks for each of the four levels of skill proficiency.
5. At the precontrol level, why do you number the balls?
6. Where does a child's foot need to contact the ball so that it travels into the air? along the ground?
7. What experiences do children have at each of the four skill levels when they're learning to punt a ball?
8. What is the outcome when a child makes contact with the ball too soon in a punt? What happens when the child makes contact too late?

REFERENCES

National Association for Sport and Physical Education (NASPE). (1995). *Moving into the future: National standards for physical education.* St. Louis, MO: Mosby.

Throwing and Catching

Throwing and catching go together just as nicely as soup and a sandwich. The two skills, however, are opposite in movement focus and unusually difficult for young children to master.

Although throwing and catching are complementary, we've learned that children have limited success in combining throwing and catching in game situations unless each skill has been given specific attention and developed in appropriate practice situations (Figure 27.1). It is important that the teacher be certain that children can throw *and* catch with relative success before progressing to the utilization and proficiency levels. Activities at those levels—throwing to a running partner or trying to prevent an opponent from catching a ball—require mature throwing and catching skills. Too often teachers neglect catching, feeling it isn't that important. But as anyone who has ever watched a professional baseball game knows, catching is a skill, a skill that often determines whether a game is won or lost. Box 27.1 contains information on throwing and catching from the *National Standards for Physical Education.*

Levels of Skill Proficiency in Throwing

Throwing is a basic movement pattern performed to propel an object away from the body. Although throwing style (overhand, underhand, sidearm) and purpose may vary, the basic pattern remains consistent:

1. An object to be sent away is grasped with one or both hands.
2. In a preparatory phase, momentum builds for the throw.
3. The actual propulsive phase—the release of the object—is performed.
4. In a follow-through phase, the body maintains control and balance while using up the momentum of the throw.

The physical educator in an elementary school setting will observe a wide range of throwing abilities among a class. Initially, the teacher should focus on ascertaining each child's skill level. When the youngsters manipulate objects such as beanbags or yarn balls, the teacher can observe individual children for significant developmental characteristics. (See the key observation points for throwing in Box 27.2 as a guide.)

After making a gross assessment of each child's development in throwing, the teacher has a basis for structuring appropriate instructional tasks. (See our progression spiral for throwing and catching activities on page 489.)

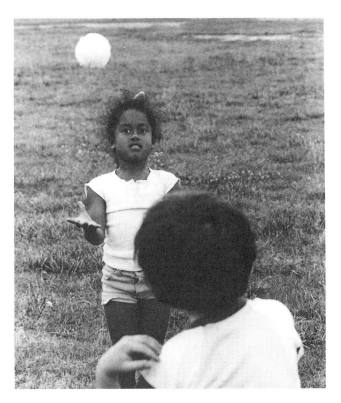

Figure 27.1 Throwing and catching complement each other and are taught together.

For children at the precontrol level, the tasks are designed to provide exploration of a multitude of throwing experiences. Many of these experiences are designed to elicit distance throws, which force children to use a more mature throwing pattern. Tasks at the level are purely explorational and include such things as:

1. Throwing against a wall
2. Catching a rolling ball
3. Catching from a skilled thrower
4. Tossing to self and catching

We expose children at the control level to various contexts so that they use throwing actions in different but relatively static situations:

1. Throwing fast/throwing slow
2. Varying the distance of throws
3. Throwing under/throwing over (a net or other obstacle)
4. Tossing a beanbag at a target
5. Throwing a yarn ball through a hoop
6. Throwing a foam ball into a basket

When children begin to focus primarily on hitting a target, they appear to regress to inefficient throwing patterns. What they are actually doing is using an effi-

BOX 27.1 THROWING AND CATCHING IN THE *NATIONAL STANDARDS FOR PHYSICAL EDUCATION*

The skill theme of throwing and catching is referenced in the *National Standards for Physical Education* (NASPE, 1995) under Standard 1: Demonstrates competency in many movement forms and proficiency in a few movement forms. The standard speaks of the child's learning the skills as simple closed skills, developing a mature motor pattern, and increasing the variety and versatility of the action.

Sample benchmarks for throwing and catching include:

▪ Tosses a ball and catches it before it bounces twice (p. 6).
▪ Throws, catches, and kicks using a mature form (p. 32).
▪ Throws a variety of objects, demonstrating both accuracy and force (e.g., basketballs, footballs, frisbees) (p. 46).

The skill theme of throwing and catching is also referenced under Standard 2: Applies movement concepts and principles to the learning and development of motor skills. This standard speaks of the child's identifying the characteristics of a quality movement pattern.

The sample benchmark states:

▪ Identifies four characteristics of a mature throw (p. 20).

---

cient pattern for accuracy—a pattern in which they control as many segments as possible and thus use as few body parts as possible. The normal characteristics of a mature throw are appropriate only for throwing for distance and speed. Asking children to use a mature throwing pattern when throwing at a close target is really an inappropriate request for the task. Generally, longer throws elicit mature throwing patterns. Therefore, it is a good idea to vary the distance of the throw, sometimes fostering success at hitting the target, other times enhancing the development of a mature throwing pattern.

Once the children are able to perform smooth throwing actions in a variety of static contexts, they're ready for utilization-level experiences. At this level, children are given tasks that encourage refinement of skills and an increase in the breadth of throwing abilities. Appropriate activities include

1. Throwing accurately while running
2. Throwing to a moving target (for example, a partner)
3. Throwing at a goal while off the ground
4. Throwing a Frisbee accurately

Children are at the proficiency level of throwing when they are able to throw effectively in unpredictable, dynamic contexts and are ready to practice throwing as it's used in the relatively complex and changing environments characterized by gamelike situations. Appropriate tasks include

1. Throwing a ball at a target (for example, as in team handball) as an opponent attempts to block and deflect the throw
2. Throwing a ball to a partner so it can be caught without being intercepted by an opposing player
3. Throwing a ball within a group of players to keep it away from another group of players.

ASSESSMENT EXAMPLES—THROWING AND CATCHING
from the National Standards for Physical Education

Peer Observations

Using an appropriate size ball, students practice throwing at a target on the wall, alternating with a partner in five-throw turns. The students should be instructed to concentrate on the critical elements of throwing as taught by the instructor (i.e., ready position, arm preparation, opposite side to the target, step with leg opposite the throwing arm, follow-through, accuracy of throw). After each bout of five throws the partner gives feedback on one of the critical elements by drawing a smiley face on a score sheet each time the element was employed as

BOX 27.2   KEY OBSERVATION POINTS: THROWING

1. Does the child take a forward step on the foot opposite the throwing arm?

2. Do the child's hips and spine rotate so that they can uncoil in forceful derotation?

3. Is the child's elbow flexed and held away from the body and extended on the backswing?

Throwing and Catching

■ **PROFICIENCY LEVEL**

Playing passball
Playing team handball (modified)
Playing four-person football
Playing Frisbee football
Playing half-court basketball (modified)
Playing Hit the Pin
Playing Keep Away
Throwing to avoid a defender
Running the bases
Playing Frisbee Stretch

■ **UTILIZATION LEVEL**

Throwing while in the air
Catching to throw quickly to a target
Catching to throw quickly to a partner
Playing Frisbee Golf
Target backaway
Throwing for distance and accuracy
Throwing to a moving target
Throwing to make a partner move to catch
Throwing on the move
Throwing and catching while traveling
Moving to catch

■ **CONTROL LEVEL**

Bench Bounce Catch
Throwing and catching over a net with a partner
Throwing and catching with a partner
Throwing for distance
Throwing a ball against a wall and catching the rebound
Catching with a scoop
Throwing a Frisbee
Throwing backhand to a target
Throwing to high targets
Throwing underhand to hoops
Bowling for targets
Hit the Can
Throwing overhand at a stationary target
Catching in different places around the body
Throwing an object to different levels and catching it
Bouncing a ball to self and catching it
Overs, Unders, and Sides
Throwing sidearm
Throwing underhand
Throwing overhand

■ **PRECONTROL LEVEL**

Tossing to self and catching
Drop—Catch
Catching from a skilled thrower
Catching a rolling ball
Throwing at a large target
Throwing a yarn ball against the wall

instructed. Note changes in performance with subsequent five-throw bouts.

Criteria for Assessment

a. Recognizes critical elements of basic movement pattern.
b. Adjusts conditions for success following feedback (p. 20).

Have partners observe the preparatory phase of a designated skill in an attempt to ascertain the correct use of critical elements. For example, student A will throw a ball toward a target five times using the overhand pattern while student B observes the performance, focusing on a single critical element during the preparatory phase (e.g., opposite foot forward, side to target, arm pulled way back). The observing student gives a "thumbs up" if the critical element is correct; if incorrect, the observing student tells what is needed to improve the movement.

Criteria for Assessment

a. Thrower displays the critical element that is the focus of the observation.
b. Observer makes an accurate judgment on the performance (p. 33).

Peer Assessment

Students are given a task of practicing the underhand throw at a target with a partner. Students may choose the type and size of ball, distance from the target (enough distance to produce a throw and not a toss), and the height of the target. Partners assist each other by marking a score sheet for accuracy for each of five throws. Partners change roles after five throws. Take as many turns as time allows.

Criteria for Assessment

a. Chooses appropriate ball and placement of target for personal competence.
b. Records partner's performance accurately and honestly.
c. Assists partner by speaking politely and taking turns.
d. Assumes personal responsibility for the results of the activity (p. 27).

Event Tasks

Have the students pretend that Rapunzel recently enrolled in your school. She knows nothing about catching a ball. Students are asked to explain what Rapunzel needs to know to catch a ball thrown to her from the front at about chest height. Instruct the students to imagine themselves practicing with Rapunzel and providing feedback after each

attempted catch. Have them imagine looking for critical elements (ready position, hand and arm position, eye contact, and absorption of force.)

Criteria for Assessment

a. Identifies critical elements of catching.
b. Uses appropriate feedback to improve performance (p. 21).

Students are requested to design a game of throwing and catching for one or two persons to play. The game must include the underhand throwing skill that has been taught in class. Students write a description of the game so students in another class could, after reading the information, play the game. They are also asked to describe how the critical elements of the skill might change when used in different conditions.

Criteria for Assessment

a. Game incorporates use of underhand throwing and catching skills.
b. Description of game adequately identifies needed skills and critical elements of each.
c. Description accurately describes how critical elements might change under varying conditions (p. 35).

Teacher Observation/Observational Record

Students are asked to receive and send a basketball pass to a partner on the move. The teacher observes the passing and uses a checklist to annotate the performance.

Criteria for Assessment

a. Receives the pass and sends it in one motion.
b. Passes ahead of the moving player (receiver does not have to stop).
c. Receiving student cuts into a space to receive the pass (p. 32).

Self-Assessment/Checklist

Following a period of working on throwing different types of objects (Frisbees, footballs, deck tennis rings) students are asked to identify the number of different objects they have thrown and the type of throwing patterns they have used with these objects. They are also asked to do a self-assessment of their throwing performance using a checklist provided by the teacher.

Criteria for Assessment

a. Recognizes difference in various types of throws.
b. Compares and contrasts throwing of different objects for different purposes.

A student teacher once embellished Throwing at a Large Target (page 494) with his own creativeness. It was Halloween, so on the target he painted the school, a full moon, corn stacks, and other autumn scenes. Did the children ever throw hard to try and hit the target once there was a little colored paint and a semblance of a drawing to aim at! You don't have to be an artist—a little tempera paint, a little imagination, and a good story to tell the children are all that it takes.

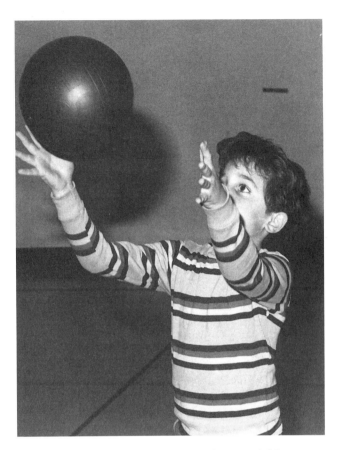

Figure 27.2 The catching abilities of young children vary.

c. Analyzes personal throwing skills accurately (p. 47).

Student Journal

Students are asked to perform a self-assessment of their progress on throwing different types of objects (e.g., Frisbee, football, softball, deck tennis rings) and record this information in their journal. Moreover, they should describe the differences and similarities in throwing these objects and discuss which objects were easy/difficult to throw.

Criteria for Assessment

a. Correctly identifies personal status on the use of critical elements of throwing.
b. Identifies differences and similarities that occur when applying principles of throwing different objects.
c. Describes which objects they found easy/difficult to throw.

NASPE (1995), p. 49

Levels of Skill Proficiency in Catching

Catching is the receiving and controlling of an object by the body or its parts. Initially, a young child's reaction to an oncoming object is to fend it off, to protect self—often by using the whole body rather than the arms and hands. Typically, a ball bounces against the young child's chest as the remainder of the body scrambles to surround it and still maintain equilibrium.

Children's catching abilities, like their throwing skills, vary immensely (Figure 27.2). The teacher who plans learning sessions in which young children manipulate soft, textured objects (such as beanbags, foam balls, or yarn balls) can observe for the developmental characteristics of catching. (See the key observation points for catching in Box 27.3 as a guide.)

The progression spiral for throwing and catching (page 489) has activities the teacher can expand while leading children from the precontrol to the proficiency level. Initially, children need experiences that let them explore the whole action of catching—trying to accurately manipulate their arms and hands into a position to receive an object. When focusing on catching at the precontrol level, we simply let children explore catching in varying contexts—with different equipment, with the ball coming from different places. At this level, it is important to note that children are often also at the precontrol level of throwing and thus have difficulty throwing an object accurately to themselves or to a partner—and an inaccurate throw is very difficult to catch. Consequently, we have found that it is helpful to find ways to minimize throwing inaccuracy. We often teach the skill of throwing before catching. More skilled throwers, such as older children or parents, and grandparents serving as teacher aides, can gently and accurately throw a ball to children who are at the precontrol level. Additionally, children can work as partners. For example, one child stands on a chair with a ball held in an out-

BOX 27.3   KEY OBSERVATION POINTS: CATCHING

1. Are the child's elbows flexed rather than extended in preparation for making the catch?

2. Does the child make the catch with the hands alone rather than by trapping the ball against the body?

stretched hand and drops the ball to the partner, who is positioned directly below, ready to catch. Children at the precontrol level generally have an easier time and experience more success when soft, textured, relatively large balls are used. The primary task for precontrol-level children is to explore the act of catching a ball thrown directly to them.

Children at the control level need opportunities to develop the skills used when catching with the right and left hands, at either side of the body, and at various levels. Appropriate tasks for children at this level include

1. Catching in different places around the body
2. Catching objects thrown to different levels
3. Moving one step in any direction to catch
4. Catching with the right hand and the left hand
5. Catching with an implement

When children are consistently able to catch a variety of objects with one or both hands, they're at the

3. Are the child's elbows extended as the catch is made so the child can absorb the force of the ball?

NO   YES

4. Do the child's eyes track the ball into the hands?

NO   YES

utilization level and can begin to use their catching skills in dynamic, unpredictable situations. Appropriate tasks include

1. Catching a passed football while traveling
2. Catching a kicked soccer ball
3. Catching a rebounding ball

Children at the proficiency level are ready to learn to catch in changing environments. They are chal-

lenged by using catching skills in combination with other skills in gamelike situations. Appropriate activities include

1. Losing a defender to catch a ball
2. Catching a rapidly thrown or hit ball that bounces against the ground
3. Catching a ball with one hand while off balance or in the air
4. Catching a ball that someone else is trying to catch

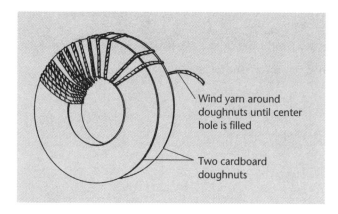

Figure 27.3   Construction of a yarn ball.

Precontrol Level: Activities for Exploration

Instructional tasks at the precontrol level give children opportunities to repeatedly explore the activities of throwing and catching. Emphasis is placed on catching throws made directly to the child and on throwing in static situations, to enable success.

THROWING A YARN BALL AGAINST THE WALL

Setting: Carpet squares about ten feet from the wall, one square for each child; one yarn ball per child (see Figure 27.3 for construction of a yarn ball)

Tasks/Challenges:

🅣 Throw the ball against the wall as hard as you can. Use the hand you hold your pencil with.

🅒 Practice until you can hit the wall three times in a row.

🅣 Practice throwing the ball with your other hand—the one you do not hold your pencil with.

🅣 This time move three steps farther away from the wall and try to hit the wall.

🅣 See how many different ways you can throw—sometimes overhand, sometimes underhand, and sometimes from the side of your body.

THROWING AT A LARGE TARGET

Setting: Several large targets suspended in various places around the room. (Old sheets work well. Attach the top of the sheet to a broom or dowel stick, and weight the bottom with heavy washers. Attach a rope

to both ends of the rod in the top of the sheet, and then hang the rope from basketball goals or rafters.) Several balls or beanbags for each child. Spaces marked on the floor about ten feet from each target for four children to throw at each target.

Tasks/Challenges:

🅣 Now you have a target at which to aim. This kind of target will soak up your ball; your ball won't come bouncing back to you. Your job is to throw at the target as hard as you can and try to make the target move. Throw all the balls you have, then bring them back and start again. Remember not to get your balls until everyone at your target has thrown and not to throw until everyone is back to the throwing space.

🅣 When you can make the target move three times in a row, take one giant step backward and try again.

🅣 Move back to your starting position, and try to make the target move by throwing with your other hand.

🅣 When you can make the target move three times, take a giant step backward and try again.

🅣 Move back to your first spot and try to throw a different way than you threw the first time. Practice that throw about fifteen times.

For children at the precontrol level, the emphasis is on providing many throwing experiences. Varying the context too early (for example, placing children in gamelike situations) causes children to use immature throwing patterns in an attempt to achieve the results called for.

CATCHING A ROLLING BALL

Setting: Partners about five feet apart; one large plastic or rubber ball per pair

Tasks/Challenges:

🅣 With your partner, you're going to practice catching the ball. You should be seated facing each other, with your legs like a V. One of you rolls the ball to the other, who catches it with the hands. The second partner then rolls the ball back to the first.

🅣 When the two of you can make five catches in a row, both of you should move backward a little and try again.

🅒 See if the two of you can make ten catches without missing.

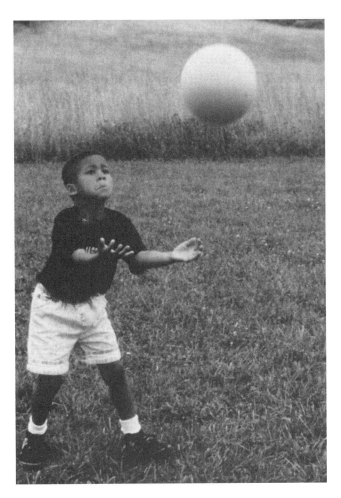

Figure 27.4 Remind youngsters to concentrate on the catching cues: Eyes on the Ball, Reach, Pull It In.

CATCHING FROM A SKILLED THROWER

Setting: A skilled thrower (older students, class-room teacher, parents, or grandparents) partnered with each child; one light, medium- to large-sized ball per pair

This activity is a wonderful way to actively involve others in the physical education program. It serves as a great public relations activity.

Tasks/Challenges:

🅣 For this task you have a "big" partner. You and your partner will stand about four to five feet apart in your own space. Your big partner will throw the ball to you so you can practice catching. When you catch the ball, throw it back to your big partner so that he or she can throw it to you again.

🅣 After you can make five catches in a row from your partner, take one giant step backward. When you

can make five more catches, take another giant step backward.

DROP—CATCH

Setting: A stable chair (one that will not move or collapse) for every pair of partners; one light, medium- to large-sized ball per pair.

Tasks/Challenges:

🅣 This is a fun task. One of you will stand on the chair and hold the ball in your hands with your arms straight out from your body. The other partner will stand close to the chair where that partner's hands and arms can be under the ball. The partner on the chair drops the ball and the other partner catches it. After five turns, switch places.

🅒 Say one letter of your name every time you catch. See if you can spell your name before missing.

TOSSING TO SELF AND CATCHING

Setting: Self-space; a yarn ball, beanbag, or light-weight ball for every child

Tasks/Challenges:

🅣 In a space by yourself, you're going to practice tossing and catching by yourself. Toss the ball (bag) very close to your body, close enough so the ball (bag) doesn't go very high over your head or very far out from your stomach. Catch it. *(Figure 27.4)*

🅣 When you can toss and catch the ball (beanbag) five times in a row, keeping it very close to your body, then toss it just a little farther away and see if you can still catch it.

🅒 This is your challenge for the day. See if you can toss and catch the ball (beanbag) ten times in a row without moving more than one step from your space.

▶ Reed and Sophie, both five years old, were playing a game in which they threw a ball under their legs to knock over a pile of tin cans. Reed placed her head a bit too far under her legs and inadvertently fell into a forward roll as she released the ball. With an expression of sheer excitement, Reed announced that she'd discovered the "flip throw."

Control Level: Learning Experiences Leading to Skill Development

Children at the control level still need practice developing mature throwing and catching patterns, yet they are also ready to focus on more complex learning experiences that still allow them to throw and catch in static situations. For example, they are challenged by catching at different levels, catching at different places around their bodies, and using either hand to catch. Throwing experiences are designed to help children learn to throw for accuracy and with varying degrees of force, and to throw a variety of objects.

A note about cues: Although several cues are listed for many of the learning experiences, it's important to focus on only one cue at a time. That way, the children can really concentrate on that cue. Once you provide feedback to the children and observe that most have learned a cue, then it's time to focus on another one.

THROWING OVERHAND

Setting: Tape marks on the floor about fifteen feet from the wall; one ball per child; children alone at first and later with a partner

Cues	
Side to Target	(Make sure the side of your body away from the hand you are throwing with is toward the wall; if you were to walk straight ahead, you would walk along the wall, not toward it.)
Arm Way Back	(Bring your throwing arm way back so that your elbow is almost above your ear and your hand is behind your head.)
Step with Opposite Foot	(Step forward on the foot opposite the hand you are using to throw.)
Follow Through	(After you throw, make your arm follow the ball. Your hand should end up almost at your knee.)

Tip: It is useful to demonstrate these cues. After the children understand them, it is easy to reduce them to one-word cues: Side, Arm, Step, Follow.

Some children have a hard time remembering which foot to step with to achieve opposition. To help these children, place an old wrist sweatband around the appropriate foot as a reminder to step with the opposite foot. You can also use a large loose-fitting rubber band for this purpose.

Tasks/Challenges:

🅣 At your own mark, practice throwing at the wall. Throw the ball overhand as hard as you can. **Remember, in an overhand throw, your arm comes above your shoulder.**

🅣 This time move three steps farther away from the wall, and practice overhand throwing.

🅣 Move back to your first spot and try to throw with your other hand—the one you don't write with.

🅒 This time you will have a partner, who is your coach. You throw three times, with your favorite hand, and your partner has to tell you if you used each of the *cues:* Side, Arm, Step, Follow. The partner gives you a thumbs-up if you did them all or a thumbs-down if you didn't. If you didn't use the cues, the partner tells you which part to practice, and you practice that two times. Then switch places.

THROWING UNDERHAND

Setting: Tape marks on the floor about fifteen feet from the wall; one ball per child

Cues	
Face Wall	(Your body should be looking straight at the wall.)
Arm Way Back	(Your throwing arm should come back behind your seat.)
Step with Opposite Foot	(Step forward on the foot opposite the hand you are using to throw.)
Follow Through	(Make your arm follow your throw straight to the wall.)

Make sure to demonstrate the throw.

Tasks/Challenges:

🅣 This time, instead of throwing overhand, you are going to practice throwing almost as if you were bowling. You are going to throw to the wall, just like before. This is called an *underhand throw.*

T Move back three steps, and practice again.

T Move back to your first spot, and try to throw with the other hand.

T Again, move back, and try to throw with the hand you don't write with.

THROWING SIDEARM

Setting: Tape marks on the floor about fifteen feet from the wall; one ball per child

Cues

Face Wall	(Your body should be looking straight at the wall.)
Arm Way Back	(Your throwing arm should come back sideways, behind your back.)
Step with Opposite Foot	(Step forward on the foot opposite the hand you are using to throw.)
Follow Through	(Make your arm follow your throw across your body.)

Demonstrate the throw.

Tasks/Challenges:

T Now you are going to try another throw. Instead of throwing overhand or underhand, you are going to throw from the side. This is called a *sidearm* throw. To do this, you bring your arm around from the side of your body. You would use a throw like this to throw a Frisbee. Remember, it's not a fling. **Let loose of the ball just as your hand faces straight at the wall.**

T After you can hit the wall eight times in a row, move back one giant step. Try again.

OVERS, UNDERS, AND SIDES

Setting: Tape marks on the floor about fifteen feet from the wall; one ball per child

Cues

Face	(Remember, depending upon your throw, your body should be looking straight at the wall or be turned sideways to it.)
Arm Way Back	(Your throwing arm should come way back behind your back, head, or seat depending upon the throw.)
Step with Opposite Foot	(Step forward on the foot opposite the hand you are using to throw.)
Follow Through	(Follow your throw.)

Tasks/Challenges:

T Now that you know the names for the three different kinds of throws, you're going to practice the throws on your own. You can practice the throws in any order you want, but make sure that you practice each one at least fifteen times.

C Here's some more practice. Pick out the throw you're having the most trouble with. Practice only that throw until you can hit the wall ten times in a row. After you can hit the wall ten times with the throw you found the most difficult, pick another throw you're having trouble with, and practice it until you can hit the wall ten times in a row.

T When you can hit the wall ten times in a row with all three throws, take three giant steps backward and try again.

 This would be a good place to include a Helping Murgatroid (see Chapter 14) exit slip that has children explain to Murgatroid how to throw correctly.

BOUNCING A BALL TO SELF AND CATCHING IT

Setting: Self-space; a playground ball or tennis ball for each child

Cues

Hands	(Always use your hands—not your arms or stomach—to catch.)
Watch the Ball	(Your eyes should be on the ball. You should see the ball as it comes into your hands.)

Tasks/Challenges:

T You're going to practice catching this time so you can get used to catching a ball that's coming down toward you. In your own space, bounce the playground ball (tennis ball) so that it barely goes over your head, and try to catch it as it comes down, before it hits the floor.

Figure 27.5 The teacher can assess catching skills by observing youngsters while they catch lightweight yarn balls.

T If you can catch the ball six times in a row, bouncing it the way that you have been, try bouncing it a little higher and still catching it using only your hands. If you have to use your body to catch the ball, you know you're bouncing the ball too high.

THROWING AN OBJECT TO DIFFERENT LEVELS AND CATCHING IT

Setting: Self-space; a beanbag or yarn ball for each child

Cues	
Watch the Ball	(Keep your eyes on the ball; see it come into your hands.)
Reach	(Reach to meet the ball; don't wait for it to come to your hands.)
Pull It In	(Pull the ball toward you so your catches are soft and quiet; give with the ball.)

Tasks/Challenges:

T This task is to give you more practice catching (Figure 27.5). In your own space, throw the beanbag

(yarn ball) up in the air and catch it. To warm up, throw the object at about head level.

T Now that you're warmed up, practice throwing the object about arm's length above your head and catching it. This makes catching a little more difficult because there's more force involved.

T Once you're able to catch the object ten times in a row using soft, quiet catches, you're ready to throw it a little higher still, maybe five feet over your head. Always remember that you must still be able to catch quietly at each level you throw to. If you can't, then you know you're throwing too high and need to bring the throw down a little.

CATCHING IN DIFFERENT PLACES AROUND THE BODY

Setting: Self-space; a beanbag or yarn ball for each child

Cues	
Watch the Ball	(Keep your eyes on the ball; see it come into your hands.)
Reach	(Reach to meet the ball; don't wait for it to come to your hands.)
Pull It In	(Pull the ball toward you so your catches are soft and quiet; give with the ball.)

Tasks/Challenges:

T You practiced catching an object that goes to different heights; now you're going to practice catching an object that goes to different places around your body. Standing in your own space, throw the beanbag (yarn ball) so you have to reach in different places around your body to catch it. This may mean catching it to the sides sometimes, or behind your head. See how many different places you can find to catch the beanbag (ball) from without leaving your self-space.

C Most of us don't like to practice places that are really hard. This time as you practice, pick out two places that you tried to catch and had the hardest time with. Practice those two places until you can catch the beanbag (yarn ball) four out of five times.

T This time practice your same catches in new places around your body. **Always try to see that the catches are as quiet as possible.**

T I'm going to make this task a little harder still. It's easy to catch the beanbag (ball) when it's fairly

▶ Two student teachers came up with a great target for Throwing Overhand at a Stationary Target. They partly filled white plastic kitchen trash bags with old aluminum cans. On the outside of each bag they drew a target and then inserted a coat hanger in the top of each bag, closed it, taped it for reinforcement, and hung each one from various things in the gym. The children loved it—the targets were big and made noise when they were hit. The cleanup was much simpler than with plates, more than one child could work at a target, and the targets were reusable.

close to your body, but now I want you to practice catching the beanbag (ball) so you have to reach to catch it. Really stretch so you feel you're almost going to fall over. It helps to think of keeping one foot glued in place all the time. You stretch from that glued foot—the foot that can't move.

🅣 Don't forget, as you're stretching to catch, to keep trying to catch in different places. So the task should be like this: stretch and reach to catch in different places around your body.

The child's success with the previous tasks depends a great deal on the child's ability to throw so that she or he has to stretch. It helps to practice stretching without the throw or simply throwing away from the body. If the students aren't catching on as you think they should, look and see if the reason is the throw.

THROWING OVERHAND AT A STATIONARY TARGET

Setting: Targets about five or six feet high on the wall, one for each student (paper plates with pictures on them make good targets), a carpet square for each child (to help maintain their spacing); a ball for each child

When drawing targets for children to throw at, we do not draw faces on the targets. Faces on targets subtly reinforces the idea of throwing at people, a violent concept we do not support in physical education programs.

Cues	
Eyes on Target	(Your eyes should be on the target all the time.)
Side, Arm, Step, Follow	(Don't forget the cues for throwing—always use them.)

Tasks/Challenges:

🅣 This time you're going to throw at targets. **You'll have to keep your eyes on the target.** Each of you has a target in your own space. See how often you can hit it.

🅣 When you can hit your target three times in a row, take a giant step backward and try from that distance.

This same task can be changed to use for underhand throwing by lowering the targets to two to three feet from the floor. The second cue would change from Side to Face, Arm, Step, Follow.)

HIT THE CAN

Setting: Partners; one ball or beanbag per pair; institutional cans stacked on benches or other objects (or on the floor) to form a can target for each pair; carpet squares as starting points

Children love this activity because of the noise. Beware of the noise level of the cans, especially if you have a tile floor.

Cues	
Eyes on Target	(Your eyes should be on the target all the time.)
Side, Arm, Step, Follow	(Always use the throwing cues.)

Tasks/Challenges:

🅣 With a partner, you're going to practice throwing at the tin cans stacked in front of you. Stand behind your carpet square as you throw. To start, one of you is the thrower, one of you the stacker. The stacker stands far enough behind the cans so as not to get hit if the thrower hits the cans but close enough to pick them up quickly if they topple. After six throws, trade places. The secret is in the stacking: The faster you stack, the faster the game goes.

🅣 If you can knock the cans over two times in a row, move your carpet square back three giant steps and try throwing from the new distance.

When practicing throwing at targets, we always try to have a throwing area for each child or group or pair of partners to maximize the number of throwing opportunities.

BOWLING FOR TARGETS

Setting: Partners, each with a target on the floor (such as several two-liter plastic bottles, weighted with sand or dirt) and a four- to six-inch playground ball

Cues

Eyes on Target	(Your eyes should be on the target all the time.)
Face, Arm, Step, Follow	(Don't forget the cues for throwing—always use them.)

Tasks/Challenges:

T With a partner, you're going to practice throwing at targets on the ground by using an underhand throw that rolls along the floor. One of you is the setter; the other, the bowler. Using an underhand throw, roll the ball and try to knock the pins over. The setter will set the pins up again and roll the ball back to you. This is like bowling. After five turns trade places.

T If you knock the pins over twice in a row, move one giant step back and try again.

THROWING UNDERHAND TO HOOPS

Setting: Partners with a hoop (on the floor between them) and a beanbag for each pair. Tape marks on the floor at various places around the hoop.

Cues

Eyes on Target	(Your eyes should be on the target all the time.)
Face, Arm, Step, Follow	(Don't forget the cues for throwing—always use them.)

Tasks/Challenges:

T This time you're going to practice throwing so your beanbag lands in the hoop that's in the middle of your space on the floor. Throw the beanbag so it lands inside the hoop. Move one giant step back each time the beanbag lands in the hoop. Your partner will collect the beanbag and throw it back to you. After five throws, switch places. Remember: The best way to do this is to throw underhand.

C A game you can play is called Around the World. Start in one place and try to hit the hoop. If you hit the hoop from that place, move to the next spot, and try to hit the hoop from there. If you miss, your partner gets a chance to toss. Whenever you miss, trade places with your partner. You can keep adding new spots to throw from as you get better.

Figure 27.6   Hoops suspended from rope as targets.

THROWING TO HIGH TARGETS

Setting: Partners, with a beanbag or ball for each pair; ropes with hoops attached strung across the space (Figure 27.6) at different heights as targets: some at chest height, others above the heads

Cues

Eyes on Target	(Your eyes should be on the target all the time.)
Side, Arm, Step, Follow	(Don't forget the cues for throwing—always use them.)

Tasks/Challenges:

T You're going to be aiming at a high target or goal—the hoops. This task will give you good practice for basketball later on. Decide how far away from your goal you want to stand. Use your overhand throw for this task.

C This time you're going to test yourself. Pick a place to stand, and see how many throws in a row you can put through the hoop (Figure 27.7). When you make eight out of ten goals, move to a new spot and try for eight out of ten goals again.

THROWING BACKHAND TO A TARGET

Setting: Individuals or partners; sticks (similar to horseshoe stakes) in the ground and plastic deck rings for each child

Cues

Eyes on Target	(Your eyes should be on the target all the time.)
Throwing Side to Target	(The side of the arm you throw with should be facing the target.)

Figure 27.7 Throwing at a large target challenges youngsters at the control level.

Arm Way across Body	(Instead of bringing it to the back, bring the arm you throw with way across your body.)
Step with Same Foot	(This is one of the few times that you step toward the target with the foot on the same side as the arm you're throwing with.)
Follow Through	(Make your arm follow your throw toward the target.)

Tasks/Challenges:

🅣 Try to throw the ring so it goes over your stick. This activity is a little different from anything you've done before, so start very close. The throwing action is also different; instead of throwing overhand or underhand, you're actually throwing sort of backward—sidearm using a flick of your wrist away from your body toward the stick. (*The teacher or a skilled child should demonstrate the throw.*)

🅣 If you can ring the stick six times in a row from where you're standing, move back a couple of steps and try it again.

THROWING A FRISBEE

Setting: Partners; one Frisbee per pair

Cues

Eyes on Target	(Your eyes should be on the target all the time.)
Throwing Side to Target	(The side of the arm you throw with should be facing the target.)
Arm Way across Body	(Instead of bringing it to the back, bring the arm you throw with way across your body.)
Step with Same Foot	(This is one of the few times that you step toward the target with the foot on the same side as the arm you're throwing with.)
Follow Through	(Make your arm follow your throw toward the target.)

Tasks/Challenges:

🅣 Now you get to practice throwing a Frisbee. The action involved is similar to the one you just did with the ring: a flick of the wrist to make the Frisbee fly. (*A demonstration is essential here.*) Practice throwing the Frisbee toward your partner, and have your partner throw it back to you. Don't worry about aiming—just try to throw to the general area where your partner is. You'll know you're getting better when the Frisbee flies flat (not tilted) each time you throw it.

🅣 Now try to throw the Frisbee so it goes fairly close to your partner. Start off pretty close together, and slowly move farther apart as you improve.

CATCHING WITH A SCOOP

Setting: Individuals alone at first, and then partners; a plastic scoop (Figure 27.8) and a beanbag for each child

Cues

Watch the Bag	(Keep your eyes on the bag; see it come into your hands.)
Reach	(Reach to meet the bag; don't wait for it to come to your hands.)
Pull It In	(Pull the bag toward you so your catches are soft and quiet—give with the ball.)

Figure 27.8   Plastic scoop. You can make scoops for throwing and catching by cutting the end and part of the side from large plastic jugs that have grip-type handles. For protection, place tape over the cut edges.

Figure 27.9   Catching with a scoop is an exciting challenge for a child at the control level.

Tasks/Challenges:

🅣 In your self-space, practice throwing the beanbag up with your hand and catching it in the scoop. To be a good catch, the beanbag must stay in the scoop and not bounce out.

🅣 Now your partner will throw the beanbag to you, and you'll catch it with the scoop (*Figure 27.9*). The partner shouldn't be very far away to begin. After seven throws, trade places.

🅣 The way you reach and pull in with the scoop as you catch the beanbag has changed a little now that a partner is throwing to you. **Instead of reaching up and pulling down, as you did when you caught from a throw you made yourself, you have to reach out and pull back.**

THROWING A BALL AGAINST A WALL AND CATCHING THE REBOUND

Setting: A wall with enough space so that the children can spread out and not be in each other's way as they throw; carpet squares as helpful reminders of self-space; one tennis ball per child; a line on the wall three feet above ground and one on the ground ten feet from the wall

Cues	
Throwing:	Eyes on Target (Your eyes should be on the target all the time.)
	Face, Arm, Step, Follow (Don't forget the cues for throwing—always use them.)
Catching:	Watch, Reach, Pull
	Get Behind (As the ball bounces off the wall, position your body so that you're behind the ball, not to the side of it.)

Tasks/Challenges:

🅣 At your carpet square, throw the ball against the wall, let it bounce on the ground on the return, and catch it.

🅣 **As you practice this time, try to catch the ball at stomach or chest level.**

🅣 As you practice now, sometimes throw the ball hard and sometimes soft so that you have to move forward and backward to catch it (*Figure 27.10*).

🅣 To make it a little harder, now try to catch the ball without letting it bounce.

🅣 Now throw from behind the line on the ground so the ball hits the wall above the line on the wall. Catch the ball as it rebounds before it hits the ground. Give it a try.

🅒 We'll make a game out of it this time. I'll time you for one minute. Count to yourself how many times you can hit the wall above the line and catch the ball in the air on the rebound. Remember the number, because we'll do it again so you can try to improve your score.

Figure 27.10 Throwing a ball against a wall and catching the rebound builds facility in both skills.

THROWING FOR DISTANCE

Setting: Partners in a large outdoor field, each pair with a bucket of about ten tennis balls; beanbags to mark where the balls land (*Often you can get old tennis balls from parents who play tennis. Send parents a note at the beginning of the year asking tennis players to save old tennis balls; collect them regularly. It doesn't take long to accumulate more balls than you need.*)

Cues

Side to Target	(Turn your hips and upper body toward your throwing hand when you pull it back in preparation to throw.)
Arm Way Back	(Pull your throwing arm way back before you begin the throw.)
Step	(Step forward on the foot opposite the hand that is throwing the ball.)
Follow Through	(Follow through toward the target, ending at your knees.)

Tasks/Challenges:

🅣 You're going to practice throwing long distances—like playing the outfield in baseball. Throw each tennis ball as far as you can. With markers, your partner will mark your farthest throw and collect the balls. Each time, try to beat your last throw. After you've thrown all the balls you have, trade places with your partner.

THROWING AND CATCHING WITH A PARTNER

Setting: Partners about ten feet apart; one ball per pair

Cues

Throwing:	Eyes on Target (Your eyes should be on the target all the time.)
	Face, Arm, Step, Follow (Don't forget the cues for throwing—always use them.)
Catching:	Watch, Reach, Pull
	Get Behind (As the ball comes toward you, position your body so that you're behind the ball, not to the side of it.)

Tasks/Challenges:

🅣 Throw the ball so that your partner doesn't have to move to catch it. You'll probably want to start with an underhand throw.

🅣 If you and your partner can make ten throws and catches from the place where you are now without missing, then both of you move back two giant steps and practice from there. Do the same thing as

▶ A baseball glove is an implement that can be used to catch an object, but generally we prefer not to use gloves in our program. When children bring their own gloves to school, there are problems. Many children prefer to not share their gloves with children who don't have gloves. We also have a hard time justifying the expense of purchasing gloves for a physical education program. In the schools we've taught in, we've always wanted other equipment that needs to be purchased and is more important than baseball gloves.

before: Make good throws so your partner doesn't have to move more than a step in either direction to catch.

🅣 Try to make sympathetic throws, which are throws that have enough force to get to your partner but are not so strong that your partner can't catch them.

🅒 From wherever you are standing, see how many throws and catches you can make without a miss. To count, the ball must be caught, not just batted back to your partner.

🅒 This time we'll play a game called One Step, which goes like this: Each time you and your partner make a catch, both of you move back one giant step; if you miss, you both move toward each other one giant step.

🅣 Change and use an overhand throw. First, just practice back and forth. When you can make ten in a row, move back two giant steps.

If children are relatively close to one another, don't expect mature throwing patterns. As the distance between the partners increases, you should start observing more mature patterns.

THROWING AND CATCHING OVER A NET WITH A PARTNER

Setting: Partners; nets or ropes between two chairs at various heights, enough for one per pair; beanbags and yarn balls

Cues

Throwing: Eyes on Target (Your eyes should be on the target all the time.)
Face, Arm, Step, Follow (Don't forget the cues for throwing—always use them.)

▶ Teachers often ask, "How do I accommodate different skill levels in one class?" More specifically, "How do I do this with little equipment?" We've found that the best way is to vary the major task for individual children according to their needs (see Chapter 13). Often you can reduce or increase the complexity of the task without substantially changing the equipment used. Consider the task of throwing a ball to a partner so that the partner is fully extended to catch. You can reduce the complexity of this task by changing the equipment from a ball to a beanbag or by having the partner use an outstretched arm as the target. Then, by changing the task so that the throw forces the partner to take a step to catch the ball, you increase the complexity of the same task.

You should make such changes by moving from group to group, observing, and modifying accordingly. In this way, the entire class is then practicing variations of the same task.

Catching: Watch, Reach, Pull
Get Behind (As the ball comes toward you, position your body so that you're behind the ball, not to the side of it.)
Thumbs/Little Fingers (When you catch over your head, make sure your thumbs are together; if the catch is low, make sure your little fingers are together.)

Tasks/Challenges:

🅣 With your partner, choose a net (rope) that you want to practice throwing and catching over and a beanbag or a yarn ball. After you've chosen your net (rope), begin throwing underhand and catching. **Try to throw so that the throw has an arch on it and your partner doesn't have to move more than one step in either direction to catch the beanbag or ball.**

🅒 See how many throws and catches you and your partner can make without missing. **Watch the object closely. Use sympathetic throws.**

🅣 If you are really good with the underhand throws over the net, change to overhand throws.

🅒 See if you or your partner can get twenty overhand throws and catches in a row without missing.

BENCH BOUNCE CATCH

Setting: Partners, each pair with a playground ball and a bench or table

Cues

Throwing: Eyes on Target and Bench (Table) (Your eyes should see your partner and the bench (table) at the same time—they are both targets.)

Catching: Watch, Reach, Pull
Get Behind (As the ball comes toward you, position your body so that you're behind the ball, not to the side of it.)
Thumbs/Little Fingers (When you catch over your head, make sure your thumbs are together; if the catch is low, make sure your little fingers are together.)

Tasks/Challenges:

🅣 Bounce the ball on your side of the bench (table) so that it travels over the bench (table) and your partner catches it. Your partner shouldn't have to move more than one step in either direction to catch the ball.

🅣 As you bounce the ball over the bench (table), sometimes bounce it with one hand and sometimes with two hands.

🅒 Try to keep the ball going back and forth as long as you can, using the bounce throw over the bench (table.) **To do this you will have to remember your quick feet.** Remember, this is a throw and catch, not a volley across the bench.

Utilization Level: Learning Experiences Leading to Skill Development

Throwing tasks at the utilization level are designed to help children learn to throw while traveling, to throw accurately at moving targets, and to jump to throw. Catching experiences include catching while traveling, while in the air, and in gamelike activities that require the ability to catch while moving in relationship to various objects and/or people.

A note about cues: Although several cues are listed for many of the learning experiences, it's important to focus on only one cue at a time. That way, the children can really concentrate on that cue. Once you provide feedback to the children and observe that most have learned a cue, then it's time to focus on another one.

MOVING TO CATCH

Setting: Individuals in self-space with a lot of extra space around each one; one ball per person

Cues

Throwing: Away, but Close (Throw away from your body so that you have to move, but don't throw so far that you can't catch the ball.)

Catching: Under or Behind Ball (Move to a position that puts you under or behind the ball, not to the side.)
Watch, Reach, Pull (As always, watch the ball, reach for it, and pull it in.)

Tasks/Challenges:

🅣 You're going to practice throwing so that you have to move to catch. Each of you has to be in your own self-space with much space around you so you don't run into others. To begin, toss the ball so you have to move just one step to catch it—put the ball just barely out of your reach. This is a skill often used in football and basketball.

🅣 Practice throwing and catching in all places around your body: forward, backward, and sideways.

🅣 I see some people catching at the same place; try to catch at different places, especially toward the back of your body.

Setting: A large area (a full-sized gymnasium or, preferably, outdoors in a large open space)

🅣 This task will take a lot of concentration on your part, not only to catch the ball, but to make sure that you do not run into or hurt others. It's fun, but it must be done with a great deal of safety. You practiced moving one or two steps to catch the ball; now you are going to practice moving a long way to catch. Throw the ball away from you so that you have to move several steps to catch it. Make the catch; then throw again so you have to move to catch the ball. Your throws should always be catchable. In other words, don't throw so far that there is absolutely no way that you could possibly catch the ball. Start out with throws that make you move only a few steps and then try longer throws. **Remember, if at all possible you should be under and behind the ball when you catch it.**

🅣 After each successful catch, see if you can throw the ball a little farther the next time. In other words, see how far you can really move to make the catch.

This would be an excellent place to use a teacher or student observation (videotape or checklist) of the critical catching cues developed at the control level. You know real learning has occurred if the children are able to catch in the dynamic situations of the utilization level using the cues.

THROWING AND CATCHING WHILE TRAVELING

Setting: Individuals in self-space with a lot of extra space around each one; one ball or beanbag per person

Cues	
	No Stopping (Both the throws and the catches should be on the move, with no stops.)
Throwing:	Away, but Not Too Far (Throw away from your body so that you have to move, but not so far that you can't catch the ball.)
Catching:	Under or Behind Ball (Move to a position that puts you under or behind the ball, not to the side.)
	Watch, Reach, Pull (As always, watch the ball, reach for it, and pull it in.)

Tasks/Challenges:

🅣 You practiced throwing that made you move to catch, but you were standing still when you threw. Now you are going to throw and catch while moving. To begin, toss the ball into the air and catch it while you walk around the space. You must be very careful while you do this and use two sets of eyes: one to watch the ball and one to watch out for other people so you don't run into them.

⚠ Mastery of space awareness—moving in relation to others—is a prerequisite to this activity.

🅣 If you can catch the ball almost all the time when you are walking and throwing and catching, try slowly jogging as you travel. Always watch closely so that you don't collide with others. (Figure 27.11)

THROWING ON THE MOVE

Setting: A large space; partners; relatively large, stationary targets (a hoop hanging from a basket, a tire hanging from a tree, a target placed on a backstop) for each pair; one ball or beanbag per pair

Cues	
Straight Pathway	(The ball should travel in a straight pathway; not curved or arched.)
No Stopping	(Both the throws and the catches should be on the move; with no stops.)

Tasks/Challenges:

🅣 With a partner, you're going to practice throwing at a target while running. Run across in front of your target, and try to throw the ball through or into your target. Your partner will give the ball back to you so you can throw again. After four throws, trade places.

🅣 Sometimes when people perform this task, they tend to run, stop, and then throw. **What you really want to be doing is throwing as you run, so the throw just seems to flow out of the run and you keep running afterward.** This time, have your partner watch you closely as you run and throw. Your partner's task is to tell you whether you stop and throw or throw on the run. Sometimes it is hard to feel what we are actually doing; partners make good observers.

THROWING TO MAKE A PARTNER MOVE TO CATCH

Setting: A large space; partners; one ball or beanbag per pair

Cues	
Throwing:	Throw Beyond (Throw beyond your partner. Pick a spot just beyond your partner and aim for it.)
Catching:	React Quickly (As soon as the ball leaves the thrower's hand, move to the spot to catch.)
	Watch, Reach, Pull (Watch the ball, reach for it, and pull it in.)

Tasks/Challenges:

🅣 With your partner, throw back and forth so that your partner has to stretch or move a few steps to catch. The idea is not to make your partner miss, but to force your partner to really stretch or move to catch so he or she can practice difficult catches (*Figures 27.11 and 27.12*).

Figure 27.11 Catching while traveling demands movement behind and under the ball.

Figure 27.12 This youngster had to move into position to make this catch.

THROWING TO A MOVING TARGET

Setting: A large space; partners; one ball per pair

> **Cues**
>
> *Throwing:*   Lead the Receiver (Throw to an open space just in front of the catcher.)
> *Catching:*   Know Where to Go (Know where the throw is supposed to go and run toward that spot.)
> Watch Passer, Then Ball (Watch the passer as you start to run, and then after the ball is thrown, track it all the way into your hands.)

Tasks/Challenges:

🕕 You're going to practice throwing the ball to your partner, who is moving. Your ultimate goal is to throw so your partner doesn't have to stop moving or turn around to catch the ball. The thrower remains still; the catcher runs away from the thrower. The thrower throws the ball to a point already decided upon so the runner can catch the ball without stopping. After six tries, trade places.

🕕 Instead of your partner running away from you, change so your partner is running across in front of you. **As before, you still throw the ball to a space in front of the runner; the runner is simply coming from a different direction.** Decide ahead of time where you are going to try and give the runner the ball.

🕕 There's one more way to practice this idea. This time the runner must be coming toward the thrower. **Again, target a space in front of the runner so that the runner doesn't have to stop and turn around to catch the ball.**

🕕 Up until now each set of partners decided where the catch was to be made. Now practice without deciding ahead of time where you'll throw the ball. This means the thrower will have to be very accurate with the throws and the catcher will have to be always on the alert to catch the ball whenever and wherever it goes. (Figure 27.13)

THROWING FOR DISTANCE AND ACCURACY

Setting: A large space; partners; one ball per pair

Figure 27.13   At the utilization level, children profit from stretching and/or jumping to catch.

Cues

Throwing: Watch the Target (Look at your partner the whole time.)
Side, Arm, Step, Follow (For long throws you really have to do all of these.)
Almost Straight (The ball should travel in a pathway that is almost halfway between the ground and straight up in the air—at about a 45-degree angle.)

Tasks/Challenges:

🅣 The object of this task is to practice throwing and catching accurately to someone far away. You and your partner need to start throwing about ten yards apart. Throw so your partner doesn't have to move to catch the ball. You want the ball to go straight to your partner.

🅣 If you can throw successfully ten times to your partner ten yards away, each of you back up two giant steps and try again. Each time you can successfully make ten throws, back up another two giant steps. Try to find your maximum distance.

TARGET BACKAWAY

Setting: A large space; stationary targets in various places (against baseball backstops, trees, or playground apparatus) around the space

Cues

Watch the Target	(Look at the target the whole time.)
Side, Arm, Step, Follow	(For long throws you really have to do all of these.)
Almost Straight	(The ball should travel in a pathway that is almost halfway between the ground and straight up in the air—at about a 45-degree angle.)

Tasks/Challenges:

🅣 The task is now to try and hit the target from far away. Start close enough so you know you can hit the target. When you hit it three times, back up about five steps and throw again. After five successful throws, back up again.

🅒 See how far you can get and still hit the target.

🅒 See how many throws out of ten you can make right to the target.

PLAYING FRISBEE GOLF

Setting: A Frisbee for each student; a Frisbee golf course: Use a hoop tied between two chairs or a hoop suspended from a tree as a target. The distance and angle of the target from the starting line can vary, depending on the amount of space available and the skill of the students. Trees, playground apparatus, fences, or backstops can be used as obstacles to throw over and around. (For a detailed analysis of Frisbee skills, write for *Frisbee: Flying Disc Manual for Students and Teachers,* International Frisbee Disc Association, PO Box 970, San Gabriel, CA 91776.)

Cues

Watch Target	(Always look at the target.)

Throwing Side to Target	(The side of the arm you throw with should be facing the target.)
Arm Way across Body	(Instead of bringing it to the back, bring the arm you throw with way across your body.)
Step with Same Foot	(This is one of the few times that you step toward the target with the foot on the same side as the arm you're throwing with.)
Follow Through	(Make your arm follow your throw toward the target.)

Tasks/Challenges:

🅣 The name of this game is Frisbee Golf, a form of golf in which you use a Frisbee instead of a golf club and ball. The object is to throw the Frisbee for distance, and often around obstacles, eventually placing it through a target hoop. You want to use as few throws as possible. Here are the rules:

1. All players make their first throw from behind the starting line.
2. Players make the second throw and all throws after that from the landing spot of the previous throw. Players are allowed to take one step in throwing.
3. Players count how many throws were needed to place the Frisbee through the hoop.

CATCHING TO THROW QUICKLY TO A PARTNER

Setting: Partners; one ball or beanbag per pair

Cues	
Move and Face	(Move toward the approaching ball and begin to face the direction you are to throw.) *It is helpful to demonstrate this cue.*
Flow	(The catch and the throw should flow together; simply move directly into the throw.)

Tasks/Challenges:

🅣 Sometimes it is necessary to throw very quickly after you catch the ball, much as baseball players do when they are trying to make a double play. With your partner you are going to practice throwing quickly after catching. Your partner will throw the ball to you; you throw it back as quickly as possible, like a hot potato. The throw to your partner

needs to be accurate as well as quick. To begin, one of you practices quick throws; the other one simply makes the first throw and is a target. After seven throws, switch places.

🅣 When most of the throws go directly to your partner, back up a few steps and try the task again.

🅣 Now, to make the task even harder, try to catch the ball with one hand and throw it with the same hand. This is almost as if you don't really want to hold the ball—as if you need to get rid of the ball quickly. You may want to use a beanbag for this task.

CATCHING TO THROW QUICKLY TO A TARGET

Setting: Partners; fairly large (two- by two-foot) targets spread around the area

Cues	
Move and Face	(Move toward the approaching ball and begin to face the direction you are to throw.) *It is helpful to demonstrate this cue.*
Flow	(The catch and the throw should flow together; simply move directly into the throw.)

Tasks/Challenges:

🅣 With your partner, you're going to practice catching and throwing quickly to a target. This skill is used, for example, in the game of team handball. Your partner throws you the ball; you catch it and quickly throw it to the target. You're trying for a quick throw so no one can block your shot. After six times, switch places.

🅒 See how many times out of ten you can hit the target. Remember: Quick throws only; ones that stop don't count. Your partner is the judge.

Many of the throwing and catching skills at the utilization level can be transformed into gamelike situations for children. Some children at this level enjoy practicing in nongame contexts, whereas others are interested in practicing only if the skill is used in a gamelike situation. Generally, these are the children who continually want to know, "When do we get to play the game?"

THROWING WHILE IN THE AIR

Setting: A large grassy space; partners; one ball or beanbag per pair

Cues

Face Target	(When you are in the air, your upper body should be facing the target.)
Follow	(Follow through to the target.)
Throw in Air	(Be in the air when you throw; don't jump, land, and then throw.)

Tasks/Challenges:

Ⓣ Sometimes when you throw, you need to be in the air. This type of throwing is harder than throwing when you're on the ground. To start, run a few steps, jump in the air, and throw the ball to your partner while you're in the air. Make the throw as accurate as possible.

Often when people practice this task, they aren't in the air when they think they are. Sometimes people run, throw, and then jump; sometimes they run, jump, land, and then throw. It's hard to tell exactly what you're doing without some help, so your partner's job is to watch you very carefully to see if you're really in the air as you throw. For now, your partner takes the place of the teacher—your partner must tell you exactly what he or she saw.

Proficiency Level: Learning Experiences Leading to Skill Development

Experiences at the proficiency level include throwing and catching in relation to an opponent who attempts to prevent the throw or the catch. These tasks foster development of consistent degrees of accuracy and distance in throwing. Children learn to catch a variety of objects while traveling rapidly and suddenly changing direction and level.

A note about cues: Although several cues are listed for many of the learning experiences, it's important to focus on only one cue at a time. That way, the children can really concentrate on that cue. Once you provide feedback to the children and observe that most have learned a cue, then it's time to focus on another one.

PLAYING FRISBEE STRETCH

Setting: A large space; partners; one Frisbee per pair

Cues

| *Catching:* | Behind and Under (Move so that you are behind and under the Frisbee when you catch it.) |

| | Watch, Reach, Pull (Watch the Frisbee, reach for it, and pull it in to your body.) |
| *Throwing:* | Throw Away (Pick a spot just barely out of your partner's reach and aim for it.) |

Tasks/Challenges:

Ⓒ This game is called Frisbee Stretch. The object is to throw the Frisbee so that your partner has to stretch to catch it. The scoring is this: If the Frisbee is caught, that counts as one point. If the body is stretched a long way while reaching to catch the Frisbee, that counts as three points. I'm going to throw a few to Mary. Let's watch to see how many points she'll get for each of her catches. (*Select a skilled catcher and throw, or have someone else throw the Frisbee so that the catcher has to stretch to make the catch.*)

Ⓒ You may want to change the way you score the game. You can work together to see how many points you can make; or you may want to play against your partner. Remember, though, that you'll have to make good throws if your partner is going to have a chance.

RUNNING THE BASES

Setting: Two teams, four players each; four bases as in baseball; one ball

Cues

Watch Target	(Your eyes should always watch the target. This time it is the chest of the catcher.)
Move and Face	(Move toward the approaching ball and begin to face the direction you are to throw.)
Flow	(The catch and the throw should flow together; simply move directly into the throw.)

Tasks/Challenges:

Ⓣ The object of Running the Bases is to throw a ball around the bases twice before a runner can circle the bases once. Here are the rules:

1. The fielding team places a player at each base—first, second, third, and home plate.

2. The player at home plate (the catcher) begins with the ball. On the signal, two runners try to run the bases before the fielders throw the ball to each base twice.
3. If the runners travel the bases before the fielders throw and catch the ball twice, they score a run. If all the fielders throw and catch twice before the runners circle the bases, it's an out.
4. After three outs *or* when all runners have had a chance to run the bases twice, the teams switch roles.

Adjust the distance between the bases according to the throwers' ability and the runners' speed.

THROWING TO AVOID A DEFENDER

Setting: A 15- by 15-foot space; groups of three; one ball or beanbag per group

Cues

Throwing:	Lead the Receiver (Throw to an open space just in front of the catcher.) Quick (Make your throw quickly, as soon as you know the receiver is open.)
Catching:	Move to Open Space (Move to a space that is at an angle from the thrower.) Watch Passer, Then Ball (Watch the passer as you start to run, and then after the ball is thrown, track it all the way into your hands.)
Intercepting:	Hips (To tell where a person is going to move, watch the hips or the belly button.) Play the Ball (Always go after the person with the ball—to force the person to pass it.)

It is very helpful to children to demonstrate the concept of moving away from the thrower at an angle of about 45 degrees (Figure 27.14).

Tip: When playing against a defense, the concept of catching changes to being able to catch while outmaneuvering the opponent. We assume that children at this point have mastered space awareness and dodging. The ability to move to an open space at an angle (approximately 45 degrees) away from the thrower is initially very difficult to understand. To get students to move away from the passer at an appropriate angle, a skilled soccer coach once provided these cues: See the Passer, See the Ball, See As Much of the Field As Possible. You may want to try using them.

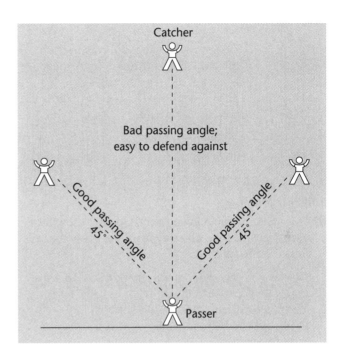

Figure 27.14 Passing angles for throwing against a defense.

Tasks/Challenges:

🅣 In this task you'll practice throwing to someone against a defense. One of you is the thrower, one is the receiver, and the other one is the interceptor. Thrower, your job is to get the ball to the receiver. **Use quick moves, and get rid of the ball when you have a chance. Receiver, move to an open space to catch the ball. Interceptor, make them throw the ball, but don't forget that you are not allowed to touch the receiver or the thrower.** After five throws, change places.

PLAYING KEEP AWAY

Setting: Self-determined space; cones for markers; groups of three; one ball

Cues

Throwing:	Lead the Receiver (Throw to an open space just in front of the catcher.) Quick (Make your throw quickly, as soon as you know the receiver is open.)
Catching:	Move to Open Space (Move to a space that is at an angle from the thrower.)

Watch Passer, Then Ball (Watch the passer as you start to run, and then after the ball is thrown, track it all the way into your hands.)

Intercepting: Hips (To tell where a person is going to move, watch the hips or the belly button.)
Play the Ball (Always go after the person with the ball—to force the person to pass it.)

Tasks/Challenges:

Ⓒ This game is called Keep Away. One of you will be trying to take the ball away from the other two. Here are the rules:

1. Decide your boundaries and mark them off with cones.
2. You can only catch the ball in the air.
3. If you get the ball, trade places with the person who threw it.
4. You may run with the ball, but you can't keep it for longer than five seconds.

PLAYING HIT THE PIN

Setting: Groups of six; two pins and one ball (Figure 27.15)

Cues

Throwing: Lead the Receiver (Throw to an open space just in front of the catcher.)
Quick (Make your throw quickly, as soon as you know the receiver is open.)

Catching: Move to Open Space (Move to a space that is at an angle from the thrower.)
Watch Passer, Then Ball (Watch the passer as you start to run, and then after the ball is thrown, track it all the way into your hands.)

Intercepting: Hips (To tell where a person is going to move, watch the hips or the belly button.)
Play the Ball (Always go after the person with the ball—to force the person to pass it.)

Tasks/Challenges:

Ⓒ The name of this game is Hit the Pin; the object is to knock over the other team's pin. Here are the rules:

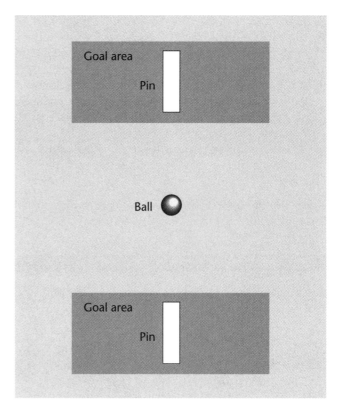

Figure 27.15   Setup for Hit the Pin.

1. There are three players on each side.
2. Players can take only two steps when they have the ball; then they must pass the ball to a teammate or shoot (throw the ball) at the pin.
3. No players are allowed in the goal area.
4. If the ball touches the ground, the last player to touch the ball loses possession. The other team begins play at that location.

PLAYING HALF-COURT BASKETBALL (MODIFIED)

Setting: Half a basketball court or comparable area around a basket; teams of three; one ball per court

Cues

Throwing: Lead the Receiver (Throw to an open space just in front of the catcher.)
Quick (Make your throw quickly, as soon as you know the receiver is open.)

Catching: Move to Open Space (Move to a space that is at an angle from the thrower.)

Watch Passer, Then Ball (Watch the passer as you start to run, and then after the ball is thrown, track it all the way into your hands.)

Intercepting: Hips (To tell where a person is going to move, watch the hips or the belly button.)

Play the Ball (Always go after the person with the ball—to force the person to pass it.)

Tasks/Challenges:

Ⓒ This is a basketball game with one exception: no dribbling or running with the ball. Here are the rules:

1. When a player has the ball, the player must shoot it to the basket or pass it to a teammate. No dribbling or steps are allowed.
2. Every player must touch the ball before a shot.

Have the children focus on traveling, with changes in direction, when they don't have the ball. When they receive the ball, have them focus on getting rid of it quickly—to a teammate or toward the goal.

SHOOTING BASKETS

In addition to throwing and catching in relation to others, the game of basketball involves a specific type of throwing at a target—shooting a basket. When children are first learning the skill of shooting baskets, the following cues will be helpful:

Preparation

- Keep eyes focused on the goal.
- Bend the knees.
- Keep elbows close to the body, not extended outward from the body.
- Place hands behind the ball, fingers (not palms) touching the ball.

Release

- "Push" the ball upward from the chest toward the basket.
- Extend legs as arms extend toward the target.
- Arch the ball upward and over the front rim of the basket.

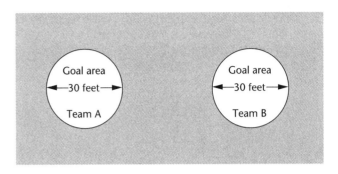

Figure 27.16   Frisbee Football field setup. There are no boundaries other than the two goal areas, each of which is thirty feet in diameter. Generally, the farther apart the goal areas can be placed, the more interesting is the game.

PLAYING FRISBEE FOOTBALL

Setting: Playing field set up as in Figure 27.16; teams of two to four; one Frisbee (alternate: a ball or a beanbag)

Cues

Throwing: Lead the Receiver (Throw to an open space just in front of the catcher.)

Quick (Make your throw quickly, as soon as you know the receiver is open.)

Catching: Move to Open Space (Move to a space that is at an angle from the thrower.)

Watch Passer, Then Ball (Watch the passer as you start to run, and then after the ball is thrown, track it all the way into your hands.)

Intercepting: Hips (To tell where a person is going to move, watch the hips or the belly button.)

Play the Ball (Always go after the person with the ball—to force the person to pass it.)

Tasks/Challenges:

Ⓒ This game is called Frisbee Football. The object is to catch the Frisbee in the other team's goal area. Here are the rules:

1. When a player has the Frisbee, he or she can take no more than three steps before passing it to a teammate.
2. A point is scored when a player catches the Frisbee in the opposing team's goal area.

3. If the Frisbee touches the ground, the team that touched the Frisbee last loses possession. The opposing team puts the Frisbee in play from that location. There is no out-of-bounds.
4. The frisbee can only be intercepted in the air. It can't be taken from someone's hands.

As you observe, you may see a need to stop the game and ask the children to practice throwing to a partner who's traveling or to reduce the difficulty by having the children practice two against two or two against one. The emphasis needs to be on leading the partner with the throw.

🅣 To make the game a little harder, this time you always have to throw to a partner who is moving.

🅣 To make the game a little easier, play two versus two or two against one.

PLAYING FOUR-PERSON FOOTBALL

Setting: A large space with goals on each end, about twenty yards from midfield (size of the field depends somewhat on the type of ball being used; children must be able to throw the football into the other team's goal area); teams of two; a foam football.

Cues	
Throwing:	Lead the Receiver (Throw to an open space just in front of the catcher.)
	Quick (Make your throw quickly, as soon as you know the receiver is open.)
Catching:	Move to Open Space (Move to a space that is at an angle from the thrower.)
	Watch Passer, Then Ball (Watch the passer as you start to run, and then after the ball is thrown, track it all the way into your hands.)
Intercepting:	Hips (To tell where a person is going to move, watch the hips or the belly button.)
	Play the Ball (Always go after the person with the ball—to force the person to pass it.)

Tasks/Challenges:

🅣 This football game has just throwing and catching, no running with the foam football. You and your partner are a team. You try to throw the ball to your partner, who's being guarded by someone on the other team. Here are the rules:

Figure 27.17 Setup for modified game of team handball. Goals can be made of stacked tires; semicircles can be spray-painted on the ground.

1. Each team has four chances to throw and catch the ball in an attempt to move the ball from their goal line to the opposing team's goal area.
2. When on offense, one player is the thrower. He or she may not move forward. The thrower tries to accurately throw the ball downfield to her or his teammate, the receiver.
3. When on defense, one player tries to stay with the receiver to block or intercept the ball. The other player remains at the location where the play starts. That player counts aloud, "One alligator, two alligators," up to "five alligators," and then rushes the thrower, trying to touch the thrower or block the thrower's pass.
4. A play is over when the ball touches the ground or when a defensive player touches the offensive player who has possession of the ball.

PLAYING TEAM HANDBALL (MODIFIED)

Setting: A large open space (see Figure 27.17 for setup); teams of three or four; a five-inch playground ball or team handball

Cues	
Throwing:	Lead the Receiver (Throw to an open space just in front of the catcher.)
	Quick (Make your throw quickly, as soon as you know the receiver is open.)
Catching:	Move to Open Space (Move to a space that is at an angle from the thrower.)
	Watch Passer, Then Ball (Watch the passer as you start to run, and then after the ball is thrown, track it all the way into your hands.)

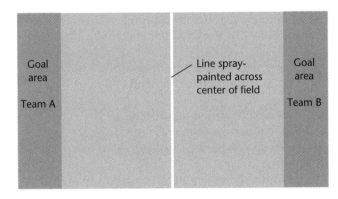

Figure 27.18 Passball field setup. Adjust the dimensions of the field according to the children's ability.

Intercepting:	Hips (To tell where a person is going to move, watch the hips or the belly button.) Play the Ball (Always go after the person with the ball—to force the person to pass it.)

Tasks/Challenges:

🅣 This game is a little like soccer because there's a goalie, but you throw the ball rather than kick it. The object is to throw the ball through the other team's goal. Here are the rules:

1. Players must stay out of the semicircle.
2. The goalie must stay in the semicircle. She or he tries to collect the ball, to prevent it from going through the goal.
3. A player who has the ball can bounce it, pass it to a teammate, or throw it toward the goal. Once a player stops bouncing the ball, he or she must pass or shoot it; she or he can no longer dribble it.

PLAYING PASSBALL

Setting: A large open space (see Figure 27.18 for setup); teams of three; any type of ball or beanbag

Cues

Throwing:	Lead the Receiver (Throw to an open space just in front of the catcher.) Quick (Make your throw quickly as soon as you know the receiver is open.)
Catching:	Move to Open Space (Move to a space that is at an angle from the thrower.) Watch Passer, Then Ball (Watch the passer as you start to run, and then after the ball is thrown, track it all the way into your hands.)
Intercepting:	Hips (To tell where a person is going to move, watch the hips or the belly button.) Play the Ball (Always go after the person with the ball—to force the person to pass it.)

Tasks/Challenges:

🅣 This game is a little like football. The object is to pass a ball to someone on your team who's in the other team's goal area. It helps to decide the type of pathways the receivers will be running before each play: straight, curved, or zigzag. Here are the rules:

1. The quarterback must remain behind the line spray-painted across the middle of the field. No defensive player may cross the line.
2. The offensive team has three plays or attempts to have successful pass completions. Then the teams switch roles.
3. A point is scored each time a receiver catches the ball. Two points are scored when a receiver catches the ball in the end zone.
4. After each play, the ball is again placed at midfield.
5. No player may purposely bump or block another.
6. All players rotate to different positions after each play.

READING COMPREHENSION QUESTIONS

1. Name the three styles of throwing. What type of task encourages children to practice overhand throws?
2. What does the term *trunk rotation* mean when throwing a ball?
3. What does throwing in a static context mean? Describe an example of a task that includes throwing in a static context and an example of a task that includes throwing in a dynamic context.
4. Why do we focus on throwing before catching?

5. Name two characteristics of an individual at the utilization level in catching.
6. What does tracking a ball mean? How can a teacher tell if a child is tracking a ball appropriately?
7. Rank the following tasks by placing the number 1 in front of the easiest (most basic) task, the number 2 in front of the next more difficult task, and so on.
   (   ) Play the game of passball.
   (   ) Toss up a beanbag and try to catch it with a plastic scoop.
   (   ) While running, throw a ball to a partner who's also running.
   (   ) Toss a yarn ball high in the air so you have to travel to catch it.
   (   ) Throw and catch with a partner.
8. What four cues do we use to remind children about the correct way of throwing a ball overhand? Explain the meaning of each cue.
9. What three cues do we use to remind children about the correct way of catching a ball? Explain the meaning of each cue.

REFERENCES

National Association for Sport and Physical Education (NASPE). (1995). *Moving into the future: National standards for physical education.* St. Louis, MO: Mosby.

C H A P T E R
28

Volleying and Dribbling

The word *volley* brings images of a high net, two teams, and the sport of volleyball, but the skill of volleying is much broader, as proven constantly by children's creative games. Games designed by youngsters, games of different cultures, and innovative equipment have opened our eyes as teachers to volleybirds, hacky sacks, bamboo balls, and balzacs, as well as to "Don't Bounce Count," "Power," and "Hand Bumping." Volleying is no longer limited to volleyball; dribbling is no longer confined to basketball.

Volleying

For our purposes, we define *volleying* as striking or giving impetus to an object by using a variety of body parts—for example, hands, arms, head, or knees. Dribbling is a subdivision of volleying. Although our discussion here is divided into two separate sections—volleying and dribbling—when teaching, you may choose to develop dribbling and volleying together. Volleying and dribbling are almost exclusively game skills and are used in such sports as soccer, volleyball, handball, basketball, and speedball. See Box 28.1 for information on volleying from the *National Standards for Physical Education.*

Levels of Skill Proficiency in Volleying

Children at the precontrol level of volleying are still struggling to achieve the hand-eye coordination required to contact the ball. They are rarely able to intentionally direct the flight of a ball when contact is made. Therefore at the precontrol level we provide a variety of activities for the exploration of volleying. Appropriate activities at this level include:

1. Striking balloons in the air
2. Striking a variety of lightweight objects
3. Striking with different body parts

At the control level, children are able to strike a ball continuously (letting it bounce) in their own space. They're able to control the amount of force that they put into the volley so that they can control the ball in their own space. At the control level, children begin:

1. Volleying balls with different body parts
2. Striking a ball using the overhand and underhand patterns
3. Striking over low nets and lines on the floor with partners

At the utilization level, children can control the direction as well as the force of their strikes. They're able, with a variety of body parts, to produce a level

surface with which to strike the ball. The children can also combine several different concepts with the skill of striking. Children at the utilization level have mastered the basic skill patterns and can concentrate on:

1. Continuously volleying with body parts
2. Playing wall and corner handball games
3. Volleying over a high net

When children are able to strike an object and simultaneously focus on the activity around them, they're able to function at the proficiency level. Appropriate tasks include:

1. Volleying with different body parts while traveling
2. Striking to targets
3. Playing competitive games involving different striking patterns

We focus on volleying as a major skill in many of our game situations. Efficient striking patterns are generally the last of the fundamental manipulative patterns to develop because of the fine perceptual and motor adjustments that the child must make. Once the child does begin to strike an object, the range of possible activities is enormous. Our progression spiral for volleying (page 520) indicates activities and experiences at various levels. The text ideas include suggestions for children at the different levels, and a range of activities and experiences within each level, stated rather directly. Remember, though, that we encourage you to modify the suggested organizational structure to satisfy your objectives (see Chapter 13).

Precontrol Level: Activities for Exploration

At the precontrol level, children need a variety of activities involving the skill of volleying. As with all skills involving sending and/or receiving an object, they will need to watch the object as it approaches (and contacts) the hand or body part used for the volley. At this exploration level, variety is the focus; contact is the measure of success.

STRIKING BALLOONS IN THE AIR

Setting: Children scattered throughout general space, each with an inflated balloon and a carpet square to designate self-space

Tasks/Challenges:

🅣 Strike the balloon upward with your open palm so it stays in the air. Try to keep the balloon from touching the floor.

BOX 28.1   THE SKILL OF VOLLEYING IN THE *NATIONAL STANDARDS FOR PHYSICAL EDUCATION*

The movement skill of volleying is referenced in the *National Standards for Physical Education* (NASPE, 1995) under Standard 1: Demonstrates competency in many movement forms and proficiency in a few movement forms. The standard speaks of the child's developing the ability to control the use of the pattern (K) and acquiring specialized skills basic to a movement form (4).

🅣 Strike the balloon high above your head. Practice striking with both your right and your left hand so you will be equally good with each hand.

🅒 See if you can volley the balloon ten times without letting it touch the floor.

🅣 Volley the balloon in the air, staying close to your carpet square.

🅒 As you volley in the self-space of your carpet square, say one letter of the alphabet for each volley. Can you get to Z?

STRIKING A BALLOON FORWARD

Setting: Children scattered throughout general space, each with an inflated balloon

Tasks/Challenges:

🅣 Strike your balloon in the air so it travels forward as you walk through general space.

🅣 Strike your balloon so it travels forward as you walk in curved pathways. Can you travel in zigzag pathways as you volley the balloon?

🅒 Travel across the gymnasium (blacktop area) as you volley the balloon forward. Can you complete your volley/travel without letting the balloon touch the ground?

STRIKING WITH DIFFERENT BODY PARTS

Setting: Children scattered throughout general space, each with an inflated balloon

Tasks/Challenges:

🅣 Keep the balloon in the air by striking it with different body parts. How many different body parts can you use to volley the balloon upward?

🅣 Volley the balloon upward by striking it with your head, then your hand. Try a combination of hand, elbow, head. Try alternate volleys from foot to hand.

🅒 Count how many times you can volley the balloon before it touches the floor. Don't use the same body part two times in a row.

🅣 Let's try a combination of more than two body parts: volley the balloon with these body parts: hand, head, knee, elbow.

🅒 Make your own combination of volleys using different body parts. You may choose a two-, three-, or four-body-part sequence.

STRIKING LIGHTWEIGHT OBJECTS

Setting: Children scattered throughout general space; a variety of lightweight objects for exploration of the volley—beach balls, lightweight plastic balls, balloons, foam balls, newspaper balls, and so forth.

▶ At the precontrol and control levels, volleying activities are best done with larger, lightweight objects, such as beach balls, balloons, or inexpensive plastic balls. They float slowly, providing more time for visual tracking. This allows children time to move under the object and volley it without the fear that accompanies heavier objects. Most equipment companies have also developed a large lightweight volleyball that provides an excellent progression between the very lightweight objects and a regulation-weight ball. These "trainer" balls are lighter in weight and larger, yet their flight is true. None of these objects work well on windy days outside, however.

Volleying

■ **PROFICIENCY LEVEL**

Playing modified volleyball
Volleying in a line formation
Spiking
Striking downward with force
Serving overhand over the net
Striking with different body parts while traveling

■ **UTILIZATION LEVEL**

Serving underhand over the net
Volleying three on three
Volleying continuously to a partner
Volleying over a net
Striking to the wall—varying levels, force, and body position
Volleying with a volleybird
Playing Aerial Soccer
Volleying with the foot
Striking a ball continuously with different body parts
Volleying game: child-designed

■ **CONTROL LEVEL**

Obstacle-Course Volley
Playing one-bounce volleyball
Playing Keep It Up
Volleying to a partner (overhead pattern)
Volleying a ball upward (overhead pattern)
Volleying to the wall (overhead pattern)
Striking over a low net (underhand pattern)
Playing Four Square, Two Square (underhand pattern)
Playing Hoop Volley (underhand pattern)
Striking a ball over a line (underhand pattern)
Striking a ball to the wall (underhand pattern)
Striking a ball upward with the forearms (the bump)
Striking a ball upward (underhand pattern)
Striking a ball noncontinuously with different body parts

■ **PRECONTROL LEVEL**

Striking lightweight objects
Striking with different body parts
Striking a balloon forward
Striking balloons in the air

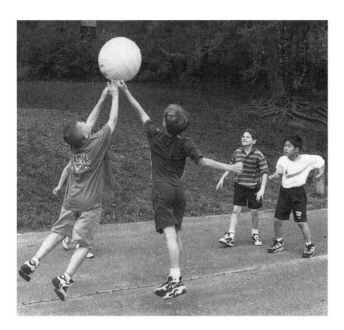

Figure 28.1 At the precontrol level, children practice volleying an object upward.

Tasks/Challenges:

🅣 You have been exploring volleying with balloons—striking them upward in self-space and forward while walking slowly through general space. Now we will try the volley with different types of lightweight balls. Select the ball (or balloon) of your choice and volley it upward in your self-space (Figure 28.1). On the signal, you will exchange that ball or balloon for a different type (rotate each two to three minutes until the children have volleyed with each type of ball or balloon).

🅣 When you begin to volley with some of the balls, you may wish to let the ball bounce after each volley; the skill then becomes "volley, bounce, volley, bounce. . . . " Remember to strike the ball or balloon upward when you volley.

🅣 Let's try one more exploration: This time the sequence will be "volley, bounce, catch; volley, bounce, catch. . . . " Are you discovering that some types of balls are better for the volley; that others require volley, bounce; and that some require volley, bounce, catch?

🅣 Count the number of times you can volley the ball or balloon before it touches the ground. Repeat the task for a second trial; remember to count your score. After two tries, switch to a different type of ball or a balloon. Which did you like best? Which one was easiest? Which gave you the highest score?

🅒 Choose your favorite type of ball or balloon to volley. Choose your type of volley: continuous volley;

volley, bounce, volley, bounce; or volley, bounce, catch. See how many times you can complete your volley sequence without a mistake.

Control Level: Learning Experiences Leading to Skill Development

At the control level, children learn an underhand and an overhead volley. They volley with different body parts, volley in relation to other people and with a variety of objects. Children at this level still find that it helps to let the ball bounce between volleys so they can gain control of the volley; they will eliminate the bounce when they are ready to do so.

A note about cues: Although several cues are listed for many of the learning experiences, it's important to focus on only one cue at a time. That way, the children can really concentrate on that cue. Once you provide feedback to the children and observe that most have learned a cue, then it's time to focus on another one.

STRIKING A BALL NONCONTINUOUSLY WITH DIFFERENT BODY PARTS

Setting: Children scattered throughout general space, each with a lightweight ball (beach ball, Nerf ball, plastic ball)

Cues	
Flat Surface	(Keep the striking surface—your leg, foot, hand—as flat as possible for contact.)
Extend to Target	(Extend upward as you contact the ball.)

Tasks/Challenges:

🅣 Strike the ball upward with different body parts: foot, elbow, upper thigh, shoulder, head, hand (Figure 28.2). Catch the ball after each volley.

🅣 Of the body parts you used for the volley, which parts can provide a flat surface for the volley? **This time as you volley the ball upward, contact the ball with the flattest surface possible—foot, upper thigh, hand.** Where is the contact surface for a head volley (Figure 28.3)?

🅒 Practice until you can do three single volleys, with a catch after each, without moving from your self-space. Practice with your foot, your thigh, your hand, your head.

Figure 28.2   This youngster experiments with using the flat surface of the thigh to volley.

🅣 Try your body-part volleys with a beach ball, a Nerf ball, a plastic ball. When you are comfortable with the upward volley, you may wish to try the skill with a playground or soccer ball.

STRIKING A BALL UPWARD (UNDERHAND PATTERN)

Setting: Children scattered throughout general space, each with a beach ball, a Nerf ball, or an eight-inch plastic ball

Cues	
Flat Surface	(Extend your hand with your palm flat, like a pancake.)
Extend to Target	(Extend your hand upward on contact.)
Quick Feet	(Move your feet quickly to always be in position to volley the ball upward.)

Figure 28.3   Volleying a ball with the head is a fun challenge for youngsters.

Tasks/Challenges:

🅣 Strike the ball with your hand, palm flat, so it travels directly upward. **Where on the ball will you need to make contact if you want the ball to travel in a straight pathway upward?**

🅣 Volley the ball directly upward so you can catch it without moving from your self-space.

🅣 Volley the ball directly upward a distance of four to five feet above your head.

🅒 Practice until you can do this underhand volley five times, never leaving your space.

🅣 Volley the ball upward continuously. **Move your feet quickly to always be in position directly "under" the ball.**

🅒 Record your personal best for today by counting the number of consecutive volleys you can complete without a mistake.

STRIKING A BALL UPWARD WITH THE FOREARMS (THE BUMP)

Setting: Children scattered throughout general space, each with a lightweight ball

Figure 28.4 Underhand striking pattern.
1. Hold ball in one hand, with feet in front-back stance.
2. Let ball bounce once. Bring hitting arm back so it's ready to hit.
3. As ball bounces back, hit it with open palm, from underneath and slightly back.

Cues

Flat Surface:	(Extend your arms forward, forearms together, to create a flat surface.)
Extend to Target	(Extend your arms upward on contact.)
Quick Feet	(Move your feet quickly to always be in position to volley the ball upward.)

Tasks/Challenges:

🅣 Toss the ball slightly upward. Quickly extend your arms, bringing your forearms together to form a flat surface. Volley the ball upward above your head so it returns to you. Catch the ball after each volley.

🅣 Toss the ball, and then volley (bump) it upward two times before you catch it again.

🅒 How many volleys (bumps) can you do without a mistake?

STRIKING A BALL TO THE WALL (UNDERHAND PATTERN)

Setting: Children spaced around the perimeter of the gymnasium, facing the wall at a distance of about six feet; a lightweight plastic ball for each child

Cues

Flat Surface	(Keep your palm flat, like a pancake.)
Extend to Target	(Extend your legs, body, striking arm toward the wall.)
Quick Feet	(Move your feet quickly to always be in position behind the ball.)

Tasks/Challenges:

🅣 Bounce the ball one time, then strike it with your open palm, underhand volley, so it travels to the wall. As the ball rebounds from the wall, let it bounce one time and then catch it (Figure 28.4). **Where on the ball do you need to make contact for it to travel forward to the wall? Right, slightly below center and behind the ball.**

Select two children who are using the correct pattern to demonstrate for the class.

🅒 Practice until you can execute the drop-hit-bounce pattern three times. Remember to catch after each sequence.

🅣 Using the underhand action, strike the ball with your open.palm so the ball contacts the wall three to four feet above the floor. Continue the volley after each bounce. The pattern will be this: volley, bounce; volley, bounce. . . . The ball will not always come back exactly to you; **move your feet quickly to be in position to extend toward the target as you volley.**

🅒 Count the number of volleys you can make without a mistake. A mistake is two bounces on the rebound or a volley that hits the ceiling.

🅣 Practice the volley with each hand. When the ball comes to your right side, contact it with your right hand; when it rebounds to your left side, use your left hand.

🅣 You have been practicing volleying to the wall by yourself. Now you are going to add a partner. The rules are the same, except after you volley the ball, the next hit will be taken by your partner. You will be alternating volleys. **Now your quick feet will really be important!**

🅒 See how many times you and your partner can volley without missing.

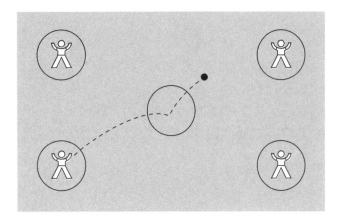

Figure 28.5   Setup for Hoop Volley.

Figure 28.6   Four-Square and Two-Square courts.

 Partner work provides an opportune time for children to observe/assess the critical cues—for example, Flat Surface, Extend to Target. See Chapter 14 for development of partner assessments.

STRIKING A BALL OVER A LINE (UNDERHAND PATTERN)

Setting: Partners; lines taped on the floor, about five feet apart

Cues	
Flat Surface	(Keep your palm flat, like a pancake.)
Extend to Target	(Extend your legs, body, striking arm toward the tape line.)
Quick Feet	(Move your feet quickly to always be in position behind the ball.)

Tasks/Challenges:

🅣 You'll be practicing underhand hits with your partner. Stand approximately three feet from the tape line and face your partner across the line. Using the underhand action, strike the ball so it crosses the line and bounces on the other side. Your partner will then volley the ball back to you so it bounces on your side.

🅣 Practice striking the ball with each hand so you will be skilled with your right and your left hand.

🅒 Cooperate with your partner to see how many times you can strike the ball back and forth over

the line. Set a personal goal for your volleys over the line.

PLAYING HOOP VOLLEY (UNDERHAND PATTERN)

Setting: Children in groups of four; five hoops and one lightweight ball for each group; arrange four of the hoops as the corners of a square or rectangle; place the fifth hoop in the middle (Figure 28.5)

Cues	
Flat Surface	(Keep your palm flat, like a pancake.)
Extend to Target	(Extend your legs, body, striking arm toward the target.)
Control	(Adjust your force to control the volley.)

Tasks/Challenges:

🅣 You have been practicing the underhand volley, striking the ball to the wall and over a line. Today you will practice striking the ball to send it to another person in your group; however, the ball must bounce inside the middle hoop on its way to that person! Remember, we are practicing the underhand pattern; that is the skill you must use in your game.

Volley the ball to someone else through the center hoop. You need to stay in your hoop, and you can volley the ball only when it bounces in your hoop or in the center hoop coming from the person directly across from you.

C See how many times you can keep the ball going without missing.

PLAYING FOUR SQUARE, TWO SQUARE (UNDERHAND PATTERN)

Setting: Children's choice: Some children in groups of four (Four Square); others in groups of two (Two Square); squares marked off on the floor for the games (Figure 28.6)

Cues	
Flat Surface	(Keep your palm flat, like a pancake.)
Extend to Target	(Extend your legs, body, striking arm toward the target.)
Quick Feet	(Move your feet quickly to always be in position behind the ball.)

Tasks/Challenges:

C Stand outside your assigned square. Serve the ball by dropping it and hitting it underhand after the bounce. The server can hit the ball to any of the other three courts (Four Square). The player receiving the ball must keep it in play by striking the ball with an underhand hit to any square. Play continues until one player fails to return the ball or commits a fault. Faults include hitting the ball sidearm or overhand, stepping in another square to play the ball, catching the ball, and letting the ball touch any part of the body other than the hands. After each mistake, rotate positions and servers. (*Use two squares for a two-person game.*)

T Play your game cooperatively by counting the number of volleys made by your group before a mistake. Hit the ball so the person will be in the best position to contact the ball.

T Play the game competitively by changing force and angles of travel for the ball; however, the volley must be underhand—no sides, no overs. **The receiver will really need quick feet to move into position for the volley.**

STRIKING OVER A LOW NET (UNDERHAND PATTERN)

Setting: Partners; nets at varying heights (lower standard nets or improvise nets from ropes: Figure 28.7) throughout the gym; one lightweight ball for each pair

Figure 28.7 Construction of a net. Suspend a rope between two chairs.

Cues	
Flat Surface	(Keep your palm flat, like a pancake.)
Extend to Target	(Extend your legs, body, striking arm toward the target.)
Quick Feet	(Move your feet quickly to always be in position behind the ball.)

Tasks/Challenges:

T You have practiced the underhand volley against the wall and over a line on the floor. Now you are ready to use the same skill to send the ball over a net to a partner. The server bounces the ball one time and then sends it over the net with the underhand volley. The partner returns the volley after the ball bounces one time.

C When you are ready, keep a collective score of how many volleys you and your partner can do before making a mistake.

T Slant your net from high to low, and repeat the skill, volleying the ball over the net at differing heights.

T Practice varying the force with which and the angles at which you volley the ball to your partner. Remember, the ball must bounce one time on each side before the contact.

C Based on your scores from the collective game, set a personal goal and see if you and your partner can attain that goal for the underhand volley over the net. Remember to volley the ball so your partner will always be in the best position for the return.

T Challenge your partner to a competitive game of volleys over the net. Add to the challenge with changes in force and angles; however, the hit must be the underhand volley you have practiced.

VOLLEYING TO THE WALL (OVERHEAD PATTERN)

Setting: Lines taped on the wall, at heights of five to seven feet; a lightweight ball or beach ball for each child

Cues	
Crab Fingers	(Curl your fingers for contact on the pads.)
Bend and Extend	(Bend your knees in preparation; extend your legs and arms upward on contact.)
Quick Feet	(Move your feet quickly to be in position behind and under the ball for contact.)

Tasks/Challenges:

🅣 Stand approximately four feet from the wall at the tape height you choose. Toss the ball slightly in front and above your head, then volley it to the wall with both hands. Catch the ball after the volley and begin again.

Select two children who are contacting the ball with their fingerpads and using their legs for the force of the volley to demonstrate the key concepts of the skill. Point out the critical cues to the children as they are demonstrated.

🅒 Practice until you can execute three overhead volleys to the wall without catching the ball or letting it drop below the tape line.

🅒 Count the number of volleys you can hit to the wall above the tape line. Remember, the volley must be with two hands; don't catch the ball.

VOLLEYING A BALL UPWARD (OVERHEAD PATTERN)

Setting: Children scattered throughout general space, each with either a beach ball or a lightweight plastic ball

Cues	
Crab Fingers	(Curl your fingers for contact on the pads.)
Bend and Extend	(Bend your knees in preparation; extend your legs and arms upward on contact.)
Quick Feet	(Move your feet quickly to always be in position under the ball.)

Tasks/Challenges:

🅣 Using your fingerpads, volley the ball upward above your head so the ball returns directly to you. Catch the ball after each volley.

🅣 Toss the ball upward, and then volley it one time two to three feet above your head.

🅣 Toss and then volley the ball upward two times before you catch it.

🅒 How many times can you volley the ball before it touches the ground?

🅣 Toss and then volley the ball from medium level: Let the ball drop until it's three to four feet from the floor; then volley. This really requires you to bend your knees!

🅒 Now that you know how to volley the ball at a lower level, count the number of times you can volley before the ball touches the floor.

VOLLEYING TO A PARTNER (OVERHEAD PATTERN)

Setting: Sets of partners scattered throughout general space; one lightweight ball for each set of partners

Cues	
Crab Fingers	(Curl your fingers for contact on the pads.)
Bend and Extend	(Bend the knees in preparation; extend the legs and arms upward on contact.)
Quick Feet	(Move your feet quickly to always be in position under the ball.)

Tasks/Challenges:

🅣 Stand three to four feet from your partner. Using the overhead skill you just learned, volley the ball back and forth to your partner. Each of you gets two hits on your side: Volley the ball first to yourself for control and then to your partner.

🅣 When you are comfortable with two volleys per side, try doing the task with only one hit per side.

🅒 On the signal, begin your partner volleys. I will time you for thirty seconds. Try to continue without a mistake for the entire time . . . and beyond!

PLAYING KEEP IT UP

Setting: Groups of four or five children (the smaller the group, the more participation/practice of the skill each child gets); a lightweight ball (or a volleyball trainer—a larger, lightweight volleyball) for each group

Cues	
Crab Fingers	(Curl your fingers for contact on the pads.)
Bend and Extend	(Bend the knees in preparation; extend the legs and arms upward on contact.)
Quick Feet	(Move your feet quickly to always be in position under the ball.)

Tasks/Challenges

T The object of the game Keep It Up is to see how many times your team can volley the ball before it touches the ground. There are only two rules: A player cannot hit the ball twice in a row, and the hit must be the overhead volley. Practice several times; then count your team volleys.

T Continue your cooperative volleys with your team, this time calling out the volley number as you contact the ball.

T This time, as your group plays Keep It Up be sure each person in the group does a volley before anyone takes a second turn.

C As a group, set a goal for the number of volleys you wish to attain, then play the game to see if you can reach that number without a mistake.

Keep It Up can be played with the forehand volley (the bump) or with a combination of the bump and the overhead volley.

PLAYING ONE-BOUNCE VOLLEYBALL

Setting: Children in teams of equal numbers (three or four per team) on either side of a low net; a lightweight ball that will bounce

Cues	
Bend and Extend	(Bend the knees in preparation; extend the legs and arms upward on contact.)
Quick Feet	(Move your feet quickly to always be in position under the ball.)

Tasks/Challenges:

T A player begins the game by bouncing the ball one time and striking it over the net with an underhand serve (much like the underhand volley action). The receiving team may let the ball bounce one time before hitting it back (or may volley the ball with no bounce). Only one bounce is permitted before the ball is volleyed back over the net; however, any number of players may volley the ball before it crosses the net. You may use either the overhead volley (crab fingers) or the forearm volley (the bump). The serving team scores a point when the receiving team fails to return the ball over the net within bounds or when the ball bounces more than one time.

OBSTACLE-COURSE VOLLEY

Setting: Prior setup: See Figure 28.8 for an example of a volley obstacle course. Once the course is ready, the class pretty much runs itself. Challenges in the obstacle course can require a student to use a number of different volleying skills. It may be helpful to provide a number of different objects to volley, to allow for differences in skill development.

Tasks/Challenges:

C Work your way through the course, following the instructions at each station. (*This activity was adapted from Mustain, 1990.*)

Utilization Level: Learning Experiences Leading to Skill Development

For continuing skill development in volleying, children must develop consistency and accuracy. They should be able to use various body parts to volley and to move in relationship to other people and objects. Strategic placement skills in a relatively stable situation are developed at the utilization level.

A note about cues: Although several cues are listed for many of the learning experiences, it's important to focus on only one cue at a time. That way, the children can really concentrate on that cue. Once you provide feedback to the children and observe that most have learned a cue, then it's time to focus on another one.

VOLLEYING GAME: CHILD-DESIGNED

Setting: A variety of lightweight balls; paper and pencils for children to record their games

Figure 28.8 Setup for Obstacle-Course Volley.

Source: Adapted from *A Manual of Physical Education Skill Theme Activities for Physical Education Specialists to Use in Collaboration with Classroom Teachers*, an unpublished master's project by Wendy Mustain, 1990, Blacksburg: Virginia Polytechnic Institute and State University. Used with permission.

Volley with hands while walking the length of the beam.

STOP! Volley from one hand to the other 10 ×.

Practice volleying using at least four different body parts.

(carpet squares)

Walk, volleying continuously while changing levels.

(jump ropes)

Volley while traveling in different pathways—zigzag and curved.

(jump ropes)

Can you sign your name with one hand and volley with the other simultaneously?

(taped X's)

Practice continuous volleying while turning 360°, touching toes, and/or doing a heel slap.

(table with paper and pencils)

STOP! Volley 10 × with eyes closed.

Walk, volley only with your nondominant hand.

(hoops)

Cues

Flat Surface	(for underhand volley) (Keep your palms flat, like a pancake.)
Extend to Target	(Extend your legs, body, striking arm towards the target.)
Quick Feet	(Move your feet quickly to always be in position under the ball.)

Tasks/Challenges:

T Earlier in our work you practiced striking the ball against the wall and over a line using the underhand volley—striking with an open palm. You are very good at that volley. Today you will use that skill in a game situation. Your task is to design an original game for two partners or a small group to provide practice of the underhand volley in a dynamic, "on-the-move" situation. You can design your game so it can be played against the wall or over a line on the floor. Remember, the focus is the underhand volley; your game must use that skill. You will need to decide the following:

1. Will your game be against the wall or over a line?
2. Will the game be cooperative or competitive?
3. Will you keep score?
4. How does a player score a point?
5. Will the game be played with a partner or in a small group? (*Not more than three.*)
6. What are the boundaries?
7. What are the rules?

Record your game on a piece of paper so you can refer to it later and others in the class can learn how to play it. You may give your game a name if you want to (*Figure 28.9*).

Children not experienced in designing games will need more direction from the teacher and fewer opportunities to make decisions; for example, the teacher decides whether the game is against the wall or over a line and whether the game is cooperative or competitive.

 This is an excellent time for teacher and/or student assessment (observation checklist, videotape analysis) of the critical cues practiced at the control level. True mastery comes when children can use the elements correctly in a dynamic, unpredictable situation. See Chapter 14 for assessment examples.

STRIKING A BALL CONTINUOUSLY WITH DIFFERENT BODY PARTS

Setting: Children scattered throughout general space, each with an object suitable for the volley—plastic ball, soccer ball, playground ball, hacky sacks

Cues

Flat Surface	(Keep the body part as flat as possible for contact.)
Bend and Extend	(Bend your knees to be in position for the head volley; extend upward on contact.)
Quick Feet	(Move your feet quickly to always be in position under the object.)

Tasks/Challenges:

T Volley the ball (hacky sack) from your thigh to your foot by striking it with your upper thigh and then with the top of your foot. Catch the ball (hacky sack) after the volley from your foot.

WHAT IS A HACKY SACK?

▶ A very popular game that has come into being in the past few years is Hacky Sack. Hacky sacks are small leather-covered beanbag-type balls. The game requires a great deal of skill but delights children and adults for hours. Utilization- and proficiency-level children will enjoy using a hacky sack at times instead of a ball. Hacky sacks are relatively inexpensive and are great on the playground or field trips.

T Practice with your right leg and foot as well as with your left. You want to be equally skilled with both.

T When you are comfortable with the volley from your thigh to your foot (three times with no mistakes), add your head: In other words, volley the ball (hacky sack) from your head—this is called heading in soccer—to your thigh to your foot or from your head to your foot to your thigh.

T Now choose any three body parts to keep the ball (hacky sack) going. See if you can keep it going from part to part without letting it touch the ground.

C This time you are going to see how well you can use different body parts for consecutive volleys. Choose the three body parts with which you like to volley. Try to keep the ball (hacky sack) going with your three parts. Can you keep it going for fifteen seconds? Thirty seconds? One minute?

VOLLEYING WITH THE FOOT

Setting: Children scattered throughout general space, with access to beach balls, vinyl balls, and/or playground balls

Cues

Flat Surface	(Make the inside, outside, top of your foot as flat as possible for the contact.)

Tasks/Challenges:

T Volley the beach ball with your foot, keeping the ball in the air for several contacts. Use the inside, outside, and top of your foot and your heel to send the ball upward.

T If consecutive volleys with the beach ball are easy, try the vinyl or the playground ball.

C On the signal, begin your foot volley. I'll give the count each ten seconds; keep the ball in the air as long as possible.

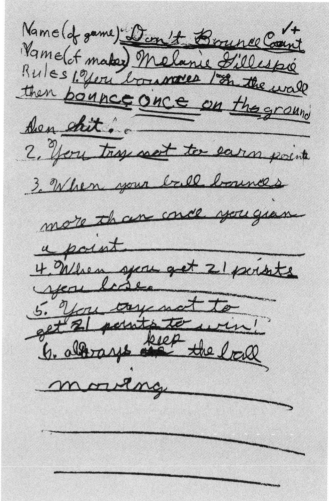

Figure 28.9 Child-designed games against the wall (Don't Bounce Count; Power) and over a line (Hand Bumping).

PLAYING AERIAL SOCCER

Setting: Children scattered throughout general space, with six-inch woven bamboo balls (or balls similar in texture, size, and weight)

Cues

Flat Surface	(Make the foot surface as flat as possible for the contact.)
Bend and Extend	(Bend the knees to be in position for the head volley; extend the legs and body upward on contact.)
Quick Feet	(Move your feet quickly to always be in position for a good volley—under and/or behind the ball.)

Tasks/Challenges:

🅣 Practice your skills of heading, foot volleys, aerial kicks, and foot-to-head volleys with the bamboo ball. When you feel comfortable with the individual skills of Aerial Soccer and can keep the ball aloft for at least ten seconds, you can play a game of Aerial Soccer with a partner or in a small group. The ball must stay aloft at all times. You will need to decide the following:

1. Is the game to be cooperative or competitive?
2. How many will be in the group? (*Not more than six—three on three.*)
3. Will you play in self-space or travel in general space?
4. What boundaries do you need?

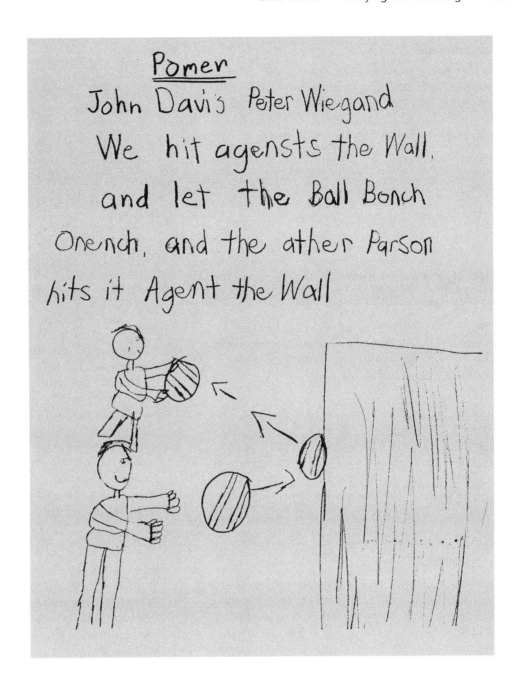

Pomer

John Davis Peter Wiegand

We hit agensts the Wall.

and let the Ball Bonch

Onench, and the ather Parson

hits it Agent the Wall

This game was observed at Regents Park in London, England. It's exciting for observers to watch and challenging for highly skilled soccer players.

VOLLEYING WITH A VOLLEYBIRD

Volleybirds are flat-bottomed shuttlecocks that have been used in Taiwan for centuries. The volleybirds are volleyed with different body parts, including hands, thighs, the instep of the foot, and the inside and outside of the foot. Because the volleybirds are flat bottomed, they can also be caught on different body parts. Young children find these relatively slow moving and brightly colored "birds" very attractive.

Setting: Children scattered in general space, each with a volleybird

Cues	
Flat Surface	(Make your hand, thigh, foot surface as flat as possible for the contact.)
Quick Feet	(Move your feet quickly to always be in position for the volley—under the volleybird.)

Tasks/Challenges:

T See how many times in a row you can strike the volleybird before it touches the ground. Start with one hand; then try your other hand. Other body parts you can use are your thigh, the instep of your foot, or the inside or outside of your foot.

C Make up a sequence that uses three different body parts. See if you can repeat the sequence without a miss.

STRIKING TO THE WALL—VARYING LEVELS, FORCE, AND BODY POSITION

Setting: Lines marked on the wall at heights of three and seven feet; a variety of balls for a combination of volleying and bouncing (plastic balls, playground balls, tennis balls)

Cues	
Flat Surface	(Flat/open palm for contact.)
Extend to Target	(Extend your legs, striking arm, and body toward the target.)
Quick Feet	(Move your feet quickly into position for the volley.)

Tasks/Challenges:

T Strike the ball to the wall between the three- and seven-foot tape marks so the ball contacts the wall at different levels. Strike the ball so it sometimes hits the wall at a high level, just below the seven-foot mark, and sometimes at a low level, just above the three-foot mark.

T Vary your striking action; sometimes use an underhand strike, sometimes an overhead one.

T Vary the amount of force you hit the ball with. Sometimes hit the ball hard so it rebounds far from the wall; sometimes use just enough force to get the ball within the tape zones. How will the ball rebound this time? Right—close to the wall.

T Strike the ball from different positions in relation to your body. Contact the ball while it's high over your head, close to the floor, on your right side, on your left side. Being able to contact the ball from different positions is important in game situations when you don't always have enough time to get in position.

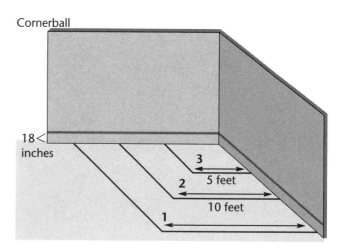

Cornerball

Figure 28.10   Setup for Hand Corner Ball.

T With a partner play handball. Your target is the area between the three- and seven-foot tape marks. Try to strike the tennis (plastic) ball to the wall so your partner can't return the shot. Challenge your partner to a game of fifteen points.

Each time you select a partner, both of you should agree on the rules, including the outside boundaries, type of hits, how to keep score, and number of bounces permitted on the rebound. Possible rules include alternating hits and hitting the ball to a certain space on the wall.

T With a group of two or four, play Hand Corner Ball. (*See Figure 28.10 for court setup.*) The rules are these:

1. It can be a singles or a doubles game.
2. You serve by dropping the ball and underhand-volleying it against the wall.
3. The ball must contact the wall above the eighteen-inch line and rebound back into one of the three activity zones.
4. Volleying alternates between teams. In doubles play, it also alternates between players. So, if player 1 on team A serves and player 1 on team B returns it, player 2 on team A takes the next volley.
5. If a team is unable to return the ball, the other team earns the number of points of the zone in which the ball landed. If a ball is mis-hit, the other team gets one point.
6. A game is fifteen points.

VOLLEYING OVER A NET

Setting: Nets at a seven-foot height; a variety of beach balls, eight-inch plastic balls, and volleyball trainers

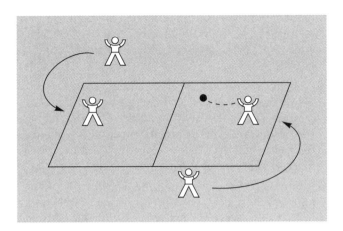

Figure 28.11   Two-person running volley.

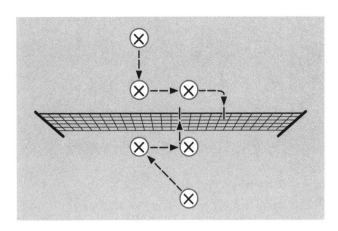

Figure 28.12   Three-on-three volleys: two patterns.

Cues

Crab Fingers	(Curl your fingers for contact on the pads.)
Bend and Extend	(Bend your knees in preparation; extend your legs and arms on contact.)
Quick Feet	(Move your feet quickly to be in position under and behind the ball.)

Tasks/Challenges:

T Select a partner; stand on either side of the net, and face each other. Partner 1 tosses the ball over the net; partner 2 volleys the ball back over the net to partner 1 with the two-hand overhead hit. Partner 1 catches the ball and then tosses again. After ten tries, partner 2 tosses, and partner 1 volleys.

T Volley the ball so your partner can catch it without moving from self-space.

T For this task, you will need four people, two on each side of the net. One of you will be on the court, and the other waits behind the end line. The activity is almost the same as the last one, with one exception: After you hit the ball, you run off the court, and the person behind comes up to return the shot. Then, that person runs off the court, and you come back on (Figure 28.11). The game goes very quickly, so you must be ready to move as soon as your partner hits the ball.

T Now that you understand the basics of the activity, let's make one change: You may choose to let the ball bounce on your side and then use an underhand volley (the bump), or you may choose to take the volley before the bounce with an overhead volley. **Remember the cue for the underhand volley—Flat Surface with Forearms.**

VOLLEYING CONTINUOUSLY TO A PARTNER

Setting: Nets at seven-foot height; a variety of beach balls, eight-inch plastic balls, and volleyball trainers

Cues

Crab Fingers	(Curl your fingers for contact on the pads.)
Bend and Extend	(Bend your knees in preparation; extend your legs and arms on contact.)
Quick Feet	(Move your feet quickly to be in position under and behind the ball.)

Tasks/Challenges:

T Partner 1 tosses the ball slightly above the head, then volleys the ball over the net to partner 2. Partner 2 volleys the ball back over the net. Continue to volley, using the overhead volley for balls at both high and medium levels.

C Set a personal best goal with your partner. See if you can attain that goal. Give your partner your best volley each time.

The above tasks/challenges can be used for continuous volleys with the underhand volley (the bump) or a combination of overhead and underhand volleys. Review with the children the differences between the critical cues for the overhead and the underhand volleys.

VOLLEYING THREE ON THREE

Setting: Children in groups of six, with three on each side of the net (Figure 28.12).

Cues

Crab Fingers	(Curl your fingers for contact on the pads.)
Bend and Extend	(Bend your knees in preparation; extend your legs and arms on contact.)
Quick Feet	(Move your feet quickly to be in ready position for the ball.)

Tasks/Challenges

🅣 Use only the overhand volley to hit the ball in the air three times on your side of the net. On the third contact, volley the ball over the net to the other team. Each team volleys the ball three times, sending it over the net on the third hit. A different player makes each one of the three hits.

🅣 Rotate positions, so that you hit the ball from different places.

🅒 Work cooperatively to keep the ball in the air as long as possible. Remember: three hits per side, one hit per person.

🅒 Challenge the other team to a three-on-three game. Rather than cooperating to keep the ball in the air, use strategies to outscore the other team. Rather than just hitting the ball over the net, direct it to a certain location; vary the amount of force on the volley, sometimes sending it just over the net, sometimes sending it deep into the court. A point is scored when the ball hits the floor or lands out of bounds.

SERVING UNDERHAND OVER THE NET

Setting: Lines marked on the wall seven feet from the floor; nets at a seven-foot height; plastic balls and volleyball trainers

Cues

Watch the Ball	(Watch the ball until the striking arm contacts it.)
Extend to Target	(Extend the striking arm toward the target—over the net.)

Tasks/Challenges:

🅣 You learned the underhand action of striking the ball with your open palm, swinging your arm forward/backward, stepping forward on your opposite foot, and contacting the ball slightly below center and back. Now you're going to learn the under-hand action of a volleyball serve. Stand ten to fifteen feet from the wall; serve the ball to the wall; your target is the area just above the seven-foot tape line.

🅣 I'll walk around and observe the underhand action of your serve. When it's correct and you feel successful, select a partner for practice over the net. Partner 1 stands ten to fifteen feet from the net and serves the ball over the net. Partner 2 retrieves the ball and then serves it back over the net.

🅣 After you feel successful serving over the net, your partner will select a position on the court and stand in that spot. Serve the ball away from your partner so your partner can't catch the ball without moving from self-space.

The last task may seem a bit backward from "what has always been done." It is. When children begin by "serving" to a partner, they tend to do the same thing in a game situation—the exact opposite response from the one required. This way, we get them to practice serving to an open space early on.

Proficiency Level: Learning Experiences Leading to Skill Development

Children at the proficiency level should be able to move consistently and accurately in relation to others and to react effectively to increasingly dynamic and unpredictable situations. They can simultaneously focus on volleying and on the game activity around them.

A note about cues: Although several cues are listed for many of the learning experiences, it's important to focus on only one cue at a time. That way, the children can really concentrate on that cue. Once you provide feedback to the children and observe that most have learned a cue, then it's time to focus on another one.

STRIKING WITH DIFFERENT BODY PARTS WHILE TRAVELING

Setting: A variety of lightweight balls: eight-inch plastic, Nerf, volleyball trainers

Cue

Quick Feet	(Move your feet quickly to always be in position to volley the ball.)

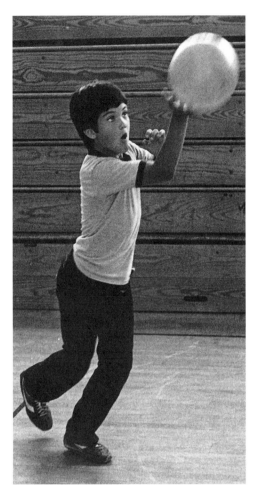

Figure 28.13 Striking a plastic ball upward while traveling requires visual tracking.

Figure 28.14 Target areas for serving.

Tasks/Challenges:

🅣 Travel the length of the gym, volleying the ball with different body parts as you go (Figure 28.13). Don't catch the ball at any time, and don't let it touch the floor.

🅣 Select a partner. Travel throughout general space, volleying the ball back and forth with different body parts. Both of you should always be moving.

🅣 This time as you travel and volley with your partner, vary the level of the volley—sometimes high, sometimes medium level.

SERVING OVERHAND OVER THE NET

Setting: Nets at a seven-foot height; the court on one side of each net divided into four areas, using tape or chalk to mark divisions (Figure 28.14), and

each of the target areas numbered; a variety of light-weight balls—plastic, Nerf, volleyball trainers—for partner practice

Cues	
Good Toss	(Toss the ball slightly in front of and above your head.)
Watch the Ball	(Watch the ball until your hand makes contact.)

Tasks/Challenges:

🅣 Earlier you learned an underhand striking action that can be used as a serve in volleyball. However, when you watch a skilled volleyball team, you will notice they serve with an overhand striking action. The opponents have less time to get ready for this serve because it travels with less of an arch.

Stand fifteen to twenty feet from the net, and face a partner on the opposite side of the net. With your nonstriking hand, toss the ball slightly above your head. Contact the ball directly behind center with the heel or palm of your hand, so the ball travels just above the net to the opposite side. Your partner will retrieve the ball and then serve it back to you. (*Demonstrate toss of ball, arm action, forward-backward stance.*)

🅣 Tell your partner where to stand in the opposite court. Serve the ball so your partner can catch it without moving from self-space.

🅣 Now serve the ball so your partner must move from self-space to catch—serve not to the person, but to the open space.

🅣 Stand fifteen to twenty feet from the net and serve the ball into each target area.

🅒 Practice serving to each target area until you can successfully serve four out of five tries to each area. Practice both your underhand and your overhead serve.

🅣 Stand fifteen to twenty feet from the net (behind the serving line). Verbally call the number of the zone to which you are going to serve. Strike the ball to that zone.

STRIKING DOWNWARD WITH FORCE

Setting: Tape lines on the wall at about ten and two feet from the floor; a variety of lightweight balls for individual practice

Cues	
Quick Feet	(Move your feet quickly to always be in position to volley the ball; transfer your weight forward as you volley.)
Up, Up, Up, Down: Soft, Soft, Soft, Hard!	(Volley the ball up, up, up, down; soft, soft, soft, hard.)

Tasks/Challenges:

🅣 Standing ten to twelve feet from the wall, begin volleying the ball between the tape lines, using the underhand pattern; you may or may not include a bounce with the volleys. After several volleys, strike the ball on top so it travels downward to the wall, contacting the wall just above the two-foot tape line. Contact the ball with your hand slightly cupped. (*Demonstrate.*).

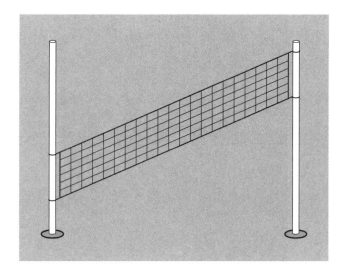

Figure 28.15   A slanted net for children who are learning to spike the ball.

🅣 Practice a pattern of three underhand volleys followed by a downward hit with force.

🅒 Challenge a partner to a handball game against the wall. Throughout the game, use a combination of forceful downward hits and underhand volleys.

🅒 Challenge the same partner to a competitive two-square game over a line. Use the forceful downward striking to create situations that move your partner/opponent out of position, making a good return more difficult.

SPIKING

Setting: Sets of partners scattered throughout general space; slanted nets (Figure 28.15) with cones to mark target area; a variety of lightweight balls

Cues	
Step Jump	(Take one step and jump high with a two-foot takeoff.)
Bend and Extend	(Bend the striking arm in preparation; extend toward the target on contact with the ball.)
Contact High, Hit Hard!	(Jump high in the air, striking the ball downward with force.)

Tasks/Challenges:

🅣 Spiking is hitting the ball downward in volleyball. It takes a lot of practice to learn to spike effectively.

We are going to begin our practice with a partner. Select a partner, and scatter throughout general space, away from the nets; we will use them later. Partner 1 tosses the ball upward. Partner 2 jumps into the air with a spring takeoff (*Jumping and Landing, Chapter 22*), and with an overhand hit tries to hit the ball toward the ground when it is still overhead. The secret to the spike is to contact the ball as high as possible. (*Select two children to demonstrate.*)

🅣 When you and your partner can spike the ball consistently (four of five times), move over to a net and continue your practice.

🅣 Now try to spike over the net and into the target area marked by the cones.

VOLLEYING IN A LINE FORMATION

Setting: Tape marks on the wall at a height of about seven feet; groups of four, each in a line formation facing the wall and three to four feet from it; a variety of lightweight balls (eight-inch plastic, Nerf, volleyball trainers)

Cues

Crab Fingers	(Curl your fingers for contact on the pads.)
Quick Feet	(Always keep your feet on the move to be in position for the volley.)
Bend and Extend	(Bend the knees in preparation; extend the arms, legs, and body toward the target on contact.)

Tasks/Challenges:

🅣 The first person in your line volleys the ball to the wall so it contacts the wall above the tape line; then that person moves quickly to the back of the line. The second person volleys the ball to the wall, moves quickly to the back, and so on. The objective is to keep the volley going. Don't let the ball touch the floor or touch the wall below the tape mark.

🅒 Count the number of volleys your team can complete without a mistake.

🅣 Continue the line volley, with each person calling "mine" just before he or she contacts the ball.

🅣 Remaining in your group of four, face another group, with approximately ten feet between the two leaders. Team members should line up behind

the leaders. One leader tosses the ball to the leader of the other team; that leader then volleys the ball back and quickly moves to the end of the line. This game is very similar to the volley against the wall: Each person volleys and then moves to the end of the line. The objective is to keep the volley going between the teams.

PLAYING MODIFIED VOLLEYBALL

Setting: Teams of four or six, depending on space available (*Place an equal number of children with comparable skills on each team; the size of the court in relation to the number of players is the crucial element; don't expect children to cover the amount of space per person that adults do in volleyball*); a beach ball, plastic ball, or large volleyball

Cues

Quick Feet	(Always keep "on the move" to be in position for the volley.)
Bend and Extend	(Bend the knees and arms in preparation; extend the arms, legs, and body toward the target on contact.)
Offense:	Open Space (Hit to the open space.)
Defense:	Ready (Bent knees, ready hands.)

Tasks/Challenges

🅣 The game begins with a serve from the back boundary line; you will have two chances to serve the ball successfully over the net. In a regulation volleyball game, the ball may be hit only three times on a side; we'll decide as a class if we want three hits per side or unlimited. (*Discuss; vote.*)

Here are the guidelines for play:

1. Remember, you score a point if your team is serving.
2. A serve that touches the net is no good; a ball in play is good even though it touches the net.
3. Although this is not an official rule, try to use the skills you learned, such as the two-hand volley. Use one hand only for the spike and the serve.
4. A skilled volleyball game shows this pattern: set, set, over the net or bump, set, over the net—not single hits back and forth. Try to use the three-part sequence for play on your side of the net.

Dribbling

Dribbling is striking downward, generally with the hands. Basketball and team handball are the tradi-

BOX 28.2   THE SKILL OF DRIBBLING IN THE *NATIONAL STANDARDS FOR PHYSICAL EDUCATION*

The skill theme of dribbling is referenced in the *National Standards for Physical Education* (NASPE, 1995) under Standard 1: Demonstrates competency in many movement forms and proficiency in a few movement forms. The standard speaks of the child's developing the mature motor skill in combination with other actions and being able to use the skill in a dynamic situation.

Sample benchmarks include:

■ Demonstrates mature motor patterns in simple combinations (e.g., dribbling while running) (p. 18).
■ Dribbles and passes a basketball to a moving receiver (p. 32).
■ Hand dribbles and foot dribbles while preventing an opponent from stealing the ball (p. 46).

tional sports in which dribbling is used. Dribbling a ball on the floor or ground, as in soccer, could have been included in this chapter, but because it's also a kicking skill, it's included in the kicking and punting discussion (Chapter 26). See Box 28.2 for information on dribbling from the *National Standards for Physical Education.*

Levels of Skill Proficiency in Dribbling

At the precontrol level of dribbling, children are satisfied with making contact with the ball so that the ball comes back to them. They explore dribbling from a stationary position with a ball that bounces back to them; they also explore walking and dribbling. Tasks that are appropriate at this level include

1. Bouncing the ball and catching it
2. Bouncing the ball with both hands
3. Dribbling the ball in self-space with either hand
4. Dribbling with limited, slow travel

At the control level, children are introduced to varying their dribble while at the same time learning to use the nondominant hand. They are also given challenges that involve dribbling and traveling. Appropriate tasks include

1. Dribbling at different heights and in different positions around the body
2. Dribbling continuously and switching hands
3. Dribbling while traveling and looking up

At the utilization level, children enjoy focusing on traveling while dribbling and on incorporating travel-

ing into dynamic gamelike situations that allow them to combine the skills of throwing, catching, dodging, and dribbling. Appropriate tasks include

1. Dribbling around obstacles
2. Dribbling in different pathways and while changing directions
3. Dribbling in one-on-one situations

When children reach the proficiency level, dribbling seems to be almost automatic. They enjoy dribbling in larger groups with more complex relationships, and the excitement of strategy development. Appropriate tasks at this level include

1. Starting and stopping, changing directions quickly while dribbling
2. Dribbling to keep the ball away from an opponent
3. Dribbling in gamelike situations

Dribbling is a skill normally developed for a basketball situation. We focus on it as one aspect of striking rather than as a basketball skill. Children enjoy working with bouncing balls. Remember, though, that dribbling—like striking upward—is one of the last fundamental skills to develop because it requires fine hand-eye coordination. Our progression spiral for dribbling appears on page 539.

ASSESSMENT EXAMPLE
from the National Standards for Physical Education
Written Test/Drawing

Students are provided with a drawing of a hand print and are asked to color the portion of the hand

Dribbling

■ PROFICIENCY LEVEL
Small-group basketball
Dribble/Pass Keep Away
Dribbling and throwing at a target
Making up fancy dribbling/passing routines
Dribbling and passing in game situations
Dribbling while dodging
Dribble Tag
Now You've Got It, Now You Don't
Dribbling against opponents: group situations

■ UTILIZATION LEVEL
Dribbling against an opponent: one on one
Dribbling and passing with a partner
Mirroring and matching while dribbling
Dribbling around stationary obstacles
Dribbling in different pathways
Starting and stopping while changing directions
Dribbling while changing directions
Dribbling and changing speed of travel

■ CONTROL LEVEL
Moving switches
Dribbling and traveling
Dribbling in different places around the body while stationary
Dribbling with the body in different positions
Switches
Dribbling and looking
Dribbling at different heights
Dribble like a basketball player
All the time dribble

■ PRECONTROL LEVEL
Dribbling and walking
Bouncing a ball down (dribbling) continuously
Bouncing a ball down and catching it

that is used in mature dribbling. Students may also be asked to draw an entire person dribbling to show the overall critical elements of this movement task.

Criteria for Assessment

a. Correctly identifies position of hand used in mature dribbling.

b. Identifies the critical elements of dribbling.

NASPE (1995, pp. 20–21)

Precontrol Level: Activities for Exploration

At the precontrol level, we want children to strike a ball down repeatedly without losing the ball from self-space. When the children are able to do this, we add limited dribbling while walking. Relatively light balls—eight-inch plastic playground balls or rubber basketballs—that bounce true (they aren't lopsided) are best for introducing children to dribbling. Be careful when inflating balls: Too much air equals too much bounce for control.

BOUNCING A BALL DOWN AND CATCHING IT

Setting: Children scattered in general space, each with a ball

Tasks/Challenges

🅣 Bounce the ball down in front of you so it comes straight back up to you. Catch it when it comes up.

🅣 Try bouncing the ball with two hands.

🅣 Now try bouncing with one hand.

🅣 Try bouncing with the other hand.

BOUNCING A BALL DOWN (DRIBBLING) CONTINUOUSLY

Setting: Children scattered in general space, each with a ball

Tasks/Challenges

🅣 Bounce the ball with both hands so that it keeps going. This bounce that keeps going is called a *dribble.*

🅣 Try dribbling the ball with one hand.

🅣 Now try the other hand.

🅒 Can you bounce three times in a row?

🅣 Try changing from one hand to the other.

DRIBBLING AND WALKING

Setting: Children scattered in general space, each with a ball

Tasks/Challenges

🅣 Bounce the ball with two hands and catch as you walk forward slowly.

🅣 Try bouncing the ball with one hand while you walk forward slowly.

🅒 See if you can take three steps without losing the ball.

Control Level: Learning Experiences Leading to Skill Development

At the control level, children learn to dribble and travel at the same time. They'll also be able to dribble in different places around their bodies and vary both direction and pathway. Some tasks very similar to those suggested for the precontrol level are repeated at the control level for continued practice and added skill development.

A note about cues: Although several cues are listed for many of the learning experiences, it's important to focus on only one cue at a time. That way, the children can really concentrate on that cue. Once you provide feedback to the children and observe that most have learned a cue, then it's time to focus on another one.

ALL THE TIME DRIBBLE

Setting: Children scattered in general space, each with a ball (either a woman's basketball or a playground ball)

Cues	
Fingerpads	(Use the soft parts of your fingers near the end to dribble, not the very ends.) *Demonstrate.*
Knees Bent	(As you dribble, bend your knees a little, keeping your

Figure 28.16   Dribbling with control requires concentration.

Figure 28.17   Dribbling a ball.

 This would be an opportune place to include an exit slip to assess student understanding of the dribbling cues. The exit slip might have students trace their hand on a piece of paper and color in the parts of the fingers used to dribble. The exit slip could later be included in a portfolio.

DRIBBLE LIKE A BASKETBALL PLAYER

Setting: Children scattered throughout general space, each with a ball

Cues	
Fingerpads	(Remember to use the soft parts of your fingers.)
Knees Bent	(As you dribble, bend your knees a little, keeping your back straight, just like you are sitting down a little.)
Hand on Top of Ball	(Make sure your hand touches the ball almost on its top.)
Forward Backward Stance	(The foot of the hand you are *not* dribbling with should be a little in front.) (See Figure 28.17.)

Tasks/Challenges:

🅣 Dribble the ball with one hand.

🅣 Dribble the ball with the other hand.

🅒 Count the number of times you can dribble without losing control.

🅣 On the signal, begin dribbling with one hand. Continue dribbling until the signal is given to stop.

Have children repeat each task with their nondominant hand throughout all levels of the skill. The proficient dribbler is equally skilled with each hand.

	back straight, just like you are sitting down a little.)
Hand on Top of Ball	(Make sure your hand touches the ball almost on its top.)

Tasks/Challenges:

🅣 Remember when we bounced a ball down so it came back up to you and then pushed it down again so the bounce continued. This continuous bounce is called a *dribble*. Practice dribbling now (Figure 28.16).

🅒 Practice until you can dribble the ball five times without losing control of it.

🅒 Say one letter of the alphabet for each time you dribble. Can you get to Z?

Tip: Children tend to dribble either with the whole palm or with the ends of the fingers. Besides using the term finger-pads, *we have also found it useful to put chalk or tape on the fingerpads to help children learn the correct part of their fingers to use.*

DRIBBLING AT DIFFERENT HEIGHTS

Setting: Children scattered throughout general space, each with a ball

Cues

Knees Bent	(Make sure that your knees are bent just slightly.)
Firm, Flexible Wrists	(Make sure that your wrists are strong and bendable.)
Hand on Top of Ball	(Make sure your hand touches the ball almost on its top.)

Tip: The preceding cues focus on the skill of dribbling. At the same time it is good to check and see if children are also dribbling at the appropriate level. The cues would then change to high, medium, and low.

Tasks/Challenges:

T Staying in self-space, dribble the ball with your preferred hand. Continue dribbling until you hear the signal to stop.

T Dribble the ball at a low level so it bounces only to your knees. Keep your body in a standing position; don't kneel or squat to the floor.

T Dribble the ball so it rebounds to a level between your waist and your knees. This medium-level dribble is the one most often used in games and the one we will concentrate on throughout our work.

T On the signal, begin dribbling the ball at waist level. Continue dribbling until you hear the drumbeat. Stay in your self-space.

DRIBBLING AND LOOKING

Setting: Children scattered in general space, alone at first and later with partners, each child with a ball for dribbling

Cues

Look Up	(You may want to find a spot on the wall to look at to help you look up. Just sometimes glance down at the ball to check on it.)

Tasks/Challenges:

T Begin dribbling the ball, then raise your head and continue dribbling without looking at the ball. Your peripheral vision enables you to look straight ahead and still see the ball. Your peripheral vision is your ability to see things at the edges of your field of vision and straight ahead at the same time. This is extremely important in a game involving dribbling.

T For this task you will need a partner and each one of you will need a ball. Face your partner; decide which one of you will be the first leader. The leader starts dribbling at any level he or she wants; the partner must follow by dribbling at any other level than the level at which the leader is dribbling. For example, if the leader is dribbling at a high level, the partner can dribble at a low or a medium level. The leader can change levels after three dribbles at the same level. Use quick changes of level to try to fake your partner. When you hear the signal (*about 30 seconds*), change leaders. How many times before the signal can you catch your partner dribbling at the same level as you are?

SWITCHES

Setting: Children scattered in general space, each with a ball for dribbling

Cues

Hand to Side of Ball	(Keep your hand a little behind and to the outside of the ball.)

Tasks:

T Begin dribbling with your preferred hand. After several dribbles, switch to the other hand and continue dribbling. Don't catch the ball; simply switch from dribbling with one hand to dribbling with the other.

T Begin dribbling with your preferred hand. Dribble five times, and then switch to your other hand. Continue to switch after five dribbles per hand. **One change here from the regular dribbling hints: Instead of having your hand directly on top of the ball, it is helpful to push the ball from the side when you want to change dribbling hands (Figure 28.18).**

C On the signal, begin dribbling with your preferred hand. Each time you hear the drumbeat, switch hands. Continue to dribble and switch hands on each drumbeat until you hear the signal to stop.

Figure 28.18   Changing hands while dribbling.

DRIBBLING WITH THE BODY IN DIFFERENT POSITIONS

Setting: Children scattered in general space, each with a ball

Cues

Firm, Flexible Wrists	(Remember the strong, bendable wrists we used before—they are really important now.)
Ball to Side, a Little in Front	(Keep the ball a little in front of your body and out to the side.)

Tasks/Challenges:

T Assume a kneeling position. Balance on one knee and one foot, with your body at a low level. Dribble with one hand while you maintain the balanced position.

T Dribble while in a squat or tuck position, balanced on both feet at a low level.

C Balance in different positions, dribbling with one hand. Create three different positions in which you can dribble with either your right or left hand.

T Begin dribbling in a standing position. Continue to dribble as you change your position to a low level—a kneeling or squatting position. Continue changing body positions while maintaining the dribble.

Choose several children to demonstrate the combinations of body positions they assume while dribbling (Figure 28.19).

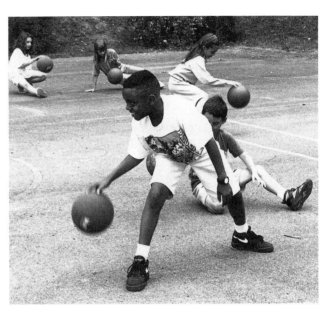

Figure 28.19   Dribbling the ball in a variety of body positions challenges skill development in children.

DRIBBLING IN DIFFERENT PLACES AROUND THE BODY WHILE STATIONARY

Setting: Children scattered in general space, each with a ball for dribbling

Cues

Ball Close to Body	(Remember, the ball should be close to your body so you don't lose it.)
Firm, Flexible Wrists	(Your wrists have to be really strong and bendable for this dribbling—floppy will not work.)

Tasks/Challenges:

T Standing in self-space, dribble the ball in different places around your body: on your right, on your left, behind your legs. **As you dribble remember to keep the ball close to your body.**

T Begin dribbling with your right hand; after several dribbles, bounce the ball under your right leg from back to front, and continue the dribble with your left hand. **The hand position will be like that for switching hands, a little to the side of the ball.**

T Practice the skill from right to left and from left to right until you can execute it in both directions.

T Dribble the ball directly in front of your body; bounce the ball between your legs from front to back. **You will need to twist your body to recover the dribble in the back.**

🅣 Can you dribble the ball from back to front?

🅒 Put together a dribbling sequence of all the ways you can dribble in self-space: in front, to the side, in back, around your body, between your legs. Remember to change levels as you go and to find different positions balanced on different parts.

 This might be a good place to include an exit slip to assess students' knowledge of different positions, places around the body, and levels, as well as a self-assessment of skill. A possible exit slip could ask children to write out the dribbling sequence they performed, indicating which positions were easy and which they will want to practice in the future.

DRIBBLING AND TRAVELING

Setting: Children scattered throughout general space, each with a ball.

Cues	
Hand a Little behind the Ball	(For walking and dribbling, your hand position changes: Keep your hand just a little behind the ball.)

Tasks/Challenges

🅣 This time start dribbling in self-space. After a few dribbles take two steps, then stop and dribble two times in self-space, then take two more steps, then stop and dribble twice. Keep traveling in general space like this until you hear the stop signal. **As you dribble push the ball slightly forward.**

Tip: This task works well when children are first learning to travel and dribble because they are able to regain control of the ball if they are close to losing it. You can gradually increase the number of steps and decrease the stationary dribbles as the skill level increases.

🅣 Begin dribbling and walking in general space. When you hear the drumbeat, stop in self-space and continue dribbling. The second drumbeat is the signal to travel again. The pattern is this: drumbeat, travel with dribble, drumbeat, stop with continued dribble, . . .

🅒 Each of you has one hundred points. On the signal begin traveling in general space. If you lose control

of the ball, subtract ten points; if you collide with another person, subtract twenty-five points. I'll time you for sixty seconds; try to keep all one hundred points. Ready? Begin.

MOVING SWITCHES

Setting: Children scattered in general space, each with a ball

Cues	
Hand behind and to Side of Ball	(Your hand position changes again, just a little: Keep your hand a little behind and to the outside of the ball.) (See Figure 28.18.)
Look Up	(Remember to look at other peoples' faces as you dribble and just sneak glances at the ball.)

Tasks/Challenges:

🅣 Start dribbling with your favorite hand while walking. On the signal, without stopping, change the dribbling to the other hand and keep walking.

🅣 Begin dribbling in general space; each time you meet someone, switch hands, and continue to travel and dribble.

Utilization Level: Learning Experiences Leading to Skill Development

At the utilization level, we increase the complexity of the dribbling by providing children with situations in which they must dribble with either hand, without looking at the ball. We also provide beginning dynamic, gamelike situations in which youngsters combine skills.

A note about cues: Although several cues are listed for many of the learning experiences, it's important to focus on only one cue at a time. That way, the children can really concentrate on that cue. Once you provide feedback to the children and observe that most have learned a cue, then it's time to focus on another one.

DRIBBLING AND CHANGING SPEED OF TRAVEL

Setting: Children scattered in general space (alone at first and later with partners), each child with a ball

Cues

Look Up (Remember to look at faces.)
Ball Low (Dribble the ball only as high as your waist.)

Tip: You may also need to refocus on speeds here as well. If so, the cues would be fast, medium, and slow. See Chapter 17.)

Tasks/Challenges:

T Travel throughout general space, maintaining a controlled dribble at all times. Travel sometimes very fast, sometimes slowly.

T Begin moving through general space with a slow, steady walk. As you're dribbling, focus your eyes on a spot on the floor fifteen to twenty feet away. Without stopping your dribble, move as quickly as possible to that spot. When you arrive, stop your travel but continue dribbling. Visually choose another spot, and repeat the sequence. The ability to change speeds and maintain a continuous dribble is a very important offensive skill in basketball.

T This time as you travel, practice quickly changing the speed of your dribble as you travel to your chosen point. It will be as if you have almost invisible stops and starts along the way. Slow down and speed up, changing the speed of travel in mid-dribble.

T Stand beside a partner whose dribbling skill is very similar to yours. Partner 1 begins the travel/dribble throughout space, changing from fast to slow speeds at will. Partner 2 attempts to stay beside partner 1 at all times. Both of you will dribble continuously. When the signal is given, rest for 10 seconds. Then partner 2 becomes the leader.

DRIBBLING WHILE CHANGING DIRECTIONS

Setting: Children scattered throughout general space, each with a ball for dribbling

Cues

Hand Position (The hand positions we used before are important here. If you want to go to the side, your hand is on the side; to go forward, hand behind; to go backward, hand in front.)

Slide (Especially when going sideways, be sure and slide your feet; don't cross them.)

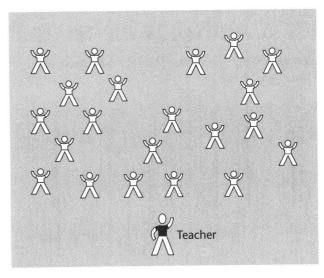

Figure 28.20 Formation for practicing dribbling and moving in the directions the teacher suggests.

Tasks/Challenges

T Dribble throughout general space, changing directions as you go: travel forward, backward, to the right, to the left. Travel slowly when you first begin the travel/dribble with a change of direction. Maintain the dribble during all your direction changes; don't stop and start again.

Traveling backward and dribbling isn't easy because the ball must move toward the body and often hits the feet. Children should develop this direction last and should be made aware of the difficulty of dribbling backward.

T Begin dribbling in general space, traveling in a forward direction. Each time you hear the drumbeat, quickly change the direction of your travel and continue the travel/dribble.

Setting: Children arranged in a scattered formation, about three to four feet apart, all facing the same direction (Figure 28.20); teacher at the front of the group, facing the children

T Begin dribbling in self-space, keeping your head up, eyes focused on me. On the first signal, I'll point to your left; dribble with your right hand as you side-step to your left. When you hear the next signal, stop your travel but continue to dribble. I'll then point forward; travel backward as you dribble. Stop on the signal. Each time the signal is given, change the direction of your travel: right, left, forward, backward.

Children need both verbal and visual directional signs as well as audible signals (via drum or whistle) for change of directions. The children will mirror your visual cues.

STARTING AND STOPPING WHILE CHANGING DIRECTIONS

Setting: Children scattered in general space, each with a ball

Cues

Ball Close	(It is important to keep the ball close to your body, within half an arm's length.)
Forward-Backward Stance	(When you stop, your feet should be about eighteen inches apart, with the foot opposite the hand you are dribbling with forward.)

Figure 28.21 Dribbling in a curved or a zigzag pathway.

Tasks/Challenges:

T Begin dribbling in general space. Travel slowly at first, and then gradually increase your speed until you are moving quickly while maintaining your dribble. On the signal, quickly stop both your travel and the dribble.

T Begin dribbling throughout general space. On the signal, stop quickly in a forward-backward stance, maintaining the dribble. Pivot by reversing the way you are facing; turn on the balls of your feet. Continue your travel/dribble. **To pivot, turn backward on the foot toward the ball hand. Remember, the ball changes hands as you turn.**

T Choose a point across the gym. Begin dribbling in general space, moving toward your point. Every time you come to a line on the floor, stop, fake as if you are going to change directions, and keep going. **To use a fake, come to a stop, quickly take a step with one foot as if you are going to change directions, and then keep going in the same direction.** It may be easier if you pretend there is an imaginary defender in your way who you have to get around. When you reach your point, choose another one and keep going.

T This time, as you travel to your point, sometimes fake and sometimes change directions. Remember, in a game you are trying to outsmart a defender.

DRIBBLING IN DIFFERENT PATHWAYS

Setting: Children scattered in general space (alone at first, then with a partner), each with a ball

Cues

Ball Close	(It is important to keep the ball close to your body, within half an arm's length.)
Ball on Outside	(In a curved or a zigzag pathway, keep the ball on the outside of the curve, the wide side.) *Demonstrate; see Figure 28.21.*

Tasks/Challenges:

T Dribble throughout general space, traveling in straight, curved, and zigzag pathways.

T Travel in a straight pathway as you dribble. Each time you meet another person or hear the drum, turn quickly to your right or left and continue to travel/dribble in a straight pathway.

T Follow the straight lines on the gym floor (or playground) as you travel/dribble.

T Travel in a series of curved pathways as you dribble. **If you curve to the left, dribble with your right hand; if you curve to the right, dribble with your left hand. Always keep the ball on the outside of the curve.**

T Travel/dribble throughout general space, quickly moving from side to side in a zigzag pathway. **Make sure the ball changes hands each time you move from side to side.**

T Travel/dribble in a straight pathway. On the signal, quickly zigzag to miss an imaginary opponent and then continue dribbling in a straight pathway.

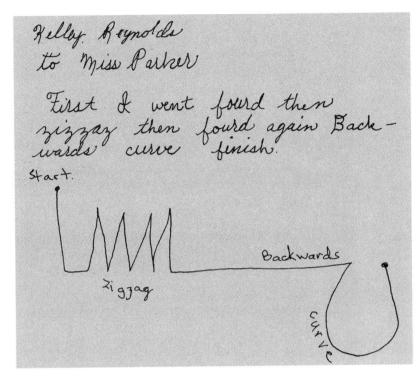

*Kelley Reynolds
to Miss Parker*

*First I went fourd then
zizzaz then fourd again Backwards curve finish.*

Start.

Zigzag

Backwards

curve

Figure 28.22   A child's pathways map.

Figure 28.23   Dribbling around obstacles/persons.

T Stand approximately three feet behind a partner; each of you has a basketball (playground ball). Partner 1 (in front) travels/dribbles throughout general space changing pathways. Partner 2 (in back) attempts to stay three feet behind the lead partner at all times. (*Give each partner several chances to be the leader.*)

C Design a traveling/dribbling strategy to move from the center of the gym (or outside blacktop) to the end line. Design the strategy using combinations of pathways to outwit imaginary opponents. Practice the traveling/dribbling strategy until you can do it three times exactly the same way. After you are done draw and write your strategy out (*Figure 28.22*).

   If I were to place three opponents in your way, could you still execute your plan?

DRIBBLING AROUND STATIONARY OBSTACLES

Setting: Marker cones or milk jugs placed randomly (not in a line) throughout general space (spots do not work well because children can go over them); with varying space between the cones or jugs (place some three feet apart, others five to six feet apart)

Cues

Body, Ball, Cone   (Remember, the cone [*jug*] is your opponent. Protect the ball by putting your body between the cone [*jug*] and the ball.)

Tasks/Challenges:

T Travel/dribble throughout general space, dribbling around the obstacles.

C See if you can dribble sixty seconds without bumping into an obstacle or another person—**Heads Up.**

Setting: The floor or blacktop divided into a series of alleys with colored tape; children in groups, one group per alley

T One person in your group will be the dribbler; that person will stand at the end of the alley. The others in your group should arrange themselves in a zigzag obstacle pattern in your alley (*Figure 28.23*).

The dribbler attempts to dribble the length of the alley, avoiding the obstacles and staying within the side boundaries. The obstacles try to gain possession of the ball. Obstacles can stretch and pivot, but one foot must remain glued in place at all times. Obstacles can touch only the ball, not the dribbler.

The difficulty of this task can be increased or decreased by adjusting the width of the alley.

Setting: Children in groups of five or six, each child with a ball

🅣 Your group will again be the obstacles. You will need to spread out in a straight line about arm's distance apart. Everybody dribbles the ball while they are in line. The first person in line starts to dribble in a zigzag pathway into and out of the line, while all the others are dribbling. When the moving dribbler gets to the end of the line, the dribbler stops and begins to dribble in place, and the next person at the beginning of the line starts zigzagging through the line. This continues until all of you have had a chance to dribble through the line.

MIRRORING AND MATCHING WHILE DRIBBLING

(See Chapter 18, "Relationships," for a discussion of mirroring and matching.)

Setting: Partners of approximately the same skill level facing each other about three to four feet apart

Cues	
Mirroring	(Remember, mirroring is like looking in a mirror. If your partner uses the left hand, you use your right hand.)
Matching	(Matching is harder than mirroring when you're facing your partner. If your partner uses the right hand, you use your right hand.)
Look Up	(For this activity it is really important to look at your partner.)

Tasks/Challenges:

🅣 Face your partner. The partner whose name comes first in the alphabet is the first leader. The leader starts dribbling, and the follower has to mirror the actions of the leader. Remember, don't make it too hard on your partner. On the signal (*about forty-five seconds*) change partners.

🅣 Now that you have gotten to be so good, try matching your partner's actions. **Remember that if your partner works with the left hand, you will use your left hand.**

🅣 This one is really hard. The leader can now travel in general space. The follower must try to copy exactly what the leader does. This is matching again.

DRIBBLING AND PASSING WITH A PARTNER

Setting: Partners, facing the same direction, about ten feet apart at one side of the gymnasium or blacktop; one partner with a basketball for dribbling and passing

Cues	
Receiver Slightly ahead of Passer	(The receiver should be ahead of the passer by about four or five steps.)
Lead Receiver	(Pass the ball to the open space just in front of the receiver so he or she doesn't have to back up to catch it.)
No Stopping	(Both the passer and the receiver should always be moving to the other side; never stop moving forward.)

Tasks/Challenges:

🅣 The object of this task is to practice passing while moving forward. You and your partner are traveling in the same direction. Your job is to move across the space to the other line. Partner 1 will dribble three or four times and then pass to partner 2, who has been traveling forward. Partner 2 receives the pass, dribbles as he or she travels forward, and then passes back to partner 1. Partners continue to travel/dribble the length of the space.

Setting: Partners about fifteen feet apart, scattered throughout general space, each pair with a ball

🅣 On the signal, begin traveling, dribbling, and passing to your partner. (*Allow about two minutes of activity, and then let the children rest for ten seconds. Repeat.*)

DRIBBLING AGAINST AN OPPONENT: ONE ON ONE

Before beginning tasks that involve offense and defense, students should be skilled with the space awareness and

dodging tasks that ask them to master the offensive and defensive skills of moving into open space; avoiding other persons; and using fakes, stops and starts, pivots, and other avoidance skills without manipulating equipment. (See Chapter 16, "Space Awareness," and Chapter 21, "Chasing, Fleeing, and Dodging.") Children need to have mastered these skills before they are asked to use them while manipulating equipment.

One key to this task—and to other initial tasks involving offense and defense—is to clearly define the boundaries of the space the students are to use. A small space gives an advantage to the defense; a large space provides an offensive advantage. Similarly, a long, narrow space gives the advantage to the defense; a wider space helps the offense. Initial tasks should generally favor the offense.

Setting: Partners facing each other, scattered throughout general space, each pair with a ball

Cues

Offense:	Look Up (You have to be able to see your partner to avoid him or her.)
	Move to Goal (Always move to your end line.)
	Ball, Body, Defense (Keep your body between the ball and your defense.)
Defense:	Body between Offense and Goal (Keep yourself between your partner and where he or she is trying to go. Your back should be to the partner's goal.)
	Watch Hips (Just like dodging, watch the hips or belly button if you want to know where your partner will move next.)
	Stay about Two or Three Feet Away (If you get too close, your partner can go right by you.)

Tasks/Challenges:

🅣 Select a partner who dribbles while traveling as well as you or slightly better. On the signal, partner 1 begins dribbling while traveling toward the end line; partner 2 (who is facing partner 1) attempts to gain possession of the ball by tapping it away (*Figure 28.24*). Neither partner should foul the other by bumping, pushing away, or reaching in. Partner 1 attempts to keep possession of the ball for thirty seconds; if partner 2 gets the ball, he or she gives it back. At the end of thirty seconds, partner 2 will dribble and partner 1 will try to take the ball away. Ready? Begin.

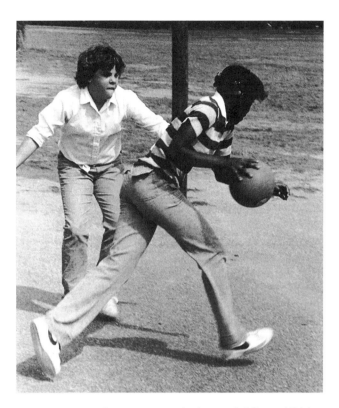

Figure 28.24   Youngsters need advanced skills to dribble while successfully avoiding an opponent.

Proficiency Level: Learning Experiences Leading to Skill Development

Children at the proficiency level seem to dribble without thinking about it. They're able to change direction, speed, and pathway at will. They're challenged by situations that involve other children as partners or as opponents who make the situation increasingly unpredictable.

A note about cues: Although several cues are listed for many of the learning experiences, it's important to focus on only one cue at a time. That way, the children can really concentrate on that cue. Once you provide feedback to the children and observe that most have learned a cue, then it's time to focus on another one.

DRIBBLING AGAINST OPPONENTS: GROUP SITUATIONS

Setting: Children divided into two equal groups, one group with playground balls for dribbling; initially, a fairly open space; later, to increase the complexity of the task, a reduced amount of space

Cues

Offense: Look Up (Remember to look up to see where your opponents are.)
Use Fakes (You'll need to use all the fakes we learned before—stopping and starting, changing speeds, changing directions—here.)

The cues at this level assume mastery of basic dribbling skills; hence, they are really strategy cues about how to use the dribble and how to stop the dribble. Many of the cues are taken from the concepts of space awareness and chasing, fleeing, and dodging. If needed, go back to and reinforce the dribbling cues and practice the basic offensive and defensive moves, but increasingly move toward children being able to use these skills in gamelike situations.

Tasks/Challenges:

🅣 Students without balls are the obstacles; you can spread out anywhere in the space. Your job is to try and steal the balls as the other group dribbles across the space. The only rules are you may not touch an offensive player, and one foot must always remain "glued" to your spot. In other words, you can step with one foot, but you cannot move from your spot. On the signal, the offense will begin dribbling from one end line and try to get to the other side without losing the ball. If the defense (the obstacles) gets a ball, just give it back. We'll trade places after three tries.

When the activity is a game situation with competing skills, it is best if you divide the children into groups, so you can place children with equal skills in a group.

NOW YOU'VE GOT IT, NOW YOU DON'T

Setting: Children divided into two groups on opposite sidelines of the gym or blacktop; one group with playground balls or basketballs

Cues

Defense: Watch Hips and Ball (The best way to tell where the dribbler is going is to look at the hips or belly button and at the same time watch the ball)
Slap Up (If you really want to knock the ball loose, slap from the bottom up.)
Offense: Look Up (Remember to look up to see where your opponents are.)

Use Fakes (You'll need to use all the fakes we learned before—stopping and starting, changing speeds, changing directions.)

Tasks/Challenges:

🅣 Each team stands on opposite sidelines of the gym (blacktop) and faces each other. Each member of team A has a playground ball for dribbling. On the signal, team A players begin dribbling toward the opposite sideline. Team B, without the playground balls, begins moving forward, trying to take away the balls. If a team B player gains possession of the ball, that player dribbles toward the opposite sideline. When the players from team A or team B make it over their goal line, they stay there until all the balls are behind one sideline. Team B is then given all the playground balls, and the game begins again.

DRIBBLE TAG

Setting: Each child with a playground ball for dribbling; two or three children designated "it" (without playground balls) wearing identifying jerseys if possible

Cues

Offense: Look Up (Remember to look up to see where your opponents are.)
Use Fakes (You'll need to use all the fakes we learned before—stopping and starting, changing speeds, changing directions.)

Tasks/Challenges:

🅣 On the signal, everyone with a ball will begin dribbling in general space. The players who are "it" will try to tag you as you're traveling and dribbling. You're caught if:

1. You're tagged by an "it."
2. You lose control of the ball.

If you're caught, stand and hold the ball above your head. You'll be free to travel if a player who is dribbling touches you. Each two minutes, we'll rest for ten seconds while I choose new "its."

DRIBBLING WHILE DODGING

Setting: Children, each with a basketball or a playground ball and a flag tucked in the waist

Cues

Look Up	(Remember to look up to see where your opponents are.)
Use Fakes	(You'll need to use all the fakes we learned before—stopping and starting, changing speeds, changing directions.)
Ball, Body, Defense	(Remember to protect the ball by keeping your body between the ball and the defense.)

Tasks/Challenges:

T You will need a partner of about your same ability level for this task. You will need to establish clear boundaries for your area, about ten feet square. Start by facing each other and dribbling. The object is to keep dribbling and pull your partner's flag. See how many times you can pull your partner's flag in two minutes.

DRIBBLING AND PASSING IN GAME SITUATIONS

Setting: A clearly defined space (the complexity of the task is increased or decreased depending upon the size of the space; initially, a larger space gives the advantage to the offense); groups of three

Cues

Offense:	Move to Open Space (When you don't have the ball, move to an open space at an angle to the passer.) (*See Chapter 27 for a detailed explanation of this idea.*) Lead the Receiver (Throw to an open space in front of the receiver.)
Defense:	Go after the Ball (Go after the person with the ball; otherwise he or she doesn't have to throw it.) Hustle (Move quickly when the ball changes players.)

Tasks/Challenges:

T Working in your group of three, two of you will dribble and pass while the third player tries to steal the ball. We'll rotate the interceptor every two minutes.

MAKING UP FANCY DRIBBLING/PASSING ROUTINES

Setting: Groups of four to six; a space about 15 feet square; any number of basketballs; music and tape players (optional)

Cues

The cues for this task are dependent upon what you want students to include in the routine. Some possibilities:

Pathways	(In your routine be sure to include at least two different pathways: straight, curved, zigzag.)
Dribbling	(The dribbling part of your routine needs to include different levels of dribbling and dribbling in different places around the body.)
Passing	(Your routine might also include passing.)

Tasks/Challenges:

T Put together a series of dribbling and passing skills in a fancy routine—kind of like a basketball warm-up drill. Design the floor pattern, ways to travel, individual tricks, and partner or group skills. Practice your routine until you have it memorized and in time with the music.

 Routines such as this are good places to use videotape for observation and assessment. The videotaping also adds incentive for students to perform well and do their best. Remember to design your scoring rubrics ahead of time so students know what is expected of their performance.

DRIBBLING AND THROWING AT A TARGET

Setting: Four-foot-square targets marked with colored tape on the wall at one end of or sides of the gym, approximately seven feet above the floor; each child with a ball at first, then later with partners and a shared ball

Cues

No Stopping	(Pick up your dribble and throw to the target without coming to a complete stop.)
Watch the Target	(To increase your accuracy, watch the target.)

Tasks/Challenges:

🔵 Beginning at the center of the gymnasium, travel/dribble toward the wall with the target on it. When you're within twelve feet of the target, throw the ball, trying to hit the wall within the target square. Collect the ball, quickly move to the side, and return to mid-court.

🔵 Select a partner who will serve as defense. Partner 1 dribbles toward the wall and attempts to score by hitting the target; partner 2 tries to gain possession of the ball on the dribble or block the throw to the target. Change partner roles after each try.

🔵 Practice the dribble/target activity with an offensive partner. Combine dribbling and passing to a partner as you travel toward the target. Alternate the throw to the target between partners.

 Here is an event task that could easily be used as an assessment: You and your partner join with another set of partners for a two-on-two game of dribbling, passing, and throwing at a target.

Tip: Place targets around the walls as space allows. Place targets on both side and end walls to provide maximum activity.

DRIBBLE/PASS KEEP AWAY

Setting: Groups of four in a space about one-quarter the size of a basketball court (or smaller)

> **Cues**
>
> *Defense:*   First Player Ball; Second Player Receiver (Play defense on the person with the ball first; then play defense on the receiver. Don't just stand in the middle. Make the passer throw the ball.)
>
> *Offense:*   Don't Pass until the Defense Commits (Until the defense plays defense on you, there is no need to pass. You might as well keep moving and dribbling the ball.)
> Receiver Move to an Open Space (Move to an open space at an angle to the passer.)
> Stay Away from the Passer. (Wherever you go, your defense goes with you. If you stay close to the passer, everyone stays together and the passer has nowhere to throw.)

Tasks/Challenges:

🔵 In your group, two of you will dribble and pass while the other two try to gain possession of the ball either by intercepting the pass or by stealing the ball on the dribble. Remember, on defense you cannot touch the other player. When you walk, you must dribble the basketball.

SMALL-GROUP BASKETBALL

Setting: Groups of no more than three; half- or short basketball court with lowered baskets

> **Cues**
>
> *Offense:*   Don't Pass until the Defense Commits (Until the defense plays defense on you, there is no need to pass. You might as well keep moving and dribbling the ball.)
> Receiver Move to an Open Space (Move to an open space at an angle to the passer.)
> Stay Away from the Passer. (Wherever you go, your defense goes with you. If you stay close to the passer, everyone stays together and the passer has nowhere to throw.)
>
> *Defense:*   Go after Ball (Force the pass by pressuring the player with the ball.)
> Ball, Body, Basket (Keep your body between the basket and the offensive player.)
> Hustle Back (After a score, run back down the court.)

Tasks/Challenges:

🟢 If you are comfortable with your skills of dribbling, passing, and throwing at a target, you may want to play a small-group basketball game. The maximum number of players on a team is three. The one rule I have is that every player must touch the ball before a shot is made. Match the skills on your team so the game will be a challenge for everyone; it's no fun if the score is a runaway.

 Here is a group project that could be used as an assessment: Before we begin the team play, let's think of all the skills we need for being successful in basketball: spatial awareness, throwing, catching, traveling, dodging, dribbling, shooting at a target. Within your group, discuss what you need to be able to do with each skill to be successful in basketball.

READING COMPREHENSION QUESTIONS

1. Discuss the difference between volleying and dribbling.
2. Name four body parts that can be used to volley a ball.
3. What is the primary focus of the tasks at the precontrol level of volleying? What is the teacher trying to accomplish before moving on to the control level?
4. List four different types of balls that can be used to practice volleying at the precontrol level.
5. What does the phrase "strike the ball with a level body part" mean? What does the phrase "meeting the ball" mean?
6. Rank the following tasks by placing the number 1 in front of the easiest (most basic) task, the number 2 in front of the next more difficult task, and so on.
   ( ) Striking a ball to different levels
   ( ) Striking a ball with two hands
   ( ) Striking a ball to outwit an opponent
   ( ) Striking a balloon
   ( ) Striking a ball to a partner
7. Explain the meaning of the phrase "the location of the hit determines the direction of travel."
8. Give two examples of dynamic and unpredictable situations related to the skill of volleying.
9. What characterizes each of the four skill levels of dribbling?
10. What does it mean to keep one's hands firm and flexible as opposed to flat and stiff when dribbling?
11. How can you teach a child to use the fingerpads while dribbling?

REFERENCES

Mustain, W. (1990). *A manual of elementary physical education skill theme activities for physical education specialists to use in collaboration with classroom teachers*. Unpublished master's project, Virginia Polytechnic Institute and State University, Blacksburg.

National Association for Sport and Physical Education (NASPE). (1995). *Moving into the future: National standards for physical education*. St. Louis, MO: Mosby.

CHAPTER 29   Striking with Rackets and Paddles

Children learning to strike with a racket or paddle must coordinate many familiar skills into one new one. They must learn to accurately toss or drop the object to be contacted, visually track the object while they're traveling to an appropriate location, and contact the object at exactly the right moment. And simultaneously they must adjust to the weight and length of the implement. A successful striker must coordinate *all* these variables. See Box 29.1 for information on striking with rackets and paddles from the *National Standards for Physical Education*.

Striking with rackets and paddles, as well as striking with long-handled implements (Chapter 30), is one of the last skills that children develop. There are two basic reasons: (1) Visual tracking is a skill that children don't refine or develop until the later elementary school years, and (2) hand-eye coordination at greater distances from the body is more difficult. Yet, striking with these implements is a skill children enjoy and can be taught at younger ages with a few simple equipment modifications (see the box on page 562). Because of the complexities of striking, we teach the skill of striking with rackets and paddles after children have been introduced to the skill of striking with body parts, specifically the hand (see Chapter 28).

Levels of Skill Proficiency

The difficulty of striking with an implement increases with the length of the implement. Children at the precontrol level struggle just to make contact between the implement and the object and are truly excited when they do—regardless of where the object goes. Children at this level benefit from exploring striking with short-handled, lightweight implements. Balloons, which travel slowly, expedite visual tracking and eye-hand coordination. Appropriate tasks for children at the precontrol level include:

1. Striking a balloon with a lightweight paddle or hose racket
2. Striking a suspended ball
3. Tossing a ball or object upward and hitting it
4. Dropping an object and contacting it underhand
5. Dropping a ball and contacting it after a bounce

When children are able to strike a ball consistently in these contexts, they're ready for control-level experiences, which include contacting a rebounding ball a number of times in succession, sending the object in a desired direction, and varying the force of the contact. We also introduce the sidearm pattern at this level. Other appropriate control-level experiences include:

1. Striking a ball at a target
2. Sending a ball high enough to travel over a net

Children at the utilization level are able to contact a ball repeatedly without a miss (bouncing it up or down with a paddle or racket) and send a ball or other object various distances and in different directions. The youngsters are now ready to apply these skills in dynamic situations, such as moving into various positions to contact an object at different places around the body and returning shots to a partner. The skill of striking is now used in such learning experiences as:

1. Striking with a variety of rackets and objects
2. Continuously hitting to a rebound wall
3. Striking cooperatively with a partner for high scores
4. Striking with overhand, forearm, backhand, and underhand strokes

When the children have attained the proficiency level, they demonstrate a mature pattern of striking: the ability to control both body and implement while traveling and to select the most effective type of striking when responding to a partner. Experiences at the proficiency level center around gamelike situations. Fast-moving, quick-reacting patterns of striking are required in both cooperative and competitive games. Appropriate experiences include:

1. Playing cooperative or competitive games
2. Offensive-defensive movements involving others

Our progression spiral (page 560) presents ideas for developing the skill of striking with rackets and paddles from the precontrol through the proficiency levels. The key observation points in Box 29.2 illustrate correct sidearm striking with rackets and paddles.

Precontrol Level: Activities for Exploration

At the precontrol level, we provide activities for the children to explore using lightweight paddles to contact balls, shuttlecocks, and other objects (Figure 29.1). These objects are often suspended from ropes at various heights to make the task easier.

We recommend balloons at the precontrol level because the flight of a balloon is longer and slower than that of a ball and the child therefore has more time for visual tracking. Heavier balloons, although a bit more expensive, are more durable than inexpensive, lightweight balloons. They also tend to be less erratic during flight and consequently are easier for children to strike successfully.

BOX 29.1 STRIKING WITH RACKETS AND PADDLES IN THE *NATIONAL STANDARDS FOR PHYSICAL EDUCATION*

The skill theme of striking with rackets and paddles is referenced in the *National Standards for Physical Education* (NASPE, 1995) under Standard 1: Demonstrates competency in many movement forms and proficiency in a few movement forms. The standard speaks of a child's learning to apply the skill in a dynamic gamelike situation. The sample benchmark states that a child "places a ball away from an opponent in a racket sport activity" (p. 46).

The skill theme of striking with rackets and paddles is also referenced under Standard 2: Applies movement concepts and principles to the learning and development of motor skills. This standard speaks of the child's recognizing and applying the concept of different grips to the striking action. The sample benchmark states that a child "consistently strikes a softly thrown ball with a bat or paddle, demonstrating an appropriate grip" (p. 34).

Figure 29.1 Youngsters at the precontrol level benefit from practice with short-handled, lightweight paddles.

 Striking is one skill theme in which safety plays an important role. Be sure to include wrist strings or guards on all rackets and paddles (and have children use them) and provide ample space for children to strike and move safely around one another.

PADDLE BALANCE

Setting: A paddle and a balloon, beanbag, and ball for each child. (Foam paddles are best because they are lightweight and easy to control.)

Tasks/Challenges:

Ⓣ You're going to practice a new skill now. Try to balance the balloon on the paddle. **As you do this, try to keep the balloon in the middle of the paddle.**

Ⓣ If you are having a little trouble with the balloon on the paddle, you may want to try balancing a beanbag on the paddle.

Ⓣ The balloon was fairly easy to balance, but this time we are going to make the task a little harder. Instead of a balloon, try to balance a ball on your paddle. Try to keep the ball on your paddle for as long as you can.

▶ Sarah. I watched her. It was at the park. Her older brothers were busy playing street hockey and tennis (on the tennis courts). She was about six, and, being ignored by her brothers, was in her own world. The boys had left a tennis racket and a ball lying aside. She picked them up, held the racket somewhere in the middle of the handle, and began to try to hit the ball. It took four tries before she even made contact, and the ball rolled away into the grass. It didn't matter; you could tell by the smile on her face that she was delighted. She ran after the ball, picked it up and (after a few attempts) hit it again, and was again off to chase it. Her game took her on a journey all over the park and continued for twenty minutes or so. Then she proudly walked over to her mother and declared, "I can play tennis!"

BOX 29.2   KEY OBSERVATION POINTS: STRIKING WITH RACKETS AND PADDLES

1. Does the child take a forward step on the foot opposite the striking arm?

2. Does the child's body coil and rotate forward as the child swings the racket?

3. Does the child draw the racket back and then swing it forward along a full arc?

Mature Striking Patterns

When children are at the mature stage of striking with rackets and paddles, do their strikes look similar to the following sequence? In the preparatory phase, weight is shifted to the back foot, the trunk rotates 45 to 90 degrees, the hip and trunk are cocked, and the racket is drawn back. This is followed by movements that occur in such quick succession that they seem almost simultaneous: The weight shifts, the body rotates forward, and the racket is swung forward along a full arc (an arc around the body).

SOURCE: Adapted from *Fundamental Motor Patterns*, 2nd ed., by R. L. Wickstrom, 1977, Philadelphia: Lea & Febiger.

Striking with Rackets and Paddles

■ PROFICIENCY LEVEL

Self-designed racket games
Badminton Volleyball
Minitennis doubles
Aerial net games
Minitennis
Racket Four Square
Racket Corner Ball
Wall Ball

■ UTILIZATION LEVEL

Racket Call Ball
Striking in various aerial pathways in gamelike situations
Striking continuously upward with a group
Striking overhead over a net
Striking overhead
Striking to different places around a partner
Hitting cooperatively and continuously with a partner
From Both Sides Now

■ CONTROL LEVEL

Striking continuously over and through a target
Striking a ball rebounding from a wall
Striking an object and sending it over a net
Striking through a target
Hitting to different places
Striking at high and low targets
To the wall again—Sideways (sidearm backhand pattern)
To the wall—Sideways (sidearm forehand pattern)
Striking for hoops (varying the distance)
Striking for distance (varying the force)
Striking to wall targets
Both Sides (of the paddle) Now
Ups, Downs, and Forwards
Up Against the Wall (striking forward)
Ups and Downs
Ups
Downs

■ PRECONTROL LEVEL

Upward Bound
Hit the wall
Striking a suspended ball
Balloon strike (lightweight paddle)
Paddle balance

Figure 29.2 Construction of nylon-hose paddles. Lightweight paddles can be made from old coat hangers, nylon socks (or stockings), and tape.

🅣 If you are really good at keeping the ball on your paddle so that it doesn't fall off very often, try rolling the ball around on the paddle but still keeping it on the paddle. At times you will really have to do some fast work to keep the ball on the paddle.

🅒 I will time you. See if you can keep your object on the paddle for fifteen seconds. Ready? Go.

🅣 This time we are going to try something even harder. Choose the object you like best. Try and walk around your self-space and balance the object on your paddle at the same time.

Volleybirds (badminton shuttlecocks with flat bottoms; see Chapter 28) also work well with children at the precontrol level. The youngsters learn to keep the paddle flat as they walk around carrying the volleybird on the paddle.

BALLOON STRIKE (LIGHTWEIGHT PADDLE)

Setting: A nylon-hose (Figure 29.2) or foam paddle and a balloon for each child. (When children first begin striking balloons with paddles, tie the balloon with string to the paddle's handle. This saves much chasing time and makes it easier for the children to remain in their self-space.) A carpet square or other way of defining self-space for each child.

PADDLES AND SAFETY

▶ Although wooden and Plexiglas paddles are very good for learning to strike, they do present a safety problem. Paddles made of foam—with both short and long handles—are available. We prefer foam paddles whenever the children are working in close spaces or in groups.

Tasks/Challenges:

🅣 In your own space with your paddle and balloon, strike the balloon up in the air. Do one hit, then catch, and start again. Find out how to make the balloon go in the air.

🅣 Now try to strike the balloon more than once— maybe twice—then catch.

🅒 How many times can you strike the balloon, keeping it in the air without missing it or moving from your space? Five would be a really good number.

🅣 So far, you've tried to stay still in your own space while you were striking the balloon. This time try and move around in your self-space.

🅣 This time we are going to try and walk while striking the balloon. Go slowly and look where you are going so you don't hit others. To be safe, the balloon should be close to you.

STRIKING A SUSPENDED BALL

Setting: A ball suspended from a string (Figure 29.3) and a paddle for each child. For the first task suspend the balls above shoulder height; place carpet squares or other markings on the floor behind each ball.

Tasks/Challenges:

🅣 In your own space you have a ball that is hanging from a string. Try to strike the ball forward while standing on your carpet square. After each strike be sure and stop the ball before you try to hit it again. Setting: Lower the balls to waist height; move the carpet squares to a position beside the suspended balls.

Tasks/Challenges:

🅣 Things have changed a little this time. Now your carpet square is beside the ball. Again, try to strike

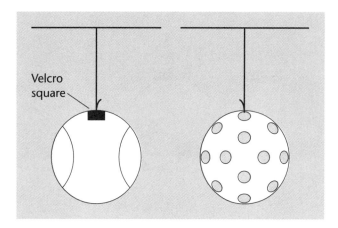

Figure 29.3   Suspending balls on strings. Glue a Velcro square to a string and another to a tennis ball to enable the ball to drop from the string when the ball is struck, or knot string or elastic into the holes of a plastic whiffle ball. Balls can be hung from climbing apparatus, from traveling rings, and between volleyball game standards, and they can be attached to walls in the corners of the gym.

the ball from your square so that it travels straight forward—like in baseball (*Figure 29.4*). Be sure and stop the ball after each hit.

Ⓒ You have been striking the ball fairly well. This time, if you strike the ball well, yell "Whacko!" If you miss, just start again.

At this point, children should be striking on their preferred side. When the children begin to strike consistently, challenge them to strike on the opposite side of their bodies (for example, backhand).

HIT THE WALL

Setting: A foam or wooden paddle and a foam ball, dead tennis ball, or volleybird for each child; spots on the floor or carpet squares about five feet away from the wall to identify self-space

Tasks/Challenges:

Ⓣ At your spot, strike the ball so that it travels to the wall. Just try for one hit at a time. Remember, if the ball goes away from you, collect it and bring it back to your spot before striking again.

Ⓣ Try hitting the ball on both sides of your body.

Ⓒ Try for five single hits; if you can do five, try seven.

UPWARD BOUND

Setting: A wooden, foam, or Plexiglas paddle (Figure 29.5); a shuttlecock or volleybird and a light-

Figure 29.4   Striking a suspended ball is an effective form of practice for many children.

weight ball; a carpet square or some way to define self-space for each child

Ⓣ This time try striking the shuttlecock (*volleybird*) upward. Drop the object, and try to strike it so it goes straight up.

Ⓣ Once you are comfortable with one hit, try to hit the shuttlecock (*volleybird*) more than once before catching it.

Ⓒ Try to hit the shuttlecock (*volleybird*) four times in a row.

Ⓣ Trade in your shuttlecock (*volleybird*) for a ball. Try to hit the ball up in the air. Remember, one hit and catch it; then hit again.

Ⓣ Try to strike the ball up more than once—maybe twice—and then catch it.

EQUIPMENT MODIFICATIONS

▶ Visual tracking is a skill that is not refined until the later elementary grades; therefore, striking, unless modified, is a difficult skill theme for children. A few simple equipment modifications allow young children to experience success in tracking. The use of large, slow-moving, easy-to-see objects, such as balloons or beach balls, makes tracking easier. The use of lightweight, short-handled, easily maneuverable rackets compensates for the developing hand-eye coordination and limited arm strength and endurance. The basic guideline to follow is that the equipment should not hamper the movement pattern; if it does, modify the equipment.

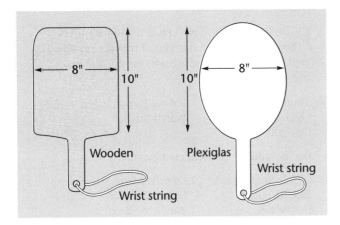

Figure 29.5 Construction of short-handled paddles. Short-handled paddles can be cut with a jigsaw from one-half-inch finished plywood or from one-fourth-inch Plexiglas. Sand plywood edges until they're smooth, and wrap the handles with fiberglass tape. *Each paddle should have a wrist string for safety.*

Control Level: Learning Experiences Leading to Skill Development

Experiences at the control level are designed to help children go beyond just contacting the ball. At this level, children learn to control the direction, force, and aerial pathway of an object. One of the first cues we give children when beginning striking activities is "watch the ball." This is hard for many youngsters because so much else is going on around them. To help children focus on the ball, paint a bright dot or letter on it, and direct their concentration toward that mark.

At the control level we introduce children to a variety of striking implements and to objects with various surfaces, lengths, and types and degrees of bounce, including Ping-Pong paddles, racquetball paddles, paddleball paddles, badminton rackets, tennis rackets, paddleballs, tennis balls, racquetballs, rubber balls, shuttlecocks, Ping-Pong balls. We also introduce children to the sidearm pattern. (At the utilization and proficiency levels, we continue to provide a variety of striking implements and objects.)

A note about cues: Although several cues are listed for many of the learning experiences, it's important to focus on only one cue at a time. That way, the children can really concentrate on that cue. Once you provide feedback to the children and observe that most have learned a cue, then it's time to focus on another one.

> ▶ The difficulty of all striking tasks can be increased or decreased by changing the object being struck. We most often start with shuttlecocks or volleybirds and progress to foam balls and dead tennis balls. We tend to stay away from "live" tennis balls because they encourage children to "hit hard" rather than use the correct pattern and move to receive the ball. Adjust the equipment for each task as appropriate for your children.

DOWNS

Setting: A wooden paddle, a dead tennis ball or a foam ball, and a carpet square or some way to define self-space for each child

Cues	
Flat Paddle	(Keep your paddle flat as a pancake.)
Watch the Ball	(Keep your eyes on the ball all the time.) *(It's helpful to paint a dot on the ball so children have something on which to focus.)*

Tasks/Challenges:

🅣 In your own space dribble the ball with your paddle. See if you can keep it going without a miss.

🅣 Once you can keep the ball going five times or more in a row without leaving your space, see if you can dribble the ball so it stays below your waist.

🅒 How many strikes can you get in a row without having to leave your self-space? These strikes don't have to be below your waist. Ready? Go.

UPS

Setting: A wooden paddle, a dead tennis ball or a foam ball, and a carpet square or some way to define self-space for each child

Cues	
Flat Paddle	(Keep your paddle flat as a pancake.)
Stiff Wrist	(Keep your wrist tight; don't let it flop around.)
Watch the Ball	(Keep your eyes on the ball all the time.) *(It's helpful to paint a dot on the ball so children have something on which to focus.)*

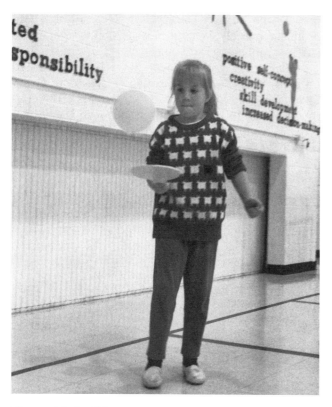

Figure 29.6   This youngster is seeing how many times she can strike her object before it touches the ground.

Tasks/Challenges:

T Now let's see if you can stay in your self-space and keep the ball going, but hit it up so that it doesn't touch the floor (Figure 29.6).

T Can you hit the ball up so that it goes above your head every time and still stay in self-space?

C Every time the paddle hits the ball, say one letter of your name. Can you spell your first name? Your last name? Your best friend's name? Remember, each time you miss you have to start spelling the word over again.

UPS AND DOWNS

Setting: A foam or wooden paddle, a dead tennis ball or a foam ball, and a carpet square or some way to define self-space for each child

Cues	
Flat Paddle	(Keep your paddle flat as a pancake.)
Stiff Wrist	(Keep your wrist tight; don't let it flop around.)

The skill of striking with rackets and paddles is complex and has a number of critical cues associated with it. These cues include, for the underarm striking pattern:

Slanted Paddle	Follow Through
Paddle Way Back	Watch the Ball
Opposite Foot	

For the sidearm pattern, cues include:

Paddle Way Back	Opposite Foot
Side to Target	Follow Through
Flat Paddle	Watch the Ball
Firm Wrist	

We have elected to highlight only some of these cues with various tasks throughout the remainder of the chapter. Feel free to interchange the cues that will best meet the needs of your students for those we have selected.

Watch the Ball	(Keep your eyes on the ball all the time.)

Tasks/Challenges:

T Now let's see if you can still stay in self-space and keep the ball going. One time bounce it off the floor, and the next time hit it into the air.

C Let's make up a sequence. For example, your sequence might be: up once, down once, up twice, down twice, up three times, down three times, and then start over. Practice until you can do your sequence two times in a row.

T Can you hit the ball up and down while walking around your self-space—without losing control of the ball?

C Try to do your sequence while you walk around in self-space.

T If that was easy, you might want to try skipping, or sliding, or galloping in self-space as you strike the ball.

T This time it becomes harder. We are going to walk in general space while striking the ball. Walk very slowly while you continue to strike the ball. For safety, be sure to look where you are going. If you think you are going to lose control of the ball, stand still for a second and catch the ball or let it bounce on the floor until you get control back; then keep going. If you do lose your ball, walk and pick it up, and start again.

When children begin moving and striking simultaneously, they tend to concentrate so much on the striking that they forget to watch out for others and for rolling balls. Besides reminding them to watch out, conduct these tasks in the largest possible space, preferably outdoors.

UP AGAINST THE WALL (STRIKING FORWARD)

Setting: A shuttlecock, a foam ball or a dead tennis ball, and a paddle for each child; children about five feet from the wall, with spots or carpet squares to remind them of their self-space

Cues

Paddle Way Back	(Start the paddle back behind your hips.)
Opposite Foot	(Just as in throwing, step forward on the foot opposite the arm you are using to strike.)
Slanted Paddle	(For this hit, keep the paddle face flat, but slant it just slightly toward the ceiling so the ball will go to the wall.)

The slight angle (slant) of the paddle face is critical here. It is helpful to demonstrate the subtle difference between it and a Flat Paddle and what the skill looks like.

Tasks/Challenges:

T Facing the wall and at your own spot, drop the shuttlecock and try to strike it so it goes straight ahead—forward toward the wall. **This strike is a little like an underhand throw; you are actually striking the shuttlecock from underneath, not from the side.**

T Now trade in your shuttlecock for a ball. This will be a little harder, but it's the same idea. Try to strike the ball with the paddle so it goes straight forward toward the wall. You may want to let the ball bounce first before you hit it. Remember, just one hit at a time. Drop, hit, catch—then go again.

C Practice until you can hit the ball so it travels to the wall five times.

C Ask the person beside you to watch you strike the ball. Your neighbor will give you a point if you step forward on the opposite foot as you hit. You'll get a second point if you swing the paddle underhand, not sidearm or overhead. Practice with your neighbor watching for a few minutes; then watch your neighbor.

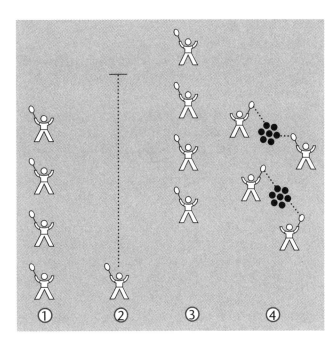

Figure 29.7 Station setup for Ups, Downs, and Forwards.

UPS, DOWN, AND FORWARDS

Setting: Four stations set up as in Figure 29.7, with children divided equally among the stations. At station 1 and 3, foam balls or dead tennis balls and paddles for every child; at station 2, balloons and paddles for each child; at station 4, yarn balls and paddles for each child, as well as seven hoops in a cloverleaf pattern for each pair

Cues

Stations 1, 2, and 3:

Flat Paddle	(Keep your paddle flat as a pancake.)
Stiff Wrist	(Keep your wrist tight; don't let it flop around.)
Watch the Ball	(Keep your eyes on the ball all the time.)

Station 4:

Paddle Way Back	(Start the paddle back behind your hips.)
Opposite Foot	(Just as in throwing, step forward on the foot opposite the arm you are using to strike.)
Slanted Paddle	(For this hit, keep the paddle face flat, but slant it just slightly toward the ceiling so the ball will go to the hoops.)

Tasks/Challenges:

T The stations today provide a chance to practice all the striking activities we have been doing. Some are just practice; others are challenges. Do your best. Change on the signal.

Station 1: How many downward hits can you do with no mistakes? Count them.
Station 2: Travel across the gym, striking the balloon upward as you go.
Station 3: Can you do five single upward hits without moving from self-space? Try continuous hits.
Station 4: Strike the ball so that it travels forward and lands in a hoop. Each time you are successful, increase your distance by taking one giant step backward.

 The preceding task could easily be turned into a self-assessment by having children record on cards how they did at each station.

BOTH SIDES (OF THE PADDLE) NOW

Setting: A wooden or foam paddle, a dead tennis ball or foam ball, and a carpet square or other way to define self-space for each child

Cues	
Flat Paddle	(Keep your paddle flat as a pancake.)
Stiff Wrist	(Keep your wrist tight; don't let it flop around.)
Watch the Ball	(Keep your eyes on the ball at all times.)

Tasks/Challenges:

T In tennis, racquetball, or badminton, players use both sides of the paddle. Let's try this. Keep hitting the ball up. Try to hit the ball with one side of the paddle, then the other.

T If that is easy, see if you can use both sides of the paddle and both sides of the body. Try not always to strike the ball when it is right in front of you.

T Can you make a rainbow with the ball? Hit it on one side of your body and then the other so the ball travels in a rainbow shape. Remember, if you miss the ball and have to chase it, go back to your self-space before you start striking again.

C How many rainbows can you make? Each time the ball goes over your head, it counts as one. Five rainbows without a miss would be excellent!

STRIKING TO WALL TARGETS

Setting: A wooden paddle and tennis ball for each student; twelve- to twenty-inch circles about six feet up on the wall in a scattered pattern

Cues	
Paddle Way Back	(Start the paddle back behind your hips.)
Opposite Foot	(Just as in throwing, step forward on the foot opposite the arm you are using to strike.)
Slanted Paddle	(For this hit, keep the paddle face flat, but slant it just slightly toward the ceiling so the ball will go to the wall.)

Tasks/Challenges:

T Find a spot about ten feet from the wall in front of a circle. Strike the ball to the wall, trying to hit the circle. Remember, this is a back-to-front swing—like an underhand throw. **If you are doing it correctly, your arm will almost brush your hip on the way forward.**

T For the next five hits, freeze your follow-through. **Check to see if you have the opposite foot forward and your arm extended, with the racket face slanted slightly toward the ceiling.**

C When you think you can do five perfect hits with opposition and slanted racket facing the target, raise your hand and I will come to observe or a friend can observe for you.

T Try to send the ball to the wall so that it touches within two to three inches of the target.

C Can you come that close five times?

T Take a giant step backward. Strike the ball so that it contacts the wall at the height of the target.

T When you are successful in hitting the target six times, take another giant step backward.

T Move back to your first space closest to the wall. See if you can use an underhand strike to make the ball drop just in front of the wall.

T When you can successfully drop the shot just in front of the wall, take a giant step backward and try the drop shoot from the longer distance.

C Pick your favorite distance. Count how many times you can hit the target without a mistake. How many times can you drop the ball just in front of the wall?

STRIKING FOR DISTANCE (VARYING THE FORCE)

Setting: Outdoors on a large field (so that children can work safely without hitting one another); children all facing the same way, either in a line or away from the center of a circle; a paddle and a variety of objects to strike for each child; objects (spots or cones) for use as markers

Cues

Opposite Foot	(Just as in throwing, step forward on the foot opposite the arm you are using to strike.)
Slanted Paddle	(For this hit, keep the paddle face flat, but slant it just slightly toward the ceiling so the ball will go to the target. Use less slant for longer hits.)
Follow Through	(Follow through with your racket so that it is aimed straight at the target.)

Tasks/Challenges:

🅣 Standing on the line, all facing the same direction so you won't hit anyone else, practice striking the objects, changing the amount of force that you use for hitting. Sometimes use a lot of force, sometimes not very much force. Each time, make sure that you use the proper underarm swing and that you follow through, no matter what amount of force you use. Use up all your objects and then go collect them.

🅒 This time you're going to play a game with yourself. First, strike an object as far as possible. Take a marker, and mark the place where your object fell. Be sure that you can see the mark from the striking line. Now try to hit an object to halfway between the striking line and your far object. Practice until you feel as if you've really figured out just exactly the right amount of force to use. Then see if you can hit the middle spot three times in a row.

🅣 After you've done this task three times in a row, hit another object as far as you can, mark it, and try the same thing all over again.

STRIKING FOR HOOPS (VARYING THE DISTANCE)

Setting: Partners; a wooden paddle and a variety of objects to hit for each child; a hoop to serve as a target for each pair

Cues

Opposite Foot	(Just as in throwing, step forward on the foot opposite the arm you are using to strike.)
Slanted Paddle	(For this hit, keep the paddle face flat, but slant it just slightly toward the ceiling so the ball will go to the target. Use less slant for longer hits and more slant for shorter hits.)
Follow Through	(Follow through with your racket so that it is aimed straight at the target.)

🅣 Place your hoop on the ground. One partner will be the hitter; the other, the catcher. The hitter strikes the object so that it lands in the hoop—hits the target. First, stay close, and then after you can hit the target three times, move back a few steps and try again. Your partner will keep the objects from going all over the place. After you take six hits, switch places with your partner for six hits and then switch back.

🅒 Now you're going to make a game out of striking into hoops. Place three hoops on the floor, one about three feet away from you, one six feet away, and one ten feet away. One partner will try to strike so that the object lands in each hoop; the other partner will collect the object after the hits. Then the partners switch places. You can make up any other rules that you wish, but you both need to practice striking into all three hoops.

TO THE WALL—SIDEWAYS (SIDEARM FOREHAND PATTERN)

Setting: A paddle and ball for each child; marks or carpet squares to define self-space; large Xs placed about three feet high on the wall in front of each space

Cues

Flat Paddle	(Keep your paddle flat as a pancake.)
Stiff Wrist	(Keep your wrist tight; don't let it flop around.)
Side to Wall	(Keep the side opposite the arm you're using to hit to the wall.)
Opposite Foot	(Just as in throwing, step forward on the foot opposite the arm you are using to strike.)

Forehand grip   Backhand grip

Figure 29.8   Examples of forehand and backhand grips.

An additional cue that is sometimes needed with the sidearm pattern is to keep the elbow away from the side. We use that cue as necessary with individuals or groups of children.

Tasks/Challenges:

🅣 Until now you have used an underhand pattern to strike the ball. Now we are going to learn a new pattern: the sidearm pattern, like what is used in tennis and racquetball. **This time your side is to the wall and your paddle is flat.** This is called the *forehand,* and you will use the forehand grip (Figure 29.8). Practice striking the ball to the wall from a mark on the floor using the sidearm pattern. Remember, these are single hits—drop, hit, and catch, and go again.

🅒 Practice until you can hit the ball so that it travels to the wall five times.

🅣 After you can hit the wall five times, take one giant step backward and try from that distance. When you can hit the wall five times, move backward again.

🅣 Return to your first spot, and try and hit the X on the wall in front of your space. When you can make five hits, move backward again.

🅒 Pick your favorite distance. How many times can you hit the target without missing?

With the forehand and backhand grips, we demonstrate the grip before the task, observe the children's grips as they practice, and provide feedback as necessary. We do not spend a lot of time teaching the grip.

TO THE WALL AGAIN—SIDEWAYS (SIDEARM BACKHAND PATTERN)

Setting: A paddle and a ball for each child; marks or carpet squares to define self-space; large Xs placed

about three feet high on the wall in front of each space

Cues	
Flat Paddle	(Keep your paddle flat toward the wall all the time.)
Stiff Wrist	(Keep your wrist tight; don't let it flop around.)
Watch the Ball	(Keep your eyes on the ball all the time. Watch it hit the paddle.)
Same Foot/ Same Shoulder	(Just as in throwing a Frisbee, step forward on the same foot and have the shoulder of the arm you are using to strike toward the wall.)

Tasks/Challenges:

🅣 This is also a sidearm pattern, but from the other side of your body. In tennis it is called the *backhand*, and you will use the backhand grip (Figure 29.8). It is the same as the forehand—except the side of your body of the arm you are using to strike is to the wall, and you step forward on the same foot as your striking arm. You reach across your body to hit. Practice striking the ball to the wall from a mark on the floor using the backhand pattern. Remember, these are single hits—drop, hit, and catch, and go again.

🅒 Practice until you can hit the ball so that it travels to the wall five times.

🅣 After you can hit the wall five times, take one giant step backward and try from that distance. When you can hit the wall five times, move backward again.

🅣 Return to your first spot, and try and hit the X on the wall in front of your space. When you can make five hits, move backward again.

🅒 Pick your favorite distance. How many times can you hit the target without missing?

▶ Place a metal gong, small bells, loose plastic jugs, or similar sound-producing objects on a wall as targets. Young children enjoy the auditory feedback when contact is made.

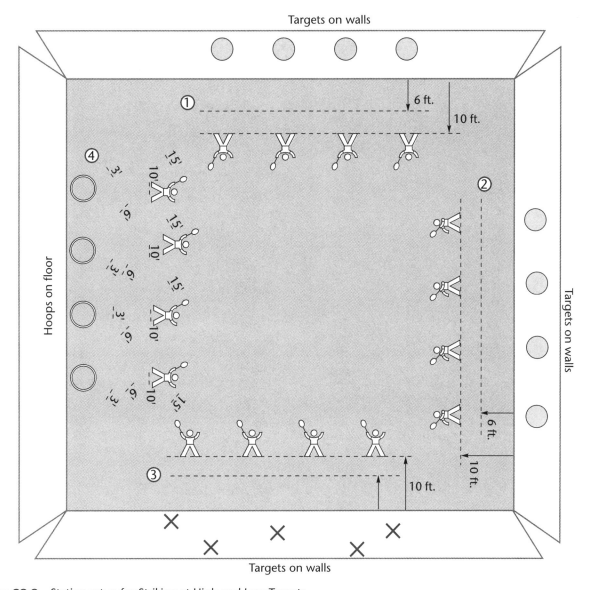

Figure 29.9   Station setup for Striking at High and Low Targets.

STRIKING AT HIGH AND LOW TARGETS

Setting: A paddle and a ball for each child. Four stations set up as in Figure 29.9. At stations 1 and 2: spots marked on the floor about six and ten feet from the wall; targets on the wall in front of each space about three feet high. At station 3: spots marked on the floor about ten feet from the wall; targets on the wall about six feet high (see Figure 29.10). At station 4: hoops on the floor against the wall; spots marked in various places around the hoops about three, six, ten, and fifteen feet away.

Cues

Paddle Face	(Your paddle will be slightly slanted or flat depending on which striking pattern you use.)
Stiff Wrist	(Keep your wrist tight: don't let it flop around.)
Watch the Ball	(Keep your eyes on the ball all the time. Watch it hit the paddle.)
Opposite Foot	(Just as in throwing, step forward on the foot opposite the arm you are using to strike.)

Figure 29.10 Target design for Striking at High and Low Targets, station 3. *(The Xs on the wall should be large enough to be hit easily.)*

Tasks/Challenges:

T You have practiced both underhand and sidearm striking patterns. You can use them both, but one is better for some things, and the other is better for other things. The underhand pattern works best when you want to send the ball to high places or make it drop low. The sidearm pattern works when you want the ball to go in a more straight forward route. Now you will get a chance to mix them up. At each station you will have to decide which striking pattern is best to use. See if you can figure out each station. I will tell you that at station 2 you have to use the backhand.

Station 1: Try to hit the target as many times as you can. When you hit the target six times, move backward to the next mark.

Station 2: Try to hit the target with a backhand pattern. What is the highest number of times you can hit the wall from each spot?

Station 3: Pick out one X on the target and see if you can hit it five times; then choose another X, and another, and finally the last X. When you can hit all of them five times, move backward one step.

Station 4: From each of the marks on the floor see if you can drop the ball into the hoop.

 It would be very appropriate here to use an exit slip to assess the children's understanding of the various striking patterns, their cues, and their uses. See Chapter 14 for examples.

HITTING TO DIFFERENT PLACES

Setting: A paddle and a ball for each child; marks or carpet squares to define self-space; large Xs about three feet high on the wall in front of each space

Cues	
Paddle Face	(Your paddle will be slightly slanted or flat depending on which striking pattern you use.)
Follow Through	(Follow through with the paddle straight toward your target.)
Watch the Ball	(Keep your eyes on the ball all the time. Watch it hit the paddle.)
Opposite Foot	(Just as in throwing, step forward on the foot opposite the arm you are using to strike.)

Tasks/Challenges:

T This time instead of trying to hit the X, pretend that the target is your opponent. Try to hit a space about two feet to the right of the X. Practice until you can hit your space six times. You can use an underhand or a sidearm pattern (Figure 29.11).

T Now practice trying to hit a space to the left of the X. Again, practice until you can hit the space six times.

T This time practice doing one hit to the right and the next hit to the left and the next hit to the X. See if you can repeat your pattern five times.

C Ask the person next to you to be your partner. You will call out where you are going to hit before the strike. Your partner gives a thumbs-up if you hit where you called out or a thumbs-down if you didn't. After eight hits, trade places.

STRIKING THROUGH A TARGET

Setting: A hoop suspended at about shoulder height for each group of two; a paddle for each child; one ball per group

Figure 29.11 Children at the control level benefit from repeatedly striking a ball against a wall.

Cues

Paddle Face	(Your paddle will be flat or slightly slanted depending on which striking pattern you use.)
Watch Ball/ Watch Target	(Keep your eyes on the ball all the time: See it hit the paddle; see it go to the target. Watch the target out of the corner of your eye.)
Opposite Foot	(Just as in throwing, step forward on the foot opposite the arm you are using to strike.)

Tasks/Challenges:

🅣 At your hoop, one of you will bounce the ball on the floor and then try to strike it through the hoop. The partner will catch the ball and return it to the striker. After ten strikes, change places.

🅣 Now that you've practiced by first letting the ball bounce, try it without letting the ball bounce. In other words, just drop the ball, hit it before it hits the ground, and try to make it go through the hoop.

🅒 Since you are so good at this, why don't we make it a game? How many hits in a row can you and your partner combined get?

STRIKING AN OBJECT TO SEND IT OVER A NET

Setting: A net (or a rope between two chairs) about two to three feet high for each group of partners; a paddle for each child; one ball per group

Cues

Paddle Face	(Your paddle will be flat or slightly slanted depending on which pattern you use.)
Watch Ball/ Watch Target	(Keep your eyes on the ball all the time: See it hit the paddle; see it go to the target. Watch the target out of the corner of your eye.)
Opposite Foot	(Just as in throwing, step forward on the foot opposite the arm you are using to strike.)

Tasks/Challenges:

🅣 With one partner on either side of the net, partner 1 strikes the ball across the net. Partner 2, instead of hitting the ball back, will catch it and throw it back to partner 1. After ten hits, change roles. It helps to bounce the ball on the floor once before you hit it across the net.

🅣 This time, use three different striking patterns to hit the ball across the net: forehand swing, backhand swing, and underhand swing. Take ten practices with one swing, and then switch; take ten practices with another swing, and then switch; take ten practices with the third swing, and then switch. Ready? Three different ways of striking, ten practices each.

🅣 You can practice any way of striking you want this time, but try to pick a spot on the opposite side of the net and hit the ball to that spot, as if you were aiming for a target. Ten practices each, then switch.

So that children in every group have their own net to work over, simply suspend a rope between two chairs. This way you can set up nets of different heights and lengths at various places around the space.

STRIKING A BALL REBOUNDING FROM A WALL

Setting: Wall space, with a line marked about three feet up the wall and a line marked on the ground six to eight feet from the wall; a paddle and a ball for each child

Cues

Quick Feet	(As the ball returns, you want to be behind it and a little to the side. You will have to move quickly to get there.)
Watch the Ball	(Keep your eyes on the ball all the time. See it hit the paddle: see it go to the wall.)
Bend Knees	(You want to contact the ball at about your waist. You'll have to bend your knees to do this.)

Tasks/Challenges:

🅣 Now you're going to have a chance to strike the ball against a wall. In your space, about six feet from the wall, practice striking the ball against the wall with a forehand strike and the forehand grip (*Figure 29.8*). **When you hit the ball, you should be slightly behind and about an arm's length to the side of the ball.**

🅒 Here comes the challenge. See how many times you can strike the ball against the wall and let the ball bounce only once before hitting it again. If you miss, just start counting over.

🅣 Now I'm going to make the activity a little harder for you. Hit the ball to different places on the wall, always trying to be ready to hit it when it comes back to you. **In other words, you'll have to figure out where the ball is coming when it bounces off the wall and be behind it so you can hit it again.** Remember, hit different places on the wall.

🅒 This time, the challenge is really hard. You need to see how many times in a row you can hit the ball above the line on the wall. The ball can bounce only once on the ground between hits. Ready? Go.

🅣 This time, you can do what you've wanted to do for a long time: hit the ball as hard as you can. But I have some rules. First, the ball must land behind the line marked on the ground; second, you're allowed only one bounce to hit the ball back. This prevents you from hitting the ball so hard that you can't get to it.

 When allowing children to strike the ball as hard as they can, make sure they are spread far apart and clearly understand the rules for retrieving a ball that has gone into another person's space.

STRIKING CONTINUOUSLY OVER AND THROUGH A TARGET

Setting: A hoop, hoop stand, two paddles, and a ball for each set of partners

Cues	
Quick Feet	(As the ball returns, you want to be behind it and a little to the side. You will have to move quickly to get there.)
Watch the Ball	(Keep your eyes on the ball all the time. See it hit the paddle; see it go over the hoop.)
Bend Knees	(You want to contact the ball at about your waist. You'll have to bend your knees to do this.)

▶ To be accomplished both safely and effectively, striking activities require a great deal of space. Unfortunately, many indoor facilities in elementary schools don't have such spaces available. If this is true at your school and there aren't any outdoor alternatives, you can have two activities going simultaneously in the space available. Some children can carry out striking activities against the walls while other children carry out activities that require less space, such as balancing or weight transference, in the center of the space or on a stage area.

Tasks/Challenges:

🅣 Now you'll play a game with your partner using all that you have learned. Set up the hoop on the hoop stand on the center line of your area. Hit the ball back and forth over the hoop, letting the ball bounce on your side before hitting it back. After five hits over the hoop, the receiver must hit the ball through the hoop so that it goes to the partner's side. If the hit through the hoop is good, play continues for another five "overs" and one "through." If the "through" is not good, the five "overs" start over again.

Utilization Level: Learning Experiences Leading to Skill Development

Experiences at the utilization level enable children to strike with an implement, not as an invariant skill, but in dynamic environments that involve partners and striking from different positions in relation to the body.

A note about cues: Although several cues are listed for many of the learning experiences, it's important to focus on only one cue at a time. That way, the children can really concentrate on that cue. Once you provide feedback to the children and observe that most have learned a cue, then it's time to focus on another one.

FROM BOTH SIDES NOW

Setting: A space about 10 feet by 10 feet; partners, each with a paddle; one ball per group

Cues	
Watch the Ball	(Keep your eyes on the ball all the time. See it hit the paddle; see your partner hit it.)

Bend Knees	(You want to contact the ball at about your waist. You'll have to bend your knees to do this.)
Side to Target	(Whether you strike forehand or backhand, your side should face your partner.)
Get Home	(Return to a position in the center and near the back of your space after each hit. This is called home. It will take quick feet to get there.)

TASKS/CHALLENGES:

🔵 This time, your partner is going to throw rather than hit to you. Partner 1 will throw the ball to partner 2 so that it bounces once before it reaches partner 2. Partner 2—the hitting partner—then tries to hit the ball straight back to partner 1—the thrower—regardless of where the ball has been sent. Partner 1 then catches the ball and throws to a new place. After ten throws, switch places. The first time, always throw the ball to your partner's right side. The next time, always throw it to your partner's left side.

🔵 This time, don't let your partner know to which side you're going to throw the ball. **Hitters, as soon as you see the ball leave the thrower's hand, adjust your position so that you can return the ball. Throw ten times, and change.**

In the beginning stages of striking a ball sent by a partner, children benefit from having the ball tossed consistently to their preferred or nonpreferred side. This way they can progress to adjusting the preparatory stage according to the direction of the oncoming ball.

 This is an excellent time for a teacher and/or student assessment (observation, videotape analysis) of the critical cues practiced at the control level. True learning occurs when children can use the cues correctly in dynamic, unpredictable situations. See Chapter 14 for assessment examples.

HITTING COOPERATIVELY AND CONTINUOUSLY WITH A PARTNER

Setting: A space about ten feet by ten feet; partners, each with a paddle and one ball

Cues

Get Home	(Return to a position in the center and near the back of your space after each hit. This is called home. It will take quick feet to get there.)
Watch the Ball	(Keep your eyes on the ball all the time. See it hit the paddle; see your partner hit it.)
Bend Knees	(You want to contact the ball at about your waist. You'll have to bend your knees to do this.)

Tasks/Challenges:

🔵 With your partner, in a space by yourselves, see if you can strike the ball back and forth to each other. The ball should bounce in the middle, but remember to get ready to hit the ball again after each hit.

🟢 Set a personal-best goal with your partner for the number of hits you can get without missing. See if you can attain your goal. Give your partner your best hit each time.

🔵 Make sure that you and your partner practice hitting on both sides of your body.

Tip: The preceding task can be used with any of the striking patterns or a combination of patterns. You may need to remind children about the cue differences for sidearm and underhand striking.

STRIKING TO DIFFERENT PLACES AROUND A PARTNER

Setting: A space about ten feet by twenty feet for each set of partners; two paddles and a ball

Cues

Get Home	(Return to a position in the center and near the back of your space after each hit. It will take quick feet to get there.)
Watch the Ball	(Keep your eyes on the ball all the time. See it hit the paddle; see your partner hit it.)
Follow Through	(Follow through with your paddle in the direction in which you want the ball to go.)

Tasks/Challenges:

🔵 With your partner, strike the ball back and forth, each time hitting to the alternate side of your partner's body. In other words, once you will hit to your partner's left and the next time to your partner's right. Try to keep the ball going for as long as possible. (*Have skilled students demonstrate what it looks like to hit to alternate sides.*)

C As you practice now, see how long you can keep the ball going, but almost try to make your partner miss.

STRIKING OVERHEAD

Setting: A wall space, with a line marked on the wall about three feet from the floor, a spot marked on the ground about ten feet from the wall, and a paddle and a ball for each child

Cues	
Toss	(Toss the ball just barely above the top of the paddle.)
Reach and Stretch	(When you hit the ball, reach and stretch as high as possible.)
Flat and Down	(Your paddle should be flat and facing slightly downward and forward as you strike the ball.)

Demonstrate the skill of striking overhead

Tasks/Challenges:

T Stand on your spot, about ten feet from the wall. Toss the ball higher than your racket can reach in the air and then stretch to hit the ball when it's at its highest point. In other words, throw the ball up, and when it reaches the very top of the throw—the point where it won't go up any farther and hasn't started to come down—hit it so it goes against the wall. Don't try to hit the ball back when it bounces off the wall; just catch it and start over.

T Now that you've caught on to this idea, try to make the ball go down so that it hits the wall near the line, about three feet above the floor. **To make it go down like that, the face of your racket must point slightly down as you hit the ball. Give it a try. Remember to watch the ball contact the racket so that you can see what you're doing.**

T This time, try to strike overhead again, but have the ball strike the wall just above the line. **Watch your racket contact the ball so that you can tell which direction your racket face is pointed.**

STRIKING OVERHEAD OVER A NET

Setting: Balls, a paddle, and a net two to three feet high for each set of partners

Cues	
Toss	(Toss the ball just barely above the top of the paddle.)
Reach and Stretch	(When you hit the ball, reach and stretch as high as possible.)
Flat and Down	(Your paddle should be flat and facing slightly down and forward as you strike the ball.)

Tasks/Challenges:

T You're going to practice hitting overhead again. Stand at the back of your court area, with your partner on the other side of the net. The partner with a paddle and some balls throws a ball in the air just above her or his reach, including the reach of the paddle, and then hits the ball down and over the net. This is like a tennis serve, only everything is smaller. The nonhitting partner should collect all the balls as they're hit. After ten times, switch places.

T As you begin to hit more balls over the net and in the court, start to try to hit the ball a little harder. But don't attempt this until you can get ten hits in a row over the net and into the court.

 Whenever children are striking over a net, always have them clearly define the boundaries of their striking area so that they don't interfere with others.

STRIKING CONTINUOUSLY UPWARD WITH A GROUP

Setting: Groups of three; a paddle for each player; one ball for each group

Cues	
Flat Paddle	(Keep your paddle flat as a pancake.)
Watch Ball/ Watch Players	(Always watch the ball. Watch the other players and the space out of the corner of your eye.)
Quick Feet	(It will take quick feet to get behind and under the ball.)

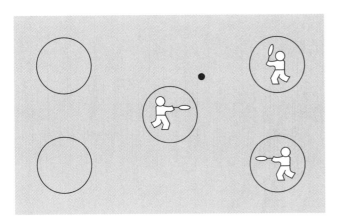

Figure 29.12   Setup for Striking Continuously Upward with a Group.

Tasks/Challenges:

C You need to clearly define the boundaries of your space; they should be approximately eight to ten feet apart. Your task is to keep the ball moving by striking it to each player without losing control. Bounces are allowed if you want them, but you do not have to use them. There is no set order in which you have to hit. See how long you can keep the ball going without losing control.

Setting: Groups of three, each group with one ball, three paddles, and five hoops; a space set up as in Figure 29.12

C This is a game that will let you practice striking in the air. The person in the center hoop begins by striking the ball in the air to a person in one of the other hoops. That person receives the ball, strikes it twice to himself or herself and sends it back to the middle person, who also has to strike it twice before sending it to the other outside person. That outside person has to strike three times to himself or herself before sending it back to the middle, where it is struck three times. This continues until the middle person has to strike seven times to himself or herself. Just to make it harder, the outside people, after striking the ball, have to move to one of the empty hoops. If anyone misses, the whole group starts over again. We will change middle hitters after seven hits or three minutes.

STRIKING IN VARIOUS AERIAL PATHWAYS IN GAMELIKE SITUATIONS

Setting: Different-colored pieces of yarn suspended one above the other—at three feet, six feet, and ten

feet—for use as nets (Figure 29.13); partners, each with a paddle; one shuttlecock or volleybird per group

Cues	
Slanted Paddle	(Your paddle needs to have a flat face that is slanted upward.)
Follow Through	(Follow through toward the string you are trying to go over.)
Get Home	(After each hit, move back to your center back position to get ready to hit again.)

Tasks/Challenges:

T Using a shuttlecock (volleybird) and an underarm swing, try to make the object go over the lowest piece of yarn. After five tries, switch with your partner.

T Now try the middle piece of yarn. Do this five times each, then switch.

T Now the highest piece. For this one, you're really going to have to use a big underarm swing to get the object over the net.

C This task will be difficult. Try to keep the shuttlecock (volleybird) going with your partner, but this time, on the first hit, make it go over the low piece of yarn; on the next hit, make it go over the middle piece; on the third hit, make it go over the top piece. Then start over and reverse the order. Practice until you can do the sequence one time all the way through.

RACKET CALL BALL

Setting: Group of up to five people, each with a paddle; one ball per group

Cues	
Flat Paddle	(Keep your paddle flat as a pancake.)
Watch Ball/ Watch Players	(Always watch the ball; watch the other players and the space out of the corner of your eye.)
Quick Feet	(It will take quick feet to get behind and under the ball.)

Tasks/Challenges:

C You are going to play a striking game. Here are the rules:

Figure 29.13 Setup for aerial pathways.

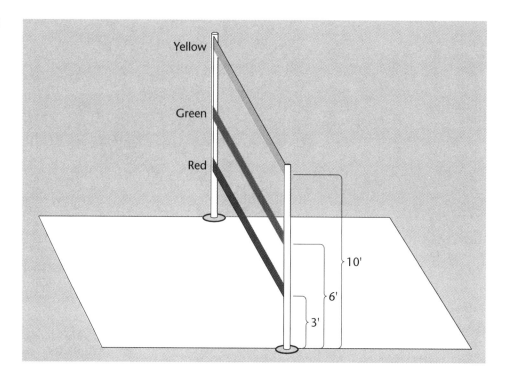

1. One person stands in the middle of a circle.
2. The person in the middle hits the ball with a paddle straight up in the air and calls out the name of another person in the group.
3. The person whose name is called out must run to the middle of the circle, hit the ball up in the air before it bounces, and call out another student's name.
4. The caller takes the place of the person whose name was called out.

The type of racket used can increase the complexity of any striking situation. A light, short-handled racket is the easiest for a child to master; a heavy, long-handled racket is the most difficult. As children begin to master the skills of striking with rackets, we gradually change the type of racket used, to make the task more difficult.

Proficiency Level: Learning Experiences Leading to Skill Proficiency

Experiences at the proficiency level encourage children to enjoy the challenge of striking with short-handled implements in game situations. These experiences involve partner or opponent relationships, spatial strategy, and the varied use of effort qualities.

A note about cues: Although several cues are listed for many of the learning experiences, it's important to focus on only one cue at a time. That way, the children can really concentrate on that cue. Once you provide feedback to the children and observe that

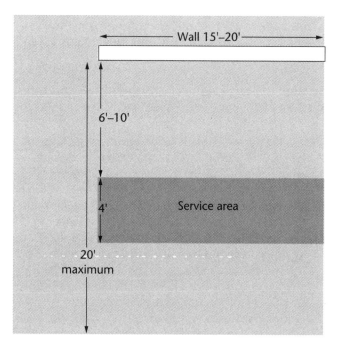

Figure 29.14 Setup for Wall Ball.

most have learned a cue, then it's time to focus on another one.

WALL BALL

Setting: Two children per group, each with a paddle; one ball per group; court set up as in Figure 29.14

Cues

Get Home	(Return to a position in the center and near the back of your space after each hit.)
Watch the Ball	(Keep your eyes on the ball all the time. See it hit the paddle; see it hit the wall; see your partner hit it.)
Mix 'Em Up	(It's time to use all your different strikes: to different spots on the wall and soft and hard strikes.)

Tasks/Challenges:

T Today you're going to play Wall Ball. The objective of this game is to hit the ball against a wall so your opponent is unable to return it. Here are the rules:

1. You may score only when you serve.
2. The ball may be returned either after one bounce or before the bounce.

The courts are marked on the floor. To start play, partner 1 serves the ball against the wall and partner 2 tries to return it. Each time partner 1 hits the ball, partner 2 tries to return it. You get points only when you serve and your partner fails to return the ball; if the server misses the ball at any time during a rally, the partner gains the serve.

RACKET CORNER BALL

Setting: Two people per group, each with a paddle; one ball per court; court set up as in Figure 29.15

Cues

Get Home	(Return to a position in the center and near the back of your space after each hit.)
Watch the Ball	(Keep your eyes on the ball all the time. See it hit the paddle; see it hit the wall; see your partner hit it.)
Mix 'Em Up	(It's time to use all your different strikes: to different spots on the wall and soft and hard strikes.)

Tasks/Challenges:

C This game is very much like the last game that you played, except that it's played in a corner instead of just flat against the wall. As you might guess, the game is called Racket Corner Ball. All the same rules apply as for Wall Ball: There are two players;

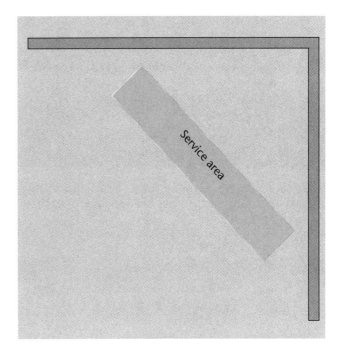

Figure 29.15   Setup for Racket Corner Ball.

points are won only when you serve; and the ball is hit either after one bounce or before it bounces. Go ahead and get used to playing in the corner.

Wall Ball and Racket Corner Ball can be played cooperatively instead of competitively. That is, children may prefer to see how many hits they can make without a miss.

RACKET FOUR SQUARE

Setting: Four square courts, each about fifteen by fifteen feet, labeled A, B, C, and D; groups of four students, with paddles and a ball

Cues

Ready Position	(Keep your weight on the balls of your feet, with your knees slightly bent.)
Paddle in Front	(To be ready, hold your paddle in front of your body about waist high.)
Back of Square	(Stay near the back of the square so you can move forward.)

Tasks/Challenges:

C This game is Racket Four Square. Here are the rules:

1. Square A starts the game.
2. You must hit the ball to another square.

3. The ball can't be hit to the person who hit it to you.
4. You must hit the ball after its first bounce.
5. The person who misses the ball goes to square D, and everyone else moves up a square.
6. All strikes must be underhanded.

MINITENNIS

Setting: Partners; a low net on a surface that allows the ball to bounce, with a marked-off court at each net area for each pair

Cues

Get Home	(Return to a position in the center and near the back of your space after each hit.)
Watch the Ball	(Keep your eyes on the ball all the time. See it hit the paddle; see your partner hit it.)
Mix 'Em Up	(It's time to use all your different strikes: to different spots on the wall and soft and hard strikes.)

Tasks/Challenges:

Ⓒ The objective of this game is to send the ball over the net so that it bounces within the court and the opponent hits the ball before it bounces twice. Here are the rules:

1. Play begins with an overhead strike behind the end line.
2. The ball can bounce no more than once on each side of the net.
3. You may hit the ball before it bounces.
4. The ball cannot be hit so hard that it is unreturnable.

You may or may not keep score; the choice is yours. If you decide to keep score, decide before you start to play how you'll do so.

AERIAL NET GAMES

Setting: Solid rackets, paddles, or badminton rackets; shuttlecocks, tennis balls, or volleybirds; one net (between children's shoulder and head height) for each set of partners; a marked-off court at each net with a serving line (Figure 29.16)

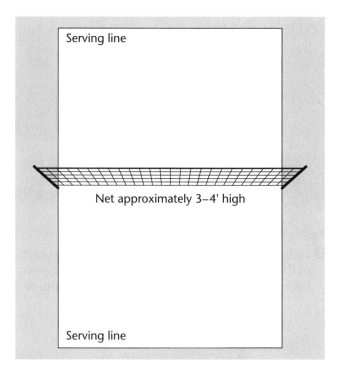

Figure 29.16   Court setup for aerial net games.

Cues

Get Home	(Return to a position in the center and near the back of your space after each hit.)
Watch the Ball	(Keep your eyes on the ball all the time: see it hit the paddle; see your partner hit it.)
Mix 'Em Up	(It's time to use all your different strikes: to different spots on the wall and soft and hard strikes.)

Tasks/Challenges:

Ⓒ The objective of this aerial net game is to send the object over the net so that the opponent can return it before it touches the floor. Here are the rules:

1. Play begins with an underhand strike behind the serve line.
2. Aerial strikes continue until the object touches the floor or goes out of bounds.
3. If you like, you can make up your own way of changing serves and keeping points.

Aerial net games using a shuttlecock can be played with regular tambourines, with old ones that are discarded from rhythm bands because the jingles have been lost, or with tambourines with rubberized heads. Children enjoy the sound made when the shuttlecock strikes the tambourine.

MINITENNIS DOUBLES

Setting: Groups of four with tennis balls, wooden paddles, and a net; a court of four equal squares, with a net running down the center

Cues

Get Home	(Return to a position in the center and near the back of your space after each hit.)
Watch the Ball	(Keep your eyes on the ball all the time. See it hit the paddle; see your opponents hit it.)
Mix 'Em Up	(It's time to use all your different strikes: to different spots on the wall and soft and hard strikes.)
Cover Space	(You want to block all the space on the court. One player usually plays near the net, and one back. When one moves, the other must adjust.)

Tasks/Challenges:

Ⓒ This game is called Minitennis Doubles. Here are the rules:

1. There are two people on each team.
2. Team A serves underhand and diagonally to team B.
3. The two teams hit the ball back and forth across the net until one team misses.
4. When the team serving misses, the other team takes over serving.
5. When the receiving team misses, the serving team keeps serving.
6. The serve always begins in the back right-hand corner behind the line, alternates to the back left-hand corner on every consecutive serve, and then back to the right.
7. The ball may be hit before it bounces or after one bounce.
8. The ball cannot be hit so hard that it is unreturnable.

BADMINTON VOLLEYBALL

Setting: Groups of six, with badminton rackets or paddles, shuttlecocks, and a net

Cues

Quick Feet	(Move quickly to get behind and under the shuttlecock.)
Close to Net	(One player should be close to the net for the last hit.)
Get Home	(After each hit, move back to your position on the court so the space is covered.)

Tasks/Challenges:

Ⓒ You're going to play Badminton Volleyball. Here are the rules:

1. There are three players on each team.
2. A player near the back of the court serves underhand to the other side of the net. The opponents hit the shuttlecock twice on their side of the net and then return it over the net.
3. The shuttlecock must be hit twice by two different players on each side of the net before it's returned.
4. The shuttlecock must be hit before it touches the ground.
5. When the serving team misses, the other team scores.
6. Keep score any way you want or not at all.

 Badminton Volleyball is an enjoyable game, but the use of long-handled rackets requires enough room to allow children to strike without hitting each other. Play the game in a space at least the size of a regulation volleyball court.

SELF-DESIGNED RACKET GAMES

Setting: Depends on the game; groups of six or fewer, each child with a foam racket

Cues

Appropriate to the game

Tasks/Challenges:

Ⓒ Today you're going to combine all that you've practiced into a game. You'll make up your games yourselves. In your groups, make up a game that involves striking with a foam racket. You can have whatever rules you want as long as you include these two: (1) The game must involve striking with foam rackets, and (2) everyone in your group must be playing at the same time. In other words, nobody sits out and waits for a turn. Remember, groups of no more than six, striking with foam rackets, and everybody plays. Go.

After you've made up your rules and started to play your game, make sure you know your rules so that you can tell somebody else how to play your game. At the end of class, I'll ask you to write down your game.

 An appropriate assessment task at this point would be to have children write down how to play their games and then share the games with others. See Chapter 14 for more assessment examples.

READING COMPREHENSION QUESTIONS

1. Students at the precontrol level benefit from striking an object suspended from a string. Describe three different ways to suspend objects.
2. What types of striking implements and objects are recommended for students at the precontrol level?
3. How does a teacher know when a child is ready to be challenged to strike the ball on the opposite side of the body (i.e., backhand)?
4. Describe the position of a child's arms and feet when the child is striking with a racket or paddle.
5. What characterizes each of the four generic levels of skill proficiency of striking with rackets and paddles?
6. What does a flat paddle look like? What does a slanted paddle face look like? What happens when an object is struck with a paddle held in each position?
7. What does it look like when children run around the ball instead of striking the ball on the opposite side of the body? Describe a task that would help them learn to not run around the ball.
8. A child swings a racket so that it remains at waist level throughout the swing. What direction does the ball travel if the child strikes the ball too early in the swing? Too late in the swing?
9. Design six tasks related to striking with rackets or paddles. Rank them in order from the easiest to the hardest. Be certain to include at least one task from each skill level. Use a different striking implement or object for each task.
10. Name the major safety cue regarding striking.

REFERENCES

National Association for Sport and Physical Education (NASPE). (1995). *Moving into the future: National standards for physical education*. St. Louis, MO: Mosby.

Striking with Long-Handled Implements

The skill of striking is used in many games. We have divided striking into various categories: kicking and punting, volleying and dribbling, striking with rackets, and striking with long-handled implements. This division allows us to cover in some detail the gamut of striking activities. The basic action in all striking is the same—giving impetus to an object with a hit, punch, or tap—although often the purpose and the equipment differ. See Box 30.1 for information on striking with long-handled implements from the *National Standards for Physical Education*.

This chapter focuses on striking using swings in horizontal (batting) and vertical (hockey and golf-type actions) planes. The implements used to accomplish these swings vary from bats to hockey sticks to golf clubs to polo sticks—yet all issue the underlying challenge of coordinating hands and eyes when striking with a long implement. Because vertical and horizontal swings have distinctive characteristics, key observation points for each are presented separately. Both swings involve striking away from the body, but the motor skills differ in relation to the purpose of the task.

Generally, striking is the last fundamental motor pattern learned because of the complexity of the hand-eye coordination involved. Children may possess a mature striking pattern before they're able to consistently make contact with the ball.

A sidearm pattern is used when striking a ball with a bat, to keep the bat at the same distance from the ground and in a horizontal plane throughout the swing. (See Box 30.2 for observation points for striking sidearm.) In contrast, a swing with a hockey stick or a golf club uses a more vertical arc—referred to as an underhand swinging pattern because in many ways it resembles the movement used to throw a ball underhand. (The key observation points for striking using an underhand pattern appear in Box 30.3.) Additionally, dribbling (stick handling) is also included as an underhand pattern.

We don't introduce children to striking with long-handled implements so that they'll become experts at golf, tennis, or hockey. We provide children opportunities to practice striking patterns they're likely to use in a variety of contexts throughout their lives. This rationale can be fully appreciated when watching an adult trying to strike with a long-handled implement. If that individual has had no previous experience with a particular striking pattern, the results can be disastrous. Frustration will result, and ultimately the person may abandon the sport. Our emphasis is on giving children a variety of movement opportunities rather than on perfecting the technical aspects of a particular swing. Specific opportunities to refine and perfect different swings are provided at the secondary level or in private instruction.

Most long-handled implements are designed for adults. Because children aren't "regulation size," they find it difficult to manipulate implements of official size, length, and weight, so we use lightweight, plastic implements in our programs, or we make implements that match the sizes of the children. This prevents the children from learning poor habits when they try to use equipment that is too heavy or too long. The equipment should never inhibit the mature striking pattern.

Levels of Skill Proficiency

Activities at the precontrol level ask children to explore all varieties of striking with long-handled implements. Due to the difficulty of the skill, tasks are developed using large and stationary objects to be struck. Initial striking tasks at this level explore:

1. Striking a large stationary object with a hockey stick
2. Striking a large ball off a batting tee with a plastic bat
3. Traveling slowly while striking an object with a hockey stick

When children are able to make contact with an object, they can be challenged to tasks that require them to include one or two other variables besides striking. Appropriate experiences at the control level include:

1. Striking on the ground to a stationary partner
2. Traveling, stopping, and controlling the ball or puck
3. Tossing a ball to oneself and striking it
4. Striking a ball while traveling in different pathways
5. Striking a ball various distances on the ground and in the air

At the utilization level children are able to control a ball in the space around them and strike consistently with the appropriate striking pattern. We challenge them to use their striking skills in more dynamic and unpredictable situations. Appropriate experiences might include:

1. Propelling an object while traveling, using changes of direction and speed to dodge an opponent
2. Striking an object on the ground against an opponent
3. Striking to open spaces, both in the air and on the ground

BOX 30.1 STRIKING WITH LONG-HANDLED IMPLEMENTS IN THE NATIONAL STANDARDS FOR PHYSICAL EDUCATION

The skill theme of striking with long-handled implements is referenced in the *National Standards for Physical Education* (NASPE, 1995) under Standard 2: Applies movement concepts and principles to the learning and development of motor skills. This standard speaks of the child's recognizing and applying the concept of different grips to the striking action. The sample benchmark states that a child "consistently strikes a softly thrown ball with a bat or paddle, demonstrating an appropriate grip" (p. 34).

4. Passing to a traveling partner

When children reach the proficiency level, many possess mature striking patterns, and striking becomes a skill that can be used in complex, unpredictable, gamelike situations. At this point, children are able to incorporate previous experiences into situations that involve strategic and split-second decisions. Appropriate tasks include:

1. Positioning the body to strike an oncoming object to an open space while traveling and while stationary
2. Striking with a golf club to targets in a strategic situation
3. Passing and receiving an object while moving and dodging other children

ASSESSMENT EXAMPLES
from the National Standards for Physical Education

Event Task/Observational Record

Students are placed in groups of five or six members and are asked to role-play the following scenario: The city Little League coach has asked your group to serve as assistant coaches this season. Specifically, the coach wants you to do a presentation of either (a) throwing and catching OR (b) striking with a bat for a bunt versus a home run. Within each group, students should prepare a presentation to include an oral presentation of the various skills, explaining the variation of each, and a demonstration of the skills. Each person within the group must be part of the presentation. Each group will present their mini-demonstrations to the class.

Criteria for Assessment

a. Demonstrates the skill correctly.

b. Compares and/or contrasts variations within the skills.
c. Presentation is organized and interesting

NASPE (1995, p. 47)

Student Report

Partners videotape each other while striking a ball resting on a batting tee (five times) and while striking a ball thrown by a pitcher (five times). They review the tape with their partner and self-assess according to criteria presented to them in class. Based on this information they write a description of one or more of the following: the critical elements of batting; the consistency of their movement patterns; the differences in cues available when striking from a tee (closed skill) versus striking a pitched ball (open skill); and practice suggestions for improvement in each skill.

Criteria for Assessment

a. Accurately describes the criteria for good batting.
b. Accurately assesses their own consistency of performance.
c. Accurately identifies cues available in open or closed skills.
d. Selects appropriate practice options based on the difference between the two skills.

NASPE (1995, pp. 48–49)

Striking skills may be the last to develop. But once children have developed the ability to consistently strike objects with long-handled implements, they can participate in fascinating activities. The tasks in this chapter are organized according to their relative difficulty. (Our progression spiral for developing the skill themes of striking with long-handled implements

BOX 30.2   KEY OBSERVATION POINTS: SIDEARM STRIKING

1. Does the child swing the bat in a horizontal plane?

NO   YES

2. Does the child take a forward step and follow it quickly with hip, trunk, and arm rotation?

NO   YES

3. Do the child's wrists uncock with contact?

NO   YES

Mature Stage

When children are at the mature stage of sidearm striking, do their strikes look similar to the following sequence? The child steps forward and then quickly rotates the hips, trunk, and arms. The forward movement of the trunk stops before contact, but the whipping rotation from the shoulders and arms continues. The pushing motion of the right arm (left arm, if the child is left-handed) and uncocking of the wrists are the final significant forces.

SOURCE: *Fundamental Motor Patterns,* 2nd ed., by R. L. Wickstrom, 1977, Philadelphia: Lea & Febiger.

BOX 30.3 KEY OBSERVATION POINTS: UNDERHAND STRIKING

1. Is the child's left arm (for right-handed children) kept firm at the top of the backswing?

2. Is the child's weight shifted to the back foot at the top of the backswing, with both knees remaining bent?

3. Is the child's weight shifted to the forward foot as the swing begins?

Mature Pattern

When children are at the mature stage of underhand striking, do their swings look similar to the following sequence? The joints are cocked—weight is shifted to the back foot, the hips and trunk rotate away from the ball, the implement is raised up and behind the back shoulder, and the wrists are cocked. The body weight is then shifted to the forward foot. The hips and spine rotate forward, the forearm swings downward, and the back arm and wrist uncock. The forward arm stays straight throughout the swing.

SOURCE: *Fundamental Motor Patterns,* 2nd ed., by R. L. Wickstrom, 1977, Philadelphia: Lea & Febiger.

Striking with Long-Handled Implements

■ **PROFICIENCY LEVEL**
Half Ball—bats
One-Base Baseball
Six-Player Teeball
Minihockey
Whiffle Ball Golf
Directing the pathway, distance, and speed of an object (Call your Hit)—bats
Directing the pathway, distance, and speed of an object —golf
Keep Away—hockey
Striking to dodge an opponent—hockey

■ **UTILIZATION LEVEL**
Two-on-one hockey
Keeping It Moving—hockey
Passing and receiving on the move—hockey
Striking from a stationary position to a moving target—hockey
One-on-one hockey
Traveling and striking for a goal—hockey
Pathways, speeds, and directions—hockey
Performing a continuous dribble and change of direction—hockey
Dribbling and changing directions backward—hockey
Directing the air pathway of the struck object—golf
Playing Hockey Bowl (small targets)
Playing Hoop Golf
Striking to targets at various distances—golf
Batting, combining distance and placement
Striking a pitched object varying the distance—bats
Hitting to open spaces—bats
Directing the placement of an object—bats
Grounders and flies—bats

■ **CONTROL LEVEL**
Striking while dodging stationary obstacles—hockey
Striking a pitched ball—bats
Striking a self-tossed ball to different distances—bats
Throwing a ball in the air and striking it—bats
Striking to varying distances—golf
Hitting a stationary ball from different places—bats
Striking to different places—hockey
Traveling and striking while changing pathways—hockey
Traveling and changing speeds—hockey
Traveling, stopping, and controlling the ball—hockey
Traveling slowly while striking a ball—hockey
Striking to a stationary partner—hockey
Hit and Run—bats
Striking suspended objects—bats
Striking a stationary ball for distance—bats
Level swings—bats
Striking a stationary ball—bats
Striking to a target (Around the World)—hockey
Striking to targets—hockey
Striking for distance—golf or hockey
Striking in the air—golf
Striking a stationary ball on the ground—hockey or golf

PRECONTROL LEVEL
Traveling slowly while striking a ball—hockey
Striking (dribbling) a ball in self-space—hockey
Striking off a batting tee—bats
Striking to large targets—hockey/golf
Striking a stationary ball—golf or hockey

appears on page 588.) We have developed tasks for both striking patterns. Each task is labeled with the equipment commonly used for the pattern. Tasks in which a sidearm pattern is called for are identified as "bats," though you could easily substitute a tennis racket or a badminton racket. Tasks which utilize an underhand pattern are largely identified as "hockey" and occasionally "golf." The only difference between a golf and a hockey swing is the length of the back swing and follow-through, so tasks could again be interchanged. We have developed most of the tasks that utilize an underhand striking pattern around the shortened hockey-type swing because it has been our experience that that is the action most often developed in elementary physical education. Numerous implements can be substituted for hockey sticks (see the box on page 590). If you choose to develop a series of lessons around one particular striking pattern, be sure to select tasks designed to develop the same pattern.

Precontrol Level: Activities for Exploration

At the precontrol level, a chopping, downward swing is typical for any striking pattern. Children struggle just to make contact between the ball and the striking instrument. Therefore, we give children activities that let them explore striking with the added length that comes with bats and hockey sticks—and the greater demands that length places on their hand-eye coordination. Children explore striking stationary objects with bats, golf clubs, and hockey sticks, and they begin to develop the ability to control a ball with a hockey stick while traveling.

All activities at this level need to be done with balls of various sizes. For beginners, yarn balls or large plastic balls are easier because they're larger and/or don't roll as fast as other balls. For tasks that involve traveling, plastic pucks are easier to control initially if the lesson is being taught on a smooth wood or tile floor. Until children become skilled and responsible, we recommend using plastic balls. The flight of the balls won't be as true, but safety is an important consideration.

 Working with long-handled implements involves some unique safety aspects. Ample space should be provided so that children can swing implements freely and with room to move around. Children should also learn to carry implements safely to their working space, to not swing them around their bodies while walking. When moving around the space, children should walk well behind others so that they will not be hit by an implement or a struck ball.

Figure 30.1 Construction of a golf club or a hockey stick (design by Tom Trimble, University of Georgia).

Materials
Hardwood dowel rod, ⅜" × 3'
Garden hose or rubber tubing, ⅜" (inside diameter)
Roll of electrical or adhesive tape (one roll is enough for at least twelve sticks)
Two flat-headed nails, ⅜"
Coat hanger

Directions
1. Cut an eighteen-inch-long piece of the garden hose and slip it approximately three-and-a-half inches onto the dowel.

2. Insert a piece of coat hanger wire into the hose so that it butts up against the bottom of the dowel and extends almost to the end of the hose.

3. Bend the hose so that the ends meet on the dowel rod. Form the hose at whatever angle you desire.

4. Use two nails to secure the hose to the dowel. One of the two nails can be used to attach the bottom portion of the hose, bent in half, to the top portion.

5. Use tape to further support the hose or the dowel.

STRIKING A STATIONARY BALL—GOLF OR HOCKEY

Setting: Preferably a large outdoor space (but can be adapted for an indoor space); golf club (Figure 30.1) or plastic field hockey stick (short-handled; long-handled street hockey sticks aren't appropriate) for each child; a variety of foam and plastic balls and

▶ Although we have associated hockey with tasks that use an underhand striking action, other sports also use the underhand swing pattern. Several striking implements may be substituted for hockey sticks or golf clubs; many times these alternatives may be more appropriate. Pilo Polo sticks are lighter and softer than hockey sticks. Short-handled broomball sticks provide a wider striking surface but unfortunately are available only in certain areas of the country. Substitution of either of these implements may not only reduce the complexity of the task, but can also take the focus away from a single sport.

pucks; each child in self-space, facing a wall or an object that will block the ball

Tasks/Challenges:

🅣 Stand beside your ball and strike it so it travels to the wall. Hit it hard so it goes all the way to the wall. Make sure to stop the ball when it comes back before you hit it again.

🅒 Practice until you can hit the wall three times in a row.

🅣 Practice hitting from both sides of your body. Each time try to make the ball go to the wall.

🅣 Try striking the ball so it sometimes goes along the floor and sometimes in the air. What makes it go in the air? On the ground?

🅣 Trade in the ball for another kind of ball or a puck. Try all the different things with your new piece of equipment.

🅣 Now move behind your ball. Try striking it to the wall from that position.

🅒 Practice until you can get the ball or puck to the wall three times.

🅣 If you are outside, practice striking the ball as far as you can. Practice strikes from the back and from the side. Which position do you like best?

STRIKING TO LARGE TARGETS—HOCKEY/GOLF

Setting: A plastic hockey stick and a foam or plastic ball or puck for each child; a large target marked on the wall within six inches of the floor for each child; children about six feet from the target and at least five feet apart

Tasks/Challenges:

🅣 Stand to the side of the ball. Strike the ball toward the target, trying to hit the target.

🅒 Your challenge is to see how many times in a row you can hit the target sin front of you. Remember to

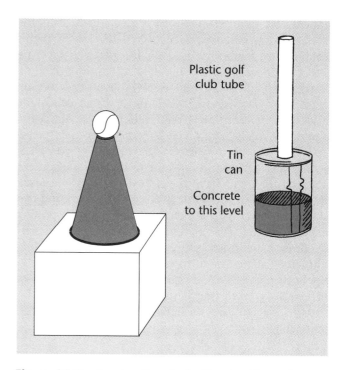

Figure 30.2   Construction of a batting tee. The easiest way to make a batting tee is to use a large (thirty-six-inch) traffic cone, which is high enough for young children. Increase the height by placing the traffic cone on a cardboard box. A batting tee can also be made out of a tin can and a plastic tube.

Materials
Large tin can (available from the school cafeteria)
Plastic golf club tube (obtained from a sporting goods store)
Sack of ready-mixed concrete (1/10 to 1/8)

Directions

1. Place the golf club tube into the tin can.

2. Add water to the concrete mix, and fill the tin can approximately half full.

3. After a few minutes, when the concrete begins to harden, make sure that the golf club tube is not leaning to the side. Once the concrete dries, the batting tee is ready to use.

You can vary the heights of the batting tees by shortening the plastic golf club tubes before inserting them into the cans. We try to have batting tees of three different heights.

stop the ball each time it comes back to you before hitting it again.

🅣 When you can hit the target three times in a row, move back one giant step and try again.

STRIKING OFF A BATTING TEE—BATS

Setting: Preferably outside in a large open space; for at least every two children (but preferably for every

Figure 30.3 Batting tees let children at precontrol and control skill levels practice independently.

child) a box containing five plastic balls or beach balls, a bat, and a batting tee (Figure 30.2)

Tasks/Challenges:

Ⓣ This time, you're going to hit a big ball off a tee with a plastic bat. Stand to the side of the tee so you are batting to the field. Now, line up facing the same way, so you won't hit one another. Hit all the balls in your box, and then wait until I give the signal before collecting them. Remember: Hit hard.

Ⓒ Practice hitting until you can hit the ball three times in a row.

Ⓣ Now see how far you can hit the ball.

Batting tees are helpful for children at the precontrol level who are unable to strike a moving ball—and for children at the control level who are practicing ball placement (Figure 30.3).

STRIKING (DRIBBLING) A BALL IN SELF-SPACE— HOCKEY

Setting: Children in self-space, each with a hoop, a hockey stick, and a foam or plastic ball or puck

Tasks/Challenges:

Ⓣ In your own space inside the hoop, use the hockey stick to gently move the ball around in as many ways as possible. Don't leave your self-space.

Ⓣ On the signal, begin striking the ball in your own space, and keep striking until you hear the signal to stop.

Ⓒ I will time you for fifteen seconds. Try to keep your strikes going for the whole time.

TRAVELING SLOWLY WHILE STRIKING A BALL— HOCKEY

Setting: A hockey stick and a foam or plastic ball or puck for each child

Tasks/Challenges:

Ⓣ Walk throughout general space tapping the ball like you did in self-space. The ball must always be very close to your stick.

Ⓣ This time as you are walking try to avoid running into others. This means you will have to keep the ball very close.

Control Level: Learning Experiences Leading to Skill Development

At the control level, children begin to develop mature striking patterns that are used in increasingly complex contexts. Traveling while striking or tapping an object along the ground is combined with one or two variables, such as changing direction and/or speed. The children also practice striking a pitched ball and striking a golf ball for distance.

A note about cues: Although several cues are listed for many of the learning experiences, it's important to focus on only one cue at a time. That way, the children can really concentrate on that cue. Once you

WHICH SWING?

▶ The underhand swings that are used in hockey and golf situations can be confusing. There is the side-to-the-target swing characteristic of golf strokes and hockey passes that are intended to travel a long distance. This is the swing illustrated in Box 30.5. The only real difference in this swing between hockey-type situations and golf is the length of the backswing and the follow-through. (In interactive settings—games like hockey, broomball, and Pilo Polo—it is unsafe for the swing to come above the waist on either the backswing or the follow-through.) Also, to complicate matters, in hockey-type situations there is also an underhand striking pattern which requires the passer to face the target. This striking action is used for most short (ten yards or less) passing situations using both a forehand and a backhand action. Consequently, given the space restrictions of physical education classes, especially when they are taught inside, it is this swing that is most frequently used. Thus, at the precontrol and control levels, we have children practice swings from both the side and the back. Other than the starting position in relation to the ball, the swings have the same critical cues. As children learn to use each swing, they will naturally select the one that fits the situation.

Figure 30.4 Hockey stick grip.

provide feedback to the children and observe that most have learned a cue, then it's time to focus on another one.

STRIKING A STATIONARY BALL ON THE GROUND—HOCKEY OR GOLF

Setting: Preferably a large outdoor space (but can be adapted for an indoor space); a golf club or plastic field hockey stick (short handled; long-handled street hockey sticks aren't appropriate) and a plastic or foam ball for each child; each child in self-space, facing a wall or an object that will block the ball; at least five feet between children

Cues

Arms Way Back	(With both hands on the stick, bring your arms way back as you swing.)
Watch the Ball	(Keep your eyes on the ball all the time.)
Opposite Foot	(Step forward on your opposite foot as you hit.)

Tasks/Challenges:

🅣 When we explored striking with hockey sticks, you practiced hitting the ball to the wall by standing beside it and behind it and having it travel on the ground. Using a hockey grip (Figure 30.4), practice striking the ball, standing beside it, so that it travels to the wall.

🅣 As you practice, bring your backswing way back over your shoulders like a golf player. Follow through so that your arms end above your other shoulder—a full swing.

🅣 Practice the same swing, but the backswing must start below your waist and end below your waist. An easy way to help it end below your waist is to turn your wrists over on the follow-through.

🅣 Using both swings—full and short—strike the ball to the wall with enough force so that it comes back to you. Which swing sends the ball harder?

🅣 Practice standing behind the ball and hitting.

🅣 From that position try to strike the ball with enough force so that it rebounds back to you off the wall.

🅒 Practice striking the ball against the wall until you can hit the wall three times in a row from each starting position.

🅣 Stand behind the ball. In this position, most of you have been hitting the ball from the preferred side of your body. That is called your *forehand*. This time we are going to practice hitting the ball from the nonpreferred side of your body. You don't change your hands; instead you use the back side of the stick to do it. Try to hit the ball to the wall this way.

🅣 Practice hitting the ball hard enough so that it rebounds back to you.

🅒 Again try for three hits in a row that are hard enough so that the ball comes back to you.

STRIKING IN THE AIR—GOLF

Setting: A striking implement (plastic hockey stick, broomball stick) and foam balls for striking placed about ten feet from the wall; marks on the wall about three feet off the floor.

Cues

Arms Way Back	(Bring your arms way back as you swing.)
Watch the Ball	(Keep your eyes on the ball all the time.)
Under the Ball	(Contact the ball below its center so it will travel upward through the air.)

Tasks/Challenges:

🅣 When we explored different ways to strike, you tried to make the ball go in the air. From a position beside the ball, with your shoulder to the wall, try to do that now. Practice striking the ball so that it travels in the air to the wall.

🅣 Practice striking the ball so that it travels through the air and hits the wall above the mark.

🅒 Try to send the ball in the air so that it hits above the mark three times in a row.

STRIKING FOR DISTANCE—GOLF OR HOCKEY

Setting: Markers of various colors (to be used for measuring) or zones at various distances from where the children are hitting; a plastic striking implement

> ▶ There is much concern over the use of hockey sticks and the teaching of related skills in the elementary school. With the increased popularity of street and ice hockey, hockey sticks are being raised above the shoulders on both the backswing and the follow-through. Because elementary school physical education classes are usually crowded, raised hockey sticks can cause injuries. We've successfully reduced the chance of such injuries by not letting youngsters raise their hockey sticks higher than their waists on *any* stroke. This restriction doesn't significantly alter the striking action; in fact, it encourages the correct field hockey striking action while at the same time providing a much safer environment for learning skills involving striking with hockey sticks.

and five or six foam, plastic, or whiffle balls for each child; children positioned in a circle in the center of a field or playground, facing out

Cues

Arms Way Back	(Bring your arms way back as you swing.)
Watch the Ball	(Keep your eyes on the ball all the time.)
Behind the Ball	(Contact directly behind the ball to make it travel on the ground or low.)
Under the Ball	(Contact the ball below its center so it will travel upward through the air.)

Tasks/Challenges:

🅣 Stand facing the outside of the circle, making sure there is enough space between you and the people next to you so that you can all swing your sticks without hitting one another. First, we are going to practice striking along the ground and in the air. There's enough room to strike as hard as you like. Practice your first strikes from behind the ball so the ball travels along the ground. Use your forehand strike. After you hit all the balls, wait for the signal, then go get your balls and quickly bring them back to your starting place for the next hits.

🅣 This time try your backhand strike—along the ground. Does the ball travel as far with your backhand?

🅣 Move beside the ball. Hit the ball as far as you can (*Figure 30.5*).

 Check for understanding: Which starting position sends the ball farther? In "face-the-target" position, which sends it farther—forehand or backhand?

🅣 This time we are going to stand beside the ball. Practice hitting the ball so that it travels through the air.

🅒 Practice striking both on the ground and through the air. Before each strike call out loud "air" or "ground." Challenge yourself to be able to do the strike you called out.

 Check for understanding: What is the key for sending the ball through the air? On the ground?

🅣 Now see with each of your strikes if you can hit the ball farther each time. The markers on the field will help you remember how far you hit the ball each time. Each time, see if you can hit the ball a little

Figure 30.5 Children are challenged to see how far they can hit the ball.

farther than the last time. Practice air and ground strikes—all from the side.

⊙ Can you hit the ball so that it lands in the same zone three times?

STRIKING TO TARGETS—HOCKEY

Setting: Plastic hockey stick or other implement and a foam or plastic ball for each child; in front of each child, a target on the floor next to the wall marked with cones or spots about four feet apart and tape marks on the floor in front of each target at about six feet, ten feet, and twelve feet

Cues	
Step	(Step forward on the opposite [front] foot.)
Watch the Ball	(Keep your eyes on the ball until it leaves your stick.)
Follow Through	(Follow through toward the target with your stick.)

Tasks/Challenges:

T Starting from behind the ball at the closest mark, try to strike the ball so it goes between the two cones.

T Practice sending the ball between the cones from your forehand and backhand sides.

⊙ Practice striking until you can hit the ball between the cones five times from each side. Remember to stop the ball each time it comes back to you before hitting it again.

T When you can hit the target five times in a row without missing from the closest mark, move back to the next mark. When you can hit the target from that spot five times without missing, move back again. If you hit the target four times and then miss, start your counting over. Practice from both the forehand and backhand sides.

T Now start back at your closest spot and strike to the target from a starting position standing beside your ball.

⚠ With this task, make sure that students are spread well apart, that they stop the ball completely on its return, and that they move in front of others only when no one is striking.

STRIKING TO A TARGET (AROUND THE WORLD)—HOCKEY

Setting: Targets, with five tape marks in a semicircle on the floor in front of each; three or fewer students per target; a hockey stick or other striking implement and ball or puck for each child (*Note:* This task is also appropriate as one of a series of stations.)

Cues	
Watch the Ball	(Keep your eyes on the ball until it leaves your stick.)
Step	(Step forward on the opposite [front] foot.)
Follow Through	(Follow through toward the target with your stick.)

T This time the striking is going to be a game. Have you ever played Around the World in basketball? This game is going to be Around the World in striking. As you see, there are five tape marks on the floor in front of you. You must hit the ball to the target from each tape mark. Strike from behind the ball. You can start on either side.

T When you make it through once, go back and hit from each mark using the backhand strike.

T Start over, striking from beside the ball.

STRIKING A STATIONARY BALL—BATS

Setting: Preferably a large, open, outdoor space, one big enough for every child to hit against a backstop or

Figure 30.6 Batting grip.

a wall; children about fifteen feet from the backstop or wall with sufficient space to swing freely without hitting others (or place a line on the ground about fifteen feet from the batting positions for children to hit over); a box of about five balls (large, light plastic or beach balls and whiffle balls), bats, and batting tees for each child or pair of children

Cues	
Side to the Field	(Turn your side to the target or field.)
Bat Back	(Bring the bat way back over your shoulder so your elbows are pointed up.)
Watch the Ball	(Keep your eyes on the ball all the time.)
Level	(Extend your arms to swing flat as a pancake.)
Shift Forward	(Shift your weight to your front leg.)

Tasks/Challenges:

T When we explored striking, you practiced hitting a ball off a tee. We're going to practice that again. Stand about a bat's length away and to the side of your batting tee. **Take a batting grip *(Figure 30.6)*, bring your bat back over your shoulder so your elbows are pointed up, extend your arms all the way so you have a level swing, shift your weight forward to your front foot, and hit.** Let's practice five times without hitting the ball. Just swing and say the cues out loud.

T Now practice striking off the tee. Use a plastic ball or a beach ball. **If you are batting the ball correctly, your swing will follow through over your other shoulder.**

T Practice until you can hit the plastic ball ten times in a row off the tee.

T When you can hit the plastic ball ten times in a row, trade it in for a whiffle ball. Now practice with that ball.

T Hit the ball so hard that it goes in the air to the wall (*over the line*).

C Practice hitting with the bat until you can hit five times in a row so the ball hits the wall (*lands over the line*).

Increasing the size of the ball reduces the complexity of the task. Increasing the size of the bat does the same thing. Some teachers also use "soap bubbles" for children to practice striking. One partner blows bubbles; the other gets to swing away trying to pop them as they fall. It works !!

LEVEL SWINGS—BATS

Setting: Ropes suspended from the ceiling or a line hung across the room to about children's shoulder height (Figure 30.7); batting tees and bats for each child

Cues	
Side to the Field	(Turn your side to the target or field.)
Bat Back	(Bring the bat way back over your shoulder so your elbows are pointed up.)
Watch the Ball	(Keep your eyes on the ball all the time.)
Level	(Extend your arms to swing flat as a pancake.)
Shift Forward	(Shift your weight to your front leg.)

Tasks/Challenges:

T Place your batting tee directly under your rope. The tee should come up to your knees. The area between the end of the rope and the top of your tee is your strike zone. Step up to the tee and swing. There is no ball for this task. Your swing should go through the strike zone without touching the rope or the tee.

T Practice until you can get three strikes in a row through the strike zone without touching the rope or the tee.

T Now both raise the tee and lower the rope one inch. Take swings through this strike zone. Again, practice until you can get three. Then make the strike zone smaller again.

Figure 30.7 Setup for level swings.

Figure 30.8 Setup for striking a stationary ball for distance

STRIKING A STATIONARY BALL FOR DISTANCE—BATS

Setting: Partners, each pair with a batting tee, three whiffle balls, and a bat; batters in a circle in the middle of the playground facing out (Figure 30.8); fielders about thirty feet (or whatever's appropriate) in front of their partner; marker cones or zones at ten-foot intervals around the center circle

Cues

Watch the Ball	(Keep your eyes on the ball all the time.)
Bat Back	(Bring the bat way back over your shoulder so your elbows are pointed up.)
Side to the Field	(Turn your side to the target or field.)

| Level | (Extend your arms to swing flat as a pancake.) |
| Shift Forward | (Shift your weight to your front leg.) |

Tasks/Challenges:

🅣 Stand inside the circle about a bat's length away from your tee with your side to the field. You are going to practice batting the ball in the air. There's enough room to hit as hard as you like. Your partner will collect the balls. After three hits, trade places. Remember to watch the ball.

🅣 This time have your partner stand where your ball landed. Try to hit the next ball farther. The partner moves to that spot. Try again to hit farther than the previous hit. After three hits, trade places with your partner.

🅣 Bat the ball as far as possible. Take note of the zone in which the ball first lands. Bat three times, each time trying to improve your distance. Trade places.

🅒 Try to bat the ball so that it lands in the same zone three times.

STRIKING SUSPENDED OBJECTS—BATS

Setting: Whiffle balls suspended about waist height from strings (see Figure 29.3) around the practice area; a bat for each child

Cues	
Side to the Field	(Turn your side to the target or field.)
Bat Back	(Bring the bat way back over your shoulder so your elbows are pointed up.)
Watch the Ball	(Keep your eyes on the ball all the time.)
Level	(Extend your arms to swing flat as a pancake.)
Shift Forward	(Shift your weight to your front leg.)

Tasks/Challenges:

🅣 This task is a little harder than the last one. Instead of hitting balls that don't move from batting tees, you're going to hit balls that are hanging from strings. Stand to the side of the ball about a bat's length away. Practice hitting the ball. Remember to stop the ball still before you hit it again.

🅒 Practice batting until you can hit five balls in a row without missing (*Figure 30.9*).

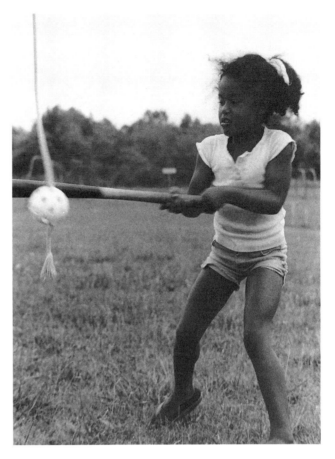

Figure 30.9   Balls suspended on strings give youngsters the opportunity to practice swinging level.

🅒 Now the game changes a little. See how many times you can strike the ball in a row without missing.

HIT AND RUN—BATS

Setting: Partners; ball, bat, and carpet square set up as in Figure 30.10

Cues	
Bat Back	(Bring the bat way back over your shoulder so your elbows are pointed up.)
Watch the Ball	(Keep your eyes on the ball all the time.)
Side to the Field	(Turn your side to the target or field.)
Level	(Extend your arms to swing flat as a pancake.)
Shift Forward	(Shift your weight to your front leg.)

Figure 30.10   Setup for Hit and Run
From: *On the Move*, by S. Holt/Hale, 1993, Mountain View, CA: Mayfield.

Tasks/Challenges:

🔵 Partner A stands at the batting tee; partner B, on the carpet square about fifteen feet away. Partner A strikes the ball off the tee, hitting it as far as possible. Then Partner A runs to the carpet square and back to the batting tee. Partner B collects the ball and runs and replaces it on the tee. Switch places after each hit. Be careful: Both of you are running.

STRIKING TO A STATIONARY PARTNER—HOCKEY

Setting: Partners about six to seven feet apart, each with a hockey stick; one ball or puck per group

Cues	
Sending:	Watch the Ball (Keep your eyes on the ball at all times.)
	Step (Step forward on the opposite foot.)
	Follow Through (Follow through toward your partner with your stick.)
Receiving:	Give (Relax your grip and move your stick back a little just as the ball hits your stick, to absorb the force.)
	Watch the Ball (Keep your eyes on the ball all the time.)

Tasks/Challenges:

🔵 Strike the ball (puck) back and forth to your partner. Hit straight to your partner so that she or he doesn't have to move. You hit the ball to your partner; your partner stops the ball completely still and then hits it back. Remember to strike easily so that your partner is able to stop the ball.

🔵 Before you worked with a partner, you practiced hitting the ball (puck) to different places. Now you're going to do that with your partner, and your partner is going to be a target for you to aim at. The partner who is to receive the ball will put his or her

hockey stick out in one place and hold it still; the partner hitting the ball will use the stick as a target and try to hit it without the receiving partner's having to move the stick. Change roles each time.

🔵 With your partner, see how many times you can hit the ball (puck) back and forth without a miss. Remember, you must stop the ball before you return it to your partner. If you miss, just start counting all over. If you get to ten, let me know.

🔵 After you hit the ball (puck) successfully to your partner ten times and your partner is able to stop the ball, move back two steps each and start again. When you're successful ten times in a row, move back again.

🔵 This will make it a little harder: Move back to your close position. After you pass the ball this time, move to a new space and stand still. The receiver must control the ball (puck), look to see where you are, and then pass. Each time after someone passes, move to a new space, stop, and then receive the ball.

🔵 Now see how many times you can keep this up without missing.

In the past few years I have learned of at least twenty-six ways that children can curve the blades of hockey sticks. Having the children keep the blade straight ensures two things: (1) The puck (ball) has a greater chance of staying on the floor, and (2) your hockey sticks last a lot longer.

TRAVELING SLOWLY WHILE STRIKING A BALL— HOCKEY

Setting: A hockey stick and a tennis ball or puck for each child

Cues	
Light Taps	(Use light taps to keep the ball close to your stick.)
Hands Apart	(Move your hands eight to ten inches apart to control the ball better.)
Ball in Front	(Keep the ball slightly in front of your body on the same side on which you are dribbling.)

Tasks/Challenges:

🔵 Before, we practiced moving around the entire space while striking a ball with the hockey stick. Let's practice again—this is called dribbling or stick-handling. To begin, go slowly. Your task is to travel

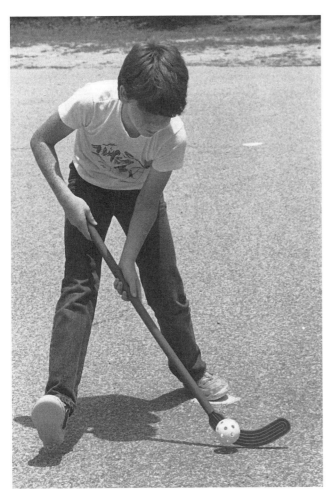

Figure 30.11 For children at the control level, traveling while manipulating a ball with a long-handled implement takes practice.

around the entire space while striking the ball and not touching anyone else (*Figure 30.11*).

T This time as you move around the room, I'm going to hold up different numbers of fingers. Tell me how many fingers I'm holding up. You'll have to look often, because I'll change the number of fingers often and try to trick you.

C You have fifty points. Your task is to keep all your points. Move around the room dribbling the ball. Every time you lose the ball, subtract five points. See how many points you have at the stop signal.

TRAVELING, STOPPING, AND CONTROLLING THE BALL—HOCKEY

Setting: A plastic hockey stick and a ball for each child

Cues

Give	(Relax your grip and bring your stick back a little to absorb the force when trying to stop the ball.) *A demonstration is helpful here.*
Light Taps	(Use light taps to keep the ball close to your stick.)
Hands Apart	(Move your hands eight to ten inches apart to control the ball better.)

Tasks/Challenges:

T Before, you practiced traveling around the room keeping the ball close to you. This time you're going to do the same thing, but with something added. Whenever you hear the signal, stop the ball, using only your stick, and wait for the signal to go again.

T This time try going a little faster and doing the same thing. Move around the space, striking the ball with your hockey stick. On the signal, stop the ball and wait for the "go" signal. I'll know you can really do this if I always see the ball close to the stick and all the balls stopped on the signal, without your having to chase them all over the room.

T Now I am going to change the task a little. Again, you should move around the entire space striking the ball. But this time on the signal, instead of stopping the ball, stand still and keep moving the ball in your self-space until you hear the signal to travel again. This is called controlling the ball. You'll know you're really good at this when, as soon as you hear the whistle, you can stop and start moving the ball in your self-space without first having to chase the ball across the room.

C This time, the stopping will be like a game. When I say "stop," I'll start counting backward from ten. When all the balls have stopped, I'll stop counting. Your goal is to get me to stop counting before I get to zero.

T You're going to play a little game with the stopping this time. Every time you come near another person, stop or control the ball and then start again. It's as if you don't want anyone to come near your ball, so you are going to protect it—and the only way you can protect it is by controlling it in your self-space or stopping it.

TRAVELING AND CHANGING SPEEDS—HOCKEY

Setting: A striking implement and a ball or puck for each child

Cues

Light Taps	(Use light taps to keep the ball close to your stick.)
Hands Apart	(Move your hands eight to ten inches apart to control the ball better.)
Ball in Front	(Keep the ball slightly in front of your body on the same side on which you are dribbling.)

Tasks/Challenges:

T One of the important things in games that use dribbling or stick-handing is the ability to change the speed at which you are traveling while you dribble. Travel in general space, and change your speed as you go. It should be easy for me to tell which speed you are using.

T This time I will call out speeds as you travel. See if you can match every speed I call out.

T Now you will practice using different speeds with a partner. It is like Follow the Leader. You will follow a partner, dribbling in general space. The first partner starts and travels, changing the speed of the travel often. The second partner follows, always trying to travel at the same speed as the first partner. On the signal, switch places.

TRAVELING AND STRIKING WHILE CHANGING PATHWAYS—HOCKEY

Setting: A hockey stick and ball or puck for each child; various pathways (the more, the better) taped or marked on the floor

Cues

Light Taps	(Use light taps to keep the ball close to your stick.)
Hands Apart	(Move your hands eight to ten inches apart to control the ball better.)
Ball in Front	(Keep the ball slightly in front of your body on the same side on which you are dribbling.)

Tasks/Challenges:

T You're going to practice something new this time: changes in pathways. Do you remember pathways: straight, curved, and zigzag? Again, you're going to move around the entire space, but whenever you come to a pathway on the floor, try to follow it

exactly. Once you finish one pathway, travel to another and follow it. As you follow the pathways, be sure you're striking the ball, not pushing it along.

T Something very different happens when you follow a zigzag pathway. What is it? That's right—you have to move your stick from one side of the ball to the other, like moving the ball in self-space to keep control of it. Practice zigzag pathways on your own. **Remember, every time you come to a zig or a zag, you have to move your stick to the other side of the ball.**

T This time we are going to practice striking while traveling in different pathways with a partner. You're going to play Follow the Leader. The leader travels in different pathways—curved, straight, and zigzag—as the follower tries to stay close behind, copying the exact pathways the leader makes. Leaders: As you begin, make easy pathways. The object is not to lose your partner but to practice striking while traveling in different pathways. On the signal, change positions as leaders and followers.

T This time, the following is going to be a little harder. Instead of staying right behind the leader, the follower is going to watch while the leader moves in a short pathway sequence. When the leader stops and freezes, the follower moves, copying the pathway of the leader until she or he catches up with the leader. When the follower catches up, the leader takes off again. This is a bit like a game of cat and mouse: Just as soon as you think you've caught someone, the person slips away again. As you move, remember that the purpose of this task is to practice different pathways, so include them in your movements. After five turns as a leader, switch places.

C This is the real pathway test. By yourself, make up a sequence of traveling and striking that involves four changes of pathways. Practice your sequence until you can do it from memory three times without stopping. Each time the sequence should look the same. Then we'll all share the sequences.

STRIKING TO DIFFERENT PLACES—HOCKEY

Setting: A hockey stick, a ball, and three targets (plastic milk bottles, two-liter soda bottles, or tennis ball cans) placed against a wall or fence for each child

Cues

Face Target	(Always face your upper body to the target.)

| Step | (Step forward on the opposite foot toward the target.) |
| Follow Through | (Follow through with your stick toward the target.) |

Tasks/Challenges:

T This time you'll practice striking from the same place each time, but trying to hit one of three different targets. Take a minute and practice striking at the three targets in front of you.

C This time, you're going to see how many points you can score in two minutes. You get one point if you hit a target and three points if you hit the particular target you call out ahead of time.

HITTING A STATIONARY BALL FROM DIFFERENT PLACES—BATS

Setting: A batting tee, ball, and bat for each child or pair of children. Place the tee so that the balls are batted into a fence or wall, or have the partner field balls; mark a home plate in the batting area.

Cues

Bat Back	(Bring the bat way back over your shoulder so your elbows are pointed up.)
Watch the Ball	(Keep your eyes on the ball all the time.)
Side to the Field	(Turn your side to the target or field.)
Level	(Extend your arms to swing flat as a pancake.)
Shift Forward	(Shift your weight to your front leg.)

Tasks/Challenges:

T Place the batting tee so the ball is on the inside corner of home plate at your knees. Hit five balls as hard as you can from this position. Switch places.

T Move the tee to the inside corner with the ball chest high. Make five hits as hard as you can. Switch.

T Move the tee to the outside corner, knee high. Go again.

T Now try the outside corner, chest high. Five and switch.

STRIKING TO VARYING DISTANCES—GOLF

Setting: Preferably a large outdoor space. A golf club and a bucket of plastic balls for each child; all children facing the same direction, with at least six feet between them; the field marked at various intervals

Cues

Full Swing	(Use a full swing—big backswing, follow-through above shoulders.)
Bend Knees	(Bend your knees throughout the whole swing.)
Watch the Ball	(Keep your eyes on the ball.)

Tasks/Challenges:

T Use the golf grip (*Figure 30.12*). You're going to be practicing a golf swing—or a full swing—by yourself in a place that is facing away from everyone else. This is like the shortened swings that you have been using with the hockey sticks, except now you'll have a full backswing and follow-through. Let's practice first without the ball. **Stand to the side of the make-believe ball, side to the target (field), and take a full backswing, bend your knees, swing, and follow through.** Practice five times on your own.

T With your golf club, practice hitting the ball on your own.

T Practice hitting the ball as far as you can.

T There are markers on the field to help you judge the length of your hits. Hit one ball, and then try to hit the next ball farther. Try to find your maximum distance.

THROWING A BALL IN THE AIR AND STRIKING IT—BATS

Setting: Preferably a large outdoor space, where children can bat against a wall or fence; large round targets on the wall; a plastic bat and a ball for each child

For this task and beginning tasks that involve hitting a pitched ball, sock balls work quite well. They won't travel too far, allowing children to focus on the swing. To make a sock ball, stuff an old sock with other socks and tie off. Cut off the tail.

Figure 30.12   Golf club grip.

Cues	
Bat Back	(Bring the bat way back over your shoulder so your elbows are pointed up.)
Watch the Ball	(Keep your eyes on the ball all the time.)
Side to the Field	(Turn your side to the target or field.)
Level	(Extend your arms to swing flat as a pancake.)
Shift Forward	(Shift your weight to your front leg.)

Tasks/Challenges:

T You're going to practice hitting a ball you throw into the air yourself. In your own space facing the wall (fence) and about ten feet from it, toss a ball up into the air and then hit it with the bat. You must have both your hands on the bat when you hit the ball, so you'll have to work quickly. (*Demonstrate.*)

T Practice now, trying to hit the large circle on the wall.

C Score five points for every ball that hits the target; three points for every ball that hits the wall, but misses the target; and one point for every ball you hit that doesn't hit the wall. Try to get to twenty-one points.

STRIKING A SELF-TOSSED BALL TO DIFFERENT DISTANCES—BATS

Setting: Lines marked on a field for distance measurement; a number of whiffle (or tennis) balls and a plastic bat for each child

Cues	
Bat Back	(Bring the bat way back over your shoulder so your elbows are pointed up.)
Watch the Ball	(Keep your eyes on the ball all the time.)
Side to the Field	(Turn your side to the target or field.)
Level	(Extend your arms to swing flat as a pancake.)
Shift Forward	(Shift your weight to your front leg.)

Tasks/Challenges:

T Now we're going to add something that you worked on before: striking to different distances. This involves using different amounts of force to hit the ball. There are a lot of lines on the field; you can use them to judge how far you hit the ball. Each time you hit a ball, see how far you can make it go. If you hit it over one line one time, try to hit it over the next line the next time you hit.

C Pick out a line you know you can hit the ball past. Try to hit the ball past that line five times in a row. After you've practiced at one line, pick another line and try again.

STRIKING A PITCHED BALL—BATS

Setting: A large outdoor space, marked as follows: a pitcher's square and a batting box for each group of two, each batter's box marked with "neat feet" in the correct batting position (Figure 30.13). A skilled thrower (older student, classroom teacher, parent or

Figure 30.13 "Neat feet" for a right-handed striking action. You can easily make "neat feet" by painting them in the correct position on a rubber mat. Challenge the children to move the left foot to the position of the dotted foot as they swing.

grandparent) as a partner for each child; one plastic or sock ball and a bat for each pair

Cues

Bat Back	(Bring the bat way back over your shoulder so your elbows are pointed up.)
Watch the Ball	(Keep your eyes on the ball all the time.)
Side to the Field	(Turn your side to the target or field.)
Level	(Extend your arms to swing flat as a pancake.)
Shift Forward	(Shift your weight to your front leg.)

Tasks/Challenges:

🅣 Before, you hit a ball off a batting tee or from a self-toss. This time you're going to practice batting a ball that's pitched by a "big" partner (*Figure 30.14*). Your big partner will be the pitcher, and you will get to bat all the time. Your partner stands on the

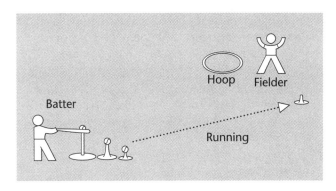

Figure 30.14 Working as partners: One child pitches a ball, the other strikes it with a bat.

pitcher's square and pitches the ball to you. You stand on the batter's square and try to hit the ball. The batter's square has a secret help in it: pictures of feet that show you exactly where to stand so you have the best chance of hitting the ball. Just try to hit the ball; it doesn't have to go far.

🅣 Each time you bat, your big partner will give you a thumbs-up if you do everything correctly. If you miss a cue, he or she will tell you so you can use it for the next swing.

C Try to hit five balls in a row.

STRIKING WHILE DODGING STATIONARY OBSTACLES—HOCKEY

Setting: An obstacle course of cones and hoops or other equipment; a hockey stick and a ball for each child

Cues	
Light Taps	(Use light taps to keep the ball close to your stick.)
Both Sides of Stick	(Use both sides of the stick to dribble around the obstacle.)
Look Up	(Look up as you travel so you can see the obstacles.)

Tasks/Challenges:

T You've traveled while dodging objects. This time, you're going to travel and dodge objects while striking a ball with a hockey stick. Your task is to travel throughout the space, striking the ball with the hockey stick. Try not to let the ball get away from you. Don't touch any of the obstacles or other people. Freeze on the signal, and have the ball with you.

T As practice for looking up, we're going to play the counting game again. I'll keep holding up a different number of fingers, and you tell me how many I'm holding up while you're striking the ball around the space.

T Dribble/stick-handle in general space. Each time you come to an obstacle, control the ball, execute a quarter turn to the right or left, and continue dribbling.

T You've all been going at fairly slow speeds. This isn't always good in game situations, so you're going to practice going at different speeds. Sometimes approach an obstacle very quickly, sometimes slowly. Make the change clear. The rules are still the same: No touching, and you must be able to stop on the signal and have the ball with you.

T Dribble in general space. As you near an obstacle, use both sides of your stick to dribble past the obstacle, then quickly continue regular dribbling. Sometimes go to the right and sometimes to the left.

C What you have just learned are called *dodges*. This time as you practice dodging, pretend you have

one hundred points. If the ball you are dribbling touches a cone, subtract ten points from your score. If you have a collision with another person, subtract twenty-five points. Try to complete your practice with one hundred points!

Utilization Level: Learning Experiences Leading to Skill Development

At the utilization level, we give the children situations in which they learn to consistently strike objects with long-handled implements. Many contexts involve more than one variable in an unpredictable or changing environment.

A note about cues: Although several cues are listed for many of the learning experiences, it's important to focus on only one cue at a time. That way, the children can really concentrate on that cue. Once you provide feedback to the children and observe that most have learned a cue, then it's time to focus on another one.

GROUNDERS AND FLIES—BATS

Setting: Groups of three or four: one batter and one pitcher per group, the rest are fielders; a space large enough for all groups to bat without interfering with the others

Cues	
Under the Ball	(Hit the ball slightly below its center for a fly ball.)
Behind the Ball	(Hit direct behind the ball for a line drive.)
Over the Ball	(Hit near the top of the ball for a grounder.)

Tasks/Challenges:

T So far you have practiced hitting from behind the ball. This usually makes the ball travel in a straight aerial pathway—a line drive. Yet, there are times when you will need to hit balls high, and others when you will need to hit grounders. That is what we will practice first—grounders. Hit the pitches so they hit the ground about six to ten yards away. After five hits switch places.

T The next practice will be for fly balls. Practice hitting these pitches so they don't hit the ground until past the baseline. They should go higher in the air than a line drive.

T Do you remember the game where the pitcher told the batter which field the batter was to hit the ball

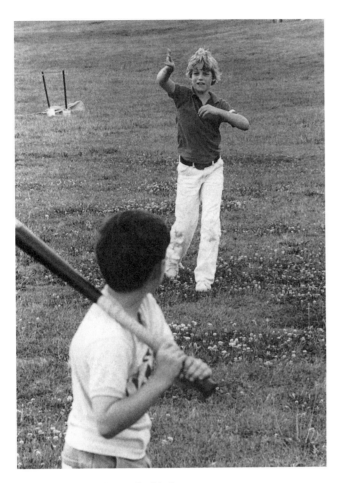

Figure 30.15 Setup for hitting to open spaces.

to? This game is similar, but here the pitcher calls out line drive, pop fly, or grounder, and the batter has to hit that kind of ball. After five hits, switch places.

Ⓒ This time the batter calls out the type of hit, before the ball is pitched. The batter gets one point for each hit that goes the way it was called. Try for four points—out of five pitches.

DIRECTING THE PLACEMENT OF AN OBJECT—BATS

Setting: Partners, each pair with a batting tee, a bat, a cone, a hoop, and a ball; each pair with enough space to bat for distance. See Figure 30.14 for setup.

Cue

Front Foot to Target	(Change your stance so your front foot points toward your target.)

Tasks/Challenges:

Ⓣ Before, you practiced hitting the ball different distances; this time, you're going to practice hitting the ball to different places. To start, one person will be at bat, and the partner will be in left field. The batter first tries to hit five balls to left field, aiming for her or his partner. If everything works correctly, the partner shouldn't have to move very far to catch the balls. After the first five hits, the partner moves to center field, and the batter tries to hit the next five balls to right field. Then switch places. You'll know you're really good when your partner doesn't have to move to catch the balls.

Ⓣ This time, the fielder is going to make it harder. After every hit, the fielder moves to a new position, and the batter tries to hit the ball exactly to the fielder. The fielder can choose any place to go. After ten hits, trade places.

Ⓣ Now that you've gotten the hang of placing the ball, you're going to try and hit where the fielder isn't. In softball, you want to be able to hit to open spaces, so you can get on base. Hit three balls off the tee, trying to send them to different places in the field. The fielder will collect them. After three hits, trade places.

Ⓒ As you hit the three balls this time, call out where the hit will go. You get one point for every hit that goes where you indicated. Try for a perfect three.

Ⓣ Now, you get to run as well. Bat the ball. As soon as you bat the ball, run around the cone and try to get home before the fielder has the ball in the hoop. After three hits, trade places.

HITTING TO OPEN SPACES—BATS

Setting: A large outdoor area; children in groups of three or four, each group with a bat and a ball (Figure 30.15)

Cue

Front Foot to Target	(Change your stance so your front foot points toward your target.)

Tasks/Challenges:

Ⓣ You're going practice hitting a pitched ball and try to make it go to open spaces. One of the fielders will become the pitcher. All pitches must be easy so they can be hit. The batter will try to hit the outfield and have the ball hit the ground before the fielder can touch it. After ten hits, switch places.

C You get one point for every ball that hits the ground untouched. Try for six points. Every ten hits, trade places.

STRIKING A PITCHED OBJECT VARYING THE DISTANCE—BATS

Setting: A large outdoor space; partners with a bat and ball

Cues	
Full Swing	(Swing hard all the way through to send the ball a long way.)
Medium Swing	(Swing at a medium speed all the way through to send the ball a shorter distance.)

Tasks/Challenges:

T This time, you're going to practice hitting a pitched ball different distances. To begin, one of you will pitch, and the other will hit. Batter, your task is sometimes to hit the ball short so it lands near the pitcher and at other times to hit it long so it goes to the outfield. Try to decide ahead of time where you want the ball to go, and then hit it there.

C Now, to show how good you are, call out where the ball is going—a short or a long distance—before you hit it. Do this ten times, and then switch places.

T This task is a little different from the last one. Instead of the batter calling out where the ball is to go, the pitcher calls out where the ball is to be hit. The batter changes places with the pitcher after five hits.

BATTING, COMBINING DISTANCE AND PLACEMENT

Setting: A large open space where children can bat balls safely; bases marked in a diamond pattern; children in groups of four or five

Cues	
Front Foot to Target	(Your front foot should be pointed to your target.)
Full Swing	(Swing hard all the way through for hits that go a long way.)
Medium Swing	(Swing at a medium speed for shorter hits.)

Tasks/Challenges:

T In your group, one of you will be the pitcher, one of you the batter, and the rest fielders. You're now going to combine hitting for distances and hitting to open spaces. The pitcher will pitch ten balls to the batter, who tries to hit the balls to where no one is standing. Some hits need to be short and others long, but all hits should be to empty spaces.

T This is a pretend baseball game. You are at bat; you get five swings. You will try to place each of the hits to advance the make-believe base runners. Your first two hits should be short, near the pitcher or third base. Your third swing is for a hit and run— try to place a ground ball between second and third so a runner could advance to second. Your fourth hit should move the runner to third—so hit a grounder between first and second. Your last swing is to score the run—hit a long fly ball to the outfield.

STRIKING TO TARGETS AT VARIOUS DISTANCES—GOLF

Setting: Targets of various sizes at different distances apart; a plastic golf club and a bucket of balls for each child

Unless "regular" golf clubs are available, children will need to use the following cues to vary the distance the ball travels. With regular clubs, they would change clubs, and the Under the Ball cue would not be applicable.

Cues	
Under the Ball	(Hit under the ball to make it travel a short distance.)
Behind the Ball	(Hit behind to ball to make it travel a long distance.)
Full Swing	(Use a swing with a big backswing and follow-through.)

Tasks/Challenges:

T This task is like target practice. There are a lot of targets set up on the field, and you have a number of balls. See if you can hit the targets from where you're standing. After you hit all your balls, wait until the signal before collecting them.

C Now see how many times in a row you can hit the target for which you are trying.

PLAYING HOOP GOLF

Setting: Hoops and other targets of various sizes placed around a field at various distances apart; a plastic golf club and a ball for each child

Figure 30.16 This youngster tries to strike the ball into the hoop using as few strokes as possible.

Cues

Under the Ball	(Hit under the ball to make it travel a short distance.)
Behind the Ball	(Hit behind the ball to make it travel a long distance.)
Full Swing	(Use a swing with a big backswing and follow-through.)

Tasks/Challenges:

T This is like a golf course, but there's no order to it. Strike the ball from hoop to hoop, using as few strokes as possible (*Figure 30.16*). You may want to go back and do the same hoop over again, to see if you can make it in fewer strokes. Be careful not to get in anyone's way.

PLAYING HOCKEY BOWL (SMALL TARGETS)

Setting: Pins (two-liter soft drink bottles or lightweight plastic bowling pins), a ball, and a hockey stick for every two children, a marked lane leading away from the pins, as for a bowling alley

Cues

Eyes on Target	(Watch the target at all times.)
Step	(Step forward on the opposite foot.)
Follow Through	(Follow through toward the target with your stick.)

Tasks/Challenges:

C This game is called Hockey Bowl. Your task is to strike the ball from behind the line and see how many pins you can knock down. After three hits, or when all the pins have been knocked down (whichever happens first), trade places.

T The first time you can knock down all the pins three times in a row, move back three steps and try it again. If you still want to make the task harder, take away some of the pins so you have a smaller target.

DIRECTING THE AIR PATHWAY OF THE STRUCK OBJECT—GOLF

Setting: A plastic golf club and ball for each child; a space with obstacles (blocks and canes, cones, boxes, cones on top of boxes) of varying heights; carpet squares mark the starting point

Cues

| Under the Ball | (Hit under the ball to make it travel over the obstacle.) |
| Short Swing | (Use a swing with a short backswing and follow-through.) |

Tasks/Challenges:

T When I say Go, find an obstacle at which to practice. Two of you may be at one obstacle. Your task at the obstacle is to see if you can gently lift the ball off the ground with the golf club so it travels in the air over the obstacle. You may want to start at some of the lower obstacles and then move on to the higher ones. You can change obstacles whenever you like, but there can never be more than two people at an obstacle.

DRIBBLING AND CHANGING DIRECTIONS BACKWARD—HOCKEY

Setting: Children scattered throughout general space, each with a hockey stick and ball

Cues

Light Taps	(Use light taps to keep the ball close to your stick.)
Back of Stick	(Use the back side of the stick to bring the ball backward.)
Pull Back	(Quickly pull the ball toward you.)

Tasks/Challenges:

 Travel in general space, dribbling the ball two to three feet in front of you as you go. **When you are comfortable with your control of the dribble, dribble the ball ahead of you; quickly put your stick in front of the ball; tap the ball lightly with the back of your stick, pulling it toward you; quickly turn; and continue the dribble.**

⚠ As hard as we try, somehow, at some time, hockey sticks and balls/pucks seem to get raised higher than they should, especially in dynamic situations. In fact, the most serious accident I've ever had while teaching involved a hockey stick and an eye. Therefore, we advocate the wearing of eye guards, especially in dynamic hockey situations.

PERFORMING A CONTINUOUS DRIBBLE AND CHANGE OF DIRECTION—HOCKEY

Setting: Children scattered throughout general space, each with a hockey stick and ball

Cues

Light Taps	(Use light taps to keep the ball close to your stick.)
Both Sides of Stick	(Use both sides of the stick to dribble when you go around an obstacle.)
Heads Up	(Look up to avoid collisions.)

Tasks/Challenges:

 You learned to change the direction of the ball by dribbling it to your right and left with both sides of the stick. You have just learned one method of changing direction from front to back. Travel within the space, using changes of direction to avoid collisions with others. Your task is continuous dribbling.

 Approach a line quickly; use the "pull back" with the stick to change the direction of the dribble at the last moment, to keep from crossing the line.

 Purposely approach others in the class; use a move to the right or left to avoid contact with each person.

 Gradually increase the speed of your travel to determine the maximum rate you can travel with a controlled dribble and frequent changes of direction.

PATHWAYS, SPEEDS, AND DIRECTIONS— HOCKEY

Setting: A hockey stick and ball for each child

Cues

Light Taps	(Use light taps to keep the ball close to your stick.)
Both Sides of Stick	(Use both sides of the stick to dribble when you go around an obstacle.)
Heads Up	(Look up to avoid collisions.)

Tasks/Challenges:

Ⓒ This is a self-testing task. The task sheet (*Figure 30.17*) lets you assess your traveling and dribbling in different directions, pathways, and speeds. Practice the tasks one by one. When you think you can do a task well, have a partner watch you. If your partner thinks you did the task successfully, the partner signs the sheet. I'll check to see how you're progressing.

 The preceding challenge is a wonderful partner observation assessment. With the date recorded, it provides an indication of when students accomplished the skill.

TRAVELING AND STRIKING FOR A GOAL— HOCKEY

Setting: Cones scattered throughout general space; markers for goals around the outside boundary; a hockey stick and ball for each child

▶ A while ago I was at a party where the hosts set up a croquet game. Adults and children alike were intrigued, and bingo, the light hit: This is a striking game. Do you remember? Croquet is a fun activity to add to physical education class as a special treat and ties together the ideas of striking at targets and varying force and distance really well. No croquet sets, you say? You'll be amazed how many families have croquet sets at home that they're willing to let you use (or sometimes even give to you). I just acquired an antique croquet set that was on its way to Goodwill. Give croquet a try sometime!

Figure 30.17 Task sheet for striking.

Name _____ Class _____

Task Sheet for Striking

Verification	Task
	I can dribble a ball with a hockey stick in a straight pathway, keeping the ball close to the stick.
	I can dribble a ball with a hockey stick in a curved pathway, keeping the ball close to the stick.
	I can dribble a ball with a hockey stick in a zigzag pathway, keeping the ball close to the stick.
	I can dribble a ball with a hockey stick around four cones set up about four feet apart, keeping the ball close to the stick.
	I can dribble a ball with a hockey stick through the cones while running, keeping the ball close to the stick.
	I can dribble a ball with a hockey stick while traveling sideways.
	I can make up a sequence including two pathways, two changes in speed, and two different directions. I have written my sequence below.
	Sequence:

Cues

Face Goal	(Your upper body must face the goal as you hit to it.)
Light Taps/Hard Strikes	(Light taps to dribble the ball; strike hard at the goal.)
Follow Through	(Follow through toward the goal with your stick.)

Tasks/Challenges:

🅣 Travel at your own speed and dribble/stick-handle the ball while avoiding the obstacles and other people. On the signal, travel quickly toward an open space, and strike for the goal. Retrieve your ball; begin dribbling again, listening for the signal to strike for the goal.

🅣 Practice dribbling around the obstacles and striking for the goal on your own; I won't give the signal.

Figure 30.18 It's a challenge to try to keep the ball away from a partner while dribbling it.

ONE-ON-ONE HOCKEY

Setting: Partners in general space, each with hockey sticks, a ball, and markers for a goal

Cues	
Light Taps/Hard Strikes	(Light taps to dribble the ball; strike hard at the goal.)
Heads Up	(Look up to avoid collisions.)
Dodges	(Use stopping/starting, both sides of the stick, and turns to avoid your partner.)

Tasks/Challenges:

🅣 Select a partner whose dribbling/stick-handling skills are about the same as yours. Cooperatively decide the boundaries for your area; a small area provides more practice. One of you begins to dribble the ball within the area; the other one tries to gain possession by using the stick to steal the ball (*Figure 30.18*). Follow these rules:

1. Contact the ball, not the person.

2. Gain possession; don't slap it away.
3. If you gain possession, begin dribbling as the offensive player; your partner is now defense.

If partners are unmatched in skill, provide a signal to change from offense to defense. Players stay on offense or defense until they hear the signal.

🅣 Within your area, set up two markers as a goal. The first partner will dribble until within scoring range (ten to twelve feet) and then shoot for a goal. The second partner will attempt to gain possession of the ball, using only the stick. After each strike for goal, switch positions.

🅒 Design your own game using the skills of stick-handling and shooting for the goal. Work with your partner to decide the rules of the game, scoring, and boundaries. Can you think of a name for your game?

STRIKING FROM A STATIONARY POSITION TO A MOVING TARGET—HOCKEY

Setting: Partners, each pair with two hockey sticks and a ball; a large enough space (about ten feet by ten yards) to send and receive the ball on the run

Cues

Lead Receiver	(Pass the ball to an open space in front of the receiver.)
Angles	(Your receiver should always be to the side and in front of you.)
Heads Up	(Always look up so you can see where your receiver is.)

Tasks/Challenges:

T You practiced striking the ball to a partner before, but then you were always standing still. When you're in a real game, how often are you able to pass to a partner who is standing still? Not very often. You're going to practice striking to a partner who is moving. One of you will be the passer, and the other the receiver. **The passer stands still and the receiver starts to run downfield, away from the passer at an angle. When the receiver is about five yards away, the passer sends the ball. The receiver should collect the ball on the run and then keep going for a few more steps.** Take five turns, and then switch positions.

T You've been passing to the same side so far. Now try passing to the other side so the receiver has to receive with the backhand. This will seem awkward at first, but stick with it. Pass ten times, and then switch.

PASSING AND RECEIVING ON THE MOVE—HOCKEY

Setting: A large, grassy outdoor area; children in pairs, with one ball for each pair and a hockey stick for each child

Cues

Lead Receiver	(Pass the ball to an open space in front of the receiver.)
Angles	(Your receiver should always be to the side and in front of you.)
Heads Up	(Always look up so you can see where your receiver is.)

Tasks/Challenges:

T Travel in the same direction as your partner, side by side, about twenty feet apart. As you're traveling, pass the ball back and forth using the hockey stick. The key is that you both must always be moving forward. When you get to the end of your area, turn around and come back.

T Now travel with your partner in general space, dribbling and passing. All the other players will be doing the same thing, so it's important that you are aware of others and of passing to open spaces. Go.

C Challenge yourself to always pass the ball ahead of your partner—to the open space. If you are successful, your partner will never have to stop to receive the pass. Try for five successful completions: open space, no stopping.

KEEPING IT MOVING—HOCKEY

Setting: Four cones marking a space five yards by five yards; four children per group, each group with four hockey sticks and a ball or puck

Cues

Lead Receiver	(Pass the ball to an open space in front of the receiver.)
Angles	(Your receiver should always be to the side of and in front of you.)
Heads Up	(Always look up so you can see where your receiver is.)

Tasks/Challenges:

C This time you're going to play a game called Keeping It Moving. One person begins by passing the ball to another player. That player passes it to someone else, and so on. The object is to never let the ball stop moving and never let it go out of bounds.

TWO-ON-ONE HOCKEY

Setting: Children in groups of three, each group with sticks, a ball, and cones to use as goals

Cues

Offense:	Lead Receiver (Strike the ball to an open space ahead of your receiver.) Light Taps/Hard Strikes (Light taps to dribble the ball; strike hard at the goal.) Angles (The receiver should be in an open space at an angle to and in front of the passer.)
Defense:	Play the Ball (Make your first move to the player with the ball.)

Tasks/Challenges:

C In your group, two of you will be the offensive players, and one will be the defensive player. The

Figure 30.19 Arrangement for dribbling and dodging activity.

Children dribbling

Children as obstacles .... Pathways made by children dribbling

two offensive players will pass and dribble to each other within the boundaries of your area. The defensive player will attempt to gain possession of the ball by intercepting passes or tapping the ball away on the dribble.

Each team will have possession of the ball for two minutes. See how many goals you can score in that time. The offensive team must execute at least two passes before attempting a goal.

Proficiency Level: Learning Experiences Leading to Skill Development

At the proficiency level, children are given situations that facilitate development of the ability to strike with implements while focusing on the strategy and outcome of the action and on their skill. The focus at this level is the attainment of consistency and accuracy while standing still or moving. Cues are focused on the *use* of the skill rather than on the skill itself.

A note about cues: Although several cues are listed for many of the learning experiences, it's important to focus on only one cue at a time. That way, the children can really concentrate on that cue. Once you provide feedback to the children and observe that most have learned a cue, then it's time to focus on another one.

Before beginning tasks that involve offense and defense, students should be skilled with the space awareness and dodging tasks that ask them to master the offensive and defensive skills of moving into open space; avoiding other persons; and using fakes, stops and starts, pivots, and

other avoidance skills without manipulating equipment. (See Chapter 16, "Space Awareness," and Chapter 21, "Chasing, Fleeing, and Dodging.") Children need to have mastered these skills before they are asked to use them while manipulating equipment.

One key to this task—and to other initial tasks involving offense and defense—is to clearly define the boundaries of the space the students are to use. A small space gives an advantage to the defense; a large space provides an offensive advantage. Similarly, a long, narow space gives the advantage to the defense; a wider space helps the offense. Initial tasks generally favor the offense.

STRIKING TO DODGE AN OPPONENT—HOCKEY

Setting: A group of ten or fewer children, several with hockey sticks and balls; the others positioned as obstacles, holding hockey sticks in their hands and wearing blue arm bands or other identifying clothing (Figure 30.19)

Cues	
Heads Up	(Always look up to avoid collisions.)
Dodges	(Use stopping/starting, both sides of the stick, changes of speed, and turns to avoid obstacles.)
Lead Receiver	(Pass to an open space ahead of the receiver.)
Angles	(The receiver should be in an open space to the side and in front of the passer.)

Tasks/Challenges:

T This is a dodging game. We've played games like this before, but without equipment. To begin, those of you wearing blue will be the obstacles; the rest of you will be dodgers. Obstacles, find a self-space and stand there. Dodgers, try to cross the room without coming near an obstacle. The obstacles have the right to steal the ball if it comes within their area. Their area is that space they can reach while keeping one foot glued to the floor. The goal of the dodgers is to get to the other end of the space without having the ball stolen. The group gets five tries and then switches places.

C We're going to change the game a little this time. Instead of all the dodgers having their own balls, they're going to have only one ball. Their job is then to get the ball to the other end, as a team. The obstacles still have the same rule: They can take the ball only when it comes into their area. After four tries, switch places.

T Now that you have the idea, let's form groups of six. Two people are dodgers; four are obstacles. Switch every time so you all get a turn.

KEEP AWAY—HOCKEY

Setting: Groups of four: three players on the outside standing about twenty feet apart and one in the middle; each player with a hockey stick; one ball or puck per group

Cues

Offense:	Don't Pass until the Defense Commits (Hold onto the ball until the defense makes you pass by coming close to you.) Receivers to Open Space (Receivers should move to an open space at an angle from the passer.) Stay Away from Passer (Receivers shouldn't go close to the passer.)
Defense:	Play the Ball (Play defense on the person with the ball.)

Tasks/Challenges:

C This is like Keep Away, except that it's played with hockey sticks. There will be four in a group: three on the outside standing about twenty feet apart, and one in the middle. The three on the outside pass the ball back and forth; the one in the middle tries to intercept the pass. After eight successful passes or four interceptions, trade places. You must

stay in the boundaries of your space. There is no contact.

DIRECTING THE PATHWAY, DISTANCE, AND SPEED OF AN OBJECT—GOLF

Setting: Boxes of various heights set up throughout the entire space; a hoop on the floor on the back side of each box; a golf club and a ball for each child. This is an appropriate station task (see Chapter 13).

Cues

Under the Ball	(Hit under the ball to make it travel a short distance.)
Short Swing	(Use a swing with a short back-swing and follow-through.)

Tasks/Challenges:

T The task is to hit the ball with the golf club so that the ball travels over the box and into the hoop. Once you're able to do this five times in a row standing close to the box, back up three steps and try it again.

T When you succeed, move to a new place and try again.

C Design your own golf game. You may have up to three players in a group. When you are finished, write down the rules for the game. Include in your write-up what skills you need to master to be able to play your game successfully. (*See Chapter 31 for details about how to help children design their own games.*)

 The written self-designed game is an appropriate assessment task to be included in a child's portfolio.

DIRECTING THE PATHWAY, DISTANCE, AND SPEED OF AN OBJECT (CALL YOUR HIT)—BATS

Setting: Groups of five: one batter, one pitcher, and three fielders; one plastic bat and ball per group; a space large enough for groups to bat without interfering with other groups

Cues

Hard Swing/ Medium Swing	(Hard swing = long hit; medium swing = shorter hit.)
Below, over, behind the Ball	(Below = fly ball; over = ground ball; behind = line drive.)

Figure 30.20   Whiffle Ball Golf course.

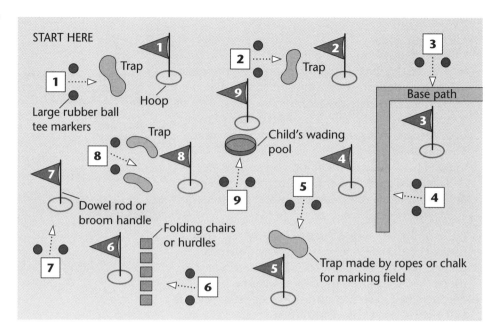

Tasks/Challenges:

Ⓖ For this game you use a plastic bat and ball. Here are the rules:

1. There are five people on a team: one batter, one pitcher, and three fielders.
2. Before the pitcher pitches the ball, she or he calls out the type of hit and the placement. The batter has to hit the ball the way the pitcher calls it.
3. Change batters after five hits.
4. Each player keeps his or her own score—one point for every ball that was hit as called out.

WHIFFLE BALL GOLF

Setting: A Whiffle Ball Golf course (Figure 30.20); a golf club and whiffle ball for each child

Cues	
Under the Ball/	(Under the ball = short distances;
Behind the Ball	behind the ball = long distances.)
Short Swing/	(Short swing = short distances;
Full Swing	full swing = long distances.)

Tasks/Challenges:

Ⓖ The game you're going to play is called Whiffle Ball Golf. It's played just as regular golf is played. The objective of the game is to get the ball to land in the hoop with as few strokes as possible. Each of you will start at the hole I assign you and then go to the next higher numbered hole. Each hole has a tee area from which to start: this area is marked with big rubber balls, to guarantee that everyone starts from the same place. When you get to hole 9, go to hole 1. Keep score by counting the shots it takes you to go around the entire course.

One of our students made the very sensible suggestion that we use old tires for the holes of the golf course, so the ball wouldn't roll out so easily. Old tires are very easy to obtain.

MINIHOCKEY

Setting: Groups of four or six, two or three players on each team; hockey sticks for every player; one ball or puck per group; milk crates, cones, or boxes for goals; a space at least twenty feet by fifteen feet

Cues	
Offense:	Don't Pass until the Defense Commits (Hold onto the ball until the defense makes you pass by coming close to you.) Receivers to Open Space (Receivers should move to an open space at an angle from the passer.) Stay Away from Passer (Receivers shouldn't go close to the passer.)

Defense: Ball First; Player Second (First play defense on the person with the ball; then cover the receivers.)
Hustle Back (When you lose the ball to the offense, hurry back on defense.)

Tasks/Challenges:

Ⓒ This game is called Minihockey. The objective is to strike the ball into the opponent's goal. Here are the rules:

1. The players on the teams decide the boundaries and width of the goal. There should be one goal on each end of the space. Use milk crates, cones, or boxes for the goals.
2. One team gets the ball first.
3. The ball can be stolen only on the pass.
4. No contact.
5. Everyone must be playing—no standing around.
6. Make up your own form of scoring (if you want to keep score.)
7. Make up any more rules you need.

Ⓣ We're going to change the game a little this time. Instead of one goal on each end of the field, there will be two.

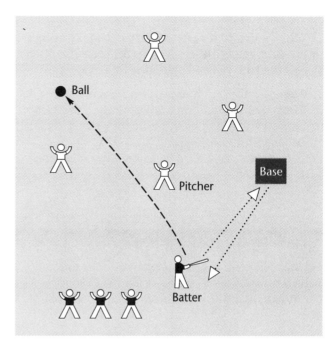

Figure 30.21 Setup for One-Base Baseball.

SIX-PLAYER TEEBALL

Setting: Groups of six players, three-person teams; bases as in softball, but with the distance between each reduced to make the game challenging for the group; one bat, ball, and tee per group; sufficient space so that children can bat without interfering with one another

> **Cues**
>
> *Batters:* Hit to Open Spaces (Always hit to open spaces.)
> *Fielders:* Throw Quickly (Throw the ball as soon as you get it.)
> Have a Plan (Know where the runners are; plan where to throw the ball.)

Tasks/Challenges:

Ⓒ This game is called Six-Player Teeball and involves the skills of striking, throwing, and catching. The objective is to place a batted ball, catch and throw, and run bases. Here are the rules:

1. There are three players on each team.

2. The batter strikes the ball from the tee and tries to run the bases.
3. The fielders try to catch or collect the ball and throw it to one another so that all three players catch the ball before the batter finishes running the bases.
4. Each player on a team bats, and then the teams switch places.

During the class, we focus on each child's individual improvements rather than on class or individual competition. Many children (and faculty!) enjoy voluntary tournaments, after school or at lunch.

ONE-BASE BASEBALL

Setting: Groups of six or eight, three- or four-person teams; one base, one bat, and one ball per group; a field set up as in Figure 30.21

> **Cues**
>
> *Batters:* Hit to Open Spaces (Always hit to open spaces.)
> *Fielders:* Throw Quickly (Throw the ball as soon as you get it.)
> Have a Plan (Know where the runners are; plan where to throw the ball.)

Tasks/Challenges:

⊤ You're going to play One-Base Baseball. The objective is to get to the base and back before the pitcher gets the ball. Here are the rules:

1. There are three or four people on each team.
2. The batter bats and then tries to run to the base and back to home plate before the pitcher gets the ball again.
3. Each person on a team bats, and then the teams trade places.

HALF BALL—BATS

Setting: Groups of six or eight; three- or four-person teams; a three- or four-inch solid rubber ball cut in half, as a ball, and a broom handle as a bat

Cues

Watch the Ball   (Keep your eyes on the ball all the time.)

Tasks/Challenges:

⊤ This game, called Half Ball, is really just for fun. It's basically played like baseball. Here are the rules that exist:

1. There are three or four players on each side.
2. Use a three- or four-inch solid rubber ball, cut in half, as a ball and a broom handle as a bat.
3. The rest is up to you.

This activity is great fun, although extremely difficult. For years, we played it on the beach at camp. It's a challenge to master, but it can be done! Kids love to try it!

READING COMPREHENSION QUESTIONS

1. What basic action is used in striking with any long-handled implement?
2. What is a sidearm pattern? What is an underhand swinging pattern? Which swings are used with which implements?
3. What is the purpose of introducing children to striking with long-handled implements?
4. What can be the long-term result when children try to swing implements that are too heavy or too long?
5. What are the observable characteristics of individuals at each level of skill proficiency in striking with long-handled implements?
6. Describe a mature striking pattern for striking a ball with a bat and with a golf club or a hockey stick.
7. Why do we recommend that children initially practice striking using yarn or plastic balls?
8. What does a level swing look like when the player is attempting to strike a ball with a bat?
9. Describe two examples, one for bats and one for hockey sticks, of contexts that are unpredictable or changing.
10. What do the terms *give* and *control* the ball with a hockey stick mean?
11. List three safety cues for striking with long-handled implements.

REFERENCES

National Association for Sport and Physical Education (NASPE). (1995). *Moving into the future: National standards for physical education.* St. Louis, MO: Mosby.

CHAPTER 31
Skill Themes in Games

All too often when it comes to the physical education of children we steal away this world of the child by dictating games to them. We do this under the assumption that it is good for all children to learn about our major sports through lead-up games involving kickball, dodgeball, Newcomb, line soccer, steal the bacon, and the like. Most of these games, however, are characterized by large groups, lack of participation, elimination, and stress on winning. Those who are not ready because of interest, motivation, strength, size or skill often turn to a search for stimulation in activities other than the game. These symptoms can be seen when children begin daydreaming, playing with dandelions in the grass, shoving, pushing, pulling, or looking for mischievous action with a friend.

——Peter Werner

ur task is to provide games experiences for children in a way that is both challenging and appropriate for all students in our classes. The manipulative skill themes, along with chasing, fleeing and dodging, are predominately the skill themes used in games.

The concept of a game holds a very different connotation for children than it does for adults. Children tend to view games as activities that use skills (most often manipulative) in a challenging, self-testing, or application fashion. These activities may or may not look like adult versions of sports. Sports are designed primarily for adults, have standardized rules and procedures, and require a level of technical expertise to which children will never aspire. Games use the same basic skills as many sports but lack the standardized rules and procedures. Quite often, children call their game activities by names similar to those of standardized sports, and their games may use equipment similar to that of standardized sports; however, the "game" is quite different. Understanding the difference between games and sports is critical to the reflective elementary school teacher: Games are appropriate elementary school content; sports, in their common form, are not.

The Council on Physical Education for Children (COPEC), in its document *Developmentally Appropriate Physical Education for Children* (1992), provides a useful analysis of when a game is appropriate and when it is not (Box 31.1). It is our responsibility as physical educators to teach developmentally appropriate games.

The instructor who teaches children to play games successfully and effectively does more than simply provide opportunities for children to play games. The successful teacher must create a variety of learning opportunities, including situations in which the children play games and situations in which they practice skills. The children in such programs acquire a foundation of movement skills that enables them to participate successfully in a broad variety of games and

sports. Once children have acquired the prerequisite game skills, sport becomes an attractive leisure-time alternative for them throughout their lives.

Some teachers view games as the easiest subject matter to teach. This is probably because game content is the content with which many of us are most comfortable; moreover, once students grasp the basic concepts of a game, it tends to be self-propelling in nature and requires little teacher intervention. Don't be deceived. Teaching games well requires the same amount of planning and skill as teaching dance and gymnastics. To teach games well, teachers need to be prepared to observe (Chapter 11) and teach (Chapter 12) in the same ways that they would with other content.

The Purpose of Games in the Elementary School

The purpose of games in the elementary school is not to develop elite athletes. Our purpose is to develop players who are versatile and skillful in game environments and who combine motor skills with basic strategic skill and knowledge to outwit opponents in dynamic, unpredictable situations. As a result of participating in physical education games experiences, all children should be excited about participating in games-playing activities on their own.

The *National Standards for Physical Education* (NASPE, 1995) support the inclusion of games in elementary physical education. Box 31.2 lists the sample benchmarks specific to games in the elementary school curriculum.

Games Experiences

Children enjoy games-playing experiences, but all too often, especially when we think in terms of sport, these experiences occur at the end—the end of a les-

BOX 31.1   APPROPRIATE AND INAPPROPRIATE PHYSICAL EDUCATION PRACTICES

Component: Games

Appropriate: Games are selected, designed, sequenced, and modified by teachers and/or children to maximize the learning and enjoyment of children.

Inappropriate: Games are taught with no obvious purpose or goal, other than to keep children "busy, happy, and good."

Component: Rules Governing Game Play

Appropriate: Teachers and/or children modify official rules, regulations, equipment, and playing space of adult sports to match the varying abilities of the children.

Inappropriate: Official, adult rules of team sports govern the activities in physical education classes, resulting in low rates of success and lack of enjoyment for many children.

Component: Forming Teams

Appropriate: Teams are formed in ways that preserve the dignity and self-respect of every child. For example, a teacher privately forms teams by using knowledge of children's skill abilities, or the children form teams cooperatively or randomly.

Inappropriate: Teams are formed by "captains" publicly selecting one child at a time, thereby exposing the lower-skilled children to peer ridicule.

Teams are formed by pitting "boys against the girls," thereby emphasizing gender differences rather than cooperation and working together.

Component: Number of Children on a Team

Appropriate: Children participate in team games (e.g., two to three per team), which allows for numerous practice opportunities while also allowing children to learn about the various aspects of the game being taught.

Inappropriate: Children participate in full-sided games (e.g., the class of thirty is split into two teams of fifteen, and these two teams play each other), which lead to few practice opportunities.

Component: Competition

Appropriate: Activities emphasize self-improvement, participation, and cooperation instead of winning and losing.

Teachers are aware of the nature of competition and do not *require* higher levels of competition from children before they are ready. For example, children are allowed to choose between a game in which score is kept and one that is just for practice.

Inappropriate: Children are *required* to participate in activities that label children as "winners" and "losers."

Children are *required* to participate in activities that compare one child's or team's performance against others (e.g., a race in which the winning child or team is clearly identified).

SOURCE: From *Developmentally Appropriate Physical Education Practices for Children: A Position Statement of the Council on Physical Education for Children* (COPEC), 1992, Reston, VA: National Association for Sport and Physical Education. Reprinted with permission.

son, the end of a unit—when we think the children have acquired all the prerequisite skills. But just as challenges need to be incorporated throughout lessons, children need games-playing experiences throughout their physical education programs, not just as a culminating activity. Yet these experiences must be adapted to the students' generic level of skill proficiency if the students are to acquire game skills and strategies as well as to enjoy playing games. In a model similar to that of Rink (1993), we organize game lessons into three types of experiences based on the children's skill levels: invariant game skill experiences, dynamic gamelike skill experiences, and games-playing experiences.

Research suggests that a child has little chance of being able actually to use basic skills in a changing or dynamic (game) situation unless he or she first practices the skills in an open, changing, or dynamic setting rather than in an unchanging situation (Arnold, 1978; Rovegno, Skonie, Charpenel, & Sieving, 1995; Schmidt, 1977). The skill acquired by a child who throws and catches a yarn ball with a partner may minimally transfer to the skill of throwing and catching used in, for example, baseball or basketball. For this reason, as soon as a child displays a minimum level of mastery in an invariant, unchanging (closed) situation, it's necessary to create open situations that are progressively and increasingly complex and in

BOX 31.2   GAMES AND THE *NATIONAL STANDARDS FOR PHYSICAL EDUCATION*

Games and game skills are referenced in the *National Standards for Physical Education* (NASPE, 1995) as sample benchmarks under Standards 1, 2, 3, 6, and 7.

The benchmarks for Standard 1: Demonstrates competency in many movement forms and proficiency in a few movement forms, state:

■ Tosses a ball and catches it before it bounces twice. (K)*
■ Kicks a stationary ball using a smooth, continuous running step. (K)
■ Demonstrates skills of chasing, fleeing, and dodging to avoid others. (2)
■ Receives and sends an object in a continuous motion. (2)
■ Strikes a ball repeatedly with a paddle. (2)
■ Throws, catches, and kicks using mature form. (4)
■ Dribbles and passes a basketball to a moving receiver. (4)
■ Throws a variety of objects, demonstrating both accuracy and force (e.g., basketball, footballs, Frisbees). (6)
■ Hand dribbles and foot dribbles while preventing an opponent from stealing the ball. (6)
■ Keeps an object going continuously with a partner using a striking pattern. (6)
■ Places the ball away from an opponent in a racket sport activity. (6)

The benchmark for Standard 2: Applies movement concepts and principles to the learning and development of motor skills, states:

■ Consistently strikes a softly thrown ball with a bat or paddle, demonstrating an appropriate grip. (4)

The benchmark for Standard 3: Exhibits a physically active lifestyle, states:

■ Participates in games, sports, dance, and outdoor pursuits both in and out of school based on individual interests and capabilities. (6)

The benchmarks for Standard 6: Demonstrates understanding and respect for differences among people in physical activity settings, state:

■ Indicates respect for persons from different backgrounds and the cultural significance they attribute to various games, dances, and physical activities. (4)
■ Recognizes the role of games, sports, and dance in getting to know and understand others of like and different backgrounds. (6)

The benchmarks for Standard 7: Understands that physical activity provides opportunities for enjoyment, challenge, self-expression, and social interaction, state:

■ Designs games, gymnastics, and dance sequences that are personally interesting. (4)
■ Recognizes the role of games, sports, and dance in getting to know and understand self and others. (6)

*Grade-level guidelines for expected student learning

which skills are used in combinations as they occur in gamelike situations. Yet, just as with the invariant situation, children must be taught the more difficult and combination skills; if the child doesn't display a minimum level of mastery, frustration again can permeate the experience.

To determine the appropriate time to switch from invariant skill experiences to dynamic situations, the teacher classifies the children's abilities according to the generic levels of skill proficiency (Chapter 7). When children reach the control/utilization level of skill proficiency, they're usually ready for dynamic gamelike skill experiences. This does *not* mean that you never return to invariant game skill experiences

(think of how many Olympic-caliber athletes practice basic skills for hours daily); it means that you can gradually make the invariant skills more complex so that they approach an increasingly open situation.

It is also at this point that simple offensive and defensive strategies are introduced as the children become more adept in the dynamic situation. Games-playing experiences allow children to focus on gaining a playing knowledge and an enthusiasm for playing a developmentally appropriate game. When children's skills have reached the automatic stage (utilization or proficiency level), they are ready for games-playing experiences (Belka, 1991). Yet, as with the dynamic experiences, introducing games-playing does

COMPETITION/COOPERATION

▶ Some children love to compete; others prefer (and seem to learn better in) games that encourage cooperation. We attempt to respect each child's preference by giving choices, trying never to place an entire class in a competitive situation. Instead, we let children choose between two or more games or ask them to make up their own games. The teachers heighten or lessen the degree of competition. Teachers who constantly shout out the score, post team won and lost records, and reward the winners (thereby punishing the losers) place an emphasis on competition for which some children aren't ready. If you don't believe us, talk to the thousands of adults who were unskilled as children and yet were placed in highly competitive situations. They can describe, in vivid detail, the feelings of begin picked last, shouted at for dropping a ball, and ridiculed for "letting the team down." Such distasteful experiences usually have lasting and negative influences on the individual's willingness to participate in sports.

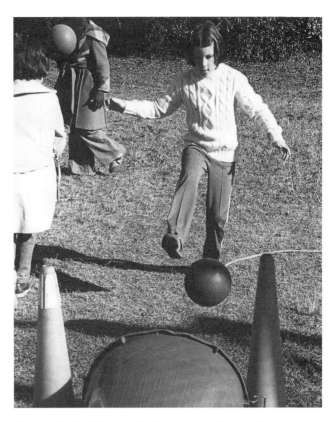

Figure 31.1 Kicking a ball at a target from behind a designated line is an example of invariant game skill experience.

not mean that you never return to the previous experiences; it means that as students become more proficient players, you gradually extend the games-playing experience to make it more complex while ensuring that it remains developmentally appropriate.

Invariant Game Skill Experiences

The first experiences we give children involve basic skills in a closed or unchanging situation (Figure 31.1). Such experiences allow the students to gain control of an object using a specific motor pattern (Rink, 1993). The experience is structured so that the task is as identical as possible each time—the experience is invariant in that the child isn't required to predict the flight of a ball or the movement of an opponent, for example. At this point, refinement is the major emphasis (Belka, 1991), and "games" experiences are limited to self-testing challenges.

Such experiences are appropriate for a child who is at the precontrol or control level of skill proficiency and would have difficulty executing a skill in a dynamic or open situation. As a child's proficiency in a skill increases, you can increase the difficulty of the tasks while retaining the relative predictability of the skill (Figure 31.2). For example, when a child is learn-

Figure 31.2 In this invariant game skill experience, the teacher has challenged the children to dribble a ball through an obstacle course.

ing to throw a ball to hit a stationary target, you can increase the distance to the target. If the child is learning to run and leap over a low obstacle, increase the height of the obstacle.

When a child who isn't able to perform a basic skill consistently (precontrol level) is placed in a game that requires that skill and the ability to perform it in a dynamic or changing situation, the results are often counterproductive. A child in that situation often fails and becomes frustrated because of continuing inability to execute the prerequisite movements of the game. The child may then become a self-proclaimed, permanently terminated games player or a teenager or adult who vows to never again play in a game situation. And the other children are frustrated when an unskilled player interrupts the flow and their enjoyment of the game.

Dynamic Gamelike Skill Experiences

When children have learned to perform skills successfully under relatively closed conditions, they need and are challenged by opportunities to practice skills in open circumstances similar to actual sports situations (control/utilization level). Shooting a basket with no opposition is a different skill from that needed to make a basket immediately after stopping a dribble or when guarded by an opponent. Children should be exposed to many experiences that relate to a variety of sports (Figure 31.3). We not only expose children to experiences from sports played in America but also attempt to expose the youngsters to gamelike experiences requiring different combinations of skills that have no apparent relationship to any sports we're familiar with. Such experiences encourage children to develop techniques and applications of skills in unique situations; no doubt they'll experience games that have yet to be invented and that require skills and abilities yet unheard of.

Rink's (1993) progression suggests that dynamic gamelike skill experiences actually involve two aspects of skill development: (1) the combining of more than one motor skill into cooperative relationships and (2) the ability to use skills in simple offensive and defensive relationships. When viewed in this manner, the progression from invariant game skill experiences to dynamic gamelike skill experiences to actual games-playing experiences is quite logical and developmental.

Tasks at the dynamic gamelike skill stage are initially self-testing activities and are usually cooperative in nature. Later, after the children develop combinations of skills, small-group activities, which can be either cooperative or competitive and which focus on decision making during increasingly complex situa-

Figure 31.3 Dribbling a ball past a defender into a goal is a dynamic gamelike skill experience.

tions, are appropriate. For example, within dynamic gamelike skill experiences, a child first practices dribbling and shooting a basketball while at the same time passing off to a partner. Then, the child practices the same skill with one person acting as a defensive player. The implication of this progression is that as the child slowly becomes more adept at using a motor skill or combination of motor skills, the child is simultaneously learning games-playing strategies to accompany the skill.

Providing experiences that require children to use gamelike skills is different from teaching games. Offensive and defensive strategies, as well as combination skills (dribble/pass), must be taught and learned just as closed skills at the invariant stage. Too often teachers skip from the invariant stage to the games-playing stage without teaching the combination skills and strategies in an open, dynamic experience.

You can create practice opportunities that simulate the way skills are used in games but don't necessarily include scoring and control or limit competition or environment. For example, ask children to try to keep a ball away from a partner using only a dribble (hand or foot) or to work in a group of three to keep a ball moving in the air without actually catching the ball. You can make these experiences more gamelike or difficult by asking the child to keep the ball away from an opponent using a dribble and to shoot at a target as soon as the child passes the opponent. The group of

Figure 31.4 Children enjoy playing a soccer-type game.

three can also increase the difficulty of their task by increasing the space in which they have to move. Tasks such as these approach the dynamic situations of games and sports.

Games-Playing Experiences

Children at the upper utilization level or proficiency level are ready for games-playing experiences. We try to acquaint these children with many different types of games-playing experiences. These activities can help children experience the enjoyment, satisfaction, excitement, and sense of accomplishment that a developmentally appropriate game can bring about (Figure 31.4).

Some skill development results from playing games, but game playing isn't the most efficient way for all children to improve the motor skills used in games. Thus it's useful to distinguish lessons in which the primary purpose is to improve skills (invariant and dynamic gamelike skill experiences) from lessons in which the primary purpose is to develop enthusiasm for and a playing knowledge of a variety of games (games-playing experiences).

Lessons devoted to skills acquisition are punctuated by a number of starts and stops. The teacher continually refocuses or redefines the tasks, giving individuals and groups feedback in an attempt to enhance the quality of their movements.

I would like to contrast the richness of children's natural play with the stultifying rigidity of play that is organized by adults. No better example can be found than that of the Little League, for what boys, left to their own devices, would ever invent such a thing? How could they make such a boneheaded error as to equate competition with play? Think of the ordinary games of boys—in sandlots, fields, parks, even stickball in the street. They are expansive and diverse, alternately intense and gay, and are filled with events of all kinds.

Between innings the boys throw themselves on the grass. They'll wrestle, do handstands, turn somersaults. They hurl twigs and stones at nearby trees, and yell at the birds that sail by. A confident player will make up dance steps as he stops a slow grounder. If an outfielder is bored, he does not stand there pulling up his pants and thumping his glove, but plays with the bugs in the grass, looks at the clouds. . . . There is almost always a dog on the field, and no part of the competition is gayer or more intense than that between the boys and the dog, who when he succeeds in snapping up their ball, leads them off in a serpentine line that is all laughter and shouts, the dog looking back over his shoulder and trotting with stiff legs, until finally he is captured and flattens his ears as they take back their ball. No one has forgotten the score or who was at bat. The game goes on. The game goes on until darkness ends it, and the winners can hardly be distinguished from the losers, for by then everyone is fumbling the ball and giggling and flopping on the grass.

George Dennison, *The Lives of Children*

The games-playing environment is somewhat different, however. The enjoyment and satisfaction derived from playing games frequently are products of playing a game without interruption. In the limited time most of us have to teach our classes, there's hardly enough time for skill practice and game playing in a single lesson.

This does not mean that the teacher does nothing during games-playing experiences. Observe the types of skill work that children need as they're playing games, and focus on those needs during later classes. Remember, games-playing experiences don't occur in every lesson; they are only a part of the total physical education program.

Take your cue from the children in determining when to provide feedback. A lull in the game, a water break, the end of class, or other natural interruption provides an opportunity to check with the children and offer guidance if needed. Try not to stop or interfere in the children's games to teach skills, unless the game has become unsatisfying and boring because of lack of ability. Adults prefer not to be interrupted during a game, even by someone who wants to provide feedback. Children share this feeling, and teachers must respect it if they want to create positive attitudes toward games.

One implication teachers often draw from the progression of invariant, dynamic, and games-playing experiences is that until children become exceedingly proficient with dynamic gamelike skills and approach the proficiency level of skill development, they shouldn't play games. This contention is only partially true. Although we don't advocate that children at the precontrol and control levels be involved in games-playing experiences, we encourage challenges, self-testing, and dynamic gamelike skill experiences. Children conceive of many of these types of experiences as games. In other words, children are playing games in their own minds; what is different is our adult conception of what a game is. Thus all children can play "games," depending on who is calling the activity a game.

The Process of Teaching Games

Teaching games to meet the developmental needs of children is not as simple as it initially appears. For many of us, it is intertwined with deeply imbedded sport experiences that make it difficult to "see differently." To see differently we must focus on the type of game we choose, the equipment used, what we call the game, the number of players involved, our role as an official or teacher, and the learning environment. It is only then that we truly start to look at the child first and the game second.

Selecting a Game

There are at least five types of game designs a teacher can use to structure games-playing experiences for the children's variety of skill levels: predesigned, modified predesigned, teacher-designed, teacher/child-designed, and child-designed. Each has its own inherent strengths and weaknesses.

Predesigned Games   Predesigned games are those described in textbooks or learned in methods classes and taught to children without modification. The textbooks imply that such games will be appropriate as well as interesting for children. Brownies and Fairies; Duck, Duck, Goose; Red Rover; Four Square; and Steal the Bacon are well-known predesigned games.

Predesigned games are easy to teach because they require little preparation or teaching skill. The teacher selects a game and explains it to the children. When the children understand the game, they start to play, and the game continues until the lesson ends or the teacher changes the activity.

It has been our experience that few predesigned games are appropriate for all the children in a class. A few skilled children often dominate such games, whereas others are minimally involved, both physically and emotionally. You may occasionally encounter a situation in which a particular predesigned game is appropriate for a class or group of children. Usually, though, you'll find that although many of the ideas in a predesigned game are worthwhile, you have to modify the structure of the game to the abilities and interests of different children.

Modified Predesigned Games   Modifying predesigned games requires greater planning and organizing ability than picking a game from a book. Yet by modifying a predesigned game, you can do much to make the game more appropriate for a particular class.

Both Rink (1993) and Morris and Stiehl (1989) provide useful ideas for modifying predesigned games. The teacher can change the rules (e.g., allow two tries instead of only one), the equipment used (e.g., larger and lighter), the number of players involved (generally, it's best to decrease the number), the playing area

---

> ▶ Nettie Wilson (1976) conducted a study to determine the number of throwing, catching, and kicking opportunities in the game of kickball as played by third- and fourth-grade children under the direction of a classroom teacher. Her findings include the following:
>
> 1. Less than half of the game was actually spent using the criterion skills.
> 2. The average number of catches attempted in the kickball games was slightly more than two—35 percent of the children never caught the ball. Of the children who didn't catch the ball, 83 percent were girls.
> 3. The average number of throws made in the kickball games, excluding those made by the pitcher and catcher, was slightly more than one—52 percent of the children never threw the ball at all during the entire game, and 67 percent of those who never threw the ball were girls.

> When I first started teaching, I was looking for games that were recommended for first-grade children and did not require a great deal of game skill. Brownies and Fairies, a simple running and chasing game, was prescribed in one text as appropriate for six-year-olds. The first time the game was played, two children fell down and bloodied their knees when they tried to run in a crowd of children. They could run by themselves without falling. But when they were placed in a dynamic situation that involved both running and dodging, they were unsuccessful. They probably forgot that experience many years ago—once their knees healed. I haven't.

(e.g., larger or smaller), or the skills involved (e.g., throwing instead of striking). Many teachers modify one aspect of the game at a time until it provides an experience appropriate for the skill level of the children. A good rule of thumb to follow is to change or eliminate anything that impedes or slows the flow of a game.

During the lesson, you may use the same teaching skills required to teach a predesigned game—explaining the game and intervening only when that's necessary to keep the game going. Evaluating the game is more complex. You'll have to decide, after observing the children, whether the game should be modified further or is satisfactory as currently structured.

Teacher-Designed Games Sometimes a teacher can't find a game appropriate for a particular class, and modifications of predesigned games don't seem effective. In such a situation, the teacher may design a game that satisfies a specific goal. Designing a game places a greater demand on a teacher's creative abilities than do either of the game lesson structures already discussed.

The teacher needs to understand the children's skill abilities and interests and be able to use this knowledge to design a game form that the children will find interesting and enjoyable. For example, a teacher could design a game to focus on striking a ball with a bat. The object would be to strike a pitched ball and then run around a cone and back before the other players catch or collect the ball and touch the home base with the ball. If the children used rather narrow boundaries and played in small groups, they would get more striking, throwing, and catching opportunities than the standardized nine-per-side version of softball provides. The teacher could design the game to be played by two teams or design it so that each

child goes back "to the field" once she or he hits the ball and runs around the cone. Once you've created the game, the teaching skills used are virtually identical to the skills needed to teach a modification of a predesigned game.

Each of these three game lesson structures places the responsibility for selecting or designing a game on the teacher. One advantage of these games structures is that the children spend most of the time—once the game has been explained and organized—playing the game. But the children don't contribute to the design of the game, nor do they have anything to say about whether they would like to continue playing the game as is or change the game to make it better. The following two game structures, by contrast, involve the children in the design of the game. They require more advanced teaching skills if they're to be effective.

Teacher/Child-Designed Games When the children and the teacher design a game together, the teacher presents the purpose of the game and the restrictions. The children and the teacher then work cooperatively to decide the rules, scoring, and equipment to be used.

You'll find that it's wise to stipulate that once the game has begun, only the team with the ball (or the advantage) can stop play to suggest a change. (Unless the children are restrained by this rule, they're likely to stop the game and suggest a change every time the other team gains an advantage.) After a brief discussion of the proposed change, the class votes, with the majority decision prevailing. If a rule needs to be made to ensure safety, offer solutions to be voted on, or ask the children to propose a solution.

One example of a teacher/child-designed game is Magladry Ball, named by the children after their school. The teacher was concerned about the children's inability to travel and pass a ball or other object to a teammate who was also traveling, particularly when an opponent attempted to intercept or prevent the pass from being made. After describing the purpose of the game, the teacher imposed two restrictions: Children couldn't touch each other, and once the ball (object) touched the ground, it was automatically in the possession of the team that didn't touch it immediately before the object hit the ground. The object of the game was to throw the ball (beanbag, Frisbee) through a hoop suspended from a goal post by a rope at either end of a field. Once the game began, children made decisions about how long one child could remain in possession of the ball (object); what type of ball (object) to play the game with; boundaries, violations, and penalties; and scoring.

> A true game is one that frees the spirit—the true game is the one that arises from the players themselves.
>
> Peter Opie and Iona Opie, *Children's Games in Street and Playground*

Teacher/child-designed games evolve slowly, and you may spend several lessons creating games that children are excited about and enjoy playing. Once the time and effort to create a game have been spent, the children will want to have opportunities to play it.

The instructor in a teacher/child-designed game serves as a facilitator, enhancing and expanding ideas rather than imposing personal ideas on the children. The teacher helps the children modify the games, offers suggestions, and manages a group of eager, charged-up children who are anxious to get the game going again. This isn't an easy task, and it often takes some time to master this approach.

Child-Designed Games   The underlying assumption of the first four game structures is that the entire class is playing the same game, either as a whole group or in small groups. With child-designed games, however, we assume that many games are being played simultaneously and that few, if any, are identical. Such an environment is a far more complex one in which to teach (Rovegno, Skonie, Charpenel, & Sieving, 1995). The teacher is assisting groups of children to develop different games and is also responsible for observing a number of different games and assisting or staying away when appropriate.

Child-designed games have some definite advantages. Children in groups of similar skill ability (given a choice, children typically choose to be with others of similar ability) are allowed to design games that are interesting and exciting to them. These may be cooperative or competitive, active or passive, depending on the children's intent.

Initially, children need help in designing their own games. Teachers who've met with success in using child-designed games have found that in the beginning it's helpful to suggest a structure for the game—that is, the purposes, boundaries, and rules (Rovegno & Bandhauer, 1994). For example, the teacher may say, "Make up your own striking game. There may be up to four people in the group. All of you must play at once; there's to be no waiting in line. And the space can be no larger than fifteen feet by fifteen feet." The teacher can also help the children organize the game

Figure 31.5   Example of a child-designed game—sixth grade.

by asking them to identify their rules, either verbally or in writing (Figures 31.5 and 31.6).

As children learn to make decisions about their games, you can decrease the amount of imposed structure. If children are to make significant and worthwhile decisions about their game, you must stay out of as many decisions as possible; this is just as important as providing proper initial guidance. Even if you're certain some idea won't work, it's no longer your role to tell them so (except in the case of safety). They'll find out soon enough.

You may consider it a disadvantage that some children take a great deal of time to design games. Children who've had little experience in designing their own games may spend as much as half of a lesson seriously working out the way they want a game to be played, perhaps without ever actually playing the game. But you'll find that as students gradually become more adept at designing games, playing time increases substantially.

Most children enjoy participating in the design of their own games. But the children must be ready—they must be able to function successfully in a small group (two or three is an appropriate number) when playing a game they know before they can begin to

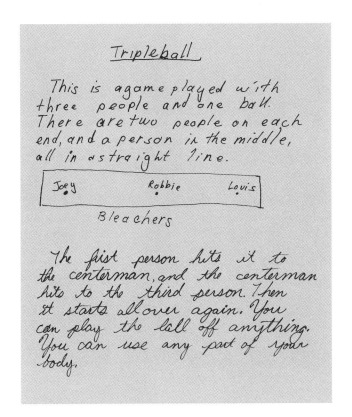

Figure 31.6 Example of a child-designed game—fifth grade.

THE FAMILY CIRCUS.   By Bil Keane

"We made it up ourselves. You don't need nine guys on a team, or grownups, or uniforms. . . . It's like baseball, only better!"

(Reprinted with special permission of King Features Syndicate.)

design games. Some teachers, even of younger children, can use child-designed games from the time they begin teaching and have exciting, successful lessons. But when a teacher—even one who believes in the philosophy represented by child-designed games—tries to have children design their own games before the children (and the teacher) are ready, the outcome can be a disaster. Start with the design that you think is most appropriate to a class and situation, and proceed from there.

The ecology of the particular teaching situation determines which game design is best. When selecting a games-playing lesson design for a class, consider the purpose for playing the game, the skills required, the children's interests and abilities, the playing area and equipment available, and your skills as a teacher. We try very carefully to match the skills required in games-playing experiences to the children's skills. Nothing is so counterproductive as having children participate in games for which they don't possess the prerequisite skills. The teacher who has closely assessed the children's skill level can discover and/or design well-matched games-playing situations to ensure the children's success and pleasure.

Games Equipment

The equipment used to play games most certainly affects the quality and difficulty of the game (Graham, 1992). Large, regulation-size sport equipment slows the play and promotes the use of incorrect skills. In recent years equipment manufacturers have begun to design equipment for children: Foam paddles, balls, and hockey sticks are three examples. Smaller, lighter, more colorful balls that don't hurt reduce the fear of catching. Basketball goals that can be adjusted to multiple heights (not just one or two) allow all children to be able to shoot at an appropriate basket. The bottom line is: Adult equipment is almost always inappropriate for elementary school children. Make sure the equipment matches the child.

The Name of the Game

By calling a game by the name of the sport its skills are usually associated with, we effectively limit children's options. The skilled children think they have to play by the rules of the sport, and the unskilled unconsciously evaluate themselves against some external standard, whether they really know much about the sport or not. As a result, some children are disenfranchised and others are frustrated. We have found that children are much more creative and open in their games playing if we refer to the experience by a new name or by the name of the skill.

Group Size

To many there is a "right" number of players for a game. Because of our conscious or unconscious sport orientation, the "right" number of players is often the number of players associated with the sport in which the skill is most commonly used. And because pre-designed games are usually designed for entire classes, they often call for fifteen, twenty, or more players. Rarely does either of the preceding scenarios contain the "right" number of players for games appropriate to the elementary school setting. Games experiences should never involve more players than can be active at any one time or so many that the flow of the game is slowed. We have found this usually means four to six (and maybe eight) players as a maximum in any games experience. Choose the "right" number of players for the children's experience.

To Ref or Not to Ref?

We do not believe in officiating children's games. Officiating does several things that detract from the ultimate value of the games-playing experience. First, officiating places the responsibility for coming to decisions about the process of the game on the teacher, thus taking away all responsibility and decision making from the children. The end result is that they can "blame the teacher" for what happened and avoid learning to cooperate and decide for themselves. Second, officiating takes the teacher out of the teaching role and limits the teacher's ability to provide feedback and instruction—our primary goal. Third, a teacher can only be in one place. If we officiate, only one game can be occurring; this means that all the children aren't active and that more than likely we have created an inappropriate games environment (Figure 31.7).

We have been very successful in letting children "call" their own games. They not only adapt the rules to fit their situation, but develop decision-making and cooperation skills. The flow of the game is also generally more continuous; they stop only when they need to.

The Learning Environment

The small group size we recommend implies that more than one game will be played simultaneously. Having several games going on at one time, however, can be uncomfortable for many of us. If this is true for you, we suggest you begin slowly. Start with a class you are confident with, and have only two games play concurrently. As you feel more confident, gradually add more games. What is amazing is that more games

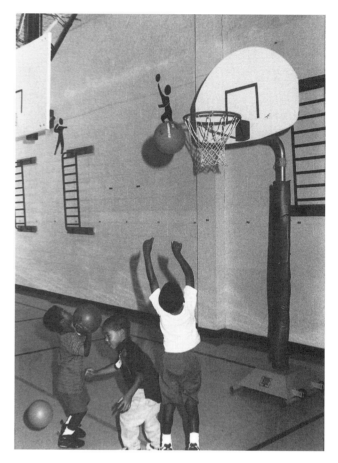

Figure 31.6 Young children's games rarely have game-playing qualities.

actually decreases many potential management problems. Because more children are actively and appropriately involved in playing and are spending less time waiting or otherwise unengaged, the amount of off-task behavior is substantially reduced.

After-School Sport Programs

Many children in your classes may be participating in various sport programs. Often these children are very skilled—many are at the proficiency level of the skills involved in their sport—and so provide an interesting dimension to games lessons. We have found that by using small groups for games experiences and varying the task, these students can be challenged in our classes just as any other student.

Child Development and Games

The research on child development (Piaget, 1962) and the development of reasoning (Kohlberg & Mayer,

1972) further supports placing children in game situations designed to accommodate their skills, interests, and abilities. Before the age of eight, children are in the egocentric stage. They have a personal conception of reality; the world centers around self. There's no sense of obligation to rules, no desire to check for accuracy. "I" am right at all times. Whatever meets the needs at the present time is what is true. Following rules is fine if it serves the purpose at the time. The concept of cheating doesn't exist, because rules constantly change to fit the child's needs. At this stage the child feels that everyone completely understands him or her and is in agreement with what the child wants or does. Imagine placing twenty-five youngsters in a traditional group game when each child thinks he or she is completely understood and in agreement with all!

Piaget (1962) described the game play of the young child (from the child's viewpoint) as a situation in which everyone plays the game as each understands it, with no concern for "checking" on others. Nobody loses and everybody wins at the same time, because the purpose is to have fun (Piaget & Inhelder, 1969).

Children between eight and eleven have a strong social need. To be a part of the group, to belong, is extremely important to children in the upper elementary years. In the early phases of this stage, however, children still have strong egocentric tendencies. Group interaction is desired, but so too is the desire to cling to the comfortable self-centered view. The earlier "absolute" view is now confronted with the viewpoints of others, viewpoints perhaps not in agreement with one's own. How many children do we see get upset and leave the game when things don't go their way or they're asked to sacrifice themselves for the good of the team? Cooperative game situations with small groups of children can facilitate establishing the child as a member of the group and foster acceptance of differing points of view.

Students entering the higher level of cognitive development, ages eleven and above, begin to create strategies and mentally test their abilities. They enjoy group activity and respect the physical and mental skills of others in the game situation. The game no longer rules the group; the game is made for the use of the group—to be adapted as needed.

A Final Thought

Much has been written about the inappropriateness of adult versions of sports for children (Orlick & Zitzelsberger, 1996; Smoll & Smith, 1996). The child who seeks sport experiences can find them outside the school. Most communities in the United States offer adequate sports at the middle and high school levels, in after-school programs, and in programs sponsored by youth agencies.

Physical educators have a responsibility to provide instruction for all children, to help them become skillful games players who enjoy participating in games and are eager to play games on their own time. We must do more than produce a few good athletes. In a successful physical education program, all the children improve their games-playing skills and are eager and excited about playing games.

SUMMARY

Because games are self-propelling, they're deceptively easier to teach than dance or gymnastics. This deceptive ease, however, is an educationally unacceptable rationale for curricular decision making. Teachers need to provide children with developmentally appropriate experiences that lead to the acquisition of games-playing skills. We give children experiences that involve invariant games skills, dynamic gamelike skills, and games-playing skills.

Invariant games experiences focus on skill acquisition in a predictable, closed environment where the movement is essentially the same each time. Dynamic gamelike experiences require children to use game skills in unpredictable, open, game-simulating situations that require more than the execution of a particular skill. Games-playing experiences are designed to expose children to the joy and satisfaction that can be found in games. In these experiences children use skill and strategy in an attempt to outwit an opponent.

Several variables affect the process of teaching games to children. The type of game selected can influence the success of the experience. Other factors to be considered when teaching games to children are the equipment used, the number of children in the game, the role of the teacher as an official, the learning environment, and what the game is called.

The role of games in elementary physical education is to provide all children the chance to be successful in playing in dynamic, unpredictable situations that challenge them to outwit their opponents. It is the teacher's responsibility to design game experiences that meet the needs of all students.

READING COMPREHENSION QUESTIONS

1. What is the difference between games and sports?
2. What are the characteristics of developmentally appropriate and inappropriate games for children? Identify one activity that you know is appropriate and one that is inappropriate.
3. Games are organized into what three types of experiences? Define the purpose of each experience.
4. What happens when we place children in dynamic situations before they're ready?
5. When is it appropriate to move children from an invariant to a dynamic situation? Why is such movement necessary?
6. How are situations that require children to use games skills different from actual games?
7. What is one difference between a games-playing lesson and a skill-development lesson? What role should a teacher take in each lesson?
8. What factors should be taken into account when teaching games?
9. What are the differences between the five game designs presented? What is the ultimate criterion for using any game in physical education?
10. Why do we recommend small group sizes and multiple games in physical education class?

REFERENCES/ SUGGESTED READINGS

Arnold, R. K. (1978) Optimizing skill learning: Moving to match the environment. *Journal of Physical Education and Recreation, 49*(9), 84–86.

Belka, D. (1991). Learning to be a games player. *Strategies, 4*(4), 8–10.

Belka, D. (1994). *Teaching games: Becoming a master teacher.* Champaign, IL: Human Kinetics.

Council on Physical Education for Children (1992). *Developmentally appropriate physical education for children.* Reston, VA: National Association for Sport and Physical Education.

Dennison, G. (1969). *The lives of children.* New York: Random House.

Graham, G. (1992). *Teaching children physical education: Becoming a master teacher.* Champaign, IL: Human Kinetics.

Kohlberg, L., & Mayer, R. (1972). Development as the aim of education. *Harvard Educational Review, 42*(4), 449–496.

Morris, G. S., & Stiehl, J. (1989). *Changing kids' games.* Champaign, IL: Human Kinetics.

National Association for Sport and Physical Education. (1995). *Moving into the future: National standards for physical education.* St. Louis, MO: Mosby.

Opie, P., & Opie, I. (1969). *Children's games in street and playground.* New York: Oxford University Press.

Orlick, T. D., & Zitzelsberger, L. (1996). Enhancing children's sport experiences. In R. E. Smith & F. L. Smoll (Eds.), *Children and youth in sport: A biopsychosocial perspective* (pp. 330–337). Dubuque, IA: Brown and Benchmark.

Piaget, J. (1962). *Play, dreams, and imitation in childhood.* New York: Norton.

Piaget, J., & Inhelder, B. (1969). *The psychology of the child.* New York: Basic Books.

Rink, J. (1993). *Teaching physical education for learning* (2nd ed.). St. Louis, MO: Mosby.

Rovegno, I., & Bandhauer, D. (1994). Child-designed games—Experience changes teachers' conceptions. *Journal of Physical Education, Recreation and Dance, 65*(6), 60–63.

Rovegno, I., Skonie, R., Charpenel, T., & Sieving, J. (1995). Learning to teach critical thinking through child-designed games. *Teaching Elementary Physical Education, 6*(1), 6–7, 15.

Schmidt, R. (1977). Schema theory: Implications for movement education. *Motor Skills: Theory into Practice, 2,* 36–48.

Smoll, F. L., & Smith, R. E. (1996). Competitive anxiety: Sources, consequences, and intervention strategies. In R. E. Smith & F. L. Smoll (Eds.), *Children and youth in sport: A biopsychosocial perspective* (pp. 359–380). Dubuque, IA: Brown and Benchmark.

Werner, P. (1979). *A movement approach to games for children.* St. Louis, MO: Mosby.

Wilson, N. (1976). *The frequency and patterns of selected motor skills by third and fourth-grade girls and boys in the game of kickball.* Unpublished master's project, University of Georgia, Athens.

PART FIVE
The Future

Our last two chapters emphasize future directions in physical education. Chapter 32, "Building Support for Your Program," describes how teachers can work with six different populations to gain support for their physical education programs. We offer practical ideas for working with other teachers in the school, the principal, parents, the school board, the children themselves, and the community at large.

Chapter 33, "Physical Education for Tomorrow's Children," is in many ways our favorite. We end the book by focusing on the future, presenting some of our thoughts. We hope our ideas will encourage you to dream too.

CHAPTER
32

Building Support for Your Program

Many parents, students, teachers, and administrators do not know how physical education contributes to an individual's growth. The lack of a public relations plan can result in an absence of communication between the physical educator and the public, thereby hampering the growth of the physical education program.

—Michael Tenoschok and Steve Sanders

One of the undisputed facts about teaching in schools is that teachers need support from a variety of sources if they're to develop the type of programs they want for their children. This is especially true in physical education, for two reasons. First, many people regard physical education as less important than other subjects, such as reading and math, for example. Second, physical education is a relatively expensive program to conduct because of the necessary equipment involved. (It's important, however, that we continually remind others that physical education is for *every* child in the school—for the entire five or six years.) Thus it's necessary to cultivate support from the various segments of a school community who have the potential to be allies in our quest for improved programs (Figure 32.1). We've identified six related populations who need to be aware of and supportive of our program: the school administration, especially the principal; other teachers in the school; parents; the school board; the community at large; and the children.

This chapter discusses ideas for building support within each of these six populations. However, note that it's important that a teacher first build as good a physical education program as possible with the support available. Even with limited resources, it's possible to begin a good program, and this should be done because much of the work that will go toward building more support involves opening the program to administrators, parents, and the community in general. Obviously, if the program doesn't get off to a good start, you don't want visitors.

Once the program is off to a reasonable start, however, the teacher can invite observers to visit the classes. It may take months before the teacher is ready, but the learning environment has to be established, with the children and teacher working together comfortably, before visitors are welcome. Once the teacher is ready, the principal and other teachers in the school will probably be the first visitors. You might want to consider your answers to the questions in Box 32.1 as you begin to build support for your program.

The Principal

Many principals, through no fault of their own, know very little about physical education—especially the approach we're advocating in *Children Moving*. Thus it's important to not take for granted that the principal knows and understands the program you're trying to develop (Schneider, 1992). We believe part of our job is to educate our principal and administrators

Figure 32.1 Thorough planning by the physical education teacher helps ensure that programs receive support.

about our physical education programs (Figure 32.2). This is probably our most important task for gaining support for our programs. Principals are extremely important. In fact, if a principal is not "on our side," the opportunity to develop our desired program is reduced considerably (Giles-Brown, 1993). We suggest the following ideas for working with your principal. The ideas aren't arranged in order of implementation, and we don't suggest that they all need to be done. We've simply listed ideas you may find helpful in your particular situation.

- Invite the principal of your school to observe a program at a nearby school with you. Sit with your principal, and be certain that she focuses on the aspects of the program that are critical to the growth of your own program. Be certain to schedule a visit with the principal at the school you're observing so that the two administrators can discuss their programs and your principal can ask questions.
- Invite your principal to your classes that are beginning to work the way you intend. Be certain to follow up this visit so that you can answer any questions that may have arisen. Some administrators, for example, are unaccustomed to seeing every child with a ball and may be concerned about the "chaotic" appearance of a class that differs from their experiences in which there was only one ball for an entire class.
- If you're able to obtain videotapes of other teachers, invite your principal to view one of the tapes

BOX 32.1   WHY SHOULD MY CHILD TAKE PHYSICAL EDUCATION?

As you consider ways to build support for your program, it helps to formulate answers to the questions that a parent (administrator, board member) might ask:

■ Why should my children take physical education?
■ What benefits is he or she gaining from participating in your program?

Think about how other teachers might respond if they were asked the same questions about math or reading or social studies. Try to be as specific as possible. Providing evidence of what your students are actually learning (not just doing) in your program by sharing some of the assessments they have completed as suggested in Chapter 14. Be sure to show how your program reflects and puts into practice the recommendations in the Surgeon General's report (U.S. Department of Health and Human Services, 1996) and the *National Standards for Physical Education* (NASPE, 1995) so that it is clear your program is contemporary and on the cutting edge.

with you. Be sure to comment on the critical aspects of the program and relate them to your needs. Remember that the principal is busy, so you may want him to watch only certain key features, not the entire videotape.

■ Occasionally give your principal a copy of an article or book you think is particularly well done and relevant to your program. Be certain to discuss the document after your principal has had a chance to read it. This is especially important if, for example, you're teaching twelve classes a day and you're able to locate a publication that recommends nine classes a day as a complete load for a physical education specialist. We recommend the publication by the Council on Physical Education for Children (COPEC), *Developmentally Appropriate Physical Education for Children*. It provides important guidelines written in an easy-to-understand format. It can be obtained from NASPE, 1900 Association Dr., Reston, VA 22091. Also be sure to share overviews of the 1996 Surgeon General's report (USDHHS) and the *National Standards for Physical Education* (NASPE, 1995) with your principal.

Try to avoid falling into the trap of thinking that your principal really doesn't like your program, or physical education in general, if she isn't initially overly enthusiastic about your program. It takes some principals several years to become active supporters of your program. In fact, we've worked with principals who took several months to find time to come view our programs. Eventually, however, they did support

our program and came to view it as an asset to the school.

Teachers in the School

As you build your program, it's important that other teachers in the school understand and support your efforts. You'll certainly want to invite these teachers to observe your classes. Some of the ideas you use with your principal can also be used with your colleagues. Physical education specialists also find the following ideas helpful:

■ Work in conjunction with a classroom teacher on certain projects. Child-designed games, for example, provide marvelous opportunities for writing, math, and art projects. Expressive dance is an excellent catalyst for creative writing.
■ If you require your students to keep student logs or do written assignments (Chapter 14), some classroom teachers will provide class time for students to do the writing immediately after physical education class (Stevens, 1994).
■ Arrange for several of the primary grades to view the last ten minutes of an intermediate grade's lesson, to show the younger children the progress that the older children have made. This motivates the younger children, encourages the older children, and also serves to "in-service" the younger children who attend the "minishow."

Figure 32.2 Open communication with the principal is one avenue leading to program support.

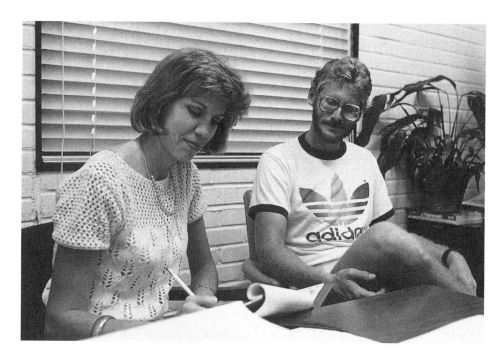

- When a classroom teacher's class has done a particularly good job on a physical education project, it's a treat for the teacher to share in the children's efforts. Invite the classroom teacher to observe the last ten minutes of a class while the children demonstrate their progress, for example, in child-designed games or gymnastics sequences. This also has the added incentive of encouraging the classroom teacher to observe your physical education program.
- When possible, try to eat with other teachers in the lunch room. This not only helps to fight isolation, but also develops rapport and helps them see you as a caring person and professional.

The classroom teacher's support of the physical education specialist is very important. Classroom teachers who understand that physical education is educational, not simply recess, won't keep children "in" to complete math or reading assignments. They also respect the fact that the physical education program has certain time limits and so make sure that their children arrive on time and are ready to return to the classroom on schedule. This may seem to be a minor point, but in fact it can be a source of considerable friction when all the teachers in a school aren't working together to provide the best possible program for children. When teachers understand the value and quality of a physical education program, their support is easier to obtain.

Parents

The physical education teacher must be sure to establish administrator and colleague support before beginning a major program to cultivate enthusiasm among parents. Parent support is important, but it's not enough without the assistance of the principal and the other teachers. If "internal" support doesn't exist, a principal might feel that you're going "over her head" by appealing to parents, which can be disastrous for a new program. Once the administration understands your program and its needs, in many instances the principal will encourage you to generate parent support. And parent support can be especially helpful in obtaining funds that aren't available in the school's budget. There are many ideas for generating support among parents. Try a few of the following ideas one year, a few the next year. Be sure to adapt the ideas to match the needs and interests of parents in your community.

- Attend PTA (PTO) meetings regularly, even if you aren't required to. Try not to sit in the back corner with the other teachers; take the time to meet some of the parents—introduce yourself, tell them what you teach, and invite them to observe your classes. This isn't necessarily the most enjoyable part of building a program, but it certainly can be a major factor in creating support.

Figure 32.3 Example of a physical education newsletter.

The Physical Education Quarterly Report

While some schools view physical education merely as a good break time for teachers or a time for students to blow off a little steam, this is not true for us at Davis. Physical Education is a necessary and integral part of the total curriculum and is viewed with the same seriousness as any other subject matter. One of my primary goals is to provide each student with specific instruction to enable them to become more skillful movers. As students become more proficient in the various motor skills taught in class, I hope that they will enjoy using these skills on a regular basis. Medical and exercise science research indicates that regular physical activity contributes to a healthier and more enjoyable lifestyle while decreasing the incidence and seriousness of various illnesses and diseases. This report will help you know more about the activities in which your child has been instructed this last quarter of the school year.

Space

The second grade students began the school year by reviewing the spatial awareness concepts related to safe, efficient movement. Some of these concepts included moving in personal and general space where students attempt to move either alone or among others without interfering with the others' movements. Additional space concepts included movement at different levels (low, medium, and high), in different directions (forward, backward, sideways, up, and down), and in pathways (straight, curved, and zigzag). A proper understanding and use of these movement concepts permit children to move more safely and effectively in all settings. Games like "Bridges & Boulders," "High-Five

Freeze Tag," and "Octopus" made this learning a lot of fun for everyone. Ask your second grader how to play these games and which one they enjoyed the most.

Throwing and Catching

The students also worked on tossing, the underhand throw, the overhand throw, and catching. To help students learn these skills, we use learning cues, key words that help students remember how to perform a skill. Learning cues can also be used to prompt students when they are practicing these skills. The learning cues for the underhand throw are:
- arm back
- step (on opposite foot)
- swing, and
- throw (the ball toward target)

The cues for the overhand throw are:
- cock (arm back in ready position, elbow out)
- step (on opposite foot)
- twist (upper body in direction of throw), and
- throw (the ball toward target)

To put these steps together into a smooth progressive action was not easy, but a lot of practice helped!

The learning cues for catching are:
- watch (the ball)
- reach (for the ball)
- grab, and
- give (with the ball to absorb the ball's force and slow it down)

Students participated in various activities to further develop throwing and catching for accuracy, distance, and with partners. "Throw and Go" and "Bombs Away" were two of the most popular games. Play these games with your students; you will have fun.

Jump Rope & Kicking

We are currently refining and extending jump rope skills during the warm-up portion of class. We work on kicking skills for the remainder of the lesson. The kicking skills students are learning are most related to soccer, such as dribbling (with the feet) trapping, juggling (thigh and foot), and kicking with various amounts of force using the instep.

The Best

As teachers and parents, we want the very best for our students. One thing we desire most is for our students to be healthy, to enjoy the benefits of good health throughout their entire lives. You can help them establish healthy levels of physical activity and support the physical education program by encouraging your children to view physical education as a place to learn, to have a serious learning aptitude, to always try their best, and to practice at home to facilitate the learning process and insure success.

Our own example is one of the most important influencing factors in the lifestyle habits passed on to our children. We must take care of ourselves. Take time to go outside and play with your children—play ball or tag, jump rope, go roller skating. These are all fun ways to stay fit and show your children that good health is in many ways a matter of what you do, as well as what you do not do.

Feel free to contact me if you would like to know more about our program. Thanks for your support!

Scott Diller, Physical Educator
Davis Elementary School

- If you're invited to do a presentation for the parents' group, try to involve as many children as possible, to ensure a large turnout for your program. Be certain to include children at all skill levels, not only the utilization- and proficiency-level youngsters—and if possible, relate your program to the 1996 Surgeon General's report (USDHHS) and the *National Standards* (NASPE, 1995).
- Send a letter home at the beginning of the year. Tell parents about your program and the general rules the children will be expected to follow (for example, shoes for physical education class). Invite parents to visit. Include a phone number where you can be reached in the evening (this will depend on your personal judgment and school policy) so that parents can call if they have questions about the program or your policies.
- A one-page monthly or quarterly newsletter is very helpful for informing parents and creating enthusiasm (Figure 32.3). Include items such as community programs of interest, books and articles to read, special accomplishments of the children, upcoming television programs of interest, and future programs that you've scheduled. Also

Figure 32.4 Bulletin boards and wall displays provide information to students, faculty, and parents.

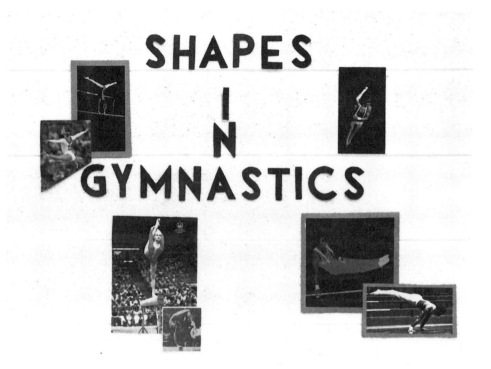

include a brief sketch of what you've been working on in physical education and suggest activities for the parents and the children to do together; for example, include the directions from this text for making a nylon-hose racket or golf club, and suggest several activities for the parents to do with their children. Be sure to have the newsletter proofread so there aren't any spelling or grammatical errors.

■ Bulletin boards are a great way to let parents know about your program (Figure 32.4). If you don't have the skills to make attractive bulletin boards, try trading with another teacher, for example, one week of bus duty for one bulletin board. In many communities there are retail stores for teachers that have very attractive bulletin board letters, pictures, backgrounds, and so on, that even the least skilled person can use to make an appealing bulletin board. Written student assessments, illustrated with their drawings, make very appealing bulletin boards.

■ Send home with the children a "good news" note, which informs the parents of their children's accomplishments in physical education class. Design and print a supply of notes at the beginning of the year, so it won't take long to send several every week (Figure 32.5). These notes are particularly effective for the children who work very hard but rarely get noticed.

■ Some teachers use positive phone calls to communicate with parents about the program. A positive phone call is just a brief phone call to tell a parent how pleased the teacher is about the child's progress (attitude, effort) in physical education. It doesn't take long, but the fact that the teacher takes the time to make the call means very much to the parent. In many instances it's also unexpected because most phone calls from the school tend to be negative. Challenge yourself to make two good phone calls a week.

■ Pete Tamm, a physical education teacher at Michael McCoy Elementary School in Orlando, Florida, writes letters to his students (Tamm, 1993). During a three-year period he has averaged more than one thousand letters a year to his children. Figure 32.6 contains several examples of his letters.

■ Several nights a year hold an open house for parents and the children. The children must have adults with them to gain admittance. At the open house, equipment is available, and the children show the adults what they've been practicing in physical education. Other ideas include mother-daughter, father-son, mother-son, and so forth, open houses. Some teachers hold these open houses on Saturday mornings because many of the parents work nights. If you schedule the open houses informally, parents are free to spend a few minutes or an hour, depending upon their schedule.

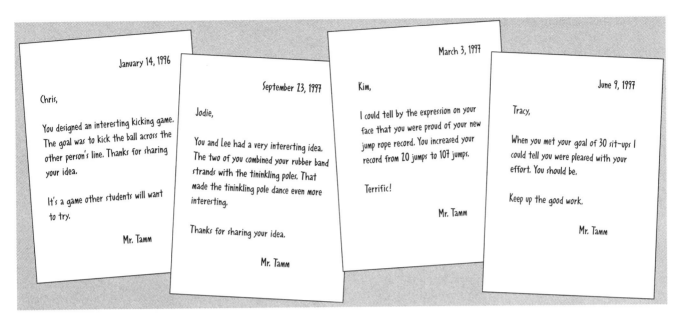

Figure 32.5 Examples of "good news" notes.

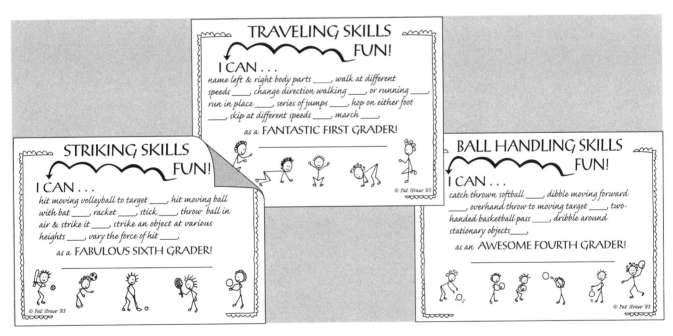

Figure 32.6 Letters to students. Source: From "Dear Physical Educator: Writing Letters Makes a Difference" by P. Tamm, 1993, *Strategies, 6*(8).

- Once a year schedule a parent work night, which is an evening in which parents can help build, repair, and paint equipment for the physical education program. The advantage of such an evening is that it gives parents an understanding of the need for physical education equipment. Make sure the evening is well organized; two hours is adequate.

- Jogging is so popular today that parents may enjoy a family run once the children have built up their ability to run a limited distance. It's important to explain that it isn't a race but just a chance to get together and run. A local celebrity runner makes an appropriate guest for such an event.

- Schedule a speaker for parents only. For example, you might invite a child psychologist, a medical doctor, a former athlete. Be certain that you've heard the speaker personally—don't trust someone else's opinion. The speaker has to be worthwhile if the parents are going to enjoy and benefit from the talk. The entire program should run a maximum of sixty minutes.

■ Invite parents with special skills to visit your physical education classes and discuss their expertise, for example, rugby player, karate expert, triathlete.

The School Board

Another obviously important factor in building support for your program is the school board. Although the board may seem far removed, the members play an extremely important role in physical education. In fact, they're the ones who ultimately determine whether a school district will employ physical education specialists for their elementary schools. The time to gain the board's support is *not* when it's considering eliminating the physical education program at the elementary schools—that's often too late. Get to know the members, and let them get to know you and your program long before then.

■ Attend several school board meetings each year. They won't be your most entertaining evenings, but you'll learn much about how decisions are made in school districts. If there's an opportunity, try to speak to one or more of the board members so that you get to know them. Don't ask for anything; just introduce yourself and talk about the current business before the board. If you ever have an occasion to speak to the board, the fact that you understand how the meetings are conducted and know a few members of the board will make things substantially easier for you.

■ Whenever you're offering a special program at your school, send the board a written invitation. Be sure you've attended enough board meetings so you can recognize the members and call them by name if they come to your program. If you know in advance that the members will attend, try to have someone, such as the principal or another teacher, available to serve as a host.

■ If you come across an article you think the school board members should read, send them a copy with a brief note. The article should be short, well written, and important to the board members.

Your relationship with the school board will be somewhat distant. It's important, however, to cultivate a relationship if your program of physical education is going to thrive within a school district.

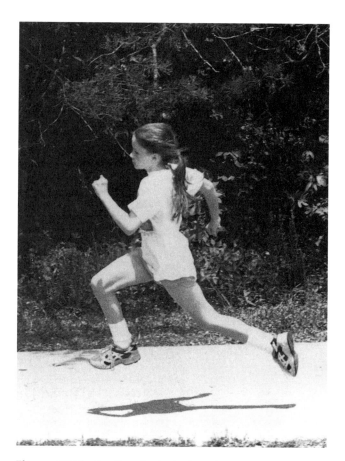

Figure 32.7   Quality physical education programs build a foundation for physically active lifestyles in children's futures.

The Community at Large

Realistically, the community at large is less important than the populations discussed so far. You can potentially enhance your program, however, by conducting a program with community appeal (Figure 32.7). Typically, however, these are major undertakings that require substantial time and effort. The workload can be lightened by conducting programs with other schools in the community.

■ If your community has a shopping mall, check with the managers; the managers of malls are often looking for demonstrations. Such a presentation will give your program a great deal of public visibility. It's a good idea to have handouts available so that people who stop by for a few minutes to watch the program know exactly what they're watching. These leaflets can be distributed by the children who aren't currently in action.

■ The halftime of basketball games is a good opportunity for displaying some of the highlights of your program. For the program to be effective, the announcer's script needs to be well done and rehearsed. Many children from different grades will make the program more appealing for the spectators. Contemporary, loud music is also stimulating. Be sure to include the younger children because they have enormous crowd appeal and can be very effective for getting across your message. Also, the children really enjoy performing, and their parents, grandparents, friends, and neighbors enjoy watching them.

Children As Advocates

We've saved the most important component until the end: the children. Obviously, if you hope to build support from the five populations just described, the chil-

dren will have to benefit from and enjoy the program. If the children aren't avid supporters of your program, you'll have difficulty gaining support from others in the immediate community.

Children become advocates and talk positively about teachers who help them learn and improve in any subject, not only physical education. In any school, the best teachers are both known and respected by the children, other teachers, and the principal. The word gets out when a teacher and a program are good.

Unfortunately, building a quality program of physical education requires more than being a successful teacher. To cultivate all the other populations that contribute to the success of a program, a teacher also needs to be part politician, part public relations director, and part fund-raiser. Some teachers find that part of the job distasteful, but it is necessary, especially when one is beginning a program of physical education.

SUMMARY

One of the roles that teachers of successful physical education programs play is that of generating support. Six different populations need to be aware and supportive of physical education if the programs are to be successful: school administration, other teachers in the school, parents, the school board, the community at large, and the children. Children are the most important advocates of a program, so a program must be of high quality if support from the other five populations is to be developed.

READING COMPREHENSION QUESTIONS

1. Why are six different populations identified for building support for a program? Can't the same ideas be used for all six groups?
2. What's the first step a teacher must take to develop a program with widespread support?
3. What does the phrase "principal education" mean?
4. Which of the suggestions for parents do you think you would use most frequently? Why?
5. Why is the school board so important to the success of a physical education program?
6. Why are the children the most important factor in developing support for a program?

REFERENCES/ SUGGESTED READINGS

Council on Physical Education for Children (COPEC). (1992). *Developmentally appropriate physical education practices for children.* Reston, VA: National Association for Sport and Physical Education.
Diller, S. (1994). Newsletters make parents and professionals take note. *Strategies, 8*(1), 18–20.
Giles-Brown, E. (1993). Teach administrators why physical education is important. *Strategies, 6 (8),* 23–25.

National Association for Sport and Physical Education (NASPE). (1995). *Moving into the future: National standards for physical education.* St. Louis, MO: Mosby.

Schneider, R. E. (1992). Don't just promote your profession—market it. *Journal of Physical Education, Recreation and Dance, 63*(5), 70–71.

Stevens, D. (1994). Movement Concepts: Stimulating cognitive development in elementary students. *Journal of Physical Education, Recreation, and Dance, 65(8),* 16–23.

Tamm, P. (1993). Dear physical educator: Writing letters makes a difference. *Strategies, 6*(8), 13–15.

Tenoschok, M., & Sanders, S. (1984). Planning an effective public relations program. *Journal of Physical Education, Recreation and Dance, 55,* 48–49.

U.S. Department of Health and Human Services. (1996). *Physical activity and health: A report of the Surgeon General.* Atlanta, GA: USDHHS, Centers for Disease Control and Prevention, National Center for Chronic Disease Prevention and Health Promotion.

CHAPTER 33

Physical Education for Tomorrow's Children

Some men see things as they are and say why. I dream things that never were and say why not.

——Robert F. Kennedy

All teachers have ideas about "the way things might be," and so do we. Since 1980, when the first edition of *Children Moving* was published, some of our dreams have become reality—in some schools, for some teachers, for some children. Some of our dreams may never become reality.

As we discussed in Chapter 1 of this edition, some of our dreams are reflected in the publication *Moving into the Future* (NASPE, 1995), which contains the first nationally endorsed definition of a physically educated person, along with the standards and benchmarks of a quality physical education program. The position statement *Developmentally Appropriate Physical Education Practices for Children* developed by the Council on Physical Education for Children (COPEC, 1992) also includes a number of our dreams (see Chapter 1). Both of these documents are important milestones in helping to improve the quality of physical education for children.

We want to go further, however, and share more of our dreams for the future. We believe that it is as important to continue to dream as it is to see our dreams realized. Perhaps our hopes for the future will stimulate you to think and dream about the way things could be. The following discussion describes the world of children's physical education as it would be if we had our way.

- Every child would have quality instruction in physical education every day.
- As a result of our programs, children would develop the healthy attitudes and habits that would lead to satisfying lifestyles as adults. Regular physical activity would become an important part of this lifestyle.
- All colleagues, parents, and administrators would understand the important contribution that a well-designed and effectively taught program of physical education can make to the quality of each individual's entire life.
- All physical education programs, recreation programs, and youth-serving agencies would cooperate to enhance the lives of children. No longer would they exist as independent agencies that serve the same children but rarely communicate or coordinate their efforts.
- Parents would become involved in their children's education. The concepts and skills introduced at school would be enhanced and embellished at home, through parent-child activity nights, after-school programs for parents, and parent volunteer programs.
- Teachers, children, and parents would all have computers that are linked through the Internet so that they could communicate whenever they needed about programs, ideas, student progress, and other topics of interest.
- Children could be grouped—by interest in a specific activity, by ability, by experience—to accomplish the specific goals of a series of lessons, then regrouped when the teacher decides to move to a new skill theme. For example, some upper grade children might be interested in putting on a dance performance for lower grade children. Those upper grade children could be grouped to meet together for two weeks, to prepare their dance and perform it. When they accomplish that goal, they could be regrouped as appropriate for another activity.
- There would be time during the day for teachers to sit down with individual children and cooperatively plan a personalized curriculum for each child. This would help children learn to make significant decisions about what they want to learn and how they want to learn it.
- Physically challenged children would benefit from programs designed specifically for them to help them lead fuller lives. This implies that programs that attempt to force children to play (and enjoy) sports they'll never be able to play (or choose to play) on their own be eliminated from physical education.
- Assistance would be readily available for those children who require special remedial attention. This program would include instruction for parents so they could help their children at home.
- There would be times during each school day, beyond scheduled physical education classes, when children could choose to come to the gymnasium to practice something in which they were interested.
- Classes would be scheduled to facilitate tutorial teaching—fifth-graders working with first-graders, or proficiency-level children working with precontrol-level children, for example.
- Classes would be scheduled so that beginnings and endings were determined by the children's interest and involvement in a lesson rather than by an impersonal and insensitive time schedule.
- Teachers would have adequate time between lessons to jot down a few notes about the progress the last class made, rearrange equipment, review lesson plans, and shift their thoughts to the next class.
- Administrators and others who schedule classes would understand that physical education is intended to be an instructional experience, not a loosely organized recess. This understanding would be reflected by scheduling only one class rather

than two or three classes with sixty or even ninety children at a time.

- Teachers would regularly use Internet sites that contain up-to-date, important information designed to enable them to remain on the cutting edge of the teaching profession. One example of such an Internet site is PE Central, which can be accessed at the following Internet address: pe.central.vt.edu.
- Teachers would use the Internet to share ideas, concerns, and successes with one another. This would dramatically enhance communication and minimize feelings of loneliness and isolation. (Teachers who are interested in this idea can join the USPE e-mail discussion group. Directions for subscribing are on PE Central.)
- Teachers would be able to arrange frequent visits to other schools and teachers easily.
- Teachers would be able to make arrangements to switch teaching assignments with other teachers for a day or a week. Then all teachers would have more experiences working in different environments and with children from various backgrounds.
- Teachers would collaborate and organize curriculum into organic, natural contexts (consistent with the way children view the world), rather than artificially separating learning into compartmentalized subjects like reading, mathematics, art, and physical education. For example, building a house involves reading, mathematics, climbing, balancing, and cooperating with others.
- *All* classroom teachers would understand that a quality program of physical education can significantly contribute to children's total development. No one would prevent children from going to physical education class because they hadn't finished their work or because they had misbehaved.
- All colleagues, parents, and administrators would be vitally interested in our teaching and physical education programs. They would demonstrate this interest by visiting our classes regularly, not only at the first PTA meeting of the year or during school lunch week.
- It would be common practice for individuals from the community to share their expertise and experiences with children. Children would learn about mountain climbing, hang gliding, hiking, human spatial ecology, and weightless gymnastics.
- Schools would become community centers that could involve parents and children in educational projects of mutual interest and benefit. These would include child/parent-designed and -constructed playscapes, child/parent-designed and

-implemented field days for preschool children or underprivileged children, and child-parent programs designed for senior citizens.

- Physical education, in both elementary and secondary schools, would receive as much emphasis as high school athletics. Communities would understand that an appropriate program of physical education for every child is at least as important as athletic programs for the gifted. And so all schools would have appropriate equipment, facilities, and budgets for physical education programs.
- All school districts would recognize the importance of providing children with quality physical education programs. None would overlook the most important years of learning and wait until junior or senior high school to provide adequate instruction, equipment, and facilities.
- All school districts would understand the differences between teaching children and teaching adolescents and would refuse to hire individuals whose primary interest and expertise is in coaching or teaching at a high school. Instead, school districts would hire, as elementary instructors, only teachers who are professionally qualified and dedicated to a career of teaching physical education to children.
- Preservice teachers would work in elementary schools for several years before going to college so that they could learn the right questions to ask about children and teaching. Then as students they would ask the kinds of questions that real-world teachers ask.
- Teacher-education institutions would offer professional preparation programs for elementary school physical education specialists; these programs would be different from those for secondary school physical education teachers.
- College teachers would regularly trade teaching assignments with public school teachers, thus allowing the public school teachers to study current theories and practices at a college and giving the college teachers realistic opportunities to translate their theories into practice.
- Teachers and professors would collaborate to discover better ways to enhance the learning experiences of children, preservice teachers, and in-service teachers.
- Teachers would be involved in conceptualizing and conducting action research. The resulting studies would have the potential for finding answers to the questions that teachers want answered.
- Research results would be disseminated in forms that teachers of children would find useful, practical, and interesting, for example, in weekly

pamphlets or newsletters or monthly television programs that would use the language of the layperson, not professional jargon or advanced concepts related to experimental design or statistics.

■ Every school would have a gymnasium designed specifically for children's physical education that would not have to be vacated for lunch, school assemblies, or plays.

■ Every school would have the quantity and variety of equipment that would allow every child maximum practice at his or her level of physical development.

■ Portable environments would be made available to schools throughout the year. Children would have opportunities to use portable swimming pools for swimming lessons, portable ski slopes for skiing lessons, and portable antigravity chambers to experience moving in a weightless atmosphere.

■ A national association designed specifically for teachers of children's physical education would be started. The meetings, newsletter, research, and other functions would be designed to specifically address and answer the questions teachers in the schools are asking.

■ Mentors would be available to teachers who want to improve their teaching effectiveness and be supported in their early years of teaching.

■ Adequate funds would be made available for resource centers operated by teachers for teachers.

Such centers would offer assistance in making materials or equipment, opportunities to hear visiting lecturers, in-service courses, discussion and sharing sessions, and up-to-date professional libraries.

■ Computers would be readily available in gyms for children to keep track of their own progress and for teachers to design better programs and report the children's progress to the parents.

■ Teachers would have access to audiovisual equipment and computer software that would facilitate valuable projects. They would be able to make continuous videotapes of classes without having to reuse tapes. Teachers could do graph-check sequence filming of complex skills to help children develop the ability to analyze their own movements. Children would be able to make and edit their own videotapes.

We continue to dream about and search for better ways of teaching children. And we'd like to hear your dreams and ideas about children, teaching, and physical education. If you'd like to communicate with us, please write to us in care of the publisher.

One other dream emerged as we were writing this book. Wouldn't it be great if the ideas from our book help you become a more effective teacher of children! We've done our part—now it's up to you.

REFERENCES

Council on Physical Education for Children (COPEC). (1992). *Developmentally appropriate physical education practices for children*. Reston, VA: National Association for Sport and Physical Education.

National Association for Sport and Physical Education (NASPE). (1995). *Moving into the future:* National standards for physical education. St. Louis, MO: Mosby.

Appendix

Sample School-Year Overviews

In this appendix we present four sample yearly overviews based on the material in *Children Moving*. The overviews are (1) a two-day-a-week program for an inexperienced class, (2) a five-day-a-week program for an inexperienced class, (3) a two-day-a-week program for an experienced class, and (4) a five-day-a-week program for an experienced class. As you study the programs, keep these important points in mind:

1. The content outlines show how we organize a year using the material in *Children Moving*. They are intended, not to be strictly followed, but rather to be used as starting points for developing your own yearly plans.

2. In this context, *inexperienced* generally refers to K–2 classes, *experienced* to grades 3–6. In your specific situation, *inexperienced* may refer to K–3 and *experienced* to grades 4–6. That's why the outlines should be used only as guides or examples and should not be taken literally.

3. The content listed for each day is intended to be the major focus of that day's lesson, but in many instances other content will be taught as well—e.g., a review of a skill theme or concept from the previous day, a skill that needs to be worked on frequently but for short periods of time, such as jumping rope and transferring weight from feet to hands.

4. In both programs, the first few days are devoted to establishing a learning environment (see Chapter 9). Several other days are devoted to "reviewing" the learning environment. The period after Christmas or spring break, for instance, is often a good time to review the learning environment. Review days give you a chance to check the environment to determine if some areas, such as immediately stopping at the stop signal and paying careful attention when the teacher is talking, need additional work.

5. The sequencing of the skill themes and movement concepts takes typical weather patterns into account. Outdoor activities are grouped at the beginning and end of the school year, indoor activities toward the middle of the year. For the most part, the movement concepts are introduced early in the year and are revisited throughout the year when time permits.

6. Fitness concepts (see Chapter 4) are taught throughout the year on Wednesdays in the five-day-a-week schedules and every other week in the two-day-a-week schedules. Obviously they could be grouped differently, but this placement allows you to teach a concept or two and set aside time for the children to incorporate the concept into their lifestyle before you introduce another fitness concept. It also allows you to review and reinforce concepts throughout the year, instead of lumping them into a block of lessons.

7. In our program, time is allowed throughout the year for special events that take time away from teaching. (In most of the elementary schools in which we have taught, there are days when physical education must be missed because of field trips, holiday shows or assemblies, voting, or picture days.)

8. Notice that skill themes tend to be massed at the beginning (several days combined) and then distributed throughout the remainder of the year. Notice too that in the programs for the experienced classes, several days in a row are sometimes spent on a single skill theme. As children improve in skill proficiency, they tend to want to spend more days on the same skill because their success rate is much higher. When success rates are low, children seem to concentrate better when the skill themes are changed frequently and reviewed regularly.

Two-Day-a-Week Program
for an Inexperienced Class

Content Outline for an Inexperienced Class That Meets Two Days a Week

Topic of Lesson/Activity	Percentage of School Year[a]	Number of Days
Establishing a Learning Environment	4	3
Space Awareness	9	6
Effort	5	4
Relationships	5	4
Traveling	7	5
Chasing/Fleeing/Dodging	4	3
Jumping and Landing	5	4
Rolling	7	5
Balancing	5	4
Transferring Weight	5	4
Kicking and Punting	7	5
Throwing and Catching	7	5
Volleying	3	2
Dribbling	3	2
Striking with Rackets	4	3
Striking with Hockey Sticks	2	1
Striking with Golf Clubs	2	1
Striking with Bats	3	2
Fitness and Wellness	8	6
Field Day and Other Events	5	3
	100	72

[a]Percentages are approximate.

Two-Day-a-Week Program for an Inexperienced Class (72 Days a Year)

Week	Chapter	Day	
1	9	1	Establishing a Learning Environment (p. 111)
	9	2	Establishing a Learning Environment (cont.) (p. 111)
2	16	1	Exploring Self-Space (p. 220)
	16	2	Exploring General Space (p. 223)
3	16	1	Traveling in Different Directions (p. 225)
	16	2	Traveling and Freezing at Different Levels (p. 226)
4	4	1	Fitness and Wellness (p. 33)
	27	2	Throwing at a Large Target (p. 494)
5	27	1	Catching a Rolling Ball; Catching from a Skilled Thrower (pp. 494, 495)
	19	2	Traveling in General Space: Sliding; Galloping; Hopping; Skipping (pp. 287, 288)
6	19	1	Performing Locomotor Sequences (p. 289)
	21	2	Traveling to Flee; Fleeing from a Partner (p. 332)
7	21	1	Traveling to Dodge; Dodging Obstacles (pp. 332, 333)
	26	2	Kicking a Stationary Ball from a Stationary Position (p. 452)
8	26	1	Approaching a Stationary Ball and Kicking; Kicking in the Air (pp. 453, 459)
	26	2	Dropping, Bouncing, and Kicking Lightweight Balls; Dropping and Punting (p. 473)
9	22	1	Jumping and Landing: Basic Patterns (p. 345)
	4	2	Fitness and Wellness (p. 33)
10	28	1	Striking Balloons in the Air (p. 518)
	28	2	Striking a Ball Upward (p. 522)
11	28	1	Striking Down (Dribbling) Continuously with Both Hands (p. 540)
	28	2	Dribbling with One Hand (p. 540)
12	17	1	Exploring Time (p. 239)
	17	2	Exploring Force (p. 243)
13	17	1	Traveling and Changing Force Qualities (p. 244)
	9	2	Establishing a Learning Environment (p. 111)
14	16	1	Exploring Pathways (p. 228)
	16	2	Exploring Extensions (p. 231)
15	19	1	Moving to Rhythms (p. 290)
	4	2	Fitness and Wellness (p. 33)
16	29	1	Downs, Ups (p. 563)
	29	2	Ups and Downs (p. 564)
17	22	1	Jumping over Low Obstacles: Hoops; Jumping over Low Obstacles: Hurdles (p. 353)
	22	2	Jumping Turned Rope; Jumping a Self-Turned Rope (p. 355)
18	18	1	Identifying Body Parts; Balancing on Matching and Nonmatching Parts (pp. 254, 256)

(continued)

Two-Day-a-Week Program for an Inexperienced Class (72 Days a Year) (continued)

Week	Chapter	Day	
	18	2	Traveling and Freezing in Different Body Shapes (p. 257)
19	4	1	Fitness and Wellness (p. 33)
	19	2	Leaping (p. 288)
20	18	1	Studying Over, Under, Around, In Front Of, and Behind Concepts (p. 263)
	19	2	The Follow Me Dance (p. 293)
21	24	1	Rocking; Twin Rockers (p. 418)
	24	2	Rolling Sideways; Rolling Forward (pp. 418, 420)
22		1	Special Event
	18	2	Matching; Mirroring; Matching and Mirroring (pp. 268, 270)
23	23	1	Balancing on Different Bases of Support (pp. 369, 373)
	23	2	Balancing in Different Body Shapes (p. 375)
24	24	1	Log Roll (p. 418)
	24	2	Back Rocker, Back Touch (pp. 419, 420)
25	24	1	Transferring Weight from Feet to Other Body Parts Without Traveling (p. 397)
	24	2	Transferring Weight from Feet to Hands Across Mats (p. 399)
26	27	1	Throwing Overhand, Underhand, and Sidearm (pp. 496, 497)
	27	2	Throwing a Ball Against a Wall and Catching the Rebound (p. 502)
27	23	1	Traveling on Low Gymnastics Equipment; Performing Stationary Balances on Equipment (pp. 371, 379)
	23	2	Balancing Sequence (p. 382)
28	17	1	Traveling and Flow (p. 246)
	24	2	Jumping off Equipment, Landing, and Rolling (p. 426)
29	24	1	Transferring Weight to Hands Across Mats (p. 399)
	24	2	Transferring off Low Apparatus (p. 402)
30	26	1	Kicking a Rolling Ball from a Stationary Position; Kicking to a Partner (pp. 461, 462)
	26	2	Punting Different Types of Balls (p. 478)
31	4	1	Fitness and Wellness (p. 33)
	21	2	Dodging Obstacles (p. 333)
32	27	1	Throwing and Catching with a Partner (p. 503)
	29	2	Striking a Ball Rebounding from a Wall (p. 571)
33	22	1	Jumping for Distance; Jumping for Height (pp. 351, 352)
	30	2	Striking a Stationary Ball on the Floor—Golf or Hockey (p. 589)
34	30	1	Striking for Distance—Golf (p. 593)
	30	2	Striking Off a Batting Tee—Bats (p. 590)
35	4	1	Fitness and Wellness (p. 33)
	30	2	Striking a Pitched Ball—Bats (p. 602)
36		1	Field Day
		2	Field Day

Two-Day-a-Week Program
for an Experienced Class

Content Outline for an Experienced Class That Meets Two Days a Week

Topic of Lesson/Activity	Percentage of School Year[a]	Number of Days
Establishing a Learning Environment	3	2
Space Awareness	3	2
Effort	5	4
Relationships	4	3
Traveling	4	3
Chasing/Fleeing/Dodging	4	3
Jumping and Landing	5	4
Rolling	7	5
Balancing	4	3
Transferring Weight	7	5
Kicking and Punting	7	5
Throwing and Catching	8	6
Volleying	5	4
Dribbling	4	3
Striking with Rackets	7	5
Striking with Hockey Sticks	3	2
Striking with Golf Clubs	3	2
Striking with Bats	3	2
Fitness and Wellness	8	6
Field Day and Other Events	4	3
	98	72

[a]Percentages are approximate.

Two-Day-a-Week Program for an Experienced Class (72 Days a Year)

Week	Chapter	Day	
1	9	1	Establishing a Learning Environment (p. 111)
	9	2	Establishing a Learning Environment (p. 111)
2	16	1	Dodging in General Space (p. 224)
	16	2	Combining Pathways, Levels, and Directions (p. 230)
3	24	1	Transferring Weight from Feet to Hands (p. 404)
	24	2	Transferring Weight to Hands: Walking (p. 405)
4	26	1	Kicking to a Partner (p. 462)
	26	2	Keeping It Perfect: Zero, Zero (p. 464)
5	27	1	Throwing Underhand, Overhand, and Sidearm (pp. 496, 497)
	27	2	Throwing for Distance (p. 503)
6	21	1	Dodging Stationary Obstacles (People Dodge) (p. 334)
	21	2	Freeze and Count Tag (p. 335)
7	26	1	Punting for Distance (p. 478)
	4	2	Fitness and Wellness (p. 33)
8	17	1	Combining Sport Skills and Time (p. 241)
	17	2	Using Imagery and Force (p. 244)
9	18	1	Creating Postcard Sculptures (p. 259)
	18	2	Creating Body Shapes in the Air (p. 259)
10	19	1	Performing Locomotor Sequences (p. 289)
	19	2	Performing Slow Motion Replay (p. 294)
11	22	1	Jumping a Self-Turned Rope (p. 355)
	22	2	Jumping and Landing Task Sheet (p. 359)
12	24	1	Jumping off Equipment, Landing, and Rolling (p. 426)
	24	2	Playing Busy Mat (p. 429)
13	28	1	Volleying a Ball Upward (p. 526)
	28	2	Volleying to a Partner (p. 526)
14	23	1	Performing Inverted Balances (p. 377)
	23	2	Balancing Symmetrically and Nonsymmetrically (p. 374)
15	18	1	Meeting and Parting in a Cooperative Group (p. 272)
	4	2	Fitness and Wellness (p. 33)
16	17	1	Following Flow Sequences (p. 247)
	17	2	Combining Time, Force, and Flow (p. 249)
17	24	1	Rolling over Low Hurdles; Rolling on Equipment (p. 430)
	24	2	Rolling, Balancing, and Rolling (p. 431)
18	28	1	Dribbling and Traveling (p. 544)
	28	2	Dribbling Against an Opponent: One on One (p. 548)
19	29	1	To the Wall, Again (p. 568)
	29	2	Striking a Ball Rebounding from a Wall (p. 571)
20	19	1	Shadowing (p. 297)
	4	2	Fitness and Wellness (p. 33)
21	22	1	Jumping to an Accented Beat (p. 363)
	24	2	Transferring Weight to Hands and Forming a Bridge (p. 405)
22	23	1	Traveling into and out of Balances (pp. 386, 387)
	24	2	Rolling to Express an Idea (p. 432)
23	24	1	Transferring Weight onto Large Apparatus (p. 406)
	24	2	Combining Weight Transfer and Balances in Sequences (p. 411)
24	28	1	Playing Once Bounce Volleyball (p. 527)
	28	2	Volleying Game: Child-Designed (p. 527)
25		1	Special Event
	4	2	Fitness and Welness (p. 33)
26	28	1	Playing Dribble Tag (p. 550)
	29	2	Hitting Cooperatively and Continuously with a Partner (p. 573)
27	29	1	Playing Racket Call Ball (p. 575)
	29	2	Playing Minitennis (p. 578)
28	27	1	Throwing and Catching with a Partner (p. 503)
	27	2	Throwing and Catching While Traveling (p. 506)

29	30	1	Striking to Targets at Varying Distances—Golf (p. 606)
	30	2	Playing Hoop Golf (p. 607)
30	21	1	Dodging and Chasing as Part of a Team (Octopus) (p. 335)
	4	2	Fitness and Wellness (p. 33)
31	26	1	Playing Soccer Golf (p. 467)
	26	2	Punting to a Partner (p. 481)
32	30	1	Traveling, Striking, and Changing Pathways with a Partner—Hockey (p. 600)
	30	2	Striking to a Stationary Partner—Hockey (p. 598)
33	27	1	Throwing for Distance and Accuracy (p. 507)
	4	2	Fitness and Wellness (p. 33)
34	27	1	Playing Keep Away (p. 511)
	22	2	Jumping to Throw; Jumping to Catch (p. 361)
35	30	1	Striking a Pitched Ball—Bats (p. 602)
	30	2	Playing One-Base Baseball (p. 615)
36		1	Field Day
		2	Field Day

Five-Day-a-Week Program
for an Inexperienced Class

Content Outline for an Inexperienced Class That Meets Five Days a Week

Topic of Lesson/Activity	Percentage of School Year[a]	Number of Days
Establishing a Learning Environment	4	7
Space Awareness	9	16
Effort	5	9
Relationships	5	9
Traveling	7	12
Chasing/Fleeing/Dodging	4	7
Jumping and Landing	5	9
Rolling	7	12
Balancing	5	9
Transferring Weight	5	9
Kicking and Punting	7	12
Throwing and Catching	7	12
Volleying	3	6
Dribbling	3	6
Striking with Rackets	4	7
Striking with Hockey Sticks	2	4
Striking with Golf Clubs	2	4
Striking with Bats	3	6
Fitness and Wellness	9	16
Field Day and Other Events	4	8
	100	180

[a]Percentages are approximate.

Five-Day-a-Week Program for an Inexperienced Class (180 Days a Year)

Week	Chapter	Day	
1	9	1	Establishing a Learning Environment (p. 111)
	9	2	Establishing a Learning Environment (p. 111)
	9	3	Establishing a Learning Environment (p. 111)
	9	4	Establishing a Learning Environment (p. 111)
	16, 18	5	Exploring Self-Space; Identifying Body Parts (pp. 220, 254)
2	16	1	Curling, Stretching, and Twisting in Self-Space (p. 221)
	16	2	Moving the Whole Body in Self-Space (p. 222)
	16, 19	3	Exploring General Space; Traveling in General Space (pp. 223, 285)
	16	4	Reducing the Size of General Space (p. 223)
	16	5	Traveling Over, Under, and Around Obstacles in General Space (p. 224)
3	16, 19	1	Traveling in Different Directions; Hopping; Skipping; Galloping; Sliding (pp. 225, 287)
	16	2	Turning While Moving in Different Directions (p. 226)
	16	3	Traveling and Freezing at Different Levels (p. 226)
	16	4	Rising and Sinking to Create Different Levels (p. 227)
	16	5	Exploring Pathways (p. 228)
4	16	1	Exploring Extensions (p. 231)
	26	2	Kicking a Stationary Ball from a Stationary Position (p. 452)
	4	3	Fitness and Wellness (p. 33)
	26	4	Dropping, Bouncing, and Kicking Lightweight Balls (p. 473)
	17	5	Exploring Time (p. 239)
5	17, 19	1	Moving at Different Speeds; Traveling at Different Speeds (pp. 240, 293)
	17	2	Exploring Force (p. 243)
	17	3	Traveling and Changing Force Qualities (p. 244)
	17	4	Traveling and Flow (p. 246)
	17	5	Eliciting Flow Qualities (p. 247)
6	18	1	Round, Narrow, Wide, and Twisted Body Shapes; Freezing in Different Body Shapes (pp. 256, 257)
	18	2	Balancing on Matching and Nonmatching Parts (p. 256)
	4	3	Fitness and Wellness (p. 33)
	18	4	Traveling Over, Close To, Far Away, Inside (p. 260)
	18	5	Studying Over, Under, Around, In Front Of, and Behind Concepts (p. 263)
7	18	1	Matching; Mirroring; Matching and Mirroring (pp. 268, 270)
	18	2	Traveling Alongside/Following (p. 270)
	19	3	Running (p. 288)
	19	4	Performing Locomotor Sequences (p. 289)
	19	5	Moving to Rhythms (p. 290)
8	27	1	Throwing a Yarn Ball Against the Wall (p. 494)
	19	2	Moving to Rhythms (cont.) (p. 290)
	4	3	Fitness and Wellness (p. 33)
	21	4	Traveling to Flee; Fleeing from a Partner (p. 332)
	21	5	Traveling to Dodge; Dodging in Response to a Signal (p. 332)
9	21	1	Dodging with Quick Changes of Direction (p. 333)
	22	2	Jumping and Landing: Basic Patterns (p. 351)
	22	3	Jumping for Distance; Jumping for Height (p. 351)
	26	4	Approaching a Stationary Ball and Kicking (p. 453)
	26	5	Dropping and Punting (p. 473)
10	24	1	Log Roll; Rolling Forward (pp. 418, 420)
	24	2	Rounds, Turn Rockers (pp. 417, 418)
	4	3	Fitness and Wellness (p. 33)

Week	Chapter	Day	
	21	4	Dodging Moving Obstacles (p. 330)
	22	5	Jumping and Landing (p. 351)
11	22	1	Jumping over a Swinging Rope (p. 351)
	9	2	Review of Learning Environment (p. 111)
	4	3	Fitness and Wellness (p. 33)
	19	4	Traveling in Confined Spaces (p. 290)
	24	5	Rolling Sideways (p. 418)
12	24	1	Rolling Backward (p. 423)
	16	2	Creating Follow the Leader Pathways (p. 229)
	16	3	Using Extensions and Imagery (p. 232)
	21	4	Overtaking a Fleeing Person (Catch-Up Chase) (p. 333)
	22	5	Jumping over Low Obstacles: Hoops; Jumping over Low Obstacles: Hurdles (p. 353)
13	22	1	Jumping Rhythmically (p. 354)
	17	2	Combining Imagery and Time (p. 240)
	4	3	Fitness and Wellness (p. 33)
	26	4	Kicking a Rolling Ball from a Stationary Position (p. 461)
	26	5	Tapping the Ball Along the Ground (p. 463)
14	19	1	Traveling Through Rope Pathways (p. 286)
	17	2	Using Imagery and Force (p. 244)
	27	3	Throwing at a Large Target (p. 494)
	24	4	Rolling in Different Directions (p. 424)
	24	5	Rolling from Different Positions (p. 421)
15	23	1	Balancing on Different Bases of Support (pp. 369, 373)
	17	2	Practicing Flow Sequences (p. 247)
	4	3	Fitness and Wellness (p. 33)
	27	4	Catching a Rolling Ball; Catching from a Skilled Thrower (p. 484)
	23	5	Traveling and Stopping in Balanced Positions; Balancing on a Wide Base of Support (p. 371)
16	23	1	Tightening the Gymnastics Muscles (p. 373)
	9	2	Review of Learning Environment (p. 111)
	18	3	Making Symmetrical and Nonsymmetrical Shapes (p. 257)
	21	4	Fleeing a Chaser: Frogs and Flies (p. 334)
	24	5	Rolling from Different Directions and Positions (p. 421)
17	24	1	Rolling at Different Speeds (p. 422)
	18	2	Going Over and Under the Obstacle Course (p. 265)
	4	3	Fitness and Wellness (p. 33)
		4	Special Event
	23	5	Balancing in Different Body Shapes (p. 371)
18	23	1	Traveling on Low Gymnastics Equipment; Stationary Balances on Equipment (pp. 371, 379)
	24	2	Locomotors; Combination Transfers (pp. 396, 399)
	19	3	Leaping (p. 288)
	18	4	Meeting/Parting (p. 271)
	22	5	Jumping a Turned Rope (p. 355)
19	22	1	Jumping a Self-Turned Rope (p. 355)
	23	2	Balancing on Boards (p. 372)
	4	3	Fitness and Wellness (p. 33)

(continued)

Five-Day-a-Week Program for an Inexperienced Class (180 Days a Year)
(continued)

Week	Chapter	Day	
	23	4	Counterbalance (p. 373)
	24	5	Rolling Using Different Directions and Speeds (p. 425)
20	24	1	Jumping off Equipment, Landing, and Rolling (p. 426)
	24	2	Transferring Weight from Feet to Back, Transferring Weight from Feet to Hands (p. 397)
	24	3	Transferring Weight Onto, Off Equipment (p. 397)
	24	4	Transferring Weight Across Mats (p. 399)
		5	Special Event
21		1	Special Event
	21	2	Dodging with Changes in Direction (p. 333)
	4	3	Fitness and Wellness (p. 33)
	22	4	Jumping Using Buoyant and Yielding Landings (p. 356)
	24	5	Jumping off Equipment, Landing, and Rolling (cont.) (p. 426)
22	27	1	Tossing to Self and Catching (p. 495)
	9	2	Review of Learning Environment (p. 111)
	26	3	Kicking to a Distance Zone (p. 460)
	26	4	Kicking to Targets (p. 460)
	24	5	Jumping for Height, Landing, and Rolling (p. 426)
23	24	1	Jumping from Different Heights and Rolling (p. 427)
	23	2	Traveling on Large Apparatus (p. 382)
	4	3	Fitness and Wellness (p. 33)
	23	4	Balancing Sequence (p. 382)
	24	5	Transferring Weight from Feet to Back (p. 427)
24	24	1	Stretching, Curling, and Twisting into Transfers (p. 400)
	28	2	Striking Balloons in the Air; Striking with Different Body Parts (pp. 518, 519)
	28	3	Striking the Ball to the Wall (p. 523)
	29	4	Balancing Objects on Paddles; Striking a Balloon with a Lightweight Paddle (pp. 557, 561)
	29	5	Upward Bound (p. 562)
25	29	1	Ups, Downs, Ups and Downs (pp. 563, 564)
	26	2	Kicking to a Partner (p. 462)
	4	3	Fitness and Wellness (p. 33)
	26	4	Tapping the Ball Along the Ground (Soccer Dribble) (p. 463)
	19	5	Traveling an Obstacle Course (p. 291)
26	30	1	Striking a Stationary Ball on the Floor—Golf or Hockey (p. 592)
	16	2	Traveling Pathways and Obstacles (p. 229)
	16	3	Combining Pathways, Levels, and Directions (p. 230)
	19	4	The Follow Me Dance (p. 293)
	24	5	Performing Step/Spring Takeoffs; Performing Spring/Step Takeoffs onto Crates and Benches (pp. 400, 401)
27	24	1	Transferring off Low Apparatus (p. 402)
	27	2	Throwing Overhand, Underhand, and Sidearm (p. 496, 497)
	4	3	Fitness and Wellness (p. 33)
	27	4	Bouncing a Ball to Self and Catching It (p. 497)
	28	5	Striking a Ball Down and Catching It; Striking Down (Dribbling) Continuously with Both Hands (p. 540)
28	28	1	Dribbling like a Basketball Player (p. 541)
	19	2	Traveling Using Different Directions, Levels, Pathways, and Locations (p. 293)
	26	3	Starting and Stopping; Traveling in Pathways (p. 463)

Week	Chapter	Day	
	26	4	Punting Different Types of Balls (p. 478)
	27	5	Throwing an Object to Different Levels and Catching It (p. 498)
29	27	1	Catching in Different Places Around the Body (p. 498)
	16	2	Review of Space Awareness Key Ideas (p. 218)
	4	3	Fitness and Wellness (p. 33)
	24	4	Traveling over Low Apparatus; Transferring onto Low Apparatus (p. 403)
	29	5	Ups and Downs (p. 564)
30		1	Special Event
	28	2	Striking Lightweight Objects (p. 519)
	28	3	Striking a Ball Upward Continuously (p. 522)
	29	4	Hitting to Different Places (p. 570)
	29	5	Varying the Force of the Hit (p. 567)
31	29	1	Striking Through a Target (p. 570)
	28	2	Dribbling at Different Heights (p. 542)
	4	3	Fitness and Wellness (p. 33)
	28	4	Switches (p. 542)
	30	5	Striking off a Batting Tee—Bats (p. 590)
32	30	1	Striking Suspended Objects—Bats (p. 597)
	30	2	Striking for Distance—Golf/Hockey (p. 593)
	30	3	Striking to Targets—Hockey (p. 594)
	30	4	Striking a Pitched Ball—Bats (p. 602)
	30	5	Striking to Varying Distance—Golf (p. 601)
33	30	1	Striking for Distance—Golf/Hockey (p. 593)
	28	2	Volleying to a Partner (p. 526)
	4	3	Fitness and Wellness (p. 33)
	28	4	Playing Keep It Up (p. 527)
	30	5	Striking a Pitched Ball—Bats (cont.) (p. 602)
34	30	1	Striking a Pitched Ball—Bats (cont.) (p. 602)
	27	2	Throwing at a Stationary Target; Hit the Can (p. 499)
	27	3	Catching with a Scoop (p. 501)
	30	4	Striking to Targets—Hockey (p. 594)
	30	5	Traveling, Stopping, and Controlling the Ball—Hockey (p. 599)
35	30	1	Throwing a Ball in the Air and Striking It—Bats (p. 601)
	27	2	Throwing a Ball Against a Wall and Catching the Rebound (p. 502)
	27	3	Throwing for Distance (p. 503)
	27	4	Throwing and Catching with a Partner (p. 503)
	28	5	Dribbling with the Body in Different Positions (p. 543)
36	28	1	Dribbling and Traveling (p. 544)
		2	Field Days and Special Events
		3	Field Days and Special Events
		4	Field Days and Special Events
		5	Field Days and Special Events

Five-Day-a-Week Program
for an Experienced Class

Content Outline for an Experienced Class That Meets Five Days a Week

Topic of Lesson/Activity	Percentage of School Year[a]	Number of Days
Establishing a Learning Environment	3	6
Space Awareness	3	6
Effort	5	9
Relationships	4	7
Traveling	4	7
Chasing/Fleeing/Dodging	4	7
Jumping and Landing	5	9
Rolling	7	12
Balancing	5	9
Transferring Weight	7	12
Kicking and Punting	7	12
Throwing and Catching	8	15
Volleying	5	9
Dribbling	4	7
Striking with Rackets	7	12
Striking with Hockey Sticks	3	6
Striking with Golf Clubs	3	6
Striking with Bats	4	7
Fitness and Wellness	9	16
Field Day and Other Events	3	6
	100	180

[a]Percentages are approximate.

Five-Day-a-Week Program for an Experienced Class (180 Days a Year)

Week	Chapter	Day	
1	9	1	Establishing a Learning Environment (p. 111)
	9	2	Establishing a Learning Environment (p. 111)
	9	3	Establishing a Learning Environment (p. 111)
	16	4	Traveling Over, Under, and Around Obstacles in General Space (p. 224)
	16	5	Turning While Moving in Different Directions (p. 226)
2	16	1	Traveling While Rising and Sinking (p. 227)
	16	2	Traveling Pathways and Obstacles (p. 229)
	17	3	Combining Imagery and Time (p. 240)
	17	4	Differentiating Among Time Words (p. 241)
	17	5	Combining Sport Skills and Time (p. 241)
3	21	1	Dodging Stationary Obstacles (People Dodge) (p. 334)
	21	2	Dodging and Faking Moves (Freeze and Count Tag) (p. 335)
	23	3	Performing Inverted Balances (p. 377)
	23	4	Performing Inverted Balances (cont.) (p. 377)
	22	5	Jumping a Self-Turned Rope (p. 355)
4	26	1	Kicking to a Partner (p. 462)
	26	2	Traveling in Pathways (p. 463)
	28	3	Dribbling Around Stationary Obstacles (p. 547)
	24	4	Transferring Weight from Feet to Hands (p. 404)
	24	5	Transferring Weight to Hands: Walking (p. 405)
5	27	1	Throwing Overhand, Underhand, and Sidearm (pp. 496, 497)
	27	2	Throwing a Ball Against a Wall and Catching the Rebound (p. 502)
	4	3	Fitness and Wellness (p. 33)
	27	4	Throwing for Distance (p. 503)
	26	5	Punting with an Approach; Punting for Distance (pp. 475, 478)
6	26	1	Punting for Accuracy; Punting for Height (p. 479)
	21	2	Dodging While Manipulating an Object (p. 337)
	21	3	Dodging While Manipulating an Object (cont.) (p. 337)
	27	4	Throwing and Catching over a Net with a Partner (p. 504)
	27	5	Throwing and Catching While Traveling (p. 506)
7	27	1	Throwing to Make a Partner Move to Catch (p. 506)
	16	2	Combining Pathways, Levels, and Directions (p. 230)
	4	3	Fitness and Wellness (p. 33)
	16	4	Traveling and Extensions (p. 232)
	26	5	Keeping it Perfect: Zero, Zero (p. 464)
8	26	1	Traveling and Kicking for a Goal (p. 466)
	29	2	Ups, Downs, and Forwards (p. 565)
	29	3	Hitting to Different Places (p. 570)
	29	4	Striking an Object to Send It over a Net (p. 571)
	29	5	Striking a Ball Rebounding from a Wall (p. 571)
9	29	1	Hitting Cooperatively and Continuously with a Partner (p. 573)
	30	2	Striking a Pitched Ball—Bats (p. 602)
	4	3	Fitness and Wellness (p. 33)
	30	4	Striking a Pitched Ball—Bats (cont.) (p. 602)
	28	5	Dribbling Continuously While Switching Hands (p. 406)
10	28	1	Dribbling and Traveling (p. 406)
	28	2	Volleying to a Partner; Playing Keep It Up (p. 526, 527)
	28	3	Obstacle Course Volley (p. 527)

(continued)

Five-Day-a-Week Program for an Experienced Class (180 Days a Year) (continued)

Week	Chapter	Day	
	28	4	Playing Four Square, Two Square (p. 525)
	28	5	Playing One Bounce Volleyball (p. 527)
11	28	1	Striking a Ball Continuously with Different Body Parts (p. 529)
	23	2	Balancing Symmetrically and Nonsymmetrically (p. 374)
	4	3	Fitness and Wellness (p. 33)
	23	4	Balancing on Crates (p. 384)
	23	5	Traveling into and out of Balances by Rolling (p. 387)
12	22	1	Jumping a Self-Turned Rope (cont.) (p. 355)
	9	2	Establishing an Environment for Learning (p. 111)
	30	3	Striking for Distance—Golf (pp. 593, 601)
	30	4	Striking for Distance—Golf (cont.) (pp. 593, 601)
	17	5	Showing Contrasts of Force; Using Imagery and Force (p. 244)
13	19	1	Changing Speeds to Music (p. 294)
	19	2	A Dance of Water, Steam, Ice (p. 294)
	4	3	Fitness and Wellness (p. 33)
	19	4	Performing Slow Motion Replay (p. 294)
	22	5	Jumping Using Buoyant and Yielding Landings; Jumping on and off Equipment Using Buoyant and Yielding Landings (pp. 356, 358)
14	22	1	Jumping and Landing Task Sheet (p. 359)
	22	2	Jumping and Landing Task Sheet (cont.) (p. 359)
	23	3	Performing Inverted Balances on Equipment (p. 387)
	23	4	Performing Sequences That Combine Stationary Balances and Traveling on Mats (p. 388)
	23	5	Balancing While Supporting the Weight of a Partner (p. 390)
15	23	1	Balancing on Hanging Ropes (p. 390)
	24	2	Transferring Weight to Hands and Forming a Bridge (p. 405)
	4	3	Fitness and Wellness (p. 33)
	24	4	Transferring Weight onto Large Apparatus (p. 406)
	30	5	Speeds, Pathways, and/or Directions—Hockey (p. 608)
16		1	Special Event
	24	2	Jumping over Equipment, Landing, and Rolling (p. 427)
	24	3	Rolling, Levels, Directions, and Jumping (p. 428)
	24	4	Traveling, Jumping, Landing, and Rolling (p. 429)
	24	5	Jumping from Different Heights and Rolling (p. 427)
17	24	1	Playing Busy Mat (p. 429)
	9	2	Establishing an Environment for Learning (p. 111)
	4	3	Fitness and Wellness (p. 33)
	19	4	Traveling with a Partner: Matching Pathways (p. 295)
	24	5	Transferring Weight to Head and Hands on Apparatus (p. 406)
18	30	1	Striking to Different Places—Hockey (p. 600)
	17	2	Following Flow Sequences; Practicing Flow Sequences (p. 247)
	17	3	Using Flow Conversations (p. 248)
	17	4	Combining Time, Force, and Flow (p. 249)
	28	5	Dribbling While Changing Directions (p. 545)
19	28	1	Dribbling Around Stationary Obstacles (p. 547)
	24	2	Practicing Touch and Go Rolls (p. 430)
	4	3	Fitness and Wellness (p. 33)
	24	4	Rolling on Equipment; Rolling over Low Hurdles (p. 430)
	19	5	Shadowing (p. 297)
20	19	1	Performing Rhythmical Patterns (p. 299)

Week	Chapter	Day	
	18	2	Creating Postcard Sculptures (p. 259)
	18	3	Creating Body Shapes in the Air (p. 259)
	24	4	Traveling and Rolling Between Pieces of Equipment (p. 431)
	24	5	Rolling, Balancing, and Rolling (p. 431)
21	18	1	Creating Postcard Sculptures (cont.) (p. 259)
	24	2	Rolling to Express an Idea (p. 432)
	4	3	Fitness and Wellness (p. 33)
	24	4	Rolling to Express an Idea (cont.) (p. 432)
	28	5	Dribbling Against an Opponent: One on One (p. 548)
22	28	1	Playing Now You've Got It, Now You Don't (p. 550)
	19	2	Traveling to Express Age: The Fountain of Youth (p. 299)
	24	3	Transferring Weight onto Bars (p. 408)
	24	4	Transferring Weight over Apparatus (p. 408)
	24	5	Transferring Weight Along Apparatus (p. 409)
23		1	Special Event
	28	2	Playing Dribble Tag (p. 550)
	4	3	Fitness and Wellness (p. 33)
	30	4	Striking to a Stationary Partner—Hockey (p. 598)
	22	5	Jumping to an Accented Beat (p. 363)
24	22	1	Jumping with a Partner to Mirror Actions; Jumping with a Partner to Match Actions (pp. 363, 364)
	30	2	Traveling and Striking; Changing Pathways (p. 600)
	18	3	Traveling Along Equipment (p. 263)
	18	4	Forming Cooperative and Collaborative Relationships (p. 271)
	18	5	Forming Cooperative and Collaborative Relationships (cont.) (p. 271)
25	18	1	Meeting and Parting in a Cooperative Group (p. 272)
	9	2	Establishing an Environment for Learning (p. 111)
	4	3	Fitness and Wellness (p. 33)
	24	4	Rolling on and off Equipment (pp. 430, 431)
	27	5	Throwing to a Moving Target (p. 507)
26	27	1	Throwing for Distance and Accuracy (p. 507)
		2	Special Event
	24	3	Transferring Weight on Bars (p. 411)
	24	4	Combining Skills on Mats (p. 411)
	24	5	Combining Weight Transfer and Balances in Sequences (p. 411)
27	24	1	Combining Weight Transfer and Balances in Sequences (cont.) (p. 411)
	22	2	Jumping to Throw; Jumping to Catch (p. 361)
	4	3	Fitness and Wellness (p. 33)
	22	4	Throwing and Catching While Jumping (p. 362)
	26	5	Playing Soccer Golf (p. 467)
28	21	1	Dodging and Chasing as Part of a Team (Octopus) (p. 335)
	28	2	Volleying with a Volleybird (p. 531)
	28	3	Striking to the Wall; Playing Hand Corner Ball (p. 532)
	28	4	Volleying Continuously to a Partner (p. 533)
	28	5	Volleying Three on Three (p. 533)
29	26	1	Playing One on One Soccer (p. 466)
	30	2	Striking and Dodging Stationary Objects—Hockey (p. 604)
	4	3	Fitness and Wellness (p. 33)
	30	4	Playing Hockey Bowl (p. 607)
	30	5	Striking to Targets at Various Distances—Golf (p. 606)
30	21	1	Dodging and Chasing One Person in a Mass (Partner Dodge) (p. 336)

(continued)

Five-Day-a-Week Program for an Experienced Class (180 Days a Year) (continued)

Week	Chapter	Day	
	27	2	Catching to Throw Quickly to a Partner (p. 509)
	27	3	Running the Bases (p. 510)
	27	4	Throwing to Avoid a Defender (p. 511)
	27	5	Playing Keep Away (p. 511)
31	27	1	Playing Hitting the Pin (p. 512)
	29	2	Striking to Different Places Around a Partner (p. 573)
	4	3	Fitness and Wellness (p. 33)
	29	4	Playing Racket Call Ball (p. 575)
	29	5	Playing Wall Ball (p. 576)
32	21	1	Dodging in a Dynamic Situation (Body Part Tag) (p. 336)
	29	2	Playing Racket Corner Ball (p. 577)
	29	3	Playing Minitennis (p. 578)
	29	4	Playing Minitennis (cont.) (p. 578)
	29	5	Playing Self-Designed Racket Games (p. 579)
33	29	1	Playing Self-Designed Racket Games (cont.) (p. 579)
	24	2	Punting Within a Limited Time (p. 481)
	4	3	Fitness and Wellness (p. 33)
	26	4	Playing Rush the Circle (p. 481)
	26	5	Playing Two on One Soccer (p. 469)
34	30	1	Directing the Air Pathway of the Object Struck—Golf (p. 607)
	30	2	Directing the Air Pathway of the Object Struck—Golf (cont.) (p. 607)
	30	3	Playing Hoop Golf (p. 606)
	30	4	Hitting to Open Places—Bats (p. 605)
	30	5	Striking a Pitched Object, Varying the Distance—Bats (p. 606)
35	30	1	Directing the Pathway Distance and Speed—Bats (p. 613)
	27	2	Playing Frisbee Golf (p. 508)
	27	3	Playing Frisbee Stretch (p. 510)
	4	4	Fitness and Wellness (p. 33)
	30	5	Playing Six-Player Teeball (p. 615)
36	30	1	Playing One-Base Baseball (p. 615)
		2	Special Event
		3	Special Event
		4	Special Event
		5	Field Day

Index

AAHPERD (American Alliance for Health, Physical Education, Recreation, and Dance), 42
abdominal strength and endurance, 38
accountability measures, 112, 122
See also assessment; content development; public recognition
Acrosport, 390
active instruction. *See* direct instruction
active participation, appropriate and inappropriate practices concerning, 9
ADD (attention deficit disorder), 81
ADHD (attention deficit hyperactivity disorder), 81
adults
  couch potatoism, causes of, 13–14
  and games, vs. children's view, 618, 623, 624
  physically uneducated, 5
Aerial Soccer, 530–531
aerobics, 49
affective development
  appropriate and inappropriate practices in, 8
  assessment of, options for, 190
  skill theme approach and, 17
African American heritage, creation of dance for, 318–319
alcohol, drug, and tobacco abuse, 53
allergies, 79
Alley Soccer, 471
American Alliance for Health, Physical Education, Recreation, and Dance (AAHPERD), 42
American Foundation for the Blind, 73
American Heart Association, 42
apparatus, gymnastic. *See under* gymnastics
applications. *See* challenges
appropriate behavior, maintaining, 128–129

corporal punishment, 139
decreasing inappropriate behavior, 132–135
  behavior contracts, 134, 135
  desists, 132–133
  letter to parents, 134, 136, 137
  planning time, 133–134
  principal, involving of, 134–135
  time-outs, 133
defined, 128
in entire class, 135–139
  behavior games, 138, 139
  responsibility, development of, 135–137
  rewards for class, 138
  token systems of reward, 138–139
increasing appropriate behavior, 129–132
  dialogue, person-to-person, 131–132
  differential treatment, eliminating, 130
  ignoring inappropriate behavior, 130–131
  nonverbal interactions, 131
  positive interaction, 118–119, 129, 130
  proactive strategies, 129–130
  prompting, 130
  reactive approaches, 130–132
teacher's behavior and, 128
See also behavior; off-task behavior
Around the World, 594
arthritis, 75, 79
assessment
  benchmarks. *See* benchmarks
  cue learning, 155
  of fitness, 45–49
  of games-playing readiness, 620–621, 626–627
  performance, methods of. *See* performance assessments
  purpose of, 176
  for remedial classes, 80–81

by teachers, of self. *See* reflection
  testing as limited, 176
asthma, 79
atlantoaxial subluxation, 69, 80
attention deficit disorder (ADD), 81
attention deficit hyperactivity disorder (ADHD), 81
audio taping. *See* tape recording
authentic assessment. *See* performance assessments
auto safety, 52

back-to-the-wall observation, 144–145, 146
Badminton Volleyball, 579
balance beams, safety on, 264
balance bench, construction of, 380
balance boards, construction of, 372
balancing, 368
  activities. *See* balancing activities
  assessment of, 371, 374–375, 383, 386, 390
  in content standards, 369
  dynamic, 368
  key teaching concepts of, 368
  levels of skills proficiency in, 368–369
  safety
    on balance beam, 264
    on body parts, inappropriate, 371
    copying more skilled students, 371
    inverted balance, 377, 388, 390
    partner balances, 390
    prerequisites and, 381, 382, 388, 390, 392
    releasing balances, 378
  sequence for skill theme development of, 370
  static, 368
  See also skill themes
balancing activities
  control level, 368, 372–373

balancing activities *(continued)*
    alignment of body parts, 377
    balance boards, 383–384
    balancing on different bases of
        support, 373
    balancing in different body
        shapes, 375–376
    balancing sequence, 382–383
    balancing on stilts, 383
    balancing symmetrically and
        nonsymmetrically, 374
    counterbalance, 373–374
    doing kickups, 377–378
    the gymnastics dance, 376–377
    performing inverted
        balances, 377
    stationary balances on
        equipment, 379–381
    tightening the gymnastics
        muscles, 373
    traveling on large
        apparatus, 382
    traveling and stopping in
        balanced positions,
        378–379
    traveling while balanced, 382
    precontrol level, 368, 369
    balance on a wide base of
        support, 371
    balancing on boards, 372
    balancing on different bases of
        support, 369, 370
    balancing in different body
        shapes, 371
    traveling on low gymnastics
        equipment, 371
    traveling and stopping in
        balanced positions, 371
    proficiency level, 369, 390
    balancing on hanging
        ropes, 390
    balancing while supporting the
        weight of a partner, 390
    performing apparatus sequences
        that combine stationary
        balances and traveling
        with movement
        concepts, 392
    transferring off equipment with
        weight on hands, 390–392
    utilization level, 368–369, 384
    balancing on boxes, 384–386
    moving out of and into
        balances by stretching,
        curling, and twisting, 386
    performing inverted balances
        on equipment, 387–388

    performing sequences that
        combine stationary
        balances and traveling on
        mats, 388–390
    traveling into and out of
        balances by rolling, 387
Ball, The, 418
baseball
    activities in
        striking with bats, 589,
            590–591, 594–598,
            601–606, 613–616
        throwing and catching. *See*
            throwing and catching
            activities
    batting grip, 595
    children's vs. adults' organization
        of, 623
    swing, 584–585, 603
baseball gloves, doing without, 504
basketball
    activities in
        dribbling. *See* dribbling
            activities
        shooting baskets, 513
        throwing and catching,
            512–513
bats, 589
batting tee, construction and use of,
    590–591
behavior
    attitude of teacher and, 113
    challenging content and, 122
    consequences of, 114, 117–118
    disorders of, 81–82
    gymnastics and, safety of, 445
    hearing impairment and, 73
    learning environment and. *See*
        learning environment
    maintaining appropriate. *See*
        appropriate behavior,
        maintaining
    off-task. *See* off-task behavior
    praise of, to parents, 134, 137
    self-reflection of teacher
        and, 202
    team or partner formation
        and, 331
behavior contracts, 134, 135
behavior disorders, 81–82
Bench Bounce Catch, 505
benchmarks
    determining of, in planning,
        103–104
    samples of, in content standards,
        29–30
    balance, 369
    chasing, fleeing, and
        dodging, 328

    dance, 309
    dribbling, 538
    effort, 236
    games, 620
    gymnastics, 439
    jumping, 312
    kicking and punting, 453
    relationships, 261
    rolling, 413
    space awareness, 218
    striking with long-handled
        implements, 583
    striking with paddles and
        rackets, 557
    throwing and catching, 487
    transferring weight, 397
    traveling, 279
    volleying, 519
benefits of physical activity, 4–6
bicycle safety, 52
blindness. *See* visual impairments
bodies, as instruments of expression,
    308, 309
body composition, 35–36
    changes in, 36
    in elementary school, 45
body parts, relationships of,
    252–253
    learning experiences, 252–260
    balancing on matching and
        nonmatching parts, 256
    balancing while using different
        body parts, 254–255
    changing from one body shape
        to another, 257
    creating body shapes in the air,
        259–260
    creating postcard
        sculptures, 259
    freezing on different body
        parts, 255
    identifying body parts, 254
    making symmetrical and
        nonsymmetrical shapes,
        257–259
    round, narrow, wide, and
        twisted body shapes,
        256–257
    traveling on different body
        parts, 255–256
    traveling and freezing in
        different body shapes, 257
Body-Part Tag, 336–337
Both Sides (of the paddle) Now, 566
bound flow. *See* flow, concept of
bowling, 499–500
broomball, 590, 592
Brownies and Fairies, 12, 624, 625
bulletin boards, 640

burns, 76, 79
Busy Mat, 429–430

Call Your Hit, 613–614
cardiovascular efficiency, 35
    activities for, 40–43, 50
        outside the gym, 43–45, 46
    in elementary school, 39–40
cartwheels, 404
catching. See throwing and catching
Catch-up Chase, 333–334
cerebral palsy, 76–78
challenges
    behavior problems and, 122
    content development and,
        156–157
    defined, 152
    function of, 122, 176–177
    icon used in text for, 156
    planning of, 106
    public, 122
chasing, fleeing, and dodging, 328
    activities. See chasing, fleeing, and
        dodging activities
    assessment of, 334
    in content standards, 328
    definitions of terms, 328
    levels of skill proficiency in,
        328, 330
    primitive tribal games and, 338
    safety in, 330, 331
    sequence of skill theme
        development of, 329
    See also skill themes
chasing, fleeing, and dodging
    activities
    control level, 330, 332
        dodging the obstacles, 333
        dodging with quick changes of
            direction, 333
        dodging in response to a
            signal, 332
        fleeing a chaser (Frogs and
            Flies), 334
        fleeing from a partner, 332–333
        overtaking a fleeing person
            (Catch-up Chase), 333–334
    precontrol level, 328–330
        Make-Believe Chase, 332
        moving obstacles, 330–331
        traveling to dodge, 332
        traveling to flee, 332
    proficiency level, 330, 337
        chasing and dodging
            simultaneously (Snatch the
            Flag), 339
        chasing and fleeing in a game
            situation, 338–339

continual fleeing and chasing
    with a large group, 338
dodging in a game situation
    (Pirate's Treasure; Safety
    Bases), 339–340
dodging while maintaining
    possession of an
    object, 338
dodging while manipulating
    an object in a game
    situation, 341
using team strategy for chasing,
    fleeing, and dodging (Rip
    Flag), 340–341
utilization level, 330, 334
    dodging and chasing one
        person in a mass (Partner
        Dodge), 336
    dodging and chasing as part of
        a team (Octopus), 335–336
    dodging in a dynamic situation
        (Body-Part Tag), 336–337
    dodging and faking moves to
        avoid a chaser (Freeze-and-
        Count Tag), 335
    dodging while manipulating an
        object, 337
    People Dodge (dodging
        stationary obstacles),
        334–335
Check for Understanding, icon used
    for, 177
child-designed games, 625–627
child-designed instruction, 170–172
child development
    appropriate and inappropriate
        educational practices and, 9,
        440, 618, 619, 637
    game-playing and, 13–15,
        628–629
    and gymnastics, nature of, 438
    skill theme approach and,
        15–16
    See also games: experiences of
children
    competition and. See competition
    development of. See child
        development
    fitness of, as declining, 34, 93–94
    games-playing by, vs. adult-
        organized, 618, 623, 624
    immediate meaning as necessary
        to, 109
    self-esteem of, 54–55
    See also students
Children's Lifetime Physical Activity
    Model, 36–37
clacker, construction of, 311
class

behavior problem of entire. See
    under appropriate behavior,
    maintaining
cooperative, and dance, 322
cooperative, and games, 628
sessions. See class sessions,
    frequency of
size of. See class size
See also groups; students; teams
classroom teachers
    building support for program
        with, 637–638
    as physical education
        teachers, 61
    playground equipment,
        discomfort with, 444
    and skill theme approach, 18
class sessions, frequency of
    skill level development and,
        93–94, 190–191
    as variable in teaching, 63, 98
    yearly overview and, 101
class size
    and game choice, 628
    in inclusion programs, 69
    as variable in teaching, 61–63, 98
clockwise and counterclockwise, as
    preferred terms, 225
closure, planning of, 107–108
cognitive development
    appropriate and inappropriate
        practices in, 8
    assessment of, options for, 190
    and right and left, understanding
        of, 232–233
    skill theme approach and, 17
cognitive strategy. See guided
    discovery
collaboration, 268, 270
collaborative relationships,
    defined, 272
communication. See interaction;
    language
community at large, building
    support with, 642–643
competence, as principle of fitness
    training, 36
competition
    as adult invention, 623
    appropriate and inappropriate
        practices in, 619
    vs. cooperation, need for choice
        of, 621
    games skill progression and, 622
    intergroup, 268, 269
    skill level deterioration and, 270
    See also cooperation
competitive games. See sports;
    traditional activities

computer games, reduced activity of children and, 5–6, 35
concepts. See movement concepts
Cone Soccer, 471–472
confidence, as principle of fitness training, 36
congruent feedback, 122, 155–156, 164
consequences of behavior, 114, 117–118
    minor offenses, guidelines for, 117–118
    See also behavior; discipline
construction of equipment
    balance bench, 380
    balance boards, 372
    balls suspended on strings, 562
    batting tee, 590
    golf club, 589
    golf holes, 614
    hockey stick, 589
    hoop, 261
    hurdles, 262
    kickballs, designating, 458
    paddles, 561, 563
    rhythm instruments, 311
    rope, 261
    rumble rhumba, 338
    scoops for throwing and catching, 502
    sock ball, 601
    standard, modification of. See equipment: modification of standard
    stilts, 383, 384
    streamers, 263
    targets, 491, 499
    tennis balls, accumulation of, 503
    tinikling poles, 301, 302
    yarn ball, 494
    See also equipment
content development, 152–158
    assessing, 157
    challenges. See challenges
    cues. See cues
    feedback. See feedback
    individual differences, accommodating, 157–158
    informing, 152–153
    overview, 152
    planning format and, 157
    tasks. See tasks
    See also lessons
content standards, 7, 27–30
    assessment examples in
        balancing, 374–375
        dribbling, 538, 540
        general space/self-space, 224

jumping, 353, 359
striking with long-handled implements, 583
throwing and catching, 487, 490–491
transferring weight, 412–413
traveling, 288–290
assessment options referenced in
    displays by students, 188
    drawings by students, 187
    event tasks, 185
    exit slips, 178
    homework, 179
    instructional approaches, 172
    journal-keeping, 177
    peer observation, 183
    portfolios, 190
    teacher observation, 189
    videotaping, 186
background of, 27–29
benchmarks in. See under benchmarks
Children Moving and, 29–31
dance in, 309
fitness and, 36
games in, 620
gymnastics in, 439
Internet site for, 7
movement concepts in
    effort, 236
    relationships, 261
    space awareness, 218
personal and social responsibility in, 53
skill themes in
    balancing, 369
    chasing, fleeing, and dodging, 328
    dribbling, 538
    jumping, 344
    kicking and punting, 453
    rolling, 413
    striking with long-handled implements, 583
    striking with rackets and paddles, 557
    throwing and catching, 487
    transferring weight, 397
    traveling, 279
    volleying, 519
contracts
    behavior, 134, 135
    child-designed instruction and, 171–172
control level, 89
    and cues, receptivity to, 154
    dance experiences for, 314
    games experiences and, 620, 621–623

gymnastics experiences for, 441, 442–443, 444
skill theme content and. See under specific skill themes (list of themes is located at skill themes: content of)
See also generic levels of skill proficiency
convergent inquiry, 167–168
Co-op, Co-op, 170
cooperation
    child development and, 629
    children officiating own games and, 628
    vs. competition, need for choice of, 621
    games skill progression and, 622
    relationship concepts of, 271–272
    See also competition
cooperative learning, 169–170
Cooperative Learning in Physical Education (Grineski), 170
Copy Cat Dance, 297
corporal punishment, 139
Council on Physical Education for Children (COPEC), 637
counterclockwise and clockwise, as preferred terms, 225
critical elements. See cues
croquet, 608
Crows and Cranes, 12
cues
    as benchmarks. See benchmarks
    content development and, 154–156
    defined, 122, 152
    direct instruction and, 164
    feedback and, 122, 155–156, 164
    objective and, planning of, 105
    observation and reiteration of, 148
    one at a time focus, 155, 275
    overview, 154–155
    skill theme vs. traditional activities approach, 14
    as valuable for students, 154
    See also specific skill theme activities
curriculum
    appropriate and inappropriate practices in, 8
    fitness in, 37
    planning. See planning
    skill theme approach to. See skill theme approach
    standards for. See content standards
    wellness in, 55

See also teaching
Curriculum Diamond, 12–13

dance
    activities
        balancing, 376–377
        expressive, 315
        jumping, 354–355, 356–358,
            363–365
        traveling, 292–293, 294–296,
            297, 298, 299–303
    aerobics, 49
    beginning themes of, 272
    content of, 316–317
    design of
        evaluation of, 316
        floor patterns, 298
        procedure for, 314–316, 317,
            318–319
    experiences of
        creative, 310, 313–314
        folk/cultural dances, 295, 296,
            310, 313, 354
        rhythmic, 310–312
    grapevine step, 295
    props and, 322
    purpose of, 17
    teaching of, 308–309, 317–323
        avoid the word "dance," 320,
            322, 323
        cooperative class and, 322
        exciting movement and, 323
        goals in, 317, 320
        imagery and, 238, 322–323
        as necessity, 323
        traveling and, skill levels in,
            283, 284
    visual impairment and, 72
    See also games; gymnastics
dance aerobics, 49
dangles, 123
deaf, as term, 73
decreasing inappropriate behavior.
        See under appropriate behavior,
        maintaining
defense
    catching in, 511
    factors affecting, in game design,
        548–549
    introduction of concept, 620, 622
demonstrations
    in direct instruction
        approach, 164
    in gymnastics, 447
    pinpointing by students, 153
    by teacher, 153
desists, 132–133
developmental level. *See* child
    development

*Developmentally Appropriate Physical
    Education for Children*
    (COPEC), 637
developmentally appropriate
    practices, 9, 440, 618, 619, 637
diabetes, 79–80
differential treatment,
    eliminating, 130
direct instruction, 162, 163–165
directions, concept of, 220,
    224–225, 232
    learning experiences
        changing directions on
            signal, 226
        combining pathways, levels,
            and directions, 230
        exploring directions, 225–226
        moving clockwise and
            counterclockwise, 225
        traveling in different
            directions, 225
        turning while moving in
            different directions, 226
    See also space awareness
disabilities, students with
    educational resources, 80
    emotional disturbance/behavior
        disorders, 81–82
    health-related impairments, 79–80
        asthma, 79
        diabetes, 79–80
    hearing impairments, 73–75
    inclusion programs, 68–69
    individualized program. *See*
        individualized education
        program (IEP)
    learning disabilities, 82–83
    least restrictive environment,
        benefits of, 68, 70
    mainstreaming of, 68
    mental retardation, 80–81
    M-Team, 69, 76
    peer acceptance and, 71, 72, 75,
        76, 80, 83
    personal interaction with, 77, 83
    physical disabilities, 75–79
        cerebral palsy, 76–78
        muscular dystrophy, 78–79
        spina bifida, 78
    visual impairments, 71–73
discipline
    corporal punishment, 139
    exercise as never used for, 132
    firmness in, 132–133
    as last resort, 128
    learning environment vs.,
        113, 128
    minor offenses, actions for,
        117–118

need for, as variable in
    teaching, 64
punishment implied by, 128, 132
teacher conduct in, 132
techniques of. *See* appropriate
    behavior, maintaining:
    decreasing inappropriate
    behavior
displays, assessment and, 186, 188
divergent inquiry, 168–169
diversity, reflective teaching and,
    60, 62
dodgeball, 12, 332
dodging. *See* chasing, fleeing, and
    dodging
Downs, 563
Down syndrome, 80
drawings, assessment and, 184–187
Dribble Tag, 550
dribbling
    activities. *See* dribbling activities
    assessment of, 538, 540
    in content standards, 538
    defined, 537–538
    levels of skill proficiency in, 538
    sequence for skill theme
        development, 539
    volleying and, 518
    See also skill themes; volleying
dribbling activities
    control level, 538, 540
        all the time dribble, 540–541
        dribble like a basketball
            player, 541
        dribbling at different
            heights, 542
        dribbling with the body in
            different positions, 543
        dribbling in different places
            around the body while
            stationary, 543–544
        dribbling and looking, 542
        dribbling and traveling, 544
        moving switches, 544
        switches, 542
    precontrol level, 538, 540
        bouncing a ball down and
            catching it, 540
        bouncing a ball down
            (dribbling)
            continuously, 540
        dribbling and walking, 540
    proficiency level, 538, 549
        Dribble/Pass Keep Away, 552
        Dribble Tag, 550
        dribbling against opponents:
            group situations, 549–550
        dribbling and passing in game
            situations, 551

dribbling activities *(continued)*
    dribbling and throwing at a
        target, 551–552
    dribbling while dodging, 551
    making up fancy
        dribbling/passing
        routines, 551
    Now You've Got It, Now You
        Don't, 550
    small-group basketball, 552
utilization level, 538, 544
    dribbling against an opponent:
        one on one, 548–549
    dribbling around stationary
        obstacles, 547–548
    dribbling and changing speed
        of travel, 544–545
    dribbling in different pathways,
        546–547
    dribbling and passing with a
        partner, 548
    dribbling while changing
        directions, 545
    mirroring and matching while
        dribbling, 548
    starting and stopping while
        changing directions, 546
See also volleying activities
Drop—Catch, 495
drug, alcohol, and tobacco abuse, 53
drums
    construction of, 311
    substitutes for, 225
    See also music; rhythm
Duck, Duck, Goose, 12, 624
"Dueling Banjos," 297
duration recording system,
    208–209, 210
dynamic gamelike skill experiences,
    619–620, 622–623

effort, concept of, 236–237
    action words and, 242
    application of, 249
    components of
        flow. *See* flow
        force. *See* force
        time. *See* time, concept of
    in content standard, 236
    See also movement concepts
egocentric stage
    game-playing and, 628–629
    and gymnastics, nature of, 438
    See also child development
elementary school
    content standards benchmarks
        for, 29, 30
    Curriculum Diamond and, 13
    dance in, purpose of, 309

movement concepts as focus
    in, 24
planning and, 99, 100
portfolios and, 186
skill levels in, 89, 90, 93
sports as inappropriate for, 618
upper grades. *See* upper grades of
    elementary
emotional disturbance, students
    with, 81–82
emotional/mental health, 54–55
endurance. *See* muscular strength
    and endurance
entrance slips. *See* exit slips
environment
    adaptations in, visual impairment
        and, 72–73
    for learning. *See* learning
        environment
    least restrictive, 68, 70
equipment
    baseball gloves, doing
        without, 504
    construction of. *See* construction
        of equipment
    cost of, and building
        programs, 636
    for gymnastics. *See under*
        gymnastics
    hockey sticks, curved vs.
        straight, 598
    modification of standard, 627
        long-handled implements, 582,
            589, 590, 595
        rackets and paddles, 562, 563
    planning for, 105
    playground, 444
    as variable in teaching, 63, 98
event tasks, assessment
    by, 185
exit slips, 178
expectations
    low vs. high, and student
        performance, 119
    setting performance standards
        and, 122–123
    See also learning environment
extensions, concept of, 220,
    230–231, 232
    learning experiences
        changing from one extension
            to another, 232
        exploring extensions,
            231–232
        traveling and extensions, 232
        using extensions and
            imagery, 232
    See also space awareness
extensions (tasks). *See* tasks

facilities, as variable in teaching, 63,
    98–99
family
    exercises with, 42, 46, 641
    fitness programs, 43
    See also parents
feedback
    congruent, 122, 155–156, 164
    examples, 223
    in games-playing, 623
    general, defined, 202
    gymnastics as self-testing and, 438
    self-reflection of teacher and,
        202–203, 207–208
    specific, defined, 202
    timing of, 123, 623
females, body composition of, 35–36
    See also gender
field hockey. *See* hockey
finger walk, 38
finish line, safety and, 330
fire safety, 52
fitness
    appropriate and inappropriate
        practices in, 8–9, 49
    Children's Lifetime Physical
        Activity Model, 36–37
    clubs for, 43
    components of, 35–36
    content standards and, 36
    decline of, in society, 34
    defined, 34–35
    guidelines for, 34
    lessons, incorporation into,
        49–50
    mental retardation and, 81
    motivation and, 36, 37
    principles of, 36
    testing for, 45–49
    wellness and. *See* wellness
fitness circuits, 49–50
fitness parcourses, 49–50
fleeing. *See* chasing, fleeing, and
    dodging
flexed-arm hang, 39
flexibility, 35
    activities for, 41, 50
    in elementary school,
        38–39, 41
    outside the gym, 42
flipflopping, 123
flow, concept of, 236, 246, 249
    learning experiences, 246–249
        combining time, force, and
            flow, 249
        eliciting flow qualities, 247
        following flow sentences, 247
        practicing flow sequences,
            247–248

studying over, under, around, in front of, and behind concepts, 263
traveling and flow, 246–247
using flow conversations, 248–249
See also effort, concept of
focus and subfocus, 105
folk/cultural dances, 295, 296, 310, 313, 354
following, 267
Follow-Me Dance, 293
football
    activities in
        punting. See punting activities
        throwing and catching, 513–514, 515
force, concept of, 236, 243, 249
    learning experiences, 243–246
        combining time, force, and flow, 249
        exploring force, 243–244
        showing contrasts of force, 244–246
        traveling and changing force qualities, 244
        using imagery and force, 244
        vs. size, 244
    See also effort, concept of
Fountain of Youth Dance, 299
Four Square, 525, 624
free flow. See flow, concept of
Freeze-and-Count Tag, 335
Frisbee, 501
Frisbee Football, 513–514
Frisbee Golf, 508–509
Frisbee Stretch, 510
Frogs and Flies, 334
From Both Sides Now, 572–573
fun, 36
future, dreams for, 646–648

galloping, 282, 287
games
    activities
        chasing, fleeing, and dodging, 332, 333–341
        dribbling, 548–551, 552
        jumping, 362
        kicking, 464–465, 467, 470–472
        punting, 481–483
        striking with long-handled implements, 594, 597–598, 606–607, 610, 611–612, 613–616
        striking with rackets and paddles, 562, 563–566, 572, 574–579

throwing and catching, 495, 497, 499, 501, 505, 508, 509, 510, 511–515
        traveling, 303
        volleying, 524–525, 527–528, 529, 530–531, 533–534, 537
    appropriate and inappropriate practices of, 619
    behavior of class, modifying with, 138, 139
    chasing, fleeing, and dodging skills and, 330
    child vs. adult view of, 618, 623, 624
    child-designed, 625–627
    child development and, 13–15, 628–629
    competition and. See competition; cooperation
    in content standards, 620
    cooperation in. See cooperation
    design types, 624–627
    experiences of, 618–624
        dynamic gamelike skills, 619–620, 622–623
        games-playing, 623–624
        invariant game skills, 619–620, 621–622
        progression of, 618–621, 622
    feedback during, 623–624
    fitness, adapted for, 50
    increasing difficulty in, 121
    for listening: noise level modulation, 120
    manipulative skill themes and, 618
    predesigned, 624–625
    See also traditional activities
    purpose of, 17, 618
    relationship concepts and, 273
    for skill theme/movement concept difference, 24
    sports, distinguished from, 618
    teacher-designed, 625–626
    teaching of, 624–628
        after-school sports, students from, 628
        equipment and, 627
        group size, 628
        naming the game, 627
        officiation in, 628
        requirements for, 618
        selecting a game, 624–627
    traditional. See traditional activities
    traveling and, skill levels in, 283, 284

See also dance; gymnastics; sports; specific games
games-playing experiences. See games: experiences of
gender
    appropriate and inappropriate practices concerning, 9
    traditional activities and, 624
general space, concept of, 219, 220, 222, 232
    assessment of, 224
    learning experiences
        city streets, crowded spaces, 223–224
        dodging in general space, 224
        exploring general space, 223
        obstacle course, 224
        reducing the size of the general space, 223
        scamper, 223
        traveling over, under, and around obstacles in general space, 224
    See also space awareness
generic levels of skill proficiency (GLSP), 88–94
    arrangement of text and, 17
    context variation and, 26–27
    force concepts and, 243
    generic as term in, 90–91
    levels of
        control. See control level
        cues as changing between, 154–155
        intratask variation and, 158
        precontrol. See precontrol level
        proficiency. See proficiency level
        utilization. See utilization level
    multiple skill levels within class, 93
    number of class sessions and, 93–94
    proficiency level as rare, 94
    relationship concepts and, 270, 273
    skills. See under specific skill themes (list of themes is located at skill themes: content of)
    tasks and. See tasks
    use of, 91–92
golf
    activities in, 589–590, 592–594, 601, 607, 613, 614
    use of, 589
    club, construction of, 589
    grip, 602
    holes, construction of, 614
    swing, 586–587, 589

good news letters, 134, 137, 640, 641
Graham, George, 27
grapevine step, 295
Grineski, Steve, 170
grips
    batting, 595
    golf, 602
    rackets, 568
groups
    decision making by, 268
    formation of, avoiding behavior problems in, 331
    relationship concepts and, 268, 271–272
    size of, and game choice, 628
    See also class; teams
guided discovery, 167–169
gymnastics
    activities
        balance. See balancing activities
        jumping. See jumping and landing activities
        rolling. See rolling activities
        transferring weight. See transferring weight activities
        traveling, 304
    apparatus
        experiences on, 441, 442–443
        playground equipment as, 444
        students transporting, 445–446
    appropriate and inappropriate practices in, 440
    balance, requirement of, 440
    beginning themes of, 272
    content of educational, 440–448
        apparatus experiences, 441, 442–443
        club gymnasts and, 413, 448
        demonstrations, 447
        floor experiences, 440–441
        learning environment, 445
        playground equipment and, 444
        sequences and notation, 441–442
        spotting and, 409, 433, 447–448
        stations, 446
        task matching/variation, 438–439, 446–447
        teaching process and, 444–448
    in content standards, 439
    educational and Olympic-style, compared, 439–440, 447, 448
    notation symbols for, 442
    purpose of, 17, 439–440
    safety

apparatus transport by students and, 445–446
assessment of skill levels and, 440
club gymnasts and, 448
concerns, avoidance of teaching and, 444
learning environment and, 445
on playground equipment, 444
prerequisites and, 438, 440, 441
rules, establishing, 446
task matching and, 438–439
See also safety
as self-testing, 438
traveling and, skill levels in, 283, 284
See also dance; games

Hacky Sack, 529
Half Ball, 616
handball, activities in, 514–515, 537–538
Hand Corner Ball, 532
Hanson, Margie, 296
Hartinger system, 192
heart defects, 76, 79
Heart Hustle, 50
Hellison's Responsibility Model, 53, 115, 116
    behavior-disordered students and, 82
    class behavior problems and, 135–137
    levels of, 54, 116
    rules and, 115–116
    See also responsibility
Helping Murgatroid, 178–179, 180
hemophilia, 76
Here, There, Everywhere, 50
high level, defined, 226
high school
    Curriculum Diamond and, 13
    teachers of, and skill theme approach, 18
Hit the Can, 499
Hit the Pin, 512
Hit and Run, 597–598
hockey
    activities in, 589–590, 591–594, 598–601, 604, 607–613, 614–615
    use of, 589
    safety and, 592, 593, 594, 598, 608
    stick
        construction of, 589
        curved vs. straight, 598
    swing, 586–587, 589, 592, 593

Hockey Bowl, 607
Holt/Hale, Shirley, 27
homework, 179–182
Hoop Golf, 606–607
hoops, construction of, 261
Hoop Volley, 524–525
hopping, 279, 287
hurdles, contruction of, 262
hurdling, 365
hyperactivity, 81, 82, 83

IDEA (Individuals with Disabilities Education Act) (1990), 68
imagery
    dance instruction and, 322–323
    distinctions necessary to, 236, 238, 286
    size and force in, 244
inappropriate behavior
    decreasing. See under appropriate behavior, maintaining
    ignoring, 130–131
inclusion, philosophy of, 68–69
individualized education program (IEP), 69–70
    implementing, 70–71
    learning disabilities and, 82
    physical disability and, 76
    See also disabilities, students with
Individuals with Disabilities Education Act (IDEA) (1990), 68
individuals, working with
    club gymnasts, 413, 448
    differences, accommodating, 157–158
    intratask variation, 158, 504
    invitation, teaching by, 158, 504
    observation and, 148
    See also class
informing students, 152–153
Ing-ly, 24
inner-city schools, testing by students of, 64
inner thigh stretch, 41
inquiry learning. See guided discovery
in-service, 637
instructional approaches, 162–172
    child-designed instruction, 170–172
    compared, 162–163
    cooperative learning, 169–170
    direct instruction, 162, 163–165
    guided discovery, 167–169
    peer teaching, 169, 172
    task teaching, 162, 165–167
instructionally appropriate practices, 9

instructional task system, 112, 121–122
interactions
    differential treatment, 130
    nagging vs. praise, determining, 129
    positive atmosphere and, 118–119, 129, 130
    prompting, 130
    self-reflection on patterns of, 206
    See also language
interactive teaching. See direct instruction
Internet
    content standards site, 7
    disabilities and health-related impairments, resources for, 80
    teacher support groups on, 69
intratask variation, 158, 504
intrinsic motivation, 36
introduction, 105–106
invariant games skill experiences, 619–620, 621–622
invariant teaching, 60, 61–64
invitation, teaching by, 158
involvement, appropriate and inappropriate practices of, 9
I See, 50
"I" stage. See egocentric stage

jigsaw, 170
jogging, 40, 42–43, 44, 641
journals
    of students, 177–178, 180–181
    of teachers, 200, 211–212
jumping and landing, 344
    activities. See jumping and landing activities
    assessment suggestions, 346–349, 352, 353, 359
    in content standards, 344
    fundamental patterns of, 344
    key observation points of, 344–345, 346–349
    levels of skill proficiency in, 344–345
    safety in, 351, 362, 427
    sequence for skill theme development of, 350
    See also skill themes
jumping and landing activities
    control level, 345, 351
        jumping for height, 352–353
        jumping and landing: basic patterns, 351–352
        jumping and landing task sheet, 359–360

jumping on and off equipment using buoyant and yielding landings, 358–359
        jumping over equipment using buoyant landings, 358
        jumping over low obstacles: hoops, 353
        jumping over low obstacles: hurdles, 353
        jumping rhythmically, 354
        jumping in rhythmical sequences, 354–355
        jumping a self-turned rope, 355
        jumping to form a body shape during flight, 356–357
        jumping a turned rope, 355
        jumping using buoyant and yielding landings, 356
        Jump, Squash, TaDa, 359
        performing jumping sequences and making body shapes, 358
        standing long jump, 352
        traveling, jumping, and body shapes, 357–358
    precontrol level, 344, 345
        jumping for distance, 351
        jumping for height, 351
        jumping and landing: different patterns, 345, 351
        jumping over a swinging rope, 351
    proficiency level, 345, 363
        hurdling jumps, 365
        jumping, dancing, and imagery, 365
        jumping as part of a dance creation, 364–365
        jumping with a partner to match actions, 364
        jumping with a partner to mirror actions, 363–364
        jumping with a springboard, 364
    utilization level, 345, 360–361
        hurdling jumps, 365
        jumping on a bench, 362
        jumping, dancing, and imagery, 365
        jumping as a part of a dance creation, 364–365
        jumping with a partner to match actions, 364
        jumping with a partner to mirror actions, 363–364
        jumping with a springboard, 364
        jumping to an accented beat, 363

jumping to catch, 361
        jumping to throw, 361–362
        throwing and catching while jumping, 362
jumping rope
    activities of, 351–352, 355
    clubs for, 41, 42
    construction of, 261
    slanty rope technique, 168
Jump Jim Joe, 354
Jump, Squash, TaDa, 359
junior high school. See middle school
Just a Piece of Paper, 39

Keep Away, 341, 511
Keep It Up, 527
key observation points
    catching, 492–493
    jumping and landing, 344–345, 346–349
    kicking, 455–457
    punting, 476–477
    rolling, 415, 416
    running, 280–281
    striking with long-handled implements, 584–587
    striking with rackets and paddles, 558–559
    throwing, 488
    See also performance assessment
kickball, 12, 624
kickballs, designating, 458
kicking, 452
    activities. See kicking activities
    in content standards, 453
    key observation points, 455–457
    levels of skill proficiency in, 452
    sequence of skill theme development for, 454
    traditional activities and, 624
    See also punting; skill themes
kicking activities
    control level, 452, 458
        dribbling around stationary objects, 464
        keeping it perfect: zero, zero, 464–465
        kicking in the air, 459
        kicking for distance, 459–460
        kicking on the ground, 458–459
        kicking a rolling ball from a stationary position, 461–462
        kicking to a distance zone, 460
        kicking to a partner, 462
        kicking to targets, 460–461
        starting and stopping, 463

kicking activities *(continued)*
tapping the ball along the
ground (soccer
dribble), 463
traveling in pathways, 463–464
precontrol level, 452
approaching a stationary ball
and kicking, 453, 458
kicking at large targets, 453
kicking a stationary ball from a
stationary position,
452–453
tapping the ball (as in
soccer), 458
proficiency level, 452, 469
kicking at a moving target, 470
kicking at small stationary
targets, 469–470
playing alley soccer, 471
playing cone soccer, 471–472
playing minisoccer, 470
playing soccer keep-away,
470–471
utilization level, 452, 465
changing directions:
tap/dribble, 465
kicking to a partner from
various angles, 467–468
kicking to a traveling partner,
468–469
passing to a partner in general
space, 469
performing a continuous
tap/dribble and change of
direction, 465–466
playing one-on-one soccer,
466–467
playing soccer golf, 467
playing two-on-one soccer, 469
traveling and kicking for a
goal, 466
kindergarten
content standard benchmarks for,
29, 30
jumping skills and, 344
skill level in, 88
KISS principle (Keep It Short and
Simple), 152
knowledge, as functional
understanding, 252

Laban, Rudolf, 442
Lambdin system, 192–193
landing. *See* jumping and landing
language
action words, in effort
concept, 242
for body parts, 254

grammar, movement concepts
and skill themes and, 24
hearing impairment and, 73–74
and imagery, use of, 238, 286
interaction with students. *See*
interaction
learning experiences and concepts
from, 247–249
mental retardation and, 80
non-English speakers, 153
notation system, 442
sign, 73, 74–75
leading, 267
leaping, 279, 282, 288
learning centers. *See* task teaching
learning disabilities, 82–83
learning environment
accountability measures, 112, 122
appropriate behavior. *See*
appropriate behavior,
maintaining
attitude of teacher in, 112–113
consistency in, maintaining, 123
discipline vs., 113, 128
as first-base skill, 112
and games, teaching of, 628
gymnastics and, 445
instructional task system, 112,
121–122
intratask variation explained
in, 158
managerial task system, 112,
113–121
beginning of school, 113–115
protocols, developing, 115
routines, 113–114, 115,
118–121
rules and expectations,
establishing, 113–114,
115–118, 133
monitoring and reacting, 123
See also observation
noise level in, games to modulate,
120–121
performance standards, setting,
122–123
reflection on, 124, 125
safety procedures, teaching,
123–125
teacher- vs. child-centered, 112
teacher's self-reflection and,
201, 202
least restrictive environment, 68, 70
left and right, cognitive
development and, 232–233
legal liability, safety and, 124, 147
lesson planning. *See* planning
lessons
appropriate, 109

content of. *See* content
development
design of, 108–109
distribution of, 101–102
games-playing vs. skills
acquisition in, 623
interesting, 109
parts of, 104–108
planning. *See* lesson planning
letters
to children, 640, 641
to parents, 134, 136, 137,
640, 641
levels, concept of, 220, 226, 232
learning experiences
combining pathways, levels,
and directions, 230
rising and sinking to create
different levels, 227
traveling with body parts at
different levels, 227
traveling and freezing at
different levels, 226–227
traveling while rising and
sinking, 227
See also space awareness
light. *See* force, concept of
line dance, 295, 296, 313
listening games, 120–121
Little League, 623
location, 219, 220
See also general space; self-space
locomotion
absence of, learning from,
220, 221
fundamental skills of, 278–282
list of types of, 25
skills. *See* traveling
See also motor skills
low level, defined, 226
low organized games. *See* traditional
activities
lying knee pull, 41

Magic Cars, 50
Magladry Ball, 625
Make-Believe Chase, 332
males, body composition of, 35–36
See also gender
managerial task system. *See under*
learning environment
manipulative skills, list of, 25
Manross, Mark, 7
Margie Dance, 296
matching, 267
mats, for rolling, 415
medical conditions, contraindicating
certain activities, 69

medium level, defined, 226
mental/emotional health, 54–55
mental retardation, 80–81
Metz system, 193–194, 195
middle school
    Curriculum Diamond and, 13
    introduction to lesson and, 106
    skill levels in, 93
    teachers of, and skill theme
        approach, 18
Minihockey, 614–615
Minisoccer, 470
Minitennis, 578
mirroring, 267
modified predesigned games,
    624–625
monitoring and reacting, 123
motivation
    for fitness, 36
    games which inhibit, 12
    intrinsic, as goal, 129
motor development
    misconceptions about, 15
    skill theme approach and, 13–15
motor skills
    appropriate and inappropriate
        development practices, 8
    assessment of, options for, 190
    demonstrations of. See
        demonstrations
    hearing impairment and, 73,
        74–75
    learning disabilities and, 82
    mental retardation and, 80–81
    physical disabilities and, 77, 79
    visual impairment and, 72
movement
    concepts of. See movement
        concepts
    imagery and. See imagery
    patterns of. See movement
        patterns
    rotation, terms for, 225
    sequences. See sequences of
        movement
    skills. See motor skills; skill
        themes
    of teacher, 123
movement analysis framework
    movement concepts. See
        movement concepts
    skill themes. See skill themes
    the wheel, 25
movement concepts, 23, 24
    appropriate and inappropriate
        development practices, 8
    categories of
        effort. See effort
        relationships. See relationships

space awareness. See space
    awareness
content standards benchmarks
    of, 30
imagery and. See imagery
preschool and primary grades
    and, 24
scope and sequence example
    for, 100
and skill themes, interaction of,
    23–25, 26, 258
the wheel and, 25
See also skill themes
movement patterns
    class, observation of, 147–148
    individual, observation of, 148
Moving into the Future: National
    Standards for Physical Education
    (NASPE)
    background of development of,
        27–29
    text and application of. See
        content standards
    Web site access to, 7
M-Team, 69, 76
multidisciplinary team (M-Team),
    69, 76
muscular dystrophy, 78–79
muscular strength and
    endurance, 35
    activities for
        abdominals, 38
        games as, 50
        outside the gym, 40
        upper body, 39
    in elementary school, 37–38,
        39, 40
    gymnastics and, 440
    rolling and, 415, 417
music
    and dance, introduction of,
        322, 323
    and flow, teaching of, 246
    and gymnastics activities, 389
    instruments, construction
        of, 311
    introduction of, 310
    and jumping activities, 354
    and rolling activities, 419–420
    sound-producing targets, 499,
        568, 578–579
    and traveling activities, 290, 293,
        294, 297
    See also drums; rhythm

narrow shape, 256
National Standards for Physical
    Education. See content
    standards; Moving into the

Future: National Standards for
    Physical Education
neat feet, construction of, 603
newsletter, 639–640
noise level modulation, 120
    See also targets: noise producing
nonmanipulative skills, list of, 25
nonsymmetrical shape, 258
nonverbal techniques
    inappropriate behavior addressed
        by, 131
    informing students with, 153
notation, gymnastics, 441–442
Now You've Got It, Now You
    Don't, 550
number of players, 628
nutrition, 51–52
nylon-hose paddles, construction
    of, 561

objectives, 105
objects, relationships with, 252, 260,
    272–273
    learning experiences, 260–266
        going over and under the
            obstacle course, 265
        learning onto/off concepts, 263
        studying over, under, around,
            in front of, and behind
            concepts, 263
        traveling along equipment,
            263–264
        traveling over, close to, far
            away, inside, 260–261
        traveling over, under, close to,
            and far away from
            equipment, 262–263
        traveling through obstacles,
            264–265
        using partners as obstacles,
            265–266
observation, 144–149
    in assessment
        by peers, 181, 183
        by teacher, 186, 189
    foci of
        class movement patterns,
            147–148
        combinations of, 148–149
        individual movement
            patterns, 148
        on-task behavior, 147
        safety, 146–147
    follow-through and, 261
    methods, during activity, 245
    in monitoring appropriate
        behavior, 123, 145, 146
    in self-assessment of teacher. See
        under reflection

observation *(continued)*
    techniques
        back-to-the-wall, 144–145, 146
        scanning, 145–146, 148
Obstacle-Course volley, 527–528
Octopus, 335–336
offense
    factors affecting, in game design,
        548–549
    introduction of concept,
        620, 622
officiation, of games, 628
off-task behavior
    in gymnastics, danger of, 445
    multiple games and reduction
        of, 628
    observation to determine, 147
    reasons for, 147
    See also behavior
Olympic-style and education
    gymnastics, compared,
    439–440, 447, 448
open house nights, 641
organizational strategies. *See*
    instructional approaches
osteogenesis imperfecta, 69
Outcomes Task Force, 27
overlap, 123
Overs, Unders, and Sides, 497

paddles
    construction of, 561, 563
    safety and, 561
    See also striking with rackets and
        paddles
pairs-check, 169–170
parcourses, 49–50
parents
    building support for program
        with, 638–642
    homework and, 179
    letters to, 134, 136, 137, 640,
        641
    phone calls to, 640
parent work night, 641
participation
    appropriate and inappropriate
        practices of, 9
    maximum, 109, 164
    and rules, establishment of, 116
    understanding problems with,
        and actions for, 131–132
Partner Dodge, 336
partners
    formation of, avoiding behavior
        problems in, 331
    relationship concepts and, 267
pathways, concept of, 220, 227,
    232–233

dance floor patterns,
    designing, 298
learning experiences
    combining pathways, levels,
        and directions, 230
    creating follow-the-leader
        pathways, 229
    designing pathways, 229
    exploring pathways, 228
    following-the-dots
        pathways, 230
    traveling pathways and
        obstacles, 229–230
    using pathway maps, 228–229
    See also space awareness
PE Central, Web site address, 7
peers
    child development and relations
        with, 629
    disabilities of students and, 71,
        72, 75, 76, 80, 83
    observation by, assessment and,
        181, 183
    teaching by, 169, 172
peer teaching, 169, 172
Pennington, Todd, 7
People Dodge, 334–335
people, relationships with, 252,
    266–268, 272–273
    competition and, 269
    learning experiences, 268–272
        following with a group, 271
        forming cooperative and
            collaborative relationships,
            271–272
        matching, 268–270
        matching and mirroring, 270
        meeting/parting, 271
        meeting and parting in a
            cooperative group, 272
        mirroring, 270
        performing solo, 272
        traveling alongside/following,
            270–271
        traveling and matching, 270
        using partners as obstacles,
            265–266
performance assessments
    content standards, examples in.
        See under content standards
    domains assessed through, 190
    dribbling, 541, 544, 551, 552
    feedback to student and. *See*
        challenges
    icon used in text for, 177
    key observation points, punting,
        476–477
    options for
        event tasks, 182–184, 185

exit slips, 178–179
homework, 179, 182
peer observation, 181, 183
portfolios, 186–187, 190
student displays, 186, 188
student drawings, 184, 187
student journals, 177–178,
    180–181
teacher observation, 186, 189
videotaping, 184, 186, 196
scoring rubrics of, 187–188, 191
suggestions for
    balancing, 371, 374–375, 383,
        386, 390
    chasing, fleeing, dodging, 334
    dribbling, 538, 540
    general space/self-space, 224
    jumping, 346–349, 352,
        353, 359
    punting, 478
    rolling, 416, 418, 424, 425, 426,
        429, 434
    running, 278–279, 280–282
    striking with long-handled
        implements, 583, 608, 613
    striking with rackets and
        paddles, 566, 570, 573, 580
    throwing and catching, 487,
        490–491, 497, 506
    transferring weight, 412–413
    traveling, 288–290
    volleying, 524, 529
    walking, 278
summarizing and reporting
    progress, 191–195
    Hartinger system, 192
    Lambdin system, 192–193
    Metz system, 193–194, 195
    similarities in systems, 194–195
time for, finding, 195–196
transferring weight, 399
weight transfer, 399, 404, 411
See also assessment
personal plan, 134
personal responsibility. *See*
    responsibility
personal safety, 52
personal space. *See* self-space
phone calls to parents, 640
phrasing. *See* sequence of movement
physical activity, benefits of, 4–6
physical activity clubs (PAC), 43, 45
Physical Activity and Health, Web site
    access to, 7
physical disabilities. *See under*
    disabilities, students with
physical education programs
    activities taught in, 4, 5
    assessment in. *See* assessment

children and. *See* children
content standards for. *See* content
    standards
disabilities and. *See* disabilities,
    students with
equipment of. *See* equipment
future of, dreams for, 646–648
goals of, 50–61
grading, 438
newsletter for, 639–640
outside others, involved in, 495,
    641–642
practices in: appropriate and
    inappropriate, 8–10, 440,
    618, 619, 637
skill theme approach to. *See* skill
    theme approach
support for, building, 636–643
teaching. *See* teaching
physical fitness. *See* fitness
Pilo Polo, 590, 592
pinpointing, 153
Pirate's Treasure, 340
planning
    of assessment, 195–196
    changes in, 103
    content. *See* content
        development; lessons
    enjoyment of, 108
    factors involved in, 98–99
    fitness, incorporation of, 49–50
    format for, content development
        and, 157
    four-step process of, 99–108
        benchmarks, determining,
            103–104
        daily lesson plans, 104–108
        scope and sequence, 99–100
        yearly overview, 100–103
    games-playing vs. skills
        acquisition lessons, 623
    hyperactive students and, 83
    importance of, 98
    lesson design, 108–109
    of observation requirements, 146
    progress, recording of, 108
    tasks, preparation of, 92
planning time (discipline),
    133–134
playground equipment, 444
"Pop Goes the Weasel," 354
portfolios, 186–187, 190
positive interaction. *See* interactions
posture, muscle tone and, 37
practice
    self-direction in, 109
    self-reflection of teacher and,
        206–208
    structure of lesson and, 164

value of, 109
precontrol level, 88, 89
    cues as absent at, 154
    dance experiences for, 313–314
    games experiences and, 619–620,
        621–622
    gymnastics experiences for, 441,
        442, 444, 446
    movement concepts and. *See*
        movement concepts
    relationship concepts and, 273
    skill theme content and. *See under*
        specific skill themes (*list of*
        themes is located at skill
        themes: content of)
    See also generic levels of skill
        proficiency
predesigned games, 624–625
    See also traditional activities
preschool
    movement concepts as focus
        in, 24
    skill level in, 88
primary school. *See* elementary
    school
principal
    building support for program
        with, 636–637, 638
    disciplinary actions and,
        134–135
problem solving. *See* guided
    discovery
proficiency level, 89, 90
    dance experiences of, 314
    effort concepts and, 236
    games experiences and, 620–621,
        623–624
    games teaching and students
        of, 628
    gymnastics experiences for, 441,
        443, 444
    as rare, 94
    rhythm and, 311–312
    skill theme content and. *See under*
        specific skill themes (*list of*
        themes is located at skill
        themes: content of)
    See also generic levels of skill
        proficiency
progression spirals, 275
    balancing, 370
    chasing, fleeing, dodging, 329
    dribbling, 539
    jumping and landing, 350
    kicking, 454
    punting, 474
    rolling, 414
    striking with long-handled
        implements, 588

striking with rackets and
    paddles, 560
throwing and catching, 489
transferring weight, 398
traveling, 284
volleying, 520
See also skill themes; *specific*
    activities
prompting, 130
proprioceptive perception,
    development of, 71–72
props, dance teaching and, 322
PTA (PTO) meetings, 638
public challenges, 122
Public Law 94–142 (1975), 68
public recognition
    behavior problems and, 138–139
    in classroom, 122
pull-ups, reverse, 39
punishment. *See* discipline
punting
    activities. *See* punting activities
    assessment suggestions, 478
    key observation points, 476–477
    levels of skill proficiency in,
        472–473
    sequence for skill theme
        development of, 474
    See also kicking
punting activities
    control level, 473
        punting for accuracy, 479
        punting with an approach, 475
        punting for consistency,
            473, 475
        punting different types of
            balls, 478
        punting for distance, 478
        punting for height, 479–480
        punting over low ropes, 475
        using punting zones, 478
    precontrol level, 472–473
        dropping, bouncing, and
            kicking lightweight
            balls, 473
        dropping and punting, 473
    proficiency level, 473, 482
        playing Punt-Over, 482–483
        punting while traveling, 482
        receiving and punting against
            opponents, 482
    utilization level, 473, 480
        playing Rush the Circle,
            481–482
        punting at angles, 480–481
        punting to a partner, 481
        punting within a limited
            time, 481

punting activities *(continued)*
   receiving a pass, then
      punting, 481
Punt-Over, 482–483

questions, teaching through. *See*
   guided discovery

Racket Call Ball, 575–576
Racket Corner Ball, 577
Racket Four Square, 577
rackets, 576
   See also striking with rackets and
      paddles
rapping, 310
recess
   appropriate and inappropriate
      practices of, 9
   physical education as, 6
   playground equipment use and
      safety during, 444
recognition, public. *See* public
   recognition
Red Rover, 12, 624
refereeing games, 628
refinements. *See* cues
reflection
   behavior problems and, 202
   on content development, 157,
      203–205
   on differential treatment,
      eliminating, 130
   duration recording system,
      208–209, 210
   on feedback, 202–203, 207–208
   on ignoring inappropriate
      behavior, 131
   on interaction patterns, 206
   on observation technique, 205
   post-lesson, 108
   on practice opportunities,
      206–208
   self-reflection, 200, 211–212
   successful teachers and, 200
   support groups, 212
   systematic observation, 201–211
      being observed, 210–211
      combining techniques, 209–210
      peer-assisted techniques,
         207–209
      performance assessment
         and, 211
      student-assisted techniques,
         205–207
      unassisted techniques, 201–205
      written instruments, 205
reflective teaching, 16–17, 60–65
   See also assessment; reflection;
      teaching

Reif, Glen, 24
relationships, concept of, 252
   application of, 272–273
   components of
      body parts. *See* body parts,
         relationships of
      objects. *See* objects,
         relationships with
      people. *See* people, relationships
         with
   in content standards, 261
   See also movement concepts
remedial physical education, 80–81
respiratory disorders, 76, 79
responsibility, personal and social,
   53–54
   accountability measures
      and, 112
   class behavior and, maintenance
      of, 135–137
   in gymnastics, 445
   Hellison's model of. *See* Hellison's
      Responsibility Model
   learning environment and,
      112, 119
   for time-out time, 133
restroom privileges, 119
reverse pull-ups, 39
rewards, behavioral problems and,
   138–139
rhythm
   dance experiences of, 310–312
   instruments, construction of, 311
   See also drums; music
right and left, cognitive
   development and, 232–233
   See also clockwise and
      counterclockwise
Rip Flag, 340–341
ripple effect, 123
Rocking Horse, 417
rolling
   activities. *See* rolling activities
   aerial: decline to teach, 432, 434
   assessment suggestions, 416, 418,
      424, 425, 426, 429, 434
   in content standards, 413
   dive: decline to teach, 432
   key observation points, 415, 416
   levels of skill proficiency in,
      413–417
   safety
      in backward rolls, 423
      Busy Mat rolling, 429
      equipment and, 409, 426, 427,
         430, 431
      general requirements of,
         415, 417
      jumping and rolling, 426, 427

multiple rolls, 425
recovery through rolling skills,
   401, 402, 408, 415
specific rolls as optional, 399,
   415, 417, 420
sequence of skill theme
   development, 414
See also skill themes; transferring
   weight
rolling activities
   control level, 415, 418
      back rocker, 419–420
      back shoulder, 422
      back touch, 420–421
      backward roll, 423–424
      egg roll, 418–419
      forward roll, 420
      handclasp backward,
         422–423
      jumping from different heights
         and rolling, 427
      jumping for height, landing,
         and rolling, 426–427
      jumping off equipment,
         landing, and rolling, 426
      jumping over equipment,
         landing, and rolling,
         427–428
      linking rolls, 425
      log roll, 418
      rolling at different speeds, 422
      rolling in different
         directions, 424
      rolling from different directions
         and positions, 424–425
      rolling, levels, directions, and
         jumping, 428–429
      rolling using different
         directions and speeds,
         425–426
      rolling from different positions,
         421–422
      shoulders sideways, 419
      through the legs, 420
      traveling, jumping, landing,
         and rolling, 429
      Twin Rockers, 418
   precontrol level, 413–415, 417
      The Ball, 418
      the Rocking Horse, 417
      rolling sideways, 418
      rounds, 417
   proficiency level, 415, 434
   utilization level, 415, 429
      balancing and rolling on
         equipment, 433
      Busy Mat, 429–430
      catching, throwing, and
         rolling, 434

rolling, balancing, and rolling, 431–432
rolling off low equipment, 431
rolling on low equipment, 430–431
rolling onto low equipment, 433
rolling over low hurdles, 430
rolling to express an idea, 432
rolling to meet and part, 433–434
striking and rolling, 434
throwing, catching, and rolling, 432–433
touch-and-go rolls, 430
traveling and rolling between pieces of equipment, 431
See also transferring weight activities
rope
    construction of, 261
    See also jumping rope
round shape, 256
routines (in learning environment), 113–114, 115, 118, 121
routines (of movement). *See* sequences of movement
rugby, activities in. *See* kicking activities; punting activities
rules
    consequences of behavior, 114, 117–118
    defined, 115
    establishing, 113–114, 115–118, 133
    of games, appropriate and inappropriate practices in, 619
    time-outs as specified in, 133
    See also learning environment
rumble rhumba, construction of, 338
running
    activities developing, 288
    process of, 278–279, 280–281
    safety and, 224
Rush the Circle, 481–482

safety
    at finish line, 330
    icon used for, 177
    in balancing. *See* balancing
    in chasing, fleeing, and dodging, 330, 331
    in gymnastics. *See* gymnastics
    jumping and landing, 351, 362, 427
    legal liability and, 124, 147

observation and correction of, 146–147
    personal, as wellness factor, 52
    playground equipment and, 444
    procedures, teaching of, 123–125
    in rolling. *See* rolling
    in running, 224, 330
    in striking. *See* striking with long-handled implements; striking with rackets and paddles
    in throwing and catching, 506
    in transferring weight. *See* transferring weight
    in traveling, 224, 565
Safety Bases, 339–340
Sanders, Steve, 442
scanning, 145–146
    vs. individual attention, 148
school board, building support for program with, 642
schools
    context of, as variable in teaching, 65, 162
    diversity in styles of, 60
    inner-city, 64
scoops, construction of, 502
scope and sequence, planning of, 99–100
scoring rubrics, 187–188, 191
self-esteem
    hearing impairment and, 75
    teacher as fostering, 54–55
self-space, concept of, 219, 220, 232
    assessment of, 224
    learning experiences
        curling, stretching, and twisting in self-space, 221–222
        exploring self-space, 220–221
        moving the whole body in self-space, 222
    See also space awareness
self-testing
    games as, 618, 624
    gymnastics as, 438
sequence of lessons, planning of, 99–100
sequence of skill theme development. *See* progression spirals
sequences of movement
    dance, 314
    designing, 241
    gymnastic, 441–442
shakers, construction of, 311
sickle cell anemia, 79
signals, anticipation of, 246
sign language, 73, 74–75
sit-ups, untimed, 38
Six-Player Teeball, 615

size, force compared with, 244
skill levels. *See* generic levels of skill proficiency (GLSP)
skill theme approach
    building support for program, 636–643
    characteristics of, distinguishing, 13–16
    context variation, 25–27
    Curriculum Diamond and, 12–13
    defined, 12
    fitness and, 17
    goals of, 12, 17, 23
    ideas of. *See* movement concepts
    integration of skills into content areas, 308, 438
    interest, maintaining, 16
    movements. *See* skill themes
    practice and. *See* practice
    reflective teaching and, 16–17
    traditional activities, avoidance of, 12
    the wheel and, 25–26
skill theme development sequence. *See* progression spirals; *specific skills*
skill themes, 23, 25
    ability in, classification of. *See* generic levels of skill proficiency
    benchmarks of. *See* benchmarks
    characteristics of, 22–23
    content of
        balancing. *See* balancing
        chasing. *See* chasing, fleeing, and dodging
        dribbling. *See* dribbling
        jumping. *See* jumping
        kicking. *See* kicking
        punting. *See* punting
        rolling. *See* rolling
        striking. *See* striking with long-handled implements; striking with rackets and paddles
        throwing and catching. *See* throwing and catching
        transferring weight. *See* transferring weight
        traveling. *See* traveling
        volleying. *See* volleying
    defined, 22
    invariant vs. dynamic, games-playing and. *See* games: experiences of
    locomotor skills, list of, 25
    manipulative skills, list of, 25
    and movement concepts, interaction of, 23–25, 26, 258

skill themes (continued)
    nonmanipulative skills, list
        of, 25
    remedial physical education
        and, 81
    scope and sequence example
        for, 100
    sequences for development of. See
        progression spirals
    in sports, 23
    See also movement concepts
skipping, 282, 287
slanty rope technique, 168
sliding, 282, 287
slippage, 123
Snatch the Flag, 339
soccer
    activities in
        kicking. See kicking activities
        volleying, 519, 521–522,
            529–531, 534–535
Soccer Golf, 467
Soccer Keep-Away, 470–471
social responsibility. See
    responsibility
social skills, hearing impairment
    and, 73
sock ball, construction of, 601
solo relationship, 267, 272
space, 25
space awareness, concept of,
    218–220
    application of, 232–233
    assessment examples in, 224
    components of
        directions. See directions
        extensions. See extensions
        levels. See levels
        location. See general space; self-
            space
        pathways. See pathways
    in content standards, 218
    the wheel and analysis of,
        218–219
    See also movement concepts
specific congruent feedback, 122,
    155–156, 164
speed. See time, concept of
spina bifida, 78
spirals, progression. See progression
    spirals
sports
    after-school
        as appropriate venue, 629
        and games-teaching, 628
    behavior disorders and, 82
    flexibility impaired in, 35,
        627, 628

games distinguished from,
    618, 627
games as preparation for, 618
names of, 627
number of players of, 628
skill themes used in, 23
See also games
Sports Dance, 294
spotting, appropriate, 409, 433,
    447–448
station teaching. See task teaching
Steal the Bacon, 624
Sticky Popcorn, 50
streamers, construction of, 263
strength. See muscular strength and
    endurance
striking, 582
striking with long-handled
    implements, 582
    activities. See striking with long-
        handled implements,
        activities in
    assessment suggestions, 583,
        608, 613
    in content standards, 583
    equipment modification/
        adjustment and, 582, 589,
        590, 595
    key observation points
        sidearm striking, 584–585
        underhand striking,
            586–587
    levels of skill proficiency in,
        582–583, 589
    safety
        eyeguards and, 608
        general requirements of, 589
        hockey swings and, 592, 593
        space required, 589
        stick straightness and, 598
        student interactions and, 594
    sequence of skill theme
        development, 588
    swings and. See swings
    See also skill themes; striking with
        rackets and paddles
striking with long-handled
    implements, activities in
    control level, 582, 591–592
        Hit and Run—bats, 597–598
        hitting a stationary ball from
            different places—
            bats, 601
        level swings—bats, 595–596
        striking in the air—golf, 593
        striking for distance—golf or
            hockey, 593–594
        striking a pitched ball—bats,
            602–604

striking a self-tossed ball to
    different distances—bats,
    602
striking a stationary ball—bats,
    594–595
striking a stationary ball for
    distance—bats, 596–597
striking a stationary ball on
    the ground—hockey or
    golf, 592
striking suspended objects—
    bats, 597
striking to different places—
    hockey, 600–601
striking to a stationary
    partner—hockey, 598
striking to a target (Around the
    World)—hockey, 594
striking to targets—hockey,
    594
striking to varying distances—
    golf, 601
striking while dodging
    stationary obstacles—
    hockey, 604
throwing a ball in the air and
    striking it—bats,
    601–602
traveling and changing
    speeds—hockey, 599–600
traveling slowly while striking a
    ball—hockey, 598–599
traveling, stopping, and
    controlling the ball—
    hockey, 599
traveling and striking while
    changing pathways—
    hockey, 600
precontrol level, 582, 589
    striking (dribbling) a ball in
        self-space—hockey, 591
    striking off a batting tee—bats,
        590–591
    striking a stationary ball—golf
        or hockey, 589–590
    striking to large targets—
        hockey/golf, 590
    traveling slowly while striking a
        ball—hockey, 591
proficiency level, 583, 612
    directing the pathway, distance,
        and speed of an object—
        golf, 613
    directing the pathway, distance,
        and speed of an object
        (Call Your Hit)—bats,
        613–614
    Keep Away—hockey, 613
    Minihockey, 614–615

striking to dodge an
opponent—hockey,
612–613
Whiffle Ball Golf, 614
utilization level, 582–583, 612
batting, combining distance
and placement, 606
directing the air pathway of the
struck object—golf, 607
directing the placement of an
object—bats, 605
dribbling and changing
directions backward—
hockey, 607–608
grounders and flies—bats,
604–605
Half Ball—bats, 616
hitting to open spaces—bats,
605–606
keeping it moving—
hockey, 611
One-Base Baseball, 615–616
one-on-one hockey, 610
passing and receiving on the
move—hockey, 611
pathways, speeds, and
directions—hockey, 608
performing a continuous
dribble and change of
direction—hockey, 608
playing Hockey Bowl (small
targets), 607
playing Hoop Golf, 606–607
Six-Player Teeball, 615
striking from a stationary
position to a moving
target—hockey, 610–611
striking a pitched object
varying the distance—
bats, 606
striking to targets at various
distances—golf, 606
traveling and striking for a
goal—hockey, 608–609
two-on-one hockey, 611–612
striking with rackets and
paddles, 556
activities. See striking with rackets
and paddles activities
assessment suggestions, 566, 570,
573, 580
in content standards, 557
cues for, additional, 564
equipment modifications/
adjustments to allow,
562, 563
key observation points, 558–559
levels of skill proficiency in, 556
safety and

general considerations, 557
nets and, 574
paddles, 557, 561
rackets, 579
space required for, 572,
574, 579
traveling, 565
sequence for skill theme
development, 560
See also skill themes; striking with
long-handled implements
striking with rackets and paddles
activities
control level, 556, 563
Both Sides (of the paddle) Now,
566
Downs, 563
hitting to different places, 570
striking a ball rebounding from
a wall, 571–572
striking at high and low targets,
569–570
striking continuously over and
through a target, 572
striking for distance (varying
the force), 567
striking for hoops (varying the
distance), 567
striking through a target,
570–571
striking to wall targets, 566
to the wall—sideways (sidearm
forehand pattern), 567–568
to the wall again—sideways
(sidearm backhand
pattern), 568
Up Against the Wall (striking
forward), 565
Ups, 563–564
Ups and Downs, 564–565
Ups, Downs, and Forwards,
565–566
precontrol level, 556–557
balloon strike (lightweight
paddle), 561
hit the wall, 562
paddle balance, 557, 561
striking a suspended ball,
561–562
Upward Bound, 562
proficiency level, 556, 576
aerial net games, 578–579
Badminton Volleyball, 579
Minitennis, 578
Racket Corner Ball, 577
Racket Four Square, 577–578
self-designed racket games,
579–580
Wall Ball, 576–577

utilization level, 556, 572
From Both Sides Now,
572–573
Racket Call Ball, 575–576
striking continuously upward
with a group, 574
striking overhead, 574
striking overhead over a
net, 574
striking in various aerial
pathways in gamelike
situations, 575, 576
strong. See force, concept of
students
as advocates for program, 639,
640, 643
apparatus, moving and setting up,
445–446
characteristics of, in class, 60, 99,
162–163
displays of, assessent and,
186, 188
drawings of, assessment and,
184, 187
follow-through in teaching
and, 261
as group. See class; groups; teams
as individuals. See individuals,
working with
journals of, assessment and,
177–178, 180–181
participation of. See participation
responsibility and. See
responsibility
self-reflection of teacher and,
205–207
skill levels of
assessment. See assessment;
performance assessment
as declining, 94
planning and, 99
See also child development;
children; teachers
studying, activities to do during,
40, 42
success rate, appropriate and
inappropriate practices in, 9
support groups for teachers,
69, 212
support for physical education
program, building, 636–643
swings
baseball, 584–585, 603
golf, 586–587, 589
hockey, 586–587, 589, 592, 593
sidearm pattern, 582, 584–585
underhand pattern, 582, 586–587,
590, 592
symmetrical shape, 258

TaDa, 259
tape-recording
    and eliminating differential
        treatment, 130
    and ignoring inappropriate
        behavior, 131
    performance assessment of
        students using, 196
    self-analysis using, 200, 201–202
    video. *See* videotaping
targeting, 123
targets
    construction of, 491, 499
    sound-producing, 499, 568,
        578–579
task development section, planning
    of, 106–107
tasks
    content development and,
        153–154
    defined, 152
    delivery of, 92
    event tasks, 182–184, 185
    grade as requiring, as
        inappropriate, 438
    gymnastics and
        matching/variation of,
        438–439, 446–447
    icon used in text for, 154
    intratask variation, 158, 504
    off-task behaviors. *See* off-task
        behaviors
    planning of, 92, 106–107
    success of, determining, 92,
        153–154
    *See also under specific concepts and
        skill theme activities*
task sheets, 165, 166
task system, 112
task teaching, 162, 165–167
    assessment during, 196
    gymnastics and, 446
teacher/child-designed games,
    625–626
teacher-designed games, 625
teachers
    actions of effective, 201
    assessment of, by self. *See*
        reflection
    building support for program,
        636–643
    classroom. *See* classroom teachers
    comfort zone of, 162
    and dance, teaching of, 308–309
    future dreams for, 646–648
    interactions with students. *See*
        interactions
    and mental/emotional health of
        students, 54–55

observation by, assessment and,
    186, 189
responsibility, guidance in,
    53–54
self-reflection in behavior
    problems, 128
and skill themes approach, 17–18
substance abuse, role modeling
    and, 53
support groups for, 69, 212
values of, 60–61, 62, 162
See also students
teaching
    approaches to. *See* instructional
        approaches
    critical demandingness in,
        122–123
    of dance. *See* dance
    effective, 60
    environment of. *See* learning
        environment
    of games. *See* games
    of gymnastics. *See* gymnastics
    invariant, 60, 61–64
    by invitation, 158
    planning. *See* planning
    reflective, 16–17, 60–65
    See also specific skills and activities;
        teachers
*Teaching Responsibility Through
    Physical Activity* (Hellison), 137
teaching strategies. *See* instructional
    approaches
teaching style
    defined, 162
    militaristic, 165
teams, formation of
    appropriate and inappropriate
        practices in, 619
    avoidance of behavior problems
        in, 331
    size of, 619
    See also class; groups
team sports, as emphasized, 4, 5
Teeball, 615
tee. *See* batting tee
television
    activities while watching, 40, 42
    reduced activity of children and,
        5–6, 35
tennis balls, accumulation of, 503
testing. *See* assessment
throwing and catching
    activities. *See* throwing and
        catching activities
    assessment suggestions, 487,
        490–491, 497, 506
    basic pattern of, 486
    as complementary skills, 486

in content standards, 487
key observation points
    of catching, 492–493
    of throwing, 488
levels of skill proficiency
    in catching, 491–493
    in throwing, 486–487
safety, 506
sequence for skill theme
    development of, 489
traditional activities and, 624
See also skill themes
throwing and catching activities
    control level, 386–387, 492,
        496
        Bench Bounce Catch, 505
        bouncing a ball to self and
            catching it, 497–498
        bowling for targets, 499–500
        catching in different places
            around the body, 498–499
        catching with a scoop, 501–502
        Hit the Can, 499
        Overs, Unders, and Sides, 497
        throwing an object to different
            levels and catching it, 498
        throwing backhand to a target,
            500–501
        throwing a ball against a wall
            and catching the
            rebound, 502
        throwing and catching over a
            net with a partner, 504
        throwing and catching with a
            partner, 503–504
        throwing for distance, 503
        throwing a Frisbee, 501
        throwing overhand, 496
        throwing overhand at a
            stationary target, 499
        throwing sidearm, 497
        throwing to high targets, 500
        throwing underhand, 496–497
        throwing underhand to
            hoops, 500
    precontrol level, 486, 491–492
        catching from a skilled
            thrower, 495
        catching a rolling ball, 494
        Drop—Catch, 495
        throwing at a large target,
            491, 494
        throwing a yarn ball against the
            wall, 494
        tossing to self and
            catching, 495
    proficiency level, 487, 493, 510
        playing four-person
            football, 514

playing Frisbee Football, 513–514
playing Frisbee Stretch, 510
playing half-court basketball, 512–513
playing Hit the Pin, 512
playing Keep Away, 511–512
playing passball, 515
playing team handball (modified), 514–515
running the bases, 510–511
utilization level, 487, 492–493, 505
catching to throw quickly to a partner, 509
catching to throw quickly to a target, 509
moving to catch, 505–506
playing Frisbee Golf, 508–509
target backaway, 508
throwing and catching while traveling, 506
throwing for distance and accuracy, 507–508
throwing on the move, 506
throwing to make a partner move to catch, 506–507
throwing to a moving target, 507
throwing while in the air, 509–510
time
for performance assessment, finding, 195–196
teacher self-assessment and, 208–209
time, concept of, 236, 237–239, 249
learning experiences, 239–243
combining imagery and time, 241
combining sport skills and time, 241, 243
combining time, force, and flow, 249
continually changing in time while traveling, 243
differentiating among time words, 241
exploring time, 239
moving at different speeds, 240
traveling and freezing by using changes in time, 240
using different speeds in self-space, 239–240
See also effort, concept of
time-outs (in discipline), 117–118, 133
timing of teacher feedback, 123, 623
tin can stilts, construction of, 383

Tinikling, 301–303
tobacco, drug, and alcohol abuse, 53
token systems of reward, 138–139
Tom Foolery rhymes, 284
traditional activities
avoidance of, 12
defined, 13
as easy fallback, 61, 94, 624
modification of, 624–625
opportunities for skill use in, 624
planning difficulties and, 108
single-level skills proficiency as assumption in, 92–93, 624, 625
vs. skill themes approach, teaching and, 17–18
transferring weight, 396
activities of. See transferring weight activities
assessment suggestions, 412–413
in content standards, 397
levels of skill proficiency in, 396
safety
equipment placement, 401
hands, taking weight on, 404, 405
in overbalance and recovery, 404, 408, 410
precontrol level as focused on, 397
prerequisites and, 401, 402, 409, 410
in rolling, 409
rolls as optional, 399
spotting, 409, 433, 447–448
transfers off equipment, 403
vaulting, 409
sequence for skill theme development of, 398
See also rolling; skill themes
transferring weight activities
control level, 396, 397
making spring/step takeoffs with sequences, 402–403
performing spring/step takeoffs, 401
performing spring/step takeoffs onto crates and/or benches, 401
stretching, curling, and twisting into transfers, 400–501
transferring off low apparatus, 402
transferring onto low apparatus, 403
transferring weight from feet to back, 399

transferring weight from feet to combinations of body parts, 399–400
transferring weight from feet to hands, 404
transferring weight to hands across mats, 399
transferring weight to hands by stepping: cartwheels, 404
traveling over low apparatus, 403
precontrol level, 396
locomotor actions, 396–397
transferring weight from feet to back, 397
transferring weight from feet to hands, 397
transferring weight onto and off equipment, 397
proficiency level, 396, 413
utilization level, 396, 404–405
combining skills on mats, 411
combining weight transfer and balances into sequences on mats and apparatus, 411
transferring weight along apparatus, 409
transferring weight on bars, 411
transferring weight from feet to hands, 410–411
transferring weight onto bars, 408
transferring weight onto large apparatus, 406
transferring weight over apparatus, 408–409
transferring weight by rolling, 409–410
transferring weight to hands: walking, 405
transferring weight to hands and forming a bridge, 405–406
transferring weight to hands and twisting, 405
transferring weight to head and hands on apparatus, 406
See also rolling activities
traveling, 278
activities. See traveling activities
assessment suggestions, 288–290
in content standards, 279
fatigue and, 239
fundamental locomotor skills, 278–282
levels of skill proficiency in, 282–284
safety in, 224, 565

traveling *(continued)*
  sequence for skill theme
    development of, 284
  See also skill themes
traveling activities
  control level, 283, 284
    changing speeds to music, 294
    combination locomotors,
      294–295
    a dance of Water, Steam, and
      Ice, 294
    the Follow-Me Dance, 293
    galloping, 287
    hopping, 287
    leaping, 288
    the locomotors dance, 292–293
    moving to rhythms, 290
    performing locomotor
      sequences, 289
    running, 288
    skipping, 287
    slidestepping, 292
    sliding, 287
    slow-motion replay: The Sports
      Dance, 294
    traveling an obstacle
      course, 291
    traveling at different
      speeds, 293
    traveling in confined
      spaces, 290
    traveling in different
      directions, 291
    traveling with different
      locomotor patterns, 287
    traveling in different
      pathways, 292
    traveling with music,
      290–291
    traveling to open spaces, 289
    traveling using different
      directions, levels,
      pathways, and locations,
      293–294
  precontrol level, 282–283, 284
    traveling among the large and
      tall, 286–287
    traveling with different
      locomotor movements, 285
    traveling in different ways,
      285–286
    traveling in general
      space, 285
    traveling with imagery, 286
    traveling through rope
      pathways, 286
  proficiency level, 283, 284, 300
    depicting primitive tribes
      through travel, 301

    performing rhythmical
      patterns: Tinikling,
      301–303
    traveling in games and sports,
      303–304
    traveling in gymnastics, 304
    traveling to show tradition vs.
      change, 301
  utilization level, 283, 284, 295
    the Copy Cat Dance, 297
    meeting and parting while
      traveling with a
      partner, 299
    performing rhythmical
      patterns, 299
    shadowing, 297, 299
    traveling in bound and free
      flow, 300
    traveling with a partner:
      changing speed and
      direction, 297
    traveling with a partner:
      matching pathways,
      295–297
    traveling to express age: The
      Fountain of Youth
      Dance, 299
    traveling to Tom Foolery
      rhymes, 300
trunk and shoulder extensions, 41
trunk and shoulder rotation, 41
Twin Rockers, 418
twisted shape, 256
Two Square, 525

unison, 267
Up Against the Wall, 565
upper-body strength and endurance,
    activities for, 39
upper grades of elementary
  game-playing and, 629
  introduction to lesson and, 106
  planning and, 99, 100
Ups, 563–564
Ups and Downs, 564–565
Ups, Downs, and Forwards,
    565–566
Upward Bound, 562
utilization level, 89–90
  dance experiences for, 314
  games experiences and, 619,
    620–621, 622–624
  gymnastics experiences for, 441,
    443, 444
  rhythm and, 311–312
  skill theme content and. *See under
    specific skill themes (list of
    themes is located at* skill
    themes: content of)

  See also generic levels of skill
    proficiency

vaulting, 408–409
videotaping
  protocol presentation, 115
  safety procedures, 124
  student assessment with, 184,
    186, 196
  See also tape-recording
violence, avoidance of
    appearance/acceptance of,
    332, 499
visual impairments, 71–73
visual learners, 153
visual tracking, development
    of, 562
voices, rapping, 310
volleyball. *See* volleying activities
volleybirds, 531–532
volleying
  activities. *See* volleying activities
  assessment suggestions, 524, 529
  in content standards, 519
  defined, 518
  dribbling and, 518
  levels of skill proficiency in, 518
  sequence for skill theme
    development, 520
  See also dribbling; skill themes
volleying activities
  control level, 518, 519, 521
    Obstacle-Course volley,
      527–528
    playing Four Square, Two
      Square (underhand
      pattern), 525
    playing Hoop Volley
      (underhand pattern),
      524–525
    playing Keep It Up, 527
    playing one-bounce
      volleyball, 527
    striking a ball noncontinuously
      with different body parts,
      521–522
    striking a ball over a line
      (underhand pattern), 524
    striking a ball to the wall
      (underhand pattern),
      523–524
    striking a ball upward with the
      forearms (the bump),
      522–523
    striking a ball upward
      (underhand pattern), 522
    striking over a low net
      (underhand pattern),
      525–526

volleying a ball upward
    (overhead pattern), 526
volleying to a partner (overhead
    pattern), 526–527
volleying to the wall (overhead
    pattern), 526
precontrol level, 518, 519
    striking a balloon forward, 519
    striking balloons in the air,
        518–519
    striking with different body
        parts, 519
    striking lightweight objects,
        519, 521
proficiency level, 518, 534
    playing modified
        volleyball, 537
    serving overhand over the net,
        535–536
    spiking, 536–537
    striking with different body
        parts while traveling,
        534–535
    striking downward with
        force, 536
    volleying in a line
        formation, 537

utilization level, 518, 527
    playing Aerial Soccer, 530–531
    serving underhand over the
        net, 534
    striking a ball continuously
        with different body
        parts, 529
    striking to the wall—varying
        levels, force, and body
        position, 532
    volleying continuously to a
        partner, 533
    volleying with the foot,
        529–530
    volleying game: child-designed,
        527–529
    volleying over a net, 532–533
    volleying three on three,
        533–534
    volleying with a volleybird,
        531–532
    See also dribbling activities

walking, process of, 278
walking hands, 39
Wall Ball, 576–577
wall push, 38

warm-up activities, general space,
    travel through, 222
water safety, 52
Water, Steam, and Ice Dance, 294
Web site
    PE Central, 7
    See also Internet
weight, body composition
    and, 36
weight, transferring. See transferring
    weight
wellness, 51–55
the wheel, 25, 26
Whiffle Ball Golf, 614
wide shape, 256
with itness, 123
wooden paddles, construction
    of, 563
wooden stilts, construction
    of, 384

yarn ball, construction
    of, 494
yearly overview, in planning,
    100–103

Zero, Zero, 464–465